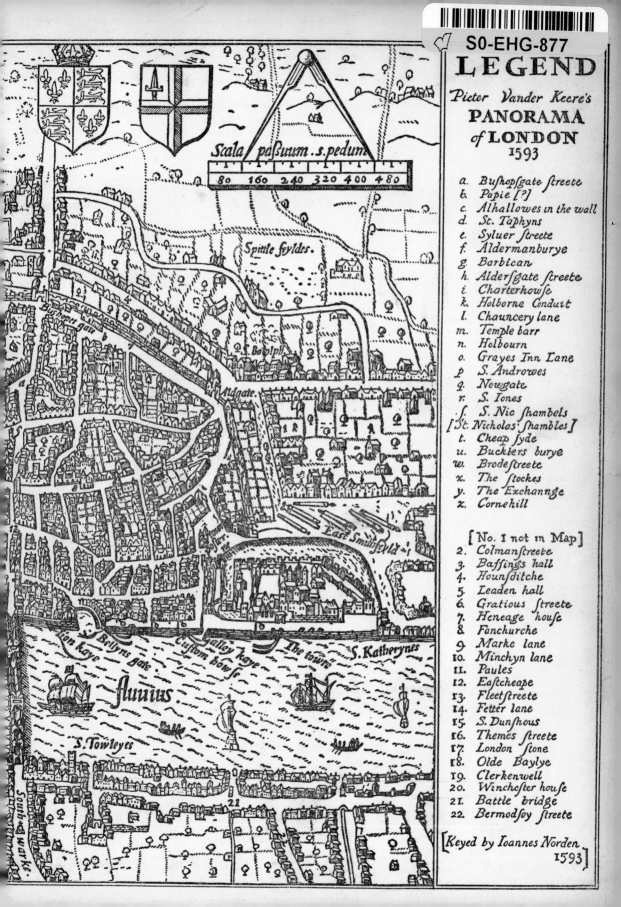

Scala passuum .s. pedum
80 160 240 320 400 480

Spittle feyldes.

S. Botolph

Aldgate.

East Smithfeyld

Bellyns gate

Lion kaye   galley kaye   The towre   S. Katherynes

Custome howse

Bushops gate

fluuius

S. Towleyes

Southwarke.

21

LEGEND

Pieter Vander Keere's
PANORAMA
of LONDON
1593

a. Bushopsgate streete
b. Papie [?]
c. Alhallowes in the wall
d. St. Taphyns
e. Syluer streete
f. Aldermanburye
g. Barbican
h. Aldersgate streete
i. Charterhowse
k. Holborne Conduit
l. Chauncery lane
m. Temple barr
n. Holbourn
o. Grayes Inn Lane
p. S. Androwes
q. Newgate
r. S. Iones
s. S. Nic shambels
[St. Nicholas' shambles]
t. Cheap syde
u. Bucklers burye
w. Brodestreete
x. The stockes
y. The Exchannge
z. Cornehill

[No. 1 not in Map]
2. Colmanstreete
3. Baffings hall
4. Hounsditche
5. Leaden hall
6. Gratious streete
7. Heneage house
8. Fanchurche
9. Marke lane
10. Minchyn lane
11. Paules
12. Eastcheape
13. Fleetstreete
14. Fetter lane
15. S. Dunshous
16. Themes streete
17. London stone
18. Olde Baylye
19. Clerkenwell
20. Winchester house
21. Battle bridge
22. Bermodsoy streete

[Keyed by Ioannes Norden
1593]

English Literature

THE MACMILLAN COMPANY
NEW YORK • CHICAGO
DALLAS • ATLANTA • SAN FRANCISCO
LONDON • MANILA
IN CANADA
BRETT-MACMILLAN LTD.
GALT, ONTARIO

FRONTISPIECE

Embroidered seventeenth-century
English binding, made for a
Bible belonging to Charles I.

Courtesy of the Pierpont Morgan Library.

ENGLISH LITERATURE

A College Anthology

Edited by

DONALD B. CLARK · LEON T. DICKINSON

CHARLES M. HUDSON · GEORGE B. PACE

of the University of Missouri

New York

The Macmillan Company

First Printing

The Macmillan Company, New York
Brett-Macmillan Ltd., Galt, Ontario

Printed in the United States of America

Library of Congress catalog card number: 60–5155

ACKNOWLEDGMENTS

Acknowledgment is gratefully made to the following authors, agents and publishers who have granted permission to use selections from their publications.

Brandt and Brandt, for:
selections from *Nineteen Eighty-Four* by George Orwell. Copyright 1949 by Harcourt, Brace and Company, Inc. Reprinted by permission also of Martin Secker and Warburg, Ltd.

J. M. Dent and Sons, Ltd., for:
"Il Conde" from *A Set of Six* by Joseph Conrad.

Harcourt, Brace and Company, Inc., for:
"The Love Song of J. Alfred Prufrock," "The Hollow Men," and "Sweeney among the Nightingales." From *Collected Poems 1909–1935* by T. S. Eliot, copyright, 1936, by Harcourt, Brace and Company, Inc., and reprinted with their permission. Reprinted by permission also of Faber and Faber Ltd.
"Macavity the Mystery Cat," from *Old Possum's Book of Practical Cats* by T. S. Eliot, copyright, 1939, by T. S. Eliot. Reprinted by permission of Harcourt, Brace and Company, Inc. Reprinted by permission also of Faber and Faber Ltd.
"Tradition and the Individual Talent." From *Selected Essays 1917–1932* by T. S. Eliot, copyright, 1932, by Harcourt, Brace and Company, Inc. and reprinted with their permission. Reprinted by permission also of Faber and Faber Ltd.
"Kew Gardens." From *A Haunted House and Other Short Stories* by Virginia Woolf, copyright, 1944, by Harcourt, Brace and Company, Inc. and reprinted with their permission. Reprinted by permission also of Mr. Leonard Woolf.

Harper and Brothers, for:
Chapters II and XVII of *Brave New World* by Aldous Huxley. Copyright, 1932, by Aldous Huxley. Reprinted by permission also of Chatto and Windus, Ltd.
Four selections from *The Collected Poetical Works of Algernon C. Swinburne.* Reprinted by permission also of William Heinemann, Ltd.

Henry Holt and Company, Inc., for:
six selections from "A Shropshire Lad." From *The Collected Poems of A. E. Housman.* Copyright, 1940, by Henry Holt and Company, Inc. By permission of the publishers. Reprinted by permission also of the Society of Authors as the Literary Representative of the Trustees of the late A. E. Housman, and of Messrs. Jonathan Cape, Ltd., publishers of A. E. Housman's *Collected Poems.*

selections from *Beowulf* by Chauncey Brewster Tinker. Copyright, 1937, by Chauncey Brewster Tinker. By permission of Henry Holt and Company, Inc.

Houghton Mifflin Company for:
the "Prologue" from Chaucer's *Canterbury Tales,* edited and revised by F. N. Robinson.

Alfred A. Knopf, Inc., for:
"The Daughters of the Late Colonel," reprinted from *The Short Stories of Katherine Mansfield* by Katherine Mansfield, by permission of Alfred A. Knopf, Inc. Copyright 1922, 1937 by Alfred A. Knopf, Inc. Reprinted by permission also of The Society of Authors as the Literary Representative of the Estate of the late Miss Katherine Mansfield.

Longmans Green and Company, Ltd., for:
"Defence of Guenevere" and "Haystack in the Flood" by William Morris.

McGraw-Hill Book Company, Inc., for:
selections from *Boswell's London Journal, 1762–1763* edited by Frederick A. Pottle. Copyright, 1950, by Yale University. Reprinted by permission of the McGraw-Hill Book Company, Inc.

The Macmillan Company, for:
"The Darkling Thrush," "Drummer Hodge," "The Man He Killed," "Channel Firing," "The Convergence of the Twain," "The Oxen." From *Collected Poems* by Thomas Hardy. Copyright 1925 by The Macmillan Company.

"The Lake Isle of Innisfree," "When You Are Old," "The Collar-Bone of a Hare," "The Second Coming," "Leda and the Swan," "The White Birds," "Never Give All the Heart," "An Irish Airman Foresees His Death," "A Prayer for My Daughter," "Sailing to Byzantium," from *The Collected Poems of William Butler Yeats.* Copyright 1903 . . 1950 by The Macmillan Company. Reprinted by permission also of the Macmillan Company Limited of Canada, and of Mrs. W. B. Yeats.

"The Tree of Knowledge" from *The Soft Side* by Henry James. Copyright © 1900 by Henry James. Reprinted by permission also of Paul R. Reynolds & Son, 599 Fifth Avenue, New York 17, N.Y.

Macmillan and Company, Ltd., for:
"Science and Culture" from *Science and Culture* by T. H. Huxley.

New Directions, for:
"The Seafarer," from *Personae* by Ezra Pound. Copyright 1926 by Ezra Pound. Reprinted by permission of New Directions.

"Fern Hill," "Do Not Go Gentle Into That Good Night," "Light Breaks Where No Sun Shines," "Poem In October," from *The Collected Poems of Dylan Thomas.* Copyright 1952, 1953 by Dylan Thomas. Reprinted by permission of New Directions.

"Old Garbo," from *Portrait of the Artist as a Young Dog* by Dylan Thomas. Copyright 1940 by New Directions. Reprinted by permission of New Directions.

Oxford University Press, Inc.:
The poems of Gerard Manley Hopkins are reprinted from *Poems* (1918) by permission of the Oxford University Press.
The letters of John Keats are reprinted from *The Letters of John Keats* edited by M. B. Forman, by permission of the Oxford University Press.

Princeton University Press, for:
"The Wanderer," from *Old English Elegies* translated by Charles F. Kennedy. Reprinted by permission of the Princeton University Press.

Random House, Inc., for:
"In Memory of W. B. Yeats" and "Musee des Beaux Arts." Copyright 1940 by W. H. Auden, from *The Collected Poetry of W. H. Auden*. Reprinted by permission of Random House, Inc.
"Doom is darker and deeper, etc." and "Epilogue." Copyright 1934 by The Modern Library, Inc. from *The Collected Poetry of W. H. Auden*. Reprinted by permission of Random House, Inc. The four poems by Auden under the titles "In Memory of W. B. Yeats," "Musee des Beaux Arts," "Something is Bound to Happen," and "Song XXV," from *Collected Shorter Poems 1930–1944* by W. H. Auden, are also published by Faber and Faber Ltd. and are reprinted with their permission.
"The Express" and "I think continually, etc." Copyright 1934 by The Modern Library, Inc. from *Collected Poems 1928–1953,* by Stephen Spender. Reprinted by permission of Random House, Inc. These two poems, from *Collected Poems* by Stephen Spender, are also published by Faber and Faber Ltd. and are reprinted with their permission.
"The Hound of Heaven" from *The Complete Poetical Works of Francis Thompson.*

Charles Scribner's Sons, for:
"Lucifer in Starlight" and "Love in the Valley" by George Meredith. Reprinted by courtesy also of Constable and Company, Ltd.

The Viking Press, Inc., for:
"The Nun's Priest's Tale," "The Pardoner's Prologue and Tale," "The Wife of Bath's Prologue and Tale," from *The Portable Chaucer,* selected and translated by Theodore Morrison. Copyright 1949 by Theodore Morrison. Reprinted by permission of the Viking Press, Inc., New York.
"A Little Cloud," from *The Portable James Joyce*. Copyright 1946, 1947 by The Viking Press, Inc. Reprinted by permission of the Viking Press, Inc., New York.
"The Rocking Horse Winner," from *The Portable D. H. Lawrence*. Copyright 1933 by the Estate of D. H. Lawrence, 1947 by The Viking Press, Inc. Reprinted by the Viking Press, Inc., New York.

Line drawings, unless otherwise credited, are taken from Garnett and Gosse, *An Illustrated History of English Literature,* Copyright, 1903, 1923, The Macmillan Company.

Preface

THIS IS A TEXTBOOK FOR THE FIRST COLLEGE COURSE IN ENGLISH LITERATURE, usually offered in the sophomore year. Although we feel it can be used successfully in courses of various types, it is best suited to the chronological survey. We are aware of the virtues of other kinds of courses, especially those that emphasize close reading and show the ways to approach imaginative literature. In fact we have emphasized these matters ourselves. But we have done so within the framework of the traditional survey, in the belief that students, particularly the nonspecialists, are entitled to experience something of the sweep, the richness, and the variety of English literature as it has developed over the years.

The book differs somewhat from other anthologies in its selections. To make a single volume of comfortable size we have omitted plays and longer prose fiction, which are available in cheap reprints. There are enough selections in the book for a year's course, however, and enough to allow a teacher considerable choice. We have represented the literature of the twentieth century rather generously; with the century's mid-point well passed, it has seemed necessary and desirable to do so. We feel, too, that the literature of our time is especially appealing to general students, or "non-English majors," who in the sophomore course often outnumber the prospective specialists. We have kept the general students in mind in other ways. Several prose writers of the early seventeenth century, interesting to advanced students, we have omitted entirely. We have reduced *Beowulf* somewhat by a careful cutting, and we have included a fresh and lively translation of *Sir Gawain and the Green Knight*. To allow students to enjoy Chaucer as a storyteller we have presented three stories from *The Canterbury Tales* in modern translation, but we have kept the General Prologue in the original Middle English. One can, however, go only so far in adapting to the needs and abilities of general readers. A student approaching English literature for the first time should make the acquaintance of those pieces which have been valued over the years. Some of this literature is admittedly difficult, some of it presents technical problems. Rather than dilute the content of the course to the point of weakness, we have chosen to include selections from most of the standard authors, even when they present difficulties, and we have provided extensive editorial aids to help the student meet those difficulties.

One of these aids is the rather extensive footnotes. Few people like footnotes, the beginning student perhaps least of all. But if his text has none, he must consult a reference shelf, he must wait to hear explanations in class that take valuable time and enlighten him *after* he has done his reading, or, as usually happens, he must read superficially or mistakenly. In an effort to provide him with what he needs when he needs it, and so to make his reading both intelligent and pleasurable, we have appended notes of various kinds: glosses, explanations of allusions and difficult points, paraphrases, and occasional questions that will urge him to read inquiringly.

Most of our questions, however, appear at the end of selections, in what we call "Study Aids." These are designed to encourage thoughtful reading and, we hope, rereading and reflection. In touching on such matters as substance, organization, language, and tone, we have tried to help the student discover what the work is in itself. But because we feel it is probably a mistake to neglect the personal reaction to a story or poem, we have included some questions that are frankly subjective. As the questions differ in content, so do they differ in difficulty. When they are hard, it is because the selection is hard. If a work is rich and complex, we feel that one does both students and literature a disservice to represent it as being otherwise. Instead of omitting the more difficult pieces or presenting them without comment, we have tried through the study aids to make them reasonably intelligible to the student. Some of the questions concern matters of technique. The casual reader, it is true, is often satisfied with the so-called content of a work, but for that very reason he needs to be shown that how a thing is said is a part of what is said. An appendix treating prosody and a glossary explaining the critical terms that appear (in small capitals) in the study aids should help the student answer the more technical questions and give him something of a critical vocabulary.

In providing these editorial aids we have no intention of trying to take the place of the teacher in the classroom, although in these days of mounting enrollments, larger classes, and harassed teachers such an aim might be welcomed. Rather, we have tried to enable the student to do more on his own, so that he will be better prepared when he comes to class. "Not enough time" is a common complaint of teachers in a survey course; we have tried to save time by helping the student read properly, thereby clearing the way for profitable class sessions.

Perhaps a word should be said about the editors' critical position. We believe that literature can profitably be read in several ways. For example, we recognize it as a revelation of the author's mind, and as a document in the social and intellectual history of its age. In a survey course, however, we prefer to emphasize it as an artistic expression of man's experience. Consequently, although we have not ignored biography and literary history, we have minimized them in the general introductions, the biographical sketches, and the headnotes to selections, as well as in the study aids. Critically we belong to no "school," except the school which insists that appreciation of literature can come only from understanding it, and that the first step toward this goal is a careful reading of the text. This book seeks to help students take the first step.

Many of the critical views and suggestions are our own. Some of them, however, have been expressed by those critics of recent years who have enriched our reading of literature. This debt will be apparent to most teachers, and we have not acknowledged it at specific places.

The problem of modernizing the texts of poems has been a difficult one. In general, we have tended to be conservative, but have kept in mind the needs of the student and have therefore cleared up some ambiguities silently, when to do so involved no appreciable violence to the meter. For example, we have followed the practice of certain modern editors in rendering Suckling's "Out upon't" as "Out upon it."

We hope, above all, that this will be a teachable text. It is based on many years of experience in teaching English literature to sophomores, and its approach, we are convinced, is a successful one. No doubt it can be improved, and to that end we sincerely invite criticisms and suggestions from teachers.

To the Student

THIS BOOK IS DESIGNED TO HELP YOU TO HELP YOURSELF IN YOUR STUDY OF ENGLISH literature. It does not seek to take the place of the teacher and the classroom session; no book can do that. Rather, it aims to provide you with the materials you need in order to study the selections intelligently. To use these materials profitably you should know what they are and how they can help you.

a. *Period Introductions.* Each of the five historical periods is preceded by a general essay. These essays sketch the political, social, and intellectual background against which the literature should be seen. From them you can get something of the "feel" of the major periods in English cultural history.

b. *Biographical Sketches.* These sketches give the salient facts in the life of an author, hints as to his personality and indications of his special significance in the history of English literature.

c. *Headnotes to Selections.* A headnote orients you to a work by indicating in broad terms its general nature.

d. *Footnotes.* The extensive footnotes are designed to explain difficult or unfamiliar matters. They include definitions of strange words, paraphrases of difficult passages, and also occasional questions to encourage you to read inquiringly. For the meanings of unfamiliar words not explained in the notes, you should consult your dictionary.

e. *Study Aids.* Probably the most important part of the editorial equipment is the study aids, in the form of questions, which follow many of the selections. These questions may not be raised in class, nor are they necessarily the only or even the most important questions relevant to the selections. What they will do is to urge you to think in significant ways about what you have read—a step often neglected in literary study. To work out answers to questions on metrics, you should refer to Appendix I, "On Prosody." Many questions include common, but possibly unfamiliar, critical terms. These are printed in small capitals, which means that they are defined in Appendix II, "A Glossary of Terms."

f. *Dates.* The date given at the end of each selection is the date of publication of the edition from which the work is taken—usually the first edition. Where two dates are given, the first is the date of composition, the second the date of publication.

Most of the literature in the book calls for intensive reading. Perhaps the best procedure is to read the headnote, then the selection itself, and then the study aids. The questions posed in the study aids probably will send you back for a second and third reading of the selection, or parts of it. It is this kind of intensive, purposeful reading that is required in literary study. Only by reading in this way can one approach understanding and full enjoyment of literature. Learn all you can from class meetings with your teacher, but take some of the responsibility yourself. You can do this if you will make full use of the editorial equipment.

The Editors.

Contents

Acknowledgments   iv
Preface   vii
To the Student   xi

The Old and Middle English Periods   1

Beowulf   7
The Seafarer   32
The Wanderer   33
Sir Gawain and the Green Knight   35

GEOFFREY CHAUCER   54

The Canterbury Tales   56

    The General Prologue   56
    The Nun's Priest's Tale   75
    The Prologue to the Pardoner's Tale   85
    The Pardoner's Tale   87
    The Prologue to the Wife of Bath's Tale   93
    The Wife of Bath's Tale   104

MIDDLE ENGLISH LYRICS   109

The Cuckoo Song   110
The Irish Dancer   110

Jesu, Swetë Sonë Derë 110
Alysoun 111
The Complaint of Chaucer to His Empty Purse 112
The Blacksmiths 112

FOLK BALLADS 113

The Twa Corbies 114
The Unquiet Grave 114
Sir Patrick Spens 115
The Demon Lover 116
The Wife at Usher's Well 117
Lord Randal 118
Get Up and Bar the Door 118

The Renaissance 121

SIR THOMAS MORE 127

From *Utopia*, The Second Book 127

SIR THOMAS WYATT 138

My Galley Chargèd with Forgetfulness 138
Divers Doth Use, As I Have Heard and Know 139
My Lute, Awake! 139
They Flee from Me 140

SIR PHILIP SIDNEY 141

Loving in Truth and Fain in Verse My Love to Show 141
With How Sad Steps, O Moon, Thou Climbest the Skies 142
Come, Sleep! O Sleep, the Certain Knot of Peace 143
Having This Day My Horse, My Hand, My Lance 143
From *The Defense of Poesy* 144

EDMUND SPENSER 152

Epithalamion 153
Prothalamion 159

MICHAEL DRAYTON 162

Ode XII: To the Cambro-Britons and Their Harp, His Ballad of Agincourt 162
Since There's No Help, Come, Let Us Kiss and Part 164

CHRISTOPHER MARLOWE 165

The Passionate Shepherd to His Love 165

SIR WALTER RALEIGH 166

The Nymph's Reply to the Shepherd 166
To His Son 167
Verses Found in His Bible in the Gate-House at Westminster .. 167

WILLIAM SHAKESPEARE 167

Sonnets 168

18.	Shall I compare thee to a summer's day?	169
23.	As an unperfect actor on the stage	169
25.	Let those who are in favor with their stars	169
29.	When, in disgrace with fortune and men's eyes	170
30.	When to the sessions of sweet silent thought	170
32.	If thou survive my well-contented day	170
33.	Full many a glorious morning have I seen	171
55.	Not marble, nor the gilded monuments	171
60.	Like as the waves make towards the pebbled shore	171
64.	When I have seen by Time's fell hand defaced	172
66.	Tired with all these, for restful death I cry	172
71.	No longer mourn for me when I am dead	172
73.	That time of year thou mayest in me behold	173
106.	When in the chronicle of wasted time	173
116.	Let me not to the marriage of true minds	173
129.	The expense of spirit in a waste of shame	174
130.	My mistress' eyes are nothing like the sun	174
146.	Pour soul, the center of my sinful earth	175

Songs 175

Winter 175
Who Is Silvia? 176
It Was a Lover and His Lass 176
O Mistress Mine, Where Are You Roaming? 176
Hark, Hark! The Lark at Heaven's Gate Sings 176
Fear No More the Heat o' the Sun 176

THOMAS CAMPION 177

My Sweetest Lesbia, Let Us Live and Love 177
Follow Your Saint, Follow with Accents Sweet 178
When Thou Must Home to Shades of Underground .. 178
Rose-cheeked Laura, Come 178

Jack and Joan 179
Young and Simple Though I Am 179
There Is a Garden in Her Face 180

FRANCIS BACON 180

Essays 181
Of Truth 181
Of Great Place 183
Of Studies 184
Of Marriage and Single Life 185

From *The Wisdom of the Ancients* 186
Preface 187
Tythonus, or Satiety 188
Daedalus, or Mechanical Skill 188
Sphinx, or Science 190

From *Novum Organum* 191
Discourse on Idols 191

THOMAS DEKKER 195

From *The Gull's Hornbook,* Chapter 6 195

JOHN DONNE 198

Song 199
The Indifferent 200
The Good-Morrow 201
The Canonization 202
Song 203
A Valediction Forbidding Mourning 204
The Holy Sonnets 205
   5. I am a little world made cunningly 205
 10. Death, be not proud, though some have callèd thee 205
 14. Batter my heart, three-personed God 206
Elegy IX 206
Hymn to God, My God, in My Sickness 207
From *Devotions upon Emergent Occasions* 208
Meditation 17 209

BEN JONSON 210

Queen and Huntress 211
Song: To Celia 211

Still to Be Neat   211
On My First Son   212
Epitaph on Elizabeth, L. H.   212
Song to Celia   212
To the Memory of My Beloved, the Author Mr. William Shakespeare   213
From Timber; or Discoveries   214

GEORGE HERBERT   222

The Collar   222
The Pulley   223
Denial   224
Love   224

RICHARD CRASHAW   225

In the Holy Nativity of Our Lord God   225

HENRY VAUGHAN   227

The Retreat   228
The World   228
I Walked the Other Day to Spend My Hour   230
The Book   231

ROBERT HERRICK   231

The Argument of His Book   232
When He Would Have His Verses Read   232
His Prayer to Ben Jonson   233
Cherry-Ripe   233
How Roses Came Red   233
How Violets Came Blue   234
Upon Julia's Clothes   234
To the Virgins to Make Much of Time   234
To Daffodils   235
Corinna's Going a-Maying   235
His Poetry His Pillar   237
The Hag   237
His Prayer for Absolution   238

SIR JOHN SUCKLING   238

Why So Pale and Wan, Fond Lover   238
O for Some Honest Lover's Ghost   239
'Tis Now, Since I Sat Down Before   239
Out upon It! I Have Loved   240

RICHARD LOVELACE 240

To Althea, from Prison 241
To Lucasta, Going to the Wars 241

ANDREW MARVELL 242

The Mower's Song 242
To His Coy Mistress 243
Bermudas 244
The Garden 245

JOHN MILTON 246

L'Allegro 248
Il Penseroso 250
Lycidas 252
Sonnets 256

How Soon Hath Time, the Subtle Thief of Youth 256
On the Late Massacre in Piedmont 257
When I Consider How My Light Is Spent 257

Paradise Lost 258

Book 1 259
Book 2 (ll. 1–889) 271
Book 9 (ll. 613–833, 853–1033, 1064–1189) 282
Book 12 (ll. 466–649) 290

From *Areopagitica* 293

The Restoration and Eighteenth Century 299

SAMUEL PEPYS 303

From *The Diary of Samuel Pepys* 304

JOHN DRYDEN 308

To My Honored Friend, Dr. Charleton 309
Prologue to "The Tempest" 311
A Song for Saint Cecilia's Day 312
Alexander's Feast; or, the Power of Music 313
From *Fables, Ancient and Modern* 316
Preface 316

DANIEL DEFOE 318

A True Relation of the Apparition of one Mrs. Veal 319
From *A Journal of the Plague Year* 324

JOSEPH ADDISON and RICHARD STEELE   332

  The Tatler   333

    181. [Recollections of Sorrow]   333
    249. [Adventures of a Shilling]   335

  The Spectator   337

      2. [The Spectator Club]   337
     10. [The Purpose of *The Spectator* Papers]   340
     18. [On Italian Opera]   343
    117. [On Witchcraft]   345
    267. [On *Paradise Lost*]   347
    323. [How Women Pass Their Time]   349

ALEXANDER POPE   352

  From *An Essay on Criticism*   353
  The Rape of the Lock   355
  Eloïsa to Abelard   368
  An Essay on Man, Epistle I   373

JONATHAN SWIFT   379

  Gulliver's Travels, Part 1   380
  A Modest Proposal   412

JAMES THOMSON   417

  From *The Seasons*   418
    Winter (ll. 1–321)   418

WILLIAM COLLINS   423

  Ode to Evening   423
  Ode Written in the Beginning of the Year 1746   424

THOMAS GRAY   425

  Elegy Written in a Country Churchyard   425
  The Bard   428
  Letters   431

    To Richard West   431
    To His Mother   432

SAMUEL JOHNSON   433

  The Rambler No. 4   434
  Letter to the Earl of Chesterfield   437

From *Preface to Shakespeare* 438
From *The Lives of the English Poets* 443

  Joseph Addison 443
  Alexander Pope 445

JAMES BOSWELL   447

From *The Life of Samuel Johnson* 448
  [Boswell's First Meeting with Johnson] 448
  [On Merit Set against Fortune] 454
  [Johnson's Peculiarities] 455
  [Johnson's Meeting with John Wilkes] 456
  [Johnson on Reading] 461
  [Johnson on Liberty] 462
  [Johnson's Death and Funeral] 463
From *The London Journal, 1762–1763* 465

OLIVER GOLDSMITH   471

The Citizen of the World 472
  Letter 11. [The Benefits of Luxury] 472
  Letter 21. [At the Play-house] 473
  Letter 54. [The Character of Beau Tibbs] 475
The Deserted Village 477

ROBERT BURNS   484

Epistle to J. Lapraik 485
To a Louse 488
The Cotter's Saturday Night 489
To a Mouse 493
Holy Willie's Prayer 494
Is There for Honest Poverty 495
O, Willie Brew'd a Peck o' Maut 496
Tam o' Shanter: A Tale 497
A Red, Red Rose 500
O, Wert Thou in the Cauld Blast 500

WILLIAM BLAKE   501

Song 502
Songs of Innocence 502
  The Lamb 502
  The Little Black Boy 503

Holy Thursday 503
The Divine Image 504

Songs of Experience 504
The Tiger 504
The Sick Rose 505
The Fly 505
A Poison Tree 505
London 506
The Chimney-Sweeper 506
Holy Thursday 506
The Clod and the Pebble 507
Infant Sorrow 507

Never Seek to Tell Thy Love 507

The Nineteenth Century 509

WILLIAM WORDSWORTH 520

Expostulation and Reply 521
The Tables Turned 522
Lines: Composed a Few Miles above Tintern Abbey 522
Strange Fits of Passion Have I Known 525
She Dwelt among the Untrodden Ways 526
I Traveled among Unknown Men 526
Three Years She Grew in Sun and Shower 526
A Slumber Did My Spirit Seal 527
Michael 527
From *The Prelude*, Book 1 534
Resolution and Independence 538
The Solitary Reaper 541
Ode: Intimations of Immortality 542
Sonnets 545

Composed upon Westminster Bridge 545
It Is a Beauteous Evening, Calm and Free 546
On the Extinction of the Venetian Republic 546
To Toussaint L'Ouverture 547
London, 1802 547
The World Is Too Much with Us 547
Nuns Fret Not at Their Convent's Narrow Room 548
Thoughts of a Briton on the Subjugation of Switzerland 548
After-Thought 549
Scorn Not the Sonnet 549

SAMUEL TAYLOR COLERIDGE   550

The Rime of the Ancient Mariner   551
Kubla Khan   569
Christabel   570
Dejection: An Ode   579
From *Biographia Literaria,* Chapter 14   582

CHARLES LAMB   586

From *Essays of Elia*   587
  A Bachelor's Complaint of the Behavior of Married People   587
  Old China   590

Letters   594
  To William Wordsworth   594
  To Mrs. William Wordsworth   595
  To Bernard Barton   596

WILLIAM HAZLITT   598

On Familiar Style   598
On Going a Journey   603

GEORGE GORDON, LORD BYRON   609

She Walks in Beauty   610
Childe Harold's Pilgrimage, Canto 3   611
Stanzas for Music   633
So We'll Go No More A-Roving   633
From *Don Juan,* Canto the First   634
On This Day I Complete My Thirty-sixth Year   657
Letters   658
  To His Mother   658
  To Miss Milbanke   660
  To Thomas Moore   661

PERCY BYSSHE SHELLEY   663

Hymn to Intellectual Beauty   665
Ozymandias   667
Stanzas Written in Dejection, near Naples   667
Song to the Men of England   668
Sonnet: England in 1819   669
Ode to the West Wind   669
The Cloud   671

To a Skylark 673
Adonais 675
Hymn of Apollo 685
To Night 686
To —— 687
To —— 687
Lines: When the Lamp Is Shattered 687

JOHN KEATS 688

The Eve of St. Agnes 689
La Belle Dame Sans Merci 696
Ode to a Nightingale 697
Ode on Melancholy 700
Ode on a Grecian Urn 701
To Autumn 702
Sonnets 703

On First Looking into Chapman's Homer 703
On the Grasshopper and the Cricket 704
On the Sea 704
When I Have Fears 705
How Fevered Is the Man 705
Bright Star, Would I Were Steadfast as Thou Art 705

Letters 706

To Benjamin Bailey 706
To John Hamilton Reynolds 707
To John Hamilton Reynolds 708
To George and Georgiana Keats 710

THOMAS CARLYLE 711

From *On Heroes, Hero-worship, and the Heroic in History* 712
The Hero as Divinity 712

From *Past and Present* 718
Gospel of Mammonism 719
Labor 722

THOMAS BABINGTON MACAULAY 724

From *Francis Bacon* 725

JOHN HENRY NEWMAN 736

From *The Idea of a University* 737
Knowledge Its Own End 737

ALFRED, LORD TENNYSON   748

The Poet   750
The Lady of Shalott   751
The Lotos-Eaters   753
St. Agnes' Eve   757
Morte d'Arthur   757
Ulysses   761
Tithonus   763
Locksley Hall   764
Break, Break, Break   770
Songs from "The Princess"   770

    The Splendor Falls on Castle Walls   770
    Tears, Idle Tears   770
    Now Sleeps the Crimson Petal   771
    Come Down, O Maid   771

  From *In Memoriam*   772
    Prologue, Sections 1, 3, 7, 19, 21, 27, 30, 34, 50, 54, 55, 56, 67, 70, 78, 95, 96, 106, 118, 124, 130, 131

The Eagle   780
Crossing the Bar   781

ROBERT BROWNING   781

My Last Duchess   783
Soliloquy of the Spanish Cloister   784
The Lost Leader   785
Meeting at Night   786
Parting at Morning   787
The Bishop Orders His Tomb at St. Praxed's Church   787
Love among the Ruins   789
"Childe Roland to the Dark Tower Came"   791
Fra Lippo Lippi   795
Andrea del Sarto   802
Prospice   806
Epilogue to Asolando   807

EDWARD FITZGERALD   808

From *The Rubáiyát of Omar Khayyám*   808

THOMAS HENRY HUXLEY   814

From *Science and Culture*   814

MATTHEW ARNOLD   823

Quiet Work   824
The Forsaken Merman   824
The Buried Life   826
To Marguerite   828
Philomela   828
The Scholar-Gypsy   829
The Progress of Poesy   834
Dover Beach   835
Rugby Chapel   836
From *Culture and Anarchy*   838
  Hebraism and Hellenism   838

From *Discourses in America*   846
  Literature and Science   846

DANTE GABRIEL ROSSETTI   858

The Blessed Damozel   858
My Sister's Sleep   861
Sister Helen   862
The House of Life   866

  The Sonnet   866
  71. The Choice—1   866
  72. The Choice—2   867
  73. The Choice—3   867
  78. Body's Beauty   867
  86. Lost Days   868
  97. A Superscription   868

GEORGE MEREDITH   868

Love in the Valley   869
Lucifer in Starlight   873

WILLIAM MORRIS   874

The Haystack in the Floods   875
The Defense of Guenevere   877

ALGERNON CHARLES SWINBURNE   883

From *Atalanta in Calydon*   884
  When the Hounds of Spring   884
  Before the Beginning of Years   885

Hymn to Proserpine 885
The Garden of Proserpine 888

FRANCIS THOMPSON 890
The Hound of Heaven 890

GERARD MANLEY HOPKINS 893
The Windhover 894
No Worst, There Is None 895
Spring and Fall: to a young child 895
Heaven-Haven 896
Felix Randal 896
Pied Beauty 897

The Twentieth Century 899

THOMAS HARDY 906
The Darkling Thrush 906
Drummer Hodge 907
The Man He Killed 908
Channel-Firing 908
The Convergence of the Twain 909
The Oxen 910

ALFRED EDWARD HOUSMAN 911
Loveliest of Trees 911
To an Athlete Dying Young 912
Is My Team Plowing? 912
Into My Heart an Air That Kills 913
With Rue My Heart Is Laden 913
Terence, This Is Stupid Stuff 913

HENRY JAMES 915
The Tree of Knowledge 916

JOSEPH CONRAD 925
Il Conde 926

WILLIAM BUTLER YEATS 935
The Lake Isle of Innisfree 936
The White Birds 936

When You Are Old   937
Never Give All the Heart   937
The Collar-Bone of a Hare   937
An Irish Airman Foresees His Death   937
The Second Coming   938
A Prayer for My Daughter   939
Leda and the Swan   940
Sailing to Byzantium   940

JAMES JOYCE   942
   A Little Cloud   943

VIRGINIA WOOLF   950
   Kew Gardens   951

KATHERINE MANSFIELD   955
   The Daughters of the Late Colonel   956

DAVID HERBERT LAWRENCE   967
   The Rocking-Horse Winner   968

THOMAS STEARNS ELIOT   977
   From *The Sacred Wood*   977
     Tradition and the Individual Talent   977
   The Love Song of J. Alfred Prufrock   982
   Sweeney among the Nightingales   985
   The Hollow Men   987
   Macavity: the Mystery Cat   989

ALDOUS HUXLEY   990
   From *Brave New World*   990
     Chapter 2   991
     Chapter 17   996

WYSTAN HUGH AUDEN   1000
   Song 25   1001
   Doom Is Dark and Deeper Than Any Sea-Dingle   1001
   Musée des Beaux Arts   1002
   In Memory of W. B. Yeats   1003

STEPHEN SPENDER 1004

I Think Continually of Those Who Were Truly Great 1005
The Express 1005

GEORGE ORWELL 1006

From *1984* 1006

    Chapter 1 1007
    Emmanuel Goldstein's Book, Chapter 1 1016

DYLAN THOMAS 1024

Light Breaks Where No Sun Shines 1025
Fern Hill 1025
Poem in October 1026
Do Not Go Gentle into That Good Night 1028
From *Portrait of the Artist as a Young Dog* 1028

    Old Garbo 1028

APPENDIX 1

On Prosody 1037

APPENDIX 2

A Glossary of Terms 1043

INDEX 1051

English Literature

The Old and Middle
English Periods

ABOUT TWO THOUSAND YEARS BEFORE THE BIRTH OF CHRIST
certain peoples in Central Europe, known as the Indo-Europeans,
began to migrate—for reasons unknown. Some went to Italy and
later became the Romans; others journeyed to Greece, to Russia,
even as far away as to India. One group trekked northwest and
settled in Germany and Scandinavia. In the third century A.D.
tribes from this Germanic group began to raid the coasts of Britain,
then a Roman colony, and by the close of the sixth century three
tribes—the Angles, the Saxons, and the Jutes—had taken possession
of England proper. Thus ended one major phase of the migration
westward of the Germanic branch of the Indo-European family,
and thus began the literature of England.

In the year 597 Pope Gregory sent Christian missionaries from
Rome to England. This was not the first time Christianity had
been introduced into Britain. In 55 B.C. Julius Caesar invaded
the British Isles, where he found a Celtic people; about one hundred years later Britain became a colony of Rome. The Romanized
Britons became Christians, and one of them, St. Patrick, carried
Christianity to Ireland. (Another, less historical, bravely resisted
the invading Angles, Saxons, and Jutes. This was the legendary
King Arthur.) In 410, however, the Emperor Honorius had
withdrawn the last of the Roman legions from Britain and had

1

left the country open to the sacking and eventual colonization by the pagan Germanic tribes.

This second introduction of Christianity, in the year 597, is in many ways the most important event in English literary history. Pope Gregory's missionaries were sent primarily, of course, to convert the heathen conquerors. But they also taught the heathens to write, to represent on parchment or vellum their native Germanic speech (Old English or Anglo-Saxon). Before 597 the Anglo-Saxons had only an oral literature, *lays* chanted to the accompaniment of a small wooden harp; shortly after 597 they began to produce a written literature also.

Their written literature was modeled on their oral. The *scop*, the royal poet, had composed his songs, usually narratives celebrating heroic deeds, in unrhymed rhythmical lines tied together internally by alliteration. When he came to write them down, he followed the same principles. A passage from the epic *Beowulf*, composed about the year 700, will illustrate both the principles on which the scop constructed his poetry and also the language in which he wrote:

> þa of wealle geseah   weard Scildinga,
> se þe holmclifu   healdan scolde,
> beran ofer bolcan   beorhte randas. . . .

[Then from the wall saw the guard of the Scildings, he who had to keep the sea-cliffs, (men) bearing over the gangplank bright shields. . . .]

The last line provides an excellent example of the way in which the words are tied together by alliteration, rather than by rhyme: *beran ofer bolcan   beorhte randas,* "*b*earing over the *b*alk [plank] *b*right shields."

[Inspection will also show something of the relationship between Old and Modern English: *beran* (bear) *ofer* (over) *bolcan* (balk) *beorhte* (bright) *randas* (obsolete; no Modern English equivalent). The relationship is analogous to that between the tiny airplane which the Wright brothers launched at Kitty Hawk, N.C., in 1903 and today's jet bombers; they hardly look alike, but one is, after all, the development of the other. Because Old English is simply an early stage of Modern English, scholars tend to prefer "Old English" for the language and "Anglo-Saxon" for the people. Interestingly, the Anglo-Saxons generally referred to their language as *Englisc* and their land as *Engla-land* (Angle-land).]

The scop, the bard or poet, held a high position in the Anglo-Saxon royal household. He was not simply an entertainer; he was also the historian, who held in his mind the tribe's past and celebrated the memorable deeds of the present:

At times one of the king's thanes [the scop], whose memory was full of songs, laden with vaunting rhymes, who knew old tales without number, invented a new story, a truthful tale; the man deftly narrated the adventures of Beowulf, and cunningly composed other skilful lays with interwoven words [*Beowulf,* Tinker translation].

The scop had indeed many stirring tales from the Germanic past of the Anglo-Saxon people to tell and retell in his songs. The continental Angles, Saxons, and Jutes had been a warlike people, brawny, fair-haired sea-rovers of the same stock as the Vikings. They had worshiped *Tiw*, the war-god; *Woden*, the wily father of the gods; *Thor*, the thunder-god; and they had brought these gods with them to England, as our *Tuesday,*

The Anglo-Irish Lindisfarne Gospels, from around A.D. 700

A page from the Lindisfarne Gospels.

Wednesday, and *Thursday* show. The scop in *Beowulf* sings the lay of Sigemund (father of the Siegfried of the *Nibelungenlied* and Wagner's opera), whose slaying of a dragon parallels Beowulf's slaying of the troll Grendel. Time and again the author of *Beowulf* reminds his hearers of historical events from their continental past—for example, the bloody Heathobard feud, which results in the burning of Heorot, the great hall of King Hrothgar, in which Beowulf fights Grendel.

By 597 the Germanic tribes had conquered nearly all of England—to the west were left the Celtic peoples in Wales and Ireland, to the north the wild Picts (whose name means "painted" because they painted themselves blue) and Celts who had fled there— and had settled down to a more peaceful way of living, predominantly agricultural, with hunting and fishing as additional ways of obtaining food. In due course they developed, for the time, a high civilization. But they were never for long at peace.

It would be impractical here to attempt to trace a path through the tangles of Anglo-Saxon political, religious, and social history. Instead, let us focus on the Anglo-Saxon ruler most significant to English literature, Alfred the Great. When Alfred came to the throne in 871, England was in danger of falling to another set of Germanic invaders called variously Danes or Vikings or Norsemen, who twenty years before had attacked with a fleet of 350 ships and had gradually occupied most of the eastern half of the country. It took Alfred seven years of desperate fighting to stop their advance. The Peace of Wedmore, which he and the Danish leader Guthrum signed in 878, did not dispel the Danes, but it did confine them within an area, the *Danelaw*. It also allowed Alfred to develop his own kingdom of Wessex, which from then on became the core of Anglo-Saxon England.

Alfred was a lover of learning, and it is for this reason especially that he is significant to English literature. He brought foreign scholars to England; he instituted the *Anglo-Saxon Chronicle,* the most important historical document of the period; above all, because there were no textbooks in English, he had important Latin works translated, and even translated some of them himself. When he died, in 901, he had done much to repair the damage wrought by the Danes.

A century later, however, England was again attacked by the Danes, who this time virtually overran the country. The extent to which England was Danish during the final years of the Anglo-Saxon era is obscured by the fact that linguistically and ethnologically invader and defender were very close. But from 1014 to 1039 England's kings were Danish, and the Danes also left their record on the land: better than fourteen hundred place-names in England are of Danish origin (e.g., *Derby* and *Rugby*). In 1066 the embattled little island finally fell to another group of invaders, the Normans under William the Conqueror, who brought the Old English period to a close. It would be naïve, of course, to think that Old English literature ceased overnight; there were entries made in the *Anglo-Saxon Chronicle* as late as 1154. By the year 1100, however, Old English literature had ceased to be produced, for all practical purposes.

Fire, war, and neglect have left us only a small portion of Old English literature. What has survived, however, shows that the literature was of a quality and a range unequaled elsewhere in Europe during the time, the so-called "Dark Ages." By common agreement, *Beowulf* is considered the earliest important poem in any of the Germanic languages. Although it is beyond doubt the most impressive work from the Old English period, it is not the only significant one. Some others are: *The Wanderer* and *The Seafarer,* meditative lyrics of high merit; *The Battle of Maldon* and *The Battle of Brunanburg*, stirring short heroic narratives (the second has been translated by Tennyson); *Widsith* and *Deor's Lament*, poems dealing with the life of the scop; *The Dream of the Rood*, an appealing religious poem in which the Cross tells its story. The list could be extended considerably, with reference to many works of poetry and also of prose. Even so, much more has probably been lost.

Most Old English literature is anonymous. It seems fitting to close this account with mention of two poets whose names we know. One of these is Cynewulf (pronounced "kin-uh-wolf"), whose signature, in runic letters arranged in acrostic fashion, is found in four poems. The other is Caedmon ("cad-mun").

We know of Caedmon only from Bede's account of him in his *Ecclesiastical History*, but this account has made him famous.

Caedmon was a poor, uneducated man living as a lay brother in a monastery. He knew nothing at all about poetry; when, at a feast, the harp was passed around for the monks to entertain each other, he would jump up from the table and run away. Then one night as he slept in the stable, it being his duty to care for the cattle, an angel appeared to him in a dream and said:

"Caedmon, sing me something."

"I know nothing to sing," Caedmon replied; "that is why I left the feast and came here."

The angel spoke again:

"Nevertheless, you *can* sing for me."

"What shall I sing?"

"Sing about the Creation."

Then Caedmon straightway began to sing.

From then on, according to Bede, Caedmon composed many poems. "None could equal him," he says, "because he received his gift from God."

Caedmon is often referred to as the first English poet. He is so, of course, only symbolically. But the divine origin claimed for his inspiration makes the symbolism especially attractive.

2

The effect of the Norman Conquest was, virtually, to put a stop to English literature for two centuries. After 1066 French was the language of the ruling class in England, and the bulk of the literature was naturally in French. The Normans seemingly made no attempt to suppress the use of English; indeed, William tried for a while to learn the tongue of his new subjects. But the fact was that literature was written primarily for the aristocracy, who looked upon themselves as French rather than as English. Gradually, however, the Normans lost their holdings on the Continent; then they began to think of themselves as Englishmen. By the fourteenth century English had become the literary language again.

This new English (Middle English) is much more like the language of today than is Old English. The opening lines of Chaucer's *The Canterbury Tales* (written probably between 1387 and 1392), except for one word, give the modern reader little difficulty:

Whan that Aprill with his shoures soote
The droghte of March hath perced to the roote. . . .
[When April with his showers sweet the drought of March hath pierced to the root. . . .]

The lines illustrate the composite nature of the vocabulary: the Normans contributed *Aprill, March,* and *perced;* the Vikings furnished *roote;* the remaining words are native English.

Not only was the language different—the literature written in it was different also. Old English literature is stark and stoical; battles very commonly are its subject matter; there is almost no mention of romantic love. In contrast, Middle English literature is lighthearted and gay; although battles do occur, they are the battles of chivalry, with love a strong element and laughter not far off. Love and humor, indeed, are two of the most prominent features of Middle English literature.

These differences must be attributed eventually to the Norman Conquest. Originally the Normans were Vikings of the same sort as those who invaded England during the latter days of the Anglo-Saxon era; the name *Norman* means "North-man." First raiding and then settling in Normandy on the coast of France in the ninth and tenth centuries, they adopted the French language and customs, and they married French wives. After the Conquest, they maintained estates both in England and France, and spent much time on the Continent. They were an admirable blend of the Germanic and the Gallic: an adaptable, versatile people, with much force and drive. Their ideas and their way of life, however, had little of the Germanic about them; the culture they brought with them to England was thoroughly French. When Geoffrey Chaucer, three centuries after the Conquest, began to seek literary models, he looked not to the North but to France and Italy. The Norman Conquest oriented England away from the Germanic North and toward the Gallic South. But the process was naturally a gradual one, and, further, exceedingly complex.

Among the factors which produced the differences between the Anglo-Saxon and the Anglo-Norman Englishman are these: the Norman Catholic Church, linked closely to Rome and pervading all aspects of life (in Middle English times, all Englishmen were Roman Catholics); the rise of Oxford and Cambridge as universities; the development of urban centers, especially London (Alfred's capital was Winchester); the practice of chivalry, a system of knighthood and also a code of conduct (well illustrated in *Sir Gawain and the Green Knight* [p. 35]).

Middle English literature can be divided into two periods, with 1300 as roughly the dividing line. Before 1300 the bulk of the literature was, as said previously, in French (and in Latin). But there was never a time when at least some writing was not done in English. Two outstanding works from this beginning period are Layamon's *Brut* and *The Owl and the Nightingale,* both written *ca.* 1200. The first of these contains the earliest account in English of King Arthur. It is an adaptation of an Anglo-French work, but it is English both in its language and in its manner of writing. Indeed, Layamon's style is very similar to that of *Beowulf* and other Old English poems, except for the addition of rhyme, a Norman contribution. *The Owl and the Nightingale,* on the other hand, is French through and through in spirit and treatment. It is a remarkably vituperative debate between two talking birds. For liveliness it is the outstanding work before Chaucer.

With the fourteenth century we come to a period of great individual writers, especially Geoffrey Chaucer, William Langland, and the anonymous author of *Sir Gawain and the Green Knight.* Each of these men deserves separate comment.

Chaucer is French in spirit, or, rather, that fusion of Norman and Saxon which is the new Englishman. His *Canterbury Tales,* unquestionably the greatest work in English before Shakespeare, has been nowhere better described than by John Dryden: "Some of his persons are vicious, and some virtuous; some are unlearned, or (as Chaucer called them) lewd, and some are learned. Even the ribaldry of the low characters is different: the Reeve, the Miller, and the Cook are several men, and distinguished from each other as much as the mincing Lady-Prioress and the broad-speaking, gap-toothed Wife of Bath. But enough of this; there is such a variety of game springing up before me that I am distracted in my choice, and know not which to follow. 'Tis sufficient to say, according to the proverb, that *here is God's plenty.*"

Chaucer was a voluminous, constantly experimenting writer. Next to *The Canterbury Tales*, his finest work is *Troilus and Criseyde*, a penetrating but sympathetic psychological study of love in wartime. In some respects the *Troilus* surpasses *The Canterbury Tales*; it is a more perfect but less varied work. It has many affinities with the modern novel, although, of course, it is written in verse, not prose. Chaucer also wrote many fine shorter works, few more delightful than his *Complaint to his Empty Purse* (p. 112). He was widely imitated in the following century.

William Langland, the reputed author of *Piers Plowman*, was seemingly a kind of wandering cleric or preacher. Nothing is known of him outside the manuscripts of his great allegorical satire, more properly entitled *The Vision of William concerning Piers the Plowman*. The poem exalts poverty and hard work, but it attacks vices wherever its author sees them. His tongue is a lash which spares none. This thorny work is written with such vividness that it ranks with *The Canterbury Tales* at least as a picture of fourteenth-century England. But it is a very different picture. Langland is the down-to-earth Englishman, scorning the graces which the Normans introduced. He writes in the old alliterative verse-form.

The anonymous author of *Sir Gawain and the Green Knight* (p. 35) is often called the Pearl Poet because of another poem by him, *The Pearl*. Like Langland, he employs the alliterative line, but he combines it with rhyme in an intricate stanzaic form. *Sir Gawain and the Green Knight* is a masterly example of the medieval genre known as the verse-romance, brilliantly constructed and written. Its vivid, colorful descriptive passages, which are almost unique in that they are never static but always move the action forward, are hardly equaled even by later writers. *Sir Gawain and the Green Knight* belongs to the cycle of stories which evolved, over centuries, around the character of King Arthur and which culminated, in the fifteenth century, in Sir Thomas Malory's *Morte d'Arthur*, Tennyson's principal source for the *Idylls of the King*, written nearly four hundred years later.

Except for Malory, the period 1400–1485 produced no great writers, possibly because of the Wars of the Roses, which kept the country in turmoil. The *Morte d'Arthur*, the most distinguished prose work before the Renaissance, was published by William Caxton, England's first printer, in 1485. It fittingly marks the end of the Middle English period. Its subject matter is medieval chivalry, by Malory's time dead, and its medium of presentation is the printing press, characteristic of the new age to come.

The Middle English period was a germinal one, in which many of the literary forms of later ages were developing. Two of these are the lyric and the drama, both of which were to be brought to perfection during the Elizabethan age.

The lyric, usually an expression of personal emotion, developed out of the song; and for some Middle English lyrics both words and music exist. An example is the delightful

Cuckoo Song (p. 110). The evolution from song to spoken poem was a natural one, and was completed within the period. The drama, however, has a much more complex history. Only its beginnings are to be found in the Middle English era.

The medieval English drama developed out of the liturgy of the Roman Catholic Church, especially the services for Easter and Christmas. Little playlets were introduced into the Mass; in due course, these playlets were elaborated upon and performed separately, often in the churchyards. Eventually they moved completely into secular hands, although their subject matter remained religious. These plays were called *miracle* or *mystery* plays, and they dealt with incidents from the Bible and the lives of the saints. In the fourteenth and fifteenth centuries they were performed by members of the craft guilds, not in theaters but on wagons in huge, out-of-door pageants. Acted by amateurs and characterized often by slapstick humor, they seem far removed from Shakespeare's *Hamlet* and other dramatic masterpieces of the sixteenth century—but the beginnings are there.

In contrast with later English literature, many of the writings of the Middle English period are imperfect; many ceased to be of literary interest with the age for which they were written. But the best—e.g., Chaucer, *Sir Gawain and the Green Knight*—despite changes in language and in customs, are among the imperishable products of the English poetic mind. Half a millennium later, they continue to delight and to instruct readers of English. Little more could be asked of the early years of the literature of any people.

Beowulf [1]

Beowulf, the earliest important literary work (eighth century) in any of the languages of northern Europe, reaches far back into the past of the Germanic peoples and at the same time marks the starting point of English literature. The setting of the poem is Denmark and southern Sweden, and the characters are people from those lands. But the poem is written in Old English, or Anglo-Saxon, and for an Anglo-Saxon audience. The poet, whose identity is unknown, has taken subject matter from the continental beginnings of his nation and fashioned it into a work designed both to entertain and to instruct the people of his own day.

Beowulf still performs these two functions. It entertains because it tells a dramatic tale of stirring adventure; it instructs because its characters behave in a manner which is psychologically true and because its hero exemplifies to the highest the ideals of his people.

The poem falls naturally into two parts. In Part 1 Beowulf rises to greatness by slaying two monsters who are ravaging a neighboring kingdom; in Part 2 he saves his own kingdom from the devastations of a dragon but in so doing dies. The narration of these two mythical events is done with vigor and dramatic effectiveness; yet it is the character of Beowulf himself which gives the work most of its impressiveness. Larger than life, gifted with phenomenal strength and courage, he is also gracious, gentle, and unselfish. He is no empty personification of virtues but a real and convincing hero whose mighty figure, in Professor Klaeber's words, "strides . . . through the epic."

Beowulf is usually called a folk epic, but the word *folk* is a misnomer. The poem is not a primitive work; it is simply in a different tradition from that of the great classical epics, e.g., *The Iliad* and *The Odyssey.* But it shares with these and other epics certain general features: (1) it is a long narrative poem, telling (2) of the heroic deeds (3) of a man of high station (4) who is of particular significance to his people.

---

[1] Although *Beowulf* is a poem, indeed a poem written with great conscious artistry, the editors have chosen to represent it by a prose translation because they feel that in an introductory course difficulties should be minimized when they can be without undue loss. Professor C. B. Tinker's lively translation is thoroughly in the spirit of the original.

The significance of Beowulf lies in his character, which exhibits the highest qualities of manhood: courage and daring and fortitude not separated from but coupled with mildness of manner and unselfishness of behavior. The true gentleman is the gentle *man*—this, in briefest form, is the meaning of Beowulf. Not without reason has he been compared to Christ.

Since the translation reprinted here is in prose, it should be emphasized that *Beowulf* is a poem. The distinctive elements of Old English versification have been discussed above on page two; the remarks made there are applicable to *Beowulf,* as well as to Old English poetry as a whole. *Beowulf,* however, is especially distinguished by its impressive rhythms and varied diction. The opening lines of the poem are as follows; we can imagine the scop striking his harp at appropriate points:

> Hwæt, we Gar-Dena   in geardagum,
> þeodcyninga   þrym gefrunon,
> hu ða æþelingas   ellen fremedon!
> Oft Scyld Scefing. . . .

PROLOGUE

[Of the Danish kings, they who were ancestors to Hrothgar, and of the passing of Scyld.]

Lo! we have learned of the glory of the kings who ruled the Spear-Danes [2] in the olden time, how those princes wrought mighty deeds. Oft did Scyld of the Sheaf wrest the mead-benches from bands of warriors, from 10 many a tribe. The hero bred awe in them from the time when first he was found helpless and outcast; for this he met with comfort, waxed great beneath the sky and throve in honors, until all the neighboring tribes be- 15 yond the ocean-paths were brought to serve him and pay him tribute. That was a good king! . . .

When at length the fated hour was come, Scyld, the valiant, departed unto the keeping 20 of the Lord. Then his dear companions bore him down to the ocean-flood, even as he himself had bidden them, while as yet the friend of the Scyldings ruled them with his words and long did reign over them, dear prince 25 of the land. There at the harbor stood a ship with curving prow, all icy, eager to be gone— meet for a prince. And in the ship's bosom,

hard by the mast, they laid that famous hero, their dear lord, the giver of treasure. Many treasures were there, abundance of ornaments brought from afar. Never have I heard men 5 tell of a ship more spendidly laden with battle-weapons and war-harness, with swords and coats of mail. Upon his breast lay many precious things which werc to go far out with him into the realm of the waters. Verily no fewer of their gifts and tribal treasures did this people bestow upon him than they who at his birth sent him forth alone over the wave, babe as he was. Moreover, they set up a golden banner, high above his head, and let 15 the sea bear him away, giving him over to the deep. Sad at heart were they, sorrowful in spirit. No man can truly say—no lord of hall, or hero under heaven—into whose hands that burden fell.[3]

PART 1. BEOWULF AND GRENDEL

1. [Of Hrothgar, son of Healfdene and king of the Scyldings, and how he built a fair mead-hall, which he named Heorot. How the merriment in the hall angered Grendel, an evil monster.]

. . . Then to Hrothgar was given success in battle, glory in warfare, so that his loyal

[2] These are the Danish people whom Beowulf saves in Part 1. They are now ruled by Hrothgar (pronounced "Roth-gar"), but the poem begins with an account of their earlier kings, notably Scyld (pronounced "Shild"), the founder of the house of Hrothgar. Only the part dealing with Scyld is given here.

[3] Ship burials were common, especially during the Viking period. Note the somber, mysterious, and almost tragic mood or ATMOSPHERE which the prologue sets. (For an account, illustrated by colored photographs, of the recently discovered Sutton-Hoo burial ship see *Life* for July 16, 1951.)

kinsmen gladly obeyed him, until the young warriors were grown, a mighty band. It came into his heart to command his men to build a hall, a mead-hall greater than any that the children of men had ever heard of, and therein to give gifts of all kinds to old and young, as God had prospered him, save the people's land and the lives of men.

And I heard men tell how the work of adorning the people's hall was allotted unto many a tribe, far and wide throughout this earth. After a season—quickly, as man's work prospereth—it came to pass that it was completed for him, this greatest of halls. And he fashioned for it the name of *Heorot*,[4] he whose word had power far and near. He broke not his promise, but gave out rings and treasure at the feast. High and pinnacled, the hall towered aloft. Yet it awaited the surging blaze of hostile fire; nor was it long thereafter that fatal hatred was destined to arise between father-in-law and son-in-law, after the deadly strife. . . .[5]

Thus the king's men lived, blissful and happy, until a certain one, a fiend of hell, began to plot mischief. This grim foe was called Grendel, a mighty stalker of the marches, who haunted the moors, the fens and fastnesses. The wretched being had long inhabited the abode of the monster kind, e'er since the Creator had condemned him. The Lord eternal wreaked vengeance upon the kindred of Cain, because of the murder— the slaying of Abel. He [6] got no pleasure in the feud, but for that wicked deed the Lord banished him far from mankind. From him there woke to life all evil broods—monsters and elves and sea-beasts, and giants too, who

long time strove with God. He gave them their reward.

2. [Grendel falls upon Heorot and slays thirty heroes. Hrothgar and his men are helpless before the monster, and the destruction is continued for twelve winters.]

As soon as night was come, he set out for the high-built hall, to see how the Ring-Danes were faring after the drinking of the mead. And he found therein a band of warrior-nobles sleeping after feast. They knew naught of sorrow, that wretched lot of all mankind. The creature of destruction, fierce and greedy, wild and furious, was ready straight. He seized thirty thanes upon their bed. Then back he returned to his abode, exulting in his booty, back to his lair with his fill of slaughter.

Then at dawn, with break of day, Grendel's deeds were manifest to men, and the voice of weeping was uplifted—a great cry at morn, after their feast. The great lord, the prince exceeding good, sat joyless, when they had looked upon the track of the monster, the accursèd foe; the mighty hero suffered, sorrowing for his thanes. Too great was that strife, too loathsome and lasting.

It was no longer than a single night ere he wrought more deeds of murder; he recked not of the feud and the crime—he was too fixed in them. Then, when the hatred of that thane of hell was fully known to them, truly told by tokens manifest, it was easy to find the man who sought him out a resting-place elsewhere more at large, a bed among the bowers of the hall. He kept himself thereafter further aloof and more secure, whosoever escaped the fiend.

Thus he held sway, and alone against them all fought accursedly, until that best of houses stood empty. Long was the time: for twelve winters the friend of the Scyldings [7] suffered distress, yea, every woe, uttermost sorrow. And so it became known to the children of men— sadly told in song—that Grendel had long been fighting against Hrothgar, and for many a season had waged a bitter war and wicked feud, an unending strife. He would not stay

---

[4] Pronounced "Hay-oh-rote." The word means hart or stag (a symbol of royalty). Heorot may also have been decorated with horns or antlers. The probable site of Heorot has been determined by modern scholars as on the north coast of Zealand, Denmark, a little southwest of Roskilde.

[5] Heorot was later burned; the reference to the fatal feud is historical. One difference between the modern reader and the Anglo-Saxon hearer is that the latter caught the many historical allusions in the poem. Note the somber, tragic ATMOSPHERE, fitting for a poem which is to deal with deeds of violence.

[6] Cain.

[7] Hrothgar.

the waste of life out of compassion toward any of the Danish race, compounding with them for tribute, and none of the wise men could look for a fair ransom from the destroyer's hands. The dread monster, like a dark shadow of death, kept pursuing warrior and youth; he trapped and ensnared them. Night after night he haunted the misty moors. Men know not whither hell's sorcerers wander in their rounds.

Thus the enemy of man, the terrible lone wanderer, oft wrought many a foul deed, much grievous affliction. In the dark of the night-tide he took up his abode in Heorot, the hall brightly adorned. . . . Hrothgar could not approach the throne, precious in the sight of God, nor did he know his love.

Mighty grief and heart-break was this for the kind lord of the Scyldings to bear. Many mighty men oft sat in council and deliberated together touching what it were best for great-hearted men to do against these sudden terrors. Sometimes they vowed sacrifices at their idol-fanes; the people prayed aloud that the Destroying Spirit [8] would aid them in the torment that had fallen upon them. Such was their custom, such their heathen faith; the thoughts of their heart were turned on hell; they knew not the Creator, Judge of deeds; they wist not of the Lord God; verily, they knew naught of the worship of the Ruler of heaven, the King of glory.

Woe unto him who through deadly hate is doomed to thrust his soul into the fiery abyss, to hope for no comfort, no change in anywise. But blessed is the man who at his death may go unto the Lord and find refuge in the Father's bosom. [9]

3. [In the far country of the Geats, Beowulf hears of Grendel's deeds, and resolves to go to the help of Hrothgar. He makes him ready a great ship and sails with his men to the country of the Danes. On landing he is accosted by the shore-guard.]

. . . A thane of Hygelac, [10] great among the Geats, heard of these deeds of Grendel in his native land. In his strength he was the best of men in the day of this life, noble and mighty. He bade make ready for him a goodly ship, saying that he would go over the ocean-road [11] unto that war-king, the great prince, since he had need of men. Little did his prudent thanes blame him for that journey, though he was dear to them; they encouraged him in his high purpose, and looked for good omens. The hero had warriors, chosen from among the Geats, the keenest he could find. Fifteen in all went down unto the ship. A skilled mariner pointed out the land-marks unto them.

Time wore on. The ship was upon the waves, the boat under the cliff. The ready warriors mounted the prow. The ocean-streams dashed the waves upon the beach. The men bore rich armor into the bosom of the ship, splendid war-harness. The warriors pushed off their tight-fitted craft on the willing adventure. So, driven by the wind, the bark most like unto a bird sped foamy-necked across the waves, until, about the same hour the second day, the curving prow had journeyed on so far that the sailors caught sight of land, saw gleaming cliffs and lofty hills, broad ocean-headlands. Thus the sea was crossed, and the voyage ended. . . .

The guard of the Scyldings, he who had been set to watch the headland, saw them from the cliff, bearing over the gangway their bright shields and ready weapons. His heart was spurred with longing to know who the men were. So the thane of Hrothgar went down to the shore, riding upon his horse. He shook his spear mightily with his hands, and asked in fitting words: "What warriors are ye, in coats of mail, who come hither, sailing

---

[8] Spirit of damnation, devil. The audience for whom the poem was written was Christian, but the poem, laid back in time, deals with near-pagan days. Hrothgar's people are depicted as Christian also; in desperation, however, they have regressed to the devil-worship of an earlier period.

[9] It is uncertain whether the author or a "monkish reviser" is responsible for the occasional passages of Christian moralizing which occur throughout the poem. The most widely held view is that the author wrote at least the majority of them.

[10] Beowulf, who is a Geat (pronounced "Gay-at"), a tribe ruled over by Hygelac ("Hee-yuh-lak").

[11] Expressions of this sort are characteristic of Old English poetry. They are a kind of METAPHOR called "kenning."

your great ship over the sea, the ocean-paths? I have been warden of the coast and have kept watch by the sea that no foe with force of ships might do harm in the Danish land. No shield-bearers have ever tried more openly to land here, nor did ye know at all the pass-word, the agreement of the warriors, our kins-men. Never have I seen a mightier hero upon earth, a mightier man in armor, than is one of you. He is no common thane decked out with weapons, unless his face, his matchless countenance, belie him.[12] But now I must know your lineage from you, ye false spies, ere ye go further in the land of the Danes. Now ye seafarers, strangers from afar, give ear to my plain counsel: it were best to make known forthwith whence ye are come."

4. [Beowulf makes answer touching the purpose of his coming, and is guided by the coast-warden to Heorot. . . .]

5. [Beowulf and his men come to Heorot. They are met by the herald, who tells their coming to King Hrothgar.]

The street was brightly set with stones; this path guided the band of men. The byrnie [13] gleamed, hard and hand-locked, the bright iron rings sang in the armor, as they came marching to the hall in battle-harness. Weary of the sea, they placed their shields, bucklers wondrous hard, against the wall of the house; they sat down upon the benches. Their byrnies rang, harness of heroes. Their ashen spears stood together, gray-shafted weapons of the seamen. This armored band was well adorned with weapons.

Then a proud warrior asked the heroes concerning their lineage: "Whence bring ye your plated shields, your gray war-shirts, and your visored helmets and this group of spears? I am Hrothgar's servant and herald. Never have I seen so great a band of strangers of more courageous mood. I think that ye have

sought out Hrothgar nowise as exiles, but from valor and out of the greatness of your hearts."

And the proud lord of the Weder people,[14] famed for his strength, answered him again; he spoke a word to him, bold under his hel-met: "We are table-companions of Hygelac. Beowulf is my name. I will tell my errand to . . . the great king thy lord, if he will grant us to draw nigh to him who is so good."

Wulfgar spoke (he was a chief of the Wendels, his boldness was known to many, his wisdom and might): "I will ask the friend of the Danes, king of the Scyldings, giver of rings, the mighty lord, touching thy jour-ney, as thou dost entreat, and will straightway make known to thee what answer the good king thinketh meet to give me."

And he went quickly to where Hrothgar was sitting, old and exceeding white-haired, with his company of thanes; the valiant man went until he stood before the face of the lord of the Danes—he knew the custom of the court. Wulfgar spoke to his friendly lord: "Hither are come across the sea-waves travel-ers, Geatish men from a far country. Warriors call their chieftain Beowulf. They beg to have speech with thee, my lord. Refuse not to converse with them, O gracious Hrothgar. In their equipment they seem worthy of the esteem of heroes, and verily the chief who led the warriors hither is a man of valor."

6. [Beowulf is graciously welcomed by the king, and thereupon tells how he will fight with Grendel.]

Then spoke Hrothgar, defense of the Scyld-ings: "I knew him when he was a child; his aged father was called Ecgtheow.[15] . . . His bold son is now come hither to a loyal friend. Moreover, seafarers, who carried thither rich gifts as good-will offerings to the Geats, have said that he, strong in battle, had in the grip of his hand the strength of thirty men.[16] Him holy God hath sent us, as I hope, to be a gracious help to the West-Danes against the

---

[12] This is an indirect characterization of Beowulf. How is it more effective than a direct statement by the author?

[13] Pronounced "burn-y." The byrnie was a corselet or linked coat of mail.

[14] Beowulf. The Geats were also called "Weders."

[15] Pronounced "Edge-thay-oh."

[16] Another example of indirect characterization.

terror of Grendel. I shall proffer the hero gifts for his boldness. Make haste and bid all the band of kinsmen come in together unto us. Say to them, moreover, that they are welcome among the Danish people."

Then Wulfgar came to the door of the hall and announced the word from within: "My victorious lord, prince of the East-Danes, bids me say that he knows your noble lineage, and that ye, as men of stout courage, are 10 welcome unto him hither over the billows of the sea. Now ye may go in unto Hrothgar in your war-array, under your helmets; but let your spears, shafts of slaughter, here await the issue of your words." 15

Then the mighty one arose with many a warrior round him—it was a noble group of thanes. Some remained and guarded the armor as the chief bade them. The heroes hastened, as the guide led them under the roof of 20 Heorot. The great-hearted man, bold under his helmet, went on until he stood within the hall. Beowulf spoke—on him gleamed his byrnie, his coat of mail linked by the smith's craft: "Hail to thee, Hrothgar! I am Hygelac's 25 kinsman and thane. Many an exploit have I undertaken in the days of my youth. In my native land I learned of Grendel's deeds; for seafarers say that this hall, this best of houses, stands empty and useless for all men, as soon 30 as evening light is hidden under the vault of heaven. And my people, even the best and wisest men among them, urged me, King Hrothgar, to come to thee, for they knew the strength of my might. They had themselves 35 beheld when I came from the fight, stained with the blood of my foes. There had I bound five of my enemies, destroyed a giant race, and slain by night the sea-beasts on the wave. . . . And now I alone will decide the fight 40 with Grendel, the giant monster. One boon I beg of thee. . . . Deny me not, thou shield of warriors, friend of the people, now I am come so far, that I alone, I and my band of thanes, this my brave company, may cleanse 45 Heorot of the evil that has come upon it. I have learned, too, that the monster in his rashness recks not of weapons. Therefore, that the heart of Hygelac my lord may be gladdened because of me, I scorn to carry sword or 50

broad shield, the yellow buckler, into the fight; but with my hands I will grapple the fiend and fight for life, foe against foe. He whom death taketh must rely upon the judgment of the Lord. . . . Thou shalt have no 5 need to bury my head if death take me, for he will have me, all red with gore; he will bear away the corpse to feast upon it; the lone wanderer will pitilessly eat it, staining his moor-haunts; thou needst not then take more 10 thought for the sustenance of my body. But send thou to Hygelac, if the fight take me, the matchless mail, best of armors, that guards my breast; it is . . . the work of Weland.[17] Wyrd [18] ever goeth her destined 15 course." [19]

7. [Hrothgar makes answer touching the deeds of Grendel. They feast in Heorot.]

Then spoke Hrothgar, defence of the Scyldings: . . . "Sorrowful am I in soul to tell to any man what shame and sudden mischief Grendel has wrought for me in Heorot out of his hateful thoughts. My hall-troop, my warrior-band, is melted away. Wyrd hath swept them away into the horrid clutch of Grendel. God alone can easily check the deeds of that mad foe. Full oft my warriors, after the drinking of the beer, have boastfully vowed [20] over their ale-cups to await with their dread swords the onset of Grendel in the hall. Then in the morning, when shone the day, this mead-hall,

[17] The blacksmith of Teutonic legend; roughly, the equivalent of Vulcan.
[18] Fate, destiny. It is uncertain whether the word *Wyrd* is to be taken as the name of a goddess (as in this translation) or simply as a term meaning "fate."
[19] Such speeches as Beowulf's are called "boasts." The Anglo-Saxon boast was a contract: This I shall do, or lose my life in trying. The boast was thus more a vow than what the word now suggests—a conceited thumping-of-the-chest. The function of the boast was seemingly psychological: in Anglo-Saxon days men *had* to take tremendous risks, to be physically brave, to be men in the fullest sense of the word. By proclaiming their intentions publicly they constructed a defense against weakness. If they failed to carry out their boasts, they either died honorably or lost face, admitting themselves to be cowards.
[20] The following lines show these are not boasts in the modern sense ("empty" boasts).

this lordly house, was all stained with blood, the benches reeking with gore—the hall was drenched in blood. So, the fewer loyal men, beloved warriors, had I then because of those whom death did snatch away. Sit now to the feast, and unseal to men as thy mind moveth thee, the thoughts of thy heart, and all thy confidence of victory."

Then in the mead-hall a bench was made ready for the Geatmen, one and all. Thither the stout-hearted men went to sit in the pride of their strength. A thane did service, who bore a chased ale-flagon in his hand, and poured out the bright mead. At times a bard sang, clear-voiced in Heorot. There was merriment among the heroes, no little company of Danes and Weders.

8 and 9. [Unferth, a thane of Hrothgar, grows jealous of Beowulf and taunts him, raking up old tales of a swimming-match with Breca. Beowulf is angered and boastfully tells the truth touching that adventure, and puts Unferth to silence. Queen Wealhtheow passes the cup. Hrothgar commends Heorot to the care of Beowulf.]

Unferth,[21] the son of Ecglaf, who sat at the feet of the lord of the Scyldings, spoke, and stirred up a quarrel; the coming of Beowulf, the brave seafarer, vexed him sore, for he would not that any other man under heaven should ever win more glories in this world than he himself. "Art thou that Beowulf who didst strive with Breca [22] on the broad sea and didst contend with him in swimming, when ye two, foolhardy, made trial of the waves and for a mad boast risked your lives in the deep water? None, friend or foe, could turn you from the sorry venture when ye two swam out upon the sea. But ye enfolded the ocean-streams with your arms, measured the sea-streets, buffeted the water with your hands, gliding over the deep. The ocean was tossing with waves, a winter's sea. Seven nights ye toiled in the power of the waters; and he overcame thee in the match, for he had the greater strength. Then at morning-tide the sea cast him up on the coast of the Heatho-ræmas, whence he, beloved of his people, went to his dear fatherland, the country of the Brondings, and his own fair city where he was lord of a stronghold, and of subjects and treasure. Verily the son of Beanstan [23] made good all his boast against thee. Wherefore, though thou hast ever been valiant in the rush of battle, I look to a grim fight, yea, and a worse issue, for thee, if thou darest for the space of one night abide near Grendel."

Beowulf, son of Ecgtheow, spoke: "Well! thou hast said a deal about Breca in thy drunkenness, Unferth my friend, and hast talked much of his adventure. The truth now I tell, that I had more sea strength, more battling with the waves, than any man else. We talked of this when boys, and boasted, being yet in the days of our youth, that we would venture our lives out at sea; and we performed it even so. Naked in our hands, we held our hard swords as we swam, purposing to defend us against the whales. He, nowise swifter on the flood, could not swim far from me through the waves, nor would I part from him. Thus we two were in the sea for the space of five nights, till the flood, the tossing waves, coldest of weathers, and darkening night drove us apart, and a fierce north wind beat down upon us;—rough were the waves. The wrath of the sea-fish was roused; then my shirt of mail, hard and hand-wrought, was of help to me against the foes; my woven armor, gold-adorned, lay upon my breast.[24] An evil monster dragged me to the

---

[21] Unferth is the royal spokesman. His name means "unpeace" or "mar-peace," and hence he is probably not historical. His father's name is pronounced "Edge-laf," which means "sword-remnant." In this passage Unferth is very unpleasant to Beowulf; later he suffers a change of heart and lends him his sword.

[22] There was an actual Breca, who was chief of the Brondingas; but the incident recounted here is of course mythical, and is comparable to the stories told about the two American folk heroes, Paul Bunyan and Mike Fink (who tried to jump across the Mississippi but, not quite halfway over, decided he could not make it and turned around in midair, landing where he started).

[23] Breca.

[24] The notion of a man in a shirt-of-mail swimming probably strains the modern reader's credulity more that it did the Anglo-Saxon's. Can you see a reason why this should be so?

bottom; the grim foe held me fast in its clutch; yet it was granted me to strike the creature with the point of my war-sword; the fierce struggle carried off the mighty sea-beast by my hand.

"Thus did the evil creatures often press me hard, but as was meet, I served them well with my war-sword; they had no joyous fill, by eating me, wicked destroyers, sitting round their feast nigh the bottom of the sea; but on the morrow, wounded by my sword, slain by the dagger, they lay up along the sea-strand so that they could nevermore hinder seafarers on their course in the deep channel.

"Light came from the east, the bright beacon of the Lord; the waves were stilled, and I could descry the sea-headlands, those wind-swept walls. Wyrd often saveth the warrior not doomed to die, if he be of good courage. Howbeit, it was granted me to slay nine sea-beasts with the sword. Never yet have I heard of a more desperate nightly struggle under the vault of heaven, nor of a man more sore beset in ocean-streams; yet I escaped with my life from the clutch of my foes, though spent with my adventure. The sea, the current of the flood, bore me on to the land of the Finns.

"Naught have I heard of like exploits on thy part, naught of the terror of thy sword. Breca never yet, nay, nor either of you, hath wrought so boldly in the play of battle with blood-stained swords—I boast not much of that—though thou wast the slayer of thine own brethren, thy next of kin; for that thou shalt be damned in hell, good though thy wit may be. I say to thee truly, thou son of Ecglaf, that Grendel, the fell monster, had never wrought against thy lord so many awful deeds, this shame in Heorot, were thy mind and heart so fierce in battle as thou thyself sayest. But he has found that he need not greatly fear the enmity, the dread attack, of thy people, the Victor-Scyldings.[25] He takes forced tribute from you; he spares none of the Danish people, but he preys at will upon you; he kills and feasts, and looks not for resistance from the Spear-Danes. I, however, will show him ere long the strength and courage of the Geats in fight. Thereafter let him who may, go proudly to the mead-drinking when the morning-light of another day, the sun in its radiance, shines from the south over the children of men."

Then rejoiced the giver of treasure, the gray-haired king, famous in battle; the prince of the Bright-Danes trusted in him for help; the shepherd of the people heard from Beowulf his firm resolve. And the laughter of the thanes arose; loud rang the din and joyous were their words.

Wealhtheow,[26] Hrothgar's queen, went forth, mindful of courtesies; in her gold array she greeted the men in the hall. The noble lady first gave the cup to him who guarded the land of the East-Danes; [27] she bade him, beloved of his people, be blithe at the beer-drinking. The victorious king partook in gladness of the feast and the hall-cup. Then the lady of the Helmings [28] moved about to old and young in every part of the hall, handing the costly cup, until the moment came when the diademed queen, noble of mind, bore the cup to Beowulf. She greeted the lord of the Geats, and thanked God, discreet in her words, that the desire of her heart was brought to pass, that she might put her trust in some hero for relief from all her affliction. That warrior, fierce in strife, received the cup from Wealhtheow; and then, eager for the fight, Beowulf, son of Ecgtheow, spoke and said: "I made this vow when I put to sea and embarked with my band of men; that I would either wholly fulfil the desire of your people, or fall in struggle, fast in the grip of the fiend. I will bravely accomplish noble deeds or abide mine end in this mead-hall." These words, these boastings of the Geat,[29] were well-pleasing to the lady; the noble queen, in her array of gold, went to sit by her lord.

[25] Another name for the Danes. Is it IRONY?

[26] Pronounced "Way-alk-thay-oh." The account of Wealhtheow is famous as one of the few pictures of woman in Anglo-Saxon literature. What qualities distinguish her? What is her principal role? How does she compare with modern woman?

[27] Hrothgar.

[28] Wealhtheow's family.

[29] Note that these are boastings only in the technical sense defined above in footnote 19 (p. 12).

Then again as of old the great word was spoken in that hall; joyous was the company —there was the sound of a mighty people— until of a sudden the son of Healfdene [30] was minded to go to his evening rest; for he knew that the monster intended war upon the high hall, as soon as men could no more see the light of the sun, and shadowy creatures came gliding forth, wan beneath the clouds, night darkening over all. The whole company arose. Hrothgar greeted Beowulf—hero greeted hero —and wished him well, wished him the mastery in the wine-hall, and spoke this word: "Never, since I could lift hand and shield, have I entrusted unto any man this royal hall of the Danes, save now to thee. Have thou and hold this best of houses; bethink thee of thy mighty deeds, show forth thy valiant strength, be watchful against the foe. Thy desires shall not be unsatisfied, if thou escape with thy life from the great adventure."

10. [They leave Beowulf and his men alone in the hall. Grendel draws nigh.]

And Hrothgar, lord of the Scyldings, went out of the hall with his company of men; for the warrior-chief was minded to go unto Wealhtheow, his queen and consort. The glorious king, as men have learned, had set a guardian in the hall to wait for Grendel; Beowulf did special service for the lord of the Danes, keeping watch against the coming of the monster. Verily, the chief of the Geats trusted surely in his mighty strength and in the favor of the Lord. Then he put off his iron byrnie and took the helmet from his head; his jeweled sword, choicest of weapons, he gave to his thane, bidding him take charge of his war-armor. Then, ere he mounted his bed, Beowulf, the great Geat, spoke a boastful word: "I deem myself nowise lesser than Grendel in my deeds of warfare; therefore, not with the sword will I quell him and take his life, though I am fully able. He knows not the use of good weapons—how to strike at me, and hew my shield—famed though he be in evil deeds; but we two this night will forego the sword if he dare come to the fight without a weapon. Thereafter let all-knowing God, the holy Lord, adjudge the victory to whichsoever it be, as seemeth meet to him."

Then the brave warrior laid him down and the pillow received the face of the hero, and round about him many a bold seaman sank down upon his bed. None of them thought ever again to reach the home he loved, his kinsfolk, or the town where he was bred; for they had heard that a bloody death had already destroyed far too many of the Danish men in that wine-hall. But the Lord wove victory for them, granting unto the Weder people comfort and help, inasmuch as they were all to overcome their foe by one man's might and by his single strength. And thus the truth is manifest that Almighty God hath ruled mankind throughout all time. . . .

11. [Grendel comes into Heorot and devours one of the men. Beowulf grapples the monster.]

Then from the moorland, beneath the misty hillsides, came Grendel drawing near; and God's wrath was on him. The deadly foe was thinking to ensnare some man in that high hall. On he strode beneath the clouds, until he could see full well the wine-hall, the gilded house of men, all bright with gold. This was not the first time that he had sought out Hrothgar's home, but never in all the days of his life, before or since, did he meet among hall-thanes, warriors more sturdy. So the creature, of all joys bereft, came roaming on unto the hall. The door, though fast in fire-hardened bands, sprang open straightway, soon as he touched it with his hands. Thus, plotting evil, he burst open the entrance to the hall, for he was swollen with rage. Quickly thereafter the fiend was treading the bright-paved floor, moving on in wrathful mood. Out of his eyes started a loathsome light, most like to flame. He saw in the hall many warriors, a kindred band together, a group of clansmen all asleep. And he laughed in his heart. The cursèd monster thought to take the life from each body, ere the day broke; for the hope of a plenteous feast was

[30] Hrothgar.

come to him. But he was not fated to devour any more of the race of men after that night.

The mighty kinsman of Hygelac was watching to see how the deadly foe would go about his swift attacks. The monster thought not of tarrying, but on a sudden, for his first move, he seized upon a sleeping thane, rent him in pieces unawares, bit into the flesh, drank the blood from the veins, and swallowed him in huge pieces. In a moment he had devoured the whole corpse, even the hands and feet. He stepped on nearer and seized with his hands the great-hearted warrior on his bed. The fiend clutched at him with his claw, but Beowulf quickly grasped it with deadly purpose, fastening upon the arm. Straightway that master of evils discovered that never in this world in all the corners of the earth, had he met in any man a mightier hand-grip. He was troubled in heart and soul; but he could get away never the faster for that. He was eager to be off; he wished to flee away into the darkness, to rejoin the horde of devils. He was not faring there as in former days.[31] Then the good kinsman of Hygelac bethought him of his speech at even; he stood up right and grappled him fast; his[32] fingers burst and bled. The giant was making off. The hero followed close. The monster was minded to fling loose, if he could, and flee away thence to the fen-hollows; but he knew that the strength of his arm was in the grasp of an angry foe. A dire journey had the destroyer made to Heorot.

Loud rang the lordly hall. All the Danes dwelling in that city, nobles and heroes every one, were struck with terror. Furious were both the maddened wrestlers. The house re-echoed. It was a great wonder that the wine-hall withstood these battling foemen, that the fair building fell not to the ground; save that all within and without it was so firmly strengthened by iron bands, cunningly forged. There, as I have heard men tell, many a mead-bench, gold-adorned, started from its base, where the fierce ones were struggling.

[31] This grim, almost "humorless" humor is characteristic of Old English literature. Its basis is UNDER-STATEMENT.

[32] Grendel's.

The wise councilors of the Scyldings had thought that none among men would ever be able to wreck by force this goodly house, bedecked with bones, nor to destroy it by craft, unless perchance the fire's embrace should swallow it in smoke.[33]

A noise arose, oft renewed; a ghastly terror fell on all the North-Danes who heard the shrieking in the house, heard God's enemy yelling out his horrid song, chant of the vanquished—Hell's captive howling o'er his wound. He held him fast who in his strength was the mightiest of men in the day of this life.

12. [Beowulf has the victory, and tears out Grendel's arm. The monster escapes to the fen with his death-wound.]

The defense of heroes would by no means let the murderer escape alive—he counted his life of no avail to any of the people. There many a warrior of Beowulf's drew his old sword; they thought to protect the life of their lord, the great prince, if so they might. They knew not, those brave warriors, when they plunged into the fight, thinking to hack the monster on every side and take his life, that not the choicest blade on earth nor battle-axe could graze that foul destroyer; for he had bound by a spell weapons of war and every edged sword. Yet he was doomed to die a wretched death in the day of this life; the outcast spirit must needs journey far away into the power of fiends. There found that foe to God, who oft ere now in mirthful mood had wrought mischief for the children of men, that his wound-proof body availed him not, for the valiant kinsman of Hygelac had got him by the hand. Hateful to each was the life of the other. The evil beast endured sore pain of body. Upon his shoulder a gaping wound appeared; the sinews sprang asunder, the flesh was rent apart. The glory of the fight was given to Beowulf. Grendel, sick to death, was doomed to flee thence and find out his joyless abode beneath the fen-banks. Full well he knew that the end of his life was come, the appointed number of his days. By that

[33] An example of FORESHADOWING.

deadly fight the desire of all the Danes was satisfied.

Thus he who came from far, wise and valiant in spirit, had cleansed Hrothgar's hall and freed it from danger. He rejoiced in the night's work, in his heroic deeds. The lord of the Geats had made good his boast to the East-Danes, for he had saved them out of all their affliction, the harrowing torment, no little sorrow, which they had suffered and were doomed to bear in sad necessity. A token of the fight was seen, when, beneath the spacious roof, the warrior flung down the hand and arm and shoulder—the whole limb and claw of Grendel.[34]

13. [The Danes rejoice. They go and look upon the mere whither Grendel escaped, and return to Heorot, racing their horses and listening to the tale of the bard.]

In the morning, as I have heard, many warriors were about the gift-hall; chieftains came from far and near to gaze upon the wonder, the traces of the foe. Grievous seemed his death to none of those who beheld the tracks of the inglorious one; how he, weary at heart, vanquished in strife, doomed and hunted, took his last steps to the Nicors'[35] mere. There the waters were seething with blood, the awful surge of the waves welled up, all mingled with blood and hot gore. Death-doomed he discolored all the flood, when, in his joyless lair, he laid down his life, his heathen soul; there Hell got him.

Thence returned the thanes and many a youth from their glad journey, proudly riding from the mere upon their horses, heroes upon white steeds. There was proclaimed the greatness of Beowulf. Full oft 'twas said that south or north, between the seas, o'er all the broad earth beneath the arch of heaven, none among shield-bearing warriors was of higher worth, none more worthy of kingdom. They did not in the least say aught against their own kind lord, gracious Hrothgar, for he was a good king.

At times the warriors made their yellow

[34] Note the dramatic effectiveness.
[35] Sea-demons.

steeds gallop or run a race, where the ways seemed good to them and known for their excellence.

At times one of the king's thanes, whose memory was full of songs, laden with vaunting rimes, who knew old tales without number, invented a new story, a truthful tale; the man deftly narrated the adventure of Beowulf, and cunningly composed other skilful lays with interwoven words. . . .

At times, in races with their steeds, they measured the yellow roads. And the morning-light was thrust forth and urged onwards. Many a stout-hearted warrior went to the high hall to see the great wonder. Likewise, the king himself, guardian of the treasure, famed for his virtues, walked forth in glory from the bower with a great company; and his queen with him, amidst a bevy of maidens, passed up the path to the mead-hall.

14. [Hrothgar and his men look upon Grendel's arm in Heorot. The king and Beowulf speak touching the fight. . . .]

15. [They adorn Heorot for the feast. Hrothgar bestows gifts upon Beowulf.]

Straightway it was bidden that Heorot be adorned within by the hand of man. Many men there were and women to prepare that hall of feasting and of guests. Along the walls shone hangings wrought with gold, many wondrous sights for all who gaze upon such things. That bright house had been greatly shattered, though all within was fast with iron bands. The hinges had been torn away. The roof alone was saved unhurt, when the monster, stained with wicked deeds, despairing of life, turned him to flight.

Death is not easily escaped, try it who will; but every living soul among the children of men dwelling upon the earth goeth of necessity unto his destined place, where the body, fast in its narrow bed, sleepeth after feast.

Now the time was come for the son of Healfdene to go into the hall; the king himself was minded to partake of the feast. Never have I heard that that people in greater company gathered more bravely about their king. Then those happy men sat them down upon the benches; they rejoiced in the feasting. Their great-hearted kinsmen, Hrothgar and Hrothulf,[36] with fair courtesy quaffed many a bowl of mead in the high hall. Heorot was filled with friends. In that day the Scylding people had done no deeds of guile.

Then the son of Healfdene gave to Beowulf, in reward of victory, a golden ensign, a broidered banner, a helmet, and a byrnie; many men saw a mighty treasure-sword borne to the hero. Beowulf quaffed the cup in the hall. He needed not to be ashamed before warriors of those sumptuous gifts. Few have I heard of at the ale-bench who gave to others in more friendly wise four treasures, gold-adorned. About the crown of the helmet there was a wreath all wrought with wires, which protected the head, so that the tempered sword could not greatly injure it, when the shielded warrior went out against his foe.

Moreover, the defense of heroes bade that eight horses with golden bridles be led into the hall under the barriers. Upon one of them there was a saddle, cunningly wrought, adorned with jewels;—it had been the battle-seat of the high king, when the son of Healfdene was minded to take part in the play of swords,[37] the might of the far-famed hero failed never at the front, while the slain were falling. And then the prince of the Ingwines gave over to Beowulf the possession of these, both the horses and the armor; bade him enjoy them well. Thus, like a true man, did the great lord, the guardian of treasure and heroes, repay the storm of the fight with horses and treasure, so that none can dispraise them, none who wills to speak the truth aright.

16 and 17. [Hrothgar bestows gifts upon Beowulf's men. The bard sings the lay of King Finn. . . .]

18. [The queen giveth gifts to Beowulf, and a fair collar which King Hygelac wore in aftertime. They feast, and the heroes rest in Heorot.]

The hall resounded. Wealhtheow spoke before the host and said: "Receive with joy this collar, dear Beowulf, beloved youth, and use this armor—treasures of our people—and prosper well; show thyself strong; and be kind in thy counsel to these youths.[38] I will be mindful of thy reward. Thou hast brought it to pass that men shall give thee honor evermore, in all the earth, far as the sea encompasseth its wind-swept walls. Be, while thou livest, a prosperous prince; much treasure truly I wish thee. Be thou friendly to my son, guarding his happy state. Here is each hero true to the other, gentle of spirit, and loyal to his lord; the thanes are obedient, the people ready at call. Ye warriors, cheered with wine, do as I bid ye."

Then she went to her seat. There was the choicest of feasts; the men drank wine. They knew not Wyrd, cruel destiny, as it had gone forth of old unto many a hero.

When even was come, and Hrothgar, the ruler, had departed to his lodge unto his evening rest, countless heroes guarded the house as they had oft of yore. They made bare the bench and spread upon it beds and pillows. Doomed and nigh unto death, one of the revelers laid him down to rest in the hall. At their heads they placed their battle-shields, bright bucklers. There upon the bench above each hero were clearly to be seen the towering helm, the ringèd coat of mail, the mighty spear. It was their wont to be ever ready for battle, whether at home or in the field, ready for either, even at the moment when their chief had need of them. That was a good people.

19. [Grendel's mother cometh to avenge her son. She seizes Æschere in Heorot.]

Then they sank to sleep. But one paid dearly for his evening rest, as had often happened when Grendel haunted that gold-hall and wrought evil till his end came, death for his sins. It now became evident to men that, though the foe was dead, there yet lived for a long time after the fierce combat, an avenger—Grendel's mother. The witch, wom-

---

[36] Hrothgar's nephew.
[37] A "kenning" for battle (cf. p. 10, fn. 11).

[38] Wealhtheow's sons.

an-monster, brooded over her woes . . . [and] determined to go a sad journey to avenge the death of her son; and she came to Heorot, where the Ring-Danes lay asleep about the hall. . . . She was in haste, for 5 she was discovered; she wished to get thence with her life. Of a sudden she clutched one of the heroes, and was off to the fen. The mighty warrior, the famed hero whom the hag murdered in his sleep, was the dearest to 10 Hrothgar of all the men in his band of comrades between the seas.[39] Beowulf was not there; for another lodging-place had been assigned to the mighty Geat after the giving of treasure. A cry arose in Heorot. All in its gore 15 she had taken the famous arm;[40] sorrow was renewed in the dwellings. . . .

20. [Hrothgar lamenteth for Æschere. He tells Beowulf of the monster and her haunt.] 20

Hrothgar, defense of the Scyldings, spoke: "Ask not after bliss,—sorrow in hall is renewed for the Danish folk. Æschere is dead, Yrmenlaf's [41] elder brother, my councilor and my 25 adviser, who stood by me, shoulder to shoulder, when we warded our heads in battle, while hosts rushed together and helmets crashed. Like Æschere should every noble be—an excellent hero. He was slain in 30 Heorot by a restless destroyer.

"I know not whither the awful monster, exulting in her prey, has turned her homeward steps, rejoicing in her fill. She has avenged the strife in which thou slewest 35 Grendel yesternight, grappling fiercely with him, for that he too long had wasted and destroyed my people. He fell in the fight, forfeiting his life, and now another is come, a mighty and a deadly foe, thinking to avenge 40 her son. She has carried the feud further; wherefore it may well seem a heavy woe to many a thane who grieveth in spirit for his treasure-giver. Low lies the hand which did satisfy all your desires. 45

"I have heard the people dwelling in my land, hall-rulers, say that they had often seen two such mighty stalkers of the marches, spirits of otherwhere, haunting the moors. One of them, as they could know full well, was like unto a woman; the other miscreated being, in the image of man, wandered in exile (save that he was larger than any man), whom in the olden time the people named Grendel. They knew not if he ever had a father among the spirits of darkness. They dwell in a hidden land amid wolf-haunted slopes and savage fen-paths, the wind-swept cliffs where the mountain-stream falleth, shrouded in the mists of the headlands, its flood flowing underground. It is not far thence in measure of miles that the mere lieth. Over it hang groves in hoary whiteness; a forest with fixed roots bendeth over the waters. There in the night-tide is a dread wonder seen—a fire on the flood. There is none of the children of men so wise that he knoweth the depths thereof. Although hard pressed by hounds, the heath-ranging stag, with mighty horns, may seek out that forest, driven from afar, yet sooner will he yield up life and breath upon the bank than hide his head within its waters. Cheerless is the place. Thence the surge riseth, wan to the clouds, when the winds stir up foul weather, till the air thicken and the heavens weep.

"Now once again help rests with thee alone. Thou knowest not yet the spot, the savage place where thou mayst find the sinful creature. Seek it out, if thou dare. I will reward thee, as I did before, with olden treasures and with twisted gold, if thou get thence alive."

21. [They track Grendel's mother to the mere. Beowulf slayeth a sea-monster.]

Then spoke Beowulf, son of Ecgtheow: "Sorrow not, thou wise man. It is better for a man to avenge his friend than mourn exceedingly. Each of us must abide the end of the worldly life, wherefore let him who may, win glory ere he die; thus shall it be best for a warrior when life is past. Arise, O guardian of the kingdom, let us straightway go and 50 look upon the tracks of Grendel's dam. I

---

[39] He is the Æschere ("Ash-hay-ruh") of the next section.
[40] Grendel's.
[41] Pronounced "Ear-men-laf."

promise thee this: she shall not escape to the covert, neither into the bosom of the earth, nor to mountain-wood, nor to the bottom of the sea, go where she will. This day do thou bear in patience every woe of thine, as I expect of thee."

Then the old man leapt up and thanked God, the mighty Lord, for what that man had said. And they bridled Hrothgar's horse, a steed with curling mane. The wise prince rode stately forth, and with him fared a troop of shielded warriors. Footprints were clearly seen along the forest-path, her track across the land. She had gone forth, over the murky moor, and borne away lifeless that best of thanes, who with Hrothgar ruled the hall.

And the offspring of princes went over steep and rocky slopes and narrow ways, straight lonely passes, an unknown course; over sheer cliffs and many a sea-beast's haunt. He, with a few prudent men, went on before to view the spot, until he suddenly came upon mountain-trees o'erhanging the gray rock—a cheerless wood. Beneath it lay a water, bloody and troubled. All the Danes, all the friends of the Scyldings, each hero and many a thane, sad at heart then suffered sore distress; for there upon the sea-cliff they found the head of Æschere. The waters were seething with blood and hot gore—the people gazed.

At times the horn sang out an eager lay. All the troop sat down. They saw in the water many of the serpent kind, strange dragons swimming the deep. Likewise they saw sea-monsters lying along the headland-slopes, serpents and wild beasts, such as oft at morning-tide make a journey, fraught with sorrow, over the sail-road. They sped away, bitter and swollen with wrath, when they heard the sound, the song of the battle-horn. But the lord of the Geats with bow and arrow took the life of one of them, as it buffeted the waves, so that the hard shaft pierced the vitals; he was then the slower in swimming the sea, for death seized him. Straightway he was hard pressed with the sharp barbs of hookèd spears, fiercely attacked, and drawn up on the cliff, a wondrous wave-tosser. The men looked on the strange and grisly beast. Then Beowulf girded him with noble ar-

mor; he took no thought for his life. His byrnie, handwoven, broad, and of many colors, was to search out the deeps. This armor could well protect his body so that the grip of the foe could not harm his breast, nor the clutch of the angry beast do aught against his life. Moreover, the white helmet guarded his head, even that which was to plunge into the depths of the mere, passing through the tumult of the waters; it was all decked with gold, encircled with noble chains, as the weapon-smith wrought it in days of yore; wondrously he made it, and set it about with boar-figures so that no brand nor battle-sword could bite it.

Nor was that the least of his mighty aids which Hrothgar's spokesman [42] lent him in his need—the name of the hilted sword was Hrunting, and it was one of the greatest among olden treasures; its blade was of iron, stained with poison-twigs, hardened with blood of battle; it had never failed any man whose hand had wielded it in fight, any who durst go on perilous adventures to the field of battle—it was not the first time that it had need to do high deeds. Surely when the son of Ecglaf, strong in his might, lent that weapon to a better swordsman, he did not remember what he had said when drunk with wine; as for him, he durst not risk his life beneath the warring waves and do a hero's deeds; there he lost the glory, the fame of valor. It was not so with the other when he had armed him for the fight.

22. [Beowulf bids farewell to Hrothgar and plunges into the mere. The monster seizes upon him. They fight.]

Then spoke Beowulf, son of Ecgtheow: "Remember, thou great son of Healfdene, wise chieftain, gracious friend of men, now that I am ready for this exploit, what we two spoke of aforetime; that, if I must needs lose my life for thee, thou wouldst ever be as a father to me when I was gone hence. Guard thou my thanes, my own comrades, if the fight take me, and do thou also send unto Hygelac the treasures that thou gavest me, beloved Hroth-

---

[42] Unferth, who has undergone a change of heart.

gar. Then, when the son of Hrethel, lord of the Geats, shall look upon that treasure, he may behold and see by the gold that I found a bountiful benefactor, and enjoyed these gifts while I might. And do thou let Unferth, that far-famed man, have the old heirloom, the wondrous wavy sword of tempered blade. I will win glory with Hrunting, or death shall take me."

After these words the lord of the Weder-Geats boldly made haste; he would await no answer, but the surging waters swallowed up the warrior. It was the space of a day ere he got sight of the bottom.

Soon the blood-thirsty creature, she who had lived for a hundred seasons, grim and greedy, in the waters' flow, found that one was there from above seeking out the abode of monsters. She seized upon the warrior and clutched him with her horrid claws; nevertheless she did no harm to his sound body, for the ringèd armor girt him round about, so that she could not pierce the byrnie, the linkèd coat of mail, with her hateful fingers. Then the mere-wolf, when she came to the bottom, bore the ring-prince to her dwelling, so that he could nowise wield his weapons, brave though he was; for many monsters came at him, many a sea-beast with awful tusks broke his battle-sark—the evil creatures pressed him hard.

Then the hero saw that he was in some dreadful hall, where the water could not harm him a whit; the swift clutch of the current could not touch him, because of the roofed hall. He saw a fire-light, a gleaming flame brightly shining. Then the hero got sight of the mighty mere-woman—the she-wolf of the deep. He made at her fiercely with his war-sword. His hand did not refuse the blow, so that the ringèd blade sang out a greedy war-song on her head. But the stranger found that the gleaming sword would make no wound, nor harm her life; so the blade failed the prince at need. It had aforetime endured many a hard fight, had often cleft the helmet and the byrnie of the doomed; this was the first time that the precious treasure ever failed of its glory. Yet the kinsman of Hygelac, heedful of great deeds, was steadfast

of purpose, not faltering in courage. Then the angry warrior threw from him the carved sword, strong and steel-edged, studded with jewels, and it lay upon the ground. He trusted to his strength, to the mighty grip of his hand. So must a brave man do when he thinketh to win lasting praise in war—he taketh no thought for his life.

Then the lord of the War-Geats, shrinking not from the fight, seized Grendel's mother by the shoulder, and full of wrath, the valiant in battle threw his deadly foe so that she fell to the floor. Speedily she paid him his reward again with fierce grapplings and clutched at him, and being wearied, he stumbled and fell, he, the champion, strongest of warriors. Then she leapt and sat upon him, and drew her dagger, broad and brown-edged, to avenge her son, her only offspring. But on his shoulder lay his woven coat of mail; it saved his life, barring the entrance against point and blade. Then the son of Ecgtheow, chief of the Geats, would have perished beneath the sea-bottom, had not his byrnie, his hard war-shirt aided him, and Holy God, the wise Lord, brought victory to pass, the King of heaven easily adjudging it aright. Thereafter he stood up again.

23. [Beowulf lays hold upon a giant sword and slays the evil beast. He finds Grendel's dead body and cuts off the head, and swims up to his thanes upon the shore. They go back to Heorot.]

Then he saw among the armor a victorious blade, an old sword of the giant-age, keen-edged, the glory of warriors; it was the choicest of weapons—save that it was larger than any other man was able to carry into battle—good, and splendidly wrought, for it was the work of the giants. And the warrior of the Scyldings seized the belted hilt; savage and angry, he drew forth the ring-sword, and, hopeless of life, smote so fiercely that the hard sword caught her by the neck, breaking the ring-bones; the blade drove right through her doomed body, and she sank upon the floor. The sword was bloody; the hero exulted in his deed.

The flame burst forth; light filled the place,

even as when the candle of heaven is shining brightly from the sky. He gazed about the place and turned him to the wall; the thane of Hygelac, angry and resolute, lifted the great weapon by the hilt. The blade was not worthless to the warrior, for he wished to repay Grendel straightway for the many attacks which he had made upon the West-Danes—oftener far than once—what time he slew Hrothgar's hearth-companions in their slumber and devoured fifteen of the sleeping Danes and carried off as many more, a horrid prey. The fierce warrior had given him his reward, so that he now saw Grendel lying lifeless in his resting-place, spent with his fight, so deadly had the combat been for him in Heorot. The body bounded far when it suffered a blow after death, a mighty sword-stroke. And thus he smote off the head.

Soon the prudent men who were watching the mere with Hrothgar saw that the surging waves were all troubled, and the water mingled with blood. The old men, white-haired, talked together of the hero, how they thought that the prince would never come again to their great lord, exultant in victory; for many believed that the sea-wolf had rent him in pieces.

Then came the ninth hour of the day. The bold Scyldings left the cliff, the bounteous friend of men departed to his home. But the strangers sat there, sick at heart, and gazed upon the mere; they longed but did not ever think to see their own dear lord again.[43]

Meanwhile the sword, that war-blade, being drenched with blood, began to waste away in icicles of steel; it melted wondrously like ice when the Father looseneth the frost, unwindeth the ropes that bind the waves; he who ruleth the times and seasons, he is a God of righteousness. The lord of the Weder-Geats took no treasure from that hall, although he saw much there, none save the head, and the hilt bright with gold; the blade had melted, the graven sword had burned away, so hot had been the blood, so venomous the strange spirit that had perished there.

[43] Note the dramatic effectiveness with which the Anglo-Saxon ideal of loyalty of retainer to lord is portrayed.

Soon he was swimming off, he who had survived the onset of his foes; he plunged up through the water. The surging waves were cleansed, the wide expanse where that strange spirit had laid down her life and the fleeting days of this world.

And the defense of seamen came to land, stoutly swimming; he rejoiced in his sea-spoil, the great burden that he bore with him. And his valiant band of thanes went unto him, giving thanks to God; they rejoiced in their chief, for that they could see him safe and sound. Then they quickly loosed helm and byrnie from the valiant man. The mere grew calm, but the water beneath the clouds was stained with the gore of battle.

They set forth along the foot-path glad at heart; the men, kingly bold, measured the earth-ways, the well-known roads. They bore away the head from the sea-cliff—a hard task for all those men, great-hearted as they were; four of them must needs bear with toil that head of Grendel upon a spear to the gold-hall. And forthwith the fourteen Geats, bold and warlike, came to the hall, and their brave lord in their midst trod the meadows. And the chief of the thanes, the valiant man crowned with glory, the warrior brave in battle went in to greet Hrothgar. And Grendel's head was borne by the hair into the hall where the men were drinking—a terror alike to heroes and to queen. The people gazed upon that wondrous sight.

24 and 25. [Beowulf tells of his fight, and Hrothgar discourses. They feast in Heorot. In the morning the Geats make ready to depart. . . .]

26. [Beowulf bids farewell to Hrothgar and the aged king weeps at his departure. He giveth him many treasures. The Geats go down to the sea. . . .]

27. [Beowulf presents to the coast-warden a golden sword. The Geats return unto their land. They bear the treasures to the hall where dwells King Hygelac with his queen, Hygd. . . .]

28, 29, and 30. [Beowulf is received by Hygelac, and telleth of his meeting with Grendel.]

Then the brave chief went forth over the sands with his companions, treading the sea-beach, the wide-stretching shores. The candle of the world was shining, the sun in its course beaming from the south. They went their ways; boldly betook them to where, as they had heard, the young and gracious war-king, shelter of heroes, slayer of Ongentheow, was giving out rings within his city. Speedily Beowulf's coming was announced to Hygelac, how that the shelter of warriors, his shield-comrade, was come back alive to the hall, come back to the court, safe from combat. Straightway the hall within was made ready for the travelers, even as the ruler bade.

Then he who had scaped from the strife sat by the king himself, kinsman by kinsman, after his lord with courtly speech had greeted the loyal hero with mighty words. And Hær-eth's daughter passed about the hall, pouring out the mead; for she loved the people; she bore the mead-cup to the hands of the heroes.

Then Hygelac began to question his companions full fairly in the lofty hall, for he was spurred with longing to know touching the adventures of the Sea-Geats: "How fared ye in your journeying, dear Beowulf, when thou on a sudden didst resolve to seek combat far away over the salt waters, battle in Heorot? Didst thou in aught lessen the well-known woe of Hrothgar, the mighty lord? I have nourished brooding care and sorrow in my heart, for I put no trust in the journey of my belovèd thane. Long did I entreat thee not to attack the deadly beast, but let the South-Danes themselves put an end to their strife with Grendel. I give thanks unto God that I am suffered to see thee safe."

Beowulf, son of Ecgtheow, spoke: "Known unto many, my lord Hygelac, is the famous meeting 'twixt Grendel and me, and our fighting there on the field where he had wrought much sorrow for the Victor-Scyldings and misery evermore. All that I avenged, so that none of Grendel's kin on earth need boast of that fray at twilight, not even he of the loathèd race who shall live the longest in the midst of the moorland. . . ."

31. [Beowulf maketh an end of his story, and giveth Hygelac all the gifts which he had of Hrothgar. Hygelac rewardeth him again.]

"So the king of that people lived in seemly wise. I lost not my reward, the meed of valor, for the son of Healfdene gave me gifts to use at mine own will, which I will bring and gladly offer thee, O hero-king. Every good thing comes from thee, and I have few bloodkinsmen saving thee, O Hyge-lac."

And he bade them bring in the boar head-crest, the helm towering in battle, the gray byrnie, and the splendid war-sword, and thereupon he uttered these words: "Hroth-gar, the wise prince, gave me this battle-ar-mor, bidding me with express words to give thee first his kindly greeting; and he said that King Heorogar, lord of the Scyldings, long possessed it, nevertheless he would not give the breast-mail to his own son, bold Heoroward, gracious though he was to him. Do thou enjoy it well."

I have learned that four dappled horses, all alike, followed upon the gift of the armor; graciously he presented unto him the horses and the treasures. So should a kinsman do, and nowise weave a cunning snare for his fellow, and plot the death of his comrade with secret craft. Full loyal was that nephew to Hygelac, the battle-strong; each took thought for the other's joy.

I have heard that he gave to Hygd the neck-lace, the wondrous jewel curiously wrought, which Wealhtheow, a king's daughter, had given him, and three horses therewith, slender and brightly saddled. Thereafter was her breast adorned, even from the time when she received the circlet.

Thus the son of Ecgtheow behaved him-self in glorious wise, he who was famed for his warfare and for his gracious deeds; full honorably he lived, nor did he slay his hearth-companions when they were drunken; his heart was not cruel, but the brave warrior with the greatest care of all mankind held fast the bounteous gift which God had given him. . . .

Then the king, the defense of heroes, strong in battle, bade them bring in the heirloom of Hrethel,[44] all decked with gold,—there was no dearer sword among the treasures of the Geats. He laid it in Beowulf's lap; and he gave to him seven thousand pieces of money, and a hall and a princely seat. The twain, by right of birth, held land in the nation, a home and its rights, but Hygelac had the broad kingdom, and therein he was the greater man.

PART 2. BEOWULF AND THE DRAGON

31. (Continued) [How Beowulf became king and reigned for fifty years, and how a great Dragon, who watched over a vast treasure-hoard, wasted his land.]

Thereafter in later days by reason of the crash of battle it fell . . . that the broad kingdom came into the hand of Beowulf. He ruled it well for fifty winters . . . until a certain dragon began to hold sway on dark nights and work his will, one who on a high mound kept watch over a treasure-hoard in a steep and rocky cave. Beneath it lay a path, unknown to men.

But a certain slave entered there and eagerly took from the heathen hoard; he seized with his hand a cup, bright with gold. Nor did he give it back, albeit he had beguiled the keeper of the hoard with thievish craft. The king, best of heroes, learned of that deed, and he was filled with wrath.[45]

32. [Of the hoard in the mound and how the Dragon came by it. The wrath of the Dragon.]

. . . Many olden treasures were lying in that cave of earth where a certain man in days of yore had hidden away the dear possessions, taking thought for the great bequest of his noble kin. Death had snatched away those men in times gone by. . . .

Then the beauteous hoard, standing all open, had been found by the old twilight foe,

the naked venomous dragon, he who, wrapped in flames, haunteth the mounds, and flies by night begirt with fire; of him the dwellers in the land are sore afraid. It is his wont to find out some hoard in the earth, where, old in winters, he may guard the heathen gold— but naught the better will he fare for that.

Thus for three hundred winters the scourge of the people had held the vast treasure-cave within the earth, until a certain man [46] angered him in his heart, and bore away the plated beaker. . . .

Soon as the dragon woke, strife was begun; fierce at heart he sniffed along the rock, and found out the tracks of his foe, for with secret craft he had gone on too far, hard by the dragon's head. So the man not doomed to die easily escapeth woe and banishment, even he whom the grace of the Lord upholdeth. The keeper of the hoard sought eagerly along the ground, he wished to find the man who had wrought him this mischief in his sleep. Wroth and hot-hearted, he circled oft about the mound without—but there was none upon the waste. Yet he rejoiced in the thought of battle, in warfare to come. At times he would turn back to the mound and seek his precious cup. Soon he was ware that some one of menfolk had found out the gold, his splendid treasure.

Impatiently the keeper of the hoard waited till even was come; the guardian of the mound was mad with wrath; the foe wished to repay them with fire and burning for the loss of his dear cup. And the day departed, even as the dragon wished. No longer, then, would he abide in his den, but went forth flaming, all girdled with fire. Fearful was the beginning for the men of that land, even as the end was bitter, which straight thereafter fell upon their gracious lord.

33. [The Dragon burneth Beowulf's hall, and the old king maketh ready to go out against him.]

. . . And forthwith the terror was made known to Beowulf, how for a truth his own home, best of halls, the gift-seat of the Geats, had melted away in waves of fire. The good

[44] Pronounced "Ray-thel." Hrethel was father of Hygelac and maternal grandfather of Beowulf.
[45] It was the function of dragons to guard treasures. Hence, when the slave steals the cup, the dragon must perforce retaliate. This Beowulf knows.

[46] The slave.

man suffered pain at heart, most grievous sorrow; the wise hero thought that, sinning against the ancient laws, he had provoked to anger the Almighty, the Lord eternal; his breast within him surged with dark thoughts, as was not his wont.

The fire-dragon with his burning coals had utterly destroyed the fortress, stronghold of the people, the water-washed fastness. Therefore the war-king, chief of the Weders, devised revenge upon him. Then the defense of warriors, lord of heroes, bade them make him a wondrous battle-shield, all of iron; for he knew full well that a shield of linden wood from the forest could avail him naught against the flame. But the valiant prince was doomed to meet the end of his fleeting days, of this worldly life, and the dragon too, though he had long held the hoarded treasure.

But the ring-prince scorned to seek out the wide-flying pest with a host of men, a great army; he had no fear of the combat for himself, nor did he esteem at all the dragon's war-might, his strength and prowess; forasmuch as aforetime, though in narrow straits, he had come safe through many a contest, many a battle-crash, since the time when, crowned with victory, he cleansed Hrothgar's hall, and closed in fight with Grendel's kin of loathèd race. . . .

34. [Beowulf goes forth. He tells of his early years and of the death of Herebeald and Hæthcyn, and how Hygelac was king.]

Thus the son of Ecgtheow had come safe through his every conflict, every perilous fight and brave adventure, even unto that great day in which he was to give battle to the dragon. Then the lord of the Geats, being filled with wrath, went forth with eleven companions to look upon the serpent. He had learned how the feud arose, and all the mischief to his men, for he had received the goodly treasure-cup from the hand of him who found it. . . .

Then the king, strong in battle, the bounteous lord of the Geats, sat him down upon the headland, while he bade farewell to his hearth-companions. His spirit was full of sorrow, wavering and ready to depart; Wyrd was upon him, she who was to come unto that aged man, to seek out the treasure of his soul and put asunder body and life; no long time was it now that the prince's soul was to be wrapped in flesh. Beowulf, son of Ecgtheow, spoke: "In my youth I passed through many a battle-onset, many an hour of strife; I remember all. I was seven winters old when the treasure-prince, dear lord of the people, received me at my father's hand; King Hrethel had me and held me as his own; he gave me of his treasure and his food, remembering our kinship. Never, while a thane in his hall, was I a whit less dear to him than any of his sons, Herebeald, Hæthcyn, or Hygelac my lord.". . .

35. [Beowulf ends his discourse, and bids farewell to his thanes. He shouts aloud, and the Dragon comes forth. The fight begins. It goes hard with Beowulf.]

Beowulf spoke; for the last time he uttered boastful words: "In the days of my youth I ventured on many battles; and even now will I, aged guardian of my people, go into fight and do memorable deeds, if the great destroyer come forth to me out of his den." Then for the last time he greeted each of the men, bold helmet-wearers, his own dear companions. "I would not bear a sword or any weapon against the serpent, if I knew how else I could make good my boast against the monster, as I did of old against Grendel. But I look for hot battle-fire there, for the venomous blast of his nostrils; therefore I have upon me shield and byrnie. I will not flee one foot's breadth from the keeper of that mound, but it shall be with us twain at the wall as Wyrd, lord of every man, allotteth. I am eager in spirit, so that I forbear boasting against the wingèd warrior. But do ye men tarry upon the mound with your armor upon you, clad in your byrnies, to see which of us twain after the strife shall survive the deadly woundings. It is no exploit for you, nor for the might of any man, save mine alone, to measure strength with the monster and do a hero's deeds. I will boldly win the gold, or else battle, yea an evil death, shall take away your lord."

Then the mighty warrior rose up with his shield, stern under his helmet; he bore his battle-mail beneath the stony cliffs. He trusted [5] in his single strength. That is no coward's way. And he beheld hard by the wall—he of noble worth, who had passed through many wars and clashing battles when armed hosts close in fight—where stood an arch of stone [10] and a stream breaking out thence from the mound; the surge of the stream was hot with fire. The hero could not anywhile endure unburned the hollow nigh the hoard, because of the dragon's flame. [15]

Then the lord of the Geats, for he was wroth, sent forth a word from his breast. The stout-hearted warrior stormed; his voice, battle-clear, entered in and rang under the hoary rock. The keeper of the hoard knew the [20] speech of men, and his hate was stirred. No further chance was there for peace. First came forth out of the rock the breath of the evil beast, the hot reek of battle. The earth resounded. The hero beneath the mound, [25] lord of the Geats, swung up his shield against the awful foe, and the heart of the coiled monster waxed eager for the strife. Already the good warrior-king had drawn his sword, that olden heirloom, undulled of edge. Either [30] destroyer struck awe in the other. But stout-hearted stood that prince of friends against his tall shield, while the dragon coiled himself quickly together; the armed man waited.

Then the flaming dragon, curving like a [35] bow, advanced upon him, hastening to his fate. A shorter time the shield warded the life and body of the mighty king than his hopes had looked for, if haply he were to prevail in the combat at that time, early in [40] the day; but Wyrd did not thus allot. The lord of the Geats lifted his hand and smote the hideous-gleaming foe with his weighty sword, in such wise that the brown blade weakened as it fell upon the bone, and bit less deeply [45] than its lord had need, when sore beset. Then, at the sword-stroke, the keeper of the mound raged furiously. He cast forth devouring fire. Far and wide shot deadly flame. The lord of the Geats nowise boasted of victory, for his [50] naked war-sword, that good blade, weakened in the fight, as was not meet. It was no easy course for the mighty son of Ecgtheow to forsake this earth for ever; yet he was doomed against his will to take up his abode in a dwelling otherwhere. So every man must quit these fleeting days.

It was not long ere the fighters closed again. The keeper of the hoard plucked up his courage; his breast heaved anew with his venomous breathing. He who erewhile ruled the people was hard put to it, being compassed with fire. In nowise did his own companions, sons of heroes, surround him in a band with warlike valor, but they took refuge in the wood to save their lives. There was but one among them whose heart surged with sorrows. Naught can ever put aside the bond of kinship in him who thinketh aright.

36. [Wiglaf, a young thane of Beowulf's, upbraids his fellows and goes to the help of the old king. Beowulf's sword is shattered in the fight, and he gets a deadly wound.]

He was called Wiglaf.[47] . . . He saw his lord suffering the heat under his helmet; and he was minded of all the benefits which Beowulf had given him in time past, the rich dwelling-place of the Wægmundings,[48] and every folk-right which his father possessed. And he could not forbear, but seized the shield, the yellow linden, with his hand, and drew forth his old sword. . . .

Wiglaf spoke many fitting words, saying to his companions—for his soul was sad within him:—"I remember the time when, as we drank the mead in hall, we promised our lord, him who gave us these rings, that we would repay him for the war-harness, for helmet and hard sword, if need like this befell him. Of his own will he chose us from his host for this adventure, urged us to do gloriously, and gave me these treasures, since he deemed us good spearmen, keen helm-bearers; albeit our lord, defender of his people, had thought to do this mighty work alone, for that he of all men hath performed

---

[47] Pronounced "Wee-laf."
[48] Beowulf's family.

most of famed exploits and daring deeds. Now the day is come when our lord needs the might of good warriors. Let us on to his help, whilst the heat is upon him, and the grim terror of fire.

"God knows of me that I would much rather that the flame enwrap my body with my king's. Methinks it unseemly that we should bear our shields back to our home, unless we can first strike down the foe and defend the life of the Weders' king. Full well I know that it is not according to his old deserts that he alone of all the Geatish force should suffer pain and sink in fight. We twain will have one sword and one helmet, one shield and one byrnie in common."

Then with his war-helmet he sped through the noisome smoke, to the aid of his lord; he spoke a few words: "Belovèd Beowulf, now do thou all things well, as thou of old sworest in the days of thy youth that thou wouldst not let thy glory wane while thou didst live. Now, O stedfast hero, famed for thy deeds, do thou defend thy life with all thy might. Lo, I will help thee."

After these words, the dragon, awful monster, flashing with blazing flames, came on all wroth a second time to meet his hated foes. Wiglaf's shield was burned away to the boss in the waves of fire; the byrnie could give no help to the young spear-warrior. But the youth went quickly under his kinsman's shield, since his own had been burned to ashes by the flames. Then again the war-king took thought for his glory; mightily he smote with his battle-sword driving fiercely so that it stood in the dragon's head. Nægling [49] was shivered in pieces; Beowulf's sword, old and gray-marked, weakened in the fight—it was not granted that the iron blade should help him in the strife. Too strong was the hand, as I have heard, which by its blow o'ertaxed all swords whatsoever; so that he fared none the better for it, when he bore into the fight a weapon wondrous hard.

Then the destroyer of people, the dread fire-dragon, for the third time was mindful

[49] The naming of prized swords was common (and also the breaking of swords in battle, because of the great strength of their wielders).

of the feud. He rushed on the brave hero, when ground was yielded him. Hot and fierce, he seized upon Beowulf's whole neck with his sharp teeth. He was all wetted with his life-blood; the gore welled forth in streams.

37. [They slay the Dragon. The king is nigh unto death.]

Then I have heard men tell how, in the king's great need, Wiglaf, the hero, showed forth unceasing courage, skill and valor, as was his nature; he heeded not the dragon's head (though the hero's hand was burned as he helped his kinsman), but the armed man smote the evil beast a little lower down, insomuch that the bright and plated sword drove into him, and the fire began to wane forthwith. Then the king recovered himself; he drew the short-sword, keen and sharp in battle, which he wore on his byrnie. The defense of the Weders cut the serpent asunder in the middle. They struck down the foe: their might drove forth his life, and thus they twain, noble kinsmen, destroyed him. Even such should a man be, a thane good at need. That was the king's last hour of victory by his own great deeds, the last of his worldly work.

But the wound which the earth-dragon had given him began to burn and swell; presently he found that poison, deadly venom, was surging in his breast. Then the prince, still wise in mind, moved along so that he might seat him by the mound; he saw that work of giants, saw how the rocky arches standing firm on their pillars, upheld within the earth-hall everlasting. Then the thane, surpassing good, taking water, with his hands bathed the great king, his own dear lord, all gory and wearied with battle, and loosed his helm.

Beowulf spoke and uttered words, despite his wound, his piteous battle-hurt; full well he knew that his life of earthly joy was spent, that the appointed number of his days was run, and death exceeding near: "Now would I give my armor to my son, had I been granted any heir, born of my body, to come after me. Fifty winters have I ruled this people; yet there was never a king of all the neighbor tribes who durst attack me with the sword or threaten me with evil. In my home I awaited what the times held in store for me, kept well mine own, sought out no wily quarrels, swore not many a false oath. In all this I can rejoice, though death-sick with my wounds, inasmuch as the Ruler of men cannot charge me with murder of kinsmen, when my life parteth from my body. Now do thou, dear Wiglaf, lightly go and view the hoard under the gray rock, now the dragon lieth low, sleepeth sore wounded, bereft of his treasure. Do thou make haste that I may behold the olden treasures, that store of gold, and gladly gaze upon those bright and curious gems; and thus, having seen the treasured wealth, I may the easier quit life and the kingdom which long I have ruled."

38. [Beowulf beholdeth the treasure, and passeth.]

And I have heard how the son of Weohstan,[50] after these words, quickly obeyed his wounded lord, sick from the battle; he bore his ringèd mail-shirt, the woven battle-sark, under the roof of the cave. And the brave thane, exultant victor, as he went by the seat, saw many precious jewels, much glistering gold lying upon the ground and wondrous treasures on the wall, and the den of the dragon, the old twilight-flier; bowls lay there, vessels of bygone men, with none to brighten them, their adornments fallen away. There was many a helmet old and rusty, many an arm-ring cunningly twisted. Treasure of gold found in the earth can easily puff with pride the heart of any man, hide it who will. Likewise he saw a banner all of gold standing there, high above the hoard, greatest of wonders, woven by skill of hand; from it there shone a ray of light, so that he could see the cavern floor, and examine the fair jewels. Naught was to be seen of the dragon there, for the sword had undone him. . . .

The messenger [51] was in haste, eager to return, urged by thought of his spoil. The great-hearted man was spurred with longing

to know whether he would find alive the lord of the Weders, grievously sick, in the place where he had left him. And bringing the treasures, he found the great prince, his lord, bleeding, at the point of death; he began to sprinkle him again with water until the word's point broke through the treasure of his heart, and Beowulf spoke, aged and sorrowful, as he gazed upon the gold: "I utter thanks unto the Ruler of all, King of Glory, everlasting Lord, for these fair things, which here I look upon, inasmuch as ere my death-day I have been able to win them for my people. I have sold and paid mine aged life for the treasure-hoard. Fulfil ye now the needs of the people. Here can I be no more. Bid the brave warriors rear a splendid mound at the seacape after my body is burned. There on Whale's Ness [52] shall it tower high as a memorial for my people, so that seafarers, they who drive from far their great ships over the misty floods, may in aftertime call it 'Beowulf's Mound.' "

The great-hearted king took from his neck the ring of gold; gave to his thane, the youthful warrior, his helmet gold-adorned, his ring and his byrnie, bade him enjoy them well.

"Thou art the latest left of all our kin, the Wægmundings. Wyrd hath swept away all my kinsmen, heroes in their might, to the appointed doom. I must after them."

That was the old king's last word from the thoughts of his heart, ere he yielded to the bale-fire and the hotly surging flames. His soul departed from out his bosom unto the reward of the righteous.

39. [Wiglaf bitterly upbraids those craven thanes.]

Thus it went full hard with the young man to see his best-beloved one lying lifeless on the ground, faring most wretchedly. His destroyer lay there too, the horrid earth-dragon, bereft of life, crushed in ruin. No longer could the coiled serpent rule over treasure-hoards, for the edge of the sword, the hard, battlenotched work of the hammer, had destroyed him, and he had fallen to the ground near

[50] Wiglaf. His father's name is pronounced "Wayoak-stan."
[51] Wiglaf.

[52] A ness is a headland.

his hoard-hall, stilled by the wounding. No more in play did he whirl through the air at midnight, and show himself forth, proud of his treasure, for he sank to earth by the mighty hand of the battle-chief. . . .

It was not long thereafter that the cowards left the wood, those craven traitors, the ten of them together, even they who in their lord's great need had not dared to brandish spear. But shamefully now they bore their shields, their war-armor, to where the old man lay. They looked upon Wiglaf. The wearied warrior was sitting by his lord's shoulder; he was trying to revive him with water, but it availed him naught. He could not stay the chieftain's life on earth, though dearly he wished it, nor change the will of God in aught. The judgment of the Lord was wont to rule the deeds of every man, even as it doth today.

And straightway the youth had a fierce and ready answer for those whose courage had failed them. Wiglaf, son of Weohstan, spoke, sad at heart, as he looked upon those hated men: "Lo! he who is minded to speak the truth may say that the liege lord, he who gave you these treasures, even the battle-armor in which ye are standing—what time at the ale-bench the king gave oft unto his thanes, sitting in the hall, helms and byrnies, the choicest far or near which he could find —utterly and wretchedly wasted that war-harness. Nowise did the king need to boast of his comrades in arms when strife overtook him; yet God, the Lord of victory, granted him unaided to avenge him with the sword, when he had need of valor. Little protection could I give him in the fight; and yet I tried what was beyond my power—to help my kinsman. It was ever the worse for the deadly foe when I smote him with the sword, the fire less fiercely flamed from his head. Too few defenders thronged about their lord when the dread moment fell. Now, all sharing of treasure, all gift of swords, all hope, all rights of home, shall cease from your kin. Every man of your house shall roam, bereft of tribal rights, as soon as the princes in far countries hear of your flight, your inglorious deed. Death is better for every man than a life of shame!"

40 and 41. [Beowulf's death is announced to the host. The messenger discourses. The people go to the place of the fight.]

Then he bade announce the issue of the fight to the stronghold up over the sea-cliff, where the sad warrior-band had been sitting by their shields the morning long, looking for either the death or the return of their dear lord. Little did he keep silence of the new tidings, he who rode up the headland, but truthfully spoke before them all: "Now the chief of the Weder people, lord of the Geats, source of all our joy, is fast in the bed of death; he lieth low in slaughter because of the dragon's deeds. Beside him lieth his deadly foe, slain by the wounding of the knife; for with the sword he could nowise wound the monster. Wiglaf, son of Weohstan, sitteth over Beowulf, the living hero by the dead; over his head with weary heart he keepeth watch o'er friend and foe." . . .

"Now we had best hasten to look upon our king, and bring our ring-bestower along his way to the pyre. No mean thing shall be burned with the hero, for the hoard of treasure, of untold riches, has been bitterly purchased; and now at the last, he has bought these jewels with his own life. Fire shall devour them, flames shall enwrap them. No warrior shall bear away any of the treasure for a memorial, no fair maiden shall wear upon her neck the jeweled adornment; but rather, bereft of gold and sad at heart, she shall tread the land of the stranger often and often, now that the chieftain has quitted laughter, mirth and glee. Therefore many a spear, cold in the morning, must needs be clasped by the fingers, uplifted in the hand; the sound of the harp shall not waken the warrior, but the wan raven, eager o'er the doomed, shall chatter freely, telling the eagle how he sped at the feast, when with the wolf he plundered the slain."

Thus the bold hero told his hated tidings: he spoke not falsely touching facts or words. All the band arose; sadly they went, with welling tears, beneath Eagle's Cliff to look upon the marvel. And they found him who had given them treasure in days gone by, found him in his resting-place, lifeless on the sand. Gone was the hero's final day, for the warrior-king, lord of the Weders, had died a wondrous death.

But first they beheld there a stranger being, the loathsome beast lying over against him on the plain; the fiery dragon, awful monster, was all scorched with flames. He was fifty feet long where he lay. At times he had been wont to rejoice in the air in the night season, thereafter down returning to his den. Now he was fast in the clutch of death; he had enjoyed the last of his caverns. By him stood bowls and flagons; dishes lay there, and precious swords, rusty and eaten through, as if they had remained in earth's bosom a thousand winters; for a spell had been wound about that vast heritage, that gold of bygone men, so that none could touch the treasure-house, save as God himself, the King of victory—he is man's defense—should grant unto whom he would, even unto whatsoever man should seem good to him, to open up the hoard.

42. [The Geats plunder the hoard and cast the Dragon into the sea.]

. . . Wiglaf, son of Weohstan, spoke: "Often, for the sake of one man, must many heroes suffer, even as we do now. We could not teach our dear lord, keeper of the realm, any counsel—that he should not go out against the guardian of the gold, but let him lie where long he had been, let him dwell in his haunts till the end of the world. He held to his high fate. The hoard is dearly bought and opened to our view; too cruel was the fate that enticed the king thither. I went within and looked upon all the riches of that cave, for a way had been opened, though not in gentle wise, and a passage granted me in under the earth-wall. Hurriedly I seized with my hands a vast burden of treasure and bore it out hither to my king. And he was yet alive, conscious still and wise of mind. Many things did the aged man speak in his sorrow; and he bade me greet you, prayed that ye would build upon the place of burning a high mound, great and glorious, in memory

of the deeds of your lord, inasmuch as he was the worthiest warrior among men over the broad earth, while he could still enjoy the wealth of his cities.

"Let us now hasten to go and see the heap of treasures cunningly wrought, the wonder beneath the wall; I will guide you that ye may behold and see, near at hand, abundance of rings and ample gold. When we come out thence, let the bier be forthwith made ready, and then let us bear our master, our beloved lord, to where he shall tarry long, safe in the keeping of the Almighty."

And the son of Weohstan, the hero bold in battle, bade that they give command to many warriors, owners of homes, rulers of men, to bring from far wood for the pyre to where the good king lay, saying: "Now shall fire consume, while the wan flame is waxing high, the chief among warriors, him who oft withstood the shower of darts, what time the storm of arrows urged by the string flew over the wall of shields, and the shaft fulfilled its duty, as, with its feather-fittings, it eagerly sped the barb."

Now the wise son of Weohstan summoned together seven of the king's best thanes from out the troop, and, himself the eighth, went with them under the hostile roof; one of the warriors, who went at the head, bore in his hand a flaming torch. And when the men had seen some portion of the treasure in the cave, lying there unguarded, and wasting away, in no wise did they choose by lot who should despoil that hoard; and little did it grieve any man among them that the precious treasures were straightway borne out thence.

Moreover, they pushed the dragon, that serpent, over the sea cliff, let the wave take him and the waters engulf the keeper of treasure.

There the twisted gold of every sort, past counting, was laden upon a wain. The prince, the hoary warrior, was borne away to Whale's Ness.

43. [They burn Beowulf.]

Then the Geatish people fashioned for him

a mighty pile upon the ground, all hung with helms, and war-shields, and bright byrnies, even as he had entreated them; and in the midst of it the sorrowing men laid their great king, their belovèd lord. Then the warriors kindled the greatest of funeral fires upon the mound. Up-rose the wood-smoke, black above the flame; blazing fire roared (mingled with a sound of weeping when the tumult of the wind was stilled), until, hot within the breast, it had consumed the bony frame. Sad at heart, with care-laden soul, they mourned the fall of their lord. Likewise the aged wife,[53] with hair upbound, sorrowing in heart, sang a dirge for Beowulf; oft said she dreaded sore that evil days would come upon her, and much bloodshed, fear of the warrior, and shame and bondage.—Heaven swallowed up the smoke.

Then the Weder people made a mound upon the cliff—it was high and broad, to be seen afar of seafaring men; and ten days they built it, the war-hero's beacon. They made a wall round about the ashes of the fire, even as the wisest of men could most worthily devise it there. Within the mound they put the rings and the jewels, all the adornments which the brave-hearted men had taken from the hoard; they let the earth hold the treasure of heroes, put the gold in the ground, where it still remains, as useless unto men as it was of yore.

Then warriors, sons of princes, twelve in all, rode about the mound; they were minded to bewail their sorrow, mourn their king, utter the dirge, and speak of their hero; they praised his courage and greatly commended his mighty deeds. Thus it is fitting that a man should praise his lord in words and cherish him in heart when he must forth from the fleeting body.

So the Geatish people, companions of his hearth, mourned the fall of their lord; said that he was a mighty king, the mildest and kindest of men, most gracious to his people, and most desirous of praise.[54]

STUDY AIDS: 1. How is the character of Beowulf made convincing? In answering this question, study sections 3, 8–9, 10–12, 35, 40–41, and 43 especially. You may be helped in your analysis by recognizing that character is revealed primarily by the following means: the speeches and actions of the character and the attitude of other characters toward him, expressed by their speeches and actions.

2. Characterize the TONE and ATMOSPHERE of *Beowulf*.

3. Briefly characterize the following: Hrothgar, Unferth, Wealhtheow, Grendel, Grendel's mother, and Wiglaf.

4. Determine the Anglo-Saxon code of conduct by analyzing the relations between Beowulf and his men, between Beowulf and Hrothgar, between Beowulf and Hygelac, and between Beowulf and Wiglaf.

5. Is *Beowulf* an organically unified poem or two poems held together only through the presence of Beowulf himself? Supply arguments on both sides of the question.

6. Are the Christian elements in *Beowulf* integral to the poem, or do they seem to be later additions to what was once a pagan poem? Cite relevant passages from the text to support your position.

7. Grendel and his mother and the dragon are hardly believable to us today. How do you account for our positive reactions to the poem? How is the incredible made credible? Is there anything universal in the poem?

8. Can Grendel and his mother and the dragon be understood symbolically? If so, what does each symbolize?

---

[53] Probably Hygd, Hygelac's widow (and perhaps later married by Beowulf to strengthen his position); but she may simply be an old prophetess predicting the evil days which are almost inevitably to come because of Beowulf's death and the cowardice of all the remaining men save Wiglaf.

[54] The Anglo-Saxon ideal: a truly gentle-*man*, courteous, unselfish, and, above all, brave, for only through courage can praise finally be gained. Does this ideal still obtain today?

The Seafarer [1]

The Seafarer belongs to a group of poems called, not very appropriately, the Old English elegies. The poem, a monologue, is especially noteworthy for the effectiveness with which its speaker presents the age-old ambivalence of men who follow the sea: loving it, yet hating it at the same time. Perhaps no work of comparable shortness gives so graphic a picture of the hardships of the sailor's life in northern waters.

The translation, by the distinguished modern poet Ezra Pound, is unusually successful in recreating the feeling of Old English poetry. It is also a memorable poem in its own right ("probably the most important" of the poems in Pound's *Ripostes,* according to T. S. Eliot).

May I for my own self song's truth reckon,
Journey's jargon,[2] how I in harsh days
Hardship endured oft.
Bitter breast-cares have I abided,
Known on my keel [3] many a care's hold,   5
And dire sea-surge, and there I oft spent
Narrow nightwatch nigh the ship's head
While she tossed close to cliffs. Coldly afflicted,
My feet were by frost benumbed.
Chill its chains are; chafing sighs   10
Hew my heart round and hunger begot
Mere-weary [4] mood. Lest man know not
That he on dry land loveliest liveth,
List [5] how I, care-wretched, on ice-cold sea,
Weathered the winter, wretched outcast   15
Deprived of my kinsmen;
Hung with hard ice-flakes, where the hail-scur [6] flew,
There I heard naught save the harsh sea
And ice-cold wave, at whiles [7] the swan cries,
Did for my games the gannet's [8] clamour,   20
Sea-fowls' loudness was for me laughter,
The mews' singing all my mead-drink.
Storms, on the stone-cliffs beaten, fell on the stern
In icy feathers; full oft the eagle screamed
With spray on his pinion.   25
                    Not any protector
May make merry man faring needy.
This he little believes, who aye in winsome life
Abides 'mid burghers [9] some heavy business,
Wealthy and wine-flushed, how I weary oft 30
Must bide above brine.
Neareth nightshade, snoweth from north,
Frost froze the land, hail fell on earth then,
Corn of the coldest. Nathless [10] there knocketh now
The heart's thought that I on high streams   35
The salt-wavy tumult traverse alone.
Moaneth always my mind's lust
That I fare forth, that I afar hence
Seek out a foreign fastness.
For this there's no mood-lofty man over earth's midst,   40
Not though he be given his good, but will have in his youth greed;
Nor his deed to the daring, nor his king to the faithful
But shall his sorrow for sea-fare
Whatever his lord will.[11]
He hath not heart for harping, nor in ring-having   45
Nor winsomeness to wife, nor world's delight
Nor any whit else save upon the wave's slash,
Yet longing comes upon him to fare forth on the water.

[1] Translated by Ezra Pound. In choosing this controversial translation, the editors place themselves on the side of John Dryden in preferring poetic fidelity to literal accuracy in translations; whatever one's views, however, the most extensive objections which have been raised to Pound's version deal with the portion here omitted (for other reasons).
[2] Roughly synonymous with "song's truth."
[3] In my ship.
[4] Sea-weary.
[5] Listen.
[6] Hail-shower.
[7] At times.
[8] A sea bird.
[9] City dwellers, i.e., landlubbers.
[10] Nevertheless.
[11] The translation is obscure here (ll. 40–44). The general sense of the original is: No man, regardless of who he is, does not have some fear of the sea. (In line 44, "lord" is more probably "Lord.")

Bosque [12] taketh blossom, cometh beauty of
berries,
Fields to fairness, land fares brisker, 50
All this admonisheth man eager of mood,
The heart turns to travel so that he then
thinks
On flood-ways to be far departing.
Cuckoo calleth with gloomy crying,
He singeth summerward, bodeth sorrow, 55
The bitter heart's blood. Burgher knows
not—
He the prosperous man—what some perform
Where wandering them widest draweth.
So that but now my heart burst from my
breastlock,
My mood 'mid the mere-flood, 60

Over the whale's acre, would wander wide.
On earth's shelter cometh oft to me,
Eager and ready, the crying lone-flyer,[13]
Whets for the whale-path the heart irresist-
ibly,
O'er tracks of ocean. . . .[14] 65

STUDY AIDS: According to an older view,
The Seafarer is a dialogue between an old
mariner and a young man who is eager to go to
sea. Which sections of the poem would you
assign to the old mariner, which to the young
man? Are these divisions equally valid for the
interpretation of the poem as a monologue expressing the ambivalent attitude of one man
towards the sea? Which interpretation do you
prefer? Why?

The Wanderer [1]

Like *The Seafarer, The Wanderer* has been interpreted in more than one way. The most
widely held view regards the poem as a monologue and the speaker as that tragic figure, a man
without a country. The speaker's lord has died; he is cut off from his clan; he has nowhere
to go but to wander. The first fifty-one lines describe his personal situation: his grief for his
dead lord and old comrades, his sense of the hopelessness of the future. The rest of the poem extends his sorrow to the world in general. *The Wanderer* is remarkable for the mood it creates.
There is a stream-of-consciousness quality to parts of it which makes it seem quite modern.

Oft to the Wanderer, weary of exile,
Cometh God's pity, compassionate love,
Though woefully toiling on wintry seas
With churning oar in the icy wave,
Homeless and helpless he fled from Fate. 5
Thus saith the Wanderer mindful of misery,
Grievous disasters, and death of kin:
"Oft when the day broke, oft at the dawning,
Lonely and wretched I wailed my woe.
No man is living, no comrade left, 10
To whom I dare fully unlock my heart.
I have learned truly the mark of a man
Is keeping his counsel and locking his lips,
Let him think what he will! For, woe of heart
Withstandeth not Fate; a failing spirit 15
Earneth no help. Men eager for honor
Bury their sorrow deep in the breast.
So have I also, often, in wretchedness
Fettered my feelings, far from my kin,

Homeless and hapless, since days of old, 20
When the dark earth covered my dear lord's
face,
And I sailed away with sorrowful heart,
Over wintry seas, seeking a gold-lord,
If far or near lived one to befriend me
With gift in the mead-hall and comfort for
grief. 25
Who bears it, knows what a bitter companion,
Shoulder to shoulder, sorrow can be,
When friends are no more. His fortune is
exile,
Not gifts of fine gold; a heart that is frozen,
Earth's winsomeness dead. And he dreams of
the hallmen, 30
The dealing of treasure, the days of his youth,
When his lord bade welcome to wassail and
feast.

so strikingly that many scholars regard the remaining
lines as a later addition and hence end the poem
here, as we do.

[12] Woods, groves.
[13] Perhaps the soul, the mood.
[14] At this point the subject matter and tone change

[1] Translated by Charles W. Kennedy.

But gone is that gladness, and never again
Shall come the loved counsel of comrade and
  king.
Even in slumber his sorrow assaileth,   35
And, dreaming, he claspeth his dear lord
  again,
Head on knee, hand on knee, loyally laying,
Pledging his liege as in days long past.
Then from his slumber he starts lonely-
  hearted,
Beholding gray stretches of tossing sea,   40
Sea-birds bathing, with wings outspread,
While hail-storms darken, and driving snow.
Bitterer then is the bane of his wretchedness,
The longing for loved one: his grief is re-
  newed.
The forms of his kinsmen take shape in the
  silence;   45
In rapture he greets them; in gladness he scans
Old comrades remembered. But they melt into
  air
With no word of greeting to gladden his
  heart.
Then again surges his sorrow upon him;
And grimly he spurs on his weary soul   50
Once more to the toil of the tossing sea.
No wonder therefore, in all the world,
If a shadow darkens upon my spirit
When I reflect on the fates of men—
How one by one proud warriors vanish   55
From the halls that knew them, and day
  by day
All this earth ages and droops unto death.
No man may know wisdom till many a win-
  ter
Has been his portion. A wise man is patient,
Not swift to anger, nor hasty of speech,   60
Neither too weak, nor too reckless, in war,
Neither fearful nor fain,[2] nor too wishful of
  wealth,
Nor too eager in vow—ere he know the event.
A brave man must bide when he speaketh his
  boast
Until he know surely the goal of his spirit.   65
A wise man will ponder how dread is that
  doom
When all this world's wealth shall be scat-
  tered and waste—
As now, over all, through the regions of earth,

[2] Eager.

Walls stand rime-covered and swept by the
  winds.
The battlements crumble, the wine-halls de-
  cay;   70
Joyless and silent the heroes are sleeping
Where the proud host fell by the wall they
  defended.[3]
Some battle launched on their long, last
  journey;
One a bird bore o'er the billowing sea;
One the gray wolf slew; one a grieving earl 75
Sadly gave to the grave's embrace.
The Warden [4] of men hath wasted this world
Till the sound of music and revel is stilled,
And these giant-built structures stand empty
  of life.
He who shall muse on these mouldering
  ruins,   80
And deeply ponder this darkling life,
Must brood on old legends of battle and
  bloodshed,
And heavy the mood that troubles his heart:
"Where now is the warrior? Where is the war-
  horse?
Bestowal of treasure, and sharing of feast? 85
Alas! the bright ale-cup, the byrny-clad [5] war-
  rior,
The prince in his splendor—those days are
  long sped
In the night of the past, as if they never had
  been!"
And now remains only, for warriors' memo-
  rial,
A wall wondrous high with serpent shapes
  carved.   90
Storms of ash-spears have smitten the earls,
Carnage of weapon, and conquering Fate.
Storms now batter these ramparts of stone;
Blowing snow and the blast of winter
Enfold the earth; night-shadows fall   95
Darkly lowering, from the north driving
Raging hail in wrath upon men.
Wretchedness fills the realm of earth,
And Fate's decrees transform the world.
Here wealth is fleeting, friends are fleet-
  ing,   100

[3] The exact reference here and in the succeeding
lines is unknown.
[4] God.
[5] Clad in coat of linked mail.

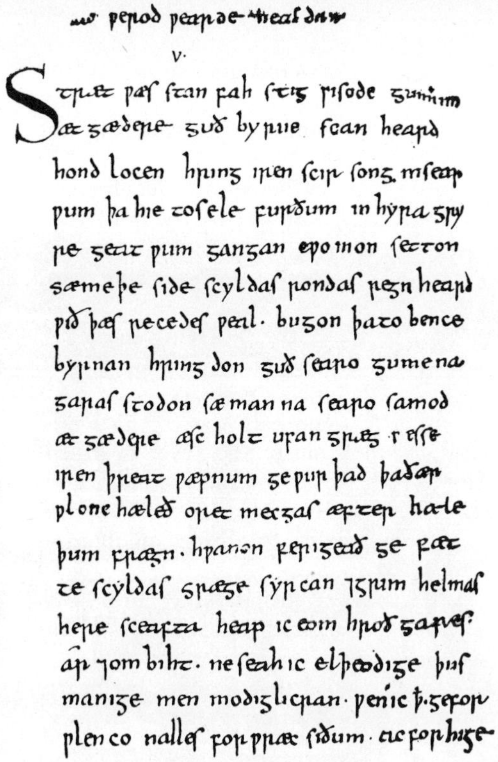

ꝩ pepod peapꝺe-heal ꝺꝛꝩ

v.

Sꞇꝩꝇꞇ paꝼ ꝼꞇan pah ꞅꞇꝭ ꝛꞇꝼoꝺe ꌞꝩmꝭꝭ
ꝼæ ꌞæꝺ�521ꝛe ꌞuꝺ byꝥꝛe ꝼꞇan heapꝺ
honꝺ locen hꝛꝛꝷ ꝥen ꞅꞇꝛꝥ ꞅonꌞ ꝥꞅꞇꝛꝥ
ꝥum ꝥa hre ꞇoꝼele ꝼuꝛꝺ11n ꝛn hyꝛa ꌞꝛꝩ
ꝥe ꌞꞇꝛꞇ ꝥum ꌞanꌞan ꝭꝩo ꝥon ꝼꞇꞇꝛon
ꞅæmeꝥe ꞅꝛꝺe ꞅcylꝺaꝼ ꝥonꝺaꝼ ꝥꝭꝛn heapꝺ
ꝥꝭꝺ ꝥꝭꝼ ꝛeceꝺeꝼ ꝥꝛꞇꝇ. buꌞon ꝥꝛꞇo benꞇo
byꝛꝛnan hꝛꝛꝷ ꝺon ꌞuꝺ ꞅꞇꝛꝥo ꌞumena
ꌞaꝛaꝼ ꞅꞇoꝺon ꞅæ man na ꞅꞇꝛꝥo ꞅamoꝺ
æ ꌞæꝺꝭꝛe aꞅꞇ holꞇ uꝥan ꌞꝥꝛꞇꌞ ꞇ ꝭꝼꞇ
ꝥen ꝥꝛꝛꞇꌞ ꝥæꝥnum ꌞeꝥꝛꝛ ꝥaꝺ ꝥaꝺꞇꝥ
ꝑlone hæleꝭ oꝥꝛꞇ meꞇꌞaꝼ æꝼꞇꝛꝛ hale
ꝥum ꝥꝛꝛꝥn. hꝛanon ꝼꝛꝛrꌞꞇꝺ ꌞe ꝥꝛꞇ
ꞇe ꞅcylꝺaꝼ ꌞꝥꝛꌞꞇ ꞅꝩꝛ can ꝛꌞꝥum helmaꝼ
heꝛꝛe ꞅcꝛꝛꝥꞇꝛꝛ heaꝛꝛ ꝛc eom hꝛꝛoꝺ ꌞaꝛꝛeꝼ
aꝛꝛ ꝛomꝛbihꞇꞇ. ne ꞅꞇah ꝛc elꝥꝛꝥꝺꝛꌞe ꝥuꝼ
manꝛꌞe men moꝺꝛɡlꝛcꝛan. ꝥenꝛc ꝥ.ꌞeꝼoꝛ
ꝑlenco nalleꝼ ꝼoꝛ ꝥꝥꝛꝛ ꞅꝛꝺum. ꞇꝛꞇ ꝼoꝛ ꝥꝛꌞe

A page from the *Beowulf* manuscript in the British Museum.

A medieval scriptorium: John Mandeville (1322–1356) seated at his desk.

A self-portrait of Jean Mielot in his scriptorium.

Man is fleeting, maid is fleeting;
All the foundation of earth shall fail!"
Thus spake the sage in solitude pondering.
Good man is he who guardeth his faith.
He must never too quickly unburden his
    breast   105
Of its sorrow, but eagerly strive for re-
    dress;
And happy the man who seeketh for mercy
From his heavenly Father, our fortress and
    strength.

STUDY AIDS: 1. Define the mood of this poem.

2. Mark the major divisions in the thought.

3. Like most Old English poetry, *The Wanderer* is a blend of the Christian and the pagan. In what ways does the poem seem pagan? In what ways, Christian? Are the two elements reconciled?

4. The translation of *The Wanderer* reproduces many of the stylistic characteristics of Old English poetry. What do some of these characteristics seem to be?

Sir Gawain and the Green Knight [1]

NO ONE KNOWS EVEN THE NAME OF THE AUTHOR OF SIR GAWAIN AND THE GREEN KNIGHT. All agree, however, that no finer work of comparable length survives from the Middle English period than this narrative which, with a richness of detail found in only a few great English poets, combines two old Celtic legends into a superbly plotted story. For color, for vividness, for atmosphere, and for suspense *Sir Gawain and the Green Knight* is almost without equal among narrative poems.

In the earliest Arthurian stories, Sir Gawain was the greatest of the Knights of the Round Table. He was famed for his prowess at arms and, above all, for his courtesy. Later writers debased him in favor of Lancelot; but it is to the earliest tradition that *Sir Gawain and the Green Knight* belongs (a tradition which, incidentally, Tennyson does not follow). Here Gawain is the perfect knight; he is so recognized by the various characters in the story and, for all his modesty, implicitly in his view of himself. To the others his greatest qualities are his knightly courtesy and his success in battle. To Gawain these are important, but he seems to set an even higher value on his courage and integrity, the two central pillars of his manhood. The story is concerned with the conflict between his conception of himself and the reality. He is not quite so brave or so honorable as he thought he was, but he is still very brave, very honorable. He cannot quite see this, but the reader can.

The character of Sir Gawain is relatively fixed by tradition; he cannot act very differently from the way he does. In consequence, his character is static—is, indeed, less interesting than that of his adversary, the Green Knight. But it is for other qualities than character interest that *Sir Gawain and the Green Knight* is valued.

The two legends upon which the work is based are known to folklorists as the Beheading Game and the Temptation. They are treated separately in various French romances but are not found combined except in *Sir Gawain and the Green Knight*. The Beheading Game forms the subject matter of Parts 1 and 4, the Temptation that of Part 3; Part 2 is a necessary transition between the two stories. What is remarkable about the combination here is that the Beheading Game leads inescapably to the Temptation, which in turn provides the solution to the Beheading Game. The result is a highly unified plot told in a series of scenes: the Christmas game at Arthur's court; the journey into Wales; the temptation at the castle; the encounter at the Green Chapel.

This method of telling a story through scenes is the method of the drama, and indeed one of the most striking qualities of the poem is its feeling for the drama, color, and pageantry of medieval life. Although the identity of the author is unknown, it is clear that he was a man with unusual powers of observation who knew at first hand and well the technical facts of arms and armor, the construction of castles and the life in them, the hunting of the deer, the boar, and the fox—and the butchering of these animals—, and nature, especially in its wilder moods.

[1] Translated especially for this volume by G. B. Pace.

He thus can describe the arming of Gawain, or the hunting of a boar, with the utmost concreteness and realism. He knows of what he writes. At the same time, his descriptions are never static; they always move the story forward. By the time Gawain is armed, he is ready to leave on his quest for the Green Chapel; by the time the boar is slain, the temptation is two-thirds over. This dynamic, dramatic quality of the descriptions gives the narrative a modernity lacking in most medieval writings.

The anonymous author of *Sir Gawain and the Green Knight* is sometimes referred to today as the Pearl Poet, from another poem believed to be by him. *Sir Gawain and the Green Knight,* however, is his masterpiece—a pearl beyond price from the literature of the late Middle Ages.

A NOTE ON THE LANGUAGE OF THE POEM: *Sir Gawain and the Green Knight* is written in an alliterative type of verse similar in many ways to that of *Beowulf.* But unlike *Beowulf* it is in stanzas. Although the poem was composed during Chaucer's lifetime, it is in much more difficult Middle English than are the writings of Chaucer, as a comparison of the opening lines with the General Prologue to *The Canterbury Tales* will show:

> Siþen þe sege and þe assaut watz sesed at Troye,
> þe borz brittened and brent to brondez and askez,
> þe tulk þat þe trammes of tresoun þer wrozt
> Watz tried for his tricherie, þe trewest on erthe. . . .

[After the siege and the assault was ceased at Troy, the city destroyed and burnt to brands and ashes, the man who wrought those treasonous tricks was tried for his treachery, the truest on earth. . . .]

These lines are the beginning of a nineteen-line stanza, which ends as follows (note the rhymes):

> And fer ouer þe French flod Felix Brutus
> On mony bonkkes ful brode Bretayn he settez
> wyth wynne,
> Where werre and wrake and wonder
> Bi syþez hatz wont þerinne,
> And oft boþe blysse and blunder
> Ful skete hatz skyfted synne.

[And far over the French flood (the English Channel) Felix Brutus (the traditional founder of Britain), on many banks full broad, establishes Britain joyously, where war and trouble and wonder from time to time have dwelt therein, and often both bliss and blunder full quickly have shifted ever since.]

Sir Gawain and the Green Knight is written in 101 stanzas of this type. The present prose translation ignores the stanzaic arrangement, regarding it as appropriate to poetry but not to prose. For a similar reason it reduces the amount of alliteration, keeping only enough to suggest the antique form. What it tries to do is to re-create for the reader of today such enduring virtues of the poem as can be rendered in modern English prose.

More marvels have occurred in Britain than in any other country that I know of; [2] and of all the kings who have ruled in this land, Arthur was beyond doubt the most unusual. At least so I have heard tell. Here is an incredibly strange adventure from among the marvels connected with this king. If you will listen, I will tell it straightway, just as I heard it told in town—just as it is set down in the book—a bold, strong story, the words 5 locked together with loyal letters,[3] as has been the custom so long in this country.

I

It was Christmas.

King Arthur lay at Camelot, and with him 10 were many noble knights, brothers of the

[2] The translation begins at l. 23. In the preceding lines the poet tries, relatively unsuccessfully, to give the story added significance by relating it to the legendary history of Britain (see the quoted passages above).

[3] The reference is to the alliterative verse in which the poem is written.

Round Table. All day long they would joust at the tournament grounds; then they would ride to the castle for singing and dancing. For a full fortnight this rich revelry continued: in the morning and afternoon a delightful din, glorious to hear; in the evening, dancing, and the finest foods that the court could devise. At Camelot, at that moment, dwelt the most renowned knights in Christ's earthly kingdom, the loveliest ladies who ever lived, and the comeliest king who ever ruled a court. (It would be hard to match any of them today, in any castle in any land; for that was in the old time, the happiest under heaven.)

Now when New Year was so fresh that it was newly come, on that day the festivities were twice as merry. The king and his knights came into the hall; the priests ended the singing of the Mass; everywhere echoed the cry, "Noel!" All the people ran forward, shouting "New Year's Gift!" and talking busily the while. Afterwards they washed their hands and went to the dining tables, seating themselves according to rank, as was fitting.

At the center of the high table sat Queen Guenever under a canopy of rich red silk; beneath her feet lay an embroidered carpet, a tapestry adorned with the finest gems. Beside her was Arthur, talking graciously to those around him. On his left was his nephew Agravain; on his right, as said, was Guenever; and next to her was Gawain, Arthur's nephew also. At the head of the table sat Bishop Baldwin; at the foot, Iwain, Urien's son. The other knights were at side tables.

A cracking of trumpets, a drumming of drums, a piping of pipes—wild warbles and loud—announced the first course. Serving men entered with an abundance of fresh foods on silver platters. Every two people had twelve silver dishes, and also good beer and bright wine. Now I will say no more of their table service; everyone must know that there was no want there.

Once again the trumpets blared, the drums rolled, the pipes piped, a signal to the company to begin eating. But they had scarcely touched the food when in at the hall door rides [4] a knight, a gigantic knight, surely the greatest on earth in stature. He is so squarely built, so thick from his neck to his middle, and his loins and his limbs are so long and so great, that I think he may well be half giant. At any rate, I declare him to be the largest of men and the most splendid. All who see him have wonder of his color, set plain in his face. He is everywhere—bright green.

Completely green [5] is this knight, as also are his garments. A green straight coat sticks full tightly to his sides; above it is a merry mantle lined with the finest of furs, as also is his hood, which is caught back from his locks and lies on his shoulders. Green hose cling to his calves; below are shining spurs of bright gold, and shoes with long pointed toes. Truly, all his garments are green, even the bars adorning his belt and the jewels sprinkled about his array and upon his saddle, which sits upon embroidered silks. It would be hard to tell even half of what is embroidered on those silks: the gayest birds and bees, green gold always in the midst. The pendants of his horse's breast trappings, the proud crupper, the studs of the bit, these are all enameled green. The stirrups, the saddle bows, and the rump trappings are all stained the same color. The whole harness glimmers and gleams with green stones.

And the horse himself is green! A green horse, great and thick, a steed full hard to restrain—well suited to the man on his back.

The green hair of the man's head fans out and covers his shoulders. His great beard is like a bush in color and size. Hair and beard are clipped all around like the eaves of a roof and fall in an "O" right above his elbows, so that half his arms are enclosed after the fashion of a king's capados.[6]

The green mane of the great horse is

---

[4] In the original the poet gains an effect of immediacy by shifting at will from past tense to present, often within a single sentence. The result is undoubtedly effective, but the practice is so at variance with modern English usage that the translator has substituted an alternate device, that of shifting certain whole sections of the poem into the present.

[5] For the medieval reader, green was symbolic of the supernatural.

[6] A short tunic of Cappadocian leather.

crisped and combed and tied into many knots. Gold threads are folded in; for each strand of green hair there is a strand of gold. The forelock and tail are plaited to match each other and are bound with bands of bright green ornamented with precious stones; to each is tied a thong in an intricate knot, from which bells of burnished gold ring.

Such a horse and such a man were never seen in that hall before. All who saw that knight swore he shone as bright as lightning. No one, they felt, might endure for long under his blows!

Yet he has no armor at all—neither helmet nor hauberk, nor breast armor nor arm armor, nor shaft nor shield. In one hand he holds a holly branch,[7] in the other an axe.

This axe is a monstrous one, a cruel battle-axe indeed. The head is forty-five inches in length; the spike is of green steel and gold and the bit is razor-sharp and burnished bright. The handle is a stiff green staff intricately carved and wound with iron; about it loops a thong, which is fastened at the head with tassels attached to buttons of bright green.

The knight holds the horse in and guides him to the high table. He greets no one. High over all he looks. He calls out:

"Who rules in this house?"

He casts his eyes to the knights and struts himself up and down. Then he stops and studies them. The whole court stares at him. They stalk nearer to him. Thinking he may be a phantom from faery land, many of them are afraid to answer him.

Now Arthur speaks, "Knight, welcome! I am King Arthur. Alight from your horse, I pray you. Afterwards we can learn what your will is."

"Nay," declines the knight, "I am not here to visit. I am here because your glory, Prince, is lifted so high, and because your knights are held to be the best—the strongest to ride on steeds in steel armor. And always ready to take part in any pure sport! You may be sure by this holly branch that I come in peace. If I had gone in fighting-wise—well, I have a hauberk at home, and a helmet, and a shield and a sharp spear, and other weapons besides. But because I wish no trouble my clothing is softer. Now, if you are as bold as men say you are, you will grant me the sport that I ask."

Arthur replies, "Sir, if you want bare battle, you will not fail to find it here."

"Nay," says the knight, "I ask for no fight, I tell you. These are but beardless children about on the bench. I crave only a Christmas game, for it is Yule and the New Year. If there is anyone in this house who will dare to strike one blow for another, he shall have the rich battle-axe as my Christmas present—and I shall take the first blow as bare as I sit here. If any of you is so brave as to test what I have said, let him come here to me and catch this weapon. I will quit-claim it forever, he can keep it as his own; and I shall stand him a stroke, right here on this floor. However, a twelvemonth to the day from now you must allow me to return the stroke. Who dares say anything?"

The knight turns in his saddle, runishly [8] rolls his red eyes about, and bends his bristling green brows. He looks around to see who will rise. When no one does, he coughs, stretches himself richly, and demands:

"What? Is this Arthur's house, the fame of which runs through so many realms? Where now are your pride and your conquests, your fierceness and your wrath, your bold speeches? Now are the revelry and the renown of the Round Table overthrown by the words of one man—for all of you cower in fear without a blow being shown!"

He grows as wrathful as the wind; so do all the knights. The king moves near him:

"Sir, by Heaven, your request is foolish;

---

[7] A sign of peace, as the Green Knight says later. The holly is of course appropriate to the Christmas season, but the poet probably has in mind also the striking color contrast made by its berries; on a color wheel red is the opposite of green. Note the great feeling for color shown throughout the poem.

[8] There is no exact equivalent in modern English for this word, which is found in a number of the alliterative poems. Here the context defines it sufficiently. What meanings are suggested to you by its use in this passage and later on (p. 39/2, l. 14)? Beware of limiting the word too precisely.

and as you have foolishly asked so it behooves you to find. I know no man who is frightened by your great words. For God's sake, give me your axe and I shall grant your wish."

Arthur leaps to him and grabs the axe by the handle. The knight lights upon his feet and stands towering above him, higher than any in the castle by a head and more. He strokes his beard and draws down his tunic.

Gawain looks to the king and cries, "I beg you that this contest may be mine! While so many bold knights sit about you on the bench, it does not seem fitting that you should answer this request. Grant it to me, since this business is so foolish that it does not become you and since I have asked you first."

Arthur commands him to rise. Gawain comes to him, kneels, and catches the weapon. Then, axe in hand, he goes to the knight, who speaks to him boldly:

"Before we pass further, let us restate our agreement. But first, knight, tell me your name."

"In good faith," Gawain replies, "I am named Gawain—and I shall give you a blow and take another from you a twelvemonth from now, with whatsoever weapon you wish."

"Sir Gawain!" exclaimed the Green Knight. "It indeed pleases me that I shall receive from your hand that which I have asked here. And you have repeated the agreement fairly, except that you must assure me, knight, that you will seek me yourself, wherever you think I may be found."

"Where shall I find you, where is your place?" Gawain queries. "I do not know where you live—nor do I know you, knight. If you will tell me your name, I shall spend all my wit to find my way to you. That I swear to you."

The Green Knight answers, "It will be sufficient if I tell you after you have struck me. If I can say nothing then, why so much the better for you! In that event, you can stay in your land and search no further. But enough of this. Let's see how you can strike."

"Gladly," replies Gawain. He caresses the axe.

The Green Knight prepares himself. He bows his head a little, lays his long lovely locks over his crown, and lets his naked neck show bare. Gawain grips the axe and, with both hands, gathers it on high. The blade comes down, sundering the bones, shrinking through the bright flesh, and biting into the ground. The green head hits the earth and rolls. The people thrust at it with their feet.

Blood spurts forth from the body, gleaming red on the green.[9] But the knight does not falter or fall. He starts forth stoutly on stiff shanks, runishly reaches out where the knights stand, and picks up his lovely head. Then he goes to his horse, catches hold of the bridle, steps into the stirrup-irons, and strides aloft. He holds his head by the hair. Many feel fear in their hearts by the time it has begun to speak.

Holding the head up in his hand, he turns its face to those at the table. The head lifts up its eyelids, stares at Gawain full broadly, and speaks thus with its mouth:

"Look you, Gawain, that you be ready to go as you promised, that you seek me faithfully till you find me, as you have sworn to do. I charge you: go to the Green Chapel, there to receive such a blow as you have given me, on next New Year's morn. I am the Knight of the Green Chapel. Many men know me. You will find me if you ask. Come, or be called recreant!"

With a runish roar he turns the reins and hales out at the hall door, his head in his hands. The fire flies under his horse's hooves. To what land he went no one knew, no more than they knew whence he came.

Arthur had wonder in his heart, but he let no sign of it show. He said most courteously to his lovely queen, "Dear lady, do not be frightened. Such tricks as this are fitting at Christmas time—the playing of interludes, laughing, singing, the comely carols of knights and ladies. I will now turn to my dinner. But that I have seen a wonder I will not deny."

Looking at Gawain, he said, "Now, sir, hang up your axe. You have cut enough."

[9] Note the color contrast.

They hung it on a tapestry above the high
table, so that all men might see it and marvel.
Then with all sorts of food and minstrelsy
they spent the rest of that day with joy, till
it came to an end in the land.

2

A year runs full quickly, and seldom does
the end match the beginning.[10] After Christmas comes the crabbed Lent, which tries the
flesh with fish and food more simple. Then
the weather of the world contends with
winter: the cold shrinks away, the clouds lift
up, the bright rain falls in showers full warm,
falls upon the fair meadow-lands. Flowers
appear. The earth and the trees are clothed
in green; birds begin to build and to sing for
joy of the soft summer which follows; blossoms swell to bloom. Now comes summer with
its soft winds; Zephirus whistles gently over
seeds and herbs. Happy are the plants that
live out of doors, when the danking dew
drops from the leaves, to await a look from
the warm sun. Then autumn nighs and hard-
ens them, warns them to wax full ripe, and
drives with drought the dust to fly full high
from the face of the earth. Wrathful winds
wrestle with the sun, leaves lance from the
trees, the grass grays that before was green.
Now all ripens and rots that rose in the
beginning, and thus runs the year in yester-
days many.[11]

Michaelmas moon [12] is come, with its pledge
of winter, and now Gawain prepares for his
wearisome voyage. Yet he lingers with
Arthur till All Saints' Day.[13]

The best of the castle—Iwain and Errik,
Sir Dodinal li Sauvage, the Duke of Clarence,
Lancelot and Lionel, and Lucan the good,
Sir Bors and Sir Bedivere, big men both, Sir
Mador de la Port, and many another noble
knight—come to counsel him, with grief in
their hearts. They sorrow that one so worthy

as Gawain should go on that errand, to
suffer a doleful blow and give none in return.
But Gawain makes light of their anxiety. He
says, "What is there to fear? Some fates are
hard, some easy. All a man can do is try."

When the morning comes he asks early
for his arms, and they are brought to him.
First, a carpet of red silk is spread on the
floor; on it a mound of gold gear gleams.
Gawain steps forward, wearing a doublet of
Turkestan silk and a capados lined with bright
white fur. His squires set the steel shoes on
his feet. They place the polished steel greaves
on his legs, with the knee pieces attached,
and fasten them with knots of gold. Then,
with thongs, they tie on the goodly thigh-
pieces, that cunningly enclose his thick
brawny thighs. Then they set on him the rest
of his armor: the broad corslet of bright steel
rings, the well-burnished arm-pieces, the el-
bow-pieces, the gloves of plate steel, the rich
coat-armor,[14] the trustworthy sword, fastened
to his side with a silken sash. His armor is
rich; every lachet and loop shines of gold.

Then clanking in his armor he goes to
Mass and worships at the high altar. Then
he meets with the king and the lords and
ladies, who kiss him and walk with him,
commending him to Christ.

By this time Gringolet is ready. His saddle
is red and studded with gold nails, specially
prepared. His red bridle is barred and bound
with gold. The breast trappings, the crupper,
the proud skirts, the cloth, the saddle bows
are all red; against this red background everywhere glint the rich gold nails.

Gawain takes up his helmet and kisses it.
It sits high on his head. Over the beaver is
a silken covering adorned with gems and
embroidery—true-love knots, preening parrots,
turtle doves. His shield is red and has a
pentangle [15] depicted on it in pure gold. His
squires hand him the shield and he hangs it
about his neck by its strap.

Even though I shall delay the story, I want
to tell you why the pentangle belongs to Sir
Gawain. The pentangle was created by Solo-

[10] Note the use of specific detail in the passage
which follows. Has the poet used specific detail
strikingly in any previous section?

[11] What is the function of this poetic passage on
the seasons?

[12] September 29; Michaelmas moon is the harvest
moon.

[13] November 1.

[14] A vest of rich material worn over the armor;
it was embroidered with heraldic devices.

[15] A five-pointed star.

mon [16] to represent truth. It has five points and each line interlocks with the others, so that everywhere it is endless. The English generally call it "the endless knot." It befitted Gawain because he was faithful in five ways and in each way five times: [17]

First, he was perfect in his five wits, and secondly in his five fingers, which never failed him. Third, all his trust was in the five wounds Christ received on the Cross, as the Creed tells. Fourth, all his fierceness in battle derived from the five joys of the Virgin Mary, which she had of her child (Gawain had her image painted on the inner side of his shield, so that when he looked at her his courage would not fail). The fifth five were these: generosity, love for fellow man, purity, chivalric courtesy, and compassion, which surpasses all virtues—these qualities were more evident in Gawain than in any other knight. Now all these various "fives" were to be found in Gawain, each joined to the other, so that they had no end; therefore this pentangle, this endless knot, was painted on his shield, in red gold on red.

Now Gawain is ready to go. He catches his lance, and gives them all good day—thinking it is to be for ever. He spurs his horse, which springs forward so vigorously that fire strikes from the stones. Those who look at him departing sigh in their hearts.

He made no stay anywhere but swiftly went his way. He rode by many a bewildering path, as the book tells. [18] . . .

Riding always alone he climbed many a cliff; at every waterfall he found an enemy, each so foul and fierce that he had to fight him. Sometimes he fought with dragons, sometimes with wolves, sometimes with the forest trolls who dwell in the crags; at other times he fought with bulls and bears and boars, and also with ogres, who puffed at him from the high rocks. But the winter weather was even worse than the fighting,

what with the clear cold water shedding from the clouds and freezing before it could reach the earth. Nearly dead from the sleet, he slept in his armor more nights than enough up among the naked rocks, with the cold streams clattering down from the crests and hanging high over his head in hard icicles. In constant peril and pain, he rode on until Christmas Eve.

He prayed to Mary to direct him to some dwelling: "I beseech thee, Lord, and Mary, that is the mildest of mothers, that you send me to some lodging where I may hear Mass, and thy Matins in the morning, and for that I pray my Pater Noster and Ave and Creed."

He rode on, signing himself and saying, "Christ's Cross speed me!" But he had scarcely crossed himself three times when he became aware of a dwelling on a knoll in a glade. Set as it was in a meadow, with a park all about, it was as fine a castle as knight ever owned. It shimmered and shone through the bright oaks. Gawain took off his helmet and thanked Jesus and Saint Julian, [19] who both are gentle. "Now good lodging," he said, "I beseech you to grant!" He spurred Gringolet and was at the main gate in no time at all.

But the drawbridge was raised, the gate fast shut. The walls sank wondrously deep in the moat and rose wondrously high. Of hard-hewn stone, that castle feared no wind's blast! Nor man's. It had watch towers evenly spaced and loop holes for the archers that locked closed. He had never seen a better fortress.

Within he could see the hall itself. Chalk-white chimneys and towers gleamed in the light. So many white pinnacles were powdered about everywhere that the castle seemed cut out of paper. [20] He thought it would be well indeed if he could spend the holy day within those walls. He called out and a porter appeared.

"Good Sir," Gawain shouted, "will you go

---

[16] The seal of Solomon was a pentangle in a circle.
[17] The passage which follows is an example of the medieval love of the schematic.
[18] Gawain's itinerary is given in some detail but is omitted here as of little interest to the modern reader. He reaches Wales.

[19] Patron saint of hospitality.
[20] This castle is not, of course, the gray structure which weathering has made of medieval castles today. It is new and gleaming white. Try to visualize it. Note the fine image in the last sentence.

to the lord of this castle and beg lodging for me?"

"Gladly, by St. Peter," said the porter.

He returned promptly, bringing others with him, who let down the great drawbridge and ran across it. They knelt down courteously on the cold earth to welcome Gawain, who bade them rise and then rode over the bridge. While he dismounted, the men held his saddle [21] and knights and squires came to bring him with joy into the hall. When he raised his helmet they rushed forward to take it from his hand; they took his sword and shield. He greeted each one of them; and then, still in his armor, he was taken to the hall, where a fine fire burned. The lord of the castle came out of his chamber to meet him with honor, and said,

"What is here is your own, to have at your will and to control."

"Gramercy," Gawain replied; "may Christ reward you."

Each folded the other in his arms. Gawain looked at the knight who greeted him so warmly. He was a huge man with a broad, beaver-hued beard. He was in the prime of life. His face was as fierce as the fire and his speech was noble. Standing firm on stalwart legs, he seemed well fit to be lord of such a castle.

The lord commanded that a servant be assigned to Gawain and went back into his chamber. Gawain was led to a bright room, where the furnishings were princely: curtains [22] of pure silk with gold hems, elegant coverlets adorned with white fur and inset with embroidered panels, tapestries on the walls and also on the floor. There he was relieved of the rest of his armor and rich robes brought for him to change into. When he had chosen a robe which became him especially, one with fur up by the face and wide flowing skirts, he seemed to them the handsomest knight that ever Christ made, a warrior without peer wherever men fought. Cushions and quilted coverings were laid on a chair before the fireplace, and he sat and warmed himself.

A table was set on trestles and covered with a clean white cloth; a salt cellar and silver spoons were put on it, and he was served most plentifully with various stews, seasoned in the best fashion, and with many kinds of fishes: one was baked in bread, a second was grilled on the coals, a third was boiled, a fourth came in a broth savored with spices. With all these were most cunningly compounded sauces.

Over and over Gawain called it a feast; but the knights, equally graciously, replied: "No, it is a penance,[23] but amends shall be made in due time." Gawain was merry because of the wine, which went to his head.

Then he was questioned, tactfully. He told that noble Arthur of the Round Table was his ruler and that he himself was Gawain, come among them by chance at Christmas time.

When the lord learned who he was he laughed loud. All the knights were delighted also to be in the presence of Gawain, the most famous on earth for prowess and refined manners. Each said softly to his companion: "We have caught the very father of courtesy. Now we shall see true courtly manners, and hear the spotless terms of noble conversation. In truth, God has granted us his grace most wondrously, that we have such a guest as Gawain at this time when men sit and sing for joy at Christ's birth."

It was nearly night before the dinner was over. Chaplains then led the way to the chapel, ringing their bells to call them to the devout Evensong. The lord went into the chapel, as did his lady also. She entered a closed pew, but the lord caught Gawain by a fold of his robe, took him to a seat aside, spoke familiarly to him, calling him by his name, and told him he was the most welcome man in all the world. Gawain thanked him from his heart and each saluted the other and sat soberly together throughout the service.

When it was over, the lady wished to see Gawain. Followed by many young maidens, she came from her pew. Another lady—much older than she, and highly honored by all

[21] Perhaps to keep it from slipping under the heavy weight of his armor.
[22] Enclosing the bed.

[23] Because it is Christmas Eve no meat is served; to that extent the meal is a penance.

the nobles about—led her by the left hand. The two ladies were most unlike: Whereas the one was young and fresh, the other was withered and yellow. A rich red appeared everywhere on the one. Rough wrinkled cheeks rolled on the other. The one had kerchiefs on her head and many shining pearls; her breast and her bright throat were bare and shone whiter than the snow that falls on the hills. The other was swathed up the neck with a gorget; her chin was wrapped around with chalk-white veils, so that only her black brows, her two eyes, her nose, and her lips were visible—and these were sour to see and wondrously bleared. A true *grande dame* one might call her, by God! Her body was short and thick; her buttocks jutted out like a bay window! The one she had in tow was the more delicious to taste. Of all women she was the fairest of skin, of flesh, of face, of figure, of expression—fairer even, he thought, than Guenever. He went through the chancel to salute them.

Gawain greeted the old woman first, bowing full low, and then clasped the younger a little in his arms and kissed her courteously. He spoke to them in a knightly fashion, asking to be allowed to be their servant. They took him between them and, conversing, led him to their sitting-room, where they called for spices and wine.

The lord of the castle leaped up graciously many a time, exhorting everyone to be merry. In high good humor, he seized off his hood, hung it on a spear, and waved it at them, putting it up as a prize to be won by whoever made the most mirth that Christmas season. "And I shall try," he said, "to contend with the best of you! Before I lose my clothes with the help of my friends!" Thus with laughing speeches the lord made merry, to amuse Sir Gawain, till it was time for bed.

On the morn joy grew in every dwelling in the world, as each person called to mind Him who for our salvation was born to die. There was much joy that day and the next and the next—St. John's day, the last of the games. There were guests who were leaving on the gray morrow, and hence they all revelled marvelously late into the night, drink-ing wine and dancing carols.[24] When Gawain went to take leave, the lord detained him, leading him to his own room and there thanking him for the great honor he had done them in visiting his house at that high season. He tried hard to persuade him to stay longer, but Gawain said that there was no way he might:

"I am bound for a place I know not where in all the world to go to find! Yet, so help me God, I would not fail to be there on New Year's morn for all the land in England. Tell me if you have ever heard of the Green Chapel, what ground it stands on; or of the Green Knight who keeps it. By solemn agreement we established a tryst between us, to meet, if I might live, at the Green Chapel on New Year's Day—and of the New Year it now lacks but a little. I have barely three days in which to busy myself, and I would as soon fall dead as fail to be there."

The lord laughed at that. "Let the Green Chapel bother you no more! You can be in your bed, man, at your ease, until well on into New Year's Day, and ride there by mid-morn! Stay until New Year's Day, then rise and leave. One of my men will set you on the way. The Green Chapel is not two miles hence!"

Then Gawain was full glad and said, "Above everything else I thank you for this! Now I shall dwell here at your will and do as you see fit."

The lord held him with his arms and called for the ladies. He made such merry sounds that he seemed out of his wits. Finally he managed to speak:

"You have promised to do as I ask? Is that true, will you keep this promise right now, right at this moment?"

"Yes. While I remain at your castle I shall do as you wish."

"Well, you have had a hard journey and have since reveled with me. You are not fully recovered yet. Tomorrow you shall stay in your bed until Mass and eat when you will. My wife will keep you company. As for me, I shall rise early and go hunting."

[24] Originally the carol was a dance and song combined.

Gawain agreed, bowing graciously.

The lord continued, "Furthermore, we shall make an agreement between us. Whatever I get hunting shall be yours; whatever you get here shall be mine. Sweet sir, so shall we swap. Swear!"

"By God," said Gawain, "I do!"

"Then the bargain is made!" cried the lord.

They drank and made merry, these lords and ladies, and afterwards with many fair speeches kissed most courteously and took their leave. Gleaming torches brought them all to bed at last.

3

Before daylight, the new day began. The guests who were leaving called their servants, who quickly saddled the horses, arranged the gear, and trussed the bags. Dressed in the richest fashion, the guests leaped on their horses, seized the bridles, and were on their way.

After he had heard Mass the lord of the castle ate a sop hastily; then, amid the sound of bugles, he and many others set out for the hunting fields. By daybreak he and his knights were high on their horses. The houndsmen leashed the dogs together in pairs, then opened the kennel door and called them out. They blew three long notes on the bugles, at which the braches [25] bayed, making a wonderful music. The houndsmen then went to the hunting stations and unleashed the greyhounds. A great and fine noise rose in the forest!

At the first sound of the hunt the wild animals quaked for dread. Mad for fear, the deer fled to the valleys, ran to the high grounds, but were quickly turned back by the shouts of a ring of beaters. They let the high-antlered harts pass through, and the broad-palmed bucks, for the lord had forbidden the hunting of the males during the closed season. They held in the hinds and the does with "Hay!" and with "Ho!" and drove them into the deep valleys, where men might see the slanting of arrows as they shot by. Under every branch whapped an arrow.

The deer cried out; they bled; they died on the slopes—and ever the hounds chased on in a rush. Blowing on horns, the hunters pursued them with such a cracking cry as though the cliffs had burst.

The lord was carried away for bliss. He galloped about. He alighted to the ground. He drove that day with joy to the dark night.

All this time Gawain lay abed, snug under a fine coverlet, curtained about. As he lay dozing, he heard a little noise at the door. He raised his hand out of the bed clothes and lifted a corner of the curtain, watching warily to see what it might be. It was the lady —and lovely she was! She closed the door after her and went to the bed. Gawain, embarrassed,[26] lay down and pretended to sleep. Stepping silently, the lady stole to his bed, lifted the curtain, and crept within. She sat down softly on the edge of the bed and waited for him to wake. Gawain pondered what her meaning might be. It seemed very strange to him—but then he said to himself, "It would be more becoming to ask straightway what she wants." He stretched himself and pretended to be amazed, crossing himself with his hand.

"Good morning, Sir Gawain!" she cried, laughing. "You are captured! Unless we make a truce, I shall bind you in your bed, that you may be sure." [27]

"Good morning!" said Gawain. "I surrender completely and cry after grace! Now, lovely lady, if you will only free your prisoner, he will get up and make himself presentable to talk with you."

"Nay—forsooth, fair sir," she answered. "I shall fasten you here on the other side also, and speak with my knight whom I have captured. I know who you are. You are Sir Gawain, whom all the world worships, whose honor and courtliness are praised by knights and ladies everywhere. I shall use my time well while it lasts. You are welcome to my

[25] Similar to beagles and used for scenting; greyhounds were used for chasing the game.

[26] In this and the subsequent bedroom, or Temptation, scenes, Gawain may be taken as sleeping nude (the usual medieval practice); so he is shown in the crude illustration to this passage in the manuscript.

[27] Note the military METAPHOR underlying this passage and try to visualize the scene.

body, to take your pleasure on it. My lord is a long way off, my maids are in their beds, the door is securely locked."

Gawain spoke modestly, "Though I am not he whom you talk of, that would indeed be a 5 pleasure—but I am unworthy of the honors you have rehearsed. By God, if it seemed good to you, I would be glad to set myself to your enjoyment. It would be a pure delight."

She replied gaily, "Sir Gawain, I would 10 show little courtesy if I found fault with the excellence which all others praise. As I love God on high, I have now in my hand what all women desire."

Gawain always answered her with the 15 purest of speeches.

"Madame," he said, "may Mary reward you for your noble generosity! The honor which people give me they exaggerate beyond my deserts. Here the honor is rather to you, who 20 are unable to think anything but good."

Thus they talked until it was past nine, and always the lady behaved as if she were much in love with him. Gawain kept on the defensive, but with the greatest courtesy.[28] 25

"Though I were the loveliest of women," she thought to herself, "the less love-making would he bring with him now—because of the disaster that he seeks, the blow that will strike him down." She said good day, and laughed. 30 Then she stood up and spoke very severely:

"Now may he who rewards every speech reward you for *this* entertainment! That you really are Gawain is debated in my mind."

"Wherefore?" said Gawain quickly, fearing 35 that somehow he had spoken amiss.

But she blessed him, saying, "One so courteous as Gawain never could have remained so long with a lady without begging for a kiss, through his courtesy, at least at 40 some place in the conversation."

"As a knight should," replied Gawain. "I kiss at your command. And, as a further reason, not to displease you."

She caught him in her arms and kissed him. Then they commended each other to Christ, and she went out the door without another word.

All this time the lord of the castle had been occupied with his games, and by sundown he had slain such a quantity of does and hinds that it was wondrous to consider them. The huntsmen quickly made a *curée* [29] of the killed deer. Then the nobles took over.[30] They gathered up the fattest animals and had them cut open. They tested them and found that even the poorest had two fingers' breadth of fat on her. Then they slit the throat, pulled out the first stomach, scraped it with a knife, and sewed it together;[31] next they cut off the legs, tore away the hide, opened the belly, and threw out the bowels; they gripped the throat and drew out the guts; then they cut out the shoulders, lifting them by a little hole to keep the sides complete. They carved the breast and then went back to the throat, slitting it to the fork in the legs. Next they removed all the edible organs in the front part and then took out the backbone; they raised it out whole, as far as the haunch. Then they removed the numbles, the thighs, the head, and the neck. At the last they detached the sides from the backbone and threw the ravens' fee [32] into the trees. They fed the hounds with the liver and lights, the tripe, and bread soaked in blood; this they spread out on a skin.

The huntsmen then blew the horns. The dogs bayed. Then the huntsmen seized the meat and turned to go home; all the way they sounded stoutly many fine notes. By the time daylight was done all were back at the castle, where Gawain waited by a bright fire.

The lord joyfully commanded everyone to gather in the hall, the ladies with their maids as well as the men, and had his share of venison brought in. He called to Gawain,

[28] Gawain's behavior is, of course, fixed to a great extent by his established character in the Gawain tradition; but he is also strongly motivated, as he makes clear later, by his obligations, as a guest, to his host. It is interesting to note that in the later tradition Gawain is often portrayed as a lecher.

[29] In a *curée* the slain deer are arranged with their heads pointing in one direction only, each deer's feet to the other's back.

[30] It was the duty of the nobility to be skilled in the butchering of game.

[31] First filling it, however, with blood and fat.

[32] A piece of gristle which custom required be thrown in the trees for the ravens and crows.

showing him the tally of the deer slain and the ribs of bright meat. "Does this please you?" he asked; "do I not deserve your praise and thanks?"

Gawain replied, "Yes, in truth."

"I give it all to you, Gawain," said the lord, "according to our agreement."

"I say the same to you," returned Gawain; "what I have won in this house is yours." He took the lord in his arms and kissed him as nicely as he could, saying: "Take now my winnings!"

"Many thanks," the lord said. "It may well be that the kiss is the better gain of the two —if you will tell me where you got it."

"That was not in the bargain," Gawain replied, laughing.

After supper, as they sat by the fire, they agreed to the same covenant as before: to exchange, when they met the next night, whatever winnings chance awarded them. Wine was brought forth, and they pledged the agreement before the whole court, then took leave of each other courteously. Each man went quickly to his bed.

By the time the cock had crowed no more than thrice the lord had leaped from his bed. The company was on its way to the hunt before day sprang. Blowing on horns, they rode across level fields until they came to thickets in a marsh. They unleashed some of the hounds there, who soon fell on a scent. Shouting, the huntsmen urged them on and unleashed others. Forty hounds landed on the trail at once, and such a din rose from them that the rocks rang.

The pack swayed together between a pool and a crag, and rushed on to a rock-heap below a cliff, at the side of the marsh. Their baying told the huntsmen that the beast must be there, and they searched both the rock heap and the crag, beating on the bushes and calling to him to come forth. Suddenly a boar swung out. Long since away from the herd, he was of great age and very fierce, and of tremendous size. He charged wildly at the men in his path and sent three of them to the earth, then rushed onward. The hunters cried "High!" and "Hay, hay!" They put their horns to their mouths and blew the recall.

Many were the merry mouths of men and dogs that pursued this boar to the kill.

The boar stood at bay. He thrust at the pack, hurting the dogs so that they yelled in pain. The men shot at him, but his hide was so tough the arrows split and shivered. Even so, the blows hurt him; and, brain-mad for a fight, he rushed at the hunters. He injured some of them; many drew back in fear. But not the lord, who, blowing boldly on his bugle, raced after him on a light horse.

All this time our courteous prince, Sir Gawain, lay at home in his richly-hued bed. The lady did not forget him but set out early to change his mind. Raising the curtain, she peeped in at him. He welcomed her graciously, and she sat by his side with a lovely look. Laughingly, she said:

"Sir, if you are Gawain, I think it is a wonder that you do not know the proper observances of good company. And if someone shows them to you, you cast them out of your mind. Have you forgotten already what I taught you yesterday?"

"What is that?" asked Gawain. "Truly, I do not know what you mean."

"Why, I taught you of kissing."

"That I dared not do," Gawain parried; "I thought you might refuse me."

"My faith, you cannot be refused!" the merry lady replied. "You are strong enough to take by force—if any could be so rude as to refuse you!"

"In my land," Gawain countered, "force does no good to the user, nor any gift that is not given with good will. I am at your command, to kiss when you like."

She bent down and kissed him, and then complained: "I would like to know why I have never heard from your mouth words that belong to love. In the romances of chivalry, the service of love is everything; it is both the title and text of these books.[33] So it is with true knights: they adventure their lives for their loves, endure for them grievous times, free them from care, and bring them to bliss. You are young, you are active, you are renowned far and wide for your knighthood. Yet I have sat by you on two separate times

[33] What is the IMAGE here?

and have not heard yet one word of love. I come here to learn from you. Teach me!—while my lord is away from home."

Gawain answered, "It is a great happiness to me that you should trouble yourself with 5 so poor a man as I. But to take it upon myself to expound to you true love, to you who have twice the skill in that art that a hundred such as I combined have, or ever shall have, would be a great folly!" 10

She made trial of him, tested him often, tried to win him to sin (whatever she may have intended besides). But he defended himself so gracefully that there was no fault to be seen, nor any sinful act, on either side: 15 nothing but happiness. At the last she kissed him and went her way, and Gawain rose to go to Mass. He played with the ladies all day.

But the lord dashed about over the countryside chasing his unlucky boar, who had bitten 20 in two the backs of his best hounds. Finally the boar was forced out in the open by the archers, who showered him with their arrows. He was so tired he could run no more. He tried to escape to a hole by a rock on the 25 bank of a stream. He got the bank at his back and began to paw the ground. His mouth foamed; he whet his white tusks. None of the hunters dared to close with him, he was so fierce and so frenzied and had hurt so many 30 already.

Then the lord came himself, urging his horse on. He saw the animal at bay with his men beside him. He jumped down from the saddle, took out his bright sword, and strode 35 forward with firm steps. He waded through the ford to where the beast stood. The boar saw him and raised up his bristles. He snorted so ferociously that the men feared for their lord's life. The boar charged. 40

Man and boar met in the swiftest part of the stream, but the boar had the worst of it. The lord marked him well, set his blade at the hollow just above the breastbone, and drove it in to the hilt. 45

Now there was a blowing of horns, a hallooing of men, a baying of dogs! A man skilled in woodcraft began to cut up the boar. First he chopped his head off and set it on high; then he slit him along the backbone 50

and pulled out the bowels. These he broiled on coals and mixed with bread, and with them he rewarded the dogs. Then he cut the flesh in broad bright slabs, tore out the haslets, fastened the two sides together, and hung them on a pole. Then the huntsmen turned home. They carried the boar's head on high.

The lord could hardly wait to see Gawain. They greeted each other with much laughter and loud talking. Then the ladies were brought, and the company gathered. The lord described to them the great size of the boar and the terribleness of the fighting. Gawain called the boar a prize, saying he had never before seen such a beast. He admired the great head.

"Now, Gawain," said the lord, "this boar is all yours, by the terms of our agreement."

"That is true," Gawain replied; "and now I shall give you my winnings." He seized the knight by the neck and kissed him graciously twice. "Now are we even," said Gawain, "of all the agreements we have made."

"By St. Giles," the lord answered, "you are the luckiest man I know! You will be rich before long if you draw such bargains."

Later, by the fireplace, they drank and made merry, and the lord proposed the same agreement for New Year's eve. But Gawain begged to be allowed to ride on in the morning, for it was near the time when he needs must go. The lord restrained him:

"As I am a true knight, I give you my word you shall be at the Green Chapel long before prime [34] on New Year's morn. Therefore lie in your bed and take your ease, and I shall hunt in the woods and keep the agreement to exchange with you the winnings when I return. I have tested you twice and have found you faithful. Now—'third time turns out best,' as they say."

Gawain agreed to stay and that night slept full still and soft.

The lord rose early. He and his men took a bit of food after Mass, and then he called for his mount. It was a fine morning. The earth was frost-covered; the sun rose red upon the clouds coasting through the sky. Soon, the dogs fell on the trail of a fox and ran

[34] Early morning.

this way and that to find where the scent was strongest. One of them cried out; all the huntsmen shouted; the rest of the pack ran to him and they all raced forth. The fox flitted on, ever before them. When the dogs saw him with their eyes they chased on even faster and denounced him with their angry barks. The fox dodged and turned across rough ground, doubled back along hedges, stopped and listened, and at last leapt over a thorn hedge by a little ditch and stole out quietly along the border of a small wood. He thought he had eluded them—but before he knew it he was at a hunting station, where three great hounds attacked him at once. He swerved quickly. With all the woe in the world upon him he went back into the woods.

Then was it life as you like it to hear the hounds! What a cursing was set on that fox's head! He was "hallooed" when the huntsmen saw him; he was damned and called thief. The greyhounds were always on his tail, so that he could never pause a moment. But he was wily, this Reynard, and he led the lord and his men a chase till midday, while at home our courteous knight slept within his comely curtains that cold morn.

But the lady did not sleep. She rose quickly and went to him. Her fair face and throat were laid all naked, her breast was bare before and behind. She came, closing the door after her, and swung open a window, calling, "Ah, man! how can you sleep? This morning is so bright and clear!"

In the heavy gloom of a dream Gawain muttered, like a man troubled with many grim matters, as indeed he was: how destiny should that next day award him his fate, when he would receive the blow without struggle. He recovered his wits, swung out of the dream, and answered her with haste. She came to him laughing softly. She bent low over his face and kissed him. When he saw her so glorious, so gaily attired, so faultless in her features, a strongly welling joy warmed his heart. Smiling courteously and gently, they fell into mirth.

There was only bliss and joy there—but great peril stood between them, unless Mary was mindful of her knight. The lovely lady

nearly pushed him to his limit. He must either take her love there or refuse her offensively. He cared much for chivalric manners and for his reputation as a knight; but even more that he should sin and be a traitor to the man in whose house he was a guest.[35]

"God forbid," he said, "that shall not happen!" With a laughing speech, he gently laid aside all the words of love that came from her mouth.

"You deserve blame," she admonished, "if you will not love the person who lies next to you, wounded in her heart more than anyone else in the world. Yes, you deserve blame, unless you have a sweetheart, someone dearer to you, who pleases you better, to whom you have plighted your troth so firmly that you will not break it. But I do not believe that. Tell me, I pray you. For all the love in the world do not hide the truth from me."

Smiling gently, Gawain said, "In faith, I have no one else—nor will I have for some time."

"That is an answer," she replied, "which is the worst of all. But I am sorry to say that I think I have been answered truly. Kiss me now, and I shall go. I can only mourn, as a woman who loves much."

Sighing, she bent down and kissed him; then she separated herself from him and, standing, asked:

"Now, beloved, do this much for me at this parting. Give me something of yours, your glove, perhaps, that I may remember you by, to lessen my grief."

Gawain replied, "I would that I had here the dearest thing I possess; you have deserved more reward than I can give. But to give you only a glove is not to your honor. I am here on a mission in a strange country, and have no men with me with bags of valuable things. Each man must do as he is circumstanced— do not take it illy."

"Nay," she said, "though I have nothing of yours, yet you shall have something of mine."

[35] The original is somewhat ambiguous here; chivalry seems at war with chastity, but Gawain's strongest reason for refusing the lady is clear: he would be violating a law of hospitality.

She handed him a ring of red gold with a great standing stone that blazed like the bright sun. But he refused it, saying:

"I will have no gifts at this time. I have none to give you nor will I take any."

Then she sighed and spoke, "If you will not take my ring, because it seems too rich to you, then I shall give you my belt. It is worth very little."

She took off a girdle that was knotted about her. It was made of green silk and gold and ornamented with pendants of gold.

"It is unworthy," she said, "but take it."

He told her he would take nothing until God granted him the achievement of his quest. "Therefore I pray you," he said, "be not displeased. Now stop pressing me, for I shall never consent. But I will always be your true servant."

"You refuse this silk because it is so simple?" she asked. "Lo, it is little, and so the less is it valuable; but anyone who knew the qualities knit into it might consider it of value, perhaps. Whoever is girt with this green belt cannot be slain by any means whatsoever. While he has it fastened about him, there is no man under heaven who can kill him."

Gawain mused a moment, and in his mind he realized what a jewel the girdle would be when he reached the Green Chapel. He suffered her to speak. She pressed the belt on him. He granted her her wish. She gave the belt to him and besought him, for her sake, never to reveal the gift, but to conceal it loyally from her lord.

He agreed that no one should ever know. She thanked him over and over, and by then she had kissed him for the third time.

When she was gone, Sir Gawain arose and dressed himself in noble array. He put away the love-token where he might find it again and then went to the chapel. He privately approached a priest and asked him to tell him how he might save his soul when he should go hence, confessed his misdeeds, besought mercy, and called for absolution. The priest absolved him, making him as clean as though Doomsday were to come that morning. Then Gawain was merrier with the ladies, with carols and all sorts of joy, than he had ever been. All were delighted with him and said, "Surely, he was never so merry since he came here." [36]

Now let us leave him in that comfortable place, surrounded by love. The lord is still in the field leading his men. He has killed the fox which he followed so long. As the lord leaped over a hedge to see the rascal, Reynard came running through the woods with the pack at his heels. The lord drew out his bright blade and cast it at him, but the fox swerved. He would have started back, except that a hound rushed him. Then the dogs all fell on him, right under the horse's hooves. The lord leaped down and snatched him from their jaws. He held him high over his head and shouted loudly. The hunters ran to him, blowing the recall on their horns. All those who had bugles blew them at once, those who did not shouted aloud, and the hounds bayed. It was a fine noise that was raised for Reynard's soul.

They rewarded the hounds, stroking them and rubbing their heads. Then they took Reynard and stripped him of his coat. As it was now nearly night, they turned towards home, blowing stoutly on horns all the way.

The lord found Sir Gawain by the fire. He wore a coat of blue that reached to the floor; his surcoat was softly furred, and a matching hood hung on his shoulder; both were bordered with white fur all about. Saying "I shall first fulfill the agreement," he embraced the good lord and, with much relish and vigor, kissed him three times.

"By Christ," said his host, "I think you got pleasure in buying this merchandise, if the price was not too high."

"No matter the price," said Gawain. "The bargain that I owed you is now fully paid."

"Marry," replied the lord, "mine is not worth much. I have hunted all day and have only this foul-smelling fox's skin—the Fiend may have it—which is poor exchange for the three kisses you have pressed so warmly on me here."

"It is enough," cried Gawain. "I thank you, by the Cross."

[36] How do you account for the change in Gawain's spirits?

With mirth and with minstrelsy, with the laughter of the ladies, with food as they liked it, Gawain and the lord passed the evening. Then Gawain humbly took his leave. First he spoke to the lord:

"May God reward you for the wonderful hospitality you have shown me at this high feast-time. I must, as you know, leave on the morrow. If you will do as you promised, give me someone to guide me to the Green Chapel, I will indeed give you myself to become one of your men."

"In good faith," the lord replied, "I shall do all that I promised you I would." At once he assigned him a servant to set him on the way.

Gawain thanked him, and then took his leave from the fair ladies. With sorrow and with kissing he spoke to them, urging upon them his heartfelt thanks. With sad sighings they commended him to Christ, and he left. He thanked each man he met for the various troubles he had gone to to serve him, and each man was as sorry to see him go as if he had lived there forever.

Surrounded by people, he was lighted to his chamber and brought merrily to bed to be at his rest. I dare not say whether he slept soundly. He had much to think of, if he would.

4

It is now almost New Year. The night passes, daylight drives away the darkness, as God commands. Outside it is storming wildly. The clouds cast to the earth the cold snow which, with all the bitterness of the north in it, sifts down, cruelly nipping all the naked wild things. From the heights the shrill wind rushes and fills every valley with great drifts of snow.

Gawain lies in his bed and listens. He sleeps very little. The crowing of each cock reminds him of his ordeal, and long before day he springs up. There is a lamp lighted in his chamber, and he calls for his groom, who brings him his armor. First he puts on his clothing, to ward off the cold; then his armor, the rings of the corslet and the plates all burnished like new; and finally his coat

with the embroidered badge set upon velvet. Gawain does not forget the belt, the lady's gift. After fastening on his sword, he winds this love-token about him; the green silk shines against the red and the gold.

Now he goes to where the household is gathered. He thanks them all. Gringolet is brought in ready to gallop. Gawain looks at the fine condition of the horse's coat and says to himself, "The people in this castle truly think about courtesy. May the man who maintains them have joy, and may the dear lady have love in this life!" He steps into the stirrup and swings aloft; he spurs Gringolet with his gilt heels. The great horse leaps forward.

Gawain cries: "I commend this castle to Christ! May he ever give it good fortune!"

He crosses himself quickly and rides over the bridge. He compliments the porter who, kneeling before him, gives him good day and prays that God may save him. Now he is on his way alone, save for the man who is to take him to the dismal place where he will receive the blow.

The way leads along hillsides covered with bare trees, along cliffs where the cold is intense. Mist drizzles on the moors, melts on the mountains. Every hill wears a hat, a cloud-cap.[37] The brooks boil and foam white as they rush down.

Now the two riders are on a high hill, and the sun rises. White snow lies around them. The man bids Gawain wait:

"You are now near the place that you have so specially asked after. But I must say the truth to you, since I know you and love you well. Take my advice and be the better for it. In that wasteland lives a man who is the very worst on earth. He is strong and stern, he loves to kill. He is larger than any man on earth, larger than the best four knights in Arthur's house, Hector,[38] or any other. He is a merciless man and a violent one. None passes by that place—churl or chaplain, monk or masspriest—who is not killed by a blow from his hand. As surely as you sit here, you will be killed if you go

[37] Note the fine descriptive IMAGE.
[38] The Trojan hero.

there. So, good Sir Gawain, let the man alone! Go by some other way! Ride through some other land, and may Christ bless you! I promise you that I shall swear by God and all his saints that you never fled from any man I ever knew of."

Gawain turns to him: "May it be well with you who so wish my good! I believe that you would keep the secret, but no matter. If I fled from here I would be a cowardly knight; there could be no excuse. I will go on to the chapel and speak with that man, for good or for ill. He may indeed be a grim fellow to deal with. But God can save His servants, if it is His will."

"Marry!" says the man. "If you wish to lose your life I cannot prevent you. Take your helmet and spear and ride down that path by the side of that rock till you come to the bottom of the valley; then look on your left and you shall see both the Green Chapel and the man who keeps it. Now farewell, noble Gawain, and God be with you! For all the gold in the earth I would not go with you one foot further!"

Gawain turns his bridle, hits his horse with his heels as hard as he can, and leaves his guide on the hill-top alone. "Before God," he says to himself, "I shall not falter; I am obedient to His will and I hold myself at one with Him."

Now he spurs Gringolet again and picks up the path, going in by a steep bank at the side of a small wood. He rides down into the valley and then looks about him, but sees no sign of the chapel: only high banks on each side, rough knuckled crags above him, clouds grazing along their tops.[39] He holds in his horse and looks for the chapel.

Now he sees a sort of knoll in the middle of a little glade, a smooth-swelling mound. It is on the bank of a stream just below a waterfall, and the stream bubbles as though it is boiling.

He urges on his horse and approaches the mound. Now he dismounts, ties the reins to a tree, and walks about the mound, debating with himself as to what it may be. It has a hole in the end and on either side, and it is over-

grown everywhere with green grass in clumps. Inside it is all hollow. "It is nothing but an old cave," he thinks, "or perhaps the crevice of an old crag." He does not know quite what to call it.

"Can this be the Green Chapel?" he asks himself. "It looks a fitting place for the devil to say his matins [40] in at midnight! And it would well suit the Green Knight, to perform his devotions here in devil's wise. I do feel it is the Fiend—feel it in all my five wits—who has forced this appointment on me, to destroy me! This is the Chapel of Disaster, the cursedest kirk I ever came in."

Helmet on head, lance in hand, he makes his way to the roof. Now he hears coming from the rocks beyond the brook, a noise, as though someone were grinding a scythe on a grindstone.

Whack! it clatters against the cliff!

Whack! it whirrs and whets!

Whack! it rushes and rings!

"By God," he says, "that is being prepared as a welcome for me! However, let God work His will. Even though I lose my life, moaning will not help me; and besides, no noise is going to make me afraid."

He calls out: "Who is here to keep an appointment with me? For now is Gawain walking right here! If any man wishes anything with him, let him come quickly, either now or never!"

"Hold!" bellows a voice from the bank over his head. "You shall soon have everything I promised you!"

The man who spoke keeps on with his noise-making. Whack! Whack! Whack!

Suddenly he whirls out of an opening in a crag. He holds before him a frightful weapon, a Danish axe newly made, with a blade, filed sharp on the whetstone, four feet wide; and he is dressed in green. Green is his face and his legs, his hair and his beard—all just as before, except that now full fairly on his feet he hastens over the earth. He comes to the water, vaults over it on his axe, and strides across the snow.

Sir Gawain stands to meet him; he does not bow. The Green man speaks: "Sweet sir, a

[39] What is the implied comparison in this IMAGE?

[40] The first prayers of the day.

man can see you keep your word! You have timed your journey like a true man, and you know the agreement between us: twelve months ago you had your opportunity, and now, at this New Year, I have mine. We are completely alone here; there are no knights to separate us; we can fight as we like. Take off your helmet and receive your payment. Give me no more resistance than I did you when you lopped off my head at one blow!"

Gawain speaks: "By God who gave me a soul, I bear you no ill will. If you limit yourself to one stroke, I shall stand still and let you work as you like."

He bows his head; the skin of his neck shows bare. He acts as though he fears nothing.

Now the Green Knight gathers up his grim tool and with all the force in his body raises it aloft. He takes aim. As the axe comes down, Gawain glances at it and flinches a little. The Green Knight swerves and withholds the axe. He rebukes Gawain with proud words:

"You are not Gawain, who is held to be so worthy! Who never showed fear before any army in valley or hill! For you flinch for fright before you even feel pain. Such cowardice of Gawain I never heard tell. Nor did I shrink when you aimed at me in Arthur's house. My head flew to my feet and yet I never moved. And you, you are frightened out of your wits before you receive any harm. Now who is the better man?"

Gawain replies:

"I flinched once, but I will not do it again. However, if you cut off *my* head I cannot put it back on again. But hurry; come to the point; deal me my fate, and do it out of hand! I shall stand you the stroke and flinch no more till your axe has hit me. Here is my word."

"Here goes then!" cries the other. He heaves the axe aloft, and looks about angrily. He aims, but he does not cut. He withholds his hand. Gawain waits; he does not flinch, but stands still as a stone, or a stump fixed in rocky ground by a hundred roots. Now the green man calls out merrily:

"So—now that you have your heart again, it behooves me to hit. Hold now the high hood that Arthur gave you, and keep your neck at this stroke—if it can recover from it!"

Gawain speaks wrathfully:

"Thrash on, you fierce fellow. You threaten too long. I suspect you have frightened your own self."

"Ah," says the other, "you speak so boldly now that I need wait no longer."

He takes his stance to strike and puckers his lips and his forehead. He raises his weapon and sends it down with all his vigor, but the blade merely nicks the skin! The bright blood shoots over Gawain's shoulder. He sees it gleaming on the snow and springs forth in a great leap, more than a spear's length, grabs his helmet, puts it on his head, raises his shield in front of him, draws out his bright sword, and cries:

"No more! I have taken one stroke, and if you offer me another I shall pay you back readily—you may trust it!—and fiercely. One stroke only belonged to you—the agreement in Arthur's house said so. Now therefore, knight, cease!"

The Green Knight rests on his axe and looks at him, how he stands armed, boldly, without fear. In his heart he is pleased with him. Now he speaks merrily, in his great, ringing voice:

"Bold fellow, do not be so fierce! No man has treated you discourteously or misused you. As the agreement had it, I promised you one stroke and you have received it; consider yourself well paid. If I had been more nimble, I might have given you a harsher blow. But here is what I did: First I threatened you, but did not hurt you. That was for the agreement we made on the first night, which you held to faithfully, giving me all you got. The second blow, also a pretended one, I gave you for the second morning on which you kissed my wife—the kisses you gave to me. If an honest man pays back honestly, he need fear no danger. But on the third day you did fail me, and therefore you took that little tap. For it is my garment that you wear, that girdle. My own wife gave it to you—I know that well. I know all about the kissing and your knightly behavior, about my wife's tempting you. I brought that all about myself. I sent her to test you, and to speak truly you seem to me to be more faultless than any other knight. But in accepting the girdle you were at fault—although you did it only because you loved your life, so I blame you very little." [41]

Gawain stands still in a deep study. Now the blood rushes to his face and he winces for shame. He cries out in anguish:

"May cowardice and covetousness be cursed for always!"

He catches at the knot, undoes it, and flings the girdle at the Green Knight:

"Lo, there lies my broken faith! For fear of your blow cowardice taught me to join hands with covetousness and forsake my own nature, which is the generosity and loyalty that belongs to a knight. Now I am false, I who have always feared treachery and untruth! Let me win back your good will."

The other laughs and says amiably:

"Any harm that I had I consider completely healed. You are confessed so clean, and have your penance so evident, that I hold you as pure as if you had never done wrong. I will give you the girdle, for it is green like my garments. It will be an excellent token of the adventure at the Green Chapel. But now you shall go back to my castle, and we shall revel away the rest of the New Year festivities. I think we can reconcile you with my wife, who was your bitter enemy!" [42]

"No," says Gawain, "I have stayed long enough. May happiness betide you. Commend me to your comely wife—to my honored ladies, both of them, who have thus beguiled their knight with their trick. But is it any wonder if a fool be won to sorrow through the wiles of women? Adam was beguiled by one, Solomon by many, Samson—Delilah gave him his—and David was blinded by Bathsheba. These were all brought to disaster by

their wiles. It would be a great gain to love women well and to believe them not, if a man could. But your girdle: God reward you for that! I will keep it gladly as a reminder of my transgression, to teach me how tender is the flesh. When pride shall prick me for my prowess at arms, I shall look at it. Now, one more word I beg of you: tell me your right name."

"Bercilak de Hautdesert," replies the Green Knight. "Through the power of Morgan le Fay,[43] who lives in my house, and the cunning of her magic, I went to Arthur's castle to put the renown of the Round Table to a test. She hoped to take away your reason and to cause Guenever to die in terror of the Green man who spoke so ghostly with his head in his hand. It is she who is at home, the ancient lady. She is also your aunt, Arthur's half-sister, the daughter of the Duchess of Tyntagel, whom noble Uther [44] afterwards had Arthur upon. Therefore I entreat you to come to your aunt and make merry in my house. All my household loves you, and I myself wish you as much good in this life as any man under God, for your great fidelity."

"No," says Gawain, "not by any means."

Now they embrace, they kiss, they commend each other to the Prince of Paradise. Now they part right there in the cold.

The knight in bright green went whithersoever he would,[45] but Gawain rode back to Arthur's castle. He had many an adventure, but I shall not at this time recount them. The cut in his neck healed, and he wore the shining girdle slantwise as a baldric, knotted under his left arm, as a sign that he was guilty of a fault. And thus he came back to the court.

Joy wakened in the castle when they knew good Gawain had returned. The king kissed him. The queen kissed him also. Then many a knight greeted him and asked him of his

---

[41] To what extent has Gawain behaved cowardly? Does he have complete faith in the girdle?

[42] How was she his "bitter enemy"? (See also ll. 3-4 above.)

[43] The enchantress, beloved by Merlin, the famous wizard of King Arthur's court, who taught her his magic. She had an affair with a knight named Guiomar; when Guenever learned of this intrigue she forced Morgan to leave the court. Ever afterwards Morgan hated Arthur's queen.

[44] King Uther Pendragon.

[45] Why is the poet so unspecific here?

journey. He told it all: about the hardships that he had, the adventure of the Green Chapel, the behavior of the knight, the love of the lady, and last of all, about the girdle. The blood shot to his face when he had to 5 tell of it.

"Lo," said he, fingering the girdle, "this is the band of cowardice and covetousness, the symbol of perfidy—and I needs must wear it as long as I live. No man can hide his harm 10 when it is one of the spirit."

They all laughed loudly at that and they all agreed—all the brotherhood of the Round Table—to wear, all of them, a baldric of the the same bright green for Gawain's sake. And 15 ever afterwards, to wear such a baldric was an honor, as is written down in the best books of romance.

In Arthur's day this adventure took place, as the books bear witness. Since Brutus,[46] that 20 bold knight, first came hither,

Many knightly adventures
Have fallen such as this;

Now may he who bore the crown of thorn
Bring us to his bliss.

Amen.

HONI SOIT QUI MAL Y PENSE [47] (*ca.* 1400)

STUDY AIDS: 1. Is Sir Gawain a coward? Study carefully his actions in all four parts to be able to give reasons in support of your answer.

2. Which is the more interesting character, Sir Gawain or the Green Knight (who is also the lord of the castle)? Analyze each character.

3. What knightly ideals does Sir Gawain exemplify? Contrast him, as the ideal knight, with Beowulf, the ideal Germanic hero. Contrast each with the ideal hero of today.

4. Analyze in detail the structure of *Sir Gawain and the Green Knight*. How many major scenes are there? How are they interrelated? How is the problem of time handled? Are any of the actions symbolic (e.g., on the day when Gawain accepts the girdle, the animal killed by the lord is a fox)?

5. Does *Sir Gawain and the Green Knight* modify in any way your mental picture of life in the Middle Ages?

Geoffrey Chaucer
(*ca.* 1344–1400)

CHAUCER'S BIOGRAPHY READS MORE LIKE THAT OF A COURTIER AND MAN-OF-AFFAIRS (both of which he was) than that of a poet. Indeed, of the many records of his life which have come down to us, not one mentions that he was a writer. Yet there is every reason to believe that he was regarded as the greatest writer of his age, for he was widely read, imitated, and quoted; even some of his success in the material world was probably a reward for his skill with his pen.

The year 1374 divides Chaucer's life into two parts. Before then, he was principally in the service of two powerful nobles: Prince Lionel and John of Gaunt (whose wife's sister he married). He was also, at times, in the service of the king. In his middle teens he was with the English army in France and was taken prisoner; he was ransomed by the king. Next he probably studied law; he also went on a number of diplomatic missions, some of them secret, which took him to France and Italy, where he became acquainted with the literature of the time. These first thirty years of his life must have been extremely broad-

---

[46] It was the medieval belief that Aeneas' grandson, Brutus, founded Britain.
[47] "Shamed be the one who thinks evil of it." This is the motto of the Order of the Garter; however, neither this nor any other knightly order seems to have worn a green band.

ening, with their opportunity for seeing all levels of society not only in his own land but in others as well.

In 1374 Chaucer was made Controller of Customs in the port of London, a post which he held for twelve years. It was during this time that he wrote his great verse romance, *Troilus and Criseyde,* a story of two star-crossed lovers which has sometimes been called the first psychological novel. In 1389 he was appointed Clerk of the King's Works. As such, he had charge of the construction and repair of the royal and public buildings, bridges, walls, and sewers. In 1391 he resigned this important and busy appointment, perhaps to have more time for writing, for by then he was well started on *The Canterbury Tales.* Whatever the reasons, he spent the remaining nine years of his life in relative quiet.

Three qualities are outstanding in his writings: a humor which is sometimes gentle, sometimes sly, often satiric, but never vicious (quite frequently he is the butt of his own jokes); an understanding of human beings which is warm and compassionate but never sentimental; and an acuteness of observation which is unfailing in its ability to discern the most significant detail. Chaucer's fame, unlike that of many writers, was great in his own lifetime and has remained consistently so for over 550 years.

A NOTE ON THE PRONUNCIATION OF CHAUCER: Much of the pleasure of reading Chaucer comes from the sound of his Middle English, a language rather different from the modern English we know. Probably the best way to become acquainted with Chaucer's English is to hear it read by a skilled reader, in person or on one of the phonograph records available. One can make a good start for himself, however, if he will observe a few suggestions. The following treatment of Middle English is considerably simplified, but it should enable you to approximate Chaucer's pronunciation. In general, there are two matters to consider: (1) the meter—that is, reading the line so as to recognize the five-beat stress that Chaucer gave it; and (2) the sounds of the individual words.

Meter. You will have no trouble giving a line the required five-beat stress if you will sound all the vowels. The most important thing to notice here is the many final –*e*'s, most of which should be sounded. Old English, like Latin, was a highly inflected language; it relied on the endings of words, rather than on word order, to show whether a word was subject or object, and so on. Most of these endings have now disappeared, although we still write some of them, such as the final *e* in *name.* In Chaucer's time the various vowel endings were in the process of disappearing, but they were still sounded, the several vowel endings having been regularized to –*e.* It is an indefinite vowel sound (*uh*), like the *a* in Cuba. In Chaucer's verse it is sounded, even in a word at the end of a line. The only time it is not sounded is when the following word begins with a vowel or an unsounded *h* (*honour*). Thus in the phrase "droghte of March" (drought of March) *droghte* is one syllable, not two; the final –*e* is not sounded, because *of* begins with a vowel. The –*e* of *droghte* and the *o* of *of* are run together, or elided.

All other vowels, too, should be sounded. This means that many words familiar to us in modern English are given more syllables in Chaucer's pronunciation. So, the modern three-syllable word *confession* (cun-fes-shun) would in Chaucer have four syllables (confessioun = con-fes-see-oon); our two-syllable word *marriage* (măr-ij) has four syllables in Chaucer (mar-ee-ahdg-uh); modern English *patience* (pay-shens) also has four syllables (pacience = pah-see-ens-uh).

Sounds. Involved here are three classes of sounds: consonants, vowels, and diphthongs.

a. Chaucer's consonants are virtually the same as those of modern English. But note the following differences: There are no silent consonants; hence the *k* of *knight* is sounded, as is the *l* in *folk* and *half,* the *g* in *king,* etc. All *r*'s are trilled. Final *–s* is unvoiced (*his* is pronounced *hiss*), as is *th* (the *th* in *that* resembles the sound in *thing* rather than in *there*). The only difficult sound is the *gh,* which is halfway between *k* and *sh.* Thus, in a word like *right* or *knight,* the *gh* resembles German *ch,* as in *Ich,* which is halfway between *–ik* and *–ish.*

b. Chaucer's short vowels are the same as in modern English; hence the vowels in *at, let, him,* etc., offer no problem. The long vowels, however, are quite different. In general they resemble the long vowels in European languages—German, French, Italian, and Spanish. The following table indicates the approximate sounds of long vowels in Middle English:

Spelling	Example	Pronunciation
a, aa	name	(nah-muh)
e, ee	sweete	(sway-tuh)
i, y	time	(teem-uh)
I		(ee)
o, oo	roote	(roh-tuh)
	good	(goad)
ou, ow	out	(oot)
	fowles	(fool-ess)

c. Diphthongs are combinations of vowels, and are pronounced very much as they look.

Spelling	Example	Pronunciation
ai, ay	day	(dă-ee)
au	cause	(cow-zuh)
eu, ew	knew	(k-nay-oo)
oi, oy	coy	(co-ee)

A little practice, especially on the final *–e*'s and the long vowels, should enable you to read Chaucer's English tolerably well.

The following respelling of the first four lines of the *General Prologue* will suggest the pronunciation:

> Whahn thaht Ahpril with hiss shoo-ress so-tuh
> The drookt of March hahth payr-sed toh the ro-tuh
> Ahnd bahth-ed every vein in switch li-koor
> Of which vair-tu engen-dred iss the floo-er.

The Canterbury Tales

GENERAL PROLOGUE [1]

The *General Prologue* to *The Canterbury Tales,* in some respects the most remarkable product of Chaucer's genius, is an extended *dramatis personae* for the collection of tales which follows.

[1] The text is that of Professor F. N. Robinson's *The Works of Geoffrey Chaucer,* Second Edition. This text incorporates the discoveries of the Manly-Rickert "Chicago" *Chaucer;* it is hence probably the definitive text of the *General Prologue.*

In it Chaucer presents his characters, one by one, in a series of vivid, detailed, and lifelike portraits, and also sets forth his plan: to have each of his characters tell two tales on the way to Canterbury and two more on the way back, to while away the time. The result is a continuous drama, for the tales give rise to altercations and other byplay and also further characterize their tellers. Chaucer did not live to complete his ambitious project. The *General Prologue,* however, shows how fully he grasped it in his own mind.

It would be a mistake to consider the *General Prologue* as merely an introduction. It is a mature and highly finished work in its own right—the liveliest, most convincing picture of life in the Middle Ages which has come down to us.

Whan that Aprill [2] with his shoures soote		*shoures soote:* sweet showers
The droghte of March hath perced to the roote,		*droghte:* drought
And bathed every veyne in swich licour		*swich licour:* such liquid
Of which vertu engendred is the flour;		*vertu:* power; *flour:* flower
Whan Zephirus [3] eek with his sweete breeth	5	*eek:* also
Inspired hath in every holt and heeth		*holt:* wood
The tendre croppes, and the yonge sonne		
Hath in the Ram his halve cours yronne,[4]		*yronne:* run
And smale foweles maken melodye,		*foweles:* birds
That slepen al the nyght with open ye	10	*ye:* eyes
(So priketh hem nature in hir corages);		*priketh hem:* stirs them; *hir corages:* their hearts
Thanne longen folk to goon on pilgrimages,[5]		
And palmeres [6] for to seken straunge strondes,		*straunge strondes:* strange shores
To ferne halwes, kowthe in sondry londes;		*ferne halwes:* far-off shrines; *kowthe:* (well) known
And specially from every shires ende	15	
Of Engelond to Caunterbury [7] they wende,		*wende:* go
The hooly blisful martir for to seke,		*seke:* seek
That hem hath holpen whan that they were seeke.		*holpen:* helped; *seeke:* sick
Bifil that in that seson on a day		
In Southwerk at the Tabard [8] as I lay	20	
Redy to wenden on my pilgrymage		*wenden:* go
To Caunterbury with ful devout corage,		
At nyght was come into that hostelrye		
Wel nyne and twenty in a compaignye,		
Of sondry folk, by aventure yfalle	25	*aventure yfalle:* chance fallen
In felaweshipe, and pilgrimes were they alle,		
That toward Caunterbury wolden ryde.[9]		*wolden:* would
The chambres and the stables weren wyde,		*wyde:* spacious
And wel we weren esed atte beste.		*esed atte beste:* well cared for
And shortly, whan the sonne was to reste,	30	*sonne was to reste:* sun was to bed
So hadde I spoken with hem everichon		*hem everichon:* them every one

[2] Why is April an appropriate month for beginning a pilgrimage? (Cf. also *Cuckoo Song,* p. 110.)

[3] The west wind, a bringer of pleasant weather in England because of the Gulf Stream.

[4] A reference to the Zodiac (cf. any farmer's almanac of today). The "young" sun has run half his course in the sign of the Ram (Aries). This astronomical reckoning of time seems to mean April 18. Why is the sun called "young"?

[5] Invariably journeys to religious shrines, usually in fulfillment of a vow made to the saint of the shrine in time of sickness or some other need.

[6] Pilgrims, so-called because of the palm branches they frequently carried.

[7] At Canterbury was the shrine of St. Thomas à Becket, who was murdered in the cathedral there in 1170.

[8] An inn or "pub," on the outskirts of London.

[9] About sixty miles from London.

That I was of hir felaweshipe anon,   *hir:* their; *anon:* straightway
And made forward erly for to ryse,   *made forward:* (we) made agreement
To take oure wey there as I yow devyse.   *as I yow devyse:* as I shall describe
    But nathelees, whil I have tyme and space,   35   *nathelees:* nevertheless
Er that I ferther in this tale pace,   *er:* ere, before; *pace:* pass
Me thynketh it acordaunt to resoun   *me thynketh:* to me it seems
To telle yow al the condicioun
Of ech of hem, so as it semed me,   *semed me:* seemed to me
And whiche they weren, and of what degree,[10] 40 *which:* what sort; *degree:* rank
And eek in what array that they were inne;   *eek:* also; *array:* dress
And at a knyght than wol I first bigynne.   *wol:* will

A KNIGHT [11] ther was, and that a worthy man,
That fro the tyme that he first bigan
To riden out, he loved chivalrie,   45   *riden out:* go on expeditions
Trouthe and honour, fredom and curteisie.   *fredom:* generosity
Ful worthy was he in his lordes werre,   *werre:* war
And therto hadde he riden, no man ferre,   *therto:* in addition; *ferre:* further
As wel in cristendom as in hethenesse,   *hethenesse:* pagan lands
And evere honoured for his worthynesse.   50
At Alisaundre [12] he was whan it was wonne.   *wonne:* won
Ful ofte tyme he hadde the bord bigonne   *he . . . begonne:* headed the table
Aboven alle nacions in Pruce;   *Pruce:* Prussia
In Lettow hadde he reysed and in Ruce,   *Lettow:* Lithuania; *reysed:* raided;
No Cristen man so ofte of his degree.   55   *Ruce:* Russia
In Gernade at the seege eek hadde he be   *Gernade:* Granada (Spain)
Of Algezir, and riden in Belmarye.   *Algezir, Belmarye:* in Morocco
At Lyeys was he and at Satalye,   *Lyeys, Satalye:* in Asia Minor
Whan they were wonne; and in the Grete See   *Grete See:* Mediterranean
At many a noble armee hadde he be.   60   *armee:* armada, armed expedition
At mortal batailles hadde he been fiftene,
And foughten for oure feith at Tramyssene   *Tramyssene:* Tlemcen (Algeria)
In lystes thries,[13] and ay slayn his foo.   *foo:* foe
This ilke worthy knyght hadde been also   *ilke:* same
Somtyme with the lord of Palatye   65   *Palatye:* Balat (Turkey)
Agayn another hethen in Turkye.
And everemoore he hadde a sovereyn prys;   *sovereyn prys:* splendid reputation
And though that he were worthy, he was wys,[14]
And of his port as meeke as is a mayde.   *port:* bearing
He nevere yet no vileynye ne sayde [15]   70   *vileynye:* rude or coarse word

[10] What difference does this suggest between medieval society and the democracies of today?
[11] Chaucer begins with the Knight, a professional soldier, because he is the highest in rank (degree). Note the qualities, scattered throughout the portrait, which are valued in the Knight.
[12] Alexandria, Egypt. The Knight has been a great fighter against the infidels. His campaigns, as given in the lines which follow, have mostly been in three areas: northeastern Europe (against the Lithuanians and Tartars), and in the eastern and western ends of the Mediterranean. The campaigns mentioned seem to represent the career of a typical knight.
[13] In tournaments thrice. The reference is to single-handed combat with the enemy.
[14] This line is commonly interpreted to mean: although he was brave, he was prudent. Can you see a reason for this interpretation?
[15] Double and triple negatives were good usage in Chaucer's time. Note the idealization of the Knight's character, and compare ll. 69–72 with the tribute paid to Beowulf at the very end of that poem.

In al his lyf unto no maner wight.   *no maner wight:* no person of any sort
He was a verray, parfit gentil knyght.   *verray:* true (adj.); *parfit:* perfect
But, for to tellen yow of his array,   *array:* apparel
His hors were goode, but he was nat gay.   *hors:* horses; *gay:* gaily dressed
Of fustian he wered a gypon   75   *fustian:* cotton cloth; *gypon:* tunic
Al bismotered with his habergeon,   *bismotered with:* discolored by;
For he was late ycome from his viage,   *habergeon:* coat of mail
And wente for to doon his pilgrymage.[16]

With hym ther was his sone, a yong SQUIER,   *squier:* squire
A lovyere and a lusty bacheler,[17]   80   *lovyere:* lover
With lokkes crulle as they were leyd in presse.   *crulle:* curled; *presse:* press (e.g.,
Of twenty yeer of age he was, I gesse.   curling iron)
Of his stature he was of evene lengthe,   *evene lengthe:* moderate height
And wonderly delyvere, and of greet strengthe.   *delyvere:* agile
And he hadde been somtyme in chyvachie   85   *chyvachie:* a cavalry raid
In Flaundres, in Artoys, and Pycardie,   *Artoys, Pycardie:* in France
And born hym weel, as of so litel space,   *hym:* himself; *space:* space of time
In hope to stonden in his lady grace.   *lady:* lady's
Embrouded was he, as it were a meede   *embrouded:* embroidered; *meede:*
Al ful of fresshe floures, whyte and reede.[18]   90   meadow
Syngynge he was, or floytynge, al the day;   *floytynge:* fluting, playing the flute
He was as fressh as is the month of May.[19]
Short was his gowne, with sleves longe and wyde.
Wel koude he sitte on hors and faire ryde.
He koude songes make and wel endite,   95   *endite:* compose
Juste and eek daunce, and weel purtreye and write.   *juste:* joust; *purtreye:* draw
So hoote he lovede that by nyghtertale   *nyghtertale:* nighttime
He sleep namoore than dooth a nyghtyngale.
Curteis he was, lowely, and servysable,
And carf biforn his fader at the table.[20]   100

A YEMAN hadde he[21] and servantz namo   *yeman:* yeoman; *namo:* no more
At that tyme, for hym liste ride so,   *liste:* he wished
And he was clad in cote and hood of grene.
A sheef of pecok arwes, bright and kene,   *pecok arwes:* peacock (feathered)
Under his belt he bar. . . .   105   arrows

Ther was also a Nonne, a PRIORESSE,[22]
That of hir smylyng was ful symple and coy;[23]

[16] Presumably he had vowed, in time of need (perhaps in battle), to make a pilgrimage to a saint's shrine. Pilgrimages could be to places as far away as Spain or even Jerusalem. Is there perhaps sly humor in having the Knight choose a very short pilgrimage?

[17] A technical term, meaning a candidate for knighthood (cf. Bachelor of Arts); the word also meant "bachelor" in the modern sense. Is this a pun?

[18] What is the IMAGE here? Why is it appropriate? Does it reveal anything of the Squire's character?

[19] What does this image reveal of the Squire's character?

[20] Make a list of the Squire's principal character traits and accomplishments. How many of these are shared by college students of today? How many are not?

[21] Which is the more logical antecedent for "he," the Squire or the Knight?

[22] What is a prioress?

[23] Neither "simple" nor "coy" has its present-day meaning: "simple" has the sense of "simplicity," "coy" that of "quietness," without any suggestion of coquetry.

Hire gretteste ooth was but by Seinte Loy; [24] 120
And she was cleped madame Eglentyne. [25]   *cleped:* called
Ful weel she soong the service dyvyne,
Entuned in hir nose ful semely,   *entuned:* intoned
And Frenssh she spak ful faire and fetisly,   *fetisly:* skilfully
After the scole of Stratford atte Bowe,[26]   125 *scole:* school
For Frenssh of Parys was to hire unknowe.
At mete wel ytaught was she with alle: *mete:* meals
She leet no morsel from hir lippes falle,   *leet:* let
Ne wette hir fyngres in hir sauce depe;
Wel koude she carie a morsel and wel kepe   130 *kepe:* keep, take care
That no drope ne fille upon hire brest.
In curteisie was set ful muchel hir lest.
Hir over-lippe wyped she so clene
That in hir coppe ther was no ferthyng sene   *coppe:* cup; *ferthyng:* bit
Of grece, whan she dronken hadde hir
    draughte.   135
Ful semely after hir mete she raughte.   *raughte:* reached
And sikerly she was of greet desport,   *sikerly:* surely; *desport:* merriment
And ful plesaunt, and amyable of port,   *port:* bearing, behavior
And peyned hire to countrefete cheere   *cheere:* appearance
Of court, and to been estatlich of manere,   140 *estatlich:* stately
And to ben holden digne of reverence.   *digne:* worthy
But, for to speken of hire conscience,   *conscience:* feeling
She was so charitable and so pitous
She wolde wepe, if that she saugh a mous
Kaught in a trappe, if it were deed or bledde. 145
Of smale houndes hadde she that she fedde   *houndes:* (simply) dogs
With rosted flessh, or milk and wastel-breed.[27] *wastel-breed:* a fine white bread
But soore wepte she if oon of hem were deed,
Or if men smoot it with a yerde smerte;
And al was conscience and tendre herte.   150
Ful semyly hir wympul pynched was,   *semyly:* comely; *wympul:* head-dress
Hir nose tretys, hir eyen greye as glas,   *tretys:* well-shaped; *eyen:* eyes
Hir mouth ful smal, and therto softe and reed;
But sikerly she hadde a fair foreheed;
It was almoost a spanne brood, I trowe;   155 *trowe:* believe
For, hardily, she was nat undergrowe.   *hardily:* surely
Ful fetys was hir cloke, as I was war.   *fetys:* handsome; *war:* aware
Of smal coral aboute hire arm she bar   *bar:* bore
A peire of bedes, gauded al with grene,   *peire of bedes:* rosary; *gauded:* with
And theron heng a brooch of gold ful sheene, 160   the gauds (large beads) all green

[24] Various attempts have been made to explain the choice of St. Loy (St. Eloi, or Eligius); perhaps the fact that he was noted for his personal beauty and courtesy, plus the rhyme, caused Chaucer to choose him for this gentle woman.

[25] Madame Eglentyne translates to "Lady Sweetbriar."

[26] The reference is presumably to the Prioress's nunnery; the French is that of England, brought in by the Norman Conquest, and not the more elegant French of Paris. Is Chaucer satirizing the Prioress? If so, what is the TONE of the SATIRE?

[27] Nuns were forbidden to have pets according to the Bishops' Registers of the time; but the literature of the period shows they did.

On which ther was first write a crowned A,   *crowned A:* (presumably) an *A*
And after *Amor vincit omnia.*[28]   surmounted by a crown

   Another NONNE with hire hadde she,
That was hir chapeleyne, and preestes thre.   *thre:* three

   A MONK [29] ther was, a fair for the maistrie, 165 *a fair for the maistrie:* a first-rate one
An outridere,[30] that lovede venerie,   *venerie:* hunting
A manly man, to been an abbot able.
Ful many a deyntee hors hadde he in stable,   *deyntee:* fine
And whan he rood, men myghte his brydel heere
Gynglen in a whistlynge wynd als cleere   170
And eek as loude as dooth the chapel belle.[31]
Ther as this lord was kepere of the celle,   *ther as:* where
The reule of seint Maure or of seint Beneit,
By cause that it was old and somdel streit
This ilke Monk leet olde thynges pace,   175
And heeld after the newe world the space.[32]
He yaf nat of that text a pulled hen,   *yaf:* gave; *pulled:* plucked
That seith that hunters ben nat hooly men,[33]
Ne that a monk, when he is recchelees,   *recchelees:* careless of duty
Is likened til a fissh that is waterlees,—   180 *til:* to
This is to seyn, a monk out of his cloystre.
But thilke text heeld he nat worth an oystre;
And I seyde his opinion was good.
What sholde he studie and make hymselven wood, *what:* why; *wood:* mad
Upon a book in cloystre alwey to poure,   185
Or swynken with his handes, and laboure,   *swynken:* work
As Austyn bit? How shal the world be served? *Austyn:* St. Augustine; *bit:* bids
Lat Austyn have his swynk to hym reserved! [34]
Therfore he was a prikasour aright: *prikasour:* fast-riding hunter
Grehoundes he hadde as swift as fowel in
   flight;   190
Of prikyng and of huntyng for the hare   *prikyng:* tracking
Was al his lust, for no cost wolde he spare.
I seigh his sleves purfiled at the hond   *purfiled:* trimmed
With grys, and that the fyneste of a lond;   *grys:* a gray fur

---

[28] "Love conquers all." The phrase could apply to spiritual love, but Chaucer leaves the matter ambiguous. What other evidences of SATIRE can you find in the description of the Prioress? What sort of person is she?

[29] Originally, monks were men who retired from the world and devoted themselves to an ascetic life in a monastery. This point is important for the satire in Chaucer's portrait of a very worldly monk.

[30] As an "out-rider," the monk supervised the monastery's estates.

[31] Is there IRONY in this image?

[32] The sentence structure of ll. 172–176 is confused: When this monk was in charge of the cell or company of monks, he did not observe the Benedictine Rule (regulations governing the Benedictine monks), because it was old and somewhat strict; he let the old (strict) things pass and held after the new (easier) world for the time being. The Benedictine Rule was also known as the Rule of St. Maur.

[33] The text referred to is a mistranslation in the medieval Bible, in which Nimrod is said to be a mighty hunter against the Lord.

[34] Is Chaucer wholly serious in his agreement with the monk's justification of his worldliness?

And, for to festne his hood under his chyn,   195
He hadde of gold ywroght a ful curious pyn;
A love-knotte in the gretter ende ther was.
His heed was balled, that shoon as any glas,
And eek his face, as he hadde been enoynt.   *enoynt:* anointed
He was a lord ful fat and in good poynt;   200   *poynt:* shape
His eyen stepe, and rollynge in his heed,   *stepe:* protruding
That stemed as a forneys of a leed;   *stemed:* shone; *forneys:* furnace, fire;
His bootes souple, his hors in greet estaat.   *leed:* caldron
Now certeinly he was a fair prelaat;
He was nat pale as a forpyned goost.   205   *forpyned goost:* tormented spirit
A fat swan loved he best of any roost.
His palfrey was as broun as is a berye.[35]

A FRERE[36] ther was, a wantowne and a merye,
A lymytour,[37] a ful solempne man.   *solempne:* festive, perhaps imposing
In alle the ordres foure[38] is noon that kan   210   *kan:* knows
So muchel of daliaunce and fair langage.   *daliaunce:* light flirtation
He hadde maad ful many a mariage
Of yonge wommen at his owene cost.[39]
Unto his ordre he was a noble post.
Ful wel biloved and famulier was he   215
With frankeleyns over al in his contree,   *frankeleynes:* franklins, well-to-do
And eek with worthy wommen of the toun;   landowners
For he hadde power of confessioun,
As seyde hymself, moore than a curat,   *curat:* priest
For of ordre he was licenciat.   220   *licenciat:* licensed by the Pope to hear
Ful swetely herde he confessioun,   confession
And plesaunt was his absolucioun:
He was an esy man to yeve penaunce,   *yeve:* give
Ther as he wiste to have a good pitaunce.   *wiste:* knew; *pitaunce:* gift
For unto a povre ordre for to yive   225   *povre:* poor; *yive:* give
Is signe that a man is wel yshryve;   *yshryve:* shriven, confessed
For if he yaf, he dorste make avaunt,   *yaf:* gave; *dorste:* dared; *avaunt:* boast
He wiste that a man was repentaunt;   *wiste:* knew
For many a man so hard is of his herte,
He may nat wepe, althogh hym soore smerte.   230   *hym soore smerte:* he smarts sorely
Therfore in stede of wepynge and preyeres
Men moote yeve silver to the povre freres.   *moote:* must
His typet was ay farsed ful of knyves   *typet:* cape; *farsed:* stuck
And pynnes, for to yeven faire wyves.

[35] What aspects of the Monk's character does Chaucer satirize? Is he wholly unsympathetic toward him? What are your reasons for your answer?

[36] In contrast to monks, friars were supposed to go out into the world, help the sick and needy, hear confessions, and even to teach. They were licensed to beg. Chaucer's Friar, however, although usually "within the law," is hardly a model. Note the irony which runs through this satiric portrait.

[37] A limiter was a friar licensed to beg within an assigned area; he usually paid for the privilege of having this monopoly (cf. ll. 252a–252b).

[38] The four principal orders of friars were the Augustinians, Carmelites, Dominicans, and Franciscans.

[39] The implication is that the Friar had seduced the young women and hence had to find husbands for them.

And certeinly he hadde a murye note: 235
Wel koude he synge and pleyen on a rote;
Of yeddynges he baar outrely the pris.
His nekke whit was as the flour-de-lys;
Therto he strong was as a champioun.
He knew the tavernes wel in every toun 240
And everich hostiler and tappestere
Bet than a lazar or a beggestere;
For unto swich a worthy man as he
Acorded nat, as by his facultee,
To have with sike lazars aqueyntaunce. 245
It is nat honest, it may nat avaunce,
For to deelen with no swich poraille,
But al with riche and selleres of vitaille.
And over al, ther as profit sholde arise,
Curteis he was and lowely of servyse. 250
Ther nas no man nowher so vertuous.
He was the beste beggere in his hous;
[And yaf a certeyn ferme for the graunt; 252ᵃ
Noon of his bretheren cam ther in his haunt;] ⁴⁰ 252ᵇ
For thogh a wydwe hadde noght a sho,
So plesaunt was his *"In principio,"* ⁴¹
Yet wolde he have a ferthyng, er he wente. 255
His purchas was wel bettre than his rente.
And rage he koude, as it were right a whelp.
In love-dayes ther koude he muchel help,
For ther he was nat lyk a cloysterer
With a thredbare cope, as is a povre scoler, 260
But he was lyk a maister or a pope.
Of double worstede was his semycope,
That rounded as a belle out of the presse.
Somwhat he lipsed, for his wantownesse,
To make his Englissh sweete upon his tonge; 265
And in his harpyng, whan that he hadde songe,
His eyen twynkled in his heed arygh,
As doon the sterres in the frosty nyght.
This worthy lymytour was cleped Huberd.

A MARCHANT was ther with a forked berd, 270
In mottelee, and hye on horse he sat;
Upon his heed a Flaundryssh bever hat,
His bootes clasped faire and fetisly.
His resons he spak ful solempnely,
Sownynge alwey th'encrees of his wynnyng. . . . 275
This worthy man ful wel his wit bisette: 279
Ther wiste no wight that he was in dette,
So estatly was he of his governaunce
With his bargaynes and with his chevyssaunce.

rote: a stringed instrument
of yeddynges: at singings; *baar
   outrely:* bore off completely
therto: in addition

tappestere: barmaid
bet: better; *lazar:* leper; *beggestere:*
   begger (female)
acorded nat: it accorded not
sike: sick; *lazars:* lepers

poraille: poor folk
riche: rich people; *vitaille:* victuals
over al: everywhere; *ther:* where

yaf: gave; *ferme:* rent

sho: shoe

ferthyng: farthing; *er:* ere
purchas: proceeds from begging
rage: romp about; *it:* he
love-dayes: days on which disputes
   were settled by arbitration

maister: university graduate
semycope: short cape
presse: mould
lipsed: lisped

eyen: eyes

cleped: called

mottelee: motley (parti-colored cloth)

fetisly: neatly
resons: remarks
sownynge: proclaiming

wiste: knew; *wight:* person
estatly: careful in dealings
chevyssaunce: profits (usury?)

⁴⁰ This couplet may have been canceled by Chaucer in his revision.
⁴¹ The opening words of the Gospel of John, believed to have magical powers.

For sothe he was a worthy man with alle,
But, sooth to seyn, I noot how men hym calle.

noot (ne wot): know not

A CLERK ther was of Oxenford also,
That unto logyk hadde longe ygo.[42]
As leene was his hors as is a rake,[43]
And he nas nat right fat, I undertake,
But looked holwe, and therto sobrely.
Ful thredbare was his overeste courtepy;
For he hadde geten hym yet no benefice,
Ne was so worldly for to have office.
For hym was levere have at his beddes heed
Twenty bookes, clad in blak or reed,
Of Aristotle and his philosophie,
Than robes riche, or fithele, or gay sautrie.
But al be that he was a philosophre,
Yet hadde he but litel gold in cofre;[44]
But al that he myghte of his freendes hente,
On bookes and on lernynge he it spente,
And bisily gan for the soules preye
Of hem that yaf hym wherwith to scoleye.
Of studie took he moost cure and moost heede.
Noght o word spak he moore than was neede,
And that was seyd in forme and reverence,
And short and quyk and ful of hy sentence;
Sownynge in moral vertu was his speche,
And gladly wolde he lerne and gladly teche.

285 clerk: cleric, scholar
ygo: gone
leene: lean
undertake: dare say
holwe: hollow
290 overeste courtepy: outer shortcoat
benefice: i.e., a church
office: i.e., secular employment
hym was levere: he'd rather

295

fithele: fiddle; sautrie: psaltery, zither

hente: get

300

gan . . . preye: did pray
hem: them; yaf: gave; scoleye: study
cure: care
o: one
305 in forme: formally
hy sentence: high matter
sownynge in: consonant with

A SERGEANT OF THE LAWE,[45] war and wys,
That often hadde been at the Parvys,
Ther was also, ful riche of excellence.
Discreet he was and of greet reverence—
He semed swich,[46] his wordes weren so wise.
Justice he was ful often in assise. . . .
Nowher so bisy a man as he ther nas,
And yet he semed bisier than he was. . . .

war and wys: wary and prudent
310 Parvys: a rendezvous for lawyers and
their clients

swich: such
assise: the court of assize
321 nas: was

A FRANKELEYN was in his compaignye.
Whit was his berd as is the dayesye;
Of his complexioun he was sangwyn.

331 frankeleyn: wealthy landowner
whit: white; dayesye: daisy
sangwyn: very ruddy

[42] He had long gone past the study of logic, which, along with grammar and rhetoric, made up the trivium, the principal subjects for the B.A. degree. Hence he was probably a graduate student, and as such he would be studying arithmetic, geometry, astronomy, and music (these being the quadrivium), and probably also natural and moral philosophy. After completing the M.A. degree, the Clerk would very likely go on to the study of theology.

[43] The horse is probably a hired nag, and hence thin. Why is the rake an appropriate IMAGE?

[44] The reference in this and the preceding line is to alchemy, the medieval chemical science which had as its aim the changing of baser metals into gold. The alchemist was a natural philosopher; the poor clerk, however, was definitely a moral philosopher, with little interest in money, except to buy books with it. The pun in "philosophre" would be more apparent to medieval readers than it is to modern ones.

[45] The sergeants-at-law were high-ranking lawyers, the king's legal servants.

[46] Note the sly humor.

Wel loved he by the morwe a sop in wyn;
To lyven in delit was evere his wone, 335
For he was Epicurus [47] owene sone,
That heeld opinioun that pleyn delit
Was verray felicitee parfit.
An housholdere, and that a greet, was he;
Seint Julian he was in his contree. 340
His breed, his ale, was always after oon;
A bettre envyned man was nowher noon.
Withoute bake mete was nevere his hous
Of fissh and flessh, and that so plentevous,
It snewed in his hous of mete and drynke,[48] 345
Of alle deyntees that men koude thynke.
After the sondry sesons of the yeer,
So chaunged he his mete and his soper.
Ful many a fat partrich hadde he in muwe,
And many a breem and many a luce in stuwe. 350
Wo was his cook but if his sauce were
Poynaunt and sharp, and redy al his geere.
His table dormant in his halle alway
Stood redy covered al the longe day.
At sessiouns ther was he lord and sire; 355
Ful ofte tyme he was knyght of the shire.
An anlaas and a gipser al of silk
Heeng at his girdel, whit as morne milk.
A shirreve hadde he been, and a contour.
Was nowher swich a worthy vavasour. 360

   An HABERDASSHERE and a CARPENTER,
A WEBBE, a DYERE, and a TAPYCER,—
And they were clothed alle in o lyveree
Of a solempne and a greet fraternitee. . . .

   A COOK they hadde with hem for the nones 379
To boille the chiknes with the marybones,
And poudre-marchant tart and galyngale.
Wel koude he knowe a draughte of Londoun ale.
He koude rooste, and sethe, and broille, and frye,
Maken mortreux, and wel bake a pye.
But greet harm was it, as it thoughte me, 385
That on his shyne a mormal hadde he.
For blankmanger, that made he with the beste.

   A SHIPMAN was ther, wonynge fer by weste;
For aught I woot, he was of Dertemouthe.[49]

morwe: morning; *sop:* bread
wone: custom

pleyn: full
verray: true; *parfit:* perfect

Julian: patron saint of hospitality
after oon: after one standard (good)
envyned: stocked with wine
bake mete: baked meats or pasties

snewed: snowed

after: according to
mete: meals; *soper:* supper
muwe: coop
luce: pike; *stuwe:* fish pond

geere: gear, equipment
table dormant: permanent table
covered: set
sessiouns: court session
knyght...: member of Parliament
anlaas: dagger; *gipser:* purse

shirreve: sheriff; *contour:* accountant
vavasour: landowner, squire

webbe: weaver; *tapycer:* tapestry
  maker; *o:* one
fraternitee: social and religious guild

nones: occasion
marybones: marrowbones
poudre-marchant, galyngale: flavor-
  ings
sethe: boil
mortreux: stew

shyne: shin; *mormal:* sore, ulcer
blankmanger: creamed fowl or meat

wonynge fer by: dwelling far in the
woot: know

[47] Epicurus, the Greek philosopher, then, as now, erroneously famed as an advocate of voluptuous living, especially with regard to food and drink.
[48] Note the image.
[49] The reference to Dartmouth (in Devonshire) is perhaps pointed to some actual person. A vessel named the *Magdaleyne* is known to have been from Dartmouth (see l. 410); her master was one Peter Risshenden.

He rood upon a rouncy, as he kouthe,[50]   390   *rouncy:* nag
In a gowne of faldyng to the knee.   *faldyng:* coarse woolen cloth
A daggere hangynge on a laas hadde he   *laas:* lanyard
Aboute his nekke, under his arm adoun.
The hoote somer hadde maad his hewe al broun;   *hewe:* complexion
And certeinly he was a good felawe.[51]   395
Ful many a draughte of wyn had he ydrawe   *ydrawe:* drawn
Fro Burdeux-ward, whil that the chapman sleep.[52]
Of nyce conscience took he no keep.   *nyce:* overly particular; *keep:* care
If that he faught, and hadde the hyer hond,   *hyer hond:* higher hand
By water he sente hem hoom to every lond.[53]   400   *hoom:* home
But of his craft to rekene wel his tydes,   *craft:* skill, ability; *tydes:* tides
His stremes, and his daungers hym bisides,   *hym bisides:* near him
His herberwe, and his moone, his lodemenage,   *herberwe:* harbor; *lodemenage:*
Ther nas noon swich from Hulle to Cartage.   piloting
Hardy he was and wys to undertake;   405   *wys to undertake:* prudent to conduct
With many a tempest hadde his berd been shake.[54]   (an enterprise)
He knew alle the havenes, as they were,
Fro Gootlond to the cape of Fynystere,   *Gootlond:* Gottland (off Sweden);
And every cryke in Britaigne and in Spayne.   *Fynystere:* cape in Spain
His barge ycleped was the Maudelayne.   410   *ycleped:* called; *Maudelayne:* Magdalen

With us ther was a DOCTOUR OF PHISIK;[55]
In al this world ne was ther noon hym lik,   *hym lik:* like him
To speke of phisik and of surgerye,
For he was grounded in astronomye.   *astronomye:* astrology
He kepte his pacient a ful greet deel   415   *kepte:* watched
In houres by his magyk natureel. . . .   *in houres:* in the proper astrological
He knew the cause of everich maladye,   419   hours
Were it of hoot, or coold, or moyste, or drye,
And where they engendered, and of what
    humour.   *humour:* fluid
He was a verray, parfit praktisour: *verray, parfit praktisour:* true, perfect
The cause yknowe, and of his harm the roote,   practitioner

[50] "As he kouthe" (as well as he knew how) suggests that the Shipman was a poor rider. Why is this appropriate?
[51] "Good felawe" is at least half-ironic, in view of the lines which follow.
[52] The implication is that the Shipman had stolen wine on the way from Bordeaux while the merchant for whom he was carrying it slept. Bordeaux, then as now, was a famous wine district.
[53] I.e., he drowned whatever prisoners he took (a common practice). Note the implied attitude toward the taking of human life in the Middle Ages.
[54] Try to account for the effectiveness of this line.
[55] To understand the portrait of the Doctor of Physic (medicine), it is necessary to realize that the medieval physician depended as much upon astrology as upon drugs. Two striking differences between medicine then and now are these: (1) the planets were believed to exert beneficial and harmful influences upon a patient and hence had to be taken into account by the physician; and (2) a person's health was thought to be dependent upon the condition of the four body fluids, called the four humors: blood, phlegm, choler (yellow bile), and melancholy (black bile). These were the product of four elementary qualities: heat, cold, moistness, and dryness. Blood was hot and moist, phlegm was cold and moist, etc. Despite the erroneousness of his theories, the physician seems to have been a good one for his time.

By permission of Mr. Francis Plimpton.

The medieval Tower of Learning, illustrating the hierarchy of academic pursuits.

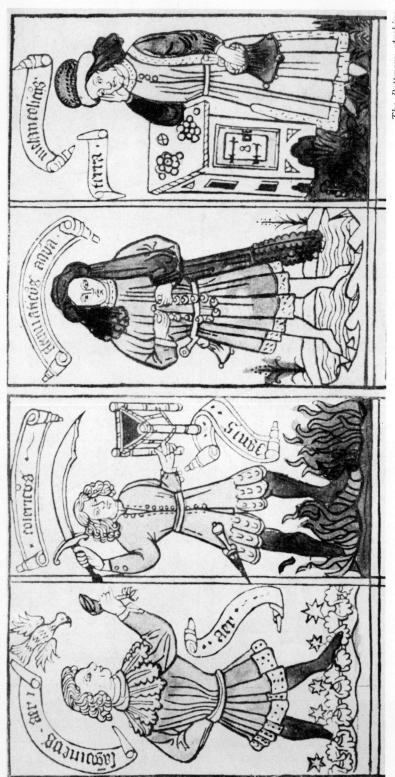

The Four Temperaments and their relation to the Four Elements. From left to right: air, fire, water, earth, corresponding to the following elements of the human body: blood (sanguine), yellow bile (choleric), phlegm (phlegmatic), black bile (melancholy).

Anon he yaf the sike man his boote.
Ful redy hadde he his apothecaries   425
To sende hym drogges and his letuaries,
For ech of hem made oother for to wynne—
Hir frendshipe nas nat newe to bigynne.[56]
Wel knew he the olde Esculapius,
And Deyscorides, and eek Rufus. . . .[57]   430
Of his diete mesurable was he,   435
For it was of no superfluitee,
But of greet norissyng and digestible.
His studie was but litel on the Bible.[58]
In sangwyn and in pers he clad was al,
Lyned with taffata and with sendal;   440
And yet he was but esy of dispence;
He kepte that he wan in pestilence.
For gold in phisik is a cordial,
Therefore he lovede gold in special.[59]

A good WIF was ther of biside BATHE,   445
But she was somdel deef, and that was scathe.
Of clooth-makyng she hadde swich an haunt,
She passed hem of Ypres and of Gaunt.
In al the parisshe wif ne was ther noon
That to the offrynge bifore hire sholde goon;   450
And if ther dide, certeyn so wrooth was she,
That she was out of alle charitee.
Hir coverchiefs ful fyne weren of ground;
I dorste swere they weyeden ten pound
That on a Sonday weren upon hir heed.   455
Hir hosen weren of fyn scarlet reed,
Ful streite yteyd, and shoes ful moyste and newe.
Boold was hir face, and fair, and reed of hewe.
She was a worthy womman al hir lyve:
Housbondes at chirche dore she hadde fyve,[60]   460
Withouten oother compaignye in youthe,—
But therof nedeth nat to speke as nowthe.
And thries hadde she been at Jerusalem;
She hadde passed many a straunge strem;
At Rome she hadde been, and at Boloigne,   465
In Galice at Seint-Jame, and at Coloigne.[61]

Glosses (right column):

anon: straightway; *yaf:* gave; *boote:* remedy
drogges: drugs; *letuaries:* remedies
wynne: profit

Esculapius: god of medicine
Deyscorides, Rufus: Greek physicians
mesurable: moderate

norissyng: nourishment

sangwyn: red; *pers:* blue
sendal: thin silk
esy of dispence: slow to spend money
wan: won; *pestilence:* the Black Death
cordial: remedy

wif: wife; *biside Bathe:* near Bath
somdel deef: a bit deaf; *scathe:* sad
haunt: skill
passed: surpassed; *Ypres, Gaunt* (Ghent): Flemish towns
sholde goon: was allowed to go

ground: texture
dorste: would dare

hosen: hose; *reed:* red
streite: tightly; *yteyd:* tied; *moyste:* i.e., new leather

withouten: in addition to
as nowthe: as for now
thries: thrice

Boloigne: Boulogne (France)
Galice: Galicia (Spain); *Jame:* James

---

[56] Note the innuendo.

[57] There follows a list of twelve famous physicians of antiquity, mostly Greek, Arabian, and English. The Doctor of Physic was well read in the standard medical authorities.

[58] The implication is that he saw little connection between religion and medicine, not necessarily that he was atheistic (note that he is on a pilgrimage).

[59] The medical use of gold (*aurum potabile*) is longstanding—but note the ironic twist given to it in Chaucer's lines.

[60] This means she was legally married (medieval marriages were customarily performed at the church door).

[61] Pilgrimages were often criticized as being merely excuses for a trip. The places mentioned were famous shrines.

She koude muchel of wandrynge by the weye.

Gat-tothed[62] was she, soothly for to seye.

Upon an amblere esily she sat,

Ywympled wel, and on hir heed an hat 470

As brood as is a bokeler or a targe;

A foot-mantel aboute hir hipes large,

And on hir feet a paire of spores sharpe.

In felaweshipe wel koude she laughe and carpe.

Of remedies of love she knew per chaunce, 475

For she koude of that art the olde daunce.[63]

koude: knew
soothly: truthfully

ywympled: covered with a wimple
bokeler: buckler; *targe*: shield
foot-mantel: skirt
spores: spurs
carpe: talk

koude: knew

A good man was ther of religioun,

And was a povre PERSOUN of a toun,[64]

But riche he was of hooly thoght and werk.

He was also a lerned man, a clerk, 480

That Cristes gospel trewely wolde preche;

His parisshens devoutly wolde he teche.

Benygne he was, and wonder diligent,

And in adversitee ful pacient.

And swich he was ypreved ofte sithes. . . . 485

Wyd was his parisshe, and houses fer asonder, 491

But he ne lefte nat, for reyn ne thonder,

In siknesse nor in meschief to visite

The ferreste in his parisshe, muche and lite,

Upon his feet, and in his hand a staf. 495

This noble ensample to his sheep he yaf,

That first he wroghte, and afterward he taughte.

Out of the gospel he tho wordes caughte,

And this figure he added eek therto,

That if gold ruste, what shal iren do? 500

For if a preest be foul, on whom we truste,

No wonder is a lewed man to ruste;

And shame it is, if a prest take keep,

A shiten shepherde and a clene sheep. . . .

To drawen folk to hevene by fairnesse, 519

By good ensample, this was his bisynesse.

But it were any persone obstinat,

What so he were, of heigh or lough estat,

Hym wolde he snybben sharply for the nonys.

A bettre preest I trowe that nowher noon ys. 525

He waited after no pompe and reverence,

Ne maked him a spiced conscience,

But Cristes loore and his apostles twelve

He taughte, but first he folwed it hymselve.

povre Persoun: poor parson

clerk: cleric, scholar

parisshens: parishioners
wonder: wondrously

swich: such; *ypreved*: proved; *ofte*
 sithes: often

meschief: misfortune
ferreste: furthest; *muche and lite*:
 high and low
ensample: example; *yaf*: gave

tho: those
figure: figure of speech
iren: iron

lewed: unlearned

shiten: befouled

heigh: high; *lough*: low; *estat*: station
snybben: rebuke; *for the nonys*: all
 right
waited after: demanded
spiced: overly fastidious
loore: lore

---

[62] "Gat-tothed," meaning widely spaced teeth, was taken as a sign of lasciviousness.

[63] The reference is to the art of love. What is the IMAGE?

[64] This is an idealized portrait of a parish priest. It is also satire of an indirect sort: Chaucer so describes the Parson as to imply that there are few like him in the land. Is it significant that the parish priest was one of the lowest members of the clergy?

With hym ther was a PLOWMAN,[65] was his
    brother
That hadde ylad of dong ful many fother;   530   *ylad:* drawn; *fother:* cartload
A trewe swynkere and a good was he,   *swynkere:* worker
Lyvynge in pees and parfit charitee.
God loved he best with al his hoole herte
At alle tymes, thogh him gamed or smerte,   535   *thogh . . . smerte:* in all circum-
And thanne his neighebor right as hymselve.   stances
He wolde thresshe, and therto dyke and delve,   *dyke:* make ditches; *delve:* dig
For Cristes sake, for every povre wight,   *povre wight:* poor person
Withouten hire, if it lay in his myght.
His tithes payde he ful faire and wel,
Bothe of his propre swynk and his catel.   540   *swynk:* work; *catel:* goods
In a tabard he rood upon a mere.   *tabard:* laborer's coat; *mere:* mare (a
                                        humble mount)

    Ther was also a REVE, and a MILLERE,   *reve:* reeve
A SOMNOUR, and a PARDONER also,   *somnour:* summoner
A MAUNCIPLE, and myself—ther were namo.[66]   *maunciple:* manciple; *namo:* no more

    The MILLERE was a stout carl for the nones; 545   *carl:* fellow; *for the nones:* all right
Ful byg he was of brawn, and eek of bones.   *brawn:* muscle
That proved wel, for over al ther he cam,   *over al ther:* wherever
At wrastlynge he wolde have alwey the ram.   *ram:* i.e., as a prize
He was short-sholdred, brood, a thikke knarre;   *knarre:* sturdy fellow (lit., knot)
Ther was no dore that he nolde heve of harre, 550   *dore:* door; *nolde:* would not; *heve:*
Or breke it at a rennyng with his heed.   heve; *harre:* hinge
His berd as any sowe or fox was reed,   *reed:* red
And therto brood, as though it were a spade.
Upon the cop right of his nose he hade   *cop:* top
A werte, and theron stood a toft of herys,   555   *werte:* wart; *toft:* tuft; *herys:* hairs
Reed as the brustles of a sowes erys;   *erys:* ears
His nosethirles blake were and wyde.[67]   *nosethirles:* nostrils
A swerd and bokeler bar he by his syde.
His mouth as greet was as a greet forneys.   *forneys:* furnace
He was a janglere and a goliardeys,   560   *janglere:* talker; *goliardeys:* coarse-
And that was moost of synne and harlotries.   spoken fellow
Wel koude he stelen corn and tollen thries;[68]
And yet he hadde a thombe of gold,[69] pardee.   *pardee:* surely (lit., by God)
A whit cote and a blew hood wered he.
A baggepipe wel koude he blowe and sowne, 565

---

[65] Another idealized portrait, a companion piece to the description of the Parson. Each represents the ideal Christian, one the professional religious man, the other the layman. What are the implications of Chaucer's choosing men from lowly walks of life for these two portraits?

[66] These remaining characters are all more or less rascals. Is there sly humor in Chaucer's placing himself among them?

[67] According to the beliefs of the time, the physical features just mentioned (short, stocky figure, red beard, warty nose, etc.) denoted a lecherous, quarrelsome, loquacious fellow.

[68] When a miller grinds grain he takes out part of it (a toll) as payment. This miller took three times as much toll as he should have.

[69] This refers to a proverb, "An honest miller has a golden thumb." As millers go, he was honest.

And therwithal he broghte us out of towne.[70]   *therwithal:* with that

A gentil MAUNCIPLE [71] was ther of a temple,
Of which achatours myghte take exemple   *which:* whom; *achatours:* buyers
For to be wise in byynge of vitaille;   *vitaille:* victuals
For wheither that he payde or took by taille,   570   *by taille:* on credit
Algate he wayted so in his achaat   *algate:* nevertheless; *wayted so:* so
That he was ay biforn and in good staat.   watched; *achaat:* purchases
Now is nat that of God a ful fair grace
That swich a lewed mannes wit shal pace   *lewed:* unlearned; *pace:* pass
The wisdom of an heep of lerned men? . . .   575

The REVE [72] was a sclendre colerik man.   587   *reve:* reeve
His berd was shave as ny as ever he kan;   *ny:* closely
His heer was by his erys full round yshorn; [73]
His top was dokked lyk a preest biforn   590
Ful longe were his legges and ful lene,   *lene:* lean
Ylyk a staf, there was no calf ysene.   *ylyk:* like
Wel koude he kepe a gerner and a bynne;   *kepe:* watch; *gerner:* granary
Ther was noon auditour koude on him wynne.   *wynne:* i.e., get the better of him
Wel wiste he by the droghte and by the reyn   595   *wiste:* knew
The yeldynge of his seed and of his greyn.   *yeldynge:* produce
His lordes sheep, his neet, his dayerye,   *neet:* cattle
His swyn, his hors, his stoor, and his pultrye   *stoor:* live-stock
Was hoolly in this Reves governynge,
And by his covenant yaf the rekenynge,   600
Syn that his lord was twenty yeer of age.   *syn:* since
Ther koude no man brynge hym in arrerage.   *arrerage:* arrears
Ther nas baillif, ne hierde, nor oother hyne,   *hierde:* herdsman; *hyne:* worker
That he ne knew his sleighte and his covyne;   *his:* bailiff's, herdsman's, etc.; *covyne:*
They were adrad of hym as of the deeth.   605   deceitfulness
His wonyng was ful faire upon an heeth;   *wonyng:* dwelling; *heeth:* heath
With grene trees yshadwed was his place.
He koude bettre than his lord purchace.
Ful riche he was astored pryvely: *astored:* provided; *pryvely:* secretly
His lord wel koude he plesen subtilly,   610
To yeve and lene [74] hym of his owene good,   *yeve:* give
And have a thank, and yet a cote and hood.
In youthe he hadde lerned a good myster;   *myster:* trade
He was a wel good wrighte, a carpenter.   *wrighte:* workman

[70] Note this vivid detail, with its appeal to the senses of sight and of hearing. Try to account for the greater vividness of the portrait of the Miller in comparison with that of the Plowman and the Parson.

[71] A manciple was a purchasing agent, in this instance for the group of lawyers who lived in the Inner or the Middle Temple (residences for societies of lawyers). The occupation of the manciple was a modest one; all that gives this manciple distinction is that he succeeded in cheating, in a minor way, his learned masters, as the last line of the portrait (omitted in the text) makes clear: "And yet this Manciple *sette hir aller cappe*" (i.e., made fools of them all).

[72] A reeve seems to have been a sort of estate manager.

[73] To show that he was a servant. Note the specific detail in the description of the Reeve.

[74] The crafty Reeve lends his lord his lord's own possessions; so he gets thanks and profit also.

This Reve sat upon a ful good stot,   615   *stot:* stallion
That was al pomely grey and highte Scot.   *pomely:* dappled; *highte:* was called
A long surcote of pers upon he hade,   *pers:* blue cloth
And by his syde he baar a rusty blade.   *baar:* bore
Of Northfolk was this Reve of which I telle,   *Northfolk:* Norfolk
Biside a toun men clepen Baldeswelle.[75]   620   *clepen:* call
Tukked he was as is a frere aboute,   *tukked:* i.e., his coat pulled up at the
And evere he rood the hyndreste of oure route.[76]   waist

A SOMONOUR [77] was ther with us in that place,
That hadde a fyr-reed cherubynnes face,[78]
For saucefleem he was, with eyen narwe.   625   *saucefleem:* pimpled; *narwe:* narrow
As hoote he was and lecherous as a sparwe,   *sparwe:* sparrow
With scalled browes blake and piled berd.   *scalled:* scabbed; *piled:* scanty (the
Of his visage children were aferd.[79]   hair falling out)
Ther nas quyk-silver, lytarge, ne brymstoon,   *lytarge:* litharge (an oxide of lead)
Boras, ceruce, ne oille of tartre noon;   630   *boras:* borax; *ceruce:* white lead
Ne oynement that wolde clense and byte,
That hym myghte helpen of his whelkes white,   *whelkes:* whelks, pustules
Nor of the knobbes sittynge on his chekes.[80]
Wel loved he garleek, oynons, and eek lekes,
And for to drynken strong wyn, reed as blood;   635
Thanne wolde he speke and crie as he were wood.   *wood:* mad, insane
And whan that he wel dronken hadde the wyn,
Thanne wolde he speke no word but Latyn.
A fewe termes hadde he, two or thre,
That he had lerned out of som decree—   640
No wonder is, he herde it al the day; [81]
And eek ye knowen wel how that a jay
Kan clepen "Watte" as wel as kan the pope.[82]
But whoso koude in oother thyng hym grope,
Thanne hadde he spent al his philosophie;   645   *philosophie:* learning
Ay *"Questio quid iuris"* wolde he crie.   *questio quid iuris:* the question is,
He was a gentil harlot and a kynde;   what part of the law applies
A bettre felawe sholde men noght fynde.[83]
He wolde suffre for a quart of wyn
A good felawe to have his concubyn   650
A twelf month, and excuse hym atte fulle;   *atte fulle:* at the full, completely

[75] This specific identification has led scholars to believe that Chaucer had a particular reeve in mind. Baldeswelle is the modern Bawdswell.

[76] In view of the enmity between the ex-carpenter Reeve and the Miller (for which see p. 74), this detail is probably significant. Why (see l. 566)?

[77] A summoner was a minor official who brought offenders to an ecclesiastical court; Chaucer's Summoner seems more corrupt than most (perhaps he had a specific summoner in mind).

[78] A "fire-red cherubim's face" primarily because cherubim were so depicted in medieval religious paintings, but the image implies other resemblances.

[79] Does this line apply to the Summoner's physical appearance only?

[80] The Summoner possibly has leprosy.

[81] In the law courts.

[82] Jays were taught to say "Wat" (Walter). What does this remark imply about the Summoner's knowledge of Latin?

[83] Note the tone in which "harlot" (rascal) and, later, "felawe" (fellow) are used.

Ful prively a fynch eek koude he pulle. . . .[84]   *fynch . . . pulle:* fornicate
In daunger hadde he at his owene gise   663   *daunger:* control; *gise:* disposal
The yonge girles [85] of the diocise,
And knew hir conseil, and was al hir reed.   665   *conseil:* secrets; *reed:* advisor
A gerland hadde he set upon his heed   *gerland:* garland
As greet as it were for an ale-stake.   *ale-stake:* signpost for an alehouse
A bokeleer hadde he maad hym of a cake.   *cake:* loaf of bread

With hym ther rood a gentil PARDONER [86]
Of Rouncivale, his freend and his compeer,   670
That streight was comen fro the court of Rome.
Ful loude he soong "Com hider, love, to me!"   *soong:* sang; *hider:* hither
This Somonour bar to hym a stif burdoun;   *bar . . . burdoun:* i.e., accompanied
Was nevere trompe of half so greet a soun.   him in a loud voice
This Pardoner hadde heer as yelow as wex,   675   *heer:* hair; *wex:* wax
But smothe it heeng as dooth a strike of flex;   *strike:* hank; *flex:* flax
By ounces henge his lokkes that he hadde,   *ounces:* small bunches
And therwith he his shuldres overspradde;
But thynne it lay, by colpons oon and oon.   *thynne:* thin; *by colpons:* in strips;
But hood, for jolitee, wered he noon,   680   *oon and oon:* one by one
For it was trussed up in his walet.
Hym thoughte he rood al of the newe jet;   *jet:* fashion
Dischevelee, save his cappe, he rood al bare.   *dischevelee:* disheveled
Swiche glarynge eyen hadde he as an hare.[87]   *eyen:* eyes
A vernycle hadde he sowed upon his cappe,   685   *vernycle:* veronica
His walet lay biforn hym in his lappe,
Bretful of pardoun, comen from Rome al hoot.   *bretful:* brimful
A voys he hadde as smal as hath a goot.   *smal:* thin; *goot:* goat
No berd hadde he, ne nevere sholde have;   *berd:* beard
As smothe it was as it were late shave.   690
I trowe he were a geldyng or a mare.[88]
But of his craft, fro Berwyk into Ware,
Ne was ther swich another pardoner.
For in his male he hadde a pilwe-beer,   *male:* bag; *pilwe-beer:* pillow case
Which that he sayde was Oure Lady veyl: 695   *Lady:* Lady's
He seyde he hadde a gobet of the seyl   *gobet:* piece
That Seint Peter hadde, whan that he wente
Upon the see, til Jhesu Crist hym hente.   *hente:* caught
He hadde a croys of latoun ful of stones,   *croys:* cross; *latoun:* latten (a cheap
And in a glas he hadde pigges bones.   700   metal)
But with thise relikes, whan that he fond

[84] I.e., the Summoner was easily bribed to overlook the sexual delinquencies for which he was employed to bring people to court, he himself being guilty of the same offenses.
[85] "Girles" might apply to young men as well as to young women, but whether it does here or not is uncertain. At any rate, the Summoner, because of his knowledge and power to bring to court, has at least the young women at his mercy.
[86] Pardoners were men who sold indulgences or pardons from the Pope; this pardoner was from the hospital of the Blessed Mary of Rouncivalle, near Charing Cross in London. Pardoners as a class were quite corrupt, selling false pardons and fake relics. Many were sheer impostors.
[87] How is the image ironic?
[88] Chaucer and the other pilgrims suspect that the Pardoner is either a eunuch or a homosexual.

A povre person dwellynge upon lond,

Upon a day he gat hym moore moneye

Than that the person gat in monthes tweye;

And thus, with feyned flaterye and japes, 705

He made the person and the peple his apes.

But trewely to tellen atte laste,

He was in chirche a noble ecclesiaste.

Wel koude he rede a lessoun or a storie,

But alderbest he song an offertorie; [89] 710

For wel he wiste, whan that song was songe,

He moste preche and wel affile his tonge

To wynne silver, as he ful wel koude;

Therefore he song the murierly and loude.

Now have I toold you soothly, in a clause, 715

Th'estaat, th'array, the nombre, and eek the cause

Why that assembled was this compaignye

In Southwerk at this gentil hostelrye

That highte the Tabard, faste by the Belle.

But now is tyme to yow for to telle 720

How that we baren us that ilke nyght,

Whan we were in that hostelrie alyght;

And after wol I telle of our viage

And al the remenaunt of oure pilgrimage.

But first I pray yow, of youre curteisye, 725

That ye n'arette it nat my vileynye, [90]

Thogh that I pleynly speke in this mateere,

To telle yow hir wordes and hir cheere,

Ne thogh I speke hir wordes proprely.

For this ye knowen al so wel as I, 730

Whoso shal telle a tale after a man,

He moot reherce as ny as evere he kan

Everich a word, if it be in his charge,

Al speke he never so rudeliche and large,

Or ellis he moot telle his tale untrewe, 735

Or feyne thyng, or fynde wordes newe.

He may nat spare, althogh he were his brother;

He moot as wel seye o word as another.

Crist spak hymself ful brode in hooly writ,

And wel ye woot no vileynye is it. 740

Eek Plato seith, whoso that kan hym rede,

The wordes moote be cosyn to the dede. . . .

Greet chiere made oure Hoost us everichon, 747

And to the soper sette he us anon.

He served us with vitaille at the beste;

Glosses:

povre person: poor parson

gat hym: got for himself

tweye: two

japes: tricks

apes: i.e., fools

alderbest: best of all

affile: file, make smooth

murierly: more merrily

in a clause: in brief

faste by: hard by

baren: bore; *ilke:* same

viage: voyage, trip

hir: their; *cheere:* appearance

proprely: literally

ny: exactly, closely

everich a: every

al: even though; *large:* freely

moot: must

feyne thyng: feign things

o: one

woot: know; *vileynye:* obscenity

eek: also

cosyn: cousin

us everichon: for each one of us

vitaille: victuals; *at the:* of the

[89] Why does the Pardoner sing the offertory best of all?

[90] "That you impute it not to any coarseness of my nature." In the lines which follow (727–742) Chaucer defends a writer's right to describe people as they are. He probably has in mind especially the tales which the cruder characters are to tell. Some of these (e.g., "The Miller's Tale" and "The Reeve's Tale"), although pornographic, are artistically among his finest works. Do you agree with his defense?

Strong was the wyn, and wel to drynke us leste. 750   *us leste:* it pleased us
A semely man OURE HOOSTE was withalle [91]   *semely:* goodly
For to han been a marchal in an halle.   *halle:* dining hall (i.e., inn)
A large man he was with eyen stepe—   *stepe:* protruding
A fairer burgeys is ther noon in Chepe—   *burgeys:* burgess, citizen; *Chepe:*
Boold of his speche, and wys, and wel ytaught, 755   Cheapside (London's old market)
And of manhod hym lakkede right naught.   *hym:* he
Eek thereto he was right a myrie man,
And after soper pleyen he bigan,   *pleyen:* to joke
And spak of myrthe amonges othere thynges,
Whan that we hadde maad oure rekenynges, 760   *maad oure rekenynges:* paid our bills
And seyde thus: "Now, lordynges, trewely,   *lordynges:* gentlemen
Ye been to me right welcome, hertely. . . .

   Ye goon to Caunterbury—God yow speede, 769   *goon:* go
The blisful martir quite yow youre meede!   *martir:* cf. l. 17; *quite . . . meede:*
And wel I woot, as ye goon by the weye,   reward you
Ye shapen yow to talen and to pleye . . .   *talen:* tell tales
And therfore wol I maken yow disport, 775   *disport:* diversion, merriment
As I seyde erst, and doon yow som confort. . . .   *erst:* before
This is the poynt, to speken short and pleyn, 790
That ech of yow, to shorte with oure weye,   *shorte:* shorten
In this viage shal telle tales tweye   *viage:* trip; *tweye:* two
To Caunterbury-ward, I mene it so,
And homward he shal tellen othere two,[92]   *othere:* another
Of aventures that whilom han bifalle. 795   *whilom:* once; *han:* have
And which of yow that bereth hym best of alle . . .,
Shal have a soper at oure aller cost 799   *soper:* supper; *oure aller cost:* the
Heere in this place, sittynge by this post,[93]   expense of all of us
Whan that we come agayn fro Caunterbury.
And for to make yow the moore mury,
I wol myselven goodly with yow ryde,
Right at myn owene cost, and be youre gyde;
And whoso wole my juggement withseye 805
Shal paye al that we spenden by the weye.
And if ye vouche sauf that it be so,   *vouche sauf:* vouchsafe
Tel me anon, withouten wordes mo,
And I wol erly shape me therfore."   *shape me:* prepare myself
   This thyng was graunted, and oure othes
     swore 810
With ful glad herte, and preyden hym also   *preyden:* we prayed
That he wolde vouche sauf for to do so. . . .
   Amorwe, whan that day bigan to sprynge, 822   *amorwe:* in the morning
Up roos oure Hoost, and was oure aller cok,   *oure aller cok:* cock of us all (i.e.,
And gadrede us togidre alle in a flok,   woke them)
And forth we riden a litel moore than paas 825

[91] Later (Cook's Prologue) the Host's name is given as Harry Bailly. Bailly actually existed, being an innkeeper in Southwark, a member of Parliament, and a tax collector, according to contemporary records.
[92] This full plan was never realized; see p. 57.
[93] Why does the Host specify "this place"? Do not miss the humor here.

Unto the wateryng of Seint Thomas;

And there oure Hoost bigan his hors areste

And seyde, "Lordynges, herkneth, if yow leste. . . .

Lat se now who shal telle the firste tale.　　831

As evere mote I drynke wyn or ale,

Whoso be rebel to my juggement

Shal paye for al that by the wey is spent.

Now draweth cut, er that we ferrer twynne;

He which that hath the shorteste shal bigynne. . . .

And whan this goode man [94] saugh that it was so, 850

As he that wys was and obedient

To kepe his foreward by his free assent,

He seyde, "Syn I shal bigynne the game,

What, welcome be the cut, a Goddes name!

Now lat us ryde, and herkneth what I seye."　　855

And with that word we ryden forth oure weye,

And he bigan with right a myrie cheere

His tale anon, and seyde as ye may heere.[95]

wateryng: watering place

areste: to arrest

leste: please

lat se: let's see

mote: may

ferrer twynne: further set out

as he that: like one who

foreward: promise

syn: since

a: in

anon: straightway

STUDY AIDS: 1. John Dryden says of *The Canterbury Tales,* "Here is God's plenty." Limiting his remark to the *Prologue,* try to justify it.

2. Chaucer is sometimes said to give a complete picture of medieval society. To what extent is this statement true? What ranks of society are omitted? Would members of them be likely to be on a pilgrimage?

3. How do the following contrast in character, motives, and ideals: the Prioress and the Wife of Bath; the Franklin and the Reeve; the Parson and the Friar? With whom do the following contrast: the Clerk, the Knight, the Monk, the Pardoner, the Doctor? Find other contrasts.

4. Which pilgrims does Chaucer satirize most sharply? Is his attitude ever wholly unsympathetic? How would you characterize his attitude toward life in general? Toward himself?

5. If the *General Prologue* were merely a series of portraits, the effect would be mechanical or wooden. How does Chaucer achieve an effect of naturalness through his organization? Is there a difference in time between beginning and end?

6. Choose a portrait which appeals to you especially and analyze it in an attempt to discover Chaucer's literary method. To what extent is the portrait general, to what extent specific? What kind of specific detail does Chaucer employ? What kind of imagery does he favor?

7. In what ways does the *General Prologue* change or expand your knowledge of life in the Middle Ages?

The Nun's Priest's Tale [1]

The first tale told is the Knight's. As befits his character, it is a courtly romance of ancient times. The Pilgrims are delighted with it, and the Host cries jovially, "Come, match the Knight's tale if you can, Sir Monk!" But the Miller, by now very drunk, insists on telling his story next, and is not to be put down. His tale of a gullible carpenter cuckolded by a student-boarder angers the Reeve, who is a carpenter by trade (cf. p. 70, l. 614); the Reeve replies with a tale of a Miller's cuckolding. Then other tellers tell their tales; and in between there is a continuous interplay of character and action, of conflicts of personality and ideas.

[94] I.e., the Knight. Since he is the highest in rank, the cut falls appropriately to him.

[95] This line indicates that Chaucer thought of his tales as being read aloud; it suggests that he is at least partly in the oral tradition (cf. above. pp. 2–3).

[1] The remaining Chaucerian selections are translated by Theodore Morrison.

In due course the Monk has another opportunity. He chooses for his tale a most doleful series of tragedies, stories of men who have risen to greatness only to be destroyed when Fortune hides her face from them. Finally the Knight, his tolerance for the lugubrious at an end, interrupts with a cry: "Stop! No more of this, good Sir!" and asks the Monk to tell a tale of hunting. "No," says the Monk, "I'll not be frivolous. Let another tell a tale, as I have told."

At this point the Host calls upon the Nun's Priest:

> Then spoke our Host, with a voice rude and bold,
> And said to the Nun's Priest, "Come over here,
> You priest, come hither, you Sir John, draw near!
> Tell us a thing to make our spirits glad.
> Be cheerful, though the jade you ride is bad.
> What if your horse is miserable and lean?
> If he will carry you, don't care a bean!
> Keep up a joyful heart, and look alive."
> "Yes, Host," he answered, "as I hope to thrive,
> If I weren't merry, I know I'd be reproached."
> And with no more ado his tale he broached,
> And this is what he told us, every one,
> This precious priest, this goodly man, Sir John.

The Nun's Priest's Tale is both a satire on marriage (ll. 62–526) and a burlesque of the epic (ll. 527–773). The central episode is the familiar fable of the cock who is caught by a fox and who tricks his captor into releasing him. But the interest of the tale lies in the characters rather than in the action. Chaucer's Chanticleer is at once a barnyard fowl and a very human husband, his Partlet a hen and a somewhat disillusioned wife. Much of the humor, which is often extremely subtle, comes from the similarity and dissimilarity between chickens and human beings. For example, Chanticleer praises the beauty of his wife's eyes, but since she is a hen it is their redness which he admires.

Once a poor widow, aging year by year,
Lived in a tiny cottage that stood near
A clump of shade trees rising in a dale.
This widow, of whom I tell you in my tale,
Since the last day that she had been a wife　5
Had led a very patient, simple life.
She had but few possessions to content her.
By thrift and husbandry of what God sent her
She and two daughters found the means to
　　dine.
She had no more than three well-fattened
　　swine,　　　　　　　　　　　　　　　　10
As many cows, and one sheep, Moll by name.
Her bower and hall were black from the
　　hearth-flame
Where she had eaten many a slender meal.
No dainty morsel did her palate feel
And no sharp sauce was needed with her
　　pottage.　　　　　　　　　　　　　　　15
Her table was in keeping with her cottage.
Excess had never given her disquiet.
Her only doctor was a moderate diet,
And exercise, and a heart that was contented.

If she did not dance, at least no gout
　　prevented;　　　　　　　　　　　　　　20
No apoplexy had destroyed her head.
She never drank wine, whether white or red.
She served brown bread and milk, loaves
　　white or black,
Singed bacon, all this with no sense of lack,
And now and then an egg or two. In short,　25
She was a dairy woman of a sort.
　　She had a yard, on the inside fenced about
With hedges, and an empty ditch without,
In which she kept a cock, called Chanticleer.
In all the realm of crowing he had no peer.　30
His voice was merrier than the merry sound
Of the church organ grumbling out its ground
Upon a saint's day. Stouter was this cock
In crowing than the loudest abbey clock.
Of astronomy instinctively aware,　　　　35
He kept the sun's hours with celestial care,
For when through each fifteen degrees it
　　moved,
He crowed so that it couldn't be improved.
His comb, like a crenelated castle wall,

Red as fine coral, stood up proud and tall. 40
His bill was black; like polished jet it glowed,
And he was azure-legged and azure-toed.
As lilies were his nails, they were so white;
Like burnished gold his hue, it shone so
    bright.
This cock had in his princely sway and
    measure 45
Seven hens to satisfy his every pleasure,
Who were his sisters and his sweethearts true,
Each wonderfully like him in her hue,
Of whom the fairest-feathered throat to see
Was fair Dame Partlet. Courteous was she, 50
Discreet, and always acted debonairly.
She was sociable, and bore herself so fairly,
Since the very time that she was seven nights
    old,
The heart of Chanticleer was in her hold
As if she had him locked up, every limb. 55
He loved her so that all was well with him.
It was a joy, when up the sun would spring,
To hear them both together sweetly sing,
"My love has gone to the country, far away!"
For as I understand it, in that day 60
The animals and birds could sing and speak.
    Now as this cock, one morning at daybreak,
With each of the seven hens that he called
    spouse,
Sat on his perch inside the widow's house,
And next him fair Dame Partlet, in his
    throat 65
This Chanticleer produced a hideous note
And groaned like a man who is having a bad
    dream;
And Partlet, when she heard her husband
    scream,
Was all aghast, and said, "Soul of my passion,
What ails you that you groan in such a
    fashion? 70
You are always a sound sleeper. Fie, for
    shame!"
    And Chanicleer awoke and answered,
    "Dame,
Take no offense, I beg you, on this score.
I dreamt, by God, I was in a plight so sore
Just now, my heart still quivers from the
    fright. 75
Now God see that my dream turns out all
    right
And keep my flesh and body from foul seizure!

I dreamed I was strutting in our yard at
    leisure
When there I saw, among the weeds and
    vines,
A beast, he was like a hound,[2] and had
    designs 80
Upon my person, and would have killed me
    dead.
His coat was not quite yellow, not quite red,
And both his ears and tail were tipped with
    black
Unlike the fur along his sides and back.
He had a small snout and a fiery eye. 85
His look for fear still makes me almost die.
This is what made me groan, I have no doubt."
    "For shame! Fie on you, faint heart!" she
    burst out.
"Alas," she said, "by the great God above,
Now you have lost my heart and all my
    love! 90
I cannot love a coward, as I'm blest!
Whatever any woman may protest,
We all want, could it be so, for our part,
Husbands who are wise and stout of heart,
No blabber, and no niggard, and no fool, 95
Nor afraid of every weapon or sharp tool,
No braggart either, by the God above!
How dare you say, for shame, to your true love
That there is anything you ever feared?
Have you no man's heart, when you have a
    beard? 100
Alas, and can a nightmare set you screaming?
God knows there's only vanity in dreaming!
Dreams are produced by such unseemly capers
As overeating; they come from stomach vapors
When a man's humors aren't behaving
    right 105
From some excess.[3] This dream you had
    tonight,
It comes straight from the superfluity
Of your red choler, certain as can be,
That causes people terror in their dreams
Of darts and arrows, and fire in red
    streams, 110
And of red beasts, for fear that they will bite,
Of little dogs, or of being in a fight;
As in the humor of melancholy lies

[2] Note the FORESHADOWING.
[3] Chaucer seems to have had a lifelong interest in dreams and their psychology.

The reason why so many a sleeper cries
For fear of a black bull or a black bear   115
Or that black devils have him by the hair.
Through other humors also I could go
That visit many a sleeping man with woe,
But I will finish as quickly as I can.
    "Cato, that has been thought so wise a
        man,   120
Didn't he tell us, 'Put no stock in dreams'?
Now, sir," she said, "when we fly down from
        our beams,
For God's sake, go and take a laxative!
On my salvation, as I hope to live,
I give you good advice, and no mere folly: 125
Purge both your choler and your melancholy!
You mustn't wait or let yourself bog down,
And since there is no druggist in this town
I shall myself prescribe for what disturbs
Your humors, and instruct you in the
        herbs   130
That will be good for you. For I shall find
Here in our yard herbs of the proper kind
For purging you both under and above.
Don't let this slip your mind, for God's own
        love!
Yours is a very choleric complexion.[4]   135
When the sun is in the ascendant, my
        direction
Is to beware those humors that are hot.
Avoid excess of them; if you should not,
I'll bet a penny, as a true believer,
You'll die of ague, or a tertian fever.   140
A day or so, if you do as I am urging,
You shall have worm-digestives,[5] before
        purging
With fumitory or with hellebore
Or other herbs that grow here by the score;
With caper-spurge, or with the goat-tree
        berry   145
Or the ground-ivy, found in our yard so merry.
Peck 'em up just as they grow, and eat 'em
        in!
Be cheerful, husband, by your father's kin!
Don't worry about a dream. I say no more."
    "Madame," he answered, "thanks for all
        your lore.   150

[4] See p. 66, l. 411.
[5] Earthworms were commonly prescribed for the
treatment of tertian fever in human beings. Note
the fusion of man and fowl in these lines.

But still, to speak of Cato,[6] though his name
For wisdom has enjoyed so great a fame,
And though he counseled us there was no
        need
To be afraid of dreams, by God, men read
Of many a man of more authority   155
Than this Don Cato could pretend to be
Who in old books declare the opposite,
And by experience they have settled it,
That dreams are omens and prefigurations
Both of good fortune and of tribulations   160
That life and its vicissitudes present.
This question leaves no room for argument.
The very upshot makes it plain, indeed.
    "One of the greatest authors that men read [7]
Informs us that two fellow travelers went,   165
Once on a time, and with the best intent,
Upon a pilgrimage, and it fell out
They reached a town where there was such a
        rout
Of people, and so little lodging space,
They could not find even the smallest
        place   170
Where they could both put up. So, for that
        night,
These pilgrims had to do as best they might,
And since they must, they parted company.
Each of them went off to his hostelry
And took his lodging as his luck might
        fall.   175
Among plow oxen in a farmyard stall
One of them found a place, though it was
        rough.
His friend and fellow was lodged well enough
As his luck would have it, or his destiny
That governs all us creatures equally.   180
And so it happened, long before the day,
He had a dream as in his bed he lay.
He dreamed that his parted friend began to
        call
And said, 'Alas, for in an ox's stall
This night I shall be murdered where I
        lie.   185
Come to my aid, dear brother, or I die.
Come to me quickly, come in haste!' he said.
He started from his sleep, this man, for
        dread,

[6] Author of a famous medieval textbook, the
Disticha.
[7] The author referred to is uncertain.

But when he had wakened, he rolled back
  once more
And on this dream of his he set no store. 190
As a vain thing he dismissed it, unconcerned.
Twice as he slept that night the dream
  returned,
And still another and third time his friend
Came in a dream and said, 'I have met my
  end!
Look on my wounds! They are bloody, deep,
  and wide. 195
Now rise up early in the morningtide
And at the west gate of the town,' said he,
'A wagon with a load of dung you'll see.
Have it arrested boldly. Do as bidden,
For underneath you'll find my body
  hidden. 200
My money caused my murder, truth to tell,'
And told him each detail of how he fell,
With piteous face, and with a bloodless hue.
And do not doubt it, he found the dream was
  true,
For on the morrow, as soon as it was day, 205
To the place where his friend had lodged he
  made his way,
And no sooner did he reach this ox's stall
Than for his fellow he began to call.
  "Promptly the stableman replied, and said,
'Your friend is gone, sir. He got out of bed 210
And left the town as soon as day began.'
  "At last suspicion overtook this man.
Remembering his dreams, he would not wait,
But quickly went and found at the west gate,
Being driven to manure a farmer's land 215
As it might seem, a dung cart close at hand
That answered the description every way,
As you yourself have heard the dead man say.
And he began to shout courageously
For law and vengeance on this felony. 220
'My friend was killed this very night! He lies
Flat in this load of dung, with staring eyes.
I call on those who should keep rule and head,
The magistrates and the governors here,' he
  said.
'Alas! Here lies my fellow, done to death!' 225
  "Why on this tale should I waste further
  breath?
The people sprang and flung the cart to
  ground
And in the middle of the dung they found

The dead man, while his murder was still new.
  "O blessed God, thou art so just and
  true, 230
Murder, though secret, ever thou wilt betray!
Murder will out, we see it day by day.
Murder so loathsome and abominable
To God is, who is just and reasonable,
That he will never suffer it to be 235
Concealed, though it hide a year, or two, or
  three.
Murder will out; to this point it comes down.
  "Promptly the magistrates who ruled that
  town
Have seized the driver, and put him to such
  pain,
And the stableman as well, that under
  strain 240
Of torture they were both led to confess
And hanged by the neck-bone for their
  wickedness.
  "Here's proof enough that dreams are things
  to dread!
And in the same book I have also read,
In the very chapter that comes right after
  this— 245
I don't speak idly, by my hope of bliss—
Two travelers who for some reason planned
To cross the ocean to a distant land
Found that the wind, by an opposing fate,
Blew contrary, and forced them both to
  wait 250
In a fair city by a harborside.
But one day the wind changed, toward
  eventide,
And blew just as it suited them instead.
Cheerfully these travelers went to bed
And planned to sail the first thing in the
  morning. 255
But to one of them befell a strange
  forewarning
And a great marvel. While asleep he lay,
He dreamed a curious dream along toward
  day.
He dreamed that a man appeared at his
  bedside
And told him not sail, but wait and
  bide. 260
'Tomorrow,' he told the man, 'if you set sail,
You shall be drowned. I have told you my
  whole tale.'

He woke, and of this warning he had met
He told his friend, and begged him to forget
His voyage, and to wait that day and bide. 265
His friend, who was lying close at his bedside,
Began to laugh, and told him in derision,
'I am not so flabbergasted by a vision
As to put off my business for such cause.
I do not think your dream is worth two
    straws! 270
For dreams are but a vain absurdity.
Of apes and owls and many a mystery
People are always dreaming, in a maze
Of things that never were seen in all their
    days
And never shall be. But I see it's clear 275
You mean to waste your time by waiting here.
I'm sorry for that, God knows; and so good
    day.'
With this he took his leave and went his way.
But not the half his course had this man
    sailed—
I don't know why, nor what it was that
    failed— 280
When by an accident the hull was rent
And ship and man under the water went
In full view of the vessels alongside
That had put out with them on the same tide.
Now then, fair Partlet, whom I love so
    well, 285
From old examples such as these I tell
You may see that none should give too little
    heed
To dreams; for I say seriously, indeed,
That many a dream is too well worth our
    dread.
    "Yes, in St. Kenelm's life I have also
    read— 290
He was the son of Cynewulf,[8] the king
Of Mercia—how this Kenelm dreamed a
    thing.
One day, as the time when he was killed
    drew near,
He saw his murder in a dream appear.
His nurse explained his dream in each
    detail, 295
And warned him to be wary without fail
Of treason; yet he was but seven years old,
And therefore any dream he could but hold
Of little weight, in heart he was so pure.

[8] Anglo-Saxon king.

I'd give my shirt, by God, you may be sure, 300
If you had read his story through like me!
    "Moreover, Partlet, I tell you truthfully,
Macrobius [9] writes—and by his book we know
The African vision of great Scipio—
Confirming dreams, and holds that they may
    be 305
Forewarnings of events that men shall see.
Again, I beg, look well at what is meant
By the Book of Daniel in the Old Testament,
Whether *he* held that dreams are vanity!
Read also about Joseph. You shall see 310
That dreams, or some of them—I don't say
    all—
Warn us of things that afterward befall.
Think of the king of Egypt, Don Pharaoh;
Of his butler and his baker think also,
Whether they found that dreams have no
    result. 315
Whoever will search through kingdoms and
    consult
Their histories reads many a wondrous thing
Of dreams. What about Croesus, Lydian
    king—
Didn't he dream he was sitting on a tree,
Which meant he would be hanged?
    Andromache, 320
The woman who was once great Hector's [10]
    wife,
On the day that Hector was to lose his life,
The very night before his blood was spilled
She dreamed of how her husband would be
    killed
If he went out to battle on that day. 325
She warned him; but he would not heed nor
    stay.
In spite of her he rode out on the plain,
And by Achilles he was promptly slain.
But all that story is too long to tell,
And it is nearly day. I must not dwell 330
Upon this matter. Briefly, in conclusion,
I say this dream will bring me to confusion
And mischief of some sort. And furthermore,
On laxatives, I say, I set no store,
For they are poisonous, I'm sure of it. 335
I do not trust them! I like them not one bit!

[9] Editor (ca. 400 A.D.) of the *Somnium Scipionis*
of Cicero. Macrobius' commentary was regarded as
the authoritative work on dreams.
[10] A hero of the Trojan War.

"Now let's talk cheerfully, and forget all
this.
My pretty Partlet, by my hope of bliss,
In one thing God has sent me ample grace,
For when I see the beauty of your face,   340
You are so scarlet-red about the eye,
It is enough to make my terrors die.
For just as true as *In principio*
Mulier est hominis confusio [11]—
And Madame, what this Latin means is
this: 345
'Woman is man's whole comfort and true
bliss' [12]—
When I feel you soft at night, and I beside
you,
Although it's true, alas, I cannot ride you
Because our perch is built so narrowly,
I am then so full of pure felicity   350
That I defy whatever sort of dream!"
   And day being come, he flew down from
the beam
And with him his hens fluttered, one and all;
And with a "cluck, cluck" he began to call
His wives to where a kernel had been
tossed.   355
He was a prince, his fears entirely lost.
The morning had not passed the hour of prime
When he treaded Partlet for the twentieth
time.
Grim as a lion he strolled to and fro,
And strutted only on his either toe.   360
He would not deign to set foot on the ground.
"Cluck, cluck," he said, whenever he had
found
A kernel, and his wives came running all.
Thus royal as a monarch in his hall
I leave to his delights this Chanticleer,   365
And presently the sequel you shall hear.
   After the month in which the world began,
The month of March, when God created man,
Had passed, and when the season had run
through
Since March began just thirty days and
two,   370
It happened that Chanticleer, in all his pride,
While his seven hens were walking by his
side,
Lifted his eyes, beholding the bright sun,

Which in the sign of Taurus had then run
Twenty and one degrees and somewhat
more,   375
And knew by instinct, not by learned lore,
It was the hour of prime. He raised his head
And crowed with lordly voice. "The sun," he
said,
"Forty and one degrees and more in height
Has climbed the sky. Partlet, my world's
delight,   380
Hear all these birds, how happily they sing,
And see the pretty flowers, how they spring.
With solace and with joy my spirits dance!"
But suddenly he met a sore mischance,
For in the end joys ever turn to woes.   385
Quickly the joys of earth are gone, God
knows,
And could a rhetorician's art indite it,
He would be on solid ground if he should
write it,
In a chronicle, as true notoriously!
Now every wise man, listen well to me.   390
This story is as true, I undertake,
As the very book of Lancelot of the Lake
On which the women set so great a store.
Now to my matter I will turn once more.
   A sly iniquitous fox, with black-tipped
ears,   395
Who had lived in the neighboring wood for
some three years,
His fated fancy swollen to a height,
Had broken through the hedges that same
night
Into the yard where in his pride sublime
Chanticleer with his seven wives passed the
time.   400
Quietly in a bed of herbs he lay
Till it was past the middle of the day,
Waiting his hour on Chanticleer to fall
As gladly do these murderers, one and all,
Who lie in wait, concealed, to murder
men.   405
O murderer, lurking traitorous in your den!
O new Iscariot, second Ganelon,
False hypocrite, Greek Sinon,[13] who brought
on

[11] As surely as Gospel truth, woman is man's ruin.
[12] What is ironic in Chanticleer's translation?

[13] Iscariot is Judas; Ganelon, the traitor in the
Chanson de Roland; Sinon, the wily Greek who allowed himself to be captured by the Trojans and
then persuaded them to take the Trojan Horse inside
the city gates.

The utter woe of Troy and all her sorrow!
O Chanticleer, accursed be that morrow   410
When to the yard you flew down from the
    beams!
That day, as you were well warned in your
    dreams,
Would threaten you with dire catastrophe.
But that which God foresees must come to be,
As there are certain scholars who aver.   415
Bear witness, any true philosopher,
That in the schools there has been great
    altercation
Upon this question,[14] and much disputation
By a hundred thousand scholars, man for
    man.
I cannot sift it down to the pure bran   420
As can the sacred Doctor, Augustine,
Or Boëthius, or Bishop Bradwardine,[15]
Whether God's high foreknowledge so
    enchains me
I needs must do a thing as it constrains me—
"Needs must"—that is, by plain necessity;   425
Or whether a free choice is granted me
To do it or not do it, either one,
Though God must know all things before
    they are done;
Or whether his foresight nowise can constrain
Except contingently, as some explain;   430
I will not labor such a high concern.
My tale is of a cock, as you shall learn,
Who took his wife's advice, to his own sorrow,
And walked out in the yard that fatal morrow.
Women have many times, as wise men
    hold,   435
Offered advice that left men in the cold.
A woman's counsel brought us first to woe
And out of Paradise made Adam go
Where he lived a merry life and one of ease.
But since I don't know whom I may
    displease   440
By giving women's words an ill report,
Pass over it; I only spoke in sport.
There are books about it you can read or skim
    in,

[14] The problem of foreordination and free will
was a much discussed topic in Chaucer's day.

[15] Augustine is St. Augustine; Boethius wrote *De
Consolatione Philosophiae*, which Chaucer translated; Bradwardine was Archbishop of Canterbury.
All of these men had written treatises dealing with
foreordination and free will.

And you'll discover what they say of women.
I'm telling you the cock's words, and not
    mine.   445
Harm in no woman at all can I divine.
    Merrily bathing where the sand was dry
Lay Partlet, with her sisters all near by,
And Chanticleer, as regal as could be,
Sang merrily as the mermaid in the sea;   450
For the *Physiologus*[16] itself declares
That they know how to sing the merriest
    airs.
And so it happened that as he fixed his eye
Among the herbs upon a butterfly,
He caught sight of this fox who crouched
    there low.   455
He felt no impulse then to strut or crow,
But cried "cucock!" and gave a fearful start
Like a man who has been frightened to the
    heart.
For instinctively, if he should chance to see
His opposite, a beast desires to flee,   460
Even the first time that it meets his eye.
    This Chanticleer, no sooner did he spy
The fox than promptly enough he would have
    fled.
But "Where are you going, kind sir?" the fox
    said.
"Are you afraid of me, who am your
    friend?   465
Truly, I'd be a devil from end to end
If I meant you any harm or villainy.
I have not come to invade your privacy.
In truth, the only reason that could bring
This visit of mine was just to hear you
    sing.   470
Beyond a doubt, you have as fine a voice
As any angel who makes heaven rejoice.
Also you have more feeling in your note
Than Boëthius, or any tuneful throat.
Milord your father once—and may God
    bless   475
His soul—your noble mother too, no less,
Have been inside my house, to my great ease.
And verily sir, I should be glad to please
You also. But for singing, I declare,
As I enjoy my eyes, that precious pair,   480
Save you, I never heard a man so sing
As your father did when night was on the
    wing.

[16] A Latin bestiary.

Straight from the heart, in truth, came all his
    song,
And to make his voice more resonant and
    strong
He would strain until he shut his either
    eye,   485
So loud and lordly would he make his cry,
And stand up on his tiptoes therewithal
And stretch his neck till it grew long and
    small.
He had such excellent discretion, too,
That whether his singing, all the region
    through,   490
Or his wisdom, there was no one to surpass.
I read in that old book, *Don Burnel the Ass,*
Among his verses once about a cock
Hit on the leg by a priest who threw a rock
When he was young and foolish; and for
    this   495
He caused the priest to lose his benefice.[17]
But no comparison, in all truth, lies
Between your father, so prudent and so wise,
And this other cock, for all his subtlety.
Sing, sir! Show me, for holy charity,   500
Can you imitate your father, that wise man?"
    Blind to all treachery, Chanticleer began
To beat his wings, like one who cannot see
The traitor, ravished by his flattery.
    Alas, you lords, about your courts there
    slips   505
Many a flatterer with deceiving lips
Who can please you more abundantly, I fear,
Than he who speaks the plain truth to your
    ear.
Read in Ecclesiastes, you will see
What flatterers are. Lords, heed their
    treachery!   510
    This Chanticleer stood tiptoe at full height.
He stretched his neck, he shut his eyelids
    tight,
And he began to crow a lordly note.
The fox, Don Russell, seized him by the
    throat
At once, and on his back bore Chanticleer 515
Off toward his den that in the grove stood
    near,
For no one yet had threatened to pursue.
    O destiny, that no man may eschew!
Alas, that he left his safe perch on the beams!

[17] Because he crowed so late the priest overslept.

Alas, that Partlet took no stock in dreams! 520
And on a Friday happened this mischance!
    Venus, whose pleasures make the whole
    world dance,
Since Chanticleer was ever your true servant,
And of your rites with all his power observant
For pleasure rather than to multiply,   525
Would you on Friday suffer him to die?
    Geoffrey,[18] dear master of the poet's art,
Who when your Richard perished by a dart
Made for your king an elegy so burning,
Why have I not your eloquence and
    learning   530
To chide, as you did, with a heart so filled,
Fridays? For on a Friday he was killed.
Then should I show you how I could complain
For Chanticleer in all his fright and pain!
    In truth, no lamentation ever rose,   535
No shriek of ladies when before its foes
Ilium fell, and Pyrrhus with drawn blade
Had seized King Priam by the beard and made
An end of him—the *Aeneid* tells the tale—
Such as the hens made with their piteous
    wail   540
In their enclosure, seeing the dread sight
Of Chanticleer. But at the shrillest height
Shrieked Partlet. She shrieked louder than the
    wife
Of Hasdrubal, when her husband lost his life
And the Romans burned down Carthage; for
    her state   545
Of torment and of frenzy was so great
She willfully chose the fire for her part,
Leaped in, and burned herself with steadfast
    heart.
    Unhappy hens, you shrieked as when for
    pity,
While the tyrant Nero put to flames the
    city   550
Of Rome, rang out the shriek of senators'
    wives
Because their husbands had all lost their
    lives;
This Nero put to death these innocent men.
But I will come back to my tale again.
    Now this good widow and her two
    daughters heard   555

[18] Geoffrey de Vinsauf, author of a treatise on
poetry containing a section dealing with the death
of Richard I.

These woeful hens shriek when the crime
   occurred,
And sprang outdoors as quickly as they could
And saw the fox, who was making for the
   wood
Bearing this Chanticleer across his back.
"Help, help!" they cried. They cried, "Alas!
   Alack!   560
The fox, the fox!" and after him they ran,
And armed with clubs came running many
   a man.
Ran Coll the dog, and led a yelping band;
Ran Malkyn, with a distaff in her hand;
Ran cow and calf, and even the very hogs, 565
By the yelping and the barking of the dogs
And men's and women's shouts so terrified
They ran till it seemed their hearts would
   burst inside;
They squealed like fiends in the pit, with none
   to still them.
The ducks quacked as if men were going to
   kill them.   570
The geese for very fear flew over the trees.
Out of the beehive came the swarm of bees.
Ah! Bless my soul, the noise, by all that's
   true,
So hideous was that Jack Straw's retinue [19]
Made never a hubbub that was half so
   shrill   575
Over a Fleming they were going to kill
As the clamor made that day over the fox.
They brought brass trumpets, and trumpets
   made of box,
Of horn, of bone, on which they blew and
   squeaked,
And those who were not blowing whooped
   and shrieked.   580
It seemed as if the very heavens would fall!
Now hear me, you good people, one and all!
Fortune, I say, will suddenly override
Her enemy in his very hope and pride!
This cock, as on the fox's back he lay,   585
Plucked up his courage to speak to him and
   say,
"God be my help, sir, but I'd tell them all,
That is, if I were you, 'Plague on you fall!
Go back, proud fools! Now that I've reached
   the wood,
I'll eat the cock at once, for all the good   590

[19] Refers to the Peasants' Revolt of 1381.

Your noise can do. Here Chanticleer shall
   stay.'"
   "Fine!" said the fox. "I'll do just what you
   say."
But the cock, as he was speaking, suddenly
Out of his jaws lurched expeditiously,
And flew at once high up into a tree.   595
And when the fox saw that the cock was free,
"Alas," he said, "alas, O Chanticleer!
Inasmuch as I have given you cause for fear
By seizing you and bearing you away,
I have done you wrong, I am prepared to
   say.   600
But, sir, I did it with no ill intent.
Come down, and I shall tell you what I meant.
So help me God, it's truth I'll offer you!"
   "No, no," said he. "We're both fools,
   through and through.
But curse my blood and bones for the chief
   dunce   605
If you deceive me oftener than once!
You shall never again by flattery persuade
   me
To sing and wink my eyes, by him that made
   me.
For he that willfully winks when he should
   see,
God never bless him with prosperity!"   610
   "Ah," said the fox, "with mischief may God
   greet
The man ungoverned, rash, and indiscreet
Who babbles when to hold his tongue were
   needful!"
   Such is it to be reckless and unheedful
And trust in flattery. But you who hold   615
That this is a mere trifle I have told,
Concerning only a fox, or a cock and hen,
Think twice, and take the moral,[20] my good
   men!
For truly, of whatever is written, all
Is written for our doctrine, says St. Paul. 620
Then take the fruit, and let the chaff lie still.
Now, gracious God, if it should be your will,
As my Lord teaches, make us all good men
And bring us to your holy bliss! Amen.

STUDY AIDS: 1. Analyze the action or
plot to show how it grows out of the characters
of Chanticleer and Partlet. What are the chief

[20] What do you think is the moral?

elements in his character? In hers? What is his view of her? What is hers of him?

2. By what means does Chaucer take a simple beast fable or animal story and make of it a masterpiece of humor? Are Chanticleer and Part-

let satirized in the same way? Does the story use IRONY in the same way for each character? What part does TONE play in the humorous effect?

3. This story is often called a MOCK EPIC. Justify the term EPIC here.

Prologue to the Pardoner's Tale

The Pardoner's prologue and tale follow closely the organization of the medieval sermon: the theme is stated in line 6; the tale which follows is an *exemplum*, or anecdote illustrative of the theme; and the tale is followed in turn (ll. 552–563) by a *peroration*, or application of the tale.

The tale itself is one of the finest short stories in English; but it is only a part of a greater whole, the portrayal which the Pardoner gives of his character. The Pardoner is a rascal whose greatest sin is greed. Ironically, he chooses to preach against this sin, but before doing so he confesses to the pilgrims just what a rascal he is, telling them, in his prologue, how he dupes the people into buying his fake relics and false pardons. Then, after telling his tale, he tries to pull his tricks on the pilgrims.

"In churches," said the Pardoner, "when I
   preach,
I use, milords, a lofty style of speech
And ring it out as roundly as a bell,
Knowing by rote all that I have to tell.
My text is ever the same, and ever was: 5
Radix malorum est cupiditas [1]
   "First I inform them whence I come; that
   done,
I then display my papal bulls,[2] each one.
I show my license first, my body's warrant,
Sealed by the bishop, for it would be
   abhorrent   10
If any man made bold, though priest or clerk,
To interrupt me in Christ's holy work.
And after that I give myself full scope.
Bulls in the name of cardinal and pope,
Of bishops and of patriarchs I show.   15
I say in Latin some few words or so
To spice my sermon; it flavors my appeal
And stirs my listeners to greater zeal.
Then I display my cases made of glass
Crammed to the top with rags and bones.
   They pass   20
For relics with all the people in the place.
I have a shoulder bone in a metal case,
Part of a sheep owned by a holy Jew.

'Good men,' I say, 'heed what I'm telling you:
Just let this bone be dipped in any well   25
And if cow, calf, or sheep, or ox should swell
From eating a worm, or by a worm be stung,
Take water from this well and wash its tongue
And it is healed at once. And furthermore
Of scab and ulcers and of every sore   30
Shall every sheep be cured, and that
   straightway,
That drinks from the same well. Heed what I
   say:
If the good man who owns the beasts will go,
Fasting, each week, and drink before cockcrow
Out of this well, his cattle shall be brought 35
To multiply—that holy Jew [3] so taught
Our elders—and his property increase.
   "'Moreover, sirs, this bone cures jealousies.
Though into a jealous madness a man fell,
Let him cook his soup in water from this
   well,   40
He'll never, though for truth he knew her sin,
Suspect his wife again, though she took in
A priest, or even two of them or three.
   "'Now here's a mitten that you all can see.
Whoever puts his hand in it shall gain,   45
When he sows his land, increasing crops of
   grain,
Be it wheat or oats, provided that he bring
His penny or so to make his offering.
   "'There is one word of warning I must say,

[1] Covetousness (or greed) is the root of evil.
[2] Indulgences from the Pope. These documents, promising remission of sins, were most probably counterfeit.
[3] Possibly Jacob.

Good men and women. If any here today 50
Has done a sin so horrible to name
He daren't be shriven of it for the shame,
Or if any woman, young or old, is here
Who has cuckolded her husband,[4] be it clear
They may not make an offering in that case 55
To these my relics; they have no power nor
    grace.
But any who is free of such dire blame,
Let him come up and offer in God's name
And I'll absolve him through the authority
That by the pope's bull has been granted
    me.'[5]   60
  "By such hornswoggling I've won, year by
    year,
A hundred marks[6] since being a pardoner.
I stand in my pulpit like a true divine,
And when the people sit I preach my line
To ignorant souls, as you have heard before, 65
And tell skullduggeries by the hundred more.
Then I take care to stretch my neck well out
And over the people I nod and peer about
Just like a pigeon perching on a shed.[7]
My hands fly and my tongue wags in my
    head   70
So busily that to watch me is a joy.
Avarice is the theme that I employ
In all my sermons, to make the people free
In giving pennies—especially to me.
My mind is fixed on what I stand to win 75
And not at all upon correcting sin.
I do not care, when they are in the grave,
If souls go berry-picking that I could save.
Truth is that evil purposes determine,
And many a time, the origin of a sermon: 80
Some to please people and by flattery
To gain advancement through hypocrisy,
Some for vainglory, some again for hate.
For when I daren't fight otherwise, I wait
And give him a tongue-lashing when I
    preach.   85

[4] Been unfaithful to him.
[5] Review the passage starting at l. 24. Is the Pardoner simply recounting what he has done in the past, or is he actually trying to sell his wares to the pilgrims?
[6] In modern purchasing power, perhaps five or six thousand dollars.
[7] Compare the IMAGE in the Pardoner's portrait (p. 72, l. 684). Are these images conflicting or complementary?

No man escapes or gets beyond the reach
Of my defaming tongue, supposing he
Has done a wrong to my brethren or to me.
For though I do not tell his proper name,
People will recognize him all the same. 90
By sign and circumstance I let them learn.
Thus I serve those who have done us an ill
    turn.
Thus I spit out my venom under hue
Of sanctity, and seem devout and true!
  "But to put my purpose briefly, I confess 95
I preach for nothing but for covetousness.
That's why my text is still and ever was
Radix malorum est cupiditas.
For by this text I can denounce, indeed,
The very vice I practice, which is greed. 100
But though that sin is lodged in my own heart,
I am able to make other people part
From avarice, and sorely to repent,
Though that is not my principal intent.
  "Then I bring in examples,[8] many a one, 105
And tell them many a tale of days long done.
Plain folk love tales that come down from of
    old.
Such things their minds can well report and
    hold.
Do you think that while I have the power to
    preach
And take in silver and gold for what I
    teach   110
I shall ever live in willful poverty?
No, no, that never was my thought, certainly.
I mean to preach and beg in sundry lands.
I won't do any labor with my hands,
Nor live by making baskets. I don't intend 115
To beg for nothing; that is not my end.
I won't ape the apostles; I must eat,
I must have money, wool, and cheese, and
    wheat,
Though I took it from the meanest wretch's
    tillage
Or from the poorest widow in a village, 120
Yes, though her children starved for want.
    In fine,
I mean to drink the liquor of the vine
And have a jolly wench in every town.
But, in conclusion, lords, I will get down

[8] *Exempla*, or illustrative anecdotes. Note that the Pardoner is following the form of the medieval sermon.

To business: you would have me tell a tale. 125
Now that I've had a drink of corny ale,
By God, I hope the thing I'm going to tell
Is one that you'll have reason to like well.
For though myself a very sinful man,
I can tell a moral tale, indeed I can, 130
One that I use to bring the profits in
While preaching. Now be still, and I'll begin."

The Pardoner's Tale

There was a company of young folk living
One time in Flanders, who were bent on
    giving
Their lives to follies and extravagances, 135
Brothels and taverns, where they held their
    dances
With lutes, harps, and guitars, diced at all
    hours,
And also ate and drank beyond their powers,
Through which they paid the devil sacrifice
In the devil's temple with their drink and
    dice, 140
Their abominable excess and dissipation.
They swore oaths that were worthy of
    damnation;
It was grisly to be listening when they swore.
The blessed body of our Lord they tore—
The Jews, it seemed to them, had failed to
    rend 145
His body enough—and each laughed at his
    friend
And fellow in sin. To encourage their pursuits
Came comely dancing girls, peddlers of fruits,
Singers with harps, bawds and confectioners
Who are the very devil's officers 150
To kindle and blow the fire of lechery
That is the follower of gluttony.
    Witness the Bible, if licentiousness
Does not reside in wine and drunkenness!
Recall how drunken Lot, unnaturally, 155
With his two daughters lay unwittingly,
So drunk he had no notion what he did.
    Herod, the stories tell us, God forbid,
When full of liquor at his banquet board
Right at his very table gave the word 160
To kill the Baptist, John, though guiltless
    he.

Seneca says a good word, certainly.[9]
He says there is no difference he can find
Between a man who has gone out of his mind
And one who carries drinking to excess, 165
Only that madness outlasts drunkenness.
O gluttony, first cause of mankind's fall,
Of our damnation the cursed original
Until Christ bought us with his blood again![10]
How dearly paid for by the race of men 170
Was this detestable iniquity!
This whole world was destroyed through
    gluttony.
    Adam our father and his wife also
From paradise to labor and to woe
Were driven for the selfsame vice, indeed. 175
As long as Adam fasted—so I read—
He was in heaven; but as soon as he
Devoured the fruit of that forbidden tree
Then he was driven out in sorrow and pain.
Of gluttony well ought we to complain! 180
Could a man know how many maladies
Follow indulgences and gluttonies
He would keep his diet under stricter measure
And sit at table with more temperate pleasure.
The throat is short and tender is the
    mouth, 185
And hence men toil east, west, and north, and
    south,
In earth, and air, and water—alas to think—
Fetching a glutton dainty meat and drink.
    This is a theme, O Paul, that you well treat:
"Meat unto belly, and belly unto meat, 190
God shall destroy them both," as Paul has
    said.
When a man drinks the white wine and the
    red—
This is a foul word, by my soul, to say,
And fouler is the deed in every way—
He makes his throat his privy through
    excess. 195
    The Apostle says, weeping for piteousness,
"There are many of whom I told you—at a
    loss
I say it, weeping—enemies of Christ's cross,
Whose belly is their god; their end is death."
O cursed belly! Sack of stinking breath 200

[9] The Roman philosopher and moralist.
[10] The humor of the situation is enhanced if one
realizes that this sermon against gluttony, drunkenness, and lechery is preached in a tavern.

In which corruption lodges, dung abounds!
At either end of you come forth foul sounds.
Great cost it is to fill you, and great pain!
These cooks, how they must grind and pound
    and strain
And transform substance into accident [11] 205
To please your cravings, though exorbitant!
From the hard bones they knock the marrow
    out.
They'll find a use for everything, past doubt,
That down the gullet sweet and soft will glide.
The spiceries of leaf and root provide   210
Sauces that are concocted for delight,
To give a man a second appetite.
But truly, he whom gluttonies entice
Is dead, while he continues in that vice.
    O drunken man, disfigured is your face, 215
Sour is your breath, foul are you to embrace!
You seem to mutter through your drunken
    nose
The sound of "Samson, Samson," yet God
    knows
That Samson never indulged himself in wine.
Your tongue is lost, you fall like a stuck
    swine,   220
And all the self-respect that you possess
Is gone, for of man's judgment, drunkenness
Is the very sepulcher and annihilation.
A man whom drink has under domination
Can never keep a secret in his head.   225
Now steer away from both the white and red,
And most of all from that white wine keep
    wide
That comes from Lepe.[12] They sell it in
    Cheapside
And Fish Street. It's a Spanish wine, and sly
To creep in other wines that grow nearby, 230
And such a vapor it has that with three drinks
It takes a man to Spain; although he thinks
He is home in Cheapside, he is far away
At Lepe. Then "Samson, Samson" will he say!
    By God himself, who is omnipotent,   235
All the great exploits in the Old Testament
Were done in abstinence, I say, and prayer.
Look in the Bible, you may learn it there.
    Attila, conqueror of many a place,

[11] A philosophical distinction: substance is the real nature of a thing, accident refers to such qualities as flavor and color.
[12] A town in Spain noted for its strong wines.

Died in his sleep in shame and in disgrace 240
Bleeding out of his nose in drunkenness.
A captain ought to live in temperateness!
And more than this, I say, remember well
The injunction that was laid on Lemuel—
Not Samuel, but Lemuel,[13] I say!   245
Read in the Bible; in the plainest way
Wine is forbidden to judges and to kings.
This will suffice; no more upon these things.
    Now that I've shown what gluttony will
        do,
Now I will warn you against gambling,
        too;   250
Gambling, the very mother of low scheming,
Of lying and forswearing and blaspheming
Against Christ's name, of murder and waste
    as well
Alike of goods and time; and, truth to tell,
With honor and renown it cannot suit   255
To be held a common gambler by repute.
The higher a gambler stands in power and
    place,
The more his name is lowered in disgrace.
If a prince gambles, whatever his kingdom be,
In his whole government and policy   260
He is, in all the general estimation,
Considered so much less in reputation.
    Stilbon, who was a wise ambassador,
From Lacedaemon once to Corinth bore
A mission of alliance. When he came   265
It happened that he found there at a game
Of hazard all the great ones of the land,
And so, as quickly as it could be planned,
He stole back, saying, "I will not lose my
    name
Nor have my reputation put to shame   270
Allying you with gamblers. You may send
Other wise emissaries to gain your end,
For by my honor, rather than ally
My countrymen to gamblers, I will die.
For you that are so gloriously renowned   275
Shall never with this gambling race be bound
By will of mine or treaty I prepare."
Thus did this wise philosopher declare.
    Remember also how the Parthians' lord
Sent King Demetrius, as the books record,   280
A pair of golden dice, by this proclaiming
His scorn, because that king was known for
    gaming,

[13] Proverbs 31:4.

And the king of Parthia therefore held his
crown
Devoid of glory, value, or renown.
Lords can discover other means of play   285
More suitable to while the time away.

Now about oaths I'll say a word or two,
Great oaths and false oaths, as the old books
do.
Great swearing is a thing abominable,
And false oaths yet more reprehensible.   290
Almighty God forbade swearing at all,
Matthew be witness; but specially I call
The holy Jeremiah on his head.
"Swear thine oaths truly, do not lie," he said.
"Swear under judgment, and
righteousness."   295
But idle swearing is a great wickedness.
Consult and see, and he that understands
In the first table of the Lord's commands
Will find the second of his commandments
this:
"Take not the Lord's name idly or amiss."   300
If a man's oaths and curses are extreme,
Vengeance shall find his house, both roof and
beam.
"By the precious heart of God," and "By his
nails"—
"My chance is seven, by Christ's blood at
Hailes,[14]
Yours five and three." "Cheat me, and if you
do,   305
By God's arms, with this knife I'll run you
through!"—
Such fruit comes from the bones, that pair
of bitches: [15]
Oaths broken, treachery, murder. For the
riches
Of Christ's love, give up curses, without fail,
Both great and small!—Now, sirs, I'll tell my
tale.   310

These three young roisterers of whom I tell
Long before prime had rung from any bell
Were seated in a tavern at their drinking,
And as they sat, they heard a bell go clinking
Before a corpse being carried to his grave.   315
One of these roisterers, when he heard it, gave

An order to his boy: "Go out and try
To learn whose corpse is being carried by.
Get me his name, and get it right. Take heed."
"Sir," said the boy, "there isn't any need.   320
I learned before you came here, by two hours.
He was, it happens, an old friend of yours,
And all at once, there on his bench upright
As he was sitting drunk, he was killed last
night.
A sly thief, Death men call him, who
deprives   325
All the people in this country of their lives,
Came with his spear and smiting his heart in
two
Went on his business with no more ado.
A thousand have been slaughtered by his hand
During this plague. And, sir, before you
stand   330
Within his presence, it should be necessary,
It seems to me, to know your adversary.
Be evermore prepared to meet this foe.
My mother taught me thus; that's all I know."
"Now by St. Mary," said the innkeeper,   335
"This child speaks truth. Man, woman,
laborer,
Servant, and child the thief has slain this
year
In a big village a mile or more from here.
I think it is his place of habitation.
It would be wise to make some preparation   340
Before he brought a man into disgrace."
"God's arms!" this roisterer said. "So that's
the case!
Is it so dangerous with this thief to meet?
I'll look for him by every path and street,
I vow it, by God's holy bones! Hear me,   345
Fellows of mine, we are all one, we three.
Let each of us hold up his hand to the other
And each of us become his fellow's brother.
We'll slay this Death, who slaughters and
betrays.
He shall be slain whose hand so many
slays,   350
By the dignity of God, before tonight!"

The three together set about to plight
Their oaths to live and die each for the other
Just as though each had been to each born
brother,
And in their drunken frenzy up they get   355
And toward the village off at once they set

---

[14] Some of Christ's blood was supposed to be
preserved in the abbey of Hailes.
[15] The original reads: *bicched bones two,* i.e., the
dice.

Which the innkeeper had spoken of before,
And many were the grisly oaths they swore.
They rent Christ's precious body limb from
 limb—
Death shall be dead, if they lay hands on
 him!   360
 When they had hardly gone the first half
 mile,
Just as they were about to cross a stile,
An old man, poor and humble, met them
 there.[16]
The old man greeted them with a meek air
And said, "God bless you, lords, and be your
 guide."   365
 "What's this?" the proudest of the three
 replied.
"Old beggar, I hope you meet with evil grace!
Why are you all wrapped up except your face?
What are you doing alive so many a year?"
 The old man at these words began to
 peer   370
Into this gambler's face. "Because I can,
Though I should walk to India, find no man,"
He said, "in any village or any town,
Who for my age is willing to lay down
His youth. So I must keep my old age still 375
For as long a time as it may be God's will.
Nor will Death take my life from me, alas!
Thus like a restless prisoner I pass
And on the ground, which is my mother's gate,
I walk and with my staff both early and
 late   380
I knock and say, 'Dear mother, let me in!
See how I vanish, flesh, and blood, and skin!
Alas, when shall my bones be laid to rest?
I would exchange with you my clothing chest,
Mother, that in my chamber long has been   385
For an old haircloth rag to wrap me in.'
And yet she still refuses me that grace.
All white, therefore, and withered is my face.
 "But, sirs, you do yourselves no courtesy
To speak to an old man so churlishly   390
Unless he had wronged you either in word or
 deed.
As you yourselves in Holy Writ may read,
'Before an aged man whose head is hoar
Men ought to rise.' I counsel you, therefore,
No harm nor wrong here to an old man do,   395

[16] Is the old man who is described in the following
lines Death, Old Age, or what?

No more than you would have men do to you
In your old age, if you so long abide.
And God be with you, whether you walk or
 ride!
I must go yonder where I have to go."
 "No, you old beggar, by St. John, not
 so,"   400
Said another of these gamblers. "As for me,
By God, you won't get off so easily!
You spoke just now of that false traitor, Death,
Who in this land robs all our friends of breath.
Tell where he is, since you must be his spy, 405
Or you will suffer for it, so say I
By God and by the holy sacrament.
You are in league with him, false thief, and
 bent
On killing us young folk, that's clear to my
 mind."
 "If you are so impatient, sirs, to find 410
Death," he replied, "turn up this crooked way,
For in that grove I left him, truth to say,
Beneath a tree, and there he will abide.
No boast of yours will make him run and hide.
Do you see that oak tree? Just there you will
 find   415
This Death, and God, who bought again
 mankind,
Save and amend you!" So said this old man;
And promptly each of these three gamblers
 ran
Until he reached the tree, and there they
 found
Florins of fine gold, minted bright and
 round,   420
Nearly eight bushels of them, as they thought.
And after Death no longer then they sought.
Each of them was so ravished at the sight,
So fair the florins glittered and so bright,
That down they sat beside the precious
 hoard.   425
The worst of them, he uttered the first word.
 "Brothers," he told them, "listen to what I
 say.
My head is sharp, for all I joke and play.
Fortune has given us this pile of treasure
To set us up in lives of ease and pleasure. 430
Lightly it comes, lightly we'll make it go.
God's precious dignity! Who was to know
We'd ever tumble on such luck today?
If we could only carry this gold away,

Home to my house, or either one of yours— 435
For well you know that all this gold is ours—
We'd touch the summit of felicity.
But still, by daylight that can hardly be.
People would call us thieves, too bold for
    stealth,
And they would have us hanged for our own
    wealth.   440
It must be done by night, that's our best plan,
As prudently and slyly as we can.
Hence my proposal is that we should all
Draw lots, and let's see where the lot will fall,
And the one of us who draws the shortest
    stick   445
Shall run back to the town, and make it quick,
And bring us bread and wine here on the
    sly,
And two of us will keep a watchful eye
Over this gold; and if he doesn't stay
Too long in town, we'll carry this gold
    away   450
By night, wherever we all agree it's best."
    One of them held the cut out in his fist
And had them draw to see where it would fall,
And the cut fell on the youngest of them all.
At once he set off on his way to town,   455
And the very moment after he was gone
The one who urged this plan said to the other:
"You know that by sworn oath you are my
    brother.
I'll tell you something you can profit by.
Our friend has gone, that's clear to any
    eye,   460
And here is gold, abundant as can be,
That we propose to share alike, we three.
But if I worked it out, as I could do,
So that it could be shared between us two,
Wouldn't that be a favor, a friendly one?" 465
    The other answered, "How that can be
    done,
I don't quite see. He knows we have the gold.
What shall we do, or what shall he be told?"
    "Will you keep the secret tucked inside your
    head?
And in a few words," the first scoundrel
    said,   470
"I'll tell you how to bring this end about."
    "Granted," the other told him. "Never
    doubt,
I won't betray you, that you can believe."

    "Now," said the first, "we are two, as you
    perceive,
And two of us must have more strength than
    one.   475
When he sits down, get up as if in fun
And wrestle with him. While you play this
    game
I'll run him through the ribs. You do the same
With your dagger there, and then this gold
    shall be
Divided, dear friend, between you and me. 480
Then all that we desire we can fulfill,
And both of us can roll the dice at will."
Thus in agreement these two scoundrels fell
To slay the third, as you have heard me tell.
    The youngest, who had started off to
    town,   485
Within his heart kept rolling up and down
The beauty of these florins, new and bright.
"O Lord," he thought, "were there some way
    I might
Have all this treasure to myself alone,
There isn't a man who dwells beneath God's
    throne   490
Could live a life as merry as mine should be!"
And so at last the fiend, our enemy,
Put in his head that he could gain his ends
If he bought poison to kill off his friends.
Finding his life in such a sinful state,   495
The devil was allowed to seal his fate.
For it was altogether his intent
To kill his friends, and never to repent.
So off he set, no longer would he tarry,
Into the town, to an apothecary,   500
And begged for poison; he wanted it because
He meant to kill his rats; besides, there was
A polecat living in his hedge, he said,
Who killed his capons; and when he went to
    bed
He wanted to take vengeance, if he might, 505
On vermin that devoured him by night.
    The apothecary answered, "You shall have
A drug that as I hope the Lord will save
My soul, no living thing in all creation,
Eating or drinking of this preparation   510
A dose no bigger than a grain of wheat,
But promptly with his death-stroke he shall
    meet.
Die, that he will, and in a briefer while
Than you can walk the distance of a mile,

This poison is so strong and virulent."   515
    Taking the poison, off the scoundrel went,
Holding it in a box, and next he ran
To the neighboring street, and borrowed from
    a man
Three generous flagons. He emptied out his
    drug
In two of them, and kept the other jug   520
For his own drink; he let no poison lurk
In that! And so all night he meant to work
Carrying off the gold. Such was his plan,
And when he had filled them, this accursed
    man
Retraced his path, still following his
    design,   525
Back to his friends with his three jugs of
    wine.
    But why dilate upon it any more?
For just as they had planned his death before,
Just so they killed him, and with no delay.
When it was finished, one spoke up to say: 530
"Now let's sit down and drink, and we can
    bury
His body later on. First we'll be merry,"
And as he said the words, he took the jug
That, as it happened, held the poisonous drug,
And drank, and gave his friend a drink as
    well,   535
And promptly they both died. But truth to
    tell,
In all that Avicenna ever wrote
He never described in chapter, rule, or note
More marvelous signs of poisoning, I suppose,
Than appeared in these two wretches at the
    close.   540
Thus they both perished for their homicide,
And thus the traitorous poisoner also died.
    O sin accursed above all cursedness,
O treacherous murder, O foul wickedness,
O gambling, lustfulness, and gluttony,   545
Traducer of Christ's name by blasphemy
And monstrous oaths, through habit and
    through pride!
Alas, mankind! Ah, how may it betide
That you to your Creator, he that wrought you
And even with his precious heart's blood
    bought you,   550
So falsely and ungratefully can live?
    And now, good men, your sins may God
    forgive

And keep you specially from avarice!
My holy pardon will avail in this,
For it can heal each one of you that brings   555
His pennies, silver brooches, spoons, or
    rings.
Come, bow your head under this holy bull!
You wives, come offer up your cloth or wool!
I write your names here in my roll, just so.
Into the bliss of heaven you shall go!   560
I will absolve you here by my high power,
You that will offer, as clean as in the hour
When you were born. —Sirs, thus I preach.[17]
    And now
Christ Jesus, our souls' healer, show you how
Within his pardon evermore to rest,   565
For that, I will not lie to you, is best.
    But in my tale, sirs, I forgot one thing.
The relics and the pardons that I bring
Here in my pouch, no man in the whole land
Has finer, given me by the pope's own
    hand.   570
If any of you devoutly wants to offer
And have my absolution, come and proffer
Whatever you have to give. Kneel down right
    here,
Humbly, and take my pardon, full and clear,
Or have a new, fresh pardon if you like   575
At the end of every mile of road we strike,
As long as you keep offering ever newly
Good coins, not counterfeit, but minted truly.
Indeed it is an honor I confer
On each of you, an authentic pardoner   580
Going along to absolve you as you ride.
For in the country mishaps may betide—
One or another of you in due course
May break his neck by falling from his horse.
Think what security it gives you all   585
That in this company I chanced to fall
Who can absolve you each, both low and
    high,
When the soul, alas, shall from the body fly!
By my advice, our Host here shall begin,
For he's the man enveloped most by sin.   590
Come, offer first, Sir Host, and once that's
    done,
Then you shall kiss the relics, every one,
Yes, for a penny! Come, undo your purse!
    "No, no," said he. "Then I should have
    Christ's curse!

[17] The end of the sermon.

I'll do nothing of the sort, for love or
    riches!   595
You'd make me kiss a piece of your old
    britches
And for a saintly relic make it pass
Although it had the tincture of your ass.
By the cross St. Helen found in the Holy
    Land,
I wish I had your balls here in my hand 600
For relics! Cut 'em off, and I'll be bound
If I don't help you carry them around.
I'll have the things enshrined in a hog's turd!"
    The Pardoner did not answer; not a word,
He was so angry, could he find to say.[18] 605
"Now," said our Host, "I will not try to
    play
With you, nor any other angry man."
    Immediately the worthy Knight began,
When he saw that all the people laughed, "No
    more,
This has gone far enough. Now as before, 610
Sir Pardoner, be gay, look cheerfully,

And you, Sir Host, who are so dear to me,
Come, kiss the Pardoner, I beg of you,
And Pardoner, draw near, and let us do
As we've been doing, let us laugh and
    play."   615
And so they kissed, and rode along their way.

STUDY AIDS: 1. Analyze the part played by
IRONY in (1) the Prologue and nonnarrative
portions of the Tale and (2) the *exemplum*
itself.

    2. Analyze the character of the Pardoner in
an effort to determine his motivation. For
example, why is he so open with his audience?
(Is he drunk? Is he proud of his rascality?)
Why is he so angry at the Host's remarks in ll.
594-603? Can he possibly have hoped to succeed?

    3. Compare the Pardoner in his Prologue and
Tale with the portrait of him in *The General
Prologue*. In what ways do the Prologue and
Tale supplement the picture in *The General
Prologue*?

The Wife of Bath's Prologue

    The Wife of Bath is one of the great comic creations of all literature. In *The General Prologue*
she appears as a striking figure with her huge mound of kerchiefs on her head on Sundays and
her scarlet stockings tightly laced. We are told that she lords it over the other ladies in church,
that she has had five husbands—not to mention "other company in youth"—, that she has been
on many pilgrimages, including three to Jerusalem, and that she knows much of the "olde daunce"
of love. She is not young, being a little over forty; but she is filled with the real stuff of life: the
capacity to bounce back, to give and take, and to laugh. She has many faults. She is lustful,
coarse, selfish, and power-driven. But she has certain supreme virtues also: she has courage and
she has integrity, and above all she is filled with the sheer joy of being alive. Chaucer obviously
loved her.

    Her Prologue is her autobiography, the first of its kind in English. In it, with complete frank-
ness and great ebullience, she tells the story of her life with each of her five husbands. Almost
incidentally, she also sets forth her ideas on love and marriage. These are principally two: that
sexual love is a good (stated by her in the medieval form: marriage is not inferior to virginity)
and that sovereignty in marriage belongs to the woman.

"Experience, though all authority
Was lacking in the world, confers on me
The right to speak of marriage, and unfold
Its woes. For, lords, since I was twelve years
    old

—Thanks to eternal God in heaven alive— 5
I have married at church door no less than
    five [1]
Husbands, provided that I can have been
So often wed,[2] and all were worthy men.

---

[18] Note that the Pardoner has been referred to as
either "a geldyng or a mare" (*General Prologue*,
l. 691).

[1] See p. 67, l. 460.
[2] I.e., if the Church recognizes so many marriages.

But I was told, indeed, and not long since,
That Christ went to a wedding only once   10
At Cana, in the land of Galilee.
By this example he instructed me
To wed only once—that's what I have heard!
Again, consider now what a sharp word,
Beside a well, Jesus, both God and man,   15
Spoke in reproving the Samaritan:
'Thou hast had five husbands'—this for a
    certainty
He said to her—'and the man that now hath
    thee
Is not thy husband.' True, he spoke this way,
But what he meant is more than I can say   20
Except that I would ask why the fifth man
Was not a husband to the Samaritan?
To just how many could she be a wife?
I have never heard this number all my life
Determined up to now. For round and
    round   25
Scholars may gloze, interpret, and expound,
But plainly, this I know without a lie,
God told us to increase and multiply.
That noble text I can well understand.
My husband—this too I have well in hand—   30
Should leave both father and mother and
    cleave to me.
Number God never mentioned, bigamy,
No, nor even octogamy; why do men
Talk of it as a sin and scandal, then? ³
    "Think of that monarch, wise King
      Solomon.   35
It strikes me that *he* had more wives than one!
To be refreshed, God willing, would please
    me
If I got it half as many times as he! ⁴
What a gift he had, a gift of God's own giving,
For all his wives! There isn't a man now
    living   40
Who has the like. By all that I make out
This king had many a merry first-night bout
With each, he was so thoroughly alive.
Blessed be God that I have married five,
And always, for the money in his chest   45
And for his nether purse, I picked the best.

In divers schools ripe scholarship is made,
And various practice in all kinds of trade
Makes perfect workmen, as the world can see.
Five husbands have had turns at schooling
    me.   50
Welcome the sixth, whenever I am faced
With yet another. I don't mean to be chaste
At all costs. When a spouse of mine is gone,
Some other Christian man shall take me on,
For then, says the Apostle,⁵ I'll be free   55
To wed, in God's name, where it pleases me.
To marry is no sin, as we can learn
From him; better to marry than to burn,
He says. Why should I care what obloquy
Men heap on Lamech and his bigamy? ⁶   60
Abraham was, by all that I can tell,
A holy man; so Jacob was as well,
And each of them took more than two as
    brides,
And many another holy man besides.
Where, may I ask, in any period,   65
Can you show in plain words that Almighty
    God
Forbade us marriage? Point it out to me!
Or where did he command virginity?
The Apostle, when he speaks of maidenhood,
Lays down no law. This I have understood   70
As well as you, milords, for it is plain.
Men may advise a woman to abstain
From marriage, but mere counsels aren't
    commands.
He left it to our judgment, where it stands.
Had God enjoined us all to maidenhood   75
Then marriage would have been condemned
    for good.
But truth is, if no seed were ever sown,
In what soil could virginity be grown?
Paul did not dare command a thing at best
On which his Master left us no behest.   80
    "But now the prize goes to virginity.⁷
Seize it whoever can, and let us see
What manner of man shall run best in the
    race!
But not all men receive this form of grace
Except where God bestows it by his will.   85

³ What differences between medieval and modern
marriage practices are implied in the preceding
thirty-four lines?
⁴ The frank sensuality is characteristic of the
Wife. Is it offensive?

⁵ St. Paul (cf. I Cor. 7:39).
⁶ Cf. Gen. 4:19–23.
⁷ According to medieval doctrine, marriage, although necessary, was inferior to chastity. To what
extent does this belief survive today?

The Apostle was a maid, I know; but still,
Although he wished all men were such as he,
It was only *counsel* toward virginity.
To be a wife he gave me his permission,
And so it is no blot on my condition   90
Nor slander of bigamy upon my state
If when my husband dies I take a mate.
A man does virtuously, St. Paul has said,
To touch no woman—meaning in his bed.
For fire and fat are dangerous friends at
          best.   95
You know what this example should suggest.
Here is the nub: he held virginity
Superior to wedded frailty,
And frailty I call it unless man
And woman both are chaste for their whole
          span.   100
  "I am not jealous if maidenhood outweighs
My marriages; I grant it all the praise.
It pleases them, these virgins, flesh and soul
To be immaculate. I won't extol
My own condition. In a lord's household   105
You know that every vessel can't be gold.
Some are of wood, and serve their master still.
God calls us variously to do his will.
Each has his proper gift, of all who live,
Some this, some that, as it pleases God to
          give.   110
  "To be virgin is a high and perfect course,
And continence is holy. But the source
Of all perfection, Jesus, never bade
Each one of us to go sell all he had
And give it to the poor; he did not say   115
That all should follow him in this one way.
He spoke to those who would live perfectly,
And by your leave, lords, that is not for me!
The flower of my best years I find it suits
To spend on the acts of marriage and its
          fruits.   120
  "Tell me this also: why at our creation
Were organs given us for generation,
And for what profit were we creatures made?
Believe me, not for nothing! Ply his trade
Of twisting texts who will, and let him
          urge [8]   125
That they [8] were only given us to purge
Our urine; say without them we should fail
To tell a female rightly from a male
And that's their only object—say you so?

[8] Organs.

It won't work, as experience will show.   130
Without offense to scholars, I say this,
They were given us for both these purposes,
That we may both be cleansed, I mean, and
          eased
Through intercourse, where God is not
          displeased.
Why else in books is this opinion met,   135
That every man should pay his wife his debt?
Tell me with what a man should hope to pay
Unless he put his instrument in play?
They were supplied us, then, for our
          purgation,
But they were also meant for generation.   140
  "But none the less I do not mean to say
That all those who were furnished in this way
Are bound to go and practice intercourse.
The world would then grant chastity no force.
Christ was a maid, yet he was formed a
          man,   145
And many a saint, too, since the world began,
And yet they lived in perfect chastity.
I am not spiteful toward virginity.
Let virgins be white bread of pure wheat-seed.
Barley we wives are called, and yet I read   150
In Mark, and tell the tale in truth he can,
That Christ with barley bread cheered many
          a man.
In the state that God assigned to each of us
I'll persevere. I'm not fastidious.
In wifehood I will use my instrument   155
As freely by my Maker it was lent.
If I hold back with it, God give me sorrow!
My husband shall enjoy it night and morrow
When it pleases him to come and pay his debt.
But a husband, and I've not been thwarted
          yet,   160
Shall always be my debtor and my slave.
From tribulation he shall never save
His flesh, not for as long as I'm his wife!
I have the power, during all my life,
Over his very body, and not he.   165
For so the Apostle has instructed me,
Who bade men love their wives for better or
          worse.
It pleases me from end to end, that verse!"
  The Pardoner, before she could go on,
Jumped up and cried, "By God and by St.
          John,   170
Upon this topic you preach nobly, Dame!

I was about to wed,[9] but now, for shame,
Why should my body pay a price so dear?
I'd rather not be married all this year!"
  "Hold on," she said. "I haven't yet
    begun.   175
You'll drink a keg of this before I'm done,
I promise you, and it won't taste like ale!
And after I have told you my whole tale
Of marriage, with its fund of tribulation—
And I'm the expert of my generation,   180
For I myself, I mean, have been the whip—
You can decide then if you want a sip
Out of the barrel that I mean to broach.
Before you come too close in your approach,
Think twice. I have examples, more than
    ten!   185
'The man who won't be warned by other men,
To other men a warning he shall be.'
These are the words we find in Ptolemy.[10]
You can read them right there in his
    Almagest."
  "Now, Madame, if you're willing, I
    suggest,"   190
Answered the Pardoner, "as you began,
Continue with your tale, and spare no man.
Teach us your practice—we young men need
    a guide."
  "Gladly, if it will please you," she replied.
"But first I ask you, if I speak my mind,   195
That all this company may be well inclined,
And will not take offense at what I say.
I only mean it, after all, in play.
  "Now, sirs, I will get onward with my tale.
If ever I hope to drink good wine or ale, 200
I'm speaking truth: the husbands I have had,
Three of them have been good, and two were
    bad.
The three were kindly men, and rich, and old.
But they were hardly able to uphold
The statute which had made them fast to
    me.   205
You know well what I mean by this, I see!
So help me God, I can't help laughing yet
When I think of how at night I made them
    sweat,
And I thought nothing of it, on my word!

Their land and wealth they had by then
    conferred   210
On me, and so I safely could neglect
Tending their love or showing them respect.
So well they loved me that by God above
I hardly set a value on their love.[11]
A woman who is wise is never done   215
Busily winning love when she has none,
But since I had them wholly in my hand
And they had given me their wealth and
    land,
Why task myself to spoil them or to please
Unless for my own profit and my ease?   220
I set them working so that many a night
They sang a dirge, so grievous was their
    plight!
They never got the bacon, well I know,
Offered as prize to couples at Dunmow [12]
Who live a year in peace, without
    repentance!   225
So well I ruled them, by my law and sentence,
They were glad to bring me fine things from
    the fair
And happy when I spoke with a mild air,
For God knows I could chide outrageously.
  "Now judge if I could do it properly!   230
You wives who understand and who are wise,
This is the way to throw dust in their eyes.
There isn't on the earth so bold a man
He can swear false or lie as a woman can.
I do not urge this course in every case,   235
Just when a prudent wife is caught off base;
Then she should swear the parrot's mad who
    tattled
Her indiscretions, and when she's once
    embattled
Should call her maid as witness, by collusion.
But listen, how I threw them in confusion: 240
  " 'Sir dotard, this is how you live?' I'd say.
'How can my neighbor's wife be dressed so
    gay?
She carries off the honors everywhere.
I sit at home. I've nothing fit to wear.
What were you doing at my neighbor's
    house?   245
Is she so handsome? Are you so amorous?

---

[9] Is there unconscious IRONY in the Pardoner's
assertion? (Cf. p. 72, ll. 689–691.)
[10] The ancient astronomer; the sayings attributed
to him by the Wife are apocryphal.

[11] Is the Wife's reaction psychologically sound?
[12] A town in Essex where an annual prize of a
flitch of bacon was given to a couple who had lived a
year without quarreling or regretting their marriage.

What do you whisper to our maid? God bless
  me,
Give up your jokes, old lecher. They depress
  me.
When I have a harmless friend myself, you
  balk
And scold me like a devil if I walk   250
For innocent amusement to his house.
You drink and come home reeling like a souse
And sit down on your bench, worse luck, and
  preach.
Taking a wife who's poor—this is the speech
That you regale me with—costs grievously, 255
And if she's rich and of good family,
It is a constant torment, you decide,
To suffer her ill humor and her pride.
And if she's fair, you scoundrel, you destroy
  her
By saying that every lecher will enjoy her; 260
For chastity at best has frail protections
If a woman is assailed from all directions.
  " 'Some want us for our wealth, so you
  declare,
Some for our figure, some think we are fair,
Some want a woman who can dance or
  sing, 265
Some want kindness, and some philandering,
Some look for hands and arms well turned and
  small.
Thus, by your tale, the devil may take us all!
Men cannot keep a castle or redoubt
Longer, you tell me, than it can hold out. 270
Or if a woman's plain, you say that she
Is one who covets each man she may see,
For at him like a spaniel she will fly
Until she finds some man that she can buy.
Down to the lake goes never a goose so
  gray 275
But it will have a mate, I've heard you say.
It's hard to fasten—this too I've been told—
A thing that no man willingly will hold.
Wise men, you tell me as you go to bed,
And those who hope for heaven should never
  wed. 280
I hope wild lightning and a thunderstroke
Will break your wizened neck! You say that
  smoke
And falling timbers and a railing wife
Drive a man from his house. Lord bless my
  life!

What ails an old man, so to make him
  chide? 285
We cover our vices till the knot is tied,
We wives, you say, and then we trot them
  out.
Here's a fit proverb for a doddering lout!
An ox or ass, you say, a hound or horse,
These we examine as a matter of course. 290
Basins and also bowls, before we buy them,
Spoons, spools, and such utensils, first we try
  them,
And so with pots and clothes, beyond denial;
But of their wives men never make a trial
Until they are married. After that, you say, 295
Old fool, we put our vices on display.
  " 'I am in a pique if you forget your duty
And fail, you tell me, to praise me for my
  beauty,
Or unless you are always doting on my face
And calling me "fair dame" in every place, 300
Or unless you give a feast on my birthday
To keep me in good spirits, fresh and gay,
Or unless all proper courtesies are paid
To my nurse and also to my chambermaid,
And my father's kin with all their family
  ties— 305
You say so, you old barrelful of lies!
  " 'Yet just because he has a head of hair
Like shining gold, and squires me everywhere,
You have a false suspicion in your heart
Of Jenkin, our apprentice. For my part 310
I wouldn't have him if you died tomorrow!
But tell me this, or go and live in sorrow:
That chest of yours, why do you hide the keys
Away from me? It's my wealth, if you please,
As much as yours. Will you make a fool of
  me, 315
The mistress of our house? You shall not be
Lord of my body and my wealth at once!
No, by St. James himself, you must renounce
One or the other, if it drives you mad!
Does it help to spy on me? You would be
  glad 320
To lock me up, I think, inside your chest.
"Enjoy yourself, and go where you think
  best,"
You ought to say; "I won't hear tales of malice.
I know you for a faithful wife, Dame Alice."
A woman loves no man who keeps close
  charge 325

Of where she goes. We want to be at large.
Blessed above all other men was he,
The wise astrologer, Don Ptolemy,
Who has this proverb in his *Almagest:*
"Of all wise men his wisdom is the best   330
Who does not care who has the world in
    hand."
Now by this proverb you should understand,
Since you have plenty, it isn't yours to care
Or fret how richly other people fare,
For by your leave, old dotard, you for one   335
Can have all you can take when day is
    done.
The man's a niggard to the point of scandal
Who will not lend his lamp to light a candle;
His lamp won't lose although the candle gain.
If you have enough, you ought not to
    complain.   340
    " 'You say, too, if we make ourselves look
    smart,
Put on expensive clothes and dress the part,
We lay our virtue open to disgrace.
And then you try to reinforce your case
By saying these words in the Apostle's
    name: 345
"In chaste apparel, with modesty and shame,
So shall you women clothe yourselves," said
    he,
"And not in rich coiffure or jewelry,
Pearls or the like, or gold, or costly wear."
Now both your text and rubric,[13] I declare,   350
I will not follow as I would a gnat!
    " 'You told me once that I was like a cat,
For singe her skin and she will stay at home,
But if her skin is smooth, the cat will roam.
No dawn but finds her on the neighbors
    calling   355
To show her skin, and go off caterwauling.[14]
If I am looking smart, you mean to say,
I'm off to put my finery on display.
    " 'What do you gain, old fool, by setting
    spies?
Though you beg Argus with his hundred
    eyes   360
To be my bodyguard, for all his skill
He'll keep me only by my own free will.
I know enough to blind him, as I live!

[13] Chapter heading.
[14] What does this IMAGE imply about the Wife's character?

    " 'There are three things, you also say, that
    give
Vexation to this world both south and
    north,   365
And you add that no one can endure the
    fourth.
Of these catastrophes a hateful wife—
You precious wretch, may Christ cut short
    your life!—
Is always reckoned, as you say, for one.
Is this your whole stock of comparison,   370
And why in all your parables of contempt
Can a luckless helpmate never be exempt?
You also liken woman's love to hell,
To barren land where water will not dwell.
I've heard you call it an unruly fire;   375
The more it burns, the hotter its desire
To burn up everything that burned will be.
You say that just as worms destroy a tree
A wife destroys her spouse, as they have found
Who get themselves in holy wedlock
    bound.'   380
    "By these devices, lords, as you perceive,
I got my three old husbands to believe
That in their cups they said things of this
    sort,
And all of it was false; but for support
Jenkin bore witness, and my niece did too.   385
These innocents, Lord, what I put them
    through!
God's precious pains! And they had no
    recourse,
For I could bite and whinny like a horse.
Though in the wrong, I kept them well
    annoyed,
Or oftentimes I would have been
    destroyed!   390
First to the mill is first to grind his grain.
I was always the first one to complain,
And so our peace was made; they gladly bid
For terms to settle things they never did!
    "For wenching I would scold them out of
    hand   395
When they were hardly well enough to stand.
But this would tickle a man; it would restore
    him
To think I had so great a fondness for him!
I'd vow when darkness came and out I
    stepped,
It was to see the girls with whom he slept.   400

The Wheel of Fortune, as applied to the choice of a husband. Late fourteenth or early fifteenth century.

The Canterbury Pilgrims leaving the Tabard Inn. From an old manuscript.

Portrait of Chaucer, from an early fifteenth-century manuscript.

Under this pretext I had plenty of mirth!
Such wit as this is given us at our birth.
Lies, tears, and needlework the Lord will give
In kindness to us women while we live.
And thus in one point I can take just pride: 405
In the end I showed myself the stronger side.
By sleight or strength I kept them in restraint,
And chiefly by continual complaint.
In bed they met their grief in fullest measure.
There I would scold; I would not do their
    pleasure.   410
Bed was a place where I would not abide
If I felt my husband's arm across my side
Till he agreed to square accounts and pay,
And after that I'd let him have his way.
To every man, therefore, I tell this tale: 415
Win where you're able, all is up for sale.
No falcon by an empty hand is lured.
For victory their cravings I endured
And even feigned a show of appetite.
And yet in old meat I have no delight;   420
It made me always rail at them and chide
    them,
For though the pope himself sat down beside
    them
I would not give them peace at their own
    board.
No, on my honor, I paid them word for word.
Almighty God so help me, if right now   425
I had to make my last will, I can vow
For every word they said to me, we're quits.
For I so handled the contest by my wits
That they gave up, and took it for the best,
Or otherwise we should have had no rest. 430
Like a mad lion let my husband glare,
In the end he got the worst of the affair.
    "Then I would say, 'My dear, you ought to
    keep
In mind how gentle Wilkin looks, our sheep.
Come here, my husband, let me kiss your
    cheek!   435
You should be patient, too; you should be
    meek.
Of Job and of his patience when you prate
Your conscience ought to show a cleaner
    slate.
He should be patient who so well can preach.
If not, then it will fall on me to teach   440
The beauty of a peaceful wedded life.
For one of us must give in, man or wife,

And since men are more reasonable creatures
Than women are, it follows that your features
Ought to exhibit patience. Why do you
    groan?   445
You want my body yours, and yours alone?
Why, take it all! Welcome to every bit!
But curse you, Peter, unless you cherish it!
Were I inclined to peddle my belle chose [15]
I could go about dressed freshly as a rose. 450
But I will keep it for your own sweet tooth.
It's your fault if we fight. By God, that's
    truth!'
    "This was the way I talked when I had
    need.
But now to my fourth husband I'll proceed.[16]
    "This fourth I married was a roisterer. 455
He had a mistress, and my passions were,
Although I say it, strong; and altogether
I was young and stubborn, pert in every
    feather.
If anyone took up his harp to play,
How I could dance! I sang as merry a lay 460
As any nightingale when of sweet wine
I had drunk my draft. Metellius, the foul
    swine,
Who beat his spouse until he took her life
For drinking wine, had I only been his wife,
He'd never have frightened me away from
    drinking!   465
But after a drink, Venus gets in my thinking,
For just as true as cold engenders hail
A thirsty mouth goes with a thirsty tail.
Drinking destroys a woman's last defense
As lechers well know by experience.   470
    "But, Lord Christ, when it all comes back
    to me,
Remembering my youth and jollity,
It tickles me to the roots. It does me good
Down to this very day that while I could
I took my world, my time, and had my
    fling.   475
But age, alas, that poisons everything
Has robbed me of my beauty and my pith.
Well, let it go! Good-by! The devil with
What cannot last! There's only this to tell:
The flour is gone, I've only chaff to sell. 480
Yet I'll contrive to keep a merry cheek!

[15] Lit. "good thing" (French); here, genitals.
[16] Characterize the Wife's relationships with her
first three husbands.

But now of my fourth husband I will speak.

"My heart was, I can tell you, full of spite
That in another he should find delight.
I paid him for his debt; I made it good.   485
I furnished him a cross of the same wood,
By God and by St. Joce [17]—in no foul fashion,
Not with my flesh; but I put on such passion
And rendered him so jealous, I'll engage
I made him fry in his own grease for rage!   490
On earth, God knows, I was his purgatory; [18]
I only hope his soul is now in glory.
God knows it was a sad song that he sung
When the shoe pinched him; sorely was he
    wrung!
Only he knew, and God, the devious
    system   495
By which outrageously I used to twist him.
He died when I came home from Jerusalem.
He is buried near the chancel, under the beam
That holds the cross. His tomb is less ornate
Than the sepulcher where Darius [19] lies in
    state   500
And which the paintings of Appelles [20] graced
With subtle work. It would have been a waste
To bury him lavishly. Farewell! God save
His soul and give him rest! He's in his grave.

"And now of my fifth husband let me
    tell.   505
God never let his soul go down to hell
Though he of all five was my scourge and
    flail!
I feel it on my ribs, right down the scale,
And ever shall until my dying day.
And yet he was so full of life and gay   510
In bed, and could so melt me and cajole me
When on my back he had a mind to roll me,
What matter if on every bone he'd beaten me!
He'd have my love, so quickly he could
    sweeten me.
I loved him best, in fact; for as you see,   515
His love was a more arduous prize for me.
We women, if I'm not to tell a lie,
Are quaint in this regard. Put in our eye
A thing we cannot easily obtain,

All day we'll cry about it and complain.   520
Forbid a thing, we want it bitterly,
But urge it on us, then we turn and flee.
We are chary of what we hope that men will
    buy.
A throng at market makes the prices high;
Men set no value on cheap merchandise,   525
A truth all women know if they are wise.

"My fifth, may God forgive his every sin,
I took for love, not money. He had been
An Oxford student once, but in our town
Was boarding with my good friend,
    Alison.   530
She knew each secret that I had to give
More than our parish priest did, as I live!
I told her my full mind, I shared it all.
For if my husband pissed against a wall
Or did a thing that might have cost his
    life,   535
To her, and to another neighbor's wife,
And to my niece, a girl whom I loved well,
His every thought I wouldn't blush to tell.
And often enough I told them, be it said.
God knows I made his face turn hot and
    red   540
For secrets he confided to his shame.
He knew he only had himself to blame.

"And so it happened once that during Lent,
As I often did, to Alison's I went,
For I have loved my life long to be gay   545
And to walk out in April or in May
To hear the talk and seek a favorite haunt.
Jenkin the student, Alice, my confidante,
And I myself into the country went.
My husband was in London all that Lent.   550
I had the greater liberty to see
And to be seen by jolly company.
How could I tell beforehand in what place
Luck might be waiting with a stroke of grace?
And so I went to every merrymaking.   555
No pilgrimage was past my undertaking.
I was at festivals, and marriages,
Processions, preachings, and at miracle
    plays,[21]
And in my scarlet clothes I made a sight.
Upon that costume neither moth nor mite   560
Nor any worm with ravening hunger fell.
And why, you ask? It was kept in use too
    well.

[17] A Breton saint.
[18] What are the implications of this IMAGE? In what ways was the Wife his purgatory?
[19] Darius III, buried by Alexander the Great, who defeated him.
[20] The great Greek artist.
[21] See p. 7.

"Now for what happened. In the fields we
    walked,
The three of us, and gallantly we talked,
The student and I, until I told him he,   565
If I became a widow, should marry me.
For I can say, and not with empty pride,
I have never failed for marriage to provide
Or other things as well. Let mice be meek;
A mouse's heart I hold not worth a leek.   570
He has one hole to scurry to, just one,
And if that fails him, he is quite undone.
   "I let this student think he had bewitched
    me.
(My mother with this piece of guile enriched
    me!)
All night I dreamed of him—this too I said; 575
He was killing me as I lay flat in bed;
My very bed in fact was full of blood;
But still I hoped it would result in good,
For blood betokens gold, as I have heard.
It was a fiction, dream and every word,   580
But I was following my mother's lore
In all this matter, as in many more.
   "Sirs—let me see; what did I mean to
    say?
Aha! By God, I have it! When he lay,
My fourth, of whom I've spoken, on his
    bier,   585
I wept of course; I showed but little cheer,
As wives must do, since custom has its place,
And with my kerchief covered up my face.
But since I had provided for a mate,
I did not cry for long, I'll freely state.   590
And so to church my husband on the morrow
Was borne away by neighbors in their sorrow.
Jenkin, the student, was among the crowd,
And when I saw him walk, so help me God,
Behind the bier, I thought he had a pair 595
Of legs and feet so cleanly turned and fair
I put my heart completely in his hold.
He was in fact some twenty winters old
And I was forty, to confess the truth;
But all my life I've still had a colt's tooth. 600
My teeth were spaced apart; [22] that was the
    seal
St. Venus printed, and became me well.
So help me God, I was a lusty one,
Pretty and young and rich, and full of fun.
And truly, as my husbands have all said, 605

[22] Cf. p. 68, l. 468.

I was the best thing there could be in bed.
For I belong to Venus [23] in my feelings,
Though I bring the heart of Mars to all my
    dealings.
From Venus come my lust and appetite,
From Mars I get my courage and my
    might,   610
Born under Taurus, while Mars stood therein.
Alas, alas, that ever love was sin!
I yielded to my every inclination
Through the predominance of my
    constellation; [24]
This made me so I never could withhold 615
My chamber of Venus, if the truth be told,
From a good fellow; yet upon my face
Mars left his mark, and in another place [25]
For never, so may Christ grant me
    intercession,
Have I yet loved a fellow with discretion, 620
But always I have followed appetite,
Let him be long or short or dark or light.
I never cared, as long as he liked me,
What his rank was or how poor he might be.
   "What should I say, but when the month
    ran out,   625
This jolly student, always much about,
This Jenkin married me in solemn state.
To him I gave land, titles, the whole slate
Of goods that had been given me before; [26]
But my repentance afterward was sore!   630
He wouldn't endure the pleasures I held dear.
By God, he gave me a lick once on the ear,
When from a book of his I tore a leaf,
So hard that from the blow my ear grew
    deaf.[27]
I was stubborn as a lioness with young, 635
And by the truth I had a rattling tongue,
And I would visit, as I'd done before,
No matter what forbidding oath he swore.
Against this habit he would sit and preach
    me

[23] The Wife was born under the planets Mars
and Venus. Venus gave her her strong sexuality,
Mars her courage and independence. For the re-
spectability of astrology in the Middle Ages, see
p. 66, l. 411.
[24] It was in her stars.
[25] The planets produced bodily marks.
[26] Note the contrast with the first three husbands.
How do you account for it?
[27] Cf. p. 67, l. 446.

Sermons enough, and he would try to teach
   me   640
Old Roman stories, how for his whole life
The man Sulpicius Gallus left his wife
Only because he saw her look one day
Bareheaded down the street from his doorway.
   "Another Roman he told me of by name   645
Who, since his wife was at a summer's game
Without his knowledge, thereupon forsook
The woman. In his Bible he would look
And find that proverb of the Ecclesiast
Where he enjoins and makes the stricture
   fast   650
That men forbid their wives to rove about.
Then he would quote me this, you needn't
   doubt:
'Build a foundation over sands or shallows,
Or gallop a blind horse across the fallows,
Let a wife traipse to shrines that some saint
   hallows,   655
And you are fit to swing upon the gallows.'
Talk as he would, I didn't care two haws
For his proverbs or his venerable saws.
Set right by him I never meant to be.
I hate the man who tells my faults to me,   660
And more of us than I do, by your pleasure.
This made him mad with me beyond all
   measure.
Under his yoke in no case would I go.
   "Now, by St. Thomas, I will let you
   know
Why from that book of his I tore a leaf,   665
For which I got the blow that made me deaf.
   "He had a book,[28] *Valerius*, he called it,
And Theophrastus, and he always hauled it
From where it lay to read both day and night
And laughed hard at it, such was his
   delight.   670
There was another scholar, too, at Rome
A cardinal, whose name was St. Jerome;
He wrote a book against Jovinian.[29]
In the same book also were Tertullian,

Chrysippus, Trotula, Abbess Héloïse [30]   675
Who lived near Paris; it contained all these,
Bound in a single volume, and many a one
Besides; the Parables of Solomon
And Ovid's *Art of Love*. On such vacation
As he could snatch from worldly
   occupation   680
He dredged this book for tales of wicked
   wives.
He knew more stories of their wretched lives
Than are told about good women in the Bible.
No scholar ever lived who did not libel
Women, believe me; to speak well of wives   685
Is quite beyond them, unless it be in lives
Of holy saints; no woman else will do.
Who was it painted the lion,[31] tell me who?
By God, if women had only written stories
Like wits and scholars in their oratories,   690
They would have pinned on men more
   wickedness
Than the whole breed of Adam can redress.
Venus's children clash with Mercury's; [32]
The two work evermore by contraries.
Knowledge and wisdom are of Mercury's
   giving,   695
Venus loves revelry and riotous living,
And with these clashing dispositions gifted
Each of them sinks when the other is uplifted.
Thus Mercury falls, God knows, in desolation
In the sign of Pisces, Venus's exaltation,   700
And Venus falls when Mercury is raised.
Thus by a scholar no woman can be praised.
The scholar, when he's old and cannot do
The work of Venus more than his old shoe,
Then sits he down, and in his dotage fond   705
Writes that no woman keeps her marriage
   bond!
   "But now for the story that I undertook—
To tell how I was beaten for a book.

[30] The famous Héloïse of the pair of lovers,
Abelard and Héloïse. Because of her, Abelard was
emasculated.
[31] In Aesop's fable.
[32] This and the next thirteen lines involve the
astrological doctrine that when one planet is in
power, another planet, of opposite nature, is out of
power. When Venus is "exalted" in the zodiacal
sign of Pisces, then Mercury, her opposite, is "dejected." Venus stands for bodily pleasures, Mercury
for science and philosophy. Since women are governed by Venus, these old scholars, governed by
Mercury, naturally cannot praise them!

[28] I.e., *Valerius and Theophrastus*. Valerius refers
to the twelfth century work by Walter Map, *Letter
of Valerius against Marriage;* Theophrastus (third
century B.C.) wrote a book on marriage. Jenkin's
book is a miscellaneous collection containing some
antifeminist writings.
[29] Jovinian maintained that marriage was not inferior to virginity; St. Jerome (fifth century) refuted
him.

"Jenkin, one night, who never seemed to
tire
Of reading in his book, sat by the fire   710
And first he read of Eve, whose wickedness
Delivered all mankind to wretchedness
For which in his own person Christ was slain
Who with his heart's blood bought us all
again.
'By this,' he said, 'expressly you may find 715
That woman was the loss of all mankind.'

"He read me next how Samson lost his hair.
Sleeping, his mistress clipped it off for fair;
Through this betrayal he lost both his eyes.
He read me then—and I'm not telling lies— 720
How Deianeira, wife of Hercules,
Caused him to set himself on fire. With these
He did not overlook the sad to-do
Of Socrates with *his* wives—he had two.
Xantippe emptied the pisspot on his head.   725
This good man sat as patient as if dead.
He wiped his scalp; he did not dare complain
Except to say 'With thunder must come rain.'

"Pasiphaë, who was the queen of Crete,
For wickedness he thought her story sweet.   730
Ugh! That's enough, it was a grisly thing,
About her lust and filthy hankering!
And Clytemnestra in her lechery
Who took her husband's life feloniously,
He grew devout in reading of her treason.   735
And then he told me also for what reason
Unhappy Amphiaraus lost his life.
My husband had the story of *his* wife,
Eriphyle, who for a clasp of gold
Went to his Grecian enemies and told   740
The secret of her husband's hiding place,
For which at Thebes he met an evil grace.
Livia and Lucilia, he went through
Their tale as well; they killed their husbands,
too.
One killed for love, the other killed for
hate.   745
At evening Livia, when the hour was late,
Poisoned her husband, for she was his foe.
Lucilia doted on her husband so
That in her lust, hoping to make him think
Ever of her, she gave him a love-drink   750
Of such a sort he died before the morrow.
And so at all turns husbands come to sorrow!

"He told me then how one Latumius,
Complaining to a friend named Arrius,

Told him that in his garden grew a tree   755
On which his wives had hanged themselves,
all three,
Merely for spite against their partnership.
'Brother,' said Arrius, 'let me have a slip
From this miraculous tree, for, begging
pardon,
I want to go and plant it in my garden.'   760
    "Then about wives in recent times he read,
How some had murdered husbands lying abed
And all night long had let a paramour
Enjoy them with the corpse flat on the floor;
Or driven a nail into a husband's brain   765
While he was sleeping, and thus he had been
slain;
And some had given them poison in their
drink.
He told more harm than anyone can think,
And seasoned his wretched stories with
proverbs
Outnumbering all the blades of grass and
herbs   770
On earth. 'Better a dragon for a mate,
Better,' he said, 'on a lion's whims to wait
Than on a wife whose way it is to chide.
Better,' he said, 'high in the loft to bide
Than with a railing wife down in the
house.   775
They always, they are so contrarious,
Hate what their husbands like,' so he would
say.
'A woman,' he said, 'throws all her shame
away
When she takes off her smock.' And on he'd
go:
'A pretty woman, unless she's chaste also,   780
Is like a gold ring stuck in a sow's nose.'
Who could imagine, who would half suppose
The gall my heart drank, raging at each
drop?
    "And when I saw that he would never stop
Reading all night from his accursed book,   785
Suddenly, in the midst of it, I took
Three leaves and tore them out in a great
pique,
And with my fist I caught him on the cheek
So hard he tumbled backward in the fire.
And up he jumped, he was as mad for ire   790
As a mad lion, and caught me on the head
With such a blow I fell down as if dead,

And seeing me on the floor, how still I lay,
He was aghast, and would have fled away,
Till I came to at length, and gave a cry.   795
'Have you killed me for my lands? Before I
    die,
False thief,' I said, 'I'll give you a last kiss!'
    "He came to me and knelt down close at
        this,
And said, 'So help me God, dear Alison,
I'll never strike you. For this thing I have
    done   800
You are to blame. Forgive me, I implore.'
So then I hit him on the cheek once more
And said, 'Thus far I am avenged, you thief.
I cannot speak. Now I shall die for grief.'
But finally, with much care and ado,   805
We reconciled our differences, we two.
He let me have the bridle in my hand
For management of both our house and land.
To curb his tongue he also undertook,
And on the spot I made him burn his
    book.   810
And when I had secured in full degree
By right of triumph the whole sovereignty,
And he had said, 'My dear, my own true wife,
Do as you will as long as you have life;
Preserve your honor and keep my estate,'   815
From that day on we had settled our debate.
I was as kind, God help me, day and dark
As any wife from India to Denmark,
And also true, and so he was to me.
I pray the Lord who sits in majesty   820
To bless his soul for Christ's own mercy
    dear.
And now I'll tell my tale, if you will hear."

"Dame," laughed the Friar, "as I hope for
    bliss,
It was a long preamble to a tale, all this!"
    "God's arms!" the Summoner said, "it is a
        sin,   825
Good people, how friars are always butting in!
A fly and a friar will fall in every dish
And every question, whatever people wish.
What do you know, with your talk about
    'preambling'?
Amble or trot or keep still or go scrambling, 830
You interrupt our pleasure."
                          "You think so,
Sir Summoner?" said the Friar. "Before I go,
I'll give the people here a chance or two
For a laugh at summoners, I promise you."
    "Curse on your face," the Summoner said,
        "curse me,   835
If I don't tell some stories, two or three,
On friars, before I get to Sittingborne,[33]
With which I'll twist your heart and make it
    mourn,
For you have lost your temper, I can see." [34]
    "Be quiet," cried our Host, "imme-
        diately   840
And ordered, "Let the woman tell her tale.
You act like people who've got drunk on ale.
Do, Madame, tell us. That is the best
    measure."
    "All ready, sir," she answered, "at your
        pleasure,
With the license of this worthy Friar
    here." [35]   845
    "Madame, tell on," he said. "You have my
        ear."

The Wife of Bath's Tale

The Wife of Bath's tale is brilliantly suited to her purpose: it rebukes the Friar, it entertains
the company, and it proves her point that women should have sovereignty in marriage.

In the old days when King Arthur ruled the
    nation,
Whom Welshmen speak of with such
    veneration,[1]
This realm we live in was a fairy land.

[1] Because Arthur was believed to have lived in
Wales.

The fairy queen danced with her jolly
    band   850

[33] About forty miles from London.
[34] This altercation results in the Friar's telling a
tale about a summoner and the Summoner replying
with one about a friar. (See p. 75 for a similar use of
this device.)
[35] Note the sarcasm.

On the green meadows where they held
dominion.
This was, as I have read, the old opinion;
I speak of many hundred years ago.
But no one sees an elf now, as you know,
For in our time the charity and prayers 855
And all the begging of these holy friars
Who swarm through every nook and every
stream
Thicker than motes of dust in a sunbeam,
Blessing our chambers, kitchens, halls, and
bowers,
Our cities, towns, and castles, our high
towers, 860
Our villages, our stables, barns, and dairies,
They keep us all from seeing any fairies,
For where you might have come upon an elf
There now you find the holy friar himself [2]
Working his district on industrious legs 865
And saying his devotions while he begs.
Women are safe now under every tree.
No incubus is there unless it's he,[3]
And all they have to fear from him is shame.
It chanced that Arthur had a knight who
came 870
Lustily riding home one day from hawking,
And in his path he saw a maiden walking
Before him, stark alone, right in his course.
This young knight took her maidenhead by
force,
A crime at which the outcry was so keen 875
It would have cost his neck, but that the
queen,
With other ladies, begged the king so long
That Arthur spared his life, for right or wrong,
And gave him to the queen, at her own will,
According to her choice, to save or kill. 880
She thanked the king, and later told this
knight,
Choosing her time, "You are still in such a
plight
Your very life has no security.
I grant your life, if you can answer me
This question: what is the thing that most of
all 885

Women desire? Think, or your neck will fall
Under the ax! If you cannot let me know
Immediately, I give you leave to go
A twelvemonth and a day, no more, in quest
Of such an answer as will meet the test. 890
But you must pledge your honor to return
And yield your body, whatever you may
learn."
The knight sighed; he was rueful beyond
measure.
But what! He could not follow his own
pleasure.
He chose at last upon his way to ride 895
And with such answer as God might provide
To come back when the year was at the close.
And so he takes his leave, and off he goes.
He seeks out every house and every place
Where he has any hope, by luck or grace, 900
Of learning what thing women covet most.
But it seemed he could not light on any coast
Where on this point two people would agree,
For some said wealth and some said jollity,
Some said position, some said sport in bed 905
And often to be widowed, often wed.
Some said that to a woman's heart what
mattered
Above all else was to be pleased and flattered.
That shaft, to tell the truth, was a close hit.
Men win us best by flattery, I admit, 910
And by attention. Some say our greatest ease
Is to be free and do just as we please,
And not to have our faults thrown in our eyes,
But always to be praised for being wise.
And true enough, there's not one of us all 915
Who will not kick if you rub us on a gall.
Whatever vices we may have within,
We won't be taxed with any fault or sin.
Some say that women are delighted well
If it is thought that they will never tell 920
A secret they are trusted with, or scandal.
But that tale isn't worth an old rake handle!
We women, for a fact, can never hold
A secret. Will you hear a story told?
Then witness Midas! For it can be read 925
In Ovid [4] that he had upon his head
Two ass's ears that he kept out of sight
Beneath his long hair with such skill and
sleight
That no one else besides his wife could guess.

[2] Note that the Friar was a limiter (cf. p. 62, l. 209).
[3] The incubus caused conception; all the friar produces is dishonor. Characterize the TONE of the SATIRE in ll. 853–869.
[4] The Roman poet.

He loved her well, and trusted her no less. 930
He begged her not to make his blemish
    known,
But keep her knowledge to herself alone.
She swore that never, though to save her skin,
Would she be guilty of so mean a sin,
And yet it seemed to her she nearly died 935
Keeping a secret locked so long inside.
It swelled about her heart so hard and deep
She was afraid some word was bound to leap
Out of her mouth, and since there was no
    man
She dared to tell, down to a swamp she
    ran— 940
Her heart, until she got there, all agog—
And like a bittern booming in the bog
She put her mouth close to the watery ground:
"Water, do not betray me with your sound!
I speak to you, and you alone," she said. 945
"Two ass's ears grow on my husband's head!
And now my heart is whole, now it is out.
I'd burst if I held it longer, past all doubt."
Safely, you see, awhile you may confide
In us, but it will out; we cannot hide 950
A secret. Look in Ovid if you care
To learn what followed; the whole tale is
    there.
    This knight, when he perceived he could
        not find
What women covet most, was low in mind;
But the day had come when homeward he
    must ride, 955
And as he crossed a wooded countryside
Some four and twenty ladies there by chance
He saw, all circling in a woodland dance,
And toward this dance he eagerly drew near
In hope of any counsel he might hear. 960
But the truth was, he had not reached the
    place
When dance and all, they vanished into space.
No living soul remained there to be seen
Save an old woman sitting on the green,
As ugly a witch as fancy could devise. 965
As he approached her she began to rise
And said, "Sir knight, here runs no
    thoroughfare.
What are you seeking with such anxious air?
Tell me! The better may your fortune be.
We old folk know a lot of things," said
    she. 970

"Good mother," said the knight, "my life's
    to pay,
That's all too certain, if I cannot say
What women covet most. If you could tell
That secret to me, I'd requite you well."
    "Give me your hand," she answered. "Swear
        me true 975
That whatsoever I next ask of you,
You'll do it if it lies within your might
And I'll enlighten you before the night."
    "Granted, upon my honor," he replied.
    "Then I dare boast, and with no empty
        pride, 980
Your life is safe," she told him. "Let me die
If the queen herself won't say the same as I.
Let's learn if the haughtiest of all who wear
A net or coverchief upon their hair
Will be so forward as to answer 'no' 985
To what I'll teach you. No more; let us go."
With that she whispered something in his
    ear,
And told him to be glad and have no fear.
    When they had reached the court, the
        knight declared
That he had kept his day, and was
    prepared 990
To give his answer, standing for his life.
Many the wise widow, many the wife,
Many the maid who rallied to the scene,
And at the head as justice sat the queen.
Then silence was enjoined; the knight was
    told 995
In open court to say what women hold
Precious above all else. He did not stand
Dumb like a beast, but spoke up at com-
    mand
And plainly offered them his answering word
In manly voice, so that the whole court
    heard. 1000
    "My liege and lady, most of all," said he,
"Women desire to have the sovereignty
And sit in rule and government above
Their husbands, and to have their way in love.
This is what most you want. Spare me or
    kill 1005
As you may like; I stand here by your will."
    No widow, wife, or maid gave any token
Of contradicting what the knight had spoken.
He should not die; he should be spared
    instead;

He was worthy of his life, the whole court
    said.   1010
    The old woman whom the knight met on
    the green
Sprang up at this. "My sovereign lady queen,
Before your court has risen, do me right!
It was I who taught this answer to the knight,
For which he pledged his honor in my
    hand,   1015
Solemnly, that the first thing I demand,
He would do it, if it lay within his might.
Before the court I ask you, then, sir knight,
To take me," said the woman, "as your wife,
For well you know that I have saved your
    life.   1020
Deny me, on your honor, if you can."
    "Alas," replied this miserable man,
"That was my promise, it must be confessed.
For the love of God, though, choose a new
    request!
Take all my wealth, and let my body be." 1025
    "If that's your tune, then curse both you
    and me,"
She said. "Though I am ugly, old, and poor,
I'll have, for all the metal and the ore
That under earth is hidden or lies above,
Nothing, except to be your wife and
    love."   1030
    "My love? No, my damnation, if you can!
Alas," he said, "that any of my clan
Should be so miserably misallied!"
    All to no good; force overruled his pride,
And in the end he is constrained to
    wed,   1035
And marries his old wife and goes to bed.
    Now some will charge me with an oversight
In failing to describe the day's delight,
The merriment, the food, the dress at least.
But I reply, there was no joy nor feast; 1040
There was only sorrow and sharp misery.
He married her in private, secretly,
And all day after, such was his distress,
Hid like an owl from his wife's ugliness.
    Great was the woe this knight had in his
    head   1045
When in due time they both were brought
    to bed.
He shuddered, tossed, and turned, and all
    the while
His old wife lay and waited with a smile.

"Is every knight so backward with a spouse?
Is it," she said, "a law in Arthur's house? 1050
I am your love, your own, your wedded wife.
I am the woman who has saved your life.
I have never done you anything but right.
Why do you treat me this way the first night?
You must be mad, the way that you
    behave!   1055
Tell me my fault, and as God's love can save,
I will amend it, truly, if I can."
    "Amend it?" answered this unhappy man.
"It can never be amended, truth to tell.
You are so loathsome and so old as well, 1060
And your low birth besides is such a cross
It is no wonder that I turn and toss.
God take my woeful spirit from my breast!"
    "Is this," she said, "the cause of your
    unrest?"
    "No wonder!" said the knight. "It truly
    is."   1065
    "Now sir," she said, "I could amend all
    this
Within three days, if it should please me to,
And if you deal with me as you should do.
    "But since you speak of that nobility
That comes from ancient wealth and
    pedigree,   1070
As if *that* constituted gentlemen,
I hold such arrogance not worth a hen!
The man whose virtue is pre-eminent,
In public and alone, always intent
On doing every generous act he can, 1075
Take him—he is the greatest gentleman!
Christ wills that we should claim nobility
From him, not from old wealth or family.
Our elders left us all that they were worth
And through their wealth and blood we claim
    high birth,   1080
But never, since it was beyond their giving,
Could they bequeath to us their virtuous
    living;
Although it first conferred on them the name
Of gentlemen, they could not leave that
    claim!
    "Dante the Florentine on this was wise: 1085
'Frail is the branch on which man's virtues
    rise'—
Thus runs his rhyme—'God's goodness wills
    that we
Should claim from him alone nobility.'

Thus from our elders we can only claim
Such temporal things as men may hurt and
 maim. 1090
 "It is clear enough that true nobility
Is not bequeathed along with property,
For many a lord's son does a deed of shame
And yet, God knows, enjoys his noble name.
But though descended from a noble
 house 1095
And elders who were wise and virtuous,
If he will not follow his elders, who are dead,
But leads, himself, a shameful life instead,
He is not noble, be he duke or earl.
It is the churlish deed that makes the
 churl. 1100
And therefore, my dear husband, I conclude
That though my ancestors were rough and
 rude,
Yet may Almighty God confer on me
The grace to live, as I hope, virtuously.
Call me of noble blood when I begin 1105
To live in virtue and to cast out sin.
 "As for my poverty, at which you grieve,
Almighty God in whom we all believe
In willful poverty chose to lead his life,
And surely every man and maid and wife 1110
Can understand that Jesus, heaven's king,
Would never choose a low or vicious thing.
A poor and cheerful life is nobly led;
So Seneca and others have well said.
The man so poor he doesn't have a stitch, 1115
If he thinks himself repaid, I count him
 rich.
He that is covetous, he is the poor man,
Pining to have the things he never can.
It is of cheerful mind, true poverty.
Juvenal [5] says about it happily: 1120
'The poor man as he goes along his way
And passes thieves is free to sing and play.'
Poverty is a good we loathe, a great
Reliever of our busy worldly state,
A great amender also of our minds 1125
As he that patiently will bear it finds.
And poverty, for all it seems distressed,
Is a possession no one will contest.
Poverty, too, by bringing a man low,
Helps him the better both God and self to
 know. 1130
Poverty is a glass where we can see
 [5] The Roman poet.

Which are our true friends, as it seems to me.
So, sir, I do not wrong you on this score;
Reproach me with my poverty no more.
 "Now, sir, you tax me with my age; but,
 sir, 1135
You gentlemen of breeding all aver
That men should not despise old age, but
 rather
Grant an old man respect, and call him
 'father.'
 "If I am old and ugly, as you have said,
You have less fear of being cuckolded, 1140
For ugliness and age, as all agree,
Are notable guardians of chastity.
But since I know in what you take delight,
I'll gratify your worldly appetite.
 "Choose now, which of two courses you will
 try: 1145
To have me old and ugly till I die
But evermore your true and humble wife,
Never displeasing you in all my life,
Or will you have me rather young and fair
And take your chances on who may repair 1150
Either to your house on account of me
Or to some other place, it well may be.
Now make your choice, whichever you
 prefer."
 The knight took thought, and sighed, and
 said to her
At last, "My love and lady, my dear wife, 1155
In your wise government I put my life.
Choose for yourself which course will best
 agree
With pleasure and honor, both for you and
 me.
I do not care, choose either of the two;
I am content, whatever pleases you." 1160
 "Then have I won from you the sovereignty,
Since I may choose and rule at will?" said
 she.
 He answered, "That is best, I think, dear
 wife."
 "Kiss me," she said. "Now we are done with
 strife,
For on my word, I will be both to you, 1165
That is to say, fair, yes, and faithful too.
May I die mad unless I am as true
As ever wife was since the world was new.
Unless I am as lovely to be seen
By morning as an empress or a queen 1170

Or any lady between east and west,
Do with my life or death as you think best.
Lift up the curtain, see what you may see."
   And when the knight saw what had come
     to be
And knew her as she was, so young, so
     fair,   1175
His joy was such that it was past compare.
He took her in his arms and gave her kisses
A thousand times on end; he bathed in blisses.
And she obeyed him also in full measure
In everything that tended to his pleasure. 1180
   And so they lived in full joy to the end.
And now to all us women may Christ send
Submissive husbands,[6] full of youth in bed,
And grace to outlive all the men we wed.
And I pray Jesus to cut short the lives   1185
Of those who won't be governed by their
     wives;
And old, ill-tempered niggards who hate
     expense,
God promptly bring them down with
     pestilence!

STUDY AIDS: 1. One of Chaucer's devices for securing unity is to have the individual prologues and tales amplify points made in the portraits of the *General Prologue.* Compare in detail the portrait of the Wife on p. 67 with her account of herself in her own prologue.

2. Define the nature of the Wife's relationships with each of her five husbands. For example, why did she marry the first three? Did she marry the fourth and fifth for different reasons? With which husband was she happiest? Was she completely happy with any? If not, why not?

3. The Wife of Bath has a complex psychological make-up. What are the elements in her personality? In answering this question, consider both her prologue and her tale, and also such matters as the following: Why does she travel on so many pilgrimages? Is she religious? If not, is she wholly irreligious? Is her view of herself different from the reader's view of her? According to her, what motivates her behavior? (See ll. 613-614.) Is she, like most great comic characters, in part a tragic figure?

MIDDLE ENGLISH LYRICS

LYRIC POETRY OF ALL TIMES HAS BEEN PRIMARILY AN EXPRESSION OF PERSONAL EMOTION, but emotion refined by art—not simply an outpouring of feeling, but feeling heightened, even refashioned, by the requirements of rhythm, meter, and verse form. The feelings expressed have commonly to do with the coming of spring, love for a beautiful girl, the experience of religion, matters of real personal concern at all times, to all people. The poet has the gift, to an especially high degree, of putting such feelings into words in a fashion which is both individual, and therefore interesting, and also general, and therefore meaningful to a variety of readers. The Middle English lyrics printed below have the two characteristics implied above: they express emotion, and they are works of art. Unlike most later lyric poems, however, they are frequently involved with another art, the art of music. Originally the lyric began as a song, and some of these Middle English lyrics were actually written to be sung. But they are all works of literature also, and some (e.g., *The Blacksmiths*) are purely so—were never sung or meant to be. They should all be studied as lyric poems: as artistic expressions of a poet's thoughts and feelings.

---

[6] The Wife's view should not be equated with Chaucer's. Her tale sets going a debate which is argued through a series of stories known to scholars as the "marriage group." The final view of the question of sovereignty is presumably that found in *The Franklin's Tale:* marriage should be based on mutual respect, courtesy, and generosity; neither partner should rule.

Cuckoo Song

In the days before well-heated houses, the coming-in of spring and summer must have been incredibly wonderful. Gone were the days of darkness and the struggle to keep warm. The cuckoo's voice symbolizes this ever-recurring miracle in this, the most famous lyric from the Middle English period. The *Cuckoo Song* was in actuality a song, a *round* (cf. "Row, row, row your boat"); the music exists. But it is equally successful as a lyric poem.

Sumer is icumen in,
Lhudë [1] sing cuccu!
Groweth sed and bloweth med [2]
And springth the wodë nu.
Sing cuccu! 5

Awë [3] bleteth after lomb,
Lhouth after calvë cu, [4]
Bulluc sterteth, buckë verteth. [5]
Murië [6] sing cuccu!
Cuccu, cuccu, 10

Wel singës thu, cuccu.
Ne swik [7] thu naver nu!

Sing cuccu nu, Sing cuccu!
Sing cuccu, Sing cuccu nu!

STUDY AIDS: What qualities make this poem a lyric? Define the emotional TONE of the poem. (For a poem with a very different tone, see Ezra Pound's amusing parody beginning, "Winter is icummen in, Lhude sing Goddamn" —*Selected Poems*, p. 95.)

The Irish Dancer

Icham [8] of Irlaundë,
Ant [9] of the holy londë
    Of Irlandë.
Gode Sire, pray ich [10] thee,
For of sayntë [11] charitë, 5
Come ant daunce wyt me
    In Irlaundë.

STUDY AIDS: This poem is deceptively simple. Is the speaker in Ireland? What is the speaker's attitude toward Ireland? How does the request in ll. 4–7 emphasize the speaker's attitude?

Jesu, Swetë Sonë Derë

Jesu, swetë sonë derë!
    On porful [12] bed liest thou herë,
And that me greveth sorë;
For thy cradel is as a berë, [13]
Oxe and asse beth thy ferë; [14] 5
Weepe ich may thereforë.

Jesu, swetë, beo not wroth,
Tho ich nabbë [15] clout ne cloth

Thee on [16] for to foldë,
Thee on to foldë ne to wrappë, 10
For ich nabbë clout ne lappë;
Bute lay thou thy fet to my pappë, [17]
And witë [18] thee from the coldë.

STUDY AIDS: 1. Who is the speaker? What is her attitude toward the infant Jesus?
2. What is the tone of the poem? What words are especially responsible for the tone?

[1] Loud. The final *-e* (see p. 55) on this word and others similarly marked is sounded lightly, very much thus: "looduh."
[2] The mead (meadow) blossoms.
[3] Ewe.
[4] The cow lows after her calf.
[5] Bullock leaps up, buck breaks wind.
[6] Merrily.
[7] Nor ceases.
[8] I am.
[9] And.
[10] I.
[11] Holy.
[12] Pitifully poor.
[13] Like a byre (cattle stall).
[14] Companions.
[15] Have not.
[16] In.
[17] Breast (child's language).
[18] Protect.

Alysoun

Much of the charm of this lyric lies in its language; the poem, if well read, is a delight to the ear. *Alysoun* is also noteworthy, however, for logical and yet natural development of thought: stanza 1—in the spring the little bird has a will to sing in her language; I live in love-longing for Alysoun; it is the greatest thing that has ever happened to me and (by implication) I too will sing in my language. Stanza 2—this is what Alysoun looks like. Stanza 3—this is the effect she has on me: I toss about at night, my cheeks grow pale. Stanza 4—although I am worn out with lying awake, tormented with jealous fears, I know that it is better to suffer a while sorely than to mourn for ever (because I lacked the courage to endure love's sorrows).

Bytuenë Mersh and Averil
When spray beginneth to springë,
The lutel foul hath hirë wyl
On hyrë lud [1] to syngë.
Ich libbe [2] in lovëlongingë   5
For semlokest [3] of allë thyngë;
He [4] may me blissë bringë,
Icham [5] in hirë baundoun.
    An hendy hap ichabbe yhent,[6]
    Ichot [7] from hevene it is me sent—   10
    From allë wymmen mi love is lent,
    And lyht on Alysoun.

On heu hire her is fayr ynoh,[8]
Hire browë brounë, hire eye blakë,
With lossum chere he on me loh; [9]   15
With middel smal and wel ymakë.
Bote he me wollë to hirë take
Fortë buen [10] hire owen makë,[11]
Longë to lyven ichullë [12] forsakë
And feyë [13] fallen adoun.   20
    An hendy hap &c.

Nihtës when y wende and wakë—
For-thi myn wongës waxeth won [14]—

Levedi,[15] al for thinë sakë,
Longinge is ylent me on.[16]   25
In world nis non so wyter mon [17]
That al hirë bounte tellë con;
Hire swyre [18] is whittorë then the swon,
And feyrest may [19] in tounë.
    An hendy hap &c.   30

Icham for wowyng al forwakë,
Wery so water in worë; [20]
Lest eny revë [21] me my makë
Ychabbe y-yyrnëd yorë.[22]
Betere is tholien [23] whylë sorë   35
Then mournen evermorë;
Geynest under gorë,[24]
Herknë to my roun.[25]
    An hendy hap &c.

STUDY AIDS: 1. Trace the progress of the thought, as outlined in the headnote, through the poem.

2. What feature of the poem suggests a connection with music? What is the effect of repeating the refrain after each stanza? Note the complexity of the rhyme scheme. What words in succeeding stanzas rhyme with *baundoun* in l. 8? Can you suggest a reason for this? Intricacy is often considered a characteristic of a work of art. In what ways is this poem intricate?

[1] In her language.
[2] I live.
[3] Loveliest.
[4] She (dialectical form; so also in l. 15).
[5] I am ("ich am").
[6] A great good fortune I have received.
[7] I wot (or, I know).
[8] In hue her hair is fair enough.
[9] With lovely look she smiles at me.
[10] For to be.
[11] Mate (note that the word is equally appropriate for a bird, as in l. 3).
[12] I will.
[13] Fated, doomed to die.
[14] Wherefore my cheeks turn pale.

[15] Lady.
[16] Come upon me.
[17] So wise a man.
[18] Neck.
[19] Maid.
[20] Uncertain meaning, perhaps millrace.
[21] Rob.
[22] I have suffered (yearned) for a long time.
[23] To suffer.
[24] Most gracious of women (lit., most gracious under gown).
[25] Speech, song.

The Complaint of Chaucer to His Empty Purse

This poem, written probably less than a year before Chaucer's death, is at once a petition to the newly elected king, Henry IV, for money and a clever parody of a love poem. Chaucer addresses his pocketbook as though it were his lady-love (blonde, of course, since that is the color of gold). Indeed, the word *complaint* at this time had the technical meaning, "love-lament." This mock love-lament to his purse was successful. On October 3, 1399, Chaucer was granted an increase in his pension.

To you, my purse, and to non other wight
Compleyne I, for ye be my lady derë!
I am so sory, now that ye be light;
For certës,[1] but ye makë me hevy cherë,[2]
Me were as leef be leyd up-on my berë;   5
For whiche un-to your mercy thus I cryë:
Beth hevy ageyn,[3] or elles mot [4] I dyë!

Now voucheth sauf [5] this day, or hit be night,
That I of you the blisful soun may herë,
Or see your colour lyk the sonnë bright,   10
That of yelownesse hadde never perë.
Ye be my lyf, ye be myn hertës sterë,[6]
Quene of comfort and of good companyë:
Beth hevy ageyn, or ellës mot I dyë!

Now purs, that be to me my lyvës light,   15
And saveour, as doun in this worlde herë,

Out of this tounë help me through your
      might,[7]
Sin that ye wole nat been my tresorerë;
For I am shave as nye as any frerë.[8]
But yit I pray un-to your curtesyë: 20
Beth hevy ageyn, or ellës mot I dyë!

LENVOY DE CHAUCER

O conquerour of Brutës Albioun! [9]
Which that by lyne and free eleccioun
Ben verray king, this song to you I sendë;
And ye, that mowen [10] al our harm
      amendë,   25
Have minde up-on my supplicacioun!

STUDY AIDS: 1. This poem is an extended IMAGE or METAPHOR. Work out the details of the metaphor. Wherein does the humor lie? What is the TONE of the poem?

The Blacksmiths

The poem translated below is a superb expression of indignation, too fine to be omitted but too difficult to be given in the original (for which see K. Sisam, *Fourteenth Century Verse and Prose,* Oxford University Press, p. 169). Except for an occasional substitution, the translation preserves the sense and approximates the alliterative meter of the original. As is true with most translations, much is lost, but the author's righteous ire at being kept awake all night by blacksmiths preparing horses and armor for a military expedition comes through.

Swart, sweaty smiths, smutched with smoke,
Drive me to death with din of their dints.

Such noise a-nights heard a man never:
What criminal cries, what clatter and
      clanging!
The cursed cow-carpenters cry after "coal!
      coal!"   5

[1] For certainly.
[2] A pun on "chere" meaning a look or expression and on good cheer.
[3] Be heavy again. What is the IRONY here?
[4] Must.
[5] Vouchsafe.
[6] Rudder, with perhaps a pun on "sterre" meaning star.

[7] Apparently a personal reference.
[8] How does this line apply to money?
[9] See p. 54 for Brutus Albion. The whole line refers to Henry IV as King of England.
[10] Can, or may.

And blow their bellows till their brains burst.
"Huff puff," says the one, "Hoff poff," the
   other.
They spit and sprawl and spell many spells;
They gnaw and gnash, they groan together,
And hold hot at it with hard hammers.   10
Of a bull's hide is their bellies' covering;
Their shanks are shackled for the spattering
   sparks;
Heavy hammers they have, that are handled
   hard.
Stark strokes they strike on a steel-stock
And batter out a burden: "Loos boos! las
   das!"   15
Such a damnable din is due only the devil.

The master lays into the links, lashing with
   his hammer,
Twists them together, and taps out a treble:
"Tic tock, hic hock, tiket taket, tic tock—
Loos boos, las das!" *This* is the life they
   lead,   20
These mare-clothers. Christ give them curses!
Not a man these nights can have his rest!

Translated by G. B. Pace

STUDY AIDS: Observe the use of concrete, specific detail and of ONOMATOPOEIA. How are these related to the poem's vivid realism? Does the poet gain anything by delaying until the end the full revelation of the cause of his annoyance?

FOLK BALLADS

No BETTER BEGINNING FOR THE STUDY OF POETRY EXISTS THAN THE BALLADS, FOR THEY ALL tell stories rich in human emotions. Indeed, they are often defined as stories told in song. They are meant to be sung, and some of them lose a great deal when taken out of a musical setting. This is not true, however, of the ballads printed here, which are poems in their own right.

Ballads could be called short stories in verse, but they differ from most short stories in that they are highly compressed. This compression is a characteristic of poetry. Because they are compressed, ballads, like all poetry, rely especially on the meaning-packed phrase, the pregnant detail; their narrative method is one of indirection, of hints. They tell us all we need to know, but no more. In this way they stimulate our imaginations.

For example, *The Twa Corbies,* the first of the ballads printed below, begins with two corbies, or crows, speculating as to where they will eat dinner. One of them says:

> In behint yon auld fail dyke,   *auld fail dyke:* old earth wall
> I wot there lies a new slain knight;   *I wot:* I know
> And naebody kens that he lies there,   *kens:* knows
> But his hawk, his hound, and lady fair.

From this hint, we realize that the crows will dine on the knight's corpse; and we ask ourselves the question, why do only the hawk, the hound, and the lady fair know? The ballad continues:

> His hound is to the hunting gane,   *gane:* gone
> His hawk to fetch the wild-fowl hame, *hame:* home
> His lady's ta'en another mate,
> So we may mak our dinner sweet.

Nowhere in the ballad are we actually told that the wife has murdered her husband, but from the hint above we have not only this knowledge but also the motivation. Indeed, we can almost reconstruct the scene: while the knight is preoccupied with his hunting, his wife slips up on him, slays him, and then goes off to her lover.

Ballads, then, are a kind of narrative poetry, but the stories they tell are rarely told directly. Furthermore, ballads are almost always more concerned with creating an emotional effect than with merely telling a tale. Mood, atmosphere become very important. *The Twa Corbies* creates a grisly atmosphere, which affects us emotionally. But this grisly atmosphere, which is somewhat childish, is not all. The ballad ends with the crow saying:

> Mony a ane for him makes mane,   *mane:* moan
> But nane sall ken where he is gane; *sall:* shall
> Oer his white banes, when they are bare, *banes:* bones
> The wind sall blaw for evermair.

We feel a very complex emotion having to do with the finality, ambiguity, and anonymity of death.

Ballads are folk poetry, and no one knows just when, how, or by whom they were composed. The subject matter of many of them suggests the later Middle Ages, but they were not written down in any quantity until the eighteenth century; they were simply passed down by word of mouth. (The language we have them in is hence not Middle English but dialectal Modern English, very frequently Scots.) Because they are folk poetry, their form is generally simple; but at their best they are true poems, expressing in brief space matters of eternal interest to human beings.

The Twa Corbies

As I was walking all alane,
I heard twa corbies making a mane;[1]
The tane[2] unto the t'other say,
"Where sall we gang[3] and dine today?"

"In behint yon auld fail dyke,[4]   5
I wot there lies a new slain knight;
And naebody kens that he lies there,
But his hawk, his hound, and lady fair.

"His hound is to the hunting gane,
His hawk to fetch the wild-fowl hame, 10
His lady's ta'en another mate,
So we may mak our dinner sweet.

"Ye'll sit on his white hause-bane,[5]
And I'll pike out his bonny blue een;[6]

Wi' ae lock o his gowden hair   15
We'll theek[7] our nest when it grows bare.

"Mony a ane for him makes mane,[8]
But nane sall ken[9] where he is gane;
Oer his white banes, when they are bare,
The wind sall blaw for evermair."

STUDY AIDS: 1. What is the story which is implied in this poem? What is the function of each stanza in the telling of the story? Are all the stanzas equally necessary for the narrative?

2. Is the reader's interest primarily in the story or in certain overtones of it? Why does the poem end with the reference to the wind blowing eternally over the white bones?

The Unquiet Grave

"The wind doth blow today, my love,
 And a few small drops of rain;[10]

I never had but one true-love,
 In cold grave she was lain.

[1] Two crows having a discussion.
[2] One.
[3] Shall we go.
[4] Old earthen wall.
[5] Neck.
[6] Eyes.

[7] Thatch.
[8] Moan.
[9] Shall know.
[10] Note the effective use of weather. Define, precisely, the kind of day.

"I'll do as much for my true-love 5
  As any young man may;
I'll sit and mourn all at her grave
  For a twelvemonth and a day."

The twelvemonth and a day being up,
  The dead began to speak; 10
"Oh who sits weeping on my grave,
  And will not let me sleep?"

" 'Tis I, my love, sits on your grave,
  And will not let you sleep;
For I crave one kiss of your clay-cold lips, 15
  And that is all I seek."

"You crave one kiss of my clay-cold lips;
  But my breath smells earthy strong;
If you have one kiss of my clay-cold lips,
  Your time will not be long.[11] 20

" 'Tis down in yonder garden green,
  Love, where we used to walk,

The finest flower that ere was seen
  Is withered to a stalk.

"The stalk is withered dry, my love, 25
  So will our hearts decay;
So make yourself content, my love,
  Till God calls you away."

STUDY AIDS: 1. Compare this ballad with *The Twa Corbies*. Which is the more tightly-knit? Does this make it a better poem, or is the easier-to-read the better?

2. Study the rhyme scheme. The typical ballad stanza rhymes *abab* or *abcb* and has alternating lines of four and three feet. How typical is the stanza here? Are the inexact rhymes a blemish on this simple folk poem?

3. Does the dead person want her lover to marry someone else? What is implied by "content" in the next-to-last line? What is the usual human feeling about remaining true to a dead wife or sweetheart?

Sir Patrick Spens

The king sits in Dumferling toune,
  Drinking the blude-reid wine:
"O whar will I get guid sailor,
  To sail this schip of mine?"

Up and spak an eldern knicht,[1] 5
  Sat at the kings richt kne:
"Sir Patrick Spens is the best sailor
  That sails upon the se."

The king has written a braid [2] letter,
  And signd it wi his hand, 10
And sent it to Sir Patrick Spens,
  Was walking on the sand.

The first line that Sir Patrick red,
  A loud lauch [3] lauched he;

The next line that Sir Patrick red, 15
  The teir blinded his ee.[4]

"O wha is this has don this deid,
  This ill deid don to me,
To send me out this time o' the yeir,
  To sail upon the se! 20

"Mak hast, mak haste, my mirry men all,
  Our guid schip sails the morne":
"O say na sae,[5] my master deir,
  For I feir a deadlie storme.

"Late late yestreen[6] I saw the new moone, 25
  Wi the auld moone in hir arme,
And I feir, I feir, my deir master,
  That we will cum to harme." [7]

[11] Note the use of repetition in this and the preceding stanza. This type of repetition, which advances the story, is called "incremental repetition." It is characteristic of the ballad.

[1] Elderly knight.
[2] Broad, apparently in the sense of "big," "impressive."
[3] Laugh.

[4] Eye. Note the IRONY in the contrast developed in this stanza.
[5] Say not so.
[6] Yesterday evening. The reference in these lines is to a superstition.
[7] Note the contrast between the lovely picture of the moon and the ominous meaning of the phenomenon (according to the superstition).

O our Scots nobles wer richt laith [8]
  To wet their cork-heild schoone; [9]   30
Bot lang owre a' the play wer playd,
  Thair hats they swam aboone.[10]

O lang, lang may their ladies sit,
  Wi thair fans into their hand,
Or eir they se Sir Patrick Spens   35
  Cum sailing to the land.

O lang, lang may the ladies stand,
  Wi thair gold kems [11] in their hair,

Waiting for thair ain deir lords,
  For they'll se thame na mair.   40

Haf owre,[12] haf owre to Aberdour,
  It's fiftie fadom deip,
And thair lies guid Sir Patrick Spens,
  Wi the Scots lords at his feit.[13]

STUDY AIDS: *Sir Patrick Spens* is generally considered one of the most artistic of the
ballads. Do you agree with this judgment?
What are your reasons for your answer?

The Demon Lover

"O where have you been, my long, long love,
  This long seven years and mair?" [1]
"O I'm com to seek my former vows
  Ye granted me before."

"O hold your tongue of your former vows, 5
  For they will breed sad strife;
O hold your tongue of your former vows,
  For I am become a wife."

He turned him right and round about,
  And the tear blinded his ee: 10
"I wad never hae trodden on Irish ground,
  If it had not been for thee.

"I might hae had a king's daughter,
  Far, far beyond the sea;
I might have had a king's daughter,   15
  Had it not been for love o thee."

"If ye might have had a king's daughter,
  Yersel ye had to blame;
Ye might have taken the king's daughter,
  For ye kend [2] that I was nane.   20

"If I was to leave my husband dear,
  And my two babes also,
O what have you to take me to,
  If with you I should go?"

"I hae seven ships upon the sea—   25
  The eighth brought me to land—
With four-and-twenty bold mariners,
  And music on every hand."

She has taken up her two little babes,
  Kissd them baith cheek and chin: 30
"O fair ye weel, my ain two babes,
  For I'll never see you again."

She set her foot upon the ship,
  No mariners could she behold;
But the sails were o the taffetie,   35
  And the masts o the beaten gold.

She had not saild a league, a league,
  A league but barely three,
When dismal grew his countenance,
  And drumlie [3] grew his ee.   40

[8] Right loath. Note the change in narrative technique beginning in this line.
[9] Cork-heeled shoes. What is the irony in this
statement (see ll. 31–32)?
[10] Their hats swam above them. Note the economy with which the shipwreck is told. Is this more
effective than a long narrative?
[11] Combs.
[12] Half over.

[13] The suggestion is that Sir Patrick Spens is still
their leader, even in death. Note the organization of
the ending of the poem: ll. 33–36 focus on Sir
Patrick, ll. 37–40 on his men, and ll. 41–44 bring
them both together.

[1] The first speaker is a woman, the second her
former lover.
[2] Knew.
[3] Dismal.

They had not saild a league, a league,
  A league but barely three,
Until she espied his cloven foot,
  And she wept right bitterlie.

"O hold your tongue of your weeping,"
    says he,   45
  "Of your weeping now let me be;
I will shew you how the lilies grow
  On the banks of Italy."

"O what hills are yon, yon pleasant hills,
  That the sun shines sweetly on?"   50
"O yon are the hills of heaven," he said,
  "Where you will never win."

"O whaten a mountain is yon," she said,
  "All so dreary wi frost and snow?"
"O yon is the mountain of hell," he cried, 55
  "Where you and I will go."

He strak the tap-mast wi his hand,
  The fore-mast wi his knee,
And he brake that gallant ship in twain,
  And sank her in the sea.[4]   60

STUDY AIDS: To what extent is this ballad concerned with the morality of the woman's actions? With what is it primarily concerned?

The Wife at Usher's Well

There lived a wife [1] at Usher's Well,
  And a wealthy wife was she;
She had three stout and stalwart sons,
  And sent them oer the sea.

They hadna been a week from her,   5
  A week but barely ane,
Whan word came to the carline wife [2]
  That her three sons were gane.

They hadna been a week from her,
  A week but barely three,   10
Whan word came to the carlin wife
  That her sons she'd never see.

"I wish the wind may never cease,
  Nor fashes [3] in the flood,
Till my three sons come hame to me,   15
  In earthly flesh and blood."

It fell about the Martinmass,
  When nights are lang and mirk,
The carlin wife's three sons came hame,
  And their hats were o the birk.[4]   20

It neither grew in syke [5] nor ditch,
  Nor yet in ony sheugh; [6]
But at the gates o Paradise,
  That birk grew fair eneugh.

"Blow up the fire, my maidens,[7]   25
  Bring water from the well;
For a' my house shall feast this night,
  Since my three sons are well."

And she has made to them a bed,
  She's made it large and wide,   30
And she's taen her mantle her about,
  Sat down at the bed-side.

Up then crew the red, red cock,[8]
  And up and crew the gray;
The eldest to the youngest said,   35
  " 'T is time we were away."

The cock he hadna crawd but once,
  And clappd his wings at a',
When the youngest to the eldest said,
  "Brother, we must awa.   40

[4] To what size has the Demon Lover grown? Can you find other reasons for the startling effectiveness of this final stanza?

---

[1] Woman.
[2] Old woman.
[3] Disturbances.

[4] Birch.
[5] Trench.
[6] Furrow.
[7] A shift in scene; the sons have arrived in the house.
[8] A shift in time; daybreak is approaching, when the spirits of the dead must take leave.

"The cock doth craw, the day doth daw,
  The channerin [1] worm doth chide;
Gin [2] we be mist out o our place,
  A sair pain we maun bide.[3]

"Faer ye weel, my mother dear! **45**
  Fareweel to barn and byre!
And fare ye weel, the bonny lass
  That kindles my mother's fire!"

Lord Randal

"O where hae ye been, Lord Randal, my son?
O where hae ye been, my handsome young
  man?"
"I hae been to the wild wood; mother, make
  my bed soon,
For I'm weary wi hunting, and fain wald [4]
  lie down."

"Where gat ye your dinner, Lord Randal, my
  son? 5
Where gat ye your dinner, my handsome
  young man?"
"I din'd wi my true-love; mother, make my
  bed soon,
For I'm weary wi hunting, and fain wald lie
  down."

"What gat ye to your dinner, Lord Randal,
  my son?
What gat ye to your dinner, my handsome
  young man?" 10
"I gat eels boild in broo; [5] mother, make my
  bed soon,
For I'm weary wi hunting, and fain wald lie
  down."

"What became of your bloodhounds, Lord
  Randal, my son?
What became of your bloodhounds, my
  handsome young man?"
"O they swelld and they died; mother, make
  my bed soon, 15
For I'm weary wi hunting, and fain wald lie
  down."

"O I fear ye are poisond, Lord Randal, my son!
O I fear ye are poisond, my handsome young
  man!"
"O yes I am poisond; mother, make my bed
  soon,
For I'm sick at the heart and I fain wald lie
  down." 20

STUDY AIDS: 1. This ballad, more than
the others printed here, has been unusually successful as a song. What qualities does it have
which might account for its success?
  2. *Lord Randal* is organized with great skill.
Study its organization carefully. Note the cumu-
lative effect of the repetition and the refrain.

Get Up and Bar the Door

It fell about the Martinmass time,
  And a gay time it was then,
When our goodwife got puddings to make,
  And she's boild them in the pan.

The wind sae cauld blew south and north, 5
  And blew into the floor;

Quoth our goodman to our goodwife,
  "Gae out and bar the door."

"My hand is in my hussyfskap,[1]
  Goodman as ye may see; 10
An [2] it shoud nae be barrd this hundred year,
  It's no be barrd for me."

---

[1] Devouring. Note the effectiveness of the alliteration in this and the preceding line.
[2] If.
[3] A sore pain we may expect.
[4] Would.

[5] Broth. Underlying this line is the belief that
the eating of snakes by human beings is fatal.

---

[1] Housewifery.
[2] If.

They made a paction [3] tween them twa,
　They made it firm and sure,
That the first word whaeer [4] shoud speak,　15
　Should rise and bar the door.

Then by there came two gentlemen,
　At twelve o clock at night,
And they could neither see house nor hall,
　Nor coal nor candle-light.　　　　　20

"Now whether is this a rich man's house,
　Or whether is it a poor?"
But neer a word wad ane o them speak,
　For barring of the door.

And first they ate the white puddings,　25
　And then they ate the black;
Tho muckle [5] thought the goodwife hersel,
　Yet neer a word she spake.

[3] Agreement.
[4] Whoever.
[5] Then much.

Then said the one unto the other,
　"Here, man, tak ye my knife;　　　30
Do ye tak aff the auld man's beard,
　And I'll kiss the goodwife."

"But there's nae water in the house,
　And what shall we do than?"
"What ails thee at the pudding-broo,[6]　35
　That boils into the pan?"

O up then started our goodman,
　An angry man was he:
"Will ye kiss my wife before my een,
　And scad [7] me wi pudding-bree?"　40

Then up and started our goodwife,
　Gied three skips on the floor:
"Goodman, you've spoken the foremost word,
　Get up and bar the door."

[6] "Why don't you use the pudding-broth?"
[7] Scald.

The Renaissance

THE RENAISSANCE IS THE TERM COMMONLY USED TO DENOTE THE period of marked cultural activity in Western Europe between 1350 and 1650. These were years of profound change, as the modern world evolved from the medieval. Basic to much of the change was the Renaissance man's desire to understand and enjoy the world he lived in. Whereas the medieval man had been taught by the Church to regard this world as a vale of tears, to be endured as a preparation for life in the next world, man in the Renaissance came to regard it as a fascinating and desirable end in itself. Study broadened his outlook and enlarged his perspectives. Columbus' discovery of a new continent doubled the size of the known world; Galileo's telescope extended man's view of the heavens. More important for literature was the new dimension to man's thinking provided by the growing interest in the writings of Greece and Rome.

Because the classics of the ancient world were instructive and entertaining accounts of men and women living in and enjoying this world, they were eagerly seized upon by such Renaissance scholars as Petrarch in Italy, Erasmus in Holland, and Thomas More in England. We call these men "humanists," and their devotion to the study of the classics "humanism," in order to indicate their concern with man's human interests and needs as distinct

121

from his obsession with the ultimate destiny of his soul. They became Europe's teachers. Through translations into the modern, native languages, widely disseminated by the newly invented printing press, the humanists made the classics available to thousands of new readers. Largely as a result of their activities learning and culture passed from the exclusive control of the Church and assumed a secular cast.

We are speaking of general tendencies. Of course men and women in the Middle Ages were flesh and blood; they never wholly succeeded in submerging their natural interests and desires, if indeed they cared to. Nor would it be proper to regard the Renaissance man as completely indifferent to matters of the spirit. Worldly the Renaissance was, even, in some of its phases, to the point of sensuality. But most of the humanists remained good churchmen, and sought to fuse the new classical learning with traditional Christianity. The break with the Middle Ages, then, was neither sudden nor complete. And yet we may think of the Renaissance as involving a decided shift of emphasis. The change is clearly reflected in the work of the Italian painters, whose childlike, ethereal saints and madonnas are in time transformed into likenesses of Italian peasants.

As the Renaissance man wakened to the riches and opportunities of this world, he became more aware of himself as an individual. The medieval Church, discouraging intellectual curiosity and demanding obedience to its authority, had not fostered self-realization. Likewise, the manorial system and the craft guilds had been organized in favor not of the individual but of the group. But as the Renaissance man's view of life expanded beyond these bounds, he came to regard himself as a creature of infinite capabilities, which he was at liberty to cultivate to the utmost. Christopher Marlowe's character, Doctor Faustus, with his insatiable desire for experience, reflects this enlarged view; so does Francis Bacon, who early in life wrote to a friend, "I have taken all knowledge to be my province"; so does Leonardo da Vinci, a genius of astonishing versatility. Versatility, indeed, became a social ideal in Elizabethan England, where a courtier could be expected to combine the talents of soldier, explorer, adventurer, scholar, musician, and poet. Men developed their skills; they also studied human nature. The English lyric poets analyzed their personal feelings, and the French essayist Montaigne wrote to reveal himself as he really was. It seems likely, too, that the great gallery of human beings that is the Elizabethan drama was created in part to satisfy the new interest in personality. At the theater an Elizabethan playgoer could not only extend his experience but also indulge his curiosity in that new and fascinating study—man in his world.

Originating in Italy, the Renaissance impulse was not fully felt in England until the sixteenth century. Civil war and war with France delayed the cultivation of scholarship and the arts until a more stable time. With the Wars of the Roses at an end in 1485, and Henry VII, first of the Tudor monarchs, on the throne, England was ready to follow Italy's lead in developing a humane culture. Indeed, Greek had already been introduced at Oxford, and William Caxton had set up his printing press in London in 1476. With peace assured, the Tudor court became a center of Renaissance influence. Both Henry VII and Henry VIII fostered commerce and encouraged exploration across the sea. Henry VIII was as absolute and ruthless as an Italian Renaissance prince; like such a prince, too, he loved splendor and he patronized the arts. But the full flowering of the Renaissance in England did not come until the time of Henry's daughter, Elizabeth I, whose long and glorious reign extended from 1558 to 1603.

The Age of Elizabeth witnessed the birth of England as a world power. Placed remotely on the northwest corner of the map of Europe, England found, with the opening of the New World, that her provincial location was a real advantage. She sent Martin Frobisher to explore the arctic areas in the West, and Walter Raleigh to encourage colonization on the American coast. Advances into the New World, however, were not unopposed. Spaniards had long been active in the Caribbean, systematically looting the natives of treasure, which they carried home in their stately galleons. These rich prizes tempted that hardy race of Devonshire sailors known as Elizabethan sea dogs, men like John Hawkins and Francis Drake, who daringly raided the Spanish Main, with the real but unofficial connivance of Elizabeth herself. Such raids were annoying to Spain, but Philip II did not act until Elizabeth executed Mary Queen of Scots, her Catholic rival to the throne. In 1588 Spain sent its fleet to subdue England, but British seamanship and a timely storm defeated the Armada in one of the great naval engagements of history.

The defeat of rival Spain, which marked the beginning of England's colonial dominance in the world, gave rise to a feeling of intense patriotism, which centered on Elizabeth. Courtiers and poets vied with each other in praising the beauty, wisdom, and talents of the Virgin Queen. Nor was this praise entirely the flattery of ambitious nobles, for Elizabeth was truly a gifted woman. Brilliant in statecraft, her feminine grace veiling the iron will of the Tudors, she was also friendly to the new culture of the age. In fact she was something of a humanist herself, tutored as she had been by the scholar Roger Ascham. She was not only fluent in French and Italian and in Latin, still the international language of learning and diplomacy, but also acquainted with the literatures of Greece and Rome. She encouraged music, eagerly followed the new drama, and was a great friend of the art of poetry. Indeed, when we use the word Elizabethan to designate that astonishing burst of creative energy in the England of the late sixteenth century, we mean it to express more than a period of time. The term also connotes the Queen's character, so firmly imprinted on the age.

Elizabeth and the humanists could read the classics in the original Greek and Latin. But when the revival of learning touched those who knew no language but English, it created a demand for translations. In casting the old thoughts into an English that was becoming flexible, vigorous, and colorful, enthusiastic translators produced a body of literature of great vitality. Notable translations from the classics include Homer's *Iliad* and *Odyssey*, Plutarch's *Lives*, Ovid's *Metamorphoses*, and Seneca's tragic dramas. An influential guide to proper courtly conduct, *The Courtier*, by the Italian writer Castiglione, was translated by Sir Thomas Hoby. John Florio's rendering of the Frenchman Montaigne's *Essays* influenced the thinking of many Englishmen. William Painter, in *The Palace of Pleasure*, translated a number of classical and Italian stories. Shakespeare probably read Painter's book, just as he drew from Sir Thomas North's translation of Plutarch, the biographer of Julius Caesar and other heroes of antiquity. The Bible that many of us are acquainted with, the King James or Authorized Version (1611), appeared in this great age of translation.

The beginnings of Renaissance poetry in England are modest. Ballads, the familiar medieval narrative poems in four-line stanzas, continued to be written, but new forms also began to appear. Sir Thomas Wyatt, for instance, introduced the sonnet form of the Italian humanist Petrarch to English readers, among them Henry Howard, Earl of Surrey, who altered the Italian form to suit the English language. For some time poets wrote in an amateur spirit, with no thought of publication. In 1557, however—a date often taken to mark the birth of poetry in Modern English—the printer Richard Tottel published a number of poems of Wyatt and Surrey and others in a collection entitled *The Book of Songs and Sonnets,* known today as "Tottel's Miscellany." Other collections appeared and the vogue for writing lyric verse spread in courtly circles, until the last decade of the century witnessed a lyric outburst perhaps unmatched, for quantity and quality, in the history of English literature.

Certain themes were especially popular. The pastoral theme, for one, was a favorite. Like Theocritus and Virgil, the classical poets whom they imitated, Elizabethan poets wrote of shepherds and their mistresses enjoying the beauties of nature and the simplicity of life in the country. Perhaps the sophisticated court poets were sincere in voicing the rural ideal; probably most of them regarded the pastoral theme as a fashionable literary convention— that is, an accepted framework within which they worked. Patriotism was another favorite theme, as was the joy of comradeship and conviviality. It was love, however, that most frequently claimed the attention of these poets. The Roman poet Ovid provided inspiration for such erotic narrative poems as Christopher Marlowe's *Hero and Leander* and Shakespeare's *Venus and Adonis.* A far more popular form of love poetry was the sonnet. The vogue of sonnet writing reached its height in the early 1590's, when "sequences" or cycles of from 50 to 154 sonnets appeared from the pens of Edmund Spenser, Sir Philip Sidney, Samuel Daniel, Michael Drayton, and William Shakespeare. A conventional form, like the pastoral, the sonnet in time became highly artificial, evidence more of poetic ingenuity than of genuine feeling. The best of the sonnets, however, transcending the limits of the convention, become poetic statements of great depth and beauty.

The Renaissance witnessed also the beginnings of modern English prose. Like all the European vernacular tongues in the Middle Ages, English had been overshadowed by Latin, the universal language of scholarship, diplomacy, and the Church. In fact English suffered under a double handicap: not only Latin but the French of William of Normandy, used in English courtly circles for generations, had tended to prevent the use of English as a literary language. Consequently, when translators discovered that their native English was not an adequate medium for expressing the thoughts of the classical writers, they thought of ways to improve it. Some wanted to enrich the language by borrowing words from Greek and Latin, whereas scholars like Roger Ascham regarded such borrowing as pedantic and "un-English." Some, like John Lyly, the author of *Euphues,* sought to improve English prose by decorating it with the devices of poetry. Such uncertainty about the proper nature of English prose gave rise to a literature of rhetorical criticism.

Another body of prose in sixteenth century England was born of the social uncertainty of men in a changing age. What was the nature of the ideal state? asked Sir Thomas More in his *Utopia*—a question that Francis Bacon asked a century later in his *New Atlantis,* and one that Shakespeare alludes to in *The Tempest.* Of even greater interest to the ambitious Elizabethan courtier was the question of personal conduct. Should he follow the formula laid down in the influential Castiglione's book, *The Courtier,* and run the risk of becoming "Italianate"? Or should he take the advice of Ascham in *The Schoolmaster* and avoid such unwholesome foreign influence? What should he study? What skills and accomplishments were expected of the ideal gentleman? Questions like these were bound to arise in an era of shifting values and ideals. The books that sought to answer such questions we call "courtesy books."

Prose appears also in the fiction of the period. Sidney's *Arcadia* was immensely popular with the court; well known, too, were Thomas Lodge's *Rosalynde* and Robert Greene's

Pandosto. Shakespeare borrowed from all three of these pastoral romances. Closer to the actualities of English life were Thomas Deloney's realistic *Jack of Newberry* and Thomas Nashe's *Unfortunate Traveller.* But these early fictions could not compete successfully with more striking forms of writing. Accounts of explorers in Richard Hakluyt's *Voyages,* for instance combined the appeal of the new and strange and remote with the vividness of eye-witness reporting. Furthermore, the main ingredients in prose fiction—characters, action, and ideas—came to be offered to the Elizabethan public, from Queen to commoner, in the popular new literary form, the drama.

The story of Renaissance drama in England is one of the great stories in all literary history, culminating as it does in the figure of William Shakespeare. So rich is the dramatic literature of the period, however, that even if Shakespeare had never lived, we would still speak of the Elizabethan age as the golden day of English drama. In general it resulted from a fusion of native and classical elements. English drama began in medieval times. Religious ritual, at first quite simple, became more elaborate and, as it moved outside to the church-yard, more secular. There followed the miracle plays and the moralities. Another strain of native dramatic activity was composed of such popular social rituals as wooing-plays, sword-plays, Christmas plays, and so on. By the early sixteenth century men were acting in simple plays called "interludes," perhaps presented at banquets or other entertainment.

The form and direction needed to develop these dramatic materials into full-fledged plays were provided by the examples of Roman drama. Schoolmasters had their boys act out the Roman comedies of Plautus and Terence; one master, Nicholas Udall, following Plautus, wrote for his boys a play entitled *Ralph Roister Doister,* usually called the first English comedy. A second comedy, *Gammer Gurton's Needle,* made use of comic rustic types. These plays, and those of such "university wits" as John Lyly, George Peele, Robert Greene, and Thomas Lodge, showed later dramatists how Roman techniques of dialogue and construction could be applied to native English materials.

Widely read, too, was Seneca, the Roman tragic playwright. Students at the Inns of Court produced *Gorboduc,* a "Senecan" tragedy in blank verse by Thomas Sackville and Thomas Norton. From Seneca later dramatists borrowed ghosts, revenge plots, bombastic rhetoric, and a fondness for violence and bloodshed. Thomas Kyd's *The Spanish Tragedy,* a tragedy of blood, foreshadowed Shakespeare's *Hamlet.* The greatest dramatist before Shakespeare was Christopher Marlowe, whose *Tamburlaine, Doctor Faustus, The Jew of Malta,* and *Edward II* showed the power of blank verse as a dramatic medium and also established the "one-man" tragedy as the most suitable mold for tragic drama. A fine dramatist in his own right, Marlowe did much to make possible the brilliant career of his contemporary, Shakespeare.

The national exuberance of Elizabeth's day was not to survive the Queen's death in 1603. If a reaction from the enthusiasm of the age was inevitable, certainly it was hastened by the character of the new Stuart monarch, James I. Playing an admittedly difficult role as successor to the fabulous Elizabeth, this ill-favored, pedantic, willful Scot failed notably in both civil and religious affairs, areas of national life where Elizabeth had been expert. For one thing he made much of the "divine right of kings." The Tudors had quietly assumed this right without talking about it; James, by noisily insisting on it, stiffened opposition to absolute power. More and more people came to support Parliament in its struggle with the Crown for power, the contest ending in civil war and the beheading of James's son and successor, Charles I. Toward the end of this turbulent century another Stuart king, James II, tried to defy Parliament. He, too, was defeated in a revolution, this one "bloodless." The principle of Parliamentary supremacy was firmly established, but only after nearly a century of turmoil and the deposition of two Stuart kings.

Closely allied with political issues in the seventeenth century were religious ones, and here James I was equally inept. After Henry VIII broke with Rome and established the Anglican Church, headship of both church and state was centered in one figure. Non-conformists in religion were therefore guilty of offenses against state as well as church. Many Catholics were martyred in Henry's reign, as were many Protestants under his daughter, "Bloody Mary," who restored Catholicism to England during her five-year rule. But most of this religious persecution ceased under Elizabeth. She was shrewd, as well as benevolent, in her tolerance, for much of her political success stemmed from her willingness to put up with nonconformity. She could condone it so long as it was no threat to the state.

The headstrong James, however, vowed he would make people conform or would "harry them out of the land, or else do worse." Some fled his despotism, notably those "separatists" who as Pilgrims came to New England in 1620; others, like the Puritans, stayed to fight it. A harmless group under Elizabeth, the Puritans seemed to thrive on James's oppression, until by midcentury they had become the dominant force in English political and religious life and had stamped their character on the New World as well.

Such changes in national life affected the intellectual and spiritual outlook in the early years of the seventeenth century. The national unity won and maintained by the Tudors gave way, under James, to an increasingly bitter factionalism. Supporters of the king, gay, worldly men, known as Cavaliers, were opposed by the zealous and dour Puritans. Renaissance and Reformation, which in sixteenth century England had been felt to be compatible impulses, now seemed to present a hopeless antithesis. The split is seen in the individual man as well as in the social body. Sidney and Spenser had sought in their work to integrate the several and often conflicting ideals of the time. Nobody made such an effort in the seventeenth century. It is true that Renaissance values are discernible in Milton's writings, but they are subordinate to the dominant strain of moral passion. Perhaps Renaissance man, dazzled by the "brave new world" uncovered before him, had entertained impossible visions, attempted too much, thought on too vast a scale. However that may be, by the seventeenth century he had come to take a more sober or even somber view of life. His mood is often melancholy, his attitude one of disenchantment. He is curious, not about whole worlds, but about limited objects; interested not in the ideal man but in the characters of individual men. His aims are modest, his mood subdued.

The temper of the time is reflected in the literature. In place of joyous and idyllic comedies, dramatists like Ben Jonson, Thomas Middleton, and Philip Massinger wrote comedies that were realistic and often satirical of the follies of London middle-class life. Violence and horror mark the plays of John Webster and John Ford. The change is clearly seen in the career of Shakespeare, who after 1600 turned to tragedy, tragicomedy, and bitter comedy. Prose, too, mirrors the new attitude. It is often sober and contemplative, as in the *Religio Medici* (ca. 1634) of Sir Thomas Browne, who wrote that "The world to me is but a dream and mock-show, and we all therein but pantaloons and antics." Indeed, so widespread was the somber mood that Robert Burton was prompted to analyze it thoroughly in *The Anatomy of Melancholy* (1621). The change in temper is plainly visible also in lyric poetry, which is always a sensitive register of spiritual climate. Although the fresh lyrics of Robert Herrick seem Elizabethan in their joy and gaiety, most of the poets of the new century reflect its dark outlook. In searching for new forms for new feeling, some followed Ben Jonson's lead in writing a chaste, severe, "classical" poetic style; others, with John Donne, developed a subtle, intellectual, and imaginatively explosive style known as "metaphysical." But both groups addressed the same themes—death, transience, mutability, and love. Several of them used poetry to express religious exaltation.

It was, then, disillusionment, doubt, uncertainty, and spiritual malaise that marked the early seventeenth century, as the modern world was being born. Because these attitudes and feelings have their counterparts in our own time, many readers today find much to interest them in English poetry and prose of the early seventeenth century.

Sir Thomas More
(1478–1535)

THOMAS MORE IS THE MOST CELEBRATED OF THE EARLY ENGLISH HUMANISTS. THE GIFTED son of a London lawyer, he was early placed in the household of Cardinal Morton, Archbishop of Canterbury, who was impressed with his mind and charmed with his affability and wit. At Oxford he studied the classics, including the newly introduced Greek, but his father thought the new study unsound and set More to reading law. Although he was soon to distinguish himself in this field, he continued his classical studies. When Erasmus visited England, the Dutch humanist was delighted with the happy, scholarly atmosphere in the big More house in Chelsea.

Another eminent visitor was King Henry VIII, who was to determine More's destiny. Henry drafted him for public service, finally appointing him Lord Chancellor to succeed Cardinal Wolsey. He filled this high office ably until he resigned when Henry broke with Rome over his divorce from Catherine of Aragon. Committed to the Tower, More was asked to subscribe to the Act of Supremacy, which denied the Pope's authority and made Henry the head of the Church of England. He refused, was charged with treason, and beheaded. Always a devout man, More met death calmly, but his martyrdom shocked all Europe. He was canonized in 1935.

Utopia

More's humanism is reflected in his *Utopia*, a work of speculative inquiry into the nature of the good society. Written in Latin (1516) and later translated into English (1551), *Utopia* is composed of two books: the first is a dialogue discussing the shortcomings of European society in More's day; the second is a discourse describing the admirable society in the imaginary land of Utopia, supposedly discovered by Renaissance navigators. The following selection is from the second book. The first book, in which More skillfully created a fiction to increase the plausibility of his tale, is briefly summarized.

The First Book of the Communication of Raphael Hythloday Concerning the Best State of a Commonwealth

[More, in Bruges on King Henry VIII's business, finding himself at leisure during a lull in diplomatic negotiations, goes to Antwerp. Here he visits his friend Peter Giles, an amiable and learned humanist, who introduces him to one Raphael Hythloday, a fictional character whose name means "relator of nonsense." A learned man, he was "well stricken in years," says More, "with a black, sun-burned face, a long beard, and a cloak cast homely about his shoulders." Sitting in Giles' garden, Hythloday tells his companions about his travels with Amerigo Vespucci to remarkable countries in the New World. More and Giles are interested and, by way of introduction to Book 2, More says he will report what Hythloday told them "of the manners, customs, laws, and ordinances of the Utopians."]

The Second Book of the Communication of Raphael Hythloday, Concerning the Best State of a Commonwealth, Containing the Description of Utopia, with a Large Declaration of the Godly Government, and of All the Good Laws and Orders of the Same Island

"The Island of Utopia[1] containeth in breadth in the middle part of it (for there it is broadest) two hundred miles; which breadth continueth through the most part of the land, saving that by little and little it cometh in, and waxeth narrower toward both the ends; which fetching about a circuit or compass[2] of five hundred miles, do fashion the whole island like to the new moon. Between these two corners the sea runneth in, dividing them asunder by the distance of eleven miles or thereabouts, and there surmounteth into a large sea, which by reason that the land on every side compasseth it about and sheltereth it from the winds, is not rough, nor mounteth not with great waves, but almost floweth quietly, not much unlike a great standing pool; and maketh well nigh all the space within the belly of the land in manner of a haven; and to the great commodity of the inhabitants receiveth in ships toward every part of the land. The forefronts or frontiers of the two corners, what with fords and shelves and what with rocks, be very jeopardous and dangerous. In the middle distance between them both standeth up above the water a great rock, which therefore is nothing perilous because it is in sight. Upon the top of this rock is a fair and a strong tower builded, which they hold with a garrison of men. Other rocks there be lying hid under the water, and therefore be dangerous. The channels be known only to themselves; and therefore it seldom chanceth that any stranger unless he be guided by an Utopian can come into this haven, insomuch that they themselves could scarcely enter without jeopardy, but that their way is directed and ruled by certain landmarks standing on the shore. By turning, translating, and removing these marks into other places, they may destroy their enemies' navies, be they never so many.

"The outside or outer circuit of the land is also full of havens; but the landing is so surely defenced, what by nature and what by workmanship of men's hands, that a few defenders may drive back many armies. Howbeit, as they say and as the fashion of the place itself doth partly shew, it was not ever compassed about with the sea. But King Utopus,[3] whose name as conqueror the island beareth (for before this time it was called Abraxa)—which also brought the rude and wild people to that excellent perfection in all good fashions, humanity, and civil gentleness, wherein they now go beyond all the people in the world—even at his arriving and entering upon the land, forthwith obtaining the victory, caused fifteen miles space of uplandish ground, where the sea had no passage, to be cut and digged up, and so brought the sea round about the land. He set to this work not only the inhabitants of this island, because[4] they should not think it done in contumely and despite,

---

[1] More coined the word; it means "the place that is not."

[2] Coming around in a circle.

[3] "King" was added by the translator.

[4] So that.

but also all his own soldiers. Thus the work, being divided into so great a number of workmen, was with exceeding marvelous speed dispatched; insomuch that the borderers, which at the first began to mock, and to jest at this vain enterprise, then turned their derision to marvel at the success, and to fear.

"There be in the island fifty-four large and fair cities, or shire towns,[5] agreeing all together in one tongue, in like manners, institutions, and laws. They be all set and situate alike, and in all points fashioned alike, as far forth as the place or plot suffereth. Of these cities, they that be nighest together be twenty-four miles asunder. Again there is none of them distant from the next, above one day's journey afoot.

"There come yearly to Amaurote[6] out of every city three old men, wise and well experienced, there to entreat and debate of the common matters of the land. For this city, because it standeth just in the midst of the island, and is therefore most meet for the ambassadors of all parts of the realm, is taken for the chief and head city. The precincts and bounds of the shires be so commodiously pointed out and set forth for the cities, that never a one of them all hath of any side less than twenty miles of ground, and of some side also much more, as of that part where the cities be of farther distance asunder. None of the cities desire to enlarge the bounds and limits of their shires, for they count themselves rather the good husbands than the owners of their lands.

"They have in the country, in all parts of the shire, houses or farms builded, well appointed and furnished with all sorts of instruments and tools belonging to husbandry. These houses be inhabited of the citizens, which come thither to dwell by course.[7] No household or farm in the country hath fewer than forty persons, men and women, besides two bondmen, which be all under the rule and order of the good man and the good wife of the house, being both very sage, discreet, and ancient persons. And every thirty farms or families have one head ruler, which is called a philarch,[8] being as it were a head bailiff. Out of every one of these families or farms cometh every year into the city twenty persons which have continued two years before in the country. In their place so many fresh be sent thither out of the city, who, of them that have been there a year already, and be therefore expert and cunning in husbandry, shall be instructed and taught. And they the next year shall teach other. This order is used for fear that either scarceness of vituals or some other like incommodity should chance through lack of knowledge, if they should be altogether new and fresh and unexpert in husbandry. This manner and fashion of yearly changing and renewing the occupiers of husbandry, though it be solemn and customably used, to the intent that no man shall be constrained against his will to continue long in that hard and sharp kind of life, yet many of them have such a pleasure and delight in husbandry that they obtain a longer space of years.

"These husbandmen plow and till the ground, and breed up cattle, and provide and make ready wood, which they carry to the city either by land or by water, as they may most conveniently. They bring up a great multitude of pullein,[9] and that by a marvelous policy. For the hens do not sit upon the eggs; but by keeping them in a certain equal heat, they bring life into them and hatch them. The chickens, as soon as they be come out of the shell, follow men and women instead of the hens. They bring up very few horses; nor none but very fierce ones, and that for none other use or purpose but only to exercise their youth in riding and feats of arms. For oxen be put to all the labor of plowing and drawing; which they grant to be not so good as horses at a sudden brunt, and, as we say, at a dead lift; but yet they hold opinion that oxen will abide and suffer much more labor, pain, and hardness than horses will. And they think that oxen be not in danger and subject

---

[5] In More's day there were 54 shire towns, or "county seats," in England and Wales.

[6] The capital of Utopia. The name is from the Greek word meaning "dim" or "obscure."

[7] In turn.

[8] Tribal chief.

[9] Poultry.

unto so many diseases, and that they be kept and maintained with much less cost and charge, and finally that they be good for meat when they be past labor.

"They sow corn only for bread. For their drink is either wine made of grapes, or else of apples, or pears, or else it is clear water. And many times mead made of honey or licorice sodden [10] in water, for thereof they have great store. And though they know certainly (for they know it perfectly, indeed) how much victuals the city with the whole country or shire round about it doth spend, yet they sow much more corn and breed up much more cattle than serveth for their own use, parting the overplus among their borderers. Whatsoever necessary things be lacking in the country, all such stuff they fetch out of the city, where without any exchange they easily obtain it of the magistrates of the city. For every month many of them go into the city on the holy day.[11] When their harvest day draweth near and is at hand, then the philarchs, which be the head officers and bailiffs of husbandry, send word to the magistrates of the city what number of harvest men is needful to be sent to them out of the city; the which company of harvest men, being ready at the day appointed, almost in one fair day dispatcheth all the harvest work."

[Of the Cities, and Namely of Amaurote]

"As for their cities, whoso knoweth one of them, knoweth them all; they be all so like one to another, as far forth as the nature of the place permitteth. I will describe therefore to you one or other of them, for it skilleth not greatly which; but which rather than Amaurote? Of them all this is the worthiest and of most dignity. For the residue 'knowledge it for the head city, because there is the Council-house. Nor to me any of them all is better beloved, as wherein I lived five whole years together.

"The city of Amaurote standeth upon the side of a low hill, in fashion almost four square;[12] for the breadth of it beginneth a little beneath the top of the hill, and still continueth by the space of two miles, until it come to the river of Anyder.[13] The length of it, which lieth by the river's side, is somewhat more.

"The river of Anyder riseth four and twenty miles above Amaurote out of a little spring; but being increased by other small rivers and brooks that run into it, and, among other, two somewhat big ones, before the city it is half a mile broad, and farther, broader. And forty miles beyond the city it falleth into the ocean sea. By all that space that lieth between the sea and the city, and certain miles also above the city, the water ebbeth and floweth six hours together with a swift tide. When the sea floweth in, for the length of thirty miles it filleth all the Anyder with salt water, and driveth back the fresh water of the river. And somewhat further it changeth the sweetness of the fresh water with saltness. But a little beyond that the river waxeth sweet, and runneth forby the city fresh and pleasant. And when the sea ebbeth and goeth back again, the fresh water followeth it almost even to the very fall into the sea. There goeth a bridge over the river, made not of piles or of timber but of stonework with gorgeous and substantial arches, at that part of the city that is farthest from the sea; to the intent that ships may pass along forby all the side of the city without let.

"They have also another river, which indeed is not very great; but it runneth gently and pleasantly. For it riseth even out of the same hill that the city standeth upon, and runneth down a slope through the midst of the city into Anyder. And because it riseth a little without the city, the Amaurotians have enclosed the head spring of it with strong fences and bulwarks, and so have joined it to the city. This is done to the intent that the water should not be stopped, nor turned away, or poisoned, if their enemies should chance to come upon them. From thence the water is derived and conveyed down in

---

[10] Boiled.
[11] The first and last days of each month were holy days.

[12] In several respects Amaurote resembles London.
[13] The name means "waterless," appropriate for an imaginary river.

canals of brick divers ways into the lower parts of the city. Where that cannot be done, by reason that the place will not suffer it, there they gather the rain-water in great cisterns, which doth them as good service.

"The city is compassed about with a high and thick stone wall, full of turrets and bulwarks. A dry ditch, but deep and broad, and overgrown with bushes, briers, and thorns, goeth about three sides or quarters of the city. To the fourth side the river itself serveth for a ditch.

"The streets be appointed and set forth very commodious and handsome, both for carriage,[14] and also against the winds. The houses be of fair and gorgeous building, and on the street side they stand joined together in a long row through the whole street without any partition or separation. The streets be twenty foot broad. On the back side of the houses, through the whole length of the street, lie large gardens, enclosed round about with the back part of the streets. Every house hath two doors, one into the street, and a postern door on the back side into the garden. These doors be made with two leaves, never locked nor bolted, so easy to be opened that they will follow the least drawing of a finger, and shut again alone. Whoso will, may go in, for there is nothing within the houses that is private, or any man's own.[15] And every tenth year they change their houses by lot.

"They set great store by their gardens. In them they have vineyards, all manner of fruit, herbs, and flowers, so pleasant, so well furnished, and so finely kept, that I never saw thing more fruitful, nor better trimmed in any place. Their study and diligence herein cometh not only of pleasure, but also of a certain strife and contention that is between street and street, concerning the trimming, husbanding, and furnishing of their gardens —every man for his own part. And verily you shall not lightly find in all the city anything that is more commodious, either for the profit of the citizens, or for pleasure. And therefore it may seem that the first founder

of the city minded nothing so much as these gardens.

"For they say that King Utopus himself, even at the first beginning, appointed and drew forth the platform of the city into this fashion and figure that it hath now; but the gallant garnishing and the beautiful setting forth of it, whereunto he saw that one man's age would not suffice, that he left to his posterity. For their chronicles, which they keep written with all diligent circumspection, containing the history of one thousand seven hundred and sixty years, even from the first conquest of the island, record and witness that the houses in the beginning were very low, and, like homely cottages or poor shepherd houses, made at all adventures [16] of every rude piece of timber that came first to hand, with mud walls, and ridged roofs, thatched over with straw. But now the houses be curiously builded after a gorgeous and gallant sort, with three stories one over another. The outsides of the walls be made either of hard flint, or of plaster, or else of brick, and the inner sides be well strengthened with timberwork. The roofs be plain and flat, covered with a certain kind of plaster that is of no cost, and yet so tempered that no fire can hurt or perish it, and withstandeth the violence of the weather better than any lead. They keep the wind out of their windows with glass, for it is there much used, and somewhere also with fine linen cloth dipped in oil or amber, and that for two commodities. For by this means more light cometh in, and the wind is better kept out. . . ."

[Of their Living and Mutual Conversation together]

"But now will I declare how the citizens use themselves one towards another, what familiar occupying and entertainment [17] there is among the people, and what fashion they use in distributing everything. First, the city consisteth of families, the families most commonly be made of kindreds. For the women, when they be married at a lawful age, they

[14] For the carrying of goods.
[15] As in Plato's ideal republic, there is no private property in Utopia.

[16] Haphazardly.
[17] Business, or intercourse.

go into their husbands' houses. But the male children with all the whole male offspring continue still in their own family and be governed of the eldest and ancientest father, unless he dote for age, for then the next to him in age is put in his room.

"But to the intent the prescript number of the citizens should neither decrease, nor above measure increase, it is ordained that no family which in every city be six thousand in the whole, besides them of the country, shall at once have fewer children of the age of fourteen years or thereabout than ten, or more than sixteen, for of children under this age no number can be appointed. This measure or number is easily observed and kept, by putting them that in fuller families be above the number into families of smaller increase. But if chance be that in the whole city the store increase above the just number, therewith they fill up the lack of other cities. But if so be that the multitude throughout the whole island pass and exceed the due number, then they choose out of every city certain citizens, and build up a town under their own laws in the next land where the inhabitants have much waste and unoccupied ground, receiving also of the inhabitants to them, if they will join and dwell with them. They thus joining and dwelling together do easily agree in one fashion of living, and that to the great wealth of both the peoples. For they so bring the matter about by their laws, that the ground which before was neither good nor profitable for the one nor for the other, is now sufficient and fruitful enough for them both. But if the inhabitants of that land will not dwell with them to be ordered by their laws, then they drive them out of those bounds which they have limited, and appointed out for themselves. And if they resist and rebel, then they make war against them. For they count this the most just cause of war, when any people holdeth a piece of ground void and vacant, to no good nor profitable use, keeping other from the use and possession of it, which notwithstanding by the law of nature ought thereof to be nourished and relieved. If any chance do so much diminish the number of any of their

cities, that it cannot be filled up again, without the diminishing of the just number of the other cities (which they say chanced but twice since the beginning of the land through a great pestilent plague) then they make up the number with citizens fetched out of their own foreign towns, for they had rather suffer their foreign towns to decay and perish, than any city of their own island to be diminished.

"But now again to the conversation of the citizens among themselves. The eldest (as I said) ruleth the family. The wives be ministers to their husbands, the children to their parents, and to be short the younger to their elders. Every city is divided into four equal parts. In the midst of every quarter there is a market-place of all manner of things. Thither the works of every family be brought into certain houses. And every kind of thing is laid up in several barns or storehouses. From hence the father of every family, or every householder, fetcheth whatsoever he and his have need of, and carrieth it away with him without money, without exchange, without any gage, or pledge. For why should any thing be denied unto him, seeing there is abundance of all things, and that it is not to be feared, lest any man will ask more than he needeth? For why should it be thought that that man would ask more than enough, which is sure never to lack? Certainly in all kinds of living creatures either fear of lack doth cause covetousness and ravin, or in man only pride, which counteth it a glorious thing to pass and excel other in the superfluous and vain ostentation of things. The which kind of vice among the Utopians can have no place.

"Next to the market-places that I spake of, stand meat-markets,[18] whither be brought not only all sorts of herbs, and the fruits of trees, with bread, but also fish, and all manner of four-footed beasts, and wild fowl that be man's meat. But first the filthiness and ordure thereof is clean washed away in the running river without the city in places appointed meet for the same purpose. From thence the beasts be brought in killed, and clean washed by the hands of their bondmen. For they permit not their free citizens to ac-

[18] Food markets.

custom themselves to the killing of beasts, through the use whereof they think that clemency, the gentlest affection of our nature, doth by little and little decay and perish. Neither they suffer any thing that is filthy, loathsome, or uncleanly, to be brought into the city, lest the air by the stench thereof infected and corrupt, should cause pestilent diseases.

"Moreover every street hath certain great large halls set in equal distance one from another, every one known by a several name. In these halls dwell the syphogrants.[19] And to every one of the same halls be appointed thirty families, on either side fifteen. The stewards of every hall at a certain hour come into the meat-markets, where they receive meat according to the number of their halls.

"But first and chiefly of all, respect is had to the sick, that be cured in the hospitals. For in the circuit of the city, a little without the walls, they have four hospitals, so big, so wide, so ample, and so large, that they may seem four little towns, which were devised of that bigness partly to the intent the sick, be they never so many in number, should not lie too throng or strait,[20] and therefore uneasily and incommodiously, and partly that they which were taken and holden with contagious diseases, such as be wont by infection to creep from one to another, might be laid apart far from the company of the residue. These hospitals be so well appointed, and with all things necessary to health so furnished, and moreover so diligent attendance through the continual presence of cunning physicians is given, that though no man be sent thither against his will, yet notwithstanding there is no sick person in all the city, that had not rather lie there than at home in his own house. When the steward of the sick hath received such meats as the physicians have prescribed, then the best is equally divided among the halls, according to the company of every one, saving that there is had a respect to the prince, the bishop, the tranibores,[21] and to ambassadors and all strangers, if there be any, which be very few and seldom. But they also, when they be there, have certain houses appointed and prepared for them.

"To these halls at the set hours of dinner and supper cometh all the whole syphogranty or ward, warned by the noise of a brazen trumpet; except such as be sick in the hospitals, or else in their own houses. Howbeit no man is prohibited or forbid, after the halls be served, to fetch home meat out of the market to his own house, for they know that no man will do it without a cause reasonable. For though no man be prohibited to dine at home, yet no man doth it willingly, because it is counted a point of small honesty.[22] And also it were a folly to take the pain to dress a bad dinner at home, when they may be welcome to good and fine fare so nigh hand at the hall. In this hall all vile service, all slavery, and drudgery, with all laborsome toil and business, is done by bondmen. But the women of every family by course [23] have the office and charge of cookery for seething and dressing the meat, and ordering all things thereto belonging. They sit at three tables or more, according to the number of their company. The men sit upon the bench next the wall, and the women against them on the other side of the table, that if any sudden evil should chance to them, as many times happeneth to women with child, they may rise without trouble or disturbance of anybody, and go thence into the nursery.

"The nurses sit several alone with their young sucklings in a certain parlor appointed and deputed to the same purpose, never without fire and clean water, nor yet without cradles, that when they will they may lay down the young infants, and at their pleasure take them out of their swathing clothes, and hold them to the fire, and refresh them with play. Every mother is nurse to her own child, unless either death, or sickness be the let. When that chanceth, the wives of the syphogrants quickly provide a nurse. And that is not hard to be done. For they that can do it, do proffer themselves to no service so gladly as to that. Because that there this kind of pity

[19] "Syphogrant" is another name for "philarch."
[20] Too crowded or confined.
[21] An older name for the chief philarchs.
[22] Somewhat dishonorable.
[23] In turn.

is much praised, and the child that is nour-ished ever after taketh his nurse for his own natural mother. Also among the nurses sit all the children that be under the age of five years. All the other children of both kinds, as well boys as girls, that be under the age of marriage, do either serve at the tables, or else if they be too young thereto, yet they stand by with marvelous silence. That which is given to them from the table they eat, and other several dinner-time they have none. The syphogrant and his wife sit in the midst of the high table, forasmuch as that is counted the honorablest place, and because from thence all the whole company is in their sight. For that table standeth overthwart the over end [24] of the hall. To them be joined two of the ancientest and eldest. For at every table they sit four at a mess. But if there be a church standing in that syphogranty or ward, then the priest and his wife sitteth with the syphogrant, as chief in the company. On both sides of them sit young men, and next unto them again old men. And thus through-out all the house equal of age be set together, and yet be mixed with unequal ages. This, they say, was ordained, to the intent that the sage gravity and reverence of the elders should keep the younger from wanton license of words and behavior. For as much as nothing can be so secretly spoken or done at the table, but either they that sit on the one side or on the other must needs perceive it. The dishes be not set down in order from the first place, but all the old men (whose places be marked with some special token to be known) be first served of their meat, and then the residue equally. The old men divide their dainties as they think best to the younger that sit on each side of them. Thus the elders be not de-frauded of their due honor, and nevertheless equal commodity cometh to every one.

"They begin every dinner and supper of reading something that pertaineth to good manners and virtue. But it is short, because no man shall be grieved therewith. Hereof the elders take occasion of honest communica-tion, but neither sad nor unpleasant. Howbe-it they do not spend all the whole dinner-time

themselves with long and tedious talks: but they gladly hear also the young men, yea, and do purposely provoke them to talk, to the intent that they may have a proof of every man's wit and towardness, or disposition to virtue, which commonly in the liberty of feast-ing doth show and utter itself. Their dinners be very short, but their suppers be somewhat longer, because that after dinner followeth labor, after supper sleep and natural rest, which they think to be of more strength and efficacy to wholesome and healthful digestion. No supper is passed without music. Nor their banquets lack no conceits [25] nor junkets.[26] They burn sweet gums and spices for per-fumes, and pleasant smells, and sprinkle about sweet ointments and waters, yea, they leave nothing undone that maketh for the cheering of the company. For they be much inclined to this opinion, to think no kind of pleasure for-bidden, whereof cometh no harm.

"Thus therefore and after this sort they live together in the city, but in the country they that dwell alone far from any neighbors, do dine and sup at home in their own houses. For no family there lacketh any kind of victuals, as from whom [27] cometh all that the citizens eat and live by. . . ."

[Of the Religions in Utopia]

"There be divers kinds of religion, not only in sundry parts of the island, but also in divers places of every city. Some worship for God the sun, some the moon, some some other of the planets.[28] There be that give worship to a man that was once of excellent virtue or of famous glory, not only as God, but also as the chiefest and highest God. But the most and the wisest part, rejecting all these, believe that there is a certain godly power, unknown, everlasting, incomprehensible, inexplicable, far above the capacity and reach of man's wit, dispersed throughout all the whole world, not in bigness, but in virtue and power. Him they call the father of all. To him alone they

[24] Across the end.

[25] Decorations.

[26] Sweetmeats.

[27] As they are those from whom.

[28] More held the prevalent Ptolemaic view that the earth was the center of the universe. Copernicus' work was not published until 1543.

attribute the beginnings, the increasings, the proceedings, the changes, and the ends of all things. Neither they give any divine honors to any other than to him.

"Yea, all the other also, though they be in divers opinions, yet in this point they agree altogether with the wisest sort, in believing that there is one principal God, the maker and ruler of the whole world, whom they call commonly, in their country language, Mythra. But in this they disagree, that among some he is counted one, and among some, another. For every one of them, whatsoever that is which he taketh for the chief God, thinketh it to be the very same nature, to whose only divine might and majesty, the sum and sovereignty of all things, by the consent of all people, is attributed and given. Howbeit, they all begin by little and little to forsake and fall from this variety of superstitions, and to agree together in that religion which seemeth by reason to pass and excel the residue. And it is not to be doubted but all the other would long ago have been abolished, but that whatsoever unprosperous thing happened to any of them, as he was minded to change his religion, the fearfulness of people did take it, not as a thing coming by chance, but as sent from God out of heaven. As though the God, whose honor he was forsaking, would have revenged that wicked purpose against him.

"But after they heard us speak of the name of Christ, of his doctrine, laws, miracles, and of the no less wonderful constancy of so many martyrs, whose blood willingly shed brought a great number of nations throughout all parts of the world into their sect—you will not believe with how glad minds they agreed unto the same! whether it were by the secret inspiration of God, or else for that they thought it nighest unto that opinion, which among them is counted the chiefest. Howbeit, I think this was no small help and furtherance in the matter, that they heard us say that Christ instituted among his, all things common: [29] and that the same community doth

yet remain amongst the rightest Christian companies.[30] Verily howsoever it came to pass, many of them consented together in our religion, and were washed in the holy water of baptism.

"But because among us four (for no more of us was left alive, two of our company being dead) there was no priest—which I am right sorry for—they being entered and instructed in all other points of our religion, lack only those sacraments, which none but priests do minister. Howbeit, they understand and perceive them, and be very desirous of the same. Yea, they reason and dispute the matter earnestly among themselves, whether, without the sending of a Christian bishop, one chosen out of their own people, may receive the order of priesthood. And truly they were minded to choose one. But at my departure thence they had chosen none.

"They also which do not agree to Christ's religion, fear no man from it, nor speak against any man that hath received it, saving that one of our company [31] in my presence was sharply punished. He, as soon as he was baptized, began against our wills, with more earnest affection [32] than wisdom, to reason of Christ's religion; and began to wax so hot in this matter, that he did not only prefer our religion before all other, but also did utterly despise and condemn all other—calling them profane, and the followers of them wicked and devilish, and the children of everlasting damnation. When he had thus long reasoned the matter, they laid hold on him, accused him, and condemned him into exile; not as a despiser of religion, but as a seditious person, and a raiser up of dissension among the people. For this is one of the ancientest laws among them: that no man shall be blamed for reasoning in the maintenance of his own religion.

"For King Utopus, even at the first beginning, hearing that the inhabitants of the land were, before his coming thither, at continual dissension and strife among themselves for their religion (perceiving also that this com-

[29] I.e., Christ approved of the principle of communal ownership.
[30] The same principle (of communal ownership) is observed among monks and friars.

[31] Christian company, i.e., a Utopian convert, not Hythloday's traveling companion.
[32] Strong feeling or zeal.

mon dissension, whilst every several sect took several parts in fighting for their country, was the only occasion of his conquest over them all) as soon as he had gotten the victory, first of all he made a decree that it should be lawful for every man to favor and follow what religion he would; and that he might do the best he could to bring other to his opinion, so that he did it peaceably, gently, quietly, and soberly, without hasty and contentious rebuking and inveighing against other. If he could not by fair and gentle speech induce them unto his opinion, yet he should use no kind of violence, and refrain from displeasant and seditious words. To him that would vehemently and fervently in this cause strive and contend, was decreed banishment or bondage.

"This law did King Utopus make, not only for the maintenance of peace, which he saw through continual contention and mortal hatred, utterly extinguished, but also because he thought this decree should make for the furtherance of religion. Whereof he durst define and determine nothing unadvisedly, as doubting whether God, desiring manifold and divers sorts of honor, would inspire sundry men with sundry kinds of religion. And this surely he thought a very unmeet and foolish thing, and a point of arrogant presumption, to compel all other by violence and threatenings to agree to the same that thou believest to be true. Furthermore, though there be one religion which alone is true, and all other vain and superstitious, yet did he well foresee (so that the matter were handled with reason and sober modesty), that the truth of the own power [33] would, at the last issue, out and come to light. But if contention and debate in that behalf should continually be used —as the worst men be most obstinate and stubborn, and in their evil opinion most constant—he perceived that then the best and holiest religion would be trodden under foot, and destroyed by most vain superstitions; even as corn is by thorns and weeds overgrown and choked. Therefore all this matter he left undiscussed, and gave to every man free liberty and choice to believe what he

[33] If its own power.

would, saving that he earnestly and straightly charged them, that no man should conceive so vile and base an opinion of the dignity of man's nature, as to think that the souls do die and perish with the body, or that the world runneth at all adventures governed by no divine providence. And therefore they believe that after this life, vices be extremely punished, and virtues bountifully rewarded. Him that is of a contrary opinion they count not in the number of men—as one that hath availed the high nature of his soul to the vileness of brute beasts' bodies: much less in the number of the citizens—whose laws and ordinances, if it were not for fear, he would nothing at all esteem. For you may be sure he will study either with craft privily to mock, or else violently to break the common laws of his country, in whom remaineth no further fear than of the laws, nor no further hope than of the body. Wherefore he that is thus minded is deprived of all honors, excluded from all offices, and rejected from all common administrations in the weal-public.

"And thus he is of all sorts despised, as of an unprofitable and of a base and vile nature. Howbeit, they put him to no punishment, because they be persuaded that it is in no man's power to believe what he list. No, nor they constrain him not with threatenings to dissemble his mind, and show countenance contrary to his thought. For deceit and falsehood, and all manner of lies, as next unto fraud, they do marvelously reject and abhor. But they suffer him not to dispute in his opinion, and that only [34] among the common people. For else apart, among the priests and men of gravity, they do not only suffer but also exhort him to dispute and argue; hoping that at the last, madness will give place to reason.

"There be also other, and of them no small number, which be not forbidden to speak their minds, as grounding their opinion upon some reason, being in their living neither evil nor vicious. Their heresy is much contrary to the other: for they believe that the souls of the brute beasts be immortal and everlasting,

[34] The prohibition against religious disputing applies only to the common people.

but nothing to be compared with others in dignity, neither ordained and predestinate to like felicity. For they all believe certainly and surely that man's bliss shall be so great, that they do mourn and lament every man's sickness, but no man's death, unless it be one whom they see depart from his life carefully [35] and against his will. For this they take for a very evil token, as though the soul being in despair, and vexed in conscience, through some privy and secret fore-feeling of the punishment now at hand, were afraid to depart. And they think he shall not be welcome to God, which, when he is called, runneth not to him gladly, but is drawn by force, and sore against his will. They therefore that see this kind of death, do abhor it; and them that so die, they bury with sorrow and silence. And when they have prayed to God to be merciful to pardon the infirmities thereof, they cover the dead corpse with earth.

"Contrarywise, all that depart merrily and full of good hope, for them no man mourneth, but followeth the hearse with joyful singing, commending the souls to God with great affection. And at the last, not with mourning sorrow, but with a great reverence, they burn the bodies. And in the same place they set up a pillar of stone, with the dead men's titles therein graved. When they be come home, they rehearse his virtuous manners and his good deeds. But no part of his life is so oft or gladly talked of, as his merry death. They think that this remembrance of the virtue and goodness of the dead doth vehemently provoke and enforce the living to virtue; and that nothing can be more pleasant and acceptable to the dead, whom they suppose to be present among them, when they talk of them, though to the dull and feeble eyesight of mortal men they be invisible. . . ."

Thus when Raphael had made an end of his tale, though many things came to my mind which in the manners and laws of that people seemed to be instituted and founded of no good reason, not only in the fashion of their chivalry [36] and in their sacrifices and religions,

and in other of their laws, but also, yea and chiefly, in that which is the principal foundation of all their ordinances, that is to say, in the community of their life and living, without any occupying of money (by the which thing only all nobility, magnificence, worship, honor, and majesty, the true ornaments and honors, as the common opinion is, of a commonwealth, utterly be overthrown and destroyed); yet, because I knew that he was weary of talking, and was not sure whether he could abide that anything should be said against his mind,[37] specially because I remembered that he had reprehended this fault in other, which be afeared lest they should seem not to be wise enough unless they could find some fault in other men's inventions; therefore I, praising both their institutions and his communication,[38] took him by the hand and led him in to supper; saying that we would choose another time to weigh and examine the same matters, and to talk with him more at large therein; which would to God it might once come to pass. In the mean time, as I cannot agree and consent to all things that he said (being else without doubt a man singularly well learned and also in all worldly matters exactly and profoundly experienced), so must I needs confess and grant that many things be in the Utopian weal public which in our cities I may rather wish for than hope after.

Thus endeth the afternoon's talk of Raphael Hythloday concerning the laws and institutions of the island of Utopia. (1516)

STUDY AIDS: 1. What features of Utopian society have been adopted by later ages? What features of the society seem undesirable to us?

2. What specific features of the story does More introduce to make his narrative seem like a factual account? (See, e.g., the realistic detail of the street and hospital of Amaurote, p. 133/1, l. 10 ff.). Why is he interested in making the story seem factual?

3. See "Utopia" in the dictionary. What conclusions do you draw from the dictionary entry?

[35] Full of care.
[36] Manner of their military operations.
[37] In opposition to his opinions.
[38] His account, or story, of Utopia.

Sir Thomas Wyatt
(1503–1542)

ENGLISH LYRIC POETRY OF THE RENAISSANCE BEGINS WITH SIR THOMAS WYATT, A VIGOR-
ous and active man of affairs in the court of Henry VIII. Soon after taking an M.A. degree
from Cambridge, Wyatt served the king on diplomatic missions to France and Italy.
He was knighted for his service, but in time suffered the king's displeasure and twice was
imprisoned in the Tower. Restored to favor, he served on the Privy Council and as am-
bassador to Spain.

Wyatt's admiration for Italian poets, gained perhaps when he visited Italy, led him to
imitate their themes and forms in his native English. From Petrarch he borrowed the
Italian, or two-part sonnet. Modified by his friend and disciple, the Earl of Surrey, this
form later enjoyed a great vogue in Elizabeth's time. If Wyatt is the father of the sonnet
in English, he is also a good poet in his own right, and deserves to be remembered for
his poems as well as for his influence.

My Galley Chargèd with Forgetfulness

My galley chargèd [1] with forgetfulness
Through sharp seas in winter nights doth pass
'Tween rock and rock; and eke mine enemy,[2]
alas,
That is my lord, steereth with cruelness;
And every oar a thought in readiness,   5
As though that death were light in such a
case.
An endless wind doth tear the sail apace,
Of forcèd sighs and trusty fearfulness;
A rain of tears, a cloud of dark disdain,
Have done the wearied cords great
hinderance;   10
Wreathèd with error and with ignorance,
The stars be hid that led me to this pain.
Drownèd is reason, that should me comfort,
And I remain despairing of the port.
(ca. 1530; 1557)

[1] Loaded.
[2] I.e., love.

STUDY AIDS: 1. The poet here tells of his
distress as a scorned lover. From first line to last,
the poem develops a single comparison, or CON-
CEIT. As a first step in analyzing the conceit,
list in one vertical column the details having to
do with a ship, the sea, and the weather; then
in an adjoining column, list the corresponding
items from the realm of love. So, "galley" = the
poet's soul or being; "cloud" = his lady's disdain, etc.

2. Line 12 tells how he got into his predicament: he was led into it by "the stars." Literally
(your left-hand column) "the stars" refers to the
actual stars in the sky, by which mariners navi-
gate; figuratively (your right-hand column) "the
[two] stars" refers to what? In what sense may
they be said to be "wreathèd with error and
with ignorance"?

Divers Doth Use, As I Have Heard and Know

Divers doth use,[1] as I have heard and know,
When that [2] to change their ladies do begin,
To moan and wail, and never for to lin,[3]
Hoping thereby to 'pease [4] their painful woe.[5]
And some there be, that when it chanceth
  so   5
That women change, and hate where love
  hath been,
They call them false, and think with words
  to win
The hearts of them which otherwhere doth
  grow.
But as for me, though that by chance indeed
Change hath outworn the favor that I had, 10
I will not wail, lament, nor yet be sad,
Nor call her false that falsely did me feed; [6]
But let it pass, and think it is of kind [7]
That often change doth please a woman's
  mind.

(ca. 1530; 1923)

STUDY AIDS: 1. In this poem Wyatt is not a slavish imitator of Petrarch. A comparison of this sonnet with the preceding one reveals several interesting differences of both content and form. Contrast the attitude of the lover toward his mistress in the two poems.

2. In a part of "Divers Doth Use" the poet is talking about himself; in another part he is talking about others. Divide the poem into parts on the basis of the person or persons being talked about. Where do your divisions come? In form, then, is this a Petrarchan or an English sonnet, or does it contain elements of both forms (see SONNET)? Are the divisions into parts in "My Galley Chargèd with Forgetfulness" as clear-cut as in "Divers Doth Use"? Why or why not?

3. Which of the two sonnets is the more regular metrically (see METER)? Which contains more FIGURATIVE LANGUAGE? How are these differences appropriate to the difference in the two poems' themes?

My Lute, Awake!

My lute, awake! perform the last
Labor that thou and I shall waste,
And end that [1] I have now begun;
For when this song is sung and past,
My lute be still, for I have done.   5

As to be heard where ear is none,
As lead to grave in marble stone,
My song may pierce her heart as soon.[2]
Should we then sigh, or sing, or moan?
No, no, my lute, for I have done.   10

The rocks do not so cruelly
Repulse the waves continually,

As she my suit and affection;
So that I am past remedy,
Whereby my lute and I have done.   15

Proud of the spoil that thou hast got
Of simple hearts through Love's shot,
By whom, unkind, thou hast them won,
Think not he hath his bow forgot,[3]
Although my lute and I have done.   20

Vengeance shall fall on thy disdain,
That makest but game of earnest pain;
Think not alone under the sun
Unquit to cause [4] thy lovers plain,
Although my lute and I have done.   25

[1] I.e., many people are accustomed.
[2] When.
[3] Stop.
[4] Appease.
[5] An elementary but necessary step in reading a poem is to determine the SYNTAX. Note, e.g., that in the clause that constitutes line 2, "ladies" is the subject of "do begin"; also, "to moan and wail" are complementary infinitives after "doth use" in line 1.

[6] I.e., feed my hopes.
[7] Natural.

---

[1] That which.
[2] I.e., my song can pierce her heart as easily as lead can engrave marble.
[3] I.e., Cupid may shoot you some day, and you will suffer.
[4] I.e., [you will be] unpunished for causing.

Perchance thee lie withered and old
The winter nights that are so cold,
Plaining in vain unto the moon;
Thy wishes then dare not be told.
Care then who list, for I have done.   30

And then may chance thee to repent
The time that thou hast lost and spent
To cause thy lovers sigh and swoon;
Then shalt thou know beauty but lent,
And wish and want as I have done.[5]   35

Now cease, my lute: this is the last
Labor that thou and I shall waste,
And ended is that we begun;
Now is thy song both sung and past.
My lute be still, for I have done.   40
(1557)

STUDY AIDS: 1. In this admired poem
Wyatt again treats the Petrarchan theme of the
scorned lover. An interesting feature of the poem
is Wyatt's use of the REFRAIN—words or phrases
more or less exactly repeated at the end of each
stanza. Note the grammatical forms of the refrains: the refrain in the first stanza is a main
clause, that in the second is a separate sentence,
given in answer to a rhetorical question. How
many different grammatical constructions can
you find in the refrains?
   2. From stanza to stanza the length of the
repeated element in the refrain ranges from three
words ("I have done") to an entire line. At what
points in the poem are entire lines repeated in
the refrain? Why at these points?
   3. In which stanza does the "I have done"
refer to something other than the poet's decision
to break with his lady?
   4. In some of the refrains the poet talks about
his lute, in others he talks directly to it, and in
still others he does not mention it at all. Notice
in which refrains he treats the lute in one or
another of these three ways. Do you discern in
the refrains a developing pattern in the poet-lute
relationship? How does this pattern fit the theme
of the poem?

They Flee from Me

They flee from me that sometime did me seek,
With naked foot stalking [1] in my chamber.
I have seen them gentle, tame, and meek,
That now are wild, and do not remember
That sometime they put themselves in
   danger [2]   5
To take bread at my hand; and now they
   range
Busily seeking with a continual change.

Thankèd be fortune, it hath been otherwise
Twenty times better; but once, in special,
In thin array, after a pleasant guise,[3]   10
When her loose gown from her shoulders did
   fall,
And she me caught in her arms long and
   small,[4]

Therewith all sweetly did me kiss,
And softly said, "Dear heart, how like you
   this?"

It was no dream; I lay broad waking.   15
But all is turned, through my gentleness,
Into a strange fashion of forsaking;
And I have leave to go, of her goodness,[5]
And she also to use newfangleness.[6]
But since that I so kindely [7] am served,   20
I would fain know what she hath deserved.[8]
(1557)

STUDY AIDS: 1. The poet, forsaken by his
fickle mistress, reminisces on how it was before
she deserted him, and contrasts his former with

[5] This entire stanza is metrically regular except
for one spot. Where is the variation? Why at this
point?

[1] Gliding stealthily.
[2] In my power (or, in a scandalous position).
[3] According to the pleasant fashion.

[4] Slender.
[5] As a result of her goodness (ironic).
[6] Fickleness.
[7] In such fashion (or, with such kindness
[ironic]).
[8] Won (with perhaps overtones of the modern
meaning).

his present lot. Notice the animal IMAGERY in the first stanza. What meanings are suggested by this imagery?

2. Some readers have regarded the erotic details in stanza 2 as a metaphoric representation of Fortune. Do you agree with them?

Sir Philip Sidney
(1554–1586)

FAVORED BY NOBLE BIRTH AND BY GREAT PERSONAL CHARM AND TALENT, SIDNEY LEARNED to do extremely well those things which his age valued. After his years at Oxford he continued to cultivate his intellectual interests during a three-year tour of the courts and universities of Europe. The tour fostered his humanism and also confirmed his Protestant belief. After witnessing the massacre of St. Bartholomew's Day in Paris he returned to Elizabeth's court, where he joined his uncle, the Earl of Leicester, in political and military efforts to strengthen England against Catholic Spain. To that end he opposed the Spanish in Holland, serving as governor of Flushing and as soldier. He died heroically in the field before Zutphen.

Sidney's writings, done in an amateur spirit and unpublished during his lifetime, were few but influential. His *Arcadia* (1590) was the first prose pastoral romance in English. His *Astrophel and Stella* (1591), a collection of 108 sonnets, probably addressed to Penelope Devereux, daughter of Lord Essex, set the fashion for "sonnet sequences" in the 1590's. His *Defense of Poesy* (1595) is the best statement by a contemporary poet-critic of the nature and value of poetry. Through personal prestige as well as literary performance Sidney greatly influenced the literature of his time.

Loving in Truth and Fain in Verse My Love to Show

Although sonnets of Wyatt and Surrey had appeared in *Tottel's Miscellany* (1557), a collection popular enough to go through eight editions in thirty years, the sonnet enjoyed no great vogue until late in the century. Then in quick succession, following publication of Sidney's *Astrophel and Stella* (1591), appeared Samuel Daniel's *Delia* (1592), Michael Drayton's *Idea's Mirror* (1594), and Edmund Spenser's *Amoretti* (1595). Shakespeare's sonnets, probably written at about this time, were published in 1609. Each of these publications is a "sonnet sequence," a collection of 50 to 154 more or less related sonnets, chronicling the progress of a courtship or praising the lady in various ways.

All of the sonneteers to some extent followed the example of the Italian poet Petrarch, whose sonnets had sung the praises of his Laura. They pictured their ladies as beautiful, often specifying their beauties and describing them in stock similes (cheeks like roses, lips like cherries, teeth like pearls); but they also showed them as cruel, disdainful, and haughty. Nevertheless they represented themselves as faithful, devoted lovers, who sighed and pined, fretted and lost sleep, but who even in their misery promised their ladies eternal devotion and possible immortality through verse. The Elizabethan sonnet, then, embodying as it does this Petrarchan ideal, was a highly conventional poetic form. Consequently it is hard to tell how sincere the poet is. Perhaps we need not ask the question. Although some of the sonnets seem like mere exercises in literary ingenuity, the best of them go beyond the convention and are poems of great beauty.

The following sonnet is the first in Sidney's sequence, *Astrophel and Stella*. Note that these proper names ("star-lover" and "star," representing the lover and his lady) are symbolically appropriate to the Petrarchan ideal.

Loving in truth, and fain in verse my love
to show,
That she, dear she, might take some pleasure
of my pain,
Pleasure might cause her read, reading might
make her know,
Knowledge might pity win, and pity grace
obtain,
I sought fit words to paint the blackest face
of woe,   5
Studying inventions fine, her wits to enter-
tain,
Oft turning others' leaves[1] to see if thence
would flow
Some fresh and fruitful showers upon my
sunburnt brain.
But words came halting forth, wanting
Invention's stay;[2]

Invention, Nature's child, fled step-dame
Study's blows,   10
And others' feet still seemed but strangers in
my way.
Thus, great with child to speak, and helpless
in my throes,
Biting my truant pen, beating myself for
spite,
"Fool," said my Muse to me, "look in thy
heart, and write."

(1591)

STUDY AIDS: 1. Two theories of literary composition are treated here. One is implied in the last line. Where is the other one treated? Which one does the poet prefer? How do you know? How does the IMAGERY of l. 10 help answer the preceding question?

2. In what way is the meter of this poem unusual?

With How Sad Steps, O Moon, Thou Climbest the Skies

In spite of the conceit (identifying moon and lover) that underlies the poem, the tone of this sonnet is neither plaintive nor witty, but surprisingly bitter.

With how sad steps, O Moon, thou climbest
the skies
How silently, and with how wan a face!
What, may it be that even in heavenly place
That busy archer[3] his sharp arrows tries?
Sure, if that long-with-love-acquainted eyes 5
Can judge of love, thou feelest a lover's
case;
I read it in thy looks; thy languished grace,
To me that feel the like, thy state descries,[4]
Then, even of fellowship,[5] O Moon, tell me,
Is constant love deemed there but want of
wit?[6]   10

Are beauties there as proud as here they be?
Do they above love to be loved, and yet
Those lovers scorn whom that love doth
possess?
Do they call virtue there ungratefulness?[7]
(1591)

STUDY AIDS: 1. What stated qualities and actions of lover and loved one are typical of the Petrarchan ideal?

2. In structure and RHYME SCHEME this sonnet is strictly neither Petrarchan nor English. Note how the last line (not the last two) is a forceful conclusion.

[1] I.e., he seeks poetic inspiration in the writings of others.
[2] I.e., the support of inspiration.
[3] Cupid.

[4] Shows.
[5] I.e., equal as we friends are.
[6] Good sense.
[7] I.e., do they call ungratefulness there a virtue?

Come, Sleep! O Sleep, the Certain Knot of Peace

Here the poet invokes sleep (strongly personified, as is the moon in the preceding poem) and even attempts to bribe him into granting him relief.

Come, Sleep! O Sleep, the certain knot of
  peace,
The baiting-place [1] of wit, the balm of woe,
The poor man's wealth, the prisoner's release,
The indifferent [2] judge between the high and
  low;
With shield of proof [3] shield me from out the
  prease [4]   5
Of those fierce darts Despair at me doth throw;
O make in me those civil wars to cease;

I will good tribute pay, if thou do so.
Take thou of me smooth pillows, sweetest
  bed,
A chamber deaf to noise and blind to light, 10
A rosy garland [5] and a weary head;
And if these things, as being thine by right,
Move not thy heavy grace, thou shalt in me,
Livelier than elsewhere, Stella's image see.
(1591)

Having This Day My Horse, My Hand, My Lance

The poem may have been prompted by an actual tournament in which Sidney took part. It was held in 1581, when French envoys were trying to arrange a marriage between Francis, Duke of Anjou, and Elizabeth.

Having this day my horse, my hand, my lance
Guided so well that I obtained the prize,
Both by the judgment of the English eyes
And of some sent from that sweet enemy
  France;
Horsemen my skill in horsemanship
  advance,[6]   5
Town folks my strength; a daintier [7] judge
  applies
His praise to sleight [8] which from good use [9]
  doth rise;
Some lucky wits impute it but to chance;
Others because of both sides I do take
My blood from them who did excel in this, 10
Think nature me a man-at-arms did make.
How far they shot awry! the true cause is,
Stella looked on, and from her heavenly face
Sent forth the beams which made so fair my
  race.
(1591)

[1] Resting place.
[2] Impartial.
[3] Protection.
[4] Press.

STUDY AIDS: 1. The structure of this sonnet is typical of Sidney; 59 of his 108 sonnets are built on this pattern. Review SONNET in the glossary and you will notice that this sonnet differs from both the Petrarchan and the English forms because the RHYME SCHEME does not correspond exactly with the pattern of thought. In the Petrarchan sonnet the OCTAVE is a thought unit, corresponding to the conventional rhyme scheme (abba, abba); Sidney observes this rhyme scheme, but his thought does not correspond to it. Lines 1–4 say he won the prize, and ll. 5–8 give offered explanations. But here, although the rhyme scheme shifts, the thought does not, since the offered explanations continue into the SESTET. The sestet reveals a similar discrepancy between rhyme scheme and thought. The rhyme scheme suggests QUATRAIN and COUPLET; the thought of the sestet, however, is expressed in two units of three lines each: ll.

[5] The rose was symbolic of secrecy (cf. sub rosa).
[6] I.e., give (as an explanation for my winning the tournament).
[7] More discriminating.
[8] Skill.
[9] Practice.

9–11 giving another offered explanation, and ll. 12–14 giving the true explanation. The final thought unit is thus not two lines (as the rhyme scheme would indicate and as the normal English sonnet requires) but three. Is this deviation from the normal pattern aesthetically pleasing?

2. Analyze "Come, Sleep!" above in a similar way.

The Defense of Poesy

Sidney's *Defense of Poesy* entered the first significant literary controversy in English literary history. Stephen Gosson, a playwright who had become convinced that the theater was sinful, attacked poetry, particularly dramatic poetry, in a pamphlet entitled *The School of Abuse* (1579). Sidney replied in his *Defense of Poesy*. From earliest times, he says, poetry has been highly valued by men, who have called poets "prophets" and "creators." It is better able than history or philosophy to achieve the end of learning—virtuous action. It is true, Sidney admits, that poetry at the moment is in a poor condition. The fault lies with the dramatic poets, who ignore the rules laid down by the authorities of Greece and Rome. Poetry itself is excellent, and the arguments in favor of it are compelling ones. If Sidney seems unduly respectful of the rules of dramatic poetry, we should remember that he was advocating the best that was then known, and that no Shakespeare had yet shown how rules could be violated successfully. Certainly the *Defense* is a lofty and spirited argument supporting the art that Sidney and many of his contemporaries were learning to master.

Since the authors of most of our sciences were the Romans, and before them the Greeks, let us a little stand upon their authorities, but even [1] so far as to see what names they have given unto this now scorned skill.[2] Among the Romans a poet was called *vates*, which is as much as a diviner, foreseer, or prophet, as by his conjoined words, *vaticinium* and *vaticinari*,[3] is manifest; so heavenly a title did that excellent people bestow upon this heart-ravishing knowledge. And so far were they carried into the admiration thereof, that they thought in the chanceable hitting upon any such verses great foretokens of their following fortunes were placed; whereupon grew the word of *Sortes Virgilianae*,[4] when by sudden opening Virgil's book they lighted upon some verse of his making. Whereof the *Histories of the Emperors' Lives*[5] are full: as of Albinus,[6] the governor of our island, who in his childhood met with this verse,

---

[1] Merely.
[2] I.e., poetry.
[3] "Prophecy" and "to prophesy."
[4] A drawing of lots from the works of Virgil. Romans consulted Virgil's poems at random as a guide to conduct.
[5] The *Augustan Histories,* by several Latin authors.
[6] Roman governor of Britain.

Arma amens capio, nec sat rationis in armis,[7] and in his age performed it. Although it were a very vain and godless superstition, as also it was to think that spirits were commanded by such verses—whereupon this word "charms," derived of *carmina,* cometh—so yet serveth it to show the great reverence those wits were held in, and altogether not without ground, since both the oracles of Delphos and Sibylla's prophecies were wholly delivered in verses; for that same exquisite observing of number and measure in words, and that high-flying liberty of conceit[8] proper to the poet, did seem to have some divine force in it.

And may not I presume a little further to show the reasonableness of this word *vates,* and say that the holy David's Psalms are a divine poem? If I do, I shall not do it without the testimony of great learned men, both ancient and modern. But even the name of Psalms will speak for me, which, being interpreted, is nothing but Songs; then, that it is fully written in meter, as all learned Hebricians[9] agree, although the rules be not yet full found; lastly and principally, his han-

---

[7] "Arms in my rage I seize, even though there is no sufficient reason for arms."
[8] Imaginative invention (see CONCEIT).
[9] Hebraic scholars.

dling his prophecy, which is merely poetical. For what else is the awaking his musical instruments, the often and free changing of persons, his notable prosopopoeias,[10] when he maketh you, as it were, see God coming in His majesty, his telling of the beasts' joyfulness and hills' leaping, but a heavenly poesy, wherein almost he showeth himself a passionate lover of that unspeakable and everlasting beauty to be seen by the eyes of the mind, only cleared by faith? But truly now having named him, I fear I seem to profane that holy name, applying it to poetry, which is among us thrown down to so ridiculous an estimation. But they that with quiet judgments will look a little deeper into it shall find the end and working of it such as, being rightly applied, deserveth not to be scourged out of the church of God.

But now let us see how the Greeks named it and how they deemed of it. The Greeks called him *poieten* [a poet] which name hath, as the most excellent, gone through other languages. It cometh of this word *poiein*, which is "to make"; wherein I know not whether by luck or wisdom we Englishmen have met with the Greeks in calling him a "maker." Which name how high and incomparable a title it is, I had rather were known by marking the scope of other sciences than by any partial allegation. There is no art delivered unto mankind that hath not the works of nature for his principal object, without which they could not consist, and on which they so depend as they become actors and players, as it were, of what nature will have set forth. So doth the astronomer look upon the stars and, by that he seeth, set down what order nature hath taken therein. So do the geometrician and arithmetician in their divers sorts of quantities. So doth the musician in times tell you which by nature agree, which not. The natural philosopher thereon hath his name, and the moral philosopher standeth upon the natural virtues, vices, and passions of man; and "follow nature," saith he, "therein, and thou shalt not err." The lawyer saith what men have determined, the historian what men have

done. The grammarian speaketh only of the rules of speech, and the rhetorician and logician, considering what in nature will soonest prove and persuade, thereon give artificial rules, which still are compassed within the circle of a question, according to the proposed matter. The physician weigheth the nature of man's body, and the nature of things helpful or hurtful unto it. And the metaphysic, though it be in the second and abstract notions, and therefore be counted supernatural, yet doth he, indeed, build upon the depth of nature.

Only the poet, disdaining to be tied to any such subjection, lifted up with the vigor of his own invention, doth grow, in effect, into another nature, in making things either better than nature bringeth forth, or, quite anew, forms such as never were in nature, as the heroes, demi-gods, cyclops, chimeras, furies, and such like; so as he goeth hand in hand with nature, not enclosed within the narrow warrant of her gifts, but freely ranging within the zodiac of his own wit. Nature never set forth the earth in so rich tapestry as divers poets have done; neither with pleasant rivers, fruitful trees, sweet-smelling flowers, nor whatsoever else may make the too-much-loved earth more lovely; her world is brazen, the poets only deliver a golden.

But let those things alone, and go to man —for whom as the other things are, so it seemeth in him her uttermost cunning is employed—and know whether she have brought forth so true a lover as Theagenes,[11] so constant a friend as Pylades;[12] so valiant a man as Orlando;[13] so right a prince as Xenophon's Cyrus; so excellent a man in every way as Virgil's Aeneas? Neither let this be jestingly conceived, because the works of the one be essential, the other in imitation or fiction; for any understanding knoweth the skill of each artificer standeth in that idea, or fore-conceit of the work, and not in the work

[10] Personifications.

[11] Hero of a romance by the Greek writer, Heliodorus.

[12] Devoted friend of Orestes in Greek legend.

[13] Hero of *Orlando Furioso*, an epic by the Italian, Ariosto.

itself.[14] And that the poet hath that idea is manifest, by delivering them forth in such excellency as he hath imagined them. Which delivering forth, also, is not wholly imaginative, as we are wont to say by [15] them that build castles in the air; but so far substantially it worketh, not only to make a Cyrus, which had been but a particular excellency, as nature might have done, but to bestow a Cyrus upon the world to make many Cyruses, if they will learn aright why and how that maker made him. Neither let it be deemed too saucy a comparison to balance the highest point of man's wit with the efficacy of nature; but rather give right honor to the heavenly maker of that maker, who, having made man to his own likeness, set him beyond and over all the works of that second nature. Which in nothing he showeth so much as in poetry, when with the force of a divine breath he bringeth things forth far surpassing her doings, with no small argument to the incredulous of that first accursed fall of Adam,—since our erected wit maketh us know what perfection is, and yet our infected will keepeth us from reaching unto it. But these arguments will by few be understood, and by fewer granted; thus much I hope will be given me, that the Greeks with some probability of reason gave him the name above all names of learning. . . .

This purifying of wit, this enriching of memory, enabling of judgment, and enlarging of conceit, which commonly we call learning, under what name soever it come forth or to what immediate end soever it be directed, the final end is to lead and draw us to as high a perfection as our degenerate souls, made worse by their clay lodgings, can be capable of. This, according to the inclination of man, bred many-formed impressions. For some that thought felicity principally to be gotten by knowledge, and no knowledge to be so high or heavenly as acquaintance with the stars, gave themselves to astronomy; others, persuading themselves to be demi-gods if they knew the causes of things, became natural and supernatural philosophers. Some an admirable delight drew to music, and some the certainty of demonstration to the mathematics; but all, one and other, having this scope:—to know, and by knowledge to lift up the mind from the dungeon of the body to the enjoying his own divine essence. But when by the balance of experience it was found that the astronomer, looking to the stars, might fall into a ditch, that the inquiring philosopher might be blind in himself, and the mathematician might draw forth a straight line with a crooked heart; then lo! did proof, the overruler of opinions, make manifest, that all these are but serving sciences, which, as they have each a private end in themselves, so yet are they all directed to the highest end of the mistress-knowledge, by the Greeks called *architectonike*, which stands, as I think, in the knowledge of a man's self, in the ethic and politic consideration, with the end of well-doing, and not of well-knowing only:—even as the saddler's next end is to make a good saddle, but his further end to serve a nobler faculty, which is horsemanship; so the horseman's to soldiery; and the soldier not only to have the skill, but to perform the practice of a soldier. So that the ending end of all earthly learning being virtuous action, those skills that most serve to bring forth that have a most just title to be princes over all the rest; wherein, if we can show, the poet is worthy to have it before any other competitors. . . .

The philosopher therefore and the historian are they which would win the goal,[16] the one by precept, the other by example; but both not having both, do both halt. For the philosopher, setting down with thorny arguments the bare rule, is so hard of utterance and so

---

[14] This sentence and the next five rest on the Platonic assumption that the essence of anything is the idea that lies behind it; hence a character in literature may be as "real" as an actual person. Do you agree?

[15] Of.

[16] I.e., win supremacy among the branches of learning. In the preceding paragraph Sidney has said that the end of learning is virtuous action; also he has shown (in a section here omitted) how philosophy and history are unable to achieve that end. In the following paragraphs he shows that virtuous action can best be taught by poetry.

misty to be conceived that one that hath no other guide but him shall wade in him till he be old, before he shall find sufficient cause to be honest. For his knowledge standeth so upon the abstract and general that happy is that man who may understand him, and more happy that can apply what he doth understand. On the other side, the historian, wanting the precept, is so tied, not to what should be but to what is, to the particular truth of things and not to the general reason of things, that his example draweth no necessary consequence, and therefore a less fruitful doctrine.

Now doth the peerless poet perform both; for whatsoever the philosopher saith should be done, he giveth a perfect picture of it in some one by whom he presupposeth it was done, so as he coupleth the general notion with the particular example. A perfect picture, I say; for he yieldeth to the powers of the mind an image of that whereof the philosopher bestoweth but a wordish description, which doth neither strike, pierce, nor possess the sight of the soul so much as that other doth. For as, in outward things, to a man that had never seen an elephant or a rhinoceros, who should tell him most exquisitely all their shapes, color, bigness, and particular marks; or of a gorgeous palace, an architector, with declaring the full beauties, might well make the hearer able to repeat, as it were by rote, all he had heard, yet should never satisfy his inward conceit with being witness to itself of a true lively knowledge; but the same man, as soon as he might see those beasts well painted, or that house well in model, should straightways grow, without need of any description, to a judicial comprehending of them: so no doubt the philosopher, with his learned definitions, be it of virtues or vices, matters of public policy or private government, replenisheth the memory with many infallible grounds of wisdom, which notwithstanding lie dark before the imaginative and judging power, if they be not illuminated or figured forth by the speaking picture of poesy. . . .

Certainly, even our Savior Christ could as well have given the moral commonplaces of uncharitableness and humbleness as the divine narration of Dives and Lazarus;[17] or of disobedience and mercy, as that heavenly discourse of the lost child and the gracious father;[18] but that his through-searching wisdom knew the estate of Dives burning in hell, and of Lazarus in Abraham's bosom, would more constantly, as it were, inhabit both the memory and judgment. Truly, for myself, meseems I see before mine eyes the lost child's disdainful prodigality, turned to envy a swine's dinner; which by the learned divines are thought not historical acts, but instructing parables.

For conclusion, I say the philosopher teacheth, but he teacheth obscurely, so as the learned only can understand him; that is to say, he teacheth them that are already taught. But the poet is the food for the tenderest stomachs; the poet is indeed the right popular philosopher. Whereof Aesop's tales give good proof; whose pretty allegories, stealing under the formal tales of beasts, make many, more beastly than beasts, begin to hear the sound of virtue from those dumb speakers.

But now may it be alleged that if this imagining of matters be so fit for the imagination, then must the historian needs surpass, who bringeth you images of true matters, such as indeed were done, and not such as fantastically or falsely may be suggested to have been done. Truly, Aristotle himself, in his *Discourse of Poesy*, plainly determineth this question, saying that poetry is . . . more philosophical and more studiously serious than history. His reason is, because poesy dealeth with . . . the universal consideration, and the history with . . . the particular. "Now," saith he, "the universal weighs what is fit to be said or done, either in likelihood or necessity—which the poesy considereth in his imposed names; and the particular only marketh whether Alcibiades did, or suffered, this or that": thus far Aristotle. Which reason of his, as all his, is most full of reason. . . .

But I that, before ever I durst aspire unto the dignity, am admitted into the company

[17] The parable of the rich man and the beggar in Luke 16: 19–31.
[18] The parable of the Prodigal Son in Luke 15: 11–32.

of the paper-blurrers, do find the very true cause of our wanting estimation is want of desert, taking upon us to be poets in despite of Pallas. Now wherein we want desert were a thankworthy labor to express; but if I knew, I should have mended myself. But as I never desired the title, so have I neglected the means to come by it; only, overmastered by some thoughts, I yielded an inky tribute unto them. Marry, they that delight in poesy itself should seek to know what they do and how they do; and especially look themselves in an unflattering glass of reason, if they be inclinable unto it. For poesy must not be drawn by the ears, it must be gently led, or rather it must lead; which was partly the cause that made the ancient learned affirm it was a divine gift, and no human skill, since all other knowledges lie ready for any that hath strength of wit; a poet no industry can make if his own genius be not carried into it. And therefore is it an old proverb: *Orator fit, poeta nascitur.* [19] Yet confess I always that, as the fertilest ground must be manured, so must the highest-flying wit have a Daedalus [20] to guide him. That Daedalus, they say, both in this and in other, hath three wings to bear itself up into the air of due commendation: that is, art, imitation, and exercise. But these, neither artificial rules nor imitative patterns, we much cumber ourselves withal. Exercise indeed we do, but that very fore-backwardly, for where we should exercise to know, we exercise as having known; and so is our brain delivered of much matter which never was begotten by knowledge. For there being two principal parts, matter to be expressed by words and words to express the matter, in neither we use art or imitation rightly. Our matter is *quodlibet* [21] indeed, though wrongly performing Ovid's verse,

Quicquid conabar dicere, versus erat,[22]

never marshaling it into any assured rank, that almost the readers cannot tell where to find themselves.

Chaucer, undoubtedly, did excellently in his *Troilus and Cressida;* of whom, truly, I know not whether to marvel more, either that he in that misty time could see so clearly, or that we in this clear age walk so stumblingly after him. Yet had he great wants, fit to be forgiven in so reverend antiquity. I account the *Mirror of Magistrates* [23] meetly furnished of beautiful parts; and in the Earl of Surrey's lyrics many things tasting of a noble birth, and worthy of a noble mind. The *Shepherd's Calendar* [24] hath much poetry in his eclogues indeed worthy the reading, if I be not deceived. That same framing of his style to an old rustic language I dare not allow, since neither Theocritus in Greek, Virgil in Latin, nor Sannazaro in Italian did affect it. Besides these, I do not remember to have seen but few (to speak boldly) printed that have poetical sinews in them. For proof whereof, let but most of the verses be put in prose, and then ask the meaning, and it will be found that one verse did but beget another, without ordering at the first what should be at the last; which becomes a confused mass of words, with a tinkling sound of rime, barely accompanied with reason.

Our tragedies and comedies, not without cause cried out against, observe rules neither of honest civility nor of skilful poetry, excepting *Gorboduc* [25] (again I say of those that I have seen); which notwithstanding as it is full of stately speeches and well-sounding phrases, climbing to the height of Seneca's [26] style, and as full of notable morality, which it doth most delightfully teach, and so obtain the very end of poesy; yet in truth it is very defectious in the circumstances, which grieveth me, because it might not remain as an exact model of all tragedies. For it is faulty both in place and time, the two necessary

[19] "An orator is made, a poet is born."
[20] Legendary Athenian who fashioned wings enabling him to fly.
[21] "What you will."
[22] "Whatever I tried to say turned out to be poetry."

[23] *A Mirror for Magistrates* (1559), chronicling the fall of eminent men, is remembered for its "Induction," by Thomas Sackville.
[24] Edmund Spenser's pastoral poems, dedicated to Sidney.
[25] One of the first English tragedies, written by Thomas Sackville and Thomas Norton, and first acted in 1561.
[26] Seneca, the Latin tragic dramatist, influenced Elizabethan tragedy.

companions of all corporal actions. For where the stage should always represent but one place, and the uttermost time presupposed in it should be, both by Aristotle's precept and common reason, but one day; there is both many days and many places inartificially imagined.

But if it be so in *Gorboduc,* how much more in all the rest? where you shall have Asia of the one side, and Afric of the other, and so many other under-kingdoms that the player, when he cometh in, must ever begin with telling where he is, or else the tale will not be conceived. Now ye shall have three ladies walk to gather flowers, and then we must believe the stage to be a garden. By and by we hear news of shipwreck in the same place, and then we are to blame if we accept it not for a rock. Upon the back of that comes out a hideous monster with fire and smoke, and then the miserable beholders are bound to take it for a cave. While in the mean time two armies fly in, represented with four swords and bucklers, and then what hard heart will not receive it for a pitched field?

Now of time they are much more liberal. For ordinary it is that two young princes fall in love; after many traverses she is got with child, delivered of a fair boy; he is lost, groweth a man, falleth in love, and is ready to get another child,—and all this in two hours' space; which how absurd it is in sense even sense may imagine, and art hath taught, and all ancient examples justified, and at this day the ordinary players in Italy will not err in. Yet will some bring in an example of *Eunuchus* in Terence, that containeth matter of two days, yet far short of twenty years. True it is, and so was it to be played in two days, and so fitted to the time it set forth. And though Plautus have in one place done amiss, let us hit with him, and not miss with him. But they will say, How then shall we set forth a story which containeth both many places and many times? And do they not know that a tragedy is tied to the laws of poesy, and not of history; not bound to follow the story, but having liberty either to feign a quite new matter, or to frame the

history to the most tragical conveniency? Again, many things may be told which cannot be showed,—if they know the difference betwixt reporting and representing. As for example, I may speak, though I am here, of Peru, and in speech digress from that to the description of Calicut; but in action I cannot represent it without Pacolet's horse.[27] And so was the manner the ancients took, by some *nuntius*[28] to recount things done in former time or other place.

Lastly, if they will represent a history, they must not, as Horace saith, begin *ab ovo,*[29] but they must come to the principal point of that one action which they will represent. By example this will be best expressed. I have a story of young Polydorus,[30] delivered for safety's sake, with great riches, by his father Priamus to Polymnestor, King of Thrace, in the Trojan war time. He, after some years, hearing the overthrow of Priamus, for to make the treasure his own murdereth the child; the body of the child is taken up by Hecuba; she, the same day, findeth a sleight to be revenged most cruelly of the tyrant. Where now would one of our tragedy-writers begin, but with the delivery of the child? Then should he sail over into Thrace, and so spend I know not how many years, and travel numbers of places. But where doth Euripides? Even with the finding of the body, leaving the rest to be told by the spirit of Polydorus. This needs no further to be enlarged; the dullest wit may conceive it.

But, besides these gross absurdities, how all their plays be neither right tragedies nor right comedies, mingling kings and clowns, not because the matter so carrieth it, but thrust in the clown by head and shoulders to play a part in majestical matters, with neither decency nor discretion; so as neither the admiration and commiseration, nor the right sportfulness, is by their mongrel tragi-comedy obtained. I know Apuleius[31] did somewhat

[27] An enchanted horse in an old romance.
[28] "Messenger."
[29] "From the very beginning."
[30] Character in *Hecuba,* by Euripides.
[31] Greek author of *Metamorphoses,* or *The Golden Ass.*

so, but that is a thing recounted with space of time, not represented in one moment; and I know the ancients have one or two examples of tragi-comedies, as Plautus hath *Amphytrio.* But, if we mark them well, we shall find that they never, or very daintily, match hornpipes and funerals. So falleth it out that, having indeed no right comedy in that comical part of our tragedy, we have nothing but scurrility, unworthy of any chaste ears, or some extreme show of doltishness, indeed fit to lift up a loud laughter, and nothing else; where the whole tract of a comedy should be full of delight, as the tragedy should be still maintained in a well-raised admiration.

But our comedians think there is no delight without laughter, which is very wrong; for though laughter may come with delight, yet cometh it not of delight, as though delight should be the cause of laughter; but well may one thing breed both together. Nay, rather in themselves they have, as it were, a kind of contrariety. For delight we scarcely do, but in things that have a conveniency to ourselves, or to the general nature; laughter almost ever cometh of things most disproportioned to ourselves and nature. Delight hath a joy in it either permanent or present; laughter hath only a scornful tickling. For example, we are ravished with delight to see a fair woman, and yet are far from being moved to laughter. We laugh at deformed creatures, wherein certainly we cannot delight. We delight in good chances; we laugh at mischances. We delight to hear the happiness of our friends and country, at which he were worthy to be laughed at that would laugh. We shall, contrarily, laugh sometimes to find a matter quite mistaken and go down the hill against the bias, in the mouth of some such men, as for the respect of them one shall be heartily sorry he cannot choose but laugh, and so is rather pained than delighted with laughter. Yet deny I not but that they may go well together. For as in Alexander's picture well set out we delight without laughter, and in twenty mad antics we laugh without delight; so in Hercules, painted, with his great beard and furious countenance, in woman's attire, spinning at

Omphale's commandment, it breedeth both delight and laughter; for the representing of so strange a power in love, procureth delight, and the scornfulness of the action stirreth laughter.

But I speak to this purpose, that all the end of the comical part be not upon such scornful matters as stir laughter only, but mixed with it that delightful teaching which is the end of poesy. And the great fault, even in that point of laughter, and forbidden plainly by Aristotle, is that they stir laughter in sinful things, which are rather execrable than ridiculous; or in miserable, which are rather to be pitied than scorned. For what is it to make folks gape at a wretched beggar or a beggarly clown, or, against law of hospitality, to jest at strangers because they speak not English so well as we do? what do we learn? since it is certain:

Nil habet infelix paupertas durius in se
Quam quod ridiculos homines facit.[32]

But rather a busy loving courtier; a heartless threatening Thraso;[33] a self-wise-seeming schoolmaster; a wry-transformed traveler: these if we saw walk in stage-names, which we play naturally, therein were delightful laughter and teaching delightfulness,—as in the other, the tragedies of Buchanan[34] do justly bring forth a divine admiration.

But I have lavished out too many words of this play-matter. I do it, because as they are excelling parts of poesy, so is there none so much used in England, and none can be more pitifully abused; which, like an unmannerly daughter, showing a bad education, causeth her mother Poesy's honesty to be called in question.

Other sorts of poetry almost have we none, but that lyrical kind of songs and sonnets, which, Lord if he gave us so good minds, how well it might be employed, and with how heavenly fruits both private and public, in singing the praises of the immortal beauty, the immortal goodness of that God who giveth us hands to write, and wits to conceive!—of

[32] "Poverty has no harder attribute than that it makes men ridiculous" (Juvenal).
[33] A boastful captain in Terence's *Eunuch.*
[34] A Scotch author of two Latin tragedies.

which we might well want words, but never matter; of which we could turn our eyes to nothing, but we should ever have new-budding occasions.

But truly, many of such writings as come under the banner of unresistible love, if I were a mistress, would never persuade me they were in love; so coldly they apply fiery speeches, as men that had rather read lovers' writings, and so caught up certain swelling phrases—which hang together like a man which once told me the wind was at northwest and by south, because he would be sure to name winds enough—than that in truth they feel those passions, which easily, as I think, may be bewrayed [35] by that same forcibleness, or *energia* (as the Greeks call it) of the writer. But let this be a sufficient, though short note, that we miss the right use of the material point of poesy.[36]

Now for the outside of it, which is words, or (as I may term it) diction, it is even well worse, so is that honey-flowing matron eloquence appareled, or rather disguised, in a courtesan-like painted affectation: one time with so far-fet words, that many seem monsters—but must seem strangers—to any poor Englishman; another time with coursing of a letter, as if they were bound to follow the method of a dictionary; another time with figures and flowers extremely winter-starved. . . .

So that since the ever praiseworthy poesy is full of virtue-breeding delightfulness, and void of no gift that ought to be in the noble name of learning; since the blames laid against it are either false or feeble; since the cause why it is not esteemed in England is the fault of poet-apes, not poets; since, lastly, our tongue is most fit to honor poesy, and to be honored by poesy; I conjure you all that have had the evil luck to read this ink-wasting toy of mine, even in the name of the Nine Muses, no more to scorn the sacred mysteries of poesy; no more to laugh

at the name of poets, as though they were next inheritors to fools; no more to jest at the reverend title of "a rimer"; but to believe, with Aristotle, that they were the ancient treasurers of the Grecians' divinity; to believe, with Bembus,[37] that they were first bringers-in of all civility; to believe, with Scaliger,[38] that no philosopher's precepts can sooner make you an honest man than the reading of Virgil; to believe, with Clauserus, the translator of Cornutus, that it pleased the heavenly deity by Hesiod and Homer, under the veil of fables, to give us all knowledge, logic, rhetoric, philosophy natural and moral, and *quid non?* [39] to believe, with me, that there are many mysteries contained in poetry which of purpose were written darkly, lest by profane wits it should be abused; to believe, with Landino,[40] that they are so beloved of the gods that whatsoever they write proceeds of a divine fury; lastly, to believe themselves, when they tell you they will make you immortal by their verses.

Thus doing, your name shall flourish in the printers' shops. Thus doing, you shall be of kin to many a poetical preface. Thus doing, you shall be most fair, most rich, most wise, most all; you shall dwell upon superlatives. Thus doing, though you be *libertino patre natus,*[41] you shall suddenly grow *Herculea proles,*[42]

> *Si quid mea carmina possunt.*[43]

Thus doing, your soul shall be placed with Dante's Beatrice or Virgil's Anchises.

But if—fie of such a but!—you be born so near the dull-making cataract of Nilus, that you cannot hear the planet-like music of poetry; if you have so earth-creeping a mind that it cannot lift itself up to look to the sky of poetry, or rather, by a certain rustical disdain, will become such a mome [44] as to be a Momus of poetry; then, though I will not wish unto you the ass's ears of Midas, nor to be driven by a poet's verses, as Bubonax [45]

---

[35] Expressed.

[36] Sidney here is speaking disparagingly of love poems; yet he wrote many fine ones.

[37] Noted Italian scholar.

[38] Italian scholar and literary critic.

[39] "What not?"

[40] Italian humanist.

[41] "The son of a freedman."

[42] "Herculean offspring."

[43] "If my songs are of any avail" (Virgil).

[44] Blockhead.

[45] Sidney probably meant Hipponax, the Greek poet.

was, to hang himself; nor to be rimed to death, as is said to be done in Ireland; yet thus much curse I must send you in the behalf of all poets:—that while you live you live in love, and never get favor for lacking skill of a sonnet; and when you die, your memory die from the earth for want of an epitaph.

(1595)

STUDY AIDS: 1. Since the treatise is an argument (i.e., the author is trying to prove something, namely, the value of poetry), try, as you study it, to isolate and identify the separate steps in Sidney's reasoning. What kind of evidence does he present in the several parts of the treatise?

2. Probably one reason Sidney's *Defense* was and still is so persuasive a statement is that, far from being a dry academic discussion, it represents the honest convictions of a man whose vigor and enthusiasm and good nature shine through to us. Pick out passages that reveal these personal qualities.

Edmund Spenser
(1552?–1599)

EDMUND SPENSER, CONSIDERED THE GREATEST NONDRAMATIC POET OF THE AGE OF Elizabeth, was born in London of middle-class parents. At the Merchant Taylors' School he came under the noted teacher, Richard Mulcaster. He continued his studies at Pembroke College, Cambridge, immersing himself in Aristotle and Plato, and reading widely in the Italian and French poets. Through Gabriel Harvey, a critic of note, he became acquainted with Sidney and his uncle, the Earl of Leicester, Elizabeth's favorite, and thus became eligible for a career at court.

In 1597 appeared his *Shepherd's Calendar,* dedicated to Sidney, whose hope for English poetry it seemed to fulfill. A series of twelve eclogues in the manner of classical and Renaissance poets, the *Calendar* includes native English scenes, customs, and names, and so marks the true beginning of the pastoral mode in English poetry. At this time, too, he expressed himself on affairs of court in political allegory. This pleased some, but not those in power; when preferment came, it was in the form of a secretaryship to Lord Grey, the new Lord Deputy of Ireland.

Spenser lived most of his remaining years in Ireland. In the midst of supporting Lord Grey's ruthless suppression of the Irish colonials, he found leisure to continue work on his masterpiece, *The Faerie Queene.* When Sir Walter Raleigh visited him in Kilcolman Castle, confiscated from the Irish and awarded to Spenser, he urged the poet to bring the poem to London. The two returned to the capital, and Spenser published the first three books of his poem. It immediately charmed readers, including Elizabeth, to whom it was dedicated, and she favored the author with a pension of fifty pounds. Somewhat disappointed, Spenser returned to Ireland, where he later married Elizabeth Boyle, celebrating his courtship in a sequence of sonnets, the *Amoretti,* and his marriage in the exquisite *Epithalamion.* A later trip to London enabled him to see three more books of *The Faerie Queene* through the press and to write for the wedding of friends the much admired *Prothalamion.* His final stay in Ireland was short, for when he arrived he found the country in revolt. With his family he fled Kilcolman Castle shortly before it was burned, and returned to London, where he took sick and suddenly died.

Some features of Spenser's art are not valued by our age as they were by his. The strain of ideality in his work, his fondness for allegory, and the archaic language he affected deter some readers from fully enjoying his verse. But the music of his lines is superb, as sensitive readers have always recognized. A model and an inspiration to poets for some three hundred years, Spenser is truly, as Charles Lamb said, a "poet's poet."

Epithalamion

Spenser wrote this beautiful song to celebrate his marriage to Elizabeth Boyle. Although concerned with a specific event at a definite time and place, the poem speaks for all bridal couples. The poet conceives of the poem as a mask (l. 26) or pageant; before his heightened consciousness pass the natural objects and creatures and the people, real and fanciful, of his world, and he addresses them directly but separately. Notice at all times who is being addressed.

Ye learnèd sisters, [1] which have oftentimes
Been to me aiding, others to adorn,
Whom ye thought worthy of your graceful
    rhymes,
That even the greatest did not greatly scorn
To hear their names sung in your simple
    lays,   5
But joyèd in their praise;
And when ye list your own mishaps to mourn,
Which death, or love, or fortune's wreck [2] did
    raise,
Your string could soon to sadder tenor turn,
And teach the woods and waters to lament 10
Your doleful dreariment.[3]
Now lay those sorrowful complaints aside,
And having all your heads with garland
    crowned,
Help me mine own love's praises to resound,
Nor let the same of any be envied: 15
So Orpheus [4] did for his own bride,
So I unto myself alone will sing,
The woods shall to me answer and my echo
    ring.

Early before the world's light-giving lamp,
His golden beam upon the hills doth spread, 20
Having dispersed the night's uncheerful damp,
Do ye awake, and with fresh lusty-head,

Go to the bower of my belovèd love,
My truest turtle dove,
Bid her awake; for Hymen [5] is awake,   25
And long since ready forth his mask to move,
With his bright tead [6] that flames with many
    a flake,
And many a bachelor [7] to wait on him,
In their fresh garments trim.
Bid her awake therefore and soon her
    dight,[8]   30
For lo the wishèd day is come at last,
That shall for all the pains and sorrows past,
Pay to her usury of long delight:
And whilst she doth her dight,
Do ye to her of joy and solace sing,   35
That all the woods may answer and your echo
    ring.

Bring with you all the nymphs that you can
    hear
Both of the rivers and the forests green:
And of the sea that neighbors to her near,[9]
All with gay garlands goodly well beseen.[10] 40
And let them also with them bring in hand,
Another gay garland
For my fair love of lilies and of roses,
Bound truelove-wise with a blue silk ribband.

[1] The nine muses.
[2] Violence.
[3] Affliction.
[4] Orpheus sang before Pluto in the underworld in order to win back his dead wife Eurydice.

[5] The god of marriage.
[6] Torch.
[7] Candidate for knighthood.
[8] Dress.
[9] Elizabeth Boyle's home was on the Irish coast.
[10] Adorned.

And let them make great store of bridal
   poses,   45
And let them eke bring store of other flowers
To deck the bridal bowers.
And let the ground whereas her foot shall
   tread,
For fear the stones her tender foot should
   wrong,
Be strewed with fragrant flowers all along, 50
And diaprèd [11] like the discolorèd mead.
Which done, do at her chamber door await,
For she will waken straight,
The whiles do ye this song unto her sing,
The woods shall to you answer and your echo
   ring.   55

Ye Nymphs of Mulla [12] which with careful
   heed,
The silver scaly trouts do tend full well,
And greedy pikes which use therein to feed,
(Those trouts and pikes all others do excel)
And ye likewise which keep the rushy lake, 60
Where none do fishes take,
Bind up the locks the which hang scattered
   light,
And in his waters which your mirror make,
Behold your faces as the crystal bright,
That when you come whereas my love doth
   lie,   65
No blemish she may spy.
And eke ye lightfoot maids which keep the
   deer,
That on the hoary mountain use to tower,[13]
And the wild wolves which seek them to
   devour,
With your steel darts do chase from coming
   near,   70
Be also present here,
To help to deck her and to help to sing,
That all the woods may answer and your echo
   ring.

Wake, now my love, awake: for it is time,
The rosy morn [14] long since left Tithones'
   bed,   75

All ready to her silver coach to climb,
And Phoebus 'gins to show his glorious head.
Hark how the cheerful birds do chant their
   lays
And carol of love's praise.
The merry lark her matins sings aloft,   80
The thrush replies, the mavis [15] descant [16]
   plays,
The ouzel [17] shrills, the ruddock [18] warbles
   soft,
So goodly all agree with sweet consent,
To this day's merriment.
Ah, my dear love, why do ye sleep thus
   long,   85
When meeter were that ye should now awake,
To await the coming of your joyous make,[19]
And hearken to the birds' love-learnèd song,
The dewy leaves among?
For they of joy and pleasance to you sing, 90
That all the woods them answer and their
   echo ring.

My love is now awake out of her dream,
And her fair eyes like stars that dimmèd
   were
With darksome cloud, now show their goodly
   beams
More bright than Hesperus [20] his head doth
   rear.   95
Come now ye damsels, daughters of delight,
Help quickly her to dight,
But first come ye fair hours which were begot
In Jove's sweet paradise, of day and night,
Which do the seasons of the year allot,   100
And all that ever in this world is fair
Do make and still repair.
And ye three handmaids [21] of the Cyprian
   queen,
The which do still adorn her beauty's pride,
Help to adorn my beautifulest bride: 105
And as ye her array, still throw between
Some graces to be seen,
And as ye use [22] to Venus, to her sing,

[11] Varied.
[12] A river in Ireland.
[13] Climb in a spiral.
[14] Aurora, goddess of the dawn, was the wife of
Tithonus.

[15] Song thrush.
[16] Accompanying melody.
[17] Blackbird.
[18] European robin.
[19] Mate.
[20] The evening star.
[21] The three Graces who served Aphrodite.
[22] Are accustomed to doing.

The whiles the woods shall answer and your
   echo ring.

Now is my love all ready forth to come,   110
Let all the virgins therefore well await,
And ye fresh boys that tend upon her groom
Prepare yourselves; for he is coming straight.
Set all your things in seemly good array
Fit for so joyful day,   115
The joyfulest day that ever sun did see.
Fair sun, show forth thy favorable ray,
And let thy lifeful [23] heat not fervent be
For fear of burning her sunshiny face,
Her beauty to disgrace.   120
O fairest Phoebus, father of the muse,
If ever I did honor thee aright,
Or sing the thing that mote [24] thy mind
   delight,
Do not thy servant's simple boon refuse,
But let this day let this one day be mine,   125
Let all the rest be thine.
Then I thy sovereign praises loud will sing,
That all the woods shall answer and their
   echo ring.

Hark how the minstrels 'gin to shrill aloud
Their merry music that resounds from far,   130
The pipe, the tabor,[25] and the trembling
   croud,[26]
That well agree withouten breach or jar.
But most of all the damsels do delight,
When they their timbrels smite,
And thereunto do dance and carol sweet,   135
That all the senses they do ravish quite,
The whiles the boys run up and down the
   street,
Crying aloud with strong confusèd noise,
As if it were one voice.
Hymen, iô Hymen, Hymen [27] they do
   shout,   140
That even to the heavens their shouting
   shrill
Doth reach, and all the firmament doth fill,
To which the people standing all about,
As in approvance do thereto applaud

And loud advance her laud,   145
And evermore they Hymen, Hymen sing,
That all the woods them answer and their
   echo ring.

Lo where she comes along with portly pace [28]
Like Phoebe [29] from her chamber of the east,
Arising forth to run her mighty race,   150
Clad all in white, that seems a virgin best.
So well it her beseems that ye would ween
Some angel she had been.
Her long loose yellow locks like golden wire,
Sprinkled with pearl, and pearling flowers
   atween,   155
Do like a golden mantle her attire,
And being crownèd with a garland green,
Seem like some maiden queen.
Her modest eyes abashèd to behold
So many gazers, as on her do stare,   160
Upon the lowly ground affixèd are.
Nor dare lift up her countenance too bold,
But blush to hear her praises sung so loud,
So far from being proud.
Nathless do ye still loud her praises sing.   165
That all the woods may answer and your
   echo ring.

Tell me ye merchants' daughters did ye see
So fair a creature in your town before,
So sweet, so lovely, and so mild as she,
Adorned with beauty's grace and virtue's
   store,   170
Her goodly eyes like sapphires shining bright,
Her forehead ivory white,
Her cheeks like apples which the sun hath
   rudded,
Her lips like cherries charming men to bite,
Her breast like to a bowl of cream
   uncrudded,[30]   175
Her paps like lilies budded,
Her snowy neck like to a marble tower,
And all her body like a palace fair,
Ascending up with many a stately stair,
To honor's seat and chastity's sweet bower.   180
Why stand ye still ye virgins in amaze,
Upon her so to gaze,
Whilst ye forget your former lay to sing,

[23] Life-giving, full of life.
[24] Might.
[25] Drum.
[26] An old stringed instrument.
[27] Refrain of a Latin nuptial song.

[28] Dignified step.
[29] Artemis, the moon goddess.
[30] Uncurdled.

To which the woods did answer and your
  echo ring?

But if ye saw that which no eyes can see, 185
The inward beauty of her lively sprite,
Garnished with heavenly gifts of high degree,
Much more then would ye wonder at that
  sight,
And stand astonished like to those which
  read [31]
Medusa's [32] mazeful head. 190
There dwells sweet love and constant
  chastity,
Unspotted faith and comely womanhood,
Regard of honor and mild modesty,
There virtue reigns as queen in royal throne,
And giveth laws alone. 195
The which the base affections do obey,
And yield their services unto her will,
No thought of thing uncomely ever may
Thereto approach to tempt her mind to ill.
Had ye once seen these her celestial
  treasures, 200
And unrevealèd pleasures,
Then would ye wonder and her praises sing,
That all the woods should answer and your
  echo ring.

Open the temple gates unto my love,
Open them wide that she may enter in, 205
And all the posts adorn as doth behoove,
And all the pillars deck with garlands trim,
For to receive this saint with honor due,
That cometh in to you.
With trembling steps and humble
  reverence, 210
She cometh in before the almighty's view:
Of her, ye virgins, learn obedience,
When so ye come into those holy places,
To humble your proud faces.
Bring her up to the high altar, that she
  may 215
The sacred ceremonies there partake,
The which do endless matrimony make:
And let the roaring organs loudly play
The praises of the Lord in lively notes,
The whiles with hollow throats 220

[31] Saw.
[32] The snaky head of the Gorgon turned observers
into stone.

The choristers the joyous anthem sing,
That all the woods may answer and their
  echo ring.

Behold, whilst she before the altar stands,
Hearing the holy priest that to her speaks,
And blesseth her with his two happy
  hands, 225
How the red roses flush up in her cheeks,
And the pure snow with goodly vermil [33] stain,
Like crimson dyed in grain: [34]
That even the angels, which continually
About the sacred altar do remain, 230
Forget their service and about her fly,
Oft peeping in her face, that seems more fair,
The more they on it stare.
But her sad [35] eyes, still fastened on the
  ground,
Are governèd with goodly modesty, 235
That suffers not one look to glance awry,
Which may let in a little thought unsound.
Why blush ye, love, to give to me your hand,
The pledge of all our band? [36]
Sing, ye sweet angels, Alleluia sing, 240
That all the woods may answer and your
  echo ring.

Now all is done; bring home the bride again,
Bring home the triumph of our victory,
Bring home with you the glory of her gain,
With joyance bring her and with jollity. 245
Never had man more joyful day than this,
Whom heaven would heap with bliss.
Make feast therefore now all this livelong
  day;
This day forever to me holy is;
Pour out the wine without restraint or
  stay, 250
Pour not by cups, but by the belly full,
Pour out to all that wull,[37]
And sprinkle all the posts and walls with
  wine,
That they may sweat, and drunken be withal.
Crown ye god Bacchus with a coronal, 255
And Hymen also crown with wreaths of vine;

[33] Crimson.
[34] A natural, not artificial dye.
[35] Serious.
[36] Bond.
[37] Wish.

And let the Graces dance unto the rest,
For they can do it best:
The whiles the maidens do their carol sing,
The which the woods shall answer and their
  echo ring.   260

Ring ye the bells, ye young men of the town,
And leave your wonted labors for this day:
This day is holy; do ye write it down,
That ye for ever it remember may.
This day the sun is in his chiefest height, 265
With Barnaby [38] the bright,
From whence declining daily by degrees,
He somewhat loseth of his heat and light,
When once the Crab [39] behind his back he
  sees.
But for this time it ill ordainèd was,   270
To choose the longest day in all the year,
And shortest night, when longest fitter were:
Yet never day so long, but late would pass.
Ring ye the bells, to make it wear away,
And bonfires make all day,   275
And dance about them, and about them sing:
That all the woods may answer and your
  echo ring.

Ah! when will this long weary day have end,
And lend me leave to come unto my love?
How slowly do the hours their numbers
  spend!   280
How slowly does sad time his feathers move!
Haste thee, O fairest planet, to thy home
Within the western foam:
Thy tired steeds long since have need of rest.
Long though it be, at last I see it gloom,   285
And the bright evening star with golden crest
Appear out of the east.
Fair child of beauty,[40] glorious lamp of love,
That all the host of heaven in ranks dost lead,
And guidest lovers through the night's
  dread,   290
How cheerfully thou lookest from above,
And seemst to laugh atween thy twinkling
  light,
As joying in the sight

[38] Spenser's wedding took place on St. Barnabas'
Day, June 11, the longest day of the year according
to the old style calendar.
[39] The zodiacal constellation of Cancer.
[40] Hesperus, the evening star.

Of these glad many, which for joy do sing,
That all the woods them answer and their
  echo ring.   295

Now cease, ye damsels, your delights forepast;
Enough is it that all the day was yours:
Now day is done, and night is nighing fast:
Now bring the bride into the bridal bowers.
Now night is come, now soon her disarray, 300
And in her bed her lay;
Lay her in lilies and in violets,
And silken curtains over her display,
And odored sheets and arras [41] coverlets.
Behold how goodly my fair love does lie 305
In proud humility!
Like unto Maia,[42] whenas Jove her took,
In Tempe, lying on the flowery grass,
'Twixt sleep and wake, after she weary was,
With bathing in the Acidalian brook.   310
Now it is night, ye damsels may be gone,
And leave my love alone,
And leave likewise your former lay to sing:
The woods no more shall answer nor your
  echo ring.

Now welcome night, thou night so long
  expected,   315
That long day's labor dost at last defray,
And all my cares, which cruel love collected,
Hast summed in one, and cancellèd for aye:
Spread thy broad wing over my love and me,
That no man may us see,   320
And in thy sable mantle us enwrap,
From fear of peril and foul horror free.
Let no false treason seek us to entrap,
Nor any dread disquiet once annoy
The safety of our joy: 325
But let the night be calm and quietsome,
Without tempestuous storms or sad affray:
Like as when Jove with fair Alcmena lay,
When he begot the great Tirynthian groom: [43]
Or like as when he with thyself did lie,   330
And begot majesty.
And let the maids and youngmen cease to
  sing:
Nor let the woods them answer nor their
  echo ring.

[41] Tapestry woven in Arras, France.
[42] One of the Pleiades.
[43] Hercules.

Let no lamenting cries nor doleful tears
Be heard all night within nor yet without: 335
Nor let false whispers, breeding hidden
    fears,
Break gentle sleep with misconceivèd doubt.
Let no deluding dreams, nor dreadful sights
Make sudden sad affrights;
Nor let housefires, nor lightning's helpless
    harms, 340
Nor let the pook,[44] nor other evil sprites,
Nor let mischievous witches with their
    charms,
Nor let hobgoblins, names whose sense we see
    not,
Fray us with things that be not.
Let not the screech owl, nor the stork be
    heard: 345
Nor the night raven that still deadly yells,
Nor damnèd ghosts called up with mighty
    spells,
Nor grisly vultures make us once affeared:
Nor let the unpleasant choir of frogs still
    croaking
Make us to wish their choking. 350
Let none of these their dreary accents sing;
Nor let the woods them answer nor their
    echo ring.

But let still silence true night watches keep,
That sacred peace may in assurance reign,
And timely sleep, when it is time to sleep, 355
May pour his limbs forth on your pleasant
    plain,
The whiles an hundred little wingèd loves,
Like divers feathered doves,
Shall fly and flutter round about your bed,
And in the secret dark, that none reproves, 360
Their pretty stealths shall work, and snares
    shall spread
To filch away sweet snatches of delight,
Concealed through covert night.
Ye sons of Venus, play your sports at will,
For greedy pleasure, careless of your toys, 365
Thinks more upon her paradise of joys,
Than what ye do, albeit good or ill.
All night therefore attend your merry play,
For it will soon be day:
Now none doth hinder you, that say or
    sing, 370

[44] An evil spirit in Irish folklore.

Nor will the woods now answer nor your
    echo ring.

Who is the same, which at my window peeps?
Or whose is that fair face, that shines so
    bright?
Is it not Cynthia,[45] she that never sleeps,
But walks about high heaven all the
    night? 375
O fairest goddess, do thou not envy
My love with me to spy:
For thou likewise didst love, though now
    unthought,
And for a fleece of wool, which privily,
The Latmian shepherd [46] once unto thee
    brought, 380
His pleasures with thee wrought.
Therefore to us be favorable now;
And since of women's labors thou hast charge,
And generation goodly dost enlarge,
Incline thy will to effect our wishful vow, 385
And the chaste womb inform with timely seed,
That may our comfort breed:
Till which we cease our hopeful hap [47] to sing,
Nor let the woods us answer nor our echo
    ring.

And thou great Juno, which with awful
    might 390
The laws of wedlock still dost patronize,
And the religion of the faith first plight
With sacred rites hast taught to solemnize:
And eke for comfort often callèd art
Of women in their smart, 395
Eternally bind thou this lovely band,
And all thy blessings unto us impart.
And thou glad genius, in whose gentle hand,
The bridal bower and genial [48] bed remain,
Without blemish or stain, 400
And the sweet pleasures of their loves' delight
With secret aid dost succor and supply,
Till they bring forth the fruitful progeny,
Send us the timely fruit of this same night.
And thou fair Hebe,[49] and thou Hymen
    free, 405

[45] The moon.
[46] Endymion, shepherd boy of Mt. Latmos, loved
by the moon goddess.
[47] Good fortune.
[48] Nuptial.
[49] Goddess of Youth.

Grant that it may so be.
Til which we cease your future praise to sing,
Nor any woods shall answer nor your echo
　ring.

And ye high heavens, the temple of the gods,
In which a thousand torches flaming
　bright　　　　　　　　　　　　　　410
Do burn, that to us wretched earthly clods,
In dreadful darkness lend desirèd light;
And all ye powers which in the same remain,
More than we men can fain,[50]
Pour out your blessing on us plenteously,　415
And happy influence upon us rain,
That we may raise a large posterity,
Which from the earth, which they may long
　possess,
With lasting happiness,
Up to your haughty palaces may mount,　420
And for the guerdon [51] of their glorious merit
May heavenly tabernacles there inherit,
Of blessed saints for to increase the count.
So let us rest, sweet love, in hope of this,
And cease till then our timely joys to sing,　425
The woods no more us answer nor our echo
　ring.

Song made in lieu of many ornaments,
With which my love should duly have been
　decked,
Which cutting off through hasty accidents,[52]
Ye would not stay your due time to expect,　430
But promised both to recompense,
Be unto her a goodly ornament,
And for short time an endless monument.
(1595)

STUDY AIDS: 1. What time span does the
poem cover? What details indicate time?
　2. Spenser could have expressed his joy in a
sustained lyric addressed to no one in particular;
instead he chose to address different persons,
creatures, and objects directly. What is the effect
of this procedure?
　3. The harmonious relation between the poet-
bridegroom and his love leads him to see all of
creation as a harmonious whole. The poem might
be said to represent a synthesis of items sometimes regarded as antithetical: Man and nature,
Christian and pagan, physical love and spiritual
love, the real and the ideal. Try to isolate these
elements in the poem and see how the poet
reconciles them.

Prothalamion [1]

Calm was the day, and through the trembling
　air
Sweet-breathing Zephyrus did softly play,
A gentle spirit, that lightly did delay [2]
Hot Titan's [3] beams, which then did glister
　fair;

When I (whom sullen care,　　　　　　5
Through discontent of my long fruitless stay
In princes' court, and expectation vain
Of idle hopes, which still do fly away
Like empty shadows, did afflict my brain)
Walked forth to ease my pain　　　　10
Along the shore of silver-streaming Thames; [4]
Whose rutty [5] bank, the which his river hems,
Was painted all with variable flowers,
And all the meads adorned with dainty gems,
Fit to deck maidens' bowers,　　　　　15
And crown their paramours
Against the bridal day, which is not long:
　Sweet Thames, run softly, till I end my
　　song.

[50] Imagine.
[51] Reward.
[52] This line suggests the wedding date may have
been advanced.

---

[1] "A Spousal Verse made by Edmund Spenser
in Honor of the Double Marriage of the Two
Honorable and Virtuous Ladies, the Lady Elizabeth
and the Lady Katherine Somerset, Daughters to the
Right Honorable the Earl of Worcester and Es-
poused to the Two Worthy Gentlemen M. Henry
Gilford and M. William Peter, Esquires."
[2] Allay.
[3] The Sun's.

[4] The Thames (pronounced *Temms*) River in
London.
[5] Rooty.

There, in a meadow by the river's side,
A flock of nymphs I chancèd to espy,   20
All lovely daughters of the flood thereby,
With goodly greenish locks all loose untied,
As each had been a bride;
And each one had a little wicker basket
Made of fine twigs, entrailèd curiously,   25
In which they gathered flowers to fill their
      flasket,
And with fine fingers cropped full feateously [6]
The tender stalks on high.[7]
Of every sort which in that meadow grew
They gathered some: the violet, pallid blue,   30
The little daisy, that at evening closes,
The virgin lily, and the primrose true,
With store of vermeil roses,
To deck their bridegrooms' posies
Against the bridal day, which was not
      long: 35
   Sweet Thames, run softly, till I end my
      song.

With that I saw two swans of goodly hue
Come softly swimming down along the lee;
Two fairer birds I yet did never see;
The snow which doth the top of Pindus [8]
      strew   40
Did never whiter shew,
Nor Jove himself, when he a swan would be
For love of Leda,[9] whiter did appear;
Yet Leda was, they say, as white as he,
Yet not so white as these, nor nothing near.   45
So purely white they were,
That even the gentle stream, the which them
      bare,
Seemed foul to them, and bade his billows
      spare
To wet their silken feathers, lest they might
Soil their fair plumes with water not so
      fair,   50
And mar their beauties bright,
That shone as heaven's light
Against their bridal day, which was not
      long:
   Sweet Thames, run softly, till I end my
      song.

Eftsoons [10] the nymphs, which now had
      flowers their fill,   55
Ran all in haste to see that silver brood,
As they came floating on the crystal flood;
Whom when they saw, they stood amazèd
      still,
Their wondering eyes to fill;
Them seemed they never saw a sight so
      fair,   60
Of fowls so lovely that they sure did deem
Them heavenly born, or to be that same pair
Which through the sky draw Venus' silver
      team.
For sure they did not seem
To be begot of any earthly seed,   65
But rather angels, or of angels' breed;
Yet were they bred of Sommers-Heat,[11] they
      say,
In sweetest season, when each flower and
      weed
The earth did fresh array;
So fresh they seemed as day,   70
Even as their bridal day, which was not long:
   Sweet Thames, run softly, till I end my
      song.

Then forth they all out of their baskets drew
Great store of flowers, the honor of the field,
That to the sense did fragrant odors yield,   75
All which upon those goodly birds they threw,
And all the waves did strew,
That like old Peneus' [12] waters they did seem
When down along by pleasant Tempe's shore,
Scattered with flowers, through Thessaly they
      stream,   80
That they appear, through lilies' plenteous
      store,
Like a bride's chamber-floor.
Two of those nymphs meanwhile two garlands
      bound,
Of freshest flowers which in that mead they
      found,
The which presenting all in trim array,   85
Their snowy foreheads therewithal they
      crowned;
Whilst one did sing this lay

---

[6] Skillfully.
[7] In haste.
[8] A mountain in Greece.
[9] Loved by Jupiter in the form of a swan.

[10] Immediately.
[11] A pun on Somerset, the bride's family name.
[12] River in Greece, that traverses the beautiful vale
of Tempe.

Prepared against that day,
Against their bridal day, which was not long:
 Sweet Thames, run softly, till I end my
  song.   90

"Ye gentle birds, the world's fair ornament
And heaven's glory, whom this happy hour
Doth lead unto your lovers' blissful bower,
Joy may you have, and gentle heart's content
Of your love's couplement;   95
And let fair Venus, that is queen of love,
With her heart-quelling son upon you smile,
Whose smile, they say, hath virtue to remove
All love's dislike, and friendship's faulty guile
For ever to assoil.[13]   100
Let endless peace your steadfast hearts accord,
And blessèd plenty wait upon your board;
And let your bed with pleasures chaste
 abound,
That fruitful issue may to you afford
Which may your foes confound,   105
And make your joys redound [14]
Upon your bridal day, which is not long:
 Sweet Thames, run softly, till I end my
  song."

So ended she, and all the rest around
To her redoubled that her undersong, 110
Which said, their bridal day should not be
 long;
And gentle echo from the neighbor ground
Their accents did resound.
So forth those joyous birds did pass along
Adown the lee [15] that to them murmured
 low,   115
As he would speak, but that he lacked a
 a tongue,
Yet did by signs his glad affection show,
Making his stream run slow.
And all the fowl which in his flood did dwell
'Gan flock about these twain that did excel 120
The rest so far as Cynthia [16] doth shend [17]
The lesser stars. So they, enrangèd well,
Did on those two attend,

---

[13] Dispel.
[14] Overflow.
[15] Stream.
[16] The moon goddess. Possibly here, as elsewhere,
a reference to Queen Elizabeth.
[17] Put to shame.

And their best service lend
Against their wedding-day, which was not
 long: 125
 Sweet Thames, run softly, till I end my
  song.

At length they all to merry London came,
To merry London, my most kindly nurse,
That to me gave this life's first native source,
Though from another place I take my
 name,   130
An house of ancient fame.
There when they came, whereas [18] those
 bricky towers,[19]
The which on Thames' broad agèd back do
 ride,
Where now the studious lawyers have their
 bowers,
There whilom wont the Templar Knights to
 bide,   135
Till they decayed through pride.
Next whereunto there stands a stately place,
Where oft I gainèd gifts and goodly grace
Of that great lord [20] which therein wont to
 dwell,
Whose want too well now feels my friendless
 case: 140
But ah! here fits not well
Old woes, but joys, to tell
Against the bridal day, which is not long:
 Sweet Thames, run softly, till I end my
  song.

Yet therein now doth lodge a noble peer,[21] 145
Great England's glory, and the world's wide
 wonder,
Whose dreadful name late through all Spain
 did thunder,[22]
And Hercules' two pillars standing near
Did make to quake and fear.
Fair branch of honor, flower of chivalry, 150
That fillest England with thy triumphs' fame,
Joy have thou of thy noble victory,

---

[18] Where.
[19] The Inner and Middle Temples near the
Thames, once inhabited by the Knights Templars
and later by law students.
[20] The Earl of Leicester.
[21] The Earl of Essex.
[22] After an English naval victory, Raleigh and
Essex occupied Cadiz, in Spain.

And endless happiness of thine own name
That promiseth the same;
That through thy prowess and victorious
    arms,   155
Thy country may be freed from foreign harms,
And great Eliza's glorious name may ring
Through all the world, filled with thy wide
    alarms,
Which some brave Muse may sing
To ages following   160
Upon the bridal day, which is not long:
  Sweet Thames, run softly, till I end my
    song.

From those high towers, this noble lord
    issuing,
Like radiant Hesper when his golden hair
In the ocean billows he hath bathèd fair, 165
Descended to the river's open viewing,
With a great train ensuing.
Above the rest were goodly to be seen
Two gentle knights [23] of lovely face and
    feature,
Beseeming well the bower of any queen, 170
With gifts of wit and ornaments of nature
Fit for so goodly stature,
That like the twins [24] of Jove they seemed in
    sight,

Which deck the baldrick of the heavens
    bright.
They two, forth pacing to the river's side, 175
Received those two fair brides, their loves'
    delight;
Which, at the appointed tide,
Each one did make his bride
Against their bridal day, which is not long:
  Sweet Thames, run softly, till I end my
    song.   180
(1596)

STUDY AIDS: 1. Spenser has inserted some autobiographical statements in this poem. What are they? Are they appropriate in a poem celebrating the weddings of others?

2. Notice the narrative line in the poem; action unfolds as in a pageant, the swans symbolizing the brides, the nymphs their attendants.

3. If you read both the *Epithalamion* and *Prothalamion* you will probably prefer one to the other. Try to justify your preference.

4. The poem is interesting technically. Notice the use of short lines and the use of refrain. What is the RHYME SCHEME of the stanzas? Is it the same in each stanza? How does the poem compare with the *Epithalamion* on these technical points?

Michael Drayton
(1563–1631)

DRAYTON DEVELOPED HIS POETIC SKILLS IN THE LATE YEARS OF ELIZABETH'S REIGN AND continued to exercise them until his death at the age of sixty-eight. He knew the leading poets of the day, admired and imitated Spenser, and tried his hand at a variety of literary forms. A skillful sonneteer, he also wrote much patriotic verse that was greatly admired in his day. Even today the trumpet blasts of his "Ballad of Agincourt" can stir the blood.

Ode XII

To the Cambro-Britons [1] and Their Harp,
His Ballad of Agincourt

    After William of Normandy conquered England in 1066 and established a state on both sides of the English Channel, England and France disputed for control of the feudal vassals in

[23] The two bridegrooms.
[24] Castor and Pollux.

[1] The Welsh.

A fruteful/

and pleasaunt worke of the
beste state of a publyqne weale, and
of the newe yle called Utopia: written
in Latine by Syr Thomas More
knyght, and translated into Englyshe
by Raphe Robynson Citizein and
Goldsmythe of London, at the
procurement, and earnest request of George Tadlowe
Citezein & Haberdassher
of the same Citie.
(∴)

¶Imprinted at London
by Abraham Vele, dwelling in Pauls
churchyarde at the sygne of
the Lambe. Anno
1551.

By permission of The Macmillan Company.

Title page of a 1551 edition of More's *Utopia*.

Queen Elizabeth, a contemporary
portrait.

Folio and quarto editions of Shakespeare, together with a modern pocket edition.

northern France. The rivalry was intense from 1337 to 1453, the period of the Hundred Years' War. Drayton's ode celebrates the decisive British victory at Agincourt in 1415, an event also treated by Shakespeare in *Henry V*.

Fair stood the wind for France,
When we our sails advance, [2]
Nor now to prove our chance [3]
  Longer will tarry;
But putting to the main,   5
At Caux, the mouth of Seine,
With all his martial train
  Landed King Harry. [4]

And taking many a fort,
Furnished in warlike sort,   10
Marcheth toward Agincourt [5]
  In happy hour;
Skirmishing, day by day,
With those that stopped his way,
Where the French general lay   15
  With all his power.

Which, [6] in his height of pride,
King Henry to deride,
His ransom to provide,
  To the King sending;   20
Which [7] he [8] neglects the while,
As from a nation vile,
Yet, with an angry smile,
  Their fall portending.

And turning to his men,   25
Quoth our brave Henry then:
"Though they to one be ten [9]
  Be not amazèd! [10]
Yet have we well begun;
Battles so bravely won   30
Have ever to the sun
  By fame been raisèd!

"And for myself," quoth he,
"This my full rest [11] shall be:
England ne'er mourn for me,   35
  Nor more esteem me!
Victor I will remain,
Or on this earth lie slain;
Never shall she sustain
  Loss to redeem me!   40
"Poitiers [12] and Cressy [13] tell,
When most their pride did swell,
Under our swords they fell.
  No less our skill is,
Than when our grandsire great, [14]   45
Claiming the regal seat,
By many a warlike feat
  Lopped the French lilies." [15]

The Duke of York so dread
The eager vanward [16] led;   50
With the main, [17] Henry sped
  Amongst his henchmen.
Exeter had the rear,
A braver man not there!
O Lord, how hot they were   55
  On the false Frenchmen!

They now to fight are gone,
Armor on armor shone,
Drum now to drum did groan;
  To hear, was wonder;   60
That, with the cries they make,
The very earth did shake;
Trumpet to trumpet spake;
  Thunder to thunder.

Well it thine age became,   65
O noble Erpingham,

[2] Hoist.
[3] Try our luck.
[4] Henry V.
[5] Drayton Anglicizes the name, as the rhyme shows.
[6] Who, i.e., the French general.
[7] The French general's demand for ransom.
[8] King Henry.
[9] Actually the British were outnumbered some four to one.
[10] Confused or panicky.

[11] Resolve.
[12] The English defeated the French at Poitiers in 1356.
[13] The French Crécy. The English were also victorious at Crécy (1346).
[14] Henry's great grandfather, Edward III.
[15] The fleurs-de-lys, royal emblem of old French kings.
[16] Vanguard.
[17] Army.

Which didst the signal aim
   To our hid forces!
When from a meadow by,
Like a storm suddenly,   70
The English archery
   Stuck the French horses.[18]

With Spanish yew [19] so strong,
Arrows a cloth-yard long,
That like to serpents stung,   75
   Piercing the weather.[20]
None from his fellow starts;
But, playing manly parts,
And like true English hearts,
   Stuck close together.   80

When down their bows they threw,
And forth their bilboes [21] drew,
And on the French they flew,
   Not one was tardy.
Arms were from shoulders sent,   85
Scalps to the teeth were rent,
Down the French peasants went;
   Our men were hardy.

This while our noble King,
His broad sword brandishing,   90
Down the French host did ding,[22]
   As to o'erwhelm it;
And many a deep wound lent,
His arms with blood besprent,
And many a cruel dent   95
   Bruisèd his helmet.

Gloucester, that duke so good,
Next of the royal blood,

For famous England stood,
   With his brave brother.[23]   100
Clarence, in steel so bright,
Though but a maiden knight,
Yet in that furious fight
   Scarce such another!

Warwick in blood did wade,   105
Oxford, the foe invade,
And cruel slaughter made,
   Still as they ran up.
Suffolk his axe did ply;
Beaumont and Willoughby   110
Bare them right doughtily,
   Ferrers, and Fanhope.

Upon Saint Crispin's day [24]
Fought was this noble fray;
Which fame did not delay   115
   To England to carry.
O when shall English men
With such acts fill a pen?
Or England breed again
   Such a King Harry?   120
(1606)

STUDY AIDS: 1. Try to determine what the following features of the poem contribute to its stirring, martial atmosphere: (a) the use of proper names, including the Anglicized French names; (b) King Henry's address to his troops; (c) repetitions in st. 8; (d) understatements in st. 11; (e) the rhyme scheme.

2. METER is important here. Mark and read aloud several stanzas as IAMBIC TRIMETER; then read some as DACTYLIC DIMETER (with perhaps a secondary accent in the second foot). Which SCANSION better suits the spirit of the poem?

Since There's No Help, Come, Let Us Kiss and Part

Since there's no help, come, let us kiss and
   part.
Nay, I have done; you get no more of me.
And I am glad, yea, glad with all my heart
That thus so cleanly I myself can free.

Shake hands for ever; cancel all our vows; 5
And when we meet at any time again,
Be it not seen in either of our brows
That we one jot of former love retain.
Now at the last gasp of Love's latest breath,

[18] Cavalry.
[19] At Crécy, Poitiers, and Agincourt the English long bow, made of the wood of the yew tree, turned the tide of battle in favor of the English.
[20] Shooting straight, and not allowing for wind.

[21] Swords.
[22] Strike.
[23] King Henry.
[24] October 25, 1415.

When, his pulse failing, Passion speechless
  lies,   10
When Faith is kneeling by his bed of death,
And Innocence is closing up his eyes—
  Now, if thou wouldst, when all have given
    him over,
  From death to life thou might'st him yet
    recover.
(1619)

STUDY AIDS: 1. The tone of the poem changes abruptly at a certain point in the poem. Where does it change? Characterize the two tones and show how the following features contribute to them: (a) length of rhetorical units; (b) diction; (c) figurative language.

2. How does the couplet function in this sonnet? Why are the FEMININE RHYMES appropriate here?

Christopher Marlowe
(1564–1593)

MARLOWE IS ONE OF THE MOST EXCITING FIGURES OF HIS AGE. AFTER TAKING A DEGREE AT Cambridge he joined a group of London playwrights known as the "university wits" and wrote in quick succession several plays that strongly influenced the new drama. In each of his major plays—*Tamburlaine, Dr. Faustus, The Jew of Malta, Edward II*—a central character of great vitality dominates the action, speaking in blank verse the splendid rhetoric that Ben Jonson characterized as "Marlowe's mighty line." A vigorous, colorful figure, who lived intensely and died violently, Marlowe is also remembered for the erotic narrative poem, *Hero and Leander,* and for the lyric here included.

The Passionate Shepherd to His Love

This poem is a pastoral lyric. Because many Elizabethan poets, even the courtly sophisticates, recognized a value in the simple life (the "quiet" as opposed to the "aspiring" mind), they borrowed forms and attitudes from such classical poets as Theocritus and Virgil, who had celebrated the joys of country living. This idealization of rural life, known as pastoralism, became a popular literary convention, used in different ways by writers of plays (Shakespeare's *As You Like It*), prose romances (Sidney's *Arcadia*), and elegies (Milton's *Lycidas*). The form and movement of Marlowe's charming lyric are appropriate to the kind of life pictured in the poet's invitation.

Come live with me, and be my love;
And we will all the pleasures prove
That hills and valleys, dales and fields,
Woods, or steepy mountain yields.

And we will sit upon the rocks,   5
Seeing the shepherds feed their flocks
By shallow rivers, to whose falls
Melodious birds sing madrigals.

And I will make thee beds of roses,
And a thousand fragrant posies;   10
A cap of flowers, and a kirtle
Embroidered all with leaves of myrtle;

A gown made of the finest wool
Which from our pretty lambs we pull;
Fair-lined slippers for the cold,   15
With buckles of the purest gold;

A belt of straw and ivy-buds,
With coral clasps and amber studs;
And if these pleasures may thee move,
Come live with me, and be my love.   20

The shepherd-swains shall dance and sing
For thy delight each May morning;
If these delights thy mind may move,
Then live with me, and be my love.
                                        (1599)

Sir Walter Raleigh
(1552?–1618)

LIKE SIDNEY, WALTER RALEIGH EMBODIES THE RENAISSANCE IDEAL OF VERSATILITY.
Voyaging to the New World, he claimed Virginia for the Queen; he was present at the
defeat of the Spanish Armada; and in search of Eldorado, he explored the Orinoco River.
He was a statesman and a favorite courtier of Elizabeth until he fell from favor and was
imprisoned. Man of letters as well as adventurer, Raleigh wrote prose accounts of his travels
and began an ambitious *History of the World.* He was also a skillful poet, whose direct
verse usually avoids the conventional modes of the day.

The Nymph's Reply to the Shepherd

Marlowe's popular poem, *The Passionate Shepherd to His Love,* inspired several poetic replies,
of which Raleigh's is the best known.

If all the world and love were young,
And truth in every shepherd's tongue,
These pretty pleasures might me move
To live with thee and be thy love.

Time drives the flocks from field to fold,   5
When rivers rage and rocks grow cold,
And Philomel becometh dumb;
The rest complains of cares to come.

The flowers do fade, and wanton fields
To wayward winter reckoning yields;   10
A honey tongue, a heart of gall,
Is fancy's spring, but sorrow's fall.

Thy gowns, thy shoes, thy beds of roses,
Thy cap, thy kirtle, and thy posies
Soon break, soon wither, soon forgotten,   15
In folly ripe, in reason rotten.

Thy belt of straw and ivy buds,
Thy coral clasps and amber studs,
All these in me no means can move
To come to thee and be thy love.   20

But could youth last and love still breed,
Had joys no date nor age no need,
Then these delights my mind might move
To live with thee and be thy love.
                                        (1599)

STUDY AIDS: Raleigh's poem, so similar to Marlowe's, is also subtly different, the
difference in general being one of TONE. The
tone of Raleigh's poem is one of cool rationality.
Note the features of the poem that contribute to
its tone—e.g., the form of ll. 11, 12, 16, and the
pace or movement of the verse, especially in
st. 4.

To His Son

Three things there be that prosper all apace
And flourish, while they are asunder far;
But on a day they meet all in a place,
And when they meet, they one another mar.
And they be these: the wood, the weed, the
    wag.   5
The wood is that that makes the gallows tree;
The weed is that that strings the hangman's
    bag;

The wag, my pretty knave, betokens thee.
Now mark, dear boy: while these assemble
    not,
Green springs the tree, hemp grows, the wag
    is wild;   10
But when they meet, it makes the timber rot,
It frets the halter, and it chokes the child.
    God bless the child!
(*ca.* 1600)

Verses Found in His Bible in the Gate-House at Westminster

Tradition says that Raleigh wrote this poem the night before his execution.

Even such is time, that takes in trust
Our youth, our joys, our all we have,
And pays us but with earth and dust;
Who, in the dark and silent grave,
When we have wandered all our ways,   5

Shuts up the story of our days;
But from this earth, this grave, this dust,
My God shall raise me up, I trust!
(1618)

William Shakespeare
(1564–1616)

It is strange that we know so little about the life of England's greatest poet. He was a popular dramatist in his day, his excellence was recognized almost immediately, and since the late eighteenth century he has been all but idolized. The known facts of his life are few, however, in spite of the diligent efforts of generations of scholars to add to them. In a way the result of our relative ignorance has been a happy one, for our attention has necessarily been focused on the plays and poems themselves, which is perhaps the way Shakespeare would have wanted it.

William Shakespeare, the eldest son of Mary Arden and John Shakespeare, a glovemaker and alderman, was born on or about April 23, 1564, in Stratford-on-Avon, Warwickshire, in the heart of England. He must have attended the town's excellent grammar school, but this was probably the extent of his formal schooling. In 1582 he married Anne Hathaway, of the nearby village of Shottery, and the following year a daughter, Susanna, was born. Hamnet and Judith, twins, were born in 1585. It is thought that he left Stratford for London about 1587, but the first record of his life there is dated 1592;

although it seems likely that during these years he was in some way connected with drama and the theater, nothing is known for certain. He published two narrative poems, *Venus and Adonis* (1593) and *The Rape of Lucrece* (1594), and was a member of the Lord Chamberlain's Company of Players. A contemporary record in 1598 lists twelve plays by Shakespeare. He must have been successful by this time, for in 1597 he bought New Place, probably the largest house in Stratford. His principal dramatic activity was writing plays, but he was also part owner of the Globe theater and apparently he acted in some of his plays. When Queen Elizabeth died in 1603, Shakespeare's company came under the patronage of her successor, James I, and was known as the King's Men. About 1610 Shakespeare retired to Stratford, a wealthy man. He died April 23, 1616, and was buried in the chancel of the parish church in Stratford.

Shakespeare's 37 plays (written from *ca.* 1590 to *ca.* 1610) are of several types. He began with comedy (*The Comedy of Errors, Two Gentlemen of Verona, Love's Labor's Lost*), a form that he soon brought to perfection in *A Midsummer Night's Dream, As You Like It,* and *Twelfth Night.* His history plays include *Richard II, Henry IV,* Parts I and II, *Henry V,* and *Julius Caesar. Romeo and Juliet* was an early venture in tragedy, but the great tragedies came later—*Hamlet, Othello, King Lear, Macbeth,* and *Antony and Cleopatra.* The notable plays of his last period, known as tragicomedies, include *Cymbeline, The Winter's Tale,* and *The Tempest.* All of his plays, except two he wrote in collaboration, were first published together in 1623 in a large, elaborate format known as the First Folio.

It is an exciting experience to read Shakespeare for the first time and to discover, as one inevitably does, that in awarding him a position of supreme eminence the world has not been wrong. Not all readers would agree as to the secret of his greatness; some would find it in the variety and depth of his characters, some in his superb poetry, some in his astonishing insight into human nature. All would agree, however, that he possesses a literary magic that is uniquely his. Shakespeare was not an innovator; his greatness lies not in his inventing new forms and methods, for he always worked within established modes. Rather, his genius is seen in his ability to take the usual and accepted, and to transcend it. Seen best in the plays, perhaps, this power is also clearly demonstrated in his sonnets, some of the best of which are here included.

Sonnets

Shakespeare's 154 sonnets were probably written between 1593 and 1596, at the height of the Elizabethan vogue for sonneteering, but they were not published until 1609. Perhaps no other work of comparable scope in all English literature has provoked so much comment as these sonnets. Much of it has been biographical speculation. Since many readers have felt that in the sonnets Shakespeare, as Wordsworth said, "unlocked his heart," they have tried to determine the identity of "W. H.," to whom the poems were dedicated, and of the dark lady and the rival poet mentioned in the poems. The value of this speculation is questionable. Today most readers value the poems not as biography but as poetry. Because like other sonneteers Shakespeare was working in an established convention, he treated the usual themes: the beauty of his lady, his love for her, his assurance of immortality for her through his verse, and so on. The excellence of the poems lies, therefore, not in what is said but in how it is said.

Questions following a sonnet are concerned with special features of that poem. It will be useful, though, to observe the following suggestions in your reading of all the sonnets: (1) Use your dictionary frequently. (2) Note the use of the three quatrains. How are they related to each other? Do they represent a progression of thought? Is the break in thought between the second and third quatrains more marked than between the first and second? (3) Note how the couplet is used in each case.

18

Shall I compare thee to a summer's day?
Thou art more lovely and more temperate:
Rough winds do shake the darling buds of
    May,
And summer's lease hath all too short a date:
Sometime too hot the eye of heaven shines, 5
And often is his gold complexion dimmed;
And every fair from fair sometime declines,[1]
By chance, or nature's changing course
    untrimmed;[2]
But thy eternal summer shall not fade,
Nor lose possession of that fair thou owest;[3] 10
Nor shall Death brag thou wanderest in his
    shade,
When in eternal lines to time thou growest:[4]
    So long as men can breathe or eyes can see,
    So long lives this, and this gives life to thee.

STUDY AIDS: 1. In what ways is the person "more temperate" than a summer's day? In the sonnet does the poet compare the person to a summer's day or does he not?

2. Which words in ll. 3–8 treat nature in personal terms? Does any word thereafter treat the person in natural terms?

23

As an unperfect actor on the stage,
Who with his fear is put besides his part,[5]
Or some fierce thing replete with too much
    rage,
Whose strength's abundance weakens his own
    heart,
So I, for fear of trust,[6] forget to say   5

[1] I.e., and every beautiful thing in time becomes less beautiful.
[2] Stripped of ornamental dress.
[3] Ownest.
[4] Conventional among Elizabethan sonneteers was the belief that the poet's verses would confer immortality on his lady or on himself or on both. The belief is a corollary of the classical observation that art is long but life is short (Ars longa, vita brevis est).
[5] Forgets his part.
[6] Fearing to trust myself.

The perfect ceremony of love's rite,
And in mine own love's strength seem to
    decay,
O'ercharged with burden of mine own love's
    might.[7]
O, let my books be then the eloquence
And dumb presagers[8] of my speaking
    breast,   10
Who plead for love and look for recompense,
More than that tongue that more hath more
    expressed.[9]
    O, learn to read what silent love hath writ:
    To hear with eyes belongs to love's fine wit.

25

Let those who are in favor with their stars
Of public honor and proud titles boast,
Whilst I, whom fortune of such triumph bars,
Unlooked for joy in that I honor most.[10]
Great princes' favorites their fair leaves
    spread   5
But as the marigold[11] at the sun's eye,
And in themselves their pride lies buried,
For at a frown they in their glory die.
The painful warrior famoused for fight,
After a thousand victories once foiled   10
Is from the book of honor razed[12] quite,
And all the rest forgot for which he toiled:
    Then happy I, that love and am beloved,
    Where I may not remove nor be removed.

STUDY AIDS: The first QUATRAIN distinguishes between the poet and others. What is the basis of the distinction? How do the second and third quatrains develop the distinction? How are they related to the final couplet?

[7] Notice that the two comparisons begun in ll. 1–4 are completed in ll. 5–8.
[8] Actors in pantomime of "dumb show," preceding a play.
[9] I.e., my books look for recognition (from you) more than does my tongue, which has expressed more things in more words than my books have.
[10] I.e., I unexpectedly take joy in that which I honor most (i.e., you).
[11] The SIMILE of ll. 5–8 is based on the heliotropic nature of the marigold.
[12] Erased.

29

When, in disgrace with fortune and men's
    eyes,
I all alone beweep my outcast state,
And trouble deaf heaven with my bootless
    cries,
And look upon myself and curse my fate,
Wishing me like to one more rich in hope, 5
Featured like him, like him with friends
    possessed,
Desiring this man's art and that man's scope,
With what I most enjoy contented least;
Yet in these thoughts myself almost despising,
Haply [1] I think on thee,—and then my
    state,   10
Like to the lark at break of day arising
From sullen earth, sings hymns at heaven's
    gate;
  For thy sweet love remembered such wealth
    brings
  That then I scorn to change my state with
    kings.

STUDY AIDS: 1. Taking "heaven" as a
monosyllable, scan l. 3. Where does the metrical
irregularity appear in this line? Note that it
coincides with a notable sound device. What is
this device called? How is the effect of this
combination of devices appropriate to the poet's
mood at this point in the poem?
   2. Do the first two quatrains perform one
function or two in the poem? What is it (or
what are they)? What, in the content (idea and
mood) of the poem, makes this handling of the
eight lines desirable?
   3. Note the distinct "turning point" in the
poem. Show how the lines following the break
differ from those that precede it, as regards
figurative expression, imagery, melodic quality,
and tempo.

30

When to the sessions of sweet silent thought
I summon up remembrance of things past,
I sigh the lack of many a thing I sought,
And with old woes new wail my dear time's
    waste: [2]

[1] By chance.
[2] Note how the weight of the SPONDEES suits the
depression the poet speaks of.

Then can I drown an eye, unused to flow, 5
For precious friends hid in death's dateless [3]
    night,
And weep afresh love's long since canceled
    woe,
And moan the expense [4] of many a vanished
    sight:
Then can I grieve at grievances foregone,[5]
And heavily from woe to woe tell [6] o'er   10
The sad account of fore-bemoanèd moan,
Which I new pay as if not paid before.
  But if the while I think on thee, dear friend,
  All losses are restored and sorrows end.

STUDY AIDS: 1. Note, between "sessions"
(l. 1) and "losses" (l. 14), the many legal and
commercial terms, which constitute a sustained
METAPHOR. Are the terms of the metaphor appropriate to the subject?
   2. SOUND DEVICES are particularly notable in
this poem. Notice how ALLITERATION and AS-
SONANCE are used. What vowel sound is prominent in ll. 1–12?
   3. Read over the third QUATRAIN to discover
a rhetorical device used in each of the four lines.
How is the device appropriate to the sense of
ll. 1–12?

32

If thou survive my well-contented day,[7]
When that churl Death my bones with dust
    shall cover,
And shalt by fortune once more re-survey
These poor rude lines of thy deceasèd lover,
Compare them with the bettering [8] of the
    time,   5
And though they be outstripped by every pen,
Reserve [9] them for my love, not for their rime,
Exceeded by the height of happier [10] men.
O, then vouchsafe me but this loving thought:
"Had my friend's Muse grown with this
    growing age,   10
A dearer birth than this his love had brought,

[3] Endless.
[4] Expenditure, loss.
[5] Past.
[6] Count.
[7] My time, or possibly the day of my death.
[8] The improvement in poetic technique.
[9] Preserve.
[10] More skillful.

To march in ranks of better equipage:
  But since he died and poets better prove,
  Theirs for their style I'll read, his for his
    love."

STUDY AIDS: 1. The contrast on which
the poem is based, made clear in l. 14, first is
suggested in l. 5. What words in ll. 5–14 refer
explicitly to the contrast?
  2. Do you think Shakespeare believes that a
technically excellent poem is insincere? Do you
think he is sincere in calling his verse "poor
rude lines" (l. 4)? Cf. sonnet 18, l. 12, and
sonnet 55, l. 2.

33

Full many a glorious morning have I seen
Flatter the mountain-tops with sovereign eye,
Kissing with golden face the meadows green,
Gilding pale streams with heavenly alchemy;
Anon permit the basest clouds to ride   5
With ugly rack [1] on his celestial face,
And from the forlorn world his visage hide,
Stealing unseen to west with this disgrace:
Even so my sun one early morn did shine
With all-triumphant splendor on my brow; 10
But out! alack! he was but one hour mine;
The region cloud hath masked him from me
    now.
  Yet him for this my love no whit disdaineth;
  Suns of the world may stain [2] when
    heaven's sun staineth.

55

Not marble, nor the gilded monuments
Of princes, shall outlive this powerful rime;
But you shall shine more bright in these
    contents [3]
Than unswept stone, besmeared with sluttish
    time.
When wasteful war shall statues overturn, 5
And broils root out the work of masonry,
Nor Mars his sword [4] nor war's quick fire shall
    burn
The living record of your memory.
'Gainst death and all-oblivious enmity [5]

[1] Thin, high-flying clouds.
[2] Become stained.
[3] This poem.
[4] Neither Mars' sword.
[5] Enmity that causes all to be forgotten.

Shall you pace forth; your praise shall still
    find room   10
Even in the eyes of all posterity
That wear this world out to the ending doom. [6]
  So, till the judgment that yourself arise,
  You live in this, and dwell in lovers' eyes.

STUDY AIDS: 1. What peculiarity do you
notice in the RHYME SCHEME?
  2. Similar in theme, sonnets 55 and 18 differ
markedly in TONE. To what extent is the difference due to IMAGERY?

60

Like as the waves make towards the pebbled
    shore,
So do our minutes hasten to their end;
Each changing place with that which goes
    before,
In sequent toil all forwards do contend.
Nativity, once in the main of light, [7]   5
Crawls to maturity, wherewith being crowned,
Crooked eclipses 'gainst his glory fight,
And Time that gave doth now his gift
    confound. [8]
Time doth transfix the flourish [9] set on youth
And delves the parallels in beauty's brow, 10
Feeds on the rarities of nature's truth,
And nothing stands but for his scythe to mow:
  And yet to times in hope [10] my verse shall
    stand,
  Praising thy worth, despite his cruel hand.

STUDY AIDS: 1. The THEME of the poem
—the power of the poet's verse to withstand the
ravages of time—is clearly stated in the concluding couplet. This statement is prepared for
and its force is enhanced by the picture (ll.
1–12) of what time normally does. In QUATRAIN
one, time is treated in terms of sea IMAGERY.
From what realms are the images in quatrains
two and three drawn? What does drawing the
imagery from these three sources allow the poet
to say about time?
  2. Perhaps the most complex imagery occurs
in quatrain two. "Nativity" and "crawls" suggest an infant; "crowned" and "glory" suggest

[6] Day of Judgment.
[7] Sea (cf. Spanish Main) of light.
[8] Destroy.
[9] Pierce the flower.
[10] I.e., in the future.

a king; "eclipses" suggests the sun. What mental picture is called to mind by ll. 5–7?

3. In which quatrain is time least felt as a personified force? In which quatrain most felt? What is the effect of the arrangement producing this feeling?

4. How do "stand" and "worth" in the couplet serve as verbal links with the rest of the poem?

64

When I have seen by Time's fell hand defaced
The rich-proud cost of outworn buried age; [1]
When sometime lofty towers I see downrazed,
And brass eternal slave to mortal rage; [2]
When I have seen the hungry ocean gain   5
Advantage on the kingdom of the shore
And the firm soil win of the watery main,
Increasing store with loss and loss with store; [3]
When I have seen such interchange of state, [4]
Or state [5] itself confounded to decay;   10
Ruin hath taught me thus to ruminate,
That Time will come and take my love away.
    This thought is as a death, which cannot
      choose [6]
    But weep to have that which it fears to lose.

STUDY AIDS: 1. After detailing several experiences the poet generalizes on them and draws an inference. In what line does he begin to do this? What use does he make of METER and SOUND DEVICES to give emphasis to the line?

2. Are love and time equal antagonists in the contest implied in the poem? If not, how has the poet conveyed a sense of their inequality?

66

Tired with all these, for restful death I cry,
As, to behold desert [7] a beggar born,
And needy nothing trimmed in jollity,
And purest faith unhappily forsworn, [8]

[1] I.e., costly things of old. Is "buried" literal or figurative?
[2] I.e., subject to the deadly fury of destruction.
[3] I.e., extending its own area by the other's loss, and losing it by the other's gain.
[4] Condition.
[5] Pomp (stateliness), or government.
[6] I.e., this thought, which cannot choose but weep, etc., is as a death.
[7] Merit or excellence (i.e., that which *deserves* help, praise, or reward).
[8] Denied.

And gilded honor shamefully misplaced, [9]   5
And maiden virtue rudely strumpeted,
And right perfection wrongfully disgraced,
And strength by limping sway [10] disabled, [11]
And art made tongue-tied by authority,
And folly, doctor-like, [12] controlling skill,   10
And simple truth miscalled simplicity, [13]
And captive good attending captain ill:
    Tired with all these, from these would I be
      gone,
    Save that, to die, I leave my love alone.

STUDY AIDS: 1. Like the famous soliloquy in *Hamlet* ("To be or not to be," III, i, 70–75), this sonnet is an extended complaint against human behavior. Although more or less personified, the human shortcomings are presented as abstractions. For each line (2–12) try to think of specific cases covered by the abstraction in question. For instance, "desert" (or "deservingness") could apply to an excellent student who had little money. What is the kind of "authority" (l. 9) that tongue-ties "art"? Censorship, perhaps? Too strict rules prescribed by theorists and critics?

2. Do the eleven shortcomings have anything in common? If so, use the common element or quality to frame a statement of the poem's THEME.

3. In what way is the unusual form of this sonnet suitable to the theme and mood of the poem?

71

No longer mourn for me when I am dead
Than you shall hear the surly sullen bell
Give warning to the world that I am fled
From this vile world, with vilest worms to
    dwell:
Nay, if you read this line, remember not   5
The hand that writ it; for I love you so,
That I in your sweet thoughts would be
    forgot [14]
If thinking on me then should make you woe.

[9] I.e., put in a high place, above what it deserves.
[10] Power or influence.
[11] Disregarding the spelling of "disabled," but considering rhyme (cf. l. 6), meter, and the sense of l. 8, do you think "disabled" should be sounded as a word of three syllables or of four?
[12] I.e., like a university scholar rather than an M.D.
[13] Ignorance.
[14] I.e., would like to be forgotten.

O, if, I say, you look upon this verse,
When I perhaps compounded am with clay, 10
Do not so much as my poor name rehearse,
But let your love even with my life decay;
   Lest the wise world should look into your
      moan
   And mock you with me after I am gone.

73

That time of year thou mayst in me behold
When yellow leaves, or none, or few, do hang
Upon those boughs which shake against the
   cold,
Bare ruined choirs, where late the sweet birds
   sang.
In me thou see'st the twilight of such day   5
As after sunset fadeth in the west,
Which by and by black night doth take away,
Death's second self, that seals up all in rest.
In me thou see'st the glowing of such fire
That on the ashes of his youth doth lie,   10
As the death-bed whereon it must expire,
Consumed with that which it was nourished
   by.
   This thou perceivest, which makes thy
      love more strong,
   To love that well which thou must leave
      ere long.

STUDY AIDS: 1. In several ways this
greatly admired poem is simple. The words are
familiar ones, requiring no annotation, and the
syntax is immediately clear. The structure, too,
is clear. The three QUATRAINS, distinctly set off
by punctuation and by the repeated phrase "in
me," enclose three clear images: fall of the year,
twilight, a dying fire. But the poem is not without subtleties, some of which are touched on in
the following questions.

2. Each quatrain implies a time relationship,
expressible as a proportion. In quatrain one, for
example, the fall of the year is to the whole year
as my present time of life is to my entire life.
Do the time spans become shorter or longer as
the poem proceeds? How is this progression related to the thought and feeling of the poem?

3. (a) If quatrain one appeals to a sense of
cold, what senses do quatrains two and three
appeal to? (b) Do the words connoting death
become more or less explicit as the poem proceeds? How are these progressions related to the
thought and feeling of the poem?

4. Although the IMAGERY is clear, it is more
complex than it seems. Quatrain one does more
than picture a fall scene, a metaphoric representation of the poet's age. How is the image enriched
by "choirs" and "sweet birds sang"?

5. Explain the PARADOX in l. 12. (Cf. sonnet 60, l. 8.)

6. What is the effect (l. 14) of the poet's
using "that" and "which" instead of "him" and
"whom"?

106

When in the chronicle of wasted time [1]
I see descriptions of the fairest wights,[2]
And beauty making beautiful old rime,[3]
In praise of ladies dead and lovely knights,
Then, in the blazon [4] of sweet beauty's best,   5
Of hand, of foot, of lip, of eye, of brow,
I see their antique pen would have expressed [5]
Even such a beauty as you master now.
So all their praises are but prophecies
Of this our time, all you prefiguring; [6]   10
And, for they looked but with divining [7] eyes,
They had not skill enough your worth to sing:
   For we, which now behold these present
      days,
   Have eyes to wonder, but lack tongues to
      praise.

STUDY AIDS: 1. The appeal of this sonnet is more intellectual than sensuous. Two
groups of people, says the poet, have tried to
portray the ideal beauty which he sees embodied
in his friend. Both have failed. Why? What,
therefore, is the THEME of the poem?

2. How do the form and rhythm of l. 6 help
characterize the "descriptions" in the old "chronicles"?

3. Are ALLITERATION and ASSONANCE used
primarily for their musical value or to bind
related words together?

116

Let me not to the marriage of true minds
Admit impediments. Love is not love
Which alters when it alteration finds,

[1] I.e., in the writings of bygone days.
[2] People.
[3] I.e., making old rhyme beautiful.
[4] Description.
[5] Would like to have expressed.
[6] Foreshadowing.
[7] Prophesying.

Or bends with the remover [1] to remove:
O, no! it is an ever-fixèd mark [2]   5
That looks on tempests and is never shaken;
It is the star to every wandering bark,
Whose worth's unknown, although his height
   be taken.[3]
Love's not Time's fool,[4] though rosy lips and
   cheeks
Within his bending sickle's compass [5]
   come;   10
Love alters not with his brief hours and weeks,
But bears it out [6] even to the edge of doom.
   If this be error and upon me proved,
   I never writ, nor no man ever loved.

STUDY AIDS: 1. This sonnet on the constancy and permanence of true love proceeds by logical definition. QUATRAIN one seeks to define love by telling what love is not. How do quatrains two and three define it? How is the couplet related to this logical pattern? What makes the couplet (and hence the whole argument) so compelling?
   2. If "rosy lips and cheeks" come within the compass of Time's "bending sickle" (cf. sonnet 60, l. 12), how can the poet say that love is permanent?
   3. "Edge of doom" (l. 12) is a haunting phrase. What does it suggest to you?

129

The expense [7] of spirit [8] in a waste of shame
Is lust [9] in action; and till action,[10] lust
Is perjured, murderous, bloody, full of blame,
Savage, extreme, rude, cruel, not to trust;
Enjoyed no sooner but despisèd straight;   5
Past reason [11] hunted; and no sooner had,
Past reason hated, as a swallowed bait,

[1] Inconstant one.
[2] A sea-mark to guide sailors (i.e., lovers; cf. Wyatt's sonnet, p. 138).
[3] I.e., although a star's altitude can be measured, its whole value (chemical or astrological?) cannot be known. So, metaphorically, with love.
[4] What is implied in the PERSONIFICATION "Time's fool"?
[5] Range or sweep.
[6] Endures.
[7] Expenditure.
[8] Vital power, life.
[9] The subject of the sentence.
[10] Until expressed in action.
[11] Beyond reason, unreasonably.

On purpose laid to make the taker mad:
Mad in pursuit, and in possession so;
Had, having, and in quest to have, extreme; 10
A bliss in proof,[12]—and proved, a very woe;
Before, a joy proposed; behind, a dream.
   All this the world well knows; yet none
      knows well
   To shun [13] the heaven that leads men to this
      hell.

STUDY AIDS: This sonnet, so startling in a collection of love poems, is a passionate tirade against sexual desire. Although it is similar in form to another of his sonnets (which one?), Shakespeare never wrote another quite like this. Notice the compression—how much meaning is packed into the fourteen lines. In what way is compression suitable to the poet's mood? To discover just how compressed the statement is, work out a close PARAPHRASE, noting each word and phrase.

130

My mistress' eyes are nothing like the sun;
Coral is far more red than her lips' red;
If snow be white, why then her breasts are
   dun;
If hairs be wires, black wires grow on her
   head.
I have seen roses damasked,[14] red and white, 5
But no such roses see I in her cheeks;
And in some perfumes is there more delight
Than in the breath that from my mistress
   reeks.[15]
I love to hear her speak, yet well I know
That music hath a far more pleasing sound; 10
I grant I never saw a goddess go;
My mistress, when she walks, treads on the
   ground:
   And yet, by heaven, I think my love as rare
   As any she belied with false compare.[16]

STUDY AIDS: What is the poet doing here with the Petrarchan convention? How does the TONE of the poem compare with that of the other sonnets?

[12] The experiencing.
[13] How to shun.
[14] Mingled white and red.
[15] Emanates.
[16] I.e., as any lady who is lied about (by poets) with false comparisons.

146

Poor soul, the center of my sinful earth,[1]
Thrall [2] to these rebel powers that thee array,[3]
Why dost thou pine within and suffer dearth,
Painting thy outward walls so costly gay?
Why so large cost, having so short a lease,   5
Dost thou upon thy fading mansion spend?
Shall worms, inheritors of this excess,
Eat up thy charge? [4] Is this thy body's end?
Then, soul, live thou upon thy servant's loss,
And let that pine to aggravate [5] thy store;   10
Buy terms [6] divine in selling hours of dross;
Within be fed, without be rich no more:

So shalt thou feed on Death, that feeds on
   men,
And Death once dead, there's no more
   dying then.
(1609)

STUDY AIDS: 1. The form of this sonnet
is unusual. Who is speaking? To whom is he
speaking? How do the questions fit the scheme
of the poem?
   2. Notice the TONE of the poem. Is it the
same at the end as at the beginning?
   3. Notice the hard core of reasoning (ll. 8–
12) leading to the conclusion in the couplet. If
the soul lives on its servant's (the body's) loss,
what happens to Death?

Songs

   Some of the finest Renaissance lyrics are the songs in the plays of the period. Songs were
not an integral part of the early plays; they were introduced, in the middle of the play or at the
end, as a kind of added attraction, often to exploit the trained voices of the boy actors in the
theatrical companies. Later, however, they were related more and more to the action, until in
Othello, for instance, Desdemona's "Willow Song" not only suits the action but does a great
deal to create a mood of pity and foreboding.
   If lyrics in the pastoral or Petrarchan convention seem limited in theme and tone, the same
cannot be said of the songs of the age, which represent an astonishingly wide range.

Winter [7]

When icicles hang by the wall,
   And Dick the shepherd blows his nail,
And Tom bears logs into the hall,
   And milk comes frozen home in pail,
When blood is nipped and ways be foul,   5
Then nightly sings the staring owl,
      Tu-who;
Tu-whit, tu-who!—a merry note,
While greasy Joan doth keel [8] the pot.

When all aloud the wind doth blow,   10
   And coughing drowns the parson's saw,[9]
And birds sit brooding in the snow,
   And Marian's nose looks red and raw,
When roasted crabs [10] hiss in the bowl,
Then nightly sings the staring owl,   15
      Tu-who;
Tu-whit, tu-who!—a merry note,
While greasy Joan doth keel the pot.
(1590–1591)

STUDY AIDS: The combination of viv-
idly rendered details evokes here a real feeling
of winter. IMAGERY is more than a matter of
visual pictures. What senses besides sight are
appealed to here? What is gained by having
Joan "greasy"?

[1] The body.
[2] Prisoner.
[3] I.e., that are arrayed against thee; or that clothe
thee.
[4] I.e., that which has cost thee so much.
[5] Increase.
[6] Long periods of time.
[7] Sung at the end of Shakespeare's *Love's Labor's
Lost* (1590–1591).
[8] Cool by stirring.

[9] Speech or maxim.
[10] Crab apples.

Who Is Silvia? [1]

Who is Silvia? what is she,
   That all our swains commend her?
Holy, fair, and wise is she;
   The heaven such grace did lend her,
That she might admirèd be.   5

Is she kind as she is fair?
   For beauty lives with kindness:
Love doth to her eyes repair
   To help him of his blindness,
And, being helped, inhabits there.   10

Then to Silvia let us sing,
   That Silvia is exceling;
She excells each mortal thing
   Upon the dull earth dwelling:
To her let us garlands bring.   15
(1591)

It Was a Lover and His Lass [2]

It was a lover and his lass,
   With a hey, and a ho, and a hey nonino,
That o'er the green corn-field did pass,
  In the spring time, the only pretty ring
     time,
When birds do sing, hey ding a ding, ding; 5
Sweet lovers love the spring.

Between the acres of the rye,
   With a hey, and a ho, and a hey nonino,
These pretty country folks would lie,
   In the spring time, etc.   10

This carol they began that hour,
   With a hey, and a ho, and a hey nonino,
How that a life was but a flower
   In the spring time, etc.

And therefore take the present time,   15
   With a hey, and a ho, and a hey nonino,
For love is crownèd with the prime [3]
   In the spring time, etc.
(1600)

[1] Sung as a serenade in Shakespeare's *Two Gentlemen of Verona* (1591).
[2] Sung, in Shakespeare's *As You Like It* (1600), to Touchstone (the court jester) and his sweetheart Audrey.
[3] Spring.

O, Mistress Mine, Where Are You Roaming? [4]

O, mistress mine, where are you roaming?
O, stay and hear; your true love's coming,
   That can sing both high and low.
Trip no further, pretty sweeting,
Journeys end in lovers meeting,   5
   Every wise man's son doth know.

What is love? 'tis not hereafter;
Present mirth hath present laughter;
   What's to come is still unsure.
In delay there lies no plenty;   10
Then come kiss me, sweet and twenty,
   Youth's a stuff will not endure.
(1601)

STUDY AIDS: This is an early instance in English of the *carpe diem* (live-for-today) theme, later to become popular. How would you describe the TONE of the poem?

Hark, Hark! The Lark at Heaven's Gate Sings [5]

Hark, hark! the lark at heaven's gate sings,[6]
   And Phoebus [7] 'gins arise,
His steeds to water at those springs
   On chaliced flowers that lies; [8]
And winking Mary-buds [9] begin   5
   To ope their golden eyes:
With every thing that pretty is,
   My lady sweet, arise:
     Arise, arise!
(1609)

Fear No More the Heat o' the Sun [1]

Fear no more the heat o' the sun,
   Nor the furious winter's rages;
Thou thy worldly task hast done,
   Home art gone, and taken thy wages.

[4] Sung by Feste, the clown in Shakespeare's *Twelfth Night* (1601).
[5] A morning serenade sung to Imogen in Shakespeare's *Cymbeline* (1609).
[6] See sonnet 29, ll. 11–12 (p. 170).
[7] Apollo, Greek god associated with the sun.
[8] Work out the SYNTAX of ll. 2–4, and analyze the CONCEIT. Elizabethans sometimes used singular verbs ("lies") with plural subjects.
[9] Marigolds.

[1] A dirge from *Cymbeline*, sung by two brothers to their sister Imogen, whom they suppose dead.

Golden lads and girls all must, 5
As chimney-sweepers, come to dust.

Fear no more the frown o' the great;
  Thou art past the tyrant's stroke;
Care no more to clothe and eat;
  To thee the reed is as the oak. 10
The sceptre, learning, physic,[2] must
All follow this, and come to dust.

Fear no more the lightning-flash,
  Nor the all-dreaded thunder-stone;[3]

Fear not slander, censure rash; 15
  Thou hast finished joy and moan.
All lovers young, all lovers must
Consign to thee,[4] and come to dust.

No exorciser harm thee!
  Nor no witchcraft charm thee![5] 20
Ghost unlaid forbear thee!
  Nothing ill come near thee!
Quiet consummation have;
And renownèd be thy grave!
(1609)

Thomas Campion
(1567–1620)

THOMAS CAMPION IS ONE OF THE MOST MUSICAL OF THE ELIZABETHAN POETS. AT A TIME when poetry and music were closely allied, he was uniquely successful in blending the words and tunes of the songs he contributed to *A Book of Airs* (1601). This was a difficult feat, he said, "for him to do that hath not power over both." Campion had such power, and although the poems are finished and delicate by themselves, they are particularly delightful when heard with their melodies, to which they are beautifully fitted. Campion writes with the ease and simplicity of the Latin poets Horace and Catullus, whom he admired and at times imitated.

My Sweetest Lesbia, Let Us Live and Love

My sweetest Lesbia, let us live and love;
And though the sager sort our deeds reprove,
Let us not weigh them: heaven's great lamps
  do dive
Into their west, and straight again revive:
But soon as once set is our little light, 5
Then must we sleep one ever-during night.

If all would lead their lives in love like me,
Then bloody swords and armor should not be;
No drum nor trumpet peaceful sleeps should
  move,
Unless alarm came from the camp of love: 10
But fools do live, and waste their little light,
And seek with pain their ever-during night.

When timely death my life and fortune ends,
Let not my hearse be vexed with mourning
  friends;
But let all lovers, rich in triumph, come 15
And with sweet pastimes grace my happy
  tomb:
And, Lesbia, close up thou my little light,
And crown with love my ever-during night.
(1601)

STUDY AIDS: SCAN ll. 3, 4, 5, 10, 16. How does the rhythm of these lines differ from the normal IAMBIC PENTAMETER of the poem? What is the effect, in each case, of the deviation from the normal meter of the poem?

[2] Medical science.
[3] Thunder-bolt.
[4] I.e., sign death's register with thee.
[5] What is the effect of the metrical variation in st. 4?

Follow Your Saint, Follow with Accents Sweet

In Campion's wistful tune for these words he succeeds in his aim "to couple words and notes lovingly together."

Follow your saint, follow with accents sweet;
Haste you, sad notes, fall at her flying feet.
There, wrapped in cloud of sorrow, pity move,
And tell the ravisher of my soul I perish for
   her love.
But if she scorns my never-ceasing pain,   5
Then burst with sighing in her sight and ne'er
   return again.

All that I sung still to her praise did tend,
Still she was first, still she my songs did end.
Yet she my love and music both doth fly,
The music that her echo is and beauty's
   sympathy.   10
Then let my notes pursue her scornful flight:
It shall suffice that they were breathed and
   died for her delight.
(1601)

When Thou Must Home to Shades of Underground

When thou must home to shades of under-
   ground,
   And there arrived, a new admirèd guest,
The beauteous spirits do engirt thee round,
   White Iope,[1] blithe Helen,[2] and the rest,
To hear the stories of thy finished love   5
From that smooth tongue whose music hell[3]
   can move,
Then wilt thou speak of banqueting delights,

Of masks and revels which sweet youth did
   make,
Of tourneys and great challenges of knights,
   And all these triumphs for thy beauty's
   sake;   10
When thou hast told these honors done to
   thee,
Then tell, O tell, how thou didst murder me.
(1601)

Rose-cheeked Laura, Come

In theory Campion favored the classical practice of avoiding end-rhyme; it was likely, he thought, to "offend the ear with tedious affectation." Although in writing his poems he usually ignored his theory, in the present poem he uses no end-rhyme. Perhaps he thought it too coarse and obvious a device for the poem's theme of harmony. Wonderfully suitable to that theme, at any rate, is the more subtle matching and near-matching of vowel sounds within the lines.

Rose-cheeked Laura, come
Sing thou smoothly with thy beauty's
Silent music, either other [4]
   Sweetly gracing.

Lovely forms do flow   5
From consent [5] divinely framèd;
Heaven is music, and thy beauty's
   Birth is heavenly.

These dull notes we sing
Discords need for helps to grace them.   10
Only beauty purely loving
   Knows no discord,

But still moves delight,
Like clear springs renewed by flowing,
Ever perfect, ever in themselves eternal.   15
(1602)

[1] Perhaps a wife of Theseus, legendary Grecian king.
[2] Helen of Troy, beautiful woman of Greek legend.

[3] Direct object of "can move."
[4] "Either" and "other" refer to her beauty and her singing.
[5] Harmony.

Jack and Joan

Jack and Joan they think no ill,
But loving live, and merry still;
Do their week-days' work and pray
Devoutly on the holy day;
Skip and trip it on the green, 5
And help to choose the summer queen;
Lash out,[1] at a country feast,
Their silver penny with the best.

Well can they judge of nappy ale,
And tell at large a winter tale; 10
Climb up to the apple loft,
And turn the crabs till they be soft.
Tib is all the father's joy,
And little Tom the mother's boy.
All their pleasure is content, 15
And care, to pay their yearly rent.

Joan can call by name her cows,
And deck her windows with green boughs;
She can wreaths and tutties [2] make,
And trim with plums a bridal cake. 20
Jack knows what brings gain or loss,
And his long flail can stoutly toss;
Make the hedge, which others break,
And ever thinks what he doth speak.

Now, you courtly dames and knights, 25
That study only strange delights,
Though you scorn the home-spun gray,
And revel in your rich array;
Though your tongues dissemble deep,
And can your heads from danger keep; 30
Yet for all your pomp and train,
Securer lives the silly swain.
(1613)

STUDY AIDS: 1. The meter is IAMBIC
TETRAMETER. Some lines (e.g., l. 4) contain
four full feet; others (e.g., l. 5), beginning with
an accented syllable, are missing the initial
unaccented syllable of the normal iambic foot.
SCAN the lines to show which opening feet are
complete and which not. What pattern do you
discover?
2. How does the poem sound rewritten in
IAMBIC PENTAMETER?

Jack and Joan they never think of ill,
But loving live, and merry they are still;
They do their week-days' work and then do pray
Devoutly in the church on holy day.

[1] Squander.
[2] Bouquets.

Young and Simple Though I Am

For several of his poems Campion drew not from literary sources but from the English life
about him. Notice here how the speech of the young lady takes on some of the compressed,
aphoristic quality of the proverbs in which she is schooled.

Young and simple though I am,
I have heard of Cupid's name;
Guess I can [1] what thing it is
Men desire when they do kiss.
Smoke can never burn, they say, 5
But the flames that follow may.

I am not so foul or fair
To be proud, nor to despair;

[1] Know.

Yet my lips have oft observed,
Men that kiss them press them hard, 10
As glad lovers use to do
When their new-met loves they woo.

Faith, 'tis but a foolish mind,
Yet methinks a heat I find,
Like thirst-longing, that doth bide 15
Ever on my weaker side,
Where they say my heart doth move.
Venus, grant it be not love.

If it be, alas, what then?
Were not women made for men?   20
As good 'twere a thing were past,
That must needs be done at last.
  Roses that are over-blown
  Grow less sweet, then fall alone.

Yet nor churl nor silken gull [2]   25
Shall my maiden blossom pull;
Who shall not I soon can tell,
Who shall, would I could as well;
  This I know, whoe'er he be,
  Love he must, or flatter me.   30

(1617)

There Is a Garden in Her Face

There is a garden in her face,
  Where roses and white lilies grow,
A heavenly paradise is that place,
  Wherein all pleasant fruits do flow.
There cherries grow, which none may buy 5
Till "Cherry ripe!" themselves do cry.

Those cherries fairly do enclose
  Of orient pearl a double row;
Which when her lovely laughter shows,
  They look like rose-buds filled with snow. 10
Yet them nor peer nor prince can buy,
Till "Cherry ripe!" themselves do cry.

Her eyes like angels watch them still;
  Her brows like bended bows do stand,
Threatening with piercing frowns to kill   15
  All that attempt with eye or hand
Those sacred cherries to come nigh,
Till "Cherry ripe!" themselves do cry.

(1618)

STUDY AIDS: The phrase "Cherry Ripe!" was the cry of London fruit vendors. In the music to which Campion set his words, this phrase, which gives distinction to the poem, is emphasized both by repetition and by a dramatic change of tonality. Lines 5–6 are a metaphoric way of saying what?

Francis Bacon
(1561–1626)

Men have interpreted Bacon's character in different ways, but all have recognized him as one of the foremost intellects of his time. He was a Renaissance scholar of great breadth; "I have taken," he wrote early in life, "all knowledge to be my province." He was also a practical man, active and influential in affairs of state.

Advancement at court was denied him during Elizabeth's reign because of his jealous uncle, Lord Burleigh, but under James he rose through several offices to become Lord Chancellor and to be named Baron Verulam and Viscount St. Albans. Although he served the state well, his final years were marred by disgrace. Convicted of bribery, he was briefly imprisoned, fined, and prohibited from sitting in Parliament. He died shortly thereafter.

Bacon probably made his greatest contribution in science, not as a practicing scientist but as a philosopher. It is often said that he changed scientific inquiry from an *a priori* method (whereby one begins with preconceived ideas about nature and argues deductively from them) to an experimental, or inductive, method (whereby one gathers data and then

[2] I.e., neither country bumpkin nor city slicker.

examines it to see what it means). Although this far-reaching change, which made possible modern technology, could hardly be the work of a single mind, there is no question that Bacon was the best interpreter of the new science. His *Novum Organum* and *Advancement of Learning* clearly and forcefully expound the value of the inductive method, and the ideal commonwealth sketched in his utopian speculation, *The New Atlantis,* has at its center a "college of philosophy," or scientific body, which may have led to the Royal Society.

These works are remembered as influential titles, but the Bacon that is read is the Bacon of the *Essays.* When in 1597 he published a collection of aphoristic sayings, he called his work *Essays,* apparently borrowing the term from the French writer, Montaigne, who in so naming his prose compositions (French "essai" = trial, attempt) had suggested their tentative, informal nature. But Bacon's "dispersed meditations," as he called them, owe less to Montaigne's intimate and humane essays than to the pithy maxims of the Roman author, Seneca. Bacon's essays are composed of meaty statements, often undeveloped by example or illustration and usually related to one another only in their bearing on a common subject. In reading them, one does well to follow Bacon's advice: he should read not "to believe and take for granted" but rather "to weigh and consider."

Some readers have deplored the shrewd, prudential character of the *Essays.* They feel that they lack nobility and human warmth. The charge has some justice, but fails to recognize the author's purpose. Bacon was deliberately writing to young men interested in getting on in the world. Since there was nothing in print on the subject, he would supply it. Like Machiavelli, like the writers of "courtesy books," Bacon offered practical advice to a particular audience. However limited he seems, his analysis of life is incisive, his expression of it definitive.

Of Truth

"What is truth?" said jesting Pilate,[1] and would not stay for an answer. Certainly there be [2] that delight in giddiness, and count it a bondage to fix a belief; affecting free-will in thinking, as well as in acting. And though the sects of philosophers of that kind [3] be gone, yet there remain certain discoursing wits which are of the same veins, though there be not so much blood in them as was in those of the ancients. But it is not only the difficulty and labor which men take in finding out of truth, nor again that when it is found it imposeth upon [4] men's thoughts, that doth bring lies in favor; but a natural though corrupt love of the lie itself. One of the later school of the Grecians examineth the matter, and is at a stand [5] to think what should be in it, that men should love lies; where neither they make for pleasure, as with poets; nor for advantage, as with the merchant; but for the lie's sake. But I cannot tell; this same truth is a naked and open daylight, that doth not show the masques and mummeries [6] and triumphs of the world, half so stately and daintily as candlelights. Truth may perhaps come to the price of a pearl, that showeth best by day; but it will not rise to the price of a diamond or carbuncle, that showeth best in varied lights.[7] A mixture of a lie doth ever

[1] Roman procurator, before whom Jesus was tried, asked this question of Jesus. See John 18:37–38.
[2] Supply "those."
[3] The Greek Skeptics, who denied that one could know anything with certainty.
[4] Affects, influences, restrains.
[5] A halt, i.e., is unable to think.
[6] Dramatic performances.
[7] In this and the preceding sentence Bacon is admitting the attractiveness of falsehood.

add pleasure. Doth any man doubt, that if there were taken out of men's minds vain opinions, flattering hopes, false valuations, imaginations as one would, and the like, but it would leave the minds of a number of men poor shrunken things, full of melancholy and indisposition, and unpleasing to themselves? One of the fathers,[8] in great severity, called poesy *vinum daemonum*,[9] because it filleth the imagination, and yet it is but with the shadow of a lie. But it is not the lie that passeth through the mind, but the lie that sinketh in and settleth in it, that doth the hurt, such as we spake of before. But howsoever these things are thus in men's depraved judgments and affections, yet truth, which only doth judge itself, teacheth that the inquiry of truth, which is the love-making or wooing of it, the knowledge of truth, which is the presence of it, and the belief of truth, which is the enjoying of it, is the sovereign good of human nature. The first creature of God, in the works of the days, was the light of the sense; the last was the light of reason; and his sabbath work, ever since, is the illumination of his spirit. First he breathed light upon the face of the matter or chaos; then he breathed light into the face of man; and still he breatheth and inspireth light into the face of his chosen. The poet [10] that beautified the sect that was otherwise inferior to the rest, saith yet excellently well: "It is a pleasure to stand upon the shore, and to see ships tossed upon the sea: a pleasure to stand in the window of a castle, and to see a battle and the adventures thereof below: but no pleasure is comparable to the standing upon the vantage ground of truth (a hill not to be commanded,[11] and where the air is always clear and serene), and to see the errors, and wanderings, and mists, and tempests, in the vale below": so [12] always that this prospect [13]

be with pity, and not with swelling or pride. Certainly, it is heaven upon earth, to have a man's mind move in charity, rest in providence, and turn upon the poles of truth.

To pass from theological and philosophical truth, to the truth of civil business: it will be acknowledged, even by those that practice it not, that clear and round [14] dealing is the honor of man's nature; and that mixture of falsehood is like alloy in coin of gold and silver; which may make the metal work the better, but it embaseth it. For these winding and crooked courses are the goings of the serpent; which goeth basely upon the belly, and not upon the feet. There is no vice that doth so cover a man with shame as to be found false and perfidious. And therefore Montaigne [15] saith prettily, when he inquired the reason, why the word of the lie should be such a disgrace and such an odious charge? Saith he, "If it be well weighed, to say that a man lieth, is as much to say as that he is brave towards God and a coward towards men." For a lie faces God, and shrinks from man. Surely the wickedness of falsehood and breach of faith cannot possibly be so highly expressed, as in that it shall be the last peal to call the judgments of God upon the generations of men; it being foretold, that when Christ cometh, *he shall not find faith upon the earth.*[16]

(1625)

STUDY AIDS: 1. The compression of Bacon's statements at times makes for difficult reading. To cover many cases he must use general, usually abstract terms. These the reader must interpret by trying to see what particular matters they include. Bacon says (p. 182/1, l. 3) that we would all suffer, in a sense, if we were not able to entertain the kind of falsehood he calls "flattering hopes." What are "flattering hopes"? Who is flattered? Think of an example of a flattering hope.

2. The first part of the essay touches on reasons why men do not always tell the truth. What are they?

---

[8] The Church Father, St. Augustine.
[9] Wine of devils.
[10] The Roman poet Lucretius, an Epicurean. The quotation is from his *De Rerum Natura* (*On the Nature of Things*).
[11] The hill of truth cannot be commanded (exceeded in height) by any other.
[12] Provided. Note Bacon's important proviso.
[13] "Prospect" in its literal sense. What is it?

[14] Plain, straightforward.
[15] The French essayist.
[16] Altered slightly from Luke 18:8.

Of Great Place [1]

Men in great place are thrice servants: servants of the sovereign or state; servants of fame; and servants of business: so as they have no freedom, neither in their persons, nor in their actions, nor in their times. It is a strange desire, to seek power, and to lose liberty; or to seek power over others, and to lose power over a man's self. The rising into place is laborious; and by pains men come to greater pains; and it is sometimes base; and by indignities men come to dignities. The standing is slippery, and the regress is either a downfall, or at least an eclipse, which is a melancholy thing. *Cum non sis qui fueris, non esse cur velis vivere.* [2] Nay, retire men cannot when they would; neither will they when it were reason: but are impatient of privateness, even in age and sickness, which require the shadow: [3] like old townsmen, that will be still sitting at their street door, though thereby they offer age to scorn. Certainly great persons had need to borrow other men's opinions to think themselves happy; for if they judge by their own feeling, they cannot find it; but if they think with themselves what other men think of them, and that other men would fain be as they are, then they are happy as it were by report, when perhaps they find the contrary within. For they are the first that find their own griefs; though they be the last that find their own faults. Certainly men in great fortunes are strangers to themselves, and while they are in the puzzle of business, they have no time to tend their health either of body or mind. *Illi mors gravis incubat, qui notus nimis omnibus, ignotus moritur sibi.* [4] In place there is license to do good and evil; whereof the latter is a curse; for in evil the best condition is not to will; the second

not to can. [5] But power to do good is the true and lawful end of aspiring. For good thoughts, though God accept them, yet towards men are little better than good dreams, except they be put in act; and that cannot be without power and place, as the vantage and commanding ground. Merit and good works is the end of man's motion; and conscience [6] of the same is the accomplishment of man's rest. For if a man can be partaker of God's theater, he shall likewise be partaker of God's rest. *Et conversus Deus, ut aspiceret opera, quæ fecerunt manus suæ, vidit quod omnia essent bona nimis;* [7] and then the Sabbath. In the discharge of thy place, set before thee the best examples; for imitation is a globe of precepts. And after a time set before thee thine own example; and examine thyself strictly, whether thou didst not best at first. Neglect not also the examples of those, that have carried themselves ill in the same place: not to set off thyself by taxing their memory; but to direct thyself what to avoid. Reform therefore, without bravery [8] or scandal of former times and persons; but yet set it down to thyself, as well to create good precedents, as to follow them. Reduce things to the first institution, and observe wherein and how they have degenerated; but yet ask counsel of both times: of the ancient time what is best; and of the latter time what is fittest. Seek to make thy course regular; that men may know beforehand what they may expect: but be not too positive and peremptory; and express thyself well when thou digressest from thy rule. Preserve the right of thy place, but stir not questions of jurisdiction: and rather assume thy right in silence, and *de facto,* than voice it with claims and challenges. Preserve likewise the rights of inferior places;

---

[1] We would say "high place," i.e., a position of authority over others.

[2] "Since you are not what you were, there is no reason why you should want to live" (Cicero).

[3] Retirement, not a place "in the sun."

[4] "Death presses heavily on him who dies well known to others but unknown to himself" (Seneca).

[5] Know, know how.

[6] Consciousness.

[7] "And God, turning back to look upon the works his hands had made, saw that all were very good" (Bacon's own Latin for Gen. 1:31).

[8] Boastfulness, ostentation.

and think it more honor to direct in chief, than to be busy in all. Embrace and invite helps and advices touching the execution of thy place; and do not drive away such as bring thee information, as meddlers, but accept of them in good part. The vices of authority are chiefly four: delays, corruption, roughness, and facility.[9] For delays: give easy access; keep times appointed; go through with that which is in hand; and interlace not business but of necessity. For corruption: do not only bind thine own hands, or thy servants' hands, from taking, but bind the hands of suitors also from offering. For integrity used doth the one; but integrity professed, and with a manifest detestation of bribery, doth the other: and avoid not only the fault, but the suspicion. Whosoever is found variable, and changeth manifestly without manifest cause, giveth suspicion of corruption. Therefore always when thou changest thine opinion or course, profess it plainly, and declare it, together with the reasons that move thee to change; and do not think to steal [10] it. A servant or a favorite, if he be inward,[11] and no other apparent cause of esteem, is commonly thought but a by-way to close [12] corruption. For roughness, it is a needless cause of discontent; severity breedeth fear, but roughness breedeth hate. Even reproofs from authority ought to be grave, and not taunting. As for facility, it is worse than bribery. For bribes come but now and then; but if importunity or idle respects lead a man, he shall never be without. As Solomon saith: "To respect persons is not good; for such a man will transgress for a piece of bread." [13] It is most true that was anciently spoken, A place showeth the man: and it showeth some to the better, and some to the worse: *Omnium consensu, capax imperii, nisi imperasset*,[14] saith Tacitus of Galba: but of Vespasian he saith: *Solus imperantium Vespasianus mutatus in melius*.[15] Though the one was meant of sufficiency,[16] the other of manners and affection.[17] It is an assured sign of a worthy and generous spirit, whom honor amends. For honor is, or should be, the place of virtue: and as in nature things move violently to their place, and calmly in their place; so virtue in ambition is violent, in authority settled and calm. All rising to great place is by a winding-stair; and if there be factions, it is good to side a man's self [18] whilst he is in the rising; and to balance himself when he is placed. Use the memory of thy predecessor fairly and tenderly; for if thou dost not, it is a debt will sure be paid when thou art gone. If thou have colleagues, respect them, and rather call them when they look not for it, than exclude them when they have reason to look to be called. Be not too sensible,[19] or too remembering of thy place in conversation, and private answers to suitors; but let it rather be said, "When he sits in place he is another man."
(1625)

STUDY AIDS: 1. Find instances, in the opening lines, of PARADOX and ANTITHESIS.

2. Is this essay more or less practical than "Of Truth"? Are Bacon's remarks cynical?

Of Studies

Studies serve for delight, for ornament, and for ability. Their chief use for delight is in privateness and retiring; for ornament, is in discourse; and for ability, is in the judgment and disposition of business; for expert [1] men can execute, and perhaps judge of particulars,

[9] Pliability, lack of firmness.
[10] Hide.
[11] Confidential.
[12] Secret.
[13] Proverbs 28:21.
[14] "In the opinion of everyone he would have been thought capable of ruling if he had never ruled."

[15] "Only Vespasian, of all the emperors, changed for the better."
[16] Ability.
[17] Disposition.
[18] To take sides.
[19] Conscious.

[1] Experienced.

one by one; but the general counsels, and the plots and marshaling of affairs come best from those that are learned. To spend too much time in studies is sloth; to use them too much for ornament is affectation; to make judgment wholly by their rules is the humor [2] of a scholar. They perfect nature, and are perfected by experience; for natural abilities are like natural plants, that need pruning by study; and studies themselves do give forth directions too much at large, except they be bounded in by experience. Crafty men contemn studies, simple men admire [3] them, and wise men use them; for they teach not their own use; but that is a wisdom without them and above them, won by observation. Read not to contradict and confute, nor to believe and take for granted, nor to find talk and discourse, but to weigh and consider. Some books are to be tasted, others to be swallowed, and some few to be chewed and digested; that is, some books are to be read only in parts; others to be read but not curiously; and some few to be read wholly, and with diligence and attention. Some books also may be read by deputy, and extracts made of them by others; but that would be only in the less important arguments and the meaner sort of books; else distilled books are, like common distilled waters, flashy [4] things. Reading maketh a full man; conference a ready man; and writing an exact man. And, therefore, if a man write little, he had need have a great memory; if he confer little, he had

need have a present wit; and if he read little, he had need have much cunning, to seem to know that [5] he doth not. Histories make men wise; poets,[6] witty; the mathematics, subtle; natural philosophy,[7] deep; moral,[8] grave; logic and rhetoric, able to contend: *Abeunt studia in mores!* [9] Nay, there is no stand [10] or impediment in the wit but may be wrought [11] out by fit studies; like as diseases of the body may have appropriate exercises. Bowling is good for the stone and reins,[12] shooting for the lungs and breast, gentle walking for the stomach, riding for the head, and the like. So if a man's wit be wandering, let him study the mathematics; for in demonstrations, if his wit be called away never so little, he must begin again. If his wit be not apt to distinguish or find differences, let him study the schoolmen; [13] for they are *cymini sectores!* [14] If he be not apt to beat over [15] matters, and to call up one thing to prove and illustrate another, let him study the lawyers' cases. So every defect of the mind may have a special receipt.[16]

(1625)

STUDY AIDS: 1. Under what headings does Bacon discuss his subject—*values* of studies, *rules* for study, etc.?

2. Notice the sentence patterns. Is Bacon fond of a particular sentence form here?

3. Bacon is a quotable writer. Which aphoristic statements here seem worth quoting? Why? What makes a saying quotable?

Of Marriage and Single Life

He that hath wife and children hath given hostages to fortune; for they are impediments to great enterprises, either of virtue or mischief. Certainly, the best works, and of greatest merit for the public, have proceeded from the unmarried or childless men, which both in affection and means have married and endowed the public. Yet it were great reason

[2] Peculiar nature.
[3] Wonder at, stand in awe of.
[4] Insipid.
[5] That which.
[6] Poets (i.e., poetry) make men imaginative.
[7] The natural sciences.
[8] Moral philosophy, or ethics, the philosophical study of ideal conduct.

[9] "Studies develop into manners" (Ovid).
[10] Halt (in the operation of), i.e., inability.
[11] Worked.
[12] Kidneys.
[13] Medieval logicians.
[14] Hair-splitters.
[15] To beat out, get to the bottom of.
[16] Prescription.

that those that have children should have greatest care of future times; unto which they know they must transmit their dearest pledges. Some there are, who though they lead a single life, yet their thoughts do end with themselves, and account future times impertinences.[1] Nay, there are some other that account wife and children but as bills of charges. Nay more, there are some foolish rich covetous men that take a pride in having no children, because they may be thought so much the richer. For perhaps they have heard some talk: "Such an one is a great rich man," and another except to it: "Yea, but he hath a great charge of children"; as if it were an abatement to his riches. But the most ordinary cause of a single life is liberty; especially in certain self-pleasing and humorous [2] minds, which are so sensible of every restraint, as they will go near to think their girdles and garters to be bonds and shackles. Unmarried men are best friends, best masters, best servants; but not always best subjects; for they are light to run away; and almost all fugitives are of that condition. A single life doth well with churchmen; for charity will hardly water the ground where it must first fill a pool. It is indifferent for judges and magistrates; for if they be facile and corrupt, you shall have a servant five times worse than a wife. For soldiers, I find the generals commonly in their hortatives put men in mind of their wives and children; and I think the despising of marriage amongst the Turks maketh the vulgar soldier more base. Certainly wife and children are a kind of discipline of humanity; and single men, though they be many times more charitable, because their means are less exhaust,[3] yet, on the other side, they are more cruel and hard-hearted (good to make severe inquisitors), because their tenderness is not so oft called upon. Grave natures, led by custom, and therefore constant, are commonly loving husbands; as was said of Ulysses, *Vetulam suam praetulit immortalitati.*[4] Chaste women are often proud and froward, as presuming upon the merit of their chastity. It is one of the best bonds both of chastity and obedience in the wife, if she think her husband wise; which she will never do if she find him jealous. Wives are young men's mistresses; companions for middle age; and old men's nurses. So as a man may have a quarrel [5] to marry when he will. But yet he [6] was reputed one of the wise men, that made answer to the question, when a man should marry? "A young man not yet, an elder man not at all." It is often seen that bad husbands have very good wives; whether it be that it raiseth the price of their husbands' kindness when it comes; or that the wives take a pride in their patience. But this never fails, if the bad husbands were of their own choosing, against their friends' consent; for then they will be sure to make good their own folly.

(1625)

The Wisdom of the Ancients

The Wisdom of the Ancients sprang from a long and honored tradition of Renaissance commentary on classic myth. Most Renaissance writers believed the myths to be allegories, or at least the media of something deeper than their apparent meaning. A few writers, however, doubted that the myths were originally intended to carry allegorical meaning. Bacon at times seems to be of this minority. But despite his occasional skepticism, he concludes, "I do certainly for my own part incline to this opinion—that beneath no small number of the fables of the ancient poets there lay from the very beginning a mystery and an allegory."

The Wisdom of the Ancients (De Sapientia Veterum) was written in Latin, the universal language of learning in the Renaissance. Of the thirty-one myths treated by Bacon, three are here reprinted.

[1] Irrelevancies.
[2] Eccentric.
[3] Exhausted.
[4] "He preferred his aged wife [Penelope] to immortality."
[5] A reason.
[6] Thales, Greek philosopher (640–546 B.C.).

Preface

The earliest antiquity lies buried in silence and oblivion, excepting the remains we have of it in sacred writ. This silence was succeeded by poetical fables, and these, at length, by the writings we now enjoy; so that the concealed and secret learning of the ancients seems separated from the history and knowledge of the following ages by a veil, or partition-wall of fables, interposing between the things that are lost and those that remain. . . .

Upon deliberate consideration, my judgment is, that a concealed instruction and allegory was originally intended in many of the ancient fables. This opinion may, in some respect, be owing to the veneration I have for antiquity, but more to observing that some fables discover a great and evident similitude, relation, and connection with the thing they signify, as well in the structure of the fable as in the propriety of the names whereby the persons or actors are characterized; insomuch, that no one could positively deny a sense and meaning to be from the first intended, and purposely shadowed out in them. . . .

But the argument of most weight with me is this, that many of these fables by no means appear to have been invented by the persons who relate and divulge them, whether Homer, Hesiod, or others; for if I were assured they first flowed from those later times and authors that transmit them to us, I should never expect any thing singularly great or noble from such an origin. But whoever attentively considers the thing, will find that these fables are delivered down and related by those writers, not as matters then first invented and proposed, but as things received and embraced in earlier ages. Besides, as they are differently related by writers nearly of the same ages, it is easily perceived that the relators drew from the common stock of ancient tradition, and varied but in point of embellishment, which is their own. And this principally raises my esteem of these fables, which I receive, not as the product of the age, or invention of the poets, but as sacred relics, gentle whispers, and the breath of better times, that from the traditions of more ancient nations came, at length, into the flutes and trumpets of the Greeks. But if any one shall, notwithstanding this, contend that allegories are always adventitious, or imposed upon the ancient fables, and no way native or genuinely contained in them, we might here leave him undisturbed in that gravity of judgment he affects (though we cannot help accounting it somewhat dull and phlegmatic), and, if it were worth the trouble, proceed to another kind of argument.

Men have proposed to answer two different and contrary ends by the use of parable; for parables serve as well to instruct or illustrate as to wrap up and envelop; so that though, for the present, we drop the concealed use, and suppose the ancient fables to be vague, undeterminate things, formed for amusement, still, the other use must remain, and can never be given up. And every man, of any learning, must readily allow that this method of instructing is grave, sober, or exceedingly useful, and sometimes necessary in the sciences, as it opens an easy and familiar passage to the human understanding, in all new discoveries that are abstruse and out of the road of vulgar opinions. Hence, in the first ages, when such inventions and conclusions of the human reason as are now trite and common were new and little known, all things abounded with fables, parables, similes, comparisons, and allusions, which were not intended to conceal, but to inform and teach, whilst the minds of men continued rude and unpracticed in matters of subtlety and speculation, or even impatient, and in a manner incapable of receiving such things as did not fall directly under and strike the senses. For as hieroglyphics were in use before writing, so were parables in use before arguments. And even to this day, if any man would let new light in upon the human understanding, and conquer prejudice, without raising contests, animosities, opposition, or disturbance, he must still go in the same path, and have recourse to the like method of allegory, metaphor, and allusion.

To conclude, the knowledge of the early ages was either great or happy; great, if they by design made this use of trope and figure; happy, if, whilst they had other views, they afforded matter and occasion to such noble contemplations. Let either be the case, our pains, perhaps, will not be misemployed, whether we illustrate antiquity or things themselves.

The like, indeed, has been attempted by others; but, to speak ingenuously, their great and voluminous labors have almost destroyed the energy, the efficacy, and grace of the thing; whilst, being unskilled in nature, and their learning no more than that of commonplace, they have applied the sense of the parables to certain general and vulgar matters, without reaching to their real purport, genuine interpretation, and full depth. For myself, therefore, I expect to appear new in these common things, because, leaving untouched such as are sufficiently plain and open, I shall drive only at those that are either deep or rich.

Tythonus, or Satiety

Explained of Predominant Passions

It is elegantly fabled by Tythonus, that being exceedingly beloved by Aurora, she petitioned Jupiter that he might prove immortal, thereby to secure herself the everlasting enjoyment of his company; but through female inadvertence she forgot to add, that he might never grow old; so that, though he proved immortal, he became miserably worn and consumed with age, insomuch that Jupiter, out of pity, at length transformed him to a grasshopper.

Explanation.—This fable seems to contain an ingenious description of pleasure; which at first, as it were in the morning of the day, is so welcome, that men pray to have it everlasting, but forget that satiety and weariness of it will, like old age, overtake them, though they think not of it; so that at length, when their appetite for pleasurable actions is gone, their desires and affections often continue; whence we commonly find that aged persons delight themselves with the discourse and remembrance of the things agreeable to them in their better days. This is very remarkable in men of a loose, and men of a military life; the former whereof are always talking over amours, and the latter the exploits of their youth; like grasshoppers, that show their vigor only by their chirping.

Daedalus, or Mechanical Skill

Explained of Arts and Artists in Kingdoms and States

The ancients have left us a description of mechanical skill, industry, and curious arts converted to ill uses, in the person of Daedalus, a most ingenious but execrable artist. This Daedalus was banished for the murder of his brother artist and rival, yet found a kind reception in his banishment from the kings and states where he came. He raised many incomparable edifices to the honor of the gods, and invented many new contrivances for the beautifying and ennobling of cities and public places, but still he was most famous for wicked inventions. Among the rest, by his abominable industry and destructive genius, he assisted in the fatal and infamous production of the monster Minotaur, that devourer of promising youths. And then, to cover one mischief with another, and provide for the security of this monster, he invented and built a labyrinth; a work infamous for its end and design, but admirable and prodigious for art and workmanship. After this, that he 5 might not only be celebrated for wicked inventions, but be sought after, as well for prevention, as for instruments of mischief, he formed that ingenious device of his clue, which led directly through all the windings 10 of the labyrinth. This Daedalus was persecuted by Minos [1] with the utmost severity, diligence, and inquiry; but he always found refuge and means of escaping. Lastly, endeavoring to teach his son Icarus [2] the art 15 of flying, the novice, trusting too much to his wings, fell from his towering flight, and was drowned in the sea.

Explanation.—The sense of the fable runs 20 thus. It first denotes envy, which is continually upon the watch, and strangely prevails among excellent artificers; for no kind of people are observed to be more implacably and destructively envious to one another than 25 these.

In the next place, it observes an impolitic and improvident kind of punishment inflicted upon Daedalus—that of banishment; for good workmen are gladly received everywhere, so 30 that banishment to an excellent artificer is scarce any punishment at all; whereas other conditions of life cannot easily flourish from home. For the admiration of artists is propagated and increased among foreigners and 35 strangers; it being a principle in the minds of men to slight and despise the mechanical operators of their own nation.

The succeeding part of the fable is plain, concerning the use of mechanic arts, whereto 40 human life stands greatly indebted, as receiving from this treasury numerous particulars for the service of religion, the ornament of civil society, and the whole provision and apparatus of life; but then the same magazine 45 supplies instruments of lust, cruelty, and death. For, not to mention the arts of luxury

[1] King of Crete.
[2] I.e., Daedalus' own son.

and debauchery, we plainly see how far the business of exquisite poisons, guns, engines of war, and such kind of destructive inventions, exceeds the cruelty and barbarity of the Minotaur himself.

The addition of the labyrinth contains a beautiful allegory, representing the nature of mechanic arts in general; for all ingenious and accurate mechanical inventions may be conceived as a labyrinth, which, by reason of their subtlety, intricacy, crossing, and interfering with one another, and the apparent resemblances they have among themselves, scarce any power of the judgment can unravel and distinguish; so that they are only to be understood and traced by the clue of experience.

It is no less prudently added, that he who invented the windings of the labyrinth, should also show the use and management of the clue; for mechanical arts have an ambiguous or double use, and serve as well to produce as to prevent mischief and destruction; so that their virtue almost destroys or unwinds itself.

Unlawful arts and indeed frequently arts themselves, are persecuted by Minos, that is, by laws, which prohibit and forbid their use among the people; but notwithstanding this, they are hid, concealed, retained, and everywhere find reception and skulking-places; a thing well observed by Tacitus of the astrologers and fortune-tellers of his time. "These," says he, "are a kind of men that will always be prohibited, and yet will always be retained in our city."

But lastly, all unlawful and vain arts, of what kind soever, lose their reputation in tract of time; grow contemptible and perish, through their over-confidence, like Icarus; being commonly unable to perform what they boasted. And to say the truth, such arts are better suppressed by their own vain pretensions, than checked or restrained by the bridle of laws.

STUDY AIDS: Bacon's attitude in this interpretation is a criticism of the applied science of his day. How? What aspects of seventeenth-century science does he condemn?

Sphinx, or Science

Explained of the Sciences [1]

They relate that Sphinx was a monster, variously formed, having the face and voice of a virgin, the wings of a bird, and the talons of a griffin.[2] She resided on the top of a mountain, near the city Thebes, and also beset the highways. Her manner was to lie in ambush and seize the travelers, and having them in her power, to propose to them certain dark and perplexed riddles, which it was thought she received from the Muses, and if her wretched captives could not solve and interpret these riddles, she, with great cruelty, fell upon them, in their hesitation and confusion, and tore them to pieces. This plague having reigned a long time, the Thebans at length offered their kingdom to the man who could interpret her riddles, there being no other way to subdue her. Oedipus, a penetrating and prudent man, though lame in his feet, excited by so great a reward, accepted the condition, and with a good assurance of mind, cheerfully presented himself before the monster, who directly asked him: "What creature that was, which, being born four-footed, afterwards became two-footed, then three-footed, and lastly four-footed again?" Oedipus, with presence of mind, replied it was man, who, upon his first birth and infant state, crawled upon all fours in endeavoring to walk; but not long after went upright upon his two natural feet; again, in old age walked three-footed, with a stick; and at last, growing decrepit, lay four-footed confined to his bed; and having by this exact solution obtained the victory, he slew the monster, and, laying the carcass upon an ass, led her away in triumph; and upon this he was, according to the agreement, made king of Thebes.

[1] In Bacon's day the word "science" had a broader meaning than it does today. Although it embraced what we call the natural (physical and biological) sciences, it was applied also to any body of systematized knowledge.

[2] A legendary monster, half lion and half eagle.

Explanation.—This is an elegant, instructive fable, and seems invented to represent science, especially as joined with practice. For science may, without absurdity, be called a monster, being strangely gazed at and admired by the ignorant and unskilful. Her figure and form is various, by reason of the vast variety of subjects that science considers; her voice and countenance are represented female, by reason of her gay appearance and volubility of speech; wings are added, because the sciences and their inventions run and fly about in a moment, for knowledge, like light communicated from one torch to another, is presently caught and copiously diffused; sharp and hooked talons are elegantly attributed to her, because the axioms and arguments of science enter the mind, lay hold of it, fix it down, and keep it from moving or slipping away. This the sacred philosopher observed, when he said: "The words of the wise are like goads or nails driven far in." Again, all science seems placed on high, as it were on the tops of mountains hard to climb; for science is justly imagined a sublime and lofty thing, looking down upon ignorance from an eminence, and at the same time taking an extensive view on all sides, as is usual on the tops of mountains. Science is said to beset the highways, because through all the journey and peregrination of human life there is matter and occasion offered of contemplation.

Sphinx is said to propose various difficult questions and riddles to men, which she received from the Muses; and these questions, so long as they remain with the Muses, may very well be unaccompanied with severity, for while there is no other end of contemplation and inquiry but that of knowledge alone, the understanding is not oppressed, or driven to straits and difficulties, but expatiates and ranges at large, and even receives a degree of pleasure from doubt and variety; but after the Muses have given over their riddles to Sphinx, that is, to practice, which urges and impels to action, choice, and determination, then it is that they become torturing, severe, and trying, and, unless solved and interpreted, strangely perplex and harass the human mind, rend it every way, and perfectly tear it to pieces. All the riddles of [5] Sphinx, therefore, have two conditions annexed, viz: laceration to those who do not solve them, and empire to those that do. For he who understands the thing proposed, obtains his end, and every artificer rules over [10] his work.

Sphinx has no more than two kinds of riddles, one relating to the nature of things, the other to the nature of man; and correspondent to these, the prizes of the solution [15] are two kinds of empire—the empire over nature, and the empire over man. For the true and ultimate end of natural philosophy is dominion over natural things, natural bodies, remedies, machines, and numberless [20] other particulars, though the schools, contented with their own discourses, neglect, and in a manner despise, both things and works.

But the riddle proposed to Oedipus, the [25] solution whereof acquired him the Theban kingdom, regarded the nature of man; for he who has thoroughly looked into and examined human nature, may in a manner command his own fortune, and seems born to acquire [30] dominion and rule. Accordingly, Virgil properly makes the arts of government to be the arts of the Romans. It was, therefore, extremely apposite in Augustus Caesar to use the image of Sphinx in his signet, whether [35] this happened by accident or by design; for he of all men was deeply versed in politics, and

through the course of his life very happily solved abundance of new riddles with regard to the nature of man; and unless he had done this with great dexterity and ready address, he would frequently have been involved in imminent danger, if not destruction.

It is with the utmost elegance added in the fable, when Sphinx was conquered, her carcass was laid upon an ass; for there is nothing so subtle and abstruse but after being once made plain, intelligible, and common, it may be received by the slowest capacity.

We must not omit that Sphinx was conquered by a lame man, and impotent in his feet; for men usually make too much haste to the solution of Sphinx's riddles; whence it happens that she prevailing, their minds are rather racked and torn by disputes, than invested with command by works and effects. (1619)

STUDY AIDS: There is considerable interest in mythology today, especially among sociologists, anthropologists, psychologists, and literary critics. Here are some definitions offered by a few of these men. Mythology is: (1) a primitive, fumbling effort to explain the world of nature (Frazer); (2) a production of poetical fantasy from prehistoric times, misunderstood by succeeding ages (Muller); (3) a repository of allegorical instruction to shape the individual to his group (Durkheim); (4) a group dream, symptomatic of archetypal urges within the depths of the human psyche (Jung); (5) a traditional vehicle of man's profoundest metaphysical insights (Coomaraswamy); (6) God's Revelation to his children (the church). With which of these definitions would Bacon agree?

Bacon's Discourse on Idols
(translated from the *Novum Organum*)

"Novum organum" means "a new instrument." The new instrument that Bacon proposed was a new method for studying natural science. The old method, used by Aristotle and by thinkers all through the Middle Ages down to Bacon's time, was to begin one's study with assumptions of general truths about nature and then to reason from these truths. Observation and experimentation played a small part in such scientific speculations. Bacon held that study should begin with the observation of particular objects and phenomena, and proceed inductively to general laws or principles—the method that experimental science has followed ever since his day.

In urging men to keep their eyes on the particular object in order to see it for what it is, Bacon recognized certain errors in thinking that men fall into. These he called "idols," which we can take to mean "misconceptions." His well-known statement lists four such idols.

The idols and false notions which have already preoccupied the human understanding, and are deeply rooted in it, not only so beset men's minds, that they become difficult of access, but even when access is obtained, will again meet and trouble us in the instauration [1] of the sciences, unless mankind, when forewarned, guard themselves with all possible care against them.

Four species of idols beset the human mind: to which (for distinction's sake) we have assigned names: calling the first, idols of the tribe; the second, idols of the den; the third, idols of the market; and the fourth, idols of the theater.

The formation of notions and axioms on the foundations of true induction, is the only fitting remedy, by which we can ward off and expel these idols. It is however of great service to point them out. For the doctrine of idols bears the same relation to the interpretation of nature, as that of the confutation of sophisms does to common logic.

The idols of the tribe are inherent in human nature, and the very tribe or race of man. For man's sense is falsely asserted to be the standard of things. On the contrary, all the perceptions, both of the senses and the mind, bear reference to man, and not to the universe, and the human mind resembles those uneven mirrors, which impart their own properties to different objects, from which rays are emitted, and distort and disfigure them.

The idols of the den are those of each individual. For every body (in addition to the errors common to the race of man) has his own individual den or cavern,[2] which intercepts and corrupts the light of nature; either from his own peculiar and singular disposition, or from his education and intercourse with others, or from his reading, and the authority acquired by those whom he reverences and admires, or from a different impression produced on the mind, as it happens to be preoccupied and predisposed, or equable and tranquil, and the like: so that the spirit of man (according to its several dispositions) is variable, confused, and as it were actuated by chance; and Heraclitus [3] said well that men search for knowledge in lesser worlds and not in the greater or common world.

There are also idols formed by the reciprocal intercourse and society of man with man, which we call idols of the market, from the commerce and association of men with each other. For men converse by means of language; but words are formed at the will of the generality; [4] and there arises from a bad and unapt formation of words a wonderful obstruction to the mind. Nor can the definitions and explanations, with which learned men are wont to guard and protect themselves in some instances, afford a complete remedy: words still manifestly force the understanding, throw everything into confusion, and lead mankind into vain and innumerable controversies and fallacies.

Lastly, there are idols which have crept into men's minds from the various dogmas of peculiar systems of philosophy, and also from the perverted rules of demonstration,[5] and these we denominate idols of the theater. For we regard all the systems of philosophy hitherto received or imagined, as so many plays brought out and performed, creating fictitious and theatrical worlds. Nor do we speak only of the present systems, or of the philosophy and sects of the ancients, since numerous other plays of a similar nature can be still composed and made to agree with each other, the causes of the most opposite errors being generally the same. Nor, again, do we allude merely to the general systems, but also to many elements and axioms of sciences, which have become inveterate by tradition,

---

[1] Restoration or renewal after decay.
[2] An allusion to the Allegory of the Cave in Plato's *Republic,* Book 7.

[3] Greek philosopher of the sixth century B.C.
[4] The general public.
[5] Process of logical proof.

implicit credence, and neglect. We must, however, discuss each species of idols more fully and distinctly in order to guard the human understanding against them. . . .

Let such, therefore, be our precautions in contemplation, that we may ward off and expel the idols of the den: which mostly owe their birth to some predominant pursuit; or, secondly, to an excess in synthesis and analysis; or, thirdly, to a party zeal in favor of certain ages; or, fourthly, to the extent or narrowness of the subject. In general he who contemplates nature should suspect whatever particularly takes and fixes his understanding, and should use so much the more caution to preserve it equable and unprejudiced.

The idols of the market are the most troublesome of all, those namely which have entwined themselves round the understanding from the associations of words and names. For men imagine that their reason governs words, whilst, in fact, words react upon the understanding; and this has rendered philosophy and the sciences sophistical and inactive. Words are generally formed in a popular sense, and define things by those broad lines which are most obvious to the vulgar mind; but when a more acute understanding, or more diligent observation, is anxious to vary those lines, and to adapt them more accurately to nature, words oppose it. Hence the great and solemn disputes of learned men often terminate in controversies about words and names, in regard to which it would be better (imitating the caution of mathematicians) to proceed more advisedly in the first instance, and to bring such disputes to a regular issue by definitions. Such definitions, however, cannot remedy the evil in natural and material objects because they consist themselves of words, and these words produce others; so that we must necessarily have recourse to particular instances, and their regular series and arrangement, as we shall mention when we come to the mode and scheme of determining notions and axioms.

The idols imposed upon the understanding by words are of two kinds. They are either the names of things which have no existence (for as some objects are from inattention left without a name, so names are formed by fanciful imaginations which are without an object), or they are the names of actual objects, but confused, badly defined, and hastily and irregularly abstracted from things. Fortune, the primum mobile, the planetary orbits, the element of fire, and the like fictions, which owe their birth to futile and false theories, are instances of the first kind. And this species of idols is removed with greater facility, because it can be exterminated by the constant refutation of the desuetude of the theories themselves. The others, which are created by vicious and unskilful abstraction, are intricate and deeply rooted. Take some word for instance, as "moist"; and let us examine how far the different significations of this word are consistent. It will be found that the word "moist" is nothing but a confused sign of different actions admitting of no settled and defined uniformity. For it means that which easily diffuses itself over another body; that which is indeterminable and cannot be brought to a consistency; that which yields easily in every direction; that which is easily united and collected; that which easily flows and is put in motion; that which easily adheres to and wets another body; that which is easily reduced to a liquid state though previously solid. When, therefore, you come to predicate or impose this name, in one sense flame is moist, in another air is not moist, in another fine powder is moist, in another glass is moist; so that it is quite clear that this notion is hastily abstracted from water only, and common ordinary liquors without any due verification of it.

There are, however, different degrees of distortion and mistake in words. One of the least faulty classes is that of the names of substances, particularly of the less abstract and more defined species (those then of "chalk" and "mud" are good, of "earth," bad); words signifying actions are more faulty, as to "generate," to "corrupt," to "change"; but the most faulty are those denoting qualities (except the immediate objects of sense), as "heavy," "light," "rare," "dense." Yet in all of these there must be some notions a little better than others, in proportion as a greater or less number of things come before the senses.

The idols of the theater are not innate, nor do they introduce themselves secretly into the understanding; but they are manifestly instilled and cherished by the fictions of theories and depraved rules of demonstrations. To attempt, however, or undertake their confutation would not be consistent with our declarations. For since we neither agree in our principles nor our demonstrations, all argument is out of the question. And it is fortunate that the ancients are left in possession of their honors. We detract nothing from them, seeing our whole doctrine relates only to the path to be pursued. The lame (as they say) in the path outstrip the swift, who wander from it, and it is clear that the very skill and swiftness of him who runs not in the right direction must increase his aberration.

Our method of discovering the sciences is such as to leave little to the acuteness and strength of wit, and indeed rather to level wit and intellect. For as in the drawing of a straight line, or accurate circle by the hand, much depends on its steadiness and practice, but if a ruler or compass be employed there is little occasion for either; so it is with our method. Although, however, we enter into no individual confutations, yet a little must be said, first, of the sects and general divisions of these species of theories; secondly, something further to show that there are external signs of their weakness, and, lastly, we must consider the causes of so great a misfortune, and so long and general a unanimity in error, that we may thus render the access to truth less difficult, and that the human understanding may the more readily be purified, and brought to dismiss its idols.

The idols of the theater or of theories are numerous, and may and perhaps will be

5 still more so. For unless men's minds had been now occupied for many ages in religious and theological considerations, and civil governments (especially monarchies) had been averse to novelties of that nature even in theory (so that men must apply to them with some risk and injury to their own fortunes, and not only without reward but subject to contumely and envy), there is no doubt that 10 many other sects of philosophers and theorists would have been introduced, like those which formerly flourished in such diversified abundance amongst the Greeks. For as many imaginary theories of the heavens can be de- 15 duced from the phenomena of the sky, so is it even more easy to found many dogmas upon the phenomena of philosophy—and the plot of this our theater resembles those of the poetical, where the plots which are in- 20 vented for the stage are more consistent, elegant, and pleasurable than those taken from real history.

In general men take for the groundwork of their philosophy either too much from a 25 few topics, or too little from many; in either case their philosophy is founded on too narrow a basis of experiment and natural history, and decides on too scanty grounds. . . .
(1620)

STUDY AIDS: 1. Bacon's four "idols," or obstacles to straight thinking, are always present to hinder men's pursuit of truth. For each of the four, state the obstacle in your own words, and 35 show how it operates today—in your personal life, in school and college, in public life.

2. Which idol does Bacon consider most troublesome? Why? Which do you consider most troublesome? Why? Is a given idol troublesome 40 to all men alike, or more so to one man than to another? Can you discover a reason for Bacon's listing the idols in the order he did?

THERE IS A GARDEN IN HER FACE

Words and Music
by Thomas Campion (1567-1620)

"There is a Garden in Her Face,"
words and music by Thomas Campion.

Arrangement by L. T. Dickinson.

FOLLOW YOUR SAINT

Words and Music
by Thomas Campion (1567-1620)

Arrangement by L. T. Dickinson.

"Follow Your Saint," words and
music by Thomas Campion.

Original notation of Thomas Campion's "There is a Garden in Her Face."

Thomas Dekker

(ca. 1572–ca. 1632)

DEKKER WAS BORN IN LONDON AND LIVED OUT HIS PRECARIOUS EXISTENCE IN THAT CITY. HE supported himself by writing, evidently a hand-to-mouth living, since he was several times in debtor's prison. The greatest contribution of his prolific pen was *The Shoemaker's Holiday* (1599), a "bourgeois" comedy of love and life among the citizens of London. It is one of forty-one plays which he wrote alone or in collaboration between 1598 and 1602. From 1603 to 1613 Dekker turned out a series of prose pamphlets which vividly describe the low and middle class society of the city.

The Gull's Hornbook

Much of the prose written during the Renaissance was highly ornamented and mannered, but there was also a less elegant style which was used for social satire and the realistic treatment of contemporary life. *The Gull's Hornbook* is one of Dekker's several pieces in this more utilitarian strain of prose. It satirizes the wealthy but foolish young men who came to London to gain experience and find a place in society, but who often were "gulls," that is, easy prey to the confidence men who cheated the "gullible." It is for these gulls that Dekker writes a "hornbook," or primer—a mock-serious book of manners, which will direct them through a day in London spent at St. Paul's, the restaurants, the theater, and the taverns.

Chapter 6

How a Gallant [1] Should Behave Himself in a Playhouse

The theater is your poets' royal exchange, upon which their muses (that are now turned to merchants) meeting, barter away that light commodity of words for a lighter ware than words, plaudities,[2] and the breath of the great beast;[3] which, like the threatenings of two cowards, vanish all into air. Players and their factors, who put away the stuff, and make the best of it they possibly can (as indeed 'tis their parts so to do), your gallant, your courtier, and your captain had wont to be the soundest paymasters; and I think are still the surest chapmen;[4] and these, by means that their heads are well stocked, deal upon this comical freight by the gross; when your groundling and gallery-commoner buys his sport by the penny and, like a haggler, is glad to utter it again by retailing.

Since then the place is so free in entertainment, allowing a stool as well to the farmer's son as to your templar; that your stinkard [5] has the selfsame liberty to be there in his tobacco fumes, which your sweet courtier hath; and that your carman [6] and tinker claim as strong a voice in their suffrage, and sit to give judgment on the play's life and death, as well as the proudest momus [7] among the tribes of critic; it is fit that he, whom the most tailors' bills do make room for, when he comes, should not be basely (like a viol) cased up in a corner.

Whether therefore the gatherers of the pub-

---

[1] A foppish young man.
[2] Applause.
[3] Audience.
[4] Merchants.

[5] The "groundling," a low-born fellow, who paid a penny to stand during the play.
[6] Laborer.
[7] Critic. Momus was the Greek god of censure.

lic or private playhouse stand to receive the afternoon's rent, let our gallant (having paid it) presently advance himself up to the throne of the stage. I mean not into the lord's room, which is now but the stage's suburbs; no, those boxes, by the iniquity of custom, conspiracy of waiting women and gentlemen ushers, that there sweat together, and the covetousness of sharers,[8] are contemptibly thrust into the rear, and much new satin is there damned by being smothered to death in darkness. But on the very rushes where the comedy is to dance, yea, and under the state of Cambyses[9] himself, must our feathered estridge,[10] like a piece of ordnance, be planted, valiantly (because impudently) beating down the mews and hisses of the opposed rascality.

For do but cast up a reckoning, what large comings-in are pursed up by sitting on the stage. First a conspicuous eminence is gotten; by which means the best and most essential parts of a gallant (good clothes, a proportionable leg, white hand, the Persian lock,[11] and a tolerable beard) are perfectly revealed.

By sitting on the stage you have a signed patent to engross [12] the whole commodity of censure; may lawfully presume to be a girder; [13] and stand at the helm to steer the passage of scenes; yet no man shall once offer to hinder you from obtaining the title of an insolent, overweening coxcomb.

By sitting on the stage, you may, without traveling for it, at the very next door ask whose play it is; and, by that quest of inquiry, the law warrants you to avoid much mistaking; if you know not the author, you may rail against him; and peradventure so behave yourself that you may enforce the author to know you.

By sitting on the stage, if you be a knight you may happily get you a mistress; if a mere Fleet-street gentleman, a wife; but assure yourself, by continual residence, you are the first and principal man in election to begin the number of We Three.[14]

By spreading your body on the stage, and by being a justice in examining of plays, you shall put yourself into such true scenical authority that some poet shall not dare to present his muse rudely upon your eyes, without having first unmasked her, rifled her, and discovered all her bare and most mystical parts before you at a tavern, when you most knightly shall, for his pains, pay for both their suppers.

By sitting on the stage, you may (with small cost) purchase the dear acquaintance of the boys; have a good stool for sixpence; at any time know what particular part any of the infants [15] present; get your match lighted, examine the play-suits' lace, and perhaps win wagers upon laying 'tis copper, etc. And to conclude, whether you be a fool or a justice of peace, a cuckold or a captain, a lord-mayor's son or a dawcock,[16] a knave or an under-sheriff; of what stamp soever you be, current or counterfeit, the stage, like time, will bring you to most perfect light and lay you open; neither are you to be hunted from thence, though the scarecrows in the yard [17] hoot at you, hiss at you, spit at you, yea, throw dirt even in your teeth; 'tis most gentlemanlike patience to endure all this and to laugh at the silly animals; but if the rabble, with a full throat, cry, "Away with the fool," you were worse than a madman to tarry by it; for the gentleman and the fool should never sit on the stage together.

Marry, let this observation go hand in hand with the rest; or rather, like a country servingman, some five yards before them. Present not yourself on the stage (especially at a new play) until the quaking prologue hath (by rubbing) got color into his cheeks, and is ready to give the trumpets their cue that he's upon point to enter; for then it is time, as though you were one of the properties, or

---

[8] Stockholders of the theater.

[9] King of the Persians and the Medes in the sixth century, B.C. He was made the hero of a bad play in 1569, and thus became a symbol of ranting drama.

[10] Ostrich.

[11] Fashionable hair style.

[12] To control by buying.

[13] A sneerer.

[14] An allusion to a humorous picture of two mules, with the caption, "We three, loggerheads be," the spectator being the third.

[15] The boy actors, who played the feminine roles.

[16] A silly fellow.

[17] Groundlings.

that you dropped out of the hangings, to creep from behind the arras, with your tripos or three-footed stool in one hand, and a teston [18] mounted between a forefinger and a thumb in the other; for, if you should bestow your person upon the vulgar when the belly of the house is but half full, your apparel is quite eaten up, the fashion lost, and the proportion of your body in more danger to be devoured than if it were served up in the Counter amongst the poultry; [19] avoid that as you would the bastone. It shall crown you with rich commendation to laugh aloud in the midst of the most serious and saddest scene of the terriblest tragedy, and to let that clapper, your tongue, be tossed so high that all the house may ring of it. Your lords use it; your knights are apes to the lords, and do so too; your Inn-o'-Court man is zany to the knights, and (many very scurvily) comes likewise limping after it; be thou a beagle to them all, and never lin [20] snuffing till you have scented them; for by talking and laughing, like a ploughman in a morris,[21] you heap Pelion upon Ossa,[22] glory upon glory; as first, all the eyes in the galleries will leave walking after the players and only follow you; the simplest dolt in the house snatches up your name, and when he meets you in the streets, or that you fall into his hands in the middle of a watch, his word shall be taken for you; he'll cry "He's such a gallant," and you pass. Secondly, you publish your temperance to the world, in that you seem not to resort thither to taste vain pleasures with a hungry appetite; but only as a gentleman to spend a foolish hour or two, because you can do nothing else; thirdly, you mightily disrelish the audience, and disgrace the author; marry, you take up, though it be at the worst hand, a strong opinion of your own judgment, and enforce the poet to take pity of your weakness, and, by some dedicated sonnet, to bring you into a better paradise, only to stop your mouth.

[18] A coin worth about six pence.
[19] A debtor's prison in the Poultry, Cheapside.
[20] Stop.
[21] Popular dance.
[22] A Greek myth which relates the Titans' efforts to scale Mt. Olympus by piling Mt. Ossa upon Mt. Pelion (not Pelion upon Ossa).

If you can, either for love or money, provide yourself a lodging by the water-side; for, above the conveniency it brings to shun shoulder-clapping, and to ship away your cockatrice [23] betimes in the morning, it adds a kind of state unto you to be carried from thence to the stairs of your playhouse. Hate a sculler [24] (remember that) worse than to be acquainted with one o' th' scullery.[25] No, your oars [26] are your only sea-crabs, board them, and take heed you never go twice together with one pair; often shifting is a great credit to gentlemen; and that dividing of your fare will make the poor water-snakes be ready to pull you in pieces to enjoy your custom. No matter whether, upon landing, you have money or no; you may swim in twenty of their boats over the river upon ticket; [27] marry, when silver comes in, remember to pay treble their fare, and it will make your flounder-catchers to send more thanks after you when you do not draw, than when you do; for they know it will be their own another day.

Before the play begins, fall to cards; you may win or lose, as fencers do in a prize, and beat one another by confederacy, yet share the money when you meet at supper; notwithstanding, to gull the ragamuffins that stand aloof gaping at you, throw the cards, having first torn four or five of them, round about the stage, just upon the third sound,[28] as though you had lost; it skills [29] not if the four knaves [30] lie on their backs, and outface the audience; there's none such fools as dare take exceptions at them, because, ere the play go off, better knaves than they will fall into the company.

Now, sir, if the writer be a fellow that hath either epigrammed you, or hath had a flirt at your mistress, or hath brought either your

[23] Prostitute.
[24] Boatman who rowed people across the Thames River.
[25] Kitchen. Dekker is punning.
[26] Boats.
[27] On credit.
[28] The last trumpet call to indicate curtain time.
[29] Matters.
[30] The four jacks in a deck of cards. This gesture would indicate that the gallant's losing at cards was of no consequence.

feather, or your red beard, or your little legs, etc., on the stage, you shall disgrace him worse than by tossing him in a blanket or giving him the bastinado [31] in a tavern, if, in the middle of his play (be it pastoral or comedy, moral or tragedy), you rise with a screwed and discontented face from your stool to be gone; no matter whether the scenes be good or no; the better they are the worse do you distaste them; and, being on your feet, sneak not away like a coward, but salute all your gentle acquaintance that are spread either on the rushes or on stools about you, and draw what troop you can from the stage after you. The mimics [32] are beholden to you for allowing them elbow-room; their poet [33] cries, perhaps, "A pox go with you," but care not for that, there's no music without frets.

Marry, if either the company or indisposition of the weather bind you to sit it out, my counsel is then that you turn plain ape, take up a rush, and tickle the earnest ears of your fellow gallants, to make other fools fall a-laughing; mew at passionate speeches, blare at merry, find fault with the music, whew at the children's action, whistle at the songs; and above all, curse the sharers, that whereas the same day you had bestowed forty shillings on an embroidered felt and feather (Scotch-fashion) for your mistress in the court or your punk [34] in the city, within two hours after you encounter with the very same block [35] on the stage, when the haberdasher swore to you the impression was extant but that morning.

To conclude, hoard up the finest play-scraps you can get, upon which your lean wit may most savorly feed, for want of other stuff, when the Arcadian and Euphuized gentlewomen [36] have their tongues sharpened to set upon you; that quality (next to your shuttlecock) is the only furniture to a courtier that's but a new beginner, and is but in his A B C of compliment. The next places that are filled, after the playhouses be emptied, are (or ought to be) taverns. Into a tavern then let us next march, where the brains of one hogshead must be beaten out to make up another. (1609)

John Donne
(1572–1631)

DONNE'S FATHER WAS A PROSPEROUS LONDON TRADESMAN, WARDEN OF THE IRONMONGER'S Company. When he died in 1576, John Donne was left in the care of his mother, a devout Catholic. She sent him to Oxford University in 1584. After three years there, Donne changed to Cambridge University, but once again, after a similar period, left without taking a degree, doubtless because of his Catholic scruples. By May, 1591, he was studying law, first at Thavies Inn, later at Lincoln's Inn.

Participation in the Expedition to Cadiz in 1596 brought Donne to the attention of the court officials. It is probable that Robert Cecil, Elizabeth's Secretary of State, sent him in 1598 to negotiate with Henry IV of France. In this same year Donne became secretary to the Lord Keeper, Thomas Egerton. His future promised to be brilliant, but he fell in love with Ann More, Egerton's niece by marriage, and in 1601 eloped with her. He was dismissed from Egerton's service, imprisoned, and when released found all doors closed to him. The fourteen years which followed were filled with poverty, illness, and despair.

[31] A blow struck with a stick.
[32] Actors.
[33] The author of the play.
[34] Prostitute.

[35] Pattern.
[36] The ladies of the court who affected the language of Sidney's *Arcadia* and Lyly's *Euphues*.

During this period James I made it clear that he would oppose any appointment for Donne except priesthood in the Anglican church. The *Essays in Divinity* (1614) record the poet's spiritual agony and eventual conversion. The following year he was ordained a priest of the Anglican church, and he moved rapidly through its hierarchy from a country parish in 1615 to the Deanship of St. Paul's in 1621.

It is one of the seventeenth century's many fascinating paradoxes that its most famous poetic amorist became its most famous preacher. Donne's audacious love poems had been written in the 1590's, but their continued circulation in manuscripts must have been a painful reminder of the worldly past to the now penitent priest. Donne the lover and Donne the priest, however, were the same man. The object of his love had changed from woman to God, but the dramatic and passionate utterance, the subtle probings of his self-awareness, and the many facets of his curiosity and learning remained the same, whether revealed in the profane poems in *Songs and Sonnets* (1633) or in the sacred *Devotions upon Emergent Occasions* (1624) and *Sermons* (1640).

Donne has been credited with founding the "metaphysical" school of poetry. The claim is true only in that Donne favored the so-called "metaphysical conceit," but it had been used earlier, perhaps with less ingenuity, by Shakespeare, Jonson, and other Elizabethans, who had tired of the Petrarchan images and the lush sensuousness of Spenser. The more traditional conceit (image) used by these poets compares one thing experienced through the senses with another thing experienced through the senses, e.g., "Shall I compare thee to a summer's day?" The metaphysical conceit, however, is more intellectual and witty, its success in communication less dependent on sensory experience. Its comparison is based on a similarity in idea or logic rather than on a similarity in sensory experience. Donne's *A Valediction Forbidding Mourning* compares the unity of love, although the lovers are physically separated, to a draughtsman's compass: when one leg moves, we know the other leg must move, whether we see it or not (see p. 205, ll. 25–28).

Dr. Johnson's well-known definition of the conceit as "a combination of dissimilar images, or discovery of occult resemblances in things apparently unlike" is fairly accurate. Certainly the metaphysical rather than the sensory image more easily brought together into one poetic whole the "dissimilar" and "occult" experiences which the seventeenth century treated in its poetry. With its aid, Donne could unify the paradoxical elements in his own personality and character; he could fuse the disparate knowledge and speculation which he and his age possessed; and he could express the uneasy rapport between the new rationalistic philosophy and the older scholasticism, still lingering in religious doctrine. It could be said that the metaphysical conceit symbolized the brilliant intellectuality and the troubled faith of the period.

Song

Go and catch a falling star,
　Get with child a mandrake root,[1]
Tell me where all times past are,

Or who cleft the Devil's foot;
Teach me to hear mermaids singing,　　5
Or to keep off envy's stinging,
　　　And find
　　　What wind
Serves to advance an honest mind.[2]

[1] Because the mandrake root was shaped like the human body, it was the object of several superstitions: (1) it flourished under the gallows; (2) it cured barrenness in women; (3) it shrieked when pulled from the ground.

[2] What do the seven injunctions listed in this stanza have in common?

If thou be'st born to strange sights,[1]   10
   Things invisible go see,
Ride ten thousand days and nights
   Till age snow white hairs on thee;
Thou, when thou return'st, wilt tell me
All strange wonders that befell thee,   15
      And swear
      No where
Lives a woman true and fair.

If thou find'st one let me know,
   Such a pilgrimage were sweet;   20
Yet [2] do not, I would not go,
   Though at next door we might meet;

Though she were true when you met her,
And last till you write your letter,
      Yet she   25
      Will be
False, ere I come, to two or three.
(1633)

STUDY AIDS: 1. Even though a man might by sorcery or supernatural aid obey the nine injunctions stated in sts. 1–2, what can he not do?

2. Does the TONE of the poem indicate that Donne's role of cynical realist is sincere or is it only an assumed literary pose?

The Indifferent [3]

I can love both [4] fair and brown;
Her whom abundance melts, and her whom want betrays;
Her who loves loneness best, and her who masks and plays;
Her whom the country formed, and whom the town;
Her who believes, and her who tries;   5
Her who still weeps with spongy eyes,
And her who is dry cork and never cries.
I can love her, and her, and you, and you;
I can love any, so she be not true.

Will no other vice [5] content you?   10
Will it not serve your turn to do as did your mothers?
Or have you all old vices spent and now would find out others?
Or doth a fear that men are true torment you?
O we are not, be not you so;
Let me—and do you—twenty know;   15
Rob me, but bind me not, and let me go.

Must I, who came to travail through you,
Grow your fixed subject, because you are true?

Venus heard me sigh this song;
And by love's sweetest part, variety, she swore   20
She heard not this till now; it should be so no more.
She went, examined, and returned ere long,
And said, "Alas! some two or three
Poor heretics [6] in love there be,
Which think to stablish dangerous con-stancy.   25
But I have told them, 'Since you will be true,
You shall be true to them, who're false to you.'"
(1633)

STUDY AIDS: 1. Does the speaker in the poem see himself as a reasonable man annoyed by the unreasonableness of women or as a flip-pant man of the world cynical about women?

[1] Are the two injunctions stated in ll. 10–13 related to sorcery and superstition? What aid is required to accomplish them?

[2] What shift in TONE does "yet" produce?

[3] I.e., the impartial one.

[4] The typical Petrarchan mistress was blonde. Much of the humor of this poem arises from Donne's poking fun at stereotyped PETRARCHAN CONCEITS, so popular in Renaissance love poetry.

[5] In st. 2 the speaker pushes his attack on woman's ability to exasperate by bluntly satirizing their sexual practices.

[6] The Petrarchan conceit used the stock analogy between love and religion. How does Donne use it in ll. 23–27?

St. 1 progresses from a catalogue of character types to "you, and you" (l. 8). Is "you" one woman or all women?

2. If the attitudes of the speaker are opposed to the conventional attitudes of Petrarchan love poems, how do Donne's METER and RHYTHM sustain this opposition?

3. Is the poem serious poetry or light verse?

The Good-Morrow

I wonder, by my troth, what thou and I
Did till we loved? [1] Were we not weaned till then,
But sucked on country pleasures, childishly?
Or snorted we in the seven sleepers' den? [2]
'Twas so; [3] but this, [4] all pleasures fancies be. 5
If ever any beauty I did see, [5]
Which I desired, and got, 'twas but a dream of thee.

And now good-morrow to our waking souls, [6]
Which watch not one another out of fear;
For love all love of other sights controls, 10
And makes one little room an everywhere.
Let sea-discoverers to new worlds have gone, [7]
Let maps to other, [8] worlds on worlds have shown;
Let us possess one world, each hath one, and is one. [9]

My face in thine eye, thine in mine appears, 15
And true plain hearts do in the faces rest;
Where can we find two better hemispheres
Without sharp north, without declining west?
Whatever dies was not mixed equally; [10]
If our two loves be one, or thou and I 20

[1] Notice how the opening is made dramatic by an oath and a burst of passion. Many of Donne's poems are dramatic soliloquies or dialogues.

[2] Like the legendary Christian youths of Ephesus, who escaped persecution by sleeping more than two centuries in a cave, so the speaker and his mistress have been asleep to the joys of love.

[3] In ll. 1–5 the lover is dramatizing the excitement of his first discovery of love. He and his mistress have been babies ("weaned," "sucked," "snorted"); they have wasted their time on naive amusements ("country pleasures") when they might have been enjoying more amorous pleasures.

[4] I.e., except for this. Notice how the phrase produces a tonal modulation from the dramatic opening to the more reflective treatment of love beginning at l. 8. Notice, e.g., the smoothness of l. 8 after the rough and tumbling metrics of ll. 1–5.

[5] What word in l. 5 is explained by ll. 6–7? Donne often uses "beauty" for a physically attractive woman. What is the implication of "desired" and "got"? It would seem, then, that the lovers are not innocents who have just discovered sex, but that they have just discovered what true love means: their souls are "waking" (l. 8); their previous experiences have been adventures in lust only ("fancies," l. 5; "dream," l. 7). Note the strong implication that the conception of love as lust is naive, scorned by the mature lover, who recognizes the psychological and intellectual qualities of true love.

[6] Donne has established a contrast between lust and love. St. 2 suggests the emotional difference between the two. What is this difference as it is stated in ll. 9–11? In true love, what happens to the world (l. 11)? Donne is also using here a philosophic commonplace of his day: man is a microcosm, or a "little world." What replaces the macrocosm, or "outer world," which is well lost for love?

[7] What word in l. 11 prepares for the expanded conceit of exploration and discovery in ll. 12–14? How does Donne use the geographical discoveries of his day to explain the way he feels about gaining a new world in his love for his mistress?

[8] "Others." "Other" as a plural was acceptable in Donne's time.

[9] The two worlds (l. 14) are one world: each lover makes a hemisphere. Their love has produced so complete a union of their souls that they have become a single personality: their souls ("hearts," l. 16) are reflected in the hemispheric mirrors of their eyes. They are now a perfect sphere (ll. 17–18), better than any other world which could be found.

[10] Lines 19–21 develop by analogy the philosophic implications of the contrast between two different worlds. The substance of the physical world is matter, not "mixed equally" (visible, mutable, gross); it is the world (or substance) of the sensual lovers. The contrasted world is celestial, without "sharp north" and "declining west" (invisible, eternal, permanent); it is the world of true love, where "none can die" (l. 21).

Love so alike that none do slacken, none can
    die.
(1633)

STUDY AIDS: 1. Donne's poems were published after his death, and we do not know with
any certainty when each was written. Some
critics believe that *The Good-Morrow* was written
after his marriage to Ann More. If we read the
poem as an expression of Donne's love for his
wife, what is the world well lost for love? Is the
poem a richer or poorer experience for the reader
when so read?

2. What do ll. 10–14 do for our understanding of Donne's new-found love for his mistress?
Can a new world be built of love to compensate
for the one passed by?

3. Is the poem about physical or spiritual love?
Does it say that both qualities are necessary in
true love?

The Canonization

This poem analyzes the point made about love in *The Good-Morrow*. It searches the philosophic
implications of renouncing the world for love, but here the world is more insistent in its claims
on the lover.

For God's sake hold your tongue, and let me
    love; [1]
Or chide my palsy, or my gout;
My five gray hairs, or ruined fortune flout;
With wealth your state, your mind with arts
    improve;
    Take you a course, get you a place,   5
    Observe his Honor, or his Grace;
Or the king's real, or his stamped [2] face
    Contemplate; what you will, approve,
    So you will let me love. [3]

Alas! alas! who's injured by my love? [4]   10
    What merchant's ships have my sighs
    drowned?
    Who says my tears have overflowed his
    ground?
When did my colds a forward spring remove?

When did the heats which my veins fill
    Add one more to the plaguy bill? [5]   15
Soldiers find wars, and lawyers find out still
    Litigious men, which quarrels move,
    Though she and I do love.

Call us what you will, we are made such by
    love; [6]
    Call her one, me another fly;   20
    We're tapers too, and at our own cost [7] die,
And we in us find the eagle and the dove. [8]

[1] To whom is the poet speaking? The poem is
obviously part of a heated argument, whose climax
has been reached at the moment the poem opens, as
the exploding oath (l. 1) indicates.

[2] I.e., on coins.

[3] Note the position of this word in ll. 1, 9, 10, 18,
19, 27, 28, 36, 37, 45. Is this an external device for
unity? Does it indicate anything about the subject
of the poem?

[4] In ll. 10–18 notice how Donne juxtaposes stock
Petrarchan love HYPERBOLES against practical concerns. Do they imply sincerity or a lack of it in the
speaker's love?

[5] Weekly lists of plague victims.

[6] From l. 19 on the TONE shifts: the speaker
seems to become concerned more with his own
inward examination than with his opponent. What
do you think the opponent has "called" the lovers
(notice the accusations the speaker seems to be
answering in the first stanza)?

[7] The speaker admits his love is sexual passion,
and according to Renaissance medical theory it
will hasten his death. The "fly" (l. 20) was a symbol
both of life's brevity and of lust. "Die" (l. 21) is a
pun with a secondary meaning for Donne's time of
sexual intercourse. "Tapers" (l. 21) is a conventional metaphor for lust.

[8] One of the conventional Renaissance antitheses
drawn from natural history was that of the "eagle"
and the "dove." They typified strength and weakness, masculinity and femininity. Coming after ll.
19–21, how does Donne use the contrast to suggest
the nature of the love? Notice, too, how the
contrast prepares for the completeness of the lovers
having become one in the following lines.

The phœnix [9] riddle hath more wit
  By us; we two being one, are it;
So, to one neutral thing both sexes fit.   25
  We die and rise the same, and prove
Mysterious by this love.

We can die by it, if not live by love, [10]
  And if unfit for tomb or hearse,
  Our legend be, it will be fit for verse;   30
And if no piece of chronicle we prove,
  We'll build in sonnets pretty rooms;
  As well a well-wrought urn becomes
The greatest ashes, as half-acre tombs,
  And by these hymns all shall approve   35
Us canonized for love;

And thus invoke us: "You, whom reverend
    love [11]
  Made one another's hermitage;

You, to whom love was peace, that now is
    rage;
Who did the whole world's soul contract, and
    drove   40
  Into the glasses of your eyes;
  So made such mirrors, and such spies,
That they did all to you epitomize,
  Countries, towns, courts, [12] beg from above
  A pattern of your love."   45
(1633)

STUDY AIDS: 1. Can the poem be read as
a SATIRE on Donne's era, concerned with "cost,"
and getting ahead, blind to spiritual values in
love and religion?
  2. Could the poem be a rationalization: an
answer by Donne to a worldly-wise friend arguing about Donne's love for Ann More, a love
which "cost" (l. 21) him fortune, ambition,
and advancement? Does the TONE of the poem
help you answer this?

Song

Izaak Walton, Donne's first biographer, states that this *Song* and *A Valediction Forbidding
Mourning* were written when Donne went to the Continent in 1612 with his patron, Sir Robert
Drury, and that they were written for Mrs. Donne, whose "divining soul boded her some ill in
his absence."

Sweetest love, I do not go,
  For weariness of thee,
Nor in hope the world can show
  A fitter love for me;

          But since that I   5
Must die at last, 'tis best,
To use myself in jest
    Thus by feigned deaths to die;

[9] A flaming bird which, according to legend,
rose from its own ashes to live another hundred
years. Lines 26–27 help explain Donne's use of
the phœnix image: consumed by fire (physical love)
the lovers rise anew to an eternal love of another
nature. They are made "mysterious" (l. 27) by the
act of love; they are "one neutral (sexless) thing,"
(l. 25), the "two being one" (l. 24). Notice what
Donne has implied about the nature of love in the
two progressive views stated in ll. 20–22 and 24–27.
Through physical love one attains spiritual love.
Notice the Christian imagery in the stanza: resurrection (l. 26); "phœnix" (Christ symbol); "mysterious" (l. 27), i.e., the Christian mysteries. Donne
thus equates physical love with Christian death and
resurrection; through the one comes spiritual love or
immortality. This imagery logically prepares for the
canonizing of the fleshly spirituality of the lovers in
the next stanza.

[10] Stanzas 4–5 contemplate the death of the lovers
and consider how posterity will remember them. Is
love presented in st. 4 as physical or spiritual? Note
ll. 35–36. Only martyrs are "canonized." To what
faith are the speaker and his mistress martyrs
(notice "we can die by it," l. 28)? Is this an answer
to the practical values urged by the speaker's opponent in ll. 1–9? Do saints renounce all worldly
values? What are the "hymns" (l. 35)?
[11] In st. 5 Donne pushes his conceit of sainthood
of the lovers. Other lovers now pray to these "saints"
("You," ll. 37, 39) to mediate for them ("beg
from above," l. 44).
[12] Notice the complete reversal from the beginning
of the poem. The practical opponent who sought
materialistic values in "countries, towns, courts"
finds these three places (the world) are in the lovers
who have become all things in their spiritualized
love.

Yesternight the sun went hence,
　And yet is here today,　　　　　　　　10
He hath no desire nor sense,
　Nor half so short a way:
　　Then fear not me,
But believe that I shall make
Speedier journeys, since I take　　　　15
　More wings and spurs than he.

O how feeble is man's power,
　That if good fortune fall,
Cannot add another hour,
　Nor a lost hour recall!　　　　　　　20
　　But come bad chance,
And we join to it our strength,
And we teach it art and length,
　Itself o'er us to advance.

When thou sighest, thou sighest not wind, 25
　But sighest my soul away,

When thou weepest, unkindly kind,
　My life's blood doth decay.
　　It cannot be
That thou lovest me, as thou sayest,　　30
If in thine my life thou waste,
　Thou art the best of me.

Let not thy divining heart
　Forethink me any ill,
Destiny may take thy part,　　　　　　35
　And may thy fears fulfill;
　　But think that we
Are but turned aside to sleep;
They who one another keep
　Alive, ne'er parted be.　　　　　　　40
(1633)

STUDY AIDS: 1. Are there any uses of
the "death-resurrection" conceit in the poem?
2. How would the poem be a comfort to Mrs.
Donne?

A Valediction [1] Forbidding Mourning

As virtuous men pass mildly away,[2]
And whisper to their souls to go,
Whilst some of their sad friends do say,
"Now his breath goes," and some say "No";

So let us meet [3] and make no noise,　　5
No tear-floods, nor sigh-tempest move,
'Twere profanation of our joys,
To tell the laity our love.

Moving of the earth brings harms and fears,[4]
Men reckon what it did and meant;　　10
But trepidation [5] of the spheres,
Though greater far, is innocent.

Dull sublunary [6] lovers' love,
(Whose soul is sense) cannot admit
Of absence, 'cause it doth remove　　　15
The thing which elemented [7] it.

But we by love so far refined,
That ourselves know not what it is,
Inter-assurèd of the mind,
Care less eyes, lips, and hands, to miss; [8]　20

Our two souls therefore, which are one,
Though I must go, endure not yet
A breach, but an expansion,
Like gold to airy thinness beat.[9]

[1] Farewell.
[2] Notice that the poem begins with a SIMILE.
How far does this extend? What two things are
compared by the simile?
[3] What does this word imply about the love of
the speaker and his mistress?
[4] In ll. 9–11 there are two kinds of movement
cited, both far greater than that made by the lovers
separating, yet these movements occasion no weeping
or sighing. What are they?
[5] In Ptolemaic astronomy, a movement of the
spheres which caused a slight change in the position
of the stars and the ecliptic.

[6] I.e., beneath the moon; material, subject to
decay.
[7] Composed. Lovers whose love is only physical
cannot stand separation, because the absence would
destroy the basis of their love.
[8] The order is inverted. Read: "[We] . . . care
less to miss eyes, lips, and hands."
[9] What approximate shape does gold leaf take
when beaten? Note the metaphysical quality of the
image. What two things are being compared?

If they be two, they are two so 25
As stiff twin compasses [10] are two;
Thy soul, the fixed foot, makes no show
To move, but doth, if the other do.

And though it in the center sit,
Yet when the other far doth roam, 30
It leans and hearkens after it,
And grows erect as that comes home.

Such wilt thou be to me, who must
Like the other foot, obliquely run;
Thy firmness makes my circle just, 35
And makes me end where I begun.
(1633)

STUDY AIDS: 1. The Renaissance regarded reasoning by analogy as a sound approach to truth. Throughout the poem true love is analogized as a circle, which to Donne's time was a symbol of infinity, immortality, perfection, and God. Find as many references as you can to the circle (note ll. 9, 11, 13, 23–24, 25–28, 35–36). What does the analogy imply about Donne's view of love?
2. The poem has the structure of a logical argument. Work out the steps of this argument.
3. Which of the following phrases best expresses the theme of the poem: (1) the eternality of true love; (2) the indissolubility of true love; (3) the ability of true love to endure separation?

The Holy Sonnets

Sonnet V

I am a little world made cunningly
Of elements,[1] and an angelic sprite;
But black sin hath betrayed to endless night
My world's both parts, and, oh, both parts
    must die.
You which beyond that heaven which was
    most high 5
Have found new spheres, and of new lands
    can write,[2]
Pour new seas in mine eyes, that so I might
Drown my world with my weeping earnestly,
Or wash it if it must be drowned no more: [3]
But oh it must be burnt! [4] Alas, the fire 10
Of lust and envy have burnt [5] it heretofore,

[10] Draughtsman's dividers. The conceit in ll. 25–36 has been condemned as bizarre and artificial. Does it express the experience of love under discussion precisely and accurately? From what field of knowledge is it drawn? Why is it METAPHYSICAL?

[1] The four qualities of matter: earth, fire, air, and water. What would the "angelic sprite" be?
[2] In ll. 5–6 notice the references to contemporary astronomical and geographical discoveries.
[3] God's promise to Noah that the world would never again be destroyed by water.
[4] The Judgment Day, when the world will be destroyed by fire (II Peter 3:5–7).
[5] What is the PARADOX based on fire in ll. 10–14 (note particularly the final clause in l. 14)?

And made it fouler; let their flames retire,
And burn me, O Lord, with a fiery zeal
Of Thee and Thy house, which doth in eating
    heal.
(1633)

STUDY AIDS: The Holy Sonnets chart the psychological analyses of Donne's fluctuating states of soul. He was always fascinated by the mystic ecstasy but was never able to achieve it. Does this sonnet reveal a TONE of assurance or torment? Is it SENTIMENTALISM? Does it contain any elements of religious self-abasement?

Sonnet X

Death, be not proud, though some have callèd
    thee
Mighty and dreadful,[6] for thou art not so;
For those whom thou think'st thou dost
    overthrow
Die not, poor Death; nor yet canst thou kill
    me.
From rest and sleep, which but thy picture
    be, 5
Much pleasure; then from thee much more
    must flow;
And soonest [7] our best men with thee do go—

[6] The poem attempts by PARADOX to show that Death is neither "mighty" nor "dreadful."
[7] Most willingly.

Rest of their bones and souls' delivery!
Thou art slave to fate, chance, kings, and
  desperate men,
And dost with poison, war, and sickness
  dwell;   10
And poppy or charms can make us sleep as
  well
And better than thy stroke. Why swellest [1]
  thou then?
One short sleep past, we wake eternally,
And Death shall be no more: Death, thou
  shalt die!
(1633)

STUDY AIDS: 1. What kind of SONNET is
this? Does the OCTAVE develop "mighty" or
"dreadful" or both? Which attribute does the
SESTET develop?
  2. In l. 14 the climactic paradox is stated in
"Death, thou shalt die!" Has the poem prepared
you to accept this statement? Upon what belief
does the truth of l. 14 rest? Are you persuaded
that death is neither "mighty" nor "dreadful"?

Sonnet XIV

Batter my heart,[2] three-personed God, for
  you
As yet but knock, breathe, shine, and seek to
  mend;
That I may rise and stand, o'erthrow [3] me;
  and bend

Your force to break, blow, burn, and make
  me new.
I, like an usurped tower to another due, 5
Labor to admit you, but oh, to no end;
Reason, your viceroy in me, me should defend,
But is captived, and proves weak or untrue.[4]
Yet dearly I love you, and would be lovèd
  fain,
But am betrothed unto your enemy: 10
Divorce me, untie or break that knot again;
Take me to you, imprison me, for I
Except you enthrall me, never shall be free,
Nor ever chaste, except you ravish me.
(1633)

STUDY AIDS: 1. Although the imagery
shifts from a vessel to a besieged town to a
woman, these images are not unrelated. What
common denominator do they have?
  2. The brazen opening of the poem has often
been commented upon. The "three-personed
God" is reinforced throughout the sonnet by the
reiteration of triple verbs in ll. 2, 4, 11, 12-14.
At least one verb in each series (except the last)
alliterates with "batter" (l. 1). Which ones?
What significance do you see in the ALLITERA-
TION?
  3. Does the poem indicate any tension between Donne's faith and reason? Does it imply
that there is a kind of violence as well as meek-
ness in the Christian faith?

Elegy IX [5]

No spring nor summer beauty hath such
  grace
As I have seen in one autumnal face.
Young beauties force our love, and that's a
  rape;
This doth but counsel, yet you cannot 'scape.
If 'twere a shame to love, here 'twere no
  shame; 5

Affection here takes reverence's name.
Were her first years the golden age? That's
  true,
  But now they are gold oft tried and ever
  new.
That was her torrid and inflaming time;
  This is her tolerable tropic clime. 10

[1] I.e., with pride (see l. 1).
[2] Donne's dramatic immediacy occasionally causes
obscurity. In ll. 1-4 he shifts from verb to verb as
if a single metaphor is not adequate to convey his
intensity. But beneath is a consistent metaphor:
God is a tinker; Donne a metal vessel in the artisan's
hands.

[3] Notice how the verb prepares for the shift in
imagery from that of an artisan to that of a town
besieged (ll. 5-8).
[4] The adjectives provide a transition from the
besieged town to the sexual imagery in ll. 9-14.
[5] This elegy, often called "The Autumnal," was
written to Magdalen Herbert, mother of George
Herbert.

Fair eyes! Who asks more heat than comes
from hence,
He in a fever wishes pestilence.
Call not these wrinkles, graves; if graves they
were,
They were Love's graves, for else he is
nowhere.
Yet lies not Love dead here, but here doth
sit   15
Vowed to this trench, like an anachorit; [1]
And here till hers, which must be his death,
come,
He doth not dig a grave, but build a tomb.
Here dwells he; though he sojourn everywhere
In progress,[2] yet his standing house is
here—   20
Here where still evening is, not noon nor
night,
Where no voluptuousness, yet all delight.
In all her words, unto all hearers fit,
You may at revels, you at council, sit.
This is Love's timber, youth his underwood; 25
There he, as wine in June, enrages blood,
Which then comes seasonabliest when our
taste
And appetite to other things is past.
Xerxes' strange love, the plantan tree,[3]
Was loved for age, none being so large as
she,   30

Or else because, being young, nature did bless
Her youth with age's glory, barrenness.
If we love things long sought, age is a thing
Which we are fifty years in compassing;
If transitory things, which soon decay,   35
Age must be loveliest at the latest day.
But name not winter's faces, whose skin's
slack,
Lank as an unthrift's purse, but a soul's
sack;
Whose eyes seem light within, for all here's
shade;
Whose mouths are holes, rather worn out
than made;   40
Whose every tooth to a several place is gone,
To vex their souls at resurrection:
Name not these living death's-heads unto
me,
For these, not ancient, but antique be.
I hate extremes, yet I had rather stay   45
With tombs than cradles, to wear out a
day.
Since love's motion natural is, may still
My love descend, and journey down the
hill,
Not panting after growing beauties; so
I shall ebb out with them who homeward
go.   50
(1633)

Hymn to God, My God, in My Sickness

Walton says this poem was written eight days before Donne's death, but modern scholarship inclines to 1623, when Donne was seriously ill. Whichever date is true, Donne casts the *Hymn* as a deathbed poem; he is trying to attain peace of mind before death, by accepting intellectually the justness of God's ways to John Donne.

The poem has three steps in its argument. Suffering and death must be accepted because: (1) heaven can be gained only through them; (2) they are necessary if God is to be just; and (3) Donne is confident of salvation through Christ.

Since I am coming to that holy room [1]
Where, with thy choir of saints for evermore

[1] Hermit.
[2] State journey of monarch or royalty.
[3] Xerxes on his march into Lydia came across
a plane tree, whose beauty so impressed him that
he decorated it with gold and appointed a soldier to
guard it.

I shall be made thy music, as I come
I tune the instrument here at the door,
And what I must do then, think here
before.   5

[1] The first stanza states the problem by presenting
the soul in an analogy with music: since heaven is
harmony, the individual soul must tune itself before
death for entrance into harmony.

Whilst my physicians by their love are grown [2]
  Cosmographers, and I their map, who lie
Flat on this bed, that by them may be shown
  That this is my southwest discovery,
  Per fretum febris,[3] by these straits to die, 10

I joy that in these straits I see my west;
  For though their currents yield return to
    none,
What shall my west hurt me? [4] As west and
    east
  In all flat maps (and I am one) are one,[5]
  So death doth touch the resurrection. 15

Is the Pacific Sea my home? Or are
  The eastern riches? Is Jerusalem?
Anyan,[6] and Magellan, and Gibraltar,
  All straits, and none but straits, are ways
    to them,

Whether where Japhet dwelt, or Cham, or
  Shem.[7] 20

We think that Paradise and Calvary,[8]
  Christ's cross and Adam's tree, stood in one
    place;
Look Lord, and find both Adams met in me; [9]
  As the first Adam's sweat [10] surrounds my
    face,
  May the last Adam's [11] blood my soul
    embrace. 25

So, in his purple wrapped receive me Lord,
  By these his thorns give me his other crown;
And as to others' souls I preached thy word,
  Be this my text, my sermon to mine own:
  Therefore, that he may raise, the Lord
    throws down. 30
(1635)

Devotions upon Emergent Occasions

These *Devotions* were written during a serious illness, a violent fever, in the winter of 1623. The siege ran its course in three weeks, and Donne chronicles its daily progress through twenty-three *Devotions,* each analyzing a successive step of the sickness. Every symptom of his bodily

[2] Stanzas 2–4 form the first logical step in the argument. Donne draws from a favorite subject for metaphor, geography and discovery, in this section: man is a "little world," a map; his doctors, who study him, are map-readers. But a map is an inadequate representation of reality. This concept allows Donne to draw in sts. 3–4 a distinction between his own full comprehension of death and the limited insight into it which his doctors have.

[3] "Through the strait of fever." The "southwest discovery" (l. 9) was made by Magellan, whose name the straits now bear. He sailed through them "to die" (l. 10) in the Philippines to the "west" (l. 11) of a fever. As Magellan did, so Donne is about to do.

[4] The west, death, is the region through which Donne must pass to reach the "Eastern riches" (l. 17), or resurrection; therefore, "I joy" (l. 11). This is the reality, the excitement of exploration, not just the map-reading, which the doctors do.

[5] In flat maps, points on the right side correspond to those on the left. Thus, like west and east, death and resurrection are not opposites but one and the same. Therefore, sickness and death are the only "straits" through which man can reach heaven.

[6] Bering Strait.

[7] Japhet, Cham, and Shem were sons of Noah. Their descendants, according to tradition, repeopled the earth: Japhet's in Asia (Bering Strait); Cham's

in Africa (Straits of Magellan); and Shem's in Europe (Straits of Gibraltar). Thus ll. 18–20 develop the idea that discovery of the world was made only through "straits." The completed metaphor of sts. 2–4 parallels Donne's emotions as he seeks heaven through death and resurrection with the excitement experienced by the explorers and discoverers of the world as they passed through uncharted straits.

[8] Notice how the excited TONE of st. 4 is replaced here by one of quiet reflection. The two final stanzas present the theological justification of the argument developed thus far. Suffering and death are not only the one way to heaven, but they are fitting punishments for original sin. Therefore, God is just; and Donne, in suffering for Adam's sin, may expect salvation.

[9] Since Donne partakes of the natures of both Adam and Christ (matter and spirit, sin and salvation through Christ's grace), he joins both death and resurrection within himself (ll. 15, 21–22).

[10] Literally, from Donne's fever, but it is also symbolic: because of the Fall, Adam was condemned to earn his daily bread by the "sweat of his face" (Gen. 3:19).

[11] Christ, the second Adam, whose blood (resurrection) atoned for the sin (death-producing) of the first Adam (I Cor. 15:45).

and mental condition is minutely detailed. Each *Devotion* is threefold: (1) Meditation; (2) Expostulation; and (3) Prayer. In almost every "Meditation" Donne passes from a consideration of his own illness to more general topics in the spiritual or intellectual realm which corresponds to his physical symptom.

Donne's prose, like his poetry, reveals a brilliant wit, far-fetched allusions, great erudition, and passionate sincerity.

Meditation 17

Nunc lento sonitu dicunt, morieris

[Now this bell tolling softly for another, says to me, Thou must die.]

Perchance he for whom this bell tolls may be so ill as that he know not it tolls for him; and perchance I may think myself so much better than I am, as that they who are about me and see my state may have caused it to toll for me, and I know not that. The church is catholic, universal, so are all her actions; all that she does belongs to all. When she baptizes a child, that action concerns me; for that child is thereby connected to that body which is my head too, and ingrafted into that body whereof I am a member. And when she buries a man, that action concerns me: all mankind is of one author and is one volume; when one man dies, one chapter is not torn out of the book, but translated into a better language; and every chapter must be so translated. God employs several translators; some pieces are translated by age, some by sickness, some by war, some by justice; but God's hand is in every translation, and his hand shall bind up all our scattered leaves again for that library where every book shall lie open to one another. As therefore the bell that rings to a sermon calls not upon the preacher only, but upon the congregation to come, so this bell calls us all; but how much more me, who am brought so near the door by this sickness. There was a contention as far as a suit (in which piety and dignity, religion and estimation,[1] were mingled) which of the religious orders should ring to prayers first in the morning; and it was determined that they should ring first that rose earliest. If

[1] Prestige.

we understand aright the dignity of this bell that tolls for our evening prayer, we would be glad to make it ours by rising early, in that application, that it might be ours as well as his whose indeed it is. The bell doth toll for him that thinks it doth; and though it intermit again, yet from that minute that that occasion wrought upon him, he is united to God. Who casts not up his eye to the sun when it rises? but who takes off his eye from a comet when that breaks out? Who bends not his ear to any bell which upon any occasion rings? but who can remove it from that bell which is passing a piece of himself out of this world? No man is an island, entire of itself; every man is a piece of the continent, a part of the main. If a clod be washed away by the sea, Europe is the less, as well as if a promontory were, as well as if a manor of thy friend's or of thine own were. Any man's death diminishes me because I am involved in mankind, and therefore never send to know for whom the bell tolls; it tolls for thee. Neither can we call this a begging of misery or a borrowing of misery, as though we were not miserable enough of ourselves but must fetch in more from the next house, in taking upon us the misery of our neighbors. Truly it were an excusable covetousness if we did; for affliction is a treasure, and scarce any man hath enough of it. No man hath affliction enough that is not matured and ripened by it and made fit for God by that affliction. If a man carry treasure in bullion, or in a wedge of gold, and have none coined into current money, his treasure will not defray him as he travels. Tribulation is treasure in the nature of it, but it is not current money in the use of it, except we get nearer and nearer our home, heaven, by it. Another man may be sick too, and sick to death, and this affliction may lie in his bowels as gold in a mine and be of no use to him; but this bell that tells me of his affliction digs out and applies that gold to me, if by this considera-5 tion of another's danger I take mine own into contemplation and so secure myself by making my recourse to my God, who is our only security.

(1624)

Ben Jonson
(1573-1637)

A LYRIC POET, A CRITIC, A DRAMATIST SECOND ONLY TO SHAKESPEARE, JONSON WAS PROBABLY the most influential literary man of his day. He was born in London and attended Westminster School, where under the great scholar William Camden he was schooled in the classics. He attended no university, but served his stepfather as bricklayer until he left for a brief turn in the army. Later he married and became both actor and playwright in a prominent dramatic company. He was imprisoned when he killed a fellow actor in a duel, but escaped hanging by reading his Latin "neck verse," a literacy test given culprits claiming benefit of clergy.

Although at times his satiric comedies offended the powerful, Jonson rose in favor with King James I, who in 1616 rewarded him with a butt of Canary wine and a pension, recognition entitling him to be called England's first poet laureate. The same year he published a folio of his collected works. His later years were less happy. His fine library was lost in a fire, his health failed, and although not without admirers, he quarreled and lost favor.

Unlike Shakespeare's comedies, set in remote or fanciful places, Jonson's comedies are laid in London. They picture realistically and often satirically the people of his own day. His characters are eccentrics, each with his own idiosyncrasy or quirk of personality, which Jonson, drawing on medieval physiology, called a "humor." This dominant trait or humor is reflected in the name, and we have Sir Epicure Mammon, Fastidious Brisk, Sir Politic Would Be, Zeal-of-the-land Busy, and so on. By thus labeling and exaggerating the foibles and vices of men, Jonson used the drama as a weapon for social criticism. *Volpone, The Alchemist,* and *Bartholomew Fair* are perhaps his most successful plays.

Less celebrated in the lyric, Jonson made important contributions to this form. His knowledge of Horace, Catullus, and other Latin lyric poets enabled him to give to the lively but often unrestrained Elizabethan lyric some of the Latin poets' feeling for form. Saying it neatly, pointedly, briefly, even if the thought were not "original," was Jonson's peculiar talent in the lyric. "What was ore in others," a contemporary said of him, "he was able to refine to himself." This attitude toward art, favoring conscious effort rather than inspiration, is implied in his own verse. It is seen also in his criticism, both theoretical, as in *Timber,* and applied, as in his poem on Shakespeare. Finally, it is the attitude which, thanks largely to Jonson's influence, came to dominate English literary thought for the next century and a half.

Queen and Huntress [1]

Queen [2] and Huntress, chaste and fair,
  Now the sun is laid to sleep,
Seated in thy silver chair
  State in wonted manner keep:
    Hesperus [3] entreats thy light,   5
    Goddess excellently bright.

Earth, let not thy envious shade
  Dare itself to interpose;
Cynthia's shining orb was made
  Heaven to clear when day did close: 10

Bless us then with wishèd sight,
Goddess excellently bright.

Lay thy bow of pearl apart
  And thy crystal-shining quiver;
Give unto the flying hart   15
  Space to breathe, how short soever:
    Thou that makest a day of night,
    Goddess excellently bright.
(1601)

Song: To Celia [4]

Come, my Celia, let us prove,
While we can, the sports of love.
Time will not be ours for ever;
He, at length, our good will sever;
Spend not then his gifts in vain.   5
Suns that set may rise again;
But if once we lose this light,
'T is with us perpetual night.
Why should we defer our joys?
Fame and rumor are but toys.[5]   10
Cannot we delude the eyes
Of a few poor household spies?
Or his [6] easier ears beguile,
Thus removèd by our wile?
'T is no sin love's fruits to steal;   15
But the sweet theft to reveal,

To be taken, to be seen,
These have crimes accounted been.
(1606)

STUDY AIDS: 1. How does the TONE of the invitation differ from that in Marlowe's *Passionate Shepherd to His Love* (p. 165)? Consider IMAGERY and METER.

2. Jonson's talent lay in stating borrowed ideas neatly. Note the formal pattern given the familiar material. The two-line pattern of the RHYME-SCHEME does not always correspond with the logical pattern: e.g., the first logical unit is ll. 1–2, but the next is ll. 3–5. Determine the logical units in relation to rhyme scheme for the rest of the poem.

Still To Be Neat [7]

Still [8] to be neat, still to be drest,
As you were going to a feast;
Still to be powdered, still perfumed;
Lady, it is to be presumed,
Though art's hid causes are not found,   5
All is not sweet, all is not sound.

Give me a look, give me a face
That makes simplicity a grace;
Robes loosely flowing, hair as free.
Such sweet neglect more taketh me   10
Than all the adulteries of art;
They strike mine eyes, but not my heart.
(1609)

[1] Song sung by Hesperus in Jonson's comedy, *Cynthia's Revels*.
[2] Cynthia, or Diana, goddess of the moon, of the hunt, and of chastity.
[3] The evening star.
[4] From Ben Jonson's comedy *Volpone* (1606).

[5] Trifles.
[6] Refers to Celia's husband.
[7] From Ben Jonson's play *Epicoene, or The Silent Woman* (1609).
[8] Always.

On My First Son

In 1616 Jonson published *Epigrams,* a collection of 133 short, pointed verses patterned somewhat after the epigrams of the Latin poet Martial. The age was beginning to favor pointed as opposed to diffuse expression, in verse as in prose (cf. Bacon's essays), and Jonson regarded his epigrams as "the ripest of my studies." A particular kind of epigrammatic poem that he excelled in was the epitaph, a short poem commemorating and usually praising one who had died.

Jonson's son died in the plague of 1603 at the age of seven. Jonson was absent from London at the time, but before the death he reported to a friend his premonition of the event.

Farewell, thou child of my right hand, and
  joy;
My sin was too much hope of thee, loved
  boy.
Seven years thou wert lent to me, and I thee
  pay,[1]
Exacted by thy fate, on the just day.
Oh, could I lose all father now! For why   5
  Will man lament the state he should envy?
To have so soon 'scaped world's and flesh's
  rage,
And if no other misery, yet age!

Rest in soft peace, and asked, say, Here doth
  lie
  Ben Jonson his best piece of poetry.   10
For whose sake henceforth all his vows be
  such,
  As what he loves may never like too much.
(1616)

STUDY AIDS: Verse we call classical often is said to show "restraint." Wherein does this poem show restraint?

Epitaph on Elizabeth, L. H. [2]

Wouldst thou hear what man can say
  In a little? Reader, stay.
Underneath this stone doth lie
  As much beauty as could die;
Which in life did harbor give   5
  To more virtue than doth live.

If at all she had a fault,
  Leave it buried in this vault.
One name was Elizabeth,
  Th'other let it sleep with death;   10
Fitter, where it died to tell,
  Than that it lived at all. Farewell.
(1616)

Song to Celia

This well known lyric illustrates Jonson's way of appropriating the work of others and making it his own. Philostratus, a Greek rhetorician, wrote what in English is as follows: "I have sent thee a wreath of roses, not honoring thee (though this also), but rather giving to the roses themselves this favor, that they should not wither." Compare this with Jonson's second stanza.

Drink to me only with thine eyes,
  And I will pledge with mine;
Or leave a kiss but in the cup,
  And I'll not look for wine.

The thirst that from the soul doth rise   5
  Doth ask a drink divine;
But might I of Jove's nectar sup,
  I would not change for thine.

[1] I.e., I pay thee ("loved boy") back to God. Explain the imagery of ll. 3–4.

[2] The identity of Elizabeth, L. H., is unknown.

I sent thee late a rosy wreath,
  Not so much honoring thee   10
As giving it a hope, that there
  It could not withered be.

But thou thereon didst only breathe,
  And sent'st it back to me;
Since when it grows, and smells, I swear, 15
  Not of itself, but thee.
(1616)

To the Memory of My Beloved, the Author
Mr. William Shakespeare,
And What He Hath Left Us

Jonson was particularly well qualified to write this tribute, which appeared in the first collected edition of Shakespeare's plays, the First Folio (1623). He knew Shakespeare as a friend and as a fellow playwright, he was a competent critic, and he had a poet's felicity of expression. His is the outstanding appreciation of Shakespeare in verse.

To draw no envy, Shakespeare, on thy name,
Am I thus ample [1] to thy book and fame;
While I confess thy writings to be such
As neither man, nor muse, can praise too
    much.
'Tis true, and all men's suffrage.[2] But these
    ways   5
Were not the paths I meant unto thy praise;
For silliest ignorance on these may light,
Which, when it sounds at best, but echoes
    right;
Or blind affection,[3] which doth ne'er advance
The truth, but gropes, and urgeth all by
    chance;   10
Or crafty malice might pretend this praise,
And think to ruin, where it seemed to raise.
These are, as some infamous bawd or whore
Should praise a matron. What could hurt her
    more?
But thou art proof against them, and,
    indeed,   15
Above the ill fortune of them, or the need.
I therefore will begin. Soul of the age!
The applause, delight, the wonder of our
    stage!
My Shakespeare, rise! I will not lodge thee
    by
Chaucer, or Spenser, or bid Beaumont lie 20
A little farther off, to make thee a room: [4]

Thou art a monument without a tomb,
And art alive still while thy book doth live
And we have wits to read and praise to give.[5]
That I not mix thee so, my brain excuses, 25
I mean with great, but disproportioned
    Muses; [6]
For if I thought my judgment were of years,
I should commit thee surely with thy peers,
And tell how far thou didst our Lily outshine,
Or sporting Kyd, or Marlowe's mighty line.[7] 30
And though thou hadst small Latin and less
    Greek, [8]
From thence to honor thee, I would not seek
For names; but call forth thundering
    Æschylus,
Euripides, and Sophocles to us; [9]
Pacuvius, Accius, him of Cordova dead,[10] 35
To life again, to hear thy buskin [11] tread,
And shake a stage; or, when thy socks [12] were
    on,
Leave thee alone for the comparison

[5] Cf. Shakespeare's sonnet 18, ll. 13–14 (p. 169).
[6] Poets of less ability.
[7] John Lyly, Thomas Kyd, and Christopher Marlowe were the dramatic predecessors of Shakespeare who most influenced his development.
[8] "Small" and "less" compared to Jonson's knowledge of classical tongues. But Shakespeare's Stratford schooling would have given him more knowledge than this line seems to imply.
[9] The three great tragic dramatists of Greece.
[10] Three Roman tragic dramatists. Seneca ("him of Cordova") greatly influenced Elizabethan tragic dramatists.
[11] Boot worn by the tragic actor.
[12] Worn by the comic actor.

[1] I.e., do I thus add.
[2] Vote.
[3] Feeling.
[4] These poets were buried in Westminster Abbey. Shakespeare needs no such burial, says Jonson, since he is his own monument.

Of all that insolent Greece or haughty Rome
Sent forth, or since did from their ashes
    come.   40
Triumph, my Britain, thou hast one to show
To whom all scenes of Europe homage owe.
He was not of an age, but for all time! [13]
And all the Muses still were in their prime,
When, like Apollo, he came forth to warm   45
Our ears, or like a Mercury to charm!
Nature herself was proud of his designs,
And joyed to wear the dressing of his lines!
Which were so richly spun, and woven so fit,
As, since, she will vouchsafe no other wit. 50
The merry Greek, tart Aristophanes,
Neat Terence, witty Plautus, now not
    please; [14]
But antiquated and deserted lie,
As they were not of Nature's family.
Yet must I not give Nature all; thy art,   55
My gentle Shakespeare, must enjoy a part.
For though the poet's matter nature be,
His art doth give the fashion; and, that he
Who casts to write a living line, must sweat,
(Such as thine are) and strike the second
    heat   60
Upon the Muses' anvil; turn the same
(And himself with it) that he thinks to frame,
Or, for the laurel, he may gain a scorn;
For a good poet's made, as well as born.
And such wert thou! Look how the father's
    face   65
Lives in his issue, even so the race
Of Shakespeare's mind and manners brightly
    shines

In his well turnèd, and true filèd lines;
In each of which he seems to shake a lance, [15]
As brandished at the eyes of ignorance.   70
Sweet Swan of Avon! [16] what a sight it were [17]
To see thee in our waters yet appear,
And make those flights upon the banks of
    Thames,
That so did take [18] Eliza, and our James! [19]
But stay, I see thee in the hemisphere   75
Advanced, and made a constellation there!
Shine forth, thou star of poets, and with rage
Or influence,[20] chide or cheer the drooping
    stage,
Which, since thy flight from hence, hath
    mourned like night,
And despairs day, but for thy volume's
    light.   80
(1623)

STUDY AIDS: 1. Major divisions in the poem appear at ll. 17, 46, and 70. What is the function of each of the four parts marked by these divisions?

2. What is notable about the following passages in the poem and in Jonson's *Timber*? (1) ll. 13–14 and *Timber*, p. 215/1, l. 35 ff.; (2) ll. 55–56, 64 and *Timber*, p. 218/2, l. 22 ff.; (3) the imagery in l. 68 and *Timber*, p. 219/1, l. 29.

3. A basic question in criticism involves the opposition between Nature and Art (ll. 55–56). What does Jonson mean by these terms? In what way are the two concepts opposed? Which does Jonson prefer? Why? Does the lyric *Still To Be Neat* (p. 211) shed any light on these questions?

Timber; or Discoveries

Jonson titled his volumes of poems *The Forest* and *Underwoods*. He gave the title *Timber* to a commonplace book full of miscellaneous sayings, or, as the subtitle says, "Discoveries Made Upon Men and Matter, As They Have Flowed out of His Daily Readings." Never finished for publication, the volume is the raw stuff of literature, but for that very reason is more vital than

[13] What does this line mean? Is it true?
[14] Three comic dramatists of antiquity. Plautus and Terence were Romans.
[15] Jonson liked to pun on names. Cf. above l. 30.
[16] This figurative epithet combines three facts or beliefs about swans: (1) their inhabiting the River Avon at Stratford; (2) their being sacred to Apollo, god of poetry and song; and hence (3) their reputedly being beautiful singers.

[17] Would be.
[18] Captivate.
[19] Queen Elizabeth and King James I.
[20] The "Swan of Avon," mounted to the heavens, has become the constellation Cygnus (Swan). In an astronomical figure the poet expresses the hope that through "rage" (poetic rapture) or "influence" the constellation (i.e., Shakespeare's spirit) will "cheer the drooping stage."

many a completed work. Jonson quotes often, and in passages purportedly his own he will give a close translation of a classical author. This is not plagiarism, but one legitimate way Renaissance writers borrowed from the classics. On page 219 he describes this process of "imitation."

Fortuna [luck, fortune].—Ill fortune never crushed that man whom good fortune deceived not. I therefore have counseled my friends never to trust to her fairer side, though she seemed to make peace with them; but to place all things she gave them so, as [1] she might ask them again without their trouble; she might take them from them, not pull them: to keep always a distance between her and themselves. He knows not his own strength that hath not met adversity. Heaven prepares good men with crosses; but no ill can happen to a good man.[2] Contraries are not mixed. Yet that which happens to any man may to every man. But it is in his reason, what he accounts it and will make it. . . .

Scientiae liberales non vulgi sunt [the liberal arts are not for everybody].—Arts that respect the mind were ever reputed nobler than those that serve the body, though we less can be without them, as tillage, spinning, weaving, building, etc., without which we could scarce sustain life a day. But these were the works of every hand; the other of the brain only, and those the most generous and exalted wits and spirits, that cannot rest or acquiesce. The mind of man is still [3] fed with labor. . . .

There is a more secret cause, and the power of liberal studies lies more hid than that it can be wrought out by profane wits.[4] It is not every man's way to hit. There are men, I confess, that set the caract [5] and value upon things as [6] they love them; but science [7] is not every man's mistress. It is as great a spite [8] to be praised in the wrong place, and by a

wrong person, as can be done to a noble nature. . . .

Censura de poetis [current opinion on poetry].—Nothing in our age, I have observed, is more preposterous than the running judgments upon poetry and poets; when we shall hear those things commended and cried up for the best writings which a man would scarce vouchsafe to wrap any wholesome drug in: he would never light his tobacco with them. And those men almost named for miracles, who yet are so vile that if a man should go about to examine and correct them, he must make all they have done but one blot. Their good is so entangled with their bad, as forcibly one must draw on the other's death with it.[9]. . . Yet their vices have not hurt them; nay, a great many they have profited, for they have been loved for nothing else. And this false opinion grows strong against the best men, if once it take root with the ignorant. Cestius,[10] in his time, was preferred to Cicero, so far as the ignorant durst. They learned him without book, and had him often in their mouths; but a man cannot imagine that thing so foolish or rude but will find and enjoy an admirer; at least a reader or spectator. The puppets are seen now in despite of the players; [11] Heath's [12] epigrams and the Sculler's [13] poems have their applause. There are never wanting [14] that dare prefer the worst preachers, the worst pleaders, the worst poets; not that the better have left to write or speak better,[15] but that they that hear them judge worse; *Non illi pejus dicunt, sed hi corruptius judicant.*[16] Nay, if it were put

[1] "So, as" = modern "so that."
[2] A doctrine of the Stoics, who believed that physical and material fortune were matters of indifference to a virtuous man.
[3] Continually.
[4] I.e., the reason for the prestige of liberal studies can not be fathomed by ordinary minds.
[5] Worth.
[6] In proportion as.
[7] Learning.
[8] Annoyance.

[9] I.e., the bad in their writing necessarily destroys the good.
[10] Rhetorician of Smyrna.
[11] I.e., some people prefer puppet shows to plays.
[12] John Heath, inferior poet of the day.
[13] John Taylor, Thames boatman called the "water poet," a prolific writer of popular verse.
[14] Supply "those."
[15] I.e., stopped ("left off") writing or speaking better.
[16] Translated in the preceding sentence.

to the question of the water-rimer's works, against Spenser's, I doubt not but they would find more suffrages; because the most favor common vices, out of a prerogative the vulgar have, to lose their judgments and like that which is naught.

Poetry, in this latter age, hath proved but a mean mistress to such as have wholly addicted themselves to her, or given their names up to her family. They who have but saluted her on the by, and now and then tendered their visits, she hath done much for, and advanced in the way of their own professions —both the law and the gospel—beyond all they could have hoped or done for themselves without her favor.[17] Wherein she doth emulate the judicious but preposterous bounty of the time's grandees,[18] who accumulate all they can upon the parasite or fresh-man in their friendship; but think an old client or honest servant bound by his place to write and starve.

Indeed, the multitude commend writers as they do fencers or wrestlers, who, if they come in robustiously and put for it with a deal of violence, are received for the braver fellows; when many times their own rudeness is a cause of their disgrace, and a slight touch of their adversary gives all that boisterous force the foil. But in these things the unskilful are naturally deceived, and judging wholly by the bulk, think rude things greater than polished, and scattered more numerous than composed. Nor think this only to be true in the sordid multitude, but the neater sort of our gallants; for all are the multitude, only they differ in clothes, not in judgment or understanding.

De Shakespeare nostrati [concerning our native Shakespeare].—I remember the players have often mentioned it as an honor to Shakespeare, that in his writing, whatsoever he penned, he never blotted out a line. My answer hath been, "Would he had blotted a thousand," which they thought a malevolent speech. I had not told posterity this but for their ignorance, who chose that circumstance to commend their friend by wherein he most

faulted;[19] and to justify mine own candor, for I loved the man, and do honor his memory on this side idolatry[20] as much as any. He was, indeed, honest, and of an open and free nature; had an excellent fancy, brave notions, and gentle expressions, wherein he flowed with that[21] facility that sometime it was necessary he should be stopped. *"Sufflaminandus erat,"*[22] as Augustus said of Haterius.[23] His wit was in his own power; would the rule of it had been so too. Many times he fell into those things, could not escape laughter,[24] as when he said in the person of Caesar, one speaking to him: "Caesar, thou dost me wrong." He replied: "Caesar did never wrong but with just cause;" and such like, which were ridiculous. But he redeemed his vices with his virtues. There was ever more in him to be praised than to be pardoned. . . .

De augmentis scientiarum [on the advancement of learning].—I have ever observed it to have been the office of a wise patriot, among the greatest affairs of the State, to take care of the commonwealth of learning. For schools, they are the seminaries of State; and nothing is worthier the study of a statesman than that part of the republic which we call the advancement of letters. Witness the care of Julius Caesar, who, in the heat of the civil war, writ his books of *Analogy,* and dedicated them to Tully.[25] This[26] made the late Lord St. Alban entitle his work *Novum Organum;*[27] which, though by the most of superficial men, who cannot get beyond the title of nominal,[28] it is not penetrated nor understood, it really

[19] I.e., I would not have told posterity this if it had not been for the ignorance of those who, in order to commend their friend, chose that circumstance wherein he most faulted.

[20] I.e., short of idolizing him.

[21] Such.

[22] "He should have been clogged (restrained)."

[23] Roman orator.

[24] I.e., those things which could not escape causing laughter.

[25] Cicero.

[26] I.e., the realization that learning is important to the state.

[27] "New Instrument" (for studying nature). Cf. pp. 191–192.

[28] Names (as opposed to the essence or "reality") of things.

[17] Jonson here discusses how poetry pays.

[18] Wealthy men, potential patrons of literature.

openeth all defects of learning whatsoever, and is a book

Qui longum noto scriptori porriget aevum.[29]

My conceit[30] of his person was never increased toward him by his place or honors. But I have and do reverence him for the greatness that was only proper to himself, in that he seemed to me ever, by his work, one of the greatest men, and most worthy of admiration, that had been in many ages. In his adversity I ever prayed that God would give him strength; for greatness he could not want.[31] Neither could I condole in a word or syllable for him, as knowing no accident could do harm to virtue, but rather help to make it manifest. . . .

De stilo, et optimo scribendi genere [about style and the best kind of writing].[32]—For a man to write well, there are required three necessaries—to read the best authors, observe the best speakers, and much exercise of his own style. In style, to consider what ought to be written, and after what manner, he must first think and excogitate his matter, then choose his words, and examine the weight of either.[33] Then take care, in placing and ranking both matter and words, that the composition be comely; and to do this with diligence and often. No matter[34] how slow the style be at first, so it be labored and accurate; seek the best, and be not glad of the forward conceits, or first words, that offer themselves to us; but judge of what we invent, and order what we approve. Repeat[35] often what we have formerly written; which beside that it helps the consequence, and makes the juncture better, it quickens the heat of imagination, that often cools in the time of setting down, and gives it new strength, as if it grew lustier by the going back. As we see in the contention[36] of leaping, they jump

farthest that fetch their race largest; or, as in throwing a dart or javelin, we force back our arms to make our loose[37] the stronger. Yet, if we have a fair gale of wind, I forbid not the steering out of our sail, so[38] the favor of the gale deceive us not. For all that we invent doth please us in the conception of birth, else we would never set it down. But the safest is to return to our judgment, and handle over again those things the easiness of which might make them justly suspected. So did the best writers in their beginnings; they imposed upon themselves care and industry; they did nothing rashly: they obtained first to write well, and then custom made it easy and a habit. By little and little their matter showed itself to them more plentifully; their words answered, their composition followed; and all, as in a well-ordered family, presented itself in the place. So that the sum of all is, ready writing[39] makes not good writing, but good writing brings on ready writing. Yet, when we think we have got the faculty, it is even then good to resist it, as to give a horse a check sometimes with a bit, which doth not so much stop his course as stir his mettle. Again, whither a man's genius is best able to reach, thither it should more and more contend, lift and dilate itself; as men of low stature raise themselves on their toes, and so ofttimes get even, if not eminent. Besides, as it is fit for grown and able writers to stand of themselves, and work with their own strength, to trust and endeavor by their own faculties, so it is fit for the beginner and learner to study others and the best. For the mind and memory are more sharply exercised in comprehending another man's things than our own; and such as accustom themselves and are familiar with the best authors shall ever and anon find somewhat of them in themselves, and in the expression of their minds, even when they feel it not, be able to utter something like theirs, which hath an authority above their own. Nay, sometimes it is the reward of a man's study, the praise of quoting another man fitly; and though a man be

[29] "Which will create a long life for its famous author."

[30] Opinion.

[31] Lack.

[32] The following passage on style is a close translation of the Roman writer Quintilian.

[33] Each (word).

[34] It is no matter.

[35] Read over.

[36] Contests.

[37] Throw.

[38] So long as.

[39] Writing done easily.

more prone and able for one kind of writing than another, yet he must exercise all. For as in an instrument, so in style, there must be a harmony and consent [40] of parts. . . .

De orationis dignitate [on the dignity of speech].— . . . Custom is the most certain mistress of language, as the public stamp makes the current money. But we must not be too frequent with the mint, every day coining, nor fetch words from the extreme and utmost ages; since the chief virtue of a style is perspicuity, and nothing so vicious in it as to need an interpreter. Words borrowed of antiquity do lend a kind of majesty to style, and are not without their delight sometimes; for they have the authority of years, and out of their intermission do win themselves a kind of gracelike newness. But the eldest of the present, and newest of the past language, is the best. For what was the ancient language, which some men so dote upon, but the ancient custom? Yet when I name custom, I understand not the vulgar custom; for that were a precept no less dangerous to language than life, if we should speak or live after the manners of the vulgar: but that I call custom of speech, which is the consent of the learned; as custom of life, which is the consent of the good. Virgil was most loving of antiquity; yet how rarely doth he insert *aquai* and *pictai!* [41] Lucretius is scabrous and rough in these; he seeks them: as some do Chaucerisms with us, which were better expunged and banished. Some words are to be culled out for ornament and color, as we gather flowers to straw houses [42] or make garlands; but they are better when they grow to our style as in a meadow, where, though the mere grass and greenness delights, yet the variety of flowers doth heighten and beautify. Marry, we must not play or riot too much with them, as in paronomasies; [43] nor use too swelling or ill-sounding words, *quae per salebras, altaque saxa cadunt.* [44] It is true, there is no sound

but shall find some lovers, as the bitterest confections are grateful to some palates. Our composition must be more accurate in the beginning and end than in the midst, and in the end more than in the beginning; for through the midst the stream bears us. And this is attained by custom, more than care or diligence. We must express readily and fully, not profusely. There is difference between a liberal and prodigal hand. As it is a great point of art, when our matter requires it, to enlarge and veer out all sail, so to take it in and contract it, is of no less praise, when the argument doth ask it. Either of them hath their fitness in the place. A good man always profits [45] by his endeavor, by his help, yea, when he is absent; nay, when he is dead, by his example and memory: so good authors in their style. A strict and succinct style is that where you can take away nothing without loss, and that loss to be manifest. . . .

De Poetica [about the art of poetry].— . . . I would lead you to the knowledge of our poet by a perfect information what he is or should be by nature, by exercise, by imitation, by study, and so bring him down through the disciplines of grammar, logic, rhetoric, and the ethics, adding somewhat out of all, peculiar to himself, and worthy of your admittance or reception.

First, we require in our poet or maker (for that title our language affords him elegantly with the Greek) a goodness of natural wit, *ingenium.* [46] For whereas all other arts consist of doctrine and precepts, the poet must be able by nature and instinct to pour out the treasure of his mind, and as Seneca saith, *Aliquando secundum Anacreontem insanire jucundum esse;* [47] by which he understands the poetical rapture. And according to that of Plato, *Frustra poeticas fores sui compos pulsavit.* [48] And of Aristotle, *Nullum magnum ingenium sine mixtura dementiae fuit. Nec potest grande aliquid, et supra caeteros loqui,*

---

[40] Agreement.
[41] Archaic Latin forms.
[42] Strew houses, i.e., decorate the rooms.
[43] Puns.
[44] "Which stumble over rough paths and lofty rocks."

[45] I.e., is of benefit (to others).
[46] Talent, ability.
[47] "According to Anacreon it is sometimes enjoyable to be crazy."
[48] "In vain does a poet of sane mind knock on the gates of the Muses."

nisi mota mens.[49] Then it riseth higher, as by a divine instinct, when it contemns common and known conceptions. It utters somewhat above a mortal mouth. Then it gets aloft and flies away with his [50] rider, whither before it was doubtful to ascend. This the poets understood by their Helicon,[51] Pegasus,[52] or Parnassus; [53] and this made Ovid to boast,

Est deus in nobis, agitante calescimus illo:
Sedibus aethereis spiritus ille venit.[54]

And Lipsius to affirm, *Scio poetam neminem praestantem fuisse, sine parte quadam uberiore divinae aurae.*[55] And hence it is that the coming up of good poets (for I mind not *mediocres* or *imos*)[56] is so thin and rare among us. Every beggarly corporation affords the State a mayor or two bailiffs yearly; but *solus rex, aut poeta, non quotannis nascitur.*[57]

To this perfection of nature in our poet we require exercise of those parts, *exercitatio,* and frequent. If his wit will not arrive suddenly at the dignity of the ancients, let him not yet fall out with it, quarrel, or be over hastily angry, offer to turn it away from study in a humor; but come to it again upon better cogitation, try another time with labor. If then it succeed not, cast not away the quills yet, nor scratch the wainscot, beat not the poor desk, but bring all to the forge and file again; torn [58] it anew. There is no statute law of the kingdom bids you be a poet against your will or [in] the first quarter; [59] if it comes in a year or two, it is well. The common rimers pour forth verses, such as they are, *ex tempore;* but there never comes from them one sense worth the life of a day. A rimer and a poet are two things. It is said of the incomparable Virgil that he brought forth his verses like a bear, and after formed them with licking. Scaliger [60] the father writes it of him, that he made a quantity of verses in the morning, which afore night he reduced to a less number. But that which Valerius Maximus [61] hath left recorded of Euripides, the tragic poet, his answer to Alcestis, another poet, is as memorable as modest; who, when it was told to Alcestis that Euripides had in three days brought forth but three verses, and those with some difficulty and throes, Alcestis, glorying he could with ease have sent forth a hundred in the space, Euripides roundly replied, "Like enough; but here is the difference: thy verses will not last those three days, mine will to all time." Which was as much as to tell him he could not write a verse. I have met many of these rattles that made a noise and buzzed. They had their hum, and no more. Indeed, things wrote with labor deserve to be so read, and will last their age.

The third requisite in our poet or maker is imitation, *imitatio,* to be able to convert the substance or riches of another poet to his own use.[62] To make choice of one excellent man above the rest, and so to follow him till he grow very he, or so like him as the copy may be mistaken for the principal. Not as a creature that swallows what it takes in, crude, raw, or undigested; but that feeds with an appetite, and hath a stomach to concoct,[63] divide, and turn all into nourishment. Not to imitate servilely, as Horace saith, and catch at vices for virtue, but to draw forth out of the best and choicest flowers, with the bee, and turn all into honey, work it into one relish and savor; make our imitation sweet;

---

[49] "There was never great genius without a tincture of madness. Nor is it possible to say anything lofty and above others unless the mind is moved."

[50] Its.

[51] Mountain sacred to the Muses.

[52] Legendary steed of poets.

[53] Chief seat of Apollo and the Muses.

[54] "There is a god in us, by whose moving we are warmed: this spirit comes from ethereal regions."

[55] "I know there is no poet (who is) really outstanding without a somewhat richer endowment of divine inspiration."

[56] "For I am not concerned with ordinary or inferior ones."

[57] "Only a king or a poet is not born every year."

[58] Turn (as on a lathe). Cf. *To the Memory of My Beloved, the Author Mr. William Shakespeare,* p. 214, l. 68.

[59] As of the moon, i.e., immediately.

[60] Julius Caesar Scaliger, Italian physician, father of the Renaissance critic and scholar, Joseph Scaliger.

[61] Roman anecdotist.

[62] When Aristotle said art is imitation, he meant that it reproduced a concept in the artist's mind. Later theorists, misinterpreting him, used "imitation" to signify mimicry of nature, or, as Jonson does here, an assimilation of the work of earlier artists.

[63] Digest.

observe how the best writers have imitated, and follow them: how Virgil and Statius have imitated Homer; how Horace, Archilochus; how Alcaeus, and the other lyrics; and so of the rest.

But that which we especially require in him is an exactness of study and multiplicity of reading, *lectio,* which maketh a full man,[64] not alone enabling him to know the history or argument of a poem and to report it, but so to master the matter and style, as to show he knows how to handle, place, or dispose of either with elegancy when need shall be. And not think he can leap forth suddenly a poet by dreaming he hath been in Parnassus, or having washed his lips, as they say, in Helicon. There goes more to his making than so; for to nature, exercise, imitation, and study, art must be added to make all these perfect. *Ars coronat opus* [art crowns the work.]— And though these challenge to themselves much in the making up of our maker, it is art only can lead him to perfection, and leave him there in possession, as planted by her hand. It is the assertion of Tully, if to an excellent nature there happen an accession or conformation [65] of learning and discipline, there will then remain somewhat noble and singular. . . . But our poet must beware that his study be not only to learn of [66] himself; for he that shall affect to do that, confesseth his ever having a fool to his master. He must read many, but ever the best and choicest; those that can teach him anything he must ever account his masters, and reverence. Among whom Horace and he that taught him, Aristotle, deserve to be the first in estimation.[67] Aristotle was the first accurate critic and truest judge, nay, the greatest philosopher the world ever had; for he noted the vices of all knowledges in all creatures; and out of many men's perfections in a science he formed still one art. So he taught us two offices together, how we ought to judge rightly of others, and what we ought to imitate specially

[64] Cf. Bacon's essay *Of Studies,* p. 185, ll. 30–31.
[65] Adaptation.
[66] By.
[67] Aristotle's *Poetics* and Horace's *Art of Poetry* were the two most influential books of literary criticism in the Renaissance.

in ourselves: but all this in vain without a natural wit and a poetical nature in chief. For no man, so soon as he knows this or reads it, shall be able to write the better; but as he is adapted to it by nature, he shall grow the perfecter writer. He must have civil prudence and eloquence, and that whole, not taken up by snatches or pieces in sentences or remnants when he will handle business or carry counsels, as if he came then out of the declaimer's gallery, or shadow furnished but out of the body of the State, which commonly is the school of men: *Virorum schola respublica.*[68] The poet is the nearest borderer upon the orator, and expresseth all his virtues, though he be tied more to numbers,[69] is his equal in ornament, and above him in his strengths. And of the kind the comic [70] comes nearest; because in moving the minds of men, and stirring of affections, in which oratory shows, and especially approves her eminence, he chiefly excels. What figure of a body was Lysippus [71] ever able to form with his graver,[72] or Apelles [73] to paint with his pencil, as [74] the comedy to life expresseth so many and various affections of the mind? There shall the spectator see some exulting with joy, others fretting with melancholy, raging with anger, mad with love, boiling with avarice, undone with riot, tortured with expectation, consumed with fear: no perturbation in common life but the orator finds an example of it in the scene. And then for the elegancy of language, read but this inscription on the grave of a comic poet:

Immortales mortales si fas esset flere,
Flerent divae Camoenae Naevium poetam;
Itaque postquam est Orcino traditus thesauro,
Obliti sunt Romae lingua loqui Latina.[75]

[68] "The state is the school of men."
[69] I.e., more concerned with meter.
[70] Comic poet. Jonson is speaking of a comic dramatic poet, or writer of comedies.
[71] Greek sculptor.
[72] Engraver, i.e., sculpturing chisel.
[73] Greek painter.
[74] Compared with.
[75] "If it were right for immortals to weep over mortals, the divine Muses would weep over Naevius; and because he had thus departed for Pluto's dungeon, the speaking of good Latin has been forgotten by Romans" (Naevius).

Or that modester testimony given by Lucius Aelius Stilo upon Plautus, who affirmed, *Musas, si Latine loqui voluissent, Plautino sermone fuisse locuturas.*[76] And that illustrious judgment by the most learned Marcus Varro of him, who pronounced him the prince of letters and elegancy in the Roman language.

I am not of that opinion to conclude a poet's liberty within the narrow limits of laws which either the grammarians or philosophers prescribe. For before they found out those laws, there were many excellent poets that fulfilled them, amongst whom none more perfect than Sophocles,[77] who lived a little before Aristotle. Which of the Greeklings durst ever give precepts to Demosthenes?[78] or to Pericles,[79] whom the age surnamed Heavenly, because he seemed to thunder and lighten with his language? or to Alcibiades,[80] who had rather Nature for his guide than Art for his master? But whatsoever nature at any time dictated to the most happy,[81] or long exercise to the most laborious, that the wisdom and learning of Aristotle hath brought into an art, because he understood the causes of things; and what other men did by chance or custom, he doth by reason; and not only found out the way not to err, but the short way we should take not to err.[82]

Many things in Euripides[83] hath Aristophanes[84] wittily reprehended, not out of art, but out of truth. For Euripides is sometimes peccant, as he is most times perfect. But judgment when it is greatest, if reason doth not accompany it, is not ever absolute.

To judge of poets is only the faculty of poets; and not of all poets, but the best. *Nemo infelicius de poetis judicavit, quam qui de poetis scripsit.*[85] But some will say critics are a kind of tinkers, that make more faults than they mend ordinarily. See their diseases and those of grammarians. It is true, many bodies are the worse for the meddling with; and the multitude of physicians hath destroyed many sound patients with their wrong practice. But the office of a true critic or censor is, not to throw by[86] a letter anywhere, or damn an innocent syllable, but lay the words together, and amend them; judge sincerely of the author and his matter, which is the sign of solid and perfect learning in a man. Such was Horace, an author of much civility,[87] and, if any one among the heathen can be, the best master both of virtue and wisdom; an excellent and true judge upon cause and reason, not because he thought so, but because he knew so out of use and experience.

(1641)

STUDY AIDS: 1. Jonson's language seems a little strange to us, but he is not a difficult writer. Try reading each section twice—once for the general drift and a second time for fuller understanding.

2. What relation do you see between Jonson's views on how to write (p. 217/1, l. 29 ff.) and his opinion of Shakespeare (p. 216/1, l. 40 ff.)?

3. Contrast Jonson's and Sidney's views on poetic inspiration vs. conscious artistry.

4. Contrast their prose styles: Whose words seem more modern? Whose sentences?

[76] "If the Muses wished to speak Latin, they would speak the language of Plautus."
[77] Greek tragic dramatist.
[78] Famous Greek orator.
[79] Greek statesman.
[80] Student of Socrates.
[81] Gifted.
[82] Jonson believed in literary rules; what he meant by "rules" is made clear in this paragraph.
[83] Greek tragic dramatist.
[84] Greek comic dramatist.

[85] "No one judged of poets more unhappily than did he who wrote about poets."
[86] Discard.
[87] Culture.

George Herbert
(1593–1633)

HERBERT WAS BORN INTO ONE OF THE OLDEST AND MOST DISTINGUISHED FAMILIES OF THE English-Welsh border. With such a family background, the usual path for a young man to follow would have led to a brilliant worldly career at Court. Even his education at Cambridge University and James I's patronage pointed in that direction. But his intellectual and pious mother, Magdalen Herbert, the friend and patroness of John Donne, had always desired her younger son to enter the church. This Herbert did in 1630 and became Vicar of Bemerton, a country parish.

If Herbert gave up a worldly career, it was not without a struggle. His poems reveal a sensitive man caught in the conflict between soul and body, between the church and the world. He even refused to publish his poetry because he feared it was evidence of worldly ambition still lurking in a spirit which had been dedicated to holy work. However, he did not destroy his poems, which he had entitled *The Temple,* but left them to his friend Nicholas Ferrar, who published them in 1633.

The Temple was immediately successful. That it has retained its popularity to the present day is due to several factors. It is the record of an individual soul in conflict with the varied interests of the world—a soul which finds its peace, not in a God of wrath and judgment, but in a personal God of tenderness and love, whose immanence can be experienced in the ordinary incidents of everyday life. Such subject matter could easily become sentimental, but Herbert never allows this. His poetry has an intellectual toughness, a precision of phrasing, and a logic of structure and imagery, all of which produce a perfection consistent throughout his work.

The Collar

I struck the board,[1] and cried, "No more; I
    will abroad!
What! shall I ever sigh and pine?
My lines and life are free; free as the road,
  Loose as the wind, as large as store.[2]
    Shall I be still in suit?[3]   5
  Have I no harvest but a thorn [4]

To let me blood, and not restore
What I have lost with cordial [5] fruit?
    Sure there was wine [6]
Before my sighs did dry it; there was corn 10
  Before my tears did drown it;
    Is the year only lost to me?
    Have I no bays to crown it,[7]

[1] Table.

[2] Abundance.

[3] Perhaps legal imagery, i.e., pleading his case before a judge.

[4] The poet is perhaps referring to the Garden of Gethsemane in ll. 6–7. Notice any later imagery in the poem which would also suggest this.

[5] Healthful.

[6] In ll. 9–16 how are "wine," "corn," and "years" denied to the speaker? Who has forbidden them? What do they metaphorically represent?

[7] Crown of laurel or flowers awarded to honor poets.

No flowers, no garlands gay? all blasted,
    All wasted?   15
  Not so, my heart, but there is fruit,
    And thou hast hands.[8]
    Recover all thy sigh-blown age
On double pleasures; leave thy cold dispute
Of what is fit and not; forsake thy cage,   20
    Thy rope of sands [9]
Which petty thoughts have made, and made
    to thee
  Good cable, to enforce and draw,
    And be thy law,
While thou didst wink and wouldst not
    see.   25
    Away! take heed;
    I will abroad.
Call in thy death's head [10] there, tie up thy
    fears;
    He that forbears

To suit and serve his need   30
    Deserves his load."
But as I raved, and grew more fierce and wild
    At every word,
  Methought I heard one calling, "Child"; [11]
    And I replied, "My Lord."   35
(1633)

STUDY AIDS: 1. The poem is a dramatized lyric. With whom is the poet arguing? Does his opponent appear in the poem? With whom is he really arguing? How is the sound of the argument produced in the poem? How do the lines, rhymes, and meter contribute to this effect?
2. At what points do shifts in TONE occur? Do they correspond to shifts in the argument? Does any repetition of lines mark these shifts?
3. Do any puns occur in the title? Of what is the collar a symbol? Is there a pun involving the doctrine of humors?

The Pulley

When God at first made man,
Having a glass of blessings standing by;
  "Let us," said he, "pour on him all we can:
Let the world's riches, which dispersèd lie,
  Contract into a span."   5

  So strength first made a way;
Then beauty flowed; then wisdom, honor,
    pleasure.
  When almost all was out, God made a stay,
Perceiving that alone, of all his treasure,
  Rest in the bottom lay.   10

  "For if I should," said he,
"Bestow this jewel also on my creature,
  He would adore my gifts instead of me,

And rest in nature, not the God of nature;
  So both should losers be.   15

  "Yet let him keep the rest,
But keep them with repining restlessness;
  Let him be rich and weary, that at least,
If goodness lead him not, yet weariness
  May toss him to my breast."   20
(1633)

STUDY AIDS: 1. The poem is one extended metaphor. What two things are compared? If the rope on one side of the pulley moves, what must be true of the other side? How is this idea developed in the poem?
2. What aspect of man's nature is revealed in the poem? Of God's? Is God lonely (see ll. 19–20)?

[8] I.e., "hands" to recover time and the world.
[9] In ll. 21–24 notice the image of the "rope of sands." Try to restate this image in prose. Does it say exactly the same thing? What does this indicate about IMAGERY? About poetry as a way of saying something compared to that of prose?
[10] A skull. I.e., don't frighten me with the terrors of death and hell.

[11] Notice how this UNDERSTATEMENT after a series of bold overstatements intensifies the climax of the poem. The poet is possibly thinking of God's calling the child Samuel to be a prophet (cf. I Sam. 3).

Denial

When my devotions could not pierce
  Thy silent ears,
Then was my heart broken, as was my verse;
  My breast was full of fears
    And disorder.   5

My bent thoughts, like a brittle bow,
  Did fly asunder.
Each took his way; some would to pleasures go,
  Some to the wars and thunder
    Of alarms.   10

As good go anywhere, they say,
  As to benumb
Both knees and heart, in crying night and
    day,
  "Come, come, my God, O come,"
    But no hearing.   15

O that Thou shouldst give dust a tongue
  To cry to Thee,
And then not hear it crying! All day long
  My heart was in my knee,
    But no hearing.   20

Therefore my soul lay out of sight,
  Untuned, unstrung;
My feeble spirit, unable to look right,
  Like a nipped blossom hung
    Discontented.   25

O cheer and tune my heartless breast,
  Defer no time;
That so Thy favors granting my request,
  They and my mind may chime,
    And mend my rhyme.   30
(1633)

STUDY AIDS: 1. What two difficulties is Herbert comparing in the poem? What does the title mean? How many "denials" are implied in the poem? How many persons do the "denying" in the poem?

2. Read the poem aloud. How is "disorder" (l. 5) echoed in the sound pattern of each stanza? Note the length of the lines (number of syllables) in sts. 1–2. In which stanza is there no disorder? Does the sound of the poem correspond to its meaning? Could this sound and meaning be copied in a prose statement of the meaning of the poem?

Love

Love bade me welcome; yet my soul drew
  back,
  Guilty of dust and sin.
But quick-eyed Love, observing me grow slack
  From my first entrance in,
Drew nearer to me, sweetly questioning   5
  If I lacked anything.

"A guest," I answered, "worthy to be here."
  Love said, "You shall be he."
"I, the unkind, ungrateful? Ah, my dear,
  I cannot look on Thee."   10
Love took my hand, and smiling, did reply,
  "Who made the eyes but I?"

"Truth, Lord, but I have marred them; let my
  shame
  Go where it doth deserve."
"And know you not," says Love, "who bore
  the blame?"   15
  "My dear, then I will serve." [1]
"You must sit down," says Love, "and taste my
  meat."
  So I did sit and eat.
(1633)

STUDY AIDS: 1. There are two situations in the poem, the storyteller's and that of the drama he narrates. Notice the different tones used by the guest and by Love. What is that of the guest (ll. 9–10, 16)? What is the tone used by Love? Does the poet-narrator speak to anyone, or is he merely reporting (see "I answered," ll. 7, 8, 15, 16)?

[1] At the table.

2. The polite restraint and intimacy of the dialogue involve the reader until the last line, at which point a reversal of feeling takes place. What is it? Is the last line UNDERSTATEMENT or OVERSTATEMENT?

3. *Love* and *The Collar* are both dramas of conversion. Are the conversions the same in both poems (see ll. 3–4)? What attribute of God appeals to Herbert in the two poems?

Richard Crashaw
(1612/13–1649)

CRASHAW WAS BORN THE SON OF AN ANTI-CATHOLIC ANGLICAN CLERGYMAN AND DIED A canon of Loreto, a priest of the Roman Catholic church. Orphaned at fourteen, he was sent by his guardians to Charterhouse and then to Pembroke College, Cambridge. While at Cambridge, Crashaw was befriended by Nicholas Ferrar and his family, who had established Little Gidding, a religious community which tried to fuse continental monasticism and Anglicanism. Ferrar had been impressed by the devotional literature and art of Italy. In becoming Catholic, Crashaw was perhaps only carrying to their conclusion sensibilities heightened by his experience at Little Gidding. When the Puritans gained control of England, Crashaw went to Holland (1644) and then to Paris (1645–1646), where he was received into the Catholic church. In 1646 Queen Henrietta Maria sent him to Rome with a letter to the Pope. After much delay, Crashaw was given a post at the Shrine of Loreto (1649). He died of a fever three months after assuming his duties there.

Almost all his poetry is devotional, characterized by an intensely emotional rather than intellectual quality. Possibly because he is a mystic, he emphasizes sensory detail and image. As his poetry becomes progressively more mystical, Crashaw relies heavily on the "emblem" or "picture," which he uses as a focal point for his emotions. In his greatest poetry, Saint Theresa, a sixteenth-century Spanish saint, serves a similar purpose.

In the Holy Nativity of Our Lord God
A Hymn Sung as by the Shepherds

Chorus

Come, we shepherds whose blest sight [1]
Hath met love's noon in nature's night;
Come, lift we up our loftier song
And wake the sun that lies too long.

To all our world of well-stol'n joy   5
He slept, and dreamed of no such thing,
While we found out heaven's fairer eye,
And kissed the cradle of our King.
Tell him he rises now too late
To show us aught worth looking at.   10

[1] In ll. 1–36, the chorus of shepherds asks its soloists, Tityrus and Thyrsis, to wake the sun and tell him of the happening of the night, seen by the light of the supernatural sun. What has happened? The two sources of light are compared throughout the poem: the earthly sun symbolizes nature; the supernatural sun symbolizes the fire of love descending from God in the form of the birth of Christ. Study the lines carefully to determine the recurrent images which make this comparison.

Tell him we now can show him more
   Then he e'er showed to mortal sight,
Than he himself e'er saw before,
   Which to be seen needs not his light.
Tell him, Tityrus, where th' hast been;   15
Tell him, Thyrsis, what th' hast seen.

Tityrus

Gloomy night embraced the place
   Where the noble Infant lay;
The Babe looked up and showed His face:
   In spite of darkness, it was day.   20
It was Thy day, Sweet, and did rise
Not from the east, but from Thine eyes.

   Chorus. It was Thy day, Sweet, [etc.]

Thyrsis

Winter chid aloud, and sent
   The angry north to wage his wars;   25
The north forgot his fierce intent,
   And left perfumes instead of scars.
By those sweet eyes' persuasive powers,
Where he meant frost, he scattered flowers.

   Chorus. By those sweet eyes' [etc.]   30

Both

We saw Thee in Thy balmy nest,
   Young Dawn of our eternal day!
We saw Thine eyes break from Their east
   And chase the trembling shades away.
We saw Thee, and we blessed the sight;   35
We saw Thee by Thine own sweet light.

Tityrus

"Poor world," [2] said I, "what wilt thou do
   To entertain this starry Stranger?
Is this the best thou canst bestow,
   A cold and not too cleanly manger?   40
Contend, ye powers of heav'n and earth,
To fit a bed for this huge birth!"

   Chorus. Contend, ye powers [etc.]

[2] Lines 37–79 develop an ancient theme from the Roman Breviary: creation (nature) cannot provide a suitable resting place for its Creator.

Thyrsis

"Proud world," said I, "cease your contest
   And let the mighty Babe alone—   45
The phoenix [3] builds the phoenix' nest,
   Love's architecture is His own;
The Babe whose birth embraves this morn
Made His own bed ere He was born."

   Chorus. The Babe whose birth [etc.]   50

Tityrus

I saw the curled drops, soft and slow,
   Come hovering o'er the place's head,
Off'ring their whitest sheets of snow [4]
   To furnish the fair Infant's bed.
"Forbear," said I, "be not too bold;   55
Your fleece is white, but 'tis too cold."

   Chorus. "Forbear," said I, [etc.]

Thyrsis

I saw the obsequious seraphims [5]
   Their rosy fleece of fire bestow;
For well they now can spare their wings   60
   Since heav'n itself lies here below.
"Well done," said I, "but are you sure
Your down so warm will pass for pure?"

   Chorus. "Well done," said I, [etc.]

Tityrus

No, no, your King's not yet to seek   65
   Where to repose His royal head;
See, see, how soon His new-bloomed cheek

[3] A mythical bird which every 100 years burst into flames. From its own ashes sprung the new phoenix. What metaphoric use does Crashaw make of the phoenix? Note the element of "fire." To what earlier use of fire in the poem does this image relate?
[4] What symbol of purity does the earth (nature) offer as a resting-place for the new-born love of God? Is it adequate?
[5] Seraphim were the "angels of fire." In one mystic tradition, the Dionysian, seraphim were the highest order of angels in the "fire of love" chain reaching down from God through the Virgin Mary to the seraphim to man. What does heaven offer as a resting place? Is it adequate?

Title page of the First Quarto of *Hamlet*.

Title page of the Second ("enlarged") Quarto of *Hamlet*.

The interior of the Swan Theatre, from a sketch made in 1596.

The interior of a print shop, from an etching made in 1619.

'Twixt mother's breasts is gone to bed.[6]
"Sweet choice!" said we, "no way but so,
Not to lie cold, yet sleep in snow."   70

Chorus. "Sweet choice!" said we, [etc.]

Both

We saw Thee in Thy balmy nest,
   Bright Dawn of our eternal day!
We saw Thine eyes break from Their east,
   And chase the trembling shades away.   75
We saw Thee, and we blessed the sight;
We saw Thee by Thine own sweet light.

Chorus. We saw Thee, [etc.]

Full Chorus

Welcome, all wonders in one sight![7]
   Eternity shut in a span,   80
Summer in winter, day in night,
   Heaven in earth, and God in man!
Great little One, whose all-embracing birth
Lifts earth to heav'n, stoops heav'n to earth.

Welcome, though nor to gold nor silk,   85
   To more than Caesar's birthright is;
Two sister-seas of virgin milk,
   With many a rarely tempered kiss,

That breathes at once both maid and mother,
Warms in the one, cools in the other.   90

Welcome, though not to those gay flies
   Gilded in the beams of earthly kings,
Slippery souls in smiling eyes;
   But to poor shepherds, homespun things,
Whose wealth's their flock, whose wit, to
      be   95
   Well read in their simplicity.
Yet when young April's husband-showers
   Shall bless the fruitful Maia's bed,
We'll bring the first-born of her flowers
   To kiss Thy feet and crown Thy head. 100
To Thee, dread Lamb, whose love must keep
   The shepherds more than they the sheep;
To Thee, meek Majesty! soft King
   Of simple graces and sweet loves,
Each of us his lamb will bring,   105
   Each his pair of silver doves;
Till burnt at last in fire of Thy fair eyes,
   Ourselves become our own best sacrifice.
(1652)

STUDY AIDS: 1. What significance does fire
have in the poem? How does it first enter? What
has it become in the conclusion? How many
images related to fire can you find in the poem?
   2. In what ways are the pastoral elements
appropriate to this poem? How does the dialogue
form enhance the effectiveness of the poem?

Henry Vaughan
(1621–1695)

OBSCURITY SURROUNDS MOST OF VAUGHAN'S LIFE, AND ONLY A FEW FACTS ARE KNOWN. He
was born of an old but impoverished Welsh family at Newton on the river Usk in Wales.
With his twin brother, Thomas, he went to Jesus College, Oxford, in 1638. After two years
Henry left for London, presumably to study law. Although there is no proof, it seems
likely that Vaughan fought on the royalist side in the Civil War. When the war was lost

[6] What is the only adequate resting place? Notice
how Crashaw is symbolizing the Catholic doctrine
of the Incarnation: the sinless Virgin Mary is the
reconciliation of the material and spiritual nature
of man, lost by man's fall.

[7] Lines 79–108 point out the significance of the
Birth to man: God's resting-place can be only in
the heart of the man who burns in the fire of love.
Thus, the man who loves God is his own best
sacrifice to God (ll. 107–108).

to the Puritans, he returned to Wales, and by 1647 he had settled his family at Newton St. Bridget, where he was practicing medicine. Where and when he received his medical training is not known.

Vaughan's first two volumes of poetry, *Poems* (1646) and *Olor Iscanus* (written in 1647 but not published until 1651), are undistinguished imitative love poems and translations. However, the extraordinary power of his third volume, *Silex Scintillans* (1650), reveals that Vaughan had undergone some profound experience, presumably religious. The volume was enlarged in 1655. Vaughan's reputation rests on *Silex Scintillans* alone, but it is secure.

Few English poets express such an intensely personal feeling for God in such an individual way as does Vaughan. Theological doctrine at this time emphasized the judgment of God and redemption through Christ; Vaughan, however, stresses the third member of the Trinity, the Holy Spirit. Vaughan sings of the presence of this Spirit in nature. Certain ideas and images become symbolic of this divine presence: reminiscences of childhood, death of loved ones, dawn, the crowing of a cock. The fall of man had drawn a veil over nature, and only momentarily can a flash of light from the other world illuminate the darkness of this one. This is Vaughan's message.

The Retreat

Happy those early days, when I
Shined in my angel-infancy!
Before I understood this place
Appointed for my second race,
Or taught my soul to fancy aught　　　　5
But a white,[1] celestial thought;
When yet I had not walked above
A mile or two from my first love,
And looking back, at that short space,
Could see a glimpse of his bright face;　10
When on some gilded cloud or flower
My gazing soul would dwell an hour,
And in those weaker glories spy
Some shadows of eternity;
Before I taught my tongue to wound　　15
My conscience with a sinful sound,
Or had the black art to dispense,

A several sin to every sense,
But felt through all this fleshly dress [2]
Bright shoots of everlastingness.　　　20
　O, how I long to travel back,
And tread again that ancient track!
That I might once more reach that plain,
Where first I left my glorious train;
From whence th' enlightened spirit sees　25
That shady city of palm trees.[3]
But ah! my soul with too much stay
Is drunk, and staggers in the way!
Some men a forward motion love,[4]
But I by backward steps would move;　　30
And when this dust falls to the urn,
In that state I came, return.
(1650)

The World

I saw Eternity the other night,
Like a great ring of pure and endless light,
　All calm, as it was bright;

And round beneath it, Time, in hours, days,
　　years,
　Driv'n by the spheres,　　　　　　　5

---

[1] Vaughan's imagery is often built on the contrast of light and dark. "White" is a favorite adjective.
[2] Lines 19-20 find a more famous restatement in Wordsworth's *Intimations of Immortality*, ll. 65-66.

[3] Moses' vision of the Promised Land (Deut. 34:3).
[4] In ll. 29-32 is the poet making a literal or figurative statement?

Like a vast shadow moved, in which the world
    And all her train were hurled.[1]
The doting lover in his quaintest [2] strain
    Did there complain;
Near him, his lute, his fancy, and his flights, 10
    Wit's sour delights,
With gloves, and knots, the silly snares of
      pleasure,
    Yet his dear treasure,
All scattered lay, while he his eyes did pour
    Upon a flower.   15

The darksome statesman, hung with weights
    and woe,
Like a thick midnight-fog, moved there so
    slow,
    He did not stay, nor go;
Condemning thoughts, like sad eclipses, scowl
    Upon his soul,   20
And clouds of crying witnesses without
    Pursued him with one shout.
Yet digged the mole,[3] and, lest his ways be
    found,
    Worked under ground,
Where he did clutch his prey; but one did
    see   25
    That policy; [4]
Churches and altars fed him; perjuries
    Were gnats and flies;
It rained about him blood and tears, but he
    Drank them as free.[5]   30

The fearful miser on a heap of rust [6]
Sat pining all his life there, did scarce trust
    His own hands with the dust,
Yet would not place one piece above, but lives
    In fear of thieves.   35

Thousands there were as frantic as himself,
    And hugged each one his pelf;
The downright epicure [7] placed heaven in
    sense,
    And scorned pretense;
While others, slipt into a wide excess,   40
    Said little less;
The weaker sort, slight, trivial wares enslave,
    Who think them brave;
And poor, despisèd Truth sat counting by [8]
    Their victory.   45

Yet some, who all this while did weep and
    sing,
And sing and weep, soared up into the ring;
    But most would use no wing.
O fools,[9] said I, thus to prefer dark night
    Before true light!   50
To live in grots and caves, and hate the day
    Because it shows the way,
The way, which from this dead and dark
    abode
    Leads up to God;
A way where you might tread the sun, and
    be   55
    More bright than he!
But, as I did their madness so discuss,
    One whispered thus:
"This ring the Bridegroom did for none
    provide,
    But for his bride." [10]   60
(1650)

STUDY AIDS: One critic has said the poem degenerates from a magnificent beginning to trite moralizing; another believes ll. 16–56 present objects from which Vaughan reacts and by which he is able to achieve a synthesis in the last line. Justify one or the other comment.

[1] Notice the contrast between the calm, eternal ring of light and the constantly turning planets of the Ptolemaic universe, at the center of which was the earth, the home of man, whose activities are then described in the poem. Why is a "ring" a good symbol for eternity?
[2] Most fanciful. The "strain" is possibly lovers' sonnets (cf. l. 11).
[3] How is the metaphor fitting?
[4] Strategy. Who is the "one" who sees?
[5] As freely as they rained.
[6] Why "rust"?
[7] Why would Vaughan place the epicure and miser in the same stanza? What do they hold in common?
[8] Watching.
[9] Who are these fools in the poem?
[10] Cf. Rev. 21:9. The Church is the bride of Christ, the Bridegroom. What is the "ring" which weds them in the poem? Are ll. 59–60 a smug statement of sectarian doctrine or are they justified in the poem?

I Walked the Other Day to Spend My Hour

This poem was inspired by the death of the poet's younger brother, William, in 1648. It was, perhaps, this experience which profoundly affected Vaughan and produced the greater depth of *Silex Scintillans.*

I walked the other day, to spend my hour,
    Into a field,
Where I sometimes had seen the soil to yield
    A gallant flower;
But winter now had ruffled all the bower   5
    And curious store
      I knew there heretofore.

Yet I, whose search loved not to peep and peer
    In the face of things,
Thought with myself, there might be other
      springs   10
    Besides this here,
Which, like cold friends, sees us but once a
      year;
    And so the flower
      Might have some other bower.

Then taking up what I could nearest spy,   15
    I digged about
That place where I had seen him to grow
      out;
    And by and by
I saw the warm recluse alone to lie,
    Where, fresh and green,   20
      He lived of us unseen.

Many a question intricate and rare
    Did I there strow;
But all I could extort was, that he now
    Did there repair   25
Such losses as befell him in this air,
    And would ere long
      Come forth most fair and young.

This past, I threw the clothes [1] quite o'er his
    head;
    And, stung with fear   30
Of my own frailty, dropped down many a tear
    Upon his bed;
Then, sighing, whispered, "Happy are the
      dead!

[1] The leaves beneath which the flower grew.

    What peace doth now
    Rock him [2] asleep below!"   35

And yet, how few believe such doctrine
    springs
    From a poor root,
Which all the winter sleeps here under foot,
    And hath no wings
To raise it to the truth and light of things,   40
    But is still trod
      By every wandering clod.

O Thou! [3] whose spirit did at first inflame
    And warm the dead,
And by a sacred incubation fed   45
    With life this frame,
Which once had neither being, form, nor
      name,
    Grant I may so [4]
      Thy steps track here below,

That in these masques and shadows I may
      see   50
    Thy sacred way;
And by those hid ascents climb to that day
    Which breaks from Thee,
Who art in all things, though invisibly;
    Show me thy peace,   55
      Thy mercy, love, and ease.

And from this care, where dreams and sorrows
      reign,
    Lead me above,
Where light, joy, leisure, and true comforts
      move
    Without all pain;   60

[2] William. Can this refer also to the flower below the leaves? Is this SENTIMENTALISM?
[3] God, whose Holy Spirit created nature (cf. Gen. 1:2), and in Vaughan's belief still gives it life.
[4] Lines 48–51 state the theme of many of Vaughan's poems: the presence of God's Spirit which can be seen in nature.

There, hid in Thee, show me his life again,
    At whose dumb urn [5]
    Thus all the year I mourn!
(1650)

STUDY AIDS: 1. What is the basic metaphor of the poem?
    2. Is this poem about nature? How does Vaughan use nature in the poem?

The Book

Eternal God! Maker of all
That have lived here since the man's fall;
The Rock of Ages! in whose shade
They live unseen, when here they fade;

Thou knew'st this paper when it was   5
Mere seed, and after that but grass;
Before 'twas dressed or spun, and when
Made linen, who did wear it then:
What were their lives, their thoughts, and
    deeds,
Whether good corn or fruitless weeds.   10

Thou knew'st this tree when a green shade
Covered it, since a cover made,
And where it flourished, grew, and spread,
As if it never should be dead.

Thou knew'st this harmless beast when he 15
Did live and feed by Thy decree
On each green thing; then slept—well fed—
Clothed with this skin which now lies spread
A covering o'er this aged book;
Which makes me wisely weep, and look   20
On my own dust; mere dust it is,
But not so dry and clean as this.
Thou knew'st and saw'st them all, and though
Now scattered thus, dost know them so.

    O knowing, glorious Spirit! when   25
Thou shalt restore trees, beasts, and men,
When thou shalt make all new again,
Destroying only death and pain,
Give him amongst Thy works a place
Who in them loved and sought Thy face! 30
(1650)

Robert Herrick
(1591–1674)

THE HERRICK FAMILY, ALTHOUGH LEICESTERSHIRE FARMERS FOR GENERATIONS, HAD BECOME London goldsmiths by the time Robert Herrick was born. At the age of sixteen, he was apprenticed to his uncle, Sir William Herrick, goldsmith to the king. After six years, however, the young man was allowed to break the agreement and go to Cambridge University, where he received the B.A. in 1617, the M.A. in 1620. By 1627 he was an ordained Anglican clergyman, and in that year he was appointed chaplain to the Duke of Buckingham on a military expedition to the Isle of Rhé. Except for this brief adventure, Herrick seems to have spent the years 1620–1629 in London, enjoying the literary fellowship to be shared there. In 1629 he was appointed Vicar of Dean Prior in Devonshire, and despite his intense dislike of the "rude" and "warty" countryside and people, he remained

---

[5] At whose "dumb urn" is the poet standing? Is it that of the flower? Can it be that of his brother (cf. ll. 1–21)?

there until ousted by the Puritans in 1647. Happy and gay with a manuscript of his poems under his arm, he returned to London to live with relatives. At the Restoration he petitioned Charles II for another clerical post and it was granted him—Dean Prior in Devonshire. He returned in 1662 and died there twelve years later.

In London, Herrick was a "son of Ben" and frequented the taverns where Ben Jonson and his disciples gathered. The group included such men as Sir John Suckling, Edmund Waller, Thomas Randolph, Richard Corbet (future bishop of Oxford and Norwich), and George Morley (future bishop of Winchester). From Jonson, the Latin poets Catullus, Martial, Horace, and the Greek poet Anacreon, Herrick learned his technique of writing verse. Like Jonson he adapted to the English countryside and idiom the Latin attitude toward life as expressed in classical forms and diction. However, he surpassed his master in sensibility and a simple lyric power, which is set free rather than caged by the artifice of its classical structure.

The Argument of His Book

I sing of brooks, of blossoms, birds, and
  bowers,
Of April, May, of June, and July flowers;
I sing of May-poles, hock-carts,[1] wassails,
  wakes,
Of bridegrooms, brides, and of their bridal
  cakes.
I write of youth, of love, and have access   5
By these, to sing of cleanly wantonness;[2]
I sing of dews, of rains, and, piece by piece,
Of balm, of oil, of spice, and ambergris;[3]
I sing of times trans-shifting; and I write
How roses first came red, and lilies white;   10
I write of groves, of twilights, and I sing
The court of Mab, and of the fairy king.

I write of hell; I sing and ever shall,
Of heaven, and hope to have it after all.
(1648)

STUDY AIDS: 1. Is this poem a sonnet? If not, how would you describe it?

2. From this summary of his subject matter, what kind of man does Herrick seem to be?

3. Notice how the poet alternates "I sing" and "I write": couplets 1 and 2 have "I sing"; 3 has "I write"; 4 and 5 have "I sing"; 6 has "I write." The reader would expect couplet 7 to have "I sing," but Herrick uses "I write." Why? What does the shift prepare for? What grammatical omissions and changes help to place emphasis?

When He Would Have His Verses Read

In sober mornings do not thou rehearse
The holy incantation of a verse;
But when that men have both well drunk
  and fed,
Let my enchantments then be sung or read.

When laurel spirts in the fire, and when the
  hearth   5
Smiles to itself, and gilds the roof with mirth;
When up thy thyrse[4] is raised, and when the
  sound

---

[1] The cart that brought in the last load of the harvest. "Wassails" were cups of wine drunk to one's health.
[2] Amorous gaiety.

[3] Waxy substance secreted by the sperm whale. It is used as a base for fine perfumes.
[4] "A javelin twined with ivy" (Herrick's note).

Of sacred orgies [1] flies—A round, a round! [2]
When the rose reigns, and locks with ointment
  shine,
Let rigid Cato [3] read these lines of mine.   10
(1648)

STUDY AIDS: "Orgies" (l. 8) was a term commonly used for the ceremonial rites of Bacchus and other deities. In connection with this word, note ll. 2, 4. What seems to be Herrick's attitude toward his poetry? In his view, what is the function of poetry?

His Prayer to Ben Jonson

When I verse shall make,
  Know I have prayed thee,
For old religion's [4] sake,
  Saint Ben, to aid me.

Make the way smooth for me,   5
  When I, thy Herrick,

Honoring thee, on my knee
  Offer my lyric.

Candles I'll give to thee,
  And a new altar;   10
And thou, Saint Ben, shalt be
  Writ in my psalter. [5]
(1648)

Cherry-Ripe [6]

Cherry-ripe, ripe, ripe, I cry,
Full and fair ones; come and buy!
If so be you ask me where
They do grow, I answer, there,
Where my Julia's [7] lips do smile;
There's the land, or cherry-isle,
Whose plantations fully show

All the year where cherries grow.
(1648)

STUDY AIDS: Which of the following adjectives best describe the TONE of the poem: frivolous, gallant, gay, sarcastic, or urbane? How does Herrick achieve this tone in the poem?

How Roses Came Red

Roses at first were white,
  Till they could not agree
Whether my Sappho's [8] breast
  Or they more white should be.

But being vanquished quite,   5
  A blush their cheeks bespread;
Since which, believe the rest,
  The roses first came red.
(1648)

[1] "Songs to Bacchus" (Herrick's note).
[2] A song sung by three or more persons in turn.
[3] Roman statesman, sometimes called "The Censor."
[4] What would the "old religion" be?
[5] The Psalms, or songs of praise. Six of Herrick's poems express his affection and admiration for Ben Jonson.

STUDY AIDS: 1. The urbanity and gallantry of Herrick's "love poems" places him in the company of the "Cavalier" poets, Suckling, Lovelace, Carew, and Waller. Try to analyze exactly how this poem is complimentary to Sappho.
2. Contrast the tone of this poem with that of Donne's love poem, The Good-Morrow (p. 201). Which seems the more sincere expression of love? Does the simplicity of Herrick's poem have anything to do with your judgment? Is simplicity a thing of art or of the heart?

[6] Herrick's poem echoes the refrain of Campion's There Is a Garden in Her Face (p. 180).
[7] Herrick wrote several poems about his "mistress," Julia. There has been much speculation whether Julia was actual or not.
[8] A fictitious mistress.

How Violets Came Blue

Love on a day, wise poets tell,
  Some time in wrangling spent,
Whether the violet should excel,
  Or she, in sweetest scent.

But Venus having lost the day,   5
  Poor girls [1] she fell on you
And beat ye so, as some dare say,
  Her blows did make ye blue.
(1648)

Upon Julia's Clothes

Whenas in silks my Julia goes,
Then, then, methinks, how sweetly flows [2]
The liquefaction of her clothes.

Next, when I cast mine eyes, and see
That brave vibration, each way free,   5
Oh, how that glittering taketh me!
(1648)

STUDY AIDS: 1. Each stanza is centered in a single quality of silk in movement and in light. In each stanza this quality is caught in a single striking word: "liquefaction" (l. 3) and "glittering" (l. 6). Notice also that the lines which describe Julia (1, 3, 5) flow smoothly and evenly; the "observer" lines (2, 4, 6) throb and are uneven in their starts and stops. Why? Is the poem about Julia's clothes or Julia?
  2. Is the second stanza about Julia in silk or out of silk? What does "Next" mean?

To The Virgins to Make Much of Time [3]

    Several of Herrick's lyrics express what is commonly regarded as an epicurean attitude toward life. However, his epicureanism is not the usual light-hearted *carpe diem* doctrine that the pursuit of pleasure is the aim of life. Behind each moment of transient beauty the death's head can be seen. It is this spirit which often gives Herrick a detachment and poise in his lyrics.

Gather ye rosebuds while ye may,
  Old Time is still a-flying;
And this same flower that smiles to-day,
  To-morrow will be dying.

The glorious lamp of heaven, the sun,   5
  The higher he's a-getting,
The sooner will his race be run,
  And nearer he's to setting.

That age is best which is the first,
  When youth and blood are warmer;   10
But being spent, the worse, and worst
  Times, still succeed the former.

Then be not coy, but use your time,
  And while ye may, go marry;
For, having lost but once your prime,   15
  You may forever tarry.
(1648)

STUDY AIDS: 1. Note the scansion of the first stanza. How many syllables are in l. 1? In l. 2? This alternation is an example of Herrick's classicism. While he uses rhyme, the beauty of the lyric lies in its strict accent and variation of line lengths rather than in variation from a metrical pattern.
  2. What is the symbolism of "rosebuds"?

[1] The violets.
[2] How is the motion of flowing produced in the poem?

[3] Like several of Herrick's poems, this one was set to music by William Lawes. In his London days, Herrick was on intimate terms with the court musicians and composers William and Henry Lawes, Robert Ramsay, and Nicholas Lanière. There is evidence that Herrick's theory of writing was influenced by that of musical composition.

To Daffodils

Fair daffodils, we weep to see
  You haste away so soon;
As yet the early-rising sun
  Has not attained his noon.
    Stay, stay,   5
    Until the hasting day
      Has run
    But to the even-song; [1]
And, having prayed together, we
  Will go with you along.   10

We have short time to stay, as you,
  We have as short a spring;
As quick a growth to meet decay,
  As you, or anything.
    We die   15

As your hours do, and dry
    Away,
  Like to the summer's rain;
Or as the pearls of morning's dew,
  Ne'er to be found again.   20
(1648)

STUDY AIDS: 1. Notice how Herrick extends his metaphor until it becomes almost a METAPHYSICAL CONCEIT. Why is it not a true one? At what point in the poem do you realize daffodils are not the subject?
2. Lines 3–8 develop a time progression. What has this progression become by the conclusion of the poem?
3. Which seems to you the more profound poem, *To Daffodils* or *To the Virgins to Make Much of Time*? Why?

Corinna's Going a-Maying

Get up, get up for shame, the blooming morn
Upon her wings presents the god unshorn.[1]
  See how Aurora [2] throws her fair
  Fresh-quilted colors through the air:
  Get up, sweet slug-a-bed, and see   5
  The dew bespangling herb and tree.
Each flower has wept and bowèd toward the
    east
Above an hour since: yet you not dressed;
  Nay! not so much as out of bed?
  When all the birds have matins said   10
  And sung their thankful hymns, 't is sin,
  Nay, profanation, to keep in,
Whenas a thousand virgins on this day
Spring, sooner than the lark, to fetch in May.

Rise, and put on your foliage,[3] and be seen 15
To come forth, like the springtime, fresh and
    green,
  And sweet as Flora.[4] Take no care

For jewels for your gown or hair:
  Fear not; the leaves will strew
  Gems in abundance upon you: 20
Besides, the childhood of the day has kept,
Against [5] you come, some orient pearls
    unwept;
  Come and receive them while the light
  Hangs on the dew-locks of the night:
  And Titan [6] on the eastern hill   25
  Retires himself, or else stands still
Till you come forth. Wash, dress, be brief in
    praying:
  Few beads [7] are best when once we go
    a-Maying.

[3] Notice how Herrick informs us through metaphor that Corinna is under the dominion of nature, as are the birds (ll. 10–11), the flowers (ll. 8–9), and the trees, which indicate their acceptance of Corinna by dropping their beads of dew upon her (ll. 17–20). If she denies this dominion of nature, it is a "sin" (ll. 11–14).
[4] Goddess of the flowers.
[5] Until.
[6] The sun.
[7] Prayers said on a rosary.

[1] Anglican service of evening prayer.

---

[1] Apollo, the sun god.
[2] Goddess of the dawn.

Come, my Corinna, come; and coming, mark
How each field turns a street, each street a
    park [8]   30
  Made green and trimmed with trees; see
    how
  Devotion gives each house a bough
  Or branch: each porch, each door ere this
  An ark,[9] a tabernacle is,
Made up of white-thorn, neatly interwove;   35
As if here were those cooler shades of love.
  Can such delights be in the street
  And open fields and we not see 't?
  Come, we'll abroad; and let's obey
  The proclamation made for May: 40
And sin no more, as we have done, by staying;
But, my Corinna, come, let's go a-Maying.

There's not a budding [10] boy or girl this day
But is got up, and gone to bring in May.
  A deal of youth, ere this, is come   45
  Back, and with white-thorn laden home.
  Some have dispatched their cakes and cream
  Before that we have left [11] to dream:
And some have wept, and wooed, and plighted
    troth,
And chose their priest, ere we can cast off
    sloth: 50
  Many a green-gown [12] has been given;
  Many a kiss, both odd and even:
  Many a glance too has been sent
  From out the eye, love's firmament;

Many a jest told of the keys betraying   55
This night, and locks picked, yet we're not
    a-Maying.

Come, let us go while we are in our prime; [13]
And take the harmless folly of the time.
  We shall grow old apace, and die
  Before we know our liberty.   60
  Our life is short, and our days run
  As fast away as does the sun;
And, as a vapor or a drop of rain, [14]
Once lost, can ne'er be found again,
  So when or you or I are made   65
  A fable, song, or fleeting shade,
  All love, all liking, all delight
  Lies drowned with us in endless night.
Then while time serves,[15] and we are but
    decaying,
Come, my Corinna, come let's go a-Maying. 70
(1648)

STUDY AIDS: 1. Notice the clash of pagan
and Christian views in sts. 1–3. For example,
the pagan view might be stated this way: "May-
day is dedicated to the worship of the nature
god. Corinna is late for this worship." What
elements in these stanzas relate to this pagan
view? Notice, however, that Herrick refers to
this pagan worship in terms of Christian worship
(see ll. 10–11, 24, 27–28, 32, 40, 50). The
fertility pagan rites and the Christian rites
come together in l. 50 with the "priest" who will
marry the "budding" boys and girls.

2. Which do you think is a most nearly
complete statement of the poem's theme: (1)
"Life is short, so let us enjoy it while we may";
(2) "the pagan view, that we are under the
dominion of nature, is part of us, so let us
recognize it when it occasionally arises, as in
the enjoyment of May-day"; or, (3) "the pagan
view is truer than the Christian view"?

[8] The village is also under nature's dominion:
streets become parks where nature is enjoyed (ll.
30–38).
[9] In primitive times, men placed baskets of boughs
over each door to ward off evil and to insure fertility of crops and family. But the word "tabernacle"
shows Herrick must be thinking of the "Ark of
the Tabernacle," the box containing the Tables of
Moses' law. It was a symbol to the Jewish people
in Old Testament times of God's constant presence
with his people.
[10] Herrick continues the metaphor noted in l. 16.
Corinna's friends are "plants" under nature's control.
[11] I.e., left off dreaming.
[12] Stained by the grass. These "budding" boys
and girls have surrendered to nature's dominion.
Like the flowers, trees, and birds, they have worshipped the "unshorn god," who is Apollo, the
bridegroom of nature, the sun god of fertility worshipped by primitive man at the coming of spring
(May-day). Lines 52–56 emphasize this surrender
to nature.

[13] Lines 57–58 perhaps form the resolution of
the conflict. May-day, since the time of primitive
man, has shown us we are a part of nature and
subject to its rule. Christianity tells us of the soul,
but nature (pagan May-day rites) tells us of the
body.
[14] Why does this metaphor succeed so well? What
imagery does it recapture from ll. 6, 20–22, 24?
What does it symbolize?
[15] Does the phrase mean "while there is still time,"
or "while time is still servant, not master"? Can it
have both meanings in the poem?

His Poetry His Pillar

Horace, the Roman poet, had said, "Life is short, but art is long." Herrick, whose classicism is always close to that of Rome, follows Horace in this view. The idea is commonplace in the Renaissance (cf. Shakespeare, *Sonnet 18*, p. 169).

Only a little more
  I have to write;
  Then I'll give o'er,
And bid the world good night.

'Tis but a flying minute   5
  That I must stay,
  Or linger in it;
And then I must away.

O Time, that cut'st down all,
  And scarce leav'st here   10
  Memorial
Of any men that were!

How many lie forgot
  In vaults beneath,

And piecemeal rot   15
Without a fame in death!

Behold this living stone
  I rear for me,
  Ne'er to be thrown
Down, envious Time, by thee.   20

Pillars let some set up,
  If so they please;
  Here is my hope,
And my pyramides.
(1648)

STUDY AIDS: 1. Can literature provide a kind of immortality? Does Herrick have an immortality because of his lyrics?
2. Is the pagan view of immortality expressed in this poem at odds with the Christian concept?

The Hag

The popular songs with their simple melodies, homely realism, and refrains ("hey-nonny-nonny") declined somewhat in Elizabeth's day. In their place rose the foreign and more consciously wrought art lyric (sonnet, madrigal, miscellany lyric), which can be seen in Tottel's Miscellany of 1557. However, while the art lyric was developing along Petrarchan, metaphysical, and classical lines, the popular song remained the property of the people. Herrick wrote several lyrics, like *The Hag*, which in their rhythms (almost syncopation) and subject matter, are clearly the descendants of the older Elizabethan songs.

The hag is astride
  This night for to ride,
The devil and she together;
  Through thick and through thin,
  Now out, and then in,   5
Though ne'er so foul be the weather.

  A thorn or a burr
  She takes for a spur,
With a lash of a bramble she rides now;

Through brakes and through briars,   10
  O'er ditches and mires,
She follows the spirit that guides now.

  No beast for his food
  Dares now range the wood,
But hushed in his lair he lies lurking: 15
  While mischiefs by these,
  On land and on seas,
At noon of night are a-working.

The storm will arise
And trouble the skies   20
This night; and, more for the wonder,
  The ghost from the tomb
  Affrighted shall come,
Called out by the clap of the thunder.
(1648)

STUDY AIDS: Scan the first stanza. What alternation of syllables do you find from line to line? What pattern of accents is in the stanza? What do the FEMININE ENDINGS do to the rhythm?

His Prayer for Absolution [1]

For those my unbaptizèd rimes,
Writ in my wild unhallowed times,
For every sentence, clause, and word,
That's not inlaid with thee, my Lord,
Forgive me, God, and blot each line   5
Out of my book that is not thine.

But if, 'mongst all, thou find'st here one
Worthy thy benediction,
That one of all the rest shall be
The glory of my work and me.   10
(1648)

Sir John Suckling
(1609–1642)

SUCKLING, ONE OF A GROUP OF COURTIERS KNOWN AS THE "CAVALIER" POETS, WAS A GAY, pleasure-loving gallant. He was the best bowler and card player at court (he is said to have invented the game of cribbage), and he spent large sums in entertainment and gambling. His later life, however, was anything but gay. At the outbreak of the Civil War he supported the King, conspired against Parliament, and was forced to flee to France, where he died, possibly by his own hand.

Poetry with Suckling was an avocation; no doubt he spoke the truth in remarking that he "prized black eyes or a lucky hit at bowls above all the trophies of wit." Certainly his verse seems unstudied. Often mocking in tone, his short lyrics combine an apparent spontaneity with great neatness and precision of phrasing.

Why So Pale and Wan, Fond Lover?

Why so pale and wan, fond lover?
  Prithee, why so pale?
Will, when looking well can't move her,
  Looking ill prevail?
  Prithee, why so pale?   5

Why so dull and mute, young sinner?
  Prithee, why so mute?

Will, when speaking well can't win her,
  Saying nothing do't?
  Prithee, why so mute?   10

Quit, quit for shame! This will not move,
  This cannot take her.
If of herself she will not love,
  Nothing can make her:
  The devil take her!   15
(1646)

[1] From *Noble Numbers* (1647), published with *Hesperides* (1648).

O for Some Honest Lover's Ghost

O for some honest lover's ghost,
  Some kind unbodied post [1]
    Sent from the shades below!
    I strangely long to know
Whether the noble chaplets wear,   5
Those that their mistress' scorn did bear
    Or those that were used kindly.

For whatsoe'er they tell us here
  To make those sufferings dear,
    'Twill there, I fear, be found   10
    That to the being crowned
T' have loved alone will not suffice,
Unless we also have been wise
    And have our loves enjoyed.

What posture can we think him in   15
  That, here unloved, again
    Departs, and is thither gone
    Where each sits by his own?

Or how can that Elysium be
Where I my mistress still must see   20
    Circled in other's arms?

For there the judges all are just,
  And Sophonisba [2] must
    Be his whom she held dear,
    Not his who loved her here.   25
The sweet Philoclea,[3] since she died,
Lies by her Pirocles [3] his side,
    Not by Amphialus. [3]

Some bays, perchance, or myrtle bough
  For difference crowns the brow   30
    Of those kind souls that were
    The noble martyrs here;
And if that be the only odds
(As who can tell?), ye kinder gods,
    Give me the woman here!   35
(1646)

'Tis Now, Since I Sat Down Before

'Tis now, since I sat down before
  That foolish fort, a heart,
(Time strangely spent) a year and more,
  And still I did my part.

Made my approaches, from her hand   5
  Unto her lip did rise,
And did already understand
  The language of her eyes;

Proceeded on with no less art,
  My tongue was engineer;   10
I thought to undermine the heart
  By whispering in the ear.

When this did nothing, I brought down
  Great cannon-oaths, and shot
A thousand thousand to the town;   15
  And still it yielded not.

I then resolved to starve the place
  By cutting off all kisses,
Praising and gazing on her face,
  And all such little blisses.   20

To draw her out and from her strength,
  I drew all batteries in,
And brought myself to lie at length
  As if no siege had been.

When I had done what man could do,   25
  And thought the place mine own,
The enemy lay quiet too,
  And smiled at all was done.

I sent to know from whence and where
  These hopes and this relief;   30
A spy informed, Honor was there,
  And did command in chief.

[1] Messenger.
[2] Carthaginian woman forced to marry against her will.
[3] Characters in Sidney's *Arcadia*.

March, march, quoth I, the word straight
   give,
   Let's lose no time, but leave her;
That giant upon air will live,   35
   And hold it out forever.

To such a place our camp remove,
   As will no siege abide;
I hate a fool that starves her love,
   Only to feed her pride.   40
(1646)

Out upon It! I Have Loved

Out upon it! I have loved
   Three whole days together!
And am like to love three more,
   If it prove fair weather.

Time shall moult away his wings,   5
   Ere he shall discover
In the whole wide world again
   Such a constant lover.

But the spite on it is, no praise
   Is due at all to me: 10
Love with me had made no stays,
   Had it any been but she.

Had it any been but she,
   And that very face,
There had been at least ere this   15
   A dozen dozen in her place.
(1659)

STUDY AIDS: 1. Suckling's verse often has a colloquial quality; "natural, easy Suckling," he has been called. What gives his verse this quality? At what place in his poems is he likely to be most pointed?

2. How does Suckling's treatment of love compare with that of the Elizabethan sonneteers? How does the dominant CONCEIT in 'Tis Now, Since I Sat Down Before differ in quality from the typical PETRARCHAN CONCEIT? From a typical conceit of Donne's?

Richard Lovelace
(1618–1658)

ALTHOUGH HIS NAME TODAY IS USUALLY PAIRED WITH SUCKLING'S, LOVELACE WAS LESS the dashing cavalier and more the model of courtesy. He was "one of the handsomest men in England," said a contemporary, "much admired and adored by the female sex." If his behavior was less spectacular than that of Suckling, like his fellow courtier he suffered for his royalism. When as representative of the Kentish nobility he petitioned Parliament in the King's behalf, he was committed to the Gatehouse in Westminster, where he composed his well-known To Althea, from Prison. Released on heavy bail, he continued to serve both King Charles and the French king, the latter in warfare that occasioned To Lucasta, Going to the Wars. The poet's last years were miserable: his king executed, his fortune gone, the elegant courtier was reduced to begging and died in poverty.

Lovelace achieved a modest but secure fame on the basis of a slender output. With something of the chivalric idealism of Sidney, something of the discipline and neatness of Jonson, and something of the wit of Donne, his lyrics represent perhaps the best of the English courtly tradition in poetry.

To Althea, from Prison

When Love with unconfinèd wings
  Hovers within my gates,
And my divine Althea brings
  To whisper at the grates;
When I lie tangled in her hair   5
  And fettered to her eye,
The gods [1] that wanton in the air
  Know no such liberty.

When flowing cups run swiftly round
  With no allaying Thames, [2]   10
Our careless heads with roses bound,
  Our hearts with loyal flames;
When thirsty grief in wine we steep,
  When healths and draughts go free,
Fishes that tipple in the deep   15
  Know no such liberty.

When, like committed [3] linnets, I
  With shriller throat will sing
The sweetness, mercy, majesty,
  And glories of my king;   20
When I shall voice aloud how good
  He is, how great should be,

Enlargèd [4] winds, that curl the flood,
  Know no such liberty.

Stone walls do not a prison make,   25
  Nor iron bars a cage:
Minds innocent and quiet take
  That for an hermitage:
If I have freedom in my love,
  And in my soul am free,   30
Angels alone, that soar above,
  Enjoy such liberty.
(1649)

STUDY AIDS: 1. This poem is built upon a
single PARADOX, made explicit in the last stanza.
How does each of the first three stanzas develop
or illustrate the paradox? Each of them also
states or implies a kind of bondage, which nevertheless is not incompatible with freedom. What
is it in each case?

2. What is the function of the last two lines
in each of the first three stanzas? Lines 31–32
differ from the concluding lines of sts. 1–3.
Is this variation a matter of form (a way of
"rounding out" the poem) or of content (the
idea of the stanza) or of both?

To Lucasta, [5] Going to the Wars

Tell me not, sweet, I am unkind,
  That from the nunnery
Of thy chaste breast and quiet mind
  To war and arms I fly.

True, a new mistress now I chase,   5
  The first foe in the field;
And with a stronger faith embrace
  A sword, a horse, a shield.

Yet this inconstancy is such
  As thou too shalt adore: 10
I could not love thee, dear, so much,
  Loved I not honor more.
(1649)

STUDY AIDS: Paralleling the logical development of the poet's reply to his lady (presumably she has called him "unkind") is a shift
of TONE—surprising in so short a poem. Where
does it occur? How would you describe it? What
does it contribute to the poem psychologically?
Aesthetically?

[1] Probably "birds."
[2] The river; hence dilution of a drink.
[3] Imprisoned, or caged.
[4] Liberated.

[5] Contracted form of lux casta, a "pure light."
Lucasta's identity is uncertain.

Andrew Marvell
(1621–1678)

RELATIVELY FEW DETAILS ARE KNOWN OF THE FIRST THIRTY YEARS OF MARVELL'S LIFE. He entered Cambridge University in 1633, withdrew for a short time to London, then returned to the University, where he remained until 1641. For the next four years he traveled on the Continent. In 1651 he became tutor to Mary Fairfax, daughter of General Fairfax, the retired leader of the Puritan army. In 1657 he was named assistant to Milton in the department of State. From 1659 until his death he was a member of Parliament from Hull, whose inhabitants expressed their satisfaction with his work by voting him a yearly barrel of ale. During this Parliamentary period, he was famous as a writer of satiric prose pamphlets defending toleration.

Probably the decade of the 1650's was the most important time for Marvell's development as a poet. It is also probable that during his sojourn in General Fairfax's house in Yorkshire, Marvell began to write the kind of poetry we now associate with his name. His earlier verse had had an exaggerated metaphysical quality. Now, his poetry began to concern itself with nature—the relationship of external and human nature, often stated in concepts of Platonism. Marvell's best poems are never as simple as they seem to be on the surface. A single word, image, or symbol can evoke a complex of moral, religious, and philosophic traditions which the poem unifies. Sensory perception, immediate and strong in Marvell, almost always leads to an intellectual understanding of man's experience.

The Mower's Song

My mind was once the true survey [1]
Of all these meadows fresh and gay,
And in the greenness of the grass
Did see its hopes as in a glass; [2]
When Juliana came, and she, 5
What I do to the grass, does to my thoughts
and me. [3]

But these, [4] while I with sorrow pine,
Grew more luxuriant still and fine,
That not one blade of grass you spied,
But had a flower on either side; 10
When Juliana came, and she,
What I do to the grass, does to my thoughts
and me.

Unthankful meadows, could you so
A fellowship [5] so true forego,
And in your gaudy May-games meet, 15
While I lay trodden under feet?
When Juliana came, and she,
What I do to the grass, does to my thoughts
and me.

But what you in compassion ought,
Shall now by my revenge be wrought; 20
And flowers, and grass, and I, and all
Will in one common ruin fall;
When Juliana comes, and she,
What I do to the grass, does to my thoughts
and me.

[1] In ll. 1–4 notice how Marvell identifies his mind with nature ("meadows").
[2] Mirror.
[3] How do the length and motion of l. 6 relate to the line's meaning?
[4] What is the antecedent of "these"?
[5] What is this "fellowship"?

And thus, ye meadows, which have
    been [6]   25
Companions of my thoughts more green,
Shall now the heraldry become
With which I shall adorn my tomb;
For Juliana comes, and she,
What I do to the grass, does to my thoughts
    and me.   30
(*ca.* 1650–1652; 1681)

STUDY AIDS: 1. On a casual reading, the poem is a love poem: the speaker's love for Juliana is unrequited. This is death to him and his love. How sincere do his feelings for Juliana seem to be? How important is Juliana in the total poem? What subject is the poem really discussing through the metaphor of love (Juliana) and nature (meadows)?

2. Is the mower a simple rustic man or is he a complicated, sophisticated individual?

To His Coy [1] Mistress

Had we but world enough, and time,
This coyness, Lady, were no crime.
We would sit down and think which way
To walk and pass our long love's day.
Thou by the Indian Ganges' side   5
Shouldst rubies find; I by the tide
Of Humber [2] would complain. I would
Love you ten years before the Flood,
And you should, if you please, refuse
Till the conversion of the Jews.   10
My vegetable [3] love should grow
Vaster than empires, and more slow;
An hundred years should go to praise
Thine eyes and on thy forehead gaze;
Two hundred to adore each breast,   15
But thirty thousand to the rest;
An age at least to every part,
And the last age should show your heart.
For, Lady, you deserve this state,
Nor would I love at lower rate.[4]   20
    But [5] at my back I always hear
Time's wingèd chariot hurrying near;
And yonder all before us lie
Deserts of vast eternity.

Thy beauty shall no more be found,   25
Nor, in thy marble vault, shall sound
My echoing song; then worms shall try
That long preserved virginity,
And your quaint [6] honor turn to dust,
And into ashes all my lust: 30
The grave's a fine and private place,
But none, I think, do there embrace.
    Now therefore, while the youthful hue
Sits on thy skin like morning dew,
And while thy willing soul transpires [7]   35
At every pore with instant [8] fires,
Now let us sport us while we may,
And now, like amorous birds of prey,
Rather at once our time devour
Than languish in his slow-chapped [9] power. 40
Let us roll all our strength and all
Our sweetness up into one ball,
And tear our pleasures with rough strife
Through the iron gates of life:
Thus, though we cannot make our sun [10] 45
Stand still, yet we will make him run.
(1650–1652; 1681)

[6] Unreasonable, old-fashioned.
[7] Breathes.
[8] Eager.
[9] Slow-jawed, or slowly-devouring. Chronos (time) devoured all his children except Zeus, who had been hidden away.
[10] Several possible sources for the final couplet have been suggested: (1) Ovid's account of Phaeton's wild ride across the sky; (2) Zeus, who bid the sun stand still so that his night with Alcmene, the wife of Amphitryon, might last longer; (3) Zeus, who escaped Chronos (time), conquered him to become chief of the gods; and (4) Joshua, whose prayer to God was answered: the sun stood still until Joshua's battle was won.

[6] Notice the identification again of "thoughts" and "meadows" in ll. 25–26.

[1] Reserved, modest.
[2] The river on whose banks Hull is situated.
[3] Lush, prolific growth characterizes the vegetable kingdom.
[4] Does the word mean "cost" or "tempo"? Which reading better fits the subject and tone of ll. 1–20?
[5] The poem has a dialectical structure: st. 1 introduces a subject; st. 2 introduces a contrast marked by "but" (l. 21); and st. 3, introduced by "therefore" (l. 33), brings the argument to a conclusion. What is the subject of ll. 1–20?

STUDY AIDS: 1. What are the three steps in the argument by which the lover tries to seduce the mistress? What is the TONE of each section?

2. The final couplet, whatever its source, states that the lovers cannot control time ("though we cannot make our sun Stand still"). But the couplet is a PARADOX. Its final statement, "Yet we will make him run," implies that the lovers are greater than time; they supply the energy which is the very power of existence, and they thus create time. They are not Joshuas—but they can be gods through their love, which is that instant in which time is devoured. Does such an interpretation fit the total poem? Where does Marvell place the emphasis in the poem, on love or on time? Is he discussing what love does to time or what time does to love? Is the poem a statement of the human dilemma?

3. Notice the images of violence in ll. 33–46. What do these imply as to the effects time works on love?

Bermudas

The song (ll. 5–36) is sung by the Puritans who settled the Bermudas in the early seventeenth century. The main influence on the poem is Psalm 104. Marvell's religious feelings are always objective rather than personal: they need some object such as a drop of dew, a garden, or the Bermuda Islands around which they can cluster. In the poem the Bermudas are a kind of earthly paradise as well as a glorified England.

Where the remote Bermudas ride,
In the ocean's bosom unespied,
From a small boat that rowed along,
The listening winds received this song:

"What should we do but sing His praise, 5
That led us through the watery maze
Unto an isle so long unknown,
And yet far kinder than our own?
Where He the huge sea-monsters wracks,[1]
That lift the deep upon their backs; 10
He lands us on a grassy stage,
Safe from the storms' and prelates' rage.
He gave us this eternal spring
Which here enamels everything,
And sends the fowls to us in care, 15
On daily visits through the air;
He hangs in shades the orange bright,
Like golden lamps in a green night,
And does in the pomegranates close
Jewels more rich than Ormus[2] shows; 20

He makes the figs our mouths to meet,
And throws the melons at our feet;
But apples[3] plants of such a price,
No tree could ever bear them twice;
With cedars, chosen by His hand, 25
From Lebanon, He stores the land;
And makes the hollow seas, that roar,
Proclaim the ambergris[4] on shore;
He cast (of which we rather boast)
The Gospel's pearl upon our coast, 30
And in these rocks for us did frame
A temple, where to sound His name.
Oh! let our voice His praise exalt,
Till it arrive at heaven's vault,
Which, thence (perhaps) rebounding, may 35
Echo beyond the Mexique Bay."

Thus sung they in the English boat,
An holy and a cheerful note;
And all the way, to guide their chime,
With falling oars they kept the time. 40
(1650; 1681)

[1] Wrecks.
[2] Hormuz, famous diamond market on the Persian Gulf.
[3] Pineapples.
[4] See footnote 3, p. 232.

The Garden

How vainly men themselves amaze,[1]
To win the palm, the oak, or bays,[2]
And their incessant labors see
Crowned from some single herb or tree,
Whose short and narrow-vergèd shade   5
Does prudently their toils upbraid;[3]
While all the flowers and trees do close
To weave the garlands of repose!

Fair Quiet, have I found thee here,[4]
And Innocence, thy sister dear?   10
Mistaken long, I sought you then
In busy companies of men.
Your sacred plants, if here below,
Only among the plants will grow;
Society is all but rude   15
To this delicious solitude.

No white nor red was ever seen[5]
So amorous as this lovely green.
Fond lovers, cruel as their flame,
Cut in these trees their mistress' name: 20
Little, alas, they know or heed
How far these beauties hers exceed!
Fair trees! wheresoe'r your barks I wound,
No name shall but your own be found.

When we have run our passion's heat,   25
Love hither makes his best retreat.
The gods, that mortal beauty chase,
Still in a tree did end their race:[6]
Apollo hunted Daphne so,
Only that she might laurel grow;   30

And Pan did after Syrinx speed,
Not as a nymph, but for a reed.

What wondrous life is this I lead![7]
Ripe apples drop about my head;
The luscious clusters of the vine   35
Upon my mouth do crush their wine;
The nectarine and curious[8] peach
Into my hands themselves do reach;
Stumbling on melons, as I pass,
Ensnared with flowers, I fall on grass.   40

Meanwhile the mind, from pleasure less,[9]
Withdraws into its happiness—
The mind, that ocean where each kind
Does straight its own resemblance find;
Yet it creates, transcending these,   45
Far other worlds and other seas,
Annihilating all that's made
To a green thought in a green shade.[10]

Here at the fountain's sliding foot,[11]
Or at some fruit-tree's mossy root,   50
Casting the body's vest aside,
My soul into the boughs does glide:
There, like a bird, it sits and sings,
Then whets and combs its silver wings,
And, till prepared for longer flight,   55
Waves in its plumes the various light.

[1] Confuse.

[2] Wreaths given for successful performance in athletics, civics, and poetry.

[3] Stanza 1 contemplates man's ambition. The ambitious man becomes narrow. Nature, by its repose, upbraids such a man and shows him how he might be complete.

[4] I.e., in the garden.

[5] Sts. 3–4 treat of the rewards of desire. First the poet surveys the polite and conventional lovers who cut their names on trees (ll. 19–22). Then he turns to the gods. Apollo hunted Daphne for the laurel crown of poetry, and Pan pursued Syrinx to capture music.

[6] A pun: "chase" and "family."

[7] Nature does not need to be chased as did Daphne and Syrinx. It woos the poet. All these eatable things give themselves so as to lose themselves like a lover, to be transformed as were Daphne and Syrinx.

[8] Exquisite.

[9] St. 6 carries the process of metamorphosis further. Even nature suffers a sea-change in the mind.

[10] I.e., there must be a green shade (the garden, matter), otherwise no green thought (transcending, spirit). "Transcending" implies something to rise from and above.

[11] St. 7 carries the metamorphosis to its ultimate completion. The "green shade" (garden) has brought the poet to a "green thought," which concentrates all existence to a point of time. At this point the soul (timeless) escapes from the body (controlled by time) and sings in the tree boughs.

Such was that happy garden-state,
While man there walked without a mate.[12]
After a place so pure and sweet,
What other help could yet be meet! 60
But 'twas beyond a mortal's share
To wander solitary there:
Two paradises 'twere in one
To live in paradise alone.

How well the skillful gardener drew 65
Of flowers and herbs this dial new,
Where, from above, the milder sun
Does through a fragrant zodiac run;
And, as it works, the industrious bee
Computes its time as well as we! [13] 70
How could such sweet and wholesome hours

Be reckoned, but with herbs and flowers!
(*ca.* 1650–1652; 1681)

STUDY AIDS: 1. What is the only permanent satisfaction which the poet finds for the passions and instincts of man (see sts. 3–4)?
2. The poem deals constantly with the problem of metamorphosis. How is metamorphosis a poetical answer to the decay of beauty (lovers) and the triumph of time (gods)?
3. There is a strain of mysticism in the poem. In which stanza does the "ecstasy" or "trance" occur? What is the Paradise or Garden of Eden attained by the poet? How is this a victory over time and decay?
4. What does Marvell think is the function of nature in man's solution of his problems?

John Milton
(1608–1674)

Paradise Lost, MILTON'S GREAT EPIC, WAS COMPOSED DURING THE POET'S OLD AGE. A lifetime of experience, literary and practical, went into its creation, which Milton deferred for years while he devoted his pen to the Puritan Commonwealth and the cause of liberty. A dedicated and skillful artist, Milton was also a man of affairs, in the thick of the political conflict of his time.

Milton's father, a notary public, destined his son "while yet a boy, for the study of humane letters" and for the Anglican ministry. After being tutored at home by Thomas Young, a Puritan divine, and attending St. Paul's School, Milton in 1625 entered Christ's College, Cambridge, where he remained until he took an M.A. degree in 1632. The next six years he spent at his father's house in the village of Horton, near London, reading and studying and debating a career. Although his university training had fitted him for the ministry, he decided to become a man of letters, and so was the first Englishman deliberately to make literature his profession. He worked hard to prepare himself for poethood, and early achieved notable success in *L'Allegro, Il Penseroso,* and *Lycidas.* To complete his training he traveled in Italy, leaving England in 1638 and returning the following year.

The period of preparation now over, Milton established a boarding school in London to support himself while he practiced his art. He felt he was ready at last to begin work on the

[12] Man and nature have achieved a union, in which Eve is an intruder. (Notice sts. 3–4, where the beauty of women was a distraction.)
[13] In the final stanza, the poet has returned from the trance and is looking at a floral sundial. The sun is "milder" (l. 67) because after this experience the poet knows that time too can be transcended: time is dependent on living things ("bee," "herbs," "flowers") rather than living things being subject to time.

great epic which for ten years had been taking shape in his mind. His profound devotion to the cause of liberty, however, caused him to put his poetic hopes in abeyance while he served his country. The conflict between Parliament and the King was growing more intense, and in the summer of 1641 Milton entered the pamphlet controversy on the side of Parliament. For four years he contributed to this clash of ideas, most of his pamphlets defending toleration—a subject which revealed his increasing disillusionment with the growing tyranny of the Puritan party. The most famous of these treatises is the *Areopagitica* (1644), which defends freedom of the press in particular and liberty in general. In fact, all of Milton's tracts are on this subject: liberty in religious affairs (anti-prelatical), in domestic affairs (pro-divorce), and in civil affairs (anti-censorship). Meanwhile, in 1642 he had married the sixteen-year-old Mary Powell, daughter of a royalist. From Milton's few references to the event and from other sources, it appears to have been an unfortunate union, which was dissolved only by Mary's death in 1652.

In 1649 Milton was appointed Latin Secretary to the Council of State, a position he held until 1659, despite the fact that he had become totally blind by 1652. At the Restoration he went into hiding, having been put under sentence of death for his defense of the execution of Charles I. An Act of Indemnity and Oblivion three months later pardoned him with other political prisoners. Not until the political conflict had been resolved did Milton feel free to resume work on his great projected poem.

Milton's poetry includes most of the forms practiced by other poets in the language. His early verse (*On the Death of a Fair Infant, On the Morning of Christ's Nativity*) is metaphysical in style, imitating the fashionable verse of the late 1620's. His next works, *L'Allegro, Il Penseroso,* and *Lycidas,* which reflect the influence of Spenser and the writers of pastoral, show Milton growing in stature as a poet. *Paradise Lost* is a work of his maturity. Its style is Milton's own: ornate, magnificent, and highly sensuous in its coloring and sound. By comparison, the language of *Paradise Regained* (1671) is decidedly austere. The poem lacks the poetic lushness and warmth of *Paradise Lost,* but it is notable for its unity and its clarity of expression. His last work, *Samson Agonistes* (1671), is considered by many readers to be his greatest. It is a tragedy, patterned after the dramas of Euripides—stark and chaste in language, classic in structure.

As one of the greatest of English poets, Milton and his poetry have been subjected to painstaking exploration and criticism. As man and writer, he has been fulsomely praised by some, severely condemned by others. Whichever judgment is passed upon Milton, it is impossible to deny certain qualities of his character which are constantly reflected in his poetry and prose. At the center of his personality was a tremendous sense of pride, which colored everything he believed and did. It motivated his ambition as a writer and demanded perfection in his poetry. It forced him to become the most learned of English poets that he might be counted among the best. It caused him to sacrifice almost two decades of his productive poetic life to politics so that he might fulfill God's work and aid the country he loved so well. And it made him conscious of the worth and dignity of the human being, a belief which finds constant expression in his insistence on the freedom of man's will.

Milton's nature was somewhat austere, which perhaps is not surprising when one considers his serious and noble view of his calling. He had many friends and admirers, however, both in Europe and in England. But whatever the defects of his personality, one who reads Milton's poetry invariably feels that he has entered the "realms of gold" and come into possession of one of the priceless treasures of English literature.

L'Allegro and Il Penseroso

These two poems were written during Milton's late years in Cambridge University. It is better to consider them as two halves of a dual poem, not as two separate poems. The contrast is not between two persons but between two sides of any one individual's personality: L'Allegro, the carefree man and Il Penseroso, the contemplative man. This contrast is presented in terms of the opposition of day and night. *Il Penseroso* proved more influential, when in the eighteenth century hundreds of imitations were written stressing melancholy, meditation, isolation, and graveyards.

L'Allegro

Hence, loathèd Melancholy,
  Of Cerberus [1] and blackest midnight born,
In Stygian cave forlorn,
    'Mongst horrid shapes, and shrieks, and sights unholy,
Find out some uncouth [2] cell,   5
  Where brooding darkness spreads his jealous wings,
And the night-raven sings;
    There under ebon shades, and low-browed rocks,
As ragged as thy locks,
  In dark Cimmerian [3] desert ever dwell. 10
But come, thou goddess fair and free,
In heaven yclept [4] Euphrosyne,
And by men, heart-easing mirth,
Whom lovely Venus at a birth
With two sister Graces more   15
To ivy-crownèd Bacchus bore;
Or whether (as some sager sing)
The frolic wind that breathes the spring,
Zephyr with Aurora playing,
As he met her once a-Maying,   20
There on beds of violets blue,
And fresh-blown roses washed in dew,
Filled her with thee, a daughter fair,
So buxom, blithe, and debonair.
  Haste thee, Nymph, and bring with thee 25
Jest and youthful jollity,
Quips, and cranks, and wanton wiles,

Nods, and becks, and wreathèd smiles,
Such as hang on Hebe's cheek,
And love to live in dimple sleek;   30
Sport that wrinkled care derides,
And laughter holding both his sides.
Come, and trip it as ye go,
On the light fantastic toe;
And in thy right hand lead with thee 35
The mountain Nymph, [5] sweet liberty;
And, if I give thee honor due,
Mirth, admit me of thy crew,
To live with her, and live with thee,
In unreprovèd pleasures free;   40
To hear the lark begin his flight, [6]
And singing startle the dull night,
From his watch-tower in the skies,
Till the dappled dawn doth rise;
Then to come, in spite of sorrow,   45
And at my window bid good-morrow,
Through the sweet-briar or the vine,
Or the twisted eglantine;
While the cock with lively din [7]
Scatters the rear of darkness thin;   50
And to the stack, or the barn-door,
Stoutly struts his dames before:
Oft listening how the hounds and horn
Cheerly rouse the slumbering morn,
From the side of some hoar hill,   55

[1] The three-headed dog that guarded the gateway to Hades.
[2] Unknown.
[3] Land of darkness beyond the ocean (*Odyssey,* xi, 13-19).
[4] Called.

[5] Why must the carefree man be accompanied by this nymph?
[6] The action begins with this line. What is the incident? What time is it? List the following episodes in order. What time progression do they present as a whole?
[7] What earlier English poet and poem is Milton possibly remembering in ll. 49-52 (see p. 76)?

Through the high wood echoing shrill:
Sometime walking, not unseen,
By hedgerow elms, on hillocks green,
Right against the eastern gate,
Where the great sun begins his state,   60
Robed in flames and amber light,
The clouds in thousand liveries dight;
While the ploughman, near at hand,[8]
Whistles o'er the furrowed land,
And the milkmaid singeth blithe,   65
And the mower whets his scythe,
And every shepherd tells his tale
Under the hawthorn in the dale.
   Straight mine eye hath caught new
     pleasures,
Whilst the landscape round it measures: 70
Russet lawns, and fallows gray,
Where the nibbling flocks do stray;
Mountains on whose barren breast
The laboring clouds do often rest;
Meadows trim with daisies pied;   75
Shallow brooks, and rivers wide.
Towers and battlements it sees
Bosomed high in tufted trees,
Where perhaps some beauty lies,
The cynosure[9] of neighboring eyes.   80
Hard by, a cottage chimney smokes
From betwixt two aged oaks,
Where Corydon and Thyrsis met
Are at their savory dinner set
Of herbs and other country messes,   85
Which the neat-handed Phillis dresses;
And then in haste her bower she leaves,
With Thestylis to bind the sheaves;
Or, if the earlier season lead,
To the tanned haycock in the mead.   90
   Sometimes with secure delight
The upland hamlets will invite,
When the merry bells ring round,
And the jocund rebecks sound
To many a youth and many a maid   95
Dancing in the chequered shade;
And young and old come forth to play
On a sunshine holiday,
Till the livelong daylight fail:

Then to the spicy nut-brown ale,   100
With stories told of many a feat,
How fairy Mab the junkets eat:
She was pinched and pulled, she said;
And he, by friar's lantern led,
Tells how the drudging goblin sweat   105
To earn his cream-bowl duly set,
When in one night, ere glimpse of morn,
His shadowy flail hath threshed the corn
That ten day-laborers could not end;
Then lies him down, the lubber fiend,[10]   110
And, stretched out all the chimney's length,
Basks at the fire his hairy strength,
And crop-full out of doors he flings,
Ere the first cock his matin rings.
Thus done the tales, to bed they creep,   115
By whispering winds soon lulled asleep.
Towered cities please us then,[11]
And the busy hum of men,
Where throngs of knights and barons bold,
In weeds of peace, high triumphs hold,   120
With store of ladies, whose bright eyes
Rain influence, and judge the prize
Of wit or arms, while both contend
To win her grace whom all commend.
There let Hymen oft appear   125
In saffron robe, with taper clear,
And pomp, and feast, and revelry,
With mask and antique pageantry;
Such sights as youthful poets dream
On summer eves by haunted stream.   130
Then to the well-trod stage anon,
If Jonson's learned sock[12] be on,
Or sweetest Shakespeare, fancy's child,[13]
Warble his native wood-notes wild.
And ever, against eating cares,   135
Lap me in soft Lydian airs,
Married to immortal verse,
Such as the meeting soul may pierce,
In notes with many a winding bout
Of linkèd sweetness long drawn out   140
With wanton heed and giddy cunning,
The melting voice through mazes running,
Untwisting all the chains that tie

[10] Clumsy elf.
[11] When darkness comes, where does L'Allegro go? Why? What light replaces that of the sun in ll. 117–130? What pleasures does L'Allegro enjoy in ll. 118–150?
[12] The light shoe of Greek comic actors.
[13] Child of the imagination or the creative faculty.

[8] In ll. 63–68 do you see any of the four characters work? Does anyone actually work in the poem? See ll. 105–110. Why do these lines not destroy the holiday mood of the poem?
[9] Focus.

The hidden soul of harmony;
That Orpheus'[14] self may heave his head   145
From golden slumber on a bed
Of heaped Elysian flowers, and hear
Such strains as would have won the ear

Of Pluto to have quite set free
His half-regained Eurydice.   150
These delights if thou canst give,
Mirth, with thee I mean to live.
(1631)

Il Penseroso

Hence, vain deluding joys,
   The brood of folly without father bred!
How little you bestèd,[1]
   Or fill the fixèd mind with all your toys!
Dwell in some idle brain,   5
   And fancies fond with gaudy shapes possess,
As thick and numberless
   As the gay motes that people the sunbeams,
Or likest hovering dreams,
   The fickle pensioners of Morpheus'[2]
      train.   10
But, hail! thou goddess sage and holy!
Hail, divinest Melancholy!
Whose saintly visage is too bright
To hit the sense of human sight,
And therefore to our weaker view   15
O'erlaid with black, staid Wisdom's hue;
Black, but such as in esteem
Prince Memnon's sister might beseem,
Or that starred Ethiop queen[3] that strove
To set her beauty's praise above   20
The sea-nymphs, and their powers offended.
Yet thou art higher far descended:
Thee bright-haired Vesta[4] long of yore
To solitary Saturn bore;
His daughter she; in Saturn's reign   25
Such mixture was not held a stain.
Oft in glimmering bowers and glades
He met her, and in secret shades
Of woody Ida's inmost grove,
Whilst yet there was no fear of Jove.   30

Come, pensive nun, devout and pure,
Sober, steadfast, and demure,
All in a robe of darkest grain,
Flowing with majestic train,
And sable stole of cypress lawn   35
Over thy decent shoulders drawn.
Come; but keep thy wonted state,
With even step, and musing gait,
And looks commercing with the skies,
Thy rapt soul sitting in thine eyes: 40
There, held in holy passion still,
Forget thyself to marble, till
With a sad leaden downward cast
Thou fix them on the earth as fast.
And join with thee calm peace and quiet,   45
Spare fast, that oft with gods doth diet,
And hears the Muses in a ring
Aye round about Jove's altar sing;
And add to these retirèd leisure,
That in trim gardens takes his pleasure;   50
But, first and chiefest, with thee bring
Him that yon soars on golden wing,
Guiding the fiery-wheelèd throne,
The cherub contemplation;[5]
And the mute silence hist along,   55
'Less Philomel[6] will deign a song,
In her sweetest saddest plight,
Smoothing the rugged brow of night,
While Cynthia[7] checks her dragon yoke
Gently o'er the accustomed oak.   60
Sweet bird, that shunn'st the noise of folly,
Most musical, most melancholy!
Thee, chauntress, oft the woods among

[14] Orpheus, on his wedding day, lost his bride, Eurydice, and followed her to Hades. His music won Pluto's consent to return with her to the world, provided he did not look back at her until they reached sunlight. Orpheus looked back.

[1] Profit.
[2] God of sleep.
[3] Cassiopeia, a constellation.
[4] Roman goddess of the hearth.

[5] Cherubs were one rank of the angels. Why is it necessary for this cherub to accompany Il Penseroso?
[6] Nightingale. Here the action begins. What time span is covered in this poem?
[7] The moon. "Dragon yoke" is perhaps the horns of the crescent moon.

I woo, to hear thy even-song;
And, missing thee, I walk unseen 65
On the dry smooth-shaven green,
To behold the wandering moon,
Riding near her highest noon,
Like one that had been led astray
Through the heaven's wide pathless way, 70
And oft, as if her head she bowed,
Stooping through a fleecy cloud.
Oft, on a plat of rising ground,
I hear the far-off curfew sound,
Over some wide-watered shore, 75
Swinging slow with sullen roar;
Or, if the air will not permit,
Some still removèd place will fit,
Where glowing embers through the room [8]
Teach light to counterfeit a gloom, 80
Far from all resort of mirth,
Save the cricket on the hearth,
Or the bellman's drowsy charm
To bless the doors from nightly harm.
Or let my lamp, at midnight hour, 85
Be seen in some high lonely tower,
Where I may oft outwatch the Bear,[9]
With thrice-great Hermes,[10] or unsphere
The spirit of Plato,[11] to unfold
What worlds or what vast regions hold 90
The immortal mind that hath forsook
Her mansion in this fleshly nook;
And of those demons that are found
In fire, air, flood, or underground,
Whose power hath a true consent 95
With planet or with element.
Sometime let gorgeous tragedy
In sceptred pall come sweeping by,
Presenting Thebes, or Pelops'[12] line,
Or the tale of Troy divine, 100
Or what (though rare) of later age
Ennobled hath the buskined[13] stage.
But, O sad virgin! that thy power

Might raise Musæus from his bower;
Or bid the soul of Orpheus sing 105
Such notes as, warbled to the string,
Drew iron tears down Pluto's cheek,
And made hell grant what love did seek;
Or call up him that left half-told
The story[14] of Cambuscan bold, 110
Of Camball, and of Algarsife,
And who had Canace to wife,
That owned the virtuous ring and glass,
And of the wondrous horse of brass
On which the Tartar king did ride; 115
And if aught else great bards beside
In sage and solemn tunes have sung,
Of tourneys, and of trophies hung,
Of forests, and enchantments drear,
Where more is meant than meets the ear.[15] 120
Thus, night, oft see me in thy pale career,
Till civil-suited morn appear,
Not tricked and frounced, as she was wont
With the Attic boy[16] to hunt,
But kerchieft in a comely cloud, 125
While rocking winds are piping loud,
Or ushered with a shower still,
When the gust hath blown his fill,
Ending on the rustling leaves,
With minute-drops from off the eaves. 130
And, when the sun begins to fling[17]
His flaring beams, me, goddess, bring
To archèd walks of twilight groves,
And shadows brown, that Sylvan loves,
Of pine, or monumental oak, 135
Where the rude axe with heavèd stroke
Was never heard the nymphs to daunt,
Or fright them from their hallowed haunt.
There, in close covert, by some brook,
Where no profaner eye may look, 140
Hide me from day's garish eye,
While the bee with honeyed thigh,
That at her flowery work doth sing,
And the waters murmuring,
With such consort as they keep, 145
Entice the dewy-feathered sleep.
And let some strange mysterious dream

[8] In ll. 79–80 notice the imagery of a peculiar half-light used throughout this poem. What kind of imagery does this parallel in *L'Allegro?*
[9] The Big Dipper.
[10] Hermes Trismegistus, the reputed author of forty-two books on Platonism.
[11] In ll. 89–120 what four kinds of reading are mentioned which appeal to the contemplative man?
[12] Subject matter of Greek tragedies.
[13] Because Greek tragic actors wore a high boot or buskin, the word came to signify tragedy.

[14] Chaucer's unfinished *Squire's Tale.*
[15] The allegory of Spenser's *Faerie Queene.*
[16] The goddess Aurora (Dawn) loved Cephalus, "the Attic boy."
[17] When daylight comes (ll. 131 and 141), where does Il Penseroso go?

Wave at his wings, in airy stream
Of lively portraiture displayed,
Softly on my eyelids laid.   150
And as I wake, sweet music breathe
Above, about, or underneath,
Sent by some spirit to mortals good,
Or the unseen genius of the wood.
But let my due feet never fail   155
To walk the studious cloister's pale,
And love the high embowèd roof,
With antique pillars massy proof,
And storied windows richly dight,
Casting a dim religious light.[18]   160
There let the pealing organ blow,
To the full voiced quire below,
In service high and anthems clear,
As may with sweetness, through mine ear,
Dissolve me into ecstasies,   165
And bring all heaven before mine eyes.
And may at last my weary age
Find out the peaceful hermitage,
The hairy gown and mossy cell,
Where I may sit and rightly spell   170
Of every star that heaven doth shew,
And every herb that sips the dew;
Till old experience do attain
To something like prophetic strain.
These pleasures, Melancholy, give,   175
And I with thee will choose to live.
(1631)

STUDY AIDS: 1. Is the contrast in the poems more one of mood or of landscape description?

2. Footnotes to the poems call attention to the almost exact paralleling of details. Which poem has material not paralleled in the other? Is this new material a part of nature, i.e., the domain of the pastoral poem? If not, into what domain does it take the contemplative man?

3. Footnotes emphasize the imagery of light used in the two poems. This use of imagery raises a vital problem: is imaginative literature true or false? In *L'Allegro*, no one really works (except the bee and goblin). Is this then a picture of the true daylight world or a false one? In *Il Penseroso* Milton could not describe action in total darkness, so he employs a half-light. He has then falsified the actual world. In doing so, has he then made his poem false? Question 1 will help in your thinking about this. Is the contemplative man, who in half-light avoids the distractions which the light of the senses brings, better prepared for the change in ll. 159–174? How then does the world created by imaginative literature differ from the actual world? Is it less true than the actual world?

4. Could these pastoral poems be answers to an earlier one (see p. 165)? If so, does Milton in his choice of a mistress continue the earlier picture of idealized nature, or could he possibly be parodying this characteristic of the pastoral poem?

Lycidas

The poem was written as an elegy mourning the death of Edward King, a Cambridge student, who drowned in 1637.

Yet once more, O ye laurels, and once more,
Ye myrtles brown, with ivy [1] never sear,
I come to pluck your berries harsh and crude,
And with forced fingers rude
Shatter your leaves before the mellowing
    year.   5
Bitter constraint and sad occasion dear

Compels me to disturb your season due;
For Lycidas is dead, dead ere his prime,
Young Lycidas, and hath not left his peer.
Who would not sing for Lycidas? He knew 10
Himself to sing, and build the lofty rime.[2]
He must not float upon his watery bier [3]
Unwept, and welter to the parching wind,

[18] What kind of light appears in the passage beginning at l. 160? In ll. 165 and 174 where does the light come from that induces "ecstasies" and "prophetic strain"?

[1] Laurels, myrtles, and ivy have traditionally been associated with the poet's crown ("poet laureate" is the "poet crowned with laurel").

[2] Notice that Milton sings for Lycidas (Edward King) because he was a poet.
[3] Here is the first of many water images, of which the poem is partly constructed. Since Edward King died by drowning, this imagery is appropriate. In keeping with this appropriateness, the pastoral elegy used the "tear" to represent the elegiac poem itself (ll. 12–14).

Without the meed of some melodious tear.
  Begin, then, sisters of the sacred well,   15
That from beneath the seat of Jove doth
    spring;
Begin, and somewhat loudly sweep the string.
Hence with denial vain and coy excuse;
So may some gentle muse
With lucky words favor my destined urn,   20
And as he passes turn
And bid fair peace be to my sable shroud!
  For we were nursed upon the selfsame hill,[4]
Fed the same flock, by fountain, shade, and
    rill;
Together both, ere the high lawns appeared   25
Under the opening eyelids of the morn,
We drove afield, and both together heard
What time the gray-fly winds her sultry
    horn,
Battening our flocks with the fresh dews of
    night,
Oft till the star that rose at evening, bright,   30
Toward heaven's descent had sloped his
    westering wheel.
Meanwhile the rural ditties were not mute,
Tempered to the oaten flute;
Rough satyrs danced, and fauns with cloven
    heel
From the glad sound would not be absent
    long;   35
And old Damoetas [5] loved to hear our song.
  But, oh! the heavy change, now thou art
    gone,
Now thou art gone, and never must return!
Thee, shepherd, thee the woods and desert
    caves,
With wild thyme and the gadding vine
    o'ergrown,   40
And all their echoes, mourn.
The willows, and the hazel copses green,
Shall now no more be seen
Fanning their joyous leaves to thy soft lays.
As killing as the canker to the rose,   45
Or taint-worm to the weanling herds that
    graze,

Or frost to flowers, that their gay wardrobe
    wear,
When first the white-thorn blows—
Such, Lycidas, thy loss to shepherd's [6] ear.
  Where were ye, nymphs,[7] when the re-
    morseless deep   50
Closed o'er the head of your loved Lycidas?
For neither were ye playing on the steep
Where your old bards, the famous Druids, lie,
Nor on the shaggy top of Mona high,
Nor yet where Deva spreads her wizard
    stream.   55
Aye me! I fondly dream
"Had ye been there"—for what could that have
    done?
What could the Muse [8] herself that Orpheus
    bore,
The Muse herself, for her enchanting son,
Whom universal nature did lament,   60
When, by the rout that made the hideous
    roar,
His gory visage down the stream was sent,
Down the swift Hebrus to the Lesbian
    shore?
  Alas! what boots [9] it with uncessant care
To tend the homely, slighted shepherd's
    trade,[10]   65
And strictly meditate the thankless muse?
Were it not better done as others [11] use,
To sport with Amaryllis in the shade,
Or with the tangles of Neaera's hair?
Fame is the spur that the clear spirit doth
    raise   70
(That last infirmity of noble mind)
To scorn delights, and live laborious days;
But, the fair guerdon when we hope to find,
And think to burst out into sudden blaze,

[4] In ll. 23–41 note how Milton associates himself
with King as a student at Cambridge ("selfsame
hill," l. 23) and as a poet (in which sense the
"hill" is the home of the Muses ["sisters of the
sacred well"], Mt. Helicon).
  [5] Pastoral name for someone at Cambridge.

[6] In the pastoral tradition a shepherd was a poet.
  [7] Lesser deities of nature represented as women
living in mountains, forests, and streams. As such
they would, in the pastoral tradition, be intermedi-
aries between the Muse (inspiration) and the poet.
  [8] Calliope, the Muse of epic poetry. She and
Apollo, the god of poetry and music, were the parents
of Orpheus, a legendary and mythological Thracian
poet and musician (cf. L'Allegro, ll. 135–150; Il
Penseroso, ll. 105–108).
  [9] Profits.
  [10] The context suggests "trade" be understood as
the writing of poetry.
  [11] Idlers. Milton may be referring to the Cavalier
poets.

Comes the blind Fury [12] with the abhorrèd
    shears,   75
And slits the thin-spun life. "But not the
    praise,"
Phoebus [13] replied, and touched my trembling
    ears;
"Fame is no plant that grows on mortal soil,
Nor in the glistering foil
Set off to the world, nor in broad rumor lies, 80
But lives and spreads aloft by those pure
    eyes
And perfect witness of all-judging Jove;
As he pronounces lastly on each deed,
Of so much fame in heaven expect thy meed."
    O fountain Arethuse,[14] and thou honored
      flood,   85
Smooth-sliding Mincius,[15] crowned with vocal
    reeds,
That strain I heard was of a higher mood.
But now my oat [16] proceeds,
And listens to the Herald of the Sea [17]
That came in Neptune's plea.   90
He asked the waves, and asked the felon
    winds,
What hard mishaps hath doomed this gentle
    swain!
And questioned every gust of rugged wings
The blows from off each beakèd promon-
    tory.
They knew not of his story;   95
And sage Hippotades [18] their answer brings,
That not a blast was from his dungeon strayed;
The air was calm, and on the level brine
Sleek Panope [19] with all her sisters played.
It was that fatal and perfidious bark,   100
Built in the eclipse, and rigged with curses
    dark,
That sunk so low that sacred head of thine.

[12] Atropos, the Fate who cut the thread of man's life as it was spun and measured by her two sister Fates.
[13] Apollo, the god of poetic inspiration.
[14] Traditional fountain of pastoral verse in Sicily, associated with Theocritus, a Greek writer of pastoral poetry.
[15] Tributary of the river Po, associated with Virgil, a Roman writer of pastoral poetry.
[16] The oaten pipe of the shepherd (poet, singer) in pastoral poetry.
[17] Triton.
[18] Aeolus, the god of winds.
[19] Daughter of Nereus, a sea god.

Next, Camus,[20] reverend sire, went footing
    slow,
His mantle hairy, and his bonnet sedge,
Inwrought with figures dim, and on the
    edge   105
Like to that sanguine flower incribed with
    woe.
"Ah! who hath reft," quoth he, "my dearest
    pledge?"
Last came, and last did go,
The Pilot of the Galilean Lake; [21]
Two massy keys he bore of metals twain 110
(The golden opes, the iron shuts amain).
He shook his mitered locks, and stern bespake:
"How well could I have spared for thee, young
    swain,
Enow of such as, for their bellies' sake,
Creep, and intrude, and climb into the
    fold!   115
Of other care they little reckoning make
Than how to scramble at the shearers' feast,
And shove away the worthy bidden guest.
Blind mouths! that scarce themselves know
    how to hold
A sheep-hook,[22] or have learned aught else
    the least   120
That to the faithful herdman's art belongs!
What recks it them? What need they? They
    are sped;
And, when they list, their lean and flashy
    songs [23]
Grate on their scrannel pipes of wretched
    straw;
The hungry sheep look up, and are not
    fed,   125
But, swoln with wind and the rank mist they
    draw,
Rot inwardly, and foul contagion spread;
Besides what the grim wolf with privy paw [24]

[20] The god of the river Cam, which runs through the campus of Cambridge University.
[21] St. Peter, to whom Jesus promised the "keys of the kingdom of heaven" (Matt. 16:19).
[22] The shepherd's crook and the bishop's insignia of office. Milton is using the word "shepherd" in its Christian connotation of "bishop" or "pastor," but in the background remains the traditional pastoral connotation of "poet."
[23] Why does Milton use the word "songs"?
[24] The phrase may refer to the Roman Catholics or to the Anglican archbishop, William Laud, then under attack by the Puritans.

Daily devours apace, and nothing said.
But that two-handed engine [25] at the door 130
Stands ready to smite once, and smite no
   more."
   Return, Alpheus,[26] the dread voice is past
That shrunk thy streams; return, Sicilian
   Muse,
And call the vales, and bid them hither cast
Their bells and flowerets of a thousand
   hues. 135
Ye valleys low, where the mild whispers use
Of shades, and wanton winds, and gushing
   brooks,
On whose fresh lap the swart star sparely
   looks,
Throw hither all your quaint enameled eyes,
That on the green turf suck the honeyed
   showers, 140
And purple all the ground with vernal
   flowers.
Bring the rathe primrose that forsaken dies,
The tufted crow-toe, and pale jessamine,
The white pink, and the pansy freaked with
   jet,
The glowing violet, 145
The musk-rose, and the well-attired woodbine,
With cowslips wan that hang the pensive
   head,
And every flower that sad embroidery wears;
Bid amaranthus [27] all his beauty shed,
And daffodillies fill their cups with tears, 150
To strew the laureate [28] hearse where Lycid
   lies.
For so, to interpose a little ease,
Let our frail thoughts dally with false surmise.
Aye me! Whilst thee the shores and sounding
   seas
Wash far away, where'er thy bones are
   hurled, 155
Whether beyond the stormy Hebrides,

Where thou perhaps under the whelming
   tide
Visit'st the bottom of the monstrous world;
Or whether thou, to our moist vows denied,
Sleep'st by the fable of Bellerus [29] old, 160
Where the great Vision of the guarded
   mount [30]
Looks toward Namancos and Bayona's [31] hold.
Look homeward, Angel, now, and melt with
   ruth;
And, O ye dolphins, waft the hapless youth.
   Weep no more, woeful shepherds, weep no
     more, 165
For Lycidas, your sorrow, is not dead,
Sunk though he be beneath the watery floor;
So sinks the day-star in the ocean bed,
And yet anon repairs his drooping head,
And tricks his beams, and with new-spangled
   ore 170
Flames in the forehead of the morning sky.
So Lycidas sunk low, but mounted high,
Through the dear might of him that walked
   the waves,
Where, other groves and other streams along,
With nectar pure his oozy locks he laves, 175
And hears the unexpressive nuptial song,
In the blest kingdoms meek of joy and love.
There entertain him all the saints above,
In solemn troops, and sweet societies,
That sing, and singing in their glory move, 180
And wipe the tears forever from his eyes.
Now, Lycidas, the shepherds weep no more;
Henceforth thou art the genius of the shore,
In thy large recompense, and shalt be good
To all that wander in that perilous flood. 185
   Thus sang the uncouth [32] swain to the oaks
     and rills,
While the still morn went out with sandals
   gray;
He touched the tender stops of various quills,
With eager thought warbling his Doric lay.

[25] No satisfactory interpretation of ll. 130–131 has ever been offered. It is usually taken to refer to the two Houses of Parliament. It is possible, however, that it refers back to the two keys given to St. Peter (ll. 110–111).
[26] The river god who loved Arethusa (l. 85) and mingled his waters with hers.
[27] "The unfading flower" in the faithful Christian's "crown of glory" (I Peter 5:4).
[28] Notice again Milton's emphasis on Lycidas as a poet.

[29] Milton's personification of *Bellerium*, the Roman name for Land's End, the southwestern tip of England.
[30] Mount St. Michael in Cornwall near Land's End. This mountain is also personified in l. 163.
[31] Districts in Spain, in which direction Mount St. Michael looks.
[32] Unknown, unlearned. Milton is undoubtedly referring to himself, as yet unprepared for or undecided upon a poetic career (cf. ll. 1–7).

And now the sun had stretched out all the
    hills,   190
And now was dropped into the western bay.
At last he rose, and twitched his mantle blue;
Tomorrow to fresh woods and pastures new.
(1638)

STUDY AIDS: 1. In view of the fact that
Edward King is constantly referred to as a
poet and that Milton has identified himself with
King in this capacity, the poem can be interpreted as a discussion of Milton's own writing
of poetry.

The poem has two judgment scenes in it: (1)
ll. 70–84, in which Apollo passes judgment
and (2) ll. 108–131, in which St. Peter passes
judgment. What are the judgments rendered?
Do they both apply to kinds of poetry? To kinds
of religion? Are ll. 108–131 a digression, which
violates the unity of the poem? Is the TONE here
consistent with that in the rest of the poem?

2. Milton is fond of the Orpheus myth. Study
ll. 50–66 carefully. What do Lycidas and
Orpheus have in common? In view of the fact
that the Muse herself could not stop the
Thracian women from tearing her son, Orpheus,
limb from limb, is Milton questioning the inspiration of pastoral poetry? In relation to this,
is the last line of the poem a farewell to pastoral
poetry?

3. Dr. Johnson and other commentators have
claimed that there is little grief for Edward King
in the poem. Do you find this to be true? If this
is true, it would follow that the poem is insincere,
yet few readers consider it insincere. What
themes and attitudes in the poem produce sincerity?

4. What kind of poetry does the poem suggest
that Milton will write in the future?

Sonnets

Milton wrote twenty-three Petrarchan sonnets, five of them in Italian, the rest in English.
The sonnets are Milton's most subjective poems: he used the form to express intimate
emotions on personal subjects.

How Soon Hath Time, the Subtle Thief of Youth

How soon hath time, the subtle thief of youth,
Stolen on his wing my three and twentieth
    year!
My hasting days fly on with full career,
But my late spring no bud or blossom shew'th.
Perhaps my semblance might deceive the
    truth   5
That I to manhood am arrived so near;
And inward ripeness doth much less appear,
That some more timely-happy spirits endu'th.
Yet be it less or more, or soon or slow,
It shall be still [1] in strictest measure even   10
To that same lot, however mean or high,

[1] Forever.

Toward which time leads me, and the will of
    heaven;
All is, if I have grace to use it so,
As ever in my great task-master's eye.
(1631–1632)

STUDY AIDS: 1. Do you think the sonnet
reflects a conflict in Milton as to whether he
should be a minister or a poet, or does it simply
reveal that Milton is disturbed by his im-
maturity?

2. Is the TONE of the sonnet religious? Pessimistic? Optimistic? Is there an air of resignation
about it?

On the Late Massacre in Piedmont

The religious practices of the Waldenses, a half-French, half-Italian community in Piedmont, had differed from those of Rome since the twelfth century. The climax of their long persecution came when, in 1655, the Duke of Savoy ordered them to become Papists or give up their property and leave the country within twenty days. When they refused, his troops marched in and terrible slaughter and atrocities followed. The Protestant world was horrified, and Milton expresses his indignation in this sonnet.

Avenge, O Lord, thy slaughtered saints, whose
    bones
Lie scattered on the Alpine mountains cold;
Even them who kept thy truth so pure of old,
When all our fathers worshiped stocks and
    stones,
Forget not: in thy book record their groans 5
Who were thy sheep, and in their ancient fold
Slain by the bloody Piedmontese, that rolled
Mother with infant down the rocks. Their
    moans
The vales redoubled to the hills, and they
To heaven. Their martyred blood and ashes
    sow   10
O'er all the Italian fields, where still doth sway
The triple Tyrant,[1] that from these may grow

A hundredfold, who, having learnt thy way,
Early may fly the Babylonian [2] woe.
(1655)

STUDY AIDS: 1. What is Milton's dominant emotion in this poem? What vowel sound predominates in the rhyme words? What does it contribute to the prevailing emotion expressed in the poem?

2. Are the OCTAVE and SESTET separated? How many of the lines are run-on? What effect does the opening trochaic foot in l. 7 create? In the run-on lines 5–8, how does the sound reinforce the meaning and emotional tone? How do these qualities help establish the emotion recorded in the sonnet?

When I Consider How My Light Is Spent

When I consider how my light is spent [3]
  Ere half my days in this dark world and
    wide,
And that one talent [4] which is death to hide
  Lodged with me useless, though my soul
    more bent
To serve therewith my Maker, and present 5
  My true account, lest he returning chide;
  "Doth God exact day-labor, light denied?"
I fondly [5] ask. But patience, to prevent
That murmur, soon replies, "God doth not
    need

Either man's work or his own gifts. Who
  best   10
Bear his mild yoke, they serve him best. His
  state
Is kingly: thousands [6] at his bidding speed,
  And post o'er land and ocean without rest;
  They also serve who only stand and wait." [7]
(1655)

STUDY AIDS: 1. Is Milton indulging in self-pity?

2. What idea does this sonnet hold in common with How Soon Hath Time . . . ?

[6] The lowest order of angels, who were God's messengers.

[7] This oft-quoted line in its context must refer to the highest orders of angels (Seraphim, Cherubim, and Thrones), who, enjoying no powers of movement, were pure contemplation, and served God in that capacity. This line, however, also carries the meaning that disabled persons like Milton also serve God with what talents they have.

[1] The Pope, so-called from his triple-tiered crown.
[2] Protestantism symbolically represented Rome, the seat of the Papacy, as the ancient Babylon (cf. Rev. 17:3–6).
[3] Has been used up.
[4] Cf. Christ's "Parable of the Talents" (Matt. 25:15–30).
[5] Foolishly.

Paradise Lost

As early as 1641 Milton projected four plans on the subject of the Fall of Man. From these notes it seems he first planned an oratorio or drama rather than an epic. Whatever his intentions were, participation in the pamphlet war of 1641 and his subsequent involvement in governmental work forced him to abandon any major literary scheme. In 1658, however, he began again on the subject, this time in epic form, and worked without serious interruption until *Paradise Lost* was completed in 1665. It was published in 1667.

The outline of the narrative is determined by its Biblical content. On this foundation Milton builds a structure of elaboration and interpretation from earlier and contemporary literary traditions and from his own experiences of sixty years. The epic begins *in medias res* (in the middle of things) in hell, where Satan and his followers have been hurled after a disastrous revolt against God in heaven. Book 2 continues this setting, as the fallen angels debate how best to revenge themselves on God. Their solution is to seek out the newly created man and seduce him. Satan begins the quest for the new world. Book 3 moves the spectator to heaven, where God and the loyal angels also debate the future of man below. The Son of God offers Himself as a sacrifice to save man. Meanwhile Satan, crossing the universe, has learned the habitat of man. Throughout the action thus far, man has been the focus of attention; in Book 4 Milton presents man in his paradise, the Garden of Eden. Satan, in the form of a cormorant sitting on the Tree of Life, listens secretly to Adam and Eve and learns the one prohibition placed on them as a test of their obedience: they shall not eat the fruit from the Tree of the Knowledge of Good and Evil. Assuming the shape of a toad, Satan tempts Eve in a dream but is routed by the angel Gabriel. In Books 5 through 8 Raphael comes from heaven to warn the couple of their imminent danger. He and Adam talk throughout the day on several learned topics. Despite the many warnings of Raphael, Eve succumbs to the temptations of Satan, and Adam chooses to perish with her rather than live alone. Thus, Book 9 recounts the Fall of Man, and the poem has reached its climax. Books 10 through 12 carry the narrative to its foregone conclusion: the Son of God pronounces judgment on man; Satan returns to hell to boast of his success; the angel Michael reveals to Adam and Eve the future history of mankind until the second coming of the Son of God; then, he leads them out of Paradise, "the fiery sword waving behind them, and the Cherubim taking their stations to guard the place."

An outline of the action of *Paradise Lost,* however, does little justice to the work as a poem. It is written in the form of an epic, a form which contributes to its greatness as a poem, but it is a greatness which in turn presents difficulties to a modern reader. For one thing its magnitude is hard to comprehend. An epic subject arises only when some event is profound enough to effect a permanent change in the world's history, such as the founding of Rome (*Aeneid*) or the fall of man (*Paradise Lost*). Milton's subject, the justification of God's ways to man, could be treated only in a long poem, and it is all too easy to become interested in the action or meaning and to lose sight of the poetry. Milton never does. No one knew better than he that sound expresses sense; no poet ever exercised more scrupulous care over related sounds in a single line or longer passages. Take for example a line which describes the dreary monotony of hell's landscape:

> Rocks, caves, lakes, fens, bogs, dens, and
> shades of death (Bk. 2, 621).

It is a line of ugly monosyllables, each ending with the harsh, hissing -s sound. The eight strong stresses and the dissonant consonants clog the line almost to a standstill. The monosyllables are related by rhyme and assonance and are grouped so that like sounds do not cluster together. Only a master poet can so weld sense to sound and give a feeling as well as a meaning to a situation.

Another element of greatness which creates difficulty is the epic's requirement that theological machinery be present in the action. We are often advised to follow Matthew Arnold's suggestion: disregard the theology and think only of the great passages of poetry. The problem, however, is not whether Milton's ideas fit into our own, but rather what they mean in the poem—how Milton

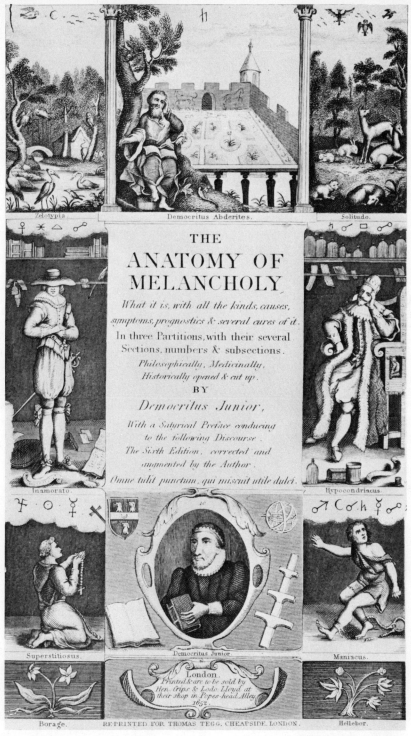

The frontispiece to the sixth edition of Burton's *Anatomy of Melancholy.*

Procession of Marie de Medici, mother-in-law of Charles I, through London in 1638.

A general view of London and the Thames, from a plan made in 1666.

uses the Biblical accounts as a myth to probe the meaning of God's dealings with mankind. The apparent contradictions are reduced to insignificance when one realizes that the story is used to embody Milton's conception of love, both divine and human. The psychology of *Paradise Lost* is sound and true for all ages. It is expressed through the action, the poetry, the characters, their relations with each other and with God. Milton's final word is not of Divine Providence. It concerns the human love, now deeper because chastened by sorrow and experience, of man and woman, who together must work out their own hazardous destiny, aided only by the power of choice:

> They hand in hand with wandering steps and slow,
> Through Eden took their solitary way.

BOOK 1

Of man's first disobedience, and the fruit
Of that forbidden tree whose mortal taste
Brought death into the world, and all our
    woe,
With loss of Eden, till one greater Man [1]
Restore us, and regain the blissful seat,   5
Sing, heavenly Muse,[2] that, on the secret top
Of Oreb, or of Sinai, didst inspire
That shepherd [3] who first taught the chosen
    seed
In the beginning how the heavens and earth
Rose out of chaos: or, if Sion hill   10
Delight thee more, and Siloa's brook that
    flowed
Fast by the oracle of God,[4] I thence
Invoke thy aid to my adventurous song,
That with no middle flight intends to soar
Above the Aonian mount, while it pursues 15
Things unattempted yet in prose or rhyme.
And chiefly Thou, O Spirit, that dost prefer
Before all temples the upright heart and pure,
Instruct me, for Thou knowest; Thou from
    the first
Wast present, and, with mighty wings out-
    spread,   20
Dove-like satst brooding on the vast abyss,
And madest it pregnant: what in me is dark
Illumine, what is low raise and support;
That, to the height of this great argument,
I may assert eternal providence,   25
And justify the ways of God to men.[5]

Say first—for heaven hides nothing from
    thy view,
Nor the deep tract of hell—say first what
    cause
Moved our grand parents,[6] in that happy state,
Favored of heaven so highly, to fall off   30
From their Creator, and transgress his will
For one restraint, lords of the world besides.
Who first seduced them to that foul revolt?
    The infernal serpent; [7] he it was whose
    guile,
Stirred up with envy and revenge, deceived 35
The mother of mankind, what time his pride
Had cast him out from heaven, with all his
    host
Of rebel angels, by whose aid, aspiring
To set himself in glory above his peers,
He trusted to have equaled the Most High, 40
If he opposed, and, with ambitious aim
Against the throne and monarchy of God,
Raised impious war in heaven and battle
    proud,
With vain attempt. Him the Almighty
    Power [8]
Hurled headlong flaming from the ethereal
    sky,   45
With hideous ruin and combustion, down
To bottomless perdition, there to dwell
In adamantine chains and penal fire,
Who durst defy the Omnipotent to arms.
    Nine times the space that measures day and
    night   50

[1] Christ.
[2] The Holy Spirit, which inspired the writers of the Bible. Note ll. 17, 21, and cf. Genesis 1:2.
[3] Moses.
[4] The Temple in Jerusalem on Mt. Zion, overlooking the stream Siloam.
[5] Lines 25-26 are a statement of the main theme. "Justify" here means "to show the justice of."

[6] Adam and Eve.
[7] The answer here to the question of the previous line is the end of the epic Invocation and Proposition and the beginning of the poem's action. Why is it fitting to begin with a characterization of Satan?
[8] Note how the sound of the verse and the run-on lines (44-49) reinforce the effect of Satan being hurled down from heaven.

To mortal men, he, with his horrid crew,
Lay vanquished, rolling in the fiery gulf,
Confounded, though immortal. But his doom
Reserved him to more wrath; for now the
    thought
Both of lost happiness and lasting pain   55
Torments him: round he throws his baleful
    eyes
That witnessed huge affliction and dismay,
Mixed with obdurate pride and steadfast hate.
At once, as far as angel's ken, he views
The dismal situation waste and wild.   60
A dungeon horrible, on all sides round,[9]
As one great furnace flamed; yet from those
    flames
No light; but rather darkness visible
Served only to discover sights of woe,
Regions of sorrow, doleful shades, where
    peace   65
And rest can never dwell, hope never comes
That comes to all, but torture without end
Still urges, and a fiery deluge, fed
With ever-burning sulphur unconsumed.
Such place eternal justice had prepared   70
For those rebellious; here their prison ordained
In utter [10] darkness, and their portion set,
As far removed from God and light of heaven
As from the center thrice to the utmost pole.
Oh, how unlike the place from whence they
    fell!   75
There the companions of his fall, o'erwhelmed
With floods and whirlwinds of tempestuous
    fire,
He soon discerns; and, weltering [11] by his
    side,
One next himself in power, and next in crime,
Long after known in Palestine, and named   80
Beëlzebub.[12] To whom the arch-enemy,
And thence in heaven called *Satan,* with bold
    words
Breaking the horrid silence, thus began:—

[9] Note ll. 60–69. What do you conclude from this passage concerning Milton's ability to describe things concretely?
[10] A half-pun: "outer" and "complete."
[11] Wallowing (cf. *Lycidas,* l. 13).
[12] The word means "Lord of Flies," from the fact that his priests foretold the future by flies attracted to the sacrificial meat. Beëlzebub is Satan's confidant in the original conspiracy against God (Bk. 5, 673) and in controlling the debate in Bk. 2.

"If thou beest he [13]—but Oh, how fallen!
    how changed
From him!—who, in the happy realms of
    light,   85
Clothed with transcendent brightness, didst
    outshine
Myriads, though bright—if he whom mutual
    league,
United thoughts and counsels, equal hope
And hazard in the glorious enterprise,
Joined with me once, now misery hath
    joined   90
In equal ruin; into what pit thou seest
From what height fallen: so much the stronger
    proved
He with his thunder: [14] and till then who
    knew
The force of those dire arms? Yet not for those,
Nor what the potent victor in his rage   95
Can else inflict, do I repent, or change,
Though changed in outward lustre, that
    fixed mind,
And high disdain from sense of injured merit,
That with the mightiest raised me to contend,
And to the fierce contention brought along   100
Innumerable force of spirits armed,
That durst dislike his reign, and, me pre-
    ferring,
His utmost power with adverse power opposed
In dubious battle on the plains of heaven,
And shook his throne. What though the field
    be lost?   105
All is not lost—the unconquerable will,[15]
And study of revenge, immortal hate,
And courage never to submit or yield:
And what is else not to be overcome;
That glory never shall his wrath or might   110
Extort from me. To bow and sue for grace
With suppliant knee, and deify his power
Who, from the terror of this arm, so late
Doubted his empire—that were low indeed;
That were an ignominy and shame be-
    neath   115

[13] Notice the effective caesura after "he." Note also how the incomplete sentences and construction of ll. 84–124 reflect the emotional turmoil of Satan.
[14] Milton constantly emphasizes Satan's spiritual blindness (cf. also l. 112). Find several other instances of this in Bk. 1.
[15] The Renaissance idea of indomitable strength and audacity in action (cf. ll. 252–255, 320).

This downfall; since, by fate, the strength of
    gods,
And this empyreal substance,[16] cannot fail;
Since, through experience of this great event,
In arms not worse, in foresight much ad-
    vanced,
We may with more successful hope resolve 120
To wage by force or guile eternal war,
Irreconcilable to our grand foe,
Who now triumphs, and in the excess of joy
Sole reigning holds the tyranny of heaven."
    So spake the apostate angel, though in
      pain,   125
Vaunting aloud, but racked with deep despair;
And him thus answered soon his bold com-
    peer:—[17]
    "O prince, O chief of many thronèd powers
That led the embattled seraphim to war
Under thy conduct, and, in dreadful deeds 130
Fearless, endangered heaven's perpetual king,
And put to proof his high supremacy,
Whether upheld by strength, or chance, or
    fate!
Too well I see and rue the dire event
That, with sad overthrow and foul defeat, 135
Hath lost us heaven, and all this mighty host
In horrible destruction laid thus low,
As far as gods and heavenly essences
Can perish: for the mind and spirit remains
Invincible, and vigor soon returns,   140
Though all our glory extinct, and happy state
Here swallowed up in endless misery.
But what if he our conqueror (whom I now
Of force believe almighty, since no less
Than such could have o'erpowered such force
    as ours)   145
Have left us this our spirit and strength
    entire,
Strongly to suffer and support our pains,
That we may so suffice his vengeful ire,
Or do him mightier service as his thralls
By right of war, whate'er his business be, 150
Here in the heart of hell to work in fire,
Or do his errands in the gloomy deep?

What can it then avail though yet we feel
Strength undiminished, or eternal being
To undergo eternal punishment?"   155
    Whereto with speedy words the arch-fiend
      replied:—
"Fallen cherub, to be weak is miserable,
Doing or suffering: but of this be sure—
To do aught good never will be our task,
But ever to do ill our sole delight,   160
As being the contrary to his high will
Whom we resist. If then his providence [18]
Out of our evil seek to bring forth good,
Our labor must be to pervert that end,
And out of good still to find means of evil; 165
Which ofttimes may succeed so as perhaps
Shall grieve him, if I fail not, and disturb
His inmost counsels from their destined aim.
But see! the angry victor hath recalled
His ministers of vengeance and pursuit   170
Back to the gates of heaven: the sulphurous
    hail,
Shot after us in storm, o'erblown hath laid
The fiery surge that from the precipice
Of heaven received us falling; and the
    thunder,
Winged with red lightning and impetuous
    rage,   175
Perhaps hath spent his shafts, and ceases now
To bellow through the vast and boundless
    deep.
Let us not slip the occasion, whether scorn
Or satiate fury yield it from our foe.
Seest thou yon dreary plain, forlorn and
    wild,   180
The seat of desolation, void of light,
Save what the glimmering of these livid flames
Casts pale and dreadful? Thither let us tend
From off the tossing of these fiery waves;
There rest, if any rest can harbor there;   185
And, re-assembling our afflicted powers,
Consult how we may henceforth most offend
Our enemy, our own loss how repair,
How overcome this dire calamity,
What reinforcement we may gain from
    hope,   190
If not what resolution from despair."

[16] Cf. "heavenly essences" in l. 138. The bodies
of angels were thought to be of "ether," a rarefied
form of air, one of the four elements.

[17] Beëlzebub. Notice in ll. 128–142 how Beëlzebub
speaks glowingly, but actually is echoing Satan's
words. What does this reveal of Beëlzebub's character?

[18] Lines 162–165 indicate that Satan already has
a vague idea for revenge in his mind (cf. ll. 650–
660). How does this passage relate to the stated
theme of the epic in ll. 25–26?

Thus Satan, talking to his nearest mate,[19]
With head uplift above the wave, and eyes
That sparkling blazed; his other parts besides
Prone on the flood, extended long and
    large,   195
Lay floating many a rood, in bulk as huge
As whom the fables name of monstrous size,
Titanian or earth-born, that warred on Jove,
Briareos or Typhon, whom the den
By ancient Tarsus held, or that sea-beast 200
Leviathan, which God of all his works
Created hugest that swim the ocean-stream.
Him, haply slumbering on the Norway foam,
The pilot of some small night-foundered skiff,
Deeming some island, oft, as seamen tell, 205
With fixèd anchor in his scaly rind,
Moors by his side under the lee, while night
Invests the sea, and wishèd morn delays.
So stretched out huge in length the arch-fiend
    lay,
Chained on the burning lake; nor ever
    thence [20]   210
Had risen, or heaved his head, but that the
    will
And high permission of all-ruling heaven
Left him at large to his own dark designs,
That with reiterated crimes he might
Heap on himself damnation, while he
    sought   215
Evil to others, and enraged might see
How all his malice served but to bring forth
Infinite goodness, grace, and mercy, shown
On man by him seduced, but on himself
Treble confusion, wrath, and vengeance
    poured.   220
    Forthwith upright he rears from off the
    pool
His mighty stature; on each hand the flames
Driven backward slope their pointing spires,
    and, rolled
In billows, leave in the midst a horrid vale.
Then with expanded wings he steers his
    flight   225
Aloft, incumbent on the dusky air,

That felt unusual weight; till on dry land
He lights—if it were land that ever burned
With solid, as the lake with liquid fire,
And such appeared in hue as when the
    force   230
Of subterranean wind transports a hill
Torn from Pelorus,[21] or the shattered side
Of thundering Aetna, whose combustible
And fueled entrails, thence conceiving fire,
Sublimed with mineral fury, aid the winds, 235
And leave a singèd bottom all involved
With stench and smoke. Such resting found
    the sole
Of unblest feet. Him followed his next mate;
Both glorying to have scaped the Stygian flood
As gods, and by their own recovered
    strength,   240
Not by the sufferance of supernal power.
  "Is this the region, this the soil, the
    clime," [22]
Said then the lost archangel, "this the seat
That we must change for heaven?—this
    mournful gloom
For that celestial light? Be it so, since he 245
Who now is sovereign can dispose and bid
What shall be right: farthest from him is
    best,
Whom reason hath equaled, force hath made
    supreme
Above his equals. Farewell, happy fields,
Where joy for ever dwells! Hail, horrors!
    hail,   250
Infernal world! and thou, profoundest hell,
Receive thy new possessor—one who brings
A mind not to be changed by place or time.
The mind is its own place, and in itself
Can make a heaven of hell, a hell of
    heaven.   255
What matter where, if I be still the same,
And what I should be, all but less than he
Whom thunder hath made greater? Here at
    least
We shall be free; the Almighty hath not built
Here for his envy, will not drive us hence: 260
Here we may reign secure; and, in my choice,
To reign is worth ambition, though in hell:
Better to reign in hell than serve in heaven.

[19] In ll. 192–210 what comparisons does Milton use to give an impression of Satan's size (cf. ll. 292–294)?

[20] Milton intrudes on the narrative in ll. 210–220 to editorialize. How does the intrusion relate to the stated theme of the epic?

[21] Promontory near Mt. Aetna.

[22] Notice the effective use of the demonstratives in ll. 242–245.

But wherefore let we then our faithful friends,
The associates and co-partners of our loss, 265
Lie thus astonished on the oblivious [23] pool,
And call them not to share with us their part
In this unhappy mansion, or once more
With rallied arms to try what may be yet
Regained in heaven, or what more lost in
    hell?"   270
   So Satan spake; and him Beëlzebub
Thus answered:—"Leader of those armies
    bright
Which, but the Omnipotent, none could have
    foiled!
If once they hear that voice, their liveliest
    pledge
Of hope in fears and dangers—heard so oft 275
In worst extremes, and on the perilous edge
Of battle, when it raged, in all assaults
Their surest signal—they will soon resume
New courage and revive, though now they
    lie
Groveling and prostrate on yon lake of
    fire,   280
As we erewhile, astounded and amazed;
No wonder, fallen such a pernicious height!"
   He scarce had ceased when the superior
    fiend
Was moving toward the shore; his ponderous
    shield,
Ethereal temper, massy, large, and round, 285
Behind him cast. The broad circumference
Hung on his shoulders like the moon, whose
    orb
Through optic glass [24] the Tuscan artist views
At evening, from the top of Fesolè,
Or in Valdarno, to descry new lands,   290
Rivers, or mountains, in her spotty globe.
His spear—to equal which the tallest pine
Hewn on Norwegian hills, to be the mast
Of some great admiral, were but a wand—
He walked with, to support uneasy steps 295
Over the burning marle, not like those steps
On heaven's azure; and the torrid clime
Smote on him sore besides, vaulted with fire.

Nathless he so endured, till on the beach
Of that inflamèd sea he stood, and called 300
His legions—angel forms, who lay entranced
Thick as autumnal leaves that strow the
    brooks
In Vallombrosa, where the Etrurian shades
High over-arched embower; or scattered sedge
Afloat,[25] when with fierce winds Orion
    armed   305
Hath vexed the Red-Sea coast, whose waves
    o'erthrew
Busiris and his Memphian chivalry,
While with perfidious hatred they pursued
The sojourners of Goshen, who beheld
From the safe shore their floating carcasses 310
And broken chariot-wheels. So thick bestrewn,
Abject and lost, lay these, covering the flood,
Under amazement of their hideous change.
He called so loud that all the hollow deep
Of hell resounded:—"Princes, potentates, 315
Warriors, the flower of heaven—once yours;
    now lost,
If such astonishment as this can seize
Eternal spirits! Or have ye chosen this place
After the toil of battle to repose
Your wearied virtue, for the ease you find 320
To slumber here, as in the vales of heaven?
Or in this abject posture have ye sworn
To adore the conqueror, who now beholds
Cherub and seraph rolling in the flood
With scattered arms and ensigns, till anon 325
His swift pursuers from heaven-gates dis-
    cern
The advantage, and, descending, tread us
    down
Thus drooping, or with linkèd thunderbolts
Transfix us to the bottom of this gulf?—
Awake, arise, or be for ever fallen!"   330
   They heard, and were abashed, and up they
    sprung
Upon the wind, as when men wont to watch,
On duty sleeping found by whom they dread,
Rouse and bestir themselves ere well awake.
Nor did they not perceive the evil plight 335

[23] Oblivion-producing.
[24] Telescope invented by Galileo, whom Milton visited at Florence, Italy in 1638. This section (ll. 287–304) is filled with Milton's memories of the Italian trip; Fiesole, Valdarno, Vallombrosa, and Etruria.

[25] In ll. 305–315 Milton seems to think of the fallen angels in metaphoric terms of the Egyptians punished by God for persecuting the Israelites, their prisoners. Twice Milton makes this association: ll. 305–315 and 338–343. In what other metaphoric terms does he conceive of the fallen angels?

In which they were, or the fierce pains not
feel;
Yet to their general's voice they soon obeyed
Innumerable. As when the potent rod
Of Amram's son, in Egypt's evil day,
Waved round the coast, up-called a pitchy
cloud   340
Of locusts, warping on the eastern wind,
That o'er the realm of impious Pharaoh hung
Like night, and darkened all the land of Nile;
So numberless were those bad angels seen
Hovering on wing under the cope of hell,   345
'Twixt upper, nether, and surrounding fires;
Till, as a signal given, the uplifted spear
Of their great sultan waving to direct
Their course, in even balance down they light
On the firm brimstone, and fill all the
plain: 350
A multitude like which the populous north
Poured never from her frozen loins to pass
Rhene or the Danaw, when her barbarous
sons
Came like a deluge on the south, and spread
Beneath Gibraltar to the Libyan sands.   355
Forthwith, from every squadron and each
band,
The heads and leaders thither haste where
stood
Their great commander—godlike shapes, and
forms
Exceling human; princely dignities;
And powers that erst in heaven sat on
thrones,   360
Though of their names in heavenly records
now
Be no memorial, blotted out and rased
By their rebellion from the books of life.
Nor had they yet among the sons of Eve
Got them new names,[26] till, wandering o'er
the earth,   365
Through God's high sufferance for the trial
of man,
By falsities and lies the greatest part
Of mankind they corrupted to forsake
God their Creator, and the invisible
Glory of him that made them to transform   370
Oft to the image of a brute, adorned

With gay religions full of pomp and gold,
And devils to adore for deities:
Then were they known to men by various
names,
And various idols through the heathen
world.   375
Say, Muse, their names then known, who
first, who last,
Roused from the slumber on that fiery couch,
At their great emperor's call, as next in worth
Came singly where he stood on the bare
strand,
While the promiscuous crowd stood yet
aloof.   380
The chief were those who, from the pit of
hell
Roaming to seek their prey on earth, durst fix
Their seats, long after, next the seat of God,
Their altars by his altar, gods adored
Among the nations round, and durst abide   385
Jehovah thundering out of Sion, throned
Between the cherubim; yea, often placed
Within his sanctuary itself their shrines,
Abominations; and with cursèd things
His holy rites and solemn feasts profaned,   390
And with their darkness durst affront his
light.
First, *Moloch*,[27] horrid king, besmeared with
blood
Of human sacrifice, and parents' tears;
Though, for the noise of drums and timbrels
loud,
Their children's cries unheard that passed
through fire   395
To his grim idol. Him the Ammonite
Worshiped in Rabba and her watery plain,
In Argob and in Basan, to the stream
Of utmost Arnon. Nor content with such
Audacious neighborhood, the wisest heart   400
Of Solomon he led by fraud to build
His temple right against the temple of God
On that opprobrious hill, and made his grove
The pleasant valley of Hinnom, Tophet
thence

[26] Milton is following the medieval practice of considering the fallen angels as the pagan gods of the ancient world, later to be created.

[27] A Moabite sun god. Children were burned in the arms of his heated idol as sacrifices. The roll call of demons which begins here is an epic device comparable to Homer's catalogue of the Greek ships at Troy (*Iliad*, 2). Milton groups his heathen gods according to nationalities which worshiped them. What are the five ethnic groups in ll. 392–521?

And black Gehenna called, the type of
hell.   405
Next *Chemos,* the obscene [28] dread of Moab's
sons,
From Aroar to Nebo and the wild
Of southmost Abarim; in Hesebon
And Horonaim, Seon's realm, beyond
The flowery dale of Sibma clad with vines, 410
And Elealè to the Asphaltic Pool:
Peor his other name, when he enticed
Israel in Sittim, on their march from Nile,
To do him wanton rites, which cost them woe.
Yet thence his lustful orgies he enlarged   415
Even to that hill of scandal, by the grove
Of Moloch homicide, lust hard by hate,
Till good Josiah drove them thence to hell.
With these came they who, from the border-
ing flood
Of old Euphrates to the brook that parts   420
Egypt from Syrian ground, had general names
Of *Baalim* and *Ashtaroth* [29]—those male,
These feminine. For spirits, when they please,
Can either sex assume, or both; so soft
And uncompounded is their essence pure,   425
Not tied or manacled with joint or limb,
Nor founded on the brittle strength of bones,
Like cumbrous flesh; but, in what shape they
choose,
Dilated or condensed, bright or obscure,
Can execute their aery purposes,   430
And works of love or enmity fulfil.
For those the race of Israel oft forsook
Their living strength, and unfrequented left
His righteous altar, bowing lowly down
To bestial gods; for which their heads, as
low   435
Bowed down in battle, sunk before the spear
Of despicable foes. With these in troop
Came *Astoreth,* [30] whom the Phœnicians called
Astarte, queen of heaven, with crescent
horns;
To whose bright image nightly by the
moon   440
Sidonian virgins paid their vows and songs;

In Sion also not unsung, where stood
Her temple on the offensive mountain, built
By that uxorious king whose heart, though
large,
Beguiled by fair idolatresses, fell   445
To idols foul. *Thammuz* [31] came next behind,
Whose annual wound in Lebanon allured
The Syrian damsels to lament his fate
In amorous ditties all a summer's day,
While smooth Adonis from his native rock 450
Ran purple to the sea, supposed with blood
Of Thammuz yearly wounded: the love-tale
Infected Sion's daughters with like heat,
Whose wanton passions in the sacred porch
Ezekiel saw, when, by the vision led,   455
His eye surveyed the dark idolatries
Of alienated Judah. Next came one
Who mourned in earnest,[32] when the captive
ark
Maimed his brute image, head and hands
lopt off,
In his own temple, on the grunsel-edge,[33] 460
Where he fell flat and shamed his worshipers:
Dagon his name, sea-monster, upward man
And downward fish; yet had his temple high
Reared in Azotus, dreaded through the coast
Of Palestine, in Gath and Ascalon,   465
And Accaron and Gaza's [34] frontier bounds.
Him followed *Rimmon,* whose delightful
seat
Was fair Damascus, on the fertile banks
Of Abbana and Pharphar, lucid streams.
He also against the house of God was bold: 470
A leper once he lost,[35] and gained a king—
Ahaz, his sottish conqueror, whom he drew
God's altar to disparage and displace
For one of Syrian mode, whereon to burn
His odious offerings, and adore the gods   475
Whom he had vanquished. After these
appeared

[31] A fertility god. The coming of autumn was
symbolized by his death and indicated by the
seasonal rains, which turned the river Adonis red
with the soil of its banks.
[32] Notice the grim humor of the phrase, "in
earnest."
[33] Threshold.
[34] The five ancient trading cities of the Phoenicians.
[35] Naaman, the leper, cleansed by immersing
himself seven times in the Jordan river (cf. 2
Kings 5).

[28] "Obscene" because he is a phallic god, comparable to the Greek god Priapus.
[29] Plural forms. There were many variants of the
Baal deity.
[30] Astarte, a goddess with a bull's head; counterpart of the Greek Aphrodite.

A crew [36] who, under names of old renown—
Osiris, Isis, Orus, and their train—
With monstrous shapes and sorceries abused
Fanatic Egypt and her priests to seek   480
Their wandering gods disguised in brutish
     forms
Rather than human. Nor did Israel scape
The infection, when their borrowed gold
     composed
The calf in Oreb; and the rebel king [37]
Doubled that sin in Bethel and in Dan,   485
Likening his Maker to the grazèd ox—
Jehovah, who, in one night, when he passed
From Egypt marching, equaled with one
     stroke
Both her first-born and all her bleating gods.
Belial came last; than whom a spirit more
     lewd   490
Fell not from heaven, or more gross to love
Vice for itself.[38] To him no temple stood
Or altar smoked; yet who more oft than he
In temples and at altars, when the priest
Turns atheist, as did Eli's sons, who filled 495
With lust and violence the house of God?
In courts and palaces he also reigns,[39]
And in luxurious cities, where the noise
Of riot ascends above their loftiest towers,
And injury and outrage; and, when night 500
Darkens the streets, then wander forth the
     sons
Of Belial, flown with insolence and wine.
Witness the streets of Sodom, and that night
In Gibeah, when the hospitable door
Exposed a matron, to avoid worse rape.   505
     These were the prime in order and in
        might:
The rest were long to tell; though far
     renowned

The Ionian [40] gods—of Javan's issue held
Gods, yet confessed later than heaven and
     earth,
Their boasted parents;—*Titan,* heaven's first-
     born,   510
With his enormous brood, and birthright
     seized
By younger *Saturn:* he from mightier Jove,
His own and Rhea's son, like measure found;
So *Jove* usurping reigned. These, first in Crete
And Ida known, thence on the snowy top 515
Of cold Olympus ruled the middle air,
Their highest heaven; or on the Delphian
     cliff,
Or in Dodona, and through all the bounds
Of Doric land; or who with Saturn old
Fled over Adria to the Hesperian fields,   520
And o'er the Celtic roamed the utmost isles.
     All these and more came flocking; but with
        looks
Downcast and damp; yet such wherein ap-
     peared
Obscure some glimpse of joy to have found
     their chief
Not in despair, to have found themselves not
     lost   525
In loss itself; which on his countenance cast
Like doubtful hue. But he, his wonted pride
Soon recollecting, with high words, that bore
Semblance of worth, not substance,[41] gently
     raised
Their fainting courage, and dispelled their
     fears: 530
Then straight commands that, at the warlike
     sound
Of trumpets loud and clarions, be upreared
His mighty standard. That proud honor
     claimed
Azazel,[42] as his right, a cherub tall:
Who forthwith from the glittering staff
     unfurled   535
The imperial ensign; which, full high
     advanced,
Shone like a meteor streaming to the wind,

[36] Egyptian gods. Notice that Milton's poetic imagination is again working in terms of the Jewish bondage in Egypt (cf. ll. 487–489).

[37] Jereboam (1 Kings 12), who divided the original twelve tribes of Israel united by David.

[38] Notice that Belial is not represented as a tribal god. He symbolizes sensuality, a quality held in common by all idolatrous worshipers. The word is used in the Bible as a name for Satan, but Milton does not follow this. "Sons of Belial" was a common Puritan epithet for courtiers.

[39] In ll. 497–505 Milton is implying that the courts of Charles I and Charles II worship Belial (cf. Genesis 19:4–11; Judges 19:22–28).

[40] Greek.

[41] Readers of *Paradise Lost* who insist that Satan is the hero overlook the dross that Milton puts into his character.

[42] Satan's standard bearer. Notice in the following lines the dramatic contrast of the glitter against darkness.

With gems and golden luster rich emblazed,
Seraphic arms and trophies; all the while
Sonorous metal blowing martial sounds: 540
At which the universal host up-sent
A shout that tore hell's concave, and beyond
Frighted the reign of Chaos and old Night.
All in a moment through the gloom were
    seen
Ten thousand banners rise into the air, 545
With orient colors waving: with them rose
A forest huge of spears; and thronging helms
Appeared, and serried shields in thick array
Of depth immeasurable. Anon they move [43]
In perfect phalanx to the Dorian mood 550
Of flutes and soft recorders—such as raised
To height of noblest temper heroes old
Arming to battle, and instead of rage
Deliberate valor breathed, firm, and unmoved
With dread of death to flight or foul
    retreat; 555
Nor wanting power to mitigate and swage
With solemn touches troubled thoughts, and
    chase
Anguish and doubt and fear and sorrow and
    pain
From mortal or immortal minds. Thus they,
Breathing united force with fixèd thought, 560
Moved on in silence to soft pipes that charmed
Their painful steps o'er the burnt soil. And
    now
Advanced in view they stand—a horrid front
Of dreadful length and dazzling arms, in guise
Of warriors old, with ordered spear and
    shield, 565
Awaiting what command their mighty chief
Had to impose. He through the armèd files
Darts his experienced eye, and soon traverse
The whole battalion views—their order due,
Their visages and stature as of gods; 570
Their number last he sums. And now his heart
Distends with pride, and, hardening in his
    strength,

Glories: for never, since created man,[44]
Met such embodied force as, named with
    these,
Could merit more than that small infantry 575
Warred on by cranes—though all the giant
    brood
Of Phlegra with the heroic race were joined
That fought at Thebes and Ilium, on each
    side
Mixed with auxiliar gods; and what resounds
In fable or romance of Uther's son, 580
Begirt with British and Armoric knights;
And all who since, baptized or infidel,
Jousted in Aspramont, or Montalban,
Damasco, or Marocco, or Trebisond,
Or whom Biserta sent from Afric shore 585
When Charlemain with all his peerage fell
By Fontarabbia. Thus far these beyond
Compare of mortal prowess, yet observed
Their dread commander. He, above the rest [45]
In shape and gesture proudly eminent, 590
Stood like a tower. His form had yet not lost
All her original brightness, nor appeared
Less than archangel ruined, and the excess
Of glory obscured: as when the sun new-
    risen
Looks through the horizontal misty air 595
Shorn of his beams, or, from behind the moon,
In dim eclipse, disastrous twilight sheds
On half the nations, and with fear of change
Perplexes monarchs. Darkened so, yet shone
Above them all the archangel: but his
    face [46] 600
Deep scars of thunder had intrenched, and
    care
Sat on his faded cheek, but under brows
Of dauntless courage, and considerate pride
Waiting revenge. Cruel his eye, but cast
Signs of remorse and passion, to behold 605
The fellows of his crime, the followers rather
(Far other once beheld in bliss), condemned
For ever now to have their lot in pain—
Millions of spirits for his fault amerced

[43] What is the picture created in ll. 549–567? Notice that the description of the army is classical, not contemporary.

[44] In ll. 573–587 Milton again proceeds by cataloguing; here, however, he describes the army of fallen angels by enumerating great battles recorded in literature: the Trojan armies at Ilium, Charlemagne's at Aspramont; Roland's at Fontarabbia.

[45] Note how the description of Satan in ll. 589–621 begins with outward appearances and moves inward to his mind and spirit. What sympathy for Satan is in the passage?

[46] Note how the impression of shattered majesty is twice conveyed by the imagery of a storm (ll. 599–602; 612–615). What does this indicate as to Milton's conception of Satan?

Of heaven, and from eternal splendors
    flung   610
For his revolt—yet faithful how they stood,
Their glory withered; as, when heaven's fire
Hath scathed the forest oaks or mountain
    pines,
With singèd top their stately growth, though
    bare,
Stands on the blasted heath. He now pre-
    pared   615
To speak; whereat their doubled ranks they
    bend
From wing to wing, and half enclose him
    round
With all his peers: attention held them
    mute.
Thrice he assayed, and thrice, in spite of
    scorn,
Tears, such as angels weep, burst forth: at
    last   620
Words interwove with sighs found out their
    way:—
"O myriads of immortal spirits! O powers
Matchless, but with the Almighty!—and that
    strife
Was not inglorious, though ,the event was
    dire,
As this place testifies, and this dire change, 625
Hateful to utter. But what power of mind,
Foreseeing or presaging, from the depth
Of knowledge past or present, could have
    feared
How such united force of gods, how such
As stood like these, could ever know re-
    pulse?   630
For who can yet believe, though after loss,
That all these puissant legions, whose exile
Hath emptied heaven, shall fail to reascend,
Self-raised, and repossess their native seat?
For me, be witness all the host of heaven, 635
If counsels different, or danger shunned
By me, have lost our hopes. But he who
    reigns
Monarch in heaven till then as one secure
Sat on his throne, upheld by old repute,
Consent or custom, and his regal state   640
Put forth at full, but still his strength
    concealed—
Which tempted our attempt, and wrought our
    fall.

Henceforth his might we know, and know our
    own,
So as not either to provoke, or dread
New war provoked: our better part
    remains   645
To work in close design, by fraud or guile,
What force effected not; that he no less
At length from us may find, who overcomes
By force hath overcome but half his foe.
Space may produce new worlds; whereof so
    rife   650
There went a fame in heaven that he ere
    long
Intended to create, and therein plant
A generation whom his choice regard
Should favor equal to the sons of heaven.
Thither, if but to pry, shall be perhaps   655
Our first eruption—thither, or elsewhere;
For this infernal pit shall never hold
Celestial spirits in bondage, nor the abyss
Long under darkness cover. But these
    thoughts
Full counsel must mature. Peace is
    despaired;   660
For who can think submission? War, then,
    war
Open or understood, must be resolved."
    He spake; and, to confirm his words, out-
    flew
Millions of flaming swords, drawn from the
    thighs
Of mighty cherubim; the sudden blaze   665
Far round illumined hell. Highly they raged
Against the Highest and fierce with graspèd
    arms
Clashed on their sounding shields the din of
    war,
Hurling defiance toward the vault of heaven.
    There stood a hill not far, whose grisly
    top   670
Belched fire and rolling smoke; the rest entire
Shone with a glossy scurf—undoubted sign
That in his womb was hid metallic ore,
The work of sulphur. Thither, winged with
    speed,
A numerous brigad hastened: as when
    bands   675
Of pioneers, with spade and pickaxe armed,
Forerun the royal camp, to trench a field,
Or cast a rampart. Mammon led them on—

Mammon,[47] the least erected spirit that fell
From heaven; for even in heaven his looks
   and thoughts   680
Were always downward bent, admiring more
The riches of heaven's pavement, trodden
   gold,
Than aught divine or holy else enjoyed
In vision beatific. By him first
Men also, and by his suggestion taught, 685
Ransacked the center, and with impious hands
Rifled the bowels of their mother earth
For treasures better hid. Soon had his crew
Opened into the hill a spacious wound,
And digged out ribs of gold. Let none
   admire [48]   690
That riches grow in hell; that soil may best
Deserve the precious bane.[49] And here let
   those
Who boast in mortal things, and wondering
   tell
Of Babel, and the works of Memphian kings,
Learn how their greatest monuments of
   fame,   695
And strength, and art, are easily outdone
By spirits reprobate, and in an hour
What in an age they, with incessant toil
And hands innumerable, scarce perform.
Nigh on the plain, in many cells prepared, 700
That underneath had veins of liquid fire
Sluiced from the lake, a second multitude
With wondrous art founded the massy ore,
Severing each kind, and scummed the
   bullion-dross.
A third as soon had formed within the
   ground   705
A various mold, and from the boiling cells
By strange conveyance filled each hollow
   nook;
As in an organ, from one blast of wind,
To many a row of pipes the sound-board
   breathes.
Anon out of the earth a fabric huge [50] 710
Rose like an exhalation, with the sound
Of dulcet symphonies and voices sweet—

[47] Like Belial, Mammon is a generic term, meaning "riches." There may be a touch of humor in the description of Mammon in the following lines.
[48] Wonder.
[49] Note the beautiful contrast in the two words.
[50] Notice ll. 710–717. Notice the architectural features of this capitol of Hell.

Built like a temple, where pilasters round
Were set, and Doric pillars overlaid
With golden architrave; nor did there
   want   715
Cornice or frieze, with bossy sculptures
   graven:
The roof was fretted gold. Not Babylon
Nor great Alcairo such magnificence
Equaled in all their glories, to enshrine
Belus or Serapis their gods, or seat 720
Their kings, when Egypt with Assyria strove
In wealth and luxury. The ascending pile [51]
Stood fixed her stately height; and straight
   the doors,
Opening their brazen folds, discover, wide
Within, her ample spaces o'er the smooth 725
And level pavement: from the archèd roof,
Pendent by subtle magic, many a row
Of starry lamps and blazing cressets, fed
With naphtha and asphaltus, yielded light
As from a sky. The hasty multitude 730
Admiring entered; and the work some praise,
And some the architect. His hand was known
In heaven by many a towered structure high,
Where sceptered angels held their residence,
And sat as princes, whom the supreme
   King   735
Exalted to such power, and gave to rule,
Each in his hierarchy, the orders bright.
Nor was his name unheard or unadored
In ancient Greece; and in Ausonian land
Men called him Mulciber; and how he fell 740
From heaven they fabled, thrown by angry
   Jove
Sheer o'er the crystal battlements: from morn
To noon he fell, from noon to dewy eve,
A summer's day, and with the setting sun
Dropt from the zenith, like a falling star, 745
On Lemnos, the Aegean isle. Thus they
   relate,
Erring; for he with this rebellious rout
Fell long before; nor aught availed him now
To have built in heaven high towers; nor did
   he scape
By all his engines, but was headlong sent, 750
With his industrious crew, to build in hell.
   Meanwhile the wingèd heralds, by
   command

[51] Notice the effect Milton achieves in ll. 722–730 without a single definite detail.

Of sovereign power, with awful ceremony
And trumpet's sound, throughout the host
    proclaim
A solemn council forthwith to be held   755
At Pandemonium,⁵² the high capitol
Of Satan and his peers. Their summons called
From every band and squarèd regiment
By place or choice the worthiest: they anon
With hundreds and with thousands trooping
    came   760
Attended. All access was thronged; the gates
And porches wide, but chief the spacious hall
(Though like a covered field, where
    champions bold
Wont ride in armed, and at the Soldan's chair
Defied the best of paynim chivalry   765
To mortal combat, or career with lance),
Thick swarmed, both on the ground and in
    the air,
Brushed with the hiss of rustling wings. As
    bees
In spring-time, when the sun with Taurus
    rides,
Pour forth their populous youth about the
    hive   770
In clusters; they among fresh dews and
    flowers
Fly to and fro, or on the smoothèd plank,
The suburb of their straw-built citadel,
New rubbed with balm, expatiate, and confer
Their state-affairs: so thick the airy crowd   775
Swarmed and were straitened; till, the signal
    given,
Behold a wonder! They but now who
    seemed ⁵³
In bigness to surpass earth's giant sons,
Now less than smallest dwarfs, in narrow
    room
Throng numberless—like that pygmean
    race   780
Beyond the Indian mount; or fairy elves,
Whose midnight revels, by a forest-side

Or fountain, some belated peasant sees,
Or dreams he sees, while overhead the moon
Sits arbitress, and nearer to the earth   785
Wheels her pale course: they, on their mirth
    and dance
Intent, with jocund music charm his ear;
At once with joy and fear his heart rebounds.
Thus incorporeal spirits to smallest forms
Reduced their shapes immense, and were at
    large,   790
Though without number still, amidst the hall
Of that infernal court. But far within,
And in their own dimensions like themselves,
The great seraphic lords and cherubim
In close recess and secret conclave sat,   795
A thousand demi-gods on golden seats,
Frequent and full. After short silence then,
And summons read, the great consult began.

STUDY AIDS: 1. What qualities make up the characterization of Satan (e.g., in ll. 105–124 he is arrogant)? What other passages can you find which develop other traits of his character? Do his physical characteristics and stature represent his internal or spiritual nature? Does Milton endow him with any good qualities?

2. Do you think Milton is fascinated with the character of Satan? Can you explain why? Does good or evil appeal more to human nature? In view of Milton's theme (ll. 25–26) and the narrative he uses to present this theme, can Satan be the hero of Paradise Lost?

3. The problem of man's freedom of will is important in the poem. Where is the first mention of it? Who is shown to have a free will? Where is this shown? Why is it necessary for this figure to have a free will? Does this passage explain man's condition as well?

4. Poetry tends to imply more than it states. What political overtones are implied in Book 1? Could these imply a changing attitude toward the Puritans on Milton's part? Could they imply a political paradise which had been lost? If so, what would it be?

5. Most of Paradise Lost was dictated by Milton when blind. Can you see any evidence of this in the poetry? I.e., has his poetic imagination compensated in any ways for his physical blindness?

6. Epic style demanded decorum or exalted dignity in language: the diction was to be heightened or solemnified (see ll. 12–16). Milton achieves this quality in such ways as the follow-

⁵² Milton coined this word, which has since been incorporated into the language. How is its present meaning related to Milton's use?
⁵³ Study ll. 777–797 carefully. Is Pandemonium so vast the fallen angels seem dwarfed, or are they actually reduced in size? Notice particularly ll. 792–794. It is possible that Milton is here satirizing the "Long Parliament's" loss of power to its dictatorial leaders.

ing: (1) elaborate phrases are drawn from a stately level of diction above that of everyday language: "grand parent" (l. 6), "mother of mankind" (l. 36); (2) language is heightened by phrases reminiscent of Greek and Latin poetry, the mixture of foreign, polysyllabic words with English monosyllabic words creating rhythmical solemnity: ll. 44–49; (3) words suggest the infinite by denying the earthly limitation: "darkness visible" (l. 63), "strength undiminished" (l. 154). Find other examples of these three devices. The eighteenth-century poet Alexander Pope distinguished two styles in *Paradise Lost:* (1) the exotic (heightened) and (2) the simple and pure. In which scenes or situations does Milton use the exotic style? In which the simple?

BOOK 2

High on a throne of royal state, which far [1]
Outshone the wealth of Ormus and of Ind,
Or where the gorgeous east with richest hand
Showers on her kings barbaric pearl and gold,
Satan exalted sat, by merit raised   5
To that bad eminence; and, from despair
Thus high uplifted beyond hope, aspires
Beyond thus high, insatiate to pursue
Vain war with heaven; and, by success untaught,
His proud imaginations thus displayed:—   10
 "Powers and dominions, deities of heaven!—
For, since no deep within her gulf can hold
Immortal vigor, though oppressed and fallen,
I give not heaven for lost: from this descent
Celestial virtues rising will appear   15
More glorious and more dread than from no fall,
And trust themselves to fear no second fate!—
Me though just right,[2] and the fixed laws of heaven,
Did first create your leader—next, free choice,
With what besides in council or in fight   20
Hath been achieved of merit—yet this loss,
Thus far at least recovered, hath much more
Established in a safe, unenvied throne,

[1] This periodic, climbing sentence symbolizes the development of Bk. 2.
[2] In ll. 18–20 what three reasons does Satan give to justify his leadership?

Yielded with full consent. The happier state [3]
In heaven, which follows dignity, might draw   25
Envy from each inferior; but who here
Will envy whom the highest place exposes
Foremost to stand against the Thunderer's aim
Your bulwark, and condemns to greatest share
Of endless pain? Where there is, then, no good   30
For which to strive, no strife can grow up there
From faction: for none sure will claim in hell
Precedence; none whose portion is so small
Of present pain that with ambitious mind
Will covet more! With this advantage, then, 35
To union, and firm faith, and firm accord,
More than can be in heaven, we now return
To claim our just inheritance of old,
Surer to prosper than prosperity
Could have assured us; and by what best way,   40
Whether of open war or covert guile,[4]
We now debate. Who can advise may speak."
 He ceased; and next him Moloch, sceptered king,
Stood up—the strongest and the fiercest spirit
That fought in heaven, now fiercer by despair.   45
His trust was with the Eternal to be deemed
Equal in strength, and rather than be less
Cared not to be at all; with that care lost
Went all his fear: of God, or hell, or worse,
He recked not, and these words thereafter spake: 50
 "My sentence is for open war.[5] Of wiles,
More unexpert, I boast not: them let those
Contrive who need, or when they need; not now.

[3] Cf. Satan's view of leadership stated in ll. 24–35 with that expressed by Bacon in "Of Great Place," p. 183/1, ll. 1–36.
[4] Lines 41–42 state the subject of the debate which forms the action of most of Bk. 2. The debate is built around four contrasting, major fallen angels introduced in Bk. 1.
[5] What adjectives would best describe the TONE of Moloch's speech (ll. 51–105)? What argument does Moloch use in support of his vote for continuing open war? What further course of action does he suggest if open war fails? What implication is here that Moloch does not believe God to be omnipotent (cf. also Bk. 1, 133, 166)?

For, while they sit contriving, shall the rest—
Millions that stand in arms, and longing
    wait   55
The signal to ascend—sit lingering here,
Heaven's fugitives, and for their dwelling-
    place
Accept this dark opprobrious den of shame,
The prison of his tyranny who reigns
By our delay? No! let us rather choose,   60
Armed with hell-flames and fury, all at once
O'er heaven's high towers to force resistless
    way,
Turning our tortures into horrid arms
Against the Torturer; when, to meet the
    noise
Of his almighty engine, he shall hear   65
Infernal thunder, and, for lightning, see
Black fire and horror shot with equal rage
Among his angels, and his throne itself
Mixed with Tartarean sulphur and strange
    fire,
His own invented torments. But perhaps 70
The way seems difficult, and steep to scale
With upright wing against a higher foe!
Let such bethink them, if the sleepy drench
Of that forgetful lake benumb not still,
That in our proper motion we ascend   75
Up to our native seat; descent and fall
To us is adverse. Who but felt of late,
When the fierce foe hung on our broken rear
Insulting, and pursued us through the deep,
With what compulsion and laborious flight 80
We sunk thus low? The ascent is easy, then;
The event is feared! Should we again provoke
Our stronger, some worse way his wrath may
    find
To our destruction, if there be in hell
Fear to be worse destroyed! What can be
    worse   85
Than to dwell here, driven out from bliss,
    condemned
In this abhorrèd deep to utter woe;
Where pain of unextinguishable fire
Must exercise us without hope of end
The vassals of his anger, when the scourge 90
Inexorably, and the torturing hour,
Calls us to penance? More destroyed than
    thus,
We should be quite abolished, and expire.
What fear we then? what doubt we to incense

His utmost ire? which, to the height
    enraged,   95
Will either quite consume us, and reduce
To nothing this essential—happier far
Than miserable to have eternal being!—
Or, if our substance be indeed divine,
And cannot cease to be, we are at worst 100
On this side nothing; and by proof we feel
Our power sufficient to disturb his heaven,
And with perpetual inroads to alarm,
Though inaccessible, his fatal throne:
Which, if not victory, is yet revenge." 105
    He ended frowning, and his look
        denounced
Desperate revenge, and battle dangerous
To less than gods. On the other side up rose
Belial, in act more graceful and humane.
A fairer person lost not heaven; he seemed 110
For dignity composed, and high exploit.
But all was false and hollow; though his
    tongue
Dropt manna, and could make the worse
    appear
The better reason, to perplex and dash
Maturest counsels: for his thoughts were
    low—   115
To vice industrious, but to nobler deeds
Timorous and slothful. Yet he pleased the ear,
And with persuasive accent thus began:—
    "I should be much for open war, O peers,[6]
As not behind in hate, if what was urged 120
Main reason to persuade immediate war
Did not dissuade me most, and seem to cast
Ominous conjecture on the whole success;
When he who most excels in fact of arms,
In what he counsels and in what excels   125
Mistrustful, grounds his courage on despair
And utter dissolution, as the scope
Of all his aim, after some dire revenge.
First, what revenge? The towers of heaven
    are filled
With armèd watch, that render all access 130
Impregnable: oft on the bordering deep
Encamp their legions, or with obscure wing

[6] How does the tone of Belial's speech (ll. 119–225) contrast to that of Moloch's? Note Belial's skill in debating: does he answer Moloch point by point? Belial urges a policy of appeasement. Upon what two contentions does he base his policy (ll. 199–214)?

Scout far and wide into the realm of night,
Scorning surprise. Or, could we break our way
By force, and at our heels all hell should
    rise   135
With blackest insurrection to confound
Heaven's purest light, yet our great enemy,
All incorruptible, would on his throne
Sit unpolluted, and the ethereal mold,
Incapable of stain, would soon expel   140
Her mischief, and purge off the baser fire,
Victorious. Thus repulsed, our final hope
Is flat despair: we must exasperate
The Almighty Victor to spend all his rage;
And that must end us; that must be our
    cure—   145
To be no more. Sad cure! for who would
    lose,[7]
Though full of pain, this intellectual being,
Those thoughts that wander through eternity,
To perish rather, swallowed up and lost
In the wide womb of uncreated night,   150
Devoid of sense and motion? And who knows,
Let this be good, whether our angry foe
Can give it, or will ever? How he can
Is doubtful; that he never will is sure.
Will he, so wise, let loose at once his ire,   155
Belike through impotence or unaware,
To give his enemies their wish, and end
Them in his anger whom his anger saves
To punish endless? 'Wherefore cease we,
    then?'
Say they who counsel war; 'we are decreed, 160
Reserved, and destined to eternal woe;
Whatever doing, what can we suffer more,
What can we suffer worse?' Is this, then,
    worst—
Thus sitting, thus consulting, thus in arms?
What when we fled amain, pursued and
    strook   165
With heaven's afflicting thunder, and be-
    sought
The deep to shelter us? This hell then seemed
A refuge from those wounds. Or when we lay
Chained on the burning lake? That sure was
    worse.
What if the breath that kindled those grim
    fires,   170

[7] Lines 146–147 have been cited as one of the best statements of humanism. What do you learn of humanism from them?

Awaked, should blow them into sevenfold
    rage,
And plunge us in the flames; or from above
Should intermitted vengeance arm again
His red right hand to plague us? What if all
Her stores were opened, and this firma-
    ment   175
Of hell should spout her cataracts of fire,
Impendent horrors, threatening hideous fall
One day upon our heads; while we perhaps,
Designing or exhorting glorious war,
Caught in a fiery tempest, shall be hurled, 180
Each on his rock transfixed, the sport and prey
Of racking whirlwinds, or for ever sunk
Under yon boiling ocean, wrapt in chains,
There to converse with everlasting groans,
Unrespited, unpitied, unreprieved,[8]   185
Ages of hopeless end? This would be worse.
War, therefore, open or concealed, alike
My voice dissuades; for what can force or
    guile
With him, or who deceive his mind, whose
    eye
Views all things at one view? He from
    heaven's height   190
All these our motions vain sees and derides,
Not more almighty to resist our might
Than wise to frustrate all our plots and wiles.
Shall we, then, live thus vile—the race of
    heaven
Thus trampled, thus expelled, to suffer
    here   195
Chains and these torments? Better these than
    worse,
By my advice; since fate inevitable
Subdues us, and omnipotent decree,
The victor's will. To suffer, as to do,
Our strength is equal; nor the law unjust 200
That so ordains. This was at first resolved,
If we were wise, against so great a foe
Contending, and so doubtful what might fall.
I laugh when those who at the spear are bold
And venturous, if that fail them, shrink, and
    fear   205
What yet they know must follow—to endure
Exile, or ignominy, or bonds, or pain,
The sentence of their conqueror. This is now
Our doom; which if we can sustain and bear,

[8] Note the unusual but effective meter of this line.

Our supreme foe in time may much remit 210
His anger, and perhaps, thus far removed,
Not mind us not offending, satisfied
With what is punished; whence these raging
    fires
Will slacken, if his breath stir not their flames.
Our purer essence then will overcome 215
Their noxious vapor; or, inured, not feel;
Or, changed at length, and to the place
    conformed
In temper and in nature, will receive
Familiar the fierce heat; and, void of pain,
This horror will grow mild, this darkness
    light; 220
Besides what hope the never-ending flight
Of future days may bring, what chance, what
    change
Worth waiting—since our present lot appears
For happy though but ill, for ill not worst,
If we procure not to ourselves more woe." 225
    Thus Belial, with words clothed in reason's
    garb,
Counseled ignoble ease and peaceful sloth,
Not peace; and after him thus Mammon
    spake:—
    "Either to disenthrone the King of Heaven [9]
We war, if war be best, or to regain 230
Our own right lost. Him to unthrone we then
May hope, when everlasting fate shall yield
To fickle chance, and chaos judge the strife.
The former, vain to hope, argues as vain
The latter; for what place can be for us 235
Within heaven's bound, unless heaven's Lord
    supreme
We overpower? Suppose he should relent,
And publish grace to all, on promise made
Of new subjection; with what eyes could we
Stand in his presence humble, and receive 240
Strict laws imposed, to celebrate his throne
With warbled hymns, and to his Godhead
    sing
Forced halleluiahs, while he lordly sits
Our envied sovereign, and his altar breathes
Ambrosial odors and ambrosial flowers, 245
Our servile offerings? This must be our task
In heaven, this our delight. How wearisome

Eternity so spent in worship paid
To whom we hate! Let us not then pursue,
By force impossible, by leave obtained 250
Unacceptable, though in heaven, our state
Of splendid vassalage; but rather seek
Our own good from ourselves, and from our
    own
Live to ourselves, though in this vast recess,
Free and to none accountable, preferring 255
Hard liberty before the easy yoke
Of servile pomp. Our greatness will appear
Then most conspicuous when great things of
    small,
Useful of hurtful, prosperous of adverse,
We can create, and in what place soe'er 260
Thrive under evil, and work ease out of pain
Through labor and endurance. This deep
    world
Of darkness do we dread? How oft amidst
Thick clouds and dark doth heaven's all-ruling
    Sire
Choose to reside, his glory unobscured, 265
And with the majesty of darkness round
Covers his throne, from whence deep thunders
    roar,
Mustering their rage, and heaven resembles
    hell!
As he our darkness, cannot we his light
Imitate when we please? This desert soil 270
Wants not her hidden luster, gems and gold;
Nor want we skill or art from whence to
    raise
Magnificence; and what can heaven show
    more?
Our torments also may, in length of time,
Become our elements,[10] these piercing fires 275
As soft as now severe, our temper changed
Into their temper; which must needs remove
The sensible of pain. All things invite
To peaceful counsels, and the settled state
Of order, how in safety best we may 280
Compose our present evils, with regard
Of what we are and where, dismissing quite
All thoughts of war. Ye have what I advise."

---

[9] Study Mammon's speech (ll. 229–283). How is
his suggestion consistent with his characterization in
Bk. 1, 679–682? How are Mammon's suggestions
more practical than those of the other speakers?

[10] Everything was believed to have been created
of the four elements—earth, air, fire, and water.
Mammon suggests that the angelic substance may
in time change from ether to fire (their present
environment) and their torment, therefore, be
lessened.

He scarce had finished, when such murmur filled
The assembly as when hollow rocks retain 285
The sound of blustering winds, which all
    night long
Had roused the sea, now with hoarse cadence
    lull
Seafaring men o'erwatched, whose bark by
    chance,
Or pinnace, anchors in a craggy bay
After the tempest. Such applause was
    heard   290
As Mammon ended, and his sentence pleased,
Advising peace: for such another field
They dreaded worse than hell; so much the
    fear
Of thunder and the sword of Michaël
Wrought still within them; and no less
    desire   295
To found this nether empire, which might
    rise,
By policy and long process of time,
In emulation opposite to heaven.
Which when Beëlzebub perceived—than
    whom,
Satan except, none higher sat—with grave 300
Aspect he rose, and in his rising seemed
A pillar of state. Deep on his front engraven
Deliberation sat, and public care;
And princely counsel in his face yet shone,
Majestic, though in ruin. Sage he stood, 305
With Atlantean shoulders, fit to bear
The weight of mightiest monarchies; his look
Drew audience and attention still as night
Or summer's noontide air, while thus he
    spake:—
    "Thrones and imperial powers, offspring of
    heaven,[11]   310
Ethereal virtues! or these titles now
Must we renounce, and, changing style, be
    called
Princes of hell? for so the popular vote
Inclines—here to continue, and build up here
A growing empire; doubtless! while we
    dream,   315

[11] What is Beëlzebub's attitude (ll. 310–378)
toward resuming war with God? Does he favor
Mammon's plan? Note the sarcasm in the word
"doubtless" (l. 315). What is his advice? Is it his
idea or Satan's?

And know not that the King of Heaven hath
    doomed
This place our dungeon—not our safe retreat
Beyond his potent arm, to live exempt
From heaven's high jurisdiction, in new
    league
Banded against his throne, but to remain 320
In strictest bondage, though thus far removed,
Under the inevitable curb, reserved
His captive multitude. For he, be sure,
In height or depth, still first and last will
    reign
Sole king, and of his kingdom lose no part 325
By our revolt, but over hell extend
His empire, and with iron scepter rule
Us here, as with his golden those in heaven.
What sit we then projecting peace and war?
War hath determined us and foiled with
    loss   330
Irreparable; terms of peace yet none
Vouchsafed or sought; for what peace will be
    given
To us enslaved, but custody severe,
And stripes and arbitrary punishment
Inflicted? and what peace can we return, 335
But, to our power, hostility and hate,
Untamed reluctance, and revenge, though
    slow,
Yet ever plotting how the conqueror least
May reap his conquest, and may least rejoice
In doing what we most in suffering feel? 340
Nor will occasion want, nor shall we need
With dangerous expedition to invade
Heaven, whose high walls fear no assault or
    siege,
Or ambush from the deep. What if we find
Some easier enterprise? There is a place 345
(If ancient and prophetic fame in heaven
Err not)—another world, the happy seat
Of some new race, called Man, about this
    time
To be created like to us, though less
In power and excellence, but favored more 350
Of him who rules above; so was his will
Pronounced among the gods, and by an oath
That shook heaven's whole circumference
    confirmed.
Thither let us bend all our thoughts, to learn
What creatures there inhabit, of what
    mold   355

Or substance, how endued, and what their
    power
And where their weakness: how attempted
    best,
By force or subtlety. Though heaven be shut,
And heaven's high arbitrator sit secure
In his own strength, this place may lie ex-
    posed,   360
The utmost border of his kingdom, left
To their defense who hold it: here, perhaps,
Some advantageous act may be achieved
By sudden onset—either with hell-fire
To waste his whole creation, or possess   365
All as our own, and drive, as we are driven,
The puny habitants; or, if not drive,
Seduce them to our party, that their God
May prove their foe, and with repenting hand
Abolish his own works. This would surpass 370
Common revenge, and interrupt his joy
In our confusion, and our joy upraise
In his disturbance; when his darling sons,
Hurled headlong to partake with us, shall
    curse
Their frail original, and faded bliss—   375
Faded so soon! Advise if this be worth
Attempting, or to sit in darkness here
Hatching vain empires." Thus Beëlzebub
Pleaded his devilish counsel—first devised
By Satan, and in part proposed: for
    whence,   380
But from the author of all ill, could spring
So deep a malice, to confound the race
Of mankind in one root, and earth with hell
To mingle and involve, done all to spite
The great Creator? But their spite still
    serves   385
His glory to augment. The bold design
Pleased highly those infernal states, and joy
Sparkled in all their eyes; with full assent
They vote: whereat his speech he thus
    renews:
    "Well have ye judged, well ended long
    debate,[12]   390
Synod of gods, and, like to what ye are,
Great things resolved, which from the lowest
    deep

[12] After the group votes in favor of Beëlzebub's proposal, he continues his speech. What important question does he raise in ll. 390–416? How is it resolved?

Will once more lift us up, in spite of fate,
Nearer our ancient seat—perhaps in view
Of those bright confines, whence, with
    neighboring arms,   395
And opportune excursion, we may chance
Re-enter heaven; or else in some mild zone
Dwell, not unvisited of heaven's fair light,
Secure, and at the brightening orient beam
Purge off this gloom: the soft delicious air, 400
To heal the scar of these corrosive fires,
Shall breathe her balm. But, first, whom shall
    we send
In search of this new world? whom shall we
    find
Sufficient? who shall tempt with wandering
    feet
The dark, unbottomed, infinite abyss,   405
And through the palpable obscure find out
His uncouth way, or spread his airy flight,
Upborne with indefatigable wings
Over the vast abrupt, ere he arrive
The happy isle? What strength, what art, can
    then   410
Suffice, or what evasion bear him safe
Through the strict senteries and stations thick
Of angels watching round? Here he had need
All circumspection: and we now no less
Choice in our suffrage; for on whom we
    send   415
The weight of all, and our last hope, relies."
    This said, he sat; and expectation held
His look suspense, awaiting who appeared
To second, or oppose, or undertake
The perilous attempt. But all sat mute, 420
Pondering the danger with deep thoughts; and
    each
In other's countenance read his own dismay,
Astonished. None among the choice and
    prime
Of those heaven-warring champions could be
    found
So hardy as to proffer or accept,   425
Alone, the dreadful voyage; till, at last,
Satan, whom now transcendent glory raised
Above his fellows, with monarchal pride
Conscious of highest worth, unmoved thus
    spake:—
    "O progeny of heaven! Empyreal
    thrones!   430
With reason hath deep silence and demur

Seized us, though undismayed. Long is the
    way
And hard, that out of hell leads up to light.
Our prison strong, this huge convex of fire,
Outrageous to devour, immures us round   435
Ninefold; and gates of burning adamant,
Barred over us, prohibit all egress.
These passed, if any pass, the void profound
Of unessential [13] night receives him next,
Wide-gaping, and with utter loss of being   440
Threatens him, plunged in that abortive [14]
    gulf.
If thence he scape, into whatever world,
Or unknown region, what remains him less
Than unknown dangers, and as hard escape?
But I should ill become this throne, O
    peers,   445
And this imperial sovereignty, adorned
With splendor, armed with power, if aught
    proposed
And judged of public moment in the shape
Of difficulty or danger, could deter
Me from attempting. Wherefore do I
    assume   450
These royalties, and not refuse to reign,
Refusing to accept as great a share
Of hazard as of honor, due alike
To him who reigns, and so much to him due
Of hazard more as he above the rest   455
High honored sits? Go, therefore, mighty
    powers,
Terror of heaven, though fallen; intend [15] at
    home,
While here shall be our home, what best may
    ease
The present misery, and render hell
More tolerable; if there be cure or charm   460
To respite, or deceive, or slack the pain
Of this ill mansion: intermit no watch
Against a wakeful foe, while I abroad
Through all the coasts of dark destruction
    seek
Deliverance for us all. This enterprise   465
None shall partake with me." Thus saying,
    rose
The monarch, and prevented all reply;
Prudent lest, from his resolution raised,

Others among the chief might offer now,
Certain to be refused, what erst they
    feared,   470
And, so refused, might in opinion stand
His rivals, winning cheap the high repute
Which he through hazard huge must earn.
    But they
Dreaded not more the adventure than his
    voice
Forbidding; and at once with him they
    rose.   475
Their rising all at once was as the sound
Of thunder heard remote. Towards him they
    bend
With awful reverence prone, and as a god
Extol him equal to the highest in heaven.
Nor failed they to express how much they
    praised   480
That for the general safety he despised
His own: for neither do the spirits damned
Lose all their virtue; lest bad men should
    boast
Their specious deeds on earth, which glory
    excites,
Or close ambition varnished o'er with zeal.   485
    Thus they their doubtful consultations dark
Ended, rejoicing in their matchless chief:
As, when from mountain-tops the dusky
    clouds
Ascending, while the north-wind sleeps, o'er-
    spread
Heaven's cheerful face, the louring ele-
    ment   490
Scowls o'er the darkened landscape snow or
    shower,
If chance the radiant sun, with farewell sweet,
Extend his evening beam, the fields revive,
The birds their notes renew, and bleating
    herds
Attest their joy, that hill and valley rings.   495
O shame to men! Devil with devil damned [16]
Firm concord holds; men only disagree
Of creatures rational, though under hope
Of heavenly grace, and, God proclaiming
    peace,
Yet live in hatred, enmity, and strife   500
Among themselves, and levy cruel wars

---

[13] Without essence.
[14] Without life or form; abortion-producing.
[15] I.e., take into consideration.

[16] Lines 496–505 are thought to have been inserted into the poem after 1664. Can you think of
any reason to support this belief?

Wasting the earth, each other to destroy:
As if (which might induce us to accord)
Man had not hellish foes enow besides,
That day and night for his destruction
    wait!   505

. . . .

   Meanwhile the adversary of God and man,
Satan, with thoughts inflamed of highest
    design,   630
Puts on swift wings, and toward the gates of
    hell
Explores his solitary flight: sometimes
He scours the right hand coast, sometimes the
    left;
Now shaves with level wing the deep, then
    soars
Up to the fiery concave towering high.   635
As when far off at sea a fleet descried
Hangs in the clouds, by equinoctial winds
Close sailing from Bengala, or the isles
Or Ternate and Tidore, whence merchants
    bring
Their spicy drugs; they on the trading
    flood,   640
Through the wide Ethiopian to the Cape,
Ply stemming nightly toward the pole: so
    seemed
Far off the flying fiend. At last appear
Hell-bounds, high reaching to the horrid [17]
    roof,
And thrice threefold the gates; three folds
    were brass,   645
Three iron, three of adamantine rock,
Impenetrable, impaled with circling fire,
Yet unconsumed. Before the gates there sat [18]
On either side a formidable shape.
The one seemed woman to the waist, and
    fair,   650
But ended foul in many a scaly fold,

[17] Used in the old meaning of "rugged" and in
the new of "terrible."
[18] Lines 648–889 form the only allegory in *Paradise Lost*. Milton is allegorizing James 1:15: "Then
lust, when it hath conceived, beareth sin; and sin,
when full-grown, bringeth forth death." Milton relates this allegory in terms of the Greek myth of
Athena springing from the head of Zeus. The
monster, Sin (ll. 648–666), is much indebted to
Spenser's monster, Error (*Faerie Queene*, 1, ix,
14 ff.).

Voluminous and vast—a serpent armed
With mortal sting. About her middle round
A cry of hell-hounds never-ceasing barked
With wide Cerberean mouths full loud, and
    rung   655
A hideous peal; yet, when they list, would
    creep,
If aught disturbed their noise, into her womb,
And kennel there; yet there still barked and
    howled
Within unseen. Far less abhorred than these
Vexed Scylla, bathing in the sea that parts 660
Calabria from the hoarse Trinacrian shore;
Nor uglier follow the night-hag, when, called
In secret, riding through the air she comes,
Lured with the smell of infant blood, to dance
With Lapland witches, while the laboring
    moon   665
Eclipses at their charms. The other shape [19]—
If shape it might be called that shape had
    none
Distinguishable in member, joint, or limb;
Or substance might be called that shadow
    seemed,
For each seemed either—black it stood as
    night,   670
Fierce as ten furies, terrible as hell,
And shook a dreadful dart: what seemed his
    head
The likeness of a kingly crown had on.
Satan was now at hand, and from his seat
The monster moving onward came as fast 675
With horrid strides; hell trembled as he
    strode.
The undaunted fiend what this might be
    admired—
Admired, not feared (God and his Son except,
Created thing naught valued he nor
    shunned),
And with disdainful look thus first
    began:—   680
   "Whence and what art thou, execrable
    shape,
That darest, though grim and terrible, advance
Thy miscreated front athwart my way
To yonder gates? Through them I mean to
    pass,

[19] Try to visualize the creature described in ll.
666–673. It is vivid and convincing, yet not a single
detail is certain or definite.

That be assured, without leave asked of
thee.   685
Retire; or taste thy folly, and learn by proof,
Hell-born, not to contend with spirits of
heaven."
    To whom the goblin, full of wrath,
replied:—
"Art thou that traitor-angel, art thou he,
Who first broke peace in heaven and faith, till
then   690
Unbroken, and in proud rebellious arms
Drew after him the third part of heaven's sons,
Conjured against the Highest—for which both
thou
And they, outcast from God, are here con-
demned
To waste eternal days in woe and pain?   695
And reckonest thou thyself with spirits of
heaven,
Hell-doomed, and breathest defiance here and
scorn,
Where I reign king, and, to enrage thee more,
Thy king and lord? Back to thy punishment,
False fugitive; and to thy speed add wings, 700
Lest with a whip of scorpions I pursue
Thy lingering, or with one stroke of this dart
Strange horror seize thee, and pangs unfelt
before."
    So spake the grisly terror, and in shape,
So speaking and so threatening, grew ten-
fold   705
More dreadful and deform. On the other side,
Incensed with indignation, Satan stood
Unterrified, and like a comet burned,
That fires the length of Ophiuchus huge
In the arctic sky, and from his horrid hair 710
Shakes pestilence and war. Each at the head
Leveled his deadly aim; their fatal hands
No second stroke intend; and such a frown
Each cast at the other as when two black
clouds,
With heaven's artillery fraught, come rattling
on   715
Over the Caspian, then stand front to front
Hovering a space, till winds the signal blow
To join their dark encounter in mid-air.
So frowned the mighty combatants that hell
Grew darker at their frown; so matched they
stood;   720
For never but once more was either like

To meet so great a foe. And now great deeds
Had been achieved, whereof all hell had rung,
Had not the snaky sorceress, that sat
Fast by hell-gate and kept the fatal key,   725
Risen, and with hideous outcry rushed
between.
    "O father, what intends thy hand," she
cried,
"Against thy only son? What fury, O son,
Possesses thee to bend that mortal dart
Against thy father's head? And knowest for
whom?   730
For him who sits above, and laughs the while
At thee, ordained his drudge to execute
Whate'er his wrath, which he calls justice,
bids—
His wrath, which one day will destroy ye
both!"
    She spake, and at her words the hellish
pest   735
Forebore: then these to her Satan returned:—
    "So strange thy outcry, and thy words so
strange
Thou interposest, that my sudden hand,
Prevented, spares to tell thee yet by deeds
What it intends, till first I know of thee 740
What thing thou art, thus double-formed, and
why,
In this infernal vale first met, thou callest
Me father, and that phantasm callest my son.
I know thee not, nor ever saw till now
Sight more detestable than him and thee." 745
    To whom thus the portress of hell-gate
replied:—
"Hast thou forgot me, then; and do I seem
Now in thine eye so foul?—once deemed so
fair
In heaven, when at the assembly, and in sight
Of all the seraphim with thee combined 750
In bold conspiracy against heaven's King,
All on a sudden miserable pain
Surprised thee, dim thine eyes, and dizzy
swum
In darkness, while thy head flames thick and
fast
Threw forth, till on the left side opening
wide,   755
Likest to thee in shape and countenance
bright,
Then shining heavenly fair, a goddess armed,

Out of thy head I sprung. Amazement seized
All the host of heaven; back they recoiled
    afraid
At first, and called me Sin, and for a sign 760
Portentous held me; but, familiar grown,
I pleased, and with attractive graces won
The most averse—thee chiefly, who, full oft
Thyself in me thy perfect image viewing,
Becamest enamored; and such joy thou
    tookest 765
With me in secret that my womb conceived
A growing burden. Meanwhile war arose,
And fields were fought in heaven: wherein
    remained
(For what could else?) to our Almighty Foe
Clear victory; to our part loss and rout 770
Through all the empyrean. Down they fell,
Driven headlong from the pitch of heaven,
    down
Into this deep; and in the general fall
I also: at which time this powerful key
Into my hands was given, with charge to
    keep 775
These gates for ever shut, which none can
    pass
Without my opening. Pensive here I sat
Alone; but long I sat not, till my womb,
Pregnant by thee, and now excessive grown,
Prodigious motion felt and rueful throes. 780
At last this odious offspring whom thou seest,
Thine own begotten, breaking violent way,
Tore through my entrails, that, with fear and
    pain
Distorted, all my nether shape thus grew
Transformed: but he my inbred enemy 785
Forth issued, brandishing his fatal dart,
Made to destroy. I fled, and cried out Death!
Hell trembled at the hideous name, and sighed
From all her caves, and back resounded Death!
I fled; but he pursued (though more, it
    seems, 790
Inflamed with lust than rage), and, swifter
    far,
Me overtook, his mother, all dismayed,
And, in embraces forcible and foul
Engendering with me, of that rape begot
These yelling monsters, that with ceaseless
    cry 795
Surround me, as thou sawest—hourly con-
    ceived

And hourly born,[20] with sorrow infinite
To me: for, when they list, into the womb
That bred them they return, and howl, and
    gnaw
My bowels, their repast; then, bursting
    forth 800
Afresh, with conscious terrors vex me round,
That rest or intermission none I find.
Before mine eyes in opposition sits
Grim Death, my son and foe, who sets them
    on,
And me, his parent, would full soon
    devour 805
For want of other prey, but that he knows
His end with mine involved, and knows that I
Should prove a bitter morsel, and his bane,
Whenever that shall be: so fate pronounced.
But thou, O father, I forewarn thee, shun 810
His deadly arrow; neither vainly hope
To be invulnerable in those bright arms,
Though tempered heavenly; for that mortal
    dint,
Save he who reigns above, none can resist."
    She finished; and the subtle fiend his
    lore 815
Soon learned, now milder, and thus answered
    smooth:—
    "Dear daughter—since thou claimest me for
    thy sire,
And my fair son here showest me, the dear
    pledge
Of dalliance had with thee in heaven, and
    joys
Then sweet, now sad to mention, through
    dire change 820
Befallen us unforeseen, unthought-of—know,
I come no enemy, but to set free
From out this dark and dismal house of pain
Both him and thee, and all the heavenly
    host
Of spirits that, in our just pretenses armed, 825
Fell with us from on high. From them I go
This uncouth errand sole, and one for all
Myself expose, with lonely steps to tread
The unfounded deep, and through the void
    immense
To search, with wandering quest, a place
    foretold 830

[20] Why are these monsters "hourly conceived And hourly born"?

Should be—and, by concurring signs, ere now
Created vast and round—a place of bliss
In the purlieus of heaven; and therein placed
A race of upstart creatures, to supply
Perhaps our vacant room, though more re-
    moved,   835
Lest heaven, surcharged with potent multi-
    tude,
Might hap to move new broils. Be this, or
    aught
Than this more secret, now designed, I haste
To know; and, this once known, shall soon
    return,
And bring ye to the place where thou and
    Death   840
Shall dwell at ease, and up and down unseen
Wing silently the buxom air, imbalmed
With odors. There ye shall be fed and filled
Immeasurably; all things shall be your prey."
    He ceased; for both seemed highly pleased,
    and Death   845
Grinned horrible a ghastly smile, to hear
His famine should be filled, and blessed his
    maw
Destined to that good hour. No less rejoiced
His mother bad, and thus bespake her sire:—
    "The key of this infernal pit, by due   850
And by command of heaven's all-powerful
    King,
I keep, by him forbidden to unlock
These adamantine gates; against all force
Death ready stands to interpose his dart,
Fearless to be o'ermatched by living might.   855
But what owe I to his commands above,
Who hates me, and hath hither thrust me
    down
Into this gloom of Tartarus profound,
To sit in hateful office here confined,
Inhabitant of heaven and heavenly-born   860
Here in perpetual agony and pain,
With terrors and with clamors compassed
    round
Of mine own brood, that on my bowels
    feed?
Thou art my father, thou my author, thou
My being gavest me; whom should I obey   865
But thee? whom follow? Thou wilt bring me
    soon
To that new world of light and bliss, among
The gods who live at ease, where I shall reign

At thy right hand [21] voluptuous, as beseems
Thy daughter and thy darling, without
    end."   870
    Thus saying, from her side the fatal key,
Sad instrument of all our woe, she took;
And, toward the gate rolling her bestial train,
Forthwith the huge portcullis high up-drew,
Which, but herself, not all the Stygian
    powers   875
Could once have moved; then in the keyhole
    turns
The intricate wards, and every bolt and bar
Of massy iron or solid rock with ease
Unfastens. On a sudden open fly,
With impetuous recoil and jarring sound,   880
The infernal doors, and on their hinges grate
Harsh thunder, that the lowest bottom shook
Of Erebus. She opened; but to shut
Excelled her power: [22] the gates wide open
    stood,
That with extended wings a bannered
    host,   885
Under spread ensigns marching, might pass
    through
With horse and chariots ranked in loose
    array;
So wide they stood, and like a furnace-mouth
Cast forth redounding smoke and ruddy
    flame. . . .

STUDY AIDS: 1. What is the subject of the debate?

2. What is the main point made by each speaker? Could the attitudes and arguments expressed by these speakers represent those of politicians? If this is plausible, could it be that Milton is satirizing the Puritan leaders, who were diverting the Reformation to gain personal ends? Are these types recognizable in today's society?

3. Is Satan in control of the situation at all times? How does he meet Mammon's threat to his leadership?

4. Notice ll. 496–505. Does the sense of frustration expressed here agree with the tone of *Areopagitica*, p. 295/1, l. 46 ff.? There are almost twenty years between the writing of these two works. What seems to be Milton's more mature

[21] In ll. 869–870 note the sacrilegious mimicry of God and Christ.
[22] Why is Sin unable to shut the gates of hell?

view of mankind? What experiences during this lapse of time might account for the change?

5. Notice ll. 345–370. How would this suggestion of Beëlzebub relate to the working out of the theme of the epic as announced in Bk. 1, 25–26?

6. What evidence do you see of Milton's reading in geography? How does his poetic imagination make use of this geographical material? I.e., how is the material used to illuminate his subject matter?

7. Does the allegory of Sin and Death contribute anything to the resolution of the stated theme of the epic?

8. Milton's metrical genius made a new poetic instrument of the blank verse line. His variations of the line are infinite. Try to analyze the following lines to find why their effect is so pronounced. Bear in mind that the effect of a line is often dependent upon the line's context: (1) Bk. 1, 247–249; (2) Bk. 2, 185; (3) Bk. 2, 582–586; (4) Bk. 2, 614–628.

BOOK 9

Now out of Hell, Satan wings his way through Chaos, skirts the approaches to Heaven, and by deceiving Uriel, the archangel who guards the sun, arrives at Earth, the habitation of newly created mankind (Adam and Eve). After an abortive first endeavor (Book 4), Satan succeeds in tempting Eve, who then wins over Adam to disobedience. The Fall of Man is thus accomplished.

On this fateful morning of the Fall, Adam recalls Raphael's final words of admonition:

> . . . stand fast; to stand or fall
> Free in thine own arbitrament it lies.
> Perfect within, no outward aid require;
> And all temptation to transgress repel.
> (Bk. 8, 640–643)

Remembering also the archangel's warning that Eve has power over Adam because he loves her, Adam is reluctant to allow her out of his sight. Eve is offended by this lack of faith (Bk. 9, 279–281) and goes off alone. Almost immediately, Satan, in the form of a serpent, confronts her and wins her confidence through flattery.

. . . .

So talked the spirited sly snake; and Eve,
Yet more amazed, unwary thus replied:[1]
"Serpent, thy overpraising leaves in
　　doubt　　　　　　　　　　　　　　615
The virtue of that fruit, in thee first proved.
But say, where grows the tree?[2] from hence
　　how far?
For many are the trees of God that grow
In Paradise, and various, yet unknown
To us; in such abundance lies our choice, 620
As leaves a greater store of fruit untouched,
Still hanging incorruptible, till men
Grow up to their provision,[3] and more
　　hands
Help to disburden nature of her birth."
　　To whom the wily adder, blithe and
　　glad:　　　　　　　　　　　　　　625
"Empress, the way is ready, and not long;
Beyond a row of myrtles, on a flat,
Fast by a fountain, one small thicket past
Of blowing myrrh and balm: if thou accept
My conduct, I can bring thee thither
　　soon."　　　　　　　　　　　　　630
　　"Lead then," said Eve. He leading swiftly
　　rolled
In tangles, and made intricate seem straight,
To mischief swift. Hope elevates, and joy
Brightens his crest. As when a wandering fire,
Compact of unctuous vapor,[4] which the
　　night　　　　　　　　　　　　　　635
Condenses, and the cold environs round,
Kindled through agitation to a flame
(Which oft, they say, some evil spirit attends),
Hovering and blazing with delusive light,
Misleads the amazed night-wanderer from his
　　way　　　　　　　　　　　　　　640
To bogs and mires, and oft through pond or
　　pool,
There swallowed up and lost, from succor far:
So glistered the dire snake, and into fraud
Led Eve, our credulous mother, to the tree[5]
Of prohibition, root of all our woe;　　　645

[1] Notice the adjective "unwary." What does it reveal?

[2] Satan has stated that eating fruit from this tree had given him the power of speech (see also l. 649).

[3] I.e., until there are enough human beings to eat what nature provides.

[4] I.e., made of oily mist.

[5] What adjective describes Eve in this line?

Which when she saw, thus to her guide she
  spake:
  "Serpent, we might have spared our coming
  hither,
Fruitless to me, though fruit be here to excess,
The credit of whose virtue rest with thee;
Wondrous indeed, if cause of such effects! 650
But of this tree we may not taste nor touch;
God so commanded, and left that command
Sole daughter of his voice: the rest, we live
Law to ourselves; our reason is our law." [6]
  To whom the tempter guilefully replied: 655
"Indeed? Hath God then said that of the fruit
Of all these garden-trees ye shall not eat,
Yet lords declared of all in earth or air?"
  To whom thus Eve, yet sinless: "Of the
  fruit
Of each tree in the garden we may eat;   660
But of the fruit of this fair tree amidst
The garden, God hath said, 'Ye shall not eat
Thereof, nor shall ye touch it, lest ye die.' "
  She scarce had said, though brief, when
  now more bold
The tempter, but with show of zeal and
  love   665
To man, and indignation at his wrong,
New part puts on, and, as to passion moved,
Fluctuates disturbed, yet comely, and in act
Raised, as of some great matter to begin.
As when of old some orator renowned   670
In Athens or free Rome, where eloquence
Flourished, since mute, to some great cause
  addressed,
Stood in himself collected, while each part,
Motion, each act, won audience [7] ere the
  tongue,
Sometimes in height began, as no delay 675
Of preface brooking through his zeal of right:
So standing, moving, or to height upgrown,
The tempter, all impassioned, thus began:
  "O sacred, wise, and wisdom-giving plant,
Mother of science! [8] now I feel thy power 680
Within me clear, not only to discern
Things in their causes, but to trace the ways

Of highest agents,[9] deemed however wise.
Queen of this universe, do not believe
Those rigid threats of death; ye shall not
  die.   685
How should ye? by the fruit? it gives you life
To knowledge.[10] By the threatener? look on
  me,
Me who have touched and tasted, yet both
  live,
And life more perfect have attained than fate
Meant me, by venturing higher than my
  lot.   690
Shall that be shut to man, which to the beast
Is open? or will God incense his ire
For such a petty trespass, and not praise
Rather your dauntless virtue,[11] whom the pain
Of death denounced, whatever thing death
  be,   695
Deterred not from achieving what might
  lead
To happier life, knowledge of good and evil?
Of good, how just? of evil, if what is evil
Be real, why not known, since easier shunned?
God therefore cannot hurt ye, and be
  just; [12]   700
Not just, not God; not feared then, nor
  obeyed:
Your fear itself of death removes the fear.
Why then was this forbid? Why but to awe,
Why but to keep ye low and ignorant,
His worshipers? He knows that in the
  day   705
Ye eat thereof, your eyes that seem so clear,
Yet are but dim, shall perfectly be then
Opened and cleared, and ye shall be as gods,
Knowing both good and evil as they know.
That ye should be as gods, since I as man, 710
Internal man, is but proportion meet,
I, of brute, human; ye, of human, gods.
So ye shall die perhaps, by putting off
Human, to put on gods, death to be wished,

[6] Notice the emphasis on reason. No laws of
God (Bible) were yet written to guide man. His
reason was divine—the breath of God breathed into
him at creation.
[7] Attention.
[8] Knowledge.

[9] Angels.
[10] I.e., life through knowledge.
[11] Notice how Satan appeals to Eve's sense of
independence which, because of Adam's lack of
faith in her strength, was foremost in her mind.
Did a belief in "dauntless virtue" have anything
to do with Satan's own character and fall from
heaven?
[12] Is the argument in ll. 700–709 in keeping with
the character of Satan as related in Book 1?

Though threatened, which no worse than this
    can bring! 715
And what are gods that man may not become
As they, participating godlike food?
The gods are first, and that advantage use
On our belief, that all from them proceeds;
I question it, for this fair earth I see, 720
Warmed by the sun, producing every kind,
Them nothing: if they all things, who en-
    closed
Knowledge of good and evil in this tree,
That whoso eats thereof forthwith attains
Wisdom without their leave? and wherein
    lies 725
The offense, that man should thus attain to
    know?
What can your knowledge hurt him, or this
    tree
Impart against his will, if all be his?
Or is it envy? and can envy dwell
In heavenly breasts? These, these and many
    more 730
Causes [13] import your need of this fair fruit.
Goddess humane, reach then, and freely
    taste!"
    He ended, and his words replete with guile
Into her heart too easy entrance won. [14]
Fixed on the fruit she gazed, which to be-
    hold 735
Might tempt alone, and in her ears the sound
Yet rung of his persuasive words, impregned [15]
With reason, to her seeming, and with truth.
Meanwhile the hour of noon drew on, and
    waked [16]
An eager appetite, raised by the smell 740
So savory of that fruit, which with desire,
Inclinable now grown to touch or taste,
Solicited her longing eye; yet first,
Pausing a while, thus to herself she mused:
    "Great are thy virtues, doubtless, best of
    fruits, 745

Though kept from man, and worthy to be
    admired,
Whose taste, too long forborne, at first assay
Gave elocution to the mute, and taught
The tongue not made for speech to speak thy
    praise.
Thy praise he also who forbids thy use, 750
Conceals not from us, naming thee the Tree
Of Knowledge, knowledge both of good and
    evil;
Forbids us then to taste. But his forbidding
Commends thee more, while it infers the
    good
By thee communicated, and our want: 755
For good unknown, sure is not had, or had
And yet unknown, is as not had at all.
In plain then, what forbids he but to know,
Forbids us good, forbids us to be wise?
Such prohibitions bind not. But if death 760
Binds us with after-bands, what profit then
Our inward freedom? In the day we eat
Of this fair fruit, our doom is, we shall die.
How dies the serpent? he hath eaten and lives,
And knows, and speaks, and reasons, and
    discerns, 765
Irrational till then. For us alone
Was death invented? or to us denied
This intellectual food, for beasts reserved?
For beasts it seems; yet that one beast which
    first
Hath tasted, envies not, but brings with
    joy 770
The good befallen him, author unsuspect, [17]
Friendly to man, far from deceit or guile.
What fear I then? rather what know to fear
Under this ignorance of good and evil,
Of God or death, of law or penalty? 775
Here grows the cure of all, this fruit divine,
Fair to the eye, inviting to the taste,
Of virtue to make wise. What hinders then
To reach, and feed at once both body and
    mind?" [18]
    So saying, her rash hand in evil hour 780
Forth reaching to the fruit, she plucked, she
    eat.
Earth felt the wound, and nature from her
    seat,

[13] What are the arguments advanced by Satan in ll. 699–732 to tempt Eve to disobedience?

[14] What comment on Eve's character is made in this line?

[15] I.e., impregned with reason. Since Eve had said "our reason is our law" (l. 654), Satan argues "reasonably."

[16] In ll. 739–744 what more immediate emotion, rather than reason, persuades Eve to believe the serpent?

[17] I.e., how then can one suspect Satan's authority?

[18] What rationalizations does Eve offer in ll. 745–779 as her reasons for eating the fruit?

Sighing through all her works, gave signs of
    woe
That all was lost. Back to the thicket slunk
The guilty serpent, and well might, for
    Eve,   785
Intent now only on her taste, naught else
Regarded; such delight till then, as seemed,
In fruit she never tasted, whether true,
Or fancied so through expectation high
Of knowledge; nor was godhead from her
    thought.[19]   790
Greedily she engorged without restraint,
And knew not eating death. Satiate at length,
And heightened as with wine, jocund and
    boon,
Thus to herself she pleasingly began:
    "O sovereign, virtuous, precious of all
        trees   795
In paradise! of operation blest
To sapience, hitherto obscured, infamed,
And thy fair fruit let hang, as to no end
Created! but henceforth my early care,
Not without song, each morning, and due
    praise,   800
Shall tend thee, and the fertile burden ease
Of thy full branches, offered free to all;
Till, dieted by thee, I grow mature
In knowledge, as the gods who all things
    know;
Though others envy what they cannot
    give—   805
For, had the gift been theirs, it had not
    here
Thus grown! Experience, next to thee I owe,
Best guide: not following thee, I had re-
    mained
In ignorance: thou openest wisdom's way,
And givest access, though secret she retire. 810
And I perhaps am secret; [20] heaven is high,
High, and remote to see from thence distinct
Each thing on earth; and other care perhaps
May have diverted from continual watch
Our great forbidder,[21] safe with all his
    spies   815

About him. But to Adam in what sort [22]
Shall I appear? Shall I to him make known
As yet my change, and give him to partake
Full happiness with me, or rather not,
But keep the odds of knowledge in my
    power   820
Without copartner? so to add what wants
In female sex, the more to draw his love,
And render me more equal, and perhaps,
A thing not undesirable, sometime
Superior; for, inferior, who is free?   825
This may be well: but what if God have seen,
And death ensue? Then I shall be no more;
And Adam, wedded to another Eve,
Shall live with her enjoying, I extinct!
A death to think! Confirmed then I resolve 830
Adam shall share with me in bliss or woe: [23]
So dear I love him, that with him all deaths
I could endure, without him live no life."

.   .   .   .

To him she hasted; in her face excuse
Came prologue, and apology to prompt,
Which, with bland words at will, she thus
    addressed: 855
    "Hast thou not wondered, Adam, at my
        stay?
Thee I have missed, and thought it long,
    deprived
Thy presence—agony of love till now
Not felt, nor shall be twice; for never more
Mean I to try, what rash untried I sought, 860
The pain of absence from thy sight.[24] But
    strange
Hath been the cause, and wonderful to hear.
This tree is not, as we are told, a tree
Of danger tasted, nor to evil unknown
Opening the way, but of divine effect   865
To open eyes, and make them gods who taste;
And hath been tasted such. The serpent wise,
Or not restrained as we, or not obeying,

[19] Some of Satan's arguments have impressed themselves on Eve's mind. How does her ambition for "godhead" relate to Satan's fall from heaven?
[20] Not seen. What does this statement indicate about Eve's spiritual maturity?
[21] Notice how Eve now regards God.

[22] In ll. 816–825 what is happening to the relationship of Adam and Eve? This is obviously an effect of Eve's fall and therefore sin. Milton's age would have so regarded woman's desire for equality with man. However, why does Eve want equality?
[23] Why does Eve decide to share her new-found "happiness" with Adam? Is there any IRONY here?
[24] Notice that Eve opens her conversation with Adam by an apology for her independent behavior of the morning.

Hath eaten of the fruit, and is become,
Not dead, as we are threatened, but thence-
   forth   870
Endued with human voice and human sense,
Reasoning to admiration, and with me
Persuasively hath so prevailed that I
Have also tasted, and have also found
The effects to correspond—opener mine
   eyes,   875
Dim erst, dilated spirits, ampler heart,
And growing up to godhead; which for thee [25]
Chiefly I sought, without thee can despise.
For bliss, as thou hast part, to me is bliss;
Tedious, unshared with thee, and odious
   soon.   880
Thou therefore also taste, that equal lot
May join us, equal joy, as equal love;
Lest, thou not tasting, different degree
Disjoin us, and I then too late renounce
Deity for thee, when fate will not permit." 885
  Thus Eve with countenance blithe her
   story told;
But in her cheek distemper flushing glowed.
On the other side, Adam, soon as he heard
The fatal trespass done by Eve, amazed,
Astonied stood and blank, while horror
   chill   890
Ran through his veins, and all his joints
   relaxed;
From his slack hand the garland wreathed for
   Eve
Down dropped, and all the faded roses shed.
Speechless he stood and pale, till thus at
   length
First to himself he inward silence broke: 895
  "O fairest of creation, last and best [26]
Of all God's works, creature in whom excelled
Whatever can to sight or thought be formed,
Holy, divine, good, amiable, or sweet!
How art thou lost! how on a sudden lost, 900
Defaced, deflowered, and now to death de-
   vote!
Rather, how hast thou yielded to transgress
The strict forbiddance, how to violate
The sacred fruit forbidden? Some cursed
   fraud

Of enemy hath beguiled thee, yet un-
   known,   905
And me with thee hath ruined; for with thee
Certain my resolution is to die:
How can I live without thee? how forgo
Thy sweet converse and love so dearly joined,
To live again in these wild woods forlorn? 910
Should God create another Eve, and I
Another rib afford, yet loss of thee
Would never from my heart; no, no! I feel
The link of nature draw me: flesh of flesh,
Bone of my bone thou art, and from thy
   state   915
Mine never shall be parted, bliss or woe."
  So having said, as one from sad dismay
Recomforted, and, after thoughts disturbed,
Submitting to what seemed remediless,
Thus in calm mood his words to Eve he
   turned: 920
  "Bold deed thou hast presumed, adventur-
   ous Eve,[27]
And peril great provoked, who thus hast dared,
Had it been only coveting to eye
That sacred fruit, sacred to abstinence;
Much more to taste it, under ban to touch. 925
But past who can recall, or done undo?
Not God omnipotent, nor fate! Yet so
Perhaps thou shalt not die; perhaps the fact
Is not so heinous now—foretasted fruit,
Profaned first by the serpent, by him first 930
Made common and unhallowed ere our taste,
Nor yet on him found deadly; he yet lives,
Lives, as thou saidst, and gains to live, as man,
Higher degree of life: inducement strong
To us, as likely, tasting, to attain   935
Proportional ascent; which cannot be
But to be gods, or angels, demi-gods.
Nor can I think that God, creator wise,
Though threatening, will in earnest so destroy
Us his prime creatures, dignified so high, 940
Set over all his works, which in our fall,
For us created, needs with us must fail,
Dependent made; so God shall uncreate,
Be frustrate, do, undo, and labor lose;
Not well conceived of God, who, though his
   power   945

---

[25] Cf. ll. 877–885 with ll. 817–825. Is Eve telling
the truth here?

[26] In ll. 896–916 what is Adam's reason for eating
the fruit?

[27] What rationalization does Adam advance in
ll. 921–959 to support his decision? Cf. especially
ll. 932–937 with ll. 703–709. Who first advanced
this view?

Creation could repeat, yet would be loath
Us to abolish, lest the adversary
Triumph and say: 'Fickle their state whom God
Most favors; who can please him long? Me first
He ruined, now mankind; whom will he next?' 950
Matter of scorn not to be given the foe,
However, I with thee have fixed my lot,
Certain to undergo like doom: if death
Consort with thee, death is to me as life;
So forcible within my heart I feel [28] 955
The bond of nature draw me to my own,
My own in thee, for what thou art is mine.
Our state cannot be severed; we are one,
One flesh; to lose thee were to lose myself."
    So Adam, and thus Eve to him replied: 960
"O glorious trial of exceeding love,
Illustrious evidence, example high!
Engaging me to emulate; but, short
Of thy perfection, how shall I attain,
Adam, from whose dear side I boast me sprung, 965
And gladly of our union hear thee speak,
One heart, one soul in both; whereof good proof
This day affords, declaring thee resolved,
Rather than death, or aught than death more dread,
Shall separate us, linked in love so dear, 970
To undergo with me one guilt, one crime,
If any be, of tasting this fair fruit;
Whose virtue (for of good still good proceeds,
Direct, or by occasion) hath presented
This happy trial of thy love, which else 975
So eminently never had been known.
Were it I thought death menaced would ensue
This my attempt, I would sustain alone
The worst, and not persuade thee, rather die
Deserted, than oblige thee with a fact 980
Pernicious to thy peace, chiefly assured
Remarkably so late of thy so true,
So faithful love unequaled. But I feel
Far otherwise the event—not death, but life

[28] Lines 955-959 summarize Adam's statement about his love for Eve made earlier to Raphael (Bk. 8, 534-560). To this, Raphael had warned Adam to allow his reason to control his emotions.

Augmented, opened eyes, new hopes, new joys, 985
Taste so divine, that what of sweet before
Hath touched my sense, flat seems to this and harsh.
On my experience, Adam, freely taste,
And fear of death deliver to the winds."
    So saying, she embraced him, and for joy 990
Tenderly wept, much won that he his love
Had so ennobled, as of choice to incur
Divine displeasure for her sake, or death.
In recompense (for such compliance bad
Such recompense best merits), from the bough 995
She gave him of that fair enticing fruit
With liberal hand; he scrupled not to eat,[29]
Against his better knowledge, not deceived,
But fondly overcome with female charm.
Earth trembled from her entrails, as again 1000
In pangs, and nature gave a second groan;
Sky loured and, muttering thunder, some sad drops
Wept at completing of the mortal sin
Original; while Adam took no thought,
Eating his fill, nor Eve to iterate 1005
Her former trespass feared, the more to soothe
Him with her loved society, that now,
As with new wine intoxicated both,[30]
They swim in mirth, and fancy that they feel
Divinity within them breeding wings 1010
Wherewith to scorn the earth. But that false fruit
Far other operation first displayed,
Carnal desire inflaming, he on Eve
Began to cast lascivious eyes, she him
As wantonly repaid; in lust [31] they burn, 1015
Till Adam thus 'gan Eve to dalliance move.

[29] Lines 997-999 recount the Fall of Man. The lines do not state what original sin is (i.e., the symbolism of the fruit), but they do state why it happened. Why?
[30] In ll. 1008-1015 what are the first two results of man's Fall? What is the third (see ll. 1024-1026)?
[31] Milton draws a firm distinction between sexual love and lust. Sexual love was enjoyed by Adam and Eve before the Fall, but here is the first instance of lust, i.e., unbridled desire not controlled by reason or will.

"Eve, now I see thou art exact of taste,
And elegant, of sapience no small part,
Since to each meaning savor we apply,
And palate call judicious; I the praise   1020
Yield thee, so well this day thou hast pur-
veyed.
Much pleasure we have lost, while we
abstained
From this delightful fruit, nor known till now
True relish, tasting. If such pleasure be
In things to us forbidden, it might be
wished,   1025
For this one tree had been forbidden ten.
But come; so well refreshed, now let us play,
As meet is, after such delicious fare;
For never did thy beauty since the day
I saw thee first and wedded thee, adorned 1030
With all perfections, so inflame my sense
With ardor to enjoy thee, fairer now
Than ever, bounty of this virtuous tree."

.   .   .   .

                          Silent, and in face
Confounded, long they sat, as stricken mute;
Till Adam, though not less than Eve
abashed,   1065
At length gave utterance to these words con-
strained:
"O Eve, in evil hour thou didst give ear
To that false worm, of whomsoever taught
To counterfeit man's voice, true in our fall,
False in our promised rising; since our
eyes [32]   1070
Opened we find indeed, and find we know
Both good and evil, good lost and evil got:
Bad fruit of knowledge, if this be to know,
Which leaves us naked thus, of honor void,
Of innocence, of faith, of purity,   1075
Our wonted ornaments now soiled and
stained,
And in our faces evident the signs
Of foul concupiscence; whence evil store,
Even shame, the last of evils; of the first
Be sure then. How shall I behold the
face   1080
Henceforth of God or angel, erst with joy
And rapture so oft beheld? those heavenly
shapes

Will dazzle now this earthly with their
blaze
Insufferably bright. Oh, might I here [33]
In solitude live savage, in some glade   1085
Obscured, where highest woods, impenetrable
To star or sunlight, spread their umbrage
broad,
And brown as evening! Cover me, ye pines!
Ye cedars, with innumerable boughs
Hide me, where I may never see them
more!   1090
But let us now, as in bad plight, devise
What best may for the present serve to hide
The parts of each from other that seem most
To shame obnoxious, and unseemliest seen;
Some tree, whose broad smooth leaves together
sewed,   1095
And girded on our loins, may cover round
Those middle parts, that this new comer,
shame,
There sit not, and reproach us as unclean."
      So counseled he, and both together went
Into the thickest wood; there soon they
chose   1100
The fig-tree—not that kind for fruit renowned,
But such as at this day, to Indians known,
In Malabar [34] or Decan spreads her arms
Branching so broad and long that in the
ground
The bended twigs take root, and daughters
grow   1105
About the mother tree, a pillared shade
High overarched, and echoing walks between:
There oft the Indian herdsman, shunning
heat,
Shelters in cool, and tends his pasturing herds
At loop-holes cut through thickest shade.
Those leaves   1110
They gathered, broad as Amazonian targe,
And with what skill they had, together sewed,
To gird their waist; vain covering, if to hide
Their guilt and dreaded shame! Oh how
unlike
To that first naked glory! Such of late   1115
Columbus found the American, so girt
With feathered cincture, naked else and
wild
Among the trees on isles and woody shores.

[32] What further effects of the Fall are given in
ll. 1070-1075?
[33] Cf. ll. 1084-1090 with ll. 908-910.
[34] Malabar and Decan were names for India.

Thus fenced, and, as they thought, their
    shame in part [35]
Covered, but not at rest or ease of mind, 1120
They sat them down to weep; nor only tears
Rained at their eyes, but high winds worse
    within
Began to rise, high passions, anger, hate,
Mistrust, suspicion, discord, and shook sore
Their inward state of mind, calm region
    once   1125
And full of peace, now tossed and turbulent:
For understanding ruled not, and the will
Heard not her lore, both in subjection now
To sensual appetite, who, from beneath
Usurping over sovereign reason, claimed 1130
Superior sway. From thus distempered breast
Adam, estranged in look and altered style,
Speech intermitted thus to Eve renewed:
    "Would thou hadst hearkened to my words,
    and stayed [36]
With me, as I besought thee, when that
    strange   1135
Desire of wandering, this unhappy morn,
I know not whence possessed thee! we had
    then
Remained still happy, not, as now, despoiled
Of all our good, shamed, naked, miserable!
Let none henceforth seek needless cause to
    approve   1140
The faith they owe; when earnestly they seek
Such proof, conclude, they then begin to fail."
    To whom, soon moved with touch of blame,
    thus Eve:
"What words have passed thy lips, Adam
    severe?
Imputest thou that to my default, or will 1145
Of wandering, as thou callest it, which who
    knows
But might as ill have happened thou being by,
Or to thyself perhaps: hadst thou been there,
Or here the attempt, thou couldst not have
    discerned

[35] Lines 1119–1131 state the most serious result
of the Fall: the emotional nature of man ("sensual
appetite") can now control man's "sovereign reason."
[36] From l. 1134 to the end of Book 9, Adam and
Eve pick up once again the disagreement of the
early morning; now, however, it is argued with
"mutual accusation," which sad situation leads
Milton through Adam to editorialize with a somewhat bitter tone in ll. 1182–1186.

Fraud in the serpent, speaking as he
    spake;   1150
No ground of enmity between us known,
Why he should mean me ill or seek to harm.
Was I to have never parted from thy side?
As good have grown there still a lifeless rib.
Being as I am, why didst not thou, the
    head,   1155
Command me absolutely not to go,
Going into such danger as thou saidst?
Too facile then, thou didst not much gainsay,
Nay, didst permit, approve, and fair dismiss.
Hadst thou been firm and fixed in thy dis-
    sent,   1160
Neither had I transgressed, nor thou with
    me."
    To whom then first incensed Adam replied:
"Is this the love, is this the recompense
Of mine to thee, ingrateful Eve, expressed
Immutable when thou wert lost, not I, 1165
Who might have lived and joyed immortal
    bliss,
Yet willingly chose rather death with thee?
And am I now upbraided as the cause
Of thy transgressing? not enough severe,
It seems, in thy restraint: what could I
    more?   1170
I warned thee, I admonished thee, foretold
The danger, and the lurking enemy
That lay in wait; beyond this had been force,
And force upon free will hath here no place.
But confidence then bore thee on, secure 1175
Either to meet no danger, or to find
Matter of glorious trial; and perhaps
I also erred in overmuch admiring
What seemed in thee so perfect, that I thought
No evil durst attempt thee, but I rue   1180
That error now, which is become my crime,
And thou the accuser. Thus it shall befall
Him who, to worth in women overtrusting,
Lets her will rule: restraint she will not brook;
And, left to herself, if evil thence ensue, 1185
She first his weak indulgence will accuse."
    Thus they in mutual accusation spent
The fruitless hours, but neither self-condemn-
    ing,
And of their vain contest appeared no end.

STUDY AIDS: 1. What kind of woman is
Eve as presented in Bk. 9?

2. Why does Eve sin? How are Adam's motives different from Eve's? How are these motives in keeping with the characterizations of Adam and Eve?

3. Who is the center of interest in Bk. 9: Satan, or Adam and Eve? How does Satan in Bk. 9 differ from the arrogant, magnificent creature he was in Bks. 1 and 2?

4. What was the sin that was committed: (1) lust; (2) longing after "godhead"; (3) control of the reason by the emotions; or (4) man's love for woman? What does Milton seem to think it was?

5. Read. ll. 684–732 carefully. Satan, in order to persuade Eve to eat the fruit, uses a subtle but insidious logic so that she thinks she is hearing reason and truth. Work out the successive steps of his argument. What is their relationship to his rationalizations about his own fall as related in Bks. 1 and 2?

BOOK 12

The angel Michael is relating to Adam the future of his offspring, mankind. When, in the course of following Old Testament history, Michael comes to Abraham, he explains the promise made to Adam, that Eve's "seed should be revenged on the serpent." The Son of God is to be born of Abraham's race, will suffer death and resurrection, and will come to the earth a second time:

> ". . . for then the earth
> Shall be all paradise, far happier place
> Than this of Eden, and far happier days."
> (Bk. 12, 463–465)

So spake the archangel Michaël; then
  paused,
As at the world's great period; and our sire,
Replete with joy and wonder, thus replied:
"O goodness infinite, goodness immense! [1]
That all this good of evil shall produce,   470
And evil turn to good; more wonderful
Than that which by creation first brought
  forth
Light out of darkness! Full of doubt I stand,
Whether I should repent me now of sin

[1] Lines 469–479 state the doctrine of the "fortunate fall." What is meant by this? How can evil become good? How does this doctrine relate to Bk. 1, 25–26?

By me done and occasioned, or rejoice   475
Much more, that much more good thereof
  shall spring;
To God more glory, more good will to men
From God, and over wrath grace shall
  abound.
But say, if our deliverer up to heaven
Must reascend, what will betide the few,   480
His faithful, left among the unfaithful herd,
The enemies of truth. Who then shall guide
His people, who defend? Will they not deal
Worse with his followers than with him they
  dealt?"
  "Be sure they will," said the angel; "but
  from heaven   485
He to his own a comforter will send,
The promise of the Father, who shall dwell,
His spirit, within them, and the law of faith,
Working through love, upon their hearts shall
  write,
To guide them in all truth, and also arm   490
With spiritual armor, able to resist
Satan's assaults, and quench his fiery darts;
What man can do against them not afraid,
Though to the death; against such cruelties
With inward consolations recompensed,   495
And oft supported so as shall amaze
Their proudest persecutors. For the spirit,
Poured first on his apostles, whom he sends
To evangelize the nations, then on all
Baptized, shall them with wondrous gifts en-
  due   500
To speak all tongues, and do all miracles,
As did their Lord before them. Thus they win
Great numbers of each nation to receive
With joy the tidings brought from heaven: at
  length
Their ministry performed, and race well
  run,   505
Their doctrine and their story written left,
They die; but in their room, as they fore-
  warn, [2]
Wolves shall succeed for teachers, grievous
  wolves,
Who all the sacred mysteries of heaven
To their own vile advantages shall turn   510
Of lucre and ambition, and the truth
With superstitions and traditions taint,

[2] Cf. ll. 507–512 with *Lycidas,* ll. 125–129 (p. 254).

Left only in those written records pure,
Though not but by the spirit understood.
Then shall they seek to avail themselves of
    names, 515
Places, and titles, and with these to join
Secular power, though feigning still to act
By spiritual; to themselves appropriating
The spirit of God, promised alike and given
To all believers; and, from that pretense, 520
Spiritual laws by carnal power shall force
On every conscience; laws which none shall
    find
Left them enrolled, or what the spirit within
Shall on the heart engrave. What will they
    then,
But force the spirit of grace itself, and
    bind 525
His consort, liberty? what but unbuild
His living temples, built by faith to stand,
Their own faith, not another's? for, on earth,
Who against faith and conscience can be
    heard
Infallible? Yet many will presume: 530
Whence heavy persecution shall arise
On all who in the worship persevere
Of spirit and truth; the rest, far greater part,
Will deem in outward rites and specious
    forms
Religion satisfied; truth shall retire 535
Bestuck with slanderous darts, and works of
    faith
Rarely be found. So shall the world go on,
To good malignant, to bad men benign,
Under her own weight groaning till the day
Appear of respiration to the just, 540
And vengeance to the wicked, at return
Of him so lately promised to thy aid,
The woman's seed—obscurely then foretold,
Now amplier known thy Savior and thy Lord;
Last in the clouds from heaven to be re-
    vealed 545
In glory of the Father, to dissolve
Satan with his perverted world; then raise
From the conflagrant mass, purged and re-
    fined,
New heavens, new earth, ages of endless date,
Founded in righteousness and peace and
    love, 550
To bring forth fruits, joy and eternal bliss."
  He ended; and thus Adam last replied:

"How soon hath thy prediction, seer blest,
Measured this transient world, the race of
    time,
Till time stand fixed! Beyond is all abyss, 555
Eternity, whose end no eye can reach.
Greatly instructed I shall hence depart,
Greatly in peace of thought, and have my fill
Of knowledge, what this vessel can contain; [3]
Beyond which was my folly to aspire. 560
Henceforth I learn that to obey is best,
And love with fear the only God, to walk
As in his presence, ever to observe
His providence, and on him sole depend,
Merciful over all his works, with good 565
Still overcoming evil, and by small
Accomplishing great things, by things deemed
    weak
Subverting worldly-strong, and worldly-wise
By simply meek; that suffering for truth's
    sake
Is fortitude to highest victory, 570
And, to the faithful, death the gate of life;
Taught this by his example whom I now
Acknowledge my Redeemer ever blest."
  To whom thus also the angel last replied:
"This having learned, thou hast attained the
    sum 575
Of wisdom; hope no higher, though all the
    stars
Thou knewest by name, and all the ethereal
    powers,
All secrets of the deep, all nature's works,
Or works of God in heaven, air, earth, or sea,
And all the riches of this world enjoyedst, 580
And all the rule, one empire. Only add
Deeds to thy knowledge answerable; add
    faith,[4]
Add virtue, patience, temperance; add love,
By name to come called charity, the soul
Of all the rest: then wilt thou not be
    loath 585
To leave this paradise, but shalt possess

[3] How could ll. 559–560 be an explanation of
the Fall?
[4] Lines 582–585 state that by building his life
on the Christian virtues enumerated by the apostle
Peter in 2 Peter 1:5–8, Adam can attain a "paradise
within." Milton's next poem, Paradise Regained,
develops this idea of the "inner paradise," and the
poem explains that it is created by reason's control
over emotion.

A paradise within thee, happier far.
Let us descend now, therefore, from this top
Of speculation; for the hour precise
Exacts our parting hence; and, see! the
    guards,   590
By me encamped on yonder hill, expect
Their motion, at whose front a flaming sword,
In signal of remove, waves fiercely round.
We may no longer stay: go, waken Eve;
Her also I with gentle dreams have
    calmed,   595
Portending good, and all her spirits composed
To meek submission: thou, at season fit,
Let her with thee partake what thou hast
    heard;
Chiefly what may concern her faith to know,
The great deliverance by her seed to come 600
(For by the woman's seed) on all mankind;
That ye may live, which will be many days,
Both in one faith unanimous; though sad
With cause for evils past, yet much more
    cheered
With meditation on the happy end."   605
  He ended, and they both descend the
    hill.
Descended, Adam to the bower where Eve
Lay sleeping ran before, but found her waked;
And thus with words not sad she him re-
    ceived:
  "Whence thou returnest, and whither went-
    est, I know;   610
For God is also in sleep, and dreams advise,
Which he hath sent propitious, some great
    good
Presaging, since with sorrow and heart's dis-
    tress
Wearied I fell asleep. But now lead on;
In me is no delay; with thee to go   615
Is to stay here; without thee here to stay
Is to go hence unwilling; thou to me
Art all things under heaven, all places thou
Who for my willful [5] crime art banished
    hence.
This further consolation yet secure   620
I carry hence; though all by me is lost,
Such favor I unworthy am vouchsafed,
By me the promised seed shall all restore."
  So spake our mother Eve, and Adam heard

[5] Notice that Eve has accepted responsibility for their Fall.

Well pleased, but answered not; for now too
    nigh   625
The archangel stood, and from the other hill
To their fixed station, all in bright array,
The cherubim descended, on the ground
Gliding meteorous, as evening mist
Risen from a river o'er the marish [6] glides, 630
And gathers ground fast at the laborer's heel
Homeward returning. High in front ad-
    vanced,
The brandished sword of God before them
    blazed
Fierce as a comet; which with torrid heat,
And vapor as the Libyan air adust, [7]   635
Began to parch that temperate clime; where-
    at
In either hand the hastening angel caught
Our lingering parents, and to the eastern gate
Led them direct, and down the cliff as fast
To the subjected [8] plain; then disap-
    peared.   640
They looking back, all the eastern side beheld
Of paradise, so late their happy seat,
Waved over by that flaming brand, the gate
With dreadful faces thronged and fiery arms.
Some natural tears they dropped, but wiped
    them soon;   645
The world was all before them, where to
    choose
Their place of rest, and providence their
    guide.
They hand in hand with wandering steps and
    slow,
Through Eden took their solitary way.
(1667)

STUDY AIDS: 1. What emotion suffuses ll. 637–648?
2. Study carefully ll. 473–478. Do you think this statement is to be taken literally or as HYPERBOLE? What does the context imply as to how it should be read? Can a person rejoice that he has done evil? Does the good which can come of evil result from man's (Adam's) actions or God's? Do Adam and Eve "pay" for their sin? What has this to do with the emotions they experience as they leave the Garden?
3. Do you feel that Milton has "justified the ways of God to men"?

[6] Marsh.
[7] Burnt.
[8] Lying below.

Areopagitica

The title is taken from an oration delivered by Isocrates to the Areopagus, a selected group of wise men who acted as a court in ancient Athens. Milton addresses his plea to the Puritan Parliament, which in 1643 had passed a law requiring all books to be censored before publication. Milton failed to change the law, but his statements remain as a manifesto for freedom of speech and the press.

This is true liberty, when free-born men,
Having to advise the public, may speak free,
Which he who can, and will, deserves high
　　praise;
Who neither can, nor will, may hold his peace:　5
What can be juster in a state than this?
　　　　　　　　　Euripides, *The Suppliants*

. . . If ye be thus resolved, as it were injury to think ye were not, I know not what should withhold me from presenting ye with 10 a fit instance wherein to show both that love of truth which ye eminently profess, and that uprightness of your judgment which is not wont to be partial to yourselves; by judging over again that order which ye have ordained 15 *to regulate printing: that no book, pamphlet, or paper shall be henceforth printed, unless the same be first approved and licensed by such, or at least one of such, as shall be thereto appointed. . . .* 20

I deny not but that it is of greatest concernment in the church and commonwealth to have a vigilant eye how books demean themselves, as well as men, and thereafter to confine, imprison, and do sharpest justice 25 on them as malefactors. For books are not absolutely dead things, but do contain a potency of life in them to be as active as that soul was whose progeny they are; nay, they do preserve as in a vial the purest efficacy 30 and extraction of that living intellect that bred them. I know they are as lively, and as vigorously productive, as those fabulous dragon's teeth; and being sown up and down, may chance to spring up armed men. And yet, 35 on the other hand, unless wariness be used, as good almost kill a man as kill a good book: who kills a man kills a reasonable creature, God's image; but he who destroys a good book, kills reason itself, kills the image of 40

God, as it were, in the eye. Many a man lives a burden to the earth; but a good book is the precious life-blood of a master spirit, embalmed and treasured up on purpose to a life beyond life. 'Tis true, no age can restore a life, whereof, perhaps, there is no great loss; and revolutions of ages do not oft recover the loss of a rejected truth, for the want of which whole nations fare the worse. We should be wary, therefore, what persecution we raise against the living labors of public men, how we spill that seasoned life of man preserved and stored up in books; since we see a kind of homicide may be thus committed, sometimes a martyrdom; and if it extend to the whole impression, a kind of massacre, whereof the execution ends not in the slaying of an elemental life, but strikes at that ethereal and fifth essence, the breath of reason itself, slays an immortality rather than a life. . . .

Good and evil we know in the field of this world grow up together almost inseparably; and the knowledge of good is so involved and interwoven with the knowledge of evil, and in so many cunning resemblances hardly to be discerned, that those confused seeds which were imposed on Psyche [1] as an incessant labor to cull out and sort asunder, were not more intermixed. It was from out the rind of one apple tasted that the knowledge of good and evil, as two twins cleaving together, leaped forth into the world. And perhaps this is that doom which Adam fell into of knowing good and evil, that is to say,

[1] Apuleius in *The Golden Ass* tells this story of Psyche. Because Psyche had won the love of Cupid, Venus in anger doomed her to sort out a mountain of mixed seeds. The ants did her work for her. How does Milton use this myth to illustrate the problem of good and evil in the world? What has censorship to do with this problem?

of knowing good by evil.[2] As therefore the state of man now is, what wisdom can there be to choose, what continence to forbear, without the knowledge of evil? He that can apprehend and consider vice with all her baits and seeming pleasures, and yet abstain, and yet distinguish, and yet prefer that which is truly better, he is the true warfaring Christian. I cannot praise a fugitive and cloistered virtue, unexercised and unbreathed, that never sallies out and sees her adversary, but slinks out of the race where that immortal garland is to be run for, not without dust and heat. Assuredly we bring not innocence into the world, we bring impurity much rather; that which purifies us is trial, and trial is by what is contrary. That virtue therefore which is but a youngling in the contemplation of evil, and knows not the utmost that vice promises to her followers, and rejects it, is but a blank virtue, not a pure; her whiteness is but an excremental[3] whiteness; which was the reason why our sage and serious poet Spenser, whom I dare be known to think a better teacher than Scotus or Aquinas,[4] describing true temperance under the person of Guyon, brings him in with his palmer through the cave of Mammon and the bower of earthly bliss, that he might see and know, and yet abstain. Since therefore the knowledge and survey of vice is in this world so necessary to the constituting of human virtue, and the scanning of error to the confirmation of truth, how can we more safely, and with less danger, scout into the regions of sin and falsity than by reading all manner of tractates and hearing all manner of reason? And this is the benefit which may be had of books promiscuously read. . . .

Seeing therefore that those books, and those in great abundance, which are likeliest to taint both life and doctrine, cannot be suppressed without the fall of learning, and of all ability in disputation; and that these books of either sort are most and soonest catching to the learned (from whom to the common people whatever is heretical or dissolute may quickly be conveyed); and that evil manners are as perfectly learned without books a thousand other ways which cannot be stopped; and evil doctrine not with books can propagate, except a teacher guide, which he might also do without writing, and so beyond prohibiting; I am not able to unfold how this cautelous[5] enterprise of licensing can be exempted from the number of vain and impossible attempts. And he who were pleasantly disposed could not well avoid to liken it to the exploit of that gallant man who thought to pound up the crows by shutting his park gate.

Besides another inconvenience, if learned men be the first receivers out of books and dispreaders both of vice and error, how shall the licensers themselves be confided in, unless we can confer upon them, or they assume to themselves above all others in the land, the grace of infallibility and uncorruptedness? And again, if it be true that a wise man, like a good refiner, can gather gold out of the drossiest volume, and that a fool will be a fool with the best book, yea, or without book, there is no reason that we should deprive a wise man of any advantage to his wisdom, while we seek to restrain from a fool that which, being restrained, will be no hindrance to his folly. For if there should be so much exactness always used to keep that from him which is unfit for his reading, we should, in the judgment of Aristotle not only, but of Solomon and of our Savior, not vouchsafe him good precepts, and by consequence not willingly admit him to good books; as being certain that a wise man will make better use of an idle pamphlet than a fool will do of sacred Scripture. . . .

It was the task which I began with, to show that no nation, or well instituted state, if they valued books at all, did ever use this way of licensing; and it might be answered that this is a piece of prudence lately discovered. To which I return that, as it was a

[2] This is Milton's interpretation of the Fall of Man. Is it the same view that he holds in *Paradise Lost?*
[3] External.
[4] John Duns Scotus and St. Thomas Aquinas were medieval philosophers. Why does Milton consider Spenser a better teacher than Scotus or Aquinas?
[5] Uncertain.

thing slight and obvious to think on, so if it had been difficult to find out, there wanted not among them long since who suggested such a course; which they not following, leave us a pattern of their judgment that it was not the not knowing, but the not approving, which was the cause of their not using it. . . .

For if they fell upon one kind of strictness, unless their care were equal to regulate all other things of like aptness to corrupt the mind, that single endeavor they knew would be but a fond [6] labor—to shut and fortify one gate against corruption and be necessitated to leave others round about wide open. If we think to regulate printing, thereby to rectify manners, we must regulate all recreations and pastimes, all that is delightful to man. No music must be heard, no song be set or sung, but what is grave and Doric. There must be licensing dancers, that no gesture, motion, or deportment be taught our youth, but what by their allowance shall be thought honest; for such Plato was provided of. It will ask more than the work of twenty licensers to examine all the lutes, the violins, and the guitars in every house; they must not be suffered to prattle as they do, but must be licensed what they may say. And who shall silence all the airs and madrigals that whisper softness in chambers? The windows also, and the balconies, must be thought on; there are shrewd books, with dangerous frontispieces, set to sale: who shall prohibit them, shall twenty licensers? The villages also must have their visitors to inquire what lectures the bagpipe and the rebeck reads even to the ballatry, and the gamut of every municipal fiddler; for these are the countryman's *Arcadias*, and his *Montemayors*. . . .

If every action which is good or evil in man at ripe years were to be under pittance [7] and prescription and compulsion, what were virtue but a name, what praise could be then due to well-doing, what gramercy [8] to be sober, just, or continent?

Many there be that complain of divine providence for suffering Adam to transgress.

Foolish tongues! when God gave him reason, he gave him freedom to choose, for reason is but choosing; he had been else a mere artificial Adam, such an Adam as he is in the motions.[9] We ourselves esteem not of that obedience, or love, or gift, which is of force; God therefore left him free, set before him a provoking object, ever almost in his eyes; herein consisted his merit, herein the right of his reward, the praise of his abstinence. Wherefore did he create passions within us, pleasures round about us, but that these, rightly tempered, are the very ingredients of virtue?[10] They are not skilful considerers of human things who imagine to remove sin by removing the matter of sin; for, besides that it is a huge heap increasing under the very act of diminishing, though some part of it may for a time be withdrawn from some persons, it cannot from all, in such a universal thing as books are; and when this is done, yet the sin remains entire. Though ye take from a covetous man all his treasure, he has yet one jewel left—ye cannot bereave him of his covetousness. Banish all objects of lust, shut up all youth into the severest discipline that can be exercised in any hermitage, ye cannot make them chaste that came not thither so: such great care and wisdom is required to the right managing of this point.

Suppose we could expel sin by this means: look how much we thus expel of sin, so much we expel of virtue, for the matter of them both is the same; remove that, and ye remove them both alike. This justifies the high providence of God, who, though he command us temperance, justice, continence, yet pours out before us even to a profuseness all desirable things, and gives us minds that can wander beyond all limit and satiety. Why should we then affect a rigor contrary to the manner of God and of nature, by abridging or scanting those means, which books freely permitted are, both to the trial of virtue and the exercise of truth?

It would be better done to learn that the law must needs be frivolous which goes to restrain things uncertainly and yet equally

[6] Foolish.
[7] Allowance.
[8] Thanks.
[9] Puppet show.
[10] How are pleasures the ingredients of virtue?

working to good and to evil. And were I the chooser, a dram of well-doing should be preferred before many times as much the forcible hindrance of evil-doing. For God sure esteems the growth and completing of one virtuous person more than the restraint of ten vicious. And albeit whatever thing we hear or see, sitting, walking, traveling, or conversing, may be fitly called our book, and is of the same effect that writings are; yet grant the thing to be prohibited were only books, it appears that this order hitherto is far insufficient to the end which it intends. Do we not see, not once or oftener, but weekly, that continued court-libel against the parliament and city printed, as the wet sheets can witness, and dispersed among us, for all that licensing can do? Yet this is the prime service, a man would think, wherein this order should give proof of itself. If it were executed, you'll say. But certain, if execution be remiss or blindfold now, and in this particular, what will it be hereafter and in other books? . . .

Another reason, whereby to make it plain that this order will miss the end it seeks, consider by the quality which ought to be in every licenser. It cannot be denied but that he who is made judge to sit upon the birth or death of books, whether they may be wafted into this world or not, had need to be a man above the common measure, both studious, learned, and judicious; there may be else no mean mistakes in the censure of what is passable or not, which is also no mean injury. If he be of such worth as behooves him, there cannot be a more tedious and unpleasing journey-work,[11] a greater loss of time levied upon his head, than to be made the perpetual reader of unchosen books and pamphlets, ofttimes huge volumes. There is no book that is acceptable unless at certain seasons; but to be enjoined the reading of that at all times, and in a hand scarce legible, whereof three pages would not down at any time in the fairest print, is an imposition which I cannot believe how he that values time and his own studies, or is but of a sensible [12] nostril, should be able to endure. . . .

[11] I.e., work paid for by the day and hence menial.
[12] I.e., sensitive to smell.

I lastly proceed from the no good it can do, to the manifest hurt it causes, in being first the greatest discouragement and affront that can be offered to learning and to learned men. . . .

If therefore ye be loath to dishearten utterly and discontent, not the mercenary crew of false pretenders to learning, but the free and ingenuous sort of such as evidently were born to study and love learning for itself, not for lucre or any other end but the service of God and of truth, and perhaps that lasting fame and perpetuity of praise which God and good men have consented shall be the reward of those whose published labors advance the good of mankind; then know, that so far to distrust the judgment and the honesty of one who hath but a common repute in learning, and never yet offended, as not to count him fit to print his mind without a tutor and examiner, lest he should drop a schism or something of corruption, is the greatest displeasure and indignity to a free and knowing spirit that can be put upon him. . . .

And how can a man teach with authority, which is the life of teaching, how can he be a doctor in his book, as he ought to be, or else had better be silent, whenas all he teaches, all he delivers, is but under the tuition, under the correction, of his patriarchal licenser, to blot or alter what precisely accords not with the hidebound humor which he calls his judgment? When every acute reader, upon the first sight of a pedantic license, will be ready with these like words to ding the book a quoit's distance from him: "I hate a pupil teacher, I endure not an instructor that comes to me under the wardship of an overseeing fist. I know nothing of the licenser, but that I have his own hand here for his arrogance; who shall warrant me his judgment?" "The state, sir," replies the stationer, but has a quick return: "The state shall be my governors, but not my critics; they may be mistaken in the choice of a licenser, as easily as this licenser may be mistaken in an author. This is some common stuff." And he might add from Sir Francis Bacon, that "such authorized books are but the language of the times." For though a licenser should happen to be judicious more than ordinary (which will be a great jeopardy of the next succession), yet his very office and his commission enjoins him to let pass [5] nothing but what is vulgarly [13] received already.

Nay, which is more lamentable, if the work of any deceased author, though never so famous in his lifetime and even to this day, [10] come to their hands for license to be printed or reprinted, if there be found in his book one sentence of a venturous edge, uttered in the height of zeal (and who knows whether it might not be the dictate of a divine spirit?), [15] yet not suiting with every low decrepit humor of their own, though it were Knox himself, the reformer of a kingdom, that spake it, they will not pardon him their dash; the sense of that great man shall to all posterity be lost, [20] for the fearfulness or the presumptuous rashness of a perfunctory licenser. And to what an author this violence hath been lately done, and in what book of greatest consequence to be faithfully published, I could now instance, [25] but shall forbear till a more convenient season. Yet if these things be not resented seriously and timely by them who have the remedy in their power, but that such ironmolds as these shall have authority to gnaw out [30] the choicest periods of exquisitest books, and to commit such a treacherous fraud against the orphan remainders of worthiest men after death, the more sorrow will belong to that hapless race of men whose misfortune it is [35] to have understanding. Henceforth let no man care to learn, or care to be more than worldly wise; for certainly in higher matters to be ignorant and slothful, to be a common steadfast dunce, will be the only pleasant life, [40] and only in request.

And as it is a particular disesteem of every knowing person alive, and most injurious to the written labors and monuments of the dead, so to me it seems an undervaluing and [45] vilifying of the whole nation. I cannot set so light by all the invention, the art, the wit, the grave and solid judgment which is in England, as that it can be comprehended in

any twenty capacities, how good soever; much less that it should not pass except their superintendence be over it, except it be sifted and strained with their strainers, that it should [5] be uncurrent without their manual stamp. Truth and understanding are not such wares as to be monopolized and traded in by tickets and statutes and standards. We must not think to make a staple commodity of all the [10] knowledge in the land, to mark and license it like our broadcloth and our woolpacks. . . .

There is yet behind of what I purposed to lay open, the incredible loss and detriment that this plot of licensing puts us to. More [15] than if some enemy at sea should stop up all our havens and ports and creeks, it hinders and retards the importation of our richest merchandise, truth. . . .

Truth indeed came once into the world with her divine master, and was a perfect shape most glorious to look on. But when he ascended, and his apostles after him were laid asleep, then straight arose a wicked race of deceivers, who (as that story goes of the Egyptian Typhon with his conspirators, how they dealt with the good Osiris) took the virgin Truth, hewed her lovely form into a thousand pieces, and scattered them to the four winds. From that time ever since, the sad friends of Truth, such as durst appear, imitating the careful search that Isis made for the mangled body of Osiris, went up and down gathering up limb by limb still as they could find them. We have not yet found them all, Lords and Commons, nor ever shall do, till her master's second coming; he shall bring together every joint and member, and shall mold them into an immortal feature of loveliness and perfection. Suffer not these licensing prohibitions to stand at every place of opportunity, forbidding and disturbing them that continue seeking, that continue to do our obsequies [14] to the torn body of our martyred saint.[15] We boast our light; but if we look not wisely on the sun itself, it smites us into darkness. Who can discern those planets that are oft combust, and those stars

[13] Commonly.

[14] Acts of reverence.
[15] How does Milton use the myth of Isis, Typhon, and Osiris to illustrate his distrust of censorship?

of brightest magnitude that rise and set with the sun, until the opposite motion of their orbs bring them to such a place in the firmament where they may be seen evening or morning? The light [16] which we have gained was given us, not to be ever staring on, but by it to discover onward things more remote from our knowledge. . . .

(1644)

STUDY AIDS: 1. Who suffers under censorship—writers, readers, teachers, censors? Milton gives several separate arguments against censorship. What are they? Which are the most telling

[16] What is the meaning of "light" in this passage?

ones? Is their effectiveness a matter of the substance of the argument or of Milton's rhetorical expression?

2. Can you think of conditions under which censorship would be justified? Milton's opposition to censorship presupposes alert, intelligent readers. Since many readers today are lazy or stupid, it may be that they are incapable of exercising the responsibility that goes with the freedom to read. Do you agree?

3. Although the *Areopagitica* is in the form of an oration, it was meant to be read, not delivered as a speech. Find illustrations of the following qualities of prose style in the "parable of truth" (p. 297/2, ll. 19–44): EUPHONY and CACOPHONY. How do the sounds agree with the sense where they are used?

The Restoration
and Eighteenth Century

SAMUEL PEPYS RECORDS IN HIS "DIARY" THE REJOICING IN ENG-
land at the return of Charles Stuart to the throne:

May 25, 1660. By the morning we were come close to the
land, and every body made ready to get on shore. The King and
the two Dukes did eat their breakfast before they went, and
there being set some ship's diet . . . they eat of nothing else but
peas and pork, and boiled beef. . . . About noon (though the
brigantine that Beale made was there ready to carry him) yet
he [the King] would go in my Lord's barge with the two Dukes.
Our captain steered, and my Lord went along bare with him. I
went, and Mr. Mansell, and one of the King's footmen, with a
dog that the King loved . . . in a boat by ourselves, and so got
on shore when the King did, who was received by General Monk
with all imaginable love and respect at his entrance upon the land
of Dover. Infinite the crowd of people and the horsemen, citizens,
and noblemen of all sorts. The mayor of the town came and gave
him his white staff, the badge of his place, which the King did give
him again. The mayor also presented him from the town a very
rich Bible, which he took and said it was the thing that he loved
above all things in the world. A canopy was provided for him to stand
under, which he did, and talked awhile with General Monk and
others, and so into a stately coach there set for him, and so away
through the town towards Canterbury, without making any stay at
Dover. The shouting and joy expressed by all is past imagination. . . .

299

Despite this jubilation, most Englishmen were hostile to Stuart absolutism, which earlier had provoked the Puritan uprising and brought Charles I to the headsman's block. Their opposition was religious as well as political. With England largely a Protestant country, Charles II's sympathy with Roman Catholicism made for suspicion and unrest. Because the Anglican church was a state church and the King its nominal head, this Protestant-Catholic controversy, troublesome since the reign of Henry VIII, was to plague England again during the latter days of the Stuart dynasty.

Its first major eruption was the "Popish Plot" of 1678. Titus Oates, an unstable and unreliable man, had returned from Spain with reports that Louis XIV's army was to invade England, depose Charles II, and replace him with the Catholic James Stuart, Duke of York. A wave of hysteria swept England. Dryden, an eyewitness of the times, records the scene in *Absalom and Achitophel*.

> From hence began that plot, the nation's curse,
> Bad in itself, but represented worse;
> Raised in extremes, and in extremes decried;
> With oaths affirmed, with dying vows denied;
> Not weighed or winnowed by the multitude;
> But swallowed in the mass, unchewed and crude.
> Some truth there was, but dashed and brewed with lies,
> To please the fools and puzzle all the wise.
> Succeeding time did equal folly call,
> Believing nothing, or believing all.
>
> (ll. 108–117)

In 1681, four years before the death of Charles II, his favorite illegitimate son, the Protestant Duke of Monmouth, inspired by his evil genius, the Earl of Shaftesbury, raised a rebellion to forestall the naming of the Catholic James Stuart as the next king. The rebellion failed but broke out again in 1685 at James II's accession to the throne. The new monarch's arrogant behavior and pro-Catholic policies caused him to be deposed and to be replaced with his Protestant daughter, Mary, and her husband, William of Orange.

This "Glorious Revolution" of 1688 settled the religious controversy of the previous two centuries by establishing a law of Protestant succession to the throne. Even more important was the political settlement, which resolved the old dispute over the location of the ultimate political power: in 1688 the supreme power of government was recognized as residing not in the Crown but in Parliament, where it has remained ever since. The last Stuart monarch, Queen Anne, ascended the throne at the death of William III in 1702 and reigned until her death in 1714. When she died without an heir, Parliament through the Act of Succession (1701) named George, the elector of Hanover, as king. The Hanoverian monarchs have occupied the English throne to this day.

Political viewpoints began to emerge quite clearly during the Restoration period, when the religious problems of England, so closely interwoven with politics, became acute. One group, composed of the aristocracy, clergy, and landed gentry, found their interests were best furthered by a strong monarchy. Eventually they became the Tory (conservative) party. Another group, the merchant middle class, largely descended from Puritans, became the Whig (liberal) party. They desired a voice in government and so favored a strong Parliament. Since both parties had to obtain the support of the "moderates," or undecided voters, in order to gain a majority in Parliament, Whig and Tory leaders employed writers to present party views to the public. Some of England's best writers in the early eighteenth century were therefore journalists, men who for the first time in English literary history were freed from living on patronage from a lord. Addison, Steele, and Defoe wrote for the Whigs; Dryden and Swift for the Tories. From this newly created journalism developed the periodical essay, which began with Defoe's *Review* (1704–1713) and continued down the century through Addison and Steele's *Tatler* (1709–1711) and *Spectator* (1711–1712), Dr. Johnson's *Rambler* (1750–1752) and *Idler* (1758–1760), to Goldsmith's *Citizen of the World* (1760–1761).

These essays, which resemble the feature stories and editorials of today, seem quite modern to us, as do the ideas and feelings reflected in the literature of the eighteenth century. The era is important to us because it gave birth to our own age. The Renaissance had extolled man's faculty of reason as one of his greatest gifts. Reason and common sense came more and more to be valued as guides to truth in the Restoration and early eighteenth century, which is why the period is often called the "Age of Reason," or "The Enlightenment." The effects of reason are to be seen in all its activities, on every page of its literature. When the age applied reason systematically to the study of nature, experimental science, earlier popularized by Francis Bacon, began to show rapid advances. In 1662 Charles II chartered the Royal Society for the advancement of this study. Men began to accept as true only that which the evidence of their senses and their reason attested. This same rationalism, when applied to religion, gave rise to Deism, or religion based on the natural (reason) rather than on the supernatural (faith). Even the language of poetry was subjected to the demands of reason and science. The result was a poetry of factual statement rather than one of imagery, a poetry based on denotation instead of connotation. Expression was controlled and restricted by the heroic couplet. Elizabethan blank verse from the pens of Shakespeare's successors had degenerated into a loose line ranging from seven to fourteen syllables. The close-knit heroic couplet tightened expression, and its compression and economy ruled out verbal excesses. Clarity of statement and plain language were the keynotes of style, replacing the Elizabethan ambiguities and richness of expression.

This application of reason to literature produced in England an age of classicism. The Renaissance had rediscovered the ancient literatures of Greece and Rome. When the eighteenth century looked at the writings of antiquity it saw many parallels between the time of Augustus Caesar in Rome and its own. That earlier literature had been rational also, and the eighteenth century liked to think of itself as "Augustan." Imitation of the earlier period was inevitable, and the age is therefore known as "neo-classic." Horace had been the literary spokesman of Rome, and Horace became the model of the English Augustan writers. When Horace had looked at his society through the eyes of reason, he had seen it as irrational in many respects and had written satire to rebuke the folly and unreason of his day. Similarly, Dryden, Pope, and Swift chastised the man who strayed from the middle of the road to an extreme on either side. Their work is the greatest satirical writing in our language. Horace had proclaimed "decorum" as a guiding principle to keep society from extremes. The Augustan satirists preached the same doctrine. Any excess was branded as "enthusiastic," or fanatical; it threatened social order and unity. Strict adherence to a social and intellectual norm was the prevailing belief of the day. This norm was established by accepting the behavior and beliefs of all civilized men, particularly those of Rome, as the model. Since the eighteenth century believed that the classical writers of antiquity had best preserved this rational norm in its literature, the genres and methods of the ancients, which had been codified into a set of "rules" by Italian and French Renaissance critics, were readily accepted by the Augustans as admirable models to be imitated. It was "reasonable" to assume that literature too had its "scientific" rules. Dryden's *Essay of Dramatic Poesy* (1668) and Pope's *Essay on Criticism* (1711) discuss at length the values and dangers inherent in these rules, which continued to influence lesser writers until Dr. Johnson, in his *Preface to Shakespeare* (1765), laid bare their fallacious assumptions.

The drama was, perhaps, the domain over which the "rules" exercised their greatest sway. When the theaters reopened in 1660, Shakespearean tragedy was replaced by the "heroic drama," a form which combined the wildly romantic subject matter of the tragi-comedies and romances of Beaumont and Fletcher with the classic structure dictated by the three unities, decorum, and propriety as observed by contemporary French drama. Possibly Charles II and his court, while in exile in France during the Commonwealth, developed a taste for the French classical drama.

If the "heroic drama" bore little relation to real life and was of an inferior quality, Restoration comedy was intensely realistic and is considered by many to be England's greatest comedy. It is a comedy of manners, and as such it is related to the social satire so prominent in the period's poetry and prose. Its writers form a galaxy of England's stellar dramatists: Dryden, Congreve, Etherege, Wycherley, Farquhar, and Vanbrugh.

Although the drama was more rigidly controlled by the "rules" than was any other form of literature, it was also the first to show a reaction against the tyranny of reason. The Restoration theater had been almost exclusively a court entertainment, but in the 1680's the theater became more a public institution. The middle class, particularly its feminine members, began attending performances. A change in the drama was almost immediately discernible. The tragedies of Thomas Otway, Thomas Southerne, and Nicholas Rowe emphasized pity, emotion, and tears. Pathetic women became the protagonists of such plays as Rowe's *Jane Shore* and *Lady Jane Grey*. Sentimentalism did not confine itself to tragedy. The hard, brilliant, and rational comedies of the Restoration competed for a hearing with sentimental comedies like Colley Cibber's *Love's Last Shift* (1696) and Richard Steele's *The Lying Lover* (1703). This new comedy proclaimed that man should be judged by his good intentions and feelings, of which tears were subjective proof, rather than by reason or an objective norm of behavior. Feeling was replacing reason as the standard of social right and wrong. Sentimentalism was heralding the coming romanticism.

Sentimentalism is to be found a little later in the poetry of the mid-eighteenth century. One of the most clearly defined feelings expressed by this poetry was melancholy, often induced by solitude. The "graveyard school" of poets (such as Robert Blair, Edward Young, Thomas Gray) and the poets of solitude, imitators of Milton's *Il Penseroso* (e.g., Thomas Warton the Elder, Thomas Warton the Younger, Joseph Warton, Mark Akenside) were widely read.

This sentimentalism found a more practical expression in dealing with social conditions produced by the industrial expansion of England in the third quarter of the eighteenth century. During the last half of the century, England changed from an agricultural to an industrial economy. Goldsmith's *Deserted Village* (1770) laments the change. Cities grew, and with them slums developed; working conditions were as appalling as housing.

A spirit of humanitarianism began to manifest itself and found its voice in Jean Jacques Rousseau, the French philosopher of romanticism. Society was corrupt and the city degraded man; a return to nature, to the simple rural life, was his hope of salvation. William Cowper confidently states, "God made the country, and man made the town" (*The Task*, 1, 749), and Blake's *Songs of Innocence* and *Songs of Experience* chronicle the urban and rural life in a symbolic portrayal of evil and good. The age was ready for a Wordsworth to trumpet a return to nature and to the simple life of the common man.

Classicism, however, was not dead throughout the latter half of the eighteenth century. Even men in sympathy with the ideals of romanticism continued to write in neoclassic forms. The heroic couplet often urged Primitivism, the return to an earlier, less complicated society; the ode often praised solitude and faraway exotic places. Even the novel, a new form, as it developed from its beginnings in Defoe through Richardson's *Pamela* (1740) and Fielding's *Joseph Andrews* (1742), while often romantic in subject matter, remained true to the classical Horatian end of literature—to instruct and to please. And over most of these men of the latter half of the century Dr. Johnson cast his huge and awesome shadow. As long as Samuel Johnson lived, the coming romanticism had a formidable opponent.

Samuel Pepys
(1633–1703)

WHILE PEPYS IS KNOWN TO THE MODERN WORLD AS THE GREATEST DIARIST OF ENGLISH literature, he was unknown as a writer in his own lifetime. His reputation at that time rested upon his abilities as an able, efficient, and honest administrator of the British navy.

He was born of an ancient and respectable family. After an undistinguished career at Cambridge university, he married a young French girl, Elizabeth St. Michel, in 1655, and five years later became secretary to his cousin, Edward Montagu (later Earl of Sandwich), the Joint Commander of the Fleet. Montagu, with Pepys in attendance, brought Charles II back to England in May, 1660. The connection with Montagu thus placed Pepys in the midst of Restoration affairs and launched his governmental career. In 1660 he was appointed Clerk of the Acts of the Navy; later he was promoted to the position of Secretary of the Admiralty, a post he held until 1688.

The *Diary* covers the years 1660–1669. Pepys wrote it in an obscure shorthand devised by Thomas Shelton in 1620. The manuscript lay unknown and undeciphered until 1825, but since that time its literary reputation has steadily increased. Its historical value is great, for Pepys gives an eyewitness account of exciting events, and he pictures many persons of the day, both famous and obscure. Its literary value is even greater. The *Diary* records an intelligent human being's emotional response to the flux of life in a colorful age. Pepys felt great joy in living; he even found some pleasure in the less happy incidents of his life. Since the manuscript was in code, he felt no reticence in frankly and honestly describing many unsavory details of his experiences. Many passages describe his marital infidelities and the consequent quarrels with his wife Betty. Pepys had many interests: music, art, literature, the theater, human beings—especially pretty women—walks in the country, the hubbub of London, his work in the Navy. As we read the *Diary* we experience with the author both the crises and the trivial incidents in the adventure of living.

The Diary of Samuel Pepys

May 25, 1660: By the morning we were come close to the land, and every body made ready to get on shore. The King and the two Dukes did eat their breakfast before they went, and there being set some ship's diet 5 before them, only to show them the manner of the ship's diet, they eat of nothing else but peas and pork, and boiled beef. I had Mr. Darcy in my cabin and Dr. Clerke, who eat with me, told me how the King had given 10 £50 to Mr. Sheply for my Lord's [1] servants, and £500 among the officers and common men of the ship. I spoke with the Duke of York about business, who called me Pepys by name, and upon my desire did promise me 15 his future favor. Great expectation of the King's making some knights, but there was none. About noon (though the brigantine that Beale made was there ready to carry him) yet he would go in my Lord's barge 20 with the two Dukes. Our captain steered, and my Lord went along bare with him. I went, and Mr. Mansell, and one of the King's footmen, with a dog that the King loved (which [dirtied] the boat, which made us laugh, and 25 methink that a King and all that belong to him are but just as others are), in a boat by ourselves, and so got on shore when the King did, who was received by General Monk with all imaginable love and respect at his 30 entrance upon the land of Dover. Infinite the crowd of people and the horsemen, citizens, and noblemen of all sorts. The mayor of the town came and gave him his white staff, the badge of his place, which the King did give 35 him again. The mayor also presented him from the town a very rich Bible, which he took and said it was the thing that he loved above all things in the world. A canopy was

provided for him to stand under, which he did, and talked awhile with General Monk and others, and so into a stately coach there set for him, and so away through the town 5 toward Canterbury, without making any stay at Dover. The shouting and joy expressed by all is past imagination. Seeing that my Lord did not stir out of his barge, I got into a boat, and so into his barge, whither Mr. John Crew stepped, and spoke a word or two to my Lord, and so returned, we back to the ship, and going did see a man almost drowned that fell out of his boat into the sea, but with much ado was got out. My Lord almost transported with joy that he had done all this without any the least blur or obstruction in the world, that could give an offense to any, and with the great honor he thought it would be to him. Being overtook by the brigantine, my Lord and we went out of our barge into it, and so went on board with Sir W. Batten and the Vice and Rear-Admirals. At night my Lord supped and Mr. Thomas Crew with Captain Stokes; I supped with the captain, who told me what the King had given us. My Lord returned late, and at his coming did give me order to cause the mark to be gilded, and a crown and C. R. to be made at the head of the coach table, where the King today with his own hand did mark his height, which accordingly I caused the painter to do, and is now done as is to be seen.

June 28, 1660: My brother Tom [2] came to me with patterns to choose for a suit. I paid him all to this day, and did give him £10 upon account. To Mr. Coventry, who told me that he would do me all right in my business. To

[1] Pepys' cousin, the Earl of Sandwich.

[2] Pepys' younger brother, Thomas, who carried on their father's tailoring business.

Sir G. Downing, the first visit I have made him since he came. He is so stingy a fellow I care not to see him; I quite cleared myself of his office, and did give him liberty to take any body in. Hawly and he are parted too; he is going to serve Sir Thos. Ingram. I went also this morning to see Mrs. Pierce, the surgeon['s wife]. I found her in bed in her house in Margaret Churchyard. Her husband returned to sea. I did invite her to go to dinner with me and my wife today. After all this to my Lord, who lay abed till eleven o'clock, it being almost five before he went to bed, they supped so late last night with the King. This morning I saw poor Bishop Wren going to chapel, it being a thanksgiving day for the King's return. After my Lord was awake, I went up to him to the nursery, where he do lie, and, having talked with him a little, I took leave and carried my wife and Mrs. Pierce to Clothworkers' Hall, to dinner, where Mr. Pierce, the purser, met us. We were invited to Mr. Chaplin, the victualer, where Nich. Osborne was. Our entertainment very good, a brave hall, good company, and very good music. Where among other things I was pleased that I could find out a man by his voice, whom I had never seen before, to be one that sang behind the curtain formerly at Sir W. Davenant's opera. Here Dr. Gauden and Mr. Gauden the victualer dined with us. After dinner to Mr. Rawlinson's, to see him and his wife, and would have gone to my aunt Wight, but that her only child, a daughter, died last night. Home and to my Lord, who supped within, and Mr. E. Montagu, Mr. Thos. Crew, and others with him sat up late. I home and to bed.

July 10, 1660: This day I put on first my new silk suit, the first that ever I wore in my life. This morning came Nan Pepys' husband Mr. Hall to see me being lately come to town. I had never seen him before. I took him to the Swan tavern with Mr. Eglin and there drank our morning draft. Home, and called my wife, and took her to Dr. Clodius's to a great wedding of Nan Hartlib to Mynheer Roder, which was kept at Goring House with very great state, cost, and noble company. But,

among all the beauties there, my wife was thought the greatest. After dinner I left the company, and carried my wife to Mrs. Turner's. I went to the Attorney General's, and had my bill, which cost me seven pieces. I called my wife, and set her home. And finding my Lord in White Hall garden, I got him to go to the Secretary's, which he did, and desired the dispatch of his and my bills to be signed by the King. His bill [3] is to be Earl of Sandwich, Viscount Hinchingbroke, and Baron of St. Neot's. Home, with my mind pretty quiet: not returning, as I said I would, to see the bride put to bed.

July 15, 1660: Lay long in bed to recover my rest. Going forth met with Mr. Sheply, and went and drank my morning draft with him at Wilkinson's, and my brother Spicer. [4] After that to Westminster Abbey, and in Henry the Seventh's Chapel heard part of a sermon, the first that ever I heard there. To my Lord's and dined all alone at the table with him. After dinner he and I alone fell to discourse, and I find him plainly to be a skeptic in all things of religion, and to make no great matter of anything therein, but to be a perfect Stoic. In the afternoon to Henry the Seventh's Chapel, where I heard service and a sermon there, and after that meeting W. Bowyer there, he and I to the park, and walked a good while till night. So to Harper's and drank together, and Captain Stokes came to us and so I fell into discourse of buying paper at the first hand in my office, and the captain promised me to buy it for me in France. After that to my Lord's lodgings, where I wrote some business and so home. My wife at home all the day, she having no clothes out, all being packed up yesterday. For this month I have wholly neglected anything of news, and so have beyond belief been ignorant how things go, but now by my patent [5] my mind is in some quiet, which God keep. I was not at my father's today, I being afraid to go for fear he should

---

[3] Title.
[4] I.e., brother clerk of the Privy Seal, not a blood relative.
[5] Appointment to office.

still solicit me to speak to my Lord for a place in the Wardrobe, which I dare not do, because of my own business yet. My wife and I mightily pleased with our new house that we hope to have. My patent has cost me a great deal of money, about £40, which is the only thing at present which do trouble me much. In the afternoon to Henry the Seventh's Chapel, where I heard a sermon and spent (God forgive me) most of my time in looking upon Mrs. Butler. After that with W. Bowyer to walk in the park. Afterwards to my Lord's lodgings, and so home to bed, having not been at my father's today.

November 22, 1660: This morning came the carpenters to make me a door at the other side of my house, going into the entry, which I was much pleased with. At noon my wife and I walked to the Old Exchange, and there she bought her a white whisk [6] and put it on, and I a pair of gloves, and so we took coach for White Hall to Mr. Fox's, where we found Mrs. Fox within, and an alderman of London paying £1,000 or £1,400 in gold upon the table for the King, which was the most gold that ever I saw together in my life. Mr. Fox came in presently and did receive us with a great deal of respect; and then did take my wife and I to the Queen's presence-chamber, where he got my wife placed behind the Queen's chair, and I got into the crowd, and by and by the Queen and the two Princesses came to dinner. The Queen a very little plain old woman, and nothing more in her presence in any respect nor garb than any ordinary woman. The Princess of Orange I had often seen before. The Princess Henrietta is very pretty, but much below my expectation; and her dressing of herself with her hair frizzed short up to her ears, did make her seem so much the less to me. But my wife standing near her with two or three black patches on, and well dressed, did seem to me much handsomer than she. Dinner being done, we went to Mr. Fox's again, where many gentlemen dined with us, and most princely dinner, all provided for me and my friends, but I bringing none but myself

[6] Scarf.

and wife, he did call the company to help to eat up so much good victuals. At the end of dinner, my Lord Sandwich's health was drunk in the gilt tankard that I did give to Mrs. Fox the other day. After dinner I had notice given me by Will my man that my Lord did inquire for me, so I went to find him, and met him and the Duke of York in a coach going toward Charing Cross. I endeavored to follow them but could not, so I returned to Mr. Fox, and after much kindness and good discourse we parted from thence. I took coach for my wife and me homewards, and I light at the Maypole in the Strand, and sent my wife home. I to the new playhouse and saw part of the "Traitor," [7] a very good tragedy; Mr. Moon did act the traitor very well. So to my Lord's, and sat there with my Lady a great while talking. Among other things, she took occasion to inquire (by Madame Dury's late discourse with her) how I did treat my wife's father and mother. At which I did give her a good account, and she seemed to be very well opinioned of my wife. From thence to White Hall at about 9 at night, and there, with Laud the page that went with me, we could not get out of Henry the Eighth's gallery into the further part of the boarded gallery, where my Lord was walking with my Lord Ormond; and we had a key of Sir S. Morland's, but all would not do; till at last, by knocking, Mr. Harrison the doorkeeper did open us the door, and, after some talk with my Lord about getting a catch to carry my Lord St. Albans' goods to France, I parted and went home on foot, it being very late and dirty, and so weary to bed.

April 27, 1663: Up betimes and to my office, where doing business alone a good while till people came about business to me. Will Griffin tells me this morning that Captain Browne, Sir W. Batten's brother-in-law, is dead of a blow given him two days ago by a seaman, a servant of his, being drunk, with a stone striking him on the forehead, for which I am sorry, he having a good woman and several small children. At the office all the morning,

[7] By James Shirley. First acted in 1635.

at noon dined at home with my wife, merry, and after dinner by water to White Hall; but found the Duke of York gone to St. James's for this summer; and thence with Mr. Coventry, to whose chamber I went, and Sir W. Pen up to the Duke's closet. And a good while with him about our Navy business; and so I to White Hall, and there alone a while with my Lord Sandwich discoursing about his debt to the navy, wherein he hath given me some things to resolve him in. Thence to my Lord's lodging, and thither came Creed to me, and he and I walked a great while in the garden, and thence to an alehouse in the market place to drink fine Lambeth ale, and so to Westminster Hall, and after walking there a great while, home by coach, where I found Mary gone from my wife, she being too high for her, though a very good servant, and my boy too will be going in a few days, for he is not for my family; he is grown so out of order and not to be ruled, and do himself, against his brother's counsel, desire to be gone, which I am sorry for, because I love the boy and would be glad to bring him to good. At home with my wife and Ashwell talking of her going into the country this year, wherein we had like to have fallen out, she thinking that I have a design to have her go, which I have not, and to let her stay here I perceive will not be convenient, for she expects more pleasure than I can give her here, and I fear I have done very ill in letting her begin to learn to dance. The Queen (which I did not know) it seems was at Windsor, at the late St. George's feast there; and the Duke of Monmouth dancing with her with his hat in hand, the King came in and kissed him, and made him put on his hat, which every body took notice of. After being a while at my office, home to supper and to bed, my Will being come home again after being at his father's all the last week taking physic.

April 28, 1663: Up betimes and to my office, and there all the morning, only stepped up to see my wife and dancing master at it, and I think after all she will do pretty well at it. So to dinner, Mr. Hunt dining with us, and so to the office, where we sat late, and then

I to my office casting up my Lord's sea accounts over again, and putting them in order for payment, and so home to supper and to bed.

August 31, 1665: Up; and, after putting several things in order to my removal, to Woolwich; the plague having a great increase this week, beyond all expectation of almost 2,000, making the general bill 7,000, odd 100; and the plague above 6,000. I down by appointment to Greenwich, to our office, where I did some business, and there dined with our company and Sir W. Boreman, and Sir The. Biddulph, at Mr. Boreman's, where a good venison pasty, and after a good merry dinner I to my office, and there late writing letters, and then to Woolwich by water, where pleasant with my wife and people, and after supper to bed. Thus this month ends with great sadness upon the public, through the greatness of the plague every where through the kingdom almost. Every day sadder and sadder news of its increase. In the city died this week 7,496 and of them 6,102 of the plague. But it is feared that the true number of the dead this week is near 10,000; partly from the poor that cannot be taken notice of, through the greatness of the number, and partly from the Quakers and others that will not have any bell ring for them. Our fleet [has in it] the Sovereign one; so that it is a better fleet than the former with the Duke was. All our fear is that the Dutch should be got in before them; which would be a very great sorrow to the public, and to me particularly, for my Lord Sandwich's sake. A great deal of money being spent, and the kingdom not in a condition to spare, nor a parliament without much difficulty to meet to give more. And to that; to have it said, what hath been done by our late fleets? As to myself I am very well, only in fear of the plague, and as much of an ague by being forced to go early and late to Woolwich, and my family to lie there continually. My late gettings have been very great to my great content, and am likely to have yet a few more profitable jobs in a little while; for which Tangier and Sir W. Warren I am wholly obliged to.

December 28: 1666: Up, and Creed and I walked (a very fine walk in the frost) to my Lord Bellasses, but missing him did find him at White Hall, and there spoke with him about some Tangier business. That done, we to Creed's lodgings, which are very pretty, but he is going from them. So we to Lincoln's Inn Fields, he to Ned Pickering's, who it seems lives there, keeping a good house, and I to my Lord Crew's, where I dined, and [10] hear the news how my Lord's brother, Mr. Nathaniel Crew, hath an estate of 6 or £700 *per annum,* left him by the death of an old acquaintance of his, but not akin to him at all. And this man is dead without will, but [15] had, above ten years since, made over his estate to this Mr. Crew, to him and his heirs for ever, and giving Mr. Crew the keeping of the deeds in his own hand all this time; by which, if he would, he might have taken [20] present possession of the estate, for he knew what they were. This is as great an act of confident friendship as this latter age, I believe, can show. From hence to the Duke's house, and there saw "Macbeth" most ex- [25] cellently acted, and a most excellent play for variety. I had sent for my wife to meet me there, who did come, and after the play was done, I out so soon to meet her at the other door that I left my cloak in the playhouse, and while I returned to get it, she was gone out and missed me, and with W. Hewer away home. I not sorry for it much did go to White Hall, and got my Lord Bellasses to get me into the playhouse; and there, after all staying above an hour for the players, the King and all waiting, which was absurd, saw "Henry the Fifth" well done by the Duke's people, and in most excellent habits, all new vests, being put on but this night. But I sat so high and far off, that I missed most of the words, and sat with a wind coming into my back and neck, which did much trouble me. The play continued till twelve at night; and then up, and a most horrid cold night it was, and frosty, and moonshine. But the worst was, I had left my cloak at Sir G. Carteret's, and they being abed I was forced to go home without it. So by chance got a coach and to the Golden Lion Tavern in the Strand, and there drank some mulled sack, and so home, where find my poor wife staying for me, and then to bed mighty cold.

John Dryden

(1631–1700)

Dryden and Pope are considered the major representatives of classicism in English literature. Dryden began his study of the classics under the famous Dr. Busby at Westminster School and continued at Trinity College, Cambridge University, from which he was graduated in 1654. A few years later he went to London, and as early as 1663 he was writing plays for the newly opened theaters. Although Dryden never felt that dramatic writing was congenial to his taste and talent, he continued to earn his living by this means until 1693. During this same period and until his death, he also produced much occasional verse, poetic satire, literary criticism, translations of the classics, and some lyric verse.

Most of Dryden's poetry and drama was written in the heroic couplet. To the untutored modern reader this verse form seems stilted and perhaps monotonous; certainly it appears restrictive and tight. These latter qualities are those which appealed to Dryden's time, which saw in the poet's sure control of his verse a parallel to the belief of the age that reason should control the emotions and thus produce order in society. Too, the couplet was felt to discipline and tighten poetic expression, which had become lax in the hands of Shakespeare's successors. The Royal Society was at that time demanding that the language be made a stable instrument of communication. Bishop Thomas Sprat, in his *History of the Royal Society* (1667), described this stabilizing as a rejection of "all amplifications, digressions, and swellings of style; to return back to the primitive purity and shortness, when men delivered so many *things* almost in an equal number of *words*. They have exacted from all their members a close, naked, natural way of speaking, positive expressions, clear senses, a native easiness, bringing all things as near the mathematical plainness as they can, and preferring the language of artisans, countrymen, and merchants, before that of wits or scholars." As a member of the Royal Society, Dryden tried to satisfy this demand and to make his poetry "scientific." The result was that in place of a poetry of actual metaphor he wrote a "poetry of statement," which reconciled the qualities of poetry with those of prose.

Dryden's personal life and the subject matter of his writing reflect the conflicting attitudes of England's most turbulent century. In politics he moved from a Whig position, seen in his first major poem, *Heroic Stanzas on the Death of Cromwell* (1659), to the Toryism of *Absalom and Achitophel* (1681). His religious development was also from left to right—from Puritanism (*Heroic Stanzas . . .*) to Anglicanism (*Religio Laici,* 1682) to Roman Catholicism (*The Hind and the Panther,* 1687).

To My Honored Friend, Dr. Charleton

Dryden's poem was written as a prefatory poetic compliment to *Chorea Gigantum* (1663), a book by Walter Charleton, well-known physician, member of the Royal Society, and writer on various scientific subjects. Charleton's book had postulated that Stonehenge was built by the Danes as a place to crown their kings. The poem is an excellent example of Dryden's "poetry of statement" and of his ability to follow a line of logical argument through a poem.

The longest tyranny [1] that ever swayed
Was that wherein our ancestors betrayed
Their free-born reason to the Stagirite,
And made his torch their universal light.
So truth, while only one supplied the state, 5
Grew scarce, and dear, and yet sophisticate; [2]
Until 'twas bought, like emp'ric [3] wares, or
    charms,
Hard words sealed up with Aristotle's arms.

[1] The pre-seventeenth-century tendency to accept as true any statement based on the authority of Aristotle ("Stagirite") rather than to test it by reason and experimentation.
[2] Refined to the point of uselessness. Members of the Royal Society often compared the speculations of the scholastics to cobwebs.
[3] Home, or natural, medical wares; hence, of dubious value as medicine.

Columbus was the first that shook his throne,
And found a temperate in a torrid zone, 10
The feverish air fanned by a cooling breeze,
The fruitful vales set round with shady trees;
And guiltless men, who danced away their
    time,
Fresh as their groves, and happy as their
    clime.
Had we still paid that homage to a name, 15
Which only God and nature justly claim,
The western seas had been our utmost bound,
Where poets still might dream the sun was
    drowned:
And all the stars that shine in southern skies
Had been admired by none but savage
    eyes. 20
    Among the asserters of free reason's claim,

The English are not the least in worth or
fame.
The world to Bacon [4] does not only owe
Its present knowledge, but its future too.
Gilbert [5] shall live, till loadstones cease to
draw,   25
Or British fleets the boundless ocean awe.
And noble Boyle,[6] not less in nature seen,
Than his great brother [7] read in states and
men.
The circling streams, once thought but pools,
of blood
(Whether life's fuel or the body's food)   30
From dark oblivion Harvey's [8] name shall
save;
While Ent [9] keeps all the honor that he
gave.
Nor are you, learned friend, the least re-
nowned;
Whose fame, not circumscribed with English
ground,
Flies like the nimble journeys of the light;   35
And is, like that, unspent too in its flight.
Whatever truths have been by art or chance
Redeemed from error, or from ignorance,
Thin in their authors, like rich veins of ore,
Your works unite, and still discover more.   40
Such is the healing virtue of your pen,
To perfect cures on books, as well as men.
Nor is this work the least: you well may give
To men new vigor, who makes stones to
live.
Through you, the Danes, their short dominion
lost,   45
A longer conquest than the Saxons boast.
Stonehenge, once thought a temple,[10] you
have found
A throne, where kings, our earthly gods, were
crowned;

Where by their wondering subjects they were
seen,
Joyed with their stature and their princely
mien.   50
Our sovereign here above the rest might
stand,
And here be chose again to rule the land.
  These ruins sheltered once his sacred
  head,[11]
Then when from Worcester's fatal field he
fled;
Watched by the genius of this royal place,   55
And mighty visions of the Danish race,
His refuge then was for a temple shown:
But, he restored, 'tis now become a throne.[12]
(1663)

STUDY AIDS. 1. The poem opens with a
generalization concerning the tyranny of scholasticism, epitomized by Aristotle, whom the age
regarded as its founder. From this generalization,
how does Dryden move to particulars to prove
that experimentation and the free use of reason
broke this tyranny (ll. 9–46)?

2. It is interesting that Dryden shows such
a strong nationalistic bias: with one exception
every illustration is British. What relation does
this have to the graceful compliment paid
Charles II in ll. 53–58? The use of free reason
had just restored the king, which meant an end
to tyranny and error. How had the use of free
reason by the British affected the long historical
development of their monarchic system?

3. In the long list of British scientists notice
Gilbert cited in ll. 25–26. This is not a simile,
metaphor, or any other figure of speech which
compares one thing to another. It is a statement
of fact. It is like prose. How does it produce
the effect of metaphoric language as it illuminates
l. 21? Although the statement is primarily
DENOTATIVE, does it have any CONNOTATIVE
qualities?

[4] Sir Francis Bacon, who popularized the new
experimental method of science and who in *The
New Atlantis* perhaps foreshadowed the Royal
Society.
[5] William Gilbert published a study of the properties of magnets in 1600.
[6] Robert Boyle, one of the founders of the Royal
Society, who specialized in the study of gases.
[7] Roger Boyle, a statesman and writer of heroic
drama.
[8] William Harvey, whose discovery (1616) of
the circulation of the blood supplanted the physiological theory of the "four humors,"

[9] Sir George Ent, one of the founders of the
Royal Society. Ent defended Harvey's theory in
several publications.
[10] Charleton's book was an answer to that of
Inigo Jones, who propounded the theory that Stonehenge had been a Roman temple.
[11] Charles II, when Prince of Wales, after the
defeat of his father's army at Worcester, had hidden
at Stonehenge on his journey into exile.
[12] Charles II has been restored *to* his throne even
as Stonehenge has been restored *as* a throne by
Charleton.

Prologue to "The Tempest"

Dryden wrote 102 known Prologues and Epilogues, which form a running commentary on the Restoration theater over a period of thirty years. These poems differ from anything else Dryden wrote in their colloquial diction and freedom from literary decorum. Taken as a whole, they form a genre in themselves, since they are not particularly relevant to the plays which they introduced or concluded, as were most of those written before Dryden's time. Any occasion might produce one from Dryden's pen: to compliment the king for attending a performance; to introduce a young playwright; to berate the audience for its low taste; or to discuss a point of literary taste or criticism.

This prologue was written for an adaptation of Shakespeare's play, The Tempest, by Dryden and Sir William Davenant. It shows Dryden's appreciation of Shakespeare, an attitude somewhat rare in an age which felt it necessary to "improve" the plays of the great dramatist.

As when a tree's cut down, the secret root
Lives under ground, and thence new branches
    shoot,
So from old Shakespeare's honored dust this
    day
Springs up and buds a new reviving play:
Shakespeare, who (taught by none) did first
    impart   5
To Fletcher [1] wit, to laboring Jonson art;
He, monarch-like, gave those his subjects law,
And is that nature [2] which they paint and
    draw.
Fletcher reached that which on his heights
    did grow,
Whilst Jonson crept and gathered all
    below.   10
This [3] did his love, and this his mirth digest:
One imitates him most, the other best.
If they have since out-writ all other men,
'Tis with the drops which fell from Shake-
    speare's pen.

The storm which vanished on the neighboring
    shore   15
Was taught by Shakespeare's Tempest first
    to roar.
That innocence and beauty, which did smile
In Fletcher, grew on this Enchanted Isle.[4]
But Shakespeare's magic [5] could not copied
    be;
Within that circle none durst walk but he. 20
I must confess 'twas bold, nor would you
    now
That liberty to vulgar wits allow,
Which works by magic supernatural things;
But Shakespeare's power is sacred as a king's.
Those legends from old priest-hood were
    received,   25
And he then writ, as people then believed.
But if for Shakespeare we your grace implore,
We for our theater shall want it more;

[1] John Fletcher, a late Elizabethan dramatist, whose plays were influential on the Restoration stage and drama. A close second to him was Ben Jonson, creator of "humor" comedies. Dryden is fond of discussing matters in terms of pairs of subjects, usually opposites or antitheses. Here Fletcher, because of his easy dialogue, represents "wit," or genius (inspiration); Jonson, because of his great learning in literary matters, particularly the neoclassic "rules," represents "art," or craftsmanship (technique).

[2] Since the time of Plato and Aristotle, it has been a commonly accepted axiom that "art is an imitation of nature." How then can art imitate art (ll. 8–10)?

[3] Notice how the original antithesis between Fletcher and Jonson (l. 6) continues through l. 12. If the comparison in ll. 9–10 is botanical, what aspect of Shakespeare's art did Fletcher best imitate? What aspect did Jonson catch best? Does this comparison have any relation to the opening simile of the poem? In l. 11, to whom does the first "this" refer? The second "this"? What writing of Shakespeare did Fletcher imitate, and what kind did Jonson follow? In l. 12, Dryden gives a judgment on the two imitators. Which one does he seem to prefer?

[4] A play by Fletcher, which was also an adaptation of Shakespeare's Tempest.

[5] Prospero, the protagonist in The Tempest, was a magician. Many critics believe that Shakespeare was portraying himself in Prospero and saying farewell to his magic, i.e., his writing.

Who by our dearth of youths are forced t'
employ
One of our women to present a boy.   30
And that's a transformation you will say
Exceeding all the magic in the play.
Let none expect in the last act to find
Her sex transformed from man to womankind.
Whate'er she was before the play began,   35
All you shall see of her is perfect man.
Or, if your fancy will be farther led
To find her woman, it must be abed.
(1667; 1670)

STUDY AIDS: 1. How many variations does
Dryden make on his opening simile? How does
he keep this process of extension from becoming
dull and uninteresting to the reader? How many
antitheses can you see in the poem?

2. How does Dryden's admiration for Shakespeare appear in the poem? Note. ll. 5–6, 8,
13–14, 19–20, 24.

3. Can you see any evidence in this poem
why the Restoration would think Shakespeare's
plays needed to be "improved"? Cf. ll. 25–28.

4. How does Dryden bring off the *double
entendre* of the last line without upsetting the
unity of the poem?

A Song for St. Cecilia's Day

Saint Cecilia was a Roman virgin, said to have been martyred in 176 A.D. According to legend,
she invented the organ, and for this reason she was honored as the patron saint of music. In 1683,
a musical society was formed in London to celebrate her feast day, November 22, with a composition. For this occasion Dryden wrote two irregular Pindaric odes: this *Song* and *Alexander's
Feast.*

From harmony, from heavenly harmony [1]
   This universal frame began;
  When nature underneath a heap
   Of jarring atoms lay,
  And could not heave her head,   5
The tuneful voice was heard from high,
  "Arise, ye more than dead."

Then cold and hot and moist and dry
  In order to their stations leap,
  And music's power obey.   10
From harmony, from heavenly harmony,
  This universal frame began:

   From harmony to harmony
Through all the compass of the notes it ran,
The diapason [2] closing full in man.   15

What passion cannot music raise and quell!
  When Jubal [3] struck the corded shell, [4]
  His listening brethren stood around,
   And, wondering, on their faces fell
To worship that celestial sound: 20
Less than a god they thought there could not
   dwell
  Within the hollow of that shell,
  That spoke so sweetly, and so well.
What passion cannot music raise and quell!

[1] Dryden, like the later American poets Edgar
Allan Poe and Sidney Lanier, was interested in the
relationship between the sounds of music and those
of words in poetry. In this poem, he tried to reproduce musical effects through words. The first
stanza is therefore similar to an overture which
introduces the main theme to be developed later in
the composition by solo instruments. This theme
is stated in figurative terms: music created the universe in the sense that God brought harmony or
order out of chaos. The implication, however, is
more than this. Note ll. 48–50. What incident in
the Orpheus myth indicates the good effect that
music and poetry, since Orpheus is god of both,
have on mankind?

[2] The highest form of creation was thought to be
man; thus the diapason, or "scale" in musical terminology, ends there. The rest of the poem then
develops the effect music has on the emotions of
man. Cf. ll. 16, 24.

[3] Cf. Genesis 4:21. Jubal, an early descendant of
Adam, invented the harp and founded the first
civilization.

[4] What is the instrument here imitated? What
liquid consonants convey the imitation of the instrument's sound in this stanza? What emotion (passion) does this instrument arouse in man, according
to Dryden?

The trumpet's[5] loud clangor   25
  Excites us to arms
With shrill notes of anger
  And mortal alarms.
The double, double, double beat
  Of the thundering drum   30
Cries, "Hark! the foes come;
Charge, charge, 'tis too late to retreat!"

The soft complaining flute
  In dying notes discovers
The woes of hopeless lovers,[6]   35
Whose dirge is whispered by the warbling
    lute.

  Sharp[7] violins proclaim
Their jealous pangs and desperation,
Fury, frantic indignation,
Depth of pains and height of passion,   40
  For the fair, disdainful dame.

But oh! what art can teach,
What human voice can reach
  The sacred organ's praise?
Notes inspiring holy love,   45
  Notes that wing their heavenly ways
To mend the choirs above.

Orpheus could lead the savage race,
And trees unrooted left their place,
  Sequacious of the lyre;   50
But bright Cecilia raised the wonder higher;
When to her organ vocal breath was given,
An angel heard, and straight appeared,
  Mistaking earth for heaven.[8]

Grand Chorus

As from the power of sacred lays   55
  The spheres began to move,
And sung the great Creator's praise
  To all the blessed above;
So, when the last and dreadful hour
This crumbling pageant shall devour,   60
The trumpet[9] shall be heard on high,
The dead shall live, the living die,
And music shall untune the sky.[10]
(1687)

STUDY AIDS: 1. How can civilization be built by the human emotions enumerated here? How can it be destroyed by these same emotions?
2. Is the poem a simple compliment to St. Cecilia, or does Dryden use her as a pretext to present a larger theme?

Alexander's Feast; or, the Power of Music
An Ode in Honor of St. Cecilia's Day

In this poem Dryden has created a new kind of lyric poem: an ode in the form of a dramatic narrative. As the subtitle indicates, the poem illustrates the power music can exert on mankind as epitomized in Alexander the Great. Dryden considered this his best piece of poetry.

'Twas at the royal feast, for Persia won
  By Philip's warlike son:
Aloft in awful state
The godlike hero sate
  On his imperial throne;   5
His valiant peers were placed around;

Their brows with roses and with myrtles
    bound:
  (So should desert in arms be crowned.)
The lovely Thaïs, by his side,
Sate like a blooming Eastern bride,   10
In flower of youth and beauty's pride.

[5] Is there a "clangor" in ll. 25–28? Why are the trumpet and drum (l. 30) linked together in the same stanza? What emotion of man is touched upon?
[6] What consonant sound prevails here? Is it representative of the sound of the flute? Why are the flute and lute (l. 36) combined into one stanza? With what emotion are these two instruments usually associated?

[7] How is the "sharpness" of the violins reproduced in the stanza? Note the punctuation.
[8] This incident was part of the legend of St. Cecilia.
[9] How does Dryden's use of the trumpet here differ from that in l. 25?
[10] The "music of the spheres" will be heard no more. This last stanza is somewhat like the coda of a musical composition.

Happy, happy, happy pair!
  None but the brave,
  None but the brave,
  None but the brave deserves the
    fair.   15

Chorus

Happy, happy, happy pair!
  None but the brave,
  None but the brave,
  None but the brave deserves the
    fair.

Timotheus,[1] placed on high   20
  Amid the tuneful quire,
  With flying fingers touched the lyre:
The trembling notes ascend the sky,
  And heavenly joys inspire.
The song began from Jove,[2]   25
Who left his blissful seats above,
(Such is the power of mighty love).
A dragon's fiery form belied the god:
Sublime on radiant spires he rode,
When he to fair Olympia pressed;   30
And while he sought her snowy breast,
Then round her slender waist he curled,
And stamped an image of himself, a sovereign
    of the world.
The listening crowd admire the lofty sound,
"A present deity," they shout around;   35
"A present deity," the vaulted roofs rebound:
  With ravished ears
  The monarch hears,
  Assumes the god,
  Affects to nod,   40
And seems to shake the spheres.

Chorus

  With ravished ears
  The monarch hears,
  Assumes the god,
  Affects to nod,   45
And seems to shake the spheres.

The praise of Bacchus then the sweet
    musician sung,[3]
  Of Bacchus ever fair, and ever young.
  The jolly god in triumph comes;
  Sound the trumpets, beat the drums; 50
    Flushed with a purple grace
  He shows his honest face:
Now give the hautboys breath; he comes, he
    comes.
  Bacchus, ever fair and young,
    Drinking joys did first ordain;   55
  Bacchus' blessings are a treasure,
  Drinking is the soldier's pleasure;
    Rich the treasure,
    Sweet the pleasure,
  Sweet is pleasure after pain.   60

Chorus

  Bacchus' blessings are a treasure,
  Drinking is the soldier's pleasure;
    Rich the treasure,
    Sweet the pleasure,
  Sweet is pleasure after pain.   65

Soothed with the sound the king grew
    vain;[4]
  Fought all his battles o'er again;
And thrice he routed all his foes, and thrice
    he slew the slain.
  The master saw the madness rise,
  His glowing cheeks, his ardent eyes;   70
  And while he heaven and earth defied,
  Changed his hand, and checked his pride.
    He chose a mournful muse,[5]
    Soft pity to infuse;
  He sung Darius great and good,   75
    By too severe a fate,
  Fallen, fallen, fallen, fallen,
    Fallen from his high estate,
  And weltering in his blood;
  Deserted at his utmost need   80
  By those his former bounty fed;

---

[1] The protagonist of the poem. He was the court musician of Alexander.

[2] The first effect Timotheus achieves by the power of music is to convince Alexander that his father was Jove, not Philip of Macedon. The name of Alexander's mother was Olympias, which Dryden changed to Olympia (l. 30), playing upon the word Olympus, the seat of the gods.

[3] Timotheus next leads Alexander into drunkenness.

[4] What is the result of Alexander's drunkenness? Note the humor in ll. 67–68.

[5] Is this next mood induced by Timotheus a natural one to follow drunkenness? What does Alexander think about while in this mood?

On the bare earth exposed he lies,
With not a friend to close his eyes.
With downcast looks the joyless victor sate,
    Revolving in his altered soul   85
        The various turns of chance be-
          low;
        And, now and then, a sigh he stole,
        And tears began to flow.

Chorus

    Revolving in his altered soul
        The various turns of chance be-
          low;   90
    And, now and then, a sigh he stole,
    And tears began to flow.

The mighty master smiled to see
That love was in the next degree; [6]
'Twas but a kindred sound to move, 95
For pity melts the mind to love.
    Softly sweet, in Lydian measures,
    Soon he soothed his soul to pleas-
        ures.
"War," he sung, "is toil and trouble;
Honor but an empty bubble;   100
    Never ending, still beginning,
Fighting still, and still destroying:
    If the world be worth thy winning,
    Think, O think it worth enjoying:
        Lovely Thaïs sits beside thee, 105
        Take the good the gods provide
        thee."
The many rend the skies with loud ap-
        plause;
So Love was crowned, but Music won the
        cause.
    The prince, unable to conceal his pain,
        Gazed on the fair   110
        Who caused his care,
    And sighed and looked, sighed and
        looked,
    Sighed and looked, and sighed again;
At length, with love and wine at once op-
        pressed,
    The vanquished victor sunk upon her
        breast.   115

[6] What is the psychological connection between the previous mood of Alexander and this one now created by Timotheus?

Chorus

    The prince, unable to conceal his pain,
        Gazed on the fair
        Who caused his care,
    And sighed and looked, sighed and
        looked,
    Sighed and looked, and sighed again; 120
At length, with love and wine at once op-
        pressed,
    The vanquished victor sunk upon her
        breast.

    Now strike the golden lyre again;
    A louder yet, and yet a louder strain.
    Break his bands of sleep asunder, 125
    And rouse him, like a rattling peal of
        thunder.
        Hark, hark, the horrid sound
          Has raised up his head;
          As awaked from the dead,
        And, amazed, he stares around. 130
"Revenge, revenge!" Timotheus cries; [7]
    "See the Furies arise;
    See the snakes that they rear,
    How they hiss in their hair,
    And the sparkles that flash from their
        eyes!   135
        Behold a ghastly band,
        Each a torch in his hand!
Those are Grecian ghosts, that in battle were
        slain,
        And unburied remain
        Inglorious on the plain: 140
        Give the vengeance due
        To the valiant crew.
Behold how they toss their torches on high,
        How they point to the Persian abodes,
And glittering temples of their hostile
        gods!"   145
The princes applaud with a furious joy;
And the king seized a flambeau with zeal to
        destroy;
        Thaïs led the way,
        To light him to his prey,
And, like another Helen, fired another
        Troy.   150

[7] What is the final emotion Timotheus calls up in the king? What is its outcome?

Chorus

And the king seized a flambeau with zeal to
　　　　destroy;
　　　Thaïs led the way,
　　　To light him to his prey,
And, like another Helen, fired another Troy.

　　　Thus long ago,　　　　　　155
　Ere heaving bellows learned to blow,
　　While organs yet were mute,
　　Timotheus, to his breathing flute
　　　And sounding lyre,
Could swell the soul to rage, or kindle soft
　　　desire.　　　　　　160
　At last divine Cecilia came,[8]
　Inventress of the vocal frame;
The sweet enthusiast, from her sacred store,
　　Enlarged the former narrow bounds,
　　And added length to solemn sounds,　165
With nature's mother wit, and arts unknown
　　　before.
　　Let old Timotheus yield the prize,
　　　Or both divide the crown:

He raised a mortal to the skies;
　She drew an angel down.　　　170

Grand Chorus

　At last divine Cecilia came,
　Inventress of the vocal frame;
The sweet enthusiast, from her sacred store,
　　Enlarged the former narrow bounds,
　　And added length to solemn sounds,　175
With nature's mother wit, and arts unknown
　　　before.
　　Let old Timotheus yield the prize,
　　　Or both divide the crown:
　He raised a mortal to the skies;
　　She drew an angel down.　　　180
(1697)

STUDY AIDS: This poem is not written in
heroic couplets. What reasons can you give for
the meter and stanzaic pattern of the poem? How
are these better fitted to the theme than the
heroic couplet would be?

Fables, Ancient and Modern

PREFACE

The *Fables, Ancient and Modern* was Dryden's last work. In a letter of February 2, 1699 to a relative, Mrs. Seward, he commented:

"In the meantime, betwixt my intervals of physic and other remedies which I am using for my gravel, I am still drudging on: always a poet, and never a good one. I pass my time sometimes with Ovid, and sometimes with our old English poet, Chaucer; translating such stories as best please my fancy; and intend besides them to add somewhat of my own: so that it is not impossible, but ere the summer be passed, I may come down to you with a volume in my hand, like a dog out of the water, with a duck in his mouth."

It may strike a modern reader as strange that Dryden would translate Chaucer. The reason lies in Dryden's view of Chaucer's language. By the seventeenth century the pronunciation of Middle English had been lost; for one thing, the final –e, pronounced in Chaucer's day, had become silent, as it is in modern English. Since Dryden had an imperfect knowledge of Middle English, he could not make Chaucer's verse scan properly, and consequently thought him a ragged metrist, whose verse would profit from being translated into the refined language of a later day. Dryden is also mistaken about some of the facts of Chaucer's life. This inaccuracy of fact, however, in no way detracts from his understanding of Chaucer as a delightful, warm human being and fellow-poet.

[8] How can Dryden justify including St. Cecilia in this poem?

. . . .

It remains that I say somewhat of Chaucer in particular.

In the first place, as he is the father of English poetry, so I hold him in the same degree of veneration as the Grecians held Homer or the Romans Virgil. He is a perpetual fountain of good sense, learned in all sciences, and therefore speaks properly on all subjects: as he knew what to say, so he knows also when to leave off, a continence which is practiced by few writers, and scarcely by any of the ancients, excepting Virgil and Horace. One of our late great poets [1] is sunk in his reputation, because he could never forgive any conceit which came in his way, but swept like a dragnet great and small. There was plenty enough, but the dishes were ill sorted; whole pyramids of sweetmeats for boys and women, but little of solid meat for men. All this proceeded not from any want of knowledge, but of judgment; neither did he want that in discerning the beauties and faults of other poets; but only indulged himself in the luxury of writing; and perhaps knew it was a fault, but hoped the reader would not find it. For this reason, though he must always be thought a great poet, he is no longer esteemed a good writer; and for ten impressions, which his works have had in so many successive years, yet at present a hundred books are scarcely purchased once a twelvemonth: for, as my last Lord Rochester said, though somewhat profanely, "Not being of God, he could not stand."

Chaucer followed nature everywhere, but was never so bold to go beyond her: and there is a great difference of being *poeta* and *nimis poeta*, [2] if we may believe Catullus, as much as betwixt a modest behavior and affectation. The verse of Chaucer, I confess, is not harmonious to us; but it is like the eloquence of one whom Tacitus commends; it was *auribus istius temporis accommodata*: [3] they who lived with him, and some time after him, thought it musical; and it continues so

[1] Abraham Cowley.
[2] "Poet" and "too much a poet."
[3] "Fitted to the ears of that time."

even in our judgment, if compared with the numbers of Lydgate and Gower, his contemporaries: there is the rude sweetness of a Scotch tune in it, which is natural and pleasing, though not perfect. It is true, I cannot go so far as he who published the last edition of him; for he would make us believe that the fault is in our ears, and that there were really ten syllables in a verse where we find but nine: but this opinion is not worth confuting; it is so gross and obvious an error that common sense (which is a rule in everything but matters of faith and revelation) must convince the reader that equality of numbers in every verse which we call heroic was either not known, or not always practiced, in Chaucer's age. It were an easy matter to produce some thousands of his verses which are lame for want of a half a foot, and sometimes a whole one, and which no pronunciation can make otherwise. We can only say that he lived in the infancy of our poetry, and that nothing is brought to perfection at the first. We must be children before we grow men. . . . But this will keep cold till another time. In the mean while I must take up Chaucer where I left him.

He must have been a man of a most wonderful comprehensive nature, because, as it has been truly observed of him, he has taken into the compass of his *Canterbury Tales* the various manners and humors (as we now call them) of the whole English nation in his age. Not a single character has escaped him. All his pilgrims are severally distinguished from each other; and not only in their inclinations, but in their very physiognomies and persons. Baptista Porta could not have described their natures better, than by the marks which the poet gives them. The matter and manner of their tales, and of their telling, are so suited to their different educations, humors, and callings, that each of them would be improper in any other mouth. Even the grave and serious characters are distinguished by their several sorts of gravity: their discourses are such as belong to their age, their calling, and their breeding; such as are becoming of them, and of them only. Some of his persons are vicious, and some virtuous; some are unlearned, or (as Chaucer calls them) lewd, and some are learned. Even the ribaldry of the low characters is different: the Reeve, the Miller, and the Cook are several men, and distinguished from each other, as much as the mincing Lady Prioress and the broad-speaking gap-toothed Wife of Bath. But enough of this: there is such a variety of game springing up before me, that I am distracted in my choice, and know not which to follow. It is sufficient to say, according to the proverb, that here is God's plenty. We have our forefathers and great-grand-dames all before us, as they were in Chaucer's day; their general characters are still remaining in mankind, and even in England, though they are called by other names than those of Monks and Friars, and Canons, and Lady Abbesses, and Nuns: for mankind is ever the same, and nothing lost out of nature, though everything is altered. May I have leave to do myself the justice—since my enemies will do me none, and are so far from granting me to be a good poet, that they will not allow me so much as to be a Christian, or a moral man—may I have leave, I say, to inform my reader that I have confined my choice to such tales of Chaucer as savor nothing of immodesty. If I had desired more to please than to instruct, the Reeve, the Miller, the Shipman, the Merchant, the Sumner, and, above all, the Wife of Bath, in the prologue to her tale, would have procured me as many friends and readers as there are beaux and ladies of pleasure in the town. But I will no more offend against good manners: I am sensible, as I ought to be, of the scandal I have given by my loose writings; and make what reparation I am able, by this public acknowledgment. If anything of this nature, or of profaneness, be crept into these poems, I am so far from defending it, that I disown it. . . . (1700)

Daniel Defoe
(1660?–1731)

DEFOE IS KNOWN TODAY AS THE AUTHOR OF *Robinson Crusoe*, BUT, IN HIS LIFETIME he was a prolific writer of more than 250 known publications on many subjects ranging from discussions of trade to treatises on the occult. He was a great journalist at a time when the foundations of the journalistic profession were being laid, and in all his writings a journalistic purpose prevails.

Defoe was born plain Daniel Foe, the son of a middle-class Puritan butcher. At the age of forty he changed his name to the more aristocratic Defoe, but he never forsook the religious and political views inherited from his family's social background. He was educated for the Puritan ministry at Newington Green Academy, and although he occasionally preached at chapels, he went into business. Twice he made a fortune and twice went bankrupt.

During this period he was writing, and in 1704 his pen attracted the attention of Robert Harley, the Whig leader in Parliament. Defoe became both his political spy in England and editor of his newspaper, *The Review*, which Defoe founded to mold public opinion in favor of Whig policies.

Because of a too busy life and a prolific pen, Defoe wrote with a haste which seldom permitted revision or correction. As a result his writings are marred by a carelessness of style and form. Nevertheless, no writer of the period better reflected its spirit of realism or endowed it with more human interest than did Defoe; and not even Addison and Steele more effectively applied common sense to the problems of the day.

A True Relation of the Apparition of One Mrs. Veal

THE NEXT DAY AFTER HER DEATH, TO
ONE MRS. BARGRAVE, AT CANTERBURY,
THE 8TH OF SEPTEMBER, 1705.

The Apparition of Mrs. Veal, which for 200 years was believed to be fiction, is true. There was a real Mrs. Bargrave living in Canterbury in 1705, who did tell anyone who would listen that Mrs. Veal had appeared to her the day she died. Defoe simply turned the contemporary ghost story to his own purpose.

THE PREFACE

This relation is matter of fact, and attended with such circumstances as may induce any reasonable man to believe it. It was sent by a 5 gentleman, a justice of peace at Maidstone, in Kent, and a very intelligent person, to his friend in London, as it is here worded; which discourse is attested by a very sober and understanding gentleman, who had it from his 10 kinswoman, who lives in Canterbury, within a few doors of the house in which the within-named Mrs. Bargrave lived; and who he believes to be of so discerning a spirit as not to be put upon by any fallacy, and who posi- 15 tively assured him that the whole matter as it is related and laid down is really true, and what she herself had in the same words, as near as may be, from Mrs. Bargrave's own mouth, who, she knows, had no reason to 20 invent and publish such a story, or any design to forge and tell a lie, being a woman of much honesty and virtue, and her whole life a course, as it were, of piety. The use which we ought to make of it is to consider that 25 there is a life to come after this, and a just God who will retribute to every one according to the deeds done in the body, and therefore to reflect upon our past course of life we have led in the world; that our time is 30 short and uncertain; and that if we would escape the punishment of the ungodly and receive the reward of the righteous, which is the laying hold of eternal life, we ought, for

the time to come to return to God by a speedy repentance, ceasing to do evil, and learning to do well; to seek after God early, if haply 5 he may be found of us, and lead such lives for the future as may be well pleasing in his sight.

A RELATION, &C.

This thing is so rare in all its circumstances, and on so good authority, that my reading and conversation have not given me anything like it. It is fit to gratify the most ingenious and serious inquirer. Mrs. Bargrave is the person 15 to whom Mrs. Veal appeared after her death; she is my intimate friend, and I can avouch for her reputation for these last fifteen or sixteen years, on my own knowledge; and I can confirm the good character she had from her youth to the time of my acquaintance; though since this relation she is calumniated by some people that are friends to the brother of Mrs. Veal who appeared, who think the relation of this appearance to be a reflection, 25 and endeavor what they can to blast Mrs. Bargrave's reputation, and to laugh the story out of countenance. But by the circumstances thereof, and the cheerful disposition of Mrs. Bargrave, notwithstanding the ill-usage of a 30 very wicked husband, there is not the least sign of dejection in her face; nor did I ever hear her let fall a desponding or murmuring expression; nay, not when actually under her husband's barbarity, which I have been wit-

ness to, and several other persons of undoubted reputation.

Now you must know Mrs. Veal was a
maiden gentlewoman of about thirty years of
age, and for some years last past had been
troubled with fits, which were perceived coming on her by her going off from her discourses very abruptly to some impertinence.
She was maintained by an only brother, and
kept his house in Dover. She was a very
pious woman, and her brother a very sober
man, to all appearance; but now he does all
he can to null or quash the story. Mrs. Veal
was intimately acquainted with Mrs. Bargrave
from her childhood. Mrs. Veal's circumstances were then mean; her father did not
take care of his children as he ought, so that
they were exposed to hardships; and Mrs.
Bargrave in those days had as unkind a father,
though she wanted neither for food nor clothing, whilst Mrs. Veal wanted for both, insomuch that she would often say, "Mrs. Bargrave, you are not only the best, but the
only friend I have in the world; and no
circumstance in life shall ever dissolve my
friendship." They would often condole each
other's adverse fortunes, and read together
Drelincourt upon death,[1] and other good
books; and so, like two Christian friends, they
comforted each other under their sorrow.

Some time after, Mr. Veal's friends got him
a place in the custom-house at Dover, which
occasioned Mrs. Veal, by little and little, to fall
off from her intimacy with Mrs. Bargrave,
though there never was any such thing as a
quarrel; but an indifferency came on by
degrees, till at last Mrs. Bargrave had not
seen her in two years and a half; though
about a twelve-month of the time Mrs. Bargrave had been absent from Dover, and this
last half-year had been in Canterbury about
two months of the time, dwelling in a house
of her own.

In this house, on the 8th of September
1705, she was sitting alone, in the forenoon,

[1] The very popular English translation of Charles
Drelincourt's *The Christian's Defense Against the
Fear of Death* was published in 1675. Throughout
the eighteenth century Defoe's *Apparition* was often
printed and bound with it.

thinking over her unfortunate life, and arguing herself into a due resignation to providence, though her condition seemed hard.
"And," said she, "I have been provided for
hitherto, and doubt not but I shall be still;
and am well satisfied that my afflictions shall
end when it is most fit for me"; and then
took up her sewing-work, which she had no
sooner done but she hears a knocking at the
door. She went to see who was there, and
this proved to be Mrs. Veal, her old friend,
who was in a riding-habit; at that moment of
time the clock struck twelve at noon.

"Madam," says Mrs. Bargrave, "I am surprised to see you, you have been so long a
stranger"; but told her she was glad to see her,
and offered to salute her, which Mrs. Veal
complied with, till their lips almost touched;
and then Mrs. Veal drew her hand across
her own eyes and said, "I am not very well,"
and so waived it. She told Mrs. Bargrave
she was going a journey, and had a great
mind to see her first. "But," says Mrs. Bargrave, "how came you to take a journey
alone? I am amazed at it, because I know you
have a good brother." "Oh," says Mrs. Veal,
"I gave my brother the slip, and came away,
because I had so great a desire to see you
before I took my journey." So Mrs. Bargrave
went in with her into another room within
the first, and Mrs. Veal set her down in an
elbow-chair, in which Mrs. Bargrave was
sitting when she heard Mrs. Veal knock.
Then says Mrs. Veal, "My dear friend, I am
come to renew our old friendship again, and
beg your pardon for my breach of it; and if
you can forgive me, you are the best of
women." "Oh," says Mrs. Bargrave, "do not
mention such a thing. I have not had an
uneasy thought about it; I can easily forgive
it." "What did you think of me?" said Mrs.
Veal. Says Mrs. Bargrave, "I thought you were
like the rest of the world, and that prosperity
had made you forget yourself and me." Then
Mrs. Veal reminded Mrs. Bargrave of the
many friendly offices she did in her former
days, and much of the conversation they had
with each other in the times of their adversity;
what books they read, and what comfort in
particular they received from Drelincourt's

book of death, which was the best, she said, on that subject ever written. She also mentioned Dr. Sherlock,[2] the two Dutch books which were translated, written upon death, and several others; but Drelincourt, she said, had the clearest notions of death and of the future state of any who had handled that subject. Then she asked Mrs. Bargrave whether she had Drelincourt. She said, "Yes." Says Mrs. Veal, "Fetch it." And so Mrs. Bargrave goes upstairs and brings it down. Says Mrs. Veal, "Dear Mrs. Bargrave, if the eyes of our faith were as open as the eyes of our body, we should see numbers of angels about us for our guard. The notions we have of heaven now are nothing like to what it is, as Drelincourt says. Therefore be comforted under your afflictions, and believe that the Almighty has a particular regard to you, and that your afflictions are marks of God's favor; and when they have done the business they are sent for, they shall be removed from you. And believe me, my dear friend, believe what I say to you, one minute of future happiness will infinitely reward you for all your sufferings; for I can never believe" (and claps her hands upon her knees with great earnestness, which indeed ran through most of her discourse) "that ever God will suffer you to spend all your days in this afflicted state; but be assured that your afflictions shall leave you, or you them, in a short time." She spake in that pathetical and heavenly manner that Mrs. Bargrave wept several times, she was so deeply affected with it.

Then Mrs. Veal mentioned Dr. Horneck's *Ascetic,* at the end of which he gives an account of the lives of the primitive Christians. Their pattern she recommended to our imitation, and said, "Their conversation was not like this of our age; for now," says she, "there is nothing but frothy, vain discourse, which is far different from theirs. Theirs was to edification, and to build one another up in faith; so that they were not as we are, nor are we as they were; but," said she, "we ought to do as they did. There was a hearty friendship among them; but where is it now to be found?" Says

Mrs. Bargrave, "It is hard indeed to find a true friend in these days." Says Mrs. Veal, "Mr. Norris has a fine copy of verses, called *Friendship in Perfection,* which I wonderfully admire. Have you seen the book?" says Mrs. Veal. "No," says Mrs. Bargrave, "but I have the verses of my own writing out." "Have you?" says Mrs. Veal; "then fetch them." Which she did from above-stairs, and offered them to Mrs. Veal to read, who refused, and waived the thing, saying holding down her head would make it ache; and then desired Mrs. Bargrave to read them to her, which she did. As they were admiring *Friendship,* Mrs. Veal said, "Dear Mrs. Bargrave, I shall love you for ever." In these verses there is twice used the word Elysian. "Ah!" says Mrs. Veal, "these poets have such names for heaven!" She would often draw her hand across her own eyes and say, "Mrs. Bargrave, do not you think I am mightily impaired by my fits?" "No," says Mrs. Bargrave, "I think you look as well as ever I knew you."

After all this discourse, which the apparition put in much finer words than Mrs. Bargrave said she could pretend to, and as much more than she can remember, for it cannot be thought that an hour and three-quarters' conversation could be retained, though the main of it she thinks she does, she said to Mrs. Bargrave she would have her write a letter to her brother, and tell him she would have him give rings to such and such, and that there was a purse of gold in her cabinet, and that she would have two broad pieces given to her cousin Watson.

Talking at this rate, Mrs. Bargrave thought that a fit was coming upon her, and so placed herself in a chair just before her knees, to keep her from falling to the ground, if her fits should occasion it (for the elbow-chair, she thought, would keep her from falling on either side); and to divert Mrs. Veal, as she thought, took hold of her gown-sleeve several times and commended it. Mrs. Veal told her it was a scoured silk, and newly made up. But for all this, Mrs. Veal persisted in her request, and told Mrs. Bargrave that she must not deny her, and she would have her tell her brother all their conversation

[2] A preacher who wrote *A Practical Discourse Concerning Death* (1689).

when she had an opportunity. "Dear Mrs. Veal," said Mrs. Bargrave, "this seems so impertinent that I cannot tell how to comply with it; and what a mortifying story will our conversation be to a young gentleman? Why," says Mrs. Bargrave, "it is much better, methinks, to do it yourself." "No," says Mrs. Veal, "though it seems impertinent to you now, you will see more reason for it hereafter." Mrs. Bargrave then, to satisfy her importunity, was going to fetch a pen and ink, but Mrs. Veal said, "Let it alone now, but do it when I am gone; but you must be sure to do it"; which was one of the last things she enjoined her at parting. So she promised her.

Then Mrs. Veal asked for Mrs. Bargrave's daughter. She said she was not at home, "But if you have a mind to see her," says Mrs. Bargrave, "I'll send for her." "Do," says Mrs. Veal. On which she left her, and went to a neighbor's to see for her; and by the time Mrs. Bargrave was returning, Mrs. Veal was got without the door into the street, in the face of the beast-market, on a Saturday (which is market-day), and stood ready to part, as soon as Mrs. Bargrave came to her. She asked why she was in such haste. She said she must be going, though perhaps she might not go her journey until Monday; and told Mrs. Bargrave she hoped she should see her again at her cousin Watson's before she went whither she was going. Then she said she would take her leave of her, and walked from Mrs. Bargrave in her view, till a turning interrupted the sight of her, which was three-quarters after one in the afternoon.

Mrs. Veal died the 7th of September, at twelve o'clock at noon, of her fits, and had not above four hours' sense before death, in which time she received the sacrament. The next day after Mrs. Veal's appearing, being Sunday, Mrs. Bargrave was so mightily indisposed with a cold and a sore throat, that she could not go out that day; but on Monday morning she sent a person to Captain Watson's to know if Mrs. Veal was there. They wondered at Mrs. Bargrave's inquiry, and sent her word that she was not there, nor was expected. At this answer, Mrs. Bargrave told the maid she had certainly mistook the name or made some blunder. And though she was ill, she put on her hood, and went herself to Captain Watson's, though she knew none of the family, to see if Mrs. Veal was there or not. They said they wondered at her asking, for that she had not been in town; they were sure, if she had, she would have been there. Says Mrs. Bargrave, "I am sure she was with me on Saturday almost two hours." They said it was impossible; for they must have seen her, if she had. In comes Captain Watson while they are in dispute, and said that Mrs. Veal was certainly dead, and her escutcheons [3] were making. This strangely surprised Mrs. Bargrave, who went to the person immediately who had the care of them, and found it true. Then she related the whole story to Captain Watson's family, and what gown she had on, and how striped, and that Mrs. Veal told her it was scoured. Then Mrs. Watson cried out, "You have seen her indeed, for none knew but Mrs. Veal and myself that the gown was scoured." And Mrs. Watson owned that she described the gown exactly, "for," said she, "I helped her to make it up." This Mrs. Watson blazed all about the town, and avouched the demonstration of the truth of Mrs. Bargrave's seeing Mrs. Veal's apparition; and Captain Watson carried two gentlemen immediately to Mrs. Bargrave's house to hear the relation from her own mouth. And when it spread so fast that gentlemen and persons of quality, the judicious and skeptical part of the world, flocked in upon her, it at last became such a task that she was forced to go out of the way; for they were in general extremely well satisfied of the truth of the thing, and plainly saw that Mrs. Bargrave was no hypochondriac, for she always appears with such a cheerful air and pleasing mien, that she has gained the favor and esteem of all the gentry, and it is thought a great favor if they can but get the relation from her own mouth. I should have told you before that Mrs. Veal told Mrs. Bargrave that her sister and brother-in-law were just come down from London to see her. Says Mrs. Bargrave, "How came you to order matters so strangely?" "It could not be helped," said Mrs.

[3] Tombstone with epitaph.

Veal. And her brother and sister did come to see her, and entered the town of Dover just as Mrs. Veal was expiring. Mrs. Bargrave asked her whether she would drink some tea. Says Mrs. Veal, "I do not care if I do; but I'll warrant you this mad fellow" (meaning Mrs. Bargrave's husband) "has broken all your trinkets." "But," says Mrs. Bargrave, "I'll get something to drink in for all that." But Mrs. Veal waived it, and said, "It is no matter; let it alone"; and so it passed.

All the time I sat with Mrs. Bargrave, which was some hours, she recollected fresh sayings of Mrs. Veal. And one material thing more she told Mrs. Bargrave—that old Mr. Breton allowed Mrs. Veal ten pounds a year, which was a secret, and unknown to Mrs. Bargrave till Mrs. Veal told it her. Mrs. Bargrave never varies in her story, which puzzles those who doubt of the truth or are unwilling to believe it. A servant in the neighbor's yard adjoining to Mrs. Bargrave's house heard her talking to somebody an hour of the time Mrs. Veal was with her. Mrs. Bargrave went out to her next neighbor's the very moment she parted with Mrs. Veal, and told her what ravishing conversation she had with an old friend, and told the whole of it. Drelincourt's book of death is, since this happened, bought up strangely. And it is to be observed that, notwithstanding all the trouble and fatigue Mrs. Bargrave has undergone upon this account, she never took the value of a farthing, nor suffered her daughter to take anything of anybody, and therefore can have no interest in telling the story.

But Mr. Veal does what he can to stifle the matter, and said he would see Mrs. Bargrave; but yet it is certain matter of fact that he has been at Captain Watson's since the death of his sister, and yet never went near Mrs. Bargrave; and some of his friends report her to be a liar, and that she knew of Mr. Breton's ten pounds a year. But the person who pretends to say so has the reputation of a notorious liar among persons whom I know to be of undoubted credit. Now, Mr. Veal is more of a gentleman than to say she lies, but says a bad husband has crazed her. But she needs only present herself and it will effectu- ally confute that pretense. Mr. Veal says he asked his sister on her deathbed whether she had a mind to dispose of anything, and she said no. Now, the things which Mrs. Veal's apparition would have disposed of were so trifling, and nothing of justice aimed at in their disposal, that the design of it appears to me to be only in order to make Mrs. Bargrave so to demonstrate the truth of her appearance, as to satisfy the world of the reality thereof as to what she had seen and heard, and to secure her reputation among the reasonable and understanding part of mankind. And then again Mr. Veal owns that there was a purse of gold; but it was not found in her cabinet, but in a comb-box. This looks improbable; for that Mrs. Watson owned that Mrs. Veal was so very careful of the key of the cabinet that she would trust nobody with it; and if so, no doubt she would not trust her gold out of it. And Mrs. Veal's often drawing her hand over her eyes, and asking Mrs. Bargrave whether her fits had not impaired her, looks to me as if she did it on purpose to remind Mrs. Bargrave of her fits, to prepare her not to think it strange that she should put her upon writing to her brother to dispose of rings and gold, which looks so much like a dying person's request; and it took accordingly with Mrs. Bargrave, as the effects of her fits coming upon her; and was one of the many instances of her wonderful love to her and care of her that she should not be affrighted, which indeed appears in her whole management, particularly in her coming to her in the daytime, waiving the salutation, and when she was alone, and then the manner of her parting to prevent a second attempt to salute her.

Now, why Mr. Veal should think this relation a reflection, as it is plain he does by his endeavoring to stifle it, I cannot imagine, because the generality believe her to be a good spirit, her discourse was so heavenly. Her two great errands were to comfort Mrs. Bargrave in her affliction, and to ask her forgiveness for the breach of friendship, and with a pious discourse to encourage her. So that after all to suppose that Mrs. Bargrave could hatch such an invention as this from Friday noon to

Saturday noon, supposing that she knew of Mrs. Veal's death the very first moment, without jumbling circumstances, and without any interest too, she must be more witty, fortunate, and wicked too than any indifferent person, I dare say, will allow. I asked Mrs. Bargrave several times if she was sure she felt the gown. She answered modestly, "If my senses are to be relied on, I am sure of it." I asked her if she heard a sound when she clapped her hands upon her knees. She said she did not remember she did, but said she appeared to be as much a substance as I did, who talked with her. "And I may," said she, "be as soon persuaded that your apparition is talking to me now as that I did not really see her; for I was under no manner of fear, and received her as a friend, and parted with her as such. I would not," says she, "give one farthing to make any one believe it; I have no interest in it. Nothing but trouble is entailed upon me for a long time, for aught I know; and had it not come to light by accident, it would never have been made public." But now she says she will make her own private use of it, and keep herself out of the way as much as she can; and so she has done since. She says she had a gentleman who came thirty miles to her to hear the relation, and that she had told it to a room full of people at a time. Several

particular gentlemen have had the story from Mrs. Bargrave's own mouth.

This thing has very much affected me, and I am as well satisfied as I am of the best grounded matter of fact. And why we should dispute matter of fact because we cannot solve things of which we have no certain or demonstrative notions, seems strange to me. Mrs. Bargrave's authority and sincerity alone would have been undoubted in any other case.

(1706)

STUDY AIDS: 1. Defoe tells this story in a dry and prosaic manner, as if he were too unimaginative to rise above the facts. What effect does this kind of narration have on the reader?

2. What do the following have to do with the credibility of the story: (1) a dress of "scoured silk"; (2) Mr. Veal; (3) Captain Watson; (4) the "Preface"; and (5) the conclusion?

3. What was Defoe's avowed purpose in writing this ghost story? How does the conversation between Mrs. Veal and Mrs. Bargrave support this purpose? Does the fact that the reader believes or disbelieves the events affect the value of the story?

4. Defoe cites four authors in the story. How do these writers fit the story and its purpose? Why does Mrs. Veal rather than Mrs. Bargrave mention these writers and their books?

A Journal of the Plague Year

A Journal of the Plague Year was inspired by an outbreak of the bubonic plague in Marseilles, France, in 1720. French shipping and merchandise were denied entrance to English ports lest the infection spread. Defoe, with a journalist's sense of impending news, wrote two articles warning Englishmen of the plague's fearsome effects. One of these was the *Journal*. It purports to be an eyewitness account by one H. F., a saddlemaker, of the plague in London in 1665. Like the *Apparition of One Mrs. Veal,* the *Journal* was long thought to be pure fiction, but modern scholars have discovered that Defoe had freely used the vital statistics of London during the troubled days. With these facts he combined fictitious incidents and other accounts from various sources.

.   .   .   .

It was now the beginning of August,[1] and the plague grew very violent and terrible in the place where I lived, and Dr. Heath coming to visit me, and finding that I ventured so

[1] 1665.

often out in the streets, earnestly persuaded me to lock myself up and my family, and not to suffer any of us to go out of doors; to keep all our windows fast, shutters and curtains close, and never to open them but first to make a very strong smoke in the room where the window or door was to be opened.

with rosin and pitch, brimstone or gun-powder, and the like; and we did this for some time. But as I had not laid in a store of provision for such a retreat, it was impossible that we could keep within doors entirely. However, I attempted, though it was so very late, to do something toward it; and first, as I had convenience both for brewing and baking, I went and bought two sacks of meal, and for several weeks, having an oven, we baked all our own bread; also I bought malt and brewed as much beer as all the casks I had would hold, and which seemed enough to serve my house for five or six weeks; also I laid in a quantity of salt butter and Cheshire cheese; but I had no flesh-meat, and the plague raged so violently among the butchers and slaughter-houses on the other side of our street, where they are known to dwell in great numbers, that it was not advisable so much as to go over the street among them.

And here I must observe again, that this necessity of going out of our houses to buy provisions was in a great measure the ruin of the whole city, for the people catched the distemper on these occasions one of another, and even the provisions themselves were often tainted; at least I have great reason to believe so; and therefore I cannot say with satisfaction what I know is repeated with great assurance, that the market-people and such as brought provisions to town were never infected. I am certain the butchers of White-chapel, where the greatest part of the flesh-meat was killed, were dreadfully visited, and that at least to such a degree that few of their shops were kept open, and those that remained of them killed their meat at Mile End and that way, and brought it to market upon horses.

However, the poor people could not lay up provisions, and there was a necessity that they must go to market to buy, and others to send servants or their children; and as this was a necessity which renewed itself daily, it brought abundance of unsound people to the markets, and a great many that went thither sound brought death home with them.

It is true people used all possible pre-caution. When any one bought a joint of meat in the market they would not take it out of the butcher's hand, but take it off the hooks themselves. On the other hand, the butcher would not touch the money, but have it put into a pot full of vinegar, which he kept for that purpose. The buyer carried always small money to make up any odd sum, that they might take no change. They carried bottles for scents and perfumes in their hands, and all the means that could be used were used. But then the poor could not do even these things, and they went at all hazards.

Innumerable dismal stories we heard every day on this very account. Sometimes a man or woman dropped down dead in the very markets, for many people that had the plague upon them knew nothing of it till the inward gangrene had affected their vitals, and they died in a few moments. This caused that many died frequently in that manner in the streets suddenly, without any warning; others perhaps had time to go to the next bulk or stall, or to any door-porch, and just sit down and die, as I have said before.

These objects were so frequent in the streets that when the plague came to be very raging on one side, there was scarce any passing by the streets but that several dead bodies would be lying here and there upon the ground. On the other hand, it is observable, that though at first the people would stop as they went along and call to the neighbors to come out on such an occasion, yet afterward no notice was taken of them; but that, if at any time we found a corpse lying, go across the way and not come near it; or, if in a narrow lane or passage, go back again and seek some other way to go on the business we were upon; and in those cases the corpse was always left till the officers had notice to come and take them away, or till night, when the bearers attending the dead-cart would take them up and carry them away. Nor did those undaunted creatures who performed these offices fail to search their pockets, and sometimes strip off their clothes if they were well dressed, as sometimes they were, and carry off what they could get.

But to return to the markets. The butchers took that care that if any person died in the market they had the officers always at hand to take them up upon hand-barrows and carry them to the next churchyard; and this was so frequent that such were not entered in the weekly bill, "Found dead in the streets or fields," as is the case now, but they went into the general articles of the great distemper.

But now the fury of the distemper increased to such a degree that even the markets were but very thinly furnished with provisions or frequented with buyers compared to what they were before; and the Lord Mayor caused the country people who brought provisions to be stopped in the streets leading into the town and to sit down there with their goods, where they sold what they brought, and went immediately away; and this encouraged the country people greatly to do so, for they sold their provisions at the very entrances into the town, and even in the fields, as particularly in the fields beyond Whitechapel, in Spitalfields; also in St. George's Fields in Southwark, in Bunhill Fields, and in a great field called Wood's Close, near Islington. Thither the Lord Mayor, aldermen, and magistrates sent their officers and servants to buy for their families, themselves keeping within doors as much as possible, and the like did many other people; and after this method was taken, the country people came with great cheerfulness, and brought provisions of all sorts, and very seldom got any harm, which I suppose added also to that report of their being miraculously preserved.

As for my little family, having thus, as I have said, laid in a store of bread, butter, cheese, and beer, I took my friend and physician's advice and locked myself up, and my family, and resolved to suffer the hardship of living a few months without flesh-meat, rather than to purchase it at the hazard of our lives.

But though I confined my family, I could not prevail upon my unsatisfied curiosity to stay within entirely myself; and though I generally came frighted and terrified home, yet I could not restrain; only that indeed I did not do it so frequently as at first.

I had some little obligations, indeed, upon me to go to my brother's house, which was in Coleman Street parish, and which he had left to my care, and I went at first every day, but afterwards only once or twice a week.

In these walks I had many dismal scenes before my eyes, as particularly of persons falling dead in the streets, terrible shrieks and screechings of women, who, in their agonies, would throw open their chamber windows and cry out in a dismal, surprising manner. It is impossible to describe the variety of postures in which the passions of the poor people would express themselves.

Passing through Tokenhouse Yard in Lothbury, of a sudden a casement violently opened just over my head, and a woman gave three frightful screeches, and then cried, "Oh! death, death, death!" in a most inimitable tone, and which struck me with horror and chillness in my very blood. There was nobody to be seen in the whole street, neither did any other window open, for people had no curiosity now in any case, nor could anybody help one another; so I went on to pass into Bell Alley.

Just in Bell Alley, on the right hand of the passage, there was a more terrible cry than that, though it was not so directed out at the window; but the whole family was in a terrible fright, and I could hear women and children run screaming about the rooms like distracted, when a garret-window opened, and somebody from a window on the other side the alley called and asked, "What is the matter?" upon which, from the first window it was answered, "O Lord, my old master has hanged himself!" The other asked again, "Is he quite dead?" and the first answered, "Ay, ay, quite dead; quite dead and cold!" This person was a merchant and a deputy alderman, and very rich. I care not to mention the name, though I knew his name too, but that would be an hardship to the family, which is now flourishing again.

But this is but one; it is scarce credible what dreadful cases happened in particular families every day. People in the rage of the distemper, or in the torment of their swellings, which was indeed intolerable, running out of their own government, raving and distracted, and oftentimes laying violent hands upon themselves, throwing themselves out at their windows, shooting themselves, &c.; mothers murdering their own children in their lunacy, some dying of mere grief as a passion, some of mere fright and surprise without any infection at all, others frighted into idiotism and foolish distractions, some into despair and lunacy, others into melancholy madness.

The pain of the swelling was in particular very violent, and to some intolerable; the physicians and surgeons may be said to have tortured many poor creatures even to death. The swellings in some grew hard, and they applied violent drawing-plasters or poultices to break them, and if these did not do they cut and scarified them in a terrible manner. In some those swellings were made hard partly by the force of the distemper and partly by their being too violently drawn, and were so hard that no instrument could cut them, and then they burnt them with caustics, so that many died raving mad with the torment, and some in the very operation. In these distresses, some, for want of help to hold them down in their beds, or to look to them, laid hands upon themselves, as above. Some broke out into the streets, perhaps naked, and would run directly down to the river, if they were not stopped by the watchmen or other officers, and plunge themselves into the water wherever they found it.

It often pierced my very soul to hear the groans and cries of those who were thus tormented, but of the two this was counted the most promising particular in the whole infection, for, if these swellings could be brought to a head, and to break and run, or, as the surgeons call it, to digest, the patient generally recovered; whereas those who, like the gentlewoman's daughter, were struck with death at the beginning, and had the tokens come out upon them, often went about indifferent easy till a little before they died, and some till the moment they dropped down, as in apoplexies and epilepsies is often the case. Such would be taken suddenly very sick, and would run to a bench or bulk, or any convenient place that offered itself, or to their own houses, if possible, as I mentioned before, and there sit down, grow faint, and die. This kind of dying was much the same as it was with those who die of common mortifications, who die swooning, and, as it were, go away in a dream. Such as died thus had very little notice of their being infected at all till the gangrene was spread through their whole body; nor could physicians themselves know certainly how it was with them, till they opened their breasts or other parts of their body, and saw the tokens.

We had at this time a great many frightful stories told us of nurses and watchmen who looked after the dying people; that is to say, hired nurses, who attended infected people, using them barbarously, starving them, smothering them, or by other wicked means hastening their end, that is to say, murdering of them. And watchmen, being set to guard houses that were shut up when there has been but one person left, and perhaps that one lying sick, that they have broke in and murdered that body, and immediately thrown them out into the dead-cart, and so they have gone scarce cold to the grave.

I cannot say but that some such murders were committed, and I think two were sent to prison for it, but died before they could be tried; and I have heard that three others, at several times, were excused for murders of that kind; but I must say I believe nothing of its being so common a crime as some have since pleased to say, nor did it seem to be so rational where the people were brought so low as not to be able to help themselves, for such seldom recovered, and there was no temptation to commit a murder, at least none equal to the fact, where they were sure persons would die in so short a time, and could not live.

That there were a great many robberies and wicked practices committed even in this dreadful time I do not deny. The power of avarice was so strong in some that they would run any hazard to steal and to plunder; and particularly in houses where all the families or inhabitants have been dead and carried out, they would break in at all hazards, and without regard to the danger of infection, take even the clothes off the dead bodies and the bed-clothes from others where they lay dead.

This, I suppose, must be the case of a family in Houndsditch, where a man and his daughter, the rest of the family being, as I suppose, carried away before by the dead-cart, were found stark naked, one in one chamber and one in another, lying dead on the floor, and the clothes of the beds, from whence 'tis supposed they were rolled off by thieves, stolen and carried quite away.

It is indeed to be observed that the women were in this calamity the most rash, fearless, and desperate creatures, and as there were vast numbers that went about as nurses to tend those that were sick, they committed a great many petty thieveries in the houses where they were employed; and some of them were publicly whipped for it, when perhaps they ought rather to have been hanged for examples, for numbers of houses were robbed on these occasions, till at length the parish officers were sent to recommend nurses to the sick, and always took an account who it was they sent, so as that they might call them to account if the house had been abused where they were placed.

But these robberies extended chiefly to wearing-clothes, linen, and what rings or money they could come at when the person died who was under their care, but not to a general plunder of the houses; and I could give an account of one of these nurses, who, several years after, being on her deathbed, confessed with the utmost horror the robberies she had committed at the time of her being a nurse, and by which she had enriched herself to a great degree. But as for murders, I do not find that there was ever any proof of the facts in the manner as it has been reported, except as above.

They did tell me, indeed, of a nurse in one place that laid a wet cloth upon the face of a dying patient whom she tended, and so put an end to his life, who was just expiring before; and another that smothered a young woman she was looking to when she was in a fainting fit, and would have come to herself; some that killed them by giving them one thing, some another, and some starved them by giving them nothing at all. But these stories had two marks of suspicion that always attended them, which caused me always to slight them, and to look on them as mere stories that people continually frighted one another with. That wherever it was that we heard it, they always placed the scene at the farther end of the town, opposite or most remote from where you were to hear it. If you heard it in Whitechapel, it happened at St. Giles', or at Westminster, or Holborn, or that end of the town. If you heard it at that end of the town, then it was done in Whitechapel, or the Minories, or about Cripplegate parish. If you heard of it in the city, why, then it happened in Southwark; and if you heard of it in Southwark, then it was done in the city, and the like.

In the next place, of what part soever you heard the story, the particulars were always the same, especially that of laying a wet double clout on a dying man's face, and that of smothering a young gentlewoman; so that it was apparent, at least to my judgment, that there was more of tale than of truth in those things.

However, I cannot say but it had some effect upon the people, and particularly that, as I said before, they grew more cautious who they took into their houses, and who they trusted their lives with, and had them always recommended if they could; and where they could not find such, for they were not very plenty, they applied to the parish officers.

But here again the misery of that time lay upon the poor, who, being infected, had neither food or physic, neither physician or apothecary to assist them, or nurse to attend them. Many of those died calling for help, and even for sustenance, out at their windows, in a most miserable and deplorable manner; but it must be added that whenever the cases of such persons or families were represented to my Lord Mayor they always were relieved.

It is true, in some houses where the people were not very poor, yet where they had sent perhaps their wives and children away, and if they had any servants they had been dismissed; I say, it is true that to save the expenses, many such as these shut themselves in, and not having help, died alone.

A neighbor and acquaintance of mine, having some money owing to him from a shopkeeper in Whitecross Street or thereabouts, sent his apprentice, a youth about eighteen years of age, to endeavor to get the money. He came to the door, and finding it shut, knocked pretty hard, and, as he thought, heard somebody answer within, but was not sure, so he waited, and after some stay knocked again, and then a third time, when he heard somebody coming downstairs.

At length the man of the house came to the door; he had on his breeches or drawers, and a yellow flannel waistcoat, no stockings, a pair of slipped-shoes,[2] a white cap on his head, and, as the young man said, death in his face.

When he opened the door, says he, "What do you disturb me thus for?" The boy, though a little surprised, replied, "I come from such a one, and my master sent me for the money which he says you know of." "Very well, child," returns the living ghost; "call as you go by at Cripple-gate Church, and bid them ring the bell"; and with these words shut the door again, and went up again, and died the same day; nay, perhaps the same hour. This the young man told me himself, and I have reason to believe it. This was while the plague was not come to a height. I think it was in June, toward the latter end of the month; it must be before the dead-carts came about, and while they used the ceremony of ringing the bell for the dead, which was over for certain, in that parish at least, before the month of July, for by the 25th of July there died 550 and upwards in a week, and then they could no more bury in form, rich or poor.

I have mentioned above that notwithstanding this dreadful calamity, yet the numbers of thieves were abroad upon all occasions where they had found any prey, and that these were generally women. It was one morning about eleven o'clock, I had walked

out to my brother's house in Coleman Street parish, as I often did, to see that all was safe.

My brother's house had a little court before it, and a brick wall and a gate in it, and within that several warehouses where his goods of several sorts lay. It happened that in one of these warehouses were several packs of women's high-crowned hats, which came out of the country, and were, as I suppose, for exportation, whither I know not.

I was surprised that when I came near my brother's door, which was in a place they called Swan Alley, I met three or four women with high-crowned hats on their heads; and, as I remembered afterwards, one, if not more, had some hats likewise in their hands; but as I did not see them come out at my brother's door, and not knowing that my brother had any such goods in his warehouse, I did not offer to say anything to them, but went across the way to shun meeting them, as was usual to do at that time, for fear of the plague. But when I came nearer to the gate, I met another woman with more hats come out of the gate. "What business, mistress," said I, "have you had there?" "There are more people there," said she; "I have had no more business there than they." I was hasty to get to the gate then, and said no more to her, by which means she got away. But just as I came to the gate, I saw two more coming across the yard to come out with hats also on their heads and under their arms; at which I threw the gate to behind me, which having a spring lock fastened itself; and turning to the women, "Forsooth," said I, "what are ye doing here?" and seized upon the hats, and took them from them. One of them, who, I confess, did not look like a thief—"Indeed," says she, "we are wrong, but we were told they were goods that had no owner. Be pleased to take them again; and look yonder, there are more such customers as we." She cried and looked pitifully, so I took the hats from her, and opened the gate, and bade them be gone, for I pitied the women indeed; but when I looked toward the warehouse, as she directed, there were six or seven more, all women, fitting themselves with hats, as

[2] House-slippers.

unconcerned and quiet as if they had been at a hatter's shop buying for their money.

I was surprised, not at the sight of so many thieves only, but at the circumstances I was in; being now to thrust myself in among so many people, who for some weeks had been so shy of myself that if I met anybody in the street I would cross the way from them.

They were equally surprised, though on another account. They all told me they were neighbors, that they had heard any one might take them, that they were nobody's goods, and the like. I talked big to them at first, went back to the gate and took out the key, so that they were all my prisoners, threatened to lock them all into the warehouse, and go and fetch my Lord Mayor's officers for them.

They begged heartily, protested they found the gate open, and the warehouse door open, and that it had no doubt been broken open by some who had expected to find goods of greater value, which indeed was reasonable to believe, because the lock was broke, and a padlock that hung to the door on the outside also loose, and not abundance of the hats carried away.

At length I considered that this was not a time to be cruel and rigorous; and besides that, it would necessarily oblige me to go much about, to have several people come to me, and I go to several whose circumstances of health I knew nothing of; and that even at this time the plague was so high as that there died 4000 a week; so that in showing my resentment, or even in seeking justice for my brother's goods, I might lose my own life; so I contented myself with taking the names and places where some of them lived, who were really inhabitants in the neighborhood, and threatening that my brother should call them to an account for it when he returned to his habitation.

Then I talked a little upon another foot with them, and asked them how they could do such things as these in a time of such general calamity, and, as it were, in the face of God's most dreadful judgments, when the plague was at their very doors, and, it may be, in their very houses, and they did not know but that the dead-cart might stop at their doors in a few hours, to carry them to their graves.

I could not perceive that my discourse made much impression upon them all that while, till it happened that there came two men of the neighborhood, hearing of the disturbance, and knowing my brother, for they had been both dependents upon his family, and they came to my assistance. These being, as I said, neighbors, presently knew three of the women, and told me who they were, and where they lived; and, it seems, they had given me a true account of themselves before.

This brings these two men to a further remembrance. The name of one was John Hayward, who was at that time under-sexton of the parish of St. Stephen, Coleman Street. By under-sexton was understood at that time gravedigger and bearer of the dead. This man carried, or assisted to carry, all the dead to their graves which were buried in that large parish, and who were carried in form, and after that form of burying was stopped, went with the dead-cart and the bell to fetch the dead bodies from the houses where they lay, and fetched many of them out of the chambers and houses; for the parish was, and is still remarkable, particularly above all the parishes in London, for a great number of alleys and thoroughfares, very long, into which no carts could come, and where they were obliged to go and fetch the bodies a very long way; which alleys now remain to witness it, such as White's Alley, Cross Key Court, Swan Alley, Bell Alley, White Horse Alley, and many more. Here they went with a kind of hand-barrow and laid the dead bodies on it, and carried them out to the carts; which work he performed and never had the distemper at all, but lived about twenty years after it, and was sexton of the parish to the time of his death. His wife at the same time was a nurse to infected people, and tended many that died in the parish, being for her honesty recommended by the parish officers, yet she never was infected neither.

He never used any preservative against the infection, other than holding garlic and rue in his mouth and smoking tobacco. This I also had from his own mouth. And his wife's remedy was washing her head in vinegar, and sprinkling her head-clothes so with vinegar as to keep them always moist; and if the smell of any of those she waited on was more than ordinary offensive, she snuffed vinegar up her nose and sprinkled vinegar upon her head-clothes, and held a handkerchief wetted with vinegar to her mouth.

It must be confessed that though the plague was chiefly among the poor, yet were the poor the most venturous and fearless of it, and went about their employment with a sort of brutal courage; I must call it so, for it was founded neither on religion or prudence; scarce did they use any caution, but ran into any business which they could get employment in, though it was the most hazardous. Such was that of tending the sick, watching houses shut up, carrying infected persons to the pesthouse, and, which was still worse, carrying the dead away to their graves.

It was under this John Hayward's care, and within his bounds, that the story of the piper, with which people have made themselves so merry, happened, and he assured me that it was true. It is said that it was a blind piper; but, as John told me, the fellow was not blind, but an ignorant, weak, poor man, and usually walked his rounds about ten o'clock at night and went piping along from door to door, and the people usually took him in at public-houses where they knew him, and would give him a drink and victuals, and sometimes farthings; and he in return would pipe and sing and talk simply, which diverted the people; and thus he lived. It was but a very bad time for this diversion while things were as I have told, yet the poor fellow went about as usual, but was almost starved; and when anybody asked how he did he would answer, the dead-cart had not taken him yet, but that they had promised to call for him next week.

It happened one night that this poor fellow, whether somebody had given him too much drink or no—John Hayward said he had not drink in his house, but that they had given him a little more victuals than ordinary at a public-house in Coleman Street; and the poor fellow, having not usually had a bellyful, or perhaps not [for] a good while, was laid all along upon the top of a bulk or stall, and fast asleep, at a door in the street near London Wall toward Cripplegate, and that upon the same bulk or stall the people of some house, in the alley of which the house was a corner, hearing a bell, which they always rang before the cart came, had laid a body really dead of the plague just by him, thinking, too, that this poor fellow had been a dead body, as the other was, and laid there by some of the neighbors.

Accordingly, when John Hayward with his bell and the cart came along, finding two dead bodies lie upon the stall, they took them up with the instrument they used and threw them into the cart; and all this while the piper slept soundly.

From hence they passed along and took in other dead bodies, till, as honest John Hayward told me, they almost buried him alive in the cart; yet all this while he slept soundly. At length the cart came to the place where the bodies were to be thrown into the ground, which, as I do remember, was at Mount Mill; and as the cart usually stopped some time before they were ready to shoot out the melancholy load they had in it, as soon as the cart stopped the fellow awaked and struggled a little to get his head out from among the dead bodies, when raising himself up in the cart, he called out, "Hey! where am I?" This frighted the fellow that attended about the work; but after some pause John Hayward, recovering himself, said, "Lord, bless us! There's somebody in the cart not quite dead!" So another called to him and said, "Who are you?" The fellow answered, "I am the poor piper. Where am I?" "Where are you?" says Hayward. "Why, you are in the dead-cart, and we are a-going to bury you." "But I an't dead though, am I?" says the piper; which made them laugh a little, though as John said, they were heartily frighted at first; so they helped the poor fellow down, and he went about his business.

I know the story goes he set up his pipes in the cart and frighted the bearers and others so that they ran away; but John Hayward did not tell the story so, nor say anything of his piping at all; but that he was a poor piper, and that he was carried away as above I am fully satisfied of the truth of.

(1722)

STUDY AIDS. 1. Notice that Defoe is skeptical of some of the stories he has heard (see p. 328/2, ll. 4–29). How does this suspicion help establish belief in other stories? What other devices does he employ to create belief in his record?

5   2. How does Defoe keep his reader's interest alive?

3. What evidence can you see that the *Journal* was written to a middle-class audience? How is Defoe's style (especially sentences and diction) adapted to his audience?

Joseph Addison
(1672–1719)

and

Richard Steele
(1672–1729)

ADDISON AND STEELE, WHOSE CAREERS WERE INTERMINGLED ALMOST FROM THE BEGINNING, were born the same year. They were fellow students at the Charterhouse and, for three years, at Oxford. When they separated in 1692, Addison remained at Oxford to pursue the scholar's life. Steele, however, with his usual gusto threw himself into a variety of activities: fighting with the army in Flanders, killing a companion in a duel, fathering an illegitimate child, writing a moral treatise, *The Christian Hero,* to quiet his conscience, then following this work with a sentimental comedy, *The Funeral,* to reestablish his reputation as a boon companion among the soldiers. In 1709 Steele began *The Tatler* to provide his family with money, a commodity always scarce because of his generous and impulsive nature.

Meanwhile, Addison had completed his education, and after four years' travel on the Continent he had entered Whig politics. His steady but unspectacular rise in this field reached its height in 1709, when he was appointed Secretary to the Lord Lieutenant of Ireland. In Dublin, Addison read issues of *The Tatler* and recognized the style of his old friend, to whom he began sending contributions. These anonymous essays appeared in *The Tatler* until it was discontinued in January, 1711. In March the two men launched *The Spectator,* which appeared six times a week until the end of 1712. Addison, always the dominant influence on the new paper, revived it for six months in 1714.

For a hundred years *The Tatler* and *The Spectator* represented the highest perfection of the journalistic essay. Their popularity and influence were due largely to their graceful style and tone—the latter a delicate blending of easy humor with good-natured satire directed against the trivia of eighteenth-century society. The essays gently laughed at the misplaced values of the growing middle class, being careful to agree with public opinion and almost never to oppose it.

Tatler 181

[Recollections of Sorrow]

Dies, ni fallor, adest, quem semper acerbum,
Semper honoratum (sic di voluistis) habebo.
Virgil, *Aeneid* V, 49-50

"And now the rising day renews the year,
A day forever sad, forever dear."

[Dryden]

There are those among mankind who can enjoy no relish of their being, except the world is made acquainted with all that relates to them, and think everything lost that passes unobserved; but others find a solid delight in stealing by the crowd, and modeling their life after such a manner, as is as much above the approbation as the practice of the vulgar. Life being too short to give instances great enough of true friendship or good-will, some sages have thought it pious to preserve a certain reverence for the *manes* [1] of their deceased friends, and have withdrawn themselves from the rest of the world at certain seasons, to commemorate in their own thoughts such of their acquaintance who have gone before them out of this life: and indeed, when we are advanced in years, there is not a more pleasing entertainment than to recollect in a gloomy moment the many we have parted with that have been dear and agreeable to us, and to cast a melancholy thought or two after those with whom, perhaps, we have indulged ourselves in whole nights of mirth and jollity. With such inclinations in my heart I went to my closet yesterday in the evening, and resolved to be sorrowful; [2] upon which occasion, I could not but look with disdain upon myself, that though all the reasons which I had to lament the loss of many of my friends, are now as forcible as at the moment of their departure, yet did not my heart swell with the same sorrow which I felt at that time; but I could, without tears, reflect upon many pleasing adventures I have had with some who have long been blended with common earth. Though it is by the benefit of nature that length of time thus blots out the violence of afflictions; yet with tempers too much given to pleasure, it is almost necessary to revive the old places of grief in our memory, and ponder step by step on past life, to lead the mind into that sobriety of thought which poises the heart, and makes it beat with due time, without being quickened with desire, or retarded with despair, from its proper and equal motion. When we wind up a clock that is out of order, to make it go well for the future, we do not immediately set the hand to the present instant, but we make it strike the round of all its hours, before it can recover the regularity of its time. "Such," thought I, "shall be my method this evening; and since it is that day of the year which I dedicate to the memory of such in another life as I much delighted in when living, an hour or two shall be sacred to sorrow and their memory, while I run over all the melancholy circumstances of this kind which have occurred to me in my whole life."

The first sense of sorrow I ever knew was upon the death of my father, at which time I was not quite five years of age; but was rather amazed at what all the house meant, than possessed with a real understanding why nobody was willing to play with me. I remember I went into the room where his body lay, and my mother sat weeping alone by it. I had my battledore [3] in my hand, and fell a beating

[1] Ancestral spirits worshiped as gods.

[2] It is often impossible to determine on the basis of style whether Steele or Addison wrote a particular essay. Steele, however, seemed to prefer a more emotional subject than did Addison. He had a strain of "sensibility," a quality which later in the eighteenth century was to become valued by the earlier romantics. To these later writers, "sensibility" and even SENTIMENTALISM was an evidence of sincerity, genius, and even goodness.

[3] Racquet or bat.

the coffin, and called "Papa"; for I know not how I had some slight idea that he was locked up there. My mother catched me in her arms, and transported beyond all patience of the silent grief she was before in, she almost smothered me in her embrace, and told me in a flood of tears, papa could not hear me, and would play with me no more, for they were going to put him under ground, whence he could never come to us again. She was a very beautiful woman, of a noble spirit, and there was a dignity in her grief amidst all the wildness of her transport, which, methought, struck me with an instinct of sorrow, which, before I was sensible of what it was to grieve, seized my very soul, and has made pity the weakness of my heart ever since. The mind in infancy is, methinks, like the body in embryo, and receives impressions so forcible, that they are as hard to be removed by reason, as any mark with which a child is born is to be taken away by any future application. Hence it is that good nature in me is no merit; but having been so frequently overwhelmed with her tears before I knew the cause of any affliction, or could draw defenses from my own judgment, I imbibed commiseration, remorse, and an unmanly gentleness of mind, which has since ensnared me into ten thousand calamities, and from whence I can reap no advantage, except it be, that in such a humor as I am now in, I can the better indulge myself in the softnesses of humanity, and enjoy that sweet anxiety which arises from the memory of past afflictions.

We that are very old, are better able to remember things which befell us in our distant youth than the passages of later days. For this reason it is, that the companions of my strong and vigorous years present themselves more immediately to me in this office of sorrow. Untimely or unhappy deaths are what we are most apt to lament, so little are we able to make it indifferent when a thing happens, though we know it must happen. Thus we groan under life, and bewail those who are relieved from it. Every object that returns to our imagination raises different passions according to the circumstance of their departure. Who can have lived in an army, and in a serious hour reflect upon the many gay and agreeable men that might long have flourished in the arts of peace, and not join with the imprecations of the fatherless and widow on the tyrant to whose ambition they fell sacrifices? But gallant men who are cut off by the sword move rather our veneration than our pity, and we gather relief enough from their own contempt of death to make it no evil, which was approached with so much cheerfulness, and attended with so much honor. But when we turn our thoughts from the great parts of life on such occasions, and instead of lamenting those who stood ready to give death to those from whom they had the fortune to receive it; I say, when we let our thoughts wander from such noble objects, and consider the havoc which is made among the tender and the innocent, pity enters with an unmixed softness, and possesses all our souls at once.

Here (were there words to express such sentiments with proper tenderness) I should record the beauty, innocence, and untimely death, of the first object my eyes ever beheld with love. The beauteous virgin! How ignorantly did she charm, how carelessly excel! O Death! thou hast right to the bold, to the ambitious, to the high, and to the haughty, but why this cruelty to the humble, to the meek, to the undiscerning, to the thoughtless? Nor age, nor business, nor distress, can erase the dear image from my imagination. In the same week, I saw her dressed for a ball, and in a shroud. How ill did the habit of death become the pretty trifler! I still behold the smiling earth——

A large train of disasters were coming on to my memory when my servant knocked at my closet door, and interrupted me with a letter, attended with a hamper of wine, of the same sort with that which is to be put to sale on Thursday next at Garraway's Coffee-house. Upon the receipt of it, I sent for three of my friends. We are so intimate that we can be company in whatever state of mind we meet, and can entertain each other without expecting always to rejoice. The wine we found to be generous and warming, but with such a heat as moved us rather to be cheerful than frolicsome. It revived the spirits without firing the blood. We commended it till two of the clock this morning, and, having today met a little before dinner, we found that, though we drank two bottles a man, we had much more reason to recollect than forget what had passed the night before.

(June 6, 1710)   (Steele)

STUDY AIDS: 1. The organization of this essay is quite simple. It consists of an introduction (paragraph 1), three illustrations (paragraphs 2–4), and a conclusion. What details in the introduction prepare for the three illustrations in the body of the essay? How do these details justify the abrupt interruption of the conclusion?

2. The "man of feeling" was usually a melancholy man. Notice how Steele emphasizes melancholy throughout this essay and how he unites it with "good nature" (p. 334/1, ll. 17–35) or "sensibility." What relations are there between "sensibility" and the medieval humor of melancholy? How does Milton's treatment of melancholy in *Il Penseroso* differ from Steele's?

3. Where and how in the essay does Steele break away from sentimentalism?

Tatler 249

[*Adventures of a Shilling*]

Per varios casus, per tot discrimina rerum,
Tendimus—

Virgil, *Aeneid* I, 209

"Through various hazards, and events, we move."

I was last night visited by a friend of mine, who has an inexhaustible fund of discourse, and never fails to entertain his company with a variety of thoughts and hints that are altogether new and uncommon. Whether it were in complaisance to my way of living, or his real opinion, he advanced the following paradox: that it required much greater talents to fill up and become a retired life than a life of business. Upon this occasion he rallied very agreeably the busy men of the age, who only value themselves for being in motion, and passing through a series of trifling and insignificant actions. In the heat of his discourse, seeing a piece of money lying on my table, "I defy," says he, "any of these active persons to produce half the adventures that this twelve-penny piece has been engaged in, were it possible for him to give us an account of his life."

My friend's talk made so odd an impression upon my mind, that soon after I was a-bed I fell insensibly into an unaccountable reverie, that had neither moral nor design in it, and cannot be so properly called a dream as a delirium.

Methought the shilling that lay upon the table reared itself upon its edge, and, turning the face toward me, opened its mouth, and in a soft silver sound, gave me the following account of his life and adventures:

"I was born," says he, "on the side of a mountain, near a little village of Peru, and made a voyage to England in an ingot under the convoy of Sir Francis Drake. I was, soon after my arrival, taken out of my Indian habit, refined, naturalized, and put into the British mode, with the face of Queen Elizabeth on one side, and the arms of the country on the other. Being thus equipped, I found in me a wonderful inclination to ramble, and visit all the parts of the new world into which I was brought. The people very much favored my natural disposition, and shifted me so fast from hand to hand, that, before I was five years old, I had traveled into almost every corner of the nation. But in the beginning of my sixth year, to my unspeakable grief, I fell into the hands of a miserable old fellow, who clapped me into an iron chest, where I found five hundred more of my own quality who lay under the same confinement. The only relief we had, was to be taken out and counted over in the fresh air every morning and evening. After an imprisonment of several years, we heard somebody knocking at our chest, and breaking it open with an hammer. This we found was the old man's heir, who, as his father lay dying, was so good as to come to our release. He separated us that very day. What was the fate of my companions I know not: as for myself, I was sent to the apothecary's shop for a pint of sack. The apothecary gave me to an herb-woman, the herb-woman to a butcher, the butcher to a brewer, and the brewer to his wife, who made a present of me to a nonconformist preacher. After this manner I made my way merrily through the world; for, as I told you before, we shillings love nothing so much as traveling. I sometimes fetched in a shoulder of mutton, sometimes a play-book, and often had the satisfaction to treat a templer at a twelve-penny ordinary, or carry him with three friends to Westminster-hall.

"In the midst of this pleasant progress which I made from place to place, I was arrested by a superstitious old woman, who shut me up in a greasy purse, in pursuance of a foolish saying, 'that while she kept a Queen Elizabeth's shilling about her, she would never be without money.' I continued here a close prisoner for many months, until at last I was exchanged for eight-and-forty farthings.

"I thus rambled from pocket to pocket until the beginning of the civil wars, when, to my shame be it spoken, I was employed in raising soldiers against the king: for, being of a very tempting breadth, a sergeant made use of me to inveigle country fellows, and lift them into the service of the Parliament.

"As soon as he had made one man sure, his way was, to oblige him to take a shilling of a more homely figure, and then practice the same trick upon another. Thus I continued doing great mischief to the crown, until my officer chancing one morning to walk abroad earlier than ordinary, sacrificed me to his pleasures, and made use of me to seduce a milk-maid. This wench bent me, and gave me to her sweetheart, applying more properly than she intended the usual form of, 'to my love and from my love.' This

ungenerous gallant marrying her within few days after, pawned me for a dram of brandy, and drinking me out next day, I was beaten flat with an hammer, and again set a running.

"After many adventures which it would be tedious to relate, I was sent to a young spendthrift, in company with the will of his deceased father. The young fellow, who I found was very extravagant, gave great demonstrations of joy at the receiving of the will: but opening it, he found himself disinherited and cut off from the possession of a fair estate, by virtue of my being made a present to him. This put him into such a passion, that after having taken me in his hand, and cursed me, he squirred me away from him as far as he could fling me. I chanced to light in an unfrequented place under a dead wall, where I lay undiscovered and useless, during the usurpation of Oliver Cromwell.

"About a year after the King's return, a poor cavalier that was walking there about dinner-time fortunately cast his eye upon me, and, to the great joy of us both, carried me to a cook's shop, where he dined upon me, and drank the King's health. When I came again into the world, I found that I had been happier in my retirement than I thought, having probably by that means escaped wearing a monstrous pair of breeches.

"Being now of great credit and antiquity, I was rather looked upon as a medal than an ordinary coin; for which reason a gamester laid hold of me, and converted me to a counter, having got together some dozens of us for that use. We led a melancholy life in his possession, being busy at those hours wherein current coin is at rest, and partaking the fate of our master, being in a few moments valued at a crown, a pound, or a sixpence, according to the situation in which the fortune of the cards placed us. I had at length the good luck to see my master break, by which means I was again sent abroad under my primitive denomination of a shilling.

"I shall pass over many other accidents of less moment, and hasten to that fatal catastrophe when I fell into the hands of an artist, who conveyed me under ground, and, with an unmerciful pair of shears, cut off my titles, clipped my brims, retrenched my shape, rubbed me to my inmost ring; and, in short, so spoiled and pillaged me, that he did not leave me worth a groat. You may think what confusion I was in to see myself thus curtailed and disfigured. I should have been ashamed to have shown my head, had not all my old acquaintance been reduced to the same shameful figure, excepting some few that were punched through the belly. In the midst of this general calamity, when everybody thought our misfortune irretrievable, and our case desperate, we were thrown into the furnace together, and, as it often happens with cities rising out of a fire, appeared with greater beauty and luster than we could ever boast of before. What has happened to me since

this change of sex which you now see, I shall take some other opportunity to relate. In the meantime, I shall only repeat two adventures, as being very extraordinary, and neither of them having ever happened to me above once in my life. The first was, my being in a poet's pocket, who was so taken with the brightness and novelty of my appearance, that it gave occasion to the finest burlesque poem in the British language, entitled, from me, *The Splendid Shilling.* The second adventure, which I must not omit, happened to me in the year 1703, when I was given away in charity to a blind man; but indeed this was by mistake, the person who gave me having thrown me heedlessly into the hat among a pennyworth of farthings."

(November 11, 1710)   (Addison)

Spectator 2
[The Spectator Club]

—Haec alii sex
Vel plures uno conclamant ore.
Juvenal

"Six more at least join their consenting voice."

The first of our society is a gentleman of Worcestershire, of ancient descent, a baronet; his name Sir Roger de Coverley.[1] His great-

[1] Although several attempts have been made to identify Sir Roger de Coverley with some contemporary figure, there can be little doubt that he is largely a creation of Steele's imagination. Sir Roger belongs to the "character-sketch" tradition, practiced first by Theophrastus (*ca.* 371–287 B.C.) and revitalized in the seventeenth century by such writers as Thomas Overbury and John Earle. From these men, the "character-sketch" descended to John Dryden, who turned the form to satiric ends in his poetry by using it to dissect political and literary foes. Still later Addison and Steele created generalized, fictitious characters, such as Sir Roger, and gave them a new and larger dimension—a social and political background. From this stage of its development the sketch moved into the novel, which was coming into existence in the first half of the eighteenth century.

grandfather was inventor of that famous country-dance which is called after him. All who know that shire are very well acquainted with the parts and merits of Sir Roger. He is a gentleman that is very singular in his behavior, but his singularities proceed from his good sense, and are contradictions to the manners of the world only as he thinks the world is in the wrong. However, this humor creates him no enemies, for he does nothing with sourness of obstinacy; and his being unconfined to modes and forms, makes him but the readier and more capable to please and oblige all who know him. When he is in town, he lives in Soho Square. It is said he keeps himself a bachelor by reason he was crossed in love by a perverse, beautiful widow of the next county to him. Before this disappointment, Sir Roger was what you call a fine gentleman, had often supped with my Lord Rochester [2] and Sir

[2] The three men in this sentence were prominent Restoration figures: Rochester was an aristocrat, minor poet, and notorious libertine; Etherege was a famous writer of comedies; and Dawson was an infamous "confidence man."

George Etherege, fought a duel upon his first coming to town, and kicked Bully Dawson in a public coffee-house for calling him "youngster." But being ill-used by the above-mentioned widow, he was very serious for a year and a half; and though, his temper being naturally jovial, he at last got over it, he grew careless of himself, and never dressed afterward. He continues to wear a coat and a doublet of the same cut that were in fashion at the time of his repulse, which, in his merry humors, he tells us, has been in and out twelve times since he first wore it. 'Tis said Sir Roger grew humble in his desires after he had forgot this cruel beauty; but this is looked upon by his friends rather as a matter of raillery than truth. He is now in his fifty-sixth year, cheerful, gay, and hearty; keeps a good house in both town and country; a great lover of mankind; but there is such a mirthful cast in his behavior that he is rather beloved than esteemed. His tenants grow rich, his servants look satisfied, all the young women profess love to him, and the young men are glad of his company; when he comes into a house he calls the servants by their names, and talks all the way upstairs to a visit. I must not omit that Sir Roger is a justice of the quorum; that he fills the chair at a quarter-session with great abilities; and, three months ago, gained universal applause by explaining a passage in the Game Act.

The gentleman next in esteem and authority among us is another bachelor, who is a member of the Inner Temple;[3] a man of great probity, wit, and understanding; but he has chosen his place of residence rather to obey the direction of an old humorsome father, than in pursuit of his own inclinations. He was placed there to study the laws of the land, and is the most learned of any of the house in those of the stage. Aristotle and Longinus are much better understood by him than Littleton or Coke.[4] The father sends up, every post, questions relating to marriage-

articles, leases, and tenures, in the neighborhood; all which questions he agrees with an attorney to answer and take care of in the lump. He is studying the passions themselves, when he should be inquiring into the debates among men which arise from them. He knows the argument of each of the orations of Demosthenes and Tully,[5] but not one case in the reports of our own courts. No one ever took him for a fool, but none, except his intimate friends, know he has a great deal of wit. This turn makes him at once both disinterested and agreeable; as few of his thoughts are drawn from business, they are most of them fit for conversation. His taste of books is a little too just for the age he lives in; he has read all, but approves of very few. His familiarity with the customs, manners, actions, and writings of the ancients makes him a very delicate observer of what occurs to him in the present world. He is an excellent critic, and the time of the play is his hour of business; exactly at five he passes through New Inn, crosses through Russell Court, and takes a turn at Will's[6] till the play begins; he has his shoes rubbed and his periwig powdered at the barber's as you go into the Rose. It is for the good of the audience when he is at a play, for the actors have an ambition to please him.

The person of next consideration is Sir Andrew Freeport,[7] a merchant of great eminence in the city of London, a person of indefatigable industry, strong reason, and great experience. His notions of trade are noble and generous, and (as every rich man has usually some sly way of jesting which would make no great figure were he not a rich man) he calls the sea the British Common. He is acquainted with commerce in all its parts, and will tell you that it is a stupid and barbarous way to extend dominion by arms; for true

[5] Cicero.

[6] Coffeehouse patronized by Dryden and his circle.

[7] Steele's audience would immediately recognize Sir Andrew Freeport as a Whig from the references to his being a merchant and holding liberal views on trade and tariff (as his name indicates). He is, then, the political opposite to Sir Roger, a landed country gentleman and by reason of that station, a Tory.

[3] The Inner Temple was one of the Inns of Court, where lawyers were trained and where they practiced.

[4] Littleton and Coke were famous legal commentators.

power is to be got by arts and industry. He will often argue that if this part of our trade were well cultivated, we should gain from one nation; and if another, from another. I have heard him prove that diligence makes more lasting acquisitions than valor, and that sloth has ruined more nations than the sword. He abounds in several frugal maxims, among which the greatest favorite is, "A penny saved is a penny got." A general trader of good sense is pleasanter company than a general scholar; and Sir Andrew having a natural unaffected eloquence, the perspicuity of his discourse gives the same pleasure that wit would in another man. He has made his fortunes himself, and says that England may be richer than other kingdoms by as plain methods as he himself is richer than other men; though at the same time I can say this of him, that there is not a point in the compass but blows home a ship in which he is an owner.

Next to Sir Andrew in the club-room sits Captain Sentry, a gentleman of great courage, good understanding, but invincible modesty. He is one of those that deserve very well, but are very awkward at putting their talents within the observation of such as should take notice of them. He was some years a captain, and behaved himself with great gallantry in several engagements and at several sieges; but having a small estate of his own, and being next heir to Sir Roger, he has quitted a way of life in which no man can rise suitably to his merit who is not something of a courtier as well as a soldier. I have heard him often lament that in a profession where merit is placed in so conspicuous a view, impudence should get the better of modesty. When he has talked to this purpose I never heard him make a sour expression, but frankly confess that he left the world because he was not fit for it. A strict honesty and an even, regular behavior are in themselves obstacles to him that must press through crowds who endeavor at the same end with himself—the favor of a commander. He will, however, in this way of talk, excuse generals for not disposing according to men's desert, or inquiring into it, "For," says he, "that great man who has a

mind to help me, has as many to break through to come at me as I have to come at him"; therefore he will conclude that the man who would make a figure, especially in a military way, must get over all false modesty, and assist his patron against the importunity of other pretenders by a proper assurance in his own vindication. He says it is a civil cowardice to be backward in asserting what you ought to expect, as it is a military fear to be slow in attacking when it is your duty. With this candor does the gentleman speak of himself and others. The same frankness runs through all his conversation. The military part of his life has furnished him with many adventures, in the relation of which he is very agreeable to the company; for he is never overbearing, though accustomed to command men in the utmost degree below him; nor ever too obsequious from an habit of obeying men highly above him.

But that our society may not appear a set of humorists [8] unacquainted with the gallantries and pleasures of the age, we have among us the gallant Will Honeycomb, a gentleman who, according to his years, should be in the decline of his life, but having ever been very careful of his person, and always had a very easy fortune, time has made but very little impression either by wrinkles on his forehead or traces in his brain. His person is well turned and of a good height. He is very ready at that sort of discourse with which men usually entertain women. He has all his life dressed very well, and remembers habits as others do men. He can smile when one speaks to him, and laughs easily. He knows the history of every mode, and can inform you from which of the French king's wenches our wives and daughters had this manner of curling their hair, that way of placing their hoods; whose frailty was covered by such a sort of petticoat, and whose vanity to show her foot made that part of the dress so short in such a year. In a word, all his conversation and knowledge has been in the female world. As other men of his age will take notice to you what such a minister said upon such and such an occasion, he will tell

[8] Eccentrics.

you when the Duke of Monmouth [9] danced at court such a woman was then smitten, another was taken with him at the head of his troop in the park. In all these important relations, he has ever about the same time received a kind glance or a blow of a fan from some celebrated beauty, mother of the present Lord Such-a-one. If you speak of a young commoner that said a lively thing in the House, he starts up: "He has good blood in his veins; Tom Mirabell, the rogue, cheated me in that affair; that young fellow's mother used me more like a dog than any woman I ever made advances to." This way of talking of his very much enlivens the conversation among us of a more sedate turn; and I find there is not one of the company but myself, who rarely speak at all, but speaks of him as of that sort of man who is usually called a well-bred, fine gentleman. To conclude his character, where women are not concerned, he is an honest, worthy man.

I cannot tell whether I am to account him whom I am next to speak of as one of our company, for he visits us but seldom; but when he does, it adds to every man else a new enjoyment of himself. He is a clergyman, a very philosophic man, of general learning, great sanctity of life, and the most exact good breeding. He has the misfortune to be of a very weak constitution, and consequently cannot accept of such cares and business as preferments in his function would oblige him to; he is therefore among divines what a

chamber-counselor is among lawyers. The probity of his mind and the integrity of his life create him followers, as being eloquent or loud advances others. He seldom introduces the subject he speaks upon; but we are so far gone in years that he observes, when he is among us, an earnestness to have him fall on some divine topic, which he always treats with much authority, as one who has no interest in this world, as one who is hastening to the object of all his wishes and conceives hope from his decays and infirmities. These are my ordinary companions.
(March 2, 1711)   (Steele)

STUDY AIDS: 1. How many characters are created here to form the Spectator Club? Notice that each one represents a distinct point of view. Is there any allegorical significance in their names? The very title of the paper, *The Spectator*, as well as its purpose which is stated in number 10, indicates the authors' desire to remain anonymous and objective in their essays. How will this club help them to do so? If they desired to discuss a matter relating to the army, who would be their spokesman? Who would comment on customs and life in the country? Through which character would they do their columns on gossip and gallantry?

2. Characterization can be direct (e.g., the author can state that the character is honest or dishonest) or indirect (the author can show by details that the character is honest or dishonest). Find examples of both methods in the characterization of Will Honeycomb.

Spectator 10
[The Purpose of The Spectator Papers]

Non aliter quam qui adverso vix flumine lembum
Remigiis subigit, si bracchia forte remisit,
Atque illum praeceps prono rapit alveus amni.
                    Virgil, *Georg.* I, 201

"So the boat's brawny crew the current stem,
And slow advancing, struggle with the stream:
But if they slack their hands, or cease to strive,
Then down the flood with headlong haste they drive."

[Dryden]

[9] An illegitimate son of Charles II. Spurred on by the Earl of Shaftesbury, Monmouth unsuccessfully attempted to seize his father's throne in 1681. Dryden recounts the rebellion in his satire, *Absalom and Achitophel.*

It is with much satisfaction that I hear this great city inquiring day by day after these my papers, and receiving my morning lectures with a becoming seriousness and attention. My publisher tells me that there are already three thousand of them distributed every day: so that if I allow twenty readers to every paper, which I look upon as a modest computation, I may reckon about threescore thousand disciples in London and Westminster, who I hope will take care to distinguish themselves from the thoughtless herd of their ignorant and unattentive brethren. Since I have raised to myself so great an audience, I shall spare no pains to make their instruction agreeable, and their diversion useful. For which reasons I shall endeavor to enliven morality with wit,[1] and to temper wit with morality, that my readers may, if possible, both ways find their account in the speculation of the day. And to the end that their virtue and discretion may not be short, transient, intermitting starts of thought, I have resolved to refresh their memories from day to day, till I have recovered them out of that desperate state of vice and folly into which the age is fallen.[2] The mind that lies fallow but a single day sprouts up in follies that are only to be killed by a constant and assiduous culture. It was said of Socrates, that he brought philosophy down from heaven, to inhabit among men; and I shall be ambitious to have it said of me that I have brought philosophy out of closets and libraries, schools and colleges, to dwell in clubs and assemblies, at tea-tables and in coffee-houses.

I would, therefore, in a very particular manner recommend these my speculations to all well-regulated families, that set apart an hour in every morning for tea and bread and butter; and would earnestly advise them for their good to order this paper to be punctually served up, and to be looked upon as a part of the tea equipage.

Sir Francis Bacon observes that a well-written book, compared with its rivals and antagonists, is like Moses' serpent, that immediately swallowed up and devoured those of the Egyptians. I shall not be so vain as to think that where the *Spectator* appears the other public prints will vanish; but shall leave it to my reader's consideration, whether is it not much better to be let into the knowledge of one's self, than to hear what passes in Muscovy or Poland; and to amuse ourselves with such writings as tend to the wearing out of ignorance, passion, and prejudice, than such as naturally conduce to inflame hatreds and make enmities irreconcilable?

In the next place, I would recommend this paper to the daily perusal of those gentlemen whom I cannot but consider as my good brothers and allies; I mean the fraternity of spectators who live in the world without having anything to do in it, and either by the affluence of their fortunes, or laziness of their dispositions, have no other business with the rest of mankind but to look upon them. Under this class of men are comprehended all contemplative tradesmen, titular physicians, fellows of the Royal Society, Templars[3] that are not given to be contentious, and statesmen that are out of business; in short, everyone that considers the world as a theater, and desires to form a right judgment of those who are the actors on it.

There is another set of men that I must likewise lay a claim to, whom I have lately called the blanks of society, as being altogether unfurnished with ideas till the business and conversation of the day has supplied them. I have often considered these poor souls with an eye of great commiseration, when I have heard them asking the first man they have met with, whether there was any news stirring? and by that means gathering together materials for thinking. These needy persons

[1] The meaning of "wit" was changing in the seventeenth and eighteenth centuries from its earlier definition as "native intelligence" or "knowledge" to something closer to our modern word "witty" or "humorous." In its newer meaning "wit" also meant literature, which was the product of artistic intelligence. Are the *Spectator* essays an attempt to "temper wit (literature) with morality"?

[2] This is the stated purpose of the *Spectator*. The preceding two sentences outline the twofold method by which this purpose would be achieved. The moral function of literature has prevailed in western civilization and was originally so stated by Horace in his phrase *utile et dulce* ("useful and pleasing"), i.e., literature should be a sugar-coated pill of wisdom.

[3] Lawyers or law students.

do not know what to talk of till about twelve o'clock in the morning; for by that time they are pretty good judges of the weather, know which way the wind sits, and whether the Dutch mail be come in. As they lie at the mercy of the first man they meet, and are grave or impertinent all the day long, according to the notions which they have imbibed in the morning, I would earnestly entreat them not to stir out of their chambers till they have read this paper, and do promise them that I will daily instill into them such sound and wholesome sentiments, as shall have a good effect on their conversation for the ensuing twelve hours.

But there are none to whom this paper will be more useful than to the female world. I have often thought there has not been sufficient pains taken in finding out proper employments and diversions for the fair ones. Their amusements seem contrived for them, rather as they are women, than as they are reasonable creatures; and are more adapted to the sex than to the species. The toilet is their great scene of business, and the right adjusting of their hair the principal employment of their lives. The sorting of a suit of ribbons is reckoned a very good morning's work; and if they make an excursion to a mercer's, or a toy-shop, so great a fatigue makes them unfit for anything else all the day after. Their more serious occupations are sewing and embroidery, and their greatest drudgery the preparation of jellies and sweet-meats. This, I say, is the state of ordinary women; though I know there are multitudes of those of a more elevated life and conversation, that move in an exalted sphere of knowledge and virtue, that join all the beauties of the mind to the ornaments of dress, and inspire a kind of awe and respect, as well as love, into their male beholders. I hope to increase the number of these by publishing this daily paper, which I shall always endeavor to make an innocent, if not an improving, entertainment, and by that means at least divert the minds of my female readers from greater

trifles. At the same time, as I would fain give some finishing touches to those which are already the most beautiful pieces in human nature, I shall endeavor to point out all those imperfections that are the blemishes, as well as those virtues which are the embellishments, of the sex. In the meanwhile I hope these my gentle readers, who have so much time on their hands, will not grudge throwing away a quarter of an hour in a day on this paper, since they may do it without any hindrance to business.

I know several of my friends and well-wishers are in great pain for me, lest I should not be able to keep up the spirit of a paper which I oblige myself to furnish every day; but to make them easy in this particular, I will promise them faithfully to give it over as soon as I grow dull. This I know will be matter of great raillery to the small wits; who will frequently put me in mind of my promise, desire me to keep my word, assure me that it is high time to give over, with many other little pleasantries of the like nature, which men of a little smart genius cannot forbear throwing out against their best friends, when they have such a handle given them of being witty. But let them remember that I do hereby enter my caveat against this piece of raillery.

(March 12, 1711) (Addison)

STUDY AIDS. 1. This essay is interesting for the knowledge it gives of Addison's reading audience. It was this audience which made possible the rise of journalism and of journalists like Defoe, Addison, and Steele. What four groups of readers does Addison list in this essay? To what social class would they belong? Why would the morality of this class need to be more witty and its wit more moral?

2. Although the *Spectator* essays are now considered literature, in their day they were journalistic. Would the purpose for which they were written be valid for journalism today? Do you know of any modern periodicals which have the same purpose?

Spectator 18
[On Italian Opera]

—Equitis quoque jam migravit ab aure voluptas
Omnis ad incertos oculos et gaudia vana.
Horace, Epistles II, i, 187

"But sound no longer pleases even the knight;
He loves the vain capricious joys of sight."
[Boscawen]

Occasionally, a deep-seated prejudice reveals itself despite Addison's objective style. Such was his feeling about opera. His stepson, the Earl of Warwick, relates that when he was a student, Addison told him that a concert of birds would entertain him with better music than could be found at the opera.

It is my design in this paper to deliver down to posterity a faithful account of the Italian opera, and of the gradual progress which it has made upon the English stage: for there is no question but our great-grand-children will be very curious to know the reason why their forefathers used to sit together like an audience of foreigners in their own country, and to hear whole plays acted before them in a tongue which they did not understand.

Arsinoe [1] was the first opera that gave us a taste of Italian music. The great success this opera met with produced some attempts of forming pieces upon Italian plans, which should give a more natural and reasonable entertainment than what can be met with in the elaborate trifles of that nation. This alarmed the poetasters and fiddlers of the town, who were used to deal in a more ordinary kind of ware; and therefore laid down an established rule, which is received as such to this day, that nothing is capable of being well set to music, that is not nonsense.

This maxim was no sooner received but we immediately fell to translating the Italian operas; and as there was no great danger of hurting the sense of those extraordinary pieces, our authors would often make words of their own which were entirely foreign to the meaning of the passages they pretended to translate; their chief care being to make the numbers of the English verse answer to those of the Italian, that both of them might go to the same tune. Thus the famous song in Camilla,[2]

Barbara si t'intendo, &c.

"Barbarous woman, yes, I know your meaning," which expresses the resentments of an angry lover, was translated into that English lamentation,

Frail are a lover's hopes, &c.

And it was pleasant enough to see the most refined persons of the British nation dying away and languishing to notes that were filled with a spirit of rage and indignation. It happened also very frequently, where the sense was rightly translated, the necessary transposition of words, which were drawn out of the phrase of one tongue into that of another, made the music appear very absurd on one tongue that was very natural in the other. I remember an Italian verse that ran thus word for word,

And turned my rage into pity:

which the English for rhyme sake translated,

And into pity turned my rage.

---

[1] A contemporary opera adapted from the Italian by Thomas Clayton. Addison had written an opera, Rosamond, for which Clayton had composed the music. It was one of Addison's few failures. This experience, perhaps, accounts for his inability to discuss opera with his usual detachment.

[2] In the London production of this Italian opera, the hero sang in Italian and the heroine in English.

By this means the soft notes that were adapted to "pity" in the Italian fell upon the word "rage" in the English, and the angry sounds that were turned to "rage" in the original were made to express "pity" in the translation. It oftentimes happened likewise that the finest notes in the air fell upon the most insignificant words in the sentence. I have known the word "and" pursued through the whole gamut, have been entertained with many a melodious "the," and have heard the most beautiful graces, quavers, and divisions bestowed upon "then," "for," and "from"; to the eternal honor of our English particles.

The next step to our refinement was the introducing of Italian actors into our opera; who sung their parts in their own language, at the same time that our countrymen performed theirs in our native tongue. The king or hero of the play generally spoke in Italian, and his slaves answered him in English: the lover frequently made his court, and gained the heart of his princess, in a language which she did not understand. One would have thought it very difficult to have carried on dialogues after this manner without an interpreter between the persons that conversed together; but this was the state of the English stage for about three years.

At length the audience grew tired of understanding half the opera and therefore, to ease themselves entirely of the fatigue of thinking, have so ordered it at present that the whole opera is performed in an unknown tongue. We no longer understand the language of our own stage; insomuch that I have often been afraid, when I have seen our Italian performers chattering in the vehemence of action, that they have been calling us names, and abusing us among themselves; but I hope, since we do put such an entire confidence in them, they will not talk against us before our faces, though they may do it with the same safety as if it were behind our backs. In the meantime, I cannot forbear thinking how naturally an historian who writes two or three hundred years hence, and does not know the taste of his wise forefathers, will make the following reflection:

In the beginning of the eighteenth century the Italian tongue was so well understood in England that operas were acted on the public stage in that language.

One scarce knows how to be serious in the confutation of an absurdity that shows itself at the first sight. It does not want any great measure of sense to see the ridicule of this monstrous practice; but what makes it the more astonishing, it is not the taste of the rabble, but of persons of the greatest politeness, which has established it.

If the Italians have a genius for music above the English, the English have a genius for other performances of a much higher nature, and capable of giving the mind a much nobler entertainment. Would one think it was possible (at a time when an author lived that was able to write the *Phaedra and Hippolytus* [3]) for a people to be so stupidly fond of the Italian opera as scarce to give a third day's hearing to that admirable tragedy? Music is certainly a very agreeable entertainment, but if it would take the entire possession of our ears, if it would make us incapable of hearing sense, if it would exclude arts that have a much greater tendency to the refinement of human nature, I must confess I would allow it no better quarter than Plato has done, who banishes it out of his commonwealth.

At present, our notions of music are so very uncertain that we do not know what it is we like; only, in general, we are transported with anything that is not English. So if it be of a foreign growth, let it be Italian, French, or High Dutch, it is the same thing. In short, our English music is quite rooted out and nothing yet planted in its stead.

When a royal palace is burned to the ground, every man is at liberty to present his plan for a new one; and though it be but indifferently put together, it may furnish several hints that may be of use to a good architect. I shall take the same liberty in a following paper, of giving my opinion upon the subject of music; which I shall lay down only

[3] Tragedy written by Edmund Smith, for which Addison wrote a prologue.

in a problematical manner, to be considered by those who are masters in the art. (March 21, 1711)   (Addison)

STUDY AIDS: 1. This essay is an example of the way Addison often uses humor to make his point. Cite three or four places in the essay where humor produces gentle satire.

2. In what indirect statements does Addison reveal his prejudice against music in general?

3. Why does Addison keep this prejudice concealed? If openly stated, how would it defeat the point he is trying to make?

Spectator 117

[On Witchcraft]

—*Ipsi sibi somnia fingunt.*
Virgil, *Eclogues* VIII, 108.

"They deceive themselves with their own dreams."

There are some opinions in which a man should stand neuter, without engaging his assent to one side or the other. Such a hovering faith as this, which refuses to settle upon any determination, is absolutely necessary to a mind that is careful to avoid errors and prepossessions. When the arguments press equally on both sides in matters that are indifferent to us, the safest method is to give up ourselves to neither.

It is with this temper of mind that I consider the subject of witchcraft. When I hear the relations that are made from all parts of the world, not only from Norway and Lapland, from the East and West Indies, but from every particular nation in Europe, I cannot forbear thinking that there is such an intercourse and commerce with evil spirits as that which we express by the name of witchcraft. But when I consider that the ignorant and credulous parts of the world abound most in these relations, and that the persons among us who are supposed to engage in such an infernal commerce are people of a weak understanding and a crazed imagination, and at the same time reflect upon the many impostures and delusions of this nature that have been detected in all ages, I endeavor to suspend my belief till I hear more certain accounts than any which have yet come to my knowledge. In short, when I consider the question whether there are such persons in the world as those we call witches, my mind is divided between the two opposite opinions; or rather (to speak my thoughts freely), I believe in general that there is, and has been, such a thing as witchcraft; but at the same time can give no credit to any particular instance of it.

I am engaged in this speculation by some occurrences that I met with yesterday, which I shall give my reader an account of at large. As I was walking with my friend Sir Roger by the side of one of his woods, an old woman applied herself to me for my charity. Her dress and figure put me in mind of the following description in Otway: [1]

In a close lane as I pursued my journey,
I spied a wrinkled hag, with age grown double,
Picking dry sticks, and mumbling to herself.
Her eyes with scalding rheum were galled and red;
Cold palsy shook her head; her hands seemed withered;
And on her crooked shoulders had she wrapped
The tattered remnants of an old striped hanging,
Which served to keep her carcase from the cold:
So there was nothing of a piece about her.
Her lower weeds were all o'er coarsely patched
With different colored rags—black, red, white, yellow—
And seemed to speak variety of wretchedness.

As I was musing on this description, and comparing it with the object before me, the knight told me that this very old woman had the reputation of a witch all over the

[1] From *The Orphan* (1680), a tragedy by Thomas Otway.

country, that her lips were observed to be always in motion, and that there was not a switch about her house which her neighbors did not believe had carried her several hundreds of miles. If she chanced to stumble, they always found sticks or straws that lay in the figure of a cross before her. If she made any mistake at church, and cried "Amen" in a wrong place, they never failed to conclude that she was saying her prayers backward. There was not a maid in the parish that would take a pin of her, though she would offer a bag of money with it. She goes by the name of Moll White, and has made the country ring with several imaginary exploits which are palmed upon her. If the dairymaid does not make her butter come so soon as she should have it, Moll White is at the bottom of the churn. If a horse sweats in the stable, Moll White has been upon his back. If a hare makes an unexpected escape from the hounds, the huntsman curses Moll White. "Nay," says Sir Roger, "I have known the master of the pack, upon such an occasion, send one of his servants to see if Moll White had been out that morning."

This account raised my curiosity so far that I begged my friend Sir Roger to go with me into her hovel, which stood in a solitary corner under the side of the wood. Upon our first entering, Sir Roger winked to me, and pointed at something that stood behind the door, which, upon looking that way, I found to be an old broomstaff. At the same time he whispered me in the ear to take notice of a tabby cat that sat in the chimney-corner, which, as the old knight told me, lay under as bad a report as Moll White herself; for besides that Moll is said often to accompany her in the same shape, the cat is reported to have spoken twice or thrice in her life, and to have played several pranks above the capacity of an ordinary cat.

I was secretly concerned to see human nature in so much wretchedness and disgrace, but at the same time could not forbear smiling to hear Sir Roger, who is a little puzzled about the old woman, advising her, as a justice of peace, to avoid all communication with the devil, and never to hurt any of her neighbor's cattle. We concluded our visit with a bounty, which was very acceptable.

In our return home, Sir Roger told me that old Moll had been often brought before him for making children spit pins, and giving maids the nightmare; and that the country people would be tossing her into a pond and trying experiments with her every day, if it was not for him and his chaplain.

I have since found, upon inquiry, that Sir Roger was several times staggered with the reports that had been brought him concerning this old woman, and would frequently have bound her over to the county sessions had not his chaplain with much ado persuaded him to the contrary.

I have been the more particular in this account because I hear there is scarce a village in England that has not a Moll White in it. When an old woman begins to dote, and grow chargeable to a parish, she is generally turned into a witch, and fills the whole country with extravagant fancies, imaginary distempers, and terrifying dreams. In the meantime the poor wretch that is the innocent occasion of so many evils begins to be frighted at herself, and sometimes confesses secret commerce and familiarities that her imagination forms in a delirious old age. This frequently cuts off charity from the greatest objects of compassion, and inspires people with a malevolence toward those poor, decrepit parts of our species in whom human nature is defaced by infirmity and dotage.

(July 14, 1711)   (Addison)

Spectator 267

[On Paradise Lost]

Cedite, Romani scriptores, cedite Graii.
                    Propertius, *Elegies* II, No. 34, 165.

"Give place, ye Roman and Greek writers."

There is nothing in nature so irksome as general discourses, especially when they turn chiefly upon words. For this reason I shall waive the discussion of that point which was started some years since, whether Milton's *Paradise Lost* may be called an heroic poem. Those who will not give it that title, may call it (if they please) a divine poem. It will be sufficient to its perfection, if it has in it all the beauties of the highest kind of poetry; and as for those who allege it is not an heroic poem, they advance no more to the diminution of it, than if they should say Adam is not Aeneas, nor Eve Helen.

I shall therefore examine it by the rules [1] of epic poetry, and see whether it falls short of the *Iliad* or *Aeneid* in the beauties which are essential to that kind of writing. The first thing to be considered in an epic poem is the fable,[2] which is perfect or imperfect according as the action which it relates is more or less so. This action should have three qualifications in it. First, it should be but one action. Secondly, it should be an entire action; and, thirdly, it should be a great action. To consider the action of the *Iliad, Aeneid,* and *Paradise Lost,* in these three several lights: Homer, to preserve the unity of his action, hastens into the midst of things,

---

[1] These "rules" have a long ancestry. Aristotle in his *Poetics* stated certain observations, not rules, about tragedy and epic. Centuries later, when interest in the *Poetics* was revived, Italian Renaissance critics accepted these observations as rules by which tragedy and epic should be written and judged. This rigid view passed into French and English criticism. The rules were accepted in theory by English neoclassic writers, but practice and theory often varied.

[2] Plot. Aristotle had called plot "the soul of tragedy."

as Horace has observed. Had he gone up to Leda's egg, or begun much later, even at the rape of Helen, or the investing of Troy, it is manifest that the story of the poem would have been a series of several actions. He therefore opens his poem with the discord of his princes and artfully interweaves, in the several succeeding parts of it, an account of everything material which relates to them and had passed before that fatal dissention. After the same manner Aeneas makes his first appearance in the Tyrrhene seas, and within sight of Italy, because the action proposed to be celebrated was that of his settling himself in Latium. But because it was necessary for the reader to know what had happened to him in the taking of Troy, and in the preceding parts of his voyage, Virgil makes his hero relate it by way of episode in the second and third books of the *Aeneid*; the contents of both which books come before those of the first book in the thread of the story, though for preserving this unity of action they follow them in the disposition of the poem. Milton, in imitation of these two great poets, opens his *Paradise Lost* with an infernal council plotting the fall of man, which is the action he proposed to celebrate; and as for those great actions, which preceded, in point of time, the battle of the angels, and the creation of the world (which would have entirely destroyed the unity of the principal action, had he related them in the same order that they happened), he cast them into the fifth, sixth, and seventh books, by way of episode to this noble poem.

Aristotle himself allows that Homer has nothing to boast of as to the unity of his fable, though at the same time that great critic and philosopher endeavors to palliate this imperfection in the Greek poet by imputing it in some measure to the very nature of an epic poem. Some have been of opinion that the *Aeneid* also labors in this particular, and has episodes which may be looked upon as excrescences rather than as parts of the action. On the contrary, the poem which we have now under our consideration hath no other episodes than such as naturally arise from the subject, and yet is filled with such a multitude of astonishing incidents that it gives us at the same time a pleasure of the greatest variety and of the greatest simplicity; uniform in its nature, though diversified in the execution.

I must observe also, that as Virgil, in the poem which was designed to celebrate the original of the Roman empire, has described the birth of its great rival, the Carthaginian commonwealth; Milton, with the like art, in his poem on the fall of man, has related the fall of those angels who are his professed enemies. Besides the many other beauties in such an episode, its running parallel with the great action of the poem hinders it from breaking the unity so much as another episode would have done, that had not so great an affinity with the principal subject. In short, this is the same kind of beauty which the critics admire in the *Spanish Friar, or the Double Discovery*,[3] where the two different plots look like counter-parts and copies of one another.

The second qualification required in the action of an epic poem is that it should be an entire action. An action is entire when it is complete in all its parts; or as Aristotle describes it, when it consists of a beginning, a middle, and an end. Nothing should go before it, be intermixed with it, or follow after it, that is not related to it. As, on the contrary, no single step should be omitted in that just and regular process which it must be supposed to take from its original[4] to its consummation. Thus we see the anger of Achilles in its birth, its continuance, and effects; and Aeneas's settlement in Italy carried on through all the oppositions in his way to it both by sea and land. The action in Milton excels (I think) both the former in this particular; we see it contrived in hell, executed upon earth, and punished by

heaven. The parts of it are told in the most distinct manner and grow out of one another in the most natural method.

The third qualification of an epic poem is its greatness. The anger of Achilles was of such consequence that it embroiled the kings of Greece, destroyed the heroes of Troy, and engaged all the gods in factions. Aeneas's settlement in Italy produced the Caesars and gave birth to the Roman empire. Milton's subject was still greater than either of the former; it does not determine the fate of single persons or nations; but of a whole species. The united powers of hell are joined together for the destruction of mankind, which they effected in part, and would have completed, had not Omnipotence itself interposed. The principal actors are man in his greatest perfection, and woman in her highest beauty. Their enemies are the fallen angels; the Messiah their friend; and the Almighty their protector. In short, everything that is great in the whole circle of being, whether within the verge of nature, or out of it, has a proper part assigned it in this admirable poem.

In poetry, as in architecture, not only the whole, but the principal members, and every part of them, should be great. I will not presume to say, that the book of games in the *Aeneid,* or that in the *Iliad,* are not of this nature; nor to reprehend Virgil's simile of the top, and many other of the same kind in the *Iliad,* as liable to any censure in this particular; but I think we may say, without derogating from those wonderful performances, that there is an unquestionable magnificence in every part of *Paradise Lost,* and indeed a much greater than could have been formed upon any pagan system.

But Aristotle, by the greatness of the action, does not only mean that it should be great in its nature, but also in its duration, or in other words, that it should have a due length in it, as well as what we properly call greatness. The just measure of this kind of magnitude he explains by the following similitude: An animal no bigger than a mite cannot appear perfect to the eye, because the sight takes it in at once and has only a

³ A tragedy by Dryden.
⁴ Beginning.

confused idea of the whole, and not a distinct idea of all its parts; if on the contrary, you should suppose an animal of ten thousand furlongs in length, the eye would be so filled with a single part of it that it could not give the mind an idea of the whole. What these animals are to the eye, a very short or a very long action would be to the memory. The first would be, as it were, lost and swallowed up by it, and the other difficult to be contained in it. Homer and Virgil have shown their principal art in this particular; the action of the *Iliad,* and that of the *Aeneid,* were in themselves exceeding short but are so beautifully extended and diversified by the invention of episodes, and the machinery of gods, with the like poetical ornaments, that they make up an agreeable story, sufficient to employ the memory without overcharging it. Milton's action is enriched with such a variety of circumstances that I have taken as much pleasure in reading the contents of his books as in the best invented story I ever met with. It is possible that the traditions on which the *Iliad* and the *Aeneid* were built had more circumstances in them than the history of the fall of man, as it is related in scripture. Besides, it was easier for Homer and Virgil to dash the truth with fiction, as they were in no danger of offending the religion of their country by it. But as for Milton, he had not only a very few circumstances upon which to raise his poem but was also obliged to proceed with the greatest caution in everything that he added out of his own invention. And indeed, notwithstanding all the restraint he was under, he has filled his story with so many surprising incidents, which bear so close an analogy with what is delivered in holy writ, that it is capable of pleasing the most delicate reader without giving offense to the most scrupulous.

The modern critics have collected from several hints in the *Iliad* and *Aeneid* the space of time which is taken up by the action of each of those poems; but as a great part of Milton's story was translated in regions that lie out of the reach of the sun and the sphere of day, it is impossible to gratify the reader with such a calculation, which indeed would be more curious than instructive, none of the critics, either ancient or modern, having laid down rules to circumscribe the action of an epic poem with any determined number of years, days, or hours.

This piece of criticism on Milton's *Paradise Lost* shall be carried on in the following Saturday's papers.[5]

(January 5, 1712)   (Addison)

STUDY AIDS: 1. Notice the structure of the essay: an introduction; a three-part proposition to be examined; the three parts examined; and a conclusion. The essay moves along a straight line with neither humor nor satire. If the essay is not satiric, what seems to be its purpose? How could it fulfil the aim stated in *Spectator* 10?

2. What does Addison mean by an "entire" action, one which has a beginning, middle, and end? Doesn't every composition have a beginning, middle, and end? Addison means more than just "length" by "greatness" (p. 384/2, l. 41 ff). What would this include? What does length have to do with a poem's greatness?

3. Addison believed that Adam (mankind), not Satan, was the hero of *Paradise Lost.* What statements in this essay indicate this belief?

Spectator 323
[How Women Pass Their Time]

—*Modo vir, modo femina*
                   Ovid, *Metamorphoses* IV, 280

"Now man, now woman"

The journal with which I presented my reader on Tuesday last, has brought me in several letters, with accounts of many private lives cast into that form. I have the *Rake's Journal,* the *Sot's Journal,* the *Whore-master's Journal,* and among several others a very

[5] There are twenty essays on Milton and *Paradise Lost* in The *Spectator.* Addison was the first eighteenth-century critic who tried to create interest in Milton's epic.

curious piece, entitled, *The Journal of a Mohock.*[1] By these instances I find that the intention of my last Tuesday's paper has been mistaken by many of my readers. I did not design so much to expose vice as idleness, and aimed at those persons who pass away their time rather in trifles and impertinence, than in crimes and immoralities. Offences of this latter kind are not to be dallied with, or treated in so ludicrous a manner. In short, my journal only holds up folly to the light, and shows the disagreeableness of such actions as are indifferent in themselves, and blameable only as they proceed from creatures endowed with reason.

My following correspondent, who calls her self Clarinda, is such a journalist as I require: she seems by her letter to be placed in a modish state of indifference between vice and virtue, and to be susceptible of either, were there proper pains taken with her. Had her journal been filled with gallantries, or such occurrences as had shown her wholly divested of her natural innocence, notwithstanding it might have been more pleasing to the generality of readers, I should not have published it; but as it is only the picture of a life filled with a fashionable kind of gaiety and laziness, I shall set down five days of it, as I have received it from the hand of my correspondent.

Dear Mr. SPECTATOR:

You having set your readers an exercise in one of your last week's papers, I have performed mine according to your orders, and herewith send it you enclosed. You must know, MR. SPECTATOR, that I am a maiden lady of a good fortune, who have had several matches offered me for these ten years last past, and have at present warm applications made to me by a very pretty fellow. As I am at my own disposal, I come up to town every winter, and pass my time in it after the manner you will find in the following journal, which I began to write upon the very day after your *Spectator* upon that subject.

TUESDAY. *Night.* Could not go to sleep till one in the morning for thinking of my journal.

WEDNESDAY. *From Eight till Ten.* Drank two dishes of chocolate in bed, and fell asleep after them.

From Ten to Eleven. Eat a slice of bread and butter, drank a dish of bohea,[2] read the *Spectator.*

From Eleven to One. At my toilette, tried a new head.[3] Gave orders for Veny[4] to be combed and washed. Mem.[5] I look best in blue.

From One till half an hour after Two. Drove to the Change. Cheapened a couple of fans.

Till Four. At dinner. Mem. Mr. Froth passed by in his new liveries.

From Four to Six. Dressed, paid a visit to old Lady Blithe and her sister, having before heard they were gone out of town that day.

From Six to Eleven. At basset. Mem. Never set again upon the ace of diamonds.

THURSDAY. *From Eleven at night to Eight in the morning.* Dreamed that I punted to Mr. Froth.

From Eight to Ten. Chocolate. Read two acts in *Aurenzebe*[6] a-bed.

From Ten to Eleven. Tea-table. Sent to borrow Lady Faddle's Cupid for Veny. Read the play-bills. Received a letter from Mr. Froth. Mem. Locked it up in my strong box.

Rest of the morning. Fontange, the tire-woman, her account of my Lady Blithe's wash. Broke a tooth in my little tortoise-shell comb. Sent Frank to know how my Lady Hectic rested after her monkey's leaping out at window. Looked pale. Fontange tells me my glass[7] is not true. Dressed by Three.

From Three to Four. Dinner cold before I sat down.

From Four to Eleven. Saw company. Mr. Froth's opinion of Milton. His account of the

---

[1] The "Mohocks" were bands of young men who roamed the streets at night, beating and insulting passers-by.

[2] Tea.

[3] Hair-do, or wig.

[4] The name of her small female dog.

[5] Memorandum; i.e., "I must remember."

[6] *Aureng-Zebe,* an heroic play by Dryden.

[7] Mirror.

Mohocks. His fancy for a pin-cushion. Picture in the lid of his snuff-box. Old Lady Faddle promises me her woman to cut my hair. Lost five guineas at crimp.

Twelve a clock at night. Went to bed.

FRIDAY. *Eight in the morning.* A-bed. Read over all Mr. Froth's letters. Cupid and Veny.

Ten a clock. Stayed within all day, not at home.

From Ten to Twelve. In conference with my mantua-maker. Sorted a suit of ribbons. Broke my blue china cup.

From Twelve to One. Shut myself up in my chamber, practiced Lady Betty Modely's skuttle.[8]

One in the afternoon. Called for my flowered handkerchief. Worked half a violet leaf in it. Eyes ached and head out of order. Threw by my work, and read over the remaining part of *Aurenzebe.*

From Three to Four. Dined.

From Four to Twelve. Changed my mind, dressed, went abroad, and played at crimp till midnight. Found Mrs. Spitely at home. Conversation Mrs. Brilliant's necklace false stones. Old Lady Loveday going to be married to a young fellow that is not worth a groat. Miss Prue gone into the country. Tom Townley has red hair. Mem. Mrs. Spitely whispered in my ear that she had something to tell me about Mr. Froth. I am sure it is not true.

Between Twelve and One. Dreamed that Mr. Froth lay at my feet, and called me Indamora.[9]

SATURDAY. Rose at eight a clock in the morning. Sat down to my toilette.

From Eight to Nine. Shifted a patch for half an hour before I could determine it. Fixed it above my left eyebrow.

From Nine to Twelve. Drank my tea, and dressed.

From Twelve to Two. At chapel. A great deal of good company. Mem. The third air in the new opera. Lady Blithe dressed frightfully.

From Three to Four. Dined. Mrs. Kitty

called upon me to go to the opera before I was risen from table.

From dinner to six. Drank tea. Turned off a footman for being rude to Veny.

Six a clock. Went to the opera. I did not see Mr. Froth till the beginning of the second act. Mr. Froth talked to a gentleman in a black wig. Bowed to a lady in the front box. Mr. Froth and his friend clapped Nicolini in the third act. Mr. Froth cried out "Ancora." Mr. Froth led me to my chair. I think he squeezed my hand.

Eleven at night. Went to bed. Melancholy dreams. Methought Nicolini said he was Mr. Froth.

SUNDAY. Indisposed.

MONDAY. *Eight a clock.* Waked by Miss Kitty. *Aurenzebe* lay upon the chair by me. Kitty repeated without book the eight best lines in the play. Went in our mobbs [10] to the dumb man,[11] according to appointment. Told me that my lover's name began with a "G." Mem. The conjurer was within a letter of Mr. Froth's name, etc.

Upon looking back into this my journal, I find that I am at a loss to know whether I pass my time well or ill; and indeed never thought of considering how I did it, before I perused your speculation upon that subject. I scarce find a single action in these five days that I can thoroughly approve of, except the working upon the violet-leaf, which I am resolved to finish the first day I am at leisure. As for Mr. Froth and Veny, I did not think they took up so much of my time and thoughts, as I find they do upon my journal. The latter of them I will turn off if you insist upon it; and if Mr. Froth does not bring matters to a conclusion very suddenly, I will not let my life run away in a dream.

Your humble servant, Clarinda.

To resume one of the morals of my first paper, and to confirm Clarinda in her good inclinations, I would have her consider what a pretty figure she would make among pos-

---

[8] Affected, mincing walk.
[9] Heroine of *Aureng-Zebe.*

[10] Informal caps.
[11] Duncan Campbell (1680–1730), a dumb astrologer.

terity, were the history of her whole life published like these five days of it. I shall conclude my paper with an epitaph written by an uncertain author [12] on Sir Philip Sidney's sister, a lady who seems to have been of a temper very much different from that of Clarinda. The last thought of it is so very noble, that I dare say my reader will pardon the quotation.

On the Countess Dowager of PEMBROKE

Underneath this marble hearse
Lies the subject of all verse:
Sidney's sister, Pembroke's mother;
Death, ere thou hast killed another,
Fair and learned and good as she,
Time shall throw a dart at thee.

(March 11, 1712)   (Addison)

Alexander Pope
(1688–1744)

WHEN POPE REFERRED TO HIS LIFE AS "THIS LONG DISEASE," HE WAS SCARCELY EXAGGERating. Born of old parents, he was a sickly, precocious child. His constitution was still further weakened by too much reading and too little exercise. When he was twelve years old he was gored by a bull, and thereafter suffered a curvature of the spine. For the remainder of his life, Pope wore an iron corset to help him stand and walk.

He was born a Roman Catholic. Because the universites required their graduates to swear allegiance to the Anglican articles of faith, he was unable to attend college. Although, as a result, his education was largely self-acquired and desultory, he was better read in earlier poetry than most of his contemporaries.

Pope began writing poetry when a child. His first publication, the *Pastorals* (1709), introduced him to the literary figures of his day, among them Addison, Steele, Swift, Wycherley, Congreve, and William Walsh. It was Walsh who advised him to try to become "the most correct poet" of England, and Pope followed the advice. The *Pastorals* were followed by the *Essay on Criticism* (1711), and *The Rape of the Lock* (1712, 1714); his translations of the *Iliad* (1715–1720) and *Odyssey* (1725–1726) made him financially independent. In 1725 he also edited the plays of Shakespeare. After this work he turned to satire and wrote *An Essay on Man* (1733–1734), *Moral Essays* (1731–1735), *An Epistle to Dr. Arbuthnot* (1735), *Satires* (1733–1738), and the revised *Dunciad* (1742–1743).

Pope claimed that he learned his versification from Dryden. Certainly, the two men are the greatest poetic satirists in English. Pope's intellectual range and vigor of expression are less than Dryden's, but his technique and subtlety are superior. Dr. Johnson's comparison of the two poets is still valid: "If the flights of Dryden therefore are higher, Pope continues longer on the wing. If of Dryden's fire the blaze is brighter, of Pope's the heat is more regular and constant. Dryden often surpasses expectation, and Pope never falls below it. Dryden is read with frequent astonishment, Pope with perpetual delight."

[12] William Browne.

An Essay on Criticism

Since this poem is an "essay"—i.e., an "attempt"—its structure is not as complex as that of *The Rape of the Lock*. Nevertheless, the thoughts are well organized, although as Addison noted, they follow "one another without that methodical regularity which would have been requisite in a prose author." The ideas are commonplace eighteenth-century critical views, but they are stated in such perfected form that the *Essay* is one of the most widely quoted pieces in English literature.

Part I

[Difficulties in being a critic, with some tenets of good writing and criticism.[1]]

.   .   .   .

But you who seek to give and merit fame,
And justly bear a critic's noble name,
Be sure yourself and your own reach to know,
How far your genius, taste, and learning go;
Launch not beyond your depth, but be discreet,   50
And mark that point where sense and dulness meet.
   Nature to all things fixed the limits fit,
And wisely curbed proud man's pretending wit.
As on the land while here the ocean gains,
In other parts it leaves wide sandy plains;   55
Thus in the soul while memory prevails,
The solid power of understanding fails;
Where beams of warm imagination play,
The memory's soft figures melt away.
One science only will one genius fit;   60
So vast is art, so narrow human wit—
Not only bounded to peculiar arts,
But oft in those confined to single parts.
Like kings we lose the conquests gained before,
By vain ambition still to make them more;   65
Each might his several province well command,
Would all but stoop to what they understand.
   First follow nature, and your judgment frame
By her just standard, which is still [2] the same:
Unerring nature, still divinely bright,   70
One clear, unchanged, and universal light,

Life, force, and beauty, must to all impart,
At once the source, and end, and test of art.
Art from that fund each just supply provides,
Works without show, and without pomp presides;   75
In some fair body thus the informing soul
With spirits feeds, with vigor fills the whole,
Each motion guides, and every nerve sustains;
Itself unseen, but in the effects remains.
Some, to whom heaven in wit has been profuse,   80
Want as much more, to turn it to its use;
For wit and judgment often are at strife,
Though meant each other's aid, like man and wife.
'Tis more to guide, than spur the muse's steed,
Restrain his fury, than provoke his speed;   85
The wingèd courser, like a generous horse,
Shows most true mettle when you check his course.
   Those rules of old discovered, not devised,
Are nature still, but nature methodized;
Nature, like liberty, is but restrained   90
By the same laws which first herself ordained.
   Hear how learned Greece her useful rules indites,
When to repress, and when indulge our flights:
High on Parnassus' top her sons she showed,
And pointed out those arduous paths they trod;   95
Held from afar, aloft, the immortal prize,
And urged the rest by equal steps to rise.
Just precepts thus from great examples given,
She drew from them what they derived from heaven.
The generous critic fanned the poet's fire, 100
And taught the world with reason to admire.

[1] Pope's headings.
[2] Always.

Then criticism the muses' handmaid proved,
To dress her charms, and make her more be-
　　loved:
But following wits from that intention
　　strayed;
Who could not win the mistress, wooed the
　　maid;　　　　　　　　　　　　　105
Against the poets their own arms they turned,
Sure to hate most the men from whom they
　　learned.
So modern 'pothecaries,[3] taught the art
By doctor's bills to play the doctor's part,
Bold in the practice of mistaken rules,　　110
Prescribe, apply, and call their masters fools.
Some on the leaves of ancient authors prey,
Nor time nor moths e'er spoiled so much as
　　they.
Some dryly plain, without invention's aid,
Write dull receipts how poems may be
　　made.　　　　　　　　　　　　　115
These leave the sense, their learning to dis-
　　play,
And those explain the meaning quite away.
　　You then whose judgment the right course
　　　would steer,
Know well each ancient's proper character;
His fable,[4] subject, scope in every page;　120
Religion, country, genius of his age:
Without all these at once before your eyes,
Cavil you may, but never criticize.
Be Homer's works your study and delight,
Read them by day, and meditate by night; 125
Thence form your judgment, thence your
　　maxims bring,
And trace the muses upward to their spring.
Still with itself compared, his text peruse,
And let your comment be the Mantuan
　　muse.[5]
　　When first young Maro[5] in his boundless
　　mind　　　　　　　　　　　　　130
A work to outlast immortal Rome designed,
Perhaps he seemed above the critic's law,
And but from nature's fountains scorned to
　　draw;
But when to examine every part he came,
Nature and Homer were, he found, the
　　same.　　　　　　　　　　　　　135

[3] Druggists.
[4] Plot.
[5] Virgil, born near Mantua.

Convinced, amazed, he checks the bold de-
　　sign;
And rules as strict his labored work confine,
As if the Stagirite[6] o'erlooked each line.
Learn hence for ancient rules a just esteem;
To copy nature is to copy them. . . .　140

Part II

*[Faults found in writing and criticism, with
the right thing implied.]*

. . . .

　　Of all the causes which conspire to blind
Man's erring judgment, and misguide the
　　mind,
What the weak head with strongest bias rules
Is pride, the never-failing vice of fools.
Whatever nature has in worth denied,　205
She gives in large recruits of needful pride;
For as in bodies, thus in souls, we find
What wants in blood and spirits, swelled
　　with wind:
Pride, where wit fails, steps in to our de-
　　fense,
And fills up all the mighty void of sense.　210
If once right reason drives that cloud away,
Truth breaks upon us with resistless day.
Trust not yourself; but your defects to know,
Make use of every friend—and every foe.
　　A little learning is a dangerous thing;　215
Drink deep, or taste not the Pierian spring:[7]
There shallow draughts intoxicate the brain,
And drinking largely sobers us again.
Fired at first sight with what the muse im-
　　parts,
In fearless youth we tempt the heights of
　　arts,　　　　　　　　　　　　　220
While from the bounded level of our mind
Short views we take, nor see the lengths be-
　　hind;
But more advanced, behold with strange sur-
　　prise
New distant scenes of endless science[8] rise!
So pleased at first the towering Alps we
　　try,　　　　　　　　　　　　　225

[6] Aristotle, born at Stagira, Macedonia.
[7] Hippocrene on Mt. Helicon, the home of the
Muses. They were first worshiped in Pieria on Mt.
Olympus, the seat of the gods.
[8] Knowledge.

Gulliver with the Lilliputians, an illustration from *Gulliver's Travels*.

An eighteenth-century coffee house.

Paris Cher Monsr Trolaria

Alexander Pope.

Alexander Pope, a self-portrait.

Mount o'er the vales, and seem to tread the
    sky;
The eternal snows appear already past,
And the first clouds and mountains seem the
    last;
But, those attained, we tremble to survey
The growing labors of the lengthened
    way;   230
The increasing prospect tires our wandering
    eyes,
Hills peep o'er hills, and Alps on Alps arise! [9]
  A perfect judge will read each work of
    wit
With the same spirit that its author writ:
Survey the whole, nor seek slight faults to
    find   235
Where nature moves, and rapture warms the
    mind;
Nor lose, for that malignant dull delight,
The generous pleasure to be charmed with
    wit.
But in such lays as neither ebb, nor flow,
Correctly cold, and regularly low,   240
That shunning faults, one quiet tenor keep,
We cannot blame indeed—but we may sleep.
In wit, as nature, what affects our hearts
Is not the exactness of peculiar parts;
'Tis not a lip, or eye, we beauty call,   245
But the joint force and full result of all.
(1711)

STUDY AIDS: 1. The only difficulty in the
poem lies in the various meanings of "nature"
and "wit." In general, "nature" is the source of
all art (i.e., human nature, experience, or even
external physical nature). However, it is also
the normal, the "natural," and is thus an objective ideal of excellence in morals as well as
in art. Underlying both meanings is the conception of nature as generic or universal.

In contrast, "wit" is specific. Its meanings also
vary: a work of art (i.e., "nature" having passed
through the mind of the artist); or pure intellect.
As "intellect," wit may mean: (1) genius, or
artistic intelligence; (2) invention, fancy, or
literary imagination; (3) witticism, or a quick
perception of resemblance.

What does "nature" mean in ll. 52, 68, 89–90,
135, 140, 236, 243?

What does "wit" mean in ll. 53, 61, 80, 82,
209, 233, 238, 243?

2. Lines 68–140 embody the eighteenth-
century and neoclassic interpretation of the
ancient doctrine that "art is an imitation of
nature." The passage illustrates the following
views: (1) Art should imitate the ideal, the
universal. As a scientist discovers the laws underlying physical phenomena, the poet should illustrate concretely the things which are universally
true in nature. (2) Art should imitate nature
by following the rules (the three unities,
decorum, etc.), which are the experience of the
ancient classical writers reduced to a method.
(3) Inasmuch as the classical writers of Greece
and Rome best followed nature in their literature,
art should imitate these classical writers.

Where in the passage does Pope state a belief
in each of these interpretations? How are the
three in agreement with each other? What function does man's reason play in this imitation of
nature?

The Rape of the Lock

This poem shows that great poetry can arise from seemingly unpoetic material. In Binfield,
Pope's village, Lord Petre cut off one of Arabella Fermor's curls, and the two families began
quarreling over the incident. When Pope's friend, John Caryll, suggested a poem to end the dispute, Pope obliged with *The Rape of the Lock* (1712). The poem is a mock-epic like Dryden's
MacFlecknoe, but it is considerably more polished and complete. This genre mocks its trivial
subject matter by making constant allusions to the epic, which traditionally presents only heroic
actions. In this way the mock-epic creates an ironic contrast between what was and what now is,
and between what ought to be and what actually exists.

In 1714, Pope expanded the poem from its original two cantos to five, by adding the super-

[9] Analyze the extended simile (ll. 219–232), which Dr. Johnson regarded as the best simile in
the language.

natural elements of sylphs and gnomes, and in a letter to Arabella Fermor he explained their significance as follows:

". . . The Rosicrucians are a people I must bring you acquainted with. The best account I know of them is in a French book called *Le Comte de Gabalis,* which both in its title and size is so like a novel, that many of the fair sex have read it for one by mistake. According to these gentlemen, the four elements are inhabited by spirits, which they call sylphs, gnomes, nymphs, and salamanders. The gnomes or daemons of earth delight in mischief; but the sylphs, whose habitation is in the air, are the best-conditioned creatures imaginable. For they say, any mortal may enjoy the most intimate familiarities with these gentle spirits, upon a condition very easy to all true adepts, an inviolate preservation of chastity."

Canto 1

What dire offense from amorous causes
   springs,
What mighty contests rise from trivial things,
I sing—This verse to Caryll, muse! is due:
This, even Belinda may vouchsafe to view:
Slight is the subject, but not so the praise, 5
If she inspire, and he approve my lays.
  Say what strange motive, Goddess! could
   compel [1]
A well-bred lord to assault a gentle belle?
O say what stranger cause, yet unexplored,
Could make a gentle belle reject a lord? 10
In tasks so bold can little men engage,
And in soft bosoms dwells such mighty rage?
  Sol through white curtains shot a timorous
   ray,
And oped those eyes that must eclipse the day.
Now lapdogs give themselves the rousing
  shake, 15
And sleepless lovers just at twelve awake:
Thrice rung the bell, the slipper knocked the
  ground,
And the pressed watch returned a silver
  sound.
Belinda still her downy pillow prest,
Her guardian sylph [2] prolonged the balmy
  rest. 20
'Twas he had summoned to her silent bed
The morning-dream that hovered o'er her
  head;

A youth more glittering than a birthnight
  beau
(That even in slumber caused her cheek to
  glow)
Seemed to her ear his winning lips to lay, 25
And thus in whispers said, or seemed to say:
  "Fairest of mortals, thou distinguished care
Of thousand bright inhabitants of air!
If e'er one vision touched thy infant thought,
Of all the nurse and all the priest have
  taught— 30
Of airy elves by moonlight shadows seen,
The silver token, and the circled green,
Or virgins visited by angel-powers,
With golden crowns and wreaths of heavenly
  flowers;
Hear and believe! thy own importance
  know, 35
Nor bound thy narrow views to things below.
Some secret truths, from learnèd pride concealed,
To maids alone and children are revealed:
What though no credit doubting wits may
  give?
The fair and innocent shall still believe. 40
Know, then, unnumbered spirits round thee
  fly,
The light militia of the lower sky.
These, though unseen, are ever on the wing,
Hang o'er the box, and hover round the ring.
Think what an equipage thou hast in air, 45
And view with scorn two pages and a chair.

[1] In ll. 7-10 Pope announces the theme of the poem: the battle of the sexes. Belinda (woman) desires to retain her chastity, yet her whole life has been a preparation for losing it (marriage).

[2] Ariel (see 1: 105-106). Pope's "Letter to Arabella Fermor, above, explains his substitution of Rosicrucian mythology for the supernatural machinery required by the mock-epic. What is the one condition upon which women can be familiar with sylphs (see "Letter," above)? Notice how Pope emphasizes this same idea in 1: 67-68, 112-114. Notice, however, it is woman's nature to seek an environment which is hostile to this one condition 1: 79-104).

As now your own, our beings were of old,
And once inclosed in woman's beauteous
    mold;
Thence, by a soft transition, we repair
From earthly vehicles to these of air.   50
Think not, when woman's transient breath is
    fled,
That all her vanities at once are dead;
Succeeding vanities she still regards,
And, though she plays no more, o'erlooks the
    cards.
Her joy in gilded chariots, when alive,   55
And love of ombre, after death survive.
For when the fair in all their pride expire,
To their first elements their souls retire.
The sprites of fiery termagants in flame
Mount up, and take a salamander's name.   60
Soft yielding minds to water glide away,
And sip, with nymphs, their elemental tea.
The graver prude sinks downward to a gnome
In search of mischief still on earth to roam.
The light coquettes in sylphs aloft repair,   65
And sport and flutter in the fields of air.
    "Know further yet: whoever fair and chaste
Rejects mankind, is by some sylph embraced;
For spirits, freed from mortal laws, with ease
Assume what sexes and what shapes they
    please.   70
What guards the purity of melting maids,
In courtly balls, and midnight masquerades,
Safe from the treacherous friend, the daring
    spark,
The glance by day, the whisper in the dark,
When kind occasion prompts their warm
    desires,   75
When music softens, and when dancing
    fires?
'Tis but their sylph, the wise celestials know,
Though honor is the word with men below.
    "Some nymphs there are, too conscious of
    their face,
For life predestined to the gnome's em-
    brace.   80
These swell their prospects and exalt their
    pride,
When offers are disdained, and love denied:
Then gay ideas crowd the vacant brain,
While peers, and dukes, and all their sweep-
    ing train,

And garters, stars, and coronets appear,   85
And in soft sounds, 'Your Grace' salutes their
    ear.
'Tis these that early taint the female soul,
Instruct the eyes of young coquettes to roll,
Teach infant cheeks a bidden blush to know,
And little hearts to flutter at a beau.   90
    "Oft, when the world imagine women
    stray,
The sylphs through mystic mazes guide their
    way;
Through all the giddy circle they pursue,
And old impertinence expel by new.
What tender maid but must a victim fall 95
To one man's treat, but for another's ball?
When Florio speaks, what virgin could with-
    stand,
If gentle Damon did not squeeze her hand?
With varying vanities, from every part,
They shift the moving toyshop of their
    heart;   100
Where wigs with wigs, with sword-knots
    sword-knots strive,
Beaux banish beaux, and coaches coaches
    drive.
This erring mortals levity may call;
Oh blind to truth! the sylphs contrive it all.
    "Of these am I, who thy protection
    claim,   105
A watchful sprite, and Ariel is my name.
Late, as I ranged the crystal wilds of air,
In the clear mirror of thy ruling star
I saw, alas! some dread event impend,
Ere to the main this morning sun descend, 110
But heaven reveals not what, or how or
    where.
Warned by the sylph, O pious maid, beware!
This to disclose is all thy guardian can:
Beware of all, but most beware of man!"
    He said; when Shock,[3] who thought she
    slept too long,   115
Leaped up, and waked his mistress with his
    tongue.
'Twas then, Belinda, if report say true,
Thy eyes first opened on a billet-doux;
Wounds, charms, and ardors were no sooner
    read,
But all the vision vanished from thy head. 120

[3] Belinda's lap-dog.

And now, unveiled, the toilet [4] stands displayed,
Each silver vase in mystic order laid.
First, robed in white, the nymph intent adores,
With head uncovered, the cosmetic powers.
A heavenly image in the glass appears; 125
To that she bends, to that her eyes she rears.
The inferior priestess,[5] at her altar's side,
Trembling begins the sacred rites of Pride.
Unnumbered treasures ope at once, and here
The various offerings of the world appear; 130
From each she nicely culls with curious toil,
And decks the goddess with the glittering spoil.
This casket India's glowing gems unlocks,
And all Arabia breathes from yonder box.
The tortoise here and elephant unite, 135
Transformed to combs, the speckled, and the white.
Here files of pins extend their shining rows,
Puffs, powders, patches, bibles, billet-doux.
Now awful beauty puts on all its arms;
The fair each moment rises in her charms, 140
Repairs her smiles, awakens every grace,
And calls forth all the wonders of her face;
Sees by degrees a purer blush arise,

[4] Lines 121–148 describe Belinda's dressing, but the passage is also an extended metaphor. Notice the following words: "mystic" (l. 122), "robed in white . . . adores" (l. 123), "head uncovered" and "powers" (l. 124), "heavenly image" (l. 125), "bends . . . rears" (l. 126), "priestess" and "altar" (l. 127), "sacred rites" (l. 128), "offerings" (l. 130), and "goddess" (l. 132). What is the other half of the metaphor in which Belinda's toilet is compared?

To develop the poem's theme (ll. 7–10), Pope thus represents Belinda as a goddess (l. 132), perhaps thinking of her as a sun-goddess. Her eyes, like the rays of the sun, eclipse all other light (1: 14; 2: 13–14) and have the power to destroy (5: 145–147; 1: 144; 3: 155–156). She has an effect on her world like sunshine on ours (2: 52). She is portrayed as the center around which her social system revolves in 2: 1–14. The Baron builds an altar to her (2: 35–46). In the card game, Belinda cries "'Let spades be trump!' and trumps they were" (3: 46) in parody of "Let there be light, and there was light." She performs miracles (2: 7–8), and she is attended by supernatural beings. To cut the lock of such a creature would be sacrilege (4: 93, 174), yet Belinda is mortal and exists that the lock might be cut.
[5] Betty, Belinda's maid (l. 148).

And keener lightnings quicken in her eyes.
The busy sylphs surround their darling care, 145
These set the head, and those divide the hair,
Some fold the sleeve, whilst others plait the gown:
And Betty's praised for labors not her own.

Canto 2

Not with more glories, in the ethereal plain,
The sun first rises o'er the purpled main,
Than, issuing forth, the rival of his beams
Launched on the bosom of the silver Thames.
Fair nymphs, and well-dressed youths around her shone, 5
But every eye was fixed on her alone.
On her white breast a sparkling cross she wore,
Which Jews might kiss, and infidels adore.
Her lively looks a sprightly mind disclose,
Quick as her eyes, and as unfixed as those: 10
Favors to none, to all she smiles extends;
Oft she rejects, but never once offends.
Bright as the sun, her eyes the gazers strike,
And, like the sun, they shine on all alike.
Yet graceful ease, and sweetness void of pride, 15
Might hide her faults, if belles had faults to hide:
If to her share some female errors fall,
Look on her face, and you'll forget 'em all.
This nymph, to the destruction of mankind,[6]

[6] Lines 19–28 explain how Belinda is a goddess. Her divinity lies in her mortality and operates through her beauty. Her beauty aids are sanctified; they receive care from heavenly spirits (1: 145–148; 2: 91–100). She nourishes her hair for the "destruction of mankind." In the passage at hand, "hair" in air, water, and earth is the means of entrapment. Since primitive times men have recognized hair as a fertility and sexual symbol; therefore, it is no wonder that "beauty draws us with a single hair."

It is Belinda's beauty which makes her like the sun; thus, she is to be worshiped by men and to slay them with a glance. She is a goddess creating and lighting the world of men. Her beauty, however, is mortal, and like the course of the sun it is destined to set in darkness (5: 145–148). Belinda, then, is faced with the human problem of 1: 9–10: she is like a flower which if picked will die, if not picked will wither on the stalk. She cannot alter her destiny; she can only choose the terms by which she will die—not rape but marriage.

Nourished two locks, which graceful hung
    behind   20
In equal curls, and well conspired to deck
With shining ringlets the smooth ivory neck.
Love in these labyrinths his slaves detains,
And mighty hearts are held in slender chains.
With hairy springes we the birds betray,   25
Slight lines of hair surprise the finny prey,
Fair tresses man's imperial race ensnare,
And beauty draws us with a single hair.

    The adventurous baron the bright locks ad-
      mired;
He saw, he wished, and to the prize as-
      pired.   30
Resolved to win, he meditates the way,
By force to ravish, or by fraud betray;
For when success a lover's toil attends,
Few ask if fraud or force attained his ends.

    For this, ere Phœbus rose, he had im-
      plored   35
Propitious heaven, and every power adored,
But chiefly Love—to Love an altar built
Of twelve vast French romances, neatly gilt.
There lay three garters, half a pair of gloves,
And all the trophies of his former loves;   40
With tender billet-doux he lights the pyre,
And breathes three amorous sighs to raise the
    fire.
Then prostrate falls, and begs with ardent
    eyes
Soon to obtain, and long possess the prize:
The powers gave ear, and granted half his
    prayer,   45
The rest the winds dispersed in empty air.

    But now secure the painted vessel glides,
The sunbeams trembling on the floating tides;
While melting music steals upon the sky,
And softened sounds along the waters die: 50
Smooth flow the waves, the zephyrs gently
    play,
Belinda smiled, and all the world was gay.
All but the sylph—with careful thoughts op-
    prest
The impending woe sat heavy on his breast.
He summons straight his denizens of air; 55
The lucid squadrons round the sails re-
    pair:
Soft o'er the shrouds aërial whispers breathe
That seemed but zephyrs to the train be-
    neath.

Some to the sun their insect-wings unfold,
Waft on the breeze, or sink in clouds of
    gold;   60
Transparent forms too fine for mortal sight,[7]
Their fluid bodies half dissolved in light,
Loose to the wind their airy garments flew,
Thin glittering textures of the filmy dew,
Dipped in the richest tincture of the skies, 65
Where light disports in ever-mingling dyes,
While every beam new transient colors flings,
Colors that change whene'er they wave their
    wings.
Amid the circle, on the gilded mast,
Superior by the head was Ariel placed;   70
His purple pinions opening to the sun,
He raised his azure wand, and thus begun:
    "Ye sylphs and sylphids, to your chief give
      ear.
Fays, fairies, genii, elves, demons, hear!
Ye know the spheres and various tasks as-
    signed   75
By laws eternal to the aërial kind.
Some in the fields of purest ether play,
And bask and whiten in the blaze of day:
Some guide the course of wandering orbs on
    high,
Or roll the planets through the boundless
    sky: 80
Some, less refined, beneath the moon's pale
    light
Pursue the stars that shoot athwart the night
Or suck the mists in grosser air below,
Or dip their pinions in the painted bow,
Or brew fierce tempests on the wintry
    main,   85
Or o'er the glebe distil the kindly rain.
Others, on earth, o'er human race preside,
Watch all their ways, and all their actions
    guide:
Of these the chief the care of nations own,
And guard with arms divine the British
    throne.   90
    "Our humbler province is to tend the fair,
Not a less pleasing, though less glorious
    care;
To save the powder from too rude a gale;

[7] Notice the predominance of the vowel *i* in ll.
61–68. Pope associates the short *i* sound with the
sylphs throughout the poem (ll. 84, 123–136), as
Drayton and Herrick had done in their fairy poems.

Nor let the imprisoned essences exhale;
To draw fresh colors from the vernal flow-
ers; 95
To steal from rainbows ere they drop in show-
ers
A brighter wash; to curl their waving hairs,
Assist their blushes and inspire their airs;
Nay oft, in dreams invention we bestow,
To change a flounce, or add a furbelow. 100
 "This day black omens threat the brightest
fair,
That e'er deserved a watchful spirit's care;
Some dire disaster, or by force or sleight;
But what, or where, the Fates have wrapped in
night.
Whether the nymph shall break Diana's
law,[8] 105
Or some frail china jar receive a flaw;
Or stain her honor, or her new brocade,
Forget her prayers, or miss a masquerade,
Or lose her heart, or necklace, at a ball;
Or whether heaven has doomed that Shock
must fall. 110
Haste, then, ye spirits! to your charge re-
pair:
The fluttering fan be Zephyretta's care;
The drops to thee, Brillante, we consign;
And, Momentilla, let the watch be thine;
Do thou, Crispissa, tend her favorite lock; 115
Ariel himself shall be the guard of Shock.
 "To fifty chosen sylphs, of special note,
We trust the important charge, the petticoat;
Oft have we known that seven-fold fence to
fail,
Though stiff with hoops, and armed with ribs
of whale. 120
Form a strong line about the silver bound,
And guard the wide circumference around.
 "Whatever spirit, careless of his charge,
His post neglects, or leaves the fair at large,
Shall feel sharp vengeance soon o'ertake his
sins: 125
Be stopped in vials, or transfixed with pins,
Or plunged in lakes of bitter washes lie,
Or wedged whole ages in a bodkin's eye;
Gums and pomatums shall his flight restrain,
While clogged he beats his silken wings in
vain, 130
Or alum styptics with contracting power
 [8] Vow of chastity.

Shrink his thin essence like a riveled [9]
flower:
Or, as Ixion [10] fixed, the wretch shall feel
The giddy motion of the whirling mill,
In fumes of burning chocolate shall glow, 135
And tremble at the sea that froths below!"
 He spoke; the spirits from the sails de-
scend;
Some, orb in orb, around the nymph extend;
Some thread the mazy ringlets of her hair;
Some hang upon the pendants of her ear; 140
With beating hearts the dire event they wait,
Anxious, and trembling for the birth of Fate.

Canto 3

Close by those meads, for ever crowned with
flowers,
Where Thames with pride surveys his rising
towers
There stands a structure of majestic frame,
Which from the neighboring Hampton [11]
takes its name.
Here Britain's statesmen oft the fall fore-
doom 5
Of foreign tyrants, and of nymphs at home;
Here, thou, great ANNA! [12] whom three realms
obey,
Dost sometimes counsel take—and sometimes
tea.
 Hither the heroes and the nymphs resort,
To taste awhile the pleasures of a court; 10
In various talk the instructive hours they past,
Who gave the ball, or paid the visit last;
One speaks the glory of the British Queen,
And one describes a charming Indian screen;
A third interprets motions, looks, and eyes; 15
At every word a reputation dies.
Snuff, or the fan, supply each pause of chat,
With singing, laughing, ogling, and all that.

 [9] Shriveled.
 [10] In mythology, Ixion was eternally bound to a
turning wheel, because he sought the love of Juno.
Here, in mock-epic style, he is tied to a coffee mill.
In like fashion, Milton's burning lake of *Paradise
Lost* has become a puddle of spilled face lotion
(1. 127), and the careless sylph struggles through
pomade as Satan did through chaos (ll. 129–130).
 [11] A royal palace.
 [12] Anne, queen of the three realms: England,
Scotland, and Wales.

Meanwhile, declining from the noon of
    day,
The sun obliquely shoots his burning ray; 20
The hungry judges soon the sentence sign,
And wretches hang that jurymen may dine;
The merchant from the Exchange returns in
    peace,
And the long labors of the toilet cease.
Belinda now, whom thirst of fame invites, 25
Burns to encounter two adventurous knights,
At ombre [13] singly to decide their doom,
And swells her breast with conquests yet to
    come.
Straight the three bands prepare in arms to
    join,
Each band the number of the sacred nine. 30
Soon as she spreads her hand, the aërial guard
Descend, and sit on each important card:
First Ariel perched upon a Matadore,
Then each according to the rank they bore;
For sylphs, yet mindful of their ancient
    race, 35
Are, as when women, wondrous fond of place.
    Behold four kings in majesty revered,
With hoary whiskers and a forky beard;
And four fair queens, whose hands sustain a
    flower,
The expressive emblem of their softer
    power; 40
Four knaves, in garbs succinct, a trusty band,
Caps on their heads, and halberts in their
    hand,
And pari-colored troops, a shining train,
Draw forth to combat on the velvet plain.
    The skilful nymph reviews her force with
    care; 45
"Let spades be trumps!" she said, and trumps
    they were.
Now move to war her sable Matadores,
In show like leaders of the swarthy Moors.
Spadillio first, unconquerable lord!

[13] A card game, which corresponds to the epic's
great battle. Who are the opposing armies here
(see ll. 25-26)? Who is the instigator of the battle
(see ll. 25-28, 139-146)? A card game is a fitting
symbol for the battle of the sexes. A card game is
played according to rules. Society ordains that
woman, by following the rules in the battle of the
sexes, may lose her lock with honor (see ll. 161-
178); otherwise, with dishonor (see 4: 103-120;
147-176).

Led off two captive trumps, and swept the
    board. 50
As many more Manillio forced to yield,
And marched a victor from the verdant field.
Him Basto followed, but his fate more hard
Gained but one trump and one plebeian card.
With his broad saber next, a chief in years, 55
The hoary Majesty of Spades appears,
Puts forth one manly leg, to sight revealed;
The rest his many-colored robe concealed.
The rebel Knave, who dares his prince en-
    gage,
Proves the just victim of his royal rage. 60
Even mighty Pam, that kings and queens
    o'erthrew,
And mowed down armies in the fights of Loo,
Sad chance of war! now destitute of aid,
Falls undistinguished by the victor spade.
    Thus far both armies to Belinda yield; 65
Now to the baron Fate inclines the field.
His warlike amazon her host invades,
The imperial consort of the crown of spades.
The club's black tyrant first her victim died,
Spite of his haughty mien and barbarous
    pride: 70
What boots the regal circle on his head,
His giant limbs, in state unwieldy spread;
That long behind he trails his pompous robe,
And of all monarchs only grasps the globe?
    The baron now his diamonds pours
    apace; 75
The embroidered King who shows but half
    his face,
And his refulgent Queen, with powers com-
    bined,
Of broken troops an easy conquest find.
Clubs, diamonds, hearts, in wild disorder
    seen,
With throngs promiscuous strew the level
    green. 80
Thus when dispersed a routed army runs,
Of Asia's troops, and Afric's sable sons,
With like confusion different nations fly,
Of various habit, and of various dye;
The pierced battalions disunited fall 85
In heaps on heaps; one fate o'erwhelms them
    all.
    The Knave of Diamonds tries his wily arts,
And wins (oh shameful chance!) the Queen
    of Hearts.

At this, the blood the virgin's cheek forsook,
A livid paleness spreads o'er all her look;   90
She sees, and trembles at the approaching ill,
Just in the jaws of ruin, and codille.
And now (as oft in some distempered state)
On one nice trick depends the general fate!
An Ace of Hearts steps forth: the King un-
    seen   95
Lurked in her hand, and mourned his cap-
    tive Queen.
He springs to vengeance with an eager pace,
And falls like thunder on the prostrate Ace.
The nymph, exulting, fills with shouts the
    sky;
The walls, the woods, and long canals re-
    ply.   100
    Oh thoughtless mortals! ever blind to fate,
Too soon dejected, and too soon elate.
Sudden these honors shall be snatched away,
And cursed for ever this victorious day.
    For lo! the board with cups and spoons is
    crowned,   105
The berries crackle, and the mill turns round;
On shining altars of japan they raise
The silver lamp; the fiery spirits blaze:
From silver spouts the grateful liquors glide,
While China's earth receives the smoking
    tide.   110
At once they gratify their scent and taste,
And frequent cups prolong the rich repast.
Straight hover round the fair her airy band;
Some, as she sipped, the fuming liquor
    fanned,
Some o'er her lap their careful plumes dis-
    played,   115
Trembling, and conscious of the rich brocade.
Coffee (which makes the politician wise,
And see through all things with his half-shut
    eyes)
Sent up in vapors to the baron's brain
New stratagems, the radiant lock to gain. 120
Ah, cease, rash youth! desist ere 'tis too late,
Fear the just gods, and think of Scylla's
    fate! [14]
Changed to a bird, and sent to flit in air,
She dearly pays for Nisus' injured hair!

[14] The mythological Scylla was changed into a bird, because she gave Nisus a lock of her father's hair, which was essential to the security of the state.

But when to mischief mortals bend their
    will,   125
How soon they find fit instruments of ill!
Just then, Clarissa drew with tempting grace
A two-edged weapon from her shining case:
So ladies in romance assist their knight,
Present the spear, and arm him for the
    fight.   130
He takes the gift with reverence, and extends
The little engine on his fingers' ends;
This just behind Belinda's neck he spread,
As o'er the fragrant steams she bends her
    head.
Swift to the lock a thousand sprites re-
    pair;   135
A thousand wings, by turns, blow back the
    hair;
And thrice they twitched the diamond in her
    ear;
Thrice she looked back, and thrice the foe
    drew near.
Just in that instant, anxious Ariel sought
The close recesses of the virgin's thought. 140
As on the nosegay in her breast reclined,
He watched the ideas rising in her mind,
Sudden he viewed, in spite of all her art,
An earthly lover lurking at her heart.
Amazed, confused, he found his power ex-
    pired,   145
Resigned to fate, and with a sigh retired.
    The peer now spreads the glittering for-
    fex [15] wide,
To inclose the lock; now joins it, to divide.
Even then, before the fatal engine closed,
A wretched sylph too fondly interposed;   150
Fate urged the shears, and cut the sylph in
    twain
(But airy substance soon unites again).
The meeting points the sacred hair dissever
From the fair head, for ever, and for ever!
    Then flashed the living lightning from her
    eyes,   155
And screams of horror rend the affrighted
    skies.
Not louder shrieks to pitying heaven are
    cast,
When husbands, or when lapdogs breathe
    their last;
Or when rich china vessels, fallen from high,

[15] Scissors.

In glittering dust and painted fragments
lie!   160
"Let wreaths of triumph now my temples
twine,"
The victor cried, "the glorious prize is mine!
While fish in streams, or birds delight in
air,
Or in a coach and six the British fair,
As long as *Atalantis* [16] shall be read,   165
Or the small pillow grace a lady's bed,
While visits shall be paid on solemn days,
When numerous wax-lights in bright order
blaze:
While nymphs take treats, or assignations
give,
So long my honor, name, and praise shall
live!   170
What time would spare, from steel receives
its date,
And monuments, like men, submit to Fate!
Steel could the labor of the gods destroy,
And strike to dust the imperial towers of
Troy;
Steel could the works of mortal pride con-
found   175
And hew triumphal arches to the ground.
What wonder, then, fair nymph! thy hairs
should feel
The conquering force of unresisted steel?"

Canto 4

But anxious cares the pensive nymph op-
pressed,
And secret passions labored in her breast.
Not youthful kings in battle seized alive,
Not scornful virgins who their charms sur-
vive,
Not ardent lovers robbed of all their bliss, 5
Not ancient ladies when refused a kiss,
Not tyrants fierce that unrepenting die,
Not Cynthia when her mantua's pinned
awry,
E'er felt such rage, resentment, and despair,
As thou, sad virgin! for thy ravished hair. 10
  For, that sad moment, when the sylphs
withdrew,
And Ariel weeping from Belinda flew.

[16] A scandalous book by Mrs. Mary Manley,
widely but secretly read by women.

Umbriel,[17] a dusky, melancholy sprite
As ever sullied the fair face of light,
Down to the central earth, his proper scene, 15
Repaired to search the gloomy Cave of
Spleen.[18]
  Swift on his sooty pinions flits the gnome,
And in a vapor reached the dismal dome.
No cheerful breeze this sullen region knows,
The dreaded east is all the wind that blows. 20
Here in a grotto sheltered close from air,
And screened in shades from day's detested
glare,
She sighs for ever on her pensive bed,
Pain at her side, and Megrim at her head.
Two handmaids wait the throne; alike in
place,   25
But differing far in figure and in face.
Here stood Ill-nature, like an ancient maid,
Her wrinkled form in black and white ar-
rayed;
With store of prayers for mornings, nights,
and noons,
Her hand is filled; her bosom with lam-
poons.   30
There Affectation, with a sickly mien,
Shows in her cheek the roses of eighteen,
Practiced to lisp, and hang the head aside,
Faints into airs, and languishes with pride;
On the rich quilt sinks with becoming woe, 35
Wrapped in a gown for sickness and for
show.
The fair ones feel such maladies as these,
When each new night-dress gives a new
disease.
  A constant vapor o'er the palace flies,
Strange phantoms rising as the mists arise; 40
Dreadful as hermits' dreams in haunted
shades,
Or bright as visions of expiring maids:
Now glaring fiends, and snakes on rolling
spires,
Pale specters, gaping tombs, and purple fires;
Now lakes of liquid gold, Elysian scenes, 45

[17] A gnome (see "Letter to Arabella Fermor,"
p. 356).
[18] In many great epics, the *Odyssey* and the
Aeneid for instance, the hero makes a journey to
the underworld, which is here being parodied as the
"hell" where the sinners (the prudish) are punished
with hysteria, headaches, melancholy, and frayed
nerves.

And crystal domes, and angels in machines.
  Unnumbered throngs on every side are seen,[19]
Of bodies changed to various forms by Spleen.
Here living teapots stand, one arm held out,
One bent; the handle this, and that the spout: 50
A pipkin there, like Homer's tripod walks;
Here sighs a jar, and there a goose-pie talks;
Men prove with child, as powerful fancy works,
And maids turned bottles call aloud for corks.
  Safe passed the gnome through this fantastic band, 55
A branch of healing spleenwort in his hand.
Then thus addressed the Power [20]—"Hail, wayward Queen!
Who rule the sex to fifty from fifteen:
Parent of vapors [21] and of female wit,
Who give the hysteric or poetic fit, 60
On various tempers act by various ways,
Make some take physic, others scribble plays;
Who cause the proud their visits to delay,
And send the godly in a pet to pray.
A nymph there is that all your power disdains, 65
And thousands more in equal mirth maintains.
But oh! if e'er thy gnome could spoil a grace,
Or raise a pimple on a beauteous face,
Like citron-waters matrons' cheeks inflame,
Or change complexions at a losing game; 70
If e'er with airy horns I planted heads,[22]
Or rumpled petticoats, or tumbled beds,
Or caused suspicion when no soul was rude,
Or discomposed the head-dress of a prude,
Or e'er to costive [23] lapdog gave disease, 75
Which not the tears of brightest eyes could ease,
Hear me, and touch Belinda with chagrin;
That single act gives half the world the spleen."
  The Goddess, with a discontented air,

Seems to reject him though she grants his prayer. 80
A wondrous bag with both her hands she binds,
Like that where once Ulysses held the winds;
There she collects the force of female lungs,
Sighs, sobs, and passions, and the war of tongues.
A vial next she fills with fainting fears, 85
Soft sorrows, melting griefs, and flowing tears.
The gnome rejoicing bears her gifts away,
Spreads his black wings, and slowly mounts to day.
  Sunk in Thalestris' [24] arms the nymph he found,
Her eyes dejected, and her hair unbound. 90
Full o'er their heads the swelling bag he rent,
And all the Furies issued at the vent.
Belinda burns with more than mortal ire,
And fierce Thalestris fans the rising fire.
"O wretched maid!" she spread her hands, and cried 95
(While Hampton's echoes, "Wretched maid!" replied),
"Was it for this you took such constant care
The bodkin, comb, and essence to prepare?
For this your locks in paper durance bound?
For this with torturing irons wreathed around? 100
For this with fillets strained your tender head,
And bravely bore the double loads of lead?
Gods! shall the ravisher display your hair,
While the fops envy, and the ladies stare!
Honor forbid! at whose unrivaled shrine 105
Ease, pleasure, virtue, all, our sex resign.
Methinks already I your tears survey,
Already hear the horrid things they say,
Already see you a degraded toast,
And all your honor in a whisper lost! 110
How shall I, then, your hapless fame defend?
'Twill then be infamy to seem your friend!
And shall this prize, the inestimable prize,
Exposed through crystal to the gazing eyes,
And heightened by the diamond's circling rays, 115
On that rapacious hand for ever blaze?
Sooner shall grass in Hyde Park Circus grow,
And wits take lodgings in the sound of Bow;

[19] In ll. 47-54 notice the unreality of the men and women who inhabit the Cave of Spleen. What does Belinda have in common with these people?
[20] I.e., Spleen.
[21] Melancholy, or "the blues," a favorite ailment of eighteenth-century women.
[22] I.e., made cuckolds.
[23] Constipated.
[24] Mrs. Morley, a friend of Arabella and sister of Sir George Brown (Sir Plume of l. 121).

Sooner let earth, air, sea, to chaos fall,
Men, monkeys, lapdogs, parrots, perish
    all!"   120
    She said; then raging to Sir Plume repairs,
And bids her beau demand the precious hairs
(Sir Plume, of amber snuff-box justly vain,
And the nice conduct of a clouded cane):
With earnest eyes, and round unthinking
    face,   125
He first the snuff-box opened, then the case,
And thus broke out—"My lord, why, what the
    devil!
Z—ds! damn the lock! 'fore Gad, you must be
    civil!
Plague on it! 'tis past a jest—nay, prithee, pox!
Give her the hair."—He spoke, and rapped
    his box.   130
    "It grieves me much," replied the peer again,
"Who speaks so well should ever speak in
    vain:
But by this lock, this sacred lock, I swear
(Which never more shall join its parted hair,
Which never more its honors shall renew, 135
Clipped from the lovely head where late it
    grew),
That, while my nostrils draw the vital air,
This hand, which won it, shall for ever wear."
He spoke, and speaking, in proud triumph
    spread
The long-contended honors of her head.   140
    But Umbriel, hateful gnome, forbears not
    so;
He breaks the vial whence the sorrows flow.
Then see! the nymph in beauteous grief
    appears,
Her eyes half-languishing, half-drowned in
    tears;
On her heaved bosom hung her drooping
    head,   145
Which with a sigh she raised, and thus she
    said:
    "For ever cursed be this detested day,
Which snatched my best, my favorite curl
    away!
Happy! ah, ten times happy had I been,
If Hampton Court these eyes had never
    seen!   150
Yet am not I the first mistaken maid,
By love of courts to numerous ills betrayed.
O had I rather unadmired remained

In some lone isle, or distant northern land;
Where the gilt chariot never marks the
    way,   155
Where none learn ombre, none e'er taste
    bohea!
There kept my charms concealed from
    mortal eye,
Like roses, that in deserts bloom and die.
What moved my mind with youthful lords to
    roam?
O had I stayed, and said my prayers at
    home;   160
'Twas this the morning omens seemed to tell,
Thrice from my trembling hand the patch-
    box fell;
The tottering china shook without a wind,
Nay, Poll sat mute, and Shock was most
    unkind!
A sylph, too, warned me of the threats of
    fate,   165
In mystic visions, now believed too late!
See the poor remnants of these slighted hairs!
My hands shall rend what even thy rapine
    spares.
These, in two sable ringlets taught to break,
Once gave new beauties to the snowy neck; 170
The sister-lock now sits uncouth alone,
And in its fellow's fate foresees its own;
Uncurled it hangs, the fatal shears demands,
And tempts once more thy sacrilegious hands.
O hadst thou, cruel! been content to seize 175
Hairs less in sight, or any hairs but these!"

Canto 5

She said: the pitying audience melt in tears;
But Fate and Jove had stopped the baron's
    ears.
In vain Thalestris with reproach assails,
For who can move when fair Belinda fails?
Not half so fixed the Trojan could remain, 5
While Anna begged and Dido raged in vain;
Then grave Clarissa graceful waved her fan;
Silence ensued, and thus the nymph began:
    "Say, why are beauties praised and honored
    most,
The wise man's passion, and the vain man's
    toast?   10
Why decked with all that land and sea
    afford,
Why angels called, and angel-like adored?

Why round our coaches crowd the white-
gloved beaux?
Why bows the side-box from its inmost rows?
How vain are all these glories, all our pains, 15
Unless good sense preserve what beauty
gains;
That men may say when we the front-box
grace,
'Behold the first in virtue as in face!'
Oh! if to dance all night, and dress all day,
Charmed the smallpox, or chased old age
away, 20
Who would not scorn what housewife's cares
produce,
Or who would learn one earthly thing of use?
To patch, nay, ogle, might become a saint,
Nor could it sure be such a sin to paint.
But since, alas! frail beauty must decay, 25
Curled or uncurled, since locks will turn
to gray;
Since painted, or not painted, all shall fade,
And she who scorns a man must die a maid;
What then remains, but well our power to
use,
And keep good humor still whate'er we
lose? 30
And trust me, dear, good humor can prevail,
When airs, and flights, and screams, and
scolding fail.
Beauties in vain their pretty eyes may roll;
Charms strike the sight, but merit wins the
soul."
So spoke the dame, but no applause en-
sued; 35
Belinda frowned, Thalestris called her prude.
"To arms, to arms!" the fierce virago cries,
And swift as lightning to the combat flies.
All side in parties, and begin the attack;
Fans clap, silks rustle, and tough whalebones
crack; 40
Heroes' and heroines' shouts confusedly rise,
And bass and treble voices strike the skies.
No common weapons in their hands are
found,
Like gods they fight nor dread a mortal
wound.
So when bold Homer makes the gods
engage, 45
And heavenly breasts with human passions
rage;

'Gainst Pallas, Mars; Latona, Hermes arms;
And all Olympus rings with loud alarms;
Jove's thunder roars, heaven trembles all
around,
Blue Neptune storms, the bellowing deeps
resound: 50
Earth shakes her nodding towers, the ground
gives way,
And the pale ghosts start at the flash of day!
Triumphant Umbriel, on a sconce's [25]
height,
Clapped his glad wings, and sat to view the
fight:
Propped on their bodkin-spears, the sprites
survey 55
The growing combat, or assist the fray.
While through the press enraged Thalestris
flies,
And scatters death around from both her eyes,
A beau and witling perished in the throng,
One died in metaphor, and one in song: 60
"O cruel nymph! a living death I bear,"
Cried Dapperwit, and sunk beside his chair.
A mournful glance Sir Fopling upwards cast,
"Those eyes are made so killing"—was his last.
Thus on Mæander's flowers margin lies 65
The expiring swan, and as he sings he dies.
When bold Sir Plume had drawn Clarissa
down,
Chloe stepped in, and killed him with a
frown;
She smiled to see the doughty hero slain,
But, at her smile, the beau revived again. 70
Now Jove suspends his golden scales in air,
Weighs the men's wits against the lady's hair;
The doubtful beam long nods from side to
side;
At length the wits mount up, the hairs sub-
side.
See, fierce Belinda on the baron flies, 75
With more than usual lightning in her eyes;
Nor feared the chief the unequal fight to try,
Who sought no more than on his foe to die.
But this bold lord, with manly strength
endued,
She with one finger and a thumb
subdued: [26] 80

[25] Candlestick holder.
[26] An echo of the epic's battle stratagem, e.g., the
wooden horse used by the Greeks to enter Troy.

Just where the breath of life his nostrils
    drew,
A charge of snuff the wily virgin threw;
The gnomes direct, to every atom just,
The pungent grains of titillating dust.
Sudden, with starting tears each eye
    o'erflows,   85
And the high dome reëchoes to his nose.
   "Now meet thy fate," incensed Belinda
    cried,
And drew a deadly bodkin from her side.
(The same, his ancient personage to deck,
Her great-great-grandsire wore about his
    neck,   90
In three seal-rings; which after, melted down,
Formed a vast buckle for his widow's gown:
Her infant grandame's whistle next it grew,
The bells she jingled, and the whistle blew;
Then in a bodkin graced her mother's hairs, 95
Which long she wore and now Belinda
    wears.)
   "Boast not my fall," he cried, "insulting
    foe!
Thou by some other shalt be laid as low;
Nor think, to die dejects my lofty mind:
All that I dread is leaving you behind!   100
Rather than so, ah, let me still survive,
And burn in Cupid's flames—but burn alive."
"Restore the lock!" she cries; and all around
"Restore the lock!" the vaulted roofs
    rebound.
Not fierce Othello in so loud a strain   105
Roared for the handkerchief that caused his
    pain.
But see how oft ambitious aims are crossed,
And chiefs contend till all the prize is lost!
The lock, obtained with guilt, and kept with
    pain,
In every place is sought, but sought in
    vain: 110
With such a prize no mortal must be blest.
So heaven decrees! with heaven who can
    contest?
   Some thought it mounted to the lunar
    sphere,
Since all things lost on earth are treasured
    there.
There heroes' wits are kept in ponderous
    vases,   115
And beaux' in snuffboxes, and tweezer-cases.

There broken vows, and deathbed alms are
    found,
And lovers' hearts with ends of ribbon bound,
The courtier's promises, and sick man's
    prayers,
The smiles of harlots, and the tears of
    heirs,   120
Cages for gnats, and chains to yoke a flea,
Dried butterflies, and tomes of casuistry.
   But trust the Muse—she saw it upward
    rise,
Though marked by none but quick poetic
    eyes
(So Rome's great founder [27] to the heavens
    withdrew,   125
To Proculus alone confessed in view):
A sudden star, it shot through liquid air,
And drew behind a radiant trail of hair.
Not Berenice's [28] locks first rose so bright,
The heavens bespangling with disheveled
    light.   130
The sylphs behold it kindling as it flies,
And pleased pursue its progress through the
    skies.
   This the beau monde shall from the Mall
    survey,
And hail with music its propitious ray;
This the blessed lover shall for Venus take, 135
And send up vows from Rosamonda's lake;
This Partridge [29] soon shall view in cloud-
    less skies,
When next he looks through Galileo's eyes;
And hence the egregious wizard shall fore-
    doom
The fate of Louis, and the fall of Rome.   140
   Then cease, bright nymph! to mourn thy
    ravished hair,
Which adds new glory to the shining sphere!
Not all the tresses that fair head can boast
Shall draw such envy as the lock you lost.
For after all the murders of your eye,   145
When, after millions slain, yourself shall die;
When those fair suns shall set, as set they
    must,

[27] Romulus, so Proculus, a senator, reported, was
translated to a star.
[28] The wife of Ptolemy III. Ovid relates that her
hair was changed into a constellation.
[29] Partridge was a widely read almanac maker,
ridiculed by Swift and by Steele in the Tatler.

And all those tresses shall be laid in dust,
This lock the muse shall consecrate to fame,
And 'midst the stars inscribe Belinda's
    name.   150
(1712; 1714)

STUDY AIDS: 1. Throughout the poem Pope satirizes the distorted sense of values held by society in his day: the disparity between what people proclaimed and what they practised, between the real and the unreal. The main burden of this theme is, of course, presented by that society's attitude toward chastity. Study Clarissa's speech and Belinda's response to it (5: 9–36). Are virtue and useful skills acceptable to Belinda as alternatives to flirting and coquetry? Is the actual loss of chastity, if unknown, as serious an infraction of morality as the loss of reputation (4: 95–120; 175–176)?

2. What attitude does Pope express when he puts the phrase "or stain her honor" in its context in 2: 101–110? What attitude does the imagery of loss of chastity = broken china convey in 2: 105–106; 3: 159–160; 4: 162–163? Is this a positive or negative attitude toward virtue? Does our present society regard virtue as the eighteenth century did, or do we agree with Pope that such a view is hypocritical?

3. How does Pope show that this distortion of moral values infects men as well as women? Study carefully 3: 21–22. What does Pope imply about the male worship of beauty in his treatment of Belinda as a goddess? What does this worship (or treatment) do to the masculine sex (note 1: 15–16; 3: 157–158; 4: 119–120)? What evidence do you see that your society worships beauty?

4. It is often said that for an age to produce satire there must be commonly accepted standards of right and wrong. Any deviation from the standard of right is a proper subject for satire. Satire is thus an instrument for producing conformity. If this is true, how does the *Rape of the Lock* illustrate it? What function does man's reason play in establishing the standard? Why is emotion ignored? How would Pope's age have determined what this "reasonable" standard was?

Eloïsa to Abelard

Pope prefaced this poem with the following statement:

"Abelard and Eloïsa flourished in the twelfth century; they were two of the most distinguished persons of their age in learning and beauty, but for nothing more famous than for their unfortunate passion. After a long course of calamities,[1] they retired each to a several convent, and consecrated the remainder of their days to religion. It was many years after this separation, that a letter of Abelard's to a friend, which contained the history of his misfortune, fell into the hands of Eloïsa. This awakening of all her tenderness, occasioned those celebrated letters (out of which the following is partly extracted) which give so lively a picture of the struggles of grace and nature, virtue and passion."

In these deep solitudes and awful cells,
Where heavenly-pensive Contemplation
    dwells,
And ever musing Melancholy reigns;
What means this tumult in a vestal's veins?
Why rove my thoughts beyond this last re-
    treat?   5
Why feels my heart its long-forgotten heat?
Yet, yet I love!—From Abelard it came,
And Eloïsa yet must kiss the name.

    Dear fatal name! rest ever unrevealed,
Nor pass these lips in holy silence sealed: 10
Hide it, my heart, within that close disguise,
Where mixed with God's, his loved idea lies:
O write it not, my hand—the name appears
Already written—wash it out, my tears!
In vain lost Eloïsa weeps and prays,   15
Her heart still dictates, and her hand obeys.
    Relentless walls! whose darksome round
        contains

[1] Peter Abelard, the great teacher and philosopher in France during the twelfth century, became the tutor and also the lover of Héloïse, niece of Canon Fulbert of Notre Dame. Because Fulbert mistreated Héloïse, Abelard moved her to a convent. Fulbert, thinking Abelard intended to abandon his niece to pursue his studies, cause ruffians to attack and emasculate him.

Repentant sighs and voluntary pains:
Ye rugged rocks! which holy knees have
    worn;
Ye grots and caverns shagged with horrid
    thorn!   20
Shrines! where their vigils pale-eyed virgins
    keep,
And pitying saints, whose statues learn to
    weep!
Though cold like you, unmoved and silent
    grown,
I have not yet forgot myself to stone.
All is not heaven's while Abelard has part, 25
Still rebel nature holds out half my heart;
Nor prayers nor fasts its stubborn pulse re-
    strain,
Nor tears for ages taught to flow in vain.
    Soon as thy letters trembling I unclose,
That well-known name awakens all my
    woes.   30
Oh name forever sad! forever dear!
Still breathed in sighs, still ushered with a
    tear.
I tremble too, where'er my own I find,
Some dire misfortune follows close behind.
Line after line my gushing eyes o'erflow, 35
Led through a sad variety of woe:
Now warm in love, now withering in my
    bloom,
Lost in a convent's solitary gloom!
There stern religion quenched the unwilling
    flame,
There died the best of passions, love and
    fame.   40
    Yet write, oh write me all, that I may join
Griefs to thy griefs, and echo sighs to thine.
Nor foes nor fortune take this power away;
And is my Abelard less kind than they?
Tears still are mine, and those I need not
    spare,   45
Love but demands what else were shed in
    prayer;
No happier task these faded eyes pursue;
To read and weep is all they now can do.
    Then share thy pain, allow that sad relief;
Ah, more than share it, give me all thy
    grief.   50
Heaven first taught letters for some wretch's
    aid,
Some banished lover or some captive maid;

They live, they speak, they breathe what love
    inspires,
Warm from the soul, and faithful to its fires,
The virgin's wish without her fears impart,
Excuse the blush, and pour out all the
    heart,   55
Speed the soft intercourse from soul to soul,
And waft a sigh from Indus to the pole.
    Thou knowest how guiltless first I met thy
    flame,
When love approached me under friend-
    ship's name;   60
My fancy formed thee of angelic kind,
Some emanation of the all-beauteous mind.
Those smiling eyes, attempering every ray,
Shone sweetly lambent with celestial day.
Guiltless I gazed; heaven listened while you
    sung;   65
And truths divine came mended from that
    tongue.
From lips like those what precept failed to
    move?
Too soon they taught me 'twas no sin to love:
Back through the paths of pleasing sense I
    ran,
Nor wished an angel whom I loved a man. 70
Dim and remote the joys of saints I see,
Nor envy them that heaven I lose for thee.
    How oft, when pressed to marriage, have I
    said,
Curse on all laws but those which love has
    made?
Love, free as air, at sight of human ties, 75
Spreads his light wings, and in a moment
    flies.
Let wealth, let honor, wait the wedded
    dame,
August her deed, and sacred be her fame;
Before true passion all those views remove,
Fame, wealth, and honor! what are you to
    love?   80
The jealous god, when we profane his fires,
Those restless passions in revenge inspires,
And bids them make mistaken mortals groan,
Who seek in love for aught but love alone.
Should at my feet the world's great master
    fall,   85
Himself, his throne, his world, I'd scorn them
    all:
Not Cæsar's empress would I deign to prove;

No, make me mistress to the man I love;
If there be yet another name more free,
More fond than mistress, make me that to
    thee!   90
Oh! happy state! when souls each other draw,
When love is liberty, and nature law:
All then is full, possessing, and possessed,
No craving void left aching in the breast:
Even thought meets thought, ere from the
    lips it part,   95
And each warm wish springs mutual from
    the heart.
This sure is bliss (if bliss on earth there be)
And once the lot of Abelard and me.
    Alas, how changed! what sudden horrors
    rise!
A naked lover bound and bleeding lies!   100
Where, where was Eloïse? her voice, her
    hand,
Her poniard, had opposed the dire com-
    mand.
Barbarian, stay! that bloody stroke restrain;
The crime was common, common be the pain.
I can no more; by shame, by rage sup-
    pressed,   105
Let tears and burning blushes speak the rest.
    Canst thou forget that sad, that solemn
    day,
When victims at yon altar's foot we lay?
Canst thou forget what tears that moment
    fell,
When, warm in youth, I bade the world fare-
    well?   110
As with cold lips I kissed the sacred veil,
The shrines all trembled, and the lamps grew
    pale:
Heaven scarce believed the conquest it sur-
    veyed,
And saints with wonder heard the vows I
    made.
Yet then, to those dread altars as I drew,   115
Not on the cross my eyes were fixed, but
    you:
Not grace, or zeal, love only was my call,
And if I lose thy love, I lose my all.
Come! with thy looks, thy words, relieve my
    woe;
Those still at least are left thee to bestow. 120
Still on that breast enamored let me lie,
Still drink delicious poison from thy eye,

Pant on thy lip, and to thy heart be pressed;
Give all thou canst—and let me dream the
    rest.
Ah no! instruct me other joys to prize,   125
With other beauties charm my partial eyes,
Full in my view set all the bright abode,
And make my soul quit Abelard for God.
    Ah, think at least thy flock deserves thy
    care,
Plants of thy hand, and children of thy
    prayer.   130
From the false world in early youth they fled,
By thee to mountains, wilds, and deserts led.
You raised these hallowed walls; the desert
    smiled,
And paradise was opened in the wild.
No weeping orphan saw his father's stores 135
Our shrines irradiate, or emblaze the floors;
No silver saints, by dying misers given,
Here bribed the rage of ill-requited heaven:
But such plain roofs as piety could raise,
And only vocal with the Maker's praise.   140
In these lone walls (their days eternal
    bound)
These moss-grown domes with spiry turrets
    crowned,
Where awful arches make a noonday night,
And the dim windows shed a solemn light;
Thy eyes diffused a reconciling ray,   145
And gleams of glory brightened all the day.
But now no face divine contentment wears,
'Tis all blank sadness, or continual tears.
See how the force of others' prayers I try,
(O pious fraud of amorous charity!)   150
But why should I on others' prayers depend?
Come thou, my father, brother, husband,
    friend!
Ah let thy handmaid, sister, daughter move,
And all those tender names in one, thy love!
The darksome pines that o'er yon rocks re-
    clined   155
Wave high, and murmur to the hollow wind,
The wandering streams that shine between
    the hills,
The grots that echo to the tinkling rills,
The dying gales that pant upon the trees,
The lakes that quiver to the curling
    breeze;   160
No more these scenes my meditation aid,
Or lull to rest the visionary maid.

But o'er the twilight groves and dusky caves,
Long-sounding aisles, and intermingled graves,
Black Melancholy sits, and round her
    throws   165
A death-like silence, and a dead repose:
Her gloomy presence saddens all the scene,
Shades every flower, and darkens every green,
Deepens the murmur of the falling floods,
And breathes a browner horror on the
    woods.   170
    Yet here forever, ever must I stay;
Sad proof how well a lover can obey!
Death, only death, can break the lasting
    chain;
And here, even then, shall my cold dust
    remain,
Here all its frailties, all its flames resign, 175
And wait till 'tis no sin to mix with thine.
    Ah wretch! believed the spouse of God in
    vain,
Confessed within the slave of love and man.
Assist me, heaven! but whence arose that
    prayer?
Sprung it from piety, or from despair?   180
Even here, where frozen chastity retires,
Love finds an altar for forbidden fires.
I ought to grieve, but cannot what I ought;
I mourn the lover, not lament the fault;
I view my crime, but kindle at the view, 185
Repent old pleasures, and solicit new;
Now turned to heaven, I weep my past
    offense,
Now think of thee, and curse my innocence.
Of all affliction taught a lover yet,
'Tis sure the hardest science to forget!   190
How shall I lose the sin, yet keep the sense,
And love the offender, yet detest the offense?
How the dear object from the crime remove,
Or how distinguish penitence from love?
Unequal task! a passion to resign,   195
For hearts so touched, so pierced, so lost as
    mine.
Ere such a soul regains its peaceful state,
How often must it love, how often hate!
How often hope, despair, resent, regret,
Conceal, disdain,—do all things but forget. 200
But let heaven seize it, all at once 'tis fired:
Not touched, but rapt; not wakened, but in-
    spired!
Oh come! oh teach me nature to subdue,

Renounce my love, my life, myself—and you.
Fill my fond heart with God alone, for he 205
Alone can rival, can succeed to thee.
    How happy is the blameless vestal's lot!
The world forgetting, by the world forgot:
Eternal sunshine of the spotless mind!
Each prayer accepted, and each wish re-
    signed;   210
Labor and rest, that equal periods keep;
"Obedient slumbers that can wake and
    weep";
Desires composed, affections ever even;
Tears that delight, and sighs that waft to
    heaven.
Grace shines around her with serenest
    beams,   215
And whispering angels prompt her golden
    dreams.
For her the unfading rose of Eden blooms,
And wings of seraphs shed divine perfumes,
For her the Spouse prepares the bridal ring,
For her white virgins hymeneals sing,   220
To sounds of heavenly harps she dies away,
And melts in visions of eternal day.
    Far other dreams my erring soul employ,
Far other raptures, of unholy joy:
When at the close of each sad, sorrowing
    day,   225
Fancy restores what vengeance snatched away,
Then conscience sleeps, and leaving nature
    free,
All my loose soul unbounded springs to thee.
Oh cursed, dear horrors of all-conscious night;
How glowing guilt exalts the keen de-
    light!   230
Provoking demons all restraint remove,
And stir within me every source of love.
I hear thee, view thee, gaze o'er all thy
    charms,
And round thy phantom glue my clasping
    arms.
I wake:—no more I hear, no more I view, 235
The phantom flies me, as unkind as you.
I call aloud; it hears not what I say:
I stretch my empty arms; it glides away.
To dream once more I close my willing eyes;
Ye soft illusions, dear deceits, arise!   240
Alas, no more! methinks we wandering go
Through dreary wastes, and weep each other's
    woe,

Where round some moldering tower pale ivy
   creeps,
And low-browed rocks hang nodding o'er the
   deeps.
Sudden you mount, you beckon from the
   skies;   245
Clouds interpose, waves roar, and winds arise.
I shriek, start up, the same sad prospect find,
And wake to all the griefs I left behind.
   For thee the fates, severely kind, ordain
A cool suspense from pleasure and from
   pain;   250
Thy life a long dead calm of fixed repose;
No pulse that riots, and no blood that glows.
Still as the sea, ere winds were taught to blow,
Or moving spirit bade the waters flow;
Soft as the slumbers of a saint forgiven, 255
And mild as opening gleams of promised
   heaven.
   Come, Abelard! for what hast thou to
   dread?
The torch of Venus burns not for the dead.
Nature stands checked; religion disapproves;
Even thou art cold—yet Eloïsa loves.   260
Ah hopeless, lasting flames! like those that
   burn
To light the dead, and warm the unfruitful
   urn.
   What scenes appear where'er I turn my
   view?
The dear ideas, where I fly, pursue,
Rise in the grove, before the altar rise, 265
Stain all my soul, and wanton in my eyes.
I waste the matin lamp in sighs for thee,
Thy image steals between my God and me,
Thy voice I seem in every hymn to hear,
With every bead I drop too soft a tear. 270
When from the censer clouds of fragrance
   roll,
And swelling organs lift the rising soul,
One thought of thee puts all the pomp to
   flight,
Priests, tapers, temples, swim before my
   sight;
In seas of flame my plunging soul is
   drowned,   275
While altars blaze, and angels tremble round.
   While prostrate here in humble grief I lie,
Kind, virtuous drops just gathering in my
   eye,

While praying, trembling, in the dust I roll,
And dawning grace is opening on my
   soul: 280
Come, if thou darest, all charming as thou
   art!
Oppose thyself to heaven; dispute my heart;
Come, with one glance of those deluding eyes
Blot out each bright idea of the skies;
Take back that grace, those sorrows, and
   those tears;   285
Take back my fruitless penitence and
   prayers;
Snatch me, just mounting, from the blest
   abode;
Assist the fiends, and tear me from my God!
   No, fly me, fly me, far as pole from pole;
Rise Alps between us! and whole oceans
   roll!   290
Ah, come not, write not, think not once of
   me,
Nor share one pang of all I felt for thee.
Thy oaths I quit, thy memory resign;
Forget, renounce me, hate whate'er was mine.
Fair eyes, and tempting looks (which yet I
   view!)   295
Long loved, adored ideas, all adieu!
Oh Grace serene! oh virtue heavenly fair!
Divine oblivion of low-thoughted care!
Fresh blooming Hope, gay daughter of the
   sky!
And Faith, our early immortality!   300
Enter, each mild, each amicable guest;
Receive, and wrap me in eternal rest!
   See in her cell sad Eloïsa spread,
Propped on some tomb, a neighbor of the
   dead.
In each low wind methinks a spirit calls, 305
And more than echoes talk along the walls.
Here, as I watched the dying lamps around,
From yonder shrine I heard a hollow sound.
"Come, sister, come!" it said, or seemed to
   say,
"Thy place is here, sad sister, come away! 310
Once like thyself, I trembled, wept, and
   prayed,
Love's victim then, though now a sainted
   maid:
But all is calm in this eternal sleep;
Here grief forgets to groan, and love to weep;
Even superstition loses every fear,   315

For God, not man, absolves our frailties
    here."
  I come, I come! prepare your roseate bowers,
Celestial palms, and ever-blooming flowers.
Thither, where sinners may have rest, I go,
Where flames refined in breasts seraphic
    glow: 320
Thou, Abelard! the last sad office pay,
And smooth my passage to the realms of day;
See my lips tremble, and my eyeballs roll,
Suck my last breath, and catch my flying
    soul!
Ah no—in sacred vestments mayst thou
    stand,   325
The hallowed taper trembling in thy hand,
Present the cross before my lifted eye,
Teach me at once, and learn of me to die.
Ah then, thy once loved Eloïsa see!
It will be then no crime to gaze on me.   330
See from my cheek the transient roses fly!
See the last sparkle languish in my eye!
Till every motion, pulse, and breath be o'er;
And even my Abelard be loved no more.
O Death all-eloquent! you only prove   335
What dust we dote on, when 'tis man we love.
  Then too, when fate shall thy fair frame
    destroy,
(That cause of all my guilt, and all my joy)
In trance ecstatic may thy pangs be drowned,
Bright clouds descend, and angels watch thee
    round,   340
From opening skies may streaming glories
    shine,
And saints embrace thee with a love like
    mine.

May one kind grave unite each hapless
    name,
And graft my love immortal on thy fame!
Then, ages hence, when all my woes are
    o'er,   345
When this rebellious heart shall beat no
    more;
If ever chance two wandering lovers brings
To Paraclete's white walls and silver springs,
O'er the pale marble shall they join their
    heads,
And drink the falling tears each other
    sheds;   350
Then sadly say, with mutual pity moved,
"Oh may we never love as these have loved!"
From the full choir when loud hosannas rise,
And swell the pomp of dreadful sacrifice,
Amid that scene if some relenting eye   355
Glance on the stone where our cold relics
    lie,
Devotion's self shall steal a thought from
    heaven,
One human tear shall drop and be forgiven.
And sure, if fate some future bard shall join
In sad similitude of griefs to mine,   360
Condemned whole years in absence to de-
    plore,
And image charms he must behold no more;
Such if there be, who loves so long, so well,
Let him our sad, our tender story tell;
The well-sung woes will soothe my pensive
    ghost;   365
He best can paint them who shall feel them
    most.
(1717)

An Essay on Man

Epistle 1 *Of the nature and state of man,
with respect to the universe* [1]

Awake, my St. John! [2] leave all meaner things
To low ambition and the pride of kings.
Let us, since life can little more supply

[1] The headings used throughout the poem are
Pope's.
[2] Henry St. John, Viscount Bolingbroke, who supplied some of the ideas which Pope here versifies.

Than just to look about us and to die,
Expatiate [3] free o'er all this scene of man; 5
A mighty maze! but not without a plan;
A wild, where weeds and flowers promis-
    cuous shoot,
Or garden, tempting with forbidden fruit.
Together let us beat this ample field,
Try what the open, what the covert yield; 10

[3] Roam, or enlarge in writing.

The latent tracts, the giddy heights, explore
Of all who blindly creep or sightless soar;
Eye nature's walks, shoot folly as it flies,
And catch the manners living as they rise.
Laugh where we must, be candid where we
    can,   15
But vindicate [4] the ways of God to man.

1. *That we can judge only with regard to our own system, being ignorant of the relations of systems and things.*

  Say first, of God above or man below
What can we reason but from what we
    know? [5]
Of man what see we but his station here,
From which to reason, or to which refer? 20
Through worlds unnumbered though the
    God be known,
'Tis ours to trace him only in our own.
He who through vast immensity can pierce,
See worlds on worlds compose one universe,
Observe how system into system runs,   25
What other planets circle other suns,
What varied being peoples every star,
May tell why heaven has made us as we are:
But of this frame, the bearings and the ties,
The strong connections, nice dependencies, 30
Gradations just, has thy pervading soul
Looked through; or can a part contain the
    whole?
  Is the great chain that draws all to agree,
And drawn supports, upheld by God or thee?

2. *That man is not to be deemed imperfect, but a being suited to his place and rank in the creation, agreeable to the general order of things, and conformable to ends and relations to him unknown.*

  Presumptuous man! the reason wouldst
    thou find,   35
Why formed so weak, so little, and so blind?
First, if thou canst, the harder reason guess
Why formed no weaker, blinder, and no less!

[4] Notice the similarity to Milton's purpose in *Paradise Lost* Bk. 1, 26.
[5] What limit is Pope here imposing on man's reason? What happens to faith and religious beliefs if this limit is accepted?

Ask of thy mother earth why oaks are made [6]
Taller or stronger than the weeds they
    shade!   40
Or ask of yonder argent fields above
Why Jove's satellites are less than Jove!
  Of systems possible, if 'tis confessed [7]
That wisdom infinite must form the best,
Where all must full or not coherent be,   45
And all that rises rise in due degree;
Then in the scale of reasoning life 'tis plain
There must be, somewhere, such a rank as
    man:
And all the question (wrangle e'er so long)
Is only this—if God has placed him
    wrong?   50
  Respecting man, whatever wrong we call,
May, must be right, as relative to all.
In human works, though labored on with pain,
A thousand movements scarce one purpose
    gain;
In God's, one single can its end produce, 55
Yet serve to second too some other use:
So man, who here seems principal alone,
Perhaps acts second to some sphere unknown,
Touches some wheel, or verges to some goal:

[6] Notice Pope's cleverness in concealing metaphor under the guise of reasoned argument in order to persuade the reader in ll. 39–42. Here and often in the *Essay,* metaphor is cast in the form of analogy: "as this is to this, so that is to that." As oaks are in size and strength to weeds, so is the universe to man. As the satellites of Jupiter (Jove) are dependent on their planet, so is man on the universe. We thus tend to accept the assumption that man must be weak and little in comparison with the universe.
[7] Lines 43–50 summarize the eighteenth-century religious view: (1) that a God of infinite wisdom exists; (2) that such a God of "wisdom" must have created the best of all possible worlds ("systems"); (3) that the "best" must be the fullest, because if not complete, it would be imperfect ("not coherent be"); and (4) that the system to be "coherent" must consist of faculties which rise in due degrees from nothingness to inanimate matter, to vegetative, then through sensitive and rational powers to God. Man is the hybrid creature which combines the animal and rational natures, allowing no gap between matter (the lower half of existence) and spirit (the upper half). This view is called the "Great Chain of Being." It was an accumulation of ideas from the time of Plato down to that of Pope, who was the last great poet to base an important poem on the concept. Science had been weakening some of its links for nearly a century before Pope wrote.

'Tis but a part we see, and not a whole.　60
　　When the proud steed shall know why
　　　　man restrains
His fiery course, or drives him o'er the plains;
When the dull ox, why now he breaks the
　　　clod,
Is now a victim, and now Egypt's god;
Then shall man's pride and dulness compre-
　　hend　　　　　　　　　　　　　　65
His actions', passions', being's, use and end;
Why doing, suffering, checked, impelled; and
　　why
This hour a slave, the next a deity.
　　Then say not man's imperfect, heaven in
　　　fault;
Say rather man's as perfect as he ought;　70
His knowledge measured to his state and
　　place,
His time a moment, and a point his space.
If to be perfect in a certain sphere,
What matter soon or late, or here or there?
The blessed to-day is as completely so　75
As who began a thousand years ago.

3. *That it is partly upon his ignorance of
future events, and partly upon the hope of a
future state, that all his happiness in the
present depends.*

　　Heaven from all creatures hides the book
　　　of fate,
All but the page prescribed, their present
　　state;
From brutes what men, from men what spirits
　　know;
Or who could suffer being here below?　80
The lamb thy riot dooms to bleed to-day,
Had he thy reason would he skip and play?
Pleased to the last he crops the flowery food,
And licks the hand just raised to shed his
　　blood.
O blindness to the future! kindly given,　85
That each may fill the circle marked by
　　heaven;
Who sees with equal eye, as God of all,[8]

[8] Notice in ll. 87–88 Pope says that God's
providence embraces both hero and sparrow; he does
not imply that they are of equal value. Both creatures
are part of the total Chain, but they are of different
links. Only in this one respect are they equal to
each other.

A hero perish or a sparrow fall,
Atoms or systems into ruin hurled,
And now a bubble burst, and now a
　　world.　　　　　　　　　　　　90
　　Hope humbly then; with trembling pinions
　　　soar;
Wait the great teacher Death, and God adore.
What future bliss he gives not thee to know,
But gives that hope to be thy blessing now.
Hope springs eternal in the human
　　breast:　　　　　　　　　　　　95
Man never is, but always to be, blest.
The soul, uneasy and confined from home,
Rests and expatiates in a life to come.
　　Lo, the poor Indian! whose untutored
　　　mind [9]
Sees God in clouds, or hears him in the
　　wind;　　　　　　　　　　　　100
His soul proud science never taught to stray
Far as the solar walk or milky way;
Yet simple nature to his hope has given,
Behind the cloud-topped hill, an humbler
　　heaven,
Some safer world in depth of woods em-
　　braced,　　　　　　　　　　　105
Some happier island in the watery waste,
Where slaves once more their native land
　　behold,
No fiends torment, no Christians thirst for
　　gold.
To be, contents his natural desire;
He asks no angel's wing, no seraph's fire;　110
But thinks, admitted to that equal sky,
His faithful dog shall bear him company.

4. *The pride of aiming at more knowledge,
and pretending to more perfection, the cause
of man's error and misery.*

　　Go, wiser thou! and in thy scale of sense
Weigh thy opinion against providence;
Call imperfection what thou fanciest
　　such;　　　　　　　　　　　　115

[9] Lines 99–112 are sometimes cited as evidence
that Pope had romantic tendencies: that he felt
primitive man more fortunate than civilized man.
Read the lines carefully and try to determine if the
Indian or the Christian is being satirized, or if the
IRONY is directed against both. Notice the phrase
"Go, wiser thou!" (l. 113). What does this phrase
indicate about Pope's view of the Indian and
Christian?

Say, here he gives too little, there too much;
Destroy all creatures for thy sport or gust,
Yet cry, if man's unhappy, God's unjust;
If man alone engross not heaven's high care,
Alone made perfect here, immortal there,   120
Snatch from his hand the balance and the
    rod,
Rejudge his justice, be the god of God.
In pride, in reasoning pride, our error lies; [10]
All quit their sphere, and rush into the skies!
Pride still is aiming at the blessed abodes,   125
Men would be angels, angels would be gods.
Aspiring to be gods if angels fell,
Aspiring to be angels men rebel:
And who but wishes to invert the laws
Of order, sins against the Eternal Cause.   130

5. *The absurdity of conceiting himself the
final cause of the creation, or expecting that
perfection in the moral world which is not in
the natural.*

   Ask for what end the heavenly bodies
    shine,
Earth for whose use—Pride answers, " 'Tis for
    mine:
For me kind nature wakes her genial power,
Suckles each herb, and spreads out every
    flower;
Annual for me the grape, the rose, renew 135
The juice nectareous and the balmy dew;
For me the mine a thousand treasures brings;
For me health gushes from a thousand springs;
Seas roll to waft me, suns to light me rise;
My footstool earth, my canopy the skies."   140
   But errs not nature from this gracious end,
From burning suns when livid deaths descend,
When earthquakes swallow, or when tempests
    sweep
Towns to one grave, whole nations to the
    deep?
"No," 'tis replied, "the first Almighty
    Cause   145

[10] Lines 123–130 state Pope's view of the source
of trouble in the universe. Like Milton, Pope believed
pride affected both the upper spiritual half of the
Chain ("angels") and the lower ("man"). Notice,
however, that Pope with typical deistic and rationalistic belief says that pride is a sin against "order,"
which is God (l. 130) or the "first Almighty
Cause" (l. 145).

Acts not by partial but by general laws;
The exceptions few; some change since all
    began;
And what created perfect?"—Why then man?
If the great end be human happiness,
Then nature deviates; and can man do
    less?   150
As much that end a constant course requires
Of showers and sunshine, as of man's desires;
As much eternal springs and cloudless skies,
As men for ever temperate, calm, and wise.
If plagues or earthquakes break not heaven's
    design,   155
Why then a Borgia or a Catiline?
Who knows but he, whose hand the lightning
    forms,
Who heaves old ocean, and who wings the
    storms;
Pours fierce ambition in a Cæsar's mind,
Or turns young Ammon loose to scourge
    mankind?   160
From pride, from pride, our very reasoning
    springs;
Account for moral as for natural things:
Why charge we heaven in those, in these
    acquit?
In both, to reason right is to submit.
   Better for us, perhaps, it might appear,   165
Were there all harmony, all virtue here;
That never air or ocean felt the wind,
That never passion discomposed the mind:
But all subsists by elemental strife;
And passions are the elements of life.   170
The general order, since the whole began,
Is kept in nature, and is kept in man.

6. *The unreasonableness of his complaints
against providence, while, on the one hand,
he demands the perfections of the angels, and,
on the other, the bodily qualifications of the
brutes; though to possess any of the sensitive
faculties in a higher degree would render
him miserable.*

   What would this man? Now upward will
    he soar,
And little less than angel, would be more;
Now looking downwards, just as grieved
    appears   175
To want the strength of bulls, the fur of bears.

Made for his use all creatures if he call,
Say what their use, had he the powers of all?
Nature to these without profusion kind,
The proper organs, proper powers as-
    signed;   180
Each seeming want compensated of course,
Here with degrees of swiftness, there of force;
All in exact proportion to the state;
Nothing to add, and nothing to abate;
Each beast, each insect, happy in its
    own: 185
Is heaven unkind to man, and man alone?
Shall he alone, whom rational we call,
Be pleased with nothing if not blessed with
    all?
    The bliss of man (could pride that blessing
    find)
Is not to act or think beyond mankind;   190
No powers of body or of soul to share,
But what his nature and his state can bear.
Why has not man a microscopic eye?
For this plain reason, man is not a fly.
Say, what the use, were finer optics
    given,   195
To inspect a mite, not comprehend the
    heaven?
Or touch, if tremblingly alive all o'er,
To smart and agonize at every pore?
Or quick effluvia darting through the brain,
Die of a rose in aromatic pain?   200
If nature thundered in his opening ears,
And stunned him with the music of the
    spheres,
How would he wish that heaven had left
    him still
The whispering zephyr and the purling rill?
Who finds not providence all good and
    wise,   205
Alike in what it gives and what denies?

7. *That throughout the whole visible world
a universal order and gradation in the sensual
and mental faculties is observed, which causes
a subordination of creature to creature, and
of all creatures to man.*

    Far as creation's ample range extends,
The scale of sensual, mental powers ascends.
Mark how it mounts to man's imperial race
From the green myriads in the peopled
    grass: 210

What modes of sight betwixt each wide
    extreme,
The mole's dim curtain and the lynx's beam:
Of smell, the headlong lioness between
And hound sagacious on the tainted green:
Of hearing, from the life that fills the
    flood   215
To that which warbles through the vernal
    wood.
The spider's touch, how exquisitely fine,
Feels at each thread, and lives along the line:
In the nice bee, what sense so subtly true
From poisonous herbs extracts the healing
    dew!   220
How instinct varies in the groveling swine,
Compared, half-reasoning elephant, with
    thine!
'Twixt that and reason what a nice barrier!
For ever separate, yet for ever near!
Remembrance and reflection how allied!   225
What thin partitions sense from thought
    divide!
And middle natures how they long to join,
Yet never pass the insuperable line!
Without this just gradation could they be
Subjected, these to those, or all to thee?   230
The powers of all subdued by thee alone,
Is not thy reason all these powers in one?

8. *How much further this order and subordination of living creatures may extend above
and below us; were any part of which broken,
not that part only, but the whole connected
creation must be destroyed.*

    See through this air, this ocean, and this
    earth
All matter quick, and bursting into birth:
Above, how high progressive life may go!   235
Around, how wide! how deep extend below!
Vast chain of being! which from God began;
Natures ethereal, human, angel, man,
Beast, bird, fish, insect, what no eye can see,
No glass can reach; from infinite to thee;   240
From thee to nothing.—On superior powers
Were we to press, inferior might on ours;
Or in the full creation leave a void,
Where, one step broken, the great scale's
    destroyed:
From nature's chain whatever link you
    strike,   245

Tenth, or ten thousandth, breaks the chain
   alike.
   And if each system in gradation roll,
Alike essential to the amazing whole,
The least confusion but in one, not all
That system only, but the whole must
   fall.   250
Let earth unbalanced from her orbit fly,
Planets and suns run lawless through the sky;
Let ruling angels from their spheres be
   hurled,
Being on being wrecked, and world on world;
Heaven's whole foundations to their center
   nod,   255
And nature tremble to the throne of God!
All this dread order break—for whom? for
   thee?
Vile worm!—O madness! pride! impiety!

*9. The extravagance, madness, and pride of
such a desire.*

   What if the foot, ordained the dust to tread,
Or hand to toil, aspired to be the head?   260
What if the head, the eye, or ear repined
To serve mere engines to the ruling mind?
Just as absurd for any part to claim
To be another in this general frame;
Just as absurd to mourn the tasks or
   pains   265
The great directing mind of all ordains.
   All are but parts of one stupendous whole,
Whose body nature is, and God the soul;
That changed through all, and yet in all the
   same,
Great in the earth as in the ethereal
   frame,   270
Warms in the sun, refreshes in the breeze,
Glows in the stars, and blossoms in the trees;
Lives through all life, extends through all
   extent,
Spreads undivided, operates unspent;
Breathes in our soul, informs our mortal
   part,   275
As full, as perfect, in a hair as heart;
As full, as perfect, in vile man that mourns,
As the rapt seraph that adores and burns.
To him no high, no low, no great, no small;
He fills, he bounds, connects, and equals
   all!   280

*10. The consequence of all, the absolute sub-
mission due to providence, both as to our
present and future state.*

   Cease, then, nor order imperfection name;
Our proper bliss depends on what we blame.
Know thy own point: this kind, this due
   degree
Of blindness, weakness, heaven bestows on
   thee.
Submit: in this or any other sphere,   285
Secure to be as blessed as thou canst bear;
Safe in the hand of one disposing Power,
Or in the natal or the mortal hour.
All nature is but art unknown to thee;
All chance, direction, which thou canst not
   see;   290
All discord, harmony not understood;
All partial evil, universal good:
And spite of pride, in erring reason's spite,
One truth is clear: Whatever is, is right.[11]
(1733–34)

STUDY AIDS: 1. In Parts 7–9 Pope describes the Great Chain of Being, which his age
inherited from past times. Do we accept any
parts of this concept today? In what ways do
we believe that man is superior to the mineral,
vegetable, and animal worlds? How is man dependent on them? Which half of the Chain has
science made less important? More important?
Why was this inevitable?

2. Pope's *Essay* invites comparison with *Paradise Lost*. Milton, in "justifying" God's ways to
man, used the Christian story of man's fall and
redemption. Pope ignores this story in his "vindication." How does Pope reflect his age's thinking
in this essential difference? What is Pope's
"vindication"?

3. There is no Satan to personify evil in the
Essay. Does Pope deny its existence? Read l. 292
in light of ll. 18–20. Why then is evil "partial"?
In ll. 141–160 Pope admits that the evil which
men experience (earthquakes, floods, Caesar,
Borgia, Catiline) is real enough, but he denies
that God can be blamed for it. How does this
help to define evil as "partial"?

[11] This statement is often misread. Notice its
immediate context. How can the statement be defended against the charges of a superficial optimism
or of hostility toward reform and progress?

Jonathan Swift
(1667–1745)

JONATHAN SWIFT, ENGLAND'S GREATEST PROSE SATIRIST, WAS BORN IN DUBLIN OF ENGLISH parents. He attended Kilkenny school, where he knew Congreve, the future playwright. At Trinity College, Dublin, he read widely in the classics, but shirked other responsibilities and took his degree by "special grace." Then followed a ten-year association with a distant relative, Sir William Temple, of Moor Park, Surrey, whom he served as secretary. Here it was that he met and tutored Temple's ward, Esther Johnson, a girl of six at the time, whom Swift called Stella and whom, of all persons in his life, he came to love the most. He enjoyed his young charge, and for a while he seems to have enjoyed his work for Temple, who recognized his talents and encouraged him to develop them. But Swift, always proud and ambitious, was eager to strike out on his own.

For several years Swift lived alternately in Ireland and in England. He had entered the church, had held small livings in Ireland, and had taken a degree in divinity from Trinity College. But he went to London when he could, and tried to advance himself politically. In 1704 he published two of his greatest works, written earlier at Moor Park: *A Tale of a Tub,* a satiric allegory directed against perversions of Christianity; and *The Battle of the Books,* a discussion of the relative merits of the ancient writers and the moderns. He lent his pen to the cause of the Whig party, but realizing that the future of the Irish Church lay with the Tories, he went over to that party, where his interest and sympathy lay. During the years of Tory rule (1710–1714) he was actively engaged in party affairs, a close record of which he kept in his *Journal to Stella.* Queen Anne did not like him, however, and the best preferment he could get was the deanery at St. Patrick's in Dublin. With the death of the Queen and the fall of the Tories, his political career was finished.

Swift spent the rest of his life in Ireland, except for two final visits to London in 1726–1727. At this time he published *Gulliver's Travels,* begun twelve years before as his contribution to the satiric program of the Scriblerus Club, which included Pope, Arbuthnot, and Gay. Many of his other writings are concerned with helping the Irish, who suffered greatly from England's colonial policy of exploitation. Most notable are *The Drapier's Letters* (1724) and *A Modest Proposal* (1729). Swift's last years were miserable. The death in 1728 of his beloved Stella, who had lived near by, but whom he had never married, affected him profoundly. He suffered increasingly from despair and melancholy, and three years before his death his mind gave way altogether. He was buried, beside Stella, in St. Patrick's.

Swift's life was a tortured one, and few writers have so lashed out at their fellow mortals. But it is not right to think of Swift as a misanthrope. To Pope, it is true, he wrote "I hate and detest that animal called man," but he added "I heartily love John, Peter, Thomas, and so forth." Furthermore, he worked tirelessly to help others; indeed, his whole satiric literary effort sprang not from a contempt for man but from a hope for his improvement. Man should not be called a rational animal, he said, but only a creature capable of reason; and in his writings he tried, by pleasing narrative, by ridicule, by invective, by cutting irony, to show man's worst side—but always in an effort to help him realize his best.

Swift wrote a prose that is clear, simple, and direct, qualities valued by the Augustan Age. It is worth remembering, however, that in virtually every one of his works Swift is speaking through a character, the purported author of the piece. Consequently the simplicity of style is not so much that of Swift himself as it is a part of the character of his fictional author.

Gulliver's Travels

A satirist is a corrector of mankind. He recognizes follies and abuses in human life and he aims to reveal them, usually in the hope of altering or destroying them. To show folly for what it is, though, is not always easy, because we are inclined to regard human life, including our foolish behavior, as perfectly normal. It is for this reason that satirists often prefer oblique methods, which in one way or another will surprise or shock readers into re-examining their world.

One such method is to create a fiction in which a total stranger, such as a man from Mars, visits the society under consideration and, out of ignorance, asks questions that reveal the society's shortcomings. Swift's method in *Gulliver's Travels* is just the opposite. He sends the Englishman Lemuel Gulliver to visit several imaginary foreign lands: Lilliput, the land of tiny people (Book 1, here included); Brobdingnag, the land of giants (Book 2); various other countries, including the flying island of Laputa, home of speculative scientists (Book 3); and the land of the Houyhnhnms, a governing race of horses who live by reason and hence are vastly superior to the manlike but bestial Yahoos (Book 4). Since the inhabitants of these lands resemble the English at many points, Swift's fiction is a distorting lens through which he permits us to view his countrymen. Their follies—and, by extension, those of mankind in general—are thus emphasized and made plain by the distortion.

Part 1

A Voyage to Lilliput [1]

Chapter 1: *The author gives some account of himself and family, his first inducements to travel. He is shipwrecked, and swims for his life, gets safe on shore in the country of Lilliput, is made a prisoner, and is carried up country.*

My father had a small estate in Nottinghamshire; I was the third of five sons. He sent me to Emanuel College in Cambridge, at fourteen years old, where I resided three years, and applied myself close to my studies; but the charge of maintaining me (although I had a very scanty allowance) being too great for a narrow fortune, I was bound apprentice to Mr. James Bates, an eminent surgeon in London, with whom I continued four years; and my father now and then sending me small sums of money, I laid them out in learning navigation, and other parts of the mathematics, useful to those who intend to travel, as I always believed it would be some time or other my fortune to do. When I left Mr. Bates, I went down to my father; where, by the assistance of him and my uncle John, and some other relations, I got forty pounds, and a promise of thirty pounds a year to maintain me at Leyden; [2] there I studied physic two years and seven months, knowing it would be useful in long voyages.

Soon after my return from Leyden, I was recommended by my good master, Mr. Bates, to be surgeon to the *Swallow*, Captain Abraham Pannell, commander; with whom I continued three years and a half, making a voyage or

[1] Probably a combination of "lilli" ("little" in the child talk that Swift at times affected) and "put," a term of contempt.

[2] Dutch university, noted for medical studies.

two into the Levant, and some other parts. When I came back I resolved to settle in London, to which Mr. Bates, my master, encouraged me, and by him I was recommended to several patients. I took part of a small house in the Old Jury;[3] and being advised to alter my condition, I married Mrs. Mary Burton, second daughter to Mr. Edmund Burton, hosier, in Newgate-street, with whom I received four hundred pounds for a portion.

But, my good master Bates dying in two years after, and I having few friends, my business began to fail; for my conscience would not suffer me to imitate the bad practice of too many among my brethren. Having therefore consulted with my wife, and some of my acquaintance, I determined to go again to sea. I was surgeon successively in two ships, and made several voyages, for six years, to the East and West Indies, by which I got some addition to my fortune. My hours of leisure I spent in reading the best authors, ancient and modern, being always provided with a good number of books; and when I was ashore, in observing the manners and dispositions of the people, as well as learning their language, wherein I had a great facility by the strength of my memory.

The last of these voyages not proving very fortunate, I grew weary of the sea, and intended to stay at home with my wife and family. I removed from the Old Jury to Fetter-Lane, and from thence to Wapping, hoping to get business among the sailors; but it would not turn to account. After three years expectation that things would mend, I accepted an advantageous offer from Captain William Prichard, master of the *Antelope,* who was making a voyage to the South Sea. We set sail from Bristol, May 4, 1699, and our voyage at first was very prosperous.

It would not be proper, for some reasons, to trouble the reader with the particulars of our adventures in those seas: let it suffice to inform him, that in our passage from thence to the East Indies, we were driven by a violent storm to the northeast of Van Diemen's Land.[4] By an observation, we found ourselves in the latitude of 30 degrees 2 minutes south. Twelve of our crew were dead by immoderate labor, and ill food; the rest were in a very weak condition. On the fifth of November, which was the beginning of summer in those parts, the weather being very hazy, the seamen spied a rock, within half a cable's length of the ship; but the wind was so strong, that we were driven directly upon it, and immediately split. Six of the crew, of whom I was one, having let down the boat into the sea, made a shift to get clear of the ship, and the rock. We rowed, by my computation, about three leagues, till we were able to work no longer, being already spent with labor while we were in the ship. We therefore trusted ourselves to the mercy of the waves, and in about half an hour the boat was overset by a sudden flurry from the north. What became of my companions in the boat, as well as of those who escaped on the rock, or were left in the vessel, I cannot tell; but conclude they were all lost. For my own part, I swam as fortune directed me, and was pushed forward by wind and tide. I often let my legs drop, and could feel no bottom: but when I was almost gone, and able to struggle no longer, I found myself within my depth; and by this time the storm was much abated. The declivity was so small, that I walked near a mile before I got to the shore, which I conjectured was about eight o'clock in the evening. I then advanced forward near half a mile, but could not discover any sign of houses or inhabitants; at least I was in so weak a condition, that I did not observe them. I was extremely tired, and with that, and the heat of the weather, and about half a pint of brandy that I drank as I left the ship, I found myself much inclined to sleep. I lay down on the grass, which was very short and soft, where I slept sounder than ever I remember to have done in my life, and, as I reckoned, above nine hours; for when I awaked, it was just daylight. I attempted to rise, but was not able to stir: for as I happened to lie on my back, I found my arms and legs were strongly fastened on each side to the ground; and my hair, which was long and thick, tied down in the same manner. I likewise felt several

[3] Old Jewry, a London street.
[4] Tasmania.

slender ligatures across my body, from my arm-pits to my thighs. I could only look upwards, the sun began to grow hot, and the light offended my eyes. I heard a confused noise about me, but in the posture I lay, could see nothing except the sky. In a little time I felt something alive moving on my left leg, which advancing gently forward over my breast, came almost up to my chin; when bending my eyes downwards as much as I could, I perceived it to be a human creature not six inches high,[5] with a bow and arrow in his hands, and a quiver at his back. In the mean time, I felt at least forty more of the same kind (as I conjectured) following the first. I was in the utmost astonishment, and roared so loud, that they all ran back in a fright; and some of them, as I was afterwards told, were hurt with the falls they got by leaping from my sides upon the ground. However, they soon returned, and one of them, who ventured so far as to get a full sight of my face, lifting up his hands and eyes by way of admiration,[6] cried out in a shrill, but distinct voice, *Hekinah degul:* [7] the others repeated the same words several times, but I then knew not what they meant. I lay all this while, as the reader may believe, in great uneasiness: at length, struggling to get loose, I had the fortune to break the strings, and wrench out the pegs that fastened my left arm to the ground: for, by lifting it up to my face, I discovered the methods they had taken to bind me, and at the same time with a violent pull, which gave me excessive pain, I a little loosened the strings that tied down my hair on the left side, so that I was just able to turn my head about two inches. But the creatures ran off a second time, before I could seize them; whereupon there was a great shout in a very shrill accent, and after it ceased, I heard one of them cry aloud *Tolgo Phonac;* when in an instant I felt above an hundred arrows discharged on my left hand, which pricked me like so many needles;

and besides, they shot another flight into the air, as we do bombs in Europe, whereof many, I suppose, fell on my body (though I felt them not), and some on my face, which I immediately covered with my left hand. When this shower of arrows was over, I fell a groaning with grief and pain, and then striving again to get loose, they discharged another volley larger than the first, and some of them attempted with spears to stick me in the sides; but, by good luck, I had on a buff jerkin, which they could not pierce. I thought it the most prudent method to lie still, and my design was to continue so till night, when my left hand being already loose, I could easily free myself: and as for the inhabitants, I had reason to believe I might be a match for the greatest armies they could bring against me, if they were all of the same size with him that I saw. But fortune disposed otherwise of me. When the people observed I was quiet, they discharged no more arrows; but, by the noise I heard, I knew their numbers increased; and about four yards from me, over-against my right ear, I heard a knocking for above an hour, like that of people at work; when turning my head that way, as well as the pegs and strings would permit me, I saw a stage erected, about a foot and a half from the ground, capable of holding four of the inhabitants, with two or three ladders to mount it: from whence one of them, who seemed to be a person of quality, made me a long speech, whereof I understood not one syllable. But I should have mentioned, that before the principal person began his oration, he cried out three times, *Langro dehul san:* (these words and the former were afterwards repeated and explained to me). Whereupon immediately about fifty of the inhabitants came and cut the strings that fastened the left side of my head, which gave me the liberty of turning it to the right, and of observing the person and gesture of him that was to speak. He appeared to be of a middle age, and taller than any of the other three who attended him, whereof one was a page that held up his train, and seemed to be somewhat longer than my middle finger; the other two stood one on each side to support

---

[5] All objects in Lilliput are 1/12 normal size.

[6] Wonder.

[7] Most of the words quoted from the imaginary language of Lilliput have no discernible meaning; a few do.

him. He acted every part of an orator, and I could observe many periods of threatenings, and others of promises, pity, and kindness. I answered in a few words, but in the most submissive manner, lifting up my left hand, and both my eyes to the sun, as calling him for a witness; and being almost famished with hunger, having not eaten a morsel for some hours before I left the ship, I found the demands of nature so strong upon me, that I could not forbear showing my impatience (perhaps against the strict rules of decency) by putting my finger frequently on my mouth, to signify that I wanted food. The *Hurgo* (for so they call a great lord, as I afterwards learned) understood me very well. He descended from the stage, and commanded that several ladders should be applied to my sides, on which above an hundred of the inhabitants mounted and walked towards my mouth, laden with baskets full of meat, which had been provided and sent thither by the King's orders, upon the first intelligence he received of me. I observed there was the flesh of several animals, but could not distinguish them by the taste. There were shoulders, legs, and loins, shaped like those of mutton, and very well dressed, but smaller than the wings of a lark. I eat [8] them by two or three at a mouthful, and took three loaves at a time, about the bigness of musket bullets. They supplied me as fast as they could, showing a thousand marks of wonder and astonishment at my bulk and appetite. I then made another sign that I wanted drink. They found by my eating, that a small quantity would not suffice me; and being a most ingenious people, they slung up with great dexterity one of their largest hogsheads, then rolled it towards my hand, and beat out the top; I drank it off at a draught, which I might well do, for it did not hold half a pint, and tasted like a small wine of Burgundy, but much more delicious. They brought me a second hogshead, which I drank in the same manner, and made signs for more, but they had none to give me. When I had performed these wonders, they shouted for joy, and danced upon my breast, repeating

[8] An old past tense of "eat," pronounced "et."

several times as they did at first, *Hekinah degul.* They made me a sign that I should throw down the two hogsheads, but first warning the people below to stand out of the way, crying aloud, *Borach mivola,* and when they saw the vessels in the air, there was an universal shout of *Hekinah degul.* I confess I was often tempted while they were passing backwards and forwards on my body, to seize forty or fifty of the first that came in my reach, and dash them against the ground. But the remembrance of what I had felt, which probably might not be the worst they could do, and the promise of honor I made them, for so I interpreted my submissive behavior, soon drove out these imaginations. Besides, I now considered myself as bound by the laws of hospitality to a people who had treated me with so much expense and magnificence. However, in my thoughts, I could not sufficiently wonder at the intrepidity of these diminutive mortals, who durst venture to mount and walk upon my body, while one of my hands was at liberty, without trembling at the very sight of so prodigious a creature as I must appear to them. After some time, when they observed that I made no more demands for meat, there appeared before me a person of high rank from his Imperial Majesty. His Excellency, having mounted on the small of my right leg, advanced forwards up to my face, with about a dozen of his retinue. And producing his credentials under the Signet Royal, which he applied close to my eyes, spoke about ten minutes, without any signs of anger, but with a kind of determinate resolution; often pointing forwards, which, as I afterwards found, was towards the capital city, about half a mile distant, whither it was agreed by his Majesty in council that I must be conveyed. I answered in few words, but to no purpose, and made a sign with my hand that was loose, putting it to the other (but over his Excellency's head for fear of hurting him or his train) and then to my own head and body, to signify that I desired my liberty. It appeared that he understood me well enough, for he shook his head by way of disapprobation, and held his hand in a posture to show that I must be carried as a prisoner.

However, he made other signs to let me understand that I should have meat and drink enough, and very good treatment. Whereupon I once more thought of attempting to break my bonds; but again, when I felt the smart of their arrows, upon my face and hands, which were all in blisters, and many of the darts still sticking in them, and observing likewise that the number of my enemies increased, I gave tokens to let them know that they might do with me what they pleased. Upon this, the *Hurgo* and his train withdrew, with much civility and cheerful countenances. Soon after I heard a general shout, with frequent repetitions of the words, *Peplom selan,* and I felt great numbers of people on my left side relaxing the cords to such a degree, that I was able to turn upon my right, and to ease myself with making water; which I very plentifully did, to the great astonishment of the people, who conjecturing by my motions what I was going to do, immediately opened to the right and left on that side to avoid the torrent which fell with such noise and violence from me. But before this, they had daubed my face and both my hands with a sort of ointment very pleasant to the smell, which in a few minutes removed all the smart of their arrows. These circumstances, added to the refreshment I had received by their victuals and drink, which were very nourishing, disposed me to sleep. I slept about eight hours, as I was afterwards assured; and it was no wonder, for the physicians, by the Emperor's order, had mingled a sleepy potion in the hogshead of wine.

It seems that upon the first moment I was discovered sleeping on the ground after my landing, the Emperor had early notice of it by an express; and determined in council that I should be tied in the manner I have related (which was done in the night while I slept), that plenty of meat and drink should be sent to me, and a machine prepared to carry me to the capital city.

This resolution perhaps may appear very bold and dangerous, and I am confident would not be imitated by any prince in Europe on the like occasion; however, in my opinion, it was extremely prudent, as well as generous: for supposing these people had endeavored to kill me with their spears and arrows while I was asleep, I should certainly have awaked with the first sense of smart, which might so far have roused my rage and strength, as to have enabled me to break the strings wherewith I was tied; after which, as they were not able to make resistance, so they could expect no mercy.

These people are most excellent mathematicians, and arrived to a great perfection in mechanics, by the countenance and encouragement of the Emperor, who is a renowned patron of learning. This prince hath several machines fixed on wheels, for the carriage of trees and other great weights. He often builds his largest men of war, whereof some are nine foot long, in the woods where the timber grows, and has them carried on these engines three or four hundred yards to the sea. Five hundred carpenters and engineers were immediately set at work to prepare the greatest engine they had. It was a frame of wood raised three inches from the ground, about seven foot long and four wide, moving upon twenty-two wheels. The shout I heard was upon the arrival of this engine, which it seems set out in four hours after my landing. It was brought parallel to me as I lay. But the principal difficulty was to raise and place me in this vehicle. Eighty poles, each of one foot high, were erected for this purpose, and very strong cords of the bigness of packthread were fastened by hooks to many bandages, which the workmen had girt round my neck, my hands, my body, and my legs. Nine hundred of the strongest men were employed to draw up these cords by many pulleys fastened on the poles, and thus, in less than three hours, I was raised and slung into the engine, and there tied fast. All this I was told, for, while the whole operation was performing, I lay in a profound sleep, by the force of that soporiferous medicine infused into my liquor. Fifteen hundred of the Emperor's largest horses, each about four inches and a half high, were employed to draw me towards the metropolis, which, as I said, was half a mile distant.

About four hours after we began our journey, I awaked by a very ridiculous accident; for the carriage being stopped a while to adjust something that was out of order, two or three of the young natives had the curiosity to see how I looked when I was asleep; they climbed up into the engine, and advancing very softly to my face, one of them, an officer in the guards, put the sharp end of his half-pike a good way up into my left nostril, which tickled my nose like a straw, and made me sneeze violently: whereupon they stole off unperceived, and it was three weeks before I knew the cause of my awaking so suddenly. We made a long march the remaining part of that day, and rested at night with five hundred guards on each side of me, half with torches, and half with bows and arrows, ready to shoot me if I should offer to stir. The next morning at sunrise we continued our march, and arrived within two hundred yards of the city gates about noon. The Emperor, and all his court, came out to meet us; but his great officers would by no means suffer his Majesty to endanger his person by mounting on my body.

At the place where the carriage stopped, there stood an ancient temple,[9] esteemed to be the largest in the whole kingdom; which having been polluted some years before by an unnatural murder, was, according to the zeal of those people, looked upon as profane, and therefore had been applied to common uses, and all the ornaments and furniture carried away. In this edifice it was determined I should lodge. The great gate fronting to the north was about four foot high, and almost two foot wide, through which I could easily creep. On each side of the gate was a small window not above six inches from the ground: into that on the left side, the King's smiths conveyed fourscore and eleven chains, like those that hang to a lady's watch in Europe, and almost as large, which were locked to my left leg with six and thirty padlocks. Over against this temple, on the other side of the great highway, at twenty foot distance, there was a turret at least five foot high. Here the Emperor ascended, with many principal lords of his court, to have an opportunity of viewing me, as I was told, for I could not see them. It was reckoned that above an hundred thousand inhabitants came out of the town upon the same errand; and, in spite of my guards, I believe there could not be fewer than ten thousand at several times, who mounted my body by the help of ladders. But a proclamation was soon issued to forbid it upon pain of death. When the workmen found it was impossible for me to break loose, they cut all the strings that bound me; whereupon I rose up, with as melancholy a disposition as ever I had in my life. But the noise and astonishment of the people at seeing me rise and walk, are not to be expressed. The chains that held my left leg were about two yards long, and gave me not only the liberty of walking backwards and forwards in a semicircle; but, being fixed within four inches of the gate, allowed me to creep in, and lie at my full length in the temple.

Chapter 2: *The Emperor of Lilliput, attended by several of the nobility, comes to see the author in his confinement. The Emperor's person and habit described. Learned men appointed to teach the author their language. He gains favor by his mild disposition. His pockets are searched, and his sword and pistols taken from him.*

When I found myself on my feet, I looked about me, and must confess I never beheld a more entertaining prospect. The country round appeared like a continued garden, and the inclosed fields, which were generally forty foot square, resembled so many beds of flowers. These fields were intermingled with woods of half a stang,[10] and the tallest trees, as I could judge, appeared to be seven foot high. I viewed the town on my left hand, which looked like the painted scene of a city in a theater.

I had been for some hours extremely

---

[9] Probably Westminster Hall, before which Charles I was condemned to death.

[10] A stang, or perche, as a measure of area, was 1/160 of an acre. Thus the little woods were about 12 feet square.

pressed by the necessities of nature; which was no wonder, it being almost two days since I had last disburthened myself. I was under great difficulties between urgency and shame. The best expedient I could think on, was to creep into my house, which I accordingly did; and shutting the gate after me, I went as far as the length of my chain would suffer, and discharged my body of that uneasy load. But this was the only time I was ever guilty of so uncleanly an action; for which I cannot but hope the candid reader will give some allowance, after he hath maturely and impartially considered my case, and the distress I was in. From this time my constant practice was, as soon as I rose, to perform that business in open air, at the full extent of my chain, and due care was taken every morning before company came, that the offensive matter should be carried off in wheelbarrows, by two servants appointed for that purpose. I would not have dwelt so long upon a circumstance, that perhaps at first sight may appear not very momentous, if I had not thought it necessary to justify my character in point of cleanliness to the world; which I am told some of my maligners have been pleased, upon this and other occasions, to call in question.

When this adventure was at an end, I came back out of my house, having occasion for fresh air. The Emperor was already descended from the tower, and advancing on horseback towards me, which had like to have cost him dear; for the beast, though very well trained, yet wholly unused to such a sight, which appeared as if a mountain moved before him, reared up on his hinder feet: but that prince, who is an excellent horseman, kept his seat, till his attendants ran in, and held the bridle, while his Majesty had time to dismount. When he alighted, he surveyed me round with great admiration, but kept beyond the length of my chain. He ordered his cooks and butlers, who were already prepared, to give me victuals and drink, which they pushed forward in a sort of vehicles upon wheels, till I could reach them. I took these vehicles, and soon emptied them all; twenty of them were filled with meat, and ten with liquor; each of the former afforded me two or three good mouthfuls, and I emptied the liquor of ten vessels, which was contained in earthen vials, into one vehicle, drinking it off at a draught; and so I did with the rest. The Empress, and young princes of the blood of both sexes, attended by many ladies, sat at some distance in their chairs; but upon the accident that happened to the Emperor's horse, they alighted, and came near his person, which I am now going to describe.[11] He is taller by almost the breadth of my nail, than any of his court; which alone is enough to strike an awe into the beholders. His features are strong and masculine, with an Austrian lip and arched nose, his complexion olive, his countenance erect, his body and limbs well proportioned, all his motions graceful, and his deportment majestic. He was then past his prime, being twenty-eight years and three quarters old, of which he had reigned about seven, in great felicity, and generally victorious. For the better convenience of beholding him, I lay on my side, so that my face was parallel to his, and he stood but three yards off: however, I have had him since many times in my hand, and therefore cannot be deceived in the description. His dress was very plain and simple, and the fashion of it between the Asiatic and the European: but he had on his head a light helmet of gold, adorned with jewels, and a plume on the crest. He held his sword drawn in his hand, to defend himself, if I should happen to break loose; it was almost three inches long, the hilt and scabbard were gold enriched with diamonds. His voice was shrill, but very clear and articulate, and I could distinctly hear it when I stood up. The ladies and courtiers were all most magnificently clad, so that the spot they stood upon seemed to resemble a petticoat spread on the ground, embroidered with figures of gold and silver. His Imperial Majesty spoke often to me, and I returned answers, but neither of us could understand a syllable. There were several of his priests

[11] Although the description of the Emperor does not tally with that of George I, it is usually assumed that Swift is alluding to the English king.

The first page of Gray's "Elegy," from the edition of 1753.

ELEGY

Written in a Country Church Yard.

 HE Curfew tolls the knell of parting day,
The lowing herd wind flowly o'er the lea,
The plowman homeward plods his weary way,
And leaves the world to darkneſs and to me.

By permission of The Macmillan Company.

"Marriage à la Mode" by William Hogarth.

The SPECTATOR.

Non fumum ex fulgore, ſed ex fumo dare lucem Cogitat, ut ſpecioſa dehinc miracula promat. Hor.

To be Continued every Day.

Opening of the first number of The Spectator.

By permission of The Macmillan Compc

Thurſday, March 1. 1711.

I Have obſerved, that a Reader ſeldom peruſes a Book with Pleaſure 'till he knows whether the Writer of it be a black or a fair Man, of a mild or cholerick Diſpoſition, Married or a Batchelor, with other Particulars of the like nature, that conduce very much to the right Underſtanding of an Author. To gratify this Curioſity, which is ſo natural to a Reader, I deſign this Paper, and my next, as Prefatory Diſcourſes to my following Writings, and ſhall give ſome Account in them of the ſeveral Perſons that are engaged in this Work. As the chief Trouble of Compiling, Digeſting and Correcting will fall to my Share, I muſt do my ſelf the Juſtice to open the Work with my own Hiſtory.

I was born to a ſmall Hereditary Eſtate, which I find, by the Writings of the Family, was bounded by the ſame Hedges and Ditches in *William* the Conqueror's Time that it is at preſent, and has been delivered down from Father to Son whole and entire, without the Loſs or Acquiſition of a ſingle Field or Meadow, during the Space of ſix hundred Years. There goes a Story in the Family, that when my Mother was gone with Child of me about three Months, ſhe dreamt that ſhe was brought to Bed of a Judge: Whether this might proceed from a Law-Suit which was then depending in the Family, or my Father's being a Juſtice of the Peace, I cannot determine; for I am not ſo vain as to think it preſaged any Dignity that I ſhould arrive at in my future Life, though that was the Interpretation which the Neighbourhood put upon it. The Gravity of my Behaviour at my very firſt Appearance in the World, and all the Time that I ſucked, ſeemed to favour my Mother's Dream: For, as ſhe has often told me, I threw away my Rattle before I was two Months old, and would not make uſe of my Coral 'till they had taken away the Bells from it.

As for the reſt of my Infancy, there being nothing in it remarkable, I ſhall paſs it over in Silence. I find, that, during my Nonage, I had the Reputation of a very ſullen Youth, but was always a Favourite of my School-Maſter, who uſed to ſay, *that my Parts were ſolid and would wear well.* I had not been long at the Univerſity, before I diſtinguiſhed my ſelf by a moſt profound Silence: For during the Space of eight Years, excepting in the publick Exerciſes of the College, I ſcarce uttered the Quantity of an hundred Words; and indeed do not remember that I ever ſpoke three Sentences together in my whole Life. Whilſt I was in this Learned Body I applied my ſelf with ſo much Diligence to my Studies, that there are very few celebrated Books, either in the Learned or the Modern Tongues, which I am not acquainted with.

Upon the Death of my Father I was reſolved to travel into Foreign Countries, and therefore left the Univerſity, with the Character of an odd unaccountable Fellow, that had a great deal of Learning, if I would but ſhow it. An inſatiable Thirſt after Knowledge carried me into all the Countries of *Europe*, where there was any thing new or ſtrange to be ſeen; nay, to ſuch a Degree was my Curioſity raiſed, that having read the Controverſies of ſome great Men concerning the Antiquities of *Egypt*, I made a Voyage to *Grand Cairo*, on purpoſe to take the Meaſure of a Pyramid; and as ſoon as I had ſet my ſelf right in that Particular, returned to my Native Country with great Satisfaction.

I have paſſed my latter Years in this City, where I am frequently ſeen in moſt publick Places, tho' there are not above half a dozen of my ſelect Friends that know me; of whom my next Paper ſhall give a more particular Account. There is no Place of Publick Reſort, wherein I do not often make my Appearance; ſometimes I am ſeen thruſting my Head into a Round of Politicians at *Will's*, and liſtning with great Attention to the Narratives that are made in thoſe little Circular Audiences. Sometimes I ſmoak a Pipe at *Child's*; and whilſt I ſeem attentive to nothing but the *Poſt-Man*, over-hear the Converſation of every Table in the Room. I appear on *Sunday* Nights at St. *James's* Coffee-Houſe, and ſometimes join the little Committee of Politicks in the Inner-Room, as one who comes there to hear and improve. My Face is likewiſe very well known at the *Grecian*, the *Cocoa-Tree*, and in the Theaters both of *Drury-Lane*, and the *Hay-Market*. I have been taken for a Merchant upon

Title page of the first volume of *The Spectator.*

THE

SPECTATOR.

VOLUME the FIRST.

LONDON:

Printed for J. and R. TONSON and S. DRAPER.

MDCCLIII.

F. Hayman delin.   *C. Grignion ſculp.*

The Bettmann Archive.

and lawyers present (as I conjectured by their habits) who were commanded to address themselves to me, and I spoke to them in as many languages as I had the least smattering of, which were High and Low Dutch, Latin, French, Spanish, Italian, and Lingua Franca; [12] but all to no purpose. After about two hours the court retired, and I was left with a strong guard, to prevent the impertinence, and probably the malice of the rabble, who were very impatient to crowd about me as near as they durst, and some of them had the impudence to shoot their arrows at me as I sat on the ground by the door of my house, whereof one very narrowly missed my left eye. But the colonel ordered six of the ringleaders to be seized, and thought no punishment so proper as to deliver them bound into my hands, which some of his soldiers accordingly did, pushing them forwards with the butt-ends of their pikes into my reach; I took them all in my right hand, put five of them into my coatpocket, and as to the sixth, I made a countenance as if I would eat him alive. The poor man squalled terribly, and the colonel and his officers were in much pain, especially when they saw me take out my penknife; but I soon put them out of fear: for, looking mildly, and immediately cutting the strings he was bound with, I set him gently on the ground, and away he ran. I treated the rest in the same manner, taking them one by one out of my pocket, and I observed both the soldiers and people were highly obliged at this mark of my clemency, which was represented very much to my advantage at court.

Toward night I got with some difficulty into my house, where I lay on the ground, and continued to do so about a fortnight, during which time the Emperor gave orders to have a bed prepared for me. Six hundred beds of the common measure were brought in carriages, and worked up in my house; an hundred and fifty of their beds sewn together made up the breadth and length, and these were four double, which however kept me but very indifferently from the hardness of

the floor, that was of smooth stone. By the same computation they provided me with sheets, blankets, and coverlets, tolerable enough for one who had been so long inured to hardships as I.

As the news of my arrival spread through the kingdom, it brought prodigious numbers of rich, idle, and curious people to see me; so that the villages were almost emptied, and great neglect of tillage and household affairs must have ensued, if his Imperial Majesty had not provided, by several proclamations and orders of state, against this inconveniency. He directed that those who had already beheld me should return home, and not presume to come within fifty yards of my house without license from court; whereby the secretaries of state got considerable fees.

In the mean time, the Emperor held frequent councils to debate what course should be taken with me; and I was afterwards assured by a particular friend, a person of great quality, who was looked upon to be as much in the secret as any, that the court was under many difficulties concerning me. They apprehended my breaking loose, that my diet would be very expensive, and might cause a famine. Sometimes they determined to starve me, or at least to shoot me in the face and hands with poisoned arrows, which would soon dispatch me; but again they considered, that the stench of so large a carcass might produce a plague in the metropolis, and probably spread through the whole kingdom. In the midst of these consultations, several officers of the army went to the door of the great council-chamber; and two of them being admitted, gave an account of my behavior to the six criminals above mentioned, which made so favorable an impression in the breast of his Majesty and the whole board, in my behalf, that an Imperial Commission was issued out, obliging all the villages nine hundred yards around the city, to deliver in every morning six beeves, forty sheep, and other victuals for my sustenance; together with a proportionable quantity of bread, and wine, and other liquors; for the due payment of which his Majesty gave assignments upon his treasury. For this prince lives chiefly upon

---

[12] A commercial jargon used in the Mediterranean area.

his own demesnes, seldom, except upon great occasions, raising any subsidies upon his subjects, who are bound to attend him in his wars at their own expense. An establishment was also made of six hundred persons to be my domestics, who had board wages allowed for their maintenance, and tents built for them very conveniently on each side of my door. It was likewise ordered, that three hundred tailors should make me a suit of clothes after the fashion of hte country: that six of his Majesty's greatest scholars should be employed to instruct me in their language: and, lastly, that the Emperor's horses, and those of the nobility, and troops of guards, should be frequently exercised in my sight, to accustom themselves to me. All these orders were duly put in execution, and in about three weeks I made a great progress in learning their language; during which time, the Emperor frequently honored me with his visits, and was pleased to assist my masters in teaching me. We began already to converse together in some sort; and the first words I learned were to express my desire that he would please to give me my liberty, which I every day repeated on my knees. His answer, as I could comprehend it, was, that this must be a work of time, not to be thought on without the advice of his council, and that first I must *Lumos kelmin pesso desmar lon emposo;* that is, swear a peace with him and his kingdom. However, that I should be used with all kindness; and he advised me to acquire, by my patience and discreet behavior, the good opinion of himself and his subjects. He desired I would not take it ill, if he gave orders to certain proper officers to search me; for probably I might carry about me several weapons, which must needs be dangerous things, if they answered the bulk of so prodigious a person. I said, his Majesty should be satisfied, for I was ready to strip myself, and turn up my pockets before him. This I delivered part in words, and part in signs. He replied, that by the laws of the kingdom I must be searched by two of his officers; that he knew this could not be done without my consent and assistance; that he had so good an opinion of my generosity and justice, as

to trust their persons in my hands: that whatever they took from me should be returned when I left the country, or paid for at the rate which I would set upon them. I took up the two officers in my hands, put them first into my coat-pockets, and then into every other pocket about me, except my two fobs, and another secret pocket which I had no mind should be searched, wherein I had some little necessaries that were of no consequence to any but myself. In one of my fobs there was a silver watch, and in the other a small quantity of gold in a purse. These gentlemen, having pen, ink, and paper about them, made an exact inventory of every thing they saw; and when they had done, desired I would set them down, that they might deliver it to the Emperor. This inventory [13] I afterwards translated into English, and is word for word as follows:

Imprimis, In the right coat-pocket of the Great Man-Mountain (for so I interpret the words *Quinbus Flestrin*) after the strictest search, we found only one great piece of coarse cloth,[14] large enough to be a foot-cloth for your Majesty's chief room of state. In the left pocket we saw a huge silver chest, with a cover of the same metal, which we, the searchers, were not able to lift. We desired it should be opened, and one of us stepping into it, found himself up to the mid leg in a sort of dust, some part whereof flying up to our faces, set us both a sneezing for several times together. In his right waistcoat-pocket we found a prodigious bundle of white thin substances, folded one over another, about the bigness of three men, tied with a strong cable, and marked with black figures; which we humbly conceive to be writings, every letter almost half as large as the palm of our hands. In the left there was a sort of engine, from the back of which were extended twenty long poles, resembling the palisadoes before

[13] The inventory probably refers to the Whigs ransacking of the house and correspondence of the Tory leader Robert Harley, whom they accused of treason for his efforts to conclude a peace treaty with defeated France.

[14] Try to identify the contents of Gulliver's pockets, described here in Lilliputian terms.

your Majesty's court; wherewith we conjecture the Man-Mountain combs his head; for we did not always trouble him with questions, because we found it a great difficulty to make him understand us. In the large pocket on the right side of his middle cover (so I translate the word *ranfu-lo*, by which they meant my breeches) we saw a hollow pillar of iron, about the length of a man, fastened to a strong piece of timber, larger than the pillar; and upon one side of the pillar were huge pieces of iron sticking out, cut into strange figures, which we know not what to make of. In the left pocket, another engine of the same kind. In the smaller pocket on the right side, were several round flat pieces of white and red metal, of different bulk; some of the white, which seemed to be silver, were so large and heavy, that my comrade and I could hardly lift them. In the left pocket were two black pillars irregularly shaped: we could not, without difficulty, reach the top of them as we stood at the bottom of his pocket. One of them was covered, and seemed all of a piece: but at the upper end of the other, there appeared a white round substance, about twice the bigness of our heads. Within each of these was enclosed a prodigious plate of steel; which, by our orders, we obliged him to show us, because we apprehended they might be dangerous engines. He took them out of their cases, and told us, that in his own country his practice was to shave his beard with one of these, and cut his meat with the other. There were two pockets which we could not enter: these he called his fobs; they were two large slits cut into the top of his middle cover, but squeezed close by the pressure of his belly. Out of the right fob hung a great silver chain, with a wonderful kind of engine at the bottom. We directed him to draw out whatever was fastened to that chain; which appeared to be a globe, half silver, and half of some transparent metal; for, on the transparent side, we saw certain strange figures circularly drawn, and thought we could touch them, till we found our fingers stopped by that lucid substance. He put this engine to our ears, which made an incessant noise like

that of a water mill. And we conjecture it is either some unknown animal, or the god that he worships; but we are more inclined to the latter opinion, because he assured us, (if we understood him right, for he expressed himself very imperfectly) that he seldom did any thing without consulting it. He called it his oracle, and said it pointed out the time for every action of his life. From the left fob he took out a net almost large enough for a fisherman, but contrived to open and shut like a purse, and served him for the same use: we found therein several massy pieces of yellow metal, which, if they be real gold, must be of immense value.

Having thus, in obedience to your Majesty's commands, diligently searched all his pockets, we observed a girdle about his waist made of the hide of some prodigious animal; from which, on the left side, hung a sword of the length of five men; and on the right, a bag or pouch divided into two cells, each cell capable of holding three of your Majesty's subjects. In one of these cells were several globes or balls of a most ponderous metal, about the bigness of our heads, and requiring a strong hand to lift them: the other cell contained a heap of certain black grains, but of no great bulk or weight, for we could hold above fifty of them in the palms of our hands.

This is an exact inventory of what we found about the body of the Man-Mountain, who used us with great civility, and due respect to your Majesty's Commission. Signed and sealed on the fourth day of the eighty-ninth moon of your Majesty's auspicious reign.

Clefrin Frelock, Marsi Frelock.

When this inventory was read over to the Emperor, he directed me, although in very gentle terms, to deliver up the several particulars. He first called for my scimitar, which I took out, scabbard and all. In the mean time he ordered three thousand of his choicest troops (who then attended him) to surround me at a distance, with their bows and arrows just ready to discharge: but I did not observe it, for my eyes were wholly fixed upon his

Majesty. He then desired me to draw my
scimitar, which, although it had got some rust
by the sea water, was in most parts exceeding
bright. I did so, and immediately all the
troops gave a shout between terror and sur- 5
prise; for the sun shone clear, and the reflection dazzled their eyes, as I waved the scimitar to and fro in my hand. His Majesty, who
is a most magnanimous prince, was less
daunted than I could expect; he ordered me 10
to return it into the scabbard, and cast it on
the ground as gently as I could, about six
foot from the end of my chain. The next
thing he demanded, was one of the hollow
iron pillars, by which he meant my pocket- 15
pistols. I drew it out, and at his desire, as well
as I could, expressed to him the use of it;
and charging it only with powder, which,
by the closeness of my pouch, happened to
escape wetting in the sea (an inconvenience 20
against which all prudent mariners take special care to provide), I first cautioned the
Emperor not to be afraid, and then I let it
off in the air. The astonishment here was
much greater than at the sight of my scimitar. 25
Hundreds fell down as if they had been
struck dead; and even the Emperor, although
he stood his ground, could not recover himself in some time. I delivered up both my
pistols in the same manner as I had done 30
my scimitar, and then my pouch of powder
and bullets; begging him that the former
might be kept from fire, for it would kindle
with the smallest spark, and blow up his
imperial palace into the air. I likewise de- 35
livered up my watch, which the Emperor
was very curious to see, and commanded two
of his tallest yeomen of the guards to bear
it on a pole upon their shoulders, as draymen
in England do a barrel of ale. He was amazed 40
at the continual noise it made, and the motion of the minute-hand, which he could
easily discern; for their sight is much more
acute than ours: and asked the opinions of
his learned men about him, which were vari- 45
ous and remote, as the reader may well
imagine without my repeating; although indeed I could not very perfectly understand
them. I then gave up my silver and copper
money, my purse, with nine large pieces of 50

gold, and some smaller ones; my knife and
razor, my comb and silver snuff-box, my handkerchief and journal-book. My scimitar, pistols, and pouch were conveyed in carriages
to his Majesty's stores; but the rest of my
goods were returned to me.

I had, as I before observed, one private
pocket which escaped their search, wherein
there was a pair of spectacles (which I sometimes use for the weakness of my eyes), a
pocket perspective, and several other little
conveniences; which being of no consequence
to the Emperor, I did not think myself bound
in honor to discover, and I apprehended
they might be lost or spoiled if I ventured
them out of my possession.

Chapter 3: *The author diverts the Emperor,
and his nobility of both sexes, in a very
uncommon manner. The diversion of the
court of* Lilliput *described. The author has
his liberty granted him upon certain conditions.*

My gentleness and good behavior had
gained so far on the Emperor and his court,
and indeed upon the army and people in
general, that I began to conceive hopes of
getting my liberty in a short time. I took all
possible methods to cultivate this favorable
disposition. The natives came by degrees to
be less apprehensive of any danger from me.
I would sometimes lie down, and let five or
six of them dance on my hand. And at last
the boys and girls would venture to come and
play at hide and seek in my hair. I had now
made a good progress in understanding and
speaking their language. The Emperor had a
mind one day to entertain me with several
of the country shows, wherein they exceed
all nations I have known, both for dexterity
and magnificence. I was diverted with none
so much as that of the rope-dancers, performed upon a slender white thread, extended about two foot, and twelve inches
from the ground. Upon which I shall desire
liberty, with the reader's patience, to enlarge
a little.

This diversion is only practiced by those
persons who are candidates for great employ-

ments, and high favor, at court. They are trained in this art from their youth, and are not always of noble birth, or liberal education. When a great office is vacant, either by death or disgrace (which often happens), five or six of those candidates petition the Emperor to entertain his Majesty and the court with a dance on the rope, and whoever jumps the highest without falling, succeeds in the office. Very often the chief ministers themselves are commanded to show their skill, and to convince the Emperor that they have not lost their faculty. Flimnap, the Treasurer,[15] is allowed to cut a caper on the straight rope, at least an inch higher than any other lord in the whole empire. I have seen him do the summerset several times together upon a trencher fixed on the rope, which is no thicker than a common packthread in England. My friend Reldresal,[16] Principal Secretary for Private Affairs, is, in my opinion, if I am not partial, the second after the Treasurer; the rest of the great officers are much upon a par.

These diversions are often attended with fatal accidents, whereof great numbers are on record. I myself have seen two or three candidates break a limb. But the danger is much greater when the ministers themselves are commanded to show their dexterity; for, by contending to excel themselves and their fellows, they strain so far, that there is hardly one of them who hath not received a fall, and some of them two or three. I was assured that a year or two before my arrival, Flimnap would have infallibly broke his neck, if one of the King's cushions,[17] that accidentally lay on the ground, had not weakened the force of his fall.

There is likewise another diversion, which is only shown before the Emperor and Empress, and first minister, upon particular occasions. The Emperor lays on the table three fine silken threads of six inches long. One is blue, the other red, and the third green.[18] These threads are proposed as prizes for those persons whom the Emperor hath a mind to distinguish by a peculiar mark of his favor. The ceremony is performed in his Majesty's great chamber of state, where the candidates are to undergo a trial of dexterity very different from the former, and such as I have not observed the least resemblance of in any other country of the old or the new world. The Emperor holds a stick in his hands, both ends parallel to the horizon, while the candidates advancing one by one, sometimes leap over the stick, sometimes creep under it backwards and forwards several times, according as the stick is advanced or depressed. Sometimes the Emperor holds one end of the stick, and his first minister the other; sometimes the minister has it entirely to himself. Whoever performs his part with most agility, and holds out the longest in leaping and creeping, is rewarded with the blue-colored silk; the red is given to the next, and the green to the third, which they all wear girt twice round about the middle; and you see few great persons about this court, who are not adorned with one of these girdles.

The horses of the army, and those of the royal stables, having been daily led before me, were no longer shy, but would come up to my very feet without starting. The riders would leap them over my hand as I held it on the ground, and one of the Emperor's huntsmen, upon a larger courser, took my foot, shoe and all; which was indeed a prodigious leap. I had the good fortune to divert the Emperor one day after a very extraordinary manner. I desired he would order several sticks of two foot high, and the thickness of an ordinary cane, to be brought me; whereupon his Majesty commanded the master of his woods to give directions accordingly; and the next morning six woodmen arrived with as many carriages, drawn by eight horses to each. I took nine of these sticks, fixing them firmly in the ground in a quadrangular figure, two

[15] Sir Robert Walpole. As the leading Whig politician under George I, he was Swift's enemy.

[16] Viscount Townshend, Swift's political ally.

[17] A reference to the Duchess of Kendal, a mistress of the King; she helped Walpole regain political power.

[18] The ribbons represent the orders of the Garter, the Bath, and the Thistle. This was a timely hit; the Order of the Bath, purportedly a revival of an old order, was founded in 1725.

foot and a half square. I took four other sticks, and tied them parallel at each corner, about two foot from the ground; then I fastened my handkerchief to the nine sticks that stood erect, and extended it on all sides, till it was tight as the top of a drum; and the four parallel sticks rising about five inches higher than the handkerchief, served as ledges on each side. When I had finished my work, I desired the Emperor to let a troop of his best horse, twenty-four in number, come and exercise upon this plain. His Majesty approved of the proposal, and I took them up, one by one, in my hands, ready mounted and armed, with the proper officers to exercise them. As soon as they got into order, they divided into two parties, performed mock skirmishes, discharged blunt arrows, drew their swords, fled and pursued, attacked and retired, and in short discovered the best military discipline I ever beheld. The parallel sticks secured them and their horses from falling over the stage; and the Emperor was so much delighted that he ordered this entertainment to be repeated several days, and once was pleased to be lifted up and give the word of command; and, with great difficulty, persuaded even the Empress herself to let me hold her in her close chair within two yards of the stage, from whence she was able to take a full view of the whole performance. It was my good fortune that no ill accident happened in these entertainments; only once a fiery horse, that belonged to one of the captains, pawing with his hoof, struck a hole in my handkerchief, and his foot slipping, he overthrew his rider and himself; but I immediately relieved them both, and covering the hole with one hand, I set down the troop with the other, in the same manner as I took them up. The horse that fell was strained in the left shoulder, but the rider got no hurt, and I repaired my handkerchief as well as I could: however, I would not trust to the strength of it any more in such dangerous enterprises.

About two or three days before I was set at liberty, as I was entertaining the court with these kind of feats, there arrived an express to inform his Majesty, that some of his sub-

jects riding near the place where I was first taken up, had seen a great black substance lying on the ground, very oddly shaped, extending its edges round as wide as his Majesty's bedchamber, and rising up in the middle as high as a man; that it was no living creature, as they at first apprehended, for it lay on the grass without motion, and some of them had walked round it several times; that by mounting upon each other's shoulders, they had got to the top, which was flat and even, and stamping upon it they found it was hollow within; that they humbly conceived it might be something belonging to the Man-Mountain; and if his Majesty pleased, they would undertake to bring it with only five horses. I presently knew what they meant, and was glad at heart to receive this intelligence. It seems upon my first reaching the shore after our shipwreck, I was in such confusion, that before I came to the place where I went to sleep, my hat, which I had fastened with a string to my head while I was rowing, and had stuck on all the time I was swimming, fell off after I came to land; the string, as I conjecture, breaking by some accident which I never observed, but thought my hat had been lost at sea. I entreated his Imperial Majesty to give orders it might be brought to me as soon as possible, describing to him the use and the nature of it: and the next day the waggoners arrived with it, but not in a very good condition; they had bored two holes in the brim, within an inch and a half of the edge, and fastened two hooks in the holes; these hooks were tied by a long cord to the harness, and thus my hat was dragged along for above half an English mile; but the ground in that country being extremely smooth and level, it received less damage than I expected.

Two days after this adventure, the Emperor having ordered that part of his army which quarters in and about his metropolis to be in readiness, took a fancy of diverting himself in a very singular manner. He desired I would stand like a colossus, with my legs as far asunder as I conveniently could. He then commanded his General (who was an old experienced leader, and a great patron of mine) to

draw up the troops in close order, and march
them under me; the foot by twenty-four in
a breast, and the horse by sixteen, with drums
beating, colors flying, and pikes advanced.
This body consisted of three thousand foot, 5
and a thousand horse. His majesty gave orders,
upon pain of death, that every soldier in his
march should observe the strictest decency
with regard to my person; which, however,
could not prevent some of the younger of- 10
ficers from turning up their eyes as they
passed under me. And, to confess the truth,
my breeches were at that time in so ill a
condition, that they afforded some opportunities for laughter and admiration. 15

I had sent so many memorials and petitions
for my liberty, that his Majesty at length
mentioned the matter, first in his cabinet,
and then in a full council; where it was opposed by none, except Skyresh Bolgolam,[19] 20
who was pleased, without any provocation,
to be my mortal enemy. But it was carried
against him by the whole board, and confirmed by the Emperor. That minister was
Galbet, or Admiral of the Realm, very much 25
in his master's confidence, and a person well
versed in affairs, but of a morose and sour
complexion. However, he was at length persuaded to comply; but prevailed that the
articles and conditions upon which I should 30
be set free, and to which I must swear, should
be drawn up by himself. These articles were
brought to me by Skyresh Bolgolam in person, attended by two under-secretaries, and
several persons of distinction. After they were 35
read, I was demanded to swear to the performance of them; first in the manner of my
own country, and afterwards in the method
prescribed by their laws; which was to hold
my right foot in my left hand, to place the 40
middle finger of my right hand on the crown
of my head, and my thumb on the tip of my
right ear. But because the reader may be
curious to have some idea of the style and
manner of expression peculiar to that people, 45
as well as to know the articles upon which
I recovered my liberty, I have made a translation of the whole instrument word for word,

as near as I was able, which I here offer to the
public.

Golbasto Momarem Evlame Gurdilo Shefin
Mully Ully Gue, most mighty Emperor of
Lilliput, delight and terror of the universe,
whose dominions extend five thousand blus-
trugs (about twelve miles in circumference)
to the extremities of the globe; monarch of all
monarchs, taller than the sons of men; whose
feet press down to the center, and whose head
strikes against the sun; at whose nod the
princes of the earth shake their knees; pleasant
as the spring, comfortable as the summer,
fruitful as autumn, dreadful as winter.[20] His
most sublime Majesty proposeth to the Man-
Mountain, lately arrived to our celestial dominions, the following articles, which by a
solemn oath he shall be obliged to perform.

First, The Man-Mountain shall not depart
from our dominions, without our license under
our great seal.

2nd, He shall not presume to come into
our metropolis, without our express order; at
which time, the inhabitants shall have two
hours warning to keep within their doors.

3rd, The said Man-Mountain shall confine
his walks to our principal high roads, and not
offer to walk or lie down in a meadow or field
of corn.

4th, As he walks the said roads, he shall
take the utmost care not to trample upon the
bodies of any of our loving subjects, their
horses, or carriages, nor take any of our subjects into his hands, without their own consent.

5th, If an express requires extraordinary dispatch, the Man-Mountain shall be obliged
to carry in his pocket the messenger and horse
a six days journey once in every moon, and
return the said messenger back (if so required) safe to our Imperial Presence.

6th, He shall be our ally against our enemies in the Island of Blefuscu, and do his
utmost to destroy their fleet, which is now
preparing to invade us.

7th, That the said Man-Mountain shall, at
his times of leisure, be aiding and assisting

[19] Probably the Earl of Nottingham, enemy of
Swift's Tory friend Robert Harley, Earl of Oxford.

[20] This address perhaps parodies the style used
in the Orient, as reported in travel books.

our workmen, in helping to raise certain great stones, towards covering the wall of the principal park, and other our royal buildings.

8th, That the said Man-Mountain shall, in two moons' time, deliver in an exact survey of the circumference of our dominions by a computation of his own paces round the coast.

Lastly, That upon his solemn oath to observe all the above articles, the said Man-Mountain shall have a daily allowance of meat and drink sufficient for the support of 1728 of our subjects, with free access to our Royal Person, and other marks of our favor. Given at our Palace at Belfaborac the twelfth day of the ninety-first moon of our reign.

I swore and subscribed to these articles with great cheerfulness and content, although some of them were not so honorable as I could have wished; which proceeded wholly from the malice of Skyresh Bolgolam, the High-Admiral: whereupon my chains were immediately unlocked, and I was at full liberty; the Emperor himself in person did me the honor to be by at the whole ceremony. I made my acknowledgments by prostrating myself at his Majesty's feet: but he commanded me to rise; and after many gracious expressions, which, to avoid the censure of vanity, I shall not repeat, he added, that he hoped I should prove a useful servant, and well deserve all the favors he had already conferred upon me, or might do for the future.

The reader may please to observe, that in the last article for the recovery of my liberty, the Emperor stipulates to allow me a quantity of meat and drink sufficient for the support of 1728 Lilliputians. Some time after, asking a friend at court how they came to fix on that determinate number, he told me that his Majesty's mathematicians, having taken the height of my body by the help of a quadrant, and finding it to exceed theirs in the proportion of twelve to one they concluded from the similarity of their bodies, that mine must contain at least 1728 of theirs, and consequently would require as much food as was necessary to support that number of Lilliputians. By which, the reader may conceive an idea of the ingenuity of that people, as well as the prudent and exact economy of so great a prince.

Chapter 4: Mildendo,[21] *the metropolis of Lilliput, described, together with the Emperor's palace. A conversation between the author and a principal Secretary, concerning the affairs of that empire. The author's offer to serve the Emperor in his wars.*

The first request I made after I had obtained my liberty, was, that I might have license to see Mildendo, the metropolis; which the Emperor easily granted me, but with a special charge to do no hurt either to the inhabitants or their houses. The people had notice by proclamation of my design to visit the town. The wall which encompassed it, is two foot and a half high, and at least eleven inches broad, so that a coach and horses may be driven very safely round it; and it is flanked with strong towers at ten foot distance. I stepped over the great Western Gate, and passed very gently, and sideling through the two principal streets, only in my short waistcoat, for fear of damaging the roofs and eaves of the houses with the skirts of my coat. I walked with the utmost circumspection, to avoid treading on any stragglers, that might remain in the streets, although the orders were very strict, that all people should keep in their houses, at their own peril. The garret windows and tops of houses were so crowded with spectators, that I thought in all my travels I had not seen a more populous place. The city is an exact square, each side of the wall being five hundred foot long. The two great streets, which run cross and divide it into four quarters, are five foot wide. The lanes and alleys, which I could not enter, but only viewed them as I passed, are from twelve to eighteen inches. The town is capable of holding five hundred thousand souls. The houses are from three to five stories. The shops and markets well provided.

The Emperor's palace is in the center of the city, where the two great streets meet. It is inclosed by a wall of two foot high, and twenty foot distant from the buildings. I had

[21] Stands for London.

his Majesty's permission to step over this wall; and the space being so wide between that and the palace, I could easily view it on every side. The outward court is a square of forty foot, and includes two other courts: in the inmost are the royal apartments, which I was very desirous to see, but found it extremely difficult; for the great gates, from one square into another, were but eighteen inches high, and seven inches wide. Now the buildings of the outer court were at least five foot high, and it was impossible for me to stride over them without infinite damage to the pile, though the walls were strongly built of hewn stone, and four inches thick. At the same time the Emperor had a great desire that I should see the magnificence of his palace; but this I was not able to do till three days after, which I spent in cutting down with my knife some of the largest trees in the royal park, about an hundreds yards distant from the city. Of these trees I made two stools, each about three foot high, and strong enough to bear my weight. The people having received notice a second time, I went again through the city to the palace, with my two stools in my hands. When I came to the side of the outer court, I stood upon one stool, and took the other in my hand: this I lifted over the roof, and gently set it down on the space between the first and second court, which was eight foot wide. I then stepped over the buildings very conveniently from one stool to the other, and drew up the first after me with a hooked stick. By this contrivance I got into the inmost court; and lying down upon my side, I applied my face to the windows of the middle stories which were left open on purpose, and discovered the most splendid apartments that can be imagined. There I saw the Empress and the young Princes, in their several lodgings, with their chief attendants about them. Her Imperial Majesty was pleased to smile very graciously upon me, and gave me out of the window her hand to kiss.

But I shall not anticipate the reader with farther descriptions of this kind, because I reserve them for a greater work, which is now almost ready for the press, containing a general description of this empire, from its first erection, through a long series of princes, with a particular account of their wars and politics, laws, learning, and religion: their plants and animals, their peculiar manners and customs, with other matters very curious and useful; my chief design at present being only to relate such events and transactions as happened to the public, or to myself, during a residence of about nine months in that empire.

One morning, about a fortnight after I had obtained my liberty, Reldresal, Principal Secretary (as they style him) of Private Affairs, came to my house attended only by one servant. He ordered his coach to wait at a distance, and desired I would give him an hour's audience; which I readily consented to, on account of his quality and personal merits, as well as the many good offices he had done me during my solicitations at court. I offered to lie down, that he might the more conveniently reach my ear; but he chose rather to let me hold him in my hand during our conversation. He began with compliments on my liberty; said he might pretend to some merit in it: but, however, added, that if it had not been for the present situation of things at court, perhaps I might not have obtained it so soon. For, said he, as flourishing a condition as we may appear to be in to foreigners, we labor under two mighty evils: a violent faction at home, and the danger of an invasion by a most potent enemy from abroad. As to the first, you are to understand, that for about seventy moons past there have been two struggling parties in this empire, under the names of *Tramecksan* and *Slamecksan*,[22] from the high and low heels on their shoes, by which they distinguish themselves. It is alleged indeed, that the high heels are most agreeable to our ancient constitution: but however this be, his Majesty hath determined to make use of only low heels in the administration of the government, and all offices in the gift of the Crown, as you cannot but observe; and particularly, that his

[22] Tories, or high church party, and Whigs, or low church party.

Majesty's Imperial heels are lower at least by a *drurr* than any of his court (*drurr* is a measure about the fourteenth part of an inch). The animosities between these two parties run so high, that they will neither eat nor drink nor talk with each other. We compute the *Tramecksan,* or High-Heels, to exceed us in number; but the power is wholly on our side. We apprehend his Imperial Highness, the Heir to the Crown, to have some tendency towards the High-Heels; at least we can plainly discover one of his heels higher than the other, which gives him a hobble in his gait.[23] Now, in the midst of these intestine disquiets, we are threatened with an invasion from the Island of Blefuscu,[24] which is the other great empire of the universe, almost as large and powerful as this of his Majesty. For as to what we have heard you affirm, that there are other kingdoms and states in the world inhabited by human creatures as large as yourself, our philosophers are in much doubt, and would rather conjecture that you dropped from the moon, or one of the stars; because it is certain, that an hundred mortals of your bulk would, in a short time, destroy all the fruits and cattle of his Majesty's dominions. Besides, our histories of six thousand moons make no mention of any other regions, than the two great empires of Lilliput and Blefuscu. Which two mighty powers have, as I was going to tell you, been engaged in a most obstinate war for six and thirty moons past. It began upon the following occasion. It is allowed on all hands, that the primitive way of breaking eggs,[25] before we eat them, was upon the larger end: but his present Majesty's grandfather,[26] while he was a boy, going to eat an egg, and breaking it according to the ancient practice, happened to cut one of his fingers. Whereupon the Emperor his father [27] published an edict, commanding all his subjects, upon great penalties, to break the smaller end of their eggs. The people so highly resented this law, that our histories tell us there have been six rebellions raised on that account; wherein one Emperor lost his life, and another his crown.[28] These civil commotions were constantly fomented by the monarchs of Blefuscu; and when they were quelled, the exiles always fled for refuge to that empire. It is computed, that eleven thousand persons have, at several times, suffered death, rather than submit to break their eggs at the smaller end. Many hundred large volumes have been published upon this controversy: but the books of the Big-Endians have been long forbidden, and the whole party rendered incapable by law of holding employments. During the course of these troubles, the Emperors of Blefuscu did frequently expostulate by their ambassadors, accusing us of making a schism in religion, by offending against a fundamental doctrine of our great prophet Lustrog, in the fifty-fourth chapter of the Blundecral (which is their Alcoran). This, however, is thought to be a mere strain upon the text: for the words are these: "That all true believers break their eggs at the convenient end:" and which is the convenient end, seems, in my humble opinion, to be left to every man's conscience, or at least in the power of the chief magistrate to determine. Now the Big-Endian exiles have found so much credit in the Emperor of Blefuscu's court, and so much private assistance and encouragement from their party here at home, that a bloody war has been carried on between the two empires for six and thirty moons with various success; during which time

[23] The Prince of Wales befriended members of both parties. He is said to have recognized this reference to himself and to have been amused by it.

[24] France. Swift's fictional geography, with Lilliput (England) the mainland and Blefuscu (France) the island, is the reverse of actuality. Is anything gained by the reversal?

[25] Specifically, this passage refers to the English Reformation. The Big-Endians are Catholic, the Little-Endians are Protestant. The reference is to the difference between the two groups in the administration of the Sacrament of Holy Communion. More generally, the passage ridicules all kinds of petty, insignificant distinctions that cause bitter controversy.

[26] King Edward VI, declared illegitimate by the Catholic Church, and hence ineligible to inherit the crown.

[27] Henry VIII, who, after quarreling with Rome over his marriages and divorce, established the Protestant Church of England.

[28] Charles I was beheaded; James II was deposed.

we have lost forty capital ships, and a much greater number of smaller vessels, together with thirty thousand of our best seamen and soldiers; and the damage received by the enemy is reckoned to be somewhat greater than ours. However, they have now equipped a numerous fleet, and are just preparing to make a descent upon us; and his Imperial Majesty, placing great confidence in your valor and strength, has commanded me to lay this account of his affairs before you.

I desired the Secretary to present my humble duty to the Emperor, and to let him know, that I thought it would not become me, who was a foreigner, to interfere with parties; [29] but I was ready, with the hazard of my life, to defend his person and state against all invaders.

Chapter 5: *The author, by an extraordinary stratagem, prevents an invasion. A high title of honor is conferred upon him. Ambassadors arrive from the emperor of Blefuscu, and sue for peace. The Empress's apartment on fire by an accident; the author instrumental in saving the rest of the palace.*

The Empire of Blefuscu is an island situated to the north north-east side of Lilliput, from whence it is parted only by a channel of eight hundred yards wide. I had not yet seen it; and upon this notice of an intended invasion, I avoided appearing on that side of the coast, for fear of being discovered by some of the enemy's ships, who had received no intelligence of me, all intercourse between the two empires having been strictly forbidden during the war, upon pain of death, and an embargo laid by our Emperor upon all vessels whatsoever. I communicated to his Majesty a project I had formed of seizing the enemy's whole fleet: which, as our scouts assured us, lay at anchor in the harbor ready to sail with the first fair wind. I consulted the most experienced seamen, upon the depth of the channel, which they had often

plumbed, who told me, that in the middle at high-water it was seventy *glumgluffs* deep, which is about six foot of European measure; and the rest of it fifty *glumgluffs* at most. I walked towards the north-east coast over against Blefuscu; and lying down behind a hillock, took out my small pocket perspective-glass, and viewed the enemy's fleet at anchor, consisting of about fifty men of war, and a great number of transports: I then came back to my house, and gave order (for which I had a warrant) for a great quantity of the strongest cable and bars of iron. The cable was about as thick as packthread, and the bars of the length and size of a knitting-needle. I trebled the cable to make it stronger, and for the same reason I twisted three of the iron bars together, binding the extremities into a hook. Having thus fixed fifty hooks to as many cables, I went back to the north-east coast, and putting off my coat, shoes, and stockings, walked into the sea in my leathern jerkin, about half an hour before high water. I waded with what haste I could, and swam in the middle about thirty yards till I felt ground; I arrived at the fleet in less than half an hour. The enemy was so frighted when they saw me, that they leaped out of their ships, and swam to shore, where there could not be fewer than thirty thousand souls. I then took my tackling, and fastening a hook to the hole at the prow of each, I tied all the cords together at the end. While I was thus employed, the enemy discharged several thousand arrows, many of which stuck in my hands and face; and besides the excessive smart, gave me much disturbance in my work. My greatest apprehension was for my eyes, which I should have infallibly lost, if I had not suddenly thought of an expedient. I kept among other little necessaries a pair of spectacles in a private pocket, which, as I observed before, had scaped the Emperor's searchers. These I took out and fastened as strongly as I could upon my nose, and thus armed went on boldly with my work in spite of the enemy's arrows, many of which struck against the glasses of my spectacles, but without any other effect, further than a little to discompose them. I had now fastened all the hooks, and taking

[29] Perhaps a reminder that George I, also a foreigner (he was German), should not "interfere with parties."

the knot in my hand, began to pull; but not a ship would stir, for they were all too fast held by their anchors, so that the boldest part of my enterprise remained. I therefore let go the cord, and leaving the hooks fixed to the ships, I resolutely cut with my knife the cables that fastened the anchors, receiving about two hundred shots in my face and hands; then I took up the knotted end of the cables, to which my hooks were tied, and with great ease drew fifty of the enemy's largest men of war after me.

The Blefuscudians, who had not the least imagination of what I intended, were at first confounded with astonishment. They had seen me cut the cables, and thought my design was only to let the ships run a-drift, or fall foul on each other: but when they perceived the whole fleet moving in order, and saw me pulling at the end, they set up such a scream of grief and despair, that it is almost impossible to describe or conceive. When I had got out of danger, I stopped awhile to pick out the arrows that stuck in my hands and face; and rubbed on some of the same ointment that was given me at my first arrival, as I have formerly mentioned. I then took off my spectacles, and waiting about an hour, till the tide was a little fallen, I waded through the middle with my cargo, and arrived safe at the royal port of Lilliput.

The Emperor and his whole court stood on the shore, expecting the issue of this great adventure. They saw the ships move forward in a large halfmoon, but could not discern me, who was up to my breast in water. When I advanced in the middle of the channel, they were yet more in pain, because I was under water to my neck. The Emperor concluded me to be drowned, and that the enemy's fleet was approaching in a hostile manner: but he was soon eased of his fears, for the channel growing shallower every step I made, I came in a short time within hearing, and holding up the end of the cable by which the fleet was fastened, I cried in a loud voice,[30] "Long live the most puissant Emperor of Lilliput!" This great prince received me at my landing with all possible encomiums, and created me a *Nardac* upon the spot, which is the highest title of honor among them.

His Majesty desired I would take some other opportunity of bringing all the rest of his enemy's ships into his ports. And so unmeasurable is the ambition of princes, that he seemed to think of nothing less than reducing the whole empire of Blefuscu into a province, and governing it by a viceroy; of destroying the Big-Endian exiles, and compelling the people to break the smaller end of their eggs, by which he would remain the sole monarch of the whole world. But I endeavored to divert him from this design, by many arguments drawn from the topics of policy as well as justice; and I plainly protested, that I would never be an instrument of bringing a free and brave people into slavery. And when the matter was debated in council, the wisest part of the ministry were of my opinion.

This open bold declaration of mine was so opposite to the schemes and politics of his Imperial Majesty, that he could never forgive it; he mentioned it in a very artful manner at council, where I was told that some of the wisest appeared, at least by their silence, to be of my opinion; but others, who were my secret enemies, could not forbear some expressions, which by a side-wind reflected on me. And from this time began an intrigue between his Majesty and a junto of ministers maliciously bent against me, which broke out in less than two months, and had like to have ended in my utter destruction. Of so little weight are the greatest services to princes, when put into the balance with a refusal to gratify their passions.

About three weeks after this exploit, there arrived a solemn embassy from Blefuscu, with humble offers of a peace; which was soon concluded upon conditions very advantageous to our Emperor, wherewith I shall not trouble the reader. There were six ambassadors, with a train of about five hundred persons, and

[30] Gulliver's capture of the Blefuscudian fleet represents the Tory ministry's success in terminating the war with France (War of the Spanish Succession) and writing the Peace of Utrecht (1713). French objections to some terms of the treaty are represented by the cries of the Blefuscudians.

their entry was very magnificent, suitable to the grandeur of their master, and the importance of their business. When their treaty was finished, wherein I did them several good offices by the credit I now had, or at least appeared to have at court, their Excellencies, who were privately told how much I had been their friend, made me a visit in form. They began with many compliments upon my valor and generosity, invited me to that kingdom in the Emperor their master's name, and desired me to show them some proofs of my prodigious strength, of which they had heard so many wonders; wherein I readily obliged them, but shall not trouble the reader with the particulars.

When I had for some time entertained their Excellencies, to their infinite satisfaction and surprise, I desired they would do me the honor to present my most humble respects to the Emperor their master, the renown of whose virtues had so justly filled the whole world with admiration, and whose royal person I resolved to attend before I returned to my own country: accordingly, the next time I had the honor to see our Emperor, I desired his general license to wait on the Blefuscudian monarch, which he was pleased to grant me, as I could perceive, in a very cold manner; but could not guess the reason, till I had a whisper from a certain person that Flimnap and Bolgolam had represented my intercourse with those ambassadors as a mark of disaffection, from which I am sure my heart was wholly free. And this was the first time I began to conceive some imperfect idea of courts and ministers.

It is to be observed, that these ambassadors spoke to me by an interpreter, the languages of both empires differing as much from each other as any two in Europe, and each nation priding itself upon the antiquity, beauty, and energy of their own tongues, with an avowed contempt for that of their neighbor; yet our Emperor, standing upon the advantage he had got by the seizure of their fleet, obliged them to deliver their credentials, and make their speech in the Lilliputian tongue. And it must be confessed, that from the great intercourse of trade and commerce between both realms, from the continual reception of exiles, which is mutual among them, and from the custom in each empire to send their young nobility and richer gentry to the other, in order to polish themselves by seeing the world, and understanding men and manners; there are few persons of distinction, or merchants, or seamen, who dwell in the maritime parts, but what can hold conversation in both tongues; as I found some weeks after, when I went to pay my respects to the Emperor of Blefuscu, which in the midst of great misfortunes, through the malice of my enemies, proved a very happy adventure to me, as I shall relate in its proper place.

The reader may remember, that when I signed those articles upon which I recovered my liberty, there were some which I disliked upon account of their being too servile; neither could anything but an extreme necessity have forced me to submit. But being now a *Nardac* of the highest rank in that empire, such offices were looked upon as below my dignity, and the Emperor (to do him justice) never once mentioned them to me. However, it was not long before I had an opportunity of doing his Majesty, at least as I then thought, a most signal service. I was alarmed at midnight with the cries of many hundred people at my door; by which being suddenly awaked, I was in some kind of terror. I heard the word *burglum* repeated incessantly: several of the Emperor's court, making their way through the crowd, entreated me to come immediately to the palace, where her Imperial Majesty's apartment was on fire, by the carelessness of a maid of honor, who fell asleep while she was reading a romance. I got up in an instant; and orders being given to clear the way before me, and it being likewise a moonshine night, I made a shift to get to the palace without trampling on any of the people. I found they had already applied ladders to the walls of the apartment, and were well provided with buckets, but the water was at some distance. These buckets were about the size of a large thimble, and the poor people supplied me with them as fast as they could; but the flame was so violent that they did little good. I might easily have stifled it with my coat, which I unfortunately left behind me for haste, and came away only in my leathern jerkin. The case seemed wholly desperate and deplorable; and this magnificent palace would have infallibly been burnt down to the ground, if, by a presence of mind, unusual to me, I had not suddenly thought of an expedient. I had the evening before drunk plentifully of a most delicious wine, called *glimigrim* (the Blefuscudians call it *flunec*, but ours is esteemed the better sort), which is very diuretic. By the luckiest chance in the world, I had not discharged myself of any part of it. The heat I had contracted by coming very near the flames, and by laboring to quench them, made the wine begin to operate by urine; which I voided in such a quantity, and applied so well to the proper places, that in three minutes the fire was wholly extinguished, and the rest of that noble pile, which had cost so many ages in erecting, preserved from destruction.

It was now daylight, and I returned to my house without waiting to congratulate with the Emperor: because, although I had done a very eminent piece of service, yet I could not tell how his Majesty might resent the manner by which I had performed it: for, by the fundamental laws of the realm, it is capital in any person, of what quality soever, to make water within the precincts of the palace. But I was a little comforted by a message from his Majesty, that he would give orders to the Grand Justiciary for passing my pardon in form; which, however, I could not obtain. And I was privately assured, that the Empress, conceiving the greatest abhorrence of what I had done, removed to the most distant side of the court, firmly resolved that those buildings should never be repaired for her use; and, in the presence of her chief confidents could not forbear vowing revenge.[31]

Chapter 6: *Of the inhabitants of* Lilliput; *their learning, laws, and customs, the man-*

[31] The Empress' abhorrence of Gulliver's method of saving the palace may refer to Queen Anne's resentment of the Earl of Oxford, or indignation at Swift's satiric methods, particularly his satire on religious differences, *A Tale of a Tub.*

ner of educating their children. The author's way of living in that country. His vindication of a great lady.

Although I intend to leave the description of this empire to a particular treatise, yet in the mean time I am content to gratify the curious reader with some general ideas. As the common size of the natives is somewhat under six inches high, so there is an exact proportion in all other animals, as well as plants and trees: for instance, the tallest horses and oxen are between four and five inches in height, the sheep an inch and a half, more or less: their geese about the bigness of a sparrow, and so the several gradations downwards till you come to the smallest, which, to my sight, were almost invisible; but nature hath adapted the eyes of the Lilliputians to all objects proper for their view: they see with great exactness, but at no great distance. And to show the sharpness of their sight towards objects that are near, I have been much pleased with observing a cook pulling a lark, which was not so large as a common fly; and a young girl threading an invisible needle with invisible silk. Their tallest trees are about seven foot high: I mean some of those in the great royal park, the tops whereof I could but just reach with my fist clinched. The other vegetables are in the same proportion; but this I leave to the reader's imagination.

I shall say but little at present of their learning, which for many ages hath flourished in all its branches among them: but their manner of writing is very peculiar, being neither from the left to the right, like the Europeans; nor from the right to the left, like the Arabians; nor from up to down, like the Chinese; nor from down to up, like the Cascagians; but aslant from one corner of the paper to the other, like ladies in England.

They bury their dead with their heads directly downwards, because they hold an opinion, that in eleven thousand moons they are all to rise again, in which period the earth (which they conceive to be flat) will turn upside down, and by this means they shall, at their resurrection, be found ready standing on their feet. The learned among them confess the absurdity of this doctrine, but the practice still continues, in compliance to the vulgar.

There are some laws and customs in this empire very peculiar; and if they were not so directly contrary to those of my own dear country, I should be tempted to say a little in their justification. It is only to be wished, that they were as well executed. The first I shall mention, relates to informers. All crimes against the state are punished here with the utmost severity; but if the person accused maketh his innocence plainly to appear upon his trial, the accuser is immediately put to an ignominious death; and out of his goods or lands, the innocent person is quadruply recompensed for the lost of his time, for the danger he underwent, for the hardship of his imprisonment, and for all the charges he hath been at in making his defense. Or, if that fund be deficient, it is largely supplied by the Crown. The Emperor does also confer on him some public mark of his favor, and proclamation is made of his innocence through the whole city.

They look upon fraud as a greater crime than theft, and therefore seldom fail to punish it with death; for they allege, that care and vigilance, with a very common understanding, may preserve a man's goods from thieves, but honesty has no fence against superior cunning; and since it is necessary that there should be a perpetual intercourse of buying and selling, and dealing upon credit, where fraud is permitted and connived at, or hath no law to punish it, the honest dealer is always undone, and the knave gets the advantage. I remember when I was once interceding with the Emperor for a criminal who had wronged his master of a great sum of money, which he had received by order, and ran away with; and happening to tell his Majesty, by way of extenuation, that it was only a breach of trust; the Emperor thought it monstrous in me to offer, as a defense, the greatest aggravation of the crime: and truly I had little to say in return, farther than the common answer, that different nations had different customs; for, I confess, I was heartily ashamed.

Although we usually call reward and punishment the two hinges upon which all government turns, yet I could never observe this maxim to be put in practice by any nation except that of Lilliput. Whoever can there bring sufficient proof that he hath strictly observed the laws of his country for seventy-three moons, hath a claim to certain privileges, according to his quality and condition of life, with a proportionable sum of money out of a fund appropriated for that use: he likewise acquires the title of *Snilpall,* or Legal, which is added to his name, but does not descend to his posterity. And these people thought it a prodigious defect of policy among us, when I told them that our laws were enforced only by penalties, without any mention of reward. It is upon this account that the image of Justice, in their courts of judicature, is formed with six eyes, two before, as many behind, and on each side one, to signify circumspection; with a bag of gold open in her right hand, and a sword sheathed in her left, to show she is more disposed to reward than to punish.

In choosing persons for all employments, they have more regard to good morals than to great abilities; for, since government is necessary to mankind, they believe that the common size of human understanding is fitted to some station or other, and that Providence never intended to make the management of public affairs a mystery, to be comprehended only by a few persons of sublime genius, of which there seldom are three born in an age: but they suppose truth, justice, temperance, and the like, to be in every man's power; the practice of which virtues, assisted by experience and a good intention, would qualify any man for the service of his country, except where a course of study is required. But they thought the want of moral virtues was so far from being supplied by superior endowments of the mind, that employments could never be put into such dangerous hands as those of persons so qualified; and at least, that the mistakes committed by ignorance in a virtuous disposition, would never be of such fatal consequence to the public weal, as the practices of a man whose inclinations led him to be corrupt, and had great abilities to manage, and multiply, and defend his corruptions.

In like manner, the disbelief of a Divine Providence renders a man uncapable of holding any public station; for, since kings avow themselves to be the deputies of Providence, the Lilliputians think nothing can be more absurd than for a prince to employ such men as disown the authority under which he acts.

In relating these and the following laws, I would only be understood to mean the original institutions, and not the most scandalous corruptions into which these people are fallen by the degenerate nature of man. For as to that infamous practice of acquiring great employments by dancing on the ropes, or badges of favor and distinction by leaping over sticks and creeping under them, the reader is to observe, that they were first introduced by the grandfather of the Emperor now reigning, and grew to the present height, by the gradual increase of party and faction.

Ingratitude is among them a capital crime, as we read it to have been in some other countries: for they reason thus, that whoever makes ill returns to his benefactor, must needs be a common enemy to the rest of mankind, from whom he hath received no obligation, and therefore such a man is not fit to live.

Their notions relating to the duties of parents and children differ extremely from ours. For, since the conjunction of male and female is founded upon the great law of nature, in order to propagate and continue the species, the Lilliputians will needs have it, that men and women are joined together like other animals, by the motives of concupiscence; and that their tenderness towards their young proceeds from the like natural principle: for which reason they will never allow, that a child is under any obligation to his father for begetting him, or to his mother for bringing him into the world, which, considering the miseries of human life, was neither a benefit in itself, nor intended so by his parents, whose thoughts in their love-encounters were otherwise employed. Upon these, and the like reasonings, their opinion is, that parents are the last of all others to be trusted with the education of their own chil-

dren; and therefore they have in every town public nurseries, where all parents, except cottagers and laborers, are obliged to send their infants of both sexes to be reared and educated when they come to the age of twenty moons, at which time they are supposed to have some rudiments of docility. These schools are of several kinds, suited to different qualities, and to both sexes. They have certain professors well skilled in preparing children for such a condition of life as befits the rank of their parents, and their own capacities as well as inclinations. I shall first say something of the male nurseries, and then of the female.

The nurseries for males of noble or eminent birth, are provided with grave and learned professors, and their several deputies. The clothes and food of the children are plain and simple. They are bred up in the principles of honor, justice, courage, modesty, clemency, religion, and love of their country; they are always employed in some business, except in the times of eating and sleeping, which are very short, and two hours for diversions, consisting of bodily exercises. They are dressed by men till four years of age, and then are obliged to dress themselves, although their quality be ever so great; and the women attendants, who are aged proportionably to ours at fifty, perform only the most menial offices. They are never suffered to converse with servants, but go together in small or greater numbers to take their diversions, and always in the presence of a professor, or one of his deputies; whereby they avoid those early bad impressions of folly and vice to which our children are subject. Their parents are suffered to see them only twice a year; the visit is to last but an hour. They are allowed to kiss the child at meeting and parting; but a professor, who always stands by on those occasions, will not suffer them to whisper, or use any fondling expressions, or bring any presents of toys, sweetmeats, and the like.

The pension from each family for the education and entertainment of a child, upon failure of due payment, is levied by the Emperor's officers.

The nurseries for children of ordinary gentlemen, merchants, traders, and handicrafts, are managed proportionably after the same manner; only those designed for trades are put out apprentices at eleven years old, whereas those of persons of quality continue in their nurseries till fifteen, which answers to one and twenty with us: but the confinement is gradually lessened for the last three years.

In the female nurseries, the young girls of quality are educated much like the males, only they are dressed by orderly servants of their own sex; but always in the presence of a professor or deputy, till they come to dress themselves, which is at five years old. And if it be found that these nurses ever presume to entertain the girls with frightful or foolish stories, or the common follies practiced by chambermaids among us, they are publicly whipped thrice about the city, imprisoned for a year, and banished for life to the most desolate part of the country. Thus the young ladies there are as much ashamed of being cowards and fools as the men, and despise all personal ornaments beyond decency and cleanliness: neither did I perceive any difference in their education, made by their difference of sex, only that the exercises of the females were not altogether so robust; and that some rules were given them relating to domestic life, and a smaller compass of learning was enjoined them: for their maxim is, that among people of quality, a wife should be always a reasonable and agreeable companion, because she cannot always be young. When the girls are twelve years old, which among them is the marriageable age, their parents or guardians take them home, with great expressions of gratitude to the professors, and seldom without tears of the young lady and her companions.

In the nurseries of females of the meaner sort, the children are instructed in all kinds of works proper for their sex, and their several degrees: those intended for apprentices are dismissed at seven years old, the rest are kept to thirteen.

The meaner families who have children at these nurseries, are obliged, besides their annual pension, which is as low as possible, to return to the steward of the nursery of a small monthly share of their gettings, to be a portion for the child; and therefore all parents are limited in their expenses by the law. For the Lilliputians think nothing can be more unjust, than for people, in subservience to their own appetites, to bring children into the world, and leave the burden of supporting them on the public. As to persons of quality, they give security to appropriate a certain sum for each child, suitable to their condition; and these funds are always managed with good husbandry, and the most exact justice.

The cottagers and laborers keep their children at home, their business being only to till and cultivate the earth, and therefore their education is of little consequence to the public; but the old and diseased among them are supported by hospitals: for begging is a trade unknown in this empire.

And here it may perhaps divert the curious reader, to give some account of my domestic, and my manner of living in this country, during a residence of nine months and thirteen days. Having a head mechanically turned, and being likewise forced by necessity, I had made for myself a table and chair convenient enough, out of the largest trees in the royal park. Two hundred sempstresses were employed to make me shirts, and linen for my bed and table, all of the strongest and coarsest kind they could get; which, however, they were forced to quilt together in several folds, for the thickest was some degrees finer than lawn. Their linen is usually three inches wide, and three foot make a piece. The sempstresses took my measure as I lay on the ground, one standing at my neck, and another at my midleg, with a strong cord extended, that each held by the end, while the third measured the length of the cord with a rule an inch long. Then they measured my right thumb, and desired no more; for by a mathematical computation, that twice round the thumb is once round the wrist, and so on to the neck and the waist, and by the help of my old shirt, which I displayed on the ground before them for a pattern, they fitted me exactly. Three hundred tailors were employed in the same manner to make me clothes; but they had another contrivance for taking my measure.

I kneeled down, and they raised a ladder from the ground to my neck; upon this ladder one of them mounted and let fall a plumbline from my collar to the floor, which just answered the length of my coat: but my waist and arms I measured myself. When my clothes were finished, which was done in my house (for the largest of theirs would not have been able to hold them), they looked like the patch-work made by the ladies in England, only that mine were all of a color.

I had three hundred cooks to dress my victuals, in little convenient huts built about my house, where they and their families lived, and prepared me two dishes a-piece. I took up twenty waiters in my hand, and placed them on the table: an hundred more attended below on the ground, some with dishes of meat, and some with barrels of wine, and other liquors, slung on their shoulders; all which the waiters above drew up as I wanted, in a very ingenious manner, by certain cords, as we draw the bucket up a well in Europe. A dish of their meat was a good mouthful, and a barrel of their liquor a reasonable draught. Their mutton yields to ours, but their beef is excellent. I have had a sirloin so large, that I have been forced to make three bites of it; but this is rare. My servants were astonished to see me eat it bones and all, as in our country we do the leg of a lark. Their geese and turkeys I usually eat at a mouthful, and I must confess they far exceed ours. Of their smaller fowl I could take up twenty or thirty at the end of my knife.

One day his Imperial Majesty, being informed of my way of living, desired that himself and his Royal Consort, with the young Princes of the blood of both sexes, might have the happiness (as he was pleased to call it) of dining with me. They came accordingly, and I placed them in chairs of state on my table, just over against me, with their guards about them. Flimnap, the Lord High Treasurer, attended there likewise with his white staff; and I observed he often looked on me with a sour countenance, which I would not seem to regard, but eat more than usual, in honor to my dear country, as well as to fill the court with admiration. I have some private reasons to believe, that this visit from his Majesty gave Flimnap an opportunity of doing me ill offices to his master. That minister had always been my secret enemy, though he outwardly caressed me more than was usual to the moroseness of his nature. He represented to the Emperor the low condition of his treasury; that he was forced to take up money at great discount; that exchequer bills would not circulate under nine per cent below par; that in short I had cost his Majesty above a million and a half of *sprugs* (their greatest gold coin, about the bigness of a spangle); and upon the whole, that it would be advisable in the Emperor to take the first fair occasion of dismissing me.

I am here obliged to vindicate the reputation of an excellent lady, who was an innocent sufferer upon my account. The Treasurer took a fancy to be jealous of his wife, from the malice of some evil tongues, who informed him that her Grace had taken a violent affection for my person; and the court-scandal ran for some time, that she once came privately to my lodging. This I solemnly declare to be a most infamous falsehood, without any grounds, farther than that her Grace was pleased to treat me with all innocent marks of freedom and friendship. I own she came often to my house, but always publicly, nor ever without three more in the coach, who were usually her sister and young daughter, and some particular acquaintance; but this was common to many other ladies of the court. And I still appeal to my servants round, whether they at any time saw a coach at my door without knowing what persons were in it. On those occasions, when a servant had given me notice, my custom was to go immediately to the door; and, after paying my respects, to take up the coach and two horses very carefully in my hands (for, if there were six horses, the postillion always unharnessed four), and place them on a table, where I had fixed a movable rim quite round, of five inches high, to prevent accidents. And I have often had four coaches and horses at once on my table full of company, while I sat in my chair leaning my face towards them; and when I was engaged with one set, the coachmen would gently drive the others round my table. I have passed many an afternoon very agreeably in these conversations. But I defy the Treasurer, or his two informers (I will name them, and let them make their best of it) Clustril and Drunlo, to prove that any person ever came to me incognito, except the secretary Reldresal, who was sent by express command of his Imperial Majesty, as I have before related. I should not have dwelt so long upon this particular, if it had not been a point wherein the reputation of a great lady is so nearly concerned, to say nothing of my own; though I then had the honor to be a *Nardac,* which the Treasurer himself is not; for all the world knows he is only a *Clumglum,* a title inferior by one degree, as that of a Marquis is to a Duke in England, although I allow he preceded me in right of his post. These false informations, which I afterwards came to the knowledge of, by an accident not proper to mention, made Flimnap, the Treasurer, show his lady for some time an ill countenance, and me a worse; and although he were at last undeceived and reconciled to her, yet I lost all credit with him, and found my interest decline very fast with the Emperor himself, who was indeed too much governed by that favorite.

Chapter 7: *The author, being informed of a design to accuse him of high-treason, makes his escape to Blefuscu. His reception there.*

Before I proceed to give an account of my leaving this kingdom, it may be proper to inform the reader of a private intrigue which had been for two months forming against me.

I had been hitherto all my life a stranger to courts, for which I was unqualified by the meanness of my condition. I had indeed heard and read enough of the dispositions of great princes and ministers; but never expected to have found such terrible effects of them in so remote a country, governed, as I thought, by very different maxims from those in Europe.

When I was just preparing to pay my attendance on the Emperor of Blefuscu, a considerable person at court (to whom I had been very serviceable at a time when he lay under the highest displeasure of his Imperial Majesty) came to my house very privately at night in a close chair, and without sending his name, desired admittance. The chairmen were dismissed; I put the chair, with his Lordship in it, into my coat-pocket: and giving orders to a trusty servant to say I was indisposed and gone to sleep, I fastened the door of my house, placed the chair on the table, according to my usual custom, and sat down by it. After the common salutations were over, observing his Lordship's countenance full of concern, and enquiring into the reason, he desired I would hear him with patience in a matter that highly concerned my honor and my life. His speech was to the following effect, for I took notes of it as soon as he left me:

"You are to know," said he, "that several Committees of Council have been lately called in the most private manner on your account; and it is but two days since his Majesty came to a full resolution.

"You are very sensible that Skyresh Bolgolam (*Galbet,* or High-Admiral) hath been your mortal enemy almost ever since your arrival. His original reasons I know not; but his hatred is much increased since your great success against Blefuscu, by which his glory, as Admiral, is obscured. This Lord, in conjunction with Flimnap the High-Treasurer, whose enmity against you is notorious on account of his lady, Limtoc the General, Lalcon the Chamberlain, and Balmuff the Grand Justiciary, have prepared articles of impeachment against you, for treason, and other capital crimes."

This preface made me so impatient, being conscious of my own merits and innocence, that I was going to interrupt; when he entreated me to be silent, and thus proceeded:

"Out of gratitude for the favors you have done me, I procured information of the whole proceedings, and a copy of the articles, wherein I venture my head for your service."

Articles of Impeachment against Quinbus
Flestrin (*the* Man-Mountain) ³²

Article I. Whereas, by a statute made in the
reign of his Imperial Majesty Calin Deffar
Plune, it is enacted, that whoever shall make
water within the precincts of the royal palace,
shall be liable to the pains and penalties of
high treason; notwithstanding, the said Quinbus Flestrin, in open breach of the said law,
under color of extinguishing the fire kindled
in the apartment of his Majesty's most dear
Imperial Consort, did maliciously, traitorously,
and devilishly, by discharge of his urine, put
out the said fire kindled in the said apartment, lying and being within the precincts
of the said royal palace, against the statute
in that case provided, *etc.* against the duty,
etc.

Article II. That the said Quinbus Flestrin
having brought the imperial fleet of Blefuscu
into the royal port, and being afterwards commanded by his Imperial Majesty to seize all
the other ships of the said empire of Blefuscu,
and reduce that empire to a province, to be
governed by a viceroy from hence, and to
destroy and put to death not only all the
Big-Endian exiles, but likewise all the people
of that empire who would not immediately
forsake the Big-Endian heresy: He, the said
Flestrin, like a false traitor against his most
Auspicious, Serene, Imperial Majesty, did
petition to be excused from the said service,
upon pretense of unwillingness to force the
consciences, or destroy the liberties and lives
of an innocent people.

Article III. That, whereas certain ambassadors arrived from the court of Blefuscu, to
sue for peace in his Majesty's court: He, the
said Flestrin, did, like a false traitor, aid, abet,
comfort, and divert the said ambassadors, although he knew them to be servants to a
Prince who was lately an open enemy to his
Imperial Majesty, and in open war against
his said Majesty.

Article IV. That the said Quinbus Flestrin,

³² The Articles of Impeachment allude to impeachment proceedings against Swift's Tory friends,
Harley and St. John, when the Tory ministry fell
in 1714.

contrary to the duty of a faithful subject, is
now preparing to make a voyage to the court
and empire of Blefuscu, for which he hath
received only verbal license from his Imperial Majesty; and under color of the said
license, doth falsely and traitorously intend to
take the said voyage, and thereby to aid,
comfort, and abet the Emperor of Blefuscu,
so late an enemy, and in open war with his
Imperial Majesty aforesaid.

"There are some other articles, but these
are the most important, of which I have read
you an abstract.

"In the several debates upon this impeachment, it must be confessed that his Majesty
gave many marks of his great lenity, often
urging the services you had done him, and
endeavoring to extenuate your crimes. The
Treasurer and Admiral insisted that you
should be put to the most painful and ignominious death, by setting fire on your house
at night, and the General was to attend with
twenty thousand men armed with poisoned
arrows to shoot you on the face and hands.
Some of your servants were to have private
orders to strew a poisonous juice on your
shirts, which would soon make you tear your
own flesh, and die in the utmost torture. The
General came into the same opinion; so that
for a long time there was a majority against
you. But his Majesty resolving, if possible, to
spare your life, at last brought off the Chamberlain.

"Upon this incident, Reldresal, Principal
Secretary for Private Affairs, who always approved himself your true friend, was commanded by the Emperor to deliver his opinion,
which he accordingly did; and therein justified the good thoughts you have of him. He
allowed your crimes to be great, but that still
there was room for mercy, the most com-
mendable virtue in a prince, and for which
his Majesty was so justly celebrated. He said,
the friendship between you and him was so
well known to the world, that perhaps the
most honorable board might think him partial:
however, in obedience to the command he
had received, he would freely offer his sentiments. That if his Majesty, in consideration

of your services, and pursuant to his own merciful disposition, would please to spare your life, and only give orders to put out both your eyes, he humbly conceived, that by this expedient, justice might in some measure be satisfied, and all the world would applaud the lenity of the Emperor, as well as the fair and generous proceedings of those who have the honor to be his counselors. That the loss of your eyes would be no impediment to your bodily strength, by which you might still be useful to his Majesty. That blindness is an addition to courage, by concealing dangers from us; that the fear you had for your eyes, was the greatest difficulty in bringing over the enemy's fleet, and it would be sufficient for you to see by the eyes of the ministers, since the greatest princes do no more.

"This proposal was received with the utmost disapprobation by the whole board. Bolgolam, the Admiral, could not preserve his temper; but rising up in fury, said, he wondered how the Secretary durst presume to give his opinion for preserving the life of a traitor; that the services you had performed were, by all true reasons of state, the great aggravation of your crimes; that you, who were able to extinguish the fire, by discharge of urine in her Majesty's apartment (which he mentioned with horror), might at another time raise an inundation by the same means, to drown the whole palace; and the same strength which enabled you to bring over the enemy's fleet, might serve, upon the first discontent, to carry it back; that he had good reasons to think you were a Big-Endian in your heart; and as treason begins in the heart, before it appears in overt acts, so he accused you as a traitor on that account, and therefore insisted you should be put to death.

"The Treasurer was of the same opinion; he showed to what straits his Majesty's revenue was reduced by the charge of maintaining you, which would soon grow insupportable: that the Secretary's expedient of putting out your eyes was so far from being a remedy against this evil, that it would probably increase it, as it is manifest from the common practice of blinding some kind of fowl, after which they fed the faster, and grew sooner fat: that his sacred Majesty and the Council, who are your judges, were in their own consciences fully convinced of your guilt, which was a sufficient argument to condemn you to death, without the formal proofs required by the strict letter of the law.

"But his Imperial Majesty, fully determined against capital punishment, was graciously pleased to say, that since the Council thought the loss of your eyes too easy a censure, some other may be inflicted hereafter. And your friend the Secretary humbly desiring to be heard again, in answer to what the Treasurer had objected concerning the great charge his Majesty was at in maintaining you, said, that his Excellency, who had the sole disposal of the Emperor's revenue, might easily provide against that evil, by gradually lessening your establishment; by which, for want of sufficient food, you would grow weak and faint, and lose your appetite, and consequently decay and consume in a few months; neither would the stench of your carcass be then so dangerous, when it should become more than half diminished; and immediately upon your death, five or six thousand of his Majesty's subjects might, in two or three days, cut your flesh from your bones, take it away by cartloads, and bury it in distant parts to prevent infection, leaving the skeleton as a monument of admiration to posterity.

"Thus by the great friendship of the Secretary, the whole affair was compromised. It was strictly enjoined, that the project of starving you by degrees should be kept a secret, but the sentence of putting out your eyes was entered on the books; none dissenting except Bolgolam the Admiral, who, being a creature of the Empress, was perpetually instigated by her Majesty to insist upon your death, she having borne perpetual malice against you, on account of that infamous and illegal method you took to extinguish the fire in her apartment.

"In three days your friend the Secretary will be directed to come to your house, and read before you the articles of impeachment; and then to signify the great lenity and favor of his Majesty and Council, whereby you are only condemned to the loss of your eyes, which his Majesty doth not question you will gratefully and humbly submit to; and twenty of his Majesty's surgeons will attend, in order to see the operation well performed, by discharging very sharp-pointed arrows into the balls of your eyes, as you lie on the ground.

"I leave to your prudence what measures you will take; and to avoid suspicion, I must immediately return in as private a manner as I came."

His Lordship did so, and I remained alone, under many doubts and perplexities of mind.

It was a custom introduced by this prince and his ministry (very different, as I have been assured, from the practices of former times), that after the court had decreed any cruel execution, either to gratify the monarch's resentment, or the malice of a favorite, the Emperor always made a speech to his whole Council, expressing his great lenity and tenderness, as qualities known and confessed by all the world. This speech was immediately published through the kingdom; nor did any thing terrify the people so much as those encomiums on his Majesty's mercy; because it was observed, that the more these praises were enlarged and insisted on, the more inhuman was the punishment, and the sufferer more innocent. And as to myself, I must confess, having never been designed for a courtier either by my birth or education, I was so ill a judge of things, that I could not discover the lenity and favor of his sentence, but conceived it (perhaps erroneously) rather to be rigorous than gentle. I sometimes thought of standing my trial, for although I could not deny the facts alleged in the several articles, yet I hoped they would admit of some extenuations. But having in my life perused many state trials, which I ever observed to terminate as the judges thought fit to direct, I durst not rely on so dangerous a decision, in so critical a juncture, and against such powerful enemies. Once I was strongly bent upon resistance, for while I had liberty, the whole strength of that empire could hardly subdue me, and I might easily with stones pelt the metropolis to pieces; but I soon rejected that project with horror, by remembering the oath I had made to the Emperor, the favors I

received from him, and the high title of *Nardac* he conferred upon me. Neither had I so soon learned the gratitude of courtiers, to persuade myself that his Majesty's present severities acquitted me of all past obligations.

At last I fixed upon a resolution, for which it is probable I may incur some censure, and not unjustly; for I confess I owe the preserving my eyes, and consequently my liberty, to my own great rashness and want of experience: because if I had then known the nature of princes and ministers, which I have since observed in many other courts, and their methods of treating criminals less obnoxious than myself, I should with great alacrity and readiness have submitted to so easy a punishment. But hurried on by the precipitancy of youth, and having his Imperial Majesty's license to pay my attendance upon the Emperor of Blefuscu, I took this opportunity, before the three days were elapsed, to send a letter to my friend the Secretary, signifying my resolution of setting out that morning for Blefuscu pursuant to the leave I had got; and without waiting for an answer, I went to that side of the island where our fleet lay. I seized a large man of war, tied a cable to the prow, and, lifting up the anchors, I stripped myself, put my clothes (together with my coverlet, which I brought under my arm) into the vessel, and drawing it after me between wading and swimming, arrived at the royal port of Blefuscu, where the people had long expected me: [33] they lent me two guides to direct me to the capital city, which is of the same name. I held them in my hands till I came within two hundred yards of the gate, and desired them to signify my arrival to one of the secretaries, and let him know, I there waited his Majesty's command. I had an answer in about an hour, that his Majesty, attended by the Royal Family, and great officers of the court, was coming out to receive me. I advanced a hundred yards. The Emperor and his train alighted from their horses, the Empress and ladies from their coaches, and I did not perceive they were in any fright or concern. I lay on the ground to kiss his Majesty's and the

[33] A reference to St. John's flight to France just before his trial.

Empress's hands. I told his Majesty, that I was come according to my promise, and with the license of the Emperor my master, to have the honor of seeing so mighty a monarch, and to offer him any service in my power, consistent with my duty to my own prince; not mentioning a word of my disgrace, because I had hitherto no regular information of it, and might suppose myself wholly ignorant of any such design; neither could I reasonably conceive that the Emperor would discover the secret while I was out of his power: wherein, however, it soon appeared I was deceived.

I shall not trouble the reader with the particular account of my reception at this court, which was suitable to the generosity of so great a prince; nor of the difficulties I was in for want of a house and bed, being forced to lie on the ground, wrapped up in my coverlet.

Chapter 8: *The author, by a lucky accident, finds means to leave* Blefuscu; *and, after some difficulties, returns safe to his native country.*

Three days after my arrival, walking out of curiosity to the north-east coast of the island, I observed, about half a league off, in the sea, somewhat that looked like a boat overturned. I pulled off my shoes and stockings, and wading two or three hundred yards, I found the object to approach nearer by force of the tide; and then plainly saw it to be a real boat, which I supposed might, by some tempest, have been driven from a ship; whereupon I returned immediately towards the city, and desired his Imperial Majesty to lend me twenty of the tallest vessels he had left after the loss of his fleet, and three thousand seamen under the command of his Vice-Admiral. This fleet sailed round, while I went back the shortest way to the coast where I first discovered the boat; I found the tide had driven it still nearer. The seamen were all provided with cordage, which I had beforehand twisted to a sufficient strength. When the ships came up, I stripped myself, and waded till I came within an hundred yards of the boat, after which I was forced to swim till I got up to it. The seamen threw me the end of the cord, which I fastened to a hole in the fore-part of the boat, and the other end to a man of war; but I found all my labor to little purpose; for being out of my depth, I was not able to work. In this necessity, I was forced to swim behind, and push the boat forwards as often as I could, with one of my hands; and the tide favoring me, I advanced so far, that I could just hold up my chin and feel the ground. I rested two or three minutes, and then gave the boat another shove, and so on till the sea was no higher than my armpits; and now the most laborious part being over, I took out my other cables, which were stowed in one of the ships, and fastening them first to the boat, and then to nine of the vessels which attended me, the wind being favorable, the seamen towed, and I shoved till we arrived within forty yards of the shore; and waiting till the tide was out, I got dry to the boat, and by the assistance of two thousand men, with ropes and engines, I made a shift to turn it on its bottom, and found it was but little damaged.

I shall not trouble the reader with the difficulties I was under by the help of certain paddles, which cost me ten days making, to get my boat to the royal port of Blefuscu, where a mighty concourse of people appeared upon my arrival, full of wonder at the sight of so prodigious a vessel. I told the Emperor that my good fortune had thrown this boat in my way, to carry me to some place from whence I might return into my native country, and begged his Majesty's orders for getting materials to fit it up, together with his license to depart; which, after some kind expostulations, he was pleased to grant.

I did very much wonder, in all this time, not to have heard of any express relating to me from our Emperor to the court of Blefuscu. But I was afterwards given privately to understand, that his Imperial Majesty, never imagining I had the least notice of his designs, believed I was only gone to Blefuscu in performance of my promise, according to the license he had given me, which was well known at our court, and would return in a few days when that ceremony was ended. But he was at last in pain at my long absence; and after consulting with the Treasurer, and the rest of that cabal, a person of quality was dispatched with the copy of the articles against me. This envoy had instructions to represent to the monarch of Blefuscu the great lenity of his master, who was content to punish me no farther than with the loss of my eyes; that I had fled from justice, and if I did not return in two hours, I should be deprived of my title of *Nardac,* and declared a traitor. The envoy further added, that in order to maintain the peace and amity between both empires, his master expected, that his brother of Blefuscu would give orders to have me sent back to Lilliput, bound hand and foot, to be punished as a traitor.

The Emperor of Blefuscu having taken three days to consult, returned an answer consisting of many civilities and excuses. He said, that as for sending me bound, his brother knew it was impossible; that, although I had deprived him of his fleet, yet he owed great obligations to me for many good offices I had done him in making the peace. That however both their Majesties would soon be made easy; for I had found a prodigious vessel on the shore, able to carry me on the sea, which he had given order to fit up with my own assistance and direction; and he hoped in a few weeks both empires would be freed from so insupportable an incumbrance.

With this answer the envoy returned to Lilliput, and the monarch of Blefuscu related to me all that had passed; offering me at the same time (but under the strictest confidence) his gracious protection, if I would continue in his service; wherein although I believed him sincere, yet I resolved never more to put any confidence in princes or ministers, where I could possibly avoid it; and therefore, with all due acknowledgments for his favorable intentions, I humbly begged to be excused. I told him, that since fortune, whether good or evil, had thrown a vessel in my way, I was resolved to venture myself in the ocean, rather than be an occasion of difference between two such mighty monarchs. Neither did I find the Emperor at all displeased; and I discovered by a certain accident, that he was very glad of my resolution, and so were most of his ministers.

These considerations moved me to hasten my departure somewhat sooner than I intended; to which the court, impatient to have me gone, very readily contributed. Five hundred workmen were employed to make two sails to my boat, according to my directions, by quilting thirteen fold of their strongest linen together. I was at the pains of making ropes and cables, by twisting ten, twenty or thirty of the thickest and strongest of theirs. A great stone that I happened to find, after a long search, by the sea-shore, served me for an anchor. I had the tallow of three hundred cows for greasing my boat, and other uses. I was at incredible pains in cutting down some of the largest timber-trees for oars and masts, wherein I was, however, much assisted by his Majesty's ship-carpenters, who helped me in smoothing them, after I had done the rough work.

In about a month, when all was prepared, I sent to receive his Majesty's commands, and take my leave. The Emperor and Royal Family came out of the palace; I lay down on my face to kiss his hand, which he very graciously gave me: so did the Empress and young Princes of the blood. His Majesty presented me with fifty purses of two hundred *sprugs* a-piece, together with his picture at full length, which I put immediately into one of my gloves, to keep it from being hurt. The ceremonies at my departure were too many to trouble the reader with at this time.

I stored the boat with the carcasses of an hundred oxen, and three hundred sheep, with bread and drink proportionable, and as much meat ready dressed as four hundred cooks could provide. I took with me six cows and two bulls alive, with as many ewes and rams, intending to carry them into my own country, and propagate the breed. And to feed them on board, I had a good bundle of hay, and a bag of corn. I would gladly have taken a dozen of the natives, but this was a thing the Emperor would by no means permit; and besides a diligent search into my pockets, his Majesty engaged my honor not to carry away any of his subjects, although with their own consent and desire.

Having thus prepared all things as well as I was able, I set sail on the twenty-fourth day of September 1701, at six in the morning; and when I had gone about four leagues to the northward, the wind being at south-east, at six in the evening I descried a small island about half a league to the north-west. I advanced forward, and cast anchor on the lee-side of the island, which seemed to be uninhabited. I then took some refreshment, and went to my rest. I slept well, and as I conjecture at least six hours, for I found the day broke in two hours after I awaked. It was a clear night. I eat my breakfast before the sun was up; and heaving anchor, the wind being favorable, I steered the same course that I had done the day before, wherein I was directed by my pocket-compass. My intention was to reach, if possible, one of those islands, which I had reason to believe lay to the north-east of Van Diemen's Land. I discovered nothing all that day; but upon the next, about three in the afternoon, when I had by my computation made twenty-four leagues from Blefuscu, I descried a sail steering to the south-east; my course was due east. I hailed her, but could get no answer; yet I found I gained upon her, for the wind slackened. I made all the sail I could, and in half an hour she spied me, then hung out her ancient, and discharged a gun. It is not easy to express the joy I was in upon the unexpected hope of once more seeing my beloved country, and the dear pledges I had left in it. The ship slackened her sails, and I came up with her between five and six in the evening, September 26; but my heart leaped within me to see her English colors. I put my cows and sheep into my coat-pockets, and got on board with all my little cargo of provisions. The vessel was an English merchantman, returning from Japan by the North and South Seas; the Captain, Mr. John Biddel of Deptford, a very civil man, and an excellent sailor. We were now in the latitude of 30 degrees south; there were about fifty men in the ship; and here I met an old comrade of mine, one Peter Williams,

who gave me a good character to the Captain. This gentleman treated me with kindness, and desired I would let him know what place I came from last, and whither I was bound; which I did in a few words, but he thought I was raving, and that the dangers I underwent had disturbed my head; whereupon I took my black cattle and sheep out of my pocket, which, after great astonishment, clearly convinced him of my veracity. I then showed him the gold given me by the Emperor of Blefuscu, together with his Majesty's picture at full length, and some other rarities of that country. I gave him two purses of two hundred *sprugs* each, and promised, when we arrived in England, to make him a present of a cow and a sheep big with young.

I shall not trouble the reader with a particular account of this voyage, which was very prosperous for the most part. We arrived in the Downs on the 13th of April, 1702. I had only one misfortune, that the rats on board carried away one of my sheep; I found her bones in a hole, picked clean from the flesh. The rest of my cattle I got safe on shore, and set them a grazing in a bowling-green at Greenwich, where the fineness of the grass made them feed very heartily, though I had always feared the contrary: neither could I possibly have preserved them in so long a voyage, if the Captain had not allowed me some of his best biscuit, which rubbed to powder, and mingled with water, was their constant food. The short time I continued in England, I made a considerable profit by showing my cattle to many persons of quality, and others: and before I began my second voyage, I sold them for six hundred pounds. Since my last return, I find the breed is considerably increased, especially the sheep; which I hope will prove much to the advantage of the woollen manufacture, by the fineness of the fleeces.

I stayed but two months with my wife and family; for my insatiable desire of seeing foreign countries would suffer me to continue no longer. I left fifteen hundred pounds with my wife, and fixed her in a good house at Redriff. My remaining stock I carried with me, part in money, and part in goods, in hopes to improve my fortunes. My eldest uncle John had left me an estate in land, near Epping, of about thirty pounds a year; and I had a long lease of the Black Bull in Fetter-Lane, which yielded me as much more; so that I was not in any danger of leaving my family upon the parish. My son Johnny, named so after his uncle, was at the Grammar School, and a towardly child. My daughter Betty (who is now well married, and has children) was then at her needle-work. I took leave of my wife, and boy and girl, with tears on both sides, and went on board the *Adventure,* a merchant-ship of three hundred tons, bound for Surat, Captain John Nicholas, of Liverpool, Commander. But my account of this voyage must be referred to the second part of my *Travels.*

(1726)

STUDY AIDS: 1. What instances of detailed, exact reporting do you find in the opening of Chapter 1 (paragraphs 1–4)? How does such reporting prepare for Gulliver's account of his life among the Lilliputians?

2. The Lilliputian scale of measurement is 1 to 12; that is, one English inch equals one Lilliputian foot. Does Swift apply the scale consistently? In what ways, besides giving dimensions, does he remind us of the minute size of everything in Lilliput?

3. As the notes suggest, Swift often used his story to satirize conditions in his own country. Is the SATIRE limited to politics? How is it we can feel the force of the satire today? What specific customs and practices are satirized?

4. What do we learn about Gulliver's character? Why is his character a suitable one for Swift's purpose?

5. Is the method of Chapter 6 in keeping with that of the book as a whole? Does the paragraph on p. 402/1, ll. 10–22 affect your opinion?

6. *Gulliver's Travels* is often enjoyed by children. Show how the features of the book that appeal to children do or do not contribute to its effectiveness as ALLEGORY.

A Modest Proposal

For Preventing the Children of Poor People in Ireland from Being a Burden to Their Parents or Country, and for Making Them Beneficial to the Public.

Swift's pamphlet was designed to bring about economic, social, and moral reform in England for the benefit of the suffering Irish. It makes clear the situation of the Irish as well as what the remedy should be. Note your reactions as you read; notice especially where you first realize what Swift is driving at.

It is a melancholy object to those who walk through this great town [1] or travel in the country, when they see the streets, the roads, and cabin doors, crowded with beggars of the female sex, followed by three, four, or six children, all in rags and importuning every passenger for an alms. These mothers, instead of being able to work for their honest livelihood, are forced to employ all their time in strolling to beg sustenance for their helpless infants: who as they grow up either turn thieves for want of work, or leave their dear native country to fight for the Pretender [2] in Spain, or sell themselves to the Barbadoes.

I think it is agreed by all parties that this prodigious number of children in the arms, or on the backs, or at the heels of their mothers, and frequently of their fathers, is in the present deplorable state of the kingdom a very

[1] Dublin.

[2] James Stuart, who as son of the deposed James II continued for years to press his claim to the throne, was known as the Pretender. His supporters, including some foreign kings, were known as "Jacobites."

great additional grievance; and, therefore, whoever could find out a fair, cheap, and easy method of making these children sound, useful members of the commonwealth, would deserve so well of the public as to have his statue set up for a preserver of the nation.

But my intention is very far from being confined to provide only for the children of professed beggars; it is of a much greater extent, and shall take in the whole number of infants at a certain age who are born of parents in effect as little able to support them as those who demand our charity in the streets.

As to my own part, having turned my thoughts for many years upon this important subject, and maturely weighed the several schemes of other projectors, I have always found them grossly mistaken in their computation. It is true, a child just dropped from its dam may be supported by her milk for a solar year, with little other nourishment; at most not above the value of 2s., which the mother may certainly get, or the value in scraps, by her lawful occupation of begging; and it is exactly at one year old that I propose to provide for them in such a manner as instead of being a charge upon their parents or the parish, or wanting food and raiment for the rest of their lives, they shall on the contrary contribute to the feeding, and partly to the clothing, of many thousands.

There is likewise another great advantage in my scheme, that it will prevent those voluntary abortions, and that horrid practice of women murdering their bastard children, alas! too frequent among us! sacrificing the poor innocent babes I doubt more to avoid the expense than the shame, which would move tears and pity in the most savage and inhuman breast.

The number of souls in this kingdom being usually reckoned one million and a half, of these I calculate there may be about 200,000 couple whose wives are breeders; from which number I subtract 30,000 couple who are able to maintain their own children (although I apprehend there cannot be so many, under the present distresses of the kingdom); but this being granted, there will remain 170,000 breeders. I again subtract 50,000 for those women who miscarry, or whose children die by accident or disease within the year. There only remains 120,000 children of poor parents annually born. The question therefore is, how this number shall be reared and provided for? which, as I have already said, under the present situation of affairs, is utterly impossible by all the methods hitherto proposed. For we can neither employ them in handicraft or agriculture; we neither build houses (I mean in the country) nor cultivate land; they can very seldom pick up a livelihood by stealing, till they arrive at six years old, except where they are of towardly parts; although I confess they learn the rudiments much earlier; during which time, they can however be properly looked upon only as probationers; as I have been informed by a principal gentleman in the county of Cavan, who protested to me that he never knew above one or two instances under the age of six, even in a part of the kingdom so renowned for the quickest proficiency in that art.

I am assured by our merchants, that a boy or a girl before twelve years old is no saleable commodity; and even when they come to this age they will not yield above 3l. or 3l. 2s. 6d. at most on the exchange; which cannot turn to account either to the parents or kingdom, the charge of nutriment and rags having been at least four times that value.

I shall now therefore humbly propose my own thoughts, which I hope will not be liable to the least objection.

I have been assured by a very knowing American of my acquaintance in London, that a young healthy child well nursed is at a year old a most delicious, nourishing, and wholesome food, whether stewed, roasted, baked, or boiled; and I make no doubt that it will equally serve in a fricassee or a ragout.

I do therefore humbly offer it to public consideration that of the 120,000 children already computed, 20,000 may be reserved for breed, whereof only one-fourth part to be males; which is more than we allow to sheep, black cattle, or swine; and my reason is, that these children are seldom the fruits of marriage, a circumstance not much regarded by our savages, therefore one male will be sufficient to serve four females. That the remaining 100,000 may, at a year old, be offered in sale to the persons of quality and fortune through the kingdom; always advising the mother to let them suck plentifully in the last month, so as to render them plump and fat for a good table. A child will make two dishes at an entertainment for friends; and when the family dines alone, the fore or hind quarter will make a reasonable dish, and seasoned with a little pepper or salt will be very good boiled on the fourth day, especially in winter.

I have reckoned upon a medium that a child just born will weigh 12 pounds, and in a solar year, if tolerably nursed, will increase to 28 pounds.

I grant this food will be somewhat dear, and therefore very proper for landlords, who, as they have already devoured most of the parents, seem to have the best title to the children.

Infant's flesh will be in season throughout the year, but more plentifully in March, and a little before and after; for we are told by a grave author, an eminent French physician, that fish being a prolific diet, there are more children born in Roman Catholic countries about nine months after Lent than at any other season; therefore, reckoning a year after Lent, the markets will be more glutted than usual, because the number of popish infants is at least three to one in this kingdom: and therefore it will have one other collateral advantage, by lessening the number of papists among us.

I have already computed the charge of nursing a beggar's child (in which list I reckon all cottagers, laborers, and four-fifths of the farmers) to be about 2s. per annum, rags included; and I believe no gentleman would repine to give 10s. for the carcass of a good fat child, which, as I have said, will make four dishes of excellent nutritive meat, when he has only some particular friend or his own family to dine with him. Thus the squire will learn to be a good landlord, and

grow popular among the tenants; the mother will have 8s. net profit, and be fit for work till she produces another child.

Those who are more thrifty (as I must confess the times require) may flay the carcass; the skin of which artificially dressed will make admirable gloves for ladies, and summer boots for fine gentlemen.

As to our city of Dublin, shambles may be appointed for this purpose in the most convenient parts of it, and butchers we may be assured will not be wanting; although I rather recommend buying the children alive, and dressing them hot from the knife as we do roasting pigs.

A very worthy person, a true lover of his country, and whose virtues I highly esteem, was lately pleased in discoursing on this matter to offer a refinement upon my scheme. He said that many gentlemen of this kingdom, having of late destroyed their deer, he conceived that the want of venison might be well supplied by the bodies of young lads and maidens, not exceeding fourteen years of age nor under twelve; so great a number of both sexes in every country being now ready to starve for want of work and service; and these to be disposed of by their parents, if alive, or otherwise by their nearest relations. But with due deference to so excellent a friend and so deserving a patriot, I cannot be altogether in his sentiments; for as to the males, my American acquaintance assured me, from frequent experience, that their flesh was generally tough and lean, like that of our school-boys by continual exercise, and their taste disagreeable; and to fatten them would not answer the charge. Then as to the females, it would, I think, with humble submission be a loss to the public, because they soon would become breeders themselves: and besides, it is not improbable that some scrupulous people might be apt to censure such a practice (although indeed very unjustly), as a little bordering upon cruelty; which, I confess, has always been with me the strongest objection against any project, how well soever intended.

But in order to justify my friend, he confessed that this expedient was put into his head by the famous Psalmanazar,[3] a native of the island Formosa, who came from thence to London about twenty years ago, and in conversation told my friend, that in his country when any young person happened to be put to death, the executioner sold the carcass to persons of quality as a prime dainty; and that in his time the body of a plump girl of fifteen, who was crucified for an attempt to poison the emperor, was sold to his imperial majesty's prime minister of state, and other great mandarins of the court, in joints from the gibbet, at 400 crowns. Neither indeed can I deny, that if the same use were made of several plump young girls in this town, who without one single groat to their fortunes cannot stir abroad without a chair, and appear at playhouse and assemblies in foreign fineries which they never will pay for, the kingdom would not be the worse.

Some persons of a desponding spirit are in great concern about that vast number of poor people, who are aged, diseased, or maimed, and I have been desired to employ my thoughts what course may be taken to ease the nation of so grievous an encumbrance. But I am not in the least pain upon the matter, because it is very well known that they are every day dying and rotting by cold and famine, and filth and vermin, as fast as can be reasonably expected. And as to the young laborers, they are now in as hopeful a condition; they cannot get work, and consequently pine away for want of nourishment, to a degree that if at any time they are accidentally hired to common labor, they have not strength to perform it; and thus the country and themselves are happily delivered from the evils to come.

I have too long digressed, and therefore shall return to my subject. I think the advantages by the proposal which I have made are obvious and many, as well as of the highest importance.

For first, as I have already observed, it would greatly lessen the number of papists, with whom we are yearly overrun, being the principal breeders of the nation as well as our most dangerous enemies; and who stay at home on purpose to deliver the kingdom to the Pretender, hoping to take their advantage by the absence of so many good protestants, who have chosen rather to leave their country than stay at home and pay tithes against their conscience to an episcopal curate.

Secondly, The poor tenants will have something valuable of their own, which by law may be made liable to distress and help to pay their landlord's rent, their corn and cattle being already seized, and money a thing unknown.

Thirdly, Whereas the maintenance of 100,-000 children, from two years old and upward, cannot be computed at less than 10s. a-piece per annum, the nation's stock will be thereby increased £50,000 per annum, beside the profit of a new dish introduced to the tables of all gentlemen of fortune in the kingdom who have any refinement in taste. And the money will circulate among ourselves, the goods being entirely of our own growth and manufacture.

Fourthly, The constant breeders, beside the gain of 8s. sterling per annum by the sale of their children, will be rid of the charge of maintaining them after the first year.

Fifthly, This food would likewise bring great custom to taverns; where the vintners will certainly be so prudent as to procure the best receipts for dressing it to perfection, and consequently have their houses frequented by all the fine gentlemen, who justly value themselves upon their knowledge in good eating: and a skilful cook, who understands how to oblige his guests, will contrive to make it as expensive as they please.

Sixthly, This would be a great inducement to marriage, which all wise nations have either encouraged by rewards or enforced by laws and penalties. It would increase the care and tenderness of mothers toward their children, when they were sure of a settlement for life to the poor babes, provided in some sort by the public, to their annual profit instead of expense. We should soon see an

[3] George Psalmanazar, born in France, was a noted impostor. He claimed to be a Japanese Christian and wrote A Description of Formosa (1705). He admitted his imposture in 1728.

honest emulation among the married women, which of them could bring the fattest child to the market. Men would become as fond of their wives during the time of their pregnancy as they are now of their mares in foal, their cows in calf, their sows when they are ready to farrow; nor offer to beat or kick them (as is too frequent a practice) for fear of a miscarriage.

Many other advantages might be enumerated. For instance, the addition of some thousand carcasses in our exportation of barreled beef, the propagation of swine's flesh, and improvement in the art of making good bacon, so much wanted among us by the great destruction of pigs, too frequent at our tables; which are no way comparable in taste or magnificence to a well-grown, fat, yearling child, which roasted whole will make a considerable figure at a lord mayor's feast or any other public entertainment. But this and many others I omit, being studious of brevity.

Supposing that 1000 families in this city would be constant customers for infants' flesh, beside others who might have it at merrymeetings, particularly at weddings and christenings, I compute that Dublin would take off annually about 20,000 carcasses; and the rest of the kingdom (where probably they will be sold somewhat cheaper) the remaining 80,000.

I can think of no one objection that will possibly be raised against this proposal, unless it should be urged that the number of people will be thereby much lessened in the kingdom. This I freely own, and it was indeed one principal design in offering it to the world. I desire the reader will observe, that I calculate my remedy for this one individual kingdom of Ireland and for no other that ever was, is, or I think ever can be upon earth. Therefore let no man talk to me of other expedients:[4] of taxing our absentees at 5s. a pound: of using neither clothes nor household furniture except what is of our own growth and manufacture: of utterly rejecting the materials and instruments that promote foreign luxury: of curing the expensiveness of pride, vanity,

idleness, and gaming in our women: of introducing a vein of parsimony, prudence, and temperance: of learning to love our country, in the want of which we differ even from *Laplanders* and the inhabitants of *Topinamboo*:[5] of quitting our animosities and factions, nor acting any longer like the Jews, who were murdering one another at the very moment their city was taken:[6] of being a little cautious not to sell our country and consciences for nothing: of teaching landlords to have at least one degree of mercy toward their tenants: lastly, of putting a spirit of honesty, industry, and skill into our shopkeepers; who, if a resolution could now be taken to buy only our native goods, would immediately unite to cheat and exact upon us in the price, the measure, and the goodness, nor could ever yet be brought to make one fair proposal of just dealing, though often and earnestly invited to it.

Therefore I repeat, let no man talk to me of these and the like expedients, till he has at least some glimpse of hope that there will be ever some hearty and sincere attempt to put them in practice.

But as to myself, having been wearied out for many years with offering vain, idle, visionary thoughts, and at length utterly despairing of success I fortunately fell upon this proposal; which, as it is wholly new, so it has something solid and real, of no expense and little trouble, full in our own power, and whereby we can incur no danger in disobliging ENGLAND. For this kind of commodity will not bear exportation, the flesh being of too tender a consistence to admit a long continuance in salt, although perhaps I could name a country which would be glad to eat up our whole nation without it.

After all, I am not so violently bent upon my own opinion as to reject any offer proposed by wise men which shall be found equally innocent, cheap, easy, and effectual. But before something of that kind shall be advanced in contradiction to my scheme, and

[4] Most of the following proposals are ones which Swift had seriously advanced in earlier pamphlets.

[5] An area in Brazil.
[6] A reference to the capture of Jerusalem by the Romans in 70 A.D., when several Jewish factions quarreled among themselves.

offering a better, I desire the author or authors will be pleased maturely to consider two points. First, as things now stand, how they will be able to find food and raiment for 100,000 useless mouths and backs. And secondly, there being a round million of creatures in human figure throughout this kingdom, whose whole subsistence put into a common stock would leave them in debt 2,000,000*l.* sterling, adding those who are beggars by profession to the bulk of farmers, cottagers, and laborers, with their wives and children who are beggars in effect; I desire those politicians who dislike my overture, and may perhaps be so bold as to attempt an answer, that they will first ask the parents of these mortals, whether they would not at this day think it a great happiness to have been sold for food at a year old in the manner I prescribe, and thereby have avoided such a perpetual scene of misfortunes as they have since gone through by the oppression of landlords, the impossibility of paying rent without money or trade, the want of common sustenance, with neither house nor clothes to cover them from the inclemencies of the weather, and the most inevitable prospect of entailing the like or greater miseries upon their breed for ever.

I profess, in the sincerity of my heart, that I have not the least personal interest in endeavoring to promote this necessary work, having no other motive than the public good of my country, by advancing our trade, providing for infants, relieving the poor, and giving some pleasure to the rich. I have no children by which I can propose to get a single penny; the youngest being nine years old, and my wife past child-bearing.
(1729)

STUDY AIDS: 1. Swift's method is one of sustained IRONY. Because irony means something different, often the exact opposite, from what it says, one must give a clue as to his real meaning. A speaker can do this with his voice or facial expression; a writer must plant the clue in his written words. What is the clue in Swift's discourse? At what point did you discover it?

2. One reason for the success of Swift's discourse is that all aspects of the presentation are controlled by the character of the author—not Swift himself, but his spokesman. Forget, for a moment, the monstrous nature of his proposal, and notice what a compelling advocate he is: (1) Is his character, as revealed here, such as to win your confidence? Is he well informed, modest, tender-hearted? Find evidence of these and other traits. (2) Is his argument logical and presented in orderly fashion? (3) Is his prose style suited to his character, his subject, and his purpose? Would you call it ornate, involved, emotional? To what extent does he use figures of speech?

James Thomson
(1700–1748)

THE POETRY OF THOMSON IS OF HISTORICAL INTEREST IN ENGLISH LITERATURE. IT IS A poetry of transition: partly neoclassic, but containing qualities which later become touchstones of romanticism. It is neoclassic in its objective description and in its avowed moral aim, achieved largely by digressions on humanity, patriotism, commerce, and the deistic belief that this is the best of all possible worlds.

The main interest of the poetry, however, lies in its foreshadowing of romantic tendencies. Thomson, living at a time when London was celebrated in English literature as the center of English life, preferred to paint external nature with an almost scientific accuracy of concrete detail. His "landscapes" are done in Miltonic blank verse rather than in the heroic couplet of his contemporaries; but, because Thomson attempted an elevated style in them, they abound in Latinisms and poetic diction. The attitude toward nature expressed in *The Seasons* is for the most part realistic, but occasionally it can be identified with primitivism. This same backward glance to an age of greater simplicity perhaps led Thomson to imitate Spenser in *The Castle of Indolence* (1748). Because of its affinity with the romantic temper, *The Seasons,* from which the following selection, "Winter," is drawn, was more widely read in the nineteenth century than the poetry of Pope and Dryden.

Winter

See, Winter comes, to rule the varied year,
Sullen and sad, with all his rising train—
Vapors, and clouds, and storms. Be these my
    theme,
These, that exalt the soul to solemn thought,
And heavenly musing. Welcome, kindred
    glooms! [1]   5
Congenial horrors, hail! with frequent foot,
Pleased have I, in my cheerful morn of life,
When nursed by careless solitude I lived,
And sung of nature with unceasing joy,
Pleased have I wandered through your rough
    domain;   10
Trod the pure virgin-snows, myself as pure;
Heard the winds roar, and the big torrent
    burst;
Or seen the deep-fermenting tempest brewed,
In the grim evening-sky. Thus passed the time,
Till through the lucid chambers of the
    south   15
Looked out the joyous Spring, looked out, and
    smiled.
    To thee, the patron of this first essay,
The Muse, O Wilmington! [2] renews her song.
Since has she rounded the revolving year:
Skimmed the gay spring; on eagle-pinions
    borne,   20
Attempted through the summer-blaze to rise;
Then swept o'er autumn with the shadowy
    gale;

And now among the wintry clouds again,
Rolled in the doubling storm, she tries to soar;
To swell her note with all the rushing
    winds;   25
To suit her sounding cadence to the floods;
As is her theme,[3] her numbers wildly great:
Thrice happy, could she fill thy judging ear
With bold description, and with manly
    thought.
Nor art thou skilled in awful schemes
    alone,   30
And how to make a mighty people thrive;
But equal goodness, sound integrity,
A firm, unshaken, uncorrupted soul
Amid a sliding age, and burning strong,
Not vainly blazing, for thy country's weal, 35
A steady spirit, regularly free—
These, each exalting each, the statesman's
    light
Into the patriot; these, the public hope
And eye to thee converting, bid the Muse
Record what envy dares not flattery call. 40
    Now when the cheerless empire of the sky
To Capricorn the Centaur-Archer yields,
And fierce Aquarius stains the inverted year;
Hung o'er the farthest verge of heaven, the
    sun
Scarce spreads o'er ether the dejected day. 45
Faint are his gleams, and ineffectual shoot
His struggling rays, in horizontal lines,
Through the thick air; as clothed in cloudy
    storm,
Weak, wan, and broad, he skirts the southern
    sky;

[1] Milton's "melancholy," which produced contemplation in *Il Penseroso,* has become sadness for its own sake in Thomson.

[2] Thomson dedicated *Winter* to the Earl of Wilmington. Since 1726 he had written *Summer* (1727), *Spring* (1728), and *Autumn* (1730).

[3] What is Thomson's aim in his poetry as expressed in ll. 27–40?

And, soon descending, to the long dark
    night,   50
Wide-shading all, the prostrate world resigns.
Nor is the night unwished; while vital heat,
Light, life, and joy the dubious day forsake.
Meantime, in sable cincture, shadows vast,
Deep tinged and damp, and congregated
    clouds,   55
And all the vapory turbulence of heaven,
Involve the face of things. Thus winter falls,
A heavy gloom oppressive o'er the world,
Through nature shedding influence malign,
And rouses up the seeds of dark disease.   60
The soul of man dies in him, loathing life,
And black with more than melancholy views.
The cattle droop; and o'er the furrowed land,
Fresh from the plough, the dun discolored
    flocks,
Untended spreading, crop the wholesome
    root.   65
Along the woods, along the moorish fens,
Sighs the sad genius of the coming storm;
And up among the loose disjointed cliffs,
And fractured mountains wild, the brawling
    brook,
And cave, presageful, send a hollow moan, 70
Resounding long in listening fancy's ear.
    Then comes the father of the tempest forth,
Wrapped in black glooms. First, joyless rains
    obscure
Drive through the mingling skies with vapor
    foul,
Dash on the mountain's brow, and shake the
    woods,   75
That grumbling wave below. The unsightly
    plain
Lies a brown deluge, as the low-bent clouds
Pour flood on flood, yet unexhausted still
Combine, and deepening into night, shut up
The day's fair face. The wanderers of heav-
    en,[4]   80
Each to his home, retire; save those that love
To take their pastime in the troubled air,
Or skimming flutter round the dimly pool.
The cattle from the untasted fields return,

And ask, with meaning low, their wonted
    stalls,   85
Or ruminate in the contiguous shade.
Thither the household feathery people crowd,
The crested cock, with all his female train.
Pensive, and dripping; while the cottage-hind
Hangs o'er the enlivening blaze, and taleful
    there   90
Recounts his simple frolic: much he talks,
And much he laughs, nor recks the storm that
    blows
Without, and rattles on his humble roof.
    Wide o'er the brim, with many a torrent
    swelled,[5]
And the mixed ruin of its banks o'erspread, 95
At last the roused-up river pours along:
Resistless, roaring, dreadful, down it comes,
From the rude mountain and the mossy wild,
Tumbling through rocks abrupt, and sound-
    ing far;
Then o'er the sanded valley floating
    spreads,   100
Calm, sluggish, silent; till again, constrained
Between two meeting hills, it bursts a way,
Where rocks and woods o'erhang the turbid
    stream;
There gathering triple force, rapid and deep,
It boils, and wheels, and foams, and thunders
    through.   105
    Nature! great parent! whose unceasing
    hand [6]
Rolls round the seasons of the changeful year,
How mighty, how majestic, are thy works!
With what a pleasing dread they swell the
    soul,
That sees astonished! and astonished sings! 110
Ye too, ye winds! that now begin to blow
With boisterous sweep, I raise my voice to
    you.
Where are your stores, ye powerful beings!
    say,
Where your aerial magazines reserved,
To swell the brooding terrors of the storm? 115

[5] How do ll. 94–105 do more than simply describe
a scene?

[6] Why are ll. 106–110 inconsistent with the TONE
of the poem? Is there any preparation for this
passage? Notice that Thomson often separates descriptive passages with these homilies. What is their
purpose? How does it relate to his poetic aim expressed in ll. 27–40?

[4] Who are these? This is an example of eighteenth-century POETIC DICTION. Is it a satisfactory
metaphor? What does a metaphor attempt to do?
What advantages does a satisfactory and exact
metaphor have over direct statement?

In what far-distant region of the sky,
Hushed in deep silence, sleep ye when 'tis
   calm?
   When from the pallid sky the sun descends,
With many a spot, that o'er his glaring orb
Uncertain wanders, stained, red fiery
   streaks   120
Begin to flush around. The reeling clouds
Stagger with dizzy poise, as doubting yet
Which master to obey; while, rising slow,
Blank in the leaden-colored east, the moon
Wears a wan circle round her blunted
   horns.   125
Seen through the turbid, fluctuating air,
The stars obtuse emit a shivering ray;
Or frequent seem to shoot athwart the gloom,
And long behind them trail the whitening
   blaze.
Snatched in short eddies, plays the withered
   leaf   130
And on the flood the dancing feather floats.
With broadened nostrils to the sky upturned,
The conscious heifer snuffs the stormy gale.
Even as the matron, at her nightly task,
With pensive labor draws the flaxen
   thread,   135
The wasted taper and the crackling flame
Foretell the blast. But chief the plumy race,
The tenants of the sky, its changes speak.
Retiring from the downs, where all day
   long
They picked their scanty fare, a blackening
   train   140
Of clamorous rooks thick-urge their weary
   flight,
And seek the closing shelter of the grove;
Assiduous, in his bower, the wailing owl
Plies his sad song. The cormorant on high
Wheels from the deep, and screams along the
   land.   145
Loud shrieks the soaring hern; and with wild
   wing
The circling sea-fowl cleave the flaky clouds.
Ocean, unequal pressed, with broken tide
And blind commotion heaves; while from the
   shore,
Eat into caverns by the restless wave,   150
And forest-rustling mountains, comes a voice
That, solemn sounding, bids the world pre-
   pare.

Then issues forth the storm with sudden
   burst,
And hurls the whole precipitated air
Down in a torrent. On the passive main   155
Descends the ethereal force, and with strong
   gust
Turns from its bottom the discolored deep.
Through the black night that sits immense
   around,
Lashed into foam, the fierce conflicting brine
Seems o'er a thousand raging waves to
   burn: 160
Meantime the mountain-billows, to the clouds
In dreadful tumult swelled, surge above
   surge,
Burst into chaos with tremendous roar,
And anchored navies from their stations
   drive,
Wild as the winds, across the howling
   waste   165
Of mighty waters: now the inflated wave
Straining they scale, and now impetuous
   shoot
Into the secret chambers of the deep,
The wintry Baltic thundering o'er their head.
Emerging thence again, before the breath   170
Of full-exerted heaven they wing their
   course,
And dart on distant coasts—if some sharp
   rock,
Or shoal insidious, break not their career,
And in loose fragments fling them floating
   round.
   Nor less at land the loosened tempest
   reigns: 175
The mountain thunders; and its sturdy sons
Stoop to the bottom of the rocks they shade.
Lone on the midnight steep, and all aghast,
The dark wayfaring stranger breathless toils,
And, often falling, climbs against the
   blast.   180
Low waves the rooted forest, vexed, and
   sheds
What of its tarnished honors yet remain—
Dashed down, and scattered by the tearing
   wind's
Assiduous fury, its gigantic limbs.
Thus struggling through the dissipated
   grove,   185
The whirling tempest raves along the plain;

And, on the cottage thatched, or lordly roof,
Keen-fastening, shakes them to the solid base.
Sleep frighted flies; and round the rocking dome,
For entrance eager, howls the savage blast. 190
Then too, they say, through all the burthened air,
Long groans are heard, shrill sounds, and distant sighs,
That, uttered by the demon of the night,
Warn the devoted [7] wretch of woe and death.
  Huge uproar lords it wide. The clouds commixed 195
With stars swift-gliding, sweep along the sky.
All nature reels: till nature's king, who oft
Amid tempestuous darkness dwells alone,
And on the wings of the careering wind
Walks dreadfully serene, commands a calm: 200
Then straight air, sea, and earth are hushed at once.
  As yet 'tis midnight deep. The weary clouds,
Slow-meeting, mingle into solid gloom.
Now, while the drowsy world lies lost in sleep,
Let me associate with the serious night, 205
And contemplation, her sedate compeer;
Let me shake off the intrusive cares of day,
And lay the meddling senses all aside.
  Where now, ye lying vanities of life!
Ye ever-tempting, ever-cheating train! 210
Where are you now? and what is your amount?
Vexation, disappointment, and remorse.
Sad, sickening thought! And yet, deluded man,
A scene of crude disjointed visions past,
And broken slumbers, rises still resolved, 215
With new-flushed hopes, to run the giddy round.
  Father of light and life! thou good supreme!
O teach me what is good! teach me thyself!
Save me from folly, vanity, and vice,
From every low pursuit; and feed my soul 220
With knowledge, conscious peace, and virtue pure—
Sacred, substantial, never-fading bliss!

    [7] Doomed.

The keener tempests come: and fuming dun
From all the livid east, or piercing north,
Thick clouds ascend, in whose capacious womb 225
A vapory deluge lies, to snow congealed.
Heavy they roll their fleecy world along;
And the sky saddens with the gathered storm.
Through the hushed air the whitening shower descends,
At first thin-wavering; till at last the flakes 230
Fall broad and wide and fast, dimming the day,
With a continual flow. The cherished fields
Put on their winter-robe of purest white.
'Tis brightness all; save where the new snow melts
Along the mazy current. Low the woods 235
Bow their hoar head; and, ere the languid sun
Faint from the west emits his evening ray,
Earth's universal face, deep-hid, and chill,
Is one wild dazzling waste, that buries wide
The works of man. Drooping, the laborer-ox 240
Stands covered o'er with snow, and then demands
The fruit of all his toil. The fowls of heaven,
Tamed by the cruel season, crowd around
The winnowing store, and claim the little boon
Which providence assigns them. One alone,[8] 245
The redbreast, sacred to the household gods,
Wisely regardful of the embroiling sky,
In joyless fields, and thorny thickets, leaves
His shivering mates, and pays to trusted man
His annual visit. Half afraid, he first 250
Against the window beats; then brisk alights
On the warm hearth; then, hopping o'er the floor,
Eyes all the smiling family askance,
And pecks, and starts, and wonders where he is—
Till, more familiar grown, the table-crumbs 255
Attract his slender feet. The foodless wilds

    [8] What two examples of winter's harshness does Thomson cite in ll. 245–261? Is the example in ll. 276–321 sentimental or true to nature?

Pour forth their brown inhabitants. The hare,
Though timorous of heart, and hard beset
By death in various forms, dark snares, and
    dogs,
And more unpitying men, the garden
    seeks,   260
Urged on by fearless want. The bleating kind
Eye the bleak heaven, and next the glisten-
    ing earth,
With looks of dumb despair; then, sad dis-
    persed,
Dig for the withered herb through heaps of
    snow.
    Now, shepherds, to your helpless charge
    be kind: 265
Baffle the raging year, and fill their pens
With food at will; lodge them below the
    storm,
And watch them strict; for from the
    bellowing east,
In this dire season, oft the whirlwind's wing
Sweeps up the burden of whole wintry
    plains   270
In one wide waft, and o'er the hapless
    flocks,
Hid in the hollow of two neighboring hills,
The billowy tempest whelms; till, upward
    urged,
The valley to a shining mountain swells,
Tipped with a wreath high-curling in the
    sky.   275
    As thus the snows arise, and, foul and
    fierce,
All winter drives along the darkened air,
In his own loose-revolving fields, the swain
Disastered stands: sees other hills ascend,
Of unknown joyless brow; and other
    scenes,   280
Of horrid prospect, shag the trackless plain:
Nor finds the river nor the forest, hid
Beneath the formless wild: but wanders on
From hill to dale, still more and more astray—
Impatient flouncing through the drifted
    heaps,   285
Stung with the thoughts of home; the
    thoughts of home
Rush on his nerves, and call their vigor forth
In many a vain attempt. How sinks his soul!
What black despair, what horror fills his
    heart,

When, for the dusky spot which fancy
    feigned   290
His tufted cottage rising through the snow,
He meets the roughness of the middle waste,
Far from the track and blest abode of man;
While round him night resistless closes fast,
And every tempest, howling o'er his head, 295
Renders the savage wilderness more wild.
Then throng the busy shapes into his mind,
Of covered pits, unfathomably deep,
A dire descent! beyond the power of frost;
Of faithless bogs; of precipices huge,   300
Smoothed up with snow; and, what is land,
    unknown,
What water, of the still unfrozen spring,
In the loose marsh or solitary lake,
Where the fresh fountain from the bottom
    boils.
These check his fearful steps; and down he
    sinks   305
Beneath the shelter of the shapeless drift,
Thinking o'er all the bitterness of death,
Mixed with the tender anguish nature shoots
Through the wrung bosom of the dying
    man—
His wife, his children, and his friends
    unseen.   310
In vain for him the officious wife prepares
The fire fair-blazing, and the vestment warm;
In vain his little children, peeping out
Into the mingling storm, demand their sire
With tears of artless innocence. Alas!   315
Nor wife, nor children, more shall he
    behold;
Nor friends, nor sacred home. On every
    nerve
The deadly winter seizes, shuts up sense,
And, o'er his inmost vitals creeping cold,
Lays him along the snows, a stiffened
    corpse!   320
Stretched out and bleaching in the northern
    blast.

. . . .

(1726)

STUDY AIDS: 1. Do you experience winter
in this poem or read only a description of it?
Why?
    2. Pick out a few scenes from the poem which

might easily be painted landscapes. How does Thomson try to "frame" these paintings?

3. Primitivism, or the romantic belief that primitive man is more noble because he has remained closer to nature and has been less subject to the corrupt influences of society, developed along two lines in the eighteenth century. (1) Chronological primitivism commended the happy virtuous state of primitive man in his early history, e.g., when in the Garden of Eden; however, (2) cultural primitivism turned in discontent from civilization to a simpler way of life, often to that of existing primitive peoples, more often to the Eden of the future which science hoped to produce. If cultural primitivism turned to primitive man enjoying his virtues in a tropical land of abundance, it was "soft"; if it believed that the struggle for existence in northern lands produced virtue in primitive man, it was "hard." Both kinds of primitivism exist in *The Seasons*. What kind is to be found in *Winter*?

4. Is our contemporary movement toward suburban life related to primitivism?

William Collins
(1721–1759)

The poetry of Collins met with little success in the poet's lifetime. Like Gray, he was a lyric poet of small output, writing in a period of transition. His poetry, however, differs from Gray's in that it is often ambiguous, with the more romantic qualities of wildness and disorder, which Dr. Johnson called Collins' "enchantment." This characteristic is perhaps the result of the poet's belief that poetry should be passionately felt, freely imagined, and possessed of "some divine excess."

Collins, like Joseph and Thomas Warton, developed a new type of ode patterned on *L'Allegro* and *Il Penseroso*: a "descriptive and allegorical ode," which treated a personified abstraction after the pictorial fashion of the landscape painters Salvator Rosa, Nicholas Poussin, and Claude Lorrain.

The central lyric achievement of Collins is the twelve *Odes on Several Descriptive and Allegorical Subjects* (1746). The volume was a failure, and Collins burned the unsold copies. In 1749 he wrote the *Ode on the Popular Superstitions of the Highlands of Scotland,* an incomplete poem which fused his scholarship with his taste for the medieval and the primitive. In 1751 Collins began to show signs of mental disorder, and the last years of his life were passed in poverty, insanity, and obscurity.

Ode to Evening

If aught of oaten stop,[1] or pastoral song,
May hope, chaste Eve, to soothe thy modest
    ear,
    Like thy own solemn springs,
    Thy springs, and dying gales;

O nymph reserved, while now the bright-
    haired sun   5
Sits in yon western tent, whose cloudy skirts,
    With brede[2] ethereal wove
    O'erhang his wavy bed:

[1] Shepherd's flute.

[2] Embroidery.

Now air is hushed, save where the weak-eyed
    bat,
With short shrill shriek, flits by on leathern
    wing;   10
    Or where the beetle winds
    His small but sullen horn,

As oft he rises 'midst the twilight path,
Against the pilgrim borne in heedless hum:
    Now teach me, maid composed,   15
    To breathe some softened strain,

Whose numbers, stealing through thy dark-
    ening vale,
May not unseemly with its stillness suit;
    As, musing slow, I hail
    Thy genial loved return!   20

For when thy folding-star [3] arising shows
His paly circlet, at his warning lamp
    The fragrant Hours, and elves
    Who slept in flowers the day,

And many a nymph who wreathes her brows
    with sedge,   25
And sheds the freshening dew, and, lovelier
    still,
    The pensive Pleasures sweet,
    Prepare thy shadowy car.

Then lead, calm votaress,[4] where some sheety
    lake
Cheers the lone heath, or some time-hallowed
    pile,   30
    Or upland fallows gray,
    Reflect its [5] last cool gleam.

But when chill blustering winds, or driving
    rain,

Forbid my willing feet, be mine the hut,
    That from the mountain's side,   35
    Views wilds, and swelling floods,

And hamlets brown, and dim-discovered
    spires,
And hears their simple bell, and marks o'er
    all
    Thy dewy fingers draw
    The gradual dusky veil.   40

While Spring shall pour his showers, as oft
    he wont,
And bathe thy breathing tresses, meekest
    Eve!
    While Summer loves to sport
    Beneath thy lingering light;

While sallow Autumn fills thy lap with
    leaves;   45
Or Winter, yelling through the troublous air.
    Affrights thy shrinking train,
    And rudely rends thy robes;

So long, sure-found beneath the sylvan shed,
Shall Fancy, Friendship, Science,[6] rose-lipped
    Health,   50
    Thy gentlest influence own,
    And hymn thy favorite name!
(1746)

STUDY AIDS: 1. Notice the syntax of the
first sentence. What is its subject? Its main
verb?
    2. What elements in the personification of
Evening indicate that Collins may have been
thinking of the Garden of Eden?
    3. What emotion suffuses the ode?

Ode Written in the Beginning of the Year 1746 [1]

How sleep the brave, who sink to rest,
By all their country's wishes blest!
When Spring, with dewy fingers cold,

Returns to deck their hallowed mold,
She there shall dress a sweeter sod   5
Than Fancy's feet have ever trod.

[3] The evening star, whose appearance marks the
time for sheep to return to their fold.
[4] One consecrated by a vow.
[5] What is the antecedent of this pronoun?
[6] Knowledge.

[1] This poem was probably written to commemorate
the Englishmen killed during the Jacobite Rebellion
in the battle of Falkland (January 17, 1746), where
they were defeated by the Young Pretender, a
descendant of James II.

By fairy hands their knell is rung;
By forms unseen their dirge is sung;
There Honor comes, a pilgrim gray,
To bless the turf that wraps their clay;　10
And Freedom shall a while repair,
To dwell a weeping hermit there!
(1746)

STUDY AIDS: 1. What is the meaning of
ll. 3–6? What is "Fancy" (l. 6)?
2. Collins uses Milton's technique of listing
PERSONIFICATIONS. How does this add to the
meaning and emotion of the poem?

Thomas Gray
(1716–1771)

THE POETRY OF THOMAS GRAY AND WILLIAM COLLINS MARKS THE RESURGENCE OF LYRIC
verse in the eighteenth century. It is indeed strange that the intimate voice of the lyric
should be heard from Gray, a man who distrusted any show of emotion. He was a
learned man, a professor of history and modern languages at Cambridge, but he was too
fastidious and self-conscious to lecture. He preferred to spend his life within the environs
of the university, reading, studying Germanic and Celtic languages, writing letters to his
friends, and working on his poetry.

His poems are few, but they show his neoclassic respect for didacticism, order, and perfection; for example, the famous and much quoted *Elegy Written in a Country Churchyard* was revised for seven years before Gray published it anonymously. However, as Gray
is a poet of the transitional period between neoclassicism and early romanticism, his poetry
also reveals romantic tendencies in its sympathy for the common man, its interest in
the past, and its melancholy mood. The most romantic of all his work are the two Pindaric
odes of 1757, *The Progress of Poesy* and *The Bard,* which describe the exalted position of
poetry in a primitive society. Even here, although romantic in impulse and temper, the
odes are neoclassic in their diction, form, and stateliness.

Elegy Written in a Country Churchyard

The curfew tolls the knell of parting day,
　The lowing herd wind slowly o'er the lea,
The ploughman homeward plods his weary
　　way,
　And leaves the world to darkness and to
　　me.[1]

[1] The structure of the poem is interesting in its
movement from the external world to the internal
world of the poet's mind. Notice here that the poet
is left alone in the world of darkness, which is conducive to melancholy and contemplation (cf. *Il
Penseroso*).

Now fades the glimmering landscape on the
　sight,　5
　And all the air a solemn stillness holds,
Save where the beetle wheels his droning
　flight,
　And drowsy tinklings lull the distant folds;

Save that from yonder ivy-mantled tower,
　The moping owl does to the moon
　　complain　10
Of such as, wandering near her secret bower,
　Molest her ancient solitary reign.

Beneath those rugged elms, that yew-tree's
    shade,
  Where heaves the turf in many a
    moldering heap,
Each in his narrow cell for ever laid,   15
  The rude forefathers of the hamlet sleep.

The breezy call of incense-breathing Morn,[2]
  The swallow twittering from the straw-built
    shed,
The cock's shrill clarion, or the echoing horn,
  No more shall rouse them from their lowly
    bed.   20

For them no more the blazing hearth shall
    burn,
  Or busy housewife ply her evening care:
No children run to lisp their sire's return,
  Or climb his knees the envied kiss to share.

Oft did the harvest to their sickle yield;   25
  Their furrow oft the stubborn glebe has
    broke;
How jocund did they drive their team afield!
  How bowed the woods beneath their sturdy
    stroke!

Let not Ambition mock their useful toil,[3]
  Their homely joys, and destiny obscure;   30
Nor Grandeur hear with a disdainful smile,
  The short and simple annals of the poor.

The boast of heraldry, the pomp of power,
  And all that beauty, all that wealth e'er
    gave,
Awaits alike the inevitable hour: 35
  The paths of glory lead but to the grave.

Nor you, ye proud, impute to these the fault,
  If Memory o'er their tomb no trophies raise,

Where through the long-drawn aisle and
    fretted vault
  The pealing anthem swells the note of
    praise.   40

Can storied urn or animated bust
  Back to its mansion call the fleeting breath?
Can Honor's voice provoke the silent dust,
  Or Flattery soothe the dull cold ear of
    Death?

Perhaps in this neglected spot [4] is laid   45
  Some heart once pregnant with celestial
    fire;
Hands that the rod of empire might have
    swayed,
  Or waked to ecstasy the living lyre.

But Knowledge to their eyes her ample page [5]
  Rich with the spoils of time did ne'er un-
    roll;   50
Chill Penury repressed their noble rage,
  And froze the genial current of the soul.

Full many a gem of purest ray serene,
  The dark unfathomed caves of ocean bear:
Full many a flower is born to blush unseen, 55
  And waste its sweetness on the desert air.

Some village-Hampden,[6] that with dauntless
    breast
  The little tyrant of his fields withstood;
Some mute inglorious Milton here may rest,
  Some Cromwell, guiltless of his country's
    blood.   60

The applause of listening senates to com-
    mand,
  The threats of pain and ruin to despise,
To scatter plenty o'er a smiling land,
  And read their history in a nation's eyes,

[2] In ll. 17–28 is the action in the external world
or in the poet's mind? What is the time of the
actions described in these lines?
[3] In ll. 29–44 what other graveyard is contrasted
to that of the country churchyard? Note especially
ll. 39–40. Who would be buried in this place? How
does Gray's use of PERSONIFICATIONS help make
this contrast, i.e., to which graveyard do the personifications belong? What do they tell us of the
people buried there? What result of the contrast
is noted in ll. 33–36?
[4] Which graveyard is "this neglected spot"?

[5] In ll. 49–52 what two things forbade fame
and fortune to those buried in the country churchyard?
[6] John Hampden opposed Charles I's attempt to
enforce an ancient tax on ships. Lines 57–76
illustrate what "Their lot forbade" (l. 65): these
"rude forefathers" might have trod the "paths of
glory" had not their "lot forbade." Had they succeeded, where would the paths have led? Since
this is true, what is the desire of all men after
death (ll. 77–92)?

Their lot forbade: nor circumscribed alone 65
  Their growing virtues, but their crimes con-
    fined;
Forbade to wade through slaughter to a
    throne,
  And shut the gates of mercy on mankind;

The struggling pangs of conscious truth to
    hide,
  To quench the blushes of ingenuous
    shame,   70
Or heap the shrine of Luxury and Pride
  With incense kindled at the Muse's flame.

Far from the madding [7] crowd's ignoble strife,
  Their sober wishes never learned to stray;
Along the cool sequestered vale of life   75
  They kept the noiseless tenor of their way.

Yet even these bones from insult to protect
  Some frail memorial still erected nigh,
With uncouth rhymes and shapeless sculpture
    decked,
  Implores the passing tribute of a sigh.   80

Their name, their years, spelt by the unlet-
    tered Muse,
  The place of fame and elegy supply;
And many a holy text around she strews,
  That teach the rustic moralist to die.

For who, to dumb Forgetfulness a prey,   85
  This pleasing anxious being e'er resigned,
Left the warm precincts of the cheerful day,
  Nor cast one longing lingering look be-
    hind?

On some fond breast the parting soul relies,
  Some pious drops the closing eye re-
    quires;   90
Even from the tomb the voice of Nature cries,
  Even in our ashes live their wonted fires.

[7] Frenzied.
[8] Who is the "thee" in ll. 93–94? The resolution
of the poem begins here. In the meditation (ll. 5–92)
the poet's identity was submerged; now it returns
to him as he applies the situation to himself.
[9] Notice the emphasis on "read" in the line. Who,
then, seems to be the "kindred spirit" (l. 96)?
[10] Gray is buried in the country churchyard at
Stoke Poges, the village where his mother lived.

For thee,[8] who, mindful of the unhonored
    dead,
  Dost in these lines their artless tale relate;
If chance, by lonely contemplation led,   95
  Some kindred spirit shall inquire thy fate,

Haply some hoary-headed swain may say,
  "Oft have we seen him at the peep of dawn
Brushing with hasty steps the dews away
  To meet the sun upon the upland lawn. 100

"There at the foot of yonder nodding beech
  That wreathes its old fantastic roots so
    high,
His listless length at noontide would he
    stretch,
  And pore upon the brook that babbles by.

"Hard by yon wood, now smiling as in
    scorn,   105
  Muttering his wayward fancies he would
    rove;
Now drooping, woeful wan, like one forlorn,
  Or crazed with care, or crossed in hopeless
    love.

"One morn I missed him on the customed
    hill,
  Along the heath and near his favorite
    tree;   110
Another came; nor yet beside the rill,
  Nor up the lawn, nor at the wood was he;

"The next, with dirges due in sad array
  Slow through the church-way path we
    saw him borne;
Approach and read [9] (for thou canst read) the
    lay,   115
  Graved on the stone beneath yon aged
    thorn."

The Epitaph

Here rests his head upon the lap of Earth,[10]
A youth, to fortune and to fame un-
* known:* [11]

[11] Is the poet "unknown to fame and fortune"
because his "lot forbade" or by deliberate choice?
Is the poet like the "rude forefathers" (l. 16)?
Is he like those who chose glory through vanity
(ll. 29–44) and are remembered only for their
mortuary sculpture?

*Fair Science frowned not on his humble
     birth,
     And Melancholy marked him for her
     own.*   120

*Large was his bounty, and his soul sincere;
     Heaven did a recompense as largely send:
He gave to Misery (all he had), a tear,
     He gained from Heaven ('twas all he
     wished) a friend.*[12]

No farther seek his merits to disclose,   125
     *Or draw his frailties from their dread
     abode,
(There they alike in trembling hope repose,)
     The bosom of his Father and his God.*

(1751)

STUDY AIDS: 1. There has been much discussion as to whether or not the "Epitaph" (ll. 117–128) is necessary to the *Elegy*. Does the "Epitaph" explain Gray's conduct? Can his "unlettered friends" understand his motives (l. 115)? Can his "friend" (who can read) understand his motives? The footnote to l. 93 implies that the "thee" is Gray. What other antecedent in the previous lines is possible for the pronoun? What interpretation would follow from this? Whose epitaph would ll. 117–128 then be? Who then would be the "kindred spirit" of l. 96? Which interpretation seems the better one to you?

2. Dr. Johnson said that the *Elegy* "abounds with images which find a mirror in every mind and with sentiments to which every bosom returns an echo." What are some of these images and sentiments? What other reasons can you offer to explain the poem's continued popularity?

The Bard

Gray is the first English poet to imitate successfully the odes of the Greek poet Pindar (522–448 B.C.). Literary tradition in the eighteenth century dictated that the Pindaric ode treat exalted subjects, in contrast to the Horatian ode, which expressed such themes as patriotism, duty, and meditative reflection. The form of the ode, as developed by Pindar, consisted of two sections similar in structure (the strophe and antistrophe) and a third (the epode) whose pattern differed from that of the first two sections. The freedom of rhyme and line lengths which Gray exercised within sections was a move toward the more relaxed poetic form as practiced by later romantic poets. Also romantic in *The Bard* are the wild scenes in Wales, the medieval setting, and the mysterious Bard, who sees the ghosts of long-dead poets about him.

The Bard "is founded on a tradition current in Wales, that Edward I, when he completed the conquest of that country, ordered all the bards that fell into his hands to be put to death" (Gray).

I · 1

"Ruin seize thee, ruthless King! [1]
Confusion on thy banners wait,
Though fanned by Conquest's crimson wing
They mock the air with idle state.
Helm, nor hauberk's twisted mail,   5
Nor even thy virtues, Tyrant, shall avail
To save thy secret soul from nightly fears,

From Cambria's curse, from Cambria's [2]
     tears!"
Such were the sounds, that o'er the crested
     pride
Of the first Edward scattered wild dismay, 10
As down the steep of Snowdon's shaggy side
He wound with toilsome march his long array.
Stout Glo'ster [3] stood aghast in speechless
     trance:
"To arms!" cried Mortimer,[4] and couched his
     quivering lance.

[12] What "passing tribute of a sigh" (l. 80) does Gray wish from posterity? See ll. 85–86. Who is this "friend" (see ll. 96, 115)? What, then, is the "tear" (l. 123)? Compare this "tear" with that Milton used in *Lycidas* (p. 253, l. 14).

[1] The bard (poet) is speaking to Edward I (see l. 18).

[2] Old name for Wales.
[3] Earl of Gloucester, son-in-law of Edward I.
[4] Edmond de Mortimer, Lord of Wigmore.

I · 2

On a rock, whose haughty brow   15
Frowns o'er old Conway's foaming flood,
Robed in the sable garb of woe,
With haggard eyes the poet stood
(Loose his beard, and hoary hair
Streamed, like a meteor, to the troubled
    air),   20
And with a master's hand, and prophet's fire,
Struck the deep sorrows of his lyre.
"Hark, how each giant-oak, and desert cave,
Sighs to the torrent's awful voice beneath!
O'er thee, oh King! their hundred arms they
    wave,   25
Revenge on thee in hoarser murmurs breathe;
Vocal no more, since Cambria's fatal day,
To high-born Hoel's harp, or soft Llewellyn's
    lay.

I · 3

"Cold is Cadwallo's [5] tongue,
That hushed the stormy main: 30
Brave Urien sleeps upon his craggy bed;
Mountains, ye mourn in vain
Modred, whose magic song
Made huge Plinlimmon [6] bow his cloud-
    topped head.
On dreary Arvon's [7] shore they lie   35
Smeared with gore, and ghastly pale:
Far, far aloof the affrighted ravens sail;
The famished eagle screams, and passes by.
Dear lost companions of my tuneful art,
Dear, as the light that visits these sad eyes, 40
Dear, as the ruddy drops that warm my heart,
Ye died amidst your dying country's cries—
No more I weep. They do not sleep.
On yonder cliffs, a grisly band,
I see them sit; they linger yet,   45
Avengers of their native land:
With me in dreadful harmony they join,
And weave with bloody hands the tissue of
    thy line.[8]

[5] Hoel (l. 28), Llewellyn (l. 28), Cadwallo (l. 29), Urien (l. 31), and Modred (l. 33) are bards murdered by Edward I.

[6] A mountain in Wales.

[7] Carnarvonshire, a county in Wales.

[8] Lines 49–100 are a chant of the dead poets prophesying the misfortunes to fall on Edward I's descendants because of his murder of the Welsh bards. Edward himself was butchered in Berkeley Castle (l. 56).

II · 1

" 'Weave the warp, and weave the woof,
The winding-sheet of Edward's race.   50
Give ample room, and verge enough
The characters of hell to trace.
Mark the year, and mark the night,
When Severn shall re-echo with affright
The shrieks of death, through Berkeley's roofs
    that ring,   55
Shrieks of an agonizing King!
She-wolf of France,[9] with unrelenting
    fangs,
That tearest the bowels of thy mangled mate,
From thee be born, who o'er thy country
    hangs,
The scourge of Heaven. What terrors round
    him wait!   60
Amazement in his van, with Flight com-
    bined,
And Sorrow's faded form, and Solitude be-
    hind.

II · 2

" 'Mighty victor, mighty lord,
Low on his funeral couch he lies!
No pitying heart, no eye, afford   65
A tear to grace his obsequies.
Is the sable warrior [10] fled?
Thy son is gone. He rests among the dead.
The swarm, that in thy noon-tide beam were
    born?
Gone to salute the rising morn.   70
Fair laughs the morn, and soft the zephyr
    blows,[11]
While proudly riding o'er the azure realm
In gallant trim the gilded vessel goes;
Youth on the prow, and Pleasure at the
    helm;
Regardless of the sweeping whirlwind's
    sway,   75
That, hushed in grim repose, expects his eve-
    ning prey.

[9] The adulterous queen of Edward II, Isabel of France, gave birth to Edward III (ll. 57–60), who died abandoned and robbed by his courtiers and mistress.

[10] Edward, the Black Prince, preceded his father, Edward III, in death.

[11] Gray said that ll. 71–76 describe the magnificence of Richard II's reign.

II · 3

" 'Fill high the sparkling bowl,[12]
The rich repast prepare,
Reft of a crown, he yet may share the feast:
Close by the regal chair   80
Fell Thirst and Famine scowl
A baleful smile upon their baffled guest.
Heard ye the din of battle bray,
Lance to lance, and horse to horse?
Long years of havoc urge their destined
        course,   85
And through the kindred squadrons mow
        their way.
Ye towers of Julius, London's lasting shame,
With many a foul and midnight murder fed,
Revere his consort's [13] faith, his father's fame,
And spare the meek usurper's holy head. 90
Above, below, the rose of snow,
Twined with her blushing foe, we spread:
The bristled boar in infant gore
Wallows beneath the thorny shade.
Now, brothers, bending o'er the accursèd
        loom,   95
Stamp we our vengeance deep, and ratify his
        doom.

III · 1

" 'Edward, lo! to sudden fate [14]
(Weave we the woof. The thread is spun.)
Half of thy heart we consecrate.
(The web is wove. The work is done.)'   100
Stay, oh stay! nor thus forlorn
Leave me unblessed, unpitied, here to mourn:
In yon bright track, that fires the western
        skies,
They melt, they vanish from my eyes.

[12] Lines 77–82 prophesy the murder of Richard II by starvation. This prophecy is followed by a forecasting of the civil wars of York and Lancaster (ll. 83–94), which occasioned the political murders of the princes Henry VI ("meek usurper," l. 90), Edward V, and Richard, Duke of York, by Richard III ("bristled boar," l. 93) in the Tower of London, built by Julius Caesar according to legend (ll. 87–88).
[13] Margaret of Anjou, queen of Henry VI. Henry VI's father was Henry V.
[14] Beginning at l. 97 (the Epode), the rest of the poem prophesies the future glories of England after the restoration of a Welsh dynasty, the Tudors ("genuine Kings," l. 110).

But oh! what solemn scenes on Snowdon's
        height   105
Descending slow their glittering skirts unroll?
Visions of glory, spare my aching sight,
Ye unborn ages, crowd not on my soul!
No more our long-lost Arthur we bewail.
All hail, ye genuine Kings, Britannia's issue,
        hail!   110

III · 2

"Girt with many a Baron bold
Sublime their starry fronts they rear;
And gorgeous dames, and statesmen old
In bearded majesty, appear.
In the midst a form divine! [15]   115
Her eye proclaims her of the Briton-line;
Her lion-port, her awe-commanding face,
Attempered sweet to virgin-grace.
What strings symphonious tremble in the air,
What strains of vocal transport round her
        play!   120
Hear from the grave, great Taliessin,[16] hear;
They breathe a soul to animate thy clay.
Bright Rapture calls, and soaring, as she sings,
Waves in the eye of Heaven her many-colored
        wings.

III · 3

"The verse adorn again [17]   125
Fierce War, and faithful Love,
And Truth severe, by fairy fiction dressed.
In buskined [18] measures move
Pale Grief, and pleasing Pain,
With Horror, tyrant of the throbbing
        breast.   130
A voice [19] as of the cherub-choir,
Gales from blooming Eden bear;
And distant warblings [20] lessen on my ear,

[15] Queen Elizabeth. The stanza describes her glittering court.
[16] "Chief of the bards who flourished in the sixth century" (Gray).
[17] Lines 125–127 refer to Spenser's description of the subject matter in The Faerie Queene.
[18] Shakespeare used this same historical subject matter in his tragedies and history plays.
[19] Milton.
[20] "The succession of poets after Milton's time" (Gray).

That lost in long futurity expire.
Fond impious man, thinkest thou yon san-
    guine cloud,   135
Raised by thy breath, has quenched the orb
    of day?
Tomorrow he repairs the golden flood,
And warms the nations with redoubled ray.
Enough for me: with joy I see
The different doom our fates assign.   140
Be thine Despair, and sceptered Care,
To triumph, and to die, are mine."

He spoke, and headlong from the mountain's
    height
Deep in the roaring tide he plunged to end-
    less night.
(1757)

STUDY AIDS: 1. What is Gray saying in *The Bard* about the power of poetry?

2. Gray's contemporaries found the poem obscure. What qualities in the poem would justify this criticism? Would this criticism argue that history is not proper subject matter for poetry?

Letter to Richard West [1]

TURIN [Italy], Nov. 16, 1739.

After eight days' journey through Greenland [i.e., the Alps], we arrived at Turin. You approach it by a handsome avenue of nine miles long, and quite straight. The entrance is 5 guarded by certain vigilant dragons, called Douâniers,[2] who mumbled us for some time. The city is not large, as being a place of strength, and consequently confined within its fortifications; it has many beauties and some 10 faults; among the first are streets all laid out by the line, regular uniform buildings, fine walks that surround the whole, and in general a good lively clean appearance. But the houses are of brick plastered, which is apt to want 15 repairing; the windows of oiled paper, which is apt to be torn; and everything very slight, which is apt to tumble down. There is an excellent opera, but it is only in the carnival; balls every night, but only in the carnival; 20 masquerades too, but only in the carnival. This carnival lasts only from Christmas to Lent; one half of the remaining part of the year is passed in remembering the last, the other in expecting the future carnival. We 25 cannot well subsist upon such slender diet, no more than upon an execrable Italian comedy, and a puppet-show, called *Rappre-sentazione d'un' anima dannata,*[3] which, I think, are all the present diversions of the 30

place; except the Marquise de Cavaillac's Conversazione, where one goes to see people play at ombre and taroc, a game with seventy-two cards all painted with suns, and moons, and devils and monks. Mr. Walpole has been at court; the family are at present at a country palace, called La Venerie. The palace here in town is the very quintessence of gilding and looking-glass; inlaid floors, carved panels, and painting, wherever they could stick a brush. I own I have not, as yet, anywhere met with those grand and simple works of art that are to amaze one, and whose sight one is to be the better for; but those of nature have astonished me beyond expression. In our little journey up to the Grande Chartreuse,[4] I do not remember to have gone ten paces without an exclamation, that there was no restraining: not a precipice, not a torrent, not a cliff, but is pregnant with religion and poetry. There are certain scenes that would awe an atheist into belief, without the help of other argument. One need not have a very fantastic imagination to see spirits there at noon-day. You have death perpetually before your eyes, only so far removed as to compose the mind without frighting it. I am well persuaded St. Bruno was a man of no common genius to choose such a situation for his retirement, and perhaps should have been a disciple of his, had I been born in his time. You may believe Abelard and Heloïse were not forgot upon this occasion. If I do not mistake, I saw you

[1] Fellow-student of Gray at Eton and a lifelong friend.
[2] Customs officials.
[3] "Representation of a damned soul."
[4] Alpine monastery founded in 1084 by St. Bruno.

too every now and then at a distance along the trees; *il me semble, que j'ai vu ce chien de visage là quelque part.*[5] You seemed to call to me from the other side of the precipice, but the noise of the river below was so great, that I really could not distinguish what you said; it seemed to have a cadence like verse. In your next you will be so good to let me know what it was. The week we have since passed among the Alps has not equaled the single day upon that mountain, because the winter was rather too far advanced, and the weather a little foggy. However, it did not want its beauties; the savage rudeness of the view is inconceivable without seeing it. I reckoned in one day thirteen cascades, the least of which was, I dare say, one hundred feet in height. . . . We set out for Genoa in two days' time.

Letter to his Mother

NAPLES, June 17, 1740.

Our journey hither was through the most beautiful part of the finest country in the world; and every spot of it, on some account or other, famous for these three thousand years past. The season has hitherto been just as warm as one would wish it; no unwholesome airs, or violent heats, yet heard of. The people call it a backward year, and are in pain about their corn, wine, and oil; but we, who are neither corn, wine, nor oil, find it very agreeable. Our road was through Velletri, Cisterna, Terracina, Capua, and Aversa, and so to Naples. The minute one leaves his holiness's dominions, the face of things begins to change from wide uncultivated plains to olive groves and well-tilled fields of corn, intermixed with ranks of elms, every one of which has its vine twining about it, and hanging in festoons between the rows from one tree to another. The great old fig-trees, the oranges in full bloom, and myrtles in every hedge, make one of the delightfullest scenes you can conceive; besides that, the roads are wide, well-kept, and full of passengers, a sight I have not beheld this long time. My wonder still increased upon entering the city, which I think, for number of people, outdoes both Paris and London. The streets are one continued market, and thronged with populace so much that a coach can hardly pass. The common sort are a jolly lively kind of animals, more industrious than Italians usually are; they work till evening; then take their lute or guitar (for they all play) and walk about the city, or upon the sea-shore with it, to enjoy the fresco. One sees their little brown children jumping about stark-naked, and the bigger ones dancing with castanets, while others play on the cymbal to them. Your maps will show you the situation of Naples; it is on the most lovely bay in the world, and one of the calmest seas. It has many other beauties besides those of nature. We have spent two days in visiting the remarkable places in the country round it, such as the bay of Baiæ, and its remains of antiquity; the lake Avernus, and the Solfatara, Charon's grotto, etc. We have been in the Sybil's cave and many other strange holes underground (I only name them, because you may consult Sandys' travels); but the strangest hole I ever was in, has been to-day at a place called Portici,[1] where his Sicilian majesty has a country-seat. About a year ago, as they were digging, they discovered some parts of ancient buildings above thirty feet deep in the ground. Curiosity led them on, and they have been digging ever since; the passage they have made, with all its turnings and windings, is now more than a mile long. As you walk, you see parts of an amphitheater, many houses adorned with marble columns, and incrusted with the same; the front of a temple, several arched vaults of rooms painted in fresco. Some pieces of painting have been taken out from hence, finer

[5] "It seems to me I have seen that dog face there somewhere."

[1] Herculaneum.

than anything of the kind before discovered, and with these the king has adorned his palace; also a number of statues, medals, and gems; and more are dug out every day. This is known to be a Roman town, that in the emperor Titus's time was overwhelmed by a furious eruption of Mount Vesuvius, which is hard by. The wood and beams remain so perfect that you may see the grain; but burnt to a coal, and dropping into dust upon the least touch. We were to-day at the foot of that mountain, which at present smokes only a little, where we saw the materials that fed 5 the stream of fire, which about four years since ran down its side. We have but a few days longer to stay here; too little in conscience for such a place. . . .

Samuel Johnson
(1709–1784)

ENGLISH LITERATURE IN THE LATTER HALF OF THE EIGHTEENTH CENTURY WAS DOMINATED by the presiding genius of Samuel Johnson. He was the last of the great neoclassicists, the staunch defender of the literary ideals of Dryden, Addison, and Pope. These ideals were finally abandoned for new ones; but the change, begun in Johnson's lifetime, was not completed until after his death.

Born the son of a Lichfield bookseller, young Johnson from an early age was exposed to books. He was well prepared when he went to Oxford, but after two years, poverty forced him to leave the University. He taught school, sold books, and in 1735 married a widow twice his age. Incidental literary chores brought little return, and in 1737 he went to London to sell his play, *Irene*.

Failing to sell it, he tried as best he could to live by his pen. This was extremely hard to do. No longer able to gain the support of wealthy patrons, writers had to rely on the general reading public, a growing but as yet small body. Like other young writers, Johnson was reduced to doing hack work and living in near poverty, a bohemian or "Grubstreet" existence, fully described in his biographical sketch of a fellow writer, the *Life of Savage*. Nevertheless he managed during these years to write two notable poems: *London* (1738), modeled on a satire of Juvenal's, and *The Vanity of Human Wishes* (1749), an expression of Johnson's pessimism.

Achievements of a different order are his scholarly works: *A Dictionary of the English Language* (1755) and the edition of *Shakespeare* (1765). For eight years he worked, virtually alone, on a dictionary that he hoped would fix the English language and establish an authoritative standard of correct usage. A few of the definitions reflect Johnson's eccentricity ("*network*: any thing reticulated, or decussated, at equal distances, with interstices between the intersections") and his prejudices ("*patriotism*: the last refuge of a scoundrel"); but the work as a whole was remarkable, particularly for its many illustrative examples drawn from reputable authors. It established his fame as a scholar. Oxford honored him with an M.A. degree shortly before publication, and in 1762 he received a royal pension of 300 pounds a year. Probably it was this financial security, combined with Johnson's usual indolence, that delayed the edition of *Shakespeare*, promised to subscribers for 1757 but not completed until 1765. It was a solid work, with useful interpretative notes and an excellent introduction, and did much to stimulate the study of Shakespeare.

Johnson's lesser works during this period reflect his moral nature. Literature should teach, he believed, and many of his 208 *Rambler* papers (1750–1752) are rich in moral precept. These periodical essays, patterned after the *Spectator* papers, exhibit the celebrated Johnson prose style: Latinate diction, and sentences abounding in paired epithets and in consciously balanced, often antithetical, elements. Sometimes ponderous, the style also has majesty and elegance. It is the medium of *Rasselas* (1759), a didactic romance embodying the author's belief in the vanity of human wishes, in man's inability to find happiness. Later periodical essays, called *The Idler* (1758–1760), are somewhat lighter in tone and in style.

In 1763 Johnson met James Boswell, his future biographer. Thereafter they were frequently together, most intimately during a three-month trip to the Hebrides. Boswell wrote an account of the tour, as did Johnson in *A Journey to the Western Islands of Scotland* (1775). The same year Oxford conferred the LL.D., making him "Doctor Johnson." His last work, *The Lives of the English Poets* (1779–1781), biographical sketches of 52 poets and commentary on their verse, is probably Johnson's major literary achievement. Death, which he had morbidly feared, came three years later, but Johnson met it with the courage and Christian devotion that had marked his life.

"Writers commonly derive their reputation from their works," Johnson said; "but there are works which owe their reputation to the character of the writer." The latter part of the statement is true of Johnson, for one feels that greater than any of his works is the man himself. Large boned and heavy, his face scarred from infancy with the scrofula contracted from a nurse, and given to nervous jerking and twitching and to odd muttering, he was almost grotesque in appearance and manner. Some facets of his character, too, were forbidding. He was often coarse, he was strongly opinionated, and he could be brusque to the point of rudeness. But his virtues and talents so outweighed his shortcomings as to make him the most eminent man of his day. Hardship and despondency he met with great courage, and beneath his bearish manner he was humble, gentle, and kind. He had a tough, vigorous mind, capable of darts of wit, but usually devoted to the large truths of common sense which his age valued. He was great in conversation, the acknowledged leader of "The Literary Club," which originally included Reynolds, Goldsmith, and Burke, and later Garrick, Bishop Percy, the Wartons, Gibbon, Fox, and Adam Smith—as brilliant a cultural galaxy as England ever produced.

The Rambler No. 4

In writing this essay on the new fiction of the day, Johnson probably had in mind such novels as Samuel Richardson's *Clarissa Harlowe* (1747–1748), Tobias Smollett's *Roderick Random* (1748), and Henry Fielding's *Tom Jones* (1749). He is considering how such fiction may affect readers.

The works of fiction, with which the present generation seems more particularly delighted, are such as exhibit life in its true state, diversified only by accidents that daily happen in the world, and influenced by passions and qualities which are really to be found in conversing with mankind.

This kind of writing may be termed, not

improperly, the comedy of romance, and is to be conducted nearly by the rules of comic poetry. Its province is to bring about natural events by easy means, and to keep up curiosity without the help of wonder: it is therefore precluded from the machines and expedients of the heroic romance, and can neither employ giants to snatch away a lady from the nuptial rites, nor knights to bring her back from captivity; it can neither bewilder its personages in deserts, nor lodge them in imaginary castles.

I remember a remark made by Scaliger [1] upon Pontanus,[2] that all his writings are filled with the same images; and that if you take from him his lilies and his roses, his satyrs and his dryads, he will have nothing left that can be called poetry. In like manner almost all the fictions of the last age will vanish, if you deprive them of a hermit and a wood, a battle and a shipwreck.

Why this wild strain of imagination found reception so long in polite and learned ages, it is not easy to conceive; but we cannot wonder that while readers could be procured, the authors were willing to continue it; for when a man had by practice gained some fluency of language, he had no further care than to retire to his closet, let loose his invention, and heat his mind with incredibilities; a book was thus produced without fear of criticism, without the toil of study, without knowledge of nature, or acquaintance with life.

The task of our present writers is very different; it requires, together with that learning which is to be gained from books, that experience which can never be attained by solitary diligence, but must arise from general converse and accurate observation of the living world. Their performances have, as Horace expresses it, *plus oneris quantum veniæ minus,* little indulgence, and therefore more difficulty. They are engaged in portraits of which everyone knows the original, and can detect any deviation from exactness of resemblance. Other writings are safe, except from the malice of learning, but these are in danger from every common reader; as the slipper ill executed was censured by a shoemaker, who happened to stop in his way at the Venus of Apelles.[3]

But the fear of not being approved as just copiers of human manners, is not the most important concern that an author of this sort ought to have before him. These books are written chiefly to the young, the ignorant, and the idle, to whom they serve as lectures of conduct, and introductions into life. They are the entertainment of minds unfurnished with ideas, and therefore easily susceptible of impressions; not fixed by principles, and therefore easily following the current of fancy: not informed by experience, and consequently open to every false suggestion and partial account.

That the highest degree of reverence should be paid to youth, and that nothing indecent should be suffered to approach their eyes or ears, are precepts extorted by sense and virtue from an ancient writer, by no means eminent for chastity of thought. The same kind, though not the same degree, of caution, is required in everything which is laid before them, to secure them from unjust prejudices, perverse opinions, and incongruous combinations of images.

In the romances formerly written, every transaction and sentiment was so remote from all that passes among men, that the reader was in very little danger of making any applications to himself; the virtues and crimes were equally beyond his sphere of activity; and he amused himself with heroes and with traitors, deliverers and persecutors, as with beings of another species, whose actions were regulated upon motives of their own, and who had neither faults nor excellencies in common with himself.

But when an adventurer is leveled with the rest of the world, and acts in such scenes of the universal drama, as may be the lot of any other man, young spectators fix their

[1] Renaissance critic.
[2] Italian poet.

[3] Noted painter of ancient times. A shoemaker criticized his painting of a shoe; when he went on to criticize the leg, too, Apelles told him not to go beyond the shoe. Hence the proverb, "Let the shoemaker stick to his last."

eyes upon him with closer attention, and hope, by observing his behavior and success, to regulate their own practices, when they shall be engaged in the like part.

For this reason these familiar histories may perhaps be made of greater use than the solemnities of professed morality, and convey the knowledge of vice and virtue with more efficacy than axioms and definitions. But if the power of example is so great as to take possession of the memory by a kind of violence, and produce effects almost without the intervention of the will, care ought to be taken, that, when the choice is unrestrained, the best examples only should be exhibited; and that which is likely to operate so strongly, should not be mischievous or uncertain in its effects.

The chief advantage which these fictions have over real life is, that their authors are at liberty, though not to invent, yet to select objects, and to cull from the mass of mankind those individuals upon which the attention ought most to be employed; as a diamond, though it cannot be made, may be polished by art, and placed in such situation, as to display that luster which before was buried among common stones.[4]

It is justly considered as the greatest excellency of art, to imitate nature; but it is necessary to distinguish those parts of nature, which are most proper for imitation: greater care is still required in representing life, which is so often discolored by passion, or deformed by wickedness. If the world be promiscuously described, I cannot see of what use it can be to read the account; or why it may not be as safe to turn the eye immediately upon mankind as upon a mirror which shows all that presents itself without discrimination.

It is therefore not a sufficient vindication of a character, that it is drawn as it appears; for many characters ought never to be drawn: nor of a narrative, that the train of events is agreeable to observation and experience; for that observation which is called knowledge of the world, will be found much more

[4] Find the terms of the ANALOGY used in this paragraph.

frequently to make men cunning than good. The purpose of these writings is surely not only to show mankind, but to provide that they may be seen hereafter with less hazard; to teach the means of avoiding the snares which are laid by treachery for innocence, without infusing any wish for that superiority with which the betrayer flatters his vanity; to give the power of counteracting fraud, without the temptation to practice it; to initiate youth by mock encounters in the art of necessary defense, and to increase prudence without impairing virtue.

Many writers, for the sake of following nature, so mingle good and bad qualities in their principal personages, that they are both equally conspicuous; and as we accompany them through their adventures with delight, and are led by degrees to interest ourselves in their favor, we lose the abhorrence of their faults, because they do not hinder our pleasure, or perhaps, regard them with some kindness, for being united with so much merit.

There have been men indeed splendidly wicked, whose endowments threw a brightness on their crimes, and whom scarce any villainy made perfectly detestable, because they never could be wholly divested of their excellencies; but such have been in all ages the great corrupters of the world, and their resemblance ought no more to be preserved, than the art of murdering without pain.

Some have advanced, without due attention to the consequence of this notion, that certain virtues have their correspondent faults, and therefore that to exhibit either apart is to deviate from probability. Thus men are observed by Swift to be "grateful in the same degree as they are resentful." This principle, with others of the same kind, supposes man to act from a brute impulse, and pursue a certain degree of inclination, without any choice of the object; for, otherwise, though it should be allowed that gratitude and resentment arise from the same constitution of the passions, it follows not that they will be equally indulged when reason is consulted; yet, unless that consequence be admitted, this sagacious maxim becomes an empty sound, without any relation to practice or to life.

Nor is it evident, that even the first motions to these effects are always in the same proportion. For pride, which produces quickness of resentment, will obstruct gratitude, by unwillingness to admit that inferiority which obligation implies; and it is very unlikely that he who cannot think he receives a favor, will acknowledge or repay it.

It is of the utmost importance to mankind, that positions of this tendency should be laid open and confuted; for while men consider good and evil as springing from the same root, they will spare the one for the sake of the other, and in judging, if not of others, at least of themselves, will be apt to estimate their virtues by their vices. To this fatal error all those will contribute, who confound the colors of right and wrong, and, instead of helping to settle their boundaries, mix them with so much art, that no common mind is able to disunite them.

In narratives where historical veracity has no place, I cannot discover why there should not be exhibited the most perfect idea of virtue; of virtue not angelical, nor above probability, for what we cannot credit, we shall never imitate, but the highest and purest that humanity can reach, which, exercised in such trials as the various revolutions of things shall bring upon it, may, by conquering some calamities, and enduring others, teach us what we may hope, and what we can perform. Vice, for vice is necessary to be shown, should always disgust; nor should the graces of gaiety, or the dignity of courage, be so united with it, as to reconcile it to the mind. Wherever it appears, it should raise hatred by the malignity of its practices, and contempt by the meanness of its stratagems: for while it is supported by either parts or spirit, it will be seldom heartily abhorred. The Roman tyrant [5] was content to be hated, if he was but feared; and there are thousands of the readers of romances willing to be thought wicked, if they may be allowed to be wits. It is therefore to be steadily inculcated, that virtue is the highest proof of understanding, and the only solid basis of greatness; and that vice is the natural consequence of narrow thoughts; that it begins in mistake, and ends in ignominy. (1750)

STUDY AIDS: 1. How does the new fiction of Johnson's day differ from earlier fiction? What responsibility to readers does the nature of the new fiction impose on writers?

2. Since vice exists in life, one can argue, a writer of fiction wanting to imitate nature will be justified in giving a lifelike picture of vice. How does Johnson meet this argument?

3. Notice the sentence structure of paragraph two. In what ways is it characteristic of Johnson's prose style?

Letter to the Earl of Chesterfield

When Johnson planned his *Dictionary* in 1747, he submitted a prospectus of the work to the Earl of Chesterfield, who seemed to encourage him in the project. The Earl gave no tangible support, however, while Johnson was at work, but he praised the work publicly just before it appeared, perhaps in the hope of winning a dedication after all. Johnson took notice of Chesterfield's belated interest by writing the following letter, often said to have ended the practice of patronage. If Chesterfield was annoyed he managed to hide his feelings, for he showed the letter about and even praised Johnson's wit.

To the Right Honorable
    the Earl of Chesterfield
            February 7, 1755.

My Lord: I have lately been informed by the proprietor [1] of *The World,* that two papers, in which my *Dictionary* is recommended to the public, were written by your lordship. To be so distinguished is an honor which, being very little accustomed to favors from the

[5] Caligula.

---

[1] Edward Moore, editor of the popular periodical *The World* (1753–1756).

great, I know not well how to receive, or in what terms to acknowledge.

When, upon some slight encouragement, I first visited your lordship, I was overpowered, like the rest of mankind, by the enchantment of your address; and I could not forbear to wish that I might boast myself *"Le vainqueur du vainqueur de la terre,"* [2] that I might obtain that regard for which I saw the world contending; but I found my attendance so little encouraged, that neither pride nor modesty would suffer me to continue it. When I had once addressed your lordship in public, I had exhausted all the art of pleasing which a retired and uncourtly scholar can possess. I had done all that I could; and no man is well pleased to have his all neglected, be it ever so little.

Seven years, my lord, have now passed, since I waited in your outward rooms, or was repulsed from your door; during which time I have been pushing on my work through difficulties, of which it is useless to complain, and have brought it at last to the verge of publication, without one act of assistance, one word of encouragement, or one smile of favor. Such treatment I did not expect, for I never had a patron before.

The shepherd in Virgil grew at last acquainted with Love, and found him a native of the rocks.

Is not a patron, my lord, one who looks with unconcern on a man struggling for life in the water, and, when he has reached ground, encumbers him with help? The notice which you have been pleased to take of my labors, had it been early, had been kind; but it has been delayed till I am indifferent, and cannot enjoy it; till I am solitary, and cannot impart it; till I am known, and do not want it. I hope it is no very cynical asperity not to confess obligations where no benefit has been received, or to be unwilling that the public should consider me as owing that to a patron, which providence has enabled me to do for myself.

Having carried on my work thus far with so little obligation to any favorer of learning, I shall not be disappointed though I should conclude it, if less be possible, with less; for I have been long wakened from that dream of hope, in which I once boasted myself with so much exaltation,

My Lord,

   Your Lordship's most humble,

    Most obedient servant,

      Sam. Johnson.

[2] "The conqueror of the conqueror of the earth" (Boileau).

Preface to Shakespeare

Because Restoration dramatists had regularized Shakespeare's plays, and some, like Nahum Tate, had given several of the tragedies happy endings in order to satisfy the taste of the audience, the eighteenth century saw the necessity of rescuing the original texts from obscurity and establishing their true readings. Nicholas Rowe was the first to edit the plays (1709). Many editions followed throughout the century, among them those of Pope (1725), Lewis Theobald (1726), and Dr. Johnson (1765). Johnson worked for ten years on his edition. While his textual emendations are not particularly noteworthy, the *Preface* is a masterpiece of good critical judgment and appreciation.

. . . .

The poet, of whose works I have undertaken the revision, may now begin to assume the dignity of an ancient, and claim the privilege of established fame and prescriptive veneration. He has long outlived his century, the term commonly fixed as the test of literary merit.[1] Whatever advantages he might once

[1] Johnson's criterion has become an axiom for us today. A work still read after a few generations is considered a "classic."

derive from personal allusions, local customs, or temporary opinions, have for many years been lost; and every topic of merriment or motive of sorrow, which the modes of artificial life afforded him, now only obscure the scenes which they once illuminated. The effects of favor and competition are at an end; the tradition of his friendships and his enmities has perished; his works support no opinion with arguments, nor supply any faction with invectives; they can neither indulge vanity nor gratify malignity, but are read without any other reason than the desire of pleasure, and are therefore praised only as pleasure is obtained; yet, thus unassisted by interest or passion, they have passed through variations of taste and changes of manners, and, as they devolved from one generation to another, have received new honors at every transmission.

But because human judgment, though it be gradually gaining upon certainty, never becomes infallible; and approbation, though long continued, may yet be only the approbation of prejudice or fashion; it is proper to inquire, by what peculiarities of excellence Shakespeare has gained and kept the favor of his countrymen.

Nothing can please many, and please long, but just representations of general nature.[2] Particular manners can be known to few, and therefore few only can judge how nearly they are copied. The irregular combinations of fanciful invention may delight a-while, by that novelty of which the common satiety of life sends us all in quest; but the pleasures of sudden wonder are soon exhausted, and the mind can only repose on the stability of truth.

[2] This is the reason Shakespeare has pleased for many generations. Johnson's sentence is also a statement of one of the foundation stones of classicism: the poet must imitate universals ("general nature") —those truths accepted by the majority of informed men of all ages—rather than "particular manners." Johnson's most striking statement on the subject is in his philosophical novel, *Rasselas*: "The business of the poet . . . is to examine, not the individual, but the species; to remark general properties and large appearances; he does not number the streaks of the tulip. . . ."

Shakespeare is above all writers, at least above all modern writers, the poet of nature;[3] the poet that holds up to his readers a faithful mirror of manners and of life. His characters are not modified by the customs of particular places, unpracticed by the rest of the world; by the peculiarities of studies or professions, which can operate but upon small numbers; or by the accidents of transient fashions or temporary opinions: they are the genuine progeny of common humanity, such as the world will always supply, and observation will always find. His persons act and speak by the influence of those general passions and principles by which all minds are agitated, and the whole system of life is continued in motion. In the writings of other poets a character is too often an individual; in those of Shakespeare it is commonly a species. . . .

The censure which he has incurred by mixing comic and tragic scenes, as it extends to all his works, deserves more consideration. Let the fact be first stated, and then examined.

Shakespeare's plays are not in the rigorous and critical sense either tragedies or comedies, but compositions of a distinct kind; exhibiting the real state of sublunary nature, which partakes of good and evil, joy and sorrow, mingled with endless variety of proportion and innumerable modes of combination; and expressing the course of the world, in which the loss of one is the gain of another; in which, at the same time, the reveler is hasting to his wine, and the mourner burying his friend; in which the malignity of one is sometimes defeated by the frolic of another; and many mischiefs and many benefits are done and hindered without design.

Out of this chaos of mingled purposes and casualties the ancient poets, according to the laws which custom had prescribed, selected some the crimes of men, and some their absurdities; some the momentous vicissitudes of life, and some the lighter occurrences; some the terrors of distress, and some the gaieties of

[3] Notice how this paragraph applies the "general vs. the particular" thesis to Shakespeare's characterizations.

prosperity. Thus rose the two modes of imitation, known by the names of "tragedy" and "comedy," compositions intended to promote different ends by contrary means, and considered as so little allied, that I do not recollect among the Greeks or Romans a single writer who attempted both.

Shakespeare has united the powers of exciting laughter and sorrow not only in one mind but in one composition. Almost all his plays are divided between serious and ludicrous characters, and, in the successive evolutions of the design, sometimes produce seriousness and sorrow, and sometimes levity and laughter.

That this is a practice contrary to the rules of criticism will be readily allowed;[4] but there is always an appeal open from criticism to nature. The end of writing is to instruct; the end of poetry is to instruct by pleasing.[5] That the mingled drama may convey all the instruction of tragedy or comedy cannot be denied, because it includes both in its alternations of exhibition, and approaches nearer than either to the appearance of life, by showing how great machinations and slender designs may promote or obviate one another, and the high and the low co-operate in the general system by unavoidable concatenation. . . .

Shakespeare engaged in dramatic poetry with the world open before him; the rules of the ancients were yet known to few; the public judgment was unformed; he had no example of such fame as might force him upon imitation, nor critics of such authority as might restrain his extravagance. He therefore indulged his natural disposition, and his disposition, as Rymer[6] has remarked, led him

to comedy. In tragedy he often writes with great appearance of toil and study, what is written at last with little felicity; but in his comic scenes, he seems to produce without labor, what no labor can improve. In tragedy he is always struggling after some occasion to be comic; but in comedy he seems to repose, or to luxuriate, as in a mode of thinking congenial to his nature. In his tragic scenes there is always something wanting, but his comedy often surpasses expectation or desire. His comedy pleases by the thoughts and the language, and his tragedy for the greater part by incident and action. His tragedy seems to be skill, his comedy to be instinct. . . .

Shakespeare with his excellencies has likewise faults, and faults sufficient to obscure and overwhelm any other merit. I shall show them in the proportion in which they appear to me, without envious malignity or superstitious veneration. No question can be more innocently discussed than a dead poet's pretensions to renown; and little regard is due to that bigotry which sets candor higher than truth.

His first defect is that to which may be imputed most of the evil in books or in men. He sacrifices virtue to convenience, and is so much more careful to please than to instruct, that he seems to write without any moral purpose. From his writings indeed a system of social duty may be selected, for he that thinks reasonably must think morally; but his precepts and axioms drop casually from him; he makes no just distribution of good or evil, nor is always careful to show in the virtuous a disapprobation of the wicked; he carries his persons indifferently through right and wrong, and at the close dismisses them without further care, and leaves their examples to operate by chance. This fault the barbarity of his age cannot extenuate; for it is always a writer's duty to make the world better, and justice is a virtue independent of time or place. . . .

It will be thought strange, that, in enumerating the defects of this writer, I have not yet mentioned his neglect of the unities; his violation of those laws which have been

[4] The rules demanded a single continuous action —either serious for tragedy or light for comedy; therefore, a tragedy could not have a comic subplot as Shakespeare's tragedies often do. Why does Johnson, a classicist, defend Shakespeare's violation of this classic practice?
[5] The end of poetry for Johnson and the other classicists. Cf. Sir Philip Sidney's end of poetry in The Defense of Poesie (p. 146/1, ll. 32–40).
[6] Thomas Rymer, a neoclassic critic who rigorously attacked Shakespeare for his violations of the rules.

instituted and established by the joint authority of poets and of critics.[7]

For his other deviations from the art of writing, I resign him to critical justice, without making any other demand in his favor than that which must be indulged to all human excellence: that his virtues be rated with his failings. But, from the censure which this irregularity may bring upon him, I shall, with due reverence to that learning which I must oppose, adventure to try how I can defend him.

His histories, being neither tragedies nor comedies, are not subject to any of their laws; nothing more is necessary to all the praise which they expect, than that the changes of action be so prepared as to be understood, that the incidents be various and affecting, and the characters consistent, natural, and distinct. No other unity is intended, and therefore none is to be sought.

In his other works he has well enough preserved the unity of action. He has not, indeed, an intrigue regularly perplexed and regularly unraveled; he does not endeavor to hide his design only to discover it, for this is seldom the order of real events, and Shakespeare is the poet of nature. But his plan has commonly what Aristotle requires, a beginning, a middle, and an end; one event is concatenated with another, and the conclusion follows by easy consequence. There are perhaps some incidents that might be spared, as in other poets there is much talk that only fills up time upon the stage; but the general system makes gradual advances, and the end of the play is the end of expectation.

To the unities of time and place he has shown no regard, and perhaps a nearer view of the principles on which they stand will diminish their value, and withdraw from them the veneration which, from the time of Corneille, they have very generally received, by discovering that they have given more trouble to the poet than pleasure to the auditor.

The necessity of observing the unities of time and place arises from the supposed necessity of making the drama credible. The critics hold it impossible, that an action of months or years can be possibly believed to pass in three hours; or that the spectator can suppose himself to sit in the theater, while ambassadors go and return between distant kings, while armies are levied and towns besieged, while an exile wanders and returns, or till he whom they saw courting his mistress shall lament the untimely fall of his son. The mind revolts from evident falsehood, and fiction loses its force when it departs from the resemblance of reality.[8]

From the narrow limitation of time necessarily arises the contraction of place. The spectator who knows that he saw the first act at Alexandria cannot suppose that he sees the next at Rome, at a distance to which not the dragons of Medea could, in so short a time, have transported him; he knows with certainty that he has not changed his place; and he knows that place cannot change itself; that what was a house cannot become a plain; that what was Thebes can never be Persepolis.

Such is the triumphant language with which a critic exults over the misery of an irregular poet, and exults commonly without resistance or reply. It is time therefore to tell him, by the authority of Shakespeare, that he assumes as an unquestionable principle a position, which, while his breath is forming it into words, his understanding pronounces

---

[7] The unities were concepts of drama formulated during the Renaissance by Italian literary critics studying the *Poetics* of Aristotle and the *Ars Poetica* of Horace. Aristotle had stated the unity of action: a play must have a beginning, middle, and end. He had casually mentioned that the length of a play should not exceed "one revolution of the sun." Various critics speculated on the time-span of "one revolution." Out of this speculation the unity of time was established, and the unity of place logically followed. The first reference in England to these so-called "rules" is in Sidney's *Defense*.

[8] Why is this statement only partially true? Is literature (fiction) real or imaginative? Are the moral values and insight into human nature in a Shakespearean play false because the shift of scene from Alexandria to Rome cannot be an imitation of reality?

to be false. It is false that any representation is mistaken for reality; that any dramatic fable in its materiality was ever credible, or, for a single moment, was ever credited.

The objection arising from the impossibility of passing the first hour at Alexandria, and the next at Rome, supposes that when the play opens the spectator really imagines himself at Alexandria, and believes that his walk to the theater has been a voyage to Egypt, and that he lives in the days of Antony and Cleopatra. Surely he that imagines this may imagine more. He that can take the stage at one time for the palace of the Ptolemies, may take it in half an hour for the promontory of Actium. Delusion, if delusion be admitted, has no certain limitation; if the spectator can be once persuaded that his old acquaintances are Alexander and Cæsar, that a room illuminated with candles is the plain of Pharsalia, or the bank of Granicus, he is in a state of elevation above the reach of reason, or of truth, and from the heights of empyrean poetry may despise the circumscriptions of terrestrial nature. There is no reason why a mind thus wandering in ecstasy should count the clock, or why an hour should not be a century in that calenture [9] of the brains that can make the stage a field.

The truth is that the spectators are always in their senses, and know, from the first act to the last, that the stage is only a stage, and that the players are only players. They came to hear a certain number of lines recited with just gesture and elegant modulation. The lines relate to some action, and an action must be in some place; but the different actions that complete a story may be in places very remote from each other; and where is the absurdity of allowing that space to represent first Athens, and then Sicily, which was always known to be neither Sicily nor Athens, but a modern theater?

By supposition, as place is introduced, time may be extended; the time required by the fable [10] elapses for the most part between the acts; for, of so much of the action as is represented, the real and poetical duration is the same. If in the first act preparations for war against Mithridates are represented to be made in Rome, the event of the war may, without absurdity, be represented in the catastrophe as happening in Pontus; we know that there is neither war, nor preparation for war; we know that we are neither in Rome nor Pontus; that neither Mithridates nor Lucullus are before us. The drama exhibits successive imitations of successive actions, and why may not the second imitation represent an action that happened years after the first, if it be so connected with it that nothing but time can be supposed to intervene? Time is, of all modes of existence, most obsequious [11] to the imagination; a lapse of years is as easily conceived as a passage of hours. In contemplation we easily contract the time of real actions, and therefore willingly permit it to be contracted when we only see their imitation.

It will be asked how the drama moves, if it is not credited. It is credited with all the credit due to a drama. It is credited, whenever it moves, as a just picture of a real original; as representing to the auditor what he would himself feel, if he were to do or suffer what is there feigned to be suffered or to be done. The reflection that strikes the heart is not, that the evils before us are real evils, but that they are evils to which we ourselves may be exposed. If there be any fallacy, it is not that we fancy the players, but that we fancy ourselves unhappy for a moment; but we rather lament the possibility than suppose the presence of misery, as a mother weeps over her babe when she remembers that death may take it from her. The delight of tragedy proceeds from our consciousness of fiction; if we thought murders and treasons real, they would please no more.

Imitations produce pain or pleasure, not because they are mistaken for realities, but because they bring realities to mind. When the imagination is recreated by a painted landscape, the trees are not supposed capable to give us shade, or the fountains coolness; but we consider how we should be pleased with such fountains playing beside us, and such woods waving over us. We are agitated in

[9] Fever.
[10] Plot.
[11] Subservient.

reading the history of *Henry the Fifth,* yet no man takes his book for the field of Agincourt. A dramatic exhibition is a book recited with concomitants that increase or diminish its effect. Familiar comedy is often more powerful in the theater, than on the page; imperial tragedy is always less. The humor of Petruchio may be heightened by grimace; but what voice or what gesture can hope to add dignity or force to the soliloquy of Cato?

A play read affects the mind like a play acted. It is therefore evident that the action is not supposed to be real, and it follows that between the acts a longer or shorter time may be allowed to pass, and that no more account of space or duration is to be taken by the auditor of a drama, than by the reader of a narrative, before whom may pass in an hour the life of a hero, or the revolutions of an empire.

(1765)

STUDY AIDS: 1. Although Johnson will contradict classicism's insistence on rules for drama, he firmly agrees with its demand for POETIC JUSTICE. Why is this? How is poetic justice related to the end of poetry? Notice the sentence (p. 440/2, ll. 41–45). Does Johnson's view have any relation to his belief that poetry should be universal rather than particular (see also p. 439, n. 2)?

2. Contemporary drama has almost freed itself from observing "poetic justice." The motion pictures, however, carefully observe it. Why? Do they observe it for the reason that Johnson approves of it? What attitude does television seem to be developing toward "poetic justice"?

3. Western civilization has long accepted as axiomatic the statement that "Art is an imitation of nature (reality)." What is Johnson's view of imitation? What, then, is the effect of literature according to Johnson?

Lives of the English Poets

When a group of London booksellers planned an edition of the English poets, they hired Johnson to write brief introductions. Many of the pieces, including those from which the following passages are drawn, grew beyond Johnson's original intention and are substantial studies. Loving "the biographical part of literature," he gave full and interesting accounts of his subjects' lives. Even more notable are his critical assessments of their writings. He may air his prejudice, as he does when he treats metaphysical poetry in his *Life of Cowley,* but in the selections here included he is more objective. The fine comparison of Dryden and Pope and the judicious comments on Addison are models of incisive criticism.

Joseph Addison

. . . .

Addison is now to be considered as a critic; a name which the present generation is scarcely willing to allow him. His criticism is condemned as tentative or experimental rather than scientific, and he is considered as deciding by taste rather than by principles.

It is not uncommon for those who have grown wise by the labor of others to add a little of their own, and overlook their masters. Addison is now despised by some who perhaps would never have seen his defects, but by the lights which he afforded them. That he always wrote as he would think it necessary to write now cannot be affirmed; his instructions were such as the character of his readers made proper. That general knowledge which now circulates in common talk was in his time rarely to be found. Men not professing learning were not ashamed of ignorance; and in the female world any acquaintance with books was distinguished only to be censured. His purpose was to infuse literary curiosity by gentle and unsuspected conveyance into the gay, the idle, and the wealthy; he therefore presented knowledge in the most alluring form, not lofty and austere, but accessible and familiar. When he showed them their defects, he showed them likewise that they might be easily supplied. His attempt succeeded; inquiry was awakened, and comprehension expanded. An emulation of intellectual elegance was excited; and from his time to our own, life has been gradually exalted, and conversation purified and enlarged.

Dryden had not many years before scattered criticism over his *Prefaces* with very little parsimony; but, though he sometimes condescended to be somewhat familiar, his manner was in general too scholastic for those who had yet their rudiments to learn, and found it not easy to understand their master. His observations were framed rather for those that were learning to write, than for those that read only to talk.

An instructor like Addison was now wanting, whose remarks being superficial, might be easily understood, and being just might prepare the mind for more attainments. Had he presented *Paradise Lost* to the public with all the pomp of system and severity of science, the criticism would perhaps have been admired, and the poem still have been neglected; but by the blandishments of gentleness and facility, he has made Milton an universal favorite, with whom readers of every class think it necessary to be pleased. . . .

As a describer of life and manners, he must be allowed to stand perhaps the first of the first rank. His humor, which, as Steele observes, is peculiar to himself, is so happily diffused as to give the grace of novelty to domestic scenes and daily occurrences. He never outsteps the modesty of nature, nor raises merriment or wonder by the violation of truth. His figures neither divert by distortion, nor amaze by aggravation. He copies life with so much fidelity, that he can be hardly said to invent; yet his exhibitions have an air so much original, that it is difficult to suppose them not merely the product of imagination.

As a teacher of wisdom, he may be confidently followed. His religion has nothing in it enthusiastic [1] or superstitious: he appears neither weakly credulous nor wantonly skep-

tical; his morality is neither dangerously lax nor impracticably rigid. All the enchantment of fancy and all the cogency of argument are employed to recommend to the reader his real interest, the care of pleasing the Author of his being. Truth is shown sometimes as the phantom of a vision; sometimes appears half-veiled in an allegory; sometimes attracts regard in the robes of fancy; and sometimes steps forth in the confidence of reason. She wears a thousand dresses, and in all is pleasing:

Mille habet ornatus, mille decenter habet.[2]

His prose is the model of the middle style; on grave subjects not formal, on light occasions not groveling; pure without scrupulosity, and exact without apparent elaboration; always equable, and always easy, without glowing words or pointed sentences. Addison never deviates from his track to snatch a grace; he seeks no ambitious ornaments, and tries no hazardous innovations. His page is always luminous, but never blazes in unexpected splendor.

It was apparently his principal endeavor to avoid all harshness and severity of diction; he is therefore sometimes verbose in his transitions and connections, and sometimes descends too much to the language of conversation; yet if his language had been less idiomatical it might have lost somewhat of its genuine Anglicism. What he attempted, he performed; he is never feeble, and he did not wish to be energetic; he is never rapid, and he never stagnates. His sentences have neither studied amplitude, nor affected brevity; his periods, though not diligently rounded, are voluble and easy. Whoever wishes to attain an English style, familiar but not coarse, and elegant but not ostentatious, must give his days and nights to the volumes of Addison.

(1779–1781)

STUDY AIDS: 1. What qualities of Addison as a critic does Johnson mention (paragraphs 1–4)? What determined the nature of Addison's criticism? What effect did it have?

2. Johnson implies that Addison's descriptions

---

[1] A term of disparagement in the eighteenth century. Johnson defined "enthusiasm" as "a vain belief in private revelation."

[2] Johnson translates the quotation in introducing it.

of life, his religion, and his prose style have a quality in common. What is it? Is the quality appropriate to a classic writer like Addison?

Alexander Pope

. . . .

[Pope] professed to have learned his poetry from Dryden, whom, whenever an opportunity was presented, he praised through his whole life with unvaried liberality; and perhaps his character may receive some illustration if he be compared with his master.

Integrity of understanding and nicety of discernment were not allotted in a less proportion to Dryden than to Pope. The rectitude of Dryden's mind was sufficiently shown by the dismission of his poetical prejudices, and the rejection of unnatural thoughts and rugged numbers. But Dryden never desired to apply all the judgment that he had. He wrote, and professed to write, merely for the people; and when he pleased others, he contented himself. He spent no time in struggles to rouse latent powers; he never attempted to make that better which was already good, nor often to mend what he must have known to be faulty. He wrote, as he tells us, with very little consideration; when occasion or necessity called upon him, he poured out what the present moment happened to supply, and, when once it had passed the press, ejected it from his mind; for when he had no pecuniary interest, he had no further solicitude.

Pope was not content to satisfy; he desired to excel, and therefore always endeavored to do his best: he did not court the candor, but dared the judgment of his reader, and, expecting no indulgence from others, he showed none to himself. He examined lines and words with minute and punctilious observation, and retouched every part with indefatigable diligence, till he had left nothing to be forgiven.

For this reason he kept his pieces very long in his hands, while he considered and reconsidered them. The only poems which can be supposed to have been written with such regard to the times as might hasten their pub-lication were the two satires of *Thirty-Eight;* [1] of which Dodsley [2] told me that they were brought to him by the author, that they might be fairly copied. "Almost every line," he said, "was then written twice over; I gave him a clean transcript, which he sent some time afterwards to me for the press, with almost every line written twice over a second time."

His declaration that his care for his works ceased at their publication was not strictly true. His parental attention never abandoned them; what he found amiss in the first edition, he silently corrected in those that followed. He appears to have revised the *Iliad,* and freed it from some of its imperfections; and the *Essay on Criticism* received many improvements after its first appearance. It will seldom be found that he altered without adding clearness, elegance, or vigor. Pope had perhaps the judgment of Dryden; but Dryden certainly wanted the diligence of Pope.

In acquired knowledge, the superiority must be allowed to Dryden, whose education was more scholastic, and who before he became an author had been allowed more time for study, with better means of information. His mind has a larger range, and he collects his images and illustrations from a more extensive circumference of science. Dryden knew more of man in his general nature, and Pope in his local manners. The notions of Dryden were formed by comprehensive speculation, and those of Pope by minute attention. There is more dignity in the knowledge of Dryden, and more certainty in that of Pope.

Poetry was not the sole praise of either; for both excelled likewise in prose; but Pope did not borrow his prose from his predecessor. The style of Dryden is capricious and varied; that of Pope is cautious and uniform. Dryden obeys the motions of his own mind; Pope constrains his mind to his own rules of composition. Dryden is sometimes vehement

[1] Two dialogues, which appeared under the title *One Thousand Seven Hundred and Thirty-Eight.* Since they dealt with the current political situation, immediate publication was essential.
[2] Robert Dodsley, author, bookseller, and publisher.

and rapid; Pope is always smooth, uniform, and gentle. Dryden's page is a natural field, rising into inequalities, and diversified by the varied exuberance of abundant vegetation; Pope's is a velvet lawn, shaven by the scythe, and leveled by the roller.

Of genius, that power which constitutes a poet; that quality without which judgment is cold, and knowledge is inert; that energy which collects, combines, amplifies, and animates; the superiority must, with some hesitation, be allowed to Dryden. It is not to be inferred that of this poetical vigor Pope had only a little, because Dryden had more; for every other writer since Milton must give place to Pope; and even of Dryden it must be said, that, if he has brighter paragraphs, he has not better poems. Dryden's performances were always hasty, either excited by some external occasion, or extorted by domestic necessity; he composed without consideration, and published without correction. What his mind could supply at call, or gather in one excursion, was all that he sought, and all that he gave. The dilatory caution of Pope enabled him to condense his sentiments, to multiply his images, and to accumulate all that study might produce or chance might supply. If the flights of Dryden therefore are higher, Pope continues longer on the wing. If of Dryden's fire the blaze is brighter, of Pope's the heat is more regular and constant. Dryden often surpasses expectation, and Pope never falls below it. Dryden is read with frequent astonishment, and Pope with perpetual delight.

This parallel will, I hope, when it is well considered, be found just; and if the reader should suspect me, as I suspect myself, of some partial fondness for the memory of Dryden, let him not too hastily condemn me; for meditation and inquiry may, perhaps, show him the reasonableness of my determination. . . .

To the praises which have been accumulated on *The Rape of the Lock* by readers of every class, from the critic to the waiting-maid, it is difficult to make any addition. Of that which is universally allowed to be the most attractive of all ludicrous compositions,

let it rather be now inquired from what sources the power of pleasing is derived.

Dr. Warburton,[3] who excelled in critical perspicacity, has remarked that the preternatural agents are very happily adapted to the purposes of the poem. The heathen deities can no longer gain attention: we should have turned away from a contest between Venus and Diana. The employment of allegorical persons always excites conviction of its own absurdity; they may produce effects, but cannot conduct actions; when the phantom is put in motion, it dissolves; thus Discord may raise a mutiny, but Discord cannot conduct a march, nor beseige a town. Pope brought into view a new race of beings, with powers and passions proportionate to their operation. The sylphs and gnomes act at the toilet and the tea-table, what more terrific and more powerful phantoms perform on the stormy ocean, or the field of battle; they give their proper help, and do their proper mischief.

Pope is said, by an objector, not to have been the inventor of this petty nation; a charge which might with more justice have been brought against the author of the *Iliad*, who doubtless adopted the religious system of his country; for what is there but the names of his agents which Pope has not invented? Has he not assigned them characters and operations never heard of before? Has he not, at least, given them their first poetical existence? If this is not sufficient to denominate his work original, nothing original ever can be written.

In this work are exhibited, in a very high degree, the two most engaging powers of an author. New things are made familiar, and familiar things are made new. A race of aerial people, never heard of before, is presented to us in a manner so clear and easy, that the reader seeks for no further information, but immediately mingles with his new acquaintance, adopts their interests, and attends their pursuits, loves a sylph, and detests a gnome.

That familiar things are made new, every

[3] William Warburton, Pope's literary executor, edited Pope's works in 1751.

paragraph will prove. The subject of the poem is an event below the common incidents of common life; nothing real is introduced that is not seen so often as to be no longer regarded, yet the whole detail of a female-day is here brought before us invested with so much art of decoration, that, though nothing is disguised, everything is striking, and we feel all the appetite of curiosity for that from which we have a thousand times turned fastidiously away.

The purpose of the poet is, as he tells us, to laugh at the little unguarded follies of the female sex. It is therefore without justice that Dennis [4] charges *The Rape of the Lock* with the want of a moral, and for that reason sets it below the *Lutrin,* which exposes the pride and discord of the clergy. Perhaps neither Pope nor Boileau [5] has made the world much better than he found it; but if they had both succeeded, it were easy to tell who would have deserved most from public gratitude. The freaks, and humors, and spleen, and vanity of women, as they embroil families in discord, and fill houses with disquiet, do more to obstruct the happiness of life in a year than the ambition of the clergy in many centuries. It has been well observed, that the misery of man proceeds not from any single crush of overwhelming evil, but from small vexations continually repeated.

It is remarked by Dennis likewise, that the machinery is superfluous; that, by all the bustle of preternatural operation, the main event is neither hastened nor retarded. To this charge an efficacious answer is not easily made. The sylphs cannot be said to help or to oppose, and it must be allowed to imply some want of art, that their power has not been sufficiently intermingled with the action. Other parts may likewise be charged with want of connection; the game of ombre might be spared, but if the lady had lost her hair while she was intent upon her cards, it might have been inferred that those who are too fond of play will be in danger of neglecting more important interests. Those perhaps are faults; but what are such faults to so much excellence! . . .

(1779–1781)

STUDY AIDS: 1. Johnson's method here is to make a point-by-point comparison, the first point (paragraphs 1–5) being the writing habits of Dryden and Pope and the reasons for them. At what other points does he compare them?

2. Johnson admits a partiality for Dryden (p. 446/1, ll. 7–44). Why does he prefer him to Pope? Is the partiality revealed in his comparative statements? If so, where?

3. Do his remarks on Dryden here agree with his remarks on Dryden in the *Life of Addison?* If not, how account for the difference?

4. What does Johnson do to gain variety of sentence pattern in his comparison of Dryden and Pope?

5. Determine, in Johnson's comment on *The Rape of the Lock,* how he answers the following questions about the supernatural creatures (sylphs, gnomes, etc.) in the poem: Did Pope originate them? Are they clearly presented? Are their doings integrated with the main action of the poem?

James Boswell
(1740–1795)

BOSWELL WAS BORN IN EDINBURGH OF AN OLD LANDED FAMILY. AFTER GRADUATING FROM the Universities of Edinburgh and Glasgow, he decided in 1763 to spend several months in London, en route to the University of Utrecht, where he was to study law. It was during this visit to London that he met Samuel Johnson. Boswell quickly cultivated

---

[4] John Dennis, literary critic in Pope's time.
[5] French critic and poet of the seventeenth century. His *Lutrin* is a satire in the mock-heroic vein.

the friendship of the famous man. After a year's sojourn in Utrecht, Boswell made the grand tour of Europe, assiduously searching out Rousseau, Voltaire, and General Paoli. He returned to Scotland in 1766, at which time he was admitted to the bar, and three years later he married Margaret Montgomerie. In 1773 he went to London, became a member of the famous Literary Club, and accompanied Dr. Johnson on a tour of the Hebrides Islands. It was on this journey that Boswell decided to write the biography of Johnson, which was not completed and published until 1791, seven years after Johnson's death.

Although one usually thinks of Boswell in connection with Dr. Johnson, he is himself a figure of considerable stature both as a writer and as a man. His writings include *An Account of Corsica* (1768), *Journal of a Tour to the Hebrides* (1789), and *The Life of Samuel Johnson* (1791). From the Boswell manuscripts discovered at Malahide Castle and Fettercairn House between 1930 and 1940 have come *The London Journal, 1762–63* (1950), *Boswell in Holland, 1763–64* (1952), *Boswell on the Grand Tour: Germany and Switzerland, 1764* (1953), *Boswell on the Grand Tour: Italy, Corsica, and France, 1765–66* (1955), and more yet to follow.

The reputation of Boswell has changed with the discovery of the manuscripts. It had suffered from remarks of Macaulay, who depicted Boswell as a fool, a toady, and a lickspittle. Now he is being recognized as a writer of consummate skill and as a man with an avid taste for experience coupled with an absorbing curiosity about human behavior, particularly his own.

The Life of Samuel Johnson

Boswell not only wrote the first modern biography and perhaps the greatest in the language but in its opening pages laid down principles which are still followed by biographers:

"Instead of melting down my materials into one mass, and constantly speaking in my own person, by which I might have appeared to have more merit in the execution of the work, I have resolved to adopt and enlarge upon the excellent plan of Mr. Mason, in his *Memoirs of Gray*. Wherever narrative is necessary to explain, connect, and supply, I furnish it to the best of my abilities; but in the chronological series of Johnson's life, which I trace as distinctly as I can, year by year, I produce, wherever it is in my power, his own minutes, letters or conversation, being convinced that this mode is more lively, and will make my readers better acquainted with him, than even most of those were who actually knew him. . . .

"Indeed I cannot conceive a more perfect mode of writing any man's life, than not only relating all the most important events of it in their order, but interweaving what he privately wrote, and said, and thought. . . .

"And he will be seen as he really was; for I profess to write, not his panegyric, which must be all praise, but his life. . . . In every picture there should be shade as well as light, and when I delineate him without reserve, I do what he himself recommended, both by his precept and his example."

[Boswell's First Meeting with Johnson (1763)]

At last, on Monday the 16th of May, when I was sitting in Mr. Davies's back-parlor, after having drunk tea with him and Mrs. Davies, 5 Johnson unexpectedly came into the shop; and Mr. Davies having perceived him through the glass-door in the room in which we were sitting, advancing towards us,—he announced his awful approach to me, somewhat in the manner of an actor in the part of Horatio, when he addresses Hamlet on the appearance of his father's ghost, "Look, my Lord, it comes." I found that I had a very perfect idea of Johnson's figure, from the portrait of him painted by Sir Joshua Reynolds soon after he had published his *Dictionary,* in the attitude of sitting in his easy chair in deep meditation, which was the first picture his friend did for him, which Sir Joshua very kindly presented to me, and from which an engraving has been made for this work. Mr. Davies mentioned my name, and respectfully introduced me to him. I was much agitated; and recollecting his prejudice against the Scotch, of which I had heard much, I said to Davies, "Don't tell where I come from."— "From Scotland," cried Davies roguishly. "Mr. Johnson," (said I) "I do indeed come from Scotland, but I cannot help it." I am willing to flatter myself that I meant this as light pleasantry to soothe and conciliate him, and not as an humiliating abasement at the expense of my country. But however that might be, this speech was somewhat unlucky; for with that quickness of wit for which he was so remarkable, he seized the expression "come from Scotland," which I used in the sense of being of that country; and, as if I had said that I had come away from it, or left it, retorted, "That, Sir, I find, is what a very great many of your countrymen cannot help." This stroke stunned me a good deal; and when we had sat down, I felt myself not a little embarrassed, and apprehensive of what might come next. He then addressed himself to Davies: "What do you think of Garrick?[1] He has refused me an order for the play for Miss Williams,[2] because he knows the house will be full, and that an order would be worth three shillings." Eager to take any opening to get into conversation with him, I ventured to say, "O, Sir, I cannot think Mr. Garrick would grudge such a trifle to you."

"Sir," (said he, with a stern look), "I have known David Garrick longer than you have done and I know no right you have to talk to me on the subject." Perhaps I deserved this check; for it was rather presumptuous in me, an entire stranger, to express any doubt of the justice of his animadversion upon his old acquaintance and pupil. I now felt myself much mortified, and began to think that the hope which I had long indulged of obtaining his acquaintance was blasted. And, in truth, had not my ardor been uncommonly strong, and my resolution uncommonly preservering, so rough a reception might have deterred me forever from making any further attempts. . . .

I was highly pleased with the extraordinary vigor of his conversation, and regretted that I was drawn away from it by an engagement at another place. I had, for a part of the evening, been left alone with him, and had ventured to make an observation now and then, which he received very civilly; so that I was satisfied that though there was a roughness in his manner, there was no ill-nature in his disposition. Davies followed me to the door, and when I complained to him a little of the hard blows which the great man had given me, he kindly took upon him to console me by saying, "Don't be uneasy. I can see he likes you very well."

A few days afterwards I called on Davies, and asked him if he thought I might take the liberty of waiting on Mr. Johnson at his chambers in the Temple. He said I certainly might, and that Mr. Johnson would take it as a compliment. So upon Tuesday the 24th of May, after having been enlivened by the witty sallies of Messieurs Thornton, Wilkes, Churchill and Lloyd,[3] with whom I had passed the morning, I boldly repaired to Johnson. His chambers were on the first floor of No. 1, Inner-Temple-lane, and I entered them with an impression given me by the

[1] David Garrick, the most famous actor of the eighteenth century. As a boy he had been a student in Johnson's school at Edial. When the school failed in 1737, he and Johnson went to London.

[2] Miss Anna Williams, friend and companion of Johnson. She was blind and lived for many years in Johnson's house with other persons whom he provided for.

[3] These men were literary figures of the day. Bonnell Thornton and Robert Lloyd are now forgotten. John Wilkes, in addition to being a notorious rake, was a friend of the American Revolution and an opponent of the English government; Charles Churchill was a virulent satirist.

Reverend Dr. Blair,[4] of Edinburgh, who had been introduced to him not long before, and described his having "found the giant in his den"; an expression, which, when I came to be pretty well acquainted with Johnson, I repeated to him, and he was diverted at this picturesque account of himself. Dr. Blair had been presented to him by Dr. James Fordyce.[5] At this time the controversy concerning the pieces published by Mr. James Macpherson, as translations of *Ossian,* was at its height. Johnson had all along denied their authenticity;[6] and, what was still more provoking to their admirers, maintained that they had no merit. The subject having been introduced by Dr. Fordyce, Dr. Blair, relying on the internal evidence of their antiquity, asked Dr. Johnson whether he thought any man of a modern age could have written such poems? Johnson replied, "Yes, Sir, many men, many women, and many children." Johnson, at this time, did not know that Dr. Blair had just published a *Dissertation,* not only defending their authenticity, but seriously ranking them with the poems of Homer and Virgil; and when he was afterwards informed of this

[4] Hugh Blair was a famous preacher and professor at the University of Edinburgh.
[5] Popular preacher and poet.
[6] James Macpherson was the alleged translator of supposedly old Gaelic manuscripts, which he claimed were written by an ancient Irish bard named Ossian. Johnson, from the beginning of the controversy, publicly claimed the manuscripts to be fraudulent and Macpherson dishonest. In 1775 Macpherson sent Johnson a challenge, which Johnson met by buying an oak club and dispatching the following letter to the challenger.

Mr. James Macpherson: I received your foolish and impudent letter. Any violence offered me I shall do my best to repel; and what I cannot do for myself the law shall do for me. I hope I shall never be deterred from detecting what I think a cheat, by the menaces of a ruffian.

What would you have me retract? I thought your book an imposture; I think it an imposture still. For this opinion I have given my reasons to the public, which I here dare you to refute. Your rage I defy. Your abilities, since your *Homer,* are not so formidable; and what I hear of your morals inclines me to pay regard not to what you shall say, but to what you shall prove. You may print this if you will.

Sam. Johnson

circumstance, he expressed some displeasure at Dr. Fordyce's having suggested the topic, and said, "I am not sorry that they got thus much for their pains. Sir, it was like leading one to talk of a book when the author is concealed behind the door."

He received me very courteously; but, it must be confessed, that his apartment, and furniture, and morning dress, were sufficiently uncouth. His brown suit of clothes looked very rusty; he had on a little old shriveled unpowdered wig, which was too small for his head; his shirt-neck and knees of his breeches were loose; his black worsted stockings ill drawn up; and he had a pair of unbuckled shoes by way of slippers. But all these slovenly particularities were forgotten the moment that he began to talk. Some gentlemen, whom I do not recollect, were sitting with him; and when they went away, I also rose; but he said to me, "Nay, don't go." "Sir," (said I), "I am afraid that I intrude upon you. It is benevolent to allow me to sit and hear you." He seemed pleased with this compliment, which I sincerely paid him, and answered, "Sir, I am obliged to any man who visits me." I have preserved the following short minute of what passed this day:—

"Madness frequently discovers itself merely by unnecessary deviation from the usual modes of the world. My poor friend Smart[7] showed the disturbance of his mind, by falling upon his knees, and saying his prayers in the street, or in any other unusual place. Now although, rationally speaking, it is greater madness not to pray at all, than to pray as Smart did, I am afraid there are so many who do not pray, that their understanding is not called in question."

Concerning this unfortunate poet, Christopher Smart, who was confined in a madhouse, he had, at another time, the following conversation with Dr. Burney:[8]—*Burney.* "How does poor Smart do, Sir; is he likely to recover?" *Johnson.* "It seems as if his mind had ceased to struggle with the disease; for he grows fat upon it." *Burney.* "Perhaps, Sir,

[7] A minor poet of the day.
[8] Musician, author, and father of Frances Burney, the novelist.

that may be from want of exercise." *Johnson.*
"No, Sir; he has partly as much exercise as
he used to have, for he digs in the garden.
Indeed, before his confinement, he used for
exercise to walk to the ale-house; but he
was *carried* back again. I did not think he
ought to be shut up. His infirmities were not
noxious to society. He insisted on people
praying with him; and I'd as lief pray with
Kit Smart as any one else. Another charge
was, that he did not love clean linen; and
I have no passion for it."—Johnson continued,
"Mankind have a great aversion to intellectual labor; but even supposing knowledge to
be easily attainable, more people would be
content to be ignorant than would take even a
little trouble to acquire it.

"The morality of an action depends on the
motive from which we act. If I fling half a
crown to a beggar with intention to break his
head, and he picks it up and buys victuals
with it, the physical effect is good; but, with
respect to me, the action is very wrong. So,
religious exercises, if not performed with an
intention to please God, avail us nothing. As
our Savior says of those who perform them
from other motives, 'Verily they have their
reward.'". . .

Before we parted, he was so good as to
promise to favor me with his company one
evening at my lodgings; and, as I took my
leave, shook me cordially by the hand. It is
almost needless to add, that I felt no little
elation at having now so happily established
an acquaintance of which I had been so long
ambitious.

My readers will, I trust, excuse me for
being thus minutely circumstantial, when it
is considered that the acquaintance of Dr.
Johnson was to me a most valuable acquisition, and laid the foundation of whatever
instruction and entertainment they may receive from my collections concerning the
great subject of the work which they are now
perusing. . . .

A revolution of some importance in my
plan of life had just taken place; for instead
of procuring a commission in the foot-
guards, which was my own inclination, I
had, in compliance with my father's wishes,
agreed to study the law; and was soon to set
out for Utrecht, to hear the lectures of an
excellent civilian in that university, and then
to proceed on my travels. Though very desirous of obtaining Dr. Johnson's advice and
instructions on the mode of pursuing my
studies, I was at this time so occupied, shall
I call it? or so dissipated, by the amusements
of London, that our next meeting was not
till Saturday, June 25, when happening to
dine at Clifton's eating-house, in Butcher-row,
I was surprised to perceive Johnson come in
and take his seat at another table. . . .

Finding him in a placid humor, and wishing to avail myself of the opportunity which
I fortunately had of consulting a sage, to hear
whose wisdom, I conceived in the ardor of
youthful imagination, that men filled with a
noble enthusiasm for intellectual improvement would gladly have resorted from distant
lands;—I opened my mind to him ingenuously, and gave him a little sketch of my life,
to which he was pleased to listen with great
attention.

I acknowledged that though educated very
strictly in the principles of religion, I had for
some time been misled into a certain degree
of infidelity; but that I was come now to a
better way of thinking, and was fully satisfied
of the truth of the Christian revelation,
though I was not clear as to every point
considered to be orthodox. Being at all times
a curious examiner of the human mind, and
pleased with an undisguised display of what
had passed in it, he called to me with warmth,
"Give me your hand; I have taken a liking
to you." He then began to descant upon the
force of testimony, and the little we could
know of final causes; so that the objections
of, why was it so? or why was it not so?
ought not to disturb us: adding, that he himself had at one period been guilty of a temporary neglect of religion, but that it was not
the result of argument, but mere absence of
thought.

After having given credit to reports of his
bigotry, I was agreeably surprised when he
expressed the following very liberal sentiment,
which has the additional value of obviating
an objection to our holy religion, founded

upon the discordant tenets of Christians themselves: "For my part, Sir, I think all Christians, whether Papists or Protestants, agree in the essential articles, and that their differences are trivial, and rather political than religious."

We talked of belief in ghosts. He said, "Sir, I make a distinction between what a man may experience by the mere strength of his imagination, and what imagination cannot possibly produce. Thus, suppose I should think that I saw a form, and heard a voice cry 'Johnson, you are a very wicked fellow, and unless you repent you will certainly be punished'; my own unworthiness is so deeply impressed upon my mind, that I might imagine I thus saw and heard, and therefore I should not believe that an external communication had been made to me. But if a form should appear, and a voice should tell me that a particular man had died at a particular place, and a particular hour, a fact which I had no apprehension of, nor any means of knowing, and this fact, with all its circumstances, should afterwards be unquestionably proved, I should, in that case, be persuaded that I had supernatural intelligence imparted to me."

Here it is proper, once for all, to give a true and fair statement of Johnson's way of thinking upon the question, whether departed spirits are ever permitted to appear in this world, or in any way to operate upon human life. He has been ignorantly misrepresented as weakly credulous upon that subject; and, therefore, though I feel an inclination to disdain and treat with silent contempt so foolish a notion concerning my illustrious friend, yet as I find it has gained ground, it is necessary to refute it. The real fact then is, that Johnson had a very philosophical mind, and such a rational respect for testimony, as to make him submit his understanding to what was authentically proved, though he could not comprehend why it was so. Being thus disposed, he was willing to inquire into the truth of any relation of supernatural agency, a general belief of which has prevailed in all nations and ages. But so far was he from being the dupe of implicit faith, that he examined the matter with a jealous attention, and no man was more ready to refute its falsehood when he had discovered it. Churchill, in his poem entitled The Ghost, availed himself of the absurd credulity imputed to Johnson, and drew a caricature of him under the name of Pomposo, representing him as one of the believers of the story of a ghost in Cock-lane, which, in the year 1762, had gained very general credit in London. Many of my readers, I am convinced, are to this hour under an impression that Johnson was thus foolishly deceived. It will therefore surprise them a good deal when they are informed upon undoubted authority, that Johnson was one of those by whom the imposture was detected. The story had become so popular, that he thought it should be investigated; and in this research he was assisted by the Reverend Dr. Douglas, now Bishop of Salisbury, the great detector of impostures; who informs me, that after the gentlemen who went and examined into the evidence were satisfied of its falsity, Johnson wrote in their presence an account of it, which was published in the newspapers and Gentleman's Magazine, and undeceived the world.

Our conversation proceeded. "Sir," (said he) "I am a friend to subordination, as most conducive to the happiness of society. There is a reciprocal pleasure in governing and being governed.

"Dr. Goldsmith is one of the first men we now have as an author, and he is a very worthy man too. He has been loose in his principles, but he is coming right.". . .

As Dr. Oliver Goldsmith will frequently appear in this narrative, I shall endeavor to make my readers in some degree acquainted with his singular character. He was a native of Ireland, and a contemporary with Mr. Burke [9] at Trinity College, Dublin, but did not then give much promise of future celebrity. He, however, observed to Mr. Malone,[10] that "though he made no great figure in mathematics, which was a study in much

[9] Edmund Burke, famous statesman and author.
[10] Edmund Malone, editor of Shakespeare and a reviser of Boswell's Life of Johnson.

repute there, he could turn an Ode of Horace into English better than any of them." He afterwards studied physic at Edinburgh, and upon the Continent; and I have been informed, was enabled to pursue his travels on foot, partly by demanding at universities to enter the lists as disputant, by which, according to the custom of many of them, he was entitled to the premium of a crown, when luckily for him his challenge was not accepted; so that, as I once observed to Dr. Johnson, he disputed his passage through Europe. He then came to England, and was employed successively in the capacities of an usher to an academy, a corrector of the press, a reviewer, and a writer for a newspaper. He had sagacity enough to cultivate assiduously the acquaintance of Johnson, and his faculties were gradually enlarged by the contemplation of such a model. To me and many others it appeared that he studiously copied the manner of Johnson, though, indeed, upon a smaller scale.

At this time I think he had published nothing with his name, though it was pretty generally known that one Dr. Goldsmith was the author of *An Enquiry into the Present State of Polite Learning in Europe,* and of *The Citizen of the World,* a series of letters supposed to be written from London by a Chinese. No man had the art of displaying with more advantage as a writer, whatever literary acquisitions he made. *"Nihil quod tetigit non ornavit."* [11] His mind resembled a fertile, but thin soil. There was a quick, but not a strong vegetation, of whatever chanced to be thrown upon it. No deep root could be struck. The oak of the forest did not grow there; but the elegant shrubbery and the fragrant parterre appeared in gay succession. It has been generally circulated and believed that he was a mere fool in conversation; but, in truth, this has been greatly exaggerated. He had, no doubt, a more than common share of that hurry of ideas which we often find in his countrymen, and which sometimes produces a laughable confusion in expressing them. He was very much what the French call *un étourdi,* [12] and from vanity and an eager desire of being conspicuous wherever he was, he frequently talked carelessly without knowledge of the subject, or even without thought. His person was short, his countenance coarse and vulgar, his deportment that of a scholar awkwardly affecting the easy gentleman. Those who were in any way distinguished, excited envy in him to so ridiculous an excess, that the instances of it are hardly credible. When accompanying two beautiful young ladies with their mother on a tour in France, he was seriously angry that more attention was paid to them than to him; and once at the exhibition of the Fantoccini in London, when those who sat next him observed with what dexterity a puppet was made to toss a pike, he could not bear that it should have such praise, and exclaimed with some warmth, "Pshaw! I can do it better myself."

He, I am afraid, had no settled system of any sort, so that his conduct must not be strictly scrutinized; but his affections were social and generous, and when he had money he gave it away very liberally. His desire of imaginary consequence predominated over his attention to truth. When he began to rise into notice, he said he had a brother who was Dean of Durham, a fiction so easily detected, that it is wonderful how he should have been so inconsiderate as to hazard it. He boasted to me at this time of the power of his pen in commanding money, which I believe was true in a certain degree, though in the instance he gave he was by no means correct. He told me that he had sold a novel for four hundred pounds. This was his *Vicar of Wakefield.* But Johnson informed me, that he had made the bargain for Goldsmith, and the price was sixty pounds. "And, Sir," (said he), "a sufficient price too, when it was sold; for then the fame of Goldsmith had not been elevated, as it afterwards was, by his *Traveler;* and the bookseller had such faint hopes of profit by his bargain, that he kept the manuscript by him a long time, and did not pub-

[11] "He touched nothing that he did not adorn" (Johnson's translation of his epitaph on Goldsmith).

[12] "A scatter brain."

lish it till after *The Traveler* had appeared. Then, to be sure, it was accidentally worth more money."

Mrs. Piozzi [13] and Sir John Hawkins have strangely misstated the history of Goldsmith's situation and Johnson's friendly interference, when this novel was sold. I shall give it authentically from Johnson's own exact narration:—"I received one morning a message from poor Goldsmith that he was in great distress, and as it was not in his power to come to me, begging that I would come to him as soon as possible. I sent him a guinea, and promised to come to him directly. I accordingly went as soon as I was dressed, and found that his landlady had arrested him for his rent, at which he was in a violent passion. I perceived that he had already changed my guinea, and had got a bottle of Madeira and a glass before him. I put the cork into the bottle, desired he would be calm, and began to talk to him of the means by which he might be extricated. He then told me that he had a novel ready for the press, which he produced to me. I looked into it, and saw its merit; told the landlady I should soon return, and having gone to a bookseller, sold it for sixty pounds. I brought Goldsmith the money, and he discharged his rent, not without rating his landlady in a high tone for having used him so ill."

My next meeting with Johnson was on Friday the 1st of July, when he and I and Dr. Goldsmith supped together at the Mitre. . . .

Talking of the eminent writers in Queen Anne's reign, he observed, "I think Dr. Arbuthnot the first man among them. He was the most universal genius, being an excellent physician, a man of deep learning, and a man of much humor. Mr. Addison was, to be sure, a great man; his learning was not profound; but his morality, his humor, and his elegance of writing, set him very high."

Mr. Ogilvie was unlucky enough to choose for the topic of his conversation the praises of his native country. He began with saying, that there was very rich land round Edinburgh. Goldsmith, who had studied physic there, contradicted this, very untruly, with a sneering laugh.[14] Disconcerted a little by this, Mr. Ogilvie then took new ground, where, I suppose, he thought himself perfectly safe; for he observed, that Scotland had a great many noble wild prospects. *Johnson.* "I believe, Sir, you have a great many. Norway, too, has noble wild prospects; and Lapland is remarkable for prodigious noble wild prospects. But, Sir, let me tell you, the noblest prospect which a Scotchman ever sees, is the high road that leads him to England!" This unexpected and pointed sally produced a roar of applause. After all, however, those who admire the rude grandeur of nature cannot deny it to Caledonia. . . .

He enlarged very convincingly upon the excellence of rhyme over blank verse in English poetry. I mentioned to him that Dr. Adam Smith,[15] in his lectures upon composition, when I studied under him in the College of Glasgow, had maintained the same opinion strenuously, and I repeated some of his arguments. *Johnson.* "Sir, I was once in company with Smith, and we did not take to each other; but had I known that he loved rhyme as much as you tell me he does, I should have hugged him.". . .

[Johnson on Merit Set against Fortune (1763)]

Rousseau's treatise on the inequality of mankind was at this time a fashionable topic.[1] It gave rise to an observation by Mr. Dempster,[2] that the advantages of fortune and rank were nothing to a wise man, who ought to

---

[14] In what ways does Boswell reveal his attitude toward Goldsmith?

[15] Noted political economist, author of *Wealth of Nations* (1776).

[1] Jean Jacques Rousseau (1712–1778), social reformer, revolutionist, and philosopher of the Romantic movement. The treatise mentioned here may be his *Discourse on Inequality* (1754) or the *Social Contract* (1762).

[2] George Dempster, politician and authority on agriculture.

---

[13] Mrs. Piozzi, formerly Mrs. Henry Thrale and intimate friend of Johnson before her marriage to the Italian Piozzi. She wrote *Anecdotes of Johnson.* Sir John Hawkins was a prominent London lawyer who wrote a *Life of Johnson.*

value only merit. *Johnson.* "If man were a savage, living in the woods by himself, this might be true; but in civilized society we all depend upon each other, and our happiness is very much owing to the good opinion of mankind. Now, Sir, in civilized society, external advantages make us more respected. A man with a good coat upon his back meets with a better reception than he who has a bad one. Sir, you may analyze this, and say what is there in it? But that will avail you nothing, for it is a part of a general system. Pound St. Paul's Church into atoms, and consider any single atom; it is, to be sure, good for nothing: but, put all these atoms together, and you have St. Paul's Church. So it is with human felicity, which is made up of many ingredients, each of which may be shown to be very insignificant. In civilized society, personal merit will not serve you so much as money will. Sir, you may make the experiment. Go into the street, and give one man a lecture on morality, and another a shilling, and see which will respect you most. If you wish only to support nature, Sir William Petty fixes your allowance at three pounds a year; but as times are much altered, let us call it six pounds. This sum will fill your belly, shelter you from the weather, and even get you a strong lasting coat, supposing it to be made of good bull's hide. Now, Sir, all beyond this is artificial, and is desired in order to obtain a greater degree of respect from our fellow-creatures. And, Sir, if six hundred pounds a year procure a man more consequence, and, of course, more happiness than six pounds a year, the same proportion will hold as to six thousand, and so on as far as opulence can be carried. Perhaps he who has a large fortune may not be so happy as he who has a small one; but that must proceed from other causes than from his having the large fortune: for, *caeteris paribus*,[3] he who is rich in a civilized society, must be happier than he who is poor; as riches, if properly used, (and it is a man's own fault if they are not), must be productive of the highest advantages. Money, to be sure, of itself is of no use; for its only use is to part

with it. Rousseau, and all those who deal in paradoxes, are led away by a childish desire of novelty. When I was a boy, I used always to choose the wrong side of a debate, because most ingenious things, that is to say, most new things, could be said upon it. Sir, there is nothing for which you may not muster up more plausible arguments, than those which are urged against wealth and other external advantages. Why, now, there is stealing; why should it be thought a crime? When we consider by what unjust methods property has been often acquired, and that what was unjustly got it must be unjust to keep, where is the harm in one man's taking the property of another from him? Besides, Sir, when we consider the bad use that many people make of their property, and how much better use the thief may make of it, it may be defended as a very allowable practice. Yet, Sir, the experience of mankind has discovered stealing to be so very bad a thing, that they make no scruple to hang a man for it. When I was running about this town a very poor fellow, I was a great arguer for the advantages of poverty; but I was, at the same time, very sorry to be poor. Sir, all the arguments which are brought to represent poverty as no evil, show it to be evidently a great evil. You never find people laboring to convince you that you may live very happily upon a plentiful fortune.—So you hear people talking how miserable a king must be; and yet they all wish to be in his place."

[Johnson's Peculiarities (1764)]

About this time he was afflicted with a very severe return of the hypochondriac disorder which was ever lurking about him. He was so ill as, notwithstanding his remarkable love of company, to be entirely averse to society, the most fatal symptom of that malady. Dr. Adams told me that as an old friend he was admitted to visit him, and that he found him in a deplorable state, sighing, groaning, talking to himself, and restlessly walking from room to room. He then used this emphatical expression of the misery which he felt: "I would consent to have a limb amputated to recover my spirits."

[3] "Other things being equal."

Talking to himself was, indeed, one of his singularities ever since I knew him. I was certain that he was frequently uttering pious ejaculations; for fragments of the Lord's Prayer have been distinctly overheard. His friend Mr. Thomas Davies, of whom Churchill says, "That Davies hath a very pretty wife," when Dr. Johnson muttered "lead us not into temptation," used with waggish and gallant humor to whisper Mrs. Davies, "You, my dear, are the cause of this."

He had another particularity, of which none of his friends ever ventured to ask an explanation. It appeared to me some superstitious habit which he had contracted early, and from which he had never called upon his reason to disentangle him. This was his anxious care to go out or in at a door or passage by a certain number of steps from a certain point, or at least so as that either his right or his left foot (I am not certain which) should constantly make the first actual movement when he came close to the door or passage. Thus I conjecture: for I have upon innumerable occasions observed him suddenly stop, and then seem to count his steps with a deep earnestness; and when he had neglected or gone wrong in this sort of magical movement, I have seen him go back again, put himself in a proper posture to begin the ceremony, and, having gone through it, break from his abstraction, walk briskly on, and join his companion. A strange instance of something of this nature, even when on horseback, happened when he was in the Isle of Skye. Sir Joshua Reynolds has observed him to go a good way about rather than cross a particular alley in Leicester Fields; but this Sir Joshua imputed to his having had some disagreeable recollection associated with it.

That the most minute singularities which belonged to him, and made very observable parts of his appearance and manner, may not be omitted, it is requisite to mention that while talking or even musing as he sat in his chair, he commonly held his head to one side towards his right shoulder, and shook it in a tremulous manner, moving his body backwards and forwards, and rubbing his left knee in the same direction with the palm of his hand. In the intervals of articulating he made various sounds with his mouth, sometimes as if ruminating, or what is called chewing the cud, sometimes giving a half whistle, sometimes making his tongue play backwards from the roof of his mouth, as if clucking like a hen, and sometimes protruding it against his upper gums in front, as if pronouncing quickly under his breath "too, too, too"; all this accompanied sometimes with a thoughtful look, but more frequently with a smile. Generally when he had concluded a period in the course of a dispute, by which time he was a good deal exhausted by violence and vociferation, he used to blow out his breath like a whale. This I supposed was a relief to his lungs; and seemed in him to be a contemptuous mode of expression, as if he had made the arguments of his opponent fly like chaff before the wind.

I am fully aware how very obvious an occasion I here give for the sneering jocularity of such as have no relish of an exact likeness; which to render complete, he who draws it must not disdain the slightest strokes. But if witlings should be inclined to attack on this account, let them have the candor to quote what I have offered in my defense. . . .

[Johnson's Meeting with
John Wilkes (1776)]

I am now to record a very curious incident in Dr. Johnson's life, which fell under my own observation; of which *pars magna fui*,[1] and which I am persuaded will, with the liberal-minded, be much to his credit.

My desire of being acquainted with celebrated men of every description, had made me, much about the same time, obtain an introduction to Dr. Samuel Johnson and to John Wilkes, Esq. Two men more different could perhaps not be selected out of all mankind. They had even attacked one another with some asperity in their writings; yet I lived in habits of friendship with both. I could fully relish the excellence of each; for

[1] "In which I played a large part." Boswell often thrust Johnson into disconcerting situations quite deliberately in order to observe his responses.

I have ever delighted in that intellectual chemistry, which can separate good qualities from evil in the same person.

Sir John Pringle, "mine own friend and my father's friend," between whom and Dr. Johnson I in vain wished to establish an acquaintance, as I respected and lived in intimacy with both of them, observed to me once, very ingeniously, "It is not in friendship as in mathematics where two things each equal to a third, are equal between themselves. You agree with Johnson as a middle quality, and you agree with me as a middle quality; but Johnson and I should not agree." Sir John was not sufficiently flexible; so I desisted; knowing, indeed, that the repulsion was equally strong on the part of Johnson; who, I know not from what cause, unless his being a Scotchman, had formed a very erroneous opinion of Sir John. But I conceived an irresistible wish, if possible, to bring Dr. Johnson and Mr. Wilkes together. How to manage it, was a nice and difficult matter.

My worthy booksellers and friends, Messieurs Dilly in the Poultry, at whose hospitable and well-covered table I have seen a greater number of literary men, than at any other, except that of Sir Joshua Reynolds, had invited me to meet Mr. Wilkes and some more gentlemen on Wednesday, May 15. "Pray" (said I), "let us have Dr. Johnson."— "What, with Mr. Wilkes? Not for the world," (said Mr. Edward Dilly): "Dr. Johnson would never forgive me."—"Come," (said I), "if you'll let me negotiate for you, I will be answerable that all shall go well." Dilly. "Nay, if you will take it upon you, I am sure I shall be very happy to see them both here."

Notwithstanding the high veneration which I entertained for Dr. Johnson, I was sensible that he was sometimes a little actuated by the spirit of contradiction, and by means of that I hoped I should gain my point. I was persuaded that if I had come upon him with a direct proposal, "Sir, will you dine in company with Jack Wilkes?" he would have flown into a passion, and would probably have answered, "Dine with Jack Wilkes, Sir! I'd as soon dine with Jack Ketch."[2] I therefore, while we were sitting quietly by ourselves at his house in an evening, took occasion to open my plan thus:—"Mr. Dilly, Sir, sends his respectful compliments to you, and would be happy if you would do him the honor to dine with him on Wednesday next along with me, as I must soon go to Scotland." Johnson. "Sir, I am obliged to Mr. Dilly. I will wait upon him—" Boswell. "Provided, Sir, I suppose, that the company which he is to have, is agreeable to you." Johnson. "What do you mean, Sir? What do you take me for? Do you think I am so ignorant of the world as to imagine that I am to prescribe to a gentleman what company he is to have at his table?" Boswell. "I beg your pardon, Sir, for wishing to prevent you from meeting people whom you might not like. Perhaps he may have some of what he calls his patriotic friends with him." Johnson. "Well, Sir, and what then? What care I for his patriotic friends?[3] Poh!" Boswell. "I should not be surprised to find Jack Wilkes there." Johnson. "And if Jack Wilkes should be there, what is that to me, Sir? My dear friend, let us have no more of this. I am sorry to be angry with you; but really it is treating me strangely to talk to me as if I could not meet any company whatever, occasionally." Boswell. "Pray forgive me, Sir: I meant well. But you shall meet whoever comes, for me." Thus I secured him, and told Dilly that he would find him very well pleased to be one of his guests on the day appointed.

Upon the much-expected Wednesday, I called on him about half an hour before dinner, as I often did when we were to dine out together, to see that he was ready in time, and to accompany him. I found him buffeting his books, as upon a former occasion, covered with dust, and making no prep-

[2] An official executioner, who died in 1686. Boswell's note states, "This has been circulated as if actually said by Johnson, when the truth is, it was only *supposed* by me."

[3] The Whigs who opposed George III and his government. Johnson was so staunch a Tory that in his *Dictionary* he defined Whig as "the name of a faction."

aration for going abroad. "How is this, Sir?" (said I). "Don't you recollect that you are to dine at Mr. Dilly's?" *Johnson.* "Sir, I did not think of going to Dilly's: it went out of my head. I have ordered dinner at home with Mrs. Williams." *Boswell.* "But, my dear Sir, you know you were engaged to Mr. Dilly, and I told him so. He will expect you, and will be much disappointed if you don't come." *Johnson.* "You must talk to Mrs. Williams about this."

Here was a sad dilemma. I feared that what I was so confident I had secured would yet be frustrated. He had accustomed himself to show Mrs. Williams such a degree of humane attention, as frequently imposed some restraint upon him; and I knew that if she should be obstinate, he would not stir. I hastened down stairs to the blind lady's room, and told her I was in great uneasiness, for Dr. Johnson had engaged to me to dine this day at Mr. Dilly's, but that he had told me he had forgotten his engagement, and had ordered dinner at home. "Yes, Sir," (said she, pretty peevishly), "Dr. Johnson is to dine at home."—"Madam," (said I), "his respect for you is such, that I know he will not leave you unless you absolutely desire it. But as you have so much of his company, I hope you will be good enough to forego it for a day; as Mr. Dilly is a very worthy man, has frequently had agreeable parties at his house for Dr. Johnson, and will be vexed if the Doctor neglects him to-day. And then, Madam, be pleased to consider my situation; I carried the message, and I assured Mr. Dilly that Dr. Johnson was to come, and no doubt he has made a dinner, and invited a company, and boasted of the honor he expected to have. I shall be quite disgraced if the Doctor is not there." She gradually softened to my solicitations, which were certainly as earnest as most entreaties to ladies upon any occasion, and was graciously pleased to empower me to tell Dr. Johnson, "that all things considered, she thought he should certainly go." I flew back to him, still in dust, and careless of what should be the event, "indifferent in his choice to go or stay"; but as soon as I had announced to him Mrs. Williams' con-

sent, he roared, "Frank,[4] a clean shirt," and was very soon dressed. When I had him fairly seated in a hackney-coach with me, I exulted as much as a fortune-hunter who has got an heiress into a postchaise with him to set out for Gretna-Green.

When we entered Mr. Dilly's drawing room, he found himself in the midst of a company he did not know. I kept myself snug and silent, watching how he would conduct himself. I observed him whispering to Mr. Dilly, "Who is that gentleman, Sir?"—"Mr. Arthur Lee."—*Johnson.* "Too, too, too," (under his breath), which was one of his habitual mutterings. Mr. Arthur Lee[5] could not but be very obnoxious to Johnson, for he was not only a patriot but an American. He was afterwards minister from the United States at the court of Madrid. "And who is the gentleman in lace?"—"Mr. Wilkes, Sir." This information confounded him still more; he had some difficulty to restrain himself, and taking up a book, sat down upon a window-seat and read, or at least kept his eye upon it intently for some time, till he composed himself. His feelings, I dare say, were awkward enough. But he no doubt recollected his having rated me for supposing that he could be at all disconcerted by any company, and he, therefore, resolutely set himself to behave quite as an easy man of the world, who could adapt himself at once to the disposition and manners of those whom he might chance to meet.

The cheering sound of "Dinner is upon the table," dissolved his reverie, and we all sat down without any symptom of ill humor. There were present, beside Mr. Wilkes, and Mr. Arthur Lee, who was an old companion of mine when he studied physic at Edinburgh, Mr. (now Sir John) Miller, Dr. Lettsom, and Mr. Slater the druggist. Mr. Wilkes placed himself next to Dr. Johnson, and behaved to him with so much attention and politeness, that he gained upon him insen-

[4] Francis Barber, Johnson's Negro servant.
[5] American lawyer and English agent for the Colony of Massachusetts. As assistant to Benjamin Franklin he helped negotiate the treaty between France and America in 1778.

sibly. No man eat more heartily than Johnson, or loved better what was nice and delicate. Mr. Wilkes was very assiduous in helping him to some fine veal. "Pray give me leave, Sir:—It is better here—A little of the brown—Some fat, Sir—A little of the stuffing—Some gravy—Let me have the pleasure of giving you some butter—Allow me to recommend a squeeze of this orange;—or the lemon, perhaps, may have more zest."—"Sir, Sir, I am obliged to you, Sir," cried Johnson, bowing, and turning his head to him with a look for some time of "surly virtue," but, in a short while, of complacency.

Foote [6] being mentioned, Johnson said, "He is not a good mimic." One of the company added, "A merry Andrew, a buffoon." *Johnson.* "But he has wit too, and is not deficient in ideas, or in fertility and variety of imagery, and not empty of reading; he has knowledge enough to fill up his part. One species of wit he has in an eminent degree, that of escape. You drive him into a corner with both hands; but he's gone, Sir, when you think you have got him—like an animal that jumps over your head. Then he has a great range for wit; he never lets truth stand between him and a jest, and he is sometimes mighty coarse. Garrick is under many restraints from which Foote is free." *Wilkes.* "Garrick's wit is more like Lord Chesterfield's." *Johnson.* "The first time I was in company with Foote was at Fitzherbert's. Having no good opinion of the fellow, I was resolved not to be pleased; and it is very difficult to please a man against his will. I went on eating my dinner pretty sullenly, affecting not to mind him. But the dog was so very comical, that I was obliged to lay down my knife and fork, throw myself back upon my chair, and fairly laugh it out. No, Sir, he was irresistible. He upon one occasion experienced, in an extraordinary degree, the efficacy of his powers of entertaining. Amongst the many and various modes which he tried of getting money, he became a partner with a small-beer brewer, and he was to have a share of the profits for procuring customers amongst his numerous acquaintance.

[6] A popular comedian and dramatist.

Fitzherbert was one who took his small-beer; but it was so bad that the servants resolved not to drink it. They were at some loss how to notify their resolution, being afraid of offending their master, who they knew liked Foote much as a companion. At last they fixed upon a little black boy, who was rather a favorite, to be their deputy, and deliver their remonstrance; and having invested him with the whole authority of the kitchen, he was to inform Mr. Fitzherbert, in all their names, upon a certain day, that they would drink Foote's small-beer no longer. On that day Foote happened to dine at Fitzherbert's, and this boy served at table; he was so delighted with Foote's stories, and merriment, and grimace, that when he went down stairs, he told them, 'This is the finest man I have ever seen. I will not deliver your message. I will drink his small-beer.'"

Somebody observed that Garrick could not have done this. *Wilkes.* "Garrick would have made the small-beer still smaller. He is now leaving the stage; but he will play Scrub [7] all his life." I knew that Johnson would let nobody attack Garrick but himself, as Garrick once said to me, and I had heard him praise his liberality; so to bring out his commendation of his celebrated pupil, I said, loudly, "I have heard Garrick is liberal." *Johnson.* "Yes, Sir, I know that Garrick has given away more money than any man in England that I am acquainted with, and that not from ostentatious views. Garrick was very poor when he began life; so when he came to have money, he probably was very unskilful in giving away, and saved when he should not. But Garrick began to be liberal as soon as he could; and I am of opinion, the reputation of avarice which he has had, has been very lucky for him, and prevented his having many enemies. You despise a man for avarice, but do not hate him. Garrick might have been much better attacked for living with more splendor than is suitable to a player: if they had had the wit to have assaulted him in that quarter, they might have galled him more. But they have kept clamor-

[7] A country servant in *The Beaux' Stratagem* by George Farquhar.

ing about his avarice, which has rescued him from much obloquy and envy."

Talking of the great difficulty of obtaining authentic information for biography, Johnson told us, "When I was a young fellow I wanted to write the *Life of Dryden,* and in order to get materials, I applied to the only two persons then alive who had seen him; these were old Swinney, and old Cibber. Swinney's information was no more than this, 'That at Will's coffee-house Dryden had a particular chair for himself, which was set by the fire in winter, and was then called his winter-chair; and that it was carried out for him to the balcony in summer, and was then called his summer-chair.' Cibber [8] could tell no more but 'that he remembered him a decent old man, arbiter of critical disputes at Will's.' You are to consider that Cibber was then at a great distance from Dryden, had perhaps one leg only in the room, and durst not draw in the other." *Boswell.* "Yet Cibber was a man of observation?" *Johnson.* "I think not." *Boswell.* "You will allow his *Apology* to be well done." *Johnson.* "Very well done, to be sure, Sir. That book is a striking proof of the justice of Pope's remark:

Each might his several province well
    command
Would all but stoop to what they under-
    stand."

Boswell. "And his plays are good." *Johnson.* "Yes; but that was his trade; *l'esprit du corps:* he had been all his life among players and play-writers. I wondered that he had so little to say in conversation, for he had kept the best company, and learned all that can be got by the ear. He abused Pindar to me, and then showed me an ode of his own, with an absurd couplet, making a linnet soar on an eagle's wing. I told him that when the ancients made a simile, they always made it like something real."

Mr. Wilkes remarked, that "among all the bold flights of Shakespeare's imagination, the boldest was making Birnam-wood march to Dunsinane; creating a wood where there

never was a shrub; a wood in Scotland! ha! ha! ha!" And he also observed, that "the clannish slavery of the Highlands of Scotland was the single exception to Milton's remark of 'The Mountain Nymph, sweet Liberty,' being worshipped in all hilly countries." —"When I was at Inverary" (said he), "on a visit to my old friend, Archibald, Duke of Argyle, his dependents congratulated me on being such a favorite of his Grace. I said, 'It is then, gentlemen, truly lucky for me; for if I had displeased the Duke, and he had wished it, there is not a Campbell among you but would have been ready to bring John Wilkes's head to him in a charger. It would have been only

Off with his head! So much for
    Aylesbury.[9]

I was then member for Aylesbury." . . .

Mr. Arthur Lee mentioned some Scotch who had taken possession of a barren part of America, and wondered why they should choose it. *Johnson.* "Why, Sir, all barrenness is comparative. The Scotch would not know it to be barren." *Boswell.* "Come, come, he is flattering the English. You have now been in Scotland, Sir, and say if you did not see meat and drink enough there." *Johnson.* "Why yes, Sir; meat and drink enough to give the inhabitants sufficient strength to run away from home." All these quick and lively sallies were said sportively, quite in jest, and with a smile, which showed that he meant only wit. Upon this topic he and Mr. Wilkes could perfectly assimilate; here was a bond of union between them, and I was conscious that as both of them had visited Caledonia, both were fully satisfied of the strange narrow ignorance of those who imagine that it is a land of famine. But they amused themselves with persevering in the old jokes. When I claimed a superiority for Scotland over England in one respect, that no man can be arrested there for a debt merely because another swears it against him; but there must

---

[8] Colley Cibber, popular actor and dramatist of the early eighteenth century.

[9] Wilkes was representative in Parliament for Aylesbury. The quotation is a parody of a line from Cibber's adaptation of Shakespeare's *Richard III.*

first be the judgment of a court of law ascertaining its justice; and that a seizure of the person, before judgment is obtained, can take place only, if his creditor should swear that he is about to fly from the country, or, as it is technically expressed, is *in meditatione fugæ*.[10] *Wilkes.* "That, I should think, may be safely sworn of all the Scotch nation." *Johnson.* (to Mr. Wilkes), "You must know, Sir, I lately took my friend Boswell and showed him genuine civilized life in an English provincial town. I turned him loose at Lichfield, my native city, that he might see for once real civility: for you know he lives among savages in Scotland, and among rakes in London." *Wilkes.* "Except when he is with grave, sober, decent people like you and me." *Johnson.* (smiling), "And we ashamed of him."

[Dr. Johnson on Reading]

[From 1763]. "Idleness is a disease which must be combatted; but I would not advise a rigid adherence to a particular plan of study. I myself have never persisted in any plan for two days together. A man ought to read just as inclination leads him; for what he reads as a task will do him little good. A young man should read five hours a day, and so may acquire a great deal of knowledge.". . .

"Sir, I love the acquaintance of young people; because in the first place, I don't like to think myself growing old. In the next place, young acquaintances must last longest, if they do last; and then, Sir, young men have more virtue than old men; they have more generous sentiments in every respect. I love the young dogs of this age: they have more wit and humor and knowledge of life than we had; but then the dogs are not so good scholars. Sir, in my early years I read very hard. It is a sad reflection, but a true one, that I knew almost as much at eighteen as I do now. My judgment, to be sure, was not so good; but I had all the facts. I remember very well, when I was at Oxford, an old gentleman said to me, 'Young man, ply your book diligently now, and acquire a stock of knowledge; for when years come upon you, you will find that

[10] "Thinking of flight."

poring upon books will be but an irksome task.' " . . .

This account of his reading, given by himself in plain words, sufficiently confirms what I have already advanced upon the disputed question as to his application. It reconciles any seeming inconsistency in his way of talking upon it at different times; and shows that idleness and reading hard were with him relative terms, the import of which, as used by him, must be gathered from a comparison with what scholars of different degrees of ardor and assiduity have been known to do. And let it be remembered, that he was now talking spontaneously, and expressing his genuine sentiments; whereas at other times he might be induced from his spirit of contradiction, or more properly from his love of argumentative contest, to speak lightly of his own application to study. It is pleasing to consider that the old gentleman's gloomy prophecy as to the irksomeness of books to men of an advanced age, which is too often fulfilled, was so far from being verified in Johnson, that his ardor for literature never failed, and his last writings had more ease and vivacity than any of his earlier productions. . . .

[From 1773]. Mr. Elphinston[1] talked of a new book that was much admired, and asked Dr. Johnson if he had read it. *Johnson.* "I have looked into it." "What, (said Elphinston) have you not read it through?" Johnson, offended at being thus pressed, and so obliged to own his cursory mode of reading, answered tartly, "No, Sir, do you read books through?"

[From 1776]. He said, that for general improvement, a man should read whatever his immediate inclination prompts him to; though, to be sure, if a man has a science to learn he must regularly and resolutely advance. He added, "What we read with inclination makes a much stronger impression. If we read without inclination, half the mind is employed in fixing the attention; so there is but one half to be employed on what we read." He told us he read Fielding's *Amelia* through without stopping. He said, "If a man

[1] James Elphinston, headmaster of an academy and publisher of the Scotch edition of *The Rambler*.

begins to read in the middle of a book, and feels an inclination to go on, let him not quit it, to go to the beginning. He may perhaps not feel again the inclination."

[From 1779]. "I am always for getting a boy forward in his learning; for that is a sure good. I would let him at first read any English book which happens to engage his attention, because you have done a great deal when you have brought him to have entertainment from a book. He'll get better books afterwards."

[From 1780]. "Snatches of reading (said he) will not make a Bentley[2] or a Clarke.[3] They are, however, in a certain degree advantageous. I would put a child into a library (where no unfit books are) and let him read at his choice. A child should not be discouraged from reading anything that he takes a liking to, from a notion that it is above his reach. If that be the case, the child will soon find it out and desist; if not, he of course gains the instruction; which is so much the more likely to come, from the inclination with which he takes up the study."

[From 1783]. On Thursday, May 1, I visited him in the evening along with young Mr. Burke.[4] He said, "It is strange that there should be so little reading in the world, and so much writing. People in general do not willingly read, if they can have anything else to amuse them. There must be an external impulse: emulation, or vanity, or avarice. The progress which the understanding makes through a book, has more pain than pleasure in it. Language is scanty, and inadequate to express the nice gradations and mixtures of our feelings. No man reads a book of science from pure inclination. The books that we do read with pleasure are light compositions, which contain a quick succession of events."

[2] Dr. Richard Bentley, royal librarian and the object of satiric attack by Swift in his *Battle of the Books*. Johnson was fond of coupling Bentley and Clarke as the most widely read men in England.
[3] Rev. Samuel Clarke, celebrated clergyman and author of *Sermons*.
[4] Richard Burke, son of Edmund Burke, author of *Reflections on the Revolution in France*.

[Dr. Johnson on Liberty]

[From 1768]. He talked in his usual style with a rough contempt of popular liberty. "They make a rout about universal liberty, without considering that all that is to be valued, or indeed can be enjoyed by individuals, is private liberty. Political liberty is good only so far as it produces private liberty. Now, Sir, there is the liberty of the press, which you know is a constant topic. Suppose you and I and two hundred more were restrained from printing our thoughts: what then? What proportion would that restraint upon us bear to the private happiness of the nation?"

This mode of representing the inconveniences of restraint as light and insignificant, was a kind of sophistry in which he delighted to indulge himself, in opposition to the extreme laxity for which it has been fashionable for too many to argue, when it is evident, upon reflection, that the very essence of government is restraint; and certain it is, that as government produces rational happiness, too much restraint is better than too little. But when restraint is unnecessary, and so close as to gall those who are subject to it, the people may and ought to remonstrate; and, if relief is not granted, to resist. Of this manly and spirited principle, no man was more convinced than Johnson himself.

[From 1772]. Happening to meet Sir Adam Fergusson, I presented him to Dr. Johnson. Sir Adam expressed some apprehension that the Pantheon would encourage luxury. "Sir, (said Johnson) I am a great friend to public amusements; for they keep people from vice. You now (addressing himself to me) would have been gone with a wench, had you not been here.—O, I forgot you were married."

Sir Adam suggested that luxury corrupts a people, and destroys the spirit of liberty. *Johnson.* "Sir, that is all visionary. I would not give half a guinea to live under one form of government rather than another. It is of no moment to the happiness of an individual. Sir, the danger of the abuse of power is nothing to a private man. What Frenchman is prevented from passing his life as he pleases?" *Sir Adam.* "But, Sir, in the British constitution it is surely of importance to keep up a spirit in the people, so as to preserve a balance against the crown." *Johnson.* "Sir, I perceive you are a vile Whig. Why all this childish jealousy of the power of the crown? The crown has not power enough. When I say that all governments are alike, I consider that in no government power can be abused long. Mankind will not bear it. If a sovereign oppresses his people to a great degree, they will rise and cut off his head. There is a remedy in human nature against tyranny that will keep us safe under every form of government. Had not the people of France thought themselves honored as sharing in the brilliant actions of Louis XIV, they would not have endured him; and we may say the same of the King of Prussia's people." Sir Adam introduced the ancient Greeks and Romans. *Johnson.* "Sir, the mass of both of them were barbarians. The mass of every people must be barbarous where there is no printing, and consequently knowledge is not generally diffused. Knowledge is diffused among our people by the newspapers."

[From 1773]. I introduced the subject of toleration. *Johnson.* "Every society has a right to preserve public peace and order, and therefore has a good right to prohibit the propagation of opinions which have a dangerous tendency. To say the magistrate has this right, is using an inadequate word: it is the society for which the magistrate is agent. He may be morally or theologically wrong in restraining the propagation of opinions which he thinks dangerous, but he is politically right." *Mayo.*[1] "I am of opinion, Sir, that every man is entitled to liberty of conscience in religion, and that the magistrate cannot restrain that right." *Johnson.* "Sir, I agree with you. Every man has a right to liberty of conscience, and with that the magistrate cannot interfere. People confound liberty of thinking with liberty of talking; nay, with liberty of preaching. Every man has a physical right to think as he pleases, for it cannot be

[1] Rev. Mayo, a dissenting minister.

discovered how he thinks. He has not a moral right, for he ought to inform himself, and think justly. But, Sir, no member of a society has the right to teach any doctrine contrary to what the society holds to be true. The magistrate, I say, may be wrong in what he thinks; but while he thinks himself right, he may and ought to enforce what he thinks." *Mayo.* "Then, Sir, we are to remain always in error, and truth can never prevail; and the magistrate was right in persecuting the first Christians." *Johnson.* "Sir, the only method by which religious truth can be established is by martyrdom. The magistrate has a right to enforce what he thinks, and he who is conscious of the truth has a right to suffer. I am afraid there is no other way of ascertaining the truth, but by persecution on the one hand and enduring it on the other."

[From 1779]. Lord Graham[2] commended Dr. Drummond at Naples, as a man of extraordinary talents, and added that he had a great love of liberty. *Johnson.* "He is young, my Lord; (looking to his Lordship with an arch smile) all boys love liberty, till experience convinces them they are not so fit to govern themselves as they imagined. We are all agreed as to our own liberty. We would have as much of it as we can get, but we are not agreed as to the liberty of others: for in proportion as we take, others must lose. I believe we hardly wish that the mob should have liberty to govern us. When that was the case some time ago, no man was at liberty not to have candles in his windows."

[Dr. Johnson's Death and Funeral (1784)]

Amidst the melancholy clouds which hung over the dying Johnson, his characteristical manner showed itself on different occasions. . . .

A man whom he had never seen before was employed one night to sit up with him. Being asked next morning how he liked his attendant, his answer was, "Not at all, Sir. The fellow's an idiot. He is as awkward as a

[2] The Marquis of Graham, Duke of Montrose. Dr. Drummond was the son of Johnson's old friend, William Drummond, a bookseller of Edinburgh.

turn-spit when first put into the wheel, and as sleepy as a dormouse.". . .

He requested three things of Sir Joshua Reynolds: to forgive him thirty pounds which he had borrowed of him; to read the Bible; 5 and never to use his pencil on a Sunday. Sir Joshua readily acquiesced. . . .

Johnson, with that native fortitude, which, amidst all his bodily distress and mental sufferings, never forsook him, asked Dr. Brock- 10 lesby, as a man in whom he had confidence, to tell him plainly whether he would recover. "Give me (said he) a direct answer." The doctor having first asked him if he could bear the whole truth which way soever it might 15 lead, and being answered that he could, declared that, in his opinion, he could not recover without a miracle. "Then (said Johnson) I will take no more physic, not even my opiates; for I have prayed that I may render 20 up my soul to God unclouded." In this resolution he persevered, and, at the same time, used only the weakest kinds of sustenance. Being pressed by Mr. Windham to take somewhat more generous nourishment, lest too 25 low a diet should have the very effect he dreaded, by debilitating his mind, he said, "I will take anything but inebriating sustenance." . . .

Having, as has already been mentioned, 30 made his will on the 8th and 9th of December, and settled all his worldly affairs, he languished till Monday, the 13th of that month, when he expired about seven o'clock in the evening, with so little apparent pain 35 that his attendants hardly perceived when his dissolution took place. . . .

A few days before his death, he had asked Sir John Hawkins, as one of his executors, where he should be buried; and on being 40 answered, "Doubtless in Westminster Abbey," seemed to feel a satisfaction, very natural to a poet; and indeed in my opinion very natural to every man of any imagination, who has no family sepulcher in which he can be laid 45 with his fathers. Accordingly, upon Monday, December 20, his remains were deposited in that noble and renowned edifice; and over his grave was placed a large blue flag-stone with this description: 50

SAMUEL JOHNSON LL.D.
Obit XIII *die Decembris,*
Anno Domini
M.DCC.LXXXIV.
Aetatis suae LXXV.

His funeral was attended by a respectable number of his friends, particularly such of the members of the Literary Club as were then in town; and was also honored with the presence of several of the Reverend Chapter of Westminster. . . .

I trust I shall not be accused of affectation, when I declare, that I find myself unable to express all that I felt upon the loss of such a "guide, philosopher, and friend." I shall, therefore, not say one word of my own, but adopt those of an eminent friend, which he uttered with an abrupt felicity, superior to all studied compositions: "He has made a chasm, which not only nothing can fill up, but which nothing has a tendency to fill up. —Johnson is dead. Let us go to the next best: there is nobody; no man can be said to put you in mind of Johnson."
(1791)

STUDY AIDS: 1. Notice the names scattered throughout the *Life*. What do they reveal of Johnson's circle of acquaintances?

2. What are the chief characteristics of Johnson's conversational methods? Of his diction?

3. Cite examples which show Boswell following the three principles he set forth for the writing of biography.

4. How does Boswell force Johnson to behave at the meeting with Wilkes? What does this reveal of Johnson's character?

5. Make an analysis of Johnson's character in terms of the following points: appearance, habits, personality, opinions and prejudices, and way of life.

6. Do you prefer Johnson's views on reading to those of modern educators? Why would Johnson's system not be feasible today? For what group of students would Johnson's system be helpful? On what group of students does modern education center its attention?

7. The section "Merit Set against Fortune" involves a basic difference between classicism and romanticism. The eighteenth century defined the term "the natural man" from two opposite

points of view: (1) that of primitivism, or man close to nature and away from corrupt society (romantic); and (2) that of civilization, or man at his highest state of social development (classic). What view of Johnson's is implied in this passage? Would this view of society preclude Johnson's sharing Gray's sympathy for the common man?

The London Journal, 1762–1763

Since Boswell had more leisure during his two-year sojourn in London than he had later in life, this *Journal*, a record of those years, is his most literary one. It possesses the organization, dramatic quality, and selectivity of material that are more likely to be found in the novel than in a diary.

The eyewitness account which the *Journal* presents of mid-eighteenth-century London is interesting; even more valuable are the glimpses of famous men Boswell knew; but most fascinating of all to the modern reader is its confessional element. As Boswell often said, he was writing a history of his own mind. It is not an apology. It is the psychological history of a young man experiencing his first hard-won freedom, wrested from a domineering father after three years of bitter struggle. As one reads the *Journal* in its entirety, the shadow of the old Laird of Auchinleck stretches across the two years and constantly threatens to engulf the raw young Scotsman come to town.

Friday 19 November. It was very cold. Stewart [1] was as effeminate [2] as I. I asked him how he, who shivered if a pane of glass was broke in a postchaise, could bear the severe hardship of a sea life. He gave me to understand that necessity made anything be endured. Indeed this is very true. For when the mind knows that it cannot help itself by struggling, it quietly and patiently submits to whatever load is laid upon it. When we [10] came upon Highgate hill and had a view of London, I was all life and joy. I repeated Cato's soliloquy on the immortality of the soul, and my soul bounded forth to a certain prospect of happy futurity. I sung all manner [15] of songs, and began to make one about an amorous meeting with a pretty girl, the burden of which was as follows:

She gave me this, I gave her that; [20]
And tell me, had she not tit for tat?

I gave three huzzas, and we went briskly in.

I got from Digges [3] a list of the best houses on the road, and also a direction to a good inn at London. I therefore made the boy drive [25] me to Mr. Hayward's, at the Black Lion, Water Lane, Fleet Street. The noise, the crowd, the glare of shops and signs agreeably confused me. I was rather more wildly struck than when I first came to London. My companion could not understand my feelings. He considered London just as a place where he was to receive orders from the East India Company. We now parted, with saying that we had agreed well and been happy, and that we should keep up the acquaintance. I then had a bit of dinner, got myself shaved and cleaned, and had my landlord, a civil jolly man, to take a glass of wine with me. I was all in a flutter at having at last got to the place which I was so madly fond of, and being restrained, had formed so many wild schemes to get back to. I had recourse to philosophy, and so rendered myself calm.

I immediately went to my friend Douglas', surgeon in Pall Mall, a kind-hearted, plain, sensible man, where I was cordially received.[4] His wife is a good-humored woman, and is that sort of character which is often met with in England: very lively without much wit. Her fault is speaking too much, which often tires people. He was my great adviser as to

[1] Boswell's fellow traveler, Duncan Stewart of Ardsheal, a sailor who was on his way to a new position as first mate of a ship.

[2] I.e., weary.

[3] Wes Digges, an actor, whose acquaintance Boswell had made in Edinburgh.

[4] Possibly a relative. Boswell had known him since 1760.

everything; and in the mean time insisted that I should have a bed in his house till I got a lodging to my mind. I agreed to come there next day. I went to Covent Garden—*Every Man in His Humor*.[5] Woodward played Bobadil finely. He entertained me much. It was fine after the fatigues of my journey to find myself snug in a theater, my body warm and my mind elegantly amused. I went to my inn, had some negus,[6] and went comfortably to bed.

Wednesday 9 February. I got up excellently well. My present life is most curious, and very fortunately is become agreeable. My affairs are conducted with the greatest regularity and exactness. I move like very clockwork. At eight in the morning Molly lights the fire, sweeps and dresses my dining-room. Then she calls me up and lets me know what o'clock it is. I lie some time in bed indulging indolence, which in that way, when the mind is easy and cheerful, is most pleasing. I then slip on my clothes loosely, easily, and quickly, and come into my dining-room. I pull my bell. The maid lays a milk-white napkin upon the table and sets the things for breakfast. I then take some light amusing book and breakfast and read for an hour or more, gently pleasing both my palate and my mental taste. Breakfast over, I feel myself gay and lively. I go to the window, and am entertained with the people passing by, all intent on different schemes. To go regularly through the day would be too formal for this my journal. Besides, every day cannot be passed exactly the same way in every particular. My day is in general diversified with reading of different kinds, playing on the violin, writing, chatting with my friends. Even the taking of medicines serves to make time go on with less heaviness. I have a sort of genius for physic and always had great entertainment in observing the changes of the human body and the effects produced by diet, labor, rest, and physical operations.

My landlord took a great anxiety that I should read the news, thought it would divert me much, and begged me to take in one of the papers. I expressed my fondness for his scheme, but said I did not choose to be at the expense of it. So I put it off. However, his anxiety was so great that he made a bold push at the office, where a number of the papers are taken in, and regularly every day does he bring home *The Public Ledger*, which is most duly served to me. I joked with him and said, "You see, Sir, when I put you to your shifts what you can do." "Indeed," said he, "I did not know before that I could do such a thing. But I find it is very easy."

As I am now in tolerable health, my appetite is very good, and I eat my slender bit of dinner with great relish. I drink a great deal of tea. Between eleven and twelve my bed is warmed and I go calmly to repose. I am not at all unsatisfied with this kind of existence. It is passing my portion of time very comfortably. Most philosophically do I reason upon this subject, being certainly the most important one to me at present. I consider that although I want many pleasures which are to be had by being abroad, yet I also want many pains. I am troubled with no dirty streets nor no jostling chairmen.[7] Multitudes of ideas float through my fancy on both sides of the question. I shall now and then put some of them down as they strike me strongly.

I now made a very near calculation of my expenses for the year, and found that I would be able to save £50 out of my allowance. This sum would be requisite for immediate necessaries in case of my getting a commission in the Guards, and I would have a pride to furnish it without any extraordinary assistance from my father, which is reasonable he should allow in that event, as everybody thinks he should rig me out. However, if I can do without him, I must be called an excellent manager. Not satisfied with saving £50, I went to work still nearer, wishing to save £20 more, and with great

[5] Comedy by Ben Jonson.
[6] A drink containing wine, hot water, sugar, nutmeg, and lemon juice.

[7] Sedan chairs were a favorite means of transportation. They were carried through the streets by two chairmen.

thought and assiduity did I compute. In short, I found myself turning very fond of money and ruminating with a kind of transport on the idea of being worth £70 at the year's end. The desire of being esteemed a clever economist was no doubt mixed with it, but I seriously think that sheer love of coin was my predominant principle.

While I was strongly possessed with this inclination, my landlord came to wait on me, and renewed a proposal which he had formerly mentioned; and that was that if I would give up one of my rooms, there should be a reasonable abatement of my rent. He said that a Mr. Smith, a gentleman of good fortune, with his lady and son, wanted to take three rooms. I told him that I should be glad to do what was convenient for him and at the same time of advantage to myself; and that I considered my having two rooms above was unnecessary, as I had the parlor below to entertain my company in. I therefore agreed to the proposal, and he engaged to have a handsome tent-bed with green and white check curtains put up in the room to the street. By this means I can save several pounds a year. The thing happened most opportunely while I was so much enamored of the money-making scheme. It gratified my passion while it was strong, which is quite the nice requisite for pleasure. A drink when a man is dry is highly relished. And in other gratifications, the analogy holds good. I have observed in some preceding period of this journal that making money is one of the greatest pleasures in life, as it is very lasting and is continually increasing. But it must be observed that a great share of anxiety is the constant concomitant of this passion, so that the mind is as much hurt in one way as it is pleased in another. I felt this now very plainly. For while I hugged myself with the prospect of my golden possessions, I was in pain lest I should not be able to fulfill my conjecture, and had disagreeable struggles between the love of many amusing schemes that gaily started up to my imagination and my principal scheme of saving.

It is a good deal diverting to consider my present views. A young fellow of life and

spirit, with an allowance extremely moderate, in so much that most people declare it must be wonderful management that can make it support a genteel appearance, yet is this fellow gravely laying down plans for making rich and being a man of wealth. The love of property is strongly implanted in mankind. Property, to be sure, gives us a power of enjoying many pleasures which it can purchase; and as society is constituted, a man has a high degree of respect from it. Let me, however, beware of allowing this passion to take a deep root. It may engross my affections and give me an appearance of meanness of spirit and a cold indifference to every manly and spirited pursuit. And when we consider what one gains, it is merely imaginary. To keep the golden mean between stinginess and prodigality is the point I should aim at. If a man is prodigal, he cannot be truly generous. His money is foolishly dissipated without any goodness on his part, and he has nothing to be generous with. On the other hand, a narrow man has a hard, contracted soul. The finer feelings are bound up, and although he has the power, he never can have the will to be generous. The character worthy of imitation is the man of economy, who with prudent attention knows when to save and when to spend, and acts accordingly. Let me pursue this system. I have done so hitherto since my setting out upon my own footing. Let me continue it. Let me lay out my money with ease and freedom, though with judgment and caution; and if at the year's end I should have a genteel sum remaining as a reward of my economy, let me congratulate myself on my felicity.

Upon my word my journal goes charmingly on at present. I was very apprehensive that there would be a dreary vacancy in it for some weeks, but by various happy circumstances I have been agreeably disappointed. I think, too, that I am making a good use of the hint which Captain Erskine [8] gave me,

[8] Andrew Erskine, younger son of the Earl of Kellie. Inasmuch as the Kellie family had been impoverished because of its loyalty to the ill-fated Jacobite Rebellion of 1745, Erskine entered the army.

and am taking more pains upon it, and consequently writing it in a more correct style. Style is to sentiment what dress is to the person. The effects of both are very great, and both are acquired and improved by habit. When once we get used to it, it is as easy to dress neatly as like a sloven; in the same way, custom makes us write in a correct style as easily as in a careless, inaccurate one.

Some time ago I left off the pamphlet shop in the passage to the Temple Exchange Coffeehouse, and took *The North Briton* from the publisher of it, Mr. Kearsley in Ludgate Street, hard by Child's. I have it now sent to me regularly by the Penny Post, and read it with vast relish. There is a poignant acrimony in it that is very relishing. Noble also sends me from time to time a fresh supply of novels from his circulating library, so that I am very well provided with entertainment.

How easily and cleverly do I write just now! I am really pleased with myself; words come skipping to me like lambs upon Moffatt Hill; and I turn my periods smoothly and imperceptibly like a skilful wheelwright turning tops in a turning-loom. There's fancy! There's simile! In short, I am at present a genius: in that does my opulence consist, and not in base metal.

My brother [9] drank tea with me and took a cordial farewell, being to set out for Scotland next day. We parted on excellent terms. He is as fond of being at home as I am of ranging freely at a distance. My friend Erskine came and supped with me. I am excellently lodged. I get anything dressed vastly well. We had a very good evening of it.

Tuesday 3 May. I walked up to the Tower in order to see Mr. Wilkes [10] come out. But he was gone. I then thought I should see prisoners of one kind or other, so went to Newgate. I stepped into a sort of court before the cells. They are surely most dismal places. There are three rows of 'em, four in a row, all above each other. They have double iron windows, and within these, strong iron rails; and in these dark mansions are the unhappy criminals confined. I did not go in, but stood in the court, where were a number of strange blackguard beings with sad countenances, most of them being friends and acquaintances of those under sentence of death. Mr. Rice the broker was confined in another part of the house. In the cells were Paul Lewis for robbery and Hannah Diego for theft. I saw them pass by to chapel. The woman was a big unconcerned being. Paul, who had been in the sea-service and was called Captain, was a genteel, spirited young fellow. He was just a Macheath.[11] He was dressed in a white coat and blue silk vest and silver, with his hair neatly queued and a silver-laced hat, smartly cocked. An acquaintance asked him how he was. He said, "Very well"; quite resigned. Poor fellow! I really took a great concern for him, and wished to relieve him. He walked firmly and with a good air, with his chains rattling upon him, to the chapel.

Erskine and I dined at the renowned Donaldson's, where we were heartily entertained. All this afternoon I felt myself still more melancholy,[12] Newgate being upon my mind like a black cloud. Poor Lewis was always coming across me. I felt myself dreary at night, and made my barber try to read me asleep with Hume's *History*,[13] of which he made very sad work. I lay in sad concern.

Wednesday 4 May. My curiosity to see the melancholy spectacle of the executions was so strong that I could not resist it, although I was sensible that I would suffer much from it. In my younger years I had read in the *Lives of the Convicts* so much about Tyburn that I had a sort of horrid eagerness to be there. I also wished to see the last behavior of Paul Lewis, the handsome fellow whom I had seen the day before. Accordingly I took Captain Temple with me, and he and I got upon a scaffold very near the fatal tree, so that we could clearly see all the dismal scene. There was a most prodigious crowd of spectators. I was most ter-

[9] John Boswell, a lieutenant in the army. This younger brother, who suffered from mental illness, had come to London the month previous to this entry.
[10] See p. 449, n. 3.

[11] Hero of Gay's *Beggar's Opera.*
[12] Boswell was often subject to fits of depression.
[13] David Hume, *History of England.*

ribly shocked, and thrown into a very deep melancholy.

I went to Lord Eglinton [14] and begged he would try to relieve me. He made me dress and dine with him, and said he would take me at night to Ranelagh and introduce me to some pretty women. Dress and dinner gave me spirits. But at seven, he proposed to take a little boy, one Barron, in the coach with us. This is a boy of great genius both as a painter and a musician, and he will probably be a man of great eminence. But at present he is a little black trifling being, so that he being in my company is a punishment to me. My Lord therefore having gone out and promised to call with the coach and take us up, I made my escape very quietly. This was perhaps being too nice and capricious.

I went home and changed my clothes. But gloomy terrors came upon me so much as night approached that I durst not stay by myself; so I went and had a bed (or rather half a one) from honest Erskine, which he most kindly gave me.

Thursday 19 May. Mr. James Coutts [15] told me that he and his brother and Mr. Cochrane were to dine with a Mr. Trotter, upholsterer, a particular friend, and that he never went thither without carrying somebody along with him; so he insisted that I should go. I accordingly went, and was introduced to Mr. Trotter, who is originally from Scotland, but has been here so long that he is become quite an Englishman. He is a bachelor, an honest, hearty, good-humored fellow. The company were all Scottish except an American lady, wife to Mr. Elliot, a son of Lord Minto's; Mr. Stewart, formerly the noted Provost of Edinburgh, and some more of these kind of old half-English gentry. We had a good dinner and plenty of wine. I resolved to be merry while I could, and soon see whether the foul fiend of the genitals had again prevailed. We were plain and hearty and comfortable; much better than the people

of high fashion. There was a Miss Rutherford there, a Scotch girl who had been long in America. She and I chatted very neatly.

We stayed and drank tea and coffee; and at seven, being in high glee, I called upon Miss Watts, [16] whom I found by herself, neatly dressed and looking very well. I was free and easy with her, and begged that she would drink a glass of wine with me at the Shakespeare, which she complied with. I told her my name was Macdonald, and that I was a Scotch Highlander. She said she liked them much, as they had always spirit and generosity. We were shown into a handsome room and had a bottle of choice sherry. We sat near two hours and became very cheerful and agreeable to each other. I told her with a polite freedom, "Madam, I tell you honestly I have no money to give you, but if you allow me favors without it, I shall be much obliged to you." She smiled and said she would. Her maid then brought her a message that a particular friend from the country was waiting for her; so that I was obliged to give her up this night, as I determined to give her no money. She left me pleased, and said she hoped to have the pleasure of my company at tea when it was convenient. This I faithfully promised and took as a good sign of her willingness to establish a friendly communication with me.

I then sallied forth to the Piazzas in rich flow of animal spirits and burning with fierce desire. I met two very pretty little girls who asked me to take them with me. "My dear girls," said I, "I am a poor fellow. I can give you no money. But if you choose to have a glass of wine and my company and let us be gay and obliging to each other without money, I am your man." They agreed with great good humor. So back to the Shakespeare I went. "Waiter," said I, "I have got here a couple of human beings; I don't know how they'll do." "I'll look, your honor," cried he, and with inimitable effrontery stared them in the face and then cried, "They'll do very well." "What," said I, "are they good fellow-creatures? Bring them up then." We were

[14] Alexander Montgomerie, Earl of Eglington, and a Scottish neighbor of Boswell's father. The older Boswell had written Eglington asking him to look up his son.

[15] A banker.

[16] A prostitute.

shown into a good room and had a bottle of
sherry before us in a minute. I surveyed my
seraglio and found them both good subjects
for amorous play. I toyed with them and
drank about and sung *Youth's the Season* and
thought myself Captain Macheath, and then
I solaced my existence with them, one after
the other, according to their seniority. I was
quite raised, as the phrase is: though I was
in a London tavern, the Shakespeare's Head,
enjoying high debauchery after my sober
winter. I parted with my ladies politely and
came home in a glow of spirits.

Friday 20 May. My blood still thrilled with
pleasure. I breakfasted with Macpherson, who
read me some of the Highland poems in the
original.[17] I then went to Lord Eglinton's,
who was highly entertained with my last
night's exploits, and insisted that I should
dine with him, after having walked in Hyde
Park with Macpherson, who was railing
against the human species, and in vast discontent.

After dinner my Lord and I went to Ranelagh in his chariot by ourselves, where he
introduced me to a Mrs. Wattman, a young
married lady, extremely pretty and agreeable.
We drank tea and chatted well. I met Lady
Margaret Hume, whom I had really used ill
in not waiting upon her one Sunday afternoon, as I engaged to do. I apologized for
myself by saying that I was an odd man. She
seemed to understand my worth, and said it
was a pity that I should just be lost in the
common stream of people here. I went home
and supped with Lord Eglinton.

Saturday 16 July. I carried Bob Temple
with me to breakfast at Dempster's and introduced him to Dempster and his sister, where
he was very well received. Since my being
honored with the friendship of Mr. Johnson,[18] I have more seriously considered the
duties of morality and religion and the dignity
of human nature. I have considered that
promiscuous concubinage is certainly wrong.
It is contributing one's share toward bringing
confusion and misery into society; and it is
a transgression of the laws of the Almighty

Creator, who has ordained marriage for the
mutual comfort of the sexes and the procreation and right educating of children. Sure
it is that if all the men and women in Britain
were merely to consult animal gratification,
society would be a most shocking scene. Nay,
it would soon cease altogether. Notwithstanding of these reflections, I have stooped to
mean profligacy even yesterday. However, I
am now resolved to guard against it.

At my last meeting with Mr. Johnson, he
said that when he came first to London and
was upon his shifts, he was told by a very
clever man who understood perfectly the common affairs of life that £30 a year was enough
to make a man live without being contemptible; that is to say, you might be always clean.
He allowed £10 for clothes and linen. He
said you might live in a garret at eighteen-
pence a week, as few people would inquire
where you lodge; and if they do, it is easy
to say, "Sir, I am to be found at such a place."
For spending threepence in a coffeehouse, you
may be for hours in very good company.
You may dine for sixpence, you may breakfast on bread and milk, and you may want
supper.

He advised me to keep a journal of my
life, fair and undisguised. He said it would
be a very good exercise, and would yield me
infinite satisfaction when the ideas were
faded from my remembrance. I told him that
I had done so ever since I left Scotland. He
said that he was very happy that I pursued
so good a plan. And now, O my journal! art
thou not highly dignified? Shalt thou not
flourish tenfold? No former solicitations or
censures could tempt me to lay thee aside;
and now is there any argument which can
outweigh the sanction of Mr. Samuel Johnson? He said indeed that I should keep it
private, and that I might surely have a friend
who would burn it in case of my death. For
my own part, I have at present such an
affection for this my journal that it shocks me
to think of burning it. I rather encourage the
idea of having it carefully laid up among the
archives of Auchinleck. However, I cannot
judge fairly of it now. Some years hence I
may. I told Mr. Johnson that I put down all

[17] *Ossian.* See p. 450, n. 6.
[18] Dr. Samuel Johnson.

sorts of little incidents in it. "Sir," said he, "there is nothing too little for so little a creature as man. It is by studying little things that we attain the great knowledge of having as little misery and as much happiness as possible."

He told me that he intended to give us some more imitations of Juvenal. When I some time ago mentioned the universality of Mr. Johnson's abilities and mentioned his Works, I am surprised how I omitted *The Idler,* which is a more easy and lively paper than *The Rambler,* but is distinguished for the same good sense and strong humor; and

his tragedy of *Irene,* which is far from deserving the indiscriminate censure of frigidity which Dempster gave it in the beginning of winter, as may be seen in a former page of my journal. *Irene* is upon the whole, perhaps, no great play, but it abounds with sentiment and with poetry. I had not read it when I marked Dempster's criticism, and I have read it now; though, to be sure, I have read it with some partiality to the work of my valuable friend. It is surprising to think how much the judgment even of the greatest may be biased in this way.

(1762–1763; 1950)

Oliver Goldsmith
(1728–1774)

ALTHOUGH MOST OF HIS FORTY-ODD VOLUMES HAVE LONG SINCE BEEN FORGOTTEN, OLIVER Goldsmith was no mere Grub Street hack. In the opinion of his good friend Samuel Johnson he was a "very great man," and since his death he has attracted and charmed more readers than any other man of his time.

Goldsmith was born and educated in Ireland. At school he was a dull student, and his career at the University of Dublin was far from distinguished. He studied medicine, first at Edinburgh, then at Leiden. There followed several aimless years of wandering about Europe, until he returned to London in 1756 and began writing for several periodicals.

The most notable of these contributions are *The Citizen of the World* papers, a series of essays resembling *The Spectator.* His first poem, *The Traveler,* was well received when it appeared in 1764. Also during that year, Boswell reports, Goldsmith's novel, *The Vicar of Wakefield,* came to light; when Johnson found Goldsmith in debt to his landlady, he sold the manuscript for sixty pounds, and it was published fourteen months later. *The Deserted Village,* Goldsmith's most admired poem, appeared in 1770. It was followed three years later by *She Stoops to Conquer.* Popular with audiences from the time it was first produced, this play, said Johnson, satisfied the "great end of comedy —making an audience merry." Thus Goldsmith did distinguished if not great work in four different genres. Few writers have done so well in so many forms. Johnson recognized this versatility; a line of his epitaph on Goldsmith's monument in Westminster Abbey reads: *Nullum quod tetigit non ornavit*—"He touched nothing which he did not adorn."

In Goldsmith's writing there is little of the studied detachment of his eighteenth-century predecessors. As writers of his time were coming more and more to do, he wrote much of himself into his work. And because he was a man of generosity, sympathy, and good nature, his writings are infused with these engaging qualities.

The Citizen of the World

In 1760–1761 Goldsmith published in the *Public Ledger* a series of 123 biweekly essays entitled "The Chinese Letters," which were collected in 1762 under the title *The Citizen of the World; or Letters from a Chinese Philosopher Residing in London, to His Friends in the East.* The eighteenth-century ideal of cosmopolitanism is reflected in Goldsmith's title and in the machinery of the letters. Lien Chi Altangi, the philosopher, is a "foreign observer"; intelligent and experienced, but unacquainted with English ways, he observes London, often with his English friend, the "man in black," and reports what he discovers.

Letter 11

[The Benefits of Luxury, in Making a People more wise and happy]

From such a picture of nature in primeval simplicity;[1] tell me, my much respected friend, are you in love with fatigue and solitude? Do you sigh for the severe frugality of the wandering Tartar, or regret being born amidst the luxury and dissimulation of the polite? Rather tell me, has not every kind of life vices peculiarly its own? Is it not a truth, that refined countries have more vices, but those not so terrible; barbarous nations few, and they of the most hideous complexion? Perfidy and fraud are the vices of civilized nations, credulity and violence those of the inhabitants of the desert. Does the luxury of the one produce half the evils of the inhumanity of the other? Certainly those philosophers who declaim against luxury have but little understood its benefits; they seem insensible, that to luxury we owe not only the greatest part of our knowledge, but even of our virtues.

It may sound fine in the mouth of a declaimer, when he talks of subduing our appetites, of teaching every sense to be content with a bare sufficiency, and of supplying only the wants of nature; but is there not more satisfaction in indulging those appetites, if with innocence and safety, than in restraining them? Am not I better pleased in enjoyment than in the sullen satisfaction of thinking that I can live without enjoyment? The more various our artificial necessities, the wider is our circle of pleasure; for all pleasure consists in obviating necessities as they rise: luxury, therefore, as it increases our wants, increases our capacity for happiness.

Examine the history of any country remarkable for opulence and wisdom, you will find they would never have been wise had they not been first luxurious; you will find poets, philosophers, and even patriots, marching in luxury's train. The reason is obvious: we then only are curious after knowledge, when we find it connected with sensual happiness. The senses ever point out the way, and reflection comments upon the discovery. Inform a native of the desert of Kobi, of the exact measure of the parallax of the moon, he finds no satisfaction at all in the information; he wonders how any could take such pains, and lay out such treasures, in order to solve so useless a difficulty: but connect it with his happiness, by showing that it improves navigation, that by such an investigation he may have a warmer coat, a better gun, or a finer knife, and he is instantly in raptures at so great an improvement. In short, we only desire to know what we desire to possess; and whatever we may talk against it, luxury adds the spur to curiosity, and gives us a desire of becoming more wise.

But not our knowledge only, but our virtues are improved by luxury. Observe the brown savage of Thibet, to whom the fruits of the spreading pomegranate supply food. and its branches an habitation. Such a character has few vices, I grant, but those he has are of the most hideous nature: rapine and cruelty are scarcely crimes in his eye; neither pity nor tenderness, which ennoble every virtue, have any place in his heart; he hates

---

[1] Letter 10 treats the religion of the Daures, a primitive people visited by the Chinese philosopher on his trip to Europe.

his enemies, and kills those he subdues. On the other hand, the polite Chinese and civilized European seem even to love their enemies. I have just now seen an instance where the English have succored those enemies, whom their own countrymen actually refused to relieve.[2]

The greater the luxuries of every country, the more closely, politically speaking, is that country united. Luxury is the child of society alone; the luxurious man stands in need of a thousand different artists to furnish out his happiness; it is more likely, therefore, that he should be a good citizen who is connected by motives of self-interest with so many, than the abstemious man who is united to none.

In whatsoever light, therefore, we consider luxury, whether as employing a number of hands naturally too feeble for more laborious employment; as finding a variety of occupation for others who might be totally idle; or as furnishing out new inlets to happiness, without encroaching on mutual property; in whatever light we regard it, we shall have reason to stand up in its defense, and the sentiment of Confucius still remains unshaken: that we should enjoy as many of the luxuries of life as are consistent with our own safety, and the prosperity of others; and that he who finds out a new pleasure is one of the most useful members of society.
(1762)

STUDY AIDS: To what extent is the last paragraph an accurate summary of the author's argument in favor of luxury?

Letter 21
[At the Play-house]

The English are as fond of seeing plays acted as the Chinese; but there is a vast difference in the manner of conducting them. We play our pieces in the open air, the English theirs under cover; we act by daylight, they by the blaze of torches. One of our plays continues eight or ten days successively; an English piece seldom takes up above four hours in the representation.

[2] At this time many Britishers were contributing to the relief of French prisoners of war.

My companion in black, with whom I am now beginning to contract an intimacy, introduced me a few nights ago to the play-house, where we placed ourselves conveniently at the foot of the stage. As the curtain was not drawn before my arrival, I had an opportunity of observing the behavior of the spectators, and indulging those reflections which novelty generally inspires.

The rich in general were placed in the lowest seats, and the poor rose above them in degrees proportioned to their poverty. The order of precedence seemed here inverted; those who were undermost all the day, now enjoyed a temporary eminence, and became masters of the ceremonies. It was they who called for the music, indulging every noisy freedom, and testifying all the insolence of beggary in exaltation.

They who held the middle region seemed not so riotous as those above them, nor yet so tame as those below: to judge by their looks, many of them seemed strangers there as well as myself; they were chiefly employed, during this period of expectation, in eating oranges, reading the story of the play, or making assignations.

Those who sat in the lowest rows, which are called the pit, seemed to consider themselves as judges of the merits of the poet and the performers; they were assembled partly to be amused, and partly to show their taste; appearing to labor under that restraint which an affectation of superior discernment generally produces. My companion, however, informed me, that not one in a hundred of them knew even the first principles of criticism; that they assumed the right of being censors because there was none to contradict their pretensions; and that every man who now called himself a connoisseur, became such to all intents and purposes.

Those who sat in the boxes appeared in the most unhappy situation of all. The rest of the audience came merely for their own amusement; these rather to furnish out a part of the entertainment themselves. I could not avoid considering them as acting parts in dumb show—not a courtesy or a nod, that was not the result of art; not a look nor a smile that was not designed for murder. Gentlemen and ladies ogled each other through spectacles; for my companion observed, that blindness was of late become fashionable; all affected indifference and ease, while their hearts at the same time burned for conquest. Upon the whole, the lights, the music, the ladies in their gayest dresses, the men with cheerfulness and expectation in their looks, all conspired to make a most agreeable picture, and to fill a heart that sympathizes at human happiness with inexpressible serenity.

The expected time for the play to begin at last arrived; the curtain was drawn, and the actors came on. A woman, who personated a queen, came in courtseying to the audience, who clapped their hands upon her appearance. Clapping of hands is, it seems, the manner of applauding in England; the manner is absurd, but every country, you know, has its peculiar absurdities. I was equally surprised, however, at the submission of the actress, who should have considered herself as a queen, as at the little discernment of the audience who gave her such marks of applause before she attempted to deserve them. Preliminaries between her and the audience being thus adjusted, the dialogue was supported between her and a most hopeful youth, who acted the part of her confidant. They both appeared in extreme distress, for it seems the queen had lost a child some fifteen years before, and still keeps its dear resemblance next to her heart, while her kind companion bore a part in her sorrows.

Her lamentations grew loud; comfort is offered, but she detests the very sound: she bids them preach comfort to the winds. Upon this her husband comes in, who, seeing the queen so much afflicted, can himself hardly refrain from tears, or avoid partaking in the soft distress. After thus grieving through three scenes, the curtain dropped for the first act.

"Truly," said I to my companion, "these kings and queens are very much disturbed at no very great misfortune: certain I am, were people of humbler stations to act in this manner, they would be thought divested of common sense." I had scarce finished this observation, when the curtain rose, and the king came on in a violent passion. His wife had, it seems, refused his proffered tenderness, had spurned his royal embrace; and he seemed resolved not to survive her fierce disdain. After he had thus fretted, and the queen had fretted through the second act, the curtain was let down once more.

"Now," says my companion, "you perceive the king to be a man of spirit; he feels at every pore: one of your phlegmatic sons of clay would have given the queen her own way, and let her come to herself by degrees; but the king is for immediate tenderness, or instant death: death and tenderness are leading passions of every modern buskined hero; this moment they embrace, and the next stab, mixing daggers and kisses in every period."

I was going to second his remarks, when my attention was engrossed by a new object: a man came in balancing a straw upon his nose, and the audience were clapping their hands in all the raptures of applause. "To what purpose," cried I, "does this unmeaning figure make his appearance? is he a part of the plot?" "Unmeaning, do you call him?" replied my friend in black; "this is one of the most important characters of the whole play; nothing pleases the people more than seeing a straw balanced: there is a great deal of meaning in the straw; there is something suited to every apprehension in the sight; and a fellow possessed of talents like these is sure of making his fortune."

The third act now began with an actor who came to inform us that he was the villain of the play, and intended to show strange things before all was over. He was joined by another, who seemed as much disposed for mischief as he; their intrigues continued through this whole division. "If that be a villain," said I, "he must be a very stupid one to tell his secrets without being asked; such soliloquies of late are never admitted in China."

The noise of clapping interrupted me once more; a child of six years old was learning to dance on the stage, which gave the ladies and mandarins infinite satisfaction. "I am sorry," said I, "to see the pretty creatures so early learning so bad a trade; dancing being, I presume, as contemptible here as in China." "Quite the reverse," interrupted my companion; "dancing is a very reputable and genteel employment here; men have a greater chance for encouragement from the merit of their heels than their heads. One who jumps up and flourishes his toes three times before he comes to the ground, may have three hundred a-year; he who flourishes them four times, gets four hundred; but he who arrives at five is inestimable, and may demand what salary he thinks proper. The female dancers, too, are valued for this sort of jumping and crossing; and it is a cant word among them, that she deserves most who shows highest. But the fourth act is begun; let us be attentive."

In the fourth act the queen finds her long-lost child, now grown up into a youth of smart parts and great qualifications; wherefore she wisely considers that the crown will fit his head better than that of her husband, whom she knows to be a driveler. The king discovers her design, and here comes on the deep distress: he loves the queen, and he loves the kingdom; he resolves, therefore, in order to possess both, that her son must die. The queen exclaims at his barbarity, is frantic with rage, and at length, overcome with sorrow, falls into a fit; upon which the curtain drops, and the act is concluded.

"Observe the art of the poet," cries my companion. "When the queen can say no more, she falls into a fit. While thus her eyes are shut, while she is supported in the arms of her Abigail, what horrors do we not fancy! We feel it in every nerve: take my word for it, that fits are the true aposiopesis of modern tragedy."

The fifth act began, and a busy piece it was. Scenes shifting, trumpets sounding, mobs hallooing, carpets spreading, guards bustling from one door to another; gods, demons, daggers, racks, and ratsbane. But whether the king was killed, or the queen was drowned, or the son poisoned, I have absolutely forgotten.

When the play was over, I could not avoid observing, that the persons of the drama ap-peared in as much distress in the first act as the last: "How is it possible," said I, "to sympathize with them through five long acts! Pity is but a short-lived passion; I hate to hear an actor mouthing trifles; neither startings, strainings, nor attitudes affect me, unless there be cause: after I have been once or twice deceived by those unmeaning alarms, my heart sleeps in peace, probably unaffected by the principal distress. There should be one great passion aimed at by the actor as well as the poet; all the rest should be subordinate, and only contribute to make that the greater; if the actor, therefore, exclaims upon every occasion in the tones of despair, he attempts to move us too soon; he anticipates the blow, he ceases to affect, though he gains our applause."

I scarcely perceived that the audience were almost all departed; wherefore mixing with the crowd, my companion and I got into the street; where, essaying an hundred obstacles from coach-wheels and palanquin poles, like birds in their flight through the branches of a forest, after various turnings we both at length got home in safety. Adieu. (1762)

STUDY AIDS: How, exactly, in this essay, does the device of the foreign observer allow Goldsmith to comment on the theater? Of what value is the presence of the man in black? Is the essay satiric?

Letter 54
[The Character of Beau Tibbs]

Though naturally pensive, yet I am fond of gay company, and take every opportunity of thus dismissing the mind from duty. From this motive, I am often found in the center of a crowd; and wherever pleasure is to be sold, am always a purchaser. In those places, without being remarked by any, I join in whatever goes forward, work my passions into a similitude of frivolous earnestness, shout as they shout, and condemn as they happen to disapprove. A mind thus sunk for a while below its natural standard, is qualified for stronger flights, as those first retire who would spring forward with greater vigor.

Attracted by the serenity of the evening, my friend and I lately went to gaze upon the company in one of the public walks near the city. Here we sauntered together for some time, either praising the beauty of such as were handsome, or the dresses of such as had nothing else to recommend them. We had gone thus deliberately forward for some time, when, stopping on a sudden, my friend caught me by the elbow, and led me out of the public walk. I could perceive by the quickness of his pace, and by his frequently looking behind, that he was attempting to avoid somebody who followed: we now turned to the right, then to the left; as we went forward he still went faster, but in vain; the person whom he attempted to escape hunted us through every doubling, and gained upon us each moment: so that at last we fairly stood still, resolving to face what we could not avoid.

Our pursuer soon came up, and joined us with all the familiarity of an old acquaintance. "My dear Drybone," cries he, shaking my friend's hand, "where have you been hiding this half a century? Positively I had fancied you were gone to cultivate matrimony and your estate in the country." During the reply, I had an opportunity of surveying the appearance of our new companion: his hat was pinched up with peculiar smartness; his looks were pale, thin, and sharp; round his neck he wore a broad black ribbon, and in his bosom a buckle studded with glass; his coat was trimmed with tarnished twist; he wore by his side a sword with a black hilt; and his stockings of silk, though newly washed, were grown yellow by long service. I was so much engaged with the peculiarity of his dress, that I attended only to the latter part of my friend's reply, in which he complimented Mr. Tibbs on the taste of his clothes, and the bloom in his countenance: "Pshaw, pshaw, Will," cried the figure, "no more of that, if you love me: you know I hate flattery, on my soul I do; and yet, to be sure, an intimacy with the great will improve one's appearance, and a course of venison will fatten; and yet, faith, I despise the great as much as you do: but there are a great many damned honest fellows among them; and we must not quarrel with one half, because the other wants breeding. If they were all such as my Lord Mudler, one of the most good-natured creatures that ever squeezed a lemon, I should myself be among the number of their admirers. I was yesterday to dine at the Duchess of Piccadilly's. My lord was there. Ned, says he to me, Ned, says he, I'll hold gold to silver, I can tell where you were poaching last night. Poaching, my lord, says I; faith you have missed already; for I stayed at home, and let the girls poach for me. That's my way; I take a fine woman as some animals do their prey—stand still, and swoop, they fall into my mouth."

"Ah, Tibbs, thou art a happy fellow," cried my companion, with looks of infinite pity; "I hope your fortune is as much improved as your understanding in such company?" "Improved," replied the other; "you shall know,—but let it go no farther,—a great secret —five hundred a-year to begin with.—My lord's word of honor for it—his lordship took me down in his own chariot yesterday, and we had a *tête-à-tête* dinner in the country, where we talked of nothing else." "I fancy you forget, Sir," cried I, "you told us but this moment of your dining yesterday in town." "Did I say so?" replied he coolly; "to be sure if I said so, it was so—dined in town: egad, now I do remember, I did dine in town, but I dined in the country too; for you must know, my boys, I eat two dinners. By the bye, I am grown as nice [1] as the devil in my eating. I'll tell you a pleasant affair about that: We were a select party of us to dine at Lady Grogram's, an affected piece, but let it go no farther; a secret: well, there happened to be no assafetida in the sauce to a turkey, upon which, says I, I'll hold a thousand guineas, and say, done first, that—but dear Drybone, you are an honest creature, lend me half-a-crown for a minute or two, or so, just till—but harkee, ask me for it the next time we meet, or it may be twenty to one but I forget to pay you."

When he left us, our conversation naturally turned upon so extraordinary a character.

[1] Fastidious.

"His very dress," cries my friend, "is not less extraordinary than his conduct. If you meet him this day, you find him in rags; if the next, in embroidery. With those persons of distinction of whom he talks so familiarly, he has scarcely a coffee-house acquaintance. However, both for the interests of society, and perhaps for his own, heaven has made him poor, and while all the world perceive his wants, he fancies them concealed from every eye. An agreeable companion, because he understands flattery; and all must be pleased with the first part of his conversation, though all are sure of its ending with a demand on their purse. While his youth countenances the levity of his conduct, he may thus earn a precarious subsistence: but when age comes on, the gravity of which is incompatible with buffoonery, then will he find himself forsaken by all; condemned in the decline of life to hang upon some rich family whom he once despised, there to undergo all the ingenuity of studied contempt, to be employed only as a spy upon the servants, or a bugbear to fright the children into obedience." Adieu.

(1762)

STUDY AIDS: Humor usually stems from some sort of incongruity. Determine the elements in this portrait of Tibbs (appearance, speech, habits, etc.). Do any of these constitute an incongruity?

The Deserted Village

During the eighteenth century, meadows and pasture lands formerly held in common came to be "enclosed." They were fenced off, that is, and restricted for the use of large landowners, who often turned them into private playgrounds. The so-called Enclosure Acts (1760–1800) worked great hardship on the small farmers; many of them failed and left their village homes. Goldsmith's poem springs from this social fact, which the poet had himself witnessed. "All my views and inquiries," he wrote, in dedicating the poem to Sir Joshua Reynolds, "have led me to believe those miseries real which I here attempt to display."

Sweet Auburn! [1] loveliest village of the plain,
Where health and plenty cheered the laboring swain,
Where smiling spring its earliest visit paid,
And parting summer's lingering blooms delayed:
Dear lovely bowers of innocence and ease, 5
Seats of my youth, when every sport could please:
How often have I loitered o'er thy green,
Where humble happiness endeared each scene!
How often have I paused on every charm,
The sheltered cot, the cultivated farm,   10
The never failing brook, the busy mill,
The decent church that topped the neighboring hill,

[1] Goldsmith's native village of Lissoy, Ireland suffered many of the changes depicted in the poem, and hence probably contributed to the picture of Auburn. There is a strong autobiographical element in the poem.

The hawthorn bush, with seats beneath the shade,
For talking age and whispering lovers made!
How often have I blessed the coming day, 15
When toil remitting lent its turn to play,
And all the village train, from labor free,
Led up their sports beneath the spreading tree;
While many a pastime circled in the shade,
The young contending as the old surveyed; 20
And many a gambol frolicked o'er the ground,
And sleights of art and feats of strength went round.
And still, as each repeated pleasure tired,
Succeeding sports the mirthful band inspired;
The dancing pair that simply sought renown,   25
By holding out to tire each other down;
The swain, mistrustless of his smutted face,
While secret laughter tittered round the place;
The bashful virgin's sidelong looks of love,

The matron's glance that would those looks
   reprove— 30
These were thy charms, sweet village! sports
   like these,
With sweet succession taught even toil to
   please;
These round thy bowers their cheerful in-
   fluence shed,
These were thy charms—but all these charms
   are fled.
   Sweet smiling village, loveliest of the
    lawn, 35
Thy sports are fled, and all thy charms with-
   drawn;
Amidst thy bowers the tyrant's hand is seen,
And desolation saddens all thy green:
One only master grasps the whole domain,
And half a tillage stints thy smiling plain; 40
No more thy glassy brook reflects the day,
But choked with sedges works its weedy way;
Along thy glades, a solitary guest,
The hollow-sounding bittern guards its nest;
Amidst thy desert walks the lapwing flies, 45
And tries their echoes with unvaried cries.
Sunk are thy bowers in shapeless ruin all,
And the long grass o'ertops the moldering
   wall;
And, trembling, shrinking from the spoiler's
   hand,
Far, far away thy children leave the land. 50
   Ill fares the land, to hastening ills a prey,
Where wealth accumulates, and men decay;
Princes and lords may flourish, or may fade;
A breath can make them, as a breath has
   made:
But a bold peasantry, their country's
   pride, 55
When once destroyed, can never be supplied.
   A time there was, ere England's griefs
   began,
When every rood of ground maintained its
   man;
For him light labor spread her wholesome
   store,
Just gave what life required, but gave no
   more: 60
His best companions, innocence and health,
And his best riches, ignorance of wealth.
   But times are altered; trade's unfeeling train

Usurp the land, and dispossess the swain;
Along the lawn, where scattered hamlets
   rose, 65
Unwieldy wealth, and cumbrous pomp re-
   pose;
And every want to opulence allied,
And every pang that folly pays to pride.
Those gentle hours that plenty bade to bloom,
Those calm desires that asked but little
   room, 70
Those healthful sports that graced the peace-
   ful scene,
Lived in each look, and brightened all the
   green;
These, far departing, seek a kinder shore,
And rural mirth and manners are no more.
   Sweet Auburn! parent of the blissful
    hour, 75
Thy glades forlorn confess the tyrant's power.
Here, as I take my solitary rounds,
Amidst thy tangling walks and ruined
   grounds,
And, many a year elapsed, return to view
Where once the cottage stood, the hawthorn
   grew, 80
Remembrance wakes with all her busy train,
Swells at my breast, and turns the past to
   pain.
   In all my wanderings round this world of
   care,
In all my griefs—and God has given my
   share—
I still had hopes, my latest hours to crown, 85
Amidst these humble bowers to lay me down;
To husband out life's taper at the close,
And keep the flame from wasting by repose:
I still had hopes, for pride attends us still,
Amidst the swains to show my book-learned
   skill, 90
Around my fire an evening group to draw,
And tell of all I felt, and all I saw;
And as a hare, whom hounds and horns pur-
   sue,
Pants to the place from whence at first she
   flew,
I still had hopes, my long vexations past, 95
Here to return—and die at home at last.
   O blest retirement, friend to life's decline,
Retreats from care, that never must be mine,

How happy he who crowns, in shades like
  these,
A youth of labor with an age of ease;   100
Who quits a world where strong temptations
  try,
And, since 'tis hard to combat, learns to fly!
For him no wretches, born to work and
  weep,
Explore the mine, or tempt the dangerous
  deep;
No surly porter stands, in guilty state,   105
To spurn imploring Famine from the gate;
But on he moves to meet his latter end,
Angels around befriending Virtue's friend;
Bends to the grave with unperceived decay,
While Resignation gently slopes the way;   110
And, all his prospects brightening to the last,
His heaven commences ere the world be
  past.
  Sweet was the sound, when oft at evening's
  close
Up yonder hill the village murmur rose;
There, as I passed with careless steps and
  slow,   115
The mingling notes came softened from
  below;
The swain responsive as the milkmaid sung,
The sober herd that lowed to meet their
  young;
The noisy geese that gabbled o'er the pool,
The playful children just let loose from
  school,   120
The watch-dog's voice that bayed the whisper-
  ing wind,
And the loud laugh that spoke the vacant [2]
  mind;
These all in sweet confusion sought the shade,
And filled each pause the nightingale had
  made.
But now the sounds of population fail,   125
No cheerful murmurs fluctuate in the gale,
No busy steps the grass-grown footway tread,
For all the bloomy flush of life is fled;
All but yon widowed solitary thing,
That feebly bends beside the plashy
  spring;   130
She, wretched matron, forced, in age, for
  bread,

[2] Carefree.

To strip the brook with mantling cresses
  spread,
To pick her wintry fagot from the thorn,
To seek her nightly shed, and weep till
  morn;
She only left of all the harmless train,   135
The sad historian of the pensive plain.
  Near yonder copse, where once the garden
  smiled,
And still where many a garden flower grows
  wild,
There, where a few torn shrubs the place
  disclose,
The village preacher's modest mansion
  rose.   140
A man he was to all the country dear,
And passing rich with forty pounds a year;
Remote from towns he ran his godly race,
Nor e'er had changed, nor wished to change
  his place;
Unpracticed he to fawn, or seek for
  power,   145
By doctrines fashioned to the varying hour;
Far other aims his heart had learned to prize,
More skilled to raise the wretched than to rise.
His house was known to all the vagrant
  train;
He chid their wanderings, but relieved their
  pain;   150
The long remembered beggar was his guest,
Whose beard descending swept his aged
  breast;
The ruined spendthrift, now no longer
  proud,
Claimed kindred there, and had his claims
  allowed;
The broken soldier, kindly bade to stay,   155
Sat by his fire, and talked the night away;
Wept o'er his wounds, or, tales of sorrow done,
Shouldered his crutch, and showed how
  fields were won.
Pleased with his guests, the good man
  learned to glow,
And quite forgot their vices in their woe;   160
Careless their merits or their faults to scan,
His pity gave ere charity began.
  Thus to relieve the wretched was his pride,
And e'en his failings leaned to Virtue's side;
But in his duty prompt, at every call,   165

He watched and wept, he prayed and felt for all:
And, as a bird each fond endearment tries,
To tempt its new-fledged offspring to the skies,
He tried each art, reproved each dull delay,
Allured to brighter worlds, and led the way.   170
   Beside the bed where parting life was laid,
And sorrow, guilt, and pain, by turns dismayed,
The reverend champion stood. At his control
Despair and anguish fled the struggling soul;
Comfort came down the trembling wretch to raise,   175
And his last faltering accents whispered praise.
   At church, with meek and unaffected grace,
His looks adorned the venerable place;
Truth from his lips prevailed with double sway,
And fools, who came to scoff, remained to pray.   180
The service past, around the pious man,
With steady zeal, each honest rustic ran:
E'en children followed, with endearing wile,
And plucked his gown, to share the good man's smile.
His ready smile a parent's warmth expressed,   185
Their welfare pleased him, and their cares distressed;
To them his heart, his love, his griefs were given,
But all his serious thoughts had rest in heaven.
As some tall cliff, that lifts its awful form,
Swells from the vale, and midway leaves the storm,   190
Though round its breast the rolling clouds are spread,
Eternal sunshine settles on its head.
   Beside yon straggling fence that skirts the way
With blossomed furze, unprofitably gay,
There, in his noisy mansion, skilled to rule,   195
The village master taught his little school:
A man severe he was, and stern to view,
I knew him well, and every truant knew;

Well had the boding tremblers learned to trace
The day's disasters in his morning face;   200
Full well they laughed with counterfeited glee
At all his jokes, for many a joke had he;
Full well the busy whisper, circling round,
Conveyed the dismal tidings when he frowned;
Yet he was kind, or if severe in aught,   205
The love he bore to learning was in fault;
The village all declared how much he knew;
'Twas certain he could write, and cipher too;
Lands he could measure, terms and tides presage,
And even the story ran that he could gauge.[3]   210
In arguing, too, the parson owned his skill,
For even though vanquished, he could argue still;
While words of learned length and thundering sound
Amazed the gazing rustics ranged around;
And still they gazed, and still the wonder grew   215
That one small head could carry all he knew.
   But past is all his fame. The very spot
Where many a time he triumphed, is forgot.
Near yonder thorn, that lifts its head on high,
Where once the sign-post caught the passing eye,   220
Low lies that house where nut-brown draughts inspired,
Where gray-beard mirth and smiling toil retired,
Where village statesmen talked with looks profound,
And news much older than their ale went round.
Imagination fondly stoops to trace   225
The parlor splendors of that festive place;
The whitewashed wall, the nicely sanded floor,
The varnished clock that clicked behind the door:
The chest contrived a double debt to pay,
A bed by night, a chest of drawers by day;   230
The pictures placed for ornament and use,
   [3] Survey.

The twelve good rules,[4] the royal game of
    goose; [5]
The hearth, except when winter chilled the
    day,
With aspen boughs, and flowers, and fennel
    gay;
While broken teacups, wisely kept for
    show,   235
Ranged o'er the chimney, glistened in a row.
  Vain transitory splendors! could not all
Reprieve the tottering mansion from its fall?
Obscure it sinks, nor shall it more impart
An hour's importance to the poor man's
    heart;   240
Thither no more the peasant shall repair
To sweet oblivion of his daily care;
No more the farmer's news, the barber's tale,
No more the woodman's ballad shall prevail;
No more the smith his dusky brow shall
    clear,   245
Relax his ponderous strength, and lean to
    hear;
The host himself no longer shall be found
Careful to see the mantling bliss go round;
Nor the coy maid, half willing to be prest,
Shall kiss the cup to pass it to the rest.   250
  Yes! let the rich deride, the proud disdain,
These simple blessings of the lowly train;
To me more dear, congenial to my heart,
One native charm, than all the gloss of art;
Spontaneous joys, where nature has its
    play,   255
The soul adopts, and owns their first-born
    sway;
Lightly they frolic o'er the vacant mind,
Unenvied, unmolested, unconfined.
But the long pomp, the midnight masquerade,
With all the freaks of wanton wealth
    arrayed,   260
In these, ere triflers half their wish obtain,
The toiling pleasure sickens into pain;
And, even while fashion's brightest arts decoy,
The heart, distrusting, asks if this be joy.
  Ye friends to truth, ye statesmen, who sur-
    vey   265

The rich man's joys increase, the poor's decay,
'Tis yours to judge how wide the limits stand
Between a splendid and a happy land.
Proud swells the tide with loads of freighted
    ore,
And shouting Folly hails them from her
    shore;   270
Hoards e'en beyond the miser's wish abound,
And rich men flock from all the world around,
Yet count our gains. This wealth is but a
    name,
That leaves our useful products still the same.
Not so the loss. The man of wealth and
    pride   275
Takes up a space that many poor supplied;
Space for his lake, his park's extended bounds,
Space for his horses, equipage, and hounds;
The robe that wraps his limbs in silken sloth
Has robbed the neighboring fields of half
    their growth;   280
His seat, where solitary sports are seen,
Indignant spurns the cottage from the green;
Around the world each needful product flies,
For all the luxuries the world supplies;
While thus the land, adorned for pleasure
    all,   285
In barren splendor feebly waits the fall.
  As some fair female, unadorned and plain,
Secure to please while youth confirms her
    reign,
Slights every borrowed charm that dress sup-
    plies,
Nor shares with art the triumph of her
    eyes;   290
But when those charms are past, for charms
    are frail,
When time advances, and when lovers fail,
She then shines forth, solicitous to bless,
In all the glaring impotence of dress:
Thus fares the land, by luxury be-
    trayed,[6]   295
In nature's simplest charms at first arrayed:
But verging to decline, its splendors rise,
Its vistas strike, its palaces surprise;

---

4 "King Charles's Twelve Good Rules," against
swearing, betting, quarreling, etc., were often hung
in taverns.

5 A game in which pieces on a board are advanced
according to a throw of the dice.

6 The author's condemnation of luxury seems
inconsistent with his praise of it in *The Citizen of
the World*, Letter 11. But note the quotation,
allegedly from Confucius, at the end of the letter:
luxury is desirable when consistent "with the
prosperity of others." The luxury mentioned in the
poem is of course ruinous to others.

While, scourged by famine, from the smiling
    land,
The mournful peasant leads his humble
    band;   300
And while he sinks, without one arm to save,
The country blooms—a garden and a grave.
    Where then, ah! where shall poverty reside,
To escape the pressure of contiguous pride?
If to some common's fenceless limits
    strayed,   305
He drives his flock to pick the scanty blade,
Those fenceless fields the sons of wealth
    divide,
And even the bare-worn common is denied.
    If to the city sped—What waits him there?
To see profusion that he must not share;   310
To see ten thousand baneful arts combined
To pamper luxury, and thin mankind:
To see those joys the sons of pleasure know,
Extorted from his fellow-creatures' woe.
Here, while the courtier glitters in
    brocade,   315
There the pale artist [7] plies the sickly trade;
Here, while the proud their long-drawn
    pomps display,
There the black gibbet glooms beside the way;
The dome where Pleasure holds her midnight
    reign,
Here, richly decked, admits the gorgeous
    train;   320
Tumultuous grandeur crowds the blazing
    square,
The rattling chariots clash, the torches glare.
Sure scenes like these no troubles e'er annoy!
Sure these denote one universal joy!
Are these thy serious thoughts?—Ah, turn
    thine eyes   325
Where the poor houseless shivering female
    lies:
She once, perhaps, in village plenty blessed,
Has wept at tales of innocence distressed;
Her modest looks the cottage might adorn,
Sweet as the primrose peeps beneath the
    thorn;   330
Now lost to all; her friends, her virtue fled,
Near her betrayer's door she lays her head,
And, pinched with cold, and shrinking from
    the shower,
With heavy heart, deplores that luckless hour,

[7] Artisan.

When idly first, ambitious of the town,   335
She left her wheel and robes of country
    brown.
    Do thine, sweet Auburn, thine, the love-
    liest train,
Do thy fair tribes participate her pain?
Even now, perhaps, by cold and hunger led,
At proud men's doors they ask a little
    bread!   340
    Ah, no. To distant climes, a dreary scene,
Where half the convex world intrudes be-
    tween,
Through torrid tracts with fainting steps
    they go,
Where wild Altama [8] murmurs to their woe.
Far different there from all that charmed be-
    fore,   345
The various terrors of that horrid shore;
Those blazing suns that dart a downward
    ray,
And fiercely shed intolerable day;
Those matted woods where birds forget to
    sing,
But silent bats in drowsy clusters cling;   350
Those poisonous fields with rank luxuriance
    crowned,
Where the dark scorpion gathers death
    around:
Where at each step the stranger fears to wake
The rattling terrors of the vengeful snake;
Where crouching tigers [9] wait their hapless
    prey,   355
And savage men more murderous still than
    they:
While oft in whirls the mad tornado flies,
Mingling the ravaged landscape with the
    skies.
Far different these from every former scene,
The cooling brook, the grassy vested
    green,   360
The breezy covert of the warbling grove,
That only sheltered thefts of harmless love.
    Good Heaven! what sorrows gloomed that
    parting day,
That called them from their native walks
    away;

[8] The Altamaha River in Georgia.
[9] "Tiger" was formerly a common term to denote
the large American cat, known as cougar, puma,
mountain lion, panther, or catamount.

Samuel Johnson, from a portrait by Sir Joshua Reynolds.

RELIQUES

OF

ANCIENT ENGLISH POETRY:

CONSISTING OF

Old Heroic BALLADS, SONGS, and ot
PIECES of our earlier POETS,

(Chiefly of the LYRIC kind.)

Together with some few of later Date.

VOLUME THE FIRST.

DURAT OPUS VATUM

·LONDON:

Printed for J. DODSLEY in Pall-Mall
M DCC LXV.

Title page of the first edition of Bishop
Thomas Percy's "Reliques."

By permission of The Macmillan Company.

A caricature of Johnson and Boswell
walking together.

When the poor exiles, every pleasure
    past,   365
Hung round the bowers, and fondly looked
    their last,
And took a long farewell, and wished in
    vain
For seats like these beyond the western main;
And, shuddering still to face the distant
    deep,
Returned and wept, and still returned to
    weep.   370
The good old sire the first prepared to go
To new-found worlds, and wept for others'
    woe;
But for himself, in conscious virtue brave,
He only wished for worlds beyond the grave.
His lovely daughter, lovelier in her tears,   375
The fond companion of his helpless years,
Silent went next, neglectful of her charms,
And left a lover's for a father's arms.
With louder plaints the mother spoke her
    woes,
And blessed the cot where every pleasure
    rose;   380
And kissed her thoughtless babes with many
    a tear,
And clasped them close, in sorrow doubly
    dear;
Whilst her fond husband strove to lend relief
In all the silent manliness of grief.
    O Luxury! thou cursed by heaven's de-
    cree,   385
How ill exchanged are things like these for
    thee!
How do thy potions, with insidious joy,
Diffuse their pleasures only to destroy!
Kingdoms by thee, to sickly greatness grown,
Boast of a florid vigor not their own: 390
At every draught more large and large they
    grow,
A bloated mass of rank unwieldy woe;
Till sapped their strength, and every part
    unsound,
Down, down they sink, and spread a ruin
    round.
    Even now the devastation is begun,   395
And half the business of destruction done;
Even now, methinks, as pondering here I
    stand,
I see the rural virtues leave the land.

Down where yon anchoring vessel spreads
    the sail,
That idly waiting flaps with every gale,   400
Downward they move, a melancholy band,
Pass from the shore, and darken all the
    strand.
Contented toil, and hospitable care,
And kind connubial tenderness are there;
And piety with wishes placed above,   405
And steady loyalty, and faithful love.
And thou, sweet Poetry, thou loveliest maid,
Still first to fly where sensual joys invade;
Unfit in these degenerate times of shame.
To catch the heart, or strike for honest
    fame;   410
Dear charming nymph, neglected and decried,
My shame in crowds, my solitary pride;
Thou source of all my bliss, and all my woe,
That foundest me poor at first, and keepest
    me so;
Thou guide, by which the nobler arts
    excel,   415
Thou nurse of every virtue, fare thee well.
Farewell! and O! where'er thy voice be tried,
On Torno's [10] cliffs, or Pambamarca's [11] side,
Whether where equinoctial fervors glow,
Or winter wraps the polar world in snow,   420
Still let thy voice, prevailing over time,
Redress the rigors of the inclement clime;
Aid slighted truth with thy persuasive strain;
Teach erring man to spurn the rage of
    gain;
Teach him, that states of native strength
    possessed,   425
Though very poor, may still be very
    blessed;
That trade's proud empire hastes to swift
    decay,
As ocean sweeps the labored mole away;
While self-dependent power can time defy,
As rocks resist the billows and the sky.   430
(1770)

STUDY AIDS: 1. Although the poet's
thought and feeling are apparent throughout
the poem, they are more prominent in the latter
part. The first part prepares for them by pre-

[10] Lake Torno, or Torneträsk, in northern Sweden,
is surrounded by precipitous mountains.
[11] Pambamarca is a mountain in Ecuador.

senting contrasting scenes. What scenes are contrasted? The poet is not a mere observer; he is also involved in what he depicts. How does his involvement contribute to his depiction? How are the passages of description related to those of moral commentary?

2. What is the greatest loss suffered from the social dislocation treated in the poem? How is this loss made vivid to us? How do the portraits of the parson, the school teacher, and the village inn make the loss vivid?

3. Although the medium is the HEROIC COUPLET, Goldsmith uses it quite differently from Pope. Contrast the two poets' use of the couplet with respect to: (1) subject treated; (2) use of particular as opposed to general statement; (3) dominant tone; (4) use of END-STOPPED couplets.

Robert Burns
(1759–1796)

IN SEVERAL WAYS BURNS WAS NOT OF HIS AGE. HE WAS NOT A COSMOPOLITAN BUT a provincial. He wrote few consciously philosophical poems, but mostly lyrics which appeal more to the heart than to the head. His usual language was not the elegant, "correct" variety demanded by neoclassic arbiters, but rather the colorful vernacular, or folk speech, of his native region.

The chief reason for this anomaly is that he was a Scot, and so somewhat apart from the main stream of English poetry. Also he was country bred. He was born in the village of Alloway, Ayrshire, where the family's poverty and the rigors of farming made for a hard life. After his father's death he continued to farm, but became discouraged and planned to emigrate to Jamaica. Partly to get passage money and partly to enlarge the local fame he had won as a poet, Burns published in nearby Kilmarnock forty-four of his poems in a volume entitled *Poems, Chiefly in the Scottish Dialect* (1786). Although the volume made him little money, it delighted Scottish readers, even the learned and cultivated of Edinburgh. He descended in triumph on the city, where for two winters he was feted and petted by the capital elite. A second, enlarged edition of the poems was published in Edinburgh in 1787, and a third in 1793.

How could the sudden emergence of this mature poet be explained? A current theory seemed to supply the answer: true genius, the critics were saying, needed no tutoring; it expressed itself naturally and spontaneously. Burns himself had said that the only learning he needed was "ae spark o' nature's fire." Henry Mackenzie spoke of him as the "Heaven-taught ploughman," a characterization that established the legend of Burns as a "natural genius." As with most legends, there is truth in this view of the poet; unquestionably he had extraordinary lyric gifts. But although fame had come quickly, Burns had not become a poet overnight, nor had he been as untaught as the legend implied. He had been rhyming, he says, almost "as soon as I could spell." And although his formal schooling had been meager, he had read much poetry—the English poets from Shakespeare to Gray, but more significantly "the glorious old Bards" of Scotland. Poetry in Scotland had flourished until the middle of the sixteenth century, when it fell under the blight of the Protestant Reformation. In the eighteenth century came a cultural revival. The poems of William Dunbar and other "Scottish Chauceri-ans," long forgotten but now reprinted, stimulated such poets as Allan Ramsay and Robert Fergusson to write in the native Scots tongue. Burns, too, was caught up in this resurgence of cultural nationalism. Indeed, because his ties with English poetry are relatively slight, it is probably more accurate historically to think of him less as a "pre-Romantic," or herald of the next great age in English poetry, than as the culmina-tion in poetry of the eighteenth-century Scottish renaissance.

Even a brief account of Burns's life would be incomplete without mention of his many loves. "I like the lasses," he said, and so, indeed, he did. His bright eye and, it is fair to imagine, his eloquent tongue made him irresistible to a surprisingly long list of them. The world has been indulgent of his conduct, though, perhaps because it was so clearly a product of his warm, generous nature.

When he returned from Edinburgh he married Jean Armour, after a stormy courtship, and settled in Dumfries, where he worked as an exciseman. He died at thirty-seven, not of drink, as his first biographer, a prohibitionist, alleged, but of rheumatic heart disease.

No man can be comprehended in a single phrase, but the term that best character-izes Burns and his poetry is vitality. He loved life intensely, and his verses are suffused with his strong feeling. He sings of love, of comradeship, of the joys of nature, of love of country. He is by turns exuberant, tender, patriotic, humorous, indignant. His themes are common ones, his treatment of them vivid and forceful. He is, in short, richly hu-man, which is why the world has taken him to its heart.

Epistle to J. Lapraik

John Lapraik was an elderly rustic poet who lived near Muirkirk, fifteen miles east of the Burns home near Mauchline. Burns's poem is a verse epistle, a poetic form popular with both Scottish and English poets of the earlier eighteenth century.

I

While briers an' woodbines budding green,
And paitricks [1] scraichin' loud at e'en,
An' morning poussie [2] whiddin' [3] seen,
    Inspire my Muse,
This freedom, in an unknown frien'   5
    I pray excuse.

2

On Fasten-e'en [4] we had a rockin',[5]
To ca' the crack [6] and weave our stockin';

And there was muckle [7] fun and jokin',
    Ye need na doubt;   10
At length we had a hearty yokin',[8]
    At 'sang about.'

3

There was ae [9] sang, amang the rest,
Aboon [10] them a' it pleased me best,
That some kind husband had addrest   15
    To some sweet wife:
It thirled [11] the heart-strings thro' the breast,
    A' [12] to the life.

[1] Partridges.
[2] Hare.
[3] Running.
[4] The eve of Ash Wednesday.
[5] Social gathering.
[6] I.e., to keep up the talk.

[7] Much.
[8] Bout.
[9] One.
[10] Above.
[11] Thrilled.
[12] All.

4

I've scarce heard ought described sae [13] weel,
What gen'rous, manly bosoms feel;
Thought I, "Can this be Pope or Steele,
Or Beattie's [14] wark?"
They tald me 'twas an odd kind chiel [15]
About Muirkirk.

5

It pat me fidgin-fain [16] to hear 't,   25
An' sae about him there I spier 't; [17]
Then a' that kent [18] him round declared
He had ingine, [19]
That nane excelled it, few cam near 't,
It was sae fine: 30

6

That, set him to a pint of ale,
An' either douce [20] or merry tale,
Or rhymes an' sangs he'd made himsel,
Or witty catches, [21]
'Tween Inverness an' Teviotdale,   35
He had few matches.

7

Then up I gat, an' swoor an aith,
Tho' I should pawn my pleugh [22] an' graith, [23]
Or die a cadger pownie's [24] death,
At some dyke-back, [25]   40
A pint an' gill I'd gie them baith,
To hear your crack. [26]

8

But, first an' foremost, I should tell,
Amaist as soon as I could spell,

[13] So.
[14] Scottish poet.
[15] An odd sort of fellow.
[16] I.e., it made me quivering-glad.
[17] Inquired.
[18] Knew.
[19] Genius.
[20] Serious.
[21] Rhymes.
[22] Plough.
[23] Harness.
[24] Hawker pony's.
[25] Stone fence.
[26] Talk.

I to the crambo-jingle [27] fell;   45
Tho' rude an' rough—
Yet crooning to a body's sel,
Does weel eneugh.

9

I am nae poet, in a sense;
But just a rhymer like by chance,   50
An' hae to learning nae pretence;
Yet, what the matter?
Whene'er my Muse does on me glance,
I jingle at her.

10

Your critic-folk may cock their nose,   55
And say, "How can you e'er propose,
You wha ken hardly verse frae prose,
To mak a sang?"
But, by your leaves, my learnèd foes,
Ye're maybe wrang.   60

11

What's a' your jargon o' your schools,
Your Latin names for horns an' stools?
If honest nature made you fools,
What sairs [28] your grammars?
Ye'd better taen up spades and shools,   65
Or knappin'-hammers.

12

A set o' dull, conceited hashes [29]
Confuse their brains in college-classes!
They gang in stirks, [30] and come out asses,
Plain truth to speak;   70
An' syne [31] they think to climb Parnassus
By dint o' Greek!

13

Gie me ae spark o' nature's fire,
That's a' the learning I desire;
Then, tho' I drudge thro' dub an' mire   75
At pleugh or cart,
My Muse, tho' hamely in attire,
May touch the heart.

[27] Rhyming.
[28] Serves.
[29] Louts.
[30] Young bulls.
[31] Then.

14

O for a spunk o' Allan's [32] glee,
Or Fergusson's,[33] the bauld an' slee, 80
Or bright Lapraik's, my friend to be,
    If I can hit it!
That would be lear [34] eneugh for me,
    If I could get it.

15

Now, sir, if ye hae friends enow, 85
Tho' real friends I b'lieve are few,
Yet, if your catalogue be fow,[35]
    I'se no insist:
But, gif ye want ae friend that's true,
    I'm on your list. 90

16

I winna blaw about mysel',
As ill I like my fauts to tell;
But friends, an' folks that wish me well,
    They sometimes roose [36] me;
Tho', I maun own,[37] as monie still 95
    As far abuse me.

17

There's ae wee faut they whyles lay to me,
I like the lasses—Gude forgie me!
For monie a plack [38] they wheedle frae me
    At dance or fair; 100
Maybe some ither thing they gie me,
    They weel can spare.

18

But Mauchline Race or Mauchline Fair,
I should be proud to meet you there:
We'se gie ae night's discharge to care, 105
    If we forgather;
And hae a swap o' rhymin'-ware
    Wi' ane anither.

19

The four-gill chap, we'se gar him clatter,
An' kirsen him wi' reekin' water; [39] 110

Syne we'll sit down an' tak our whitter,[40]
    To cheer our heart;
An' faith, we'se be acquainted better
    Before we part.

20

Awa ye selfish, warly [41] race, 115
Wha think that havins,[42] sense, an' grace,
Ev'n love an' friendship should give place
    To catch-the-plack! [43]
I dinna like to see your face,
    Nor hear your crack.[44] 120

21

But ye whom social pleasure charms,
Whose hearts the tide of kindness warms,
Who hold your being on the terms,
    "Each aid the others,"
Come to my bowl, come to my arms, 125
    My friends, my brothers!

22

But, to conclude my lang epistle,
As my auld pen's worn to the grissle,
Twa lines frae you wad gar me fissle,[45]
    Who am, most fervent, 130
While I can either sing or whistle,
    Your friend and servant.

(1785)

STUDY AIDS: 1. Although the poem is in formal stanzas, the expression follows the procedure of a personal letter. After a polite opening, the writer states what moved him to write the letter, introduces himself (since presumably he is not personally acquainted with Lapraik), hopes for a meeting, and gracefully closes. Which stanzas perform each of these functions?

2. The portion of the epistle in which the writer introduces himself comes close to summing up Burns's poetic creed. What are the important features of his creed? Find passages that best state them.

[32] Allan Ramsay, Scottish poet.
[33] Robert Fergusson, Scottish poet.
[34] Learning.
[35] Full.
[36] Praise.
[37] I.e., I must admit.
[38] Penny.
[39] I.e., christen him with steaming water.
[40] Drink.
[41] Worldly.
[42] Good manners.
[43] Money-making.
[44] Talk.
[45] I.e., make me tingle.

To a Louse: On Seeing One on a Lady's Bonnet at Church

1

Ha! whare ye gaun, ye crowlin' ferlie? [1]
Your impudence protects you sairly; [2]
I canna say but ye strunt [3] rarely
      Owre gauze and lace,
Tho' faith! I fear ye dine but sparely   5
      On sic a place.

2

Ye ugly, creepin', blastit wonner, [4]
Detested, shunn'd by saunt an' sinner,
How daur ye set your fit upon her—
      Sae fine a lady!   10
Gae somewhere else and seek your dinner
      On some poor body.

3

Swith! [5] in some beggar's hauffet [6] squattle: [7]
There ye may creep, and sprawl, and sprattle, [8]
Wi' ither kindred, jumping cattle,   15
      In shoals and nations;
Whare horn [9] nor bane [10] ne'er daur unsettle
      Your thick plantations.

4

Now haud you there! ye're out o' sight,
Below the fatt'rils, [11] snug an' tight;   20
Na, faith ye yet! ye'll no be right,
      Till ye've got on it—
The vera tapmost, tow'ring height
      O' Miss's bonnet.

5

My sooth! right bauld ye set your nose out,   25
As plump an' gray as onie grozet: [12]

[1] Crawling wonder.
[2] Greatly.
[3] Strut.
[4] Blasted wonder.
[5] Quick.
[6] Temple.
[7] Settle.
[8] Scramble.
[9] Horn comb.
[10] Bone comb.
[11] Ribbon ends.
[12] Gooseberry.

O for some rank, mercurial rozet, [13]
      Or fell, red smeddum, [14]
I'd gie ye sic a hearty dose o 't,
      Wad dress your drod-
        dum. [15]   30

6

I wad na been surpriz'd to spy
You on an auld wife's flainen toy; [16]
Or aiblins [17] some bit duddie [18] boy,
      On 's wyliecoat; [19]
But Miss's fine Lunardi! [20] fye!   35
      How daur ye do 't?

7

O Jenny, dinna toss your head,
An' set your beauties a' abread!
Ye little ken what cursèd speed
      The blastie's makin'!   40
Thae winks an' finger-ends, I dread,
      Are notice takin'!

8

O wad some Power the giftie gie us
To see oursels as ithers see us!
It wad frae monie a blunder free us,   45
      An' foolish notion:
What airs in dress an' gait wad lea'e us,
      An' ev'n devotion!

(1786)

STUDY AIDS: 1. The poem is rich in incongruity. Try to state the incongruities by considering the poet's attitude and behavior, Jenny's behavior, the setting, etc.

2. Burns had a talent for deriving far-reaching truths from trivial, unpromising subjects. What often-quoted lines contain a proverbial truth drawn from the episode of the louse?

[13] Rosin.
[14] Powder.
[15] Bottom.
[16] Flannel cap.
[17] Perhaps.
[18] Ragged.
[19] Flannel vest.
[20] Balloon bonnet.

The Cotter's Saturday Night

Inscribed to R. Aiken, Esq.

Let not Ambition mock their useful toil,
  Their homely joys, and destiny obscure;
Nor Grandeur hear with a disdainful smile
  The short and simple annals of the poor.
             —Gray

My loved, my honored, much respected
    friend! [1]
  No mercenary bard his homage pays:
With honest pride I scorn each selfish end,
  My dearest meed a friend's esteem and
    praise:
  To you I sing, in simple Scottish lays, 5
The lowly train in life's sequestered scene;
  The native feelings strong, the guileless
    ways;
What Aiken in a cottage would have been—
Ah! though his worth unknown, far happier
    there, I ween!

November chill blaws loud wi' angry
    sugh; [2]   10
  The shortening winter-day is near a close;
The miry beasts retreating frae the pleugh;
  The blackening trains o' craws to their
    repose:
The toil-worn cotter frae his labor goes,
This night his weekly moil is at an end, 15
  Collects his spades, his mattocks, and his
    hoes,
Hoping the morn in ease and rest to spend,
And weary, o'er the moor, his course does
    hameward bend.

At length his lonely cot appears in view,
  Beneath the shelter of an agèd tree; 20
The expectant wee things, toddlin', stacher [3]
    through
  To meet their dad, wi' flichterin' [4] noise
    an' glee.

His wee bit ingle,[5] blinkin bonnilie,
His clean hearth-stane, his thrifty wifie's
    smile,
  The lisping infant prattling on his
    knee,   25
Does a' his weary kiaugh [6] and care be-
    guile,
An' makes him quite forget his labor an' his
    toil.

Belyve [7] the elder bairns come drapping
    in,
  At service out, amang the farmers roun';
Some ca' the pleugh, some herd, some
    tentie [8] rin   30
  A cannie errand to a neibor town:
  Their eldest hope, their Jenny, woman-
    grown,
In youthfu' bloom, love sparkling in her e'e,
  Comes hame, perhaps, to shew a braw [9]
    new gown,
Or deposite her sair-won [10] penny-fee, 35
To help her parents dear, if they in hardship
    be.

With joy unfeigned brothers and sisters
    meet,
  An' each for other's weelfare kindly
    spiers: [11]
The social hours, swift-winged, unnoticed
    fleet;
  Each tells the uncos [12] that he sees or
    hears;   40
  The parents, partial, eye their hopeful
    years;
Anticipation forward points the view.
  The mother, wi' her needle an' her
    sheers,

[1] Robert Aiken, a lawyer of Ayr and friend of
Burns.
[2] Moaning of the wind.
[3] Stagger.
[4] Fluttering.

[5] Fireplace.
[6] Anxiety.
[7] Soon.
[8] Watchful.
[9] Fine.
[10] Hard-won.
[11] Asks.
[12] Uncommon things.

Gars [13] auld claes look amaist as weel's the new;
The father mixes a' wi' admonition due.   45

Their master's an' their mistress's command,
    The younkers a' are warnèd to obey;
An' mind their labors wi' an eydent [14] hand,
    An' ne'er, though out o' sight, to jauk [15] or play;
"And O! be sure to fear the Lord alway,   50
An' mind your duty, duly, morn an' night!
    Lest in temptation's path ye gang [16] astray,
Implore His counsel and assisting might:
They never sought in vain that sought the Lord aright!"

But hark! a rap comes gently to the door;   55
    Jenny, wha kens [17] the meaning o' the same,
Tells how a neibor lad cam o'er the moor,
    To do some errands, and convoy her hame.
The wily mother sees the conscious flame
Sparkle in Jenny's e'e, and flush her cheek;   60
    Wi' heart-struck anxious care, inquires his name,
While Jenny hafflins [18] is afraid to speak;
Weel pleased the mother hears, it's nae wild, worthless rake.

Wi' kindly welcome, Jenny brings him ben; [19]
    A strappin' youth, he takes the mother's eye;   65
Blythe Jenny sees the visit's no ill ta'en;
    The father cracks [20] of horses, pleughs, and kye.[21]

[13] Makes.
[14] Diligent.
[15] Dally.
[16] Go.
[17] Knows.
[18] Half.
[19] Inside.
[20] Chats.
[21] Cattle.

The youngster's artless heart o'erflows wi' joy,
But blate and laithfu', [22] scarce can weel behave;
    The mother, wi' a woman's wiles, can spy   70
What makes the youth sae bashfu' an' sae grave;
Weel-pleased to think her bairn's respected like the lave.[23]

O happy love! where love like this is found!
    O heart-felt raptures! bliss beyond compare!
I've pacèd much this weary, mortal round,   75
    And sage experience bids me this declare—
"If heaven a draught of heavenly pleasure spare,
One cordial in this melancholy vale,
'Tis when a youthful, loving, modest pair
In other's arms breathe out the tender tale,   80
Beneath the milk-white thorn that scents the evening gale."

Is there, in human form, that bears a heart—
    A wretch, a villain, lost to love and truth—
That can, with studied, sly, ensnaring art,
    Betray sweet Jenny's unsuspecting youth?   85
    Curse on his perjured arts! dissembling smooth!
Are honor, virtue, conscience, all exiled?
    Is there no pity, no relenting ruth,
Points to the parents fondling o'er their child?
Then paints the ruined maid, and their distraction wild?   90

But now the supper crowns their simple board,
    The halesome parritch,[24] chief of Scotia's food:

[22] Bashful and sheepish.
[23] Rest.
[24] Wholesome porridge.

The sowpe [25] their only hawkie [26] does af-
ford,
    That 'yont the hallan [27] snugly chows her
    cood;
The dame brings forth in complimental
    mood,   95
To grace the lad, her weel-hained keb-
buck,[28] fell; [29]
    An' aft [30] he's prest, and aft he ca's it
    guid;
The frugal wifie, garrulous, will tell
How 'twas a towmond [31] auld sin' lint was i'
    the bell.[32]

The cheerfu' supper done, wi' serious
    face,   100
    They round the ingle form a circle wide;
The sire turns o'er, wi' patriarchal grace,
The big ha'-bible, ance his father's
    pride:
    His bonnet reverently is laid aside,
His lyart haffets [33] wearing thin an'
    bare;   105
    Those strains that once did sweet in Zion
    glide—
He wales [34] a portion with judicious care;
And "Let us worship God!" he says with sol-
    emn air.

They chant their artless notes in simple
    guise;
    They tune their hearts, by far the noblest
    aim: 110
Perhaps Dundee's wild warbling measures
    rise,
    Or plaintive martyrs, worthy of the
    name;
    Or noble Elgin beets [35] the heavenward
    flame,
The sweetest far of Scotia's holy lays:

Compared with these, Italian trills are
    tame;   115
The tickled ears no heartfelt raptures raise;
Nae unison hae they with our Creator's
    praise.

The priest-like father reads the sacred
    page,—
    How Abram was the friend of God on
    high;
Or Moses bade eternal warfare wage   120
    With Amalek's ungracious progeny;
    Or how the royal bard did groaning lie
Beneath the stroke of heaven's avenging
    ire;
    Or Job's pathetic plaint, and wailing
    cry;
Or rapt Isaiah's wild, seraphic fire;   125
Or other holy seers that tune the sacred lyre.

Perhaps the Christian volume is the
    theme,—
    How guiltless blood for guilty man was
    shed;
How He, who bore in heav'n the second
    name,
    Had not on earth whereon to lay His
    head: 130
    How His first followers and servants
    sped;
The precepts sage they wrote to many a
    land;
    How he, who lone in Patmos banishèd,[36]
Saw in the sun a mighty angel stand,
And heard great Bab'lon's doom pronounced
    by heav'n's command.   135

Then kneeling down to heaven's eternal
    king,
    The saint, the father, and the husband
    prays:
Hope "springs exulting on triumphant
    wing," [37]
    That thus they all shall meet in future
    days:
    There ever bask in uncreated rays,   140
No more to sigh or shed the bitter tear,
    Together hymning their Creator's praise,

[25] Small portion.
[26] Cow.
[27] Beyond the partition.
[28] Well-saved cheese.
[29] Strong.
[30] Oft.
[31] Twelvemonth.
[32] Since flax was in bloom.
[33] Gray locks.
[34] Chooses.
[35] Kindles.
[36] The Apostle John.
[37] Slightly misquoted from Pope's *Windsor Forest*.

In such society, yet still more dear,
While circling time moves round in an
    eternal sphere.

Compared with this, how poor religion's
    pride   145
  In all the pomp of method and of art,
When men display to congregations
    wide
  Devotion's every grace except the
    heart!
  The power, incensed, the pageant will
    desert,
The pompous strain, the sacerdotal
    stole;   150
  But haply in some cottage far apart
May hear, well pleased, the language of the
    soul,
And in His book of life the inmates poor
    enroll.

Then homeward all take off their several
    way;
  The youngling cottagers retire to
    rest;   155
  The parent-pair their secret homage pay,
  And proffer up to heaven the warm
    request,
  That He who stills the raven's clamor-
    ous nest
And decks the lily fair in flowery pride,
  Would, in the way His wisdom sees the
    best,   160
For them and for their little ones provide;
But chiefly, in their hearts with grace divine
    preside.

From scenes like these old Scotia's grandeur
    springs,
  That makes her loved at home, revered
    abroad:
Princes and lords are but the breath of
    kings,   165

"An honest man's the noblest work of
    God": [38]
  And certes, in fair virtue's heavenly road,
The cottage leaves the palace far behind:
  What is a lordling's pomp? a cumbrous
    load,
Disguising oft the wretch of human
    kind,   170
Studied in arts of hell, in wickedness re-
    fined!

O Scotia! my dear, my native soil!
  For whom my warmest wish to heaven
    is sent!
Long may thy hardy sons of rustic toil
  Be blest with health, and peace, and
    sweet content!   175
  And, oh! may heaven their simple lives
    prevent
From luxury's contagion, weak and vile!
  Then, however crowns and coronets be
    rent,
A virtuous populace may rise the while,
And stand a wall of fire around their much-
    loved isle.   180

O Thou! who poured the patriotic tide
  That streamed through Wallace's [39] un-
    daunted heart,
Who dared to nobly stem tyrannic pride,
  Or nobly die, the second glorious part,—
  (The patriot's God peculiarly thou
    art,   185
  His friend, inspirer, guardian, and re-
    ward!)
  O never, never Scotia's realm desert,
  But still the patriot, and the patriot-bard,
In bright succession raise, her ornament and
    guard!
(1786)

[38] Slightly misquoted from Pope's *Essay on Man.*
[39] Sir William Wallace led the Scots to victory
over the British in 1297.

To a Mouse: On Turning Her up in Her Nest with the Plough, November, 1785

1

Wee, sleekit,[1] cowrin', tim'rous beastie,
O, what a panic's in thy breastie!
Thou need na start awa sae hasty
   Wi' bickering brattle![2]
I wad be laith to rin an' chase thee, 5
   Wi' murdering pattle![3]

2

I'm truly sorry man's dominion
Has broken nature's social union,
An' justifies that ill opinion
   Which makes thee startle 10
At me, thy poor, earth-born companion
   An' fellow mortal!

3

I doubt na, whyles,[4] but thou may thieve;
What then? poor beastie, thou maun live!
A daimen icker in a thrave[5] 15
   'S a sma' request;
I'll get a blessin' wi' the lave,[6]
   An' never miss 't!

4

Thy wee-bit housie, too, in ruin!
Its silly wa's the win's are strewin'! 20
An' naething, now, to big[7] a new ane,
   O' foggage[8] green!
An' bleak December's win's ensuin',
   Baith snell[9] an' keen!

5

Thou saw the fields laid bare an' waste, 25
An' weary winter comin' fast,

An' cozie here, beneath the blast,
   Thou thought to dwell,
Till crash! the cruel coulter past
   Out through thy cell. 30

6

That wee bit heap o' leaves an' stibble,
Has cost thee monie a weary nibble!
Now thou's turned out, for a' thy trouble,
   But house or hald,[10]
To thole[11] the winter's sleety dribble, 35
   An' cranreuch[12] cauld!

7

But Mousie, thou art no thy lane,[13]
In proving foresight may be vain:
The best-laid schemes o' mice an' men
   Gang aft agley,[14] 40
An' lea'e us nought but grief an' pain,
   For promised joy!

8

Still thou art blest, compared wi' me!
The present only toucheth thee:
But och! I backward cast my e'e, 45
   On prospects drear!
An' forward, though I canna see,
   I guess an' fear!

(1786)

STUDY AIDS: 1. It would be easy for a poem on this subject to become excessively sentimental. What keeps this poem from being so: The fact that the spokesman is a husky ploughman, his attitude toward the mouse, or what?

2. How do sts. 1–6 prepare for the moral observation in sts. 7–8? The celebrated moral in ll. 39–40 is addressed to the mouse. Does this make it more or less palatable to us than if Burns were speaking directly to the reader?

[1] Sleek.
[2] Hurrying scamper.
[3] Spade for cleaning the plough.
[4] Sometimes.
[5] I.e., an occasional ear of grain in a shock.
[6] Rest.
[7] Build.
[8] Coarse grass.
[9] Bitter.
[10] I.e., without house or home.
[11] Endure.
[12] Hoarfrost.
[13] Not alone.
[14] Go often astray.

Holy Willie's Prayer

Burns had little sympathy with the prevailing theology of Calvinism, which often produced self-righteous hypocrites like "Holy Willie." Willie was William Fisher, who hounded Burns's friend Gavin Hamilton for such lapses as missing a few church services. Condemned by the Kirk Session in Mauchline, Hamilton was acquitted by the Synods at Ayr (cf. st. 14) and at Glasgow.

In his prayer Willie mentions some of the tenets of Calvinism: God is all-powerful (l. 7); because of the inherited sin of Adam (l. 18) God condemns many people to hell (l. 3); but some he saves, not as a reward for good conduct (ll. 5–6), but simply because he chooses to favor them with his grace. Since a Calvinist could not be sure he was "elected" by God to be saved, he was obliged to search his soul humbly for inner assurance. Willie, however, blandly assumes God has elected him. And in the last stanza he has the monstrous effrontery to propose a bargain to God: If God will favor him with "gear [wealth] and grace," he is willing to allow the gift to redound to God's glory.

O thou wha in the heavens does dwell,
Wha, as it pleases best thysel',
Sends ane to heaven an' ten to hell
    A' for thy glory,
And no for onie guid or ill   5
    They've done before thee!

I bless and praise thy matchless might
When thousands thou hast left in night,
That I am here before thy sight,
    For gifts an' grace   10
A burning and a shining light
    To a' this place.

What was I, or my generation,
That I should get sic exaltation?
I, wha deserv'd most just damnation   15
    For broken laws
Sax thousand years ere my creation,
    Through Adam's cause!

When from my mither's womb I fell,
Thou might hae plung'd me deep in hell,   20
To gnash my gooms, and weep, and wail
    In burning lakes,
Where damnèd devils roar and yell,
    Chained to their stakes.

Yet I am here, a chosen sample,   25
To show thy grace is great and ample;
I'm here a pillar in thy temple,
    Strong as a rock,
A guide, a buckler, an example
    To a' thy flock.   30

O Lord, thou kens what zeal I bear,
When drinkers drink, and swearers swear,
And singin' there and dancin' here,
    Wi' great an' sma':
For I am keepit by thy fear,   35
    Free frae them a'.

But yet, O Lord! confess I must:
At times I'm fash'd [1] wi' fleshly lust;
An' sometimes, too, wi' warldly trust,
    Vile self gets in;   40
But thou remembers we are dust,
    Defil'd in sin.

O Lord! yestreen, thou kens, wi' Meg—
Thy pardon I sincerely beg,
O! may it ne'er be a livin' plague   45
    To my dishonor!
An' I'll ne'er lift a lawless leg
    Again upon her.

Besides, I farther maun allow,
Wi' Lizzie's lass, three times, I trow;   50
But, Lord, that Friday I was fou, [2]
    When I came near her,
Or else, thou kens, thy servant true
    Wad ne'er hae steered [3] her.

May be thou lets this fleshly thorn   55
Beset thy servant e'en and morn,

[1] Beset.
[2] Drunk.
[3] Meddled with.

Lest he owre high and proud should turn,
　　'Cause he's sae gifted;
If sae, thy hand maun e'en be borne,
　　Until thou lift it.　　　　　　　60

Lord, bless thy chosen in this place,
For here thou hast a chosen race;
But God confound their stubborn face,
　　And blast their name,
Wha bring thy elders to disgrace　　65
　　An' public shame!

Lord, mind Gau'n Hamilton's deserts:
He drinks, an' swears, an' plays at cartes,
Yet has sae monie takin' arts
　　Wi' grit and sma',　　　　　　70
Frae God's ain priest the people's hearts
　　He steals awa'.

An' whan we chasten'd him therefore,
Thou kens how he bred sic a splore,[4]
As set the warld in a roar　　　　75
　　O' laughin' at us;
Curse thou his basket and his store,
　　Kail and potatoes!

Lord, hear my earnest cry an' pray'r
Against that Presbyt'ry o' Ayr!　　80
Thy strong right hand, Lord, make it bare
　　Upo' their heads;

Lord, weigh it down, an' dinna spare,
　　For their misdeeds!

O Lord my God! that glib-tongu'd Aiken,[5]　85
My very heart and flesh are quakin',
To think how we stood sweatin', shakin',
　　An' piss'd wi' dread,
While he, wi' hingin' lip an' snakin',[6]
　　Held up his head.　　　　　　90

Lord, in the day of vengeance try him;
Lord, visit them wha did employ him,
And pass not in thy mercy by 'em,
　　Nor hear their pray'r:
But, for thy people's sake, destroy 'em,　95
　　An' dinna spare.

But, Lord, remember me and mine
Wi' mercies temp'ral and divine,
That I for gear[7] and grace may shine,
　　Excell'd by nane;　　　　　　100
And a' the glory shall be thine,
　　Amen, Amen.

(1799)

STUDY AIDS: 1. Burns stays out of the poem; Willie does all the talking. "The muse," Burns said, "overheard him at his devotions." What advantages for SATIRE result from this arrangement? How does it enhance the IRONY? 2. Is the poem a DRAMATIC MONOLOGUE? Why or why not?

Is There for Honest Poverty

It is not hard to see how the French Revolution, with its watchwords "Liberty, Equality, Fraternity," would appeal to a warm, benevolent nature like Burns's. This poem is one of several that express his sympathy with the liberal cause of his day. The refrain and the slogan-like phrases make it an ideal poem for public recitation, its ringing words serving as a group affirmation of the democratic faith.

I

Is there for honest poverty
　　That hings his head,[1] an' a' that?
The coward slave, we pass him by—
　　We dare be poor for a' that!

For a' that, an' a' that,　　　　5
　　Our toils obscure, an' a' that,
The rank is but the guinea's stamp,
　　The man's the gowd[2] for a' that.

[6] Sneering.
[7] Wealth.

[4] I.e., made such a fuss.
[5] Robert Aiken had defended Hamilton before the Synod at Ayr.

[1] The syntax here is elliptical. What word or words should be supplied?
[2] Gold.

2

What though on hamely fare we dine,
  Wear hoddin grey,[3] an' a' that?   10
Gie fools their silks, and knaves their wine—
  A man's a man for a' that.
For a' that, an' a' that,
  Their tinsel show, an' a' that,
The honest man, though e'er sae poor,   15
  Is king o' men for a' that.

3

Ye see yon birkie [4] ca'd "a lord,"
  Wha struts, an' stares, an' a' that?
Though hundreds worship at his word,
  He's but a cuif [5] for a' that.   20
For a' that, an' a' that,
  His ribband, star, an' a' that,
The man o' independent mind,
  He looks an' laughs at a' that.

4

A prince can mak a belted knight,   25
  A marquis, duke, an' a' that!
But an honest man's aboon his might—
  Guid faith, he mauna fa' that! [6]
For a' that, an' a' that,
  Their dignities, an' a' that,   30
The pith o' sense an' pride o' worth
  Are higher rank than a' that.

5

Then let us pray that come it may
  (As come it will for a' that)
That sense and worth o'er a' the earth   35
  Shall bear the gree [7] an' a' that!
For a' that, an' a' that,
  It's comin' yet for a' that,
That man to man the world o'er
  Shall brithers be for a' that.   40
(1794)

O, Willie Brew'd a Peck o' Maut

After a gay visit to their friend William Nicol, Allan Masterton and Burns felt they should commemorate the occasion. Masterton composed a tune and Burns these infectious words.

O, Willie brew'd a peck o' maut,[1]
And Rob an' Allan cam to see:
Three blyther hearts that lee-lang [2] night
Ye wad na found in Christendie.

  Chorus

We are na fou,[3] we're nae that fou,   5
But just a drappie [4] in our ee;
The cock may craw, the day may daw,
And ay we'll taste the barley bree.[5]

Here are we met, three merry boys,
Three merry boys, I trow, are we;   10
And monie a night we've merry been,
And monie mae [6] we hope to be!

It is the moon, I ken her horn,
That's blinkin in the lift [7] sae hic;
She shines sae bright to wyle [8] us hame,   15
But, by my sooth, she'll wait a wee!

Wha first shall rise to gang awa',
A cuckold, coward loun [9] is he!
Wha first beside his chair shall fa',
He is the king amang us three!   20

  Chorus

We are na fou, we're nae that fou,
But just a drappie in our ee;
The cock may craw, the day may daw,
And ay we'll taste the barley bree.
(1790)

---

[3] Coarse gray woolen cloth.
[4] Young chap.
[5] Or "coof," i.e., a ninny.
[6] I.e., a prince cannot raise the rank of an "honest man."
[7] Win the victory.

---

[1] Malt.
[2] Live-long.

---

[3] Drunk.
[4] Little drop.
[5] Brew.
[6] More.
[7] Sky.
[8] Entice.
[9] Low fellow.

Tam o' Shanter: A Tale

In *Tam o' Shanter*, Burns's only extended narrative poem, the poet was retelling a well-known folk legend associated with Alloway Kirk.

When chapman billies[1] leave the street,
And drouthy[2] neebors neebors meet;
As market-days are wearing late,
An' folk begin to tak the gate;
While we sit bousing at the nappy,[3]   5
An' getting fou and unco[4] happy,
We think na on the lang Scots miles,
The mosses, waters, slaps,[5] and styles,
That lie between us and our hame,
Whare sits our sulky, sullen dame,   10
Gathering her brows like gathering storm,
Nursing her wrath to keep it warm.

This truth fand honest Tam o' Shanter,
As he frae Ayr ae night did canter:
(Auld Ayr, wham ne'er a town surpasses,   15
For honest men and bonie lasses).

O Tam, hadst thou but been sae wise,
As taen thy ain wife Kate's advice!
She tauld thee weel thou was a skellum,[6]
A blethering, blustering, drunken blel-
    lum;[7]   20
That frae November till October,
Ae market-day thou was nae sober;
That ilka melder[8] wi' the miller,
Thou sat as lang as thou had siller;[9]
That ev'ry naig was ca'd a shoe on,[10]   25
The smith and thee gat roaring fou on;
That at the Lord's house, even on Sunday,
Thou drank wi' Kirkton Jean till Monday.
She prophesied, that, late or soon,
Thou would be found deep drowned in
    Doon,   30

Or catched wi' warlocks[11] in the mirk[12]
By Alloway's auld, haunted kirk.

Ah! gentle dames, it gars me greet,[13]
To think how monie counsels sweet,
How monie lengthened, sage advices   35
The husband frae the wife despises!

But to our tale: Ae market-night,
Tam had got planted unco right,
Fast by an ingle,[14] bleezing finely,
Wi' reaming swats,[15] that drank divinely;   40
And at his elbow, Souter[16] Johnie,
His ancient, trusty, drouthy cronie:[17]
Tam lo'ed him like a very brither;
They had been fou for weeks thegither.
The night drave on wi' sangs and clatter;   45
And ay the ale was growing better:
The landlady and Tam grew gracious
Wi' favors secret, sweet, and precious:
The Souter tauld his queerest stories;
The landlord's laugh was ready chorus: 50
The storm without might rair and rustle,
Tam did na mind the storm a whistle.

Care, mad to see a man sae happy,
E'en drowned himsel amang the nappy.
As bees flee hame wi' lades o' treasure,   55
The minutes winged their way wi' pleasure:
Kings may be blest but Tam was glorious,
O'er a' the ills o' life victorious!

But pleasures are like poppies spread:
You seize the flower, its bloom is shed;   60
Or like the snow falls in the river,
A moment white—then melts for ever:
Or like the borealis race,

[1] Peddler fellows.
[2] Thirsty.
[3] Strong ale.
[4] Very.
[5] Gates.
[6] Good-for-nothing.
[7] Babbler.
[8] Every meal-grinding.
[9] Silver.
[10] I.e., every time a horse was shod.
[11] Wizards.
[12] Dark.
[13] Makes me weep.
[14] Fireplace.
[15] Foaming ale.
[16] Shoemaker.
[17] Thirsty companion.

That flit ere you can point their place;
Or like the rainbow's lovely form　　65
Evanishing amid the storm.
Nae man can tether time or tide;
The hour approaches Tam maun ride:
That hour, o' night's black arch the keystane,
That dreary hour Tam mounts his beast
　　in;　　70
And sic a night he taks the road in,
As ne'er poor sinner was abroad in.

The wind blew as 't wad blawn its last;
The rattling showers rose on the blast;
The speedy gleams the darkness swal-
　　lowed;　　75
Loud, deep, and lang the thunder bellowed:
That night, a child might understand,
The Deil [18] had business on his hand.

Weel mounted on his gray mare Meg,
A better never lifted leg,　　80
Tam skelpit [19] on thro' dub and mire,
Despising wind, and rain, and fire;
Whiles holding fast his guid blue bonnet,
Whiles crooning o'er some auld Scots sonnet,
Whiles glow'ring round wi' prudent
　　cares,　　85
Lest bogles [20] catch him unawares:
Kirk-Alloway was drawing nigh,
Whare ghaists and houlets [21] nightly cry.

By this time he was cross the ford,
Whare in the snaw the chapman
　　smoor'd; [22]　　90
And past the birks [23] and meikle stane, [24]
Whare drunken Charlie brak's neck-bane;
And thro' the whins, [25] and by the cairn, [26]
Whare hunters fand the murdered bairn; [27]
And near the thorn, aboon the well,　　95
Whare Mungo's mither hanged hersel.
Before him Doon pours all his floods;

The doubling storm roars thro' the woods;
The lightnings flash from pole to pole;
Near and more near the thunders roll:　　100
When, glimmering thro' the groaning trees,
Kirk-Alloway seemed in a bleeze; [28]
Thro' ilka bore [29] the beams were glancing,
And loud resounded mirth and dancing.

Inspiring bold John Barleycorn,　　105
What dangers thou canst make us scorn!
Wi' tippenny, [30] we fear nae evil;
Wi' usquabae, [31] we'll face the Devil!
The swats sae reamed in Tammie's noddle,
Fair play, he cared na deils a boddle. [32]　　110
But Maggie stood, right sair astonished,
Till, by the heel and hand admonished,
She ventured forward on the light;
And, vow! Tam saw an unco sight!

Warlocks and witches in a dance:　　115
Nae cotillion, brent [33] new frae France,
But hornpipes, jigs, strathspeys, and reels,
Put life and mettle in their heels.
A winnock-bunker [34] in the east,
There sat Auld Nick, in shape o' beast;　　120
A tousie tyke, [35] black, grim, and large,
To gie them music was his charge:
He screwed the pipes and gart them skirl, [36]
Till roof and rafters a' did dirl. [37]
Coffins stood round, like open presses,　　125
That shawed the dead in their last dresses;
And, by some devilish cantraip sleight, [38]
Each in its cauld hand held a light:
By which heroic Tam was able
To note upon the haly table,　　130
A murderer's banes, in gibbet-airns; [39]
Twa span-lang, wee, unchristened bairns;
A thief new-cutted frae a rape—
Wi' his last gasp his gab [40] did gape;

[18] Devil.
[19] Dashed.
[20] Bogies, ghosts.
[21] Owls.
[22] Smothered.
[23] Birches.
[24] Great stone.
[25] Gorse bushes.
[26] Stone pile.
[27] Child.

[28] Blaze.
[29] Every chink.
[30] Twopenny ale.
[31] Whisky.
[32] I.e., he cared not a farthing for devils.
[33] Brand.
[34] Window-seat.
[35] Shaggy dog.
[36] Made them scream.
[37] Ring.
[38] Magic trick.
[39] Irons.
[40] Mouth.

Five tomahawks wi' bluid red-rusted;   135
Five scymitars wi' murder crusted;
A garter which a babe had strangled;
A knife a father's throat had mangled—
Whom his ain son o' life bereft—
The grey hairs yet stack to the heft;   140
Wi' mair o' horrible and awfu',
Which even to name wad be unlawfu'.

As Tammie glowered, amazed, and curious,
The mirth and fun grew fast and furious;
The piper loud and louder blew,   145
The dancers quick and quicker flew,
They reeled, they set, they crossed, they
      cleekit,[41]
Till ilka carlin [42] swat and reekit,[43]
And coost her duddies [44] to the wark,
And linket [45] at it in her sark! [46]   150

Now Tam, O Tam! had thae been
      queans,[47]
A' plump and strapping in their teens!
Their sarks, instead o' creeshie [48] flannen,
Been snaw-white seventeen hunder linen!—
Thir [49] breeks [50] o' mine, my only pair,   155
That ance were plush, o' guid blue hair,
I wad hae gi'en them aff my hurdies [51]
For ae blink o' the bonie burdies!

But withered beldams, auld and droll,
Rigwoodie hags wad spean a foal,[52]   160
Louping and flinging on a crummock,[53]
I wonder did na turn thy stomach!

But Tam kend what was what fu'
      brawlie: [54]
There was ae winsome wench and wawlie,[55]

That night enlisted in the core,   165
Lang after kend on Carrick shore
(For monie a beast to dead she shot,
An' perished monie a bonie boat,
And shook baith meikle corn and bear,[56]
And kept the country-side in fear).   170
Her cutty sark,[57] o' Paisley harn,[58]
That while a lassie she had worn,
In longitude tho' sorely scanty,
It was her best, and she was vauntie.[59]
Ah! little kend thy reverend grannie,   175
That sark she coft [60] for her wee Nannie,
Wi' twa pund Scots ('twas a' her riches),
Wad ever graced a dance of witches!

But here my Muse her wing maun cour,[61]
Sic flights are far beyond her power: 180
To sing how Nannie lap and flang
(A souple jade she was and strang),
And how Tam stood like ane bewitched,
And thought his very een enriched;
Even Satan glowered, and fidged [62] fu'
      fain,   185
And hotched [63] and blew wi' might and
      main;
Till first ae caper, syne anither,
Tam tint [64] his reason a' thegither,
And roars out: "Weel done, Cutty-sark!"
And in an instant all was dark;   190
And scarcely had he Maggie rallied,
When out the hellish legion sallied.

As bees bizz out wi' angry fyke,[65]
When plundering herds assail their byke; [66]
As open pussie's [67] mortal foes,   195
When, pop! she starts before their nose;
As eager runs the market-crowd,
When "Catch the thief!" resounds aloud:
So Maggie runs, the witches follow,

[41] Joined hands.
[42] Hag.
[43] Steamed.
[44] Cast off her clothes.
[45] Danced.
[46] Shirt.
[47] Girls.
[48] Greasy.
[49] These.
[50] Breeches.
[51] Hips.
[52] I.e., bony hags, who would wean a foal.
[53] Crooked staff.
[54] Well.
[55] Choice.

[56] Barley.
[57] Short shirt.
[58] Yarn.
[59] Proud.
[60] Bought.
[61] Curb.
[62] Fidgeted.
[63] Jerked.
[64] Lost.
[65] Fuss.
[66] Hive.
[67] The rabbit's.

Wi' monie an eldritch skriech [68] and
  hollo.   200

Ah, Tam! ah, Tam! thou'll get thy fairin'! [69]
In hell they'll roast thee like a herrin'!
In vain thy Kate awaits thy comin'!
Kate soon will be a woefu' woman!
Now, do thy speedy utmost, Meg,   205
And win the key-stane of the brig; [70]
There, at them thou thy tail may toss,
A running stream they dare na cross! [71]
But ere the key-stane she could make,
The fient [72] a tail she had to shake;   210
For Nannie, far before the rest,
Hard upon noble Maggie prest,
And flew at Tam wi' furious ettle; [73]
But little wist she Maggie's mettle!
Ae spring brought off her master hale,   215
But left behind her ain grey tail:
The carlin [74] claught her by the rump,
And left poor Maggie scarce a stump.

Now, wha this tale o' truth shall read,
Ilk man, and mother's son, take heed: 220
Whene'er to drink you are inclined,
Or cutty sarks run in your mind,
Think! ye may buy the joys o'er dear:
Remember Tam o' Shanter's mare.
(1791)

STUDY AIDS: 1. The narrative progresses through a series of verse paragraphs. At what points does the poet interrupt the narrative with commentary (e.g., ll. 105–108)? Why does he interrupt it at these points?

2. Much of the fun of the tale results from the narrator's attitude toward his story? What is his attitude? Does he believe that drink caused Tam to "see things"? Is he against drink (cf. ll. 219–224)?

3. The poem could be described as a succession of pictures. Which scenes are particularly vivid?

A Red, Red Rose

O, my luve's like a red, red rose,
  That's newly sprung in June.
O, my luve's like the melodie,
  That's sweetly played in tune.

As fair art thou, my bonie lass,   5
  So deep in luve am I,
And I will luve thee still, my dear,
  Till a' the seas gang dry.

Till a' the seas gang dry, my dear,
  And the rocks melt wi' the sun!   10
And I will luve thee still, my dear,
  While the sands o' life shall run.

And fare thee weel, my only luve,
  And fare thee weel a while!
And I will come again, my luve,   15
  Though it were ten thousand mile!
(1796)

O, Wert Thou in the Cauld Blast

A poem about protective love, these lines take on an added poignancy when it is remembered that Burns wrote them to the woman, the sister of a friend, who was nursing him in his final illness.

O, wert thou in the cauld blast
  On yonder lea, on yonder lea,
My plaidie to the angry airt,[1]
  I'd shelter thee, I'd shelter thee.

Or did misfortune's bitter storms   5
  Around thee blaw, around thee blaw,
Thy bield [2] should be my bosom,
  To share it a', to share it a'.

[68] Unearthly yell.
[69] Deserts.
[70] I.e., get to the keystone (middle) of the bridge.
[71] Superstition held that witches could not cross a running stream.

[72] The devil.
[73] Intent.
[74] Hag.

---

[1] Wind.
[2] Shelter.

Or were I in the wildest waste,
  Sae black and bare, sae black and bare, 10
The desert were a paradise,
  If thou wert there, if thou wert there.

Or were I monarch o' the globe,
  Wi' thee to reign, wi' thee to reign,
The brightest jewel in my crown   15
  Wad be my queen, wad be my queen.
(1796)

William Blake
(1757–1827)

No English poet has been the object of such opposing critical opinions as Blake. In his lifetime some considered him only a madman, others the greatest genius who had ever lived. Opposed as they are, these judgments follow from a single fact: Blake lived and wrote in the life of the imagination.

He was born in London, the son of a hosier, who could afford no formal education for his son. Nevertheless, Blake's father gave the boy much through love and understanding; and the religious mysticism of Swedenborg, which permeated the household, encouraged eccentric and unorthodox beliefs. Young Blake's flights of imagination were never curbed: he attended a fairy's funeral; he saw the soul of his dead brother fly away and heard its wings flapping; he walked in the meadow and touched God with his finger. Later, when he showed interest in design, he was encouraged in it and was sent to a drawing school. Then he was apprenticed to an engraver who sent him to sketch the Gothic features of Westminster Abbey. After his apprenticeship he studied art at the Royal Academy. In 1782, after his marriage to Catherine Boucher, he opened a print shop.

Blake, a professional engraver who illustrated his own books with striking drawings perfectly suited to the poems they accompany, began writing poems at the age of twelve. These early lyrics were published in 1783 as *Poetical Sketches*. Somewhat mystical in subject and Elizabethan in form, they show little of the prevailing classic temper. *Songs of Innocence* and the first of many "prophetic" works, *The Book of Thel*, followed in 1789. Five years later *Songs of Experience* marked the end of Blake's work as a lyrist.

Like most mystics, Blake found language incapable of communicating his visions. To free his imagination from time, space, reason, and nature ("I fear Wordsworth loves nature, and nature is the work of the devil"), he relied more and more on symbolism. As a result, his work became more intuitive, mystical, and "prophetic." Among these writings are *The Marriage of Heaven and Hell* (1790), *The Vision of the Daughters of Albion* (1793), and *Milton* (1804). The last is particularly interesting, because in it Blake argues that Satan as a symbol of man's revolt against restriction should be regarded as the hero of *Paradise Lost*.

After a happy life, Blake died poor and relatively obscure. Although completely misunderstood by most of his contemporaries, he was mourned by his friends and admirers, who considered him a great creative genius.

Song: "How Sweet I Roamed" [1]

How sweet I roamed from field to field,
  And tasted all the summer's pride;
Till I the Prince of Love beheld,
  Who in the sunny beams did glide.

He showed me lilies for my hair,   5
  And blushing roses for my brow;
And led me through his gardens fair,
  Where all his golden pleasures grow.

With sweet May-dews my wings were wet,
  And Phœbus fired my vocal rage;   10
He caught me in his silken net,
  And shut me in his golden cage.

He loves to sit and hear me sing,
  Then laughing sports and plays with me;
Then stretches out my golden wing,   15
  And mocks my loss of liberty.
(1783)

Songs of Innocence and Songs of Experience

Blake perhaps would have agreed with Wordsworth's statement, "The child is father of the man." Childhood, to Blake, is the state of imaginative existence. The child inhabits not a hostile but a helpful world, made intelligible and reassuring by the imagination. Childhood is the state of innocence. But Blake is not sentimental. His children, while symbolizing the innocence of the imagination, are not in themselves symbols of innocence. Like all human beings, they have their jealousies and vanities. Nevertheless, the child's world is an ideal one, and Blake presents it in the pastoral tradition, which had long been used to image the unfallen state of man.

But the child must grow. The time soon comes when his imagination finds the world not good enough. This condition receives a terrible indictment in the Songs of Experience. Here innocence has been lost; civilization has tarnished the original luster of man; nature is terrifying. Man's good instincts have been perverted by social restrictions into a cold law of morality enforced by churches. However, outgrowing the child's world does not mean abandoning what it stands for. Reason cannot answer the demands of the state of experience: man cannot abandon his civilization. Only the imagination, lingering on into the state of experience, can give man a vision, which alone can understand and cope with evil which burns "in the forests of the night." Songs of Innocence presents the ideal world; Songs of Experience, the actual. Each parallels and satirizes the other.

Songs of Innocence

The Lamb

Little Lamb, who made thee?
Dost thou know who made thee?
Gave thee life, and bid thee feed,
By the stream and o'er the mead;
Gave thee clothing of delight,   5

Softest clothing, woolly, bright;
Gave thee such a tender voice,
Making all the vales rejoice?
Little Lamb, who made thee?
Dost thou know who made thee? [2]   10

Little Lamb, I'll tell thee,
Little Lamb, I'll tell thee:
He is callèd by thy name, [3]

[1] This poem, from Poetical Sketches, is said to have been written by Blake at the age of fourteen. What suggestions of symbolism can you see in the poem?
[2] Notice the childlike language which describes the lamb. The poem's structure is equally childlike: in stanza one the child asks a question; in stanza two, he himself answers it.

[3] The second stanza becomes symbolic by a series of identifications: the actual lamb is identified with the Lamb of God, then with a child (l. 16; cf. Luke 18:16–17), then both lamb and child with the Lamb of God.

For He calls Himself a Lamb,
He is meek, and He is mild;   15
He became a little child.
I a child, and thou a lamb,
We are callèd by His name.
    Little Lamb, God bless thee!
    Little Lamb, God bless thee!   20
(1789)

STUDY AIDS: 1. What relationship does the child see between himself and nature? Does he see nature as divine, good, evil, or indifferent?
2. What does the child symbolize? Can the poem be suggesting that the imagination, which sees the world as innocent, is divine as well as childlike?

The Little Black Boy

My mother bore me in the southern wild,
    And I am black, but O my soul is white!
White as an angel is the English child,
    But I am black, as if bereaved of light.

My mother taught me underneath a tree,   5
    And, sitting down before the heat of day,
She took me on her lap and kissèd me,
    And, pointing to the east, began to say:

"Look on the rising sun;—there God does live,
    And gives his light, and gives his heat
    away;   10
And flowers and trees and beasts and men
    receive [1]
    Comfort in morning, joy in the noonday.

"And we are put on earth a little space,
    That we may learn to bear the beams of
    love; [2]
And these black bodies and this sunburnt
    face [3]   15
    Is but a cloud, and like a shady grove.

"For when our souls have learned the heat to
    bear,

[1] Apart from ll. 11–12, the METER of the whole poem is a child's sing-song chant. What effect does the shift in meter here produce?
[2] Lines 14 and 17 state the central idea of the poem. What is it?
[3] Lines 15–16 present a METAPHOR. What is it? What is its relation to the more important metaphor expressed in ll. 14, 17?

The cloud will vanish; we shall hear his
    voice,
Saying: 'Come out from the grove, my love
    and care,
    And round my golden tent like lambs re-
    joice.' "   20

Thus did my mother say, and kissèd me;
    And thus I say to little English boy: [4]
When I from black, and he from white cloud
    free,
    And round the tent of God like lambs we
    joy,

I'll shade him from the heat, till he can
    bear   25
    To lean in joy upon our father's knee;
And then I'll stand and stroke his silver hair,
    And be like him, and he will then love
    me.[5]
(1789)

STUDY AIDS: 1. Is the poem a protest against race discrimination? Suggest other themes treated by the poem.
2. The idea that God's love, like the sun's heat, can nourish, Blake translates into a metaphor: skins shade us from God's love as clouds shade us from the sun's heat. What difficulties do you encounter if you push this metaphor too far, literally or logically? What can you say about the nature of METAPHOR from this?

Holy Thursday

'Twas on a Holy Thursday, their innocent
    faces clean,
The children walking two and two, in red
    and blue and green,
Grey-headed beadles [6] walked before, with
    wands as white as snow,
Till into the high dome of Paul's [7] they like
    Thames' waters flow.

[4] What effect is produced by omitting the article "the" and the verbs in l. 23?
[5] Will the white boy love the colored boy because he has lost his dark skin? Is the poem written for the benefit of the white boy or black boy? Which will learn of God's love?
[6] Officials who head church processions.
[7] St. Paul's Cathedral.

Oh, what a multitude they seemed, these
   flowers of London town!   5
Seated in companies they sit with radiance
   all their own.
The hum of multitudes was there, but multitudes of lambs,
Thousands of little boys and girls raising their
   innocent hands.

Now like a mighty wind they raise to heaven
   the voice of song,
Or like harmonious thunderings the seats of
   heaven among.   10
Beneath them sit the agèd men, wise guardians of the poor;
Then cherish pity, lest you drive an angel
   from your door.[1]
(1789)

The Divine Image

To Mercy, Pity, Peace, and Love
All pray in their distress;
And to these virtues of delight
Return their thankfulness.

For Mercy, Pity, Peace, and Love   5
Is God, our Father dear,
And Mercy, Pity, Peace, and Love
Is man, his child and care.

For Mercy has a human heart,
Pity a human face,   10
And Love, the human form divine,
And Peace, the human dress.

Then every man, of every clime,
That prays in his distress,
Prays to the human form divine,   15
Love, Mercy, Pity, Peace.

And all must love the human form,
In heathen, Turk, or Jew;
Where Mercy, Love, and Pity dwell
There God is dwelling too.   20
(1789)

STUDY AIDS: 1. Why is man divine? How is he an image of God in the poem?

2. What does Blake mean when he says we pray to "the human form divine" (l. 15)?

3. What do you think Dr. Johnson would have thought of this poem? Thomas Gray?

Songs of Experience

The Tiger

Tiger! Tiger! burning bright [2]
In the forests of the night,
What immortal hand or eye
Could frame thy fearful symmetry?

In what distant deeps or skies   5
Burned the fire of thine eyes?
On what wings dare he aspire?
What the hand dare seize the fire?

And what shoulder, and what art,
Could twist the sinews of thy heart?   10

And when thy heart began to beat,
What dread hand and what dread feet?

What the hammer? what the chain?
In what furnace was thy brain?
What the anvil? what dread grasp   15
Dare its deadly terrors clasp?

When the stars [3] threw down their spears,
And watered heaven with their tears,
Did he smile his work to see? [4]
Did he who made the lamb make thee?   20

[1] The TONE shifts in this final line. To whom is the line addressed? What should the "aged" do for the children? How does this shift strengthen or weaken the poem? What is the hint of "experience" here?

[2] What qualities of the tiger are emphasized in ll. 1–12?

[3] When did the "stars" throw down their spears? See Rev. 12:3–4, 7–9; Isa. 14:12; Paradise Lost, Bk. 1, 44–49. Since these lines seem to refer to the origin of evil, what does the tiger symbolize? Is it the opposite of the symbolic "Lamb"?

[4] Lines 19–20 push the problem of evil as far as it can go: did God create both good and evil? Blake seems to agree with Milton (cf. Areopagitica, p. 293/2, l. 21 ff.).

Tiger! Tiger! burning bright
In the forests of the night,
What immortal hand or eye
Dare frame thy fearful symmetry? [5]

(1794)

STUDY AIDS: 1. What poem in *Songs of Innocence* does this poem parallel?

2. What is Blake's view of nature in *The Tiger*? What is his view in *The Lamb*? The two views seem contradictory. Can both be true? If so, how?

3. What do the qualities emphasized in the description of the physical tiger indicate as to Blake's feelings about the symbolic tiger?

The Sick Rose

O Rose, thou art sick!
The invisible worm
That flies in the night,
In the howling storm,

Has found out thy bed   5
Of crimson joy;
And his dark secret love
Does thy life destroy.

(1794)

STUDY AIDS: 1. How is the theme of this poem similar to that of *The Tiger*? How do the basic images, which present the theme in both poems, differ? In what respects are they alike?

2. Study the imaginative design of this poem —i.e., the interconnectedness of a large number of different items of experience (any response which a printed word elicits): a sick rose, a rose eaten by a worm, a worm flying in the night, an invisible worm, the sensation of "crimson," the hint of illicit love, the rhyme, the sounds, and the meter. Although the poem is about a rose, notice how "worm" dominates it: the word is stressed; it rhymes with "storm"; and its predicate does not appear until the last word. How does "worm" relate to each item of experience listed above? What chronological development is suggested by the verb forms?

3. What is the symbolism of the "worm" which loves (illicitly) and yet kills? What is Blake saying about nature? How can the poem also be exploring the nature of love?

[5] Compare this line with l. 4. What does the change imply as to Blake's conception of the symbolic tiger?

The Fly

Little fly,
Thy summer's play
My thoughtless hand
Has brushed away.

Am not I   5
A fly like thee?
Or art not thou
A man like me?

For I dance,
And drink, and sing,   10
Till some blind hand
Shall brush my wing.

If thought is life
And strength and breath,
And the want   15
Of thought is death;

Then am I
A happy fly,
If I live
Or if I die.   20

(1794)

A Poison Tree

I was angry with my friend:
I told my wrath, my wrath did end.
I was angry with my foe:
I told it not, my wrath did grow.

And I watered it in fears   5
Night and morning with my tears,
And I sunnèd it with smiles
And with soft deceitful wiles.

And it grew both day and night,
Till it bore an apple bright,   10
And my foe beheld it shine,
And he knew that it was mine—

And into my garden stole
When the night had veiled the pole;
In the morning, glad, I see   15
My foe outstretched beneath the tree.

(1794)

STUDY AIDS: 1. In what garden does this tree grow? Is there a hint here that Blake considers this related to the fall of man?

2. Are the speaker's last words intended to be the reader's reaction?

3. How is the poem a study of the effect of hatred? Who is most affected?

London

I wander [1] through each chartered street,
Near where the chartered [2] Thames does
   flow,
And mark in every face I meet
Marks of weakness, marks of woe.

In every cry [3] of every man,   5
In every infant's cry of fear,
In every voice, in every ban,
The mind-forged manacles I hear:

How the chimney-sweeper's cry [4]
Every blackening [5] church appalls,   10
And the hapless soldier's sigh
Runs in blood down palace walls.[6]

But most,[7] through midnight streets I hear
How the youthful harlot's curse
Blasts the newborn infant's tear,   15
And blights with plagues the marriage
   hearse.[8]
(1794)

[1] Blake's poem is built on what he sees and hears as he walks the streets of London.
[2] This word is used with more than one meaning. What various meanings apply? Charters once gave men freedom, but in time they became oppressive. In what ways can a river and street be "chartered"?
[3] The poem progresses to a climax through the meanings of these cries heard in the streets. What does Blake hear behind the cries of stanza two?
[4] Blake now makes specific the "cry" of ll. 5–6.
[5] What are the meanings of this word as Blake uses it?
[6] Soldiers at this time were hired to fight.
[7] Up to this point Blake has vividly pictured a London bought and enslaved. In this last stanza he states that the very source of life is enslaved ("chartered"). How? How does l. 13 indicate that this is the climax of the poem? What words would best complete the unfinished phrase?
[8] What is the PARADOX implicit in "marriage hearse"?

STUDY AIDS: 1. In each of the last two stanzas, how are both the adult and child (from st. 2) brought into the poem?

2. For several words in the poem, the primary meaning (DENOTATION) of each fits its immediate literal context, but its secondary meanings (CONNOTATION) fit the condemnation of London created by the total poem. How do the following words illustrate this dual function: "ban" (l. 7), "midnight" (l. 13), "curse" (l. 14)?

The Chimney-Sweeper

A little black thing among the snow,
Crying "weep! [9] weep!" in notes of woe!
"Where are thy father and mother, say?"—
"They are both gone up to the church to pray.

"Because I was happy upon the heath,   5
And smiled among the winter's snow,
They clothed me in the clothes of death,
And taught me to sing the notes of woe.

"And because I am happy and dance and sing,
They think they have done me no injury,   10
And are gone to praise God and his priest
   and king,
Who make up a heaven of our misery."
(1794)

STUDY AIDS: 1. This poem is built on contrasts which point out its theme. What are some of these? What theme do they point out?

2. What are the "notes of woe" (l. 8)? What does the final stanza mean?

Holy Thursday

Is this a holy thing to see
In a rich and fruitful land,
Babes reduced to misery,
Fed with cold and usurous hand?

Is that trembling cry a song?   5
Can it be a song of joy?
And so many children poor?
It is a land of poverty!

[9] Chimney sweeps were small children who made their living by climbing down the insides of chimneys in order to clean them. They advertised their business by crying "Sweep, Sweep," as they went about the streets. Notice how Blake changes this cry to fit his purpose.

And their sun does never shine,
And their fields are bleak and bare,   10
And their ways are filled with thorns:
It is eternal winter there.

For where'er the sun does shine,
And where'er the rain does fall,
Babe can never hunger there,   15
Nor poverty the mind appall.
(1794)

STUDY AIDS: In what ways is this poem a contrast to its counterpart in *Songs of Innocence*?

The Clod and the Pebble

"Love seeketh not itself to please,
Nor for itself hath any care,
But for another gives its ease,
And builds a heaven in hell's despair."

So sung a little clod of clay,   5
Trodden with the cattle's feet,
But a pebble of the brook
Warbled out these meters meet:

"Love seeketh only self to please,
To bind another to its delight,   10

Joys in another's loss of ease,
And builds a hell in heaven's despite."
(1794)

STUDY AIDS: What relationship does the poem present between egoistic and altruistic love?

Infant Sorrow

My mother groaned! my father wept.
Into the dangerous world I leapt:
Helpless, naked, piping loud:
Like a fiend hid in a cloud.

Struggling in my father's hands,   5
Striving against my swaddling-bands,
Bound and weary I thought best
To sulk upon my mother's breast.
(1794)

STUDY AIDS: 1. Why does the father weep (l. 1)?
2. What is the "cloud" (l. 4)? Why a "fiend" (l. 4)?
3. How long does the process of "struggling" and "striving" (ll. 5–6) continue? What aspect of human nature does an infant's sorrow symbolize for Blake? What is the significance of "sulk" (l. 8)?

Never Seek to Tell Thy Love

This poem is from the Rossetti MS., first published in 1863. It is not from *Songs of Innocence* or *Songs of Experience*.

Never seek to tell thy love,
Love that never told can be; [1]
For the gentle wind does move
Silently, invisibly.

I told my love, I told my love,   5
I told her all my heart;

[1] Presumably, "Love that can never be uttered or told" (for it is on the deepest level).

Trembling, cold, in ghastly fears,
Ah! she doth depart.

Soon as she was gone from me,
A traveler came by,   10
Silently, invisibly:
He took her with a sigh.
(1863)

The Nineteenth Century

THE ROMANTIC PERIOD (1798-1832)

DURING THE CLOSING YEARS OF THE EIGHTEENTH CENTURY AND
the early years of the nineteenth century, England was deeply
affected by three revolutions—one political, one social, one literary.

The first was the French Revolution and its aftermath. When,
on July 14, 1789, a mob stormed the Bastille, a prison for political
criminals, the revolt of the French people against their tyrannical
masters officially began. The Revolution rapidly increased in
violence, which reached a climax in the Reign of Terror under
Robespierre in 1793-1794. After the fall of Robespierre, the
government passed to the Directory (1795), and thereafter to
Napoleon Bonaparte, who overthrew the Directory in 1799 and
crowned himself Emperor of the French in 1804. There followed
a series of Napoleonic Wars which did not end until Napoleon's
defeat at Waterloo in 1815.

In England the initial reaction of English liberals, like the
young Wordsworth and Coleridge, was one of enthusiasm and
optimistic expectancy. The old corrupt order was being swept
away; the new order of "liberty, equality, and fraternity" was
being established. Even when England joined the alliance against
the French in 1793, many Englishmen opposed their country's
policy and remained loyal to the Revolution.

But as the violence and bloodshed increased, and the French

509

Republic turned to aggression and conquest, most of the English partisans of the Revolution became more and more disillusioned and were finally forced to admit that one form of tyranny had merely been exchanged for another. The advent of Napoleon with his autocratic rule and schemes for world power served only to intensify the conservative reaction. Indeed, for more than thirty years—from 1790 to the 1820's—the various rights and freedoms long enjoyed by Englishmen were continually subjected to severe governmental restrictions because of the French Revolution and the Napoleonic Wars. Much of the liberalism of English Romantic literature is an expression of protest against the curtailment of rights and liberties by a Tory government fearful of possible uprising at home.

The second revolution that greatly affected England during these years was the Industrial Revolution, inaugurated by the application of steam power to machinery and by the increasing use of that machinery in the production of goods. The factory system, gradually replacing that of small hand workers' shops, brought in its wake abrupt shifts of population, the growth of urban centers unfairly represented in Parliament, gross abuses in conditions of work, and an increasing conflict between capital and labor. Reform was blocked by private interests, by a conservative social philosophy of laissez faire ("let things alone") that condemned any sort of interference with the sacred laws of supply and demand, and by a religious philosophy (inherited from the eighteenth century) of a well-ordered world which man tampered with at his peril. Since the workers had no vote, and unions were outlawed, the only recourse was to mass meetings, petitions, and occasional riots. Although in the 1820's the tide began to turn and more reforms were instituted, the problems created by the Industrial Revolution continued into the Victorian period, where they influenced the literature much more powerfully than they did in the early nineteenth century. Romantic writers were by no means indifferent to the miseries caused by the industrial upheaval, but in general they preferred to deal with such evils indirectly, working by means of literature upon the mind and heart to produce the moral and spiritual changes necessary to any enduring practical reform.

The third revolution was that literary revolution to which we attach the label "Romantic." This is a difficult word. As a critical term it may be used to define a particular literary method or attitude (as opposed to the "Classic"), which may be traced throughout the whole history of literature. Or it may refer specifically to that group of authors in the late eighteenth and early nineteenth centuries who broke away from the literary standards followed by neoclassical writers and who established a fresh set of values and criteria for literature. It is in this second sense that we shall consider the terms "Romantic" and "Romanticism."

Even with the field so narrowed, the difficulties are great. A precise definition escapes us and should not be sought, for a movement so vital and many-sided as the Romantic movement cannot be imprisoned in a neat formula. Indeed, there seem to be about as many definitions of Romanticism as there are definers. A return to nature, a return to the Middle Ages, the renascence of wonder, the addition of strangeness to beauty, liberalism in literature, emotion placed above reason, a revolt against rules, the cult of subjectivity, the apotheosis of the imagination, escape from actuality, sentimental melancholy, the fairy way of writing, the love of the picturesque, the substitution of faith in a dynamic, organic universe for belief in a static, mechanical cosmos—these are only some of the many approaches to a definition which have been advanced by critics and scholars.

Perhaps the key word to an understanding of Romanticism is individualism. A statement by Jean Jacques Rousseau, the eighteenth-century French thinker whose influence on English Romanticism was considerable, could be taken as a motto of Romantic individualism: "I am not made like anyone I have ever seen; I dare believe that I am not made like anyone in existence. If I am not better, at least I am different." The nonconformist element in all the Romantic writers—in their lives and personalities as well as in their works—is usually very strong indeed. They cherished the right to be different; and it is this very individualism that makes it difficult to sum up their philosophies and accomplishments in one neat, compact, all-embracing definition. It is instructive to note that one of Pope's major poems is the *Essay on Man*—Man in general, not a particular man, not Alexander Pope. But Wordsworth's greatest long poem is *The Prelude,* which is subtitled the "Growth of a Poet's Mind"—not any poet, not poet-in-general, but William Wordsworth. Coleridge, Shelley, and Keats gave us their personal vision. And when Byron wrote an epic, *Don Juan,* the principal character was not, as in the classical epics, the wandering hero, but Byron himself.

This cult of personal individualism is paralleled by an aesthetic preference for the particular over against the general. Samuel Johnson said that it was not the business of the poet to number the streaks of a tulip; it was rather to deal with general, universal truths. But to a poet like Wordsworth the streaks of a tulip are quite worthy of poetical treatment. And William Hazlitt, Romantic essayist, once wrote: "I hate people who have no notion of anything but generalities, and forms, and creeds, and naked propositions. . . ."

The philosophy of intense individualism helps to explain the Romantic rebellion against many of the principles and practices of eighteenth-century, or neoclassical, authors. Being individualists, Romantic writers were impatient of the rules and regulations that appealed to the neoclassical mind; they tended to be nonconformists rather than conformists, and decorum was not one of their idols. And so they went back to forms (such as the popular ballad, the Spenserian stanza, blank verse, and the sonnet) and subject matters (such as simple, everyday subjects or wild, fanciful subjects or medieval subjects) which had been slighted by the Age of Reason. Since the previous age placed such a high value upon reason and common sense, the Romantic Age emphasized the importance of intuition and the emotions and tended to distrust the analytical, logical faculty of the human mind. The neoclassical period stressed the delights of social life in urban centers; the Romantic period preferred country life and the joys of solitude. Both ages exalted nature. But for neoclassical writers nature meant either the great chain of ordered being with everything in its proper place, or what was in accordance with human nature and common sense and thus was "natural." To "follow nature" was thus to do what was reasonable, what was defined by traditional norms. To Romantic writers nature was the wild, unregulated creaton of the great out-of-doors, an external nature filled with a spirit with which man could have helpful communion.

If the individual is important, if he is indeed something more than a link in a chain-of-being with the primary duty of accepting his place in the scheme of things, then the creative power of the individual is a real and vital force, capable of introducing significant novelty and change into a universe by no means static and mechanical. To this creative power the Romantics gave the name imagination, a term which they invested with a dignity and importance that it had never had before in the literary world. For Hobbes, the seventeenth-century English philosopher, "imagination . . . is nothing but decaying sense"; and for Pascal, the French writer of the same century, "imagination is the deceptive part in man, the mistress of error and falsehood." For the neoclassical authors, imagination was a wild, unregulated kind of day-dreaming, vivid with unearthly images, or at best a nimble fancy making new and attractive combinations out of old elements. But for the Romantics the imagination is the very reproduction in man of the divine creativity ("the repetition in the finite mind of the eternal act of creation in the infinite I AM," Coleridge calls it); it is the God in man, producing order out of chaos, piercing beneath the appearances of things into the underlying truth, harmonizing disparate elements into trumphant new wholes greater than the sums of their parts. For Wordsworth, imagination

> Is but another name for absolute power
> And clearest insight, amplitude of mind,
> And Reason in her most exalted mood.

For Shelley poetry has moral influence because it is "the expression of the imagination," which is "the great instrument of moral good." Keats was "certain of nothing but the holiness of the heart's affections, and the truth of imagination. What the imagination seizes as beauty must be truth—whether it existed before or not. . . ." And even though Byron pretended to be contemptuous of such metaphysical notions, much of his poetry shows that he practiced what he did not care to preach.

Setting dates for the Romantic Period is a task almost as difficult as definition. Such chronological limits are arbitrary at best. The truth of the matter is, of course, that English Romanticism did not begin, or end, in any specific year. We have already seen how, down through the eighteenth century, certain men and writings and new ideas prepared the way for the full flowering of Romanticism in the nineteenth century: the blank verse and nature poetry of Thomson; the school of graveyard poetry; the increased appreciation of older English authors, of the Middle Ages, of the folk ballads; the cults of melancholy and sentimentalism and primitivism; lyrical qualities in the poetry of Gray and Collins; the emotional influence of the Methodist revival; the Gothic novel; a deepening humanitarianism; and the almost full-blown romanticism of Burns and Blake. The English Romantic movement was an evolutionary development.

Nevertheless, when William Wordsworth and Samuel Taylor Coleridge formed their famous poetical partnership in 1798 and published the first edition of the *Lyrical Ballads*, they brought to a focus many of those eighteenth-century principles and practices that were opposed to neoclassical standards. They were deliberately trying to produce poems unlike the poetry of the Age of Reason, poems, to quote Wordsworth, "materially different from those upon which general approbation is at present bestowed," poems which give pleasure "of a kind very different from that which is supposed by many persons to be the proper object of poetry." The experimental poetry of the *Lyrical Ballads* is of two kinds, rising (as Coleridge tells us in the *Biographia Literaria*) out of the "two cardinal points of poetry" as the two men conceived them—namely, "the power of exciting the sympathy of the reader by a faithful adherence to the truth of nature, and the power of giving the interest of novelty by the modifying colors of the imagination." Thus two sorts of poems might be composed:

In the one, the incidents and agents were to be, in part at least, supernatural; and the excellence aimed at was to consist in the interesting of the affections by the dramatic truth of such emotions, as would naturally accompany such situations, supposing them real. . . . For the second class, subjects were to be chosen from ordinary life; the characters and incidents were to be such as will be found in every village and its vicinity, where there is a meditative and feeling mind to seek after them, or to notice them when they present themselves.

Coleridge would write poems of the first sort, Wordsworth of the second.

To the second edition of the *Lyrical Ballads* in 1800 Wordsworth prefixed his famous preface, which is more than a mere attempt to justify the experimental poetry (especially the Wordsworthian kind) of the collection. It is a strong declaration of independence against the poetical canons of the neoclassical age and thus a kind of literary manifesto for the early years of the Romantic movement.

The glory of English Romanticism is in its poetry, and especially in the work of the five great Romantic poets: Wordsworth, Coleridge, Byron, Shelley, and Keats. Other poets of the age are, in comparison, "as moonlight unto sunlight, and as water unto wine." Of these might be mentioned Walter Scott, who wrote some stirring ballads and vigorous long narrative poems; Robert Southey, who turned out a number of creditable ballads and four ambitious epics that are not entirely without merit; and Walter Savage Landor, who produced many fine lyrics, the best of which are memorable for their quiet, restrained beauty.

In prose the age did not attain the distinction that it did in poetry. Criticism is best represented by Coleridge, one of the truly great philosophical critics of English literary history, who influenced the whole trend of later criticism, and by Hazlitt, a vigorous critic notable for his sanity and gusto. The informal personal essay reached a high level with Lamb and Hazlitt. Both men are typically romantic in their strongly individualistic reactions to their topics. Lamb is quaint and flavorful, with oddities of style appropriate to his genial quixotism. Hazlitt is more forthright, expressing himself with clarity and wit, and with an amazing command of allusion and concrete illustration. Excellent essays both critical and personal were also written by Leigh Hunt and Thomas DeQuincey, the latter in a style distinguished for its long, ornate, and sonorous sentences, the direct descendant of the seventeenth-century prose of Milton and Thomas Browne.

The Romantic Period produced only two really outstanding novelists, quite opposed in their technique and subject matter. Walter Scott is regarded as the father of the historical novel. A true Romantic, he wrote colorful novels (frequently laid in medieval times) emphasizing sweep, panorama, pageant, and stirring episodes, with little concern for subtleties of character or tightness of plot. On the other hand Jane Austen had the neoclassical love of order and neatness. Her six, carefully constructed novels are the prose equivalent of comedies of manners, stressing character portrayal, dramatic objectivity, tidiness of plot.

In drama the age is altogether undistinguished. The only two licensed theaters were rebuilt on a large scale that favored grandiose productions and flamboyant acting, not literary merit. The other theaters, not allowed to produce legitimate plays, resorted to vaudeville acts, German and French melodramas (with music), and various sorts of burlettas, light operas, extravaganzas. All the great Romantic poets tried their hand at drama, but they were more interested in the poetry than in the demands of the stage, and were unable to achieve the objectivity demanded of a successful playwright. The greatest of these efforts—and perhaps the most notable piece of dramatic writing between Sheridan and Shaw—was *The Cenci,* a powerful play of violence, incest, and murder. It was created, oddly enough, by that poet apparently least likely to succeed in dramatic composition—Percy Bysshe Shelley.

This poverty in drama continued down through the century. Although there are Victorian playwrights whose work is of more than average interest, it was not until the 1890's that real literary genius returned to the English stage in the plays of Oscar Wilde and especially those of George Bernard Shaw.

THE VICTORIAN PERIOD (1832–1901)

Although Victoria did not become Queen of England until 1837, the Victorian Period is commonly regarded as beginning with the Reform Bill of 1832. This bill illustrates one of the striking tendencies of the age: a tendency toward evolutionary progress and reform by solving conflicts through compromise. From 1783 to 1830 the reactionary Tories had been in control; from 1830 to 1870 the more liberal Whigs were the dominant party. The Whigs began their reign with a program of cautious reforms, which set the pattern for a series of similar measures down through the century.

One of the major conflicts of the age was that between the property owners (consisting of the old, landed aristocracy and the prospering upper middle class) and a rising workers' class with a developing political consciousness. The political solution of this conflict is marked by the steady advance of democracy in the nineteenth century. The three Reform Bills of the age—those of 1832, 1867, and 1884—expanded the electorate until most of the laboring class had been given the vote. Property qualifications for voters were first reduced and then done away with altogether. Electoral districts were gradually equalized. Other measures brought democratic control to local governments and introduced the secret ballot. In the first three decades of the century England was an oligarchy, governed by a Parliament made up of aristocrats and property owners, with millions of Englishmen not allowed to vote and with vast centers of population totally unrepresented; by the end of the century England was almost a true democracy, needing only the later Reform Bills of 1917 and 1928 to complete the process.

One good illustration of how revolutionary programs yielded to slow evolutionary progress is found in the failure of the Chartist movement, which flourished between 1838 and 1848. The working people, dissatisfied with the modest extension of the suffrage afforded by the Reform Bill of 1832, presented a People's Charter to Parliament in the form of a lengthy petition. The Charter advocated six measures: universal suffrage, annual Parliaments, abolition of the property qualification for members of Parliament, payment of members, equal electoral districts, and the secret ballot. This petition and a later one were turned down; the demands were too radical for the time. However, although there were riots and agitations, England never became a stage for armed rebellion, and the movement died in 1848, a year which saw a series of violent Continental revolutions. Four of the six points advocated by the Chartists were achieved by legislative action before the end of the century.

Though Chartism failed, it did publicize the plight of the worker and helped to educate him politically. To achieve his ends, he now turned to less radical means such as trade unions and cooperative societies. Unions, outlawed by the Combinations Act of 1800, were legalized by the repeal of that act in 1824 (though strikes were still forbidden); but the period of greatest growth was after 1850. By the end of the century, unions had

William Blake's illustration for "The Grave," a poem by Robert Blair.

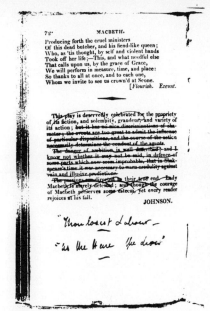

A page of the original manuscript of Keats's "Eve of St. Agnes."

A coalman in the early nineteenth century. This print shows one of the first railroads powered by coal.

Keats's comments on Samuel Johnson's criticism of *Macbeth*.

And kettle drums and far heard clarinet
Reach'd his scar'd ears   in
Affray'd his ears though but with faintest tones;
                                          is
The Hall door shuts again and all the noise ⩘ gone;
But
And still she slept:
And still she slept an azure-lidded sleep
  In blanched linen smooth and lavender'd;
While he from frorth the closet brought a heap
                  fruit
  Of candied sweets sweets with and plumb and gourd
                  apple Quince   creamed
With jellies soother than the dairy curd
                  tinct
  And lucent syrups smooth with ciannamons [?]
  And sugar'd dates from that o'er Euphrates fard *
            Manna and daites in [?] [?]   [?]
  And Manna and   and peaches [?] transferred
                  and Bragantine
                        sugar'd dates transferred
  In Brigantine from Fez
    From Fez—and spiced dainties every one
    glutted [?]
From wealthy Saſmarchand to cedard lebanon
    silken
                        he heap'd
These Delicates with ∧ glowing ∧ hand he
  On golden salvers and in baskets bright
Of· twisted wreathed silver—sumptuous they stand
Amid the quiet of St. Agnes' night,
Filling the chilly room
And now saith he my Seraph with perfume light
Teeming my Love   fair
And now saith he my Seraph now awake,
Thou art my heaven and I thine Eremite
Open thine eyes for meek St. Agnes' sake

A transcription of the manuscript page of Keats's "Eve of St. Agnes."

* This portion of the manuscript is almost impossible to decip

become very powerful and measures had been passed for their benefit. Cooperative societies, too, stemming from the work of Robert Owen, had a steady expansion throughout the period, with the final years of the century seeing the rise of many socialistic groups dedicated to the common ownership of the means of production.

Another area in which the worker gradually won his way against the entrenched opposition of wealth and conservatism was that of laboring conditions. The first Factory Act of 1819, forbidding children under nine to work in cotton mills, was poorly enforced and did not go far enough. The Factory Act of 1833 (the so-called "Children's Charter") went further, fixing the working hours of children and appointing inspectors to secure enforcement. Later factory legislation limited working hours and ages still more; and various bills (the first in 1848) aimed at improving public health conditions were passed. In 1846 the repeal of the Corn Laws (a tax on imported wheat to protect the English farmer) made cheap bread available to the laborer and, establishing the principle of free trade, was one of the causes for the high prosperity of England during the third quarter of the century. In the beginning the proponents of laissez faire, urging a hands-off policy for government and preaching the virtues of the untouchable laws of supply and demand, put up a strong fight; but it gradually became obvious even to the most conservative that great social and political abuses could not be left to correct themselves and that government interference and regulation had to come.

The progress in education is similar. The Reform Parliament of 1830 made a gesture toward education by making a grant to the private, voluntary schools, and a system of such aids was set up in 1851, with grants dependent upon results achieved. Workers undertook to educate themselves through colleges, cooperative libraries, and debating clubs. The first Working Men's College was founded in 1854. Cheap books, newspapers (the tax on newspapers was completely abolished in 1855), and magazines played an important role in both education and democracy. But with the passage of the Second Reform Bill (1867), which gave the vote to a million more workers, men came to realize that an ignorant electorate was a threat to good government, and in the next few years giant strides were taken to meet the threat. In 1870 an Elementary Education Act established a system of public schools; in 1880 such education was made compulsory; and in 1891 it was made free.

Another major conflict in the Victorian Period was that between science and religion. The nineteenth century was an age of remarkable scientific growth, both in applied and in theoretical science, and England was in the forefront of the advance. In applied science, the story is a part of the expanding industrial revolution, as more and better machinery strengthened the factory system and as railroads made possible the rapid and efficient transportation of large quantities of coal, iron, raw materials, and manufactured goods. The first railroad in England was built in 1825; by midcentury there were over 5,000 miles of railway in Great Britain, with 2,000 miles more under construction. The railroad was an important factor in England's prosperity between 1850 and 1870. Gas lighting, the telegraph, photography, ether and chloroform, new methods in medicine and surgery, the dynamo, steamboats, the submarine cable, the telephone, the lucifer match—these are only some of the accomplishments in scientific technology during the nineteenth century.

But the conflict was not due primarily to this aspect of scientific expansion—though many writers and thinkers decried the materialism, the smugness, the superficial optimism and faith in progress which such triumphs over nature induced in the mass of the people.

The great battle was between the church and theoretical science, particularly geology and biology, which broke more sharply with previous theory than did the disciplines of chemistry or physics, where the progress was equally remarkable but not so revolutionary.

Between 1830 and 1833 Charles Lyell published his *Principles of Geology*, which challenged the prevailing theory of catastrophism—the belief that earth forms came into being through some sudden convulsion, a belief that was compatible with the Biblical account of creation. Lyell substituted the theory of uniformitarianism, which stated that earth forms are the results of thousands of years of slow, evolutionary forces just like the forces now in operation. This seemed to contradict the belief in special, divine creation which the orthodox held sacred.

Then came Darwin's *Origin of Species* in 1859, one of the most influential books in man's intellectual history. Darwin extended the theory of evolution to organic life, demonstrating through cogent argument and convincing evidence that the complex organisms of today were evolved through a long, slow process from simpler organisms of far-off eons, and that the principle of what Herbert Spencer called the "survival of the fittest" in the struggle for survival was enough to explain the natural selection and continuance of certain species. Organic evolution was not new with Darwin, but it was he who supported it with the fullest data and buttressed it with the corollary theory of natural selection through the "survival of the fittest."

The effect of Darwin's book was electric. Here was a direct challenge to supernatural miracles, to the Biblical account of the special creation of each species, and—though Darwin did not specifically include the human organism in his theory, the inference was plain—to man's dignity as a creature made in the image of God. For many years the battle raged between the champions of Darwin, like Thomas Huxley, and the defenders of the imperiled faith, like Bishop Wilberforce.

Meanwhile the scientific method had invaded the study of the Scriptures. From Germany came the new "higher criticism" of the Bible, applying the same rigorous, rational analysis to Biblical texts as to any other writings. Through this analysis much of the Old Testament was branded as legend, supernaturalism and miracle were questioned, and the humanity of Jesus was stressed. David F. Strauss' *Leben Jesu* ("The Life of Jesus"), published in 1835 and translated by George Eliot in 1846, substituted a human, historical Jesus for the divine Christ of the theologians; and later studies by Renan and Seeley bore a similar emphasis. In the early 1860's England was shocked by the Colenso controversy, caused by Bishop Colenso's questioning of scriptural accuracy and by a series of articles, *Essays and Reviews,* which took a critically rationalistic attitude toward the Bible.

In the face of this invasion by science and the scientific method of a realm hitherto held invulnerable to human criticism, reactions were varied. Some persons went over into the camp of the skeptics and agnostics. Many retreated into an even more obstinate orthodoxy. Others attempted to reconcile the new science and the old faith, believing, like Tennyson, that evolution is evidence of God's developing purpose for man, or insisting, like Matthew Arnold, that the moral and literary values of the Bible are not dependent upon its literal accuracy or upon one's uncritical acceptance of its recounted miracles.

We have spoken of religious England as if there were a single faith presenting a united front against its secular enemies. Actually there were three broad religious divisions in Victorian England, each with its particular character. At one extreme was the Roman

Catholic Church, a strong minority faithful to Rome, to the Pope, to a religion of ritual and authority. At the other extreme were the Dissenters, or Nonconformists (subdivided into a number of denominations), proponents of an infallible Bible, the priesthood of individual believers, and a congregational type of church organization. In the middle was the Establishment, or state-supported Anglican church, itself composed of three fairly well-defined groups: the High Church party, close to Roman Catholicism in its emphasis on liturgy, sacraments, and formality; the Low Church, or Evangelical, party, the Anglican counterpart of the Dissenters, stressing like them the saving of souls and the rewards and punishments of the after-life; and finally the Broad Church, or Latitudinarian, party, the "modernists" of the Establishment, indifferent to dogma, liberal and social in their outlook. Only this last group was sympathetic to the new science and criticism. The rest were dismayed, frightened, and hostile.

One of the earliest countermeasures to the growing liberalism of the nineteenth century was the Oxford Movement, inaugurated by the High Church party and led by John Henry Newman to combat the mounting indifference within the Establishment by a return to the ornaments and rituals of the pre-Reformation Church. This movement, begun in 1833, came to an end in 1845 with Newman's conversion to Roman Catholicism, but its influence in terms of a more serious dedication by churchmen was felt down through the century.

In the midst of all these conflicts Great Britain grew richer, larger, more powerful. This is the century of the rapid development of the Empire, in which England, needing new markets for her expanding economy, extended her control over an area five times as large as Europe, annexing new colonies and setting up commonwealths in Canada, Australia, and New Zealand.

All these currents and cross-currents in the Victorian era are reflected in its literature, which is unsurpassed for richness and variety. It is a mistake to characterize the age as a solemn, humorless age (the robust humor of Browning and Dickens alone would invalidate the characterization), but the fact is that the period is one of great moral earnestness, whose writers—with due exceptions to be noted—took seriously Shelley's dictum that creative artists are "the unacknowledged legislators of the world." Most of the poets had a message as well as a song; the essayists tended to be "prose prophets"; and the novelists were usually unsatisfied merely to tell a story.

Victorian poetry makes no radical break with Romantic poetry; indeed, the early Victorian poets are heirs of the Romantics, often imitating their manner, following their lead in subject matter and technique, and carrying even further their experimentation with new forms. But there is an added realism; the escapism, subjectivity, and visionary idealism characteristic of much of Romantic verse is not typical of Victorian poetry, which is more directly responsive to the major issues of the age. Tennyson, the poetical high priest of Victorianism, is an excellent example. Beginning his career as a disciple of Keats, he soon put his superb lyrical gifts to the service of a social conscience. In poem after poem he denounces an "art-for-art's sake" philosophy, reworks classical myths with Victorian motifs, makes a Victorian allegory of the Arthurian legends, illustrates the Victorian faith in progress ("Better fifty years of Europe than a cycle of Cathay"), makes an uneasy peace with evolution, and offers typically Victorian compromise solutions to the problems raised by advancing education, democracy, and science.

Browning might be called a psychological realist. He quickly renounced an early subjectivism induced by his love for Shelley and found his characteristic utterance in the dramatic monologue, in which he probes character with keen psychological insight. English social and political problems interest Browning very little; but religious issues concern him deeply. Many of his poems explain and defend his faith in a God of love, his belief in a success-through-failure doctrine, and his conviction that there is a compensatory after-life. Browning was particularly disturbed by the higher criticism of the Bible and by the attempt of the rationalists to reduce Christ to a merely good man.

Matthew Arnold turned in midcareer from poetry to prose criticism because he believed that he could thereby speak more effectively to contemporary issues. But even in his poetry, a poetry largely of doubt and questioning, he felt that he had represented the "main movement of mind" in his generation. Later poets, like Hardy and Meredith, reflect the impact of the new science, especially evolution, on literature. In Hardy's verse man is presented as a tragic, ironic figure in a universe hostile or indifferent to his aspirations. Meredith, on the other hand, though dismissing the orthodox conception of divine providence, welcomes the evolutionary doctrine as pointing the way to man's further development in a world where struggle is necessary for discipline and growth.

There was a reaction, of course, to this moral earnestness, this emphasis on the poet-as-prophet. D. G. Rossetti expressed in his poetry a revolt similar to that expressed in art by the Pre-Raphaelite Brotherhood, of which he was the leader—a revolt against the typical Victorian product. He was primarily a medievalist, a colorist, and a recorder of intense personal emotion. William Morris called himself "the idle singer of an empty day"; his best poems are stories in verse, untouched by the socialistic doctrines that are found in his prose and in his life. Edward Fitzgerald's *Rubáiyát of Omar Khayyám* upholds an eat-drink-and-be-melancholy creed in a universe in which man's philosophical ignorance is irremediable and his fate inexorably determined. A. C. Swinburne's foremost appeal is that of a musician in verse, though he is a stirring poet of freedom, and he is as zealous in the expression of his neopagan views as Browning is in the presentation of his essentially Christian ones.

The novel attained high distinction in the Victorian Period, and the novelists, too, are usually close to their age. Most of them followed the lead of Walter Scott and wrote one or more historical novels, but few of them concentrated exclusively on this type of fiction. Charles Dickens was a crusader as well as a storyteller; his reforming zeal plays a part in many of his novels, which are noted for their pathos, their vivid character portrayal amounting frequently to caricature, their robust humor, their graphic settings, and their episodic plot structure. W. M. Thackeray tends to take a satirical, somewhat cynical view of the upper-class society about which he writes. In contrast to these two authors are the Brontë sisters, Charlotte and Emily, who go against the current of Victorian realism by producing poetic, highly introspective novels characterized by a brooding, somber quality. Perhaps the greatest of the women novelists of the period is George Eliot, a conscious realist whose well-constructed novels are often laid in rural communities, excel in psychological analysis, and reveal a strong ethical bias. Another careful craftsman was Anthony Trollope, called by one critic "the first truly professional novelist," who portrays with sincerity and mild humor ordinary people in ordinary settings and situations.

The most noteworthy of the later novelists are George Meredith and Thomas Hardy. Meredith neglects plot for subtle psychological probing, prefers implication to explication in his difficult style, and takes a highly intellectual view of life and people. The world of Thomas Harry is grim and forbidding; he depicts characters frustrated in a universe where freedom of the human will has little meaning.

The essential difference between Romantic and Victorian literature is well illustrated in nonfictional prose. The informal personal essay, practiced so delightfully by Lamb and Hazlitt, gives way to long, critical essays on serious subjects. Many of these essays make up a massive protest against the dominant attitudes and outstanding abuses of the period. Carlyle, Newman, Ruskin, and Arnold are one in their condemnation of the selfishness, the superficial faith in progress, and the crass materialism which they saw around them, and in their suspicion of science or democracy as panaceas. Carlyle turned from his interpretation of German literature to become the most violent of the Victorian "prose prophets," denouncing the mammonism and cash-payment philosophy of the day in vehement prose. Newman calls for a liberal education which will truly develop the well-rounded intelligence and decries instruction based on the ignoble creed of practical utility. Arnold, dismayed by the shallow and complacent Philistinism of the age, preaches his religion of culture—the harmonious development of all the worth-while powers of human life—urging his fellow countrymen to cultivate their best selves instead of their ordinary class selves. John Ruskin shifted from art criticism to sharp social criticism, convinced that there could be no great art without a sound national life, which for him meant abandoning the worship of the "Goddess of Getting-on" and following the ideals of love and service. Among the great essayists only T. B. Macaulay seems satisfied with the material progress of his day—with the science which made that progress possible and with the advancing democracy which was distributing its benefits more widely. Thomas Huxley, too, was a spokesman for science, though he was more critical than Macaulay of other aspects of Victorian life.

A few decades ago it was fashionable to take a patronizing attitude toward the Victorian Period, and "Victorianism" became a synonym for prudery, superficial optimism, excessive moral seriousness, a shallow faith in progress, and a total insensitivity to aesthetic values. These qualities, to be sure, are found in Victorian society, and some of them are reflected in its writers. But we must not forget that these writers are often as critical of that society as we are and denounced its shortcomings with a vigor even greater than our own. We must remember, too, that the Victorians faced giant problems which are still plaguing the twentieth century—problems of education, science and religion, labor and capital, government regulation and interference, and a society dedicated to materialistic values. Concerning these enduring problems Victorian authors say many wise things relevant to our own age; and in addition they are great creative artists whose literary performance commands our attention and our admiration.

William Wordsworth
(1770–1850)

WILLIAM WORDSWORTH WAS BORN AND REARED IN THE LAKE DISTRICT OF ENGLAND, A beautiful country of hills, meadows, woods, and waters—a natural setting that deeply affected his personality, philosophy, and poetry. His mother died when he was seven, his father six years later. After his early schooling at Penrith and Hawkshead, he attended Cambridge, from which he received his degree in 1791.

The year 1792 was an important one for Wordsworth. He went over to France, where his sympathy for the French Revolution was strengthened by his associations with the Girondist party (one of the revolutionary groups), and where he fell in love with Annette Vallon, a French girl of Royalist background. Their daughter, Caroline, was born in December.

Wordsworth returned to England in the winter of 1792–1793 to raise money so that he could marry Annette. But when in February, 1793, England declared war on France, crossing the Channel became impossible. It was ten years before he saw Annette again; by that time their lives had grown far apart.

As Wordsworth saw the French Revolution taking a more violent and militant turn, he became increasingly disillusioned. The early promise of the Revolution was being drowned in blood as a new, aggressive tyranny took the place of the old Bourbon autocracy. Wordsworth turned from the Revolution to abstract philosophy, especially to the philosophy of William Godwin, a rationalistic thinker who deplored the role of emotion in human affairs and who taught that salvation lay only in reason perfected by education. Since Godwinism, however, was radically opposed to Wordsworth's basic make-up, he sank further into spiritual confusion until finally, as he confesses in *The Prelude,* he "yielded up moral questions in despair."

From this despair Wordsworth was saved by his sister Dorothy, by nature and poetry, and by the friendship of Samuel Taylor Coleridge. Realizing the futility of external revolutions, he started to write those poems of simple tragedy which might arouse in readers the emotions of benevolence and sympathy needful for any ultimate and lasting social reform. In 1797 the acquaintance with Coleridge ripened into close friendship. As the two men roamed the Quantock hills together, discussing their common disillusionment, and talking philosophy and poetry, they began the joint venture which was to be the *Lyrical Ballads* of 1798. Wordsworth wrote his finest poetry between 1797 and 1808. Thereafter the quality of his verse declined.

The rest of Wordsworth's long life, most of it lived in the Lake Country, may be summarized briefly. He was married in 1802. In 1813 he was appointed to a government post in Westmoreland, a post which he resigned in 1842, receiving an annual pension. From 1843 until his death in 1850 he was Poet Laureate of England. After the turbulence of the 1790's these were quiet years for Wordsworth. He traveled abroad, went on many a walking tour, and enjoyed the company of a few friends.

The key to much of Wordsworth's poetry is his anti-rationalism—his distrust of the logical, analytical faculty of the mind as a means for either discovering the deepest truths or attaining the more abundant life. This hostility to rationalism accounts for many of Wordsworth's attitudes: his suspicion of science, which "murders to dissect"; his faith in the intuitive wisdom of children and of unsophisticated human types; his reliance on feeling and emotion, on the "genial impulses" of the spirit; his exaltation of imagination, "reason in her most exalted mood"; his confidence in those times of quiet awareness, ranging from a simple "wise passiveness" to moments of mystical insight, when we are "laid asleep in body and become a living soul"; his worship of nature, both of the beauty of her external forms and of the spirit within her; his preference for solitude and solitary places; his hatred of show and materialism, and his attachment to the grand simplicities of life, to "plain living and high thinking."

Expostulation and Reply

Wordsworth says that this poem and the following one "arose out of a conversation with a friend who was somewhat unreasonably attached to modern books of moral philosophy." The friend was probably William Hazlitt. The two poems are good illustrations of Wordsworth's anti-intellectual tendency, especially (1) his distrust of bookishness and scientific analysis, and (2) his upholding of a "wise passiveness" in the presence of nature as the best way to truth and moral betterment.

"Why, William, on that old gray stone,
Thus for the length of half a day,
Why, William, sit you thus alone,
And dream your time away?

"Where are your books?—that light bequeathed   5
To beings else forlorn and blind!
Up! up! and drink the spirit breathed
From dead men to their kind.

"You look round on your mother earth,
As if she for no purpose bore you;   10
As if you were her first-born birth,
And none had lived before you!"

One morning thus, by Esthwaite lake,
When life was sweet, I knew not why,
To me my good friend Matthew spake,   15
And thus I made reply:—

"The eye,—it cannot choose but see;
We cannot bid the ear be still;

Our bodies feel, where'er they be,
Against or with our will.   20

"Nor less I deem that there are powers
Which of themselves our minds impress;
That we can feed this mind of ours
In a wise passiveness.

"Think you, 'mid all this mighty sum   25
Of things forever speaking,
That nothing of itself will come
But we must still be seeking?

"Then ask not wherefore, here, alone,
Conversing as I may,   30
I sit upon this old gray stone,
And dream my time away."
(1798)

STUDY AIDS: 1. Distinguish between Wordsworth's "wise passiveness" and sheer idleness.

2. What does Wordsworth mean by "powers" (l. 21)? Why is it plural?

The Tables Turned:

An Evening Scene on the Same Subject

Up! up! my friend, and quit your books;
Or surely you'll grow double:
Up! up! my friend, and clear your looks;
Why all this toil and trouble?

The sun, above the mountain's head,   5
A freshening luster mellow
Through all the long green fields has spread,
His first sweet evening yellow.

Books! 'tis a dull and endless strife:
Come, hear the woodland linnet,   10
How sweet his music! on my life,
There's more of wisdom in it.

And hark! how blithe the throstle sings!
He, too, is no mean preacher:
Come forth into the light of things,   15
Let nature be your teacher.

She has a world of ready wealth,
Our minds and hearts to bless—
Spontaneous wisdom breathed by health,
Truth breathed by cheerfulness.   20

One impulse from a vernal wood
May teach you more of man,

Of moral evil and of good,
Than all the sages can.

Sweet is the lore which nature brings;   25
Our meddling intellect
Mis-shapes the beauteous forms of things:—
We murder to dissect.[1]

Enough of science and of art;
Close up those barren leaves;   30
Come forth, and bring with you a heart
That watches and receives.[2]
(1798)

STUDY AIDS: 1. What ideas not found in *Expostulation and Reply* are found in this poem? How are "the tables turned"? Is the tone different or the same in the two poems? Explain.

2. Line 28 is often quoted. What does it mean? How does the meddling intellect misshape the beauteous form of things? Is this a valid attack upon scientific analysis?

3. In st. 6, Wordsworth suggests that one will derive more moral benefit from a walk in the woods (bringing a "heart that watches and receives") than he will from reading a book on ethics. Does Wordsworth explain in the poem how he arrives at this opinion? How does he arrive at it?

Lines:

Composed a Few Miles above Tintern Abbey

In the summer of 1798 Wordsworth and his sister, Dorothy, walking from Alfoxden to Bristol, visited the beautiful ruins of Tintern Abbey, located on the Wye River in Monmouthshire. Wordsworth had been there in 1793, and in this poem he records his impressions after a five-year absence. Summing up Wordsworth's creed of the ministering power of nature (especially through the function of memory) and the development of his appreciation of nature from childhood to maturity, *Tintern Abbey* is a key poem to any understanding of Wordsworth's nature-philosophy.

Five years have past; five summers, with the length
Of five long winters! and again I hear

These waters, rolling from their mountain-springs
With a soft inland murmur.—Once again

[1] Stanzas 6 and 7 are the key stanzas of the poem and the core of Wordsworth's nature-philosophy.

[2] Compare "watches" and "receives" with "wise" and "passiveness" in *Expostulation and Reply*.

Do I behold these steep and lofty cliffs, 5
That on a wild, secluded scene impress
Thoughts of more deep seclusion; and connect
The landscape with the quiet of the sky.
The day is come when I again repose
Here, under this dark sycamore, and view 10
These plots of cottage-ground, these orchard-tufts,
Which at this season, with their unripe fruits,
Are clad in one green hue, and lose themselves
'Mid groves and copses. Once again I see
These hedge-rows, hardly hedge-rows, little lines 15
Of sportive wood run wild: these pastoral farms,
Green to the very door; and wreaths of smoke
Sent up, in silence, from among the trees!
With some uncertain notice, as might seem
Of vagrant dwellers in the houseless woods, 20
Or of some hermit's cave, where by his fire
The hermit sits alone. These beauteous forms,
Through a long absence, have not been to me
As is a landscape to a blind man's eye:
But oft, in lonely rooms, and 'mid the din 25
Of towns and cities, I have owed to them,
In hours of weariness, sensations sweet,
Felt in the blood, and felt along the heart;
And passing even into my purer mind,
With tranquil restoration:—feelings too 30
Of unremembered pleasure: such, perhaps,
As have no slight or trivial influence
On that best portion of a good man's life,
His little, nameless, unremembered acts
Of kindness and of love. Nor less, I trust, 35
To them I may have owed another gift,
Of aspect more sublime; that blessed mood,
In which the burden of the mystery,
In which the heavy and the weary weight
Of all this unintelligible world, 40
Is lightened:—that serene and blessed mood,
In which the affections gently lead us on,—
Until, the breath of this corporeal frame
And even the motion of our human blood
Almost suspended, we are laid asleep 45
In body, and become a living soul:
While with an eye made quiet by the power
Of harmony, and the deep power of joy,

We see into the life of things.
 If this
Be but a vain belief, yet, oh! how oft— 50
In darkness and amid the many shapes
Of joyless daylight; when the fretful stir
Unprofitable, and the fever of the world,
Have hung upon the beatings of my heart—
How oft, in spirit, have I turned to thee, 55
O sylvan Wye! thou wanderer through the woods,
How often has my spirit turned to thee!
And now, with gleams of half-extinguished thought,
With many recognitions dim and faint,
And somewhat of a sad perplexity, 60
The picture of the mind revives again:
While here I stand, not only with the sense
Of present pleasure, but with pleasing thoughts
That in this moment there is life and food
For future years. And so I dare to hope, 65
Though changed, no doubt, from what I was when first
I came among these hills; when like a roe
I bounded o'er the mountains, by the sides
Of the deep rivers, and the lonely streams,
Wherever nature led: more like a man 70
Flying from something that he dreads, than one
Who sought the thing he loved. For nature then
(The coarser pleasures of my boyish days,
And their glad animal movements all gone by)
To me was all in all.—I cannot paint 75
What then I was. The sounding cataract
Haunted me like a passion: the tall rock,
The mountain, and the deep and gloomy wood,
Their colors and their forms, were then to me
An appetite; a feeling and a love, 80
That had no need of a remoter charm,
By thought supplied, nor any interest
Unborrowed from the eye.—That time is past,
And all its aching joys are now no more,
And all its dizzy raptures. Not for this 85
Faint I, nor mourn nor murmur; other gifts
Have followed; for such loss, I would believe,
Abundant recompense. For I have learned
To look on nature, not as in the hour

Of thoughtless youth; but hearing often-
    times   90
The still, sad music of humanity,
Nor harsh nor grating, though of ample power
To chasten and subdue. And I have felt
A presence that disturbs me with the joy
Of elevated thoughts; a sense sublime   95
Of something far more deeply interfused,
Whose dwelling is the light of setting suns,
And the round ocean and the living air,
And the blue sky, and in the mind of man;
A motion and a spirit, that impels   100
All thinking things, all objects of all thought,
And rolls through all things.[1] Therefore am I
    still
A lover of the meadows and the woods,
And mountains; and of all that we behold
From this green earth; of all the mighty
    world   105
Of eye, and ear—both what they half create,
And what perceive; well pleased to recognize
In nature and the language of the sense
The anchor of my purest thoughts, the nurse,
The guide, the guardian of my heart, and
    soul   110
Of all my moral being.   Nor perchance,
If I were not thus taught, should I the more
Suffer my genial spirits to decay:
For thou art with me here upon the banks
Of this fair river; thou my dearest friend,   115
My dear, dear friend; and in thy voice I catch
The language of my former heart, and read
My former pleasures in the shooting lights
Of thy wild eyes. Oh! yet a little while
May I behold in thee what I was once,   120
My dear, dear sister! and this prayer I make,
Knowing that nature never did betray
The heart that loved her; 'tis her privilege,
Through all the years of this our life, to
    lead
From joy to joy: for she can so inform   125
The mind that is within us, so impress
With quietness and beauty, and so feed

With lofty thoughts, that neither evil tongues,
Rash judgments, nor the sneers of selfish men,
Nor greetings where no kindness is, nor
    all   130
The dreary intercourse of daily life,
Shall e'er prevail against us, or disturb
Our cheerful faith, that all which we behold
Is full of blessings. Therefore let the moon
Shine on thee in thy solitary walk;   135
And let the misty mountain-winds be free
To blow against thee: and, in after years,
When these wild ecstasies shall be matured
Into a sober pleasure; when thy mind
Shall be a mansion for all lovely forms,   140
Thy memory be as a dwelling-place
For all sweet sounds and harmonies; oh! then,
If solitude, or fear, or pain, or grief,
Should be thy portion, with what healing
    thoughts
Of tender joy wilt thou remember me,   145
And these my exhortations! Nor, perchance—
If I should be where I no more can hear
Thy voice, nor catch from thy wild eyes these
    gleams
Of past existence—wilt thou then forget
That on the banks of this delightful
    stream   150
We stood together; and that I, so long
A worshiper of nature, hither came
Unwearied in that service: rather say
With warmer love—oh! with far deeper zeal
Of holier love. Nor wilt thou then forget,   155
That after many wanderings, many years
Of absence, these steep woods and lofty cliffs,
And this green pastoral landscape, were to me
More dear, both for themselves and for thy
    sake!
(1798)

STUDY AIDS: 1. The following broad outline may be of help in a careful re-reading of
the poem: (1) the scene recaptured (ll. 1–22);
(2) the ministry of remembered natural beauty
(ll. 23–57); (3) the development of the poet's
appreciation of nature (ll. 58–111); (4) a
prayer for Dorothy (ll. 111–159).

2. In the second division (ll. 26–49), how
many different kinds of ministration of nature
(or of the memory of natural scenery) are suggested? Note the climactic order in which they
are arranged.

[1] Lines 93–102 are often quoted as an illustration
of Wordsworth's early pantheism (the belief that
the sum total of creation is God). Perhaps a better
term for Wordsworth's belief here would be "pan-
psychism"; the belief in an all-pervading soul of
the universe.

3. In the third division (ll. 58–111), Wordsworth defines three stages in the growth of his appreciation of nature: the first is suggested briefly in ll. 73–74; the second is described in ll. 67–85 (except ll. 73–74); the third is given in ll. 88–102. Try to explain these stages in your own words, giving particular attention to the third stage, which Wordsworth regards as "abundant recompense" for the loss of the other two.

4. In the fourth division (ll. 111–159) just what is Wordsworth's prayer for his sister? (Note especially ll. 116–119, 125–134, 137–146.)

5. What are some of the qualities of the blank verse used in this poem? Note, for instance, the long rhythmical sentences, the RUN-ON LINES,

the heightened diction. Coleridge speaks of the "lofty and sustained diction" of *Tintern Abbey*. What lines or passages particularly illustrate this quality?

6. One critic says that the central meaning of *Tintern Abbey* is that "the beauty of nature enables the poet to feel, despite the apparent evils of life, that the universe is fundamentally harmonious." Do you agree that this is the central meaning of the poem? In this connection note ll. 121–134. Is this an expression of superficial optimism? Is there any difference between the conviction expressed in these lines and that in Pope's famous couplet: "And, spite of pride, in erring reason's spite, One truth is clear: Whatever is, is right"?

Strange Fits of Passion Have I Known

This lyric and the four that follow are commonly referred to as the "Lucy poems," since they concern a girl named Lucy, whose identity has been the subject of much speculation.

Strange fits of passion have I known:
And I will dare to tell,
But in the lover's ear alone,
What once to me befell.

When she I loved looked every day   5
Fresh as a rose in June,
I to her cottage bent my way,
Beneath an evening-moon.

Upon the moon I fixed my eye,
All over the wide lea;   10
With quickening pace my horse drew nigh
Those paths so dear to me.

And now we reached the orchard-plot;
And, as we climbed the hill,
The sinking moon to Lucy's cot [1]   15
Came near, and nearer still.

In one of those sweet dreams I slept,
Kind nature's gentlest boon!

[1] Cottage.

And all the while my eyes I kept
On the descending moon.   20

My horse moved on; hoof after hoof
He raised, and never stopped:
When down behind the cottage roof,
At once, the bright moon dropped.

What fond and wayward thoughts will
   slide   25
Into a lover's head!
"O mercy!" to myself I cried,
"If Lucy should be dead!"
(1799; 1800)

STUDY AIDS: 1. Wordsworth had recently been reading Percy's *Reliques of Ancient English Poetry,* a collection of old English ballads. What evidence of ballad influence can you find in this lyric?

2. What purpose is served by the repeated references to the moon in the poem?

She Dwelt among the Untrodden Ways

She dwelt among the untrodden ways
  Beside the springs of Dove,
A maid whom there were none to praise
  And very few to love:

A violet by a mossy stone   5
  Half hidden from the eye!

—Fair as a star, when only one
  Is shining in the sky.[1]

She lived unknown, and few could know
  When Lucy ceased to be;   10
But she is in her grave, and, oh,
  The difference to me!
    (1799; 1800)

I Traveled among Unknown Men

I traveled among unknown men,
  In lands beyond the sea;
Nor, England! did I know till then
  What love I bore to thee.

'Tis past, that melancholy dream!   5
  Nor will I quit thy shore
A second time; for still I seem
  To love thee more and more.

Among thy mountains did I feel
  The joy of my desire;   10
And she I cherished turned her wheel
  Beside an English fire.

Thy mornings showed, thy nights concealed,
  The bowers where Lucy played;
And thine too is the last green field   15
  That Lucy's eyes surveyed.
    (1799; 1807)

Three Years She Grew in Sun and Shower

Three years she grew in sun and shower,
Then Nature said, "A lovelier flower
On earth was never sown;
This child I to myself will take;
She shall be mine, and I will make   5
A lady of my own.

"Myself will to my darling be
Both law and impulse: and with me
The girl, in rock and plain,
In earth and heaven, in glade and bower, 10
Shall feel an overseeing power
To kindle or restrain.

"She shall be sportive as the fawn
That wild with glee across the lawn,
Or up the mountain springs;   15

And hers shall be the breathing balm,
And hers the silence and the calm
Of mute insensate things.

"The floating clouds their state shall lend
To her; for her the willow bend;   20
Nor shall she fail to see
Even in the motions of the storm
Grace that shall mold the maiden's form
By silent sympathy.

"The stars of midnight shall be dear   25
To her; and she shall lean her ear
In many a secret place
Where rivulets dance their wayward round,
And beauty born of murmuring sound
Shall pass into her face.   30

"And vital feelings of delight
Shall rear her form to stately height,

[1] How is the imagery of this stanza appropriate to the central idea of the poem?

Her virgin bosom swell;
Such thoughts to Lucy I will give
While she and I together live   35
Here in this happy dell."

Thus Nature spake.—The work was done.—
How soon my Lucy's race was run!
She died, and left to me

This heath, this calm, and quiet scene;   40
The memory of what has been,
And never more will be.
(1799; 1800)

STUDY AIDS: In l. 8 note the key words "law" and "impulse." How are their meanings repeated in l. 12 and in the first and last parts of the next stanza?

A Slumber Did My Spirit Seal

A slumber did my spirit seal;
    I had no human fears:
She seemed a thing that could not feel
    The touch of earthly years.

No motion has she now, no force;
    She neither hears nor sees;
Rolled round in earth's diurnal course
    With rocks, and stones, and trees.
(1799; 1800)

STUDY AIDS: 1. What is the tone of this poem? How does it differ in this respect from ll. 125–134 of *Tintern Abbey*? How is this tone achieved? (What is the effect, for example, of the emphasis on monosyllables, and, in the final line, of the two strong pauses?)

2. What is the difference in time between the two stanzas? (Note the tenses of the main verbs.) Is there a change in intensity between the two stanzas corresponding to the shift in time?

3. Is there a conflict between the thought of the last stanza and ll. 93–102 of *Tintern Abbey*?

Michael

A Pastoral Poem

"I have attempted to give a picture of a man, of strong mind and lively sensibility, agitated by two of the most powerful affections of the human heart: the parental affection, and the love of property (*landed* property), including the feelings of inheritance, home, and personal and family independence . . . " (Wordsworth).

If from the public way you turn your steps
Up the tumultuous brook of Greenhead
    Ghyll,[1]
You will suppose that with an upright path
Your feet must struggle; in such bold ascent
The pastoral mountains front you, face to
    face.   5
But, courage! for around that boisterous brook
The mountains have all opened out them-
    selves,
And made a hidden valley of their own.
No habitation can be seen; but they

Who journey thither find themselves
    alone   10
With a few sheep, with rocks and stones,
    and kites
That overhead are sailing in the sky.
It is in truth an utter solitude;
Nor should I have made mention of this dell
But for one object which you might pass
    by,   15
Might see and notice not. Beside the brook
Appears a straggling heap of unhewn stones!
And to that simple object appertains
A story—unenriched with strange events,
Yet not unfit, I deem, for the fireside,   20

[1] A ghyll is a ravine with a stream running through it.

Or for the summer shade. It was the first [2]
Of those domestic tales that spake to me
Of shepherds, dwellers in the valleys, men
Whom I already loved; not verily
For their own sakes, but for the fields and
    hills   25
Where was their occupation and abode.
And hence this tale, while I was yet a boy
Careless of books, yet having felt the power
Of nature, by the gentle agency
Of natural objects, led me on to feel   30
For passions that were not my own, and think
(At random and imperfectly indeed)
On man, the heart of man, and human life.
Therefore, although it be a history
Homely and rude, I will relate the same   35
For the delight of a few natural hearts;
And, with yet fonder feeling, for the sake
Of youthful poets, who among these hills
Will be my second self when I am gone.

    Upon the forest-side in Grasmere Vale [3]   40
There dwelt a shepherd, Michael was his
    name;
An old man, stout of heart, and strong of limb.
His bodily frame had been from youth to
    age
Of an unusual strength: his mind was keen,
Intense, and frugal, apt for all affairs,   45
And in his shepherd's calling he was prompt
And watchful more than ordinary men.
Hence had he learned the meaning of all
    winds,
Of blasts of every tone; and, oftentimes,
When others heeded not, he heard the
    south   50
Make subterraneous music, like the noise
Of bagpipers on distant Highland hills.
The shepherd, at such warning, of his flock
Bethought him, and he to himself would say,

"The winds are now devising work for
    me!"   55
And, truly, at all times, the storm, that drives
The traveler to a shelter, summoned him
Up to the mountains: he had been alone
Amid the heart of many thousand mists,
That came to him, and left him, on the
    heights.   60
So lived he till his eightieth year was past;
And grossly that man errs, who should sup-
    pose
That the green valleys, and the streams and
    rocks,
Were things indifferent to the shepherd's
    thoughts.
Fields, where with cheerful spirits he had
    breathed   65
The common air; hills, which with vigorous
    step
He had so often climbed; which had impressed
So many incidents upon his mind
Of hardship, skill or courage, joy or fear;
Which, like a book, preserved the memory 70
Of the dumb animals, whom he had saved,
Had fed or sheltered, linking to such acts
The certainty of honorable gain;
Those fields, those hills—what could they
    less?—had laid
Strong hold on his affections, were to him 75
A pleasurable feeling of blind love,
The pleasure which there is in life itself. [4]

    His days had not been passed in single-
    ness.
His helpmate was a comely matron, old,
Though younger than himself full twenty
    years.   80
She was a woman of a stirring life,
Whose heart was in her house: two wheels
    she had
Of antique form; this large, for spinning wool;
That small, for flax; and if one wheel had rest,
It was because the other was at work.   85
The pair had but one inmate in their house,
An only child, who had been born to them
When Michael, telling o'er his years, began
To deem that he was old,—in shepherd's
    phrase,

[2] Lines 21-33 constitute a significant passage, indicating how Wordsworth's love of nature led him to a love of English shepherds and thus to a love of man in general. This theme is developed at length in *The Prelude,* where Wordsworth emphasizes the actuality of the shepherds he knew and contrasts them with the unreal shepherds of traditional pastoral poetry. Thus, although Wordsworth's poem is subtitled a PASTORAL, it breaks sharply with the classical pastoral tradition.
[3] A valley in the county of Westmoreland.

[4] What qualities of Michael are brought out in ll. 40-77?

With one foot in the grave. This only son, 90
With two brave sheep-dogs tried in many a
    storm,
The one of an inestimable worth,
Made all their household. I may truly say,
That they were as a proverb in the vale
For endless industry. When day was
    gone, 95
And from their occupations out of doors
The son and father were come home, even
    then,
Their labor did not cease; unless when all
Turned to the cleanly supper-board, and
    there,
Each with a mess of pottage and skimmed
    milk, 100
Sat round the basket piled with oaten cakes,
And their plain home-made cheese. Yet
    when the meal
Was ended, Luke (for so the son was named)
And his old father both betook themselves
To such convenient work as might
    employ 105
Their hands by the fireside; perhaps to card
Wool for the housewife's spindle, or repair
Some injury done to sickle, flail, or scythe,
Or other implement of house or field.

Down from the ceiling, by the chimney's
    edge, 110
That in our ancient uncouth country style
With huge and black projection overbrowed
Large space beneath, as duly as the light
Of day grew dim, the housewife hung a
    lamp;
An aged utensil, which had performed 115
Service beyond all others of its kind.
Early at evening did it burn—and late,
Surviving comrade of uncounted hours,
Which, going by from year to year, had
    found,
And left, the couple neither gay perhaps 120
Nor cheerful, yet with objects and with hopes,
Living a life of eager industry.
And now, when Luke had reached his
    eighteenth year,
There by the light of this old lamp they sat,
Father and son, while far into the night 125
The housewife plied her own peculiar work,
Making the cottage through the silent hours

Murmur as with the sound of summer flies.
This light was famous in its neighborhood,
And was a public symbol of the life 130
That thrifty pair had lived. For, as it chanced,
Their cottage on a plot of rising ground
Stood single, with large prospect, north and
    south,
High into Easedale, up to Dunmail-Raise,
And westward to the village near the
    lake; 135
And from this constant light, so regular
And so far seen, the house itself, by all
Who dwelt within the limits of the vale,
Both old and young, was named *The
    Evening Star.*

Thus living on through such a length of
    years, 140
The shepherd, if he loved himself, must needs
Have loved his helpmate; but to Michael's
    heart
This son of his old age was yet more dear—
Less from instinctive tenderness, the same
Fond spirit that blindly works in the blood
    of all— 145
Than that a child, more than all other gifts
That earth can offer to declining man,
Brings hope with it, and forward-looking
    thoughts,
And stirrings of inquietude, when they
By tendency of nature needs must fail. 150
Exceeding was the love he bare to him,
His heart and his heart's joy! For oftentimes
Old Michael, while he was a babe in arms,
Had done him female service, not alone
For pastime and delight, as is the use 155
Of fathers, but with patient mind enforced
To acts of tenderness; and he had rocked
His cradle, as with a woman's gentle hand.

And, in a later time, ere yet the boy
Had put on boy's attire, did Michael
    love, 160
Albeit of a stern unbending mind,
To have the young-one in his sight, when he
Wrought in the field, or on his shepherd's
    stool
Sat with a fettered sheep before him stretched
Under the large old oak, that near his
    door 165

Stood single, and, from matchless depth of
    shade,
Chosen for the shearer's covert from the sun,
Thence in our rustic dialect was called
The *Clipping Tree,* a name which yet it bears.
There, while they two were sitting in the
    shade,   170
With others round them, earnest all and
    blithe,
Would Michael exercise his heart with looks
Of fond correction and reproof bestowed
Upon the child, if he disturbed the sheep
By catching at their legs, or with his
    shouts   175
Scared them, while they lay still beneath the
    shears.

    And when by heaven's good grace the
    boy grew up
A healthy lad, and carried in his cheek
Two steady roses that were five years old;
Then Michael from a winter coppice cut   180
With his own hand a sapling, which he
    hooped
With iron, making it throughout in all
Due requisites a perfect shepherd's staff,
And gave it to the boy; wherewith equipped
He as a watchman oftentimes was placed 185
At gate or gap, to stem or turn the flock;
And, to his office prematurely called,
There stood the urchin, as you will divine,
Something between a hindrance and a help;
And for this cause not always, I believe, 190
Receiving from his father hire of praise;
Though nought was left undone which staff,
    or voice,
Or looks, or threatening gestures, could per-
    form.

    But soon as Luke, full ten years old, could
    stand
Against the mountain blasts; and to the
    heights,   195
Not fearing toil, nor length of weary ways,
He with his father daily went, and they
Were as companions, why should I relate
That objects which the shepherd loved before
Were dearer now? that from the boy
    there came   200
Feelings and emanations—things which were

Light to the sun and music to the wind;
And that the old man's heart seemed born
    again?

    Thus in his father's sight the boy grew up:
And now, when he had reached his eight-
    eenth year,   205
He was his comfort and his daily hope.

    While in this sort the simple household
    lived
From day to day, to Michael's ear there came
Distressful tidings. Long before the time
Of which I speak, the shepherd had been
    bound   210
In surety for his brother's son, a man
Of an industrious life, and ample means;
But unforeseen misfortunes suddenly
Had pressed upon him; and old Michael now
Was summoned to discharge the for-
    feiture,   215
A grievous penalty, but little less
Than half his substance. This unlooked-for
    claim,
At the first hearing, for a moment took
More hope out of his life than he supposed
That any old man ever could have lost.   220
As soon as he had armed himself with strength
To look his trouble in the face, it seemed
The shepherd's sole resource to sell at once
A portion of his patrimonial fields.
Such was his first resolve; he thought
    again,   225
And his heart failed him. "Isabel," said he,
Two evenings after he had heard the news,
"I have been toiling more than seventy years,
And in the open sunshine of God's love
Have we all lived; yet, if these fields of
    ours   230
Should pass into a stranger's hand, I think
That I could not lie quiet in my grave.
Our lot is a hard lot; the sun himself
Has scarcely been more diligent than I;
And I have lived to be a fool at last   235
To my own family. An evil man
That was, and made an evil choice, if he
Were false to us; and, if he were not false,
There are ten thousand to whom loss like this
Had been no sorrow. I forgive him;—but 240
'Twere better to be dumb than to talk thus.

"When I began, my purpose was to speak
Of remedies and of a cheerful hope.
Our Luke shall leave us, Isabel; the land
Shall not go from us, and it shall be free;   245
He shall possess it, free as is the wind
That passes over it. We have, thou know'st,
Another kinsman—he will be our friend
In this distress. He is a prosperous man,
Thriving in trade—and Luke to him
     shall go,   250
And with his kinsman's help and his own
     thrift
He quickly will repair this loss, and then
He may return to us. If here he stay,
What can be done? Where every one is poor,
What can be gained?"   255
           At this the old man paused,
And Isabel sat silent, for her mind
Was busy, looking back into past times.
There's Richard Bateman, thought she to her-
     self,
He was a parish-boy—at the church-door
They made a gathering for him, shillings,
     pence,   260
And halfpennies, wherewith the neighbors
     bought
A basket, which they filled with pedlar's
     wares;
And, with this basket on his arm, the lad
Went up to London, found a master there,
Who, out of many, chose the trusty boy   265
To go and overlook his merchandise
Beyond the seas; where he grew wondrous
     rich,
And left estates and monies to the poor,
And, at his birth-place, built a chapel floored
With marble, which he sent from foreign
     lands.   270
These thoughts, and many others of like
     sort,
Passed quickly through the mind of Isabel,
And her face brightened. The old man was
     glad,
And thus resumed:—"Well, Isabel! this
     scheme
These two days has been meat and drink
     to me.   275
Far more than we have lost is left us yet.
—We have enough—I wish indeed that I
Were younger;—but this hope is a good hope.

Make ready Luke's best garments, of the best
Buy for him more, and let us send him
     forth   280
To-morrow, or the next day, or to-night:
—If he *could* go, the boy should go to-night."

     Here Michael ceased, and to the fields went
     forth
With a light heart. The housewife for five
     days
Was restless morn and night, and all day
     long   285
Wrought on with her best fingers to prepare
Things needful for the journey of her son.
But Isabel was glad when Sunday came
To stop her in her work: for, when she lay
By Michael's side, she through the last two
     nights   290
Heard him, how he was troubled in his
     sleep:
And when they rose at morning she could see
That all his hopes were gone. That day at
     noon
She said to Luke, while they two by them-
     selves
Were sitting at the door, "Thou must not
     go: 295
We have no other child but thee to lose,
None to remember;—do not go away,
For if thou leave thy father he will die."
The youth made answer with a jocund voice;
And Isabel, when she had told her fears,   300
Recovered heart. That evening her best fare
D:d she bring forth, and all together sat
Like happy people round a Christmas fire.

     With daylight Isabel resumed her work;
And all the ensuing week the house ap-
     peared   305
As cheerful as a grove in spring: at length
The expected letter from their kinsman came,
With kind assurances that he would do
His utmost for the welfare of the boy;
To which, requests were added, that forth-
     with   310
He might be sent to him. Ten times or more
The letter was read over; Isabel
Went forth to show it to the neighbors
     round;
Nor was there at that time on English land

A prouder heart than Luke's. When
    Isabel   315
Had to her house returned, the old man said,
"He shall depart to-morrow." To this word
The housewife answered, talking much of
    things
Which, if at such short notice he should go,
Would surely be forgotten. But at length 320
She gave consent, and Michael was at ease.

    Near the tumultuous brook of Greenhead
    Ghyll,
In that deep valley, Michael had designed
To build a sheepfold; and, before he heard
The tidings of his melancholy loss,   325
For this same purpose he had gathered up
A heap of stones, which by the streamlet's
    edge
Lay thrown together, ready for the work.
With Luke that evening thitherward he
    walked:
And soon as they had reached the place he
    stopped,   330
And thus the old man spake to him:—"My
    son,
To-morrow thou wilt leave me: with full heart
I look upon thee, for thou art the same
That wert a promise to me ere thy birth,
And all thy life has been my daily joy.   335
I will relate to thee some little part
Of our two histories; 'twill do thee good
When thou art from me, even if I should
    touch
On things thou canst not know of.—After
    thou
First camest into the world—as ofte befalls 340
To new-born infants—thou didst sleep away
Two days, and blessings from thy father's
    tongue
Then fell upon thee. Day by day passed on,
And still I loved thee with increasing love.
Never to living ear came sweeter sounds 345
Than when I heard thee by our own fireside
First uttering, without words, a natural
    tune;
While thou, a feeding babe, didst in thy joy
Sing at thy mother's breast. Month followed
    month,
And in the open fields my life was
    passed   350

And on the mountains; else I think that thou
Hadst been brought up upon thy father's
    knees.
But we were playmates, Luke; among these
    hills,
As well thou knowest, in us the old and young
Have played together, nor with me didst
    thou   355
Lack any pleasure which a boy can know."
Luke had a manly heart; but at these words
He sobbed aloud. The old man grasped his
    hand,
And said, "Nay, do not take it so—I see
That these are things of which I need not
    speak.   360
—Even to the utmost I have been to thee
A kind and a good father: and herein
I but repay a gift which I myself
Received at others' hands; for, though now
    old
Beyond the common life of man, I still   365
Remember them who loved me in my youth.
Both of them sleep together: here they lived,
As all their forefathers had done; and when
At length their time was come, they were not
    loth
To give their bodies to the family mold.   370
I wished that thou shouldst live the life they
    lived,
But 'tis a long time to look back, my son,
And see so little gain from threescore years.
These fields were burdened when they came
    to me;
Till I was forty years of age, not more   375
Than half of my inheritance was mine.
I toiled and toiled; God blessed me in my
    work,
And till these three weeks past the land was
    free.
—It looks as if it never could endure
Another master. Heaven forgive me,
    Luke,   380
If I judge ill for thee, but it seems good
That thou shouldst go."
                  At this the old man paused;
Then, pointing to the stones near which they
    stood,
Thus, after a short silence, he resumed:
"This was a work for us; and now, my
    son,   385

It is a work for me. But, lay one stone—
Here, lay it for me, Luke, with thine own
    hands.
Nay, boy, be of good hope;—we both may
    live
To see a better day. At eighty-four
I still am strong and hale;—do thou thy
    part;   390
I will do mine.—I will begin again
With many tasks that were resigned to thee:
Up to the heights, and in among the storms,
Will I without thee go again, and do
All works which I was wont to do alone, 395
Before I knew thy face.—Heaven bless thee,
    boy!
Thy heart these two weeks has been beating
    fast
With many hopes; it should be so—yes—
    yes—
I knew that thou couldst never have a wish
To leave me, Luke: thou hast been bound
    to me   400
Only by links of love: when thou art gone,
What will be left to us!—But I forget
My purposes. Lay now the corner-stone,
As I requested; and hereafter, Luke,
When thou art gone away, should evil
    men   405
Be thy companions, think of me, my son,
And of this moment; hither turn thy thoughts,
And God will strengthen thee: amid all
    fear
And all temptation, Luke, I pray that thou
Mayst bear in mind the life thy fathers
    lived,   410
Who, being innocent, did for that cause
Bestir them in good deeds. Now, fare thee
    well;
When thou returnest, thou in this place wilt
    see
A work which is not here: a covenant
'Twill be between us; but, whatever fate   415
Befall thee, I shall love thee to the last,
And bear thy memory with me to the grave."

The shepherd ended here; and Luke
    stooped down,
And, as his father had requested, laid
The first stone of the sheepfold. At the
    sight   420

The old man's grief broke from him; to his
    heart
He pressed his son, he kissèd him and wept;
And to the house together they returned.
—Hushed was that house in peace, or seeming
    peace,
Ere the night fell:—with morrow's dawn the
    boy   425
Began his journey, and when he had reached
The public way, he put on a bold face;
And all the neighbors, as he passed their
    doors,
Came forth with wishes and with farewell
    prayers,
That followed him till he was out of
    sight.   430

    A good report did from their kinsman
    come,
Of Luke and his well-doing: and the boy
Wrote loving letters, full of wondrous news,
Which, as the housewife phrased it, were
    throughout
"The prettiest letters that were ever
    seen."   435
Both parents read them with rejoicing hearts.
So, many months passed on: and once again
The shepherd went about his daily work
With confident and cheerful thoughts; and
    now
Sometimes when he could find a leisure
    hour   440
He to that valley took his way, and there
Wrought at the sheep-fold. Meantime Luke
    began
To slacken in his duty; and, at length,
He in the dissolute city gave himself
To evil courses: ignominy and shame   445
Fell on him, so that he was driven at last
To seek a hiding-place beyond the seas.[5]

    There is a comfort in the strength of
    love;
'Twill make a thing endurable, which else
Would overset the brain, or break the
    heart: 450
I have conversed with more than one who
    well

[5] Why does Wordsworth treat Luke's misadventures so briefly?

Remember the old man, and what he was
Years after he had heard this heavy news.
His bodily frame had been from youth to
    age
Of an unusual strength. Among the
    rocks   455
He went, and still looked up to sun and
    cloud,
And listened to the wind; and, as before,
Performed all kinds of labor for his sheep,
And for the land, his small inheritance.
And to that hollow dell from time to
    time   460
Did he repair, to build the fold of which
His flock had need. 'Tis not forgotten yet
The pity which was then in every heart
For the old man—and 'tis believed by all
That many and many a day he thither
    went,   465
And never lifted up a single stone.

There, by the sheepfold, sometimes was he
    seen
Sitting alone, or with his faithful dog,
Then old, beside him, lying at his feet.
The length of full seven years, from time
    to time,   470
He at the building of this sheepfold wrought,
And left the work unfinished when he died.
Three years, or little more, did Isabel
Survive her husband: at her death the estate
Was sold and went into a stranger's
    hand.   475
The cottage which was named *The Evening
    Star*
Is gone;—the ploughshare has been through
    the ground
On which it stood; great changes have been
    wrought
In all the neighborhood:—yet the oak is left
That grew beside their door; and the re-
    mains   480
Of the unfinished sheepfold may be seen
Beside the boisterous brook of Greenhead
    Ghyll.[6]
(1800)

STUDY AIDS: 1. Show how this poem illustrates Wordsworth's remark: ". . . the feeling therein developed [in the poems of the *Lyrical Ballads*] gives importance to the action and situation, and not the action and situation to the feeling."

2. Compare the blank verse of *Michael* with that of *Tintern Abbey*. Which medium is nearer to the "language really used by men"? In each case, show how the poetic style is appropriate to the subject matter.

3. What is the dramatic conflict centering in Michael? How does Wordsworth bring out this conflict? Why is the slowness of the narrative in keeping with the kind of story that is being told? Why does Wordsworth use so many homely details?

The Prelude

Although *The Prelude* in its final form was not published until 1850 (after Wordsworth's death in that year), the first draft was completed in 1805. It was intended as an introductory poem to a much more ambitious work on "Man, Nature, and Society," in which Wordsworth hoped to achieve the great philosophical poem that Coleridge was confident his friend could write. *The Recluse*—for so the master work was to be called—was never finished; of the three projected divisions only the second was completed (*The Excursion*, 1814). Of the first part 860 lines were written, and nothing at all was done on part three.

The Prelude traces the "growth of a poet's mind" (the subtitle) from boyhood to maturity (1798). Thus, although it does no great violence to chronology, the emphasis is not upon things, people, and events as such, but upon their influence in the development of Wordsworth's poetic imagination. The result, in fourteen books, is not only a treasure house of some of Wordsworth's finest poetry but also a psychological document of interest and importance.

[6] What is the IRONY of the concluding lines (473–482)?

Book 1. Introduction
Childhood and School-Time

. . . .

Fair seed-time had my soul, and I grew
up   301
Fostered alike by beauty and by fear:
Much favored in my birthplace, and no less
In that belovèd vale [1] to which erelong
We were transplanted—there were we let
loose   305
For sports of wider range. Ere I had told
Ten birthdays, when among the mountain-
slopes
Frost, and the breath of frosty wind, had
snapped
The last autumnal crocus, 'twas my joy
With store of springes [2] o'er my shoulder
hung   310
To range the open heights where woodcocks
run
Among the smooth green turf. Through half
the night,
Scudding away from snare to snare, I plied
That anxious visitation;—moon and stars
Were shining o'er my head. I was alone,   315
And seemed to be a trouble to the peace
That dwelt among them. Sometimes it befell
In these night wanderings, that a strong desire
O'erpowered my better reason, and the bird
Which was the captive of another's toil   320
Became my prey; and when the deed was
done,
I heard among the solitary hills
Low breathings coming after me, and sounds
Of undistinguishable motion, steps
Almost as silent as the turf they trod.   325

Nor less when spring had warmed the
cultured vale,
Roved we as plunderers where the mother-
bird
Had in high places built her lodge; though
mean
Our object and inglorious, yet the end
Was not ignoble. Oh! when I have hung 330

Above the raven's nest, by knots of grass
And half-inch fissures in the slippery rock
But ill sustained, and almost (so it seemed)
Suspended by the blast that blew amain,
Shouldering the naked crag, oh, at that
time   335
While on the perilous ridge I hung alone,
With what strange utterance did the loud day
wind
Blow through my ear! the sky seemed not a
sky
Of earth—and with what motion moved the
clouds!

Dust as we are, the immortal spirit
grows   340
Like harmony in music; there is a dark
Inscrutable workmanship that reconciles
Discordant elements,[3] makes them cling to-
gether
In one society. How strange that all
The terrors, pains, and early miseries,   345
Regrets, vexations, lassitudes interfused
Within my mind, should e'er have borne a
part,
And that a needful part, in making up
The calm existence that is mine when I
Am worthy of myself! Praise to the end!   350
Thanks to the means which nature deigned
to employ;
Whether her fearless visitings, or those
That came with soft alarm, like hurtless light
Opening the peaceful clouds; or she may
use
Severer interventions,[4] ministry   355
More palpable, as best might suit her aim.

One summer evening (led by her) I found
A little boat tied to a willow tree
Within a rocky cave, its usual home.
Straight I unloosed her chain, and stepping
in   360

[1] Esthwaite vale, in Lancashire, the location of
Hawkshead, Wordsworth's boyhood home.

[2] Snares for bird-catching.

[3] What are the "discordant elements" in ll. 340–
350 and how are they reconciled? Does this analysis
seem psychologically valid?

[4] An illustration of "severer interventions" follows
(ll. 357–400). The two illustrations already given—
stealing the other boys' birds (ll. 317–321) and
robbing the birds' nests of eggs (ll. 326–328)—
are likewise examples of the "ministry of fear"
(see l. 302), but in a milder form.

Pushed from the shore. It was an act of
   stealth
And troubled pleasure, nor without the voice
Of mountain-echoes did my boat move on;
Leaving behind her still, on either side,
Small circles glittering idly in the moon, 365
Until they melted all into one track
Of sparkling light. But now, like one who
   rows,
Proud of his skill, to reach a chosen point
With an unswerving line, I fixed my view
Upon the summit of a craggy ridge,   370
The horizon's utmost boundary; for above
Was nothing but the stars and the gray sky.
She was an elfin pinnace,[5] lustily
I dipped my oars into the silent lake,
And, as I rose upon the stroke, my boat   375
Went heaving through the water like a swan;
When, from behind that craggy steep till then
The horizon's bound, a huge peak, black and
   huge,
As if with voluntary power instinct
Upreared its head. I struck and struck
   again,   380
And growing still in stature the grim shape
Towered up between me and the stars, and
   still,
For so it seemed, with purpose of its own
And measured motion like a living thing,
Strode after me. With trembling oars I
   turned,   385
And through the silent water stole my way
Back to the covert of the willow tree;
There in her mooring-place I left my bark—
And through the meadows homeward went,
   in grave
And serious mood; but after I had seen   390
That spectacle, for many days, my brain
Worked with a dim and undetermined sense
Of unknown modes of being; o'er my
   thoughts
There hung a darkness, call it solitude
Or blank desertion. No familiar shapes   395
Remained, no pleasant images of trees,
Of sea or sky, no colors of green fields;
But huge and mighty forms, that do not live
Like living men, moved slowly through the
   mind
By day, and were a trouble to my dreams. 400
  [5] A light sailing boat.

Wisdom and spirit of the universe! [6]
Thou soul that art the eternity of thought,
That givest to forms and images a breath
And everlasting motion, not in vain
By day or star-light thus from my first
   dawn   405
Of childhood didst thou intertwine for me
The passions that build up our human soul; [7]
Not with the mean and vulgar works of man,
But with high objects, with enduring things—
With life and nature—purifying thus   410
The elements of feeling and of thought,
And sanctifying, by such discipline,
Both pain and fear, until we recognize
A grandeur in the beatings of the heart.
Nor was this fellowship vouchsafed to me 415
With stinted kindness. In November days,
When vapors rolling down the valley made
A lonely scene more lonesome, among woods,
At noon and 'mid the calm of summer nights,
When, by the margin of the trembling
   lake,   420
Beneath the gloomy hills homeward I went
In solitude, such intercourse was mine;
Mine was it in the fields both day and night,
And by the waters, all the summer long.

   And in the frosty season, when the sun 425
Was set, and visible for many a mile
The cottage windows blazed through twilight
   gloom,
I heeded not their summons: happy time
It was indeed for all of us—for me
It was a time of rapture! Clear and loud   430
The village clock tolled six—I wheeled about,
Proud and exulting like an untired horse
That cares not for his home. All shod with
   steel,
We hissed along the polished ice in games
Confederate, imitative of the chase   435
And woodland pleasures—the resounding
   horn,
The pack loud chiming, and the hunted hare.
So through the darkness and the cold we flew,

  [6] Lines 401–463 were published separately in
1809 with this significant title: "Growth of Genius
from the Influence of Natural Objects on the
Imagination in Boyhood and Early Youth."
  [7] In Wordsworth there is no enmity between
flesh and spirit, between the "passions" and the
"human soul."

And not a voice was idle; with the din
Smitten, the precipices rang aloud;   440
The leafless trees and every icy crag
Tinkled like iron; while far distant hills
Into the tumult sent an alien sound
Of melancholy not unnoticed, while the stars
Eastward were sparkling clear, and in the
     west   445
The orange sky of evening died away.
Not seldom from the uproar I retired
Into a silent bay, or sportively
Glanced sideway, leaving the tumultuous
     throng,
To cut across the reflex of a star   450
That fled, and, flying still before me, gleamed
Upon the glassy plain; and oftentimes,
When we had given our bodies to the wind,
And all the shadowy banks on either side
Came sweeping through the darkness, spin-
     ning still   455
The rapid line of motion, then at once
Have I, reclining back upon my heels,
Stopped short; yet still the solitary cliffs
Wheeled by me—even as if the earth had
     rolled
With visible motion her diurnal round!   460
Behind me did they stretch in solemn train,
Feebler and feebler, and I stood and watched
Till all was tranquil as a dreamless sleep. . . .[8]

Nor, sedulous as I have been to trace
How nature by extrinsic [9] passion first   545
Peopled the mind with forms sublime or
     fair,
And made me love them, may I here omit
How other pleasures have been mine, and
     joys
Of subtler origin; how I have felt,
Not seldom even in that tempestuous
     time,   550
Those hallowed and pure emotions of the
     sense

Which seem, in their simplicity, to own
An intellectual [10] charm; that calm delight
Which, if I err not, surely must belong
To those first-born affinities that fit   555
Our new existence to existing things,
And, in our dawn of being, constitute
The bond of union between life and joy.[11]

Yes, I remember when the changeful earth,
And twice five summers on my mind had
     stamped   560
The faces of the moving year, even then
I held unconscious intercourse with beauty
Old as creation, drinking in a pure
Organic pleasure from the silver wreaths
Of curling mist, or from the level plain   565
Of waters colored by impending clouds.

The sands of Westmoreland, the creeks
     and bays
Of Cumbria's rocky limits, they can tell
How, when the sea threw off his evening
     shade
And to the shepherd's hut on distant hills 570
Sent welcome notice of the rising moon,
How I have stood, to fancies such as these
A stranger, linking with the spectacle
No conscious memory of a kindred sight,
And bringing with me no peculiar sense 575
Of quietness or peace; yet have I stood,
Even while mine eye hath moved o'er many
     a league
Of shining water, gathering as it seemed,
Through every hair-breadth in that field of
     light,
New pleasure like a bee among the
     flowers.   580

Thus oft amid those fits of vulgar joy
Which, through all seasons, on a child's pur-
     suits
Are prompt attendants, 'mid that giddy bliss
Which, like a tempest, works along the
     blood
And is forgotten; even then I felt   585
Gleams like the flashing of a shield; the earth
And common face of nature spake to me

---

[8] Coleridge pointed to ll. 425–463 as an illustration of one of the excellences of Wordsworth's
poetry—namely, "the perfect truth of nature in his
images and descriptions." What kind of imagery
predominates in this passage? Note the realism of
ll. 447–463.
[9] Because it was not directed to nature for her
own sake, but arose in connection with boyish
sports.

[10] Spiritual.
[11] What do ll. 553–558 mean? Is the soul's pre-
existence implied?

Rememberable things; sometimes, 'tis true,
By chance collisions and quaint accidents
(Like those ill-sorted unions, work sup-
posed   590
Of evil-minded fairies), yet not vain
Nor profitless, if haply they impressed
Collateral objects and appearances,
Albeit lifeless then, and doomed to sleep
Until maturer seasons called them forth   595
To impregnate and to elevate the mind.
—And if the vulgar joy by its own weight
Wearied itself out of the memory,
The scenes which were a witness of that
joy
Remained in their substantial lineaments 600
Depicted on the brain, and to the eye
Were visible, a daily sight; and thus
By the impressive discipline of fear,
By pleasure and repeated happiness,
So frequently repeated, and by force   605
Of obscure feelings representative
Of things forgotten, these same scenes so
bright,
So beautiful, so majestic in themselves,
Though yet the day was distant, did become
Habitually dear, and all their forms   610
And changeful colors by invisible links
Were fastened to the affections. . . .[12]
(1798–1805; 1850)

STUDY AIDS: 1. It has been said that in *The Prelude* Wordsworth almost places psychology above poetry, that "poetical psychology is his triumph." How true is this of Book I of *The Prelude?* Does Wordsworth's interest in the psychology of his boyhood hurt his poetry or make it more effective? In this connection consider Wordsworth's statement in the 1805 note to *The Thorn:* "Poetry is passion: it is the history or science of feelings."

2. Lines 357–400 constitute a striking passage. Like the two incidents that precede, the passage treats an "act of stealth." Point out the descriptive images and show how they contribute to the TONE of the passage. What is that tone? What is the climax of the incident? What effect did the episode have upon the boy Wordsworth? Is this a normal reaction for a child?

Lines 559–596 illustrate the "beauty" in "fostered alike by beauty and by fear" (l. 302). Why does Wordsworth pay more attention to the "ministry of fear"? How do all the "terrors," "pains," "miseries," etc. (see ll. 345 ff.) play a "needful part" in the development of Wordsworth's adult poise?

3. Is there any connection among the objects of Wordsworth's love: "enduring things" (l. 409), solitude and the solitary, twilight and gloomy weather?

4. What is the conception of God in this Book? Compare ll. 401–404 with ll. 100–102 of *Tintern Abbey.*

Resolution and Independence

"I describe myself as having been exalted to the highest pitch of delight by the joyousness and beauty of nature; and then as depressed, even in the midst of those beautiful objects, to the lowest dejection and despair. . . . What is brought forward? A lonely place, 'a pond by which an old man *was,* far from all house or home': not *stood,* nor *sat,* but *was*—the figure presented in the most naked simplicity possible. This feeling of spirituality or supernaturalness is again referred to as being strong in my mind in this passage. How came he here? thought I, or what can he be doing? I then describe him. . . . Though I believe God has given me a strong imagination, I cannot conceive a figure more impressive than that of an old man like this, the survivor of a wife and ten children, traveling alone among the mountains and all lonely places, carrying with him his own fortitude, and the necessities which an unjust state of society has laid upon him" (Wordsworth).

There was a roaring in the wind all night;
The rain came heavily and fell in floods;
But now the sun is rising calm and bright;

The birds are singing in the distant woods:
Over his own sweet voice the stock-dove
broods;   5

[12] Lines 581–612: The "vulgar joy" and "giddy bliss" are soon forgotten, but the "gleams like the flashing of a shield" are not; nor are the "collateral objects"—"the scenes which were a witness of that joy." Do ll. 601–602 seem to contradict ll. 594–596?

The jay makes answer as the magpie chatters;
And all the air is filled with pleasant noise of
   waters.

All things that love the sun are out of doors;
The sky rejoices in the morning's birth;
The grass is bright with raindrops;—on the
   moors   10
The hare is running races in her mirth;
And with her feet she from the plashy [1] earth
Raises a mist, that, glittering in the sun,
Runs with her all the way wherever she doth
   run.

I was a traveler then upon the moor;   15
I saw the hare that raced about with joy;
I heard the woods and distant waters roar,
Or heard them not, as happy as a boy:
The pleasant season did my heart employ:
My old remembrances went from me
   wholly;   20
And all the ways of men so vain and melan-
   choly.

But, as it sometimes chanceth, from the might
Of joy in minds that can no further go,
As high as we have mounted in delight
In our dejection do we sink as low;   25
To me that morning did it happen so;
And fears, and fancies, thick upon me came;
Dim sadness—and blind thoughts, I knew
   not, nor could name.

I heard the skylark warbling in the sky;
And I bethought me of the playful hare: 30
Even such a happy child of earth am I;
Even as these blissful creatures do I fare;
Far from the world I walk, and from all care;
But there may come another day to me—
Solitude, pain of heart, distress, and pov-
   erty.   35

My whole life I have lived in pleasant
   thought,
As if life's business were a summer mood;
As if all needful things would come unsought
To genial faith, still rich in genial good;
But how can he expect that others should 40
Build for him, sow for him, and at his call

[1] Marshy.

Love him, who for himself will take no heed
   at all?

I thought of Chatterton,[2] the marvelous boy,
The sleepless soul that perished in his pride;
Of him [3] who walked in glory and in joy 45
Following his plow, along the mountain side:
By our own spirits are we deified:
We poets in our youth begin in gladness;
But thereof come in the end despondency and
   madness.

Now, whether it were by peculiar grace,   50
A leading from above, a something given,
Yet it befell, that, in this lonely place,
When I with these untoward thoughts had
   striven,
Beside a pool bare to the eye of heaven
I saw a man before me unawares: 55
The oldest man he seemed that ever wore gray
   hairs.

As a huge stone is sometimes seen to lie
Couched on the bald top of an eminence;
Wonder to all who do the same espy,
By what means it could thither come, and
   whence;   60
So that it seems a thing endued with sense:
Like a sea-beast crawled forth, that on a shelf
Of rock or sand reposeth, there to sun itself; [4]

Such seemed this man, not all alive nor dead,
Nor all asleep—in his extreme old age: 65
His body was bent double, feet and head
Coming together in life's pilgrimage;
As if some dire constraint of pain, or rage

[2] Eighteenth-century English poet who committed
suicide when he was 17.
[3] Burns.
[4] Wordsworth used this stanza to illustrate the
workings of the poetic imagination: "The stone is
endowed with something of the power of life to
approximate it to the sea-beast; and the sea-beast
stripped of some of its vital qualities to assimilate
it to the stone; which intermediate image is thus
treated for the purpose of bringing the original
image, that of the stone, to a nearer resemblance
to the figure and condition of the aged man; who
is divested of so much of the indications of life
and motion as to bring him to the point where the
two objects coalesce in just comparison" (Preface
of 1815).

Of sickness felt by him in times long past,
A more than human weight upon his frame
   had cast. 70

Himself he propped, limbs, body, and pale
   face,
Upon a long gray staff of shaven wood:
And, still as I drew near with gentle pace,
Upon the margin of that moorish flood
Motionless as a cloud the old man stood; 75
That heareth not the loud winds when they
   call,
And moveth altogether, if it move at all.

At length, himself unsettling, he the pond
Stirred with his staff and fixedly did look
Upon the muddy water, which he conned, 80
As if he had been reading in a book:
And now a stranger's privilege I took;
And, drawing to his side, to him did say,
"This morning gives us promise of a glorious
   day."

A gentle answer did the old man make, 85
In courteous speech which forth he slowly
   drew;
And him with further words I thus bespake:
"What occupation do you there pursue?
This is a lonesome place for one like you."
Ere he replied, a flash of mild surprise 90
Broke from the sable orbs of his yet vivid
   eyes.

His words came feebly, from a feeble chest,
But each in solemn order followed each,
With something of a lofty utterance dressed;
Choice word, and measured phrase, above the
   reach 95
Of ordinary men; a stately speech;
Such as grave Livers [5] do in Scotland use,
Religious men, who give to God and man
   their dues.

He told, that to these waters he had come
To gather leeches, being old and poor: 100
Employment hazardous and wearisome!
And he had many hardships to endure:
From pond to pond he roamed, from moor to
   moor;

[5] A Scottish religious sect.

Housing, with God's good help, by choice or
   chance;
And in this way he gained an honest maintenance. 105

The old man still stood talking by my side;
But now his voice to me was like a stream
Scarce heard; nor word from word could I
   divide;
And the whole body of the man did seem
Like one whom I had met with in a
   dream; 110
Or like a man from some far region sent,
To give me human strength, by apt admon-
   ishment. [6]

My former thoughts returned: the fear that
   kills;
And hope that is unwilling to be fed;
Cold, pain and labor, and all fleshly ills; 115
And mighty poets in their misery dead.
Perplexed, and longing to be comforted,
My question eagerly did I renew,
"How is it that you live, and what is it you
   do?"

He with a smile did then his words repeat; 120
And said that, gathering leeches, far and
   wide
He traveled; stirring thus about his feet
The waters of the pools where they abide.
"Once I could meet with them on every side;
But they have dwindled long by slow
   decay; 125
Yet still I persevere, and find them where I
   may."

While he was talking thus, the lonely place,
The old man's shape, and speech, all troubled
   me:
In my mind's eye I seemed to see him pace
About the weary moors continually, 130
Wandering about alone and silently.
While I these thoughts within myself pur-
   sued,
He, having made a pause, the same discourse
   renewed.

[6] In ll. 106–112 Wordsworth has something
closely akin to a mystical experience as the old man
becomes larger than life. Note also ll. 127–131.

And soon with this he other matter blended,
Cheerfully uttered, with demeanor kind, 135
But stately in the main; and when he ended,
I could have laughed myself to scorn to find
In that decrepit man so firm a mind.
"God," said I, "be my help and stay secure;
I'll think of the leech-gatherer on the lonely
   moor!" 140
(1802; 1807)

STUDY AIDS: 1. Coleridge, in listing Wordsworth's faults as a poet, points out his frequently excessive "matter-of-factness." *Resolution and Independence* has a bare, realistic quality. By what means does Wordsworth raise it above drab matter-of-factness? In this connection, critics of Wordsworth's day often condemned him for his use of pedlars, vagrants, leech-gatherers, and other "low-life" characters as the central figures in many of his poems. Is such criticism justified? What are the limits to permissible subject matter in poetry?

2. Note the metrical form of this poem. What effect is gained by the final six-foot line in each stanza?

3. What is the theme of the poem?

The Solitary Reaper

In 1803 Wordsworth and his sister took a walking trip through the Scottish Highlands. Although Dorothy records in her journal an experience that could have suggested this poem to her brother, he was specifically indebted to Thomas Wilkinson's *Tour in Scotland*, especially to this passage: "Passed a female who was reaping alone. She sung in Erse, as she bended over her sickle; the sweetest human voice I ever heard; her strains were tenderly melancholy, and felt delicious long after they were heard no more."

Behold her, single in the field,
Yon solitary Highland lass!
Reaping and singing by herself;
Stop here, or gently pass!
Alone she cuts and binds the grain,[1] 5
And sings a melancholy strain;
O listen! for the vale profound
Is overflowing with the sound.

No nightingale did ever chaunt
More welcome notes to weary bands 10
Of travelers in some shady haunt,
Among Arabian sands:
A voice so thrilling ne'er was heard
In springtime from the cuckoo-bird,
Breaking the silence of the seas 15
Among the farthest Hebrides.[2]

Will no one tell me what she sings?—
Perhaps the plaintive numbers flow

For old, unhappy, far-off things,[3]
And battles long ago: 20
Or is it some more humble lay,
Familiar matter of today?
Some natural sorrow, loss, or pain,
That has been, and may be again?[4]

Whate'er the theme, the maiden sang[5] 25
As if her song could have no ending;
I saw her singing at her work,
And o'er the sickle bending;—
I listened, motionless and still;
And, as I mounted up the hill, 30
The music in my heart I bore,
Long after it was heard no more.
(1805; 1807)

STUDY AIDS: 1. Mark Van Doren has said of this poem: ". . . each stanza is inferior to the one before it. The first . . . is the best . . . and in fact contains or expresses the whole of the impulse that was moving Wordsworth as

[1] Lines 1–5 afford another illustration of the fascination that solitude and the solitary had for Wordsworth. Note the repetition of the idea: "single," "solitary," "by herself," "alone."

[2] Islands just off the northwest coast of Scotland.

[3] Justify Wordsworth's use of the vague, general word "things" here.

[4] Lines 21–24 present Wordsworth's own theory of the best subject matter for poetry.

[5] Why the shift of tense in this final stanza?

he wrote. . . . The second stanza is noble, yet less so than the one that rendered it unnecessary. And the rest of the poem goes steadily downhill" (*Introduction to Poetry*, 1951, pp. 51, 53). How would you support or refute Van Doren's criticism?

2. Reread the passage from Wilkinson, quoted in the headnote. Show how Wordsworth has incorporated all of the elements of the prose statement into the four stanzas of his poem, elaborating them and making them more meaningful.

Ode:
Intimations of Immortality from Recollections of Early Childhood

In *Tintern Abbey* Wordsworth says that it is the privilege of nature "Through all the years of this our life, to lead From joy to joy." The *Ode: Intimations of Immortality* is an elaboration of this theme, an attempt to show that in going from childhood to maturity, although there is a loss of one kind of joy, there is compensation in the gain of another.

The child is father of the man;
And I could wish my days to be
Bound each to each by natural piety.[1]

I

There was a time when meadow, grove, and stream,
    The earth, and every common sight,
      To me did seem
    Appareled in celestial light,
The glory and the freshness of a dream.   5
It is not now as it hath been of yore;—
    Turn wheresoe'er I may,
      By night or day,
The things which I have seen I now can see no more.[2]

2

    The rainbow comes and goes,   10
    And lovely is the rose;
    The moon doth with delight
Look round her when the heavens are bare;
    Waters on a starry night

Are beautiful and fair;   15
    The sunshine is a glorious birth;
    But yet I know, where'er I go,
That there hath passed away a glory from the earth.

3

Now, while the birds thus sing a joyous song,
    And while the young lambs bound 20
      As to the tabor's sound,
To me alone there came a thought of grief:
A timely utterance [3] gave that thought relief,
    And I again am strong:
The cataracts blow their trumpets from the steep; 25
No more shall grief of mine the season wrong;
I hear the echoes through the mountains throng,
The winds come to me from the fields of sleep,
    And all the earth is gay;
      Land and sea 30
    Give themselves up to jollity,
    And with the heart of May
      Doth every beast keep holiday;—
      Thou child of joy,
Shout round me, let me hear thy shouts, thou happy shepherd-boy! 35

[1] This three-line motto is a quotation from a short poem by Wordsworth. What is the meaning of the first line and of the phrase "natural piety" in the third line? Keep these meanings in mind as you read the *Ode* and try to determine their relation to the content.

[2] How does the emphasis on monosyllabic words reinforce the TONE of ll. 6–9?

[3] The "timely utterance" probably refers to one of Wordsworth's poems.

4

Ye blessèd creatures, I have heard the call
    Ye to each other make; I see
The heavens laugh with you in your jubilee;
    My heart is at your festival,
    My head hath its coronal,   40
The fulness of your bliss, I feel—I feel it all.
    Oh, evil day! If I were sullen
    While earth herself is adorning,
      This sweet May-morning,
    And the children are culling   45
      On every side,
    In a thousand valleys far and wide,
Fresh flowers; while the sun shines warm,
And the babe leaps up on his mother's arm—
    I hear, I hear, with joy I hear! 50
    —But there's a tree, of many, one,
A single field which I have looked upon,
Both of them speak of something that is gone:
    The pansy at my feet
    Doth the same tale repeat: 55
Whither is fled the visionary gleam?
Where is it now, the glory and the dream?

5

Our birth is but a sleep and a forgetting:
The soul that rises with us, our life's star,
    Hath had elsewhere its setting, 60
    And cometh from afar:
    Not in entire forgetfulness,
    And not in utter nakedness,
But trailing clouds of glory do we come
    From God, who is our home: 65
Heaven lies about us in our infancy!
Shades of the prison-house begin to close
    Upon the growing boy,
But he beholds the light, and whence it flows,
    He sees it in his joy;   70
The youth, who daily farther from the east
    Must travel, still is nature's priest,
    And by the vision splendid
    Is on his way attended;
At length the man perceives it die away 75
And fade into the light of common day.[4]

6

Earth fills her lap with pleasures of her own;
Yearnings she hath in her own natural kind,
And even with something of a mother's mind,
    And no unworthy aim,   80
    The homely nurse doth all she can
To make her foster-child, her inmate man,
    Forget the glories he hath known,
And that imperial palace whence he came.

7

Behold the child among his new-born
    blisses,   85
A six years' darling of a pigmy size!
See, where 'mid work of his own hand he lies,
Fretted by sallies of his mother's kisses,
With light upon him from his father's eyes!
See, at his feet, some little plan or chart, 90
Some fragment from his dream of human life,
Shaped by himself with newly-learnèd art;
    A wedding or a festival,
    A mourning or a funeral,
      And this hath now his heart, 95
      And unto this he frames his song:
      Then will he fit his tongue
To dialogues of business, love, or strife;
    But it will not be long
    Ere this be thrown aside,   100
    And with new joy and pride
The little actor cons another part;
Filling from time to time his "humorous
    stage"
With all the persons, down to palsied Age,
That life brings with her in her equip-
    page;   105
    As if his whole vocation
    Were endless imitation.[5]

8

Thou, whose exterior semblance doth belie
    Thy soul's immensity;
Thou best philosopher, who yet dost keep 110
Thy heritage, thou eye [6] among the blind,
That, deaf and silent, read'st the eternal deep,

[4] We ordinarily think of light as gradually fading into darkness. Why is it more effective here to have the light of the "glory" fade into another kind of light, the light of "common day"? What is the PARADOX here?

[5] What is the change of tone in this stanza (note especially l. 86), and why is it made?

[6] Note the startling figure: the child is an eye; moreover, he is a "deaf and silent" eye. Literally, this is impossible. Why is it poetically effective?

Haunted forever by the eternal mind—
    Mighty prophet! Seer blest!
      On whom those truths do rest,   115
Which we are toiling all our lives to find,
In darkness lost, the darkness of the grave;
Thou, over whom thy immortality
Broods like the day, a master o'er a slave,
A presence which is not to be put by;   120
Thou little child, yet glorious in the might
Of heaven-born freedom on thy being's
    height,
Why with such earnest pains dost thou pro-
    voke
The years to bring the inevitable yoke,
Thus blindly with thy blessedness at
    strife?   125
Full soon thy soul shall have her earthly
    freight,
And custom lie upon thee with a weight,
Heavy as frost, and deep almost as life!

9

    Oh, joy! that in our embers
    Is something that doth live,   130
    That nature yet remembers
    What was so fugitive!
The thought of our past years in me doth
    breed
Perpetual benediction: not indeed
For that which is most worthy to be blest— 135
Delight and liberty, the simple creed
Of childhood, whether busy or at rest,
With new-fledged hope still fluttering in his
    breast—
    Not for these I raise
    The song of thanks and praise;   140
    But for those obstinate questionings
    Of sense and outward things,
    Fallings from us, vanishings;
    Blank misgivings of a creature
Moving about in worlds not realized,   145
High instincts before which our mortal nature
Did tremble like a guilty thing surprised:
    But for those first affections,
    Those shadowy recollections,
    Which, be they what they may,   150
Are yet the fountain light of all our day,
Are yet a master light of all our seeing;
    Uphold us, cherish, and have power to
    make

Our noisy years seem moments in the being
Of the eternal silence: truths that wake, 155
    To perish never;
Which neither listlessness, nor mad endeavor,
    Nor man nor boy,
Nor all that is at enmity with joy,
Can utterly abolish or destroy!   160
    Hence in a season of calm weather
    Though inland far we be,
Our souls have sight of that immortal sea
    Which brought us hither,
    Can in a moment travel thither,   165
And see the children sport upon the shore,
And hear the mighty waters rolling evermore.

10

Then sing, ye birds, sing, sing a joyous song!
    And let the young lambs bound
    As to the tabor's sound!   170
We in thought will join your throng,
    Ye that pipe and ye that play,
    Ye that through your hearts today
    Feel the gladness of the May!
What though the radiance which was once so
    bright   175
Be now forever taken from my sight,
   Though nothing can bring back the hour
Of splendor in the grass, of glory in the
    flower;
    We will grieve not, rather find
    Strength in what remains behind; 180
    In the primal sympathy
    Which having been must ever be;
    In the soothing thoughts that spring
    Out of human suffering;
    In the faith that looks through
    death,   185
In years that bring the philosophic mind.

11

And O, ye fountains, meadows, hills, and
    groves,
Forebode not any severing of our loves!
Yet in my heart of hearts I feel your might;
I only have relinquished one delight   190
To live beneath your more habitual sway.
I love the brooks which down their channels
    fret,
Even more than when I tripped lightly as
    they;

The innocent brightness of a new-born day
    Is lovely yet;   195
The clouds that gather round the setting sun
Do take a sober coloring from an eye
That hath kept watch o'er man's mortality.
Another race hath been, and other palms are
    won.
Thanks to the human heart by which we
    live,   200
Thanks to its tenderness, its joys, and fears,
To me the meanest flower that blows can give
Thoughts that do often lie too deep for tears.
(1802–04; 1807)

STUDY AIDS: 1. The *Ode* may be divided
into three large sections: (1) the statement of a
loss; (2) the explanation of the loss; (3) the
compensation for the loss. Define these sections
precisely by stanza divisions.

2. What is the loss that Wordsworth is
lamenting? Is this a loss we all suffer as we grow
older, or does it seem to be peculiar to Wordsworth?

3. What is Wordsworth's explanation of the
loss? Plato says in the *Phaedo*: "Your favorite
doctrine, Socrates, that knowledge is simply
recollection, if true, also necessarily implies a
previous time in which we learned that which
we now recollect. But this would be impossible
unless our soul was in some place before existing
in the human form. . . ." Consider the relation
of this quotation to the *Ode*.

4. What is the compensation for the loss?

What does Wordsworth mean by "the philosophic mind"? How are man and nature brought
together in the last part of the *Ode*? (Compare
the "third stage" in *Tintern Abbey*, a stage per-
vaded by "the still, sad music of humanity.")
What is the difference between the poet's love
of nature in maturity and that in childhood
(see ll. 187–203)?

Many critics regard the last division of the
poem as receiving the poet's major emphasis.
Others think that the fact of a loss is more important and that the attempt to find compensation
is weaker by comparison. What is your opinion
here?

5. Note how images of light, and images
related to light, run throughout the poem. Find
examples. What shift, however, in the dominant
type of imagery takes place in ll. 19–51 as
Wordsworth attempts to recapture the lost glory?
Why is the shift appropriate? In this respect,
note the climactic effect of l. 51.

6. Is there any conflict between the account
of childhood given in the *Ode* and that suggested by ll. 73–74 of *Tintern Abbey* or that
developed in Book 1 of *The Prelude*? Is the
child himself conscious of this supernatural glory
in his response to nature, or is it only realized
in the retrospection of maturity? In what sense
is the child "thou best philosopher" (l. 110)?

7. Is the complicated verse structure and
syntax of the *Ode* better suited to the subject
matter than blank verse would be (cf. *Tintern
Abbey*)? How does this poem fit the definition
of an ODE?

Sonnets

One afternoon in May, 1802, Dorothy Wordsworth read to her brother some of the sonnets of
Milton. Although he had long been familiar with them, Wordsworth says, "I took fire . . . and
produced three sonnets the same afternoon." Before this time he had written very few sonnets;
from this date on, the sonnet was one of his favorite metrical forms, and by 1850 (the year of his
death) he had written more than 500 of them. Of this great number many are prosaic and
undistinguished; but the best have put Wordsworth among the English sonneteers of
unquestioned excellence, in the company of Shakespeare, Milton, and Keats.

Composed upon Westminster Bridge

This sonnet gives the effect upon Wordsworth of seeing London in the early morning from
Westminster Bridge. The first three lines present the poet's reaction; the rest of the sonnet shows
why he had that reaction.

Earth has not anything to show more fair:
Dull would he be of soul who could pass by

A sight so touching in its majesty:
This city now doth like a garment wear

The beauty of the morning: silent, bare,   5
Ships, towers, domes, theaters, and temples
  lie
Open unto the fields, and to the sky—
All bright and glittering in the smokeless air.
Never did sun more beautifully steep
In his first splendor valley, rock, or hill;   10
Ne'er saw I, never felt, a calm so deep!
The river glideth at his own sweet will:
Dear God! the very houses seem asleep;
And all that mighty heart is lying still!
(1802; 1807)

STUDY AIDS: 1. What effect do the RUN-ON
LINES 4 and 6, and the series of words (two
adjectives, five nouns) in ll. 5 and 6, have upon
the reader? In ll. 9–10, why does Wordsworth
make a comparison with natural scenery?

2. Line 12 seems to stand by itself. Why is
this appropriate? Does the moving river (the
Thames) destroy the calm immobility of the
preceding description, or does it reinforce the
static and dreamlike quality? In this connection,
note the effect of the verb "glideth."

3. In the last two lines, Wordsworth focuses
all the elements of the scene in the image of
the "mighty heart" which now lies still. Not
only the outer form of this being ("the very
houses") seems asleep, but its inner life is for a
time suspended. Has Wordsworth's comment in
the first three lines now been "proved"?

It Is a Beauteous Evening, Calm and Free

It is a beauteous evening, calm and free.
The holy time is quiet as a nun
Breathless with adoration: the broad sun
Is sinking down in its tranquility;
The gentleness of heaven broods o'er the
  sea;   5
Listen! the mighty being is awake,
And doth with his eternal motion make
A sound like thunder—everlastingly.
Dear child! [1] dear girl! that walkest with me
  here,
If thou appear untouched by solemn
  thought,   10
Thy nature is not therefore less divine:
Thou liest in Abraham's bosom [2] all the year,
And worship'st at the temple's inner shrine,
God being with thee when we know it not.
(1802; 1807)

STUDY AIDS: 1. This sonnet observes the
usual division of an Italian sonnet into an octave
and a sestet. The octave describes a scene; the
sestet comments upon a ten-year-old girl. What
is the relation between the two subjects?

2. How does the first simile, that of a "nun
breathless with adoration," define the theme
of the entire sonnet?

3. What is Wordsworth saying about Caroline
in ll. 9–14? What is the relation of these lines
to the second division of the Ode: Intimations of
Immortality (especially st. 5)?

On the Extinction of the Venetian Republic

The Venetian Republic, under the threat of Napoleon's armies, was dissolved by treaty in 1797
after a long and glorious history. Venice had become a republic in 997 (l. 4); in the thirteenth
century she was one of the wealthiest cities of the world (l. 1); and for many years she stood
as a bulwark against the Turks (l. 2). From the sixteenth century on, her power gradually
declined (ll. 9–10).

Once did she hold the gorgeous East in fee
And was the safeguard of the West; the worth
Of Venice did not fall below her birth,
Venice, the eldest child of liberty.

She was a maiden city, bright and free;   5
No guile seduced, no force could violate;

[1] Caroline, the natural daughter of Wordsworth
and Annette.

[2] Luke 16:22: "The poor man died and was
carried by the angels to Abraham's bosom." The
line means that Caroline is continually close to
God. What is the effect of using the Biblical
image here?

And when she took unto herself a mate,[1]
She must espouse the everlasting sea.
And what if she had seen those glories fade,
Those titles vanish, and that strength de-
cay,—   10

Yet shall some tribute of regret be paid
When her long life hath reached its final day:
Men are we, and must grieve when even the
shade
Of that which once was great is passed away.
(1802; 1807)

To Toussaint L'Ouverture

François Dominique Toussaint (called "L'Ouverture" because of his ability to "open up" enemy lines) liberated Haiti and later resisted Napoleon when the Emperor attempted to reintroduce slavery into the island. He was arrested, brought to France, and died in prison in 1803.

Toussaint, the most unhappy man of men!
Whether the whistling rustic tend his plough
Within thy hearing, or thy head be now
Pillowed in some deep dungeon's earless
den;—
O miserable chieftain! where and when   5
Wilt thou find patience? Yet die not; do thou
Wear rather in thy bonds a cheerful brow:
Though fallen thyself, never to rise again,

Live, and take comfort. Thou hast left be-
hind
Powers that will work for thee; air, earth,
and skies;   10
There's not a breathing of the common wind
That will forget thee; thou hast great allies;
Thy friends are exultations, agonies,
And love, and man's unconquerable mind.
(1802; 1807)

London, 1802

Milton! thou shouldst be living at this hour:
England hath need of thee: she is a fen
Of stagnant waters: altar, sword, and pen,
Fireside, the heroic wealth of hall and bower,
Have forfeited their ancient English dower 5
Of inward happiness. We are selfish men:
Oh! raise us up, return to us again;
And give us manners, virtue, freedom, power.
Thy soul was like a star, and dwelt apart:
Thou hadst a voice whose sound was like the
sea,   10
Pure as the naked heavens, majestic, free;
So didst thou travel on life's common way

In cheerful godliness; and yet thy heart
The lowliest duties on herself did lay.
(1802; 1807)

STUDY AIDS: 1. What does Wordsworth think is wrong with the England of his day? What specific groups of people are referred to by the five terms in ll. 3–4? What does Wordsworth mean by "inward happiness"?

2. Why does Wordsworth choose Milton as the type of person England needs in 1802? What qualities of Milton's character are summed up in the SESTET? Do ll. 13–14 contradict l. 9?

3. In what ways does Wordsworth achieve something of the Miltonic style in this sonnet?

The World Is Too Much with Us

The world is too much with us; late and soon,
Getting and spending, we lay waste our
powers:

[1] Lines 7–8: In 1177 the Pope, in gratitude for service rendered him by the Venetian navy, gave the Doge of Venice a ring and told him to wed the Adriatic Sea as a symbol of Venetian rule thereof. Each year this ceremony was performed, the ring being cast into the sea during a splendid naval procession.

Little we see in nature that is ours;
We have given our hearts away, a sordid
boon!
The sea that bares her bosom to the moon; 5
The winds that will be howling at all hours
And are up-gathered now like sleeping flow-
ers;
For this, for every thing, we are out of tune;
It moves us not.—Great God! I'd rather be

A pagan suckled in a creed outworn;   10
So might I, standing on this pleasant lea,
Have glimpses that would make me less for-
   lorn;
Have sight of Proteus rising from the sea;
Or hear old Triton [1] blow his wreathèd horn.
(1806; 1807)

STUDY AIDS: 1. A conflict is developed in
this sonnet between materialism ("the world")
and religion. But what kind of religion is Wordsworth talking about? How is the conflict resolved?

2. Compare this sonnet with the previous one,

which has a similar content. Which do you
think is the more effective poem, and why?
Analyze carefully the imagery of this sonnet.
Is it consistent throughout? What changes in
TONE occur in the sonnet?

3. What is unusual about the division between
OCTAVE and SESTET? In what way does this
division help to convey the meaning of the
poem?

4. Precisely what is Wordsworth saying in
the sestet? In a Christian country this is an
extravagant statement. What comment does this
extravagance make on the poet's opinion in ll.
1–9?

Nuns Fret Not at Their Convent's Narrow Room

Nuns fret not at their convent's narrow room;
And hermits are contented with their cells;
And students with their pensive citadels;
Maids at the wheel, the weaver at his loom,
Sit blithe and happy; bees that soar for
   bloom,   5
High as the highest peak of Furness-fells,
Will murmur by the hour in foxglove bells:
In truth the prison, into which we doom
Ourselves, no prison is: and hence for me,
In sundry moods, 'twas pastime to be
   bound   10

Within the sonnet's scanty plot of ground;
Pleased if some souls (for such there needs
   must be)
Who have felt the weight of too much liberty,
Should find brief solace there, as I have
   found.
(1806; 1807)

STUDY AIDS: This is a sonnet in defense
of the sonnet form. What is the central idea of
the poem? How does the succession of images
in ll. 1–7 illustrate this idea?

Thoughts of a Briton on the Subjugation of Switzerland

In 1807 Napoleon, now master of Europe, was preparing to cross the channel for an invasion
of England. Wordsworth, remembering Napoleon's conquest of Switzerland in 1798, considers
the terrible possibility of England's fall and expresses his fears in this sonnet, which he regarded
as his best.

Two voices [2] are there; one is of the sea,
One of the mountains; each a mighty voice:
In both from age to age thou didst rejoice,
They were thy chosen music, Liberty!
There came a tyrant,[3] and with holy glee   5
Thou fought'st against him; but hast vainly
   striven:
Thou from thy Alpine holds at length art
   driven,

[1] Proteus and Triton are Greek sea gods. How
are the predominant consonant sounds of ll. 13–14
appropriate to these figures?
[2] England (the voice of the sea) and Switzerland
(the voice of the mountains).
[3] Napoleon.

Where not a torrent murmurs heard by thee.
Of one deep bliss thine ear hath been bereft:
Then cleave, O cleave to that which still is
   left;   10
For, high-souled maid, what sorrow would it
   be
That mountain floods should thunder as be-
   fore,
And ocean bellow from his rocky shore,
And neither awful voice be heard by thee!
(1807)

STUDY AIDS: Show how the PERSONIFICA-
TION of Liberty unifies the entire sonnet.

After-Thought

I thought of thee,[1] my partner and my guide,
As being passed away.—Vain sympathies!
For, backward, Duddon! as I cast my eyes,
I see what was, and is, and will abide;
Still glides the stream, and shall for ever
    glide;   5
The form remains, the function never dies;
While we, the brave, the mighty, and the
    wise,
We men, who in our morn of youth defied
The elements, must vanish;—be it so!

Enough, if something from our hands have
    power   10
To live, and act, and serve the future hour;
And if, as toward the silent tomb we go,
Through love, through hope, and faith's tran-
    scendent dower,
We feel that we are greater than we know.
(1820)

STUDY AIDS: This sonnet is made up of
a contrast and a consolation. Identify them.

Scorn Not the Sonnet

Scorn not the sonnet;[2] critic, you have
    frowned,
Mindless of its just honors; with this key
Shakespeare unlocked his heart;[3] the melody
Of this small lute gave ease to Petrarch's
    wound;[4]
A thousand times this pipe did Tasso[5]
    sound;   5
With it Camoëns[6] soothed an exile's grief;
The sonnet glittered a gay myrtle leaf
Amid the cypress with which Dante[7]
    crowned
His visionary brow: a glow-worm lamp,
It cheered mild Spenser,[8] called from faery-
    land   10
To struggle through dark ways; and, when a
    damp
Fell round the path of Milton, in his hand

The thing became a trumpet; whence he blew
Soul-animating strains—alas, too few![9]
(1827)

STUDY AIDS: 1. Show how this sonnet is
built up through a succession of appropriate
metaphors. How is the brevity of the sonnet
form suggested by the chosen images? How does
Wordsworth try to persuade us that the sonnet,
despite its brevity, is an effective instrument?

2. This sonnet should be compared with
Nuns Fret Not (p. oo), which also defends
the sonnet form. Is the method of development
the same? What are the differences in tone and
in choice of images? Which to you is the more
effective, and why?

[5] Tasso wrote two volumes of sonnets.
[6] Because of one of his satires Camoëns was exiled
to Macao in 1556, where he wrote many sonnets.
[7] Dante's *Vita Nuova*, commemorating his lady
Beatrice, contains many sonnets.
[8] In the 80th sonnet of his sonnet sequence,
Amoretti, Spenser says that the writing of the
sonnets was a relaxation after his labors on *The
Faerie Queene*.
[9] Milton wrote only twenty-three sonnets, eighteen in English and five in Italian. Why is the
sonnet called a "trumpet" in Milton's hands?

[1] The River Duddon.
[2] From the time of Milton to the Romantic period,
the sonnet was a neglected lyric form.
[3] Shakespeare's sonnets are more personal and
autobiographical than his other works, though he
hardly "unlocked his heart" with them.
[4] "Petrarch's wound" was his hopeless love for
his lady Laura, who inspired his sonnets.

Samuel Taylor Coleridge
(1772–1834)

COLERIDGE DESCRIBED HIMSELF AS "INDOLENCE CAPABLE OF ENERGIES." THE INDOLENCE often kept him from finishing what he started. The energies, when harnessed, enabled him to produce a few of the most magical poems in our literature, and to write and speak what Emerson called "the only high criticism of his time."

Samuel Taylor Coleridge was the youngest of thirteen children, the son of a scholarly, eccentric preacher. Sent to school at Christ's Hospital in London, "the inspired charity boy," as Lamb called him, became a voracious reader and a student of the classics. At Cambridge, which he entered on a scholarship in 1791, his exposure to radical influences led him to form a Utopian social scheme with his friend Robert Southey. The two young idealists envisioned a "Pantisocracy," a small communal society to be established in the United States on the banks of the Susquehanna as an "experiment of human perfectibility."

Coleridge left Cambridge without taking a degree, and when the dream of Pantisocracy faded in the hard light of financial demands, he turned to other projects. He lectured on politics, published a volume of verses, and launched a periodical, which soon failed. Distressed over its failure and suffering with neuralgia, he took opium for relief and so began a habit that plagued him for twenty years.

Friendship with Wordsworth, begun in 1797, brought out Coleridge's finest poetical gifts. He and William and Dorothy became "three persons with one soul," and under the stimulus of this sympathetic relationship Coleridge wrote his greatest poems—*The Ancient Mariner, Kubla Khan,* and *Christabel.* When the three went to Germany in 1798, Coleridge steeped himself in German language, literature, and philosophy, and returned to become one of the foremost disseminators of German thought in England in the early nineteenth century.

The years 1800–1816 were unhappy ones. His marriage was a failure, his creative energies flagged, and he fell out with Wordsworth. The two were later reconciled, but never again enjoyed their old intimacy. All the while he became more and more enslaved to opium.

To cure his addiction, Coleridge put himself in the hands of a doctor at Highgate. He went for a month's stay in 1816 and remained until his death. It was a happy arrangement, Coleridge for the first time in years enjoying a measure of health and contentment. He also was able to write again and to publish—*Biographia Literaria* (1817), *Sybilline Leaves* (1817), and other volumes. He lectured occasionally, and enjoyed talking with friends. Coleridge was a brilliant talker. Highgate became a gathering-place for youthful disciples, who sat awestruck at the feet of this enchanting monologist, who held forth, Carlyle says, "like a sage escaped from the inanity of life's battle."

Coleridge's chief claim to poetical fame rests upon those poems of magic and witchery in which actions and characters are often supernatural. Such a poem is *The Rime of the Ancient Mariner,* the greatest of all literary ballads. Fully to enjoy poems of this kind, said

Coleridge in a remark that has become famous, one must bring to a reading of them "that willing suspension of disbelief for the moment, which constitutes poetic faith."

Coleridge's literary criticism, influential in the nineteenth century and in our own, is undeniably brilliant. It is true that his work in this field was sporadic and fragmentary; even the *Biographia Literaria,* his one "complete" volume of criticism, is something of a hodgepodge. But his ideas, fully developed or not, are always suggestive. Although contemptuous of artistic "rules," he sought to ground his critical evaluations on philosophical principles, such as his "organic theory" of art, which holds that a true work of art is, like a plant, an organic whole. Whether analyzing Wordsworth's poetry, distinguishing between fancy and imagination, or probing the depths of Hamlet or Othello, Coleridge displays a penetrating intellect. Often he comes close to saying the final critical word.

The Rime of the Ancient Mariner
In Seven Parts

The Ancient Mariner is an excellent example of a great poet's ability to fuse, in the "deep well of imagination," the materials derived from extensive reading, and to bring them forth as an organic work of art. With all the indefinable magic of a superbly told fairy tale, the poem creates a sense of the reality of the unreal, such as we know in vivid dreams.

Wordsworth and Coleridge planned *The Ancient Mariner* together, but Wordsworth soon withdrew himself "from an undertaking upon which I could only have been a clog." Coleridge continued to work on the poem, his part in a joint program in which he would contribute poems of the supernatural and Wordsworth poems of everyday life. The result was the *Lyrical Ballads* (1798), to which *The Ancient Mariner* was Coleridge's major contribution.

The marginal prose glosses were added by Coleridge in a later edition.

Argument: How a Ship having passed the Line was driven by storms to the cold Country towards the South Pole, and how from thence she made her course to the tropical Latitude of the Great Pacific Ocean, and of the strange things that befell; and in what manner the Ancient Mariner came back to his own Country.

Part I

It is an ancient Mariner,
And he stoppeth one of three.
"By thy long gray beard and glittering eye,
Now wherefore stopp'st thou me?

"The bridegroom's doors are opened wide,   5
And I am next of kin;
The guests are met, the feast is set:
May'st hear the merry din."

He holds him with his skinny hand;
"There was a ship," quoth he.   10
"Hold off! unhand me, gray-beard loon!"
Eftsoons[1] his hand dropt he.

An ancient Mariner meeteth three gallants bidden to a wedding-feast, and detaineth one.

[1] Immediately.

He holds him with his glittering eye—
The Wedding-Guest stood still,
And listens like a three years' child.   15
The Mariner hath his will.

The Wedding-Guest sat on a stone:
He cannot choose but hear;
And thus spake on that ancient man,
The bright-eyed Mariner.   20

The Wedding-Guest is spellbound by the eye of the old seafaring man and constrained to hear his tale.

"The ship was cheered, the harbor cleared,
Merrily did we drop
Below the kirk, below the hill,
Below the light-house top.

"The sun came up upon the left,   25
Out of the sea came he!
And he shone bright, and on the right
Went down into the sea.

The Mariner tells how the ship sailed southward with a good wind and fair weather, till it reached the Line.

"Higher and higher every day,
Till over the mast at noon—"   30
The Wedding-Guest here beat his breast,
For he heard the loud bassoon.

The bride hath paced into the hall,
Red as a rose [2] is she;
Nodding their heads before her goes   35
The merry minstrelsy.

The Wedding-Guest heareth the bridal music; but the Mariner continueth his tale.

The Wedding-Guest he beat his breast,
Yet he cannot choose but hear;
And thus spake on that ancient man,
The bright-eyed Mariner.   40

"And now the storm-blast came, and he
Was tyrannous and strong:
He struck with his o'ertaking wings,
And chased us south along.

The ship driven by a storm toward the south pole.

"With sloping masts and dipping prow,[3]   45
As who pursued with yell and blow
Still treads the shadow of his foe,
And forward bends his head,
The ship drove fast, loud roared the blast,
And southward aye we fled.   50

[2] "Red as a rose" is a stock comparison in the old ballads.
[3] This stanza is the first deviation from the QUATRAIN. Why is a longer stanza appropriate here?

"And now there came both mist and snow,
And it grew wondrous cold:
And ice, mast-high, came floating by,
As green as emerald.

"And through the drifts the snowy clifts   55   *The land of ice, and of fearful sounds where no living thing was to be seen.*
Did send a dismal sheen:
Nor shapes of men nor beasts we ken—
The ice was all between.

"The ice was here, the ice was there,
The ice was all around: 60
It cracked and growled, and roared and howled,
Like noises in a swound! [4]

"At length did cross an albatross,   *Till a great sea-bird, called the albatross, came through the snow-fog, and was received with great joy and hospitality.*
Thorough the fog it came;
As if it had been a Christian soul,   65
We hailed it in God's name.

"It ate the food it ne'er had eat,[5]
And round and round it flew.
The ice did split with a thunder-fit;
The helmsman steered us through!   70

"And a good south wind sprung up behind;   *And lo! the albatross proveth a bird of good omen, and followeth the ship as it returned northward through fog and floating ice.*
The albatross did follow,
And every day, for food or play,
Came to the mariners' hollo!

"In mist or cloud, on mast or shroud,   75
It perched for vespers [6] nine;
Whiles all the night, through fog-smoke white,
Glimmered the white moon-shine."

"God save thee, ancient Mariner!   *The ancient Mariner inhospitably killeth the pious bird of good omen.*
From the fiends, that plague thee thus!—   80
Why look'st thou so?" [7]—"With my cross-bow
I shot the albatross!"

---

[4] Swoon (dream). What does the occasional use of archaic words add to the poem?
[5] The first version is more specific: "The Marineres gave it biscuit-worms." Why do you think Coleridge changed the line?
[6] Evening church services—here with the general meaning of "evenings." Why does Coleridge use religious terminology here?
[7] Lines 78–81: The enormity of the act is enhanced by shifting the point of view from the Mariner to the Wedding-Guest and having him comment upon the Mariner's facial expression.

Part 2

"The sun now rose upon the right:
Out of the sea came he,
Still hid in mist, and on the left   85
Went down into the sea.

"And the good south wind still blew behind,
But no sweet bird did follow,
Nor any day for food or play
Came to the mariners' hollo!   90

"And I had done a hellish thing,
And it would work 'em woe:
For all averred, I had killed the bird
That made the breeze to blow.
Ah, wretch! said they, the bird to slay   95
That made the breeze to blow!

His shipmates cry out against the ancient Mariner, for killing the bird of good luck.

"Nor dim nor red, like God's own head,
The glorious sun uprist:
Then all averred, I had killed the bird
That brought the fog and mist.   100
'Twas right, said they, such birds to slay,
That bring the fog and mist.

But when the fog cleared off they justify the same, and thus make themselves accomplices in the crime.

"The fair breeze blew, the white foam flew,
The furrow followed free;
We were the first that ever burst   105
Into that silent sea.

The fair breeze continues; the ship enters the Pacific Ocean, and sails northward, even till it reaches the Line.

"Down dropt the breeze, the sails [8] dropt down,
'Twas sad as sad could be;
And we did speak only to break
The silence of the sea!   110

The ship hath been suddenly becalmed.

"All in a hot and copper sky,
The bloody sun, at noon,
Right up above the mast did stand,
No bigger than the moon.

"Day after day, day after day,   115
We stuck, nor breath nor motion;
As idle as a painted ship
Upon a painted ocean.

[8] From this point on, note the arrangement of the punishments in the order of increasing severity: the becalming of the ship; physical tortures; mental and spiritual agonies.

"Water, water, everywhere,
And all the boards did shrink;   120
Water, water, everywhere,
Nor any drop to drink.

"The very deep did rot: O Christ!
That ever this should be!
Yea, slimy things did crawl with legs   125
Upon the slimy sea.

"About, about, in reel and rout
The death-fires[9] danced at night;
The water, like a witch's oils,
Burnt green, and blue and white.   130

"And some in dreams assurèd were
Of the spirit that plagued us so;
Nine fathom deep he had followed us
From the land of mist and snow.

"And every tongue, through utter drought,   135
Was withered at the root;
We could not speak, no more than if
We had been choked with soot.

"Ah! well-a-day! what evil looks
Had I from old and young!   140
Instead of the cross,[10] the albatross
About my neck was hung."

Part 3

"There passed a weary time. Each throat
Was parched, and glazed each eye.
A weary time! a weary time!   145
How glazed each weary eye,
When looking westward, I beheld
A something in the sky.[11]

"At first it seemed a little speck,
And then it seemed a mist;   150
It moved and moved, and took at last
A certain shape, I wist.[12]

And the albatross begins to be avenged.

A spirit had followed them; one of the invisible inhabitants of this planet, neither departed souls nor angels; concerning whom the learned Jew, Josephus, and the Platonic Constantinopolitan, Michael Psellus, may be consulted. They are very numerous, and there is no climate or element without one or more.

The shipmates, in their sore distress, would fain throw the whole guilt on the ancient Mariner: in sign whereof they hang the dead seabird round his neck.

The ancient Mariner beholdeth a sign in the element afar off.

---

[9] Phosphorescent lights ("St. Elmo's fire"), an electrical phenomenon which superstitious seamen regarded as foreboding death.

[10] According to some legends, the Wandering Jew (who had forbidden Jesus to rest on the way to Golgotha) was branded with a cross; and so too was Cain.

[11] Lines 143–148: What means does Coleridge use in this stanza to intensify the Mariner's weariness?

[12] Knew.

"A speck, a mist, a shape, I wist!
And still it neared and neared:
As if it dodged a water-sprite,   155
It plunged and tacked and veered.

"With throats unslaked, with black lips baked,
We could nor laugh nor wail;
Through utter drought all dumb we stood!
I bit my arm, I sucked the blood,   160
And cried, A sail! a sail! [13]

At its nearer approach, it seemeth him to be a ship; and at a dear ransom he freeth his speech from the bonds of thirst.

"With throats unslaked, with black lips baked,
Agape they heard me call:
Gramercy! they for joy did grin,
And all at once their breath drew in,   165
As they were drinking all.

A flash of joy;

"See! see! (I cried) she tacks no more!
Hither to work us weal [14]—
Without a breeze, without a tide,
She steadies with upright keel!   170

And horror follows. For can it be a ship that comes onward without wind or tide?

"The western wave was all aflame,
The day was well nigh done!
Almost upon the western wave
Rested the broad bright sun;
When that strange shape drove suddenly   175
Betwixt us and the sun.

"And straight the sun was flecked with bars,
(Heaven's Mother send us grace!)
As if through a dungeon-grate he peered
With broad and burning face.   180

It seemeth him but the skeleton of a ship.

"Alas! (thought I, and my heart beat loud)
How fast she nears and nears!
Are those her sails that glance in the sun,
Like restless gossameres?

"Are those her ribs through which the sun   185
Did peer, as through a grate?
And is that woman all her crew?
Is that a Death? and are there two?
Is Death that woman's mate?

And its ribs are seen as bars on the face of the setting sun.

The specter-woman and her death-mate, and no other on board the skeleton ship.

[13] In ll. 147–161, note the artistic and suspenseful handling of the approach of the phantom ship (a common item in travelers' tales): first "a something"; then "a little speck"; then "a mist"; then "a certain shape"; then the repetition of "a speck, a mist, a shape"; and finally, after an interval of graphic description, "A sail! a sail!"

[14] Good.

"Her lips were red, her looks were free,
Her locks were yellow as gold:
Her skin was as white as leprosy,
The night-mare Life-in-Death was she,
Who thicks man's blood with cold.

190

Like vessel, like crew!

"The naked hulk alongside came,
And the twain were casting dice;[15]
'The game is done! I've won! I've won!'
Quoth she, and whistles thrice.

195

Death and Life-in-Death have diced for the ship's crew, and she (the latter) winneth the ancient Mariner.

"The sun's rim dips; the stars rush out:
At one stride comes the dark;
With far-heard whisper, o'er the sea,
Off shot the specter-bark.

200

No twilight within the courts of the sun.

"We listened and looked sideways up!
Fear at my heart, as at a cup,
My life-blood seemed to sip!
The stars were dim, and thick the night,
The steersman's face by his lamp gleamed white;
From the sails the dew did drip—
Till clomb above the eastern bar
The hornèd moon, with one bright star
Within the nether tip.[16]

205

210

At the rising of the moon,

"One after one, by the star-dogged moon,
Too quick for groan or sigh,
Each turned his face with a ghastly pang,
And cursed me with his eye.

215

One after another,

"Four times fifty living men,
(And I heard nor sigh nor groan)
With heavy thump, a lifeless lump,
They dropt down one by one.

His shipmates drop down dead.

"The souls did from their bodies fly—
They fled to bliss or woe!
And every soul, it passed me by
Like the whizz of my cross-bow!"

220

But Life-in-Death begins her work on the ancient Mariner.

Part 4

"I fear thee, ancient Mariner!
I fear thy skinny hand!
And thou art long, and lank, and brown,
As is the ribbed sea-sand.

225

The Wedding-Guest feareth that a spirit is talking to him;

[15] "A tale of two spectral figures casting dice on a phantom ship for the soul of an eternal wanderer was current on the seas" (J. L. Lowes, *The Road to Xanadu*, 1927, p. 277).

[16] This stanza is the only 9-line stanza in the poem. Why is the extra length appropriate here? (The "hornèd moon" of l. 210 is the waning moon, which may rise at dawn.)

"I fear thee and thy glittering eye,
And thy skinny hand, so brown."—
"Fear not, fear not, thou Wedding-Guest! 230
This body dropt not down.

But the ancient Mariner assureth him of his bodily life, and proceedeth to relate his horrible penance.

"Alone, alone, all, all alone,
Alone on a wide, wide sea!
And never a saint took pity on
My soul in agony. 235

"The many men, so beautiful!
And they all dead did lie:
And a thousand thousand slimy things
Lived on; and so did I.

He despiseth the creatures of the calm.

"I looked upon the rotting sea, 240
And drew my eyes away;
I looked upon the rotting deck,
And there the dead men lay.

And envieth that they should live, and so many lie dead.

"I looked to heaven, and tried to pray;
But or ever a prayer had gusht, 245
A wicked whisper came, and made
My heart as dry as dust.

"I closed my lids, and kept them close,
And the balls like pulses beat;
For the sky and the sea, and the sea and the sky 250
Lay like a load on my weary eye,
And the dead were at my feet.

"The cold sweat melted from their limbs,
Nor rot nor reek did they: [17]
The look with which they looked on me 255
Had never passed away.

But the curse liveth for him in the eye of the dead men.

"An orphan's curse would drag to hell
A spirit from on high;
But oh! more horrible than that
Is a curse in a dead man's eye! 260
Seven days, seven nights, I saw that curse,
And yet I could not die.

"The moving moon went up the sky,
And nowhere did abide:
Softly she was going up, 265
And a star or two beside—

In his loneliness and fixedness he yearneth towards the journeying moon, and the stars that still sojourn, yet still move onward; and everywhere the blue sky belongs to them, and is their appointed rest, and their native country and their own natural homes, which they enter unannounced, as lords that are certainly expected, and yet there is a silent joy at their arrival.

[17] Travel tales described regions where the dead would lie uncorrupted.

"Her beams bemocked the sultry main,
Like April hoar-frost spread;
But where the ship's huge shadow lay,
The charmèd water burnt alway   270
A still and awful red.

"Beyond the shadow of the ship,
I watched the water-snakes:
They moved in tracks of shining white,   275
And when they reared, the elfish light
Fell off in hoary flakes.

"Within the shadow of the ship
I watched their rich attire:
Blue, glossy green, and velvet black,
They coiled and swam; and every track   280
Was a flash of golden fire.

"O happy living things! no tongue
Their beauty might declare:
A spring of love gushed from my heart,
And I blessed them unaware; [18]   285
Sure my kind saint took pity on me,
And I blessed them unaware.

"The selfsame moment I could pray;
And from my neck so free
The albatross fell off, and sank   290
Like lead into the sea."

By the light of the moon he beholdeth God's creatures of the great calm.

Their beauty and their happiness.

He blesseth them in his heart.

The spell begins to break.

Part 5

"Oh sleep! it is a gentle thing,
Beloved from pole to pole!
To Mary Queen the praise be given!
She sent the gentle sleep from heaven,   295
That slid into my soul.

"The silly [19] buckets on the deck,
That had so long remained,
I dreamt that they were filled with dew;
And when I awoke, it rained.   300

"My lips were wet, my throat was cold,
My garments all were dank;
Sure I had drunken in my dreams,
And still my body drank.

By grace of the holy Mother, the ancient Mariner is refreshed with rain.

[18] This is the moral turning point of the poem. From here on the torments are abated, though the guilty Mariner must still do penance and undergo punishment.
[19] Useless, because they were empty.

"I moved, and could not feel my limbs: 305
I was so light—almost
I thought that I had died in sleep,
And was a blessèd ghost.

"And soon I heard a roaring wind:
It did not come anear;   310
But with its sound it shook the sails,
That were so thin and sere.

He heareth sounds and seeth strange sights and commotions in the sky and the element.

"The upper air burst into life!
And a hundred fire-flags sheen,
To and fro they were hurried about!   315
And to and fro, and in and out,
The wan stars danced between.[20]

"And the coming wind did roar more loud,
And the sails did sigh like sedge;
And the rain poured down from one black cloud; 320
The moon was at its edge.

"The thick black cloud was cleft, and still
The moon was at its side:
Like waters shot from some high crag,
The lightning fell with never a jag,   325
A river steep and wide.

"The loud wind never reached the ship,
Yet now the ship moved on!
Beneath the lightning and the moon
The dead men gave a groan.   330

The bodies of the ship's crew are inspirited, and the ship moves on;

"They groaned, they stirred, they all uprose,
Nor spake, nor moved their eyes;
It had been strange, even in a dream,
To have seen those dead men rise.

"The helmsman steered, the ship moved on;   335
Yet never a breeze up blew;
The mariners all 'gan work the ropes,
Where they were wont to do;
They raised their limbs like lifeless tools—
We were a ghastly crew.   340

"The body of my brother's son
Stood by me, knee to knee:
The body and I pulled at one rope,
But he said nought to me."

[20] Lines 314–317: Stars seen through the aurora borealis.

"I fear thee, ancient Mariner!"
"Be calm, thou Wedding-Guest!
'Twas not those souls that fled in pain,
Which to their corses came again,
But a troop of spirits blessed: [21]

345

But not by the souls of the men, nor by demons of earth or middle air, but by a blessed troop of angelic spirits, sent down by the invocation of the guardian saint.

"For when it dawned—they dropped their arms,
And clustered round the mast;
Sweet sounds rose slowly through their mouths,
And from their bodies passed.

350

"Around, around, flew each sweet sound,
Then darted to the sun;
Slowly the sounds came back again,
Now mixed, now one by one.

355

"Sometimes a-dropping from the sky
I heard the skylark sing;
Sometimes all little birds that are,
How they seemed to fill the sea and air
With their sweet jargoning!

360

"And now 'twas like all instruments,
Now like a lonely flute;
And now it is an angel's song,
That makes the heavens be mute.[22]

365

"It ceased; yet still the sails made on
A pleasant noise till noon,
A noise like of a hidden brook
In the leafy month of June,
That to the sleeping woods all night
Singeth a quiet tune.

370

"Till noon we quietly sailed on,
Yet never a breeze did breathe:
Slowly and smoothly went the ship,
Moved onward from beneath.

375

"Under the keel nine fathom deep,
From the land of mist and snow,
The spirit slid: and it was he
That made the ship to go.
The sails at noon left off their tune,
And the ship stood still also.

380

The lonesome spirit from the South Pole carries on the ship as far as the Line, in obedience to the angelic troop, but still requireth vengeance.

[21] Why is it appropriate that a troop of angelic spirits should take over the ship (through controlling the bodies of the dead men) at this point?

[22] In what metaphoric terms (ll. 358–366) does the Mariner describe the voices of the angelic spirits?

"The sun, right up above the mast,
Had fixed her to the ocean:
But in a minute she 'gan stir,   385
With a short uneasy motion—
Backwards and forwards half her length
With a short uneasy motion.

"Then like a pawing horse let go,
She made a sudden bound: 390
It flung the blood into my head,
And I fell down in a swound.

"How long in that same fit I lay,
I have not [23] to declare;
But ere my living life returned,   395
I heard, and in my soul discerned,
Two voices in the air.

The polar spirit's fellow demons, the invisible inhabitants of the element, take part in his wrong; and two of them relate, one to the other that penance long and heavy for the ancient Mariner hath been accorded to the polar spirit, who returneth southward.

" 'Is it he?' quoth one, 'Is this the man?
By Him who died on cross,
With his cruel bow he laid full low   400
The harmless albatross.

" 'The spirit who bideth by himself
In the land of mist and snow,
He loved the bird that loved the man
Who shot him with his bow.'   405

"The other was a softer voice,
As soft as honey-dew:
Quoth he, 'The man hath penance done,
And penance more will do.' "

Part 6

FIRST VOICE

" 'But tell me, tell me! speak again,
Thy soft response renewing—   410
What makes that ship drive on so fast?
What is the ocean doing?'

SECOND VOICE

" 'Still as a slave before his lord,
The ocean hath no blast;   415
His great bright eye most silently
Up to the moon is cast—

[23] Have not power.

" 'If he may know which way to go;
For she guides him smooth or grim.
See, brother, see! how graciously   420
She looketh down on him.'

FIRST VOICE

" 'But why drives on that ship so fast,   *The Mariner hath been cast into a trance;*
Without or wave or wind?'   *for the angelic power causeth the vessel to*
                                              drive northward faster than human life could
                                              endure.

SECOND VOICE

" 'The air is cut away before,
And closes from behind.'   425

" 'Fly, brother, fly! more high, more high!
Or we shall be belated:
For slow and slow that ship will go,
When the Mariner's trance is abated.'

"I woke, and we were sailing on   430   *The supernatural motion is retarded; the*
As in a gentle weather: *Mariner awakes, and his penance begins*
'Twas night, calm night, the moon was high;   *anew.*
The dead men stood together.

"All stood together on the deck,
For a charnel-dungeon fitter: 435
All fixed on me their stony eyes,
That in the moon did glitter.

"The pang, the curse, with which they died,
Had never passed away:
I could not draw my eyes from theirs,   440
Nor turn them up to pray.

"And now this spell was snapt: once more   *The curse is finally expiated.*
I viewed the ocean green,
And looked far forth, yet little saw
Of what had else been seen—   445

"Like one, that on a lonesome road
Doth walk in fear and dread,
And having once turned round, walks on,
And turns no more his head;
Because he knows, a frightful fiend   450
Doth close behind him tread.

"But soon there breathed a wind on me,
Nor sound nor motion made:
Its path was not upon the sea,
In ripple or in shade.   455

"It raised my hair, it fanned my cheek
Like a meadow-gale of spring—
It mingled strangely with my fears,
Yet it felt like a welcoming.

"Swiftly, swiftly flew the ship,   460
Yet she sailed softly too:
Sweetly, sweetly blew the breeze—
On me alone it blew.

"Oh! dream of joy! is this indeed   *And the ancient Mariner beholdeth his native*
The light-house top I see?   465   *country.*
Is this the hill? is this the kirk?
Is this mine own countree?

"We drifted o'er the harbor-bar,
And I with sobs did pray—
O let me be awake, my God!   470
Or let me sleep alway.

"The harbor-bay was clear as glass,
So smoothly it was strewn!
And on the bay the moonlight lay,
And the shadow of the moon.   475

"The rock shone bright, the kirk no less,
That stands above the rock:
The moonlight steeped in silentness
The steady weathercock.

"And the bay was white with silent light   480
Till, rising from the same,   *The angelic spirits leave the dead bodies,*
Full many shapes, that shadows were,
In crimson colors came.

"A little distance from the prow
Those crimson shadows were: 485
I turned my eyes upon the deck—
Oh, Christ! what saw I there!

"Each corse lay flat, lifeless and flat,
And, by the holy rood! [24]
A man all light, a seraph-man,   490   *And appear in their own forms of light.*
On every corse there stood.

"This seraph-band, each waved his hand:
It was a heavenly sight!
They stood as signals to the land,
Each one a lovely light;   495

[24] Cross.

"This seraph-band, each waved his hand,
No voice did they impart—
No voice; but oh! the silence sank
Like music on my heart.

"But soon I heard the dash of oars,   500
I heard the pilot's cheer;
My head was turned perforce away,
And I saw a boat appear.

"The pilot and the pilot's boy,
I heard them coming fast: 505
Dear Lord in Heaven! it was a joy
The dead men could not blast.

"I saw a third—I heard his voice:
It is the hermit good!
He singeth loud his godly hymns   510
That he makes in the wood.
He'll shrieve my soul, he'll wash away
The albatross's blood."

Part 7

"This hermit good lives in that wood   *The hermit of the wood,*
Which slopes down to the sea.   515
How loudly his sweet voice he rears!
He loves to talk with marineres
That come from a far countree.

"He kneels at morn, and noon, and eve—
He hath a cushion plump: 520
It is the moss that wholly hides
The rotted old oak-stump.

"The skiff-boat neared: I heard them talk,
'Why, this is strange, I trow!
Where are those lights so many and fair,   525
That signal made but now?'

" 'Strange, by my faith!' the hermit said—   *Approacheth the ship with wonder.*
'And they answered not our cheer!
The planks looked warped! and see those sails,
How thin they are and sere!   530
I never saw aught like to them,
Unless perchance it were

" 'Brown skeletons of leaves that lag
My forest-brook along;
When the ivy-tod [25] is heavy with snow,   535
And the owlet whoops to the wolf below,
That eats the she-wolf's young.'

" 'Dear Lord! it hath a fiendish look—
(The pilot made reply)
I am a-feared'—'Push on, push on!'   540
Said the hermit cheerily.

"The boat came closer to the ship,
But I nor spake nor stirred;
The boat came close beneath the ship,
And straight a sound was heard.   545

"Under the water it rumbled on,
Still louder and more dread:
It reached the ship, it split the bay;
The ship went down like lead.

The ship suddenly sinketh.

"Stunned by that loud and dreadful sound,   550
Which sky and ocean smote,
Like one that hath been seven days drowned
My body lay afloat;
But swift as dreams, myself I found
Within the pilot's boat.   555

The ancient Mariner is saved in the pilot's boat.

"Upon the whirl, where sank the ship,
The boat spun round and round;
And all was still, save that the hill
Was telling of the sound.

"I moved my lips—the pilot shrieked   560
And fell down in a fit;
The holy hermit raised his eyes,
And prayed where he did sit.

"I took the oars: the pilot's boy,
Who now doth crazy go,   565
Laughed loud and long, and all the while
His eyes went to and fro.
'Ha! ha!' quoth he, 'full plain I see,
The devil knows how to row.'

"And now, all in my own countree,   570
I stood on the firm land!
The hermit stepped forth from the boat,
And scarcely he could stand.

[25] Ivy-bush.

"'O shrieve me, shrieve me, holy man!'
The hermit crossed [26] his brow.
'Say quick,' quoth he, 'I bid thee say—
What manner of man art thou?'

575   *The ancient Mariner earnestly entreateth the hermit to shrieve him; and the penance of life falls on him.*

"Forthwith this frame of mine was wrenched
With a woful agony,
Which forced me to begin my tale;
And then it left me free.

580

"Since then, at an uncertain hour,
That agony returns;
And till my ghastly tale is told,
This heart within me burns.

    And ever and anon throughout his future life an agony constraineth him to travel from land to land,

585

"I pass, like night, from land to land;
I have strange power of speech;
That moment that his face I see,
I know the man that must hear me:
To him my tale I teach. [27]

590

"What loud uproar bursts from that door!
The wedding-guests are there:
But in the garden-bower the bride
And bride-maids singing are:
And hark the little vesper bell,
Which biddeth me to prayer!

595

"O Wedding-Guest! this soul hath been
Alone on a wide, wide sea:
So lonely 'twas, that God himself
Scarce seemèd there to be.

600

"Oh sweeter than the marriage-feast,
'Tis sweeter far to me,
To walk together to the kirk
With a goodly company!—

"To walk together to the kirk,
And all together pray,
While each to his great Father bends,
Old men, and babes, and loving friends,
And youths and maidens gay!

605

"Farewell, farewell! but this I tell
To thee, thou Wedding-Guest!
He prayeth well, who loveth well
Both man and bird and beast.

610   *And to teach by his own example love and reverence to all things that God made and loveth.*

[26] Made the sign of the cross upon.
[27] Lines 582–590: The Ancient Mariner has to undergo a penance like that of the Wandering Jew.

"He prayeth best, who loveth best
All things both great and small;   615
For the dear God who loveth us,
He made and loveth all." [28]

The Mariner, whose eye is bright,
Whose beard with age is hoar,
Is gone: and now the Wedding-Guest   620
Turned from the bridegroom's door.

He went like one that hath been stunned,
And is of sense forlorn: [29]
A sadder and a wiser man,
He rose the morrow morn.   625
(1798)

STUDY AIDS: 1. J. L. Lowes says that *The Ancient Mariner* has three main structural elements: (1) the voyage itself ("as austerely true to fact as an Admiralty report"); (2) the balance of angelic and demonic forces; (3) the crime-and-punishment theme. How are these three elements interrelated and how do they reinforce one another? Is any one of them stressed more than the others?

2. The poem is a literary ballad and thus attempts to suggest many of the qualities of the old folk ballads, which were usually written in a simple 4-line stanza form, dealt with fundamental human passions and situations, were direct and somewhat (unconsciously) naïve, tended toward the dramatic and objective, used a great deal of repetition, and were frequently concerned with the supernatural. Show how Coleridge has used all these elements in *The Ancient Mariner*. In the case of the versification, how has he relieved the monotony of the simple ballad quatrain?

3. There has been much discussion of the "moral" of *The Ancient Mariner*, and of the possible symbolism by which this moral is developed. Here are some interpretations for you to consider: (1) Everything is really a delusion of the childlike Mariner. (2) There is no moral; for killing a bird, 200 men die in agony and another is condemned to eternal punishment. (3) The moral is simply that we cannot escape the consequences of our sins; in *The Ancient Mariner* both the sin and the consequences are exaggerated because they take place in a dream world, where things are always distorted. (4) The shooting of the albatross represents an abuse of human reason; the Mariner must learn the meaning of love for all life before he can begin his expiation. (5) "The killing of the albatross is a sin against the great sentimental principle that the universe is one loving Whole." The Mariner's "blessing of the water snakes reaffirms the benevolistic Unity and makes possible his salvation in the religion of Nature." (6) The albatross represents a redeeming Christ-like force guiding humanity from its primitive origins, and the death of the bird "may correspond to the death of Christ in racial history." (7) The poem is no more than a fairy tale: the Mariner violates the hospitality of the region by killing one of its creatures; whereupon the tutelary spirits of the place wreak vengeance upon the criminal and his accomplices.

[28] Lines 612–617: A lady complained that *The Ancient Mariner* has no moral. Coleridge replied that in his judgment the poem has too much, and that the chief fault is "the intrusion of the moral sentiment so openly on the reader as a principle or cause of action in a work of pure imagination." Coleridge was probably thinking of ll. 612–617. Are they objectionable—out of place in a "work of pure imagination"? Can they be justified?

[29] Deprived.

Kubla Khan

"In the summer of the year 1797, the author, then in ill health, had retired to a lonely farmhouse between Porlock and Linton, on the Exmoor confines of Somerset and Devonshire. In consequence of a slight indisposition, an anodyne [1] had been prescribed, from the effects of which he fell asleep in his chair at the moment he was reading the following sentence, or words of the same substance, in 'Purchas's Pilgrimage': [2] 'Here the Khan Kubla [3] commanded a palace to be built, and a stately garden thereunto. And thus ten miles of fertile ground were inclosed with a wall.' The author continued for about three hours in a profound sleep, at least of the external senses, during which time he has the most vivid confidence, that he could not have composed less than from two to three hundred lines; if that indeed can be called composition in which all the images rose up before him as *things,* with a parallel production of the correspondent expressions, without any sensation or consciousness of effort. On awaking he appeared to himself to have a distinct recollection of the whole, and taking his pen, ink, and paper, instantly and eagerly wrote down the lines that are here preserved. At this moment he was unfortunately called out by a person on business from Porlock, and detained by him above an hour, and on his return to his room, found, to his no small surprise and mortification, that though he still retained some vague and dim recollection of the general purport of the vision, yet, with the exception of some eight or ten scattered lines and images, all the rest had passed away like the images on the surface of a stream into which a stone has been cast, but,

alas! without the after restoration of the latter! . . ."

(Coleridge, Preface to *Kubla Khan,* 1816)

In Xanadu [4] did Kubla Khan
A stately pleasure-dome decree:
Where Alph,[5] the sacred river, ran
Through caverns measureless to man
    Down to a sunless sea.   5

So twice five miles of fertile ground
With walls and towers were girdled round:
And here were gardens bright with sinuous
    rills,
Where blossomed many an incense-bearing
    tree;
And here were forests ancient as the hills,   10
Enfolding sunny spots of greenery.

But oh! that deep romantic chasm which
    slanted
Down the green hill athwart a cedarn cover!
A savage place! as holy and enchanted [6]
As e'er beneath a waning moon was
    haunted   15
By woman wailing for her demon-lover!
And from this chasm, with ceaseless turmoil
    seething,
As if this earth in fast thick pants were breath-
    ing,
A mighty fountain momently was forced;
Amid whose swift half-intermitted burst   20
Huge fragments vaulted like rebounding hail,
Or chaffy grain beneath the thresher's flail:
And 'mid these dancing rocks at once and
    ever
It flung up momently the sacred river.

[1] Laudanum, a tincture of opium.
[2] The precise reading of the passage from Samuel Purchas's *Pilgrimage* is as follows: "In Xamdu did Cubla Can build a stately Palace, encompassing sixteen miles of plaine ground with a wall, wherein are fertile Meddowes, pleasant springs, delightful Streames, and all sorts of beasts of chace and game, and in the middest thereof a sumptuous house of pleasure, which may be removed from place to place."
[3] Chinese emperor, founder of the Mogul dynasty in China in the thirteenth century.

[4] A region in Tartary (China).
[5] Virgil and other ancient writers tell of the Alpheus, a river that sank beneath the earth and arose again in a fountain. See Milton's *Lycidas,* p. 225, l. 132.
[6] Of these lines and two from Keats's *Ode to a Nightingale* (ll. 69–70) Kipling said: "These are the magic. These are the vision. The rest is only poetry." On the other hand, another critic finds the association of "holy" with demonic love objectionable. What is your reaction to these lines?

Five miles meandering with a mazy
    motion   25
Through wood and dale the sacred river ran,
Then reached the caverns measureless to man,
And sank in tumult to a lifeless ocean:
And 'mid this tumult Kubla heard from far
Ancestral voices prophesying war!   30

    The shadow of the dome of pleasure
    Floated midway on the waves;
    Where was heard the mingled measure
    From the fountain and the caves.
It was a miracle of rare device,   35
A sunny pleasure-dome with caves of ice!

    A damsel with a dulcimer
    In a vision once I saw:
    It was an Abyssinian maid,
    And on her dulcimer she played,   40
    Singing of Mount Abora.
    Could I revive within me
    Her symphony and song,
    To such a deep delight 'twould win me,
That with music loud and long,   45
I would build that dome in air,
That sunny dome! those caves of ice!
And all who heard should see them there,
And all should cry, Beware! Beware!
His flashing eyes, his floating hair!   50

Weave a circle round him thrice,
And close your eyes with holy dread,
For he on honey-dew hath fed,
And drunk the milk of paradise.
(1798?–1816)

STUDY AIDS: 1. The poem could be said to consist of three clearly defined parts, which relate logically to each other and which make good sense as far as the poem goes. First the poet attempts to describe the palace and environs of the great emperor Kubla Khan, as suggested in the passage from Purchas. Second, the poet breaks off, dissatisfied with his attempt and revealing that if he could only recapture the inspiration once afforded him by the music of the "Abyssinian maid," he could succeed in his effort. Finally, so succeeding, he would be held in awe as an inspired poet-prophet, even a god, by all who heard him. Locate these three parts. Do you find such a pattern of organization and meaning convincing, or do you prefer to regard the poem as merely beautiful but meaningless nonsense?
2. The rhythms of the poem are quite different from the artful simplicity of versification in *The Ancient Mariner*. Note the rhymes, the metrical patterns, the run-on lines, the onomatopoeic effects, and the shifts in tempo and TONE (e.g., from l. 30 to 31). Point out other qualities in the music of the poem. How are the sound effects in keeping with the content?

Christabel

    Coleridge never finished this poem; it was published in its fragmentary form in 1816. We do not know how Coleridge intended to carry on and complete the work, although he insisted more than once that he had had the whole plan in his mind from the very beginning.
    The poem as we have it is an enigmatic vision of evil, and the key to the enigma lies in the complex figure of Geraldine, a weird composite of witch, vampire, and lamia (snake-woman). The stage is set for a war between the supernatural forces of good and evil, with the ministering angels guarding Christabel (including the spirit of her dead mother) opposing the powers of darkness centered around Geraldine. But in the poem as far as it goes, evil has triumphed as Geraldine has brought Christabel under her spell and has turned her wiles upon the susceptible Sir Leoline.

Part 1

'Tis the middle of night by the castle clock,
And the owls have awakened the crowing
    cock,
Tu—whit!——Tu—whoo!

And hark, again! the crowing cock,
How drowsily it crew.   5

Sir Leoline, the baron rich,
Hath a toothless mastiff bitch;
From her kennel beneath the rock

She maketh answer to the clock,
Four for the quarters, and twelve for the
   hour;   10
Ever and aye, by shine and shower,
Sixteen short howls, not over loud;
Some say, she sees my lady's shroud.

Is the night chilly and dark?
The night is chilly, but not dark.   15
The thin gray cloud is spread on high,
It covers but not hides the sky.
The moon is behind, and at the full;
And yet she looks both small and dull.
The night is chill, the cloud is gray: 20
'Tis a month before the month of May,
And the spring comes slowly up this
   way.

The lovely lady, Christabel,
Whom her father loves so well,
What makes her in the wood so late,   25
A furlong from the castle gate?
She had dreams all yesternight
Of her own betrothèd knight;
And she in the midnight wood will pray
For the weal of her lover that's far away.   30

She stole along, she nothing spoke,
The sighs she heaved were soft and low,
And naught was green upon the oak
But moss and rarest mistletoe:
She kneels beneath the huge oak tree   35
And in silence prayeth she.

The lady sprang up suddenly,
The lovely lady, Christabel!
It moaned as near, as near can be,
But what it is she cannot tell.—   40
On the other side it seems to be,
Of the huge, broad-breasted, old oak tree.

The night is chill; the forest bare;
Is it the wind that moaneth bleak?
There is not wind enough in the air   45
To move away the ringlet curl
From the lovely lady's cheek—
There is not wind enough to twirl
The one red leaf, the last of its clan,
That dances as often as dance it can,   50
Hanging so light, and hanging so high,

On the topmost twig that looks up at the
   sky.[1]

Hush, beating heart of Christabel!
Jesu, Maria, shield her well!
She folded her arms beneath her cloak,   55
And stole to the other side of the oak.
   What sees she there?

There she sees a damsel bright,
Drest in a silken robe of white,
That shadowy in the moonlight shone: 60
The neck that made that white robe wan,
Her stately neck, and arms were bare;
Her blue-veined feet unsandaled were,
And wildly glittered here and there
The gems entangled in her hair.   65
I guess, 'twas frightful there to see
A lady so richly clad as she—
Beautiful exceedingly!

"Mary mother, save me now!"
(Said Christabel) "And who art thou?"   70

The lady strange made answer meet,
And her voice was faint and sweet:
"Have pity on my sore distress,
I scarce can speak for weariness:
Stretch forth thy hand,[2] and have no
   fear!"   75
Said Christabel, "How camest thou here?"
And the lady, whose voice was faint and
   sweet,
Did thus pursue her answer meet:

"My sire is of a noble line,
And my name is Geraldine: 80
Five warriors seized me yestermorn.
Me, even me, a maid forlorn:
They choked my cries with force and
   fright,
And tied me on a palfrey white.
The palfrey was as fleet as wind,   85
And they rode furiously behind.

[1] SCAN this line and compare, say, l. 58. How are
the lines metrically alike? How different? How is
the metrical effect of l. 52 related to its meaning?
(In this connection, how would you scan line 57?)
[2] Note the eagerness of Geraldine to establish
physical contact. See also ll. 102, 130-134, 263,
449-450. The vampire-motif is strongly suggested.

They spurred amain, their steeds were white:
And once we crossed the shade of night.
As sure as heaven shall rescue me,
I have no thought what men they be;   90
Nor do I know how long it is
(For I have lain entranced, I wis)
Since one, the tallest of the five,
Took me from the palfrey's back,
A weary woman, scarce alive.   95
Some muttered words his comrades spoke:
He placed me underneath this oak;
He swore they would return with haste;
Whither they went I cannot tell—
I thought I heard, some minutes past,   100
Sounds as of a castle bell.
Stretch forth thy hand (thus ended she),
And help a wretched maid to flee."

Then Christabel stretched forth her hand,
And comforted fair Geraldine: 105
"Oh well, bright dame! may you command
The service of Sir Leoline:
And gladly our stout chivalry
Will he send forth, and friends withal,
To guide and guard you safe and free   110
Home to your noble father's hall."

She rose: and forth with steps they passed
That strove to be, and were not, fast.
Her gracious stars the lady blessed,
And thus spake on sweet Christabel: 115
"All our household are at rest,
The hall as silent as the cell;
Sir Leoline is weak in health,
And may not well awakened be,
But we will move as if in stealth,   120
And I beseech your courtesy,
This night, to share your couch with me."

They crossed the moat, and Christabel
Took the key that fitted well;
A little door she opened straight,   125
All in the middle of the gate;
The gate that was ironed within and with-
    out,
Where an army in battle array had marched
    out.
The lady sank, belike through pain,
And Christabel with might and main   130
Lifted her up, a weary weight,

Over the threshold of the gate: [3]
Then the lady rose again,
And moved, as she were not in pain.

So free from danger, free from fear,   135
They crossed the court: right glad they were.
And Christabel devoutly cried
To the lady by her side:
"Praise we the Virgin all divine
Who hath rescued thee from thy dis-
    tress!"   140
"Alas, alas!" said Geraldine,
"I cannot speak for weariness."
So free from danger, free from fear,
They crossed the court: right glad they were.

Outside her kennel the mastiff old   145
Lay fast asleep, in moonshine cold.
The mastiff old did not awake,
Yet she an angry moan did make!
And what can ail the mastiff bitch?
Never till now she uttered yell   150
Beneath the eye of Christabel.
Perhaps it is the owlet's scritch:
For what can ail the mastiff bitch? [4]

They passed the hall, that echoes still,
Pass as lightly as you will!   155
The brands were flat, the brands were dying,
Amid their own white ashes lying;
But when the lady passed, there came
A tongue of light, a fit of flame; [5]
And Christabel saw the lady's eye,   160
And nothing else saw she thereby,
Save the boss of the shield of Sir Leoline tall,
Which hung in a murky old niche in the
    wall.
"O softly tread," said Christabel,
"My father seldom sleepeth well."   165

Sweet Christabel her feet doth bare,
And jealous of the listening air,
They steal their way from stair to stair,

[3] Lines 129–132: Evil spirits cannot cross Christian
thresholds under their own power.
[4] Lines 145–153: According to an old superstition, animals can sense the presence of a witch or
other evil being.
[5] Lines 158–159 present another phenomenon
traditionally associated with the presence of a witch
or evil spirit.

Now in glimmer, and now in gloom,
And now they pass the baron's room,   170
As still as death, with stifled breath!
And now have reached her chamber door;
And now doth Geraldine press down
The rushes of the chamber floor.

The moon shines dim in the open air,   175
And not a moonbeam enters here.
But they without its light can see
The chamber carved so curiously,
Carved with figures strange and sweet,
All made out of the carver's brain,   180
For a lady's chamber meet:
The lamp with twofold silver chain
Is fastened to an angel's feet.

The silver lamp burns dead and dim;
But Christabel the lamp will trim.   185
She trimmed the lamp, and made it bright,
And left it swinging to and fro,
While Geraldine, in wretched plight,
Sank down upon the floor below.

"O weary lady, Geraldine,   190
I pray you, drink this cordial wine!
It is a wine of virtuous powers;
My mother made it of wild flowers."

"And will your mother pity me,
Who am a maiden most forlorn?"   195
Christabel answered—"Woe is me!
She died the hour that I was born.
I have heard the gray-haired friar tell,
How on her death-bed she did say,
That she should hear the castle-bell   200
Strike twelve upon my wedding-day.
O mother dear! that thou wert here!"
"I would," said Geraldine, "she were!"

But soon with altered voice, said she—
"Off, wandering mother! Peak and pine!   205
I have power to bid thee flee."
Alas! what ails poor Geraldine?
Why stares she with unsettled eye?
Can she the bodiless dead espy?
And why with hollow voice cries she,   210
"Off, woman, off! this hour is mine—
Though thou her guardian spirit be,
Off, woman, off! 'tis given to me."

Then Christabel knelt by the lady's side,
And raised to heaven her eyes so blue—   215
"Alas!" said she, "this ghastly ride—
Dear lady! it hath wildered you!"
The lady wiped her moist cold brow,
And faintly said, "'Tis over now!"

Again the wild-flower wine she drank: 220
Her fair large eyes 'gan glitter bright,
And from the floor whereon she sank,
The lofty lady stood upright;
She was most beautiful to see,
Like a lady of a far countree.   225

And thus the lofty lady spake—
"All they, who live in the upper sky,
Do love you, holy Christabel!
And you love them, and for their sake
And for the good which me befell,   230
Even I in my degree will try,
Fair maiden, to requite you well.
But now unrobe yourself; for I
Must pray, ere yet in bed I lie."

Quoth Christabel, "So let it be!"   235
And as the lady bade, did she.
Her gentle limbs did she undress,
And lay down in her loveliness.

But through her brain of weal and woe
So many thoughts moved to and fro,   240
That vain it were her lids to close:
So half-way from the bed she rose,
And on her elbow did recline
To look at the lady Geraldine.

Beneath the lamp the lady bowed,   245
And slowly rolled her eyes around;
Then drawing in her breath aloud,
Like one that shuddered, she unbound
The cincture [6] from beneath her breast:
Her silken robe, and inner vest,   250
Dropt to her feet, and full in view,
Behold! her bosom and half her side— [7]

[6] Belt, or girdle.
[7] Between ll. 252 and 253, three manuscript
versions have this added line: "Are lean and old
and foul of hue," and there is also some authority
for "Hideous, deformed, and pale of hue." Witches
often had beautiful faces and hideous bodies.

A sight to dream of, not to tell!
Oh, shield her! shield sweet Christabel!

Yet Geraldine nor speaks nor stirs; 255
Ah! what a stricken look was hers!
Deep from within she seems half-way
To lift some weight with sick assay,
And eyes the maid and seeks delay;
Then suddenly, as one defied, 260
Collects herself in scorn and pride,
And lay down by the maiden's side!—
And in her arms the maid she took,
        Ah, well-a-day!
And with low voice and doleful look 265
        These words did say:
"In the touch of this bosom there worketh a
        spell,
Which is lord of thy utterance, Christabel!
Thou knowest tonight, and wilt know to-
        morrow,
This mark of my shame, this seal of my sor-
        row: 270
    But vainly thou warrest,
        For this is alone in
    Thy power to declare,
        That in the dim forest
    Thou heard'st a low moaning, 275
And found'st a bright lady, surpassingly
        fair:
And didst bring her home with thee in love
        and in charity,
To shield her and shelter her from the damp
        air."

The Conclusion to Part 1

It was a lovely sight to see
The lady Christabel, when she 280
Was praying at the old oak tree.
    Amid the jagged shadows
    Of mossy leafless boughs,
    Kneeling in the moonlight,
        To make her gentle vows; 285
Her slender palms together pressed,
Heaving sometimes on her breast;
Her face resigned to bliss or bale—
Her face, oh call it fair not pale,
And both blue eyes more bright than
        clear, 290
Each about to have a tear.

With open eyes (ah, woe is me!)
Asleep, and dreaming fearfully,
Fearfully dreaming, yet, I wis
Dreaming that alone, which is— 295
O sorrow and shame! Can this be she,
The lady, who knelt at the old oak tree?
And lo! the worker of these harms,
That holds the maiden in her arms,
Seems to slumber still and mild, 300
As a mother with her child.

A star hath set, a star hath risen,
O Geraldine! since arms of thine
Have been the lovely lady's prison.
O Geraldine! one hour was thine— 305
Thou'st had thy will! By tairn [8] and rill,
The night-birds all that hour were still.
But now they are jubilant anew,
From cliff and tower, tu—whoo! tu—whoo!
Tu—whoo! tu!—whoo! from wood and
        fell! 310

And see! the lady Christabel
Gathers herself from out her trance;
Her limbs relax, her countenance
Grows sad and soft; the smooth thin lids
Close o'er her eyes; and tears she sheds— 315
Large tears that leave the lashes bright!
And oft the while she seems to smile
As infants at a sudden light!

Yea, she doth smile, and she doth weep,
Like a youthful hermitess, 320
Beauteous in a wilderness,
Who, praying always, prays in sleep.
And, if she move unquietly,
Perchance, 'tis but the blood so free
Comes back and tingles in her feet. 325
No doubt she hath a vision sweet.
What if her guardian spirit 'twere?
What if she knew her mother near?
But this she knows, in joys and woes,
That saints will aid if men will call: 330
For the blue sky bends over all!

Part 2

Each matin bell, the baron saith,
Knells us back to a world of death.

[8] Mountain pool.

These words Sir Leoline first said,
When he rose and found his lady dead: 335
These words Sir Leoline will say,
Many a morn to his dying day!

And hence the custom and law began,
That still at dawn the sacristan,
Who duly pulls the heavy bell,   340
Five and forty beads must tell
Between each stroke—a warning knell,
Which not a soul can choose but hear
From Bratha Head to Wyndermere.

Saith Bracy the bard, "So let it knell!   345
And let the drowsy sacristan
Still count as slowly as he can!
There is no lack of such, I ween,
As well fill up the space between."
In Langdale Pike [9] and Witch's lair,   350
And Dungeon-ghyll so foully rent,
With ropes of rock and bells of air
Three sinful sextons' ghosts are pent,
Who all give back, one after t' other,
The death-note to their living brother;   355
And oft too, by the knell offended,
Just as their one! two! three! is ended,
The devil mocks the doleful tale
With a merry peal from Borodale.

The air is still! through mist and cloud   360
That merry peal comes ringing loud;
And Geraldine shakes off her dread,
And rises lightly from the bed;
Puts on her silken vestments white,
And tricks her hair in lovely plight,[10]   365
And nothing doubting of her spell
Awakens the lady Christabel.
"Sleep you, sweet lady Christabel?
I trust that you have rested well."

And Christabel awoke and spied   370
The same who lay down by her side—
Oh, rather say, the same whom she
Raised up beneath the old oak tree!
Nay, fairer yet; and yet more fair!
For she belike hath drunken deep   375
Of all the blessedness of sleep!

[9] Peak. All the places mentioned in this section are in the Lake Country.
[10] Plait.

And while she spake, her looks, her air,
Such gentle thankfulness declare,
That (so it seemed) her girded vests
Grew tight beneath her heaving breasts.   380
"Sure I have sinned!" said Christabel,
"Now heaven be praised if all be well!"
And in low faltering tones, yet sweet,
Did she the lofty lady greet,
With such perplexity of mind   385
As dreams too lively leave behind.

So quickly she rose, and quickly arrayed
Her maiden limbs, and having prayed
That He, who on the cross did groan,
Might wash away her sins unknown,   390
She forthwith led fair Geraldine
To meet her sire, Sir Leoline.

The lovely maid and lady tall
Are pacing both into the hall,
And pacing on through page and groom,   395
Enter the baron's presence-room.

The baron rose, and while he prest
His gentle daughter to his breast,
With cheerful wonder in his eyes
The lady Geraldine espies,   400
And gave such welcome to the same,
As might beseem so bright a dame!

But when he heard the lady's tale,
And when she told her father's name,
Why waxed Sir Leoline so pale,   405
Murmuring o'er the name again,
Lord Roland de Vaux of Tryermaine?

Alas! they had been friends in youth;
But whispering tongues can poison truth;
And constancy lives in realms above;   410
And life is thorny; and youth is vain;
And to be wroth with one we love
Doth work like madness in the brain.
And thus it chanced, as I divine,
With Roland and Sir Leoline.   415
Each spake words of high disdain
And insult to his heart's best brother:
They parted—ne'er to meet again!
But never either found another
To free the hollow heart from paining—   420
They stood aloof, the scars remaining,

Like cliffs which had been rent asunder;
A dreary sea now flows between—
But neither heat, nor frost, nor thunder,
Shall wholly do away, I ween,   425
The marks of that which once hath been.[11]

Sir Leoline, a moment's space,
Stood gazing on the damsel's face:
And the youthful Lord of Tryermaine
Came back upon his heart again.   430

Oh then the baron forgot his age,
His noble heart swelled high with rage;
He swore by the wounds in Jesu's side,
He would proclaim it far and wide,
With trump and solemn heraldry,   435
That they, who thus had wronged the dame,
Were base as spotted infamy!
"And if they dare deny the same,
My herald shall appoint a week,
And let the recreant traitors seek   440
My tourney court—that there and then
I may dislodge their reptile souls
From the bodies and forms of men!"
He spake: his eye in lightning rolls!
For the lady was ruthlessly seized; and he
    kenned   445
In the beautiful lady the child of his friend!

And now the tears were on his face,
And fondly in his arms he took
Fair Geraldine, who met the embrace,
Prolonging it with joyous look.   450
Which when she viewed, a vision fell
Upon the soul of Christabel,
The vision of fear, the touch and pain!
She shrunk and shuddered, and saw again—
(Ah, woe is me! Was it for thee,   455
Thou gentle maid! such sights to see?)

Again she saw that bosom old,
Again she felt that bosom cold,
And drew in her breath with a hissing
    sound:[12]

[11] Lines 408–426: "The best and sweetest lines
that I ever wrote" (Coleridge).
[12] The snake-woman or lamia motif seems to
begin here, as Christabel betrays the "infection" of
Geraldine's touch. Note also ll. 549–554, 583–585,
591, and 602.

Whereat the knight turned wildly
    round,   460
And nothing saw but his own sweet maid
With eyes upraised, as one that prayed.

The touch, the sight, had passed away,
And in its stead that vision blessed,
Which comforted her after-rest   465
While in the lady's arms she lay,
Had put a rapture in her breast,
And on her lips and o'er her eyes
Spread smiles like light!
                        With new surprise,
"What ails then my belovèd child?"   470
The baron said—His daughter mild
Made answer, "All will yet be well!"
I ween, she had no power to tell
Aught else: so mighty was the spell.

Yet he, who saw this Geraldine,   475
Had deemed her sure a thing divine.
Such sorrow with such grace she blended,
As if she feared she had offended
Sweet Christabel, that gentle maid!
And with such lowly tones she prayed,   480
She might be sent without delay
Home to her father's mansion.

                                        "Nay!
Nay, by my soul!" said Leoline.
"Ho! Bracy, the bard, the charge be thine!
Go thou, with music sweet and loud,   485
And take two steeds with trappings proud,
And take the youth whom thou lov'st best
To bear thy harp, and learn thy song,
And clothe you both in solemn vest,
And over the mountains haste along,   490
Lest wandering folk, that are abroad,
Detain you on the valley road.

"And when he has crossed the Irthing flood,
My merry bard! he hastes, he hastes
Up Knorren Moor, through Halegarth
    Wood,   495
And reaches soon that castle good
Which stands and threatens Scotland's wastes.

"Bard Bracy! bard Bracy! your horses are
    fleet,
Ye must ride up the hall, your music so sweet,

More loud than your horses' echoing
    feet!   500
And loud and loud to Lord Roland call,
Thy daughter is safe in Langdale hall!
Thy beautiful daughter is safe and free—
Sir Leoline greets thee thus through me.
He bids thee come without delay   505
With all thy numerous array;
And take thy lovely daughter home:
And he will meet thee on the way
With all his numerous array
White with their panting palfreys' foam: 510
And by mine honor! I will say,
That I repent me of the day
When I spake words of fierce disdain
To Roland de Vaux of Tryermaine!—
For since that evil hour hath flown,   515
Many a summer's sun hath shone;
Yet ne'er found I a friend again
Like Roland de Vaux of Tryermaine."

The lady fell, and clasped his knees,
Her face upraised, her eyes o'erflowing;   520
And Bracy replied, with faltering voice,
His gracious hail on all bestowing!—
"Thy words, thou sire of Christabel,
Are sweeter than my harp can tell;
Yet might I gain a boon of thee,   525
This day my journey should not be,
So strange a dream hath come to me;
That I had vowed with music loud
To clear yon wood from thing unblessed,
Warned by a vision in my rest!   530
For in my sleep I saw that dove,
That gentle bird, whom thou dost love,
And call'st by thy own daughter's name—
Sir Leoline! I saw the same
Fluttering, and uttering fearful moan,   535
Among the green herbs in the forest alone.
Which when I saw and when I heard,
I wondered what might ail the bird;
For nothing near it could I see,
Save the grass and green herbs underneath
    the old tree.   540

"And in my dream methought I went
To search out what might there be found;
And what the sweet bird's trouble meant,
That thus lay fluttering on the ground.
I went and peered, and could descry   545

No cause for her distressful cry;
But yet for her dear lady's sake
I stooped, methought, the dove to take,
When lo! I saw a bright green snake
Coiled around its wings and neck.   550
Green as the herbs on which it couched,
Close by the dove's its head it crouched;
And with the dove it heaves and stirs,
Swelling its neck as she swelled hers!
I woke; it was the midnight hour,   555
The clock was echoing in the tower;
But though my slumber was gone by,
This dream it would not pass away—
It seems to live upon my eye!
And thence I vowed this self-same day,   560
With music strong and saintly song
To wander through the forest bare,
Lest aught unholy loiter there."

Thus Bracy said: the baron, the while,
Half-listening heard him with a smile;   565
Then turned to Lady Geraldine,
His eyes made up of wonder and love;
And said in courtly accents fine,
"Sweet maid, Lord Roland's beauteous dove,
With arms more strong than harp or
    song,   570
Thy sire and I will crush the snake!"
He kissed her forehead as he spake,
And Geraldine, in maiden wise,
Casting down her large bright eyes,
With blushing cheek and courtesy fine   575
She turned her from Sir Leoline;
Softly gathering up her train,
That o'er her right arm fell again;
And folded her arms across her chest,
And couched her head upon her breast,   580
And looked askance at Christabel—
Jesu, Maria, shield her well!

A snake's small eye blinks dull and shy,
And the lady's eyes they shrunk in her head,
Each shrunk up to a serpent's eye,   585
And with somewhat of malice, and more of
    dread,
At Christabel she looked askance!—
One moment—and the sight was fled!
But Christabel in dizzy trance
Stumbling on the unsteady ground   590
Shuddered aloud, with a hissing sound;

And Geraldine again turned round,
And like a thing that sought relief,
Full of wonder and full of grief,
She rolled her large bright eyes divine   595
Wildly on Sir Leoline.

The maid, alas! her thoughts are gone,
She nothing sees—no sight but one!
The maid, devoid of guile and sin,
I know not how, in fearful wise   600
So deeply had she drunken in
That look, those shrunken serpent eyes,
That all her features were resigned
To this sole image in her mind;
And passively did imitate   605
That look of dull and treacherous hate!
And thus she stood, in dizzy trance,
Still picturing that look askance
With forced unconscious sympathy
Full before her father's view—   610
As far as such a look could be
In eyes so innocent and blue!

And when the trance was o'er, the maid
Paused awhile, and inly prayed:
Then falling at the baron's feet,   615
"By my mother's soul do I entreat
That thou this woman send away!"
She said: and more she could not say:
For what she knew she could not tell,
O'ermastered by the mighty spell.   620

Why is thy cheek so wan and wild,
Sir Leoline? Thy only child
Lies at thy feet, thy joy, thy pride,
So fair, so innocent, so mild;
The same, for whom thy lady died!   625
O, by the pangs of her dear mother
Think thou no evil of thy child!
For her, and thee, and for no other,
She prayed the moment ere she died:
Prayed that the babe for whom she died,   630
Might prove her dear lord's joy and pride!
That prayer her deadly pangs beguiled,
   Sir Leoline!
And wouldst thou wrong thy only child,
   Her child and thine?   635

Within the baron's heart and brain
If thoughts, like these, had any share,
They only swelled his rage and pain,
And did but work confusion there.
His heart was cleft with pain and rage,   640
His cheeks they quivered, his eyes were wild,
Dishonored thus in his old age;
Dishonored by his only child,
And all his hospitality
To the wronged daughter of his friend   645
By more than woman's jealousy
Brought thus to a disgraceful end—
He rolled his eye with stern regard
Upon the gentle minstrel bard,
And said in tones abrupt, austere—   650
"Why, Bracy! dost thou loiter here?
I bade thee hence!" The bard obeyed;
And turning from his own sweet maid,
The agèd knight, Sir Leoline,
Led forth the lady Geraldine!   655
(1798–1802; 1816)

Here is the planned continuation as reported by Coleridge's good friend Dr. Gilman, who said it represented the poet's intention:

Over the mountains, the bard, as directed by Sir Leoline, hastes with his disciple; but in consequence of one of those inundations supposed to be common to this country, the spot only where the castle once stood is discovered—the edifice itself being washed away. He determines to return. Geraldine, being acquainted with all that is passing, like the weird sisters in *Macbeth*, vanishes. Reappearing, however, she awaits the return of the bard, exciting in the meantime, by her wily arts, all the anger she could rouse in the baron's breast, as well as that jealousy of which he is described to have been susceptible. The old bard and the youth at length arrive, and therefore she can no longer personate the character of Geraldine, the daughter of Lord Roland de Vaux, but changes her appearance to that of the accepted though absent lover of Christabel. Now ensues a courtship most distressing to Christabel, who feels, she knows not why, great disgust for her once favored knight. This coldness is very painful to the baron, who has no more conception than herself of the supernatural transformation. She at last yields to her father's entreaties, and consents to approach the altar with this hated suitor. The real lover, returning, enters at this moment, and produces the ring which she had once given him in sign of her betrothment. Thus defeated, the super-natural being Geraldine disappears. As predicted, the castle bell tolls, the mother's voice is heard, and, to the exceeding great joy of the parties, the rightful marriage takes place, after which follows a reconciliation and explanation between the father and daughter.

STUDY AIDS: 1. Coleridge said that the meter of *Christabel* was "founded on a new principle: namely, that of counting in each line the accents, not the syllables. Though the latter may vary from seven to twelve, yet in each line the accents will be found to be only four. Nevertheless, this occasional variation of syllables is not introduced wantonly, or for the mere ends of convenience, but in correspondence with some transition in the nature of the imagery or passion." How many illustrations can you find of such purposeful variation? What does this metrical principle add to the over-all effect of the poem? (It was not, however, a "new principle"; it is the basis, for example, of Old English verse and is found occasionally in later English poetry.)

2. How does Coleridge's treatment of the supernatural in *Christabel* compare with his treatment in *The Ancient Mariner*? Which poem has the more effective use of appropriate imagery?

3. What do you think of the continuation of the poem as reported by James Gilman? Does this continuation seem to you to be in keeping with the poem?

Dejection: An Ode

Dejection: An Ode has been called Coleridge's farewell to poetry. Although he continued to write poetry until his death, his interests turned more and more to criticism and philosophy (the "abstruse research" of l. 89), and he never again displayed the poetic power that he showed during the years 1797–1802.

In the ode Coleridge explains why he is losing his poetic creativity. Various "afflictions" (l. 82) have robbed him of joy, the motivating power of the imagination, which in turn is the mainspring of true poetry. As a result he can no longer feel the beauty of the world, though he can still see it (ll. 37–38); and it is what is inside the poet that counts, the "shaping spirit of imagination" (l. 86), not the external world.

Late, late yestreen I saw the new moon,
With the old moon in her arms;
And I fear, I fear, my master dear!
We shall have a deadly storm.
Ballad of Sir Patrick Spence

I

Well! If the bard was weather-wise, who made
The grand old ballad of Sir Patrick Spence,
This night, so tranquil now, will not go
    hence
Unroused by winds, that ply a busier trade
Than those which mold yon cloud in lazy
    flakes,   5
Or the dull sobbing draft, that moans and
    rakes
Upon the strings of this Æolian lute[1]
Which better far were mute.

[1] A box fitted with strings, which makes music as the wind blows over them. The Aeolian lute was a favorite image with the Romantic poets. Why?

For lo! the new-moon winter-bright!
And overspread with phantom light,   10
(With swimming phantom light o'erspread
But rimmed and circled by a silver thread)
I see the old moon in her lap,[2] foretelling
    The coming-on of rain and squally blast.
And oh! that even now the gust were
    swelling,   15
And the slant night-shower driving loud
    and fast!
Those sounds which oft have raised me, whilst
    they awed,
    And sent my soul abroad,
Might now perhaps their wonted impulse
    give,
Might startle this dull pain, and make it
    move and live!   20

[2] During the time of the new moon, the faint outline of the entire moon can often be seen. Such a phenomenon used to be regarded as forecasting a storm. Why does Coleridge want the storm to come?

2

A grief without a pang, void, dark, and drear,
A stifled, drowsy, unimpassioned grief,
Which finds no natural outlet, no relief,
In word, or sigh, or tear—
O lady! in this wan and heartless mood,   25
To other thoughts by yonder throstle wooed,
All this long eve, so balmy and serene,
Have I been gazing on the western sky,
And its peculiar tint of yellow green:
And still I gaze—and with how blank an
eye!   30
And those thin clouds above, in flakes and
bars,
That give away their motion to the stars;
Those stars, that glide behind them or be-
tween,
Now sparkling, now bedimmed, but always
seen:
Yon crescent moon, as fixed as if it grew   35
In its own cloudless, starless lake of blue;
I see them all so excellently fair,
I see, not feel, how beautiful they are!

3

My genial spirits fail;
And what can these avail   40
To lift the smothering weight from off my
breast?
It were a vain endeavor,
Though I should gaze for ever
On that green light that lingers in the west:
I may not hope from outward forms to
win   45
The passion and the life, whose fountains
are within.

4

O lady! we receive but what we give,
And in our life alone does nature live:
Ours is her wedding-garment, ours her
shroud!
And would we aught behold, of higher
worth,   50
Than that inanimate cold world allowed
To the poor loveless ever-anxious crowd,
Ah! from the soul itself must issue forth
A light, a glory, a fair luminous cloud
Enveloping the earth—   55

And from the soul itself must there be sent
A sweet and potent voice, of its own birth,
Of all sweet sounds the life and element! [3]

5

O pure of heart! thou need'st not ask of me
What this strong music in the soul may
be!   60
What, and wherein it doth exist,
This light, this glory, this fair luminous mist,
This beautiful and beauty-making power.
Joy, virtuous lady! Joy that ne'er was given,
Save to the pure, and in their purest hour,   65
Life, and life's effluence, cloud at once and
shower,—
Joy, lady! is the spirit and the power,
Which, wedding nature to us, gives in dower
A new earth and new heaven,
Undreamt of by the sensual and the
proud;   70
Joy is the sweet voice, joy the luminous
cloud:—
We in ourselves rejoice!
And thence flows all that charms or ear or
sight,
All melodies the echoes of that voice,
All colors a suffusion from that light.   75

6

There was a time when, though my path was
rough,
This joy within me dallied with distress,
And all misfortunes were but as the stuff
Whence fancy made me dreams of hap-
piness:
For hope grew round me, like the twining
vine,   80
And fruits, and foliage, not my own, seemed
mine.
But now afflictions [4] bow me down to earth:

[3] Lines 45-58 give the reason why natural beauty
cannot rid the poet of his grief. We impose our life
and feelings upon nature, not she upon us; and
we can wed nature to us only through joy,
which is the motivating power of the creative
imagination (st. 5).

[4] In the first, and much longer, version of this
ode, these "afflictions" are made embarrassingly
clear, particularly Coleridge's unhappiness with his
wife and his hopeless love for Sarah Hutchinson,
Wordsworth's sister-in-law, to whom the original
version was addressed.

Nor care I that they rob me of my mirth;
   But oh! each visitation
Suspends what nature gave me at my
      birth,   85
   My shaping spirit of imagination.[5]
For not to think of what I needs must feel,
   But to be still and patient, all I can;
And haply by abstruse research to steal
   From my own nature all the natural
      man—   90
   This was my sole resource, my only plan:
Till that which suits a part infects the whole,
And now is almost grown the habit of my
   soul.

7

Hence, viper thoughts, that coil around my
   mind,
   Reality's dark dream!   95
I turn from you, and listen to the wind,
   Which long has raved unnoticed. What a
   scream
Of agony by torture lengthened out
That lute sent forth! Thou wind, that ravest
   without,
   Bare crag, or mountain-tairn,[6] or
      blasted tree,   100
Or pine-grove whither woodman never clomb,
Or lonely house, long held the witches' home,
   Methinks were fitter instruments for thee,
Mad lutanist! who in this month of showers,
Of dark-brown gardens, and of peeping
      flowers,   105
Mak'st devils' yule, with worse than wintry
   song,
The blossoms, buds, and timorous leaves
   among.
Thou actor, perfect in all tragic sounds!
Thou mighty poet, e'en to frenzy bold!
   What tellest thou now about?   110
      'Tis of the rushing of an host in rout,
With groans, of trampled men, with smart-
   ing wounds—
At once they groan with pain, and shudder
   with the cold!

But hush! there is a pause of deepest silence!
   And all that noise, as of a rushing
      crowd,   115
With groans, and tremulous shudderings—all
   is over—
It tells another tale, with sounds less deep
   and loud!
   A tale of less affright,
   And tempered with delight,
As Otway's [7] self had framed the tender
      lay,—   120
   'Tis of a little child
   Upon a lonesome wild,
Not far from home, but she hath lost her
   way:
And now moans low in bitter grief and fear,
And now screams loud, and hopes to make her
      mother hear.   125

8

'Tis midnight, but small thoughts have I of
   sleep:
Full seldom may my friend such vigils keep!
Visit her, gentle sleep! with wings of healing,
   And may this storm be but a mountain-
   birth,
May all the stars hang bright above her
   dwelling,   130
   Silent as though they watched the sleeping
   earth!
   With light heart may she rise,
   Gay fancy, cheerful eyes,
   Joy lift her spirit, joy attune her voice;
To her may all things live, from pole to
      pole,   135
Their life the eddying of her living soul!
   O simple spirit, guided from above,
Dear lady! friend devoutest of my choice,
Thus mayest thou ever, evermore rejoice.
(1802)

STUDY AIDS: 1. Both Wordsworth's *Ode:
Intimations of Immortality* and his *Resolution
and Independence* have been regarded as answers

---

[5] An important tenet of the Romantic creed:
The imagination creates; it is not just a passive
receiver of impressions.
   [6] A small lake or pool.

[7] Otway was a seventeenth-century English
dramatist. But the story referred to in ll. 121–125 is
obviously a poem (*Lucy Gray*) by Wordsworth;
and indeed, in the original version of the *Ode,*
"William" was used instead of "Otway."

to Coleridge's *Dejection: An Ode*. How do they answer it? How much of Wordsworth's *Ode* is a kind of repetition of the mood of Coleridge's *Ode*? Which one of the "answers" do you regard as the more satisfactory?

2. Coleridge wants to find an outlet for his "stifled, drowsy, unimpassioned grief" through the storm. Does he find such an outlet through the poem itself? Does the ending of the poem seem to indicate such a resolution of his problem?

Biographia Literaria

The *Biographia Literaria* began as a preface to Coleridge's *Sibylline Leaves*, a book of poems published in 1817. It soon outgrew its original purpose, however, expanding into two volumes of philosophy and criticism and containing little of the literary biography, or autobiography, suggested by the title. The *Biographia Literaria* is both general and specific in its topics, passing from a consideration of the nature of poetry and of the poetical genius to a detailed analysis of Wordsworth's particular faults and excellences as a poet. Despite its somewhat disorganized nature, its frequently abstruse argument ("I wish he would explain his explanation," complained Byron), and its miscellaneous content, it remains the best and most sustained expression of Coleridge's critical powers.

The famous fourteenth chapter begins with the well-known account of the Wordsworth-Coleridge partnership in the production of the *Lyrical Ballads*. Then it passes on to a broader consideration of what makes a poet and a poem. In this discussion Coleridge takes issue with Wordsworth's treatment of meter in the *Preface*, emphasizing the organic nature of a poem and the unifying power of the poetic imagination.

Chapter 14

During the first year [1] that Mr. Wordsworth and I were neighbors, our conversations turned frequently on the two cardinal points of poetry: the power of exciting the sympathy of the reader by a faithful adherence to the truth of nature, and the power of giving the interest of novelty by the modifying colors of imagination. The sudden charm, which ac- 10 cidents of light and shade, which moonlight or sunset, diffused over a known and familiar landscape, appeared to represent the practicability of combining both. These are the poetry of nature. The thought suggested 15 itself (to which of us I do not recollect) that a series of poems might be composed of two sorts. In the one, the incidents and agents were to be, in part at least, supernatural; and the excellence aimed at was to consist in the 20 interesting of the affections by the dramatic truth of such emotions as would naturally

accompany such situations, supposing them real. And real in this sense they have been to every human being who, from whatever source of delusion, has at any time believed 5 himself under supernatural agency. For the second class, subjects were to be chosen from ordinary life; the characters and incidents were to be such as will be found in every village and its vicinity where there is a medita- 10 tive and feeling mind to seek after them or to notice them when they present themselves.

In this idea originated the plan of the *Lyrical Ballads*; in which it was agreed that my endeavors should be directed to 15 persons and characters supernatural, or at least romantic; yet so as to transfer from our inward nature a human interest and a semblance of truth sufficient to procure for these shadows of imagination that willing sus- 20 pension of disbelief for the moment, which constitutes poetic faith. Mr. Wordsworth, on the other hand, was to propose to himself as his object, to give the charm of novelty to things of every day, and to excite a feeling 25 analogous to the supernatural by awakening the mind's attention from the lethargy of

[1] 1797–1798. The first two and a half paragraphs are the best account we have of the division of labor which Wordsworth and Coleridge set for themselves in composing the *Lyrical Ballads*.

custom and directing it to the loveliness and the wonders of the world before us; an inexhaustible treasure, but for which, in consequence of the film of familiarity and selfish solicitude, we have eyes, yet see not, ears that hear not, and hearts that neither feel nor understand.

With this view I wrote the *Ancient Mariner,* and was preparing, among other poems, the *Dark Ladie* and the *Christabel,* in which I should have more nearly realized my ideal than I had done in my first attempt. But Mr. Wordsworth's industry had proved so much more successful, and the number of his poems so much greater,[2] that my compositions, instead of forming a balance, appeared rather an interpolation of heterogeneous matter. Mr. Wordsworth added two or three poems[3] written in his own character, in the impassioned, lofty, and sustained diction which is characteristic of his genius. In this form the *Lyrical Ballads* were published; and were presented by him, as an experiment, whether subjects, which from their nature rejected the usual ornaments and extracolloquial style of poems in general, might not be so managed in the language of ordinary life as to produce the pleasurable interest which it is the peculiar business of poetry to impart. To the second edition he added a preface of considerable length; in which, notwithstanding some passages of apparently a contrary import, he was understood to contend for the extension of this style to poetry of all kinds, and to reject as vicious and indefensible all phrases and forms of style that were not included in what he (unfortunately, I think, adopting an equivocal expression) called the language of real life. From this preface prefixed to poems in which it was impossible to deny the presence of original genius, however mistaken its direction might be deemed, arose the whole long-continued controversy.[4] For from the

conjunction of perceived power with supposed heresy I explain the inveteracy and in some instances, I grieve to say, the acrimonious passions, with which the controversy has been conducted by the assailants.

Had Mr. Wordsworth's poems been the silly, the childish things which they were for a long time described as being; had they been really distinguished from the compositions of other poets merely by meanness of language and inanity of thought; had they indeed contained nothing more than what is found in the parodies and pretended imitations of them; they must have sunk at once, a dead weight, into the slough of oblivion, and have dragged the preface along with them. But year after year increased the number of Mr. Wordsworth's admirers. They were found, too, not in the lower classes of the reading public, but chiefly among young men of strong sensibility and meditative minds; and their admiration (inflamed perhaps in some degree by opposition) was distinguished by its intensity, I might almost say, by its religious fervor. These facts and the intellectual energy of the author, which was more or less consciously felt where it was outwardly and even boisterously denied, meeting with sentiments of aversion to his opinions, and of alarm at their consequences, produced an eddy of criticism, which would of itself have borne up the poems by the violence with which it whirled them round and round. With many parts of this preface, in the sense attributed to them, and which the words undoubtedly seem to authorize, I never concurred; but, on the contrary, objected to them as erroneous in principle and as contradictory (in appearance at least) both to other parts of the same preface and to the author's own practice in the greater number of the poems themselves. Mr. Wordsworth, in his recent collection, has, I find, degraded this prefatory disquisition to the end of his second volume, to be read or not at the reader's choice. But he has not, as far as I can discover, announced any change in his poetic creed. At all events, considering it as the source of a controversy in which I have been honored more than I deserve by the frequent conjunction of my

[2] Of the twenty-three poems in the first edition of the *Lyrical Ballads* (1798), nineteen were by Wordsworth, only four by Coleridge—but one of the four was *The Ancient Mariner,* the longest poem in the volume.
[3] Especially *Tintern Abbey.*
[4] Over Wordsworth's poetical creed as expressed in the *Preface.*

name with his, I think it expedient to declare, once for all, in what points I coincide with his opinions and in what points I altogether differ. But in order to render myself intelligible, I must previously, in as few words as possible, explain my ideas, first, of a poem; and secondly, of poetry itself, in kind and in essence.

The office of philosophical disquisition consists in just distinction; while it is the privilege of the philosopher to preserve himself constantly aware that distinction is not division. In order to obtain adequate notions of any truth, we must intellectually separate its distinguishable parts; and this is the technical process of philosophy. But having so done, we must then restore them in our conceptions to the unity in which they actually co-exist; and this is the result of philosophy. A poem contains the same elements as a prose composition; the difference, therefore, must consist in a different combination of them, in consequence of a different object proposed. According to the difference of the object will be the difference of the combination. It is possible that the object may be merely to facilitate the recollection of any given facts or observations by artificial arrangement; and the composition will be a poem, merely because it is distinguished from prose by meter, or by rime, or by both conjointly. In this, the lowest sense, a man might attribute the name of a poem to the well-known enumeration of the days in the several months:

Thirty days hath September,
April, June, and November, etc.

and others of the same class and purpose. And as a particular pleasure is found in anticipating the recurrence of sounds and quantities, all compositions that have this charm superadded, whatever be their contents, *may* be entitled poems.

So much for the superficial form. A difference of object and contents supplies an additional ground of distinction. The immediate purpose may be the communication of truths: either of truth absolute and demonstrable, as in works of science; or of facts experienced and recorded, as in history. Pleasure, and that of the highest and most permanent kind, may result from the attainment of the end; but it is not itself the immediate end. In other works the communication of pleasure may be the immediate purpose; and though truth, either moral or intellectual, ought to be the ultimate end, yet this will distinguish the character of the author, not the class to which the work belongs. Blessed indeed is that state of society, in which the immediate purpose would be baffled by the perversion of the proper ultimate end; in which no charm of diction or imagery could exempt the Bathyllus even of an Anacreon, or the Alexis of Virgil, from disgust and aversion!

But the communication of pleasure may be the immediate object of a work not metrically composed; and that object may have been in a high degree attained, as in novels and romances. Would then the mere superaddition of meter, with or without rime, entitle these to the name of poems? The answer is, that nothing can permanently please which does not contain in itself the reason why it is so, and not otherwise. If meter be superadded, all other parts must be made consonant with it. They must be such as to justify the perpetual and distinct attention to each part which an exact correspondent recurrence of accent and sound are calculated to excite. The final definition then, so deduced, may be thus worded. A poem is that species of composition which is opposed to works of science by proposing for its immediate object pleasure, not truth; and from all other species (having this object in common with it) it is discriminated by proposing to itself such delight from the whole as is compatible with a distinct gratification from each component part.

Controversy is not seldom excited in consequence of the disputants' attaching each a different meaning to the same word; and in few instances has this been more striking than in disputes concerning the present subject. If a man chooses to call every composition a poem which is rime, or measure, or both, I must leave his opinion uncontroverted. The distinction is at least competent to characterize the writer's intention. If it were subjoined, that the whole is likewise entertaining or affecting as a tale, or as a series of interesting reflections, I of course admit this as another fit ingredient of a poem and an additional merit. But if the definition sought for be that of a legitimate poem, I answer, it must be one the parts of which mutually support and explain each other; all in their proportion harmonizing with and supporting the purpose and known influences of metrical arrangement. The philosophic critics of all ages coincide with the ultimate judgment of all countries in equally denying the praises of a just poem, on the one hand, to a series of striking lines or distichs, each of which, absorbing the whole attention of the reader to itself, disjoins it from its context and makes it a separate whole, instead of a harmonizing part; and on the other hand, to an unsustained composition from which the reader collects rapidly the general result unattracted by the component parts. The reader should be carried forward, not merely or chiefly by the mechanical impulse of curiosity, or by a restless desire to arrive at the final solution; but by the pleasurable activity of mind excited by the attractions of the journey itself. Like the motion of a serpent, which the Egyptians made the emblem of intellectual power; or like the path of sound through the air, at every step he pauses and half recedes, and from the retrogressive movement collects the force which again carries him onward. *Praecipitandus est liber spiritus*,[5] says Petronius Arbiter most happily. The epithet, *liber*, here balances the preceding verb; and it is not easy to conceive more meaning condensed in fewer words.

But if this should be admitted as a satisfactory character of a poem, we have still to seek for a definition of poetry. The writings of Plato and Bishop Taylor, and the *Theoria Sacra* of Burnet furnish undeniable proofs that poetry of the highest kind may exist without meter, and even without the contradistinguishing objects of a poem. The first chapter of

Isaiah (indeed a very large proportion of the whole book) is poetry in the most emphatic sense; yet it would be not less irrational than strange to assert that pleasure, and not truth, was the immediate object of the prophet. In short, whatever specific import we attach to the word poetry, there will be found involved in it, as a necessary consequence, that a poem of any length neither can be, nor ought to be, all poetry. Yet if a harmonious whole is to be produced, the remaining parts must be preserved in keeping with the poetry; and this can be not otherwise effected than by such a studied selection and artificial arrangement as will partake of one, though not a peculiar property of poetry. And this again can be no other than the property of exciting a more continuous and equal attention than the language of prose aims at, whether colloquial or written.

My own conclusions of the nature of poetry, in the strictest use of the word, have been in part anticipated in the preceding disquisition on the fancy and imagination. What is poetry? is so nearly the same question with, what is a poet? that the answer to the one is involved in the solution of the other. For it is a distinction resulting from the poetic genius itself, which sustains and modifies the images, thoughts, and emotions of the poet's own mind. The poet,[6] described in ideal perfection, brings the whole soul of man into activity, with the subordination of its faculties to each other, according to their relative worth and dignity. He diffuses a tone and spirit of unity that blends and (as it were) fuses each into each, by that synthetic and magical power to which we have exclusively appropriated the name of imagination. This power, first put in action by the will and understanding, and retained under their irremissive, though gentle and unno-

[5] "The free spirit should be impelled onward." Petronius was a Roman satirist of the first century A.D.

[6] The rest of this paragraph contains Coleridge's famous definition of a poet and thus of poetry. For Coleridge the key to the poet's power lies in the "balance or reconciliation of opposite or discordant qualities" he attains. This reconciliation is made through the fusing power of the imagination, a power that is achieved partly through metaphorical language. (Cf. *Dejection: An Ode*, l. 86: the "shaping spirit of imagination.")

ticed, control (*laxis effertur habenis* [7]) reveals itself in the balance or reconciliation of opposite or discordant qualities: of sameness, with difference; of the general, with the concrete; the idea, with the image; the individual, with the representative; the sense of novelty and freshness, with old and familiar objects; a more than usual state of emotion, with more than usual order; judgment ever awake and steady self-possession with enthusiasm and feeling profound or vehement; and while it blends and harmonizes the natural and the artificial, still subordinates art to nature; the manner to the matter; and our admiration of the poet to our sympathy with the poetry. "Doubtless," as Sir John Davies observes of the soul (and his words may with slight alteration be applied, and even more appropriately, to the poetic imagination)— [8]

Doubtless this could not be, but that she turns 20
Bodies to spirit by sublimation strange,
As fire converts to fire, the things it burns,
As we our food into our nature change.

From their gross matter she abstracts their
    forms, 25

And draws a kind of quintessence from things;
Which to her proper nature she transforms
To bear them light on her celestial wings.

Thus does she, when from individual states 5
She doth abstract the universal kinds;
Which then re-clothed in divers names and
    fates
Steal access through our senses to our minds.

Finally, good sense is the body of poetic genius, fancy its drapery, motion its life, and imagination the soul that is everywhere, and in each; and forms all into one graceful and intelligent whole.
(1815–16; 1817)

STUDY AIDS: 1. What are the "two cardinal points of poetry" as stated by Coleridge? Can you think of others not covered by these two?
2. Wordsworth had said in his preface to the *Lyrical Ballads* that there is no essential difference between poetry and good prose—that poetry is only good prose with meter "superadded." What is Coleridge's opinion on this point? To Coleridge, what is a poem, and what are the principal aims of poetry? What is the function of imagination in the creation of poetry?

Charles Lamb
(1775–1834)

"GENTLE-HEARTED CHARLES," COLERIDGE CALLED HIM; AND WORDSWORTH WROTE OF HIM: "O, he was good, if e'er a good man lived." Lamb's goodness and gentleness shine through all his writing, especially the informal essays by which he is best remembered.

"You may extract honey from everything," Lamb advised a friend; "do not go a-gathering after gall." Charles Lamb seldom did. And yet his life was filled with tragedy that would have conquered a less gallant spirit. Poverty prevented him from continuing his schooling beyond his fourteenth year. Although he fell in love when he was twenty, marriage proved impossible because of the insanity that ran in his family. Lamb himself had an attack of madness in 1795 and was temporarily confined to an institution. The next

---

[7] "Carried along with slack reins."
[8] The following poem is from Sir John Davies' "On the Soul of Man," a section of *Nosce Teipsum* (1599).

year, in a fit of lunacy, his sister Mary stabbed and killed their mother. Although Mary regained her sanity, she was subject to recurrent attacks all her life; and Charles, unaided by a richer brother, took upon himself the burden of caring for her, facing the responsibility without complaint and with his characteristic quiet courage. He did not allow his monotonous work as a bookkeeper for the East India Company to keep him from the pursuit of culture and a program of wide reading and steady writing, writing which culminated in the *Essays of Elia* ("Elia" being Lamb's pen name) of 1823 and 1833. Whimsical, romantic, and sentimental, filled with odd turns of thought and phrase, these essays make up in graciousness and insight what they lack in weight and high seriousness. Usually they are as unsystematic as a rambling walk through a fragrant meadow, but in them there is the charm of the man himself, "the prince of English essayists."

A Bachelor's Complaint of the Behavior of Married People

As a single man, I have spent a good deal of my time in noting down the infirmities of married people, to console myself for those superior pleasures, which they tell me I have lost by remaining as I am.

I cannot say that the quarrels of men and their wives ever made any great impression upon me, or had much tendency to strengthen me in those anti-social resolutions, which I took up long ago upon more substantial considerations. What oftenest offends me at the houses of married persons where I visit, is an error of quite a different description;—it is that they are too loving.

Not too loving neither: that does not explain my meaning. Besides, why should that offend me? The very act of separating themselves from the rest of the world, to have the fuller enjoyment of each other's society, implies that they prefer one another to all the world.

But what I complain of is, that they carry this preference so undisguisedly, they perk it up in the faces of us single people so shamelessly, you cannot be in their company a moment without being made to feel, by some indirect hint or open avowal, that *you* are not the object of this preference. Now there are some things which give no offense, while implied or taken for granted merely; but expressed, there is much offense in them. If a man were to accost the first homely-featured or plain-dressed young woman of

his acquaintance, and tell her bluntly, that she was not handsome or rich enough for him, and he could not marry her, he would deserve to be kicked for his ill manners; yet no less is implied in the fact, that having access and opportunity of putting the question to her, he has never yet thought fit to do it. The young woman understands this as clearly as if it were put into words; but no reasonable young woman would think of making this a ground of a quarrel. Just as little right have a married couple to tell me by speeches and looks that are scarce less plain than speeches, that I am not the happy man,—the lady's choice. It is enough that I know that I am not: I do not want this perpetual reminding.

The display of superior knowledge or riches may be made sufficiently mortifying: but these admit of a palliative. The knowledge which is brought out to insult me, may accidentally improve me; and in the rich man's houses and pictures,—his parks and gardens, I have a temporary usufruct at least. But the display of married happiness has none of these palliatives; it is throughout pure, unrecompensed, unqualified insult.

Marriage by its best title is a monopoly, and not of the least invidious sort. It is the cunning of most possessors of any exclusive privilege to keep their advantage as much out of sight as possible, that their less favored neighbors, seeing little of the benefit, may the less be disposed to question the right. But these married monopolists thrust the most obnoxious part of their patent into our faces.

Nothing is to me more distasteful than that entire complacency and satisfaction which beam in the countenances of a new-married couple,—in that of the lady particularly; it tells you, that her lot is disposed of in this world; that *you* can have no hopes of her. It is true, I have none; nor wishes either, perhaps; but this is one of those truths which ought, as I said before, to be taken for granted, not expressed.

The excessive airs which those people give themselves, founded on the ignorance of us unmarried people, would be more offensive if they were less irrational. We will allow them to understand the mysteries belonging to their own craft better than we who have not had the happiness to be made free of the company: but their arrogance is not content within these limits. If a single person presume to offer his opinion in their presence, though upon the most indifferent subject, he is immediately silenced as an incompetent person. Nay, a young married lady of my acquaintance who, the best of the jest was, had not changed her condition above a fortnight before, in a question on which I had the misfortune to differ from her, respecting the properest mode of breeding oysters for the London market, had the assurance to ask with a sneer, how such an old bachelor as I could pretend to know anything about such matters.

But what I have spoken of hitherto is nothing to the airs these creatures give themselves when they come, as they generally do, to have children. When I consider how little of a rarity children are—that every street and blind alley swarms with them—that the poorest people commonly have them in most abundance—that there are few marriages that are not blest with at least one of these bargains —how often they turn out ill, and defeat the fond hopes of their parents, taking to vicious courses, which end in poverty, disgrace, the gallows, etc.—I cannot for my life tell what cause for pride there can possibly be in having them. If they were young phœnixes, in-

deed, that were born but one in a year, there might be a pretext. But when they are so common——

I do not advert to the insolent merit which they assume with their husbands on these occasions. Let *them* look to that. But why *we,* who are not their natural-born subjects, should be expected to bring our spices, myrrh, and incense—our tribute and homage of admiration—I do not see.

"Like as the arrows in the hand of the giant, even so are the young children": so says the excellent office in our prayer-book appointed for the churching of women. "Happy is the man that hath his quiver full of them": So say I; but then don't let him discharge his quiver upon us that are weaponless;—let them be arrows, but not to gall and stick us. I have generally observed that these arrows are double-headed: they have two forks, to be sure to hit with one or the other. As for instance, where you come into a house which is full of children, if you happen to take no notice of them (you are thinking of something else, perhaps, and turn a deaf ear to their innocent caresses), you are set down as untractable, morose, a hater of children. On the other hand, if you find them more than usually engaging—if you are taken with their pretty manners, and set about in earnest to romp and play with them, some pretext or other is sure to be found for sending them out of the room; they are too noisy or boisterous, or Mr.—— does not like children. With one or other of these forks the arrow is sure to hit you.

I could forgive their jealousy, and dispense with toying with their brats, if it gives them any pain; but I think it unreasonable to be called upon to *love* them, where I see no occasion—to love a whole family, perhaps eight, nine, or ten, indiscriminately—to love all the pretty dears, because children are so engaging!

I know there is a proverb, "Love me, love my dog": that is not always so very practicable, particularly if the dog be set upon you to tease you or snap at you in sport. But a dog, or a lesser thing—any inanimate substance, as a keepsake, a watch or a ring, a tree, or the place where we last parted when my friend went away upon a long absence, I can make shift to love, because I love him, and anything that reminds me of him; provided it be in its nature indifferent, and apt to receive whatever hue fancy can give it. But children have a real character, and an essential being of themselves: they are amiable or unamiable *per se*; I must love or hate them as I see cause for either in their qualities. A child's nature is too serious a thing to admit of its being regarded as a mere appendage to another being, and to be loved or hated accordingly: they stand with me upon their own stock, as much as men and women do. Oh! but you will say, sure it is an attractive age—there is something in the tender years of infancy that of itself charms us? This is the very reason why I am more nice about them. I know that a sweet child is the sweetest thing in nature, not even excepting the delicate creatures which bear them; but the prettier the kind of a thing is, the more desirable it is that it should be pretty of its kind. One daisy differs not much from another in glory; but a violet should look and smell the daintiest.—I was always rather squeamish in my women and children.

But this is not the worst: one must be admitted into their familiarity at least, before they can complain of inattention. It implies visits, and some kind of intercourse. But if the husband be a man with whom you have lived on a friendly footing before marriage—if you did not come in on the wife's side—if you did not sneak into the house in her train, but were an old friend in fast habits of intimacy before their courtship was so much as thought on,—look about you—your tenure is precarious—before a twelvemonth shall roll over your head, you shall find your old friend gradually grow cool and altered towards you, and at last seek opportunities of breaking with you. I have scarce a married friend of my acquaintance, upon whose firm faith I can rely, whose friendship did not commence *after the period of his marriage*. With some limitations, they can endure that: but that the good man should have dared to enter into a solemn league of friendship in which they were not consulted, though it happened be-fore they knew him—before they that are now man and wife ever met—this is intolerable to them. Every long friendship, every old authentic intimacy, must be brought into their office to be new stamped with their currency, as a sovereign prince calls in the good old money that was coined in some reign before he was born or thought of, to be new marked and minted with the stamp of his authority, before he will let it pass current in the world. You may guess what luck generally befalls such a rusty piece of metal as I am in these *new mintings*.

Innumerable are the ways which they take to insult and worm you out of their husband's confidence. Laughing at all you say with a kind of wonder, as if you were a queer kind of fellow that said good things, *but an oddity*, is one of the ways—they have a particular kind of stare for the purpose—till at last the husband, who used to defer to your judgment, and would pass over some excrescences of understanding and manner for the sake of a general vein of observation (not quite vulgar) which he perceived in you, begins to suspect whether you are not altogether a humorist,—a fellow well enough to have consorted with in his bachelor days, but not quite so proper to be introduced to ladies. This may be called the staring way; and is that which has oftenest been put in practice against me.

Then there is the exaggerating way, or the way of irony: that is, where they find you an object of especial regard with their husband, who is not so easily to be shaken from the lasting attachment founded on esteem which he has conceived towards you; by never-qualified exaggerations to cry up all that you say or do, till the good man, who understands well enough that it is all done in compliment to him, grows weary of the debt of gratitude which is due to so much candor, and by relaxing a little on his part, and taking down a peg or two in his enthusiasm, sinks at length to that kindly level of moderate esteem—that "decent affection and complacent kindness" towards you, where she herself can join in sympathy with him without much stretch and violence to her sincerity.

Another way (for the ways they have to accomplish so desirable a purpose are infinite) is, with a kind of innocent simplicity, continually to mistake what it was which first made their husbands fond of you. If an esteem for something excellent in your moral character was that which riveted the chain she is to break, upon any imaginary discovery of a want of poignancy in your conversation, she will cry, "I thought, my dear, you describe your friend, Mr. ——, as a great wit." If, on the other hand, it was for some supposed charm in your conversation that he first grew to like you, and was content for this to overlook some trifling irregularities in your moral deportment, upon the first notice of any of these she as readily exclaims, "This, my dear, is your good Mr. ——." One good lady whom I took the liberty of expostulating with for not showing me quite so much respect as I thought due to her husband's old friend, had the candor to confess to me that she had often heard Mr. —— speak of me before marriage, and that she had conceived a great desire to be acquainted with me, but that the sight of me had very much disappointed her expectations; for from her husband's representations of me, she had formed a notion that she was to see a fine, tall, officer-like looking man (I use her very words); the very reverse of which proved to be the truth. This was candid; and I had the civility not to ask her in return, how she came to pitch upon a standard of personal accomplishments for her husband's friends which differed so much from his own; for my friend's dimensions as near as possible approximate to mine; he standing five feet five in his shoes, in which I have the advantage of him by about half an inch; and he no more than myself exhibiting any indications of a martial character in his air or countenance.

These are some of the mortifications which I have encountered in the absurd attempt to visit at their houses. To enumerate them all would be a vain endeavor; I shall therefore just glance at the very common impropriety of which married ladies are guilty—of treating us as if we were their husbands, and *vice versa.* I mean, when they use us with familiarity, and their husbands with ceremony. *Testacea,* for instance, kept me the other night two or three hours beyond my usual time of supping, while she was fretting because Mr. —— did not come home, till the oysters were all spoiled, rather than she would be guilty of the impoliteness of touching one in his absence. This was reversing the point of good manners: for ceremony is an invention to take off the uneasy feeling which we derive from knowing ourselves to be less the object of love and esteem with a fellow-creature than some other person is. It endeavors to make up, by superior attentions in little points, for that invidious preference which it is forced to deny in the greater. Had *Testacea* kept the oysters back for me, and withstood her husband's importunities to go to supper, she would have acted according to the strict rules of propriety. I know no ceremony that ladies are bound to observe to their husbands, beyond the point of a modest behavior and decorum: therefore I must protest against the vicarious gluttony of *Cerasia,* who at her own table sent away a dish of Morellas,[1] which I was applying to with great good-will, to her husband at the other end of the table, and recommended a plate of less extraordinary gooseberries to my unwedded palate in their stead. Neither can I excuse the wanton affront of ——

But I am weary of stringing up all my married acquaintances by Roman denominations. Let them amend and change their manners, or I promise to record the full-length English of their names, to the terror of all such desperate offenders in future. (1823)

Old China

I have an almost feminine partiality for old china. When I go to see any great house, I

[1] A kind of sour cherry.

enquire for the china-closet, and next for the picture gallery. I cannot defend the order of preference, but by saying, that we have all some taste or other, of too ancient a date to admit of our remembering distinctly that it was an acquired one. I can call to mind the first play, and the first exhibition, that I was taken to; but I am not conscious of a time when china jars and saucers were introduced into my imagination.

I had no repugnance then—why should I now have?—to those little, lawless, azure-tinctured grotesques, that under the notion of men and women, float about, uncircumscribed by any element, in that world before perspective—a china tea-cup.

I like to see my old friends—whom distance cannot diminish—figuring up in the air (so they appear to our optics), yet on *terra firma* still—for so we must in courtesy interpret that speck of deeper blue,—which the decorous artist, to prevent absurdity, had made to spring up beneath their sandals.

I love the men with women's faces, and the women, if possible, with still more womanish expressions.

Here is a young and courtly mandarin, handing tea to a lady from a salver—two miles off. See how distance seems to set off respect! And here the same lady, or another—for likeness is identity on tea-cups—is stepping into a little fairy boat, moored on the hither side of this calm garden river, with a dainty mincing foot, which in a right angle of incidence (as angles go in our world) must infallibly land her in the midst of a flowery mead— a furlong off on the other side of the same strange stream!

Farther on—if far or near can be predicated of their world—see horses, trees, pagodas, dancing the hays.[1]

Here—a cow and rabbit couchant, and co-extensive—so objects show, seen through the lucid atmosphere of fine Cathay.

I was pointing out to my cousin last evening over our Hyson[2] (which we are old fashioned enough to drink unmixed still of an afternoon) some of these *speciosa miracula*[3] upon a set of extraordinary old blue china (a recent purchase) which we were now for the first time using; and could not help remarking, how favorable circumstances had been to us of late years, that we could afford to please the eye sometimes with trifles of this sort—when a passing sentiment seemed to overshade the brows of my companion. I am quick at detecting these summer clouds in Bridget.[4]

"I wish the good old times would come again," she said, "when we were not quite so rich. I do not mean, that I want to be poor; but there was a middle state"—so she was pleased to ramble on,—"in which I am sure we were a great deal happier. A purchase is but a purchase, now that you have money enough and to spare. Formerly it used to be a triumph. When we coveted a cheap luxury (and, O! how much ado I had to get you to consent in those times!)—we were used to have a debate two or three days before, and to weigh the *for* and *against,* and think what we might spare it out of, and what saving we could hit upon, that should be an equivalent. A thing was worth buying then, when we felt the money that we paid for it.

"Do you remember the brown suit, which you made to hang upon you, till all your friends cried shame upon you, it grew so thread-bare—and all because of that folio Beaumont and Fletcher,[5] which you dragged home late at night from Barker's in Covent Garden? Do you remember how we eyed it for weeks before we could make up our minds to the purchase, and had not come to a determination till it was near ten o'clock of the Saturday night, when you set off from Islington, fearing you should be too late—and when the old bookseller with some grumbling opened his shop, and by the twinkling taper (for he was setting bedwards) lighted out the relic from his dusty treasures—and when you lugged it home, wishing it were twice as cumbersome—and when you presented it to me—and when we were exploring the perfectness of it (*collating* you called it)—and while I was repairing some of the loose leaves with paste, which your impatience would not suffer to be left till daybreak—was there no

[1] An old English country dance.
[2] Green tea.
[3] "Glorious wonders."

[4] Lamb's sister, Mary, earlier called his "cousin."
[5] Elizabethan dramatists.

pleasure in being a poor man? or can those neat black clothes which you wear now, and are so careful to keep brushed, since we have become rich and finical, give you half the honest vanity, with which you flaunted it about in that overworn suit—your old corbeau [6]—for four or five weeks longer than you should have done, to pacify your conscience for the mighty sum of fifteen—or sixteen shillings was it?—a great affair we thought it then—which you had lavished on the old folio. Now you can afford to buy any book that pleases you, but I do not see that you ever bring me home any nice old purchases now.

"When you came home with twenty apologies for laying out a less number of shillings upon that print after Lionardo,[7] which we christened the 'Lady Blanche'; when you looked at the purchase, and thought of the money—and thought of the money, and looked again at the picture—was there no pleasure in being a poor man? Now, you have nothing to do but to walk into Colnaghi's,[8] and buy a wilderness of Lionardos. Yet do you?

"Then, do you remember our pleasant walks to Enfield, and Potter's Bar, and Waltham, when we had a holiday—holidays, and all other fun, are gone, now we are rich—and the little hand-basket in which I used to deposit our day's fare of savory cold lamb and salad—and how you would pry about at noon-tide for some decent house, where we might go in, and produce our store—only paying for the ale that you must call for—and speculate upon the looks of the landlady, and whether she was likely to allow us a tablecloth—and wish for such another honest hostess, as Izaak Walton has described [9] many a one on the pleasant banks of the Lea, when he went a fishing—and sometimes they would prove obliging enough, and sometimes they would look grudgingly upon us—but we had cheerful looks still for one another, and would eat our plain food savorily, scarcely grudging

Piscator [10] his Trout Hall? Now,—when we go out a day's pleasuring, which is seldom moreover, we *ride* part of the way—and go into a fine inn, and order the best of dinners, never debating the expense—which, after all, never has half the relish of those chance country snaps, when we were at the mercy of uncertain usage, and a precarious welcome.

"You are too proud to see a play anywhere now but in the pit. Do you remember where it was we used to sit, when we saw the *Battle of Hexham* and the *Surrender of Calais*,[11] and Bannister and Mrs. Bland in the *Children in the Wood* [12]—when we squeezed out our shillings a-piece to sit three or four times in a season in the one-shilling gallery—where you felt all the time that you ought not to have brought me—and more strongly I felt obligation to you for having brought me—and the pleasure was the better for a little shame—and when the curtain drew up, what cared we for our place in the house, or what mattered it where we were sitting, when our thoughts were with Rosalind [13] in Arden, or with Viola [14] at the Court of Illyria? You used to say, that the gallery was the best place of all for enjoying a play socially—that the relish of such exhibitions must be in proportion to the infrequency of going—that the company we met there, not being in general readers of plays, were obliged to attend the more, and did attend, to what was going on, on the stage—because a word lost would have been a chasm, which it was impossible for them to fill up. With such reflections we consoled our pride then—and I appeal to you, whether, as a woman, I met generally with less attention and accommodation, than I have done since in more expensive situations in the house? The getting in indeed, and the crowding up those inconvenient staircases, was bad enough,—but there was still a law of civility to woman recognized to quite as great an

[10] The leading character in *The Compleat Angler*, who often stopped at Trout Hall, an ale-house.
[11] Plays by George Colman the Younger.
[12] A musical play by Thomas Morton. John Bannister was a famous actor, Maria Theresa Bland a well-known actress.
[13] Heroine of Shakespeare's *As You Like It*.
[14] Heroine of Shakespeare's *Twelfth Night*.

[6] Dark coat.
[7] Leonardo da Vinci.
[8] Dealer in prints.
[9] In *The Compleat Angler*.

extent as we ever found in the other passages—and how a little difficulty overcome, heightened the snug seat, and the play, afterwards. Now we can only pay our money and walk in. You cannot see, you say, in the galleries now. I am sure we saw, and heard too, well enough then—but sight, and all, I think, is gone with our poverty.

"There was pleasure in eating strawberries, before they became quite common—in the first dish of peas, while they were yet dear—to have them for a nice supper, a treat. What treat can we have now? If we were to treat ourselves now—that is, to have dainties a little above our means, it would be selfish and wicked. It is the very little more that we allow ourselves beyond what the actual poor can get at, that makes what I call a treat—when two people living together, as we have done, now and then indulge themselves in a cheap luxury, which both like; while each apologizes, and is willing to take both halves of the blame to his single share. I see no harm in people making much of themselves in that sense of the word. It may give them a hint how to make much of others. But now—what I mean by the word—we never do make much of ourselves. None but the poor can do it. I do not mean the veriest poor of all, but persons as we were, just above poverty.

"I know what you were going to say, that it is mighty pleasant at the end of the year to make all meet,—and much ado we used to have every thirty-first night of December to account for our exceedings—many a long face did you make over your puzzled accounts, and in contriving to make it out how we had spent so much—or that we had not spent so much—or that it was impossible we should spend so much next year—and still we found our slender capital decreasing—but then, betwixt ways, and projects, and compromises of one sort or another, and talk of curtailing this charge, and doing without that for the future—and the hope that youth brings, and laughing spirits (in which you were never poor till now) we pocketed up our loss, and in conclusion, with 'lusty brimmers'[15] (as you used to quote it out of *hearty cheerful Mr.*

[15] Brimming cups.

Cotton, as you called him), we used to welcome in the 'coming guest.' Now we have no reckoning at all at the end of the old year—no flattering promises about the new year doing better for us."

Bridget is so sparing of her speech on most occasions, that when she gets into a rhetorical vein, I am careful how I interrupt it. I could not help, however, smiling at the phantom of wealth which her dear imagination had conjured up out of a clear income of poor—hundred pounds a year. "It is true we were happier when we were poorer, but we were also younger, my cousin. I am afraid we must put up with the excess, for if we were to shake the superflux into the sea, we should not much mend ourselves. That we had much to struggle with, as we grew up together, we have reason to be most thankful. It strengthened, and knit our compact closer. We could never have been what we have been to each other, if we had always had the sufficiency which you now complain of. The resisting power—those natural dilations of the youthful spirit, which circumstances cannot straiten—with us are long since passed away. Competence to age is supplementary youth, a sorry supplement indeed, but I fear the best that is to be had. We must ride, where we formerly walked: live better, and lie softer—and shall be wise to do so—than we had means to do in those good old days you speak of. Yet could those days return—could you and I once more walk our thirty miles a-day—could Bannister and Mrs. Bland again be young, and you and I be young to see them—could the good old one-shilling gallery days return—they are dreams, my cousin, now—but could you and I at this moment, instead of this quiet argument, by our well-carpeted fireside, sitting on this luxurious sofa—be once more struggling up those inconvenient staircases, pushed about, and squeezed, and elbowed by the poorest rabble or poor gallery scramblers—could I once more hear those anxious shrieks of yours—and the delicious *Thank God, we are safe,* which always followed when the topmost stair, conquered, let in the first light of the whole cheerful theater down beneath us—I know not the fathom

line that ever touched a descent so deep as I would be willing to bury more wealth in than Crœsus [16] had, or the great Jew R—— [17] is supposed to have, to purchase it. And now do just look at that merry little Chinese waiter 5 holding an umbrella, big enough for a bed-tester,[18] over the head of that pretty insipid half-Madonna-ish chit of a lady in that very blue summer house."
(1823)

STUDY AIDS: 1. This essay is entitled *Old China;* how much of it is about old china? What is the relation between the old china and the long monologue of Bridget? What is the theme of Bridget's talk?

2. What qualities of Romanticism are found in this essay? What characteristics of the author are suggested? What characteristics of Mary Lamb (Bridget)?

3. How would you describe Lamb's prose 10 style?

Letters

To William Wordsworth
Jan. 30, 1801

I ought before this to have replied to your very kind invitation into Cumberland. With 15 you and your sister I could gang anywhere; but I am afraid whether I shall ever be able to afford so desperate a journey. Separate from the pleasure of your company, I don't much care if I never see a mountain in my life. I 20 have passed all my days in London, until I have formed as many and intense local attachments as any of you mountaineers can have done with dead nature. The lighted shops of the Strand and Fleet Street; the innumerable 25 trades, tradesmen, and customers, coaches, waggons, playhouses; all the bustle and wickedness round about Covent Garden; the very women of the Town; the watchmen, drunken scenes, rattles; life awake, if you awake, at 30 all hours of the night; the impossibility of being dull in Fleet Street; the crowds, the very dirt and mud, the sun shining upon houses and pavements, the print shops, the old bookstalls, parsons cheapening books, cof- 35 fee-houses, steams of soups from kitchens, the pantomimes—London itself a pantomime and a masquerade—all these things work themselves into my mind, and feed me, without a power of satiating me. The wonder of these 40 sights impels me into night-walks about her crowded streets, and I often shed tears in the

[16] Extremely rich king of Lydia.
[17] Rothschild, famous banker.
[18] Bed-canopy.

motley Strand from fulness of joy at so much life. All these emotions must be strange to you; so are your rural emotions to me. But consider, what must I have been doing all 15 my life, not to have lent great portions of my heart with usury to such scenes?

My attachments are all local, purely local. I have no passion (or have had none since I was in love, and then it was the spurious 20 engendering of poetry and books) for groves and valleys. The rooms where I was born, the furniture which has been before my eyes all my life, a book-case which has followed me about like a faithful dog (only exceeding 25 him in knowledge), wherever I have moved, old chairs, old tables, streets, squares, where I have sunned myself, my old school—these are my mistresses. Have I not enough, without your mountains? I do not envy you. I 30 should pity you, did I not know that the mind will make friends of anything. Your sun, and moon, and skies, and hills, and lakes, affect me no more, or scarcely come to me in more venerable characters, than as 35 a gilded room with tapestry and tapers, where I might live with handsome visible objects. I consider the clouds above me but as a roof beautifully painted, but unable to satisfy the mind: and at last, like the pictures of the 40 apartment of a connoisseur, unable to afford him any longer a pleasure. So fading upon me, from disuse, have been the beauties of nature, as they have been confinedly called; so ever fresh, and green, and warm are all the 45 inventions of men, and assemblies of men in this great city. I should certainly have laughed with dear Joanna.[1]

Give my kindest love, and my sister's, to D. and yourself; and a kiss from me to little Barbara Lewthwaite.[2] Thank you for liking my play.

To Mrs. Wordsworth
Feb. 18, 1818

My dear Mrs. Wordsworth—I have repeatedly taken pen in hand to answer your kind letter. My sister should more properly have done it, but she having failed, I consider myself answerable for her debts. I am now trying to do it in the midst of commercial noises, and with a quill which seems more ready to glide into arithmetical figures and names of gourds, cassia, cardamoms, aloes, ginger, or tea,[1] than into kindly responses and friendly recollections. The reason why I cannot write letters at home is, that I am never alone. Plato's—(I write to W. W. now)—Plato's double-animal[2] parted never longed more to be reciprocally re-united in the system of its first creation than I sometimes do to be but for a moment single and separate. Except my morning's walk to the office, which is like treading on sands of gold for that reason, I am never so. I cannot walk home from office but some officious friend offers his unwelcome courtesies to accompany me. All the morning I am pestered. I could sit and gravely cast up sums in great books, or compare sum with sum, and write "paid" against this, and "unpaid" against t'other, and yet reserve in some corner of my mind "some darling thoughts all my own"—faint memory of some passage

[1] A reference to a passage in Wordsworth's poem *To Joanna,* in which Joanna, Mary Hutchinson's youngest sister, laughs at Wordsworth's rapture over a scene of natural beauty.

[2] A beautiful little girl celebrated in Wordsworth's poem *The Pet Lamb.*

[1] All these items were imported by the East India Company, of which Lamb was a bookkeeper. Cassia and cardamoms are spices.

[2] In the *Symposium,* Plato has Aristophanes put forward the theory that the present sexual division of the race is a result of the splitting of a single man-woman creature by the gods.

in a book, or the tone of an absent friend's voice—a snatch of Miss Burrell's singing, or a gleam of Fanny Kelly's divine plain face. The two operations might be going on at the same time without thwarting, as the sun's two motions (earth's, I mean), or as I sometimes turn round till I am giddy, in my back parlor, while my sister is walking longitudinally in the front; or as the shoulder of veal twists round with the spit, while the smoke wreathes up the chimney. But there are a set of amateurs of the belles lettres—the gay science—who come to me as a sort of rendezvous, putting questions of criticism, of British Institutions, Lalla Rookhs,[3] etc.—what Coleridge said at the lecture last night—who have the form of reading men, but, for any possible use reading can be to them, but to talk of, might as well have been ante-Cadmeans[4] born, or have lain sucking out the sense of an Egyptian hieroglyph as long as the pyramids will last, before they should find it. These pests worrit me at business, and in all its intervals, perplexing my accounts, poisoning my little salutary warming-time at the fire, puzzling my paragraphs if I take a newspaper, cramming in between my own free thoughts and a column of figures, which had come to an amicable compromise but for them. Their noise ended, one of them, as I said, accompanies me home, lest I should be solitary for a moment; he at length takes his welcome leave at the door; up I go, mutton on table, hungry as hunter, hope to forget my cares, and bury them in the agreeable abstraction of mastication; knock at the door, in comes Mr. Hazlitt, or Mr. Martin Burney, or Morgan Demigorgon, or my brother, or somebody, to prevent my eating alone—a process absolutely necessary to my poor wretched digestion. O the pleasure of eating alone!—eating my dinner alone! let me think of it. But in they come, and make it absolutely necessary that I should open a bottle of orange; for my meat turns into stone when any one dines with me, if I have not wine.

[3] *Lalla Rookh* (1817) is a poem by Tom Moore.

[4] Cadmus was the legendary founder of Thebes; so "ante-Cadmean" (before Cadmus) would refer to very ancient times.

Wine can mollify stones; then *that* wine turns into acidity, acerbity, misanthropy, a hatred of my interrupters—(God bless 'em! I love some of 'em dearly), and with the hatred, a still greater aversion to their going away. Bad is the dead sea they bring upon me, choking and deadening, but worse is the deader dry sand they leave me on, if they go before bed-time. Come never, I would say to these spoilers of my dinner; but if you come, never go! The fact is, this interruption does not happen very often; but every time it comes by surprise, that present bane of my life, orange wine, with all its dreary stifling consequences, follows. Evening company I should always like had I any mornings, but I am saturated with human faces (*divine* [5] forsooth!) and voices all the golden morning; and five evenings in a week would be as much as I should covet to be in company; but I assure you that is a wonderful week in which I can get two, or one to myself. I am never C. L., but always C. L. and Co. He who thought it not good for man to be alone, preserve me from the more prodigious monstrosity of being never by myself! I forget bed-time, but even there these sociable frogs clamber up to annoy me. Once a week, generally some singular evening that, being alone, I go to bed at the hour I ought always to be a-bed; just close to my bedroom window is the club-room of a public-house, where a set of singers, I take them to be chorus-singers of the two theaters (it must be *both of them*), begin their orgies. They are a set of fellows (as I conceive) who, being limited by their talents to the burthen [6] of the song at the playhouses, in revenge have got the common popular airs by Bishop, or some cheap composer, arranged for choruses; that is, to be sung all in chorus. At least I never can catch any of the text of the plain song, nothing but the Babylonish choral howl at the tail on't. "That fury being quenched"— the howl, I mean—a burden succeeds of shouts and clapping, and knocking of the table. At length overtasked nature drops

under it, and escapes for a few hours into the society of the sweet silent creatures of dreams, which go away with mocks and mows [7] at cockcrow. And then I think of the words Christabel's father used (bless me, I have dipped in the wrong ink!) to say every morning by way of variety when he awoke:

> Every knell, the Baron saith,
> Wakes up as to a world of death [8]

or something like it. All I mean by this senseless interrupted tale, is, that by my central situation I am a little over-companied. Not that I have any animosity against the good creatures that are so anxious to drive away the happy solitude from me. I like 'em, and cards, and a cheerful glass; but I mean merely to give you an idea, between office confinement and after-office society, how little time I can call my own. I mean only to draw a picture, not to make an inference. I would not that I know of have it otherwise. I only wish sometimes I could exchange some of my faces and voices for the faces and voices which a late visitation brought most welcome and carried away, leaving regret, but more pleasure, even a kind of gratitude, at being so often favored with that kind northern visitation. My London faces and noises don't hear me—I mean no disrespect, or I should explain myself, that instead of their return 220 times a year, and the return of W. W., etc., seven times in 104 weeks, some more equal distribution might be found. I have scarce room to put in Mary's kind love, and my poor name.

To Bernard Barton

Jan. 9, 1824

Dear B. B.,

Do you know what it is to succumb under an insurmountable day mare—whoreson lethargy, Falstaff [1] calls it—an indisposition to do any thing, or be any thing—a total deadness and distaste—a suspension of vitality—an indifference to locality—a numb soporifical [2]

---

[5] "Human face divine" (Milton, *Paradise Lost* Bk. 3, 44).
[6] Refrain.

[7] Derisive actions and grimaces.
[8] See *Christabel*, ll. 332–333. Lamb misquotes.

[1] Shakespeare's *Henry IV*, Part 2.
[2] Sleep-producing.

goodfornothingness—an ossification all over—an oysterlike insensibility to the passing events—a mind-stupor—a brawny defiance to the needles of a thrusting-in conscience—did you ever have a very bad cold with a total irresolution to submit to water gruel [3] processes?—this has been for many weeks my lot, and my excuse—my fingers drag heavily over this paper, and to my thinking it is three and twenty furlongs from here to the end of this demi-sheet—I have not a thing to say—nothing is of more importance than another—I am flatter than a denial or a pancake—emptier than Judge Park's [4] wig when the head is in it—duller than a country stage when the actors are off it—a cypher—an O—I acknowledge life at all only by an occasional convulsional cough and a permanent phlegmatic pain in the chest—I am weary of the world—Life is weary of me—My day is gone into twilight and I don't think it worth the expense of candles—my wick hath a thief in it, but I can't muster courage to snuff it—I inhale suffocation—I can't distinguish veal from mutton—nothing interests me—'tis 12 o'clock and Thurtell [5] is just coming out upon the New Drop [6]—Jack Ketch [7] alertly tucking up his sleeves to do the last office of mortality, yet cannot I elicit a groan or a moral reflection—if you told me the world will be at end tomorrow, I should just say, "Will it?"—I have not volition enough to dot my *i's*—much less to comb my eyebrows—my eyes are set in my head—my brains are gone out to see a poor

relation in Moorfields, and they did not say when they'd come back again—my scull [8] is a Grub street attic, to let—not so much as a joint stool or a cracked jordan [9] left in it—my hand writes, not I, from habit, as chickens run about a little when their heads are cut off—O for a vigorous fit of gout, cholic, tooth ache—an earwig [10] in my auditory, a fly in my visual organs—pain is life—the sharper, the more evidence of life—but this apathy, this death—did you ever have an obstinate cold, a six or seven weeks' unintermitting chill and suspension of hope, fear, conscience, and everything—yet do I try all I can to cure it. I try wine, and spirits, and smoking, and snuff in unsparing quantities, but they all only seem to make me worse instead of better —I sleep in a damp room, but it does me no good; I come home late o' nights, but do not find any visible amendment.

Who shall deliver me from the body of this death? [11] It is just fifteen minutes after twelve. Thurtell is by this time a good way on his journey, baiting at Scorpion [12] perhaps, Ketch is bargaining for his cast coat and waistcoat, [13] the Jew demurs at first at three half crowns, but on consideration that he may get somewhat by showing 'em in the Town, finally closes.—

STUDY AIDS: How do the style, the syntax, and the punctuation of this letter fit the contents? Is there any seriousness at all in the letter? What characteristics of the writer emerge?

---

[3] A thin liquid food made of water and meal.

[4] Judge Park was the judge who tried the notorious murderer Thurtell.

[5] Thurtell was hanged on the day this letter was written.

[6] The gallows.

[7] The standard name for an English executioner. (John Ketch beheaded the Duke of Monmouth in 1685.)

[8] Skull.

[9] A chamber pot.

[10] A harmless insect mistakenly believed to creep into the human ear.

[11] Romans 7:24.

[12] Stopping for rest ("baiting") at the eighth sign of the zodiac (Scorpio) on his way to the next world.

[13] The clothes of the executed man were given to the hangman.

William Hazlitt
(1778–1830)

ABOUT THE ONLY THING THAT LAMB AND HAZLITT HAD IN COMMON WAS THEIR MASTERY of the personal essay. Temperamentally they were poles apart. Lamb was, for the most part, a genial person, friendly to all. Hazlitt was a quarrelsome, hot-tempered man who made many enemies, could not stay happily married, and, at one time or another, fell out with most of his friends.

Hazlitt had trouble finding his proper life work. He attended a theological school but decided the ministry did not interest him. He returned to his native village in Shropshire, where he painted, read, philosophized. Thereafter he spent four years—partly in Paris —trying to become a painter. Finally he turned to writing, his first book being *An Essay on the Principles of Human Action* (1805).

As a writer he tried his hand at many prose forms: reporting, political pamphleteering, dramatic criticism, biography, literary and informal essays. He also delivered many lectures—on English poets and dramatists, on philosophy, on the arts.

As an essayist Hazlitt is vigorous and keen-minded. His criticism is not systematic, but he has good taste and reliable intuitional judgment, qualities that do much to compensate for the lack of logically developed criteria. His style is clear and lively; illustrations make it concrete and it bristles with colloquial energy. Profundity of thought he does not have; wit and gusto he has in abundance. His highly opinionated pronouncements are always readable and most often right. "We are mighty fine fellows nowadays," said Robert Louis Stevenson, himself a craftsman in prose, "but we cannot write like William Hazlitt."

On Familiar Style

It is not easy to write a familiar style. Many people mistake a familiar for a vulgar style, and suppose that to write without affectation is to write at random. On the contrary, there is nothing that requires more precision, and, if I may so say, purity of expression, than the style I am speaking of. It utterly rejects not only all unmeaning pomp, but all low, cant phrases, and loose, unconnected, *slipshod* allusions. It is not to take the first word that offers, but the best word in common use; it is not to throw words together in any combinations we please, but to follow and avail ourselves of the true idiom of the language.

To write a genuine familiar or truly English style, is to write as any one would speak in common conversation, who had a thorough command and choice of words, or who could discourse with ease, force, and perspicuity, setting aside all pedantic and oratorical flourishes. Or to give another illustration, to write naturally is the same thing in regard to common conversation, as to read naturally is in regard to common speech. It does not follow that it is an easy thing to give the true accent and inflection to the words you utter, because you do not attempt to rise above the level of ordinary life and colloquial speaking. You do not assume indeed the solemnity of the pulpit, or the tone of stage-declamation; neither are you at liberty to gabble on at a venture, without emphasis or discretion, or to resort to vulgar dialect or clownish pronunciation. You must steer a middle course. You are tied down to a given and appropriate articulation, which is determined by the habitual associations between sense and sound, and which you can only hit by entering into the author's meaning, as you must find the proper words and style to express yourself by fixing your thoughts on the subject you have to write about. Any one may mouth out a passage with a theatrical cadence, or get upon stilts to tell his thoughts: but to write or speak with propriety and simplicity is a more difficult task. Thus it is easy to affect a pompous style, to use a word twice as big as the thing you want to express: it is not so easy to pitch upon the very word that exactly fits it. Out of eight or ten words equally common, equally intelligible, with nearly equal pretensions, it is a matter of some nicety and discrimination to pick out the very one, the preferableness of which is scarcely perceptible, but decisive. The reason why I object to Dr. Johnson's style is, that there is no discrimination, no selection, no variety in it. He uses none but "tall, opaque words," [1] taken from the "first row of the rubric" [2]—words with the greatest number of syllables, or Latin phrases with merely English terminations. If a fine style depended on this sort of arbitrary pretension, it would be fair to judge of an author's elegance by the measurement of his words, and the substitution of foreign circumlocutions (with no precise associations) for the mother-tongue. How simple it is to be dignified without ease, to be pompous without meaning! Surely, it is but a mechanical rule for avoiding what is low to be always pedantic and affected. It is clear you cannot use a vulgar English word, if you never use a common English word at all. A fine tact is shown in adhering to those which are perfectly common, and yet never falling into any expressions which are debased by disgusting

circumstances, or which owe their significance and point to technical or professional allusions. A truly natural or familiar style can never be quaint or vulgar, for this reason, that it is of universal force and applicability, and that quaintness and vulgarity arise out of the immediate connection of certain words with coarse and disagreeable, or with confined ideas. The last form what we understand by *cant* or *slang* phrases.—To give an example of what is not very clear in the general statement. I should say that the phrase *To cut with a knife,* or *To cut a piece of wood,* is perfectly free from vulgarity, because it is perfectly common: but to *cut an acquaintance* [3] is not quite unexceptionable, because it is not perfectly common or intelligible, and has hardly yet escaped out of the limits of slang phraseology. I should hardly therefore use the word in this sense without putting it in italics as a license of expression, to be received *cum grano salis.* [4] All provincial or bye-phrases come under the same mark of reprobation—all such as the writer transfers to the page from his fireside or a particular *coterie,* or that he invents for his own sole use and convenience. I conceive that words are like money, not the worse for being common, but that it is the stamp of custom alone that gives them circulation or value. I am fastidious in this respect, and would almost as soon coin the currency of the realm as counterfeit the King's English. I never invented or gave a new and unauthorized meaning to any word but one single one (the term *impersonal* applied to feelings) and that was in an abstruse metaphysical discussion to express a very difficult distinction. I have been (I know) loudly accused of reveling in vulgarisms and broken English. I cannot speak to that point: but so far I plead guilty to the determined use of acknowledged idioms and common elliptical expressions. [5] I am not sure that the critics in question know the one from the other, that is, can distinguish any

[1] From Laurence Sterne's *Tristram Shandy.*
[2] From *Hamlet.*

[3] Is "cut an acquaintance" still slang?
[4] "With a grain of salt."
[5] An elliptical expression is one in which understood words are omitted. E.g., "I liked it as well as he [liked it]."

medium between formal pedantry and the most barbarous solecism.[6] As an author, I endeavor to employ plain words and popular modes of construction, as were I a chapman [7] and dealer, I should common weights and measures.

The proper force of words lies not in the words themselves, but in their application. A word may be a fine-sounding word, of an unusual length, and very imposing from its learning and novelty, and yet in the connection in which it is introduced, may be quite pointless and irrelevant. It is not pomp or pretension, but the adaptation of the expression to the idea that clenches a writer's meaning:—as it is not the size or glossiness of the materials, but their being fitted each to its place, that gives strength to the arch; or as the pegs and nails are as necessary to the support of the building as the larger timbers, and more so than the mere showy, unsubstantial ornaments. I hate anything that occupies more space than it is worth. I hate to see a load of band-boxes go along the street, and I hate to see a parcel of big words without anything in them. A person who does not deliberately dispose of all his thoughts alike in cumbrous draperies and flimsy disguises, may strike out twenty varieties of familiar everyday language, each coming somewhat nearer to the feeling he wants to convey, and at last not hit upon that particular and only one, which may be said to be identical with the exact impression in his mind. This would seem to show that Mr. Cobbett [8] is hardly right in saying that the first word that occurs is always the best. It may be a very good one; and yet a better may present itself on reflection or from time to time. It should be suggested naturally, however, and spontaneously, from a fresh and lively conception of the subject. We seldom succeed by trying at improvement, or by merely substituting one word for another that we are not satisfied with, as we cannot recollect the name of a place or person by merely plaguing ourselves about it. We

wander farther from the point by persisting in a wrong scent; but it starts up accidentally in the memory when we least expected it, by touching some link in the chain of previous association.

There are those who hoard up and make a cautious display of nothing but rich and rare phraseology;—ancient medals, obscure coins, and Spanish pieces of eight. They are very curious to inspect; but I myself would neither offer nor take them in the course of exchange. A sprinkling of archaisms is not amiss: but a tissue of obsolete expressions is more fit *for keep than wear*. I do not say I would not use any phrase that had been brought into fashion before the middle or the end of the last century; but I should be shy of using any that had not been employed by any approved author during the whole of that time. Words, like clothes, get old-fashioned, or mean and ridiculous, when they have been for some time laid aside. Mr. Lamb is the only imitator of old English style I can read with pleasure; and he is so thoroughly imbued with the spirit of his authors, that the idea of imitation is almost done away. There is an inward unction, a marrowy vein both in the thought and feeling, an intuition, deep and lively, of his subject, that carries off any quaintness or awkwardness arising from an antiquated style and dress. The matter is completely his own, though the manner is assumed. Perhaps his ideas are altogether so marked and individual as to require their point and pungency to be neutralized by the affectation of a singular but traditional form of conveyance. Tricked out in the prevailing costume, they would probably seem more startling and out of the way. The old English authors, Burton, Fuller, Coryate, Sir Thomas Browne,[9] are a kind of mediators between us and the more eccentric and whimsical modern, reconciling us to his peculiarities. I do not, however, know how far this is the case or not, till he condescends to write like one of us. I must confess that what I like best of his papers under the signature of Elia (still I do not presume, amidst such excellence, to de-

[6] An ungrammatical combination of words.
[7] Peddler.
[8] Contemporary English political writer.

[9] Seventeenth-century writers who influenced Lamb's style.

cide what is most excellent) is the account of "Mrs. Battle's Opinions on Whist," which is also the most free from obsolete allusions and turns of expression—

A well of native English undefiled.[10] To those acquainted with his admired proto- types, these essays of the ingenious and highly gifted author have the same sort of charm and relish that Erasmus's Colloquies[11] or a fine piece of modern Latin have to the classical scholar. Certainly, I do not know any borrowed pencil that has more power or felicity of execution than the one of which I have here been speaking.

It is as easy to write a gaudy style without ideas as it is to spread a pallet of showy colors, or to smear in a flaunting transparency. "What do you read?"—"Words, words, words." —"What is the matter?"[12]—"Nothing," it might be answered. The florid style is the reverse of the familiar. The last is employed as an unvarnished medium to convey ideas; the first is resorted to as a spangled veil to conceal the want of them. When there is nothing to be set down but words, it costs little to have them fine. Look through the dictionary, and cull out a *florilegium*,[13] rival the *tulippomania*.[14] *Rouge* high enough, and never mind the natural complexion. The vul- gar, who are not in the secret, will admire the look of preternatural health and vigor; and the fashionable, who regard only appear- ances, will be delighted with the imposition. Keep to your sounding generalities, your tinkling phrases, and all will be well. Swell out an unmeaning truism to a perfect tym- pany[15] of style. A thought, a distinction is the rock on which all this brittle cargo of verbiage splits at once. Such writers have merely *verbal* imaginations, that retain noth-

ing but words. Or their puny thoughts have dragon-wings, all green and gold. They soar far above the vulgar failing of the *Sermo humi obrepens*[16]—their most ordinary speech is never short of an hyperbole, splendid, im- posing, vague, incomprehensible, magnilo- quent, a cento[17] of sounding common-places. If some of us, whose "ambition is more lowly,"[18] pry a little too narrowly into nooks and corners to pick up a number of "uncon- sidered trifles,"[19] they never once direct their eyes or lift their hands to seize on any but the most gorgeous, tarnished, threadbare, patch-work set of phrases, the left-off finery of poetic extravagance, transmitted down through successive generations of barren pre- tenders. If they criticize actors and actresses, a huddled phantasmagoria of feathers, spangles, floods of light, and oceans of sound float be- fore their morbid sense, which they paint in the style of Ancient Pistol.[20] Not a glimpse can you get of the merits or defects of the performers: they are hidden in a profusion of barbarous epithets and wilful rhodomontade. Our hypercritics are not thinking of these little fantoccini[21] beings—

That strut and fret their hour
Upon the stage[22]—,

but of tall phantoms of words, abstractions, *genera* and *species,* sweeping clauses, periods that unite the Poles, forced alliterations, astounding antitheses—

And on their pens *Fustian* sits plumed.[23]

If they describe kings and queens, it is an Eastern pageant. The Coronation at either House is nothing to it. We get at four re- peated images—a curtain, a throne, a scepter, and a footstool. These are with them the wardrobe of a lofty imagination; and they

[10] In *The Faerie Queene* Spenser spoke of Chaucer as a "well of English undefiled."

[11] The *Colloquia* of Erasmus, famous Dutch humanist.

[12] The three previous quotations are all from *Hamlet.*

[13] List of flowers.

[14] Mania for growing tulips. What is the TONE of the next four sentences?

[15] Condition of being puffed up or inflated; a metaphor from "tympani," meaning kettledrums.

[16] "Speech that creeps along the ground" (Horace).

[17] A composition made up of scraps from other authors.

[18] From *The Tempest.*

[19] From *The Winter's Tale.*

[20] A braggart in three of Shakespeare's plays.

[21] Puppets.

[22] From *Macbeth.*

[23] Cf. Milton's "And on his crest Sat horror plumed" (*Paradise Lost*). "Fustian" means "bom- bast" or "claptrap."

turn their servile strains to servile uses. Do we read a description of pictures? It is not a reflection of tones and hues which "nature's own sweet and cunning hand laid on," [24] but piles of precious stones, rubies, pearls, emeralds, Golconda's [25] mines, and all the blazonry of art. Such persons are in fact besotted with words, and their brains are turned with the glittering but empty and sterile phantoms of things. Personifications, capital letters, seas of sunbeams, visions of glory, shining inscriptions, the figures of a transparency, Britannia with her shield, or Hope leaning on an anchor, make up their stock-in-trade. They may be considered as *hieroglyphical* [26] writers. Images stand out in their minds isolated and important merely in themselves, without any ground-work of feeling—there is no context in their imaginations. Words affect them in the same way, by the mere sound, that is, by their possible, not by their actual application to the subject in hand. They are fascinated by first appearances, and have no sense of consequences. Nothing more is meant by them than meets the ear: they understand or feel nothing more than meets their eye. The web and texture of the universe, and of the heart of man, is a mystery to them: they have no faculty that strikes a chord in unison with it. They cannot get beyond the daubings of fancy, the varnish of sentiment. Objects are not linked to feelings, words to things, but images revolve in splendid mockery, words represent themselves in their strange rhapsodies. The categories of such a mind are pride and ignorance—pride in outside show, to which they sacrifice every thing, and ignorance of the true worth and hidden structure both of words and things. With a sovereign contempt for what is familiar and natural, they are the slaves of vulgar affectation—of a routine of high-flown phrases.

[24] From *Twelfth Night*.
[25] Golconda is a city in India once noted for its diamonds.
[26] I.e., writers of unintelligible symbols.

Scorning to imitate realities, they are unable to invent any thing, to strike out one original idea. They are not copyists of nature, it is true; but they are the poorest of all plagiarists, the plagiarists of words. All is far-fetched, dear-bought, artificial, oriental in subject and allusion; all is mechanical, conventional, vapid, formal, pedantic in style and execution. They startle and confound the understanding of the reader by the remoteness and obscurity of their illustrations; they soothe the ear by the monotony of the same everlasting round of circuitous metaphors. They are the *mock-school* in poetry and prose. They flounder about between fustian in expression and bathos in sentiment. They tantalize the fancy, but never reach the head nor touch the heart. Their Temple of Fame is like a shadowy structure raised by Dulness to Vanity, or like Cowper's description of the Empress of Russia's palace of ice, "as worthless as in show 'twas glittering"—

It smiled, and it was cold! [27]
(1821)

STUDY AIDS: 1. What major qualities of a familiar or informal style does Hazlitt discuss? Does he leave out some important ones?

2. What are some of the qualities of Hazlitt's prose style? Pick out some good examples of the CONCRETE in his writing. What images and comparisons suggest that he was interested in the visual arts, especially painting? How does his style compare with that of Lamb?

3. What is Hazlitt's advice concerning big words, flowery language, new words, slang expressions, roundabout phrasing? How does his own style stand up according to these principles? Hazlitt has in this essay many literary allusions (most of them from Shakespeare), some Latin expressions, and some rather unusual words (such as "florilegium," "tulippomania," "cento," "phantasmagoria," "rhodomontade," "fantoccini," "hieroglyphical," and "fustian"). Is he violating his own principles by his use of such words, expressions, and allusions?

[27] From Cowper's *The Task*.

On Going a Journey

One of the pleasantest things in the world is going a journey; but I like to go by myself. I can enjoy society in a room; but out of doors nature is company enough for me. I am then never less alone than when alone.

The fields his study, nature was his book.[1]

I cannot see the wit of walking and talking at the same time. When I am in the country, I wish to vegetate like the country. I am not for criticizing hedge-rows and black cattle. I go out of town in order to forget the town and all that is in it. There are those who for this purpose go to watering-places, and carry the metropolis with them. I like more elbow-room, and fewer incumbrances. I like solitude, when I give myself up to it, for the sake of solitude; nor do I ask for

> . . . a friend in my retreat,
> Whom I may whisper, solitude is sweet.[2]

The soul of a journey is liberty, perfect liberty, to think, feel, do, just as one pleases. We go a journey chiefly to be free of all impediments and of all inconveniences; to leave ourselves behind, much more to get rid of others. It is because I want a little breathing-space to muse on indifferent matters, where contemplation

> May plume her feathers and let grow her wings,
> That in the various bustle of resort
> Were all too ruffled, and sometimes impaired,[3]

that I absent myself from the town for awhile, without feeling at a loss the moment I am left by myself. Instead of a friend in a post-chaise or in a Tilbury,[4] to exchange good things with, and vary the same stale topics over again, for once let me have a truce with impertinence. Give me the clear blue sky over my head, and the green turf beneath my feet, a winding road before me, and a three hours' march to dinner—and then to thinking! It is hard if I cannot start some game on these lone heaths. I laugh, I run, I leap, I sing for joy. From the point of yonder rolling cloud, I plunge into my past being, and revel there, as the sunburnt Indian plunges headlong into the wave that wafts him to his native shore. Then long-forgotten things, like "sunken wrack and sumless treasuries,"[5] burst upon my eager sight, and I begin to feel, think, and be myself again. Instead of an awkward silence, broken by attempts at wit or dull common-places, mine is that undisturbed silence of the heart which alone is perfect eloquence. No one likes puns, alliterations, antitheses, argument, and analysis better than I do; but I sometimes had rather be without them. "Leave, oh, leave me to my repose!"[6] I have just now other business in hand, which would seem idle to you, but is with me "very stuff of the conscience."[7] Is not this wild rose sweet without a comment? Does not this daisy leap to my heart set in its coat of emerald? Yet if I were to explain to you the circumstance that has so endeared it to me, you would only smile. Had I not better then keep it to myself, and let it serve me to brood over, from here to yonder craggy point, and from thence onward to the far-distant horizon? I should be but bad company all that way, and therefore prefer being alone. I have heard it said that you may, when the moody fit comes on, walk or ride on by yourself, and indulge your reveries. But this looks like a breach of manners, a neglect of others, and you are thinking all the time that you ought to rejoin your party. "Out upon such half-faced fellowship,"[8] say I. I like to be either entirely to myself, or entirely at the dis-

---

[1] Bloomfield, The Farmer's Boy.
[2] Cowper, Retirement.
[3] Milton, Comus.
[4] A two-wheeled carriage with no top.
[5] Shakespeare, Henry V.
[6] Gray, The Descent of Odin.
[7] Shakespeare, Othello.
[8] Shakespeare, I Henry IV.

posal of others; to talk or be silent, to walk or sit still, to be sociable or solitary. I was pleased with an observation of Mr. Cobbett's, that "he thought it a bad French custom to drink our wine with our meals, and that an Englishman ought to do only one thing at a time." So I cannot talk and think, or indulge in melancholy musing and lively conversation by fits and starts. "Let me have a companion of my way," says Sterne, "were it but to remark how the shadows lengthen as the sun declines." [9] It is beautifully said: but in my opinion, this continual comparing of notes interferes with the involuntary impression of things upon the mind, and hurts the sentiment. If you only hint what you feel in a kind of dumb show, it is insipid: if you have to explain it, it is making a toil of a pleasure. You cannot read the book of nature, without being perpetually put to the trouble of translating it for the benefit of others. I am for the synthetical method on a journey, in preference to the analytical. I am content to lay in a stock of ideas then, and to examine and anatomize them afterwards. I want to see my vague notions float like the down of the thistle before the breeze, and not to have them entangled in the briars and thorns of controversy. For once, I like to have it all my own way; and this is impossible unless you are alone, or in such company as I do not covet. I have no objection to argue a point with anyone for twenty miles of measured road, but not for pleasure. If you remark the scent of a bean-field crossing the road, perhaps your fellow-traveler has no smell. If you point to a distant object, perhaps he is short-sighted, and has to take out his glass to look at it. There is a feeling in the air, a tone in the color of a cloud, which hits your fancy, but the effect of which you are unable to account for. There is then no sympathy, but an uneasy craving after it, and a dissatisfaction which pursues you on the way, and in the end probably produces ill humor. Now I never quarrel with myself, and take all my own conclusions for granted till I find it necessary to defend them against objections. It is not merely that you may

[9] Sermons.

not be of accord on the objects and circumstances that present themselves before you— they may recall a number of ideas, and lead to associations too delicate and refined to be possibly communicated to others. Yet these I love to cherish, and sometimes still fondly clutch them, when I can escape from the throng to do so. To give way to our feelings before company, seems extravagance or affectation; on the other hand, to have to unravel this mystery of our being at every turn, and to make others take an equal interest in it (otherwise the end is not answered) is a task to which few are competent. We must "give it an understanding, but no tongue." [10] My old friend C——, [11] however, could do both. He could go on in the most delightful explanatory way over hill and dale, a summer's day, and convert a landscape into a didactic poem or a Pindaric ode. "He talked far above singing." [12] If I could so clothe my ideas in sounding and flowing words, I might perhaps wish to have some one with me to admire the swelling theme; or I could be more content, were it possible for me still to hear his echoing voice in the woods of All-Foxden. They had "that fine madness in them which our first poets had"; [13] and if they could have been caught by some rare instrument, would have breathed such strains as the following:

　　　　　　　—Here be woods as green
As any, air likewise as fresh and sweet
As when smooth Zephyrus [14] plays on the fleet
Face of the curlèd stream, with flowers as many
As the young spring gives, and as choice as any;
Here be all new delights, cool streams and wells,
Arbors o'ergrown with woodbines, caves and
　　dells:
Choose where thou wilt, while I sit by and sing,
Or gather rushes to make many a ring
For thy long fingers; tell thee tales of love,
How the pale Phoebe, [15] hunting in a grove,
First saw the boy Endymion, from whose eyes

[10] Shakespeare, Hamlet.
[11] Coleridge.
[12] Beaumont and Fletcher, Philaster.
[13] Drayton, Elegy to Henry Reynolds.
[14] The west wind.
[15] Diana.

She took eternal fire that never dies;
How she conveyed him softly in a sleep,
His temples bound with poppy, to the steep
Head of old Latmos,[16] where she stoops each
   night,
Gilding the mountain with her brother's [17] light,
To kiss her sweetest.—[18]

Had I words and images at command like these, I would attempt to wake the thoughts that lie slumbering on golden ridges in the evening clouds: but at the sight of nature my fancy, poor as it is, droops and closes up its leaves, like flowers at sunset. I can make nothing out on the spot:—I must have time to collect myself.

In general, a good thing spoils out-of-door prospects: [19] it should be reserved for table-talk. L—— [20] is for this reason, I take it, the worst company in the world out of doors; because he is the best within. I grant, there is one subject on which it is pleasant to talk on a journey; and that is, what one shall have for supper when we get to our inn at night. The open air improves this sort of conversation or friendly altercation, by setting a keener edge on appetite. Every mile of the road heightens the flavor of the viands we expect at the end of it. How fine it is to enter some old town, walled and turreted, just at the approach of night-fall, or to come to some straggling village, with the lights streaming through the surrounding gloom; and then after inquiring for the best entertainment that the place affords, to "take one's ease at one's inn"! [21] These eventful moments in our lives are in fact too precious, too full of solid, heartfelt happiness, to be frittered and dribbled away in imperfect sympathy. I would have them all to myself, and drain them to the last drop: they will do to talk of or to write about afterwards. What a delicate speculation it is, after drinking whole goblets of tea,

The cups that cheer, but not inebriate,[22]

and letting the fumes ascend into the brain, to sit considering what we shall have for supper—eggs and a rasher, a rabbit smothered in onions, or an excellent veal-cutlet! Sancho [23] in such a situation once fixed upon cow-heel; and his choice, though he could not help it, is not to be disparaged. Then in the intervals of pictured scenery and Shandean [24] contemplation, to catch the preparation and the stir in the kitchen—*Procul, O procul este profani!* [25] These hours are sacred to silence and to musing, to be treasured up in the memory, and to feed the source of smiling thoughts hereafter. I would not waste them in idle talk; or if I must have the integrity of fancy broken in upon, I would rather it were by a stranger than a friend. A stranger takes his hue and character from the time and place; he is a part of the furniture and costume of an inn. If he is a Quaker, or from the West Riding [26] of Yorkshire, so much the better. I do not even try to sympathize with him, and he *breaks no squares.*[27] I associate nothing with my traveling companion but present objects and passing events. In his ignorance of me and my affairs, I in a manner forget myself. But a friend reminds one of other things, rips up old grievances, and destroys the abstraction of the scene. He comes in ungraciously between us and our imaginary character. Something is dropped in the course of conversation that gives a hint of your profession and pursuits; or from having some one with you that knows the less sublime portions of your history, it seems that other people do. You are no longer a citizen of the world: but your "unhousèd, free condition is put into circumscription and confine." [28] The *incognito* of an inn is one of its striking privileges—"lord of one's-self, un-

---

[16] A mountain in Asia Minor.
[17] Apollo's.
[18] Fletcher, *The Faithful Shepherdess.*
[19] I.e., an interesting or witty remark spoils the views of the scenery.
[20] Lamb.
[21] Shakespeare, *I Henry IV.*

[22] Cowper, *The Task.*
[23] Don Quixote's comic squire.
[24] Rambling, discursive, like Sterne's *Tristram Shandy.*
[25] "Get away, get away, O ye unsanctified!"
[26] A remote division of Yorkshire.
[27] Does not violate the regular order; hence, is harmless.
[28] Shakespeare, *Othello.*

cumber'd with a name." [29] Oh! it is great to shake off the trammels of the world and of public opinion—to lose our importunate, tormenting, everlasting personal identity in the elements of nature, and become the creature of the moment, clear of all ties—to hold to the universe only by a dish of sweet-breads, and to owe nothing but the score [30] of the evening—and no longer seeking for applause and meeting with contempt, to be known by no other title than *the Gentleman in the parlor!* One may take one's choice of all characters in this romantic state of uncertainty as to one's real pretensions, and become indefinitely respectable and negatively right-worshipful. We baffle prejudice and disappoint conjecture; and from being so to others, begin to be objects of curiosity and wonder even to ourselves. We are no more those hackneyed common-places that we appear in the world: an inn restores us to the level of nature, and quits scores with society! I have certainly spent some enviable hours at inns —sometimes when I have been left entirely to myself, and have tried to solve some metaphysical problem, as once at Witham-common,[31] where I found out the proof that likeness is not a case of the association of ideas— at other times, when there have been pictures in the room, as at St. Neot's [32] (I think it was) where I first met with Gribelin's engravings of the Cartoons,[33] into which I entered at once; and at a little inn on the borders of Wales, where there happened to be hanging some of Westall's [34] drawings, which I compared triumphantly (for a theory that I had, not for the admired artist) with the figure of a girl who had ferried me over the Severn, standing up in a boat between me and the fading twilight—at other times I might mention luxuriating in books, with a peculiar interest in this way, as I remember sitting up half the night to read Paul and

Virginia,[35] which I picked up at an inn at Bridgewater,[36] after being drenched in the rain all day; and at the same place I got through two volumes of Madame d'Arblay's Camilla.[37] It was on the tenth of April, 1798, that I sat down to a volume of the New Eloise,[38] at the inn at Llangollen,[39] over a bottle of sherry and a cold chicken. The letter I chose was that in which St. Preux describes his feelings as he first caught a glimpse from the heights of the Jura [40] of the Pays de Vaud, which I had brought with me as a *bonne bouche* [41] to crown the evening with. It was my birthday, and I had for the first time come from a place in the neighborhood to visit this delightful spot. The road to Llangollen turns off between Chirk and Wrexham; and on passing a certain point, you come all at once upon the valley, which opens like an amphitheater, broad, barren hills rising in majestic state on either side, with "green, upland swells that echo to the bleat of flocks" [42] below, and the river Dee babbling over its stony bed in the midst of them. The valley at this time "glittered green with sunny showers," [43] and a budding ash-tree dipped its tender branches in the chiding stream. How proud, how glad I was to walk along the high road that commanded the delicious prospect, repeating the lines which I have just quoted from Mr. Coleridge's poems! But besides the prospect which opened beneath my feet, another also opened to my inward sight, a heavenly vision, on which were written, in letters large as hope could make them, these four words, LIBERTY, GENIUS, LOVE, VIRTUE; which have since faded into the light of common day,[44] or mock my idle gaze.

[36] Town in Somersetshire.
[37] Novel by Fanny Burney, who married a French general, d'Arblay.
[38] Novel in letter form by Rousseau.
[39] Town in Wales.
[40] A mountain range between France and Switzerland.
[41] "Choice morsel."
[42] Coleridge, *Ode on the Departing Year.*
[43] Coleridge, *Ode on the Departing Year.*
[44] See Wordsworth, *Ode: Intimations of Immortality,* l. 76. What is Hazlitt referring to here and in the rest of the paragraph?

[29] Dryden, *Epistle to My Honor'd Kinsman, John Driden.*
[30] Bill.
[31] A town in Somersetshire.
[32] A town in Huntingdonshire.
[33] Religious drawings by Raphael.
[34] Painter and book illustrator.
[35] Romance by Bernardin de St. Pierre.

The beautiful is vanished and returns not.[45]

Still I would return some time or other to this enchanted spot; but I would return to it alone. What other self could I find to share that influx of thoughts, of regret, and delight, the fragments of which I could hardly conjure up to myself, so much have they been broken and defaced! I could stand on some tall rock, and overlook the precipice of years that separates me from what I then was. I was at that time going shortly to visit the poet whom I have above named. Where is he now? Not only I myself have changed; the world, which was then new to me, has become old and incorrigible. Yet will I turn to thee in thought, O sylvan Dee, in joy, in youth and gladness as thou then wert; and thou shalt always be to me the river of Paradise, where I will drink of the waters of life freely! [46]

There is hardly anything that shows the short-sightedness or capriciousness of the imagination more than traveling does. With change of place we change our ideas; nay, our opinions and feelings. We can by an effort indeed transport ourselves to old and long-forgotten scenes, and then the picture of the mind revives again; but we forget those that we have just left. It seems that we can think but of one place at a time. The canvas of the fancy is but of a certain extent, and if we paint one set of objects upon it, they immediately efface every other. We cannot enlarge our conceptions, we only shift our point of view. The landscape bares its bosom to the enraptured eye, we take our fill of it, and seem as if we could form no other image of beauty or grandeur. We pass on, and think no more of it: the horizon that shuts it from our sight, also blots it from our memory like a dream. In traveling through a wild barren country, I can form no idea of a woody and cultivated one. It appears to me that all the world must be barren, like what I see of it. In the country we forget the town, and in

town we despise the country. "Beyond Hyde Park," says Sir Fopling Flutter, "all is a desert." [47] All that part of the map that we do not see before us is a blank. The world in our conceit of it is not much bigger than a nutshell. It is not one prospect expanded into another, county joined to county, kingdom to kingdom, land to seas, making an image voluminous and vast;—the mind can form no larger idea of space than the eye can take in at a single glance. The rest is a name written in a map, a calculation of arithmetic. For instance, what is the true signification of that immense mass of territory and population, known by the name of China to us? An inch of pasteboard on a wooden globe, of no more account than a China orange! Things near us are seen of the size of life: things at a distance are diminished to the size of the understanding. We measure the universe by ourselves, and even comprehend the texture of our own being only piecemeal. In this way, however, we remember an infinity of things and places. The mind is like a mechanical instrument that plays a great variety of tunes, but it must play them in succession. One idea recalls another, but it at the same time excludes all others. In trying to renew old recollections, we cannot as it were unfold the whole web of our existence; we must pick out the single threads. So in coming to a place where we have formerly lived and with which we have intimate associations, everyone must have found that the feeling grows more vivid the nearer we approach the spot, from the mere anticipation of the actual impression: we remember circumstances, feelings, persons, faces, names that we had not thought of for years; but for the time all the rest of the world is forgotten! —To return to the question I have quitted above.

I have no objection to go to see ruins, aqueducts, pictures, in company with a friend or a party, but rather the contrary, for the former reason reversed. They are intelligible matters, and will bear talking about. The sentiment here is not tacit, but communicable

[45] Coleridge, *The Death of Wallenstein.*
[46] Throughout this and the following paragraphs, Hazlitt is incorporating phrases from Wordsworth's poems.

[47] Etherege, *The Man of Mode, or Sir Fopling Flutter.*

and overt. Salisbury Plain is barren of criticism, but Stonehenge [48] will bear a discussion antiquarian, picturesque, and philosophical. In setting out on a party of pleasure, the first consideration always is where we shall go to: in taking a solitary ramble, the question is what we shall meet with by the way. The mind then is "its own place"; [49] nor are we anxious to arrive at the end of our journey. I can myself do the honors indifferently [50] well to works of art and curiosity. I once took a party to Oxford with no mean *éclat* [51] —showed them the seat of the Muses at a distance,

With glistering spires and pinnacles adorn'd— [52]

descanted on the learned air that breathes from the grassy quadrangles and stone walls of halls and colleges—was at home in the Bodleian; [53] and at Blenheim [54] quite superseded the powdered Cicerone [55] that attended us, and that pointed in vain with his wand to common-place beauties in matchless pictures.—As another exception to the above reasoning, I should not feel confident in venturing on a journey in a foreign country without a companion. I should want at intervals to hear the sound of my own language. There is an involuntary antipathy in the mind of an Englishman to foreign manners and notions that requires the assistance of social sympathy to carry it off. As the distance from home increases, this relief, which was at first a luxury, becomes a passion and an appetite. A person would almost feel stifled to find himself in the deserts of Arabia without friends and countrymen: there must be allowed to be something in the view of Athens or old Rome that claims the utterance of

speech; and I own that the Pyramids are too mighty for any single contemplation. In such situations, so opposite to all one's ordinary train of ideas, one seems a species by one's-self, a limb torn off from society, unless one can meet with instant fellowship and support.—Yet I did not feel this want or craving very pressing once, when I first set my foot on the laughing shores of France. Calais was peopled with novelty and delight. The confused, busy murmur of the place was like oil and wine poured into my ears; nor did the mariners' hymn, which was sung from the top of an old crazy vessel in the harbor, as the sun went down, send an alien sound into my soul. I breathed the air of general humanity. I walked over "the vine-covered hills and gay regions of France," [56] erect and satisfied; for the image of man was not cast down and chained to the foot of arbitrary thrones. I was at no loss for language, for that of all the great schools of painting was open to me. The whole is vanished like a shade. Pictures, heroes, glory, freedom, all are fled: nothing remains but the Bourbons [57] and the French people!— There is undoubtedly a sensation in traveling into foreign parts that is to be had nowhere else: but it is more pleasing at the time than lasting. It is too remote from our habitual associations to be a common topic of discourse or reference, and, like a dream or another state of existence, does not piece into our daily modes of life. It is an animated but a momentary hallucination. It demands an effort to exchange our actual for our ideal identity; and to feel the pulse of our old transports revive very keenly, we must "jump" [58] all our present comforts and connections. Our romantic and itinerant character is not to be domesticated. Dr. Johnson remarked how little foreign travel added to the facilities of conversation in those who had been abroad. In fact, the time we have spent there is both delightful and in one sense instructive; but it appears to be cut out

[48] A group of prehistoric stones on Salisbury Plain in southern England.

[49] Milton, *Paradise Lost.*

[50] Moderately.

[51] Brilliance of success.

[52] *Paradise Lost.*

[53] Oxford University library.

[54] The Duke of Marlborough's palace, near Oxford.

[55] Sight-seers' guide (so called because he is a talkative "orator," like Cicero).

[56] Roscoe, *Song . . . on the Anniversary of the 14th of August, 1791.*

[57] The reactionary French royal house, restored to power after the fall of Napoleon.

[58] Risk. From *Macbeth.*

of our substantial, downright existence, and never to join kindly [59] on to it. We are not the same, but another, and perhaps more enviable individual, all the time we are out of our own country. We are lost to ourselves, as well as our friends. So the poet somewhat quaintly sings,

Out of my country and myself I go.[60]

Those who wish to forget painful thoughts, do well to absent themselves for a while from the ties and objects that recall them; but we can be said only to fulfil our destiny in the place that gave us birth. I should on this account like well enough to spend the whole of my life in traveling abroad, if I could anywhere borrow another life to spend afterwards at home!

(1822)

STUDY AIDS: 1. What opinions about traveling does Hazlitt express in this essay? Do you agree with them?

2. What characteristics of the writer are revealed? Would he make a good traveling companion? What political philosophy is displayed?

3. One critic has said that Hazlitt has the knack "for bringing out unnoticed sides of familiar truth." How does this essay illustrate that ability? Point out striking images and picturesque phrases. What does he mean, for instance, by saying "we baffle prejudice and disappoint conjecture" (p. 606/1, ll. 16–17)?

George Gordon, Lord Byron
(1788–1824)

He taught us little; but our soul
Had *felt* him like the thunder's roll.

IN THESE TWO LINES MATTHEW ARNOLD PUT HIS FINGER ON THE ESSENTIAL ELEMENT in Byron's poetical appeal. The reader of Byron's verse is quickly aware of the poet's tremendous energy, his dramatic intensity, his declamatory style, his quick wit and sharp (though not profound) intellect, and the fascination of a towering ego. Byron lacks the meditative depth of Wordsworth, the witchery of Coleridge, the intense lyricism of Shelley, the full richness of Keats—but he excels them all in sheer personal force.

Byron's is a many-sided genius, but two facets of his brilliance stand out. One is the classical-satirical, expressing itself in poems of bite and humor from the *jeux d'esprit* of boyhood through the sardonic thrusts, playful or savage, in *Don Juan* and *The Vision of Judgment,* and in a few plays exhibiting his concern for classic control. The other facet is the romantic-sentimental, emerging in the many melodramatic lyrics, in the Spenserian stanzas of *Childe Harold's Pilgrimage,* in the fustian of the Oriental Tales, and in the Titanism of *Manfred* (1817) and *Cain* (1821). Both facets shine harmoniously in *Don Juan.*

There are no dull biographies of Byron, for his life is as variegated as his poetry. Both his parents were capricious, quick-tempered, and unstable. He was born with a twisted foot, a deformity that intensified his proud and sensitive nature. His early Calvinistic training gave him a curious streak of puritanism that his later immorality could never completely submerge. From Harrow school, where he excelled in cricket, boxing, and declamation, Byron entered Cambridge. Here he indulged his interests. He became an

[59] Naturally.
[60] Unidentified quotation.

expert swimmer, read what he pleased, and published a youthful volume of verse, *Hours of Idleness,* which was unfavorably reviewed. Byron replied to his critics in his first major satire, *English Bards and Scotch Reviewers* (1809), which lashed out, in Popean couplets, both at contemporary critics and at authors as well.

Byron had hardly taken his seat in the House of Lords when he and a friend set sail for an extended tour of the Spanish peninsula, the Mediterranean, and the Near East. The most important result of this adventurous trip was the first two cantos of *Childe Harold's Pilgrimage* (1812), which made Byron famous overnight and inaugurated four years of high and loose living in London. He was the darling of society, engaging in various amours (including an affair with his half-sister, Augusta) and writing oriental tales to please the popular taste.

Byron thought that marriage to the decorous Anne Milbanke might reform him, but the union was doomed from the outset. She was a conventional woman with little understanding of her husband's dissolute ways, and Byron made no effort to accept the necessary compromises of a marital partnership. The result: separation and divorce, with the fickle public mind turned violently against the once fawned-upon idol. Byron had had enough. He left England in April, 1816, never to return.

Byron's eight years of self-exile were divided chiefly among Switzerland, Italy, and Greece. He and Shelley sailed on Lake Geneva, rode horseback in Venice, and started a magazine in Pisa. Byron's self-indulgence became extreme in Venice, from which he wrote back to Tom Moore blasé letters describing his amorous intrigues. Later he settled down to a single mistress, Teresa Guiccioli, an Italian woman of beauty and intellect. In Ravenna he joined the movement of Italian resistance against Austria, and in Greece he trained troops to fight the Turks.

During these adventurous years he was writing and publishing: Cantos 3 (1816) and 4 (1818) of *Childe Harold's Pilgrimage,* eight poetical dramas, *Beppo* (1818), *The Vision of Judgment* (1822), and sixteen-plus cantos of *Don Juan* (1818–1824). He was still at work on *Don Juan* when, serving with the Greek army in their fight for independence, he contracted a fever and died. The news of his death shocked all of Europe. It seemed incredible that this titanic rebel, a beloved champion of freedom, could be dead.

She Walks in Beauty

She [1] walks in beauty, like the night
  Of cloudless climes and starry skies;
And all that's best of dark and bright
  Meet in her aspect and her eyes:
Thus mellowed to that tender light   5
  Which heaven to gaudy day denies.

One shade the more, one ray the less,
  Had half impaired the nameless grace

Which waves in every raven tress,
  Or softly lightens o'er her face;   10
Where thoughts serenely sweet express
  How pure, how dear their dwelling-place.

And on that cheek, and o'er that brow,
  So soft, so calm, yet eloquent,
The smiles that win, the tints that glow,   15
  But tell of days in goodness spent,
A mind at peace with all below,
  A heart whose love is innocent!
(1814; 1815)

[1] Lady Wilmot Horton, Byron's cousin. Byron saw her, dressed in mourning with spangles on her dress, at a party; he wrote this poem the next morning.

Childe Harold's Pilgrimage

"I awoke one morning and found myself famous," Byron said after the publication of the first two cantos of Childe [1] Harold's Pilgrimage in 1812, soon after his return from an adventurous tour of the Mediterranean and the Near East. The reading public was in the mood for a romantic poetical travelogue, dealing with faraway places and people and centering around a vague, gloomy figure who found his wanderings an antidote for some nameless pain.

The poem was resumed after a four-year interlude, an interlude which saw the rise and fall of Byron in London society, the marriage with Lady Byron, the separation, and finally Byron's self-banishment from the country where he had known so much of both triumph and travail. These tempestuous years made their mark upon the continued poem. For in cantos three and four the mood of bitterness and disillusionment has deepened, and the personality of the poet himself—proud, defiant, cynical, sentimental—looms larger than ever. There are passages of lyric beauty, vivid description, dramatic narrative, philosophic comment, and shrewd estimations of men, places, and events. Most of all there is Byron himself, and "the pageant of his bleeding heart."

Canto 3

1

Is thy face like thy mother's, my fair child! [2]
Ada! sole daughter of my house and heart?
When last I saw thy young blue eyes they
   smiled,
And then we parted—not as now we part,
But with a hope.[3]—Awaking with a start, 5
The waters heave around me; and on high
The winds lift up their voices: I depart,
Whither I know not, but the hour's gone by,
When Albion's [4] lessening shores could grieve
   or glad mine eye.

2

Once more upon the waters! yet once more! 10
And the waves bound beneath me as a steed
That knows his rider. Welcome to their roar!
Swift be their guidance, wheresoe'er it lead!
Though the strained mast should quiver as a
   reed,

And the rent canvas fluttering strew the
   gale, 15
Still must I on; for I am as a weed,
Flung from the rock, on ocean's foam to sail
Where'er the surge may sweep, the tempest's
   breath prevail.

3

In my youth's summer [5] I did sing of one,
The wandering outlaw of his own dark
   mind; 20
Again I seize the theme, then but begun,
And bear it with me, as the rushing wind
Bears the cloud onwards: in that tale I find
The furrows of long thought, and dried-up
   tears,
Which, ebbing, leave a sterile track behind, 25
O'er which all heavily the journeying years
Plod the last sands of life—where not a flower
   appears.

4

Since my young days of passion—joy, or pain,
Perchance my heart and harp have lost a
   string,
And both may jar: it may be, that in vain 30
I would essay as I have sung to sing.
Yet, though a dreary strain, to this I cling,

[1] A young nobleman awaiting knighthood.
[2] Stanzas 1–16 are introductory. They constitute a transition from Cantos 1 and 2.
[3] Ada was five weeks old when Lady Byron left Byron in January, 1816. Byron hoped for a reunion, but he never saw Ada again. Note the dramatic effect of the sudden shift in this line. Watch for similar shifts throughout the poem (e.g., ll. 145 and 860).
[4] Poetical name for Britain.
[5] Byron was 21 (1809) when he began the first canto of Childe Harold's Pilgrimage.

So that it wean me from the weary dream
Of selfish grief or gladness—so it fling
Forgetfulness around me—it shall seem   35
To me, though to none else, a not ungrateful
   theme.

5

He, who grown agèd in this world of woe,
In deeds, not years, piercing the depths of life,
So that no wonder waits him; nor below
Can love or sorrow, fame, ambition, strife,   40
Cut to his heart again with the keen knife
Of silent, sharp endurance: he can tell
Why thought seeks refuge in lone caves, yet
   rife
With airy images, and shapes which dwell
Still unimpaired, though old, in the soul's
   haunted cell.   45

6

'Tis to create, and in creating live
A being more intense that we endow
With form our fancy, gaining as we give
The life we image, even as I do now.[6]
What am I? Nothing: but not so art thou,   50
Soul of my thought! with whom I traverse
   earth,
Invisible but gazing, as I glow
Mixed with thy spirit, blended with thy birth,
And feeling still with thee in my crushed
   feelings' dearth.

7

Yet must I think less wildly—I *have*
   thought   55
Too long and darkly, till my brain became,
In its own eddy boiling and o'erwrought,
A whirling gulf of phantasy and flame:
And thus, untaught in youth my heart to
   tame,
My springs of life were poisoned. 'Tis too
   late!   60
Yet am I changed; though still enough the
   same
In strength to bear what time cannot abate,
And feed on bitter fruits without accusing
   fate.

[6] Lines 46–49 give Byron's answer to the question: Why do people write poetry? Note the egoism of the creed.

8

Something too much of this—but now 'tis
   past,
And the spell closes with its silent seal.   65
Long absent HAROLD[7] reappears at last;
He of the breast which fain no more would
   feel,
Wrung with the wounds which kill not, but
   ne'er heal;
Yet time, who changes all, had altered him
In soul and aspect as in age: years steal   70
Fire from the mind as vigor from the limb;
And life's enchanted cup but sparkles near
the brim.

9

His had been quaffed too quickly, and he
   found
The dregs were wormwood;[8] but he filled
   again,
And from a purer fount, on holier ground,   75
And deemed its spring perpetual; but in
   vain!
Still round him clung invisibly a chain
Which galled forever, fettering though un-
   seen,
And heavy though it clanked not; worn with
   pain,
Which pined although it spoke not, and grew
   keen,   80
Entering with every step he took through
   many a scene.

10

Secure in guarded coldness, he had mixed
Again in fancied safety with his kind,
And deemed his spirit now so firmly fixed
And sheathed with an invulnerable mind,   85
That, if no joy, no sorrow lurked behind;
And he, as one, might 'midst the many stand
Unheeded, searching through the crowd to
   find
Fit speculation; such as in strange land
He found in wonder-works of God and Na-
   ture's hand.   90

[7] Byron now turns from himself to Harold, but the disguise is thin.
[8] A bitter-tasting plant.

11

But who can view the ripened rose, nor seek
To wear it? who can curiously behold
The smoothness and the sheen of beauty's
cheek,
Nor feel the heart can never all grow old?
Who can contemplate fame through clouds
unfold 95
The star which rises o'er her steep, nor climb?
Harold, once more within the vortex, rolled
On with the giddy circle, chasing time,
Yet with a nobler aim than in his youth's
fond [9] prime.

12

But soon he knew himself the most unfit 100
Of men to herd with man; with whom he
held
Little in common; untaught to submit
His thoughts to others, though his soul was
quelled
In youth by his own thoughts; still uncom-
pelled,
He would not yield dominion of his mind 105
To spirits against whom his own rebelled;
Proud though in desolation; which could find
A life within itself, to breathe without man-
kind.[10]

13

Where rose the mountains, there to him were
friends;
Where rolled the ocean, thereon was his
home; 110
Where a blue sky, and glowing clime, ex-
tends,
He had the passion and the power to roam;
The desert, forest, cavern, breaker's foam,
Were unto him companionship; they spake
A mutual language, clearer than the tome 115
Of his land's tongue, which he would oft for-
sake
For nature's pages glassed by sunbeams on
the lake.[11]

14

Like the Chaldean,[12] he could watch the
stars,
Till he had peopled them with beings bright
As their own beams; and earth, and earth-
born jars, 120
And human frailties, were forgotten quite:
Could he have kept his spirit to that flight
He had been happy; but this clay will sink
Its spark immortal, envying it the light
To which it mounts, as if to break the link 125
That keeps us from yon heaven which woos
us to its brink.

15

But in man's dwellings he became a thing
Restless and worn, and stern and wearisome,
Drooped as a wild-born falcon with clipped
wing,
To whom the boundless air alone were
home: 130
Then came his fit again, which to o'ercome,
As eagerly the barred-up bird will beat
His breast and beak against his wiry dome
Till the blood tinge his plumage, so the heat
Of his impeded soul would through his bosom
eat. 135

16

Self-exiled Harold wanders forth again,
With nought of hope left, but with less of
gloom,
The very knowledge that he lived in vain,
That all was over on this side the tomb,
Had made despair a smilingness assume, 140
Which, though 'twere wild—as on the plun-
dered wreck
When mariners would madly meet their doom
With draughts intemperate on the sinking
deck—
Did yet inspire a cheer, which he forbore to
check.

[9] Foolish.
[10] This stanza embodies a dominant theme of this poem and of much of Byron's poetry. Cf. especially st. 113.
[11] This stanza also states a recurrent idea of the canto: A soul hating society seeks the solace of nature. Find similar expressions throughout the poem. How does Byron's reaction to nature here differ from Wordsworth's?
[12] The Chaldeans were expert astrologers.

17

Stop!—for thy tread is on an empire's dust!   145
An earthquake's spoil is sepulchered below!
Is the spot marked with no colossal bust?
Nor column trophied for triumphal show?
None; but the moral's truth tells simpler so,
As the ground was before, thus let it be;—   150
How that red rain hath made the harvest
   grow!
And is this all the world has gained by thee,
Thou first and last of fields! king-making
   victory? [13]

18

And Harold stands upon this place of skulls,
The grave of France, the deadly Water-
   loo!   155
How in an hour the power which gave an-
   nuls
Its gifts, transferring fame as fleeting too!
In "pride of place" [14] here last the eagle flew,
Then tore with bloody talon the rent plain;
Pierced by the shaft of banded nations
   through;   160
Ambition's life and labors all were vain;
He wears the shattered links of the world's
   broken chain.

19

Fit retribution! Gaul may champ the bit
And foam in fetters;—but is earth more free? [15]
Did nations combat to make *one* submit;   165
Or league to teach all kings true sovereignty?
What! shall reviving thralldom again be
The patched-up idol of enlightened days?
Shall we, who struck the lion [16] down, shall
   we

[13] The victory over Napoleon at Waterloo simply made more secure the thrones of various European kings. Thus, for Byron, the appropriateness of the absence of a monument (at the time he visited the battlefield) at Waterloo (ll. 147–150).

[14] At the highest point of flight (falconry).

[15] Note the dramatic and oratorical effectiveness of the five rhetorical questions in ll. 164–171. In school Byron was an excellent orator, and his poetical style abounds in oratorical flourishes. Cf. the disillusionment after World War I, a war "to make the world safe for democracy."

[16] Napoleon.

Pay the wolf [17] homage? proffering lowly
   gaze   170
And servile knees to thrones? No; *prove* before ye praise!

20

If not, o'er one fallen despot boast no more!
In vain fair cheeks were furrowed with hot
   tears
For Europe's flowers long rooted up before
The trampler of her vineyards; in vain
   years   175
Of death, depopulation, bondage, fears,
Have all been borne, and broken by the ac-
   cord
Of roused-up millions; all that most endears
Glory, is when the myrtle wreathes a sword
Such as Harmodius [18] drew on Athens' ty-
   rant lord.   180

21

There was a sound of revelry by night, [19]
And Belgium's capital [20] had gathered then
Her beauty and her chivalry, and bright
The lamps shone o'er fair women and brave
   men;
A thousand hearts beat happily; and when   185
Music arose with its voluptuous swell,
Soft eyes looked love to eyes which spake
   again,
And all went merry as a marriage bell;
But hush! hark! a deep sound strikes like a
   rising knell!

22

Did ye not hear it?—No; 'twas but the
   wind,   190

[17] Any lesser tyrant, like the Austrian emperor.

[18] Harmodius and other assassins killed an Athenian tyrant by means of daggers hidden in myrtle branches.

[19] Stanzas 21–28: The ball at Brussels. These stanzas constitute one of the most striking passages of the canto, a passage in which Byron's flair for dramatic incident is fully displayed. Search out the ways by which Byron achieves suspense, vividness, and IRONY.

[20] Brussels. The ball was given on the evening before the battle of Quatre-Bras, which took place two days before Waterloo.

Or the car rattling o'er the stony street;
On with the dance! let joy be unconfined;
No sleep till morn, when youth and pleasure
    meet
To chase the glowing hours with flying feet—
But hark!—that heavy sound breaks in once
    more,   195
As if the clouds its echo would repeat;
And nearer, clearer, deadlier than before!
Arm! Arm! it is—it is—the cannon's opening
    roar!

23

Within a windowed niche of that high hall
Sat Brunswick's fated chieftain;[21] he did
    hear   200
That sound the first amidst the festival,
And caught its tone with death's prophetic
    ear;
And when they smiled because he deemed it
    near,
His heart more truly knew that peal too well
Which stretched his father on a bloody
    bier,   205
And roused the vengeance blood alone could
    quell;
He rushed into the field, and, foremost fight-
    ing, fell.

24

Ah! then and there was hurrying to and fro,
And gathering tears, and tremblings of dis-
    tress,
And cheeks all pale, which but an hour
    ago   210
Blushed at the praise of their own loveliness;
And there were sudden partings, such as press
The life from out young hearts, and choking
    sighs
Which ne'er might be repeated; who could
    guess
If ever more should meet those mutual
    eyes,   215
Since upon night so sweet such awful morn
    could rise!

[21] Frederick William, Duke of Brunswick. His
father (l. 205) had been killed in the battle of
Auerstädt in 1806. What is the effect gained by
this sudden concentration upon a single individual
who is to be slain in the coming battle?

25

And there was mounting in hot haste: the
    steed,
The mustering squadron, and the clattering
    car,
Went pouring forward with impetuous speed,
And swiftly forming in the ranks of war; 220
And the deep thunder peal on peal afar;
And near, the beat of the alarming drum
Roused up the soldier ere the morning star;
While thronged the citizens with terror dumb,
Or whispering, with white lips—"The foe!
    they come! they come!"   225

26

And wild and high the "Cameron's gather-
    ing"[22] rose!
The war-note of Lochiel,[23] which Albyn's[24]
    hills
Have heard, and heard, too, have her Saxon
    foes[25]—
How in the noon of night that pibroch[26]
    thrills,
Savage and shrill! But with the breath which
    fills   230
Their mountain-pipe, so fill the mountain-
    eers
With the fierce native daring which instills
The stirring memory of a thousand years,
And Evan's, Donald's[27] fame rings in each
    clansman's ears!

27

And Ardennes[28] waves above them her green
    leaves,   235
Dewy with nature's teardrops as they pass,
Grieving, if aught inanimate e'er grieves,
Over the unreturning brave—alas!
Ere evening to be trodden like the grass
Which now beneath them, but above shall
    grow   240

[22] Battle song of the Cameron clan (in Scotland).
[23] Chief of the Cameron clan.
[24] Scotland's.
[25] The English.
[26] Bagpipe music.
[27] Famous Cameron clansmen.
[28] Byron's error for Soignies, a forest near Waterloo.

In its next verdure, when this fiery mass
Of living valor, rolling on the foe
And burning with high hope, shall molder
cold and low.

28

Last noon beheld them full of lusty life,
Last eve in beauty's circle proudly gay; 245
The midnight brought the signal-sound of
strife,
The morn the marshaling in arms—the day
Battle's magnificently stern array!
The thunder-clouds close o'er it, which when
rent
The earth is covered thick with other clay, 250
Which her own clay shall cover, heaped and
pent,
Rider and horse—friend, foe—in one red
burial blent!

29

Their praise is hymned to loftier harps [29]
than mine; [30]
Yet one [31] I would select from that proud
throng,
Partly because they blend me with his
line, 255
And partly that I did his sire some wrong,
And partly that bright names will hallow
song;
And his was of the bravest, and when
showered
The death-bolts deadliest the thinned files
along,
Even where the thickest of war's tempest
lowered, 260
They reached no nobler breast than thine,
young gallant Howard!

30

There have been tears and breaking hearts
for thee,

[29] A tribute to Walter Scott and his *Field of
Waterloo* (1815).
[30] Stanzas 29-35: The tragedy of the war dead.
[31] Frederick Howard, who was killed at Waterloo.
He was Byron's second cousin (l. 255), whose
father, the Earl of Carlisle (l. 256), Byron satirized
in *English Bards and Scotch Reviewers.*

And mine were nothing had I such to give;
But when I stood beneath the fresh green
tree,
Which living waves where thou didst cease
to live, 265
And saw around me the wide field revive
With fruits and fertile promise, and the
spring
Came forth her work of gladness to con-
trive,
With all her reckless birds upon the wing,
I turned from all she brought to those she
could not bring. 270

31

I turned to thee, to thousands, of whom
each
And one as all a ghastly gap did make
In his own kind and kindred, whom to
teach
Forgetfulness were mercy for their sake;
The archangel's trump, not glory's, must
awake 275
Those whom they thirst for; though the
sound of fame
May for a moment soothe, it cannot slake
The fever of vain longing, and the name
So honored but assumes a stronger, bitterer
claim.

32

They mourn, but smile at length—and,
smiling, mourn: [32] 280
The tree will wither long before it fall;
The hull drives on, though mast and sail
be torn;
The roof-tree sinks, but molders on the hall
In massy hoariness; the ruined wall
Stands when its wind-worn battlements are
gone; 285
The bars survive the captive they enthrall;
The day drags through, though storms keep
out the sun;
And thus the heart will break, yet brokenly
live on:

[32] What is the single point made by this succession of items in ll. 280-287? Are they all
equally effective?

33

Even as a broken mirror, which the glass
In every fragment multiplies—and
makes   290
A thousand images of one that was
The same—and still the more, the more it
breaks;
And thus the heart will do which not for-
sakes,
Living in shattered guise; and still, and
cold,
And bloodless, with its sleepless sorrow
aches,   295
Yet withers on till all without is old,
Showing no visible sign, for such things are
untold.

34

There is a very life in our despair,[33]
Vitality of poison,—a quick root
Which feeds these deadly branches; for it
were   300
As nothing did we die; but life will suit
Itself to sorrow's most detested fruit,
Like to the apples on the Dead Sea's shore,
All ashes to the taste: Did man compute
Existence by enjoyment, and count o'er 305
Such hours 'gainst years of life,—say, would
he name threescore?

35

The psalmist numbered out the years [34] of
man:
They are enough; and if thy tale be *true,*
Thou, who didst grudge him even that
fleeting span,
More than enough, thou fatal Water-
loo!   310
Millions of tongues record thee, and anew
Their children's lips shall echo them, and
say—
"Here, where the sword united nations
drew,

Our countrymen were warring on that day!"
And this is much—and all—which will not
pass away.   315

36

There sunk the greatest, nor the worst of
men,[35]
Whose spirit, antithetically mixed,
One moment of the mightiest, and again
On little objects with like firmness fixed;
Extreme in all things! hadst thou been be-
twixt,   320
Thy throne had still been thine, or never
been;
For daring made thy rise as fall: thou
seekest
Even now to re-assume the imperial mien,[36]
And shake again the world, the thunderer of
the scene!

37

Conqueror and captive of the earth art
thou!   325
She trembles at thee still, and thy wild
name
Was ne'er more bruited in men's minds
than now
That thou art nothing, save the jest of
fame,
Who wooed thee once, thy vassal, and be-
came
The flatterer of thy fierceness, till thou
wert   330
A god unto thyself; nor less the same
To the astounded kingdoms all inert,
Who deemed thee for a time whate'er thou
didst assert.

38

Oh, more or less than man—in high or
low—

---

[33] Note how the poet identifies himself, through their common despair, with those bereft of their loved ones by Waterloo. This theme of "life in our despair" is frequent in Byron's poetry.
[34] Threescore and ten (Psalms 90:10).
[35] Stanzas 36-45: Napoleon and kindred spirits. Byron makes a penetrating analysis of the complex personality that was Napoleon. Note how he immediately (l. 317) strikes the keynote of his analysis: "spirit antithetically mixed." How do the succeeding lines (especially st. 38) develop this phrase?
[36] Napoleon was at this time exiled at St. Helena, but Byron suggests that he might return.

Battling with nations, flying from the
    field,   335
Now making monarchs' necks thy footstool,
    now
More than thy meanest soldier taught to
    yield;
An empire thou couldst crush, command,
    rebuild,
But govern not thy pettiest passion, nor,
However deeply in men's spirits skilled, 340
Look through thine own, nor curb the lust
    of war,
Nor learn that tempted fate will leave the
    loftiest star.

39

Yet well thy soul hath brooked the turning
    tide
With that untaught innate philosophy,
Which, be it wisdom, coldness, or deep
    pride,   345
Is gall and wormwood to an enemy.[37]
When the whole host of hatred stood hard
    by,
To watch and mock thee shrinking, thou
    hast smiled
With a sedate and all-enduring eye;—
When fortune fled her spoiled and favorite
    child,   350
He stood unbowed beneath the ills upon
    him piled.

40

Sager than in thy fortunes; for in them
Ambition steeled thee on too far to show
That just habitual scorn, which could con-
    temn
Men and their thoughts; 'twas wise to feel,
    not so   355
To wear it ever on thy lip and brow,
And spurn the instruments thou wert to use
Till they were turned unto thine over-
    throw:
'Tis but a worthless world to win or lose;
So hath it proved to thee, and all such lot
    who choose.   360

[37] Lines 343–346: Stoical acceptance of defeat is
vexing to a conqueror, who would rather see his
enemy squirm.

41

If, like a tower upon a headland rock,
Thou hadst been made to stand or fall
    alone,
Such scorn of man had helped to brave
    the shock;
But men's thoughts were the steps which
    paved thy throne,
Their admiration thy best weapon
    shone;   365
The part of Philip's son [38] was thine, not
    then
(Unless aside thy purple had been thrown)
Like stern Diogenes to mock at men;
For sceptered cynics earth were far too wide
    a den.

42

But quiet to quick bosoms is a hell,   370
And *there* hath been thy bane; there is a
    fire
And motion of the soul which will not
    dwell
In its own narrow being, but aspire
Beyond the fitting medium of desire;
And, but once kindled, quenchless ever
    more,   375
Preys upon high adventure, nor can tire
Of aught but rest; a fever at the core,
Fatal to him who bears, to all who ever bore.

43

This makes the madmen who have made
    men mad
By their contagion; conquerors and
    kings,   380
Founders of sects and systems, to whom add
Sophists, bards, statesmen, all unquiet
    things
Which stir too strongly the soul's secret
    springs,
And are themselves the fools to those they
    fool;

[38] Alexander the Great. Byron is saying in sts.
40–41 that Napoleon should have modeled his
handling of men upon the magnanimity of Alexander, not on the cynicism of the Athenian philosopher Diogenes. A retiring philosopher can afford
to be cynical and to show it, but not a ruler of men.

Envied, yet how unenviable! what
   stings   385
Are theirs! One breast laid open were a
   school
Which would unteach mankind the lust to
   shine or rule:

44

Their breath is agitation, and their life
A storm whereon they ride, to sink at last,
And yet so nursed and bigoted to strife, 390
That should their days, surviving perils
   past,
Melt to calm twilight, they feel overcast
With sorrow and supineness, and so die;
Even as a flame unfed, which runs to
   waste
With its own flickering, or a sword laid
   by,   395
Which eats into itself, and rusts inglori-
   ously.

45

He who ascends to mountain tops, shall
   find
The loftiest peaks most wrapped in clouds
   and snow;
He who surpasses or subdues mankind,
Must look down on the hate of those be-
   low.   400
Though high *above* the sun of glory glow,
And far *beneath* the earth and ocean
   spread,
Round him are icy rocks, and loudly blow
Contending tempests on his naked head,
And thus reward the toils which to those
   summits led.   405

46

Away with these! true wisdom's world will
   be [39]
Within its own creation, or in thine,
Maternal Nature! for who teems like thee,
Thus on the banks of thy majestic Rhine?
There Harold gazes on a work divine,   410
A blending of all beauties; streams and
   dells,

[39] Stanzas 46–51: The Rhine and its castles.

Fruit, foliage, crag, wood, cornfield, mountain, vine,
And chiefless castles breathing stern fare-
   wells
From gray but leafy walls, where ruin
   greenly dwells.

47

And there they stand, as stands a lofty
   mind,   415
Worn, but unstooping to the baser
   crowd,
All tenantless, save to the crannying wind,
Or holding dark communion with the
   cloud.
There was a day when they were young
   and proud;
Banners on high, and battles [40] passed below;   420
But they who fought are in a bloody
   shroud,
And those which waved are shredless dust
   ere now,
And the bleak battlements shall bear no
   future blow.

48

Beneath those battlements, within those
   walls,
Power dwelt amidst her passions; in proud
   state   425
Each robber chief upheld his armèd
   halls,
Doing his evil will, nor less elate
Than mightier heroes of a longer date.
What want these outlaws conquerors
   should have,
But history's purchased page to call them
   great?   430
A wider space—an ornamented grave?
Their hopes were not less warm, their souls
   were full as brave.

49

In their baronial feuds and single fields,
What deeds of prowess unrecorded died!
And love, which lent a blazon to their
   shields   435

[40] Battalions.

With emblems well devised by amorous
    pride,
Through all the mail of iron hearts would
    glide;
But still their flame was fierceness, and
    drew on
Keen contest and destruction near allied,
And many a tower for some fair mischief
    won,   440
Saw the discolored Rhine beneath its ruin
    run.

50

But thou, exulting and abounding river!
Making thy waves a blessing as they flow
Through banks whose beauty would en-
    dure for ever
Could man but leave thy bright creation
    so,   445
Nor its fair promise from the surface mow
With the sharp scythe of conflict,—then to
    see
Thy valley of sweet waters, were to know
Earth paved like heaven—and to seem such
    to me,
Even now what wants thy stream?—that it
    should Lethe [41] be.   450

51

A thousand battles have assailed thy banks,
But these and half their fame have passed
    away,
And slaughter heaped on high his weltering
    ranks:
Their very graves are gone, and what are
    they?
Thy tide washed down the blood of yester-
    day,   455
And all was stainless, and on thy clear
    stream
Glassed, with its dancing light, the sunny
    ray;
But o'er the blackened memory's blighting
    dream
Thy waves would vainly roll, all sweeping
    as they seem.

[41] River of forgetfulness in Hades. What does this
line mean?

52

Thus Harold inly said, and passed
    along,[42]   460
Yet not insensible to all which here
Awoke the jocund birds to early song
In glens which might have made even exile
    dear:
Though on his brow were graven lines
    austere,
And tranquil sternness, which had ta'en the
    place   465
Of feelings fierier far but less severe—
Joy was not always absent from his face,
But o'er it in such scenes would steal with
    transient trace.

53

Nor was all love shut from him, though his
    days
Of passion had consumed themselves to
    dust.   470
It is in vain that we would coldly gaze
On such as smile upon us; the heart must
Leap kindly back to kindness, though dis-
    gust
Hath weaned it from all worldlings: thus
    he felt,
For there was soft remembrance, and sweet
    trust   475
In one fond breast, to which his own would
    melt,
And in its tenderer hour on that his bosom
    dwelt.

54

And he had learned to love,—I know not
    why,
For this in such as him seems strange of
    mood,—
The helpless looks of blooming infancy, 480
Even in its earliest nurture; what subdued,
To change like this, a mind so far imbued,
With scorn of man, it little boots to know;
But thus it was; and though in solitude
Small power the nipped affections have to
    grow,   485
In him this glowed when all beside had
    ceased to glow.

[42] Stanzas 52-55: Comments on Childe Harold.

55

And there was one soft breast,[43] as hath
  been said,
Which unto his was bound by stronger ties
Than the church links withal; and, though
  unwed,
That love was pure—and, far above dis-
  guise,   490
Had stood the test of mortal enmities,
Still undivided, and cemented more
By peril, dreaded most in female eyes;
But this was firm, and from a foreign shore
Well to that heart might his these absent
  greetings pour!   495

(1)

The castled crag of Drachenfels
Frowns o'er the wide and winding Rhine,
Whose breast of waters broadly swells
Between the banks which bear the vine;
And hills all rich with blossomed trees,   500
And fields which promise corn and wine,
And scattered cities crowning these,
Whose far white walls along them shine,
Have strewed a scene, which I should see
With double joy wert *thou* with me.   505

(2)

And peasant girls, with deep blue eyes,
And hands which offer early flowers,
Walk smiling o'er this paradise;
Above, the frequent feudal towers
Through green leaves lift their walls of gray; **510**
And many a rock which steeply lowers,
And noble arch in proud decay,
Look o'er this vale of vintage-bowers;
But one thing want these banks of Rhine,—
Thy gentle hand to clasp in mine!   515

(3)

I send the lilies given to me—
Though long before thy hand they touch,
I know that they must withered be,
But yet reject them not as such;
For I have cherished them as dear,   520

Because they yet may meet thine eye,
And guide thy soul to mine even here—
When thou beholdest them drooping nigh,
And knowest them gathered by the Rhine,
And offered from my heart to thine!   525

(4)

The river nobly foams and flows—
The charm of this enchanted ground,
And all its thousand turns disclose
Some fresher beauty varying round:
The haughtiest breast its wish might bound   530
Through life to dwell delighted here;
Nor could on earth a spot be found
To nature and to me so dear—
Could thy dear eyes in following mine
Still sweeten more these banks of Rhine!   535

56

By Coblentz, on a rise of gentle ground,[44]
There is a small and simple pyramid,
Crowning the summit of the verdant
  mound;
Beneath its base are heroes' ashes hid—
Our enemy's—but let not that forbid   540
Honor to Marceau![45] o'er whose early
  tomb
Tears, big tears, gushed from the rough
  soldier's lid,
Lamenting and yet envying such a doom,
Falling for France, whose rights he battled
  to resume.

57

Brief, brave, and glorious was his young
  career,—   545
His mourners were two hosts, his friends and
  foes;
And fitly may the stranger lingering here
Pray for his gallant spirit's bright repose;
For he was freedom's champion, one of
  those,
The few in number, who had not o'er-
  stepped   550

[43] Byron's half-sister, Augusta, who had stood by
him during his days of unpopularity in London
(ll. 491–493).

[44] Stanzas 56–61: Coblentz and Marceau; Ehrenbreitstein; farewell to the Rhine.

[45] French general who was killed near Coblentz
in 1796.

The charter to chastise which she bestows
On such as wield her weapons; he had kept
The whiteness of his soul—and thus men
o'er him wept.

58

Here Ehrenbreitstein,[46] with her shattered
wall
Black with the miner's blast, upon her
height   555
Yet shows of what she was, when shell and
ball
Rebounding idly on her strength did light:
A tower of victory! from whence the flight
Of baffled foes was watched along the
plain:
But peace destroyed what war could never
blight,[47]   560
And laid those proud roofs bare to sum-
mer's rain—
On which the iron shower for years had
poured in vain.

59

Adieu to thee, fair Rhine! How long de-
lighted
The stranger fain would linger on his way!
Thine is a scene alike where souls
united,   565
Or lonely contemplation thus might stray;
And could the ceaseless vultures cease to
prey
On self-condemning bosoms, it were here,
Where nature, nor too somber nor too gay,
Wild but not rude, awful yet not
austere,   570
Is to the mellow earth as autumn to the
year.

60

Adieu to thee again! a vain adieu!
There can be no farewell to scene like
thine;
The mind is colored by thy every hue;
And if reluctantly the eyes resign   575

[46] A hill fortress opposite Coblentz.
[47] By "the miner's blast" (l. 555).

Their cherished gaze upon thee, lovely
Rhine!
'Tis with the thankful heart of parting
praise;
More mighty spots may rise—more glaring
shine,
But none unite in one attaching maze,
The brilliant, fair, and soft,—the glories of
old days.   580

61

The negligently grand, the fruitful bloom
Of coming ripeness, the white city's sheen,
The rolling stream, the precipice's gloom,
The forest's growth, and Gothic walls be-
tween,—
The wild rocks shaped, as they had turrets
been,   585
In mockery of man's art; and these withal
A race of faces happy as the scene,
Whose fertile bounties here extend to all,
Still springing o'er thy banks, though em-
pires near them fall.

62

But these recede. Above me are the
Alps,[48]   590
The palaces of nature, whose vast walls
Have pinnacled in clouds their snowy
scalps,
And throned eternity in icy halls
Of cold sublimity, where forms and falls
The avalanche—the thunderbolt of
snow!   595
All that expands the spirit, yet appalls,
Gather around these summits, as to show
How earth may pierce to heaven, yet leave
vain man below.

63

But ere these matchless heights I dare to
scan,
There is a spot should not be passed in
vain,—   600
Morat![49] the proud, the patriot field! where
man

[48] Stanzas 62–67: The Alps; the field of Morat;
Julia Alpinula.
[49] A small Swiss town near which the invading
Duke of Burgundy was defeated in 1476.

May gaze on ghastly trophies of the slain,
Nor blush for those who conquered on
  that plain;
Here Burgundy bequeathed his tombless
  host,
A bony heap, through ages to remain, 605
Themselves their monument;—the Stygian
  coast [50]
Unsepulchered they roamed, and shrieked
  each wandering ghost.

64

While Waterloo with Cannæ's [51] carnage
  vies,
Morat and Marathon [52] twin names shall
  stand;
They were true glory's stainless victories, 610
Won by the unambitious heart and hand
Of a proud, brotherly, and civic band,
All unbought champions in no princely
  cause
Of vice-entailed corruption; they no land
Doomed to bewail the blasphemy of
  laws 615
Making kings' rights divine, by some Dra-
  conic [53] clause.

65

By a lone wall a lonelier column rears
A gray and grief-worn aspect of old days;
'Tis the last remnant of the wreck of years,
And looks as with the wild-bewildered
  gaze 620
Of one to stone converted by amaze,
Yet still with consciousness; and there it
  stands
Making a marvel that it not decays,

[50] Lines 606–607: According to superstition, the spirits of the unburied could not pass over the Styx into Hades.
[51] Cannæ was the site of Hannibal's defeat of the Romans in 216 B.C.
[52] The site of the victory of the Athenian general Miltiades over the Persians in 490 B.C. Waterloo and Cannæ represent for Byron modern and ancient examples of futile carnage; Morat and Marathon, on the other hand, illustrate worth-while battles for freedom. Again the dramatic contrast.
[53] Severe—derived from the harsh penal code drawn up by Draco for Athens.

When the coeval pride of human hands,
Leveled Aventicum,[54] hath strewed her subject lands. 625

66

And there—oh! sweet and sacred be the
  name!
Julia [55]—the daughter—the devoted—gave
Her youth to heaven; her heart, beneath a
  claim
Nearest to heaven's, broke o'er a father's
  grave.
Justice is sworn 'gainst tears, and hers
  would crave 630
The life she lived in—but the judge was
  just—
And then she died on him she could not
  save.
Their tomb was simple, and without a bust,
And held within their urn one mind—one
  heart—one dust.

67

But these are deeds which should not pass
  away, 635
And names that must not wither, though
  the earth
Forgets her empires with a just decay,
The enslavers and the enslaved—their death
  and birth;
The high, the mountain-majesty of worth
Should be—and shall, survivor of its
  woe, 640
And from its immortality, look forth
In the sun's face, like yonder Alpine snow,
Imperishably pure beyond all things below.

68

Lake Leman [56] woos me with its crystal
  face,[57]

[54] The modern Avenches, capital of Switzerland in Roman times.
[55] Julia Alpinula, who, according to legend, died in a vain effort to save the life of her father, condemned to death as a traitor.
[56] Lake Geneva.
[57] Stanzas 68–75: Lake Leman; the ministry of nature.

The mirror where the stars and mountains
view   645
The stillness of their aspect in each trace
Its clear depth yields of their far height
and hue:
There is too much of man here, to look
through
With a fit mind the might which I behold;
But soon in me shall loneliness renew 650
Thoughts hid, but not less cherished than
of old,
Ere mingling with the herd had penned me
in their fold.

69

To fly from, need not be to hate, mankind:
All are not fit with them to stir and toil,
Nor is it discontent to keep the mind 655
Deep in its fountain, lest it overboil
In the hot throng, where we become the
spoil
Of our infection, till too late and long,
We may deplore and struggle with the coil,
In wretched interchange of wrong for
wrong   660
Midst a contentious world, striving where
none are strong.

70

There, in a moment, we may plunge our
years
In fatal penitence, and in the blight
Of our own soul turn all our blood to tears,
And color things to come with hues of
night;   665
The race of life becomes a hopeless flight
To those that walk in darkness: on the sea
The boldest steer but where their ports
invite—
But there are wanderers o'er eternity,
Whose bark drives on and on, and anchored
ne'er shall be.   670

71

Is it not better, then, to be alone,
And love earth only for its earthly sake?
By the blue rushing of the arrowy Rhone,
Or the pure bosom of its nursing lake,

Which feeds it as a mother who doth
make   675
A fair but froward infant her own care,
Kissing its cries away as these awake;—
Is it not better thus our lives to wear,
Than join the crushing crowd, doomed to
inflict or bear?

72

I live not in myself, but I become   680
Portion of that around me; and to me
High mountains are a feeling, but the hum
Of human cities torture: [58] I can see
Nothing to loathe in nature, save to be
A link reluctant in a fleshy chain,   685
Classed among creatures, when the soul can
flee,
And with the sky—the peak—the heaving
plain
Of ocean, or the stars, mingle—and not in
vain.

73

And thus I am absorbed, and this is life:
I look upon the peopled desert past,   690
As on a place of agony and strife,
Where, for some sin, to sorrow I was cast,
To act and suffer, but remount at last
With a fresh pinion; which I feel to spring,
Though young, yet waxing vigorous as the
blast   695
Which it would cope with, on delighted
wing,
Spurning the clay-cold bonds which round
our being cling.

74

And when, at length, the mind shall be all
free
From what it hates in this degraded form,
Reft of its carnal life, save what shall be 700
Existent happier in the fly and worm,—

[58] The Wordsworthian quality of ll. 680–683 and
of much of the following meditation is not accidental. In the summer of 1816, when Canto 2 was
written, Shelley was reading to Byron Wordsworth's
poetry and arousing in him at least a temporary
admiration for it.

When elements to elements conform,
And dust is as it should be, shall I not
Feel all I see, less dazzling, but more warm?
The bodiless thought? the spirit of each
    spot?   705
Of which, even now, I share at times the
    immortal lot?

75

Are not the mountains, waves, and skies, a
    part
Of me and of my soul, as I of them?
Is not the love of these deep in my heart
With a pure passion? should I not con-
    temn   710
All objects, if compared with these? and
    stem
A tide of suffering, rather than forego
Such feelings for the hard and worldly
    phlegm
Of those whose eyes are only turned below,
Gazing upon the ground, with thoughts
    which dare not glow?   715

76

But this is not my theme; and I return [59]
To that which is immediate, and require
Those who find contemplation in the urn,[60]
To look on one,[61] whose dust was once all
    fire,
A native of the land where I respire   720
The clear air for a while—a passing guest,
Where he became a being,—whose desire
Was to be glorious; 'twas a foolish quest,
The which to gain and keep, he sacrificed
    all rest.

77

Here the self-torturing sophist, wild Rous-
    seau,   725
The apostle of affliction, he who threw

Enchantment over passion, and from woe
Wrung overwhelming eloquence, first drew
The breath which made him wretched; yet
    he knew
How to make madness beautiful, and
    cast   730
O'er erring deeds and thoughts a heavenly
    hue
Of words, like sunbeams, dazzling as they
    passed
The eyes, which o'er them shed tears feel-
    ingly and fast.

78

His love was passion's essence—as a tree
On fire by lighning; with ethereal flame 735
Kindled he was, and blasted; for to be
Thus, and enamored, were in him the
    same.
But his was not the love of living dame,
Nor of the dead who rise upon our dreams,
But of ideal beauty, which became   740
In him existence, and o'erflowing teems
Along his burning page, distempered though
    it seems.

79

This breathed itself to life in Julie,[62] *this*
Invested her with all that's wild and sweet;
This hallowed, too, the memorable
    kiss [63]   745
Which every morn his fevered lip would
    greet,
From hers, who but with friendship his
    would meet;
But to that gentle touch through brain and
    breast
Flashed the thrilled spirit's love-devouring
    heat;
In that absorbing sigh perchance more
    blessed   750
Than vulgar minds may be with all they
    seek possessed.

[59] Stanzas 76-84: Rousseau and the French Revolution.
[60] What is the meaning of this line?
[61] Jean Jacques Rousseau, eighteenth-century French philosopher, born in Geneva. Byron sees Rousseau primarily as a romanticist and a revolutionist.

[62] The heroine of Rousseau's novel *La Nouvelle Héloïse*.
[63] A kiss from a lady celebrated in the *Confessions*, Rousseau's frank autobiography. To her the kiss was merely the common form of French greeting.

80

His life was one long war with self-sought
foes,
Or friends by him self-banished; for his
mind
Had grown suspicion's sanctuary, and
chose,
For its own cruel sacrifice, the kind,   755
'Gainst whom he raged with fury strange
and blind.
But he was frenzied,—wherefore, who may
know?
Since cause might be which skill could
never find;
But he was frenzied by disease or woe,
To that worst pitch of all, which wears a
reasoning show.   760

81

For then he was inspired, and from him
came,
As from the Pythian's mystic cave [64] of
yore,
Those oracles [65] which set the world in
flame,
Nor ceased to burn till kingdoms were no
more: [66]
Did he not this for France? which lay, be-
fore,   765
Bowed to the inborn tyranny of years?
Broken and trembling to the yoke she bore,
Till by the voice of him and his compeers
Roused up to too much wrath, which fol-
lows o'ergrown fears?

82

They made themselves a fearful monument!   770
The wreck of old opinions—things which
grew,
Breathed from the birth of time: the veil
they rent,
And what behind it lay, all earth shall
view;

[64] Apollo's oracle at Delphi.
[65] Especially *The Social Contract*, Rousseau's
most famous essay of political philosophy.
[66] The reference here and in the following lines
is to Rousseau's influence on the French Revolution.

But good with ill they also overthrew,
Leaving but ruins, wherewith to rebuild 775
Upon the same foundation, and renew
Dungeons and thrones, which the same
hour refilled,
As heretofore, because ambition was self-
willed.

83

But this will not endure, nor be endured! [67]
Mankind have felt their strength, and made
it felt.   780
They might have used it better, but, al-
lured
By their new vigor, sternly have they dealt
On one another; pity ceased to melt
With her once natural charities. But
they,
Who in oppression's darkness caved had
dwelt,   785
They were not eagles, nourished with the
day;
What marvel then, at times, if they mistook
their prey?

84

What deep wounds ever closed without a
scar?
The heart's bleed longest, and but heal to
wear
That which disfigures it; and they who
war   790
With their own hopes, and have been vanquished, bear
Silence, but not submission: in his lair
Fixed passion holds his breath, until the
hour
Which shall atone for years; none need
despair:
It came—it cometh—and will come,—the
power   795
To punish or forgive—in *one* we shall be
slower.

[67] In ll. 779–796 rings the voice of the Byron
who cried out (in *Don Juan*): "I will teach, if
possible, the stones To rise against earth's tyrants."
The Continental influence of Byron, the champion
of freedom, was very strong in the nineteenth
century.

85

Clear, placid Leman! thy contrasted lake,[68]
With the wild world I dwelt in, is a thing
Which warns me, with its stillness, to for-
sake
Earth's troubled waters for a purer
spring.   800
This quiet sail is as a noiseless wing
To waft me from distraction; once I loved
Torn ocean's roar, but thy soft murmuring
Sounds sweet as if a sister's voice reproved,
That I with stern delights should e'er have
been so moved.   805

86

It is the hush of night, and all between
Thy margin and the mountains, dusk, yet
clear,
Mellowed and mingling, yet distinctly
seen,
Save darkened Jura,[69] whose capped
heights appear
Precipitously steep; and drawing near, 810
There breathes a living fragrance from the
shore,
Of flowers yet fresh with childhood; on the
ear
Drops the light drip of the suspended oar,
Or chirps the grasshopper one good-night
carol more.[70]

87

He is an evening reveler, who makes 815
His life an infancy, and sings his fill;
At intervals, some bird from out the brakes
Starts into voice a moment, then is still.
There seems a floating whisper on the hill,
But that is fancy, for the starlight dews 820

[68] Stanzas 85–91: Lake Leman at nightfall. Note the abrupt shift in tone and mood. Like a versatile actor, Byron moves easily from one role to another. Now for awhile he will be the quiet, introspective meditator. He once said of himself: "I am so changeable, being everything by turns and nothing long. . . ."
[69] A mountain range northwest of Lake Geneva.
[70] This stanza concentrates the mood of the whole section. Note the handling of the meter (particularly l. 813) and the contribution made by images of sight, smell, and sound.

All silently their tears of love instill,
Weeping themselves away, till they infuse
Deep into nature's breast the spirit of her
hues.

88

Ye stars! which are the poetry of heaven!
If in your bright leaves we would read the
fate   825
Of men and empires,—'tis to be forgiven,
That in our aspirations to be great,
Our destinies o'erleap their mortal state,
And claim a kindred with you; [71] for ye are
A beauty and a mystery, and create   830
In us such love and reverence from afar,
That fortune, fame, power, life, have named
themselves a star.

89

All heaven and earth are still—though not
in sleep,
But breathless, as we grow when feeling
most;
And silent, as we stand in thoughts too
deep:—   835
All heaven and earth are still. From the
high host
Of stars, to the lulled lake and mountain-
coast,
All is concentered in a life intense,
Where not a beam, nor air, nor leaf is lost,
But hath a part of being, and a sense 840
Of that which is of all Creator and defense.

90

Then stirs the feeling infinite, so felt
In solitude, where we are *least* alone;
A truth, which through our being then
doth melt,
And purifies from self: it is a tone,   845
The soul and source of music, which makes
known
Eternal harmony, and sheds a charm
Like to the fabled Cytherea's zone,[72]

[71] Byron can understand how the pseudo-science of astrology arose.
[72] The girdle of Aphrodite (Venus), which con-ferred upon the wearer the power to attract love.

Binding all things with beauty;—'twould dis-
arm
The specter death, had he substantial power
to harm.   850

91

Not vainly did the early Persian make
His altar the high places, and the peak
Of earth-o'ergazing mountains, and thus
take
A fit and unwalled temple, there to seek
The spirit, in whose honor shrines are
weak,   855
Upreared of human hands. Come, and
compare
Columns and idol-dwellings—Goth or
Greek—
With nature's realms of worship, earth and
air—
Nor fix on fond abodes to circumscribe thy
prayer!

92

The sky is changed!—and such a change!
Oh, night,[73]   860
And storm, and darkness, ye are wondrous
strong,
Yet lovely in your strength, as is the light
Of a dark eye in woman! Far along,
From peak to peak, the rattling crags
among
Leaps the live thunder! Not from one lone
cloud,   865
But every mountain now hath found a
tongue,
And Jura answers, through her misty
shroud,
Back to the joyous Alps, who call to her
aloud!

93

And this is in the night:—Most glorious
night!
Thou wert not sent for slumber! let me
be   870

[73] Stanzas 92–97: Storm in the Alps. Note again
the quick change of tone, mood, and tempo.

A sharer in thy fierce and far delight,—
A portion of the tempest and of thee!
How the lit lake shines, a phosphoric
sea,
And the big rain comes dancing to the
earth!
And now again 'tis black,—and now, the
glee   875
Of the loud hills shakes with its mountain-
mirth,
As if they did rejoice o'er a young earth-
quake's birth.

94

Now, where the swift Rhone cleaves his
way between
Heights which appear as lovers who have
parted
In hate, whose mining depths so inter-
vene,   880
That they can meet no more, though
broken-hearted:
Though in their souls, which thus each
other thwarted,
Love was the very root of the fond rage
Which blighted their life's bloom, and
then departed:—
Itself expired, but leaving them an age   885
Of years all winters,—war within themselves
to wage:

95

Now, where the quick Rhone thus hath
cleft his way,
The mightiest of the storms hath taken his
stand:
For here, not one, but many, make their
play,
And fling their thunder-bolts from hand to
hand,   890
Flashing and cast around: of all the
band,
The brightest through these parted hills
hath forked
His lightnings,—as if he did understand,
That in such gaps as desolation worked,
There the hot shaft should blast whatever
therein lurked.   895

96

Sky, mountains, river, winds, lake, light-
     nings! ye!
With night, and clouds, and thunder, and
     a soul
To make these felt and feeling, well may be
Things that have made me watchful; the
     far roll
Of your departing voices, is the knoll [74]   900
Of what in me is sleepless,—if I rest.
But where of ye, O tempests! is the goal?
Are ye like those within the human breast?
Or do ye find, at length, like eagles, some
     high nest?

97

Could I embody and unbosom now   905
That which is most within me,—could I
     wreak
My thoughts upon expression, and thus
     throw
Soul, heart, mind, passions, feelings, strong
     or weak,
All that I would have sought, and all I seek,
Bear, know, feel—and yet breathe—into *one*
     word,   910
And that one word were lightning, I would
     speak;
But as it is, I live and die unheard,
With a most voiceless thought, sheathing it
     as a sword.

98

The morn is up again, the dewy morn,[75]
With breath all incense, and with cheek
     all bloom—   915
Laughing the clouds away with playful
     scorn,
And living as if earth contained no tomb,—
And glowing into day: we may resume
The march of our existence: and thus I,
Still on thy shores, fair Leman! may find
     room   920
And food for meditation, nor pass by
Much, that may give us pause, if pondered
     fittingly.

[74] Knell.
[75] Stanzas 98–104: Clarens; Rousseau again.

99

Clarens! sweet Clarens,[76] birthplace of deep
     love!
Thine air is the young breath of passionate
     thought;
Thy trees take root in love; the snows
     above,   925
The very glaciers have his colors caught,
And sun-set into rose-hues sees them
     wrought
By rays which sleep there lovingly: the
     rocks,
The permanent crags, tell here of love, who
     sought
In them a refuge from the worldly
     shocks,   930
Which stir and sting the soul with hope
     that woos, then mocks.

100

Clarens! by heavenly feet thy paths are
     trod,—
Undying love's, who here ascends a throne
To which the steps are mountains; where
     the god
Is a pervading life and light,—so shown 935
Not on those summits solely, nor alone
In the still cave and forest; o'er the flower
His eye is sparkling, and his breath hath
     blown,
His soft and summer breath, whose tender
     power
Passes the strength of storms in their most
     desolate hour.   940

101

All things are here of *him;* from the black
     pines,
Which are his shade on high, and the
     loud roar
Of torrents, where he listeneth, to the
     vines
Which slope his green path downward to
     the shore,

[76] A town on Lake Geneva, the setting of *La
Nouvelle Héloïse.* It is as "the birthplace of deep
love" that Byron celebrates Clarens in the next
six stanzas.

Where the bowed waters meet him, and
adore,   945
Kissing his feet with murmurs; and the
wood,
The covert of old trees, with trunks all
hoar,
But light leaves, young as joy, stands where
it stood,
Offering to him, and his, a populous solitude.

102

A populous solitude of bees and birds   950
And fairy-formed and many-colored things,
Who worship him with notes more sweet
than words,
And innocently open their glad wings,
Fearless and full of life: the gush of springs,
And fall of lofty fountains, and the
bend   955
Of stirring branches, and the bud which
brings
The swiftest thought of beauty, here extend
Mingling, and made by love, unto one
mighty end.

103

He who hath loved not, here would learn
that lore,
And make his heart a spirit; he who
knows   960
That tender mystery, will love the more;
For this is love's recess, where vain men's
woes,
And the world's waste, have driven him
far from those,
For 'tis his nature to advance or die;
He stands not still, but or decays, or
grows   965
Into a boundless blessing, which may vie
With the immortal lights, in its eternity!

104

'Twas not for fiction chose Rousseau this
spot,
Peopling it with affections; but he found
It was the scene which passion must
allot   970

To the mind's purified beings; 'twas the
ground
Where early Love his Psyche's zone un-
bound,[77]
And hallowed it with loveliness: 'tis lone,
And wonderful, and deep, and hath a
sound,
And sense, and sight of sweetness; here the
Rhone   975
Hath spread himself a couch, the Alps have
reared a throne.

105

Lausanne![78] and Ferney![79] ye have been
the abodes
Of names which unto you bequeathed a
name;
Mortals, who sought and found, by danger-
ous roads,
A path to perpetuity of fame: 980
They were gigantic minds, and their steep
aim
Was, Titan-like, on daring doubts[80] to pile
Thoughts which should call down thunder
and the flame
Of heaven again assailed—if heaven the
while
On man and man's research could deign do
more than smile.   985

106

The one[81] was fire and fickleness, a child
Most mutable in wishes, but in mind
A wit as various,—gay, grave, sage, or wild,—
Historian, bard, philosopher, combined;
He multiplied himself among mankind, 990
The Proteus[82] of their talents: But his own
Breathed most in ridicule,—which, as the
wind,

[77] Lines 972–973 refer to the myth of Cupid and
Psyche.
[78] A Swiss town where Edward Gibbon lived for
a long time and finished his monumental *History of
the Decline and Fall of the Roman Empire* (1787).
[79] A Swiss village founded by Voltaire, who lived
there from 1759 to 1777. Stanzas 105–108: Lausanne and Ferney; Voltaire and Gibbon.
[80] Both Voltaire and Gibbon were skeptics.
[81] Voltaire. This stanza, like the one following, is
a vivid "thumb-nail" sketch.
[82] A sea-god who could take any shape at will.

Blew where it listed, laying all things
prone,—
Now to o'erthrow a fool, and now to shake a
throne.

107

The other,[83] deep and slow, exhausting
thought,   995
And hiving wisdom with each studious
year,
In meditation dwelt, with learning wrought,
And shaped his weapon with an edge
severe,
Sapping a solemn creed with solemn
sneer; [84]
The lord of irony,—that master spell,   1000
Which stung his foes to wrath, which grew
from fear,
And doomed him to the zealot's ready hell,
Which answers to all doubts so eloquently
well.

108

Yet, peace be with their ashes,—for by them,
If merited, the penalty is paid;   1005
It is not ours to judge,—far less condemn;
The hour must come when such things
shall be made
Known unto all,—or hope and dread allayed
By slumber, on one pillow, in the dust,
Which, thus much we are sure, must lie
decayed;   1010
And when it shall revive, as is our trust,
'Twill be to be forgiven—or suffer what is
just.

109

But let me quit man's works, again to
read [85]
His Maker's, spread around me, and suspend
This page, which from my reveries I
feed,   1015

[83] Gibbon.
[84] In his *Decline and Fall*, Gibbon took an antag-
onistic attitude toward Christianity. What effect is
gained by the four initial s-sounds?
[85] Stanzas 109-110: To Italy.

Until it seems prolonging without end.
The clouds above me to the white Alps
tend,
And I must pierce them, and survey
whate'er
May be permitted, as my steps I bend
To their most great and growing region,
where   1020
The earth to her embrace compels the
powers of air.

110

Italia! too, Italia! looking on thee,
Full flashes on the soul the light of ages,
Since the fierce Carthaginian [86] almost won
thee,
To the last halo of the chiefs and sages   1025
Who glorify thy consecrated pages;
Thou wert the throne and grave of empires;
still
The fount at which the panting mind as-
suages
Her thirst of knowledge, quaffing there
her fill,
Flows from the eternal source of Rome's im-
perial hill.   1030

111

Thus far have I proceeded in a theme [87]
Renewed with no kind auspices:—to feel
We are not what we have been, and to
deem
We are not what we should be,—and to
steel
The heart against itself; and to conceal, 1035
With a proud caution, love, or hate, or
aught,—
Passion or feeling, purpose, grief, or zeal,
Which is the tyrant spirit of our thought,
Is a stern task of soul:—No matter,—it is
taught.

112

And for these words, thus woven into
song,   1040
It may be that they are a harmless wile,—

[86] Hannibal.
[87] Stanzas 111-118: Conclusion.

The coloring of the scenes which fleet
along,
Which I would seize, in passing, to beguile
My breast, or that of others, for a while.
Fame is the thirst of youth,—but I am
not   1045
So young as to regard men's frown or smile,
As loss or guerdon of a glorious lot;—
I stood and stand alone,—remembered or
forgot.

113

I have not loved the world, nor the world
me; [88]
I have not flattered its rank breath, nor
bowed   1050
To its idolatries a patient knee,
Nor coined my cheek to smiles,—nor cried
aloud
In worship of an echo: in the crowd
They could not deem me one of such—I
stood
Among them, but not of them; in a
shroud   1055
Of thoughts which were not their thoughts,
and still could,
Had I not filed [89] my mind, which thus
itself subdued.

114

I have not loved the world, nor the world
me,—
But let us part fair foes; I do believe,
Though I have found them not, that there
may be   1060
Words which are things,—hopes which will
not deceive,
And virtues which are merciful, nor weave
Snares for the failing: I would also deem
O'er others' griefs that some sincerely
grieve—
That two, or one, are almost what they
seem,—   1065

[88] Stanzas 113 and 114 are two of the bitterest
stanzas in Byron's poetry. How does the preponderance of monosyllables contribute to the tone of the
stanzas?
[89] Defiled.

That goodness is no name—and happiness
no dream.

115

My daughter! with thy name this song be-
gun!
My daughter! with thy name thus much
shall end!—
I see thee not—I hear thee not—but none
Can be so wrapped in thee; thou art the
friend   1070
To whom the shadows of far years ex-
tend:
Albeit my brow thou never shouldst behold,
My voice shall with thy future visions
blend,
And reach into thy heart,—when mine is
cold,—
A token and a tone, even from thy father's
mold.   1075

116

To aid thy mind's development, to watch
Thy dawn of little joys, to sit and see
Almost thy very growth, to view thee catch
Knowledge of objects,—wonders yet to thee!
To hold thee lightly on a gentle knee, 1080
And print on thy soft cheek a parent's
kiss,—
This, it should seem, was not reserved for
me—
Yet this was in my nature: as it is,
I know not what is there, yet something like
to this.

117

Yet, though dull hate as duty should be
taught,   1085
I know that thou wilt love me—though my
name
Should be shut from thee, as a spell still
fraught
With desolation,—and a broken claim:
Though the grave closed between us,—
'twere the same,
I know that thou wilt love me—though to
drain   1090
My blood from out thy being were an aim,

And an attainment,—all would be in vain,—
Still thou wouldst love me, still that more
than life retain.[90]

118

The child of love, though born in bitter-
ness,
And nurtured in convulsion of thy
sire   1095
These were the elements,—and thine no
less.
As yet such are around thee,—but thy fire
Shall be more tempered, and thy hope far
higher.
Sweet be thy cradled slumbers! O'er the sea
And from the mountains where I now
respire,   1100
Fain would I waft such blessing upon thee,

As, with a sigh, I deem thou might'st have
been to me.
(1816)

STUDY AIDS: 1. What are the various kinds
of subject matter found in this canto? Does Byron
seem more effective in dealing with some of
these than with others?
2. Wherein lies the unity of a poem with
such a variety of content as this canto? Does
Byron master the diversity of material (if so,
how?), or does it master him?
3. Try to formulate Byron's views on poetical
creation, nature, society, Waterloo, Napoleon,
war in general, the Rhine and its castles, Marceau, the Alps, immortality, Rousseau, Lake
Leman, astrology, Clarens, Gibbon, Voltaire, and
Ada.
4. Sum up the personality of Byron as revealed in this poem. What elements of his
character does he himself bring out?

Stanzas for Music

There be none of beauty's daughters
  With a magic like thee;[1]
And like music on the waters
  Is thy sweet voice to me:
When, as if its sound were causing   5
The charmèd ocean's pausing,
The waves lie still and gleaming,
And the lulled winds seem dreaming:

And the midnight moon is weaving
  Her bright chain o'er the deep;   10

Whose breast is gently heaving,
  As an infant's asleep:
So the spirit bows before thee,
To listen and adore thee;
With a full but soft emotion,   15
Like the swell of summer's ocean.
(1816)

STUDY AIDS: What musical effect is gained
by the many FEMININE RHYMES in this lyric?

So We'll Go No More A-Roving

So, we'll go no more a-roving
  So late into the night,
Though the heart be still as loving,
  And the moon be still as bright.

90 This stanza was unfair to Lady Byron, who
made no attempt to turn Ada's mind against her
father.

---

1 According to tradition, Claire Clairmont, the
stepdaughter of William Godwin and the mother
of Byron's child Allegra. Byron was inspired by
her voice to write this lyric.

For the sword outwears its sheath,   5
  And the soul wears out the breast,
And the heart must pause to breathe,
  And love itself have rest.

Though the night was made for loving,
  And the day returns too soon,   10
Yet we'll go no more a-roving
  By the light of the moon.
(1817; 1830)

STUDY AIDS: Byron put this lyric in a letter
to his friend Tom Moore soon after Carnival
time in Venice. What mood is expressed?

Don Juan

Don Juan has rightly been called a "monument of egotism." The unity behind this vast miscellany is the ever-present personality of the author. In the poem all the diverse elements of Byron's protean character are brought together and bound by the magnetic power of the poet himself. Not Juan but Byron is the real hero, and the asides and digressions, which make up perhaps half the poem, are in many ways its chief attraction.

Early in the poem the poet announces that

> The regularity of my design
> Forbids all wandering as the worst of sinning.

He speaks in mock seriousness, of course; the poem is planless, but its very planlessness is a part of its wayward genius. "The soul of such writing is its license," Byron said; he will stand on no ceremony and abide by no rules. Much of the haphazard quality is due to the way the poem was composed—at intervals from the summer of 1818 to Byron's death in 1824. Although Byron's first plan called for the traditional dozen cantos, he later said he might "canter gently through a hundred." That the poem remains a giant fragment of sixteen-plus cantos is entirely fitting to a work of such inviolable freedom.

Byron called the poem an "Epic Satire," which is as good a label as any for a work that defies labeling. It is epic in the grand scale of its narration of a wandering hero, and in its dealing expansively with such large themes as love, sex, war, shipwreck, royal courts, and high society. And it is unquestionably a satire, growing from a work "meant to be a little quietly facetious on everything" (1818) to a "satire on the abuses of the present state of society" (1822).

Byron uses the ottava rima stanza, packing it with outrageous rhymes that anticipate those of our own Ogden Nash. Writes Byron:

> But—Oh! ye lords of ladies *intellectual,*
> Inform us truly, have they not *hen-peck'd you all?*

This verbal fooling, which makes light of the honored poetic convention of rhyme, sets the tone of mockery that pervades the entire poem.

Canto the First

1

I want a hero: an uncommon want,
  When every year and month sends forth a
  new one,
Till, after cloying the gazettes with cant,
  The age discovers he is not the true one:
Of such as these I should not care to vaunt, 5
  I'll therefore take our ancient friend Don
  Juan [1]—
We all have seen him, in the pantomime,[2]
Sent to the devil somewhat ere his time. . . .

[1] The resemblance between Byron's hero and the legendary Don Juan is slight; Byron seems to have known little of the Spanish figure. Note that Byron's "Juan" must be given the Anglicized pronunciation of the name.
[2] A brief version of Shadwell's *Libertine,* in which the Furies consign Don Juan to the flames.

6

Most epic poets plunge "in medias res"[3]
  (Horace makes this the heroic turnpike
  road),
And then your hero tells, whene'er you please,
  What went before—by way of episode,
While seated after dinner at his ease, 45
  Beside his mistress in some soft abode,
Palace, or garden, paradise, or cavern,
Which serves the happy couple for a tavern.

7

That is the usual method, but not mine—
  My way is to begin with the beginning; 50

[3] "In the middle of things." According to Horace's *The Art of Poetry,* an epic poet should begin in the middle of the action and later on tell what went before.

The regularity of my design
  Forbids all wandering as the worst of sin-
    ning,
And therefore I shall open with a line
  (Although it cost me half an hour in spin-
    ning)
Narrating somewhat of Don Juan's father, 55
And also of his mother, if you'd rather.

8

In Seville was he born, a pleasant city,
  Famous for oranges and women—he
Who has not seen it will be much to pity,
  So says the proverb—and I quite agree; 60
Of all the Spanish towns is none more pretty,
  Cadiz, perhaps—but that you soon may
    see:—
Don Juan's parents lived beside the river,
A noble stream, and called the Guadalquivir.

9

His father's name was Jóse—*Don,* of course, 65
  A true Hidalgo,[4] free from every stain
Of Moor or Hebrew blood, he traced his
    source
  Through the most Gothic gentlemen of
    Spain;
A better cavalier ne'er mounted horse,
  Or, being mounted, e'er got down again, 70
Than Jóse, who begot our hero, who
Begot—but that's to come—— Well, to renew:

10

His mother was a learned lady, famed [5]
  For every branch of every science
    known—
In every Christian language ever named, 75
  With virtues equaled by her wit alone:
She made the cleverest people quite ashamed,
  And even the good with inward envy groan,
Finding themselves so very much exceeded
In their own way by all the things that she
    did. . . .   80

[4] A Spanish nobleman of lower class.
[5] The portrait of Donna Inez which follows is obviously a caricature of Lady Byron, though Byron protested the identification.

17

Oh! she was perfect past all parallel—
  Of any modern female saint's compari-
    son;   130
So far above the cunning powers of hell,
  Her guardian angel had given up his gar-
    rison;
Even her minutest motions went as well
  As those of the best time-piece made by
    Harrison:
In virtues nothing earthly could surpass
    her,   135
Save thine "incomparable oil," Macassar! [6]

18

Perfect she was, but as perfection is
  Insipid in this naughty world of ours,
Where our first parents never learned to kiss
  Till they were exiled from their earlier
    bowers,   140
Where all was peace, and innocence, and bliss
  (I wonder how they got through the twelve
    hours),
Don Jóse, like a lineal son of Eve,
Went plucking various fruit without her
    leave.

19

He was a mortal of the careless kind,   145
  With no great love for learning, or the
    learned,
Who chose to go where'er he had a mind,
  And never dreamed his lady was concerned;
The world, as usual, wickedly inclined
  To see a kingdom or a house o'erturned, 150
Whispered he had a mistress, some said *two,*
But for domestic quarrels *one* will do. . . .

22

'Tis pity learned virgins ever wed
  With persons of no sort of education,   170
Or gentlemen, who, though well born and
    bred,
  Grow tired of scientific conversation;
I don't choose to say much upon this head,
  I'm a plain man, and in a single station,

[6] A hair oil.

But—Oh! ye lords of ladies intellectual,   175
Inform us truly, have they not hen-pecked
   you all?

23

Don Jóse and his lady quarreled—*why*,
   Not any of the many could divine,
Though several thousand people chose to try,
   'Twas surely no concern of theirs nor
      mine;   180
I loathe that low vice—curiosity;
   But if there's anything in which I shine,
'Tis in arranging all my friends' affairs,
Not having, of my own, domestic cares.

24

And so I interfered, and with the best   185
   Intentions, but their treatment was not
      kind;
I think the foolish people were possessed,
   For neither of them could I ever find,
Although their porter afterwards confessed—
   But that's no matter, and the worst's be-
      hind,   190
For little Juan o'er me threw, down stairs,
A pail of housemaid's water unawares.

25

A little curly-headed, good-for-nothing,
   And mischief-making monkey from his
      birth;
His parents ne'er agreed except in doting   195
   Upon the most unquiet imp on earth;
Instead of quareling, had they been but both
      in
   Their senses, they'd have sent young master
      forth
To school, or had him soundly whipped at
      home,
To teach him manners for the time to
      come.   200

26

Don Jóse and the Donna Inez led
   For some time an unhappy sort of life,
Wishing each other, not divorced, but dead;
   They lived respectably as man and wife,
Their conduct was exceedingly well-bred,   205
   And gave no outward signs of inward strife,

Until at length the smothered fire broke out,
And put the business past all kind of doubt.

27

For Inez called some druggists and physi-
      cians,[7]
   And tried to prove her loving lord was
      mad,   210
But as he had some lucid intermissions,
   She next decided he was only *bad*;
Yet when they asked her for her depositions,
   No sort of explanation could be had,
Save that her duty both to man and God   215
Required this conduct—which seemed very
      odd.

28

She kept a journal, where his faults were
      noted,
   And opened certain trunks of books and
      letters,
All which might, if occasion served, be
      quoted;
   And then she had all Seville for abettors,   220
Besides her good old grandmother (who
      doted);
   The hearers of her case became repeaters,
Then advocates, inquisitors, and judges,
Some for amusement, others for old
      grudges. . . .

32

Their friends had tried at reconciliation,
   Then their relations, who made matters
      worse,   250
('Twere hard to tell upon a like occasion
   To whom it may be best to have recourse—
I can't say much for friend or yet relation):
   The lawyers did their utmost for divorce,
But scarce a fee was paid on either side   255
Before, unluckily, Don Jóse died. . . .

37

Dying intestate, Juan was sole heir
   To a chancery suit, and messuages and
      lands,   290

[7] Lines 209–210: Lady Byron asked a doctor
to report on Byron's sanity.

Which, with a long minority and care,
　Promised to turn out well in proper hands:
Inez became sole guardian, which was fair,
　And answered but to nature's just demands;
An only son left with an only mother　295
Is brought up much more wisely than another.

38

Sagest of women, even of widows, she
　Resolved that Juan should be quite a para-
　　gon,
And worthy of the noblest pedigree:
　(His sire was of Castile, his dam from
　　Aragon).　300
Then for accomplishments of chivalry,
　In case our lord the king should go to war
　　again,
He learned the arts of riding, fencing, gun-
　nery,
And how to scale a fortress—or a nunnery.

39

But that which Donna Inez most desired,　305
　And saw into herself each day before all
The learned tutors whom for him she hired,
　Was, that his breeding should be strictly
　　moral:
Much into all his studies she inquired,
　And so they were submitted first to her,
　　all,　310
Arts, sciences, no branch was made a mystery
To Juan's eyes, excepting natural history.

40

The languages, especially the dead,
　The sciences, and most of all the abstruse,
The arts, at least all such as could be said　315
　To be the most remote from common use,
In all these he was much and deeply read:
　But not a page of anything that's loose,
Or hints continuation of the species,
　Was ever suffered, lest he should grow vi-
　　cious.　320

41

His classic studies made a little puzzle,
　Because of filthy loves of gods and god-
　　desses,

Who in the earlier ages raised a bustle,
　But never put on pantaloons or bodices;
His reverend tutors had at times a tussle,　325
　And for their Æneids, Iliads, and Odysseys,
Were forced to make an odd sort of apology,
But Donna Inez dreaded the mythology. . . .

47

Sermons he read, and lectures he endured,
　And homilies and lives of all the saints;　370
To Jerome and to Chrysostom [8] inured,
　He did not take such studies for restraints;
But how faith is acquired, and then insured,
　So well not one of the aforesaid paints
As Saint Augustine in his fine Confes-
　sions,[9]　375
Which make the reader envy his transgres-
　sions. . . .

52

For my part I say nothing—nothing—but
　This I will say—my reasons are my
　　own—　410
That if I had an only son to put
　To school (as God be praised that I have
　　none),
'Tis not with Donna Inez I would shut
　Him up to learn his catechism alone,
No—no—I'd send him out betimes to col-
　lege,　415
For there it was I picked up my own knowl-
　edge.

53

For there one learns—'tis not for me to boast,
　Though I acquired—but I pass over *that,*
As well as all the Greek I since have lost:
　I say that there's the place—but *"Verbum
　　sat,"*　420
I think I picked up too, as well as most,
　Knowledge of matters—but no matter
　　what—
I never married—but, I think, I know
That sons should not be educated so.[10]

[8] Latin church fathers.
[9] In a note Byron says that from the *Confessions*
(Augustine's frank autobiography) "it is easy to
see that he was what we should call a rake."
[10] Note the extremely colloquial tone of sts. 52–53.
How is this easy conversational quality achieved?

54

Young Juan now was sixteen years of age, 425
  Tall, handsome, slender, but well knit: he
    seemed
Active, though not so sprightly, as a page;
  And everybody but his mother deemed
Him almost man; but she flew in a rage
  And bit her lips (for else she might have
    screamed) 430
If any said so, for to be precocious
Was in her eyes a thing the most atrocious.

55

Amongst her numerous acquaintance, all
  Selected for discretion and devotion,
There was the Donna Julia, whom to call 435
  Pretty were but to give a feeble notion
Of many charms in her as natural
  As sweetness to the flower, or salt to ocean,
Her zone to Venus, or his bow to Cupid,
  (But this last simile is trite and
    stupid). . . . 440

62

Wedded she was some years, and to a man
  Of fifty, and such husbands are in
    plenty; 490
And yet, I think, instead of such a one
  'Twere better to have two of five-and-
    twenty,
Especially in countries near the sun:
  And now I think on it, "mi vien in
    mente,"[11]
Ladies even of the most uneasy virtue 495
Prefer a spouse whose age is short of thirty.

63

'Tis a sad thing, I cannot choose but say,
  And all the fault of that indecent sun,
Who cannot leave alone our helpless clay,
  But will keep baking, broiling, burning
    on, 500
That howsoever people fast and pray,
  The flesh is frail, and so the soul undone:
What men call gallantry, and gods adultery,
Is much more common where the climate's
  sultry. . . .
  [11] "It comes to mind."

69

Juan she saw, and, as a pretty child, 545
  Caressed him often—such a thing might be
Quite innocently done, and harmless styled,
  When she had twenty years, and thirteen
    he;
But I am not so sure I should have smiled
  When he was sixteen, Julia twenty-
    three; 550
These few short years make wondrous altera-
  tions,
Particularly amongst sun-burnt nations.

70

Whatever the cause might be, they had
    become
  Changed; for the dame grew distant, the
    youth shy,
Their looks cast down, their greetings almost
    dumb, 555
  And much embarrassment in either eye;
There surely will be little doubt with some
  That Donna Julia knew the reason why,
But as for Juan, he had no more notion
Than he who never saw the sea of ocean. 560

71

Yet Julia's very coldness still was kind,
  And tremulously gentle her small hand
Withdrew itself from his, but left behind
  A little pressure, thrilling, and so bland
And slight, so very slight, that to the mind 565
  'Twas but a doubt; but ne'er magician's
    wand
Wrought change with all Armida's [12] fairy art
Like what this light touch left on Juan's heart.

72

And if she met him, though she smiled no
    more,
  She looked a sadness sweeter than her
    smile, 570
As if her heart had deeper thoughts in store
  She must not own, but cherished more the
    while

[12] The sorceress in Tasso's *Jerusalem Delivered,*
who captures Rinaldo with her magic.

For that compression in its burning core;
  Even innocence itself has many a wile,
And will not dare to trust itself with truth, 575
And love is taught hypocrisy from youth.

73

But passion most dissembles, yet betrays
  Even by its darkness; as the blackest sky
Foretells the heaviest tempest, it displays
  Its workings through the vainly guarded
    eye, 580
And in whatever aspect it arrays
  Itself, 'tis still the same hypocrisy:
Coldness or anger, even disdain or hate,
Are masks it often wears, and still too late.

74

Then there were sighs, the deeper for suppres-
    sion, 585
  And stolen glances, sweeter for the theft,
And burning blushes, though for no trans-
    gression,
  Tremblings when met, and restlessness
    when left;
All these are little preludes to possession,
  Of which young passion cannot be be-
    reft, 590
And merely tend to show how greatly love is
Embarrassed at first starting with a novice.

75

Poor Julia's heart was in an awkward state;
  She felt it going, and resolved to make
The noblest efforts for herself and mate, 595
  For honor's, pride's, religion's, virtue's sake.
Her resolutions were most truly great,
  And almost might have made a Tarquin [13]
    quake:
She prayed the Virgin Mary for her grace,
As being the best judge of a lady's case. 600

76

She vowed she never would see Juan more,
  And next day paid a visit to his mother
And looked extremely at the opening door,
  Which, by the Virgin's grace, let in another;

[13] The rapist in Shakespeare's *Rape of Lucrece.*

Grateful she was, and yet a little sore— 605
  Again it opens, it can be no other,
'Tis surely Juan now—No! I'm afraid
That night the Virgin was no further prayed.

77

She now determined that a virtuous woman
  Should rather face and overcome tempta-
    tion, 610
That flight was base and dastardly, and no
    man
  Should ever give her heart the least sensa-
    tion;
That is to say, a thought beyond the common
  Preference, that we must feel upon oc-
    casion,
For people who are pleasanter than others, 615
But then they only seem so many brothers.

78

And even if by chance—and who can tell?
  The devil's so very sly—she should discover
That all within was not so very well,
  And, if still free, that such or such a
    lover 620
Might please perhaps, a virtuous wife can
    quell
  Such thoughts, and be the better when
    they're over;
And if the man should ask, 'tis but denial:
I recommend young ladies to make trial.

79

And then there are such things as love di-
    vine, 625
  Bright and immaculate, unmixed and pure,
Such as the angels think so very fine,
  And matrons, who would be no less secure,
Platonic, perfect, "just such love as mine":
  Thus Julia said—and thought so, to be
    sure; 630
And so I'd have her think, were I the man
On whom her reveries celestial ran.

80

Such love is innocent, and may exist
  Between young persons without any dan-
    ger:

A hand may first, and then a lip be kissed; 635
  For my part, to such doings I'm a stranger,
But *hear* these freedoms form the utmost list
  Of all o'er which such love may be a ranger:
If people go beyond, 'tis quite a crime,
But not my fault—I tell them all in time. 640

81

Love, then, but love within its proper limits
  Was Julia's innocent determination
In young Don Juan's favor, and to him its
  Exertion might be useful on occasion;
And, lighted at too pure a shrine to dim its 645
  Ethereal luster, with what sweet persuasion
He might be taught, by love and her to-
  gether—
I really don't know what, nor Julia either.

82

Fraught with this fine intention, and well
  fenced
  In mail of proof—her purity of soul, 650
She, for the future of her strength convinced,
  And that her honor was a rock, or mole,
Exceeding sagely from that hour dispensed
  With any kind of troublesome control;
But whether Julia to the task was equal 655
  Is that which must be mentioned in the
  sequel.

83

Her plan she deemed both innocent and feasi-
  ble,
  And, surely, with a stripling of sixteen
Not scandal's fangs could fix on much that's
  seizable,
  Or if they did so, satisfied to mean   660
Nothing but what was good, her breast was
  peaceable:
  A quiet conscience makes one so serene!
Christians have burnt each other, quite per-
  suaded
That all the Apostles would have done as they
  did.

84

And if in the mean time her husband died, 665
  But heaven forbid that such a thought
  should cross

Her brain, though in a dream! (and then she
  sighed)
  Never could she survive that common loss;
But just suppose that moment should betide,
  I only say suppose it—*inter nos.*   670
(This should be *entre nous,* for Julia thought
In French, but then the rhyme would go for
  nought.)

85

I only say, suppose this supposition:
  Juan being then grown up to man's estate
Would fully suit a widow of condition,   675
  Even seven years hence it would not be
  too late;
And in the interim (to pursue this vision)
  The mischief, after all, could not be great,
For he would learn the rudiments of love,
I mean the seraph way of those above.   680

86

So much for Julia. Now we'll turn to Juan.
  Poor little fellow! he had no idea
Of his own case, and never hit the true
  one;
  In feelings as quick as Ovid's Miss Medea,[14]
He puzzled over what he found a new one, 685
  But not as yet imagined it could be a
Thing quite in course, and not at all alarming,
Which, with a little patience, might grow
  charming.

87

Silent and pensive, idle, restless, slow,
  His home deserted for the lonely wood, 690
Tormented with a wound he could not know,
  His, like all deep grief, plunged in solitude:
I'm fond myself of solitude or so,
  But then, I beg it may be understood,
By solitude I mean a Sultan's, not   695
A hermit's, with a harem for a grot. . . .

90

Young Juan wandered by the glassy brooks,
  Thinking unutterable things; he threw
Himself at length within the leafy nooks 715

[14] A legendary Greek sorceress, whose story is
told by Ovid in his *Metamorphoses.*

Where the wild branch of the cork forest
 grew;
There poets find materials for their books,
 And every now and then we read them
  through,
So that their plan and prosody are eligible,
Unless, like Wordsworth, they prove unin-
 telligible.   720

91

He, Juan (and not Wordsworth), so pursued
 His self-communion with his own high
  soul,
Until his mighty heart, in its great mood,
 Had mitigated part, though not the whole
Of its disease; he did the best he could 725
 With things not very subject to control,
And turned, without perceiving his condition,
Like Coleridge, into a metaphysician.

92

He thought about himself, and the whole
 earth,
 Of man the wonderful, and of the stars, 730
And how the deuce they ever could have
 birth;
 And then he thought of earthquakes, and
  of wars,
How many miles the moon might have in
 girth,
 Of air-balloons, and of the many bars
To perfect knowledge of the boundless
 skies—   735
And then he thought of Donna Julia's eyes.

93

In thoughts like these true wisdom may dis-
 cern
 Longings sublime, and aspirations high,
Which some are born with, but the most part
 learn
 To plague themselves withal, they know
  not why: 740
'Twas strange that one so young should thus
 concern
 His brain about the action of the sky;
If *you* think 'twas philosophy that this did,
I can't help thinking puberty assisted.

94

He pored upon the leaves, and on the
 flowers,   745
 And heard a voice in all the winds; and
  then
He thought of wood-nymphs and immortal
 bowers,
 And how the goddesses came down to men:
He missed the pathway, he forgot the hours,
 And when he looked upon his watch
  again,   750
He found how much old Time had been a
 winner—
He also found that he had lost his dinner.[15]

95

Sometimes he turn'd to gaze upon his book,
 Boscan, or Garcilasso; [16]—by the wind
Even as the page is rustled while we look, 755
 So by the poesy of his own mind
Over the mystic leaf his soul was shook,
 As if 'twere one whereon magicians bind
Their spells, and give them to the passing gale
According to some good old woman's tale. 760

96

Thus would he while his lonely hours away
 Dissatisfied, nor knowing what he wanted;
Nor glowing revery, nor poet's lay,
 Could yield his spirit that for which it
  panted,
A bosom whereon he his head might lay, 765
 And hear the heart beat with the love it
  granted,
With——several other things, which I forget,
Or which, at least, I need not mention yet.[17]

97

Those lonely walks, and lengthening reveries,
 Could not escape the gentle Julia's eyes; 770
She saw that Juan was not at his ease;

[15] Note the anticlimax of this line, a common
practice of Byron in *Don Juan*. Find other examples.
What is the function of such anticlimax? How does
it affect the TONE of the stanza?

[16] Early sixteenth-century Spanish poets.

[17] Note Byron's subtle analysis of the psychology
of Julia in sts. 71–85, and then of Juan in 86–96.

But that which chiefly may, and must sur-
   prise,
Is, that the Donna Inez did not tease
   Her only son with question or surmise;
Whether it was she did not see, or would
   not,   775
Or, like all very clever people, could not.

98

This may seem strange, but yet 'tis very com-
   mon;
   For instance—gentlemen, whose ladies take
Leave to o'erstep the written rights of woman,
   And break the—— Which commandment
   is it they break?   780
(I have forgot the number, and think no man
   Should rashly quote, for fear of a mistake.)
I say, when these same gentlemen are jeal-
   ous,
They make some blunder, which their ladies
   tell us.

99

A real husband always is suspicious,   785
   But still no less suspects in the wrong place,
Jealous of some one who had no such wishes,
   Or pandering blindly to his own disgrace,
By harboring some dear friend extremely
   vicious;
   The last indeed's infallibly the case: 790
And when the spouse and friend are gone off
   wholly,
He wonders at their vice, and not his
   folly. . . .

102

It was upon a day, a summer's day;—
   Summer's indeed a very dangerous sea-
   son,   810
And so is spring about the end of May;
   The sun, no doubt, is the prevailing reason;
But whatsoe'er the cause is, one may say,
   And stand convicted of more truth than
   treason,
That there are months which nature grows
   more merry in—   815
March has its hares, and May must have its
   heroine.

103

'Twas on a summer's day—the sixth of June—
   I like to be particular in dates,
Not only of the age, and year, but moon;
   They are a sort of post-house, where the
   fates   820
Change horses, making history change its
   tune,
   Then spur away o'er empires and o'er states,
Leaving at last not much besides chronology,
Excepting the post-obits of theology.

104

'Twas on the sixth of June, about the hour 825
   Of half-past six—perhaps still nearer seven—
When Julia sat within as pretty a bower
   As e'er held houri in that heathenish
   heaven
Described by Mahomet, and Anacreon
   Moore,[18]
   To whom the lyre and laurels have been
   given,   830
With all the trophies of triumphant song—
He won them well, and may he wear them
   long!

105

She sat, but not alone; I know not well
   How this same interview had taken place,
And even if I knew, I should not tell— 835
   People should hold their tongues in any
   case;
No matter how or why the thing befell,
   But there were she and Juan, face to face—
When two such faces are so, 'twould be wise,
But very difficult, to shut their eyes.   840

106

How beautiful she looked! her conscious heart
   Glowed in her cheek, and yet she felt no
   wrong,
Oh Love! how perfect is thy mystic art,
   Strengthening the weak, and trampling on
   the strong!
How self-deceitful is the sagest part   845
   Of mortals whom thy lure hath led along!—

[18] Tom Moore, Byron's friend, translated the *Odes*
of Anacreon, a Greek poet.

The precipice she stood on was immense,
So was her creed in her own innocence. . . .

109

Julia had honor, virtue, truth, and love   865
  For Don Alfonso; and she inly swore,
By all the vows below to powers above,
  She never would disgrace the ring she wore,
Nor leave a wish which wisdom might re-
      prove;
  And while she pondered this, besides much
      more,   870
One hand on Juan's carelessly was thrown,
Quite by mistake—she thought it was her
      own;

110

Unconsciously she leaned upon the other,
  Which played within the tangles of her
      hair;
And to contend with thoughts she could not
      smother   875
  She seemed, by the distraction of her air.
'Twas surely very wrong in Juan's mother
  To leave together this imprudent pair,
She who for many years had watched her son
      so—
I'm very certain mine would not have done
      so.   880

111

The hand which still held Juan's by degrees
  Gently, but palpably confirmed its grasp,
As if it said, "Detain me, if you please";
  Yet there's no doubt she only meant to clasp
His fingers with a pure Platonic squeeze;   885
  She would have shrunk as from a toad, or
      asp,
Had she imagined such a thing could rouse
A feeling dangerous to a prudent spouse.

112

I cannot know what Juan thought of this,
  But what he did, is much what you would
      do;   890
His young lip thanked it with a grateful kiss,
  And then, abashed at its own joy, with-
      drew

In deep despair, lest he had done amiss,—
  Love is so very timid when 'tis new:
She blushed, and frowned not, but she strove
      to speak,   895
And held her tongue, her voice was grown so
      weak.

113

The sun set, and up rose the yellow moon:
  The devil's in the moon for mischief; they
Who called her CHASTE, methinks, began too
      soon
  Their nomenclature; there is not a day,   900
The longest, not the twenty-first of June,
  Sees half the business in a wicked way,
On which three single hours of moonshine
      smile—
And then she looks so modest all the while.

114

There is a dangerous silence in that hour,   905
  A stillness, which leaves room for the full
      soul
To open all itself, without the power
  Of calling wholly back its self-control;
The silver light which, hallowing tree and
      tower,
  Sheds beauty and deep softness o'er the
      whole,   910
Breathes also to the heart, and o'er it throws
A loving languor, which is not repose.

115

And Julia sat with Juan, half embraced
  And half retiring from the glowing arm,
Which trembled like the bosom where 'twas
      placed;   915
  Yet still she must have thought there was
      no harm,
Or else 'twere easy to withdraw her waist;
  But then the situation had its charm,
And then—— God knows what next—I can't
      go on;
I'm almost sorry that I e'er begun.   920

116

Oh Plato! Plato! you have paved the way,
  With your confounded fantasies, to more

Immoral conduct by the fancied sway
   Your system feigns o'er the controlless
      core
Of human hearts, than all the long array 925
   Of poets and romancers:—You're a bore,
A charlatan, a coxcomb—and have been,
At best, no better than a go-between.

117

And Julia's voice was lost, except in sighs,
   Until too late for useful conversation; 930
The tears were gushing from her gentle
      eyes,
   I wish, indeed, they had not had occasion;
But who, alas! can love, and then be wise?
   Not that remorse did not oppose temptation;
A little still she strove, and much re-
      pented, 935
And whispering "I will ne'er consent"—con-
      sented.

118

'Tis said that Xerxes [19] offered a reward
   To those who could invent him a new
      pleasure;
Methinks the requisition's rather hard,
   And must have cost his majesty a treas-
      ure: 940
For my part, I'm a moderate-minded bard
   Fond of a little love (which I call leisure);
I care not for new pleasures, as the old
Are quite enough for me, so they but hold.

119

Oh Pleasure! you're indeed a pleasant
      thing, 945
   Although one must be damned for you,
      no doubt:
I make a resolution every spring
   Of reformation, ere the year run out,
But somehow, this my vestal vow takes wing,
   Yet still, I trust, it may be kept through-
      out: 950
I'm very sorry, very much ashamed,
And mean, next winter, to be quite reclaimed.

[19] Ancient king of Persia.

120

Here my chaste Muse a liberty must take—
   Start not! still chaster reader—she'll be nice
      hence-
Forward, and there is no great cause to
      quake; 955
   This liberty is a poetic license,
Which some irregularity may make
   In the design, and as I have a high sense
Of Aristotle and the Rules, 'tis fit
To beg his pardon when I err a bit. 960

121

This license is to hope the reader will
   Suppose from June the sixth (the fatal day
Without whose epoch my poetic skill
   For want of facts would all be thrown
      away),
But keeping Julia and Don Juan still 965
   In sight, that several months have passed;
      we'll say
'Twas in November, but I'm not so sure
About the day—the era's more obscure.

122

We'll talk of that anon.—'Tis sweet to hear
   At midnight on the blue and moonlit
      deep 970
The song and oar of Adria's gondolier,
   By distance mellowed, o'er the waters
      sweep;
'Tis sweet to see the evening star appear;
   'Tis sweet to listen as the night-winds creep
From leaf to leaf; 'tis sweet to view on
      high 975
The rainbow, based on ocean, span the sky.

123

'Tis sweet to hear the watch-dog's honest bark
   Bay deep-mouthed welcome as we draw
      near home;
'Tis sweet to know there is an eye will mark
   Our coming, and look brighter when we
      come; 980
'Tis sweet to be awakened by the lark,
   Or lulled by falling waters; sweet the hum
Of bees, the voice of girls, the song of birds,
The lisp of children, and their earliest words.

124

Sweet is the vintage when the showering
    grapes   985
In Bacchanal profusion reel to earth,
Purple and gushing; sweet are our escapes
    From civic revelry to rural mirth;
Sweet to the miser are his glittering heaps,
    Sweet to the father is his first-born's
    birth,   990
Sweet is revenge—especially to women,
Pillage to soldiers, prize-money to seamen.

125

Sweet is a legacy, and passing sweet
    The unexpected death of some old lady
Or gentleman of seventy years complete, 995
    Who've made "us youth" wait too—too long
    already
For an estate, or cash, or country seat,
    Still breaking, but with stamina so steady
That all the Israelites are fit to mob its
    Next owner for their double-damned post-
    obits.   1000

126

'Tis sweet to win, no matter how, one's
    laurels,
    By blood or ink; 'tis sweet to put an end
To strife; 'tis sometimes sweet to have our
    quarrels,
    Particularly with a tiresome friend:
Sweet is old wine in bottles, ale in bar-
    rels;   1005
    Dear is the helpless creature we defend
Against the world; and dear the schoolboy
    spot
We ne'er forget, though there we are forgot.

127

But sweeter still than this, than these, than
    all,
    Is first and passionate love—it stands
    alone,   1010
Like Adam's recollection of his fall;
    The tree of knowledge has been plucked
    —all's known—
And life yields nothing further to recall
    Worthy of this ambrosial sin, so shown,

No doubt in fable, as the unforgiven   1015
Fire which Prometheus filched for us from
    heaven.

128

Man's a strange animal, and makes strange
    use
    Of his own nature, and the various arts,
And likes particularly to produce
    Some new experiment to show his
    parts;   1020
This is the age of oddities let loose,
    Where different talents find their different
    marts;
You'd best begin with truth, and when you've
    lost your
Labor, there's a sure market for imposture.

129

What opposite discoveries we have seen! 1025
    (Signs of true genius, and of empty
    pockets.)
One makes new noses, one a guillotine,
    One breaks your bones, one sets them in
    their sockets;
But vaccination certainly has been
    A kind of antithesis to Congreve's
    rockets,[20]   1030
With which the doctor paid off an old pox,
By borrowing a new one from an ox.

130

Bread has been made (indifferent) from po-
    tatoes;
    And galvanism[21] has set some corpses grin-
    ning,
But has not answered like the apparatus 1035
    Of the Humane Society's beginning,
By which men are unsuffocated gratis:
    What wondrous new machines have late
    been spinning!
I said the small pox has gone out of late;
Perhaps it may be followed by the
    great. . . .   1040

[20] A new kind of explosive shell invented by Sir William Congreve, a nineteenth-century scientist.
[21] The science of the effects of electric currents. In 1803 experiments in galvanism were made on a murderer's corpse.

132

This is the patent age of new inventions
 For killing bodies, and for saving souls, 1050
All propagated with the best intentions;
 Sir Humphrey Davy's lantern,[22] by which coals
Are safely mined for in the mode he mentions,
 Timbuctoo travels, voyages to the Poles,
Are ways to benefit mankind, as true, 1055
Perhaps, as shooting them at Waterloo.

133

Man's a phenomenon, one knows not what,
 And wonderful beyond all wondrous measure;
'Tis pity, though, in this sublime world, that
 Pleasure's a sin, and sometimes sin's a pleasure; 1060
Few mortals know what end they would be at,
 But whether glory, power, or love, or treasure,
The path is through perplexing ways, and when
The goal is gained, we die, you know—and then——

134

What then?—I do not know, no more do you—— 1065
 And so good night.—Return we to our story:
'Twas in November, when fine days are few,
 And the far mountains wax a little hoary,
And clap a white cape on their mantles blue;
 And the sea dashes round the promontory, 1070
And the loud breaker boils against the rock,
And sober suns must set at five o'clock.

135

'Twas, as the watchmen say, a cloudy night;
 No moon, no stars, the wind was low or loud
By gusts, and many a sparkling hearth was bright 1075

[22] Safety lamp for miners, invented in 1815.

With the piled wood, round which the family crowd;
There's something cheerful in that sort of light,
 Even as a summer sky's without a cloud:
I'm fond of fire, and crickets, and all that,
A lobster salad, and champagne, and chat. 1080

136

'Twas midnight—Donna Julia was in bed,
 Sleeping, most probably—when at her door
Arose a clatter might awake the dead,
 If they had never been awoke before,
And that they have been so we all have read, 1085
 And are to be so, at the least, once more;—
The door was fastened, but with voice and fist
First knocks were heard, then "Madam—Madam—hist!

137

"For God's sake, Madam—Madam—here's my master,
 With more than half the city at his back— 1090
Was ever heard of such a cursed disaster!
 'Tis not my fault—I kept good watch—Alack!
Do pray undo the bolt a little faster—
 They're on the stair just now, and in a crack
Will all be here; perhaps he yet may fly—1095
Surely the window's not so very high!"

138

By this time Don Alfonso was arrived,
 With torches, friends, and servants in great number;
The major part of them had long been wived,
 And therefore paused not to disturb the slumber 1100
Of any wicked woman, who contrived
 By stealth her husband's temples to encumber:
Examples of this kind are so contagious,
Were one not punished, all would be outrageous.

139

I can't tell how, or why, or what suspi-
cion   1105
    Could enter into Don Alfonso's head;
But for a cavalier of his condition
    It surely was exceedingly ill-bred,
Without a word of previous admonition,
    To hold a levee round his lady's bed, 1110
And summon lackeys, armed with fire and
    sword,
To prove himself the thing he most abhorred.

140

Poor Donna Julia! starting as from sleep
    (Mind—that I do not say—she had not
    slept),
Began at once to scream, and yawn, and
    weep;   1115
    Her maid, Antonia, who was an adept,
Contrived to fling the bed-clothes in a heap,
    As if she had just now from out them
    crept;
I can't tell why she should take all this
    trouble
To prove her mistress had been sleeping
    double.   1120

141

But Julia mistress, and Antonia maid,
    Appeared like two poor harmless women,
    who
Of goblins, but still more of men afraid,
    Had thought one man might be deterred
    by two,
And therefore side by side were gently
    laid,   1125
    Until the hours of absence should run
    through,
And truant husband should return, and say,
"My dear, I was the first who came away."

142

Now Julia found at length a voice, and cried,
    "In heaven's name, Don Alfonso, what d'ye
    mean?   1130
Has madness seized you? would that I had
    died
    Ere such a monster's victim I had been!

What may this midnight violence betide,
    A sudden fit of drunkenness or spleen?
Dare you suspect me, whom the thought
    would kill?   1135
Search, then, the room!"—Alfonso said, "I
will."

143

He searched, *they* searched, and rummaged
    everywhere,
    Closet and clothes-press, chest and window-
    seat,
And found much linen, lace, and several pair
    Of stockings, slippers, brushes, combs, com-
    plete,   1140
With other articles of ladies fair,
    To keep them beautiful, or leave them
    neat:
Arras they pricked and curtains with their
    swords,
And wounded several shutters, and some
    boards.

144

Under the bed they searched, and there they
    found—   1145
    No matter what—it was not that they
    sought;
They opened windows, gazing if the ground
    Had signs or footmarks, but the earth said
    nought;
And then they stared each other's faces
    round:
    'Tis odd, not one of all these seekers
    thought,   1150
And seems to me almost a sort of blunder,
Of looking *in* the bed as well as under.

145

During this inquisition Julia's tongue
    Was not asleep—"Yes, search and search,"
    she cried,
"Insult on insult heap, and wrong on
    wrong!   1155
    It was for this that I became a bride!
For this in silence I have suffered long
    A husband like Alfonso at my side;
But now I'll bear no more, nor here remain,
If there be law or lawyers in all Spain. 1160

146

"Yes, Don Alfonso! husband now no more,
　If ever you indeed deserved the name,
Is it worthy of your years?—you have three-
　score—
　Fifty, or sixty, it is all the same—
Is it wise or fitting, causeless to explore　　1165
　For facts against a virtuous woman's fame?
Ungrateful, perjured, barbarous Don Alfonso,
How dare you think your lady would go on
　so?

147

"Is it for this I have disdained to hold
　The common privileges of my sex?　　1170
That I have chosen a confessor so old
　And deaf, that any other it would vex,
And never once he has had cause to scold,
　But found my very innocence perplex
So much, he always doubted I was
　married—　　1175
How sorry you will be when I've miscarried!

148

"Was it for this that no Cortejo [23] e'er
　I yet have chosen from out the youth of
　Seville?
Is it for this I scarce went anywhere,
　Except to bull-fights, mass, play, rout, and
　revel?　　1180
Is it for this, whate'er my suitors were,
　I favored none—nay, was almost uncivil?
Is it for this that General Count O'Reilly,
Who took Algiers,[24] declares I used him vilely?

149

"Did not the Italian Musico Cazzani [25]　1185
　Sing at my heart six months at least in
　vain?
Did not his countryman, Count Corniani,
　Call me the only virtuous wife in Spain?
Were there not also Russians, English, many?

[23] Lover.
[24] In a note Byron says Julia erred; O'Reilly
actually retreated.
[25] Julia's harangue reaches a farcical climax in this
stanza, with its ridiculous proper names.

The Count Strongstroganoff I put in
　pain,　　1190
And Lord Mount Coffeehouse, the Irish peer,
Who killed himself for love (with wine) last
　year.

150

"Have I not had two bishops at my feet?
　The Duke of Ichar, and Don Fernan
　Nunez?
And is it thus a faithful wife you treat?　1195
　I wonder in what quarter now the moon
　is:
I praise your vast forbearance not to beat
　Me also, since the time so opportune is—
Oh, valiant man! with sword drawn and
　cocked trigger,
Now, tell me, don't you cut a pretty fig-
　ure?　　1200

151

"Was it for this you took your sudden journey,
　Under pretense of business indispensable,
With that sublime of rascals your attorney,
　Whom I see standing there, and looking
　sensible
Of having played the fool? though both I
　spurn, he　　1205
　Deserves the worst, his conduct's less de-
　fensible,
Because, no doubt, 'twas for his dirty fee,
And not from any love to you nor me.

152

"If he comes here to take a deposition,
　By all means let the gentleman pro-
　ceed;　　1210
You've made the apartment in a fit condi-
　tion:—
　There's pen and ink for you, sir, when you
　need—
Let everything be noted with precision,
　I would not you for nothing should be
　fee'd—
But as my maid's undressed, pray turn your
　spies out."　　1215
"Oh!" sobbed Antonia, "I could tear their
　eyes out."

153

"There is the closet, there the toilet, there
  The antechamber—search them under, over;
There is the sofa, there the great arm-chair,
  The chimney—which would really hold a
    lover.   1220
I wish to sleep, and beg you will take care
  And make no further noise, till you discover
The secret cavern of this lurking treasure—
And when 'tis found, let me, too, have that
  pleasure.

154

"And now, Hidalgo! now that you have
    thrown   1225
  Doubt upon me, confusion over all,
Pray have the courtesy to make it known
  Who is the man you search for? how d'ye
    call
Him? what's his lineage? let him but be
    shown—
  I hope he's young and handsome—is he
    tall?   1230
Tell me—and be assured, that since you stain
Mine honor thus, it shall not be in vain.

155

"At least, perhaps, he has not sixty years,
  At that age he would be too old for slaugh-
    ter,
Or for so young a husband's jealous fears—   1235
  (Antonia! let me have a glass of water.)
I am ashamed of having shed these tears,
  They are unworthy of my father's daughter;
My mother dreamed not in my natal hour,
That I should fall into a monster's power.   1240

156

"Perhaps 'tis of Antonia you are jealous,
  You saw that she was sleeping by my side,
When you broke in upon us with your fel-
    lows;
  Look where you please—we've nothing, sir,
    to hide;
Only another time, I trust, you'll tell us,   1245
  Or for the sake of decency abide
A moment at the door, that we may be
Dressed to receive so much good company.

157

"And now, sir, I have done, and say no
    more;
  The little I have said may serve to show   1250
The guileless heart in silence may grieve
    o'er
  The wrongs to whose exposure it is slow:—
I leave you to your conscience as before,
  'Twill one day ask you, why you used me
    so?
God grant you feel not then the bitterest
    grief!   1255
Antonia! where's my pocket-handkerchief?"

158

She ceased, and turned upon her pillow; pale
  She lay, her dark eyes flashing through their
    tears,
Like skies that rain and lighten; as a veil,
  Waved and o'ershading her wan cheek,
    appears   1260
Her streaming hair; the black curls strive, but
    fail,
  To hide the glossy shoulder, which up-
    rears
Its snow through all;—her soft lips lie apart,
And louder than her breathing beats her
  heart.

159

The Senor Don Alfonso stood confused;   1265
  Antonia bustled round the ransacked room,
And, turning up her nose, with looks abused
  Her master, and his myrmidons, of whom
Not one, except the attorney, was amused;
  He, like Achates,[26] faithful to the
    tomb,   1270
So there were quarrels, cared not for the
  cause,
Knowing they must be settled by the laws.

160

With prying snub-nose, all small eyes, he
  stood,
  Following Antonia's motions here and
    there,

[26] Loyal companion to Aeneas, in the *Aeneid*.

With much suspicion in his attitude;   1275
  For reputations he had little care;
So that a suit or action were made good,
  Small pity had he for the young and fair,
And ne'er believed in negatives, till these
Were proved by competent false wit-
  nesses.   1280

161

But Don Alfonso stood with downcast looks,
  And, truth to say, he made a foolish fig-
  ure;
When, after searching in five hundred nooks,
  And treating a young wife with so much
  rigor,
He gained no point, except some self-re-
  bukes,   1285
  Added to those his lady with such vigor
Had poured upon him for the last half hour,
Quick, thick, and heavy—as a thunder-shower.

162

At first he tried to hammer an excuse,
  To which the sole reply was tears and
  sobs,   1290
And indications of hysterics, whose
  Prologue is always certain throes, and
  throbs,
Gasps, and whatever else the owners choose:
  Alfonso saw his wife, and thought of Job's;
He saw too, in perspective, her relations,   1295
And then he tried to muster all his pa-
  tience.

163

He stood in act to speak, or rather stammer,
  But sage Antonia cut him short before
The anvil of his speech received the hammer,
  With "Pray, sir, leave the room, and say
  no more,   1300
Or madam dies."—Alfonso muttered, "D—n
  her."
  But nothing else, the time of words was
  o'er;
He cast a rueful look or two, and did,
He knew not wherefore, that which he was
  bid.

164

With him retired his *posse comitatus*,[27]   1305
  The attorney last, who lingered near the
  door
Reluctantly, still tarrying there as late as
  Antonia let him—not a little sore
At this most strange and unexplained *hiatus*
  In Don Alfonso's facts, which just now
  wore   1310
An awkward look; as he revolved the case,
The door was fastened in his legal face.

165

No sooner was it bolted, than—Oh shame!
  Oh sin! Oh sorrow! and Oh womankind!
How can you do such things and keep your
  fame,   1315
  Unless this world, and t'other too, be blind?
Nothing so dear as an unfilched good name!
  But to proceed—for there is more behind:
With much heartfelt reluctance be it said,
Young Juan slipped, half-smothered, from the
  bed.   1320

166

He had been hid—I don't pretend to say
  How, nor can I indeed describe the where—
Young, slender, and packed easily, he lay,
  No doubt, in little compass, round or
  square;
But pity him I neither must nor may   1325
  His suffocation by that pretty pair;
'Twere better, sure, to die so, than be shut
With maudlin Clarence in his Malmsey
  butt.[28]

167

And, secondly, I pity not, because
  He had no business to commit a sin,   1330
Forbid by heavenly, fined by human laws,
  At least 'twas rather early to begin;
But at sixteen the conscience rarely gnaws
  So much as when we call our old debts in

[27] The full legal term for posse.
[28] After being stabbed, the Duke of Clarence was thrown into a large container (butt) of wine (Malmsey) and left to drown.

At sixty years, and draw the accounts of
    evil,   1335
And find a deuced balance with the devil.

168

Of his position I can give no notion:
   'Tis written in the Hebrew Chronicle,
How the physicians, leaving pill and potion,
   Prescribed, by way of blister, a young
      belle,   1340
When old King David's blood grew dull in
    motion,
   And that the medicine answered very well;
Perhaps 'twas in a different way applied,
For David lived, but Juan nearly died.

169

What's to be done? Alfonso will be back 1345
   The moment he has sent his fools away.
Antonia's skill was put upon the rack,
   But no device could be brought into play—
And how to parry the renewed attack?
   Besides, it wanted but few hours of
      day: 1350
Antonia puzzled; Julia did not speak,
But pressed her bloodless lip to Juan's cheek.

170

He turned his lip to hers, and with his hand
   Called back the tangles of her wandering
      hair;
Even then their love they could not all com-
    mand,   1355
   And half forgot their danger and despair:
Antonia's patience now was at a stand—
   "Come, come, 'tis no time now for fooling
      there,"
She whispered, in great wrath—"I must de-
    posit
This pretty gentleman within the
    closet. . . ."   1360

173

Now, Don Alfonso entering, but alone,
   Closed the oration of the trusty maid:
She loitered, and he told her to be gone,
   An order somewhat sullenly obeyed;   1380
However, present remedy was none,

And no great good seemed answered if she
    stayed;
Regarding both with slow and sidelong view,
She snuffed the candle, curtsied, and with-
    drew.

174

Alfonso paused a minute—then begun   1385
   Some strange excuses for his late proceed-
    ing;
He would not justify what he had done,
   To say the best, it was extreme ill-breeding;
But there were ample reasons for it, none
   Of which he specified in this his plead-
    ing: 1390
His speech was a fine sample, on the whole,
Of rhetoric, which the learned call *"rigma-
    role."* . . .

180

Alfonso closed his speech, and begged her
    pardon,
   Which Julia half withheld, and then half
    granted,
And laid conditions, he thought very hard,
    on,   1435
   Denying several little things he wanted:
He stood like Adam lingering near his garden,
   With useless penitence perplexed and
    haunted,
Beseeching she no further would refuse,
When, lo! he stumbled o'er a pair of
    shoes.   1440

181

A pair of shoes!—what then? not much, if they
   Are such as fit with ladies' feet, but these
(No one can tell how much I grieve to say)
   Were masculine; to see them, and to seize,
Was but a moment's act.—Ah! well-a-
    day!   1445
   My teeth begin to chatter, my veins freeze—
Alfonso first examined well their fashion,
And then flew out into another passion.

182

He left the room for his relinquished sword,
   And Julia instant to the closet flew. 1450

"Fly, Juan, fly! for heaven's sake—not a
   word—
The door is open—you may yet slip through
The passage you so often have explored—
   Here is the garden-key—Fly—fly—Adieu!
Haste—haste! I hear Alfonso's hurrying
   feet—   1455
Day has not broke—there's no one in the
   street."

183

None can say that this was not good advice,
   The only mischief was, it came too late;
Of all experience 'tis the usual price,
   A sort of income-tax laid on by fate: 1460
Juan had reached the room-door in a trice,
   And might have done so by the garden-
      gate,
But met Alfonso in his dressing-gown,
Who threatened death—so Juan knocked him
   down.

184

Dire was the scuffle, and out went the
   light;   1465
   Antonia cried out "Rape!" and Julia "Fire!"
But not a servant stirred to aid the fight.
   Alfonso, pommeled to his heart's desire,
Swore lustily he'd be revenged this night;
   And Juan, too, blasphemed an octave
    higher;   1470
His blood was up: though young, he was a
   Tartar,[29]
And not at all disposed to prove a martyr.

185

Alfonso's sword had dropped ere he could
   draw it,
   And they continued battling hand to hand,
For Juan very luckily ne'er saw it;   1475
   His temper not being under great com-
    mand,
If at that moment he had chanced to claw it,
   Alfonso's days had not been in the land
Much longer.—Think of husbands', lovers'
   lives!
And how ye may be doubly widows—
   wives!   1480

[29] A person of violent temper.

186

Alfonso grappled to detain the foe,
   And Juan throttled him to get away,
And blood ('twas from the nose) began to
   flow;
   At last, as they more faintly wrestling lay,
Juan contrived to give an awkward blow, 1485
   And then his only garment quite gave
    way;
He fled, like Joseph, leaving it; but there,
I doubt, all likeness ends between the pair.

187

Lights came at length, and men, and maids,
   who found
   An awkward spectacle their eyes before; 1490
Antonia in hysterics, Julia swooned,
   Alfonso leaning, breathless, by the door;
Some half-torn drapery scattered on the
   ground,
   Some blood, and several footsteps, but no
    more:
Juan the gate gained, turned the key
   about,   1495
And liking not the inside, locked the out.

188

Here ends this canto.—Need I sing, or say,
   How Juan, naked, favored by the night,
Who favors what she should not, found his
   way,
   And reached his home in an unseemly
    plight?   1500
The pleasant scandal which arose next day,
   The nine days' wonder which was brought
    to light,
And how Alfonso sued for a divorce,
Were in the English newspapers, of
   course. . . .

190

But Donna Inez, to divert the train
   Of one of the most circulating scandals
That had for centuries been known in
   Spain,   1515
   At least since the retirement of the Van-
    dals,

First vowed (and never had she vowed in
    vain)
    To Virgin Mary several pounds of candles;
And then, by the advice of some old ladies,
She sent her son to be shipped off from
    Cadiz.   1520

191

She had resolved that he should travel through
    All European climes, by land or sea,
To mend his former morals, and get new,
    Especially in France and Italy
(At least this is the thing most people
    do).   1525
    Julia was sent into a convent: she
Grieved, but, perhaps, her feelings may be
    better
Shown in the following copy of her letter:—

192

"They tell me 'tis decided you depart:
    'Tis wise—'tis well, but not the less a
    pain;   1530
I have no further claim on your young heart,
    Mine is the victim, and would be again:
To love too much has been the only art
    I used;—I write in haste, and if a stain
Be on this sheet, 'tis not what it appears; 1535
My eyeballs burn and throb, but have no
    tears.

193

"I loved, I love you, for this love have lost
    State, station, heaven, mankind's, my own
    esteem,
And yet cannot regret what it hath cost,
    So dear is still the memory of that
    dream;   1540
Yet, if I name my guilt, 'tis not to boast,
    None can deem harshlier of me than I
    deem:
I trace this scrawl because I cannot rest—
I've nothing to reproach or to request.

194

"Man's love is of man's life a thing apart, 1545
    'Tis woman's whole existence; man may
    range

The court, camp, church, the vessel, and the
    mart;
    Sword, gown, gain, glory, offer in exchange
Pride, fame, ambition, to fill up his heart,
    And few there are whom these cannot
    estrange;   1550
Men have all these resources, we but one,
To love again, and be again undone.

195

"You will proceed in pleasure, and in pride,
    Beloved and loving many; all is o'er
For me on earth, except some years to
    hide   1555
    My shame and sorrow deep in my heart's
    core:
These I could bear, but cannot cast aside
    The passion which still rages as before,—
And so farewell—forgive me, love me—No,
That word is idle now—but let it go.   1560

196

"My breast has been all weakness, is so yet:
    But still I think I can collect my mind;
My blood still rushes where my spirit's set,
    As roll the waves before the settled wind;
My heart is feminine, nor can forget—   1565
    To all, except one image, madly blind;
So shakes the needle, and so stands the
    pole,
As vibrates my fond heart to my fixed soul.

197

"I have no more to say, but linger still,
    And dare not set my seal upon this
    sheet,   1570
And yet I may as well the task fulfil,
    My misery can scarce be more complete:
I had not lived till now, could sorrow kill;
    Death shuns the wretch who fain the blow
    would meet,
And I must even survive this last adieu,   1575
And bear with life to love and pray for
    you!" [30] . . .

[30] Shelley called this love-letter (sts. 192–197)
"altogether a masterpiece of portraiture."

199

This was Don Juan's earliest scrape; but
    whether   1585
I shall proceed with his adventures is
Dependent on the public altogether;
    We'll see, however, what they say to this,
Their favor in an author's cap's a feather,
    And no great mischief's done by their ca-
        price;   1590
And if their approbation we experience,
Perhaps they'll have some more about a year
    hence.

200

My poem's epic, and is meant to be
    Divided in twelve books; each book con-
        taining,
With love, and war, a heavy gale at sea, 1595
    A list of ships, and captains, and kings
        reigning,
New characters; the episodes are three:
    A panoramic view of hell's in training,
After the style of Virgil and of Homer,
So that my name of epic's no misnomer. 1600

201

All these things will be specified in time,
    With strict regard to Aristotle's rules,
The *Vade Mecum*[31] of the true sublime,
    Which makes so many poets, and some
        fools:
Prose poets like blank-verse,[32] I'm fond of
        rhyme,   1605
    Good workmen never quarrel with their
        tools;
I've got new mythological machinery,
And very handsome supernatural scenery.

202

There's only one slight difference between
    Me and my epic brethren gone before, 1610
And here the advantage is my own, I ween
    (Not that I have not several merits more,
But this will more peculiarly be seen);
    They so embellish, that 'tis quite a bore

[31] Literally "go with me"; thus, a handbook.
[32] A dig at Wordsworth.

Their labyrinth of fables to thread
    through,   1615
Whereas this story's actually true.

203

If any person doubt it, I appeal
    To history, tradition, and to facts,
To newspapers, whose truth all know and
        feel,
    To plays in five, and operas in three
        acts;   1620
All these confirm my statement a good deal,
    But that which more completely faith exacts
Is, that myself, and several now in Seville,
    Saw Juan's last elopement with the devil.

204

If ever I should condescend to prose,   1625
    I'll write poetical commandments, which
Shall supersede beyond all doubt all those
    That went before; in these I shall enrich
My text with many things that no one knows,
    And carry precept to the highest pitch: 1630
I'll call the work "Longinus[33] o'er a Bottle,
Or, Every Poet his *own* Aristotle."

205

Thou shalt believe in Milton, Dryden, Pope;
    Thou shalt not set up Wordsworth, Cole-
        ridge, Southey;
Because the first is crazed beyond all hope, 1635
    The second drunk, the third so quaint and
        mouthy:
With Crabbe[34] it may be difficult to cope,
    And Campbell's Hippocrene[35] is somewhat
        drouthy:
Thou shalt not steal from Samuel Rogers, nor
Commit—flirtation with the muse of
    Moore. . . .   1640

207

If any person should presume to assert
    This story is not moral, first, I pray, 1650
That they will not cry out before they're
    hurt,

[33] First-century literary critic and rhetorician.
[34] English poet—as were Campbell, Rogers, and
Moore in the following three lines.
[35] Fountain on Mt. Helicon, whose waters were
said to impart poetic inspiration.

Then that they'll read it o'er again, and
say
(But, doubtless, nobody will be so pert),
  That this is not a moral tale, though gay;
Besides, in Canto Twelfth, I mean to
  show   1655
The very place where wicked people go.[36]

208

If, after all, there should be some so blind
  To their own good this warning to despise,
Led by some tortuosity of mind,
  Not to believe my verse and their own
  eyes,   1660
And cry that they "the moral cannot find,"
  I tell him, if a clergyman, he lies;
Should captains the remark, or critics, make,
They also lie too—under a mistake.

209

The public approbation I expect,   1665
  And beg they'll take my word about the
  moral,
Which I with their amusement will connect
  (So children cutting teeth receive a coral);
Meantime they'll doubtless please to recol-
  lect
  My epical pretensions to the laurel: 1670
For fear some prudish readers should grow
  skittish,
I've bribed my grandmother's review—the
  British.

210

I sent it in a letter to the Editor,
  Who thanked me duly by return of post—
I'm for a handsome article his creditor;   1675
  Yet, if my gentle Muse he please to roast,
And break a promise after having made it her,
  Denying the receipt of what it cost,
And smear his page with gall instead of
  honey,
All I can say is—that he had the money.[37] 1680

[36] Byron wrote that it was his plan, perhaps, to
finish his poem by sending Don Juan to Hell or get
him married; he regarded the two destinations as
quite similar.
[37] In ll. 1671–1680 Byron is merely having a
bit of fun at the expense of the staid *British Review*,
but the magazine found it necessary to disavow any
bribe.

211

I think that with this holy new alliance
  I may ensure the public, and defy
All other magazines of art or science,
  Daily, or monthly or three monthly; I
Have not essayed to multiply their clients, 1685
  Because they tell me 'twere in vain to try,
And that the Edinburgh Review and Quar-
  terly
Treat a dissenting author very martyrly.

212

"*Non ego hoc ferrem calida juventâ
  Consule Planco,*"[38] Horace said, and
  so   1690
Say I; by which quotation there is meant a
  Hint that some six or seven good years ago
(Long ere I dreamt of dating from the
  Brenta [39])
  I was most ready to return a blow,
And would not brook at all this sort of
  thing   1695
In my hot youth—when George the Third
  was King.

213

But now at thirty years my hair is gray—
  (I wonder what it will be like at forty?
I thought of a peruke the other day)—
  My heart is not much greener; and, in
  short, I   1700
Have squandered my whole summer while
  'twas May,
  And feel no more the spirit to retort; I
Have spent my life, both interest and princi-
  pal,
And deem not, what I deemed, my soul in-
  vincible.

214

No more—no more—Oh! never more on
  me   1705
  The freshness of the heart can fall like dew,

[38] "I should not have endured this in the heat
of my youth when Plancus was consul" (Horace,
Odes, 3: 14). Byron is saying that he is too old
to fight the reviewers.
[39] An Italian river that flows into the Gulf of
Venice.

Which out of all the lovely things we see
  Extracts emotions beautiful and new;
Hived in our bosoms like the bag o' the bee.
  Thinkest thou the honey with those ob-
    jects grew?   1710
Alas! 'twas not in them, but in thy power
To double even the sweetness of a flower.

215

No more—no more—Oh! never more, my
    heart,
  Canst thou be my sole world, my universe!
Once all in all, but now a thing apart,   1715
  Thou canst not be my blessing or my
    curse:
The illusion's gone for ever, and thou art
  Insensible, I trust, but none the worse,
And in thy stead I've got a deal of judgment,
  Though heaven knows how it ever found a
    lodgment.   1720

216

My days of love are over, me no more
  The charms of maid, wife, and still less of
    widow
Can make the fool of which they made be-
    fore,—
  In short, I must not lead the life I did do;
The credulous hope of mutual minds is
    o'er.   1725
  The copious use of claret is forbid too,
So for a good old gentlemanly vice,
I think I must take up with avarice.

217

Ambition was my idol, which was broken
  Before the shrines of sorrow, and of pleas-
    ure;   1730
And the two last have left me many a token
  O'er which reflection may be made at
    leisure;
Now, like Friar Bacon's brazen head, I've
    spoken,
  "Time is, Time was, Time's past:" [40]—a
    chemic treasure

[40] From Robert Greene's *Friar Bacon and Friar
Bungay,* an Elizabethan play.

Is glittering youth, which I have spent be-
    times—   1735
My heart in passion, and my head on rhymes.

218

What is the end of fame? 'tis but to fill
  A certain portion of uncertain paper:
Some liken it to climbing up a hill,
  Whose summit, like all hills, is lost in
    vapor;   1740
For this men write, speak, preach, and heroes
    kill,
  And bards burn what they call their "mid-
    night taper,"
To have, when the original is dust,
A name, a wretched picture, and worse bust.

219

What are the hopes of man? Old Egypt's
    King   1745
  Cheops erected the first pyramid
And largest, thinking it was just the thing
  To keep his memory whole, and mummy
    hid:
But somebody or other rummaging,
  Burglariously broke his coffin's lid.   1750
Let not a monument give you or me hopes,
Since not a pinch of dust remains of Cheops.

220

But I, being fond of true philosophy,
  Say very often to myself, "Alas!
All things that have been born were born to
    die,   1755
  And flesh (which Death mows down to
    hay) is grass;
You've passed your youth not so unpleasantly,
  And if you had it o'er again—'twould pass—
So thank your stars that matters are no worse,
And read your Bible, sir, and mind your
    purse."   1760

221

But for the present, gentle reader! and
  Still gentler purchaser! the bard—that's I—
Must, with permission, shake you by the
    hand,
  And so your humble servant, and good-
    bye!

We meet again, if we should understand 1765
  Each other; and if not, I shall not try
Your patience further than by this short
  sample—
'Twere well if others followed my example.

222

"Go, little book, from this my solitude!
  I cast thee on the waters—go thy ways! 1770
And if, as I believe, thy vein be good,
  The world will find thee after many
    days." [41]
When Southey's read, and Wordsworth un-
  derstood,
  I can't help putting in my claim to praise—
The four first rhymes are Southey's, every
  line: 1775
For God's sake, reader! take them not for
  mine!
(1818; 1819)

STUDY AIDS: 1. Wordsworth recommended for poetry a selection of language really used by men. Byron's poetical style in *Don Juan* is frequently colloquial. Would Wordsworth approve or disapprove of Byron's language? What is the difference between the simple style of *Michael* and the simplicity of *Don Juan*?

2. What do the ingenious rhymes add to the poem? Note that you often have to mispronounce the words to get them to rhyme (e.g., "widow"—"did do"). Is this annoying to the reader?

3. In what respects is *Don Juan* a MOCK-EPIC? What qualities of the epic does Byron parody or burlesque? One critic has said that the method of *Don Juan* is the only way that an epic can be written in modern times. What does he mean?

4. Keats said that *Don Juan* had only a "paltry originality" and exclaimed: "How horrible an example of human nature is the man who has no pleasure left him but to gloat over and jeer at the most awful incidents of life!" Do you agree with Keats? How would you defend Byron against this charge?

On This Day I Complete My Thirty-sixth Year [1]

'Tis time this heart should be unmoved,
  Since others it hath ceased to move:
Yet, though I cannot be beloved,
      Still let me love!

My days are in the yellow leaf;   5
  The flowers and fruits of love are gone;
The worm, the canker, and the grief
      Are mine alone!

The fire that on my bosom preys
  Is lone as some volcanic isle;   10
No torch is kindled at its blaze—
      A funeral pile.

The hope, the fear, the jealous care,
  The exalted portion of the pain
And power of love, I cannot share,   15
      But wear the chain.

But 'tis not *thus*—and 'tis not *here*— [2]
  Such thoughts should shake my soul, nor
      now,
Where glory decks the hero's bier,
      Or binds his brow.   20

The sword, the banner, and the field,
  Glory and Greece,[3] around me see!
The Spartan, borne upon his shield,
      Was not more free.[4]

Awake! (not Greece—she *is* awake!)   25
  Awake, my spirit! Think through *whom* [5]

[41] These quoted lines (1769–1772) are from Robert Southey's *Epilogue to the Lay of the Laureate*. Byron hated Southey for personal and political reasons. Their long-standing feud came to a climax in Byron's most devastating personal satire, *The Vision of Judgment* (1822).

[1] This was Byron's last poem, written on January 22, 1824. He died at Missolonghi three months later.

[2] The poet shifts his mood at this point. How?
[3] The Greeks were engaged in a war of independence against the Turks. Byron went to Greece to help.
[4] Free from selfish concerns.
[5] His warrior forebears.

Thy life-blood tracks its parent lake,
    And then strike home!

Tread those reviving passions [6] down,
    Unworthy manhood!—unto thee   30
Indifferent should the smile or frown
    Of Beauty be.

If thou regret'st thy youth, *why live?*
    The land of honorable death
Is here:—up to the field, and give   35
    Away thy breath!

Seek out—less often sought than found—
    A soldier's grave,[7] for thee the best;
Then look around, and choose thy ground,
    And take thy rest.   40
(1824)

STUDY AIDS: One critic says that Byron, in his final years, was moving toward a stoical acceptance of life and its troubles. How does this poem bear out this opinion? How does its TONE differ from that of *So We'll Go No More A-Roving* (p. 633)?

Letters

To His Mother

Prevesa, November 12, 1809

My dear Mother,

I have now been some time in Turkey: this place is on the coast, but I have traversed the interior of the province of Albania on a visit to the Pacha. I left Malta in the *Spider,* a brig of war, on the 21st of September, and arrived in eight days at Prevesa. I thence have been about 150 miles, as far as Tepaleen, his Highness's country palace, where I stayed three days. The name of the Pacha is *Ali,* and he is considered a man of the first abilities: he governs the whole of Albania (the ancient Illyricum), Epirus, and part of Macedonia. His son, Vely Pacha, to whom he has given me letters, governs the Morea,[1] and has great influence in Egypt; in short, he is one of the most powerful men in the Ottoman empire. When I reached Yanina, the capital, after a journey of three days over the mountains, through a country of the most picturesque beauty, I found that Ali Pacha was with his army in Illyricum, besieging Ibrahim Pacha in the castle of Berat He had heard that an Englishman of rank was in his dominions, and had left orders in Yanina with the commandant to provide a house, and supply me with every kind of necessary *gratis;* and, though I have been allowed to make presents to the slaves, etc., I have not been permitted to pay for a single article of household consumption.

I rode out on the vizier's horses, and saw the palaces of himself and grandsons: they are splendid, but too much ornamented with silk and gold. I then went over the mountains through Zitza, a village with a Greek monastery (where I slept on my return), in the most beautiful situation (always excepting Cintra, in Portugal) I ever beheld. In nine days I reached Tepaleen. Our journey was much prolonged by the torrents that had fallen from the mountains, and intersected the roads. I shall never forget the singular scene on entering Tepaleen at five in the afternoon, as the sun was going down. It brought to my mind (with some change of *dress* however) Scott's description of Branksome Castle in his *Lay,*[2] and the feudal system. The Albanians, in their dresses (the most magnificent in the world, consisting of a long *white kilt,* gold-worked cloak, crimson velvet gold-laced jacket and waistcoat, silver-mounted pistols and daggers), the Tartars with their high caps, the Turks in their vast

[6] Of the first four stanzas.

[7] Though Byron did not actually fall in battle as he hoped to do, he was engaged in training troops at the time of his death and so found "a soldier's grave." What effect is gained by the three brief imperatives of the last two lines? Note the rhythm, especially the pauses before the two "and's."

[1] Peninsula in southern Greece.

[2] *The Lay of the Last Minstrel.*

pelisses [3] and turbans, the soldiers and black slaves with the horses, the former in groups in an immense large open gallery in front of the palace, the latter placed in a kind of cloister below it, two hundred steeds ready caparisoned to move in a moment, couriers entering or passing out with despatches, the kettledrums beating, boys calling the hour from the minaret of the mosque, altogether, with the singular appearance of the building itself, formed a new and delightful spectacle to a stranger. I was conducted to a very handsome apartment, and my health inquired after by the vizier's secretary, "a-la-mode Turque!" [4]

The next day I was introduced to Ali Pacha. I was dressed in a full suit of staff uniform, with a very magnificent saber, etc. The vizier received me in a large room paved with marble; a fountain was playing in the center; the apartment was surrounded by scarlet ottomans. He received me standing, a wonderful compliment from a Mussulman, and made me sit down on his right hand. I have a Greek interpreter for general use, but a physician of Ali's, named Femlario, who understands Latin, acted for me on this occasion. His first question was, why, at so early an age, I left my country?—(the Turks have no idea of traveling for amusement). He then said, the English minister, Captain Leake, had told him I was of a great family, and desired his respects to my mother; which I now, in the name of Ali Pacha, present to you. He said he was certain I was a man of birth, because I had small ears, curling hair, and little white hands, and expressed himself pleased with my appearance and garb. He told me to consider him as a father whilst I was in Turkey, and said he looked on me as his son. Indeed, he treated me like a child, sending me almonds and sugared sherbet, fruit and sweetmeats, twenty times a day. He begged me to visit him often, and at night, when he was at leisure. I then, after coffee and pipes, retired for the first time. I saw him thrice afterwards. It is singular, that the Turks, who have no hereditary dignities, and few great families, except the Sultans, pay so much respect to birth; for I found my pedigree more regarded than my title. . . .

To-day I saw the remains of the town of Actium, near which Antony lost the world,[5] in a small bay, where two frigates could hardly maneuver: a broken wall is the sole remnant. On another part of the gulf stand the ruins of Nicopolis, built by Augustus in honor of his victory. Last night I was at a Greek marriage; but this and a thousand things more I have neither time nor space to describe.

I am going to-morrow, with a guard of fifty men, to Patras in the Morea, and thence to Athens, where I shall winter. Two days ago I was nearly lost in a Turkish ship of war, owing to the ignorance of the captain and crew, though the storm was not violent. Fletcher [6] yelled after his wife, the Greeks called on all the saints, the Mussulmans on Alla; the captain burst into tears and ran below deck, telling us to call on God; the sails were split, the main-yard shivered, the wind blowing fresh, the night setting in, and all our chance was to make Corfu, which is in possession of the French, or (as Fletcher pathetically termed it) "a watery grave." I did what I could to console Fletcher, but finding him incorrigible, wrapped myself up in my Albanian capote (an immense cloak), and lay down on deck to wait the worst. I have learned to philosophize in my travels, and if I had not, complaint was useless. Luckily the wind abated, and only drove us on the coast of Suli, on the main land, where we landed, and proceeded, by the help of the natives, to Prevesa again; but I shall not trust Turkish sailors in future, though the Pacha had ordered one of his own galliots [7] to take me to Patras. I am therefore going as far as Missolonghi by land, and there have only to cross a small gulf to get to Patras.

Fletcher's next epistle will be full of marvels: we were one night lost for nine hours in the mountains in a thunder-storm, and since

[3] Fur-lined coat
[4] In Turkish style.
[5] In 31 B.C. Octavian (the future emperor Augustus) defeated Mark Antony and Cleopatra in a naval battle near Actium.
[6] Byron's manservant.
[7] Small, swift boats.

nearly wrecked. In both cases Fletcher was sorely bewildered, from apprehensions of famine and banditti in the first, and drowning in the second instance. His eyes were a little hurt by the lightning, or crying (I don't know which), but are now recovered. When you write, address to me at Mr. Strané's, English consul, Patras, Morea.

I could tell you I know not how many incidents that I think would amuse you, but they crowd on my mind as much as they would swell my paper, and I can neither arrange them in the one, nor put them down on the other, except in the greatest confusion. I like the Albanians much; they are not all Turks; some tribes are Christians. But their religion makes little difference in their manner or conduct. They are esteemed the best troops in the Turkish service. I lived on my route, two days at once, and three days again, in a barrack at Salora, and never found soldiers so tolerable, though I have been in the garrisons of Gibraltar and Malta, and seen Spanish, French, Sicilian, and British troops in abundance. I have had nothing stolen, and was always welcome to their provision and milk. Not a week ago an Albanian chief (every village has its chief, who is called Primate), after helping us out of the Turkish galley in her distress, feeding us, and lodging my suite, consisting of Fletcher, a Greek, two Athenians, a Greek priest, and my companion, Mr. Hobhouse, refused any compensation but a written paper stating that I was well received; and when I pressed him to accept a few sequins,[8] "No," he replied; "I wish you to love me, not to pay me." These are his words. . . .

I am going to Athens to study modern Greek, which differs much from the ancient, though radically similar. I have no desire to return to England, nor shall I, unless compelled by absolute want, and Hanson's neglect; but I shall not enter into Asia for a year or two, as I have much to see in Greece, and I may perhaps cross into Africa, at least the Egyptian part. Fletcher, like all Englishmen, is very much dissatisfied, though a little reconciled to the Turks by a present of eighty

[8] Gold coins.

piastres from the vizier, which, if you consider every thing, and the value of specie here, is nearly worth ten guineas English. He has suffered nothing but from cold, heat, and vermin, which those who lie in cottages and cross mountains in a cold country must undergo, and of which I have equally partaken with himself; but he is not valiant, and is afraid of robbers and tempests. I have no one to be remembered to in England, and wish to hear nothing from it, but that you are well, and a letter or two on business from Hanson,[9] whom you may tell to write. I will write when I can, and beg you to believe me

Your affectionate son.

To Miss Milbanke

Sept. 26, 1813.

My dear Friend,—for such you will permit me to call you—On my return to town I find some consolation for having left a number of pleasant people in your letter—the more so as I begun to doubt if I should ever receive another. You ask me some questions, and as they are about myself, you must pardon the egotism into which my answers must betray me. I am glad that you know any "good deed" that I am supposed ever to have blundered upon, simply because it proves that you have not heard me invariably ill spoken of. If true I am sufficiently rewarded by a short step towards your good opinion. You don't like my "restless" doctrines—I should be very sorry if you did; but I can't stagnate nevertheless. If I must sail let it be on the ocean no matter how stormy—any thing but a dull cruise on a land lake without ever losing sight of the same insipid shores by which it is surrounded.

"Gay" but not "content"—very true. You say I never attempt to justify myself. You are right. At times I can't and occasionally I won't defend by explanation; life is not worth having on such terms. The only attempt I ever made at defense was in a poetical point of view [1]—and what did it end in? not an ex-

[9] John Hanson, Byron's lawyer.

[1] English Bards and Scotch Reviewers.

culpation of me, but an attack on all other persons whatsoever. I should make a pretty scene indeed if I went on defending—besides, by proving myself (supposing it possible) a good sort of quiet country gentleman, to how many people should I give more pain than pleasure? Do you think accusers like one the better for being confuted? You have detected a laughter "false to the heart"—allowed—yet I have been tolerably sincere with you and I fear sometimes troublesome. To the charge of pride I suspect I must plead guilty, because when a boy and a very young one it was the constant reproach of schoolfellows and tutors. Since I grew up I have heard less about it— probably because I have now neither school-fellow nor tutor. It was, however, originally defensive—for at that time my hand like Ishmael's was against every one's and every one's against mine. I now come to a subject of your inquiry which you must have per-ceived I always hitherto avoided—an awful one—"Religion." I was bred in Scotland among Calvinists in the first part of my life, which gave me a dislike to that persuasion. Since that period I have visited the most bigoted and credulous of countries—Spain, Greece, Turkey. As a spectacle the Catholic is more fascinating than the Greek or the Moslem; but the last is the only believer who practices the precepts of his Prophet to the last chapter of his creed. My opinions are quite undecided. I may say so sincerely, since, when given over at Patras in 1810, I rejected and ejected three Priest-loads of spiritual con-solation by threatening to turn Mussulman if they did not leave me in quiet. I was in great pain and looked upon death as in that respect a relief—without much regret for the past, and few speculations on the future. In-deed so indifferent was I to my bodily situa-tion, that, though I was without any attend-ant but a young Frenchman as ill as myself, two barbarous Arnouts, and a deaf and des-perate Greek Quack—and my English servant (a man with me) within two days journey— I would not allow the last to be sent for— worth all the rest as he would because been in attendance at such a time, was a se—I really don't know why—unless it an in-

difference to which I am certainly not subject when in good health. I believe doubtless in God, and should be happy to be convinced of much more. If I do not at present place implicit faith in tradition and revelation of any human creed, I hope it is not from want of reverence for the Creator but the created, and when I see a man publishing a pamphlet to prove that Mr. Pitt [2] is risen from the dead (as was done a week ago), perfectly positive in the truth of his assertion, I must be permitted to doubt more miracles equally well attested; but the moral of Chris-tianity is perfectly beautiful—and the very sublime of virtue—yet even there we find some of its finer precepts in the earlier axioms of the Greeks—particulary "do unto others as you would they should do unto you"—the forgiveness of injuries and more which I do not remember. Good night; I have sent you a long prose; I hope your answer will be equal in length—I am sure it will be more amusing —You write remarkably well—which you won't like to hear, so I shall say no more about it.

Ever yours most sincerely.

To Thomas Moore

Venice, January 28, 1817.

Your letter of the 8th is before me. The remedy for your plethora [1] is simple—abstin-ence. I was obliged to have recourse to the like some years ago, I mean in point of *diet*, and, with the exception of some convivial weeks and days (it might be months, now and then), have kept to Pythagoras [2] ever since. For all this, let me hear that you are better. You must not *indulge* in "filthy beer," nor in porter,[3] nor eat *suppers*—the last are the devil to those who swallow dinner. . . .

I am truly sorry to hear of your father's misfortune [4]—cruel at any time, but doubly

[2] English statesman who died in 1806.

---

[1] A morbid condition thought in Byron's time to be due to over-fullness of the blood.

[2] A Greek philosopher who aimed at the purifica-tion of the soul.

[3] A weak, sweet beer.

[4] Moore's father was dismissed from his job.

cruel in advanced life. However, you will, at least, have the satisfaction of doing your part by him, and, depend upon it, it will not be in vain. Fortune, to be sure, is a female, but not such a b— as the rest (always excepting your wife and my sister from such sweeping terms); for she generally has some justice in the long run. I have no spite against her, though, between her and Nemesis,[5] I have had some sore gauntlets to run—but then I have done my best to deserve no better. But to *you,* she is a good deal in arrear, and she will come round—mind if she don't: you have the vigor of life, of independence, of talent, spirit, and character all with you. What you can do for yourself, you have done and will do; and surely there are some others in the world who would not be sorry to be of use, if you would allow them to be useful, or at least attempt it.

I think of being in England in the spring. If there is a row, by the scepter of King Ludd,[6] but I'll be one;[7] and if there is none, and only a continuance of "this meek, piping time of peace,"[8] I will take a cottage a hundred yards to the south of your abode, and become your neighbor; and we will compose such canticles, and hold such dialogues, as shall be the terror of the *Times* (including the newspaper of that name), and the wonder, and honor, and praise of the *Morning Chronicle*[9] and posterity.

I rejoice to hear of your forthcoming in February[10]—though I tremble for the "magnificence" which you attribute to the new *Childe Harold.*[11] I am glad you like it; it is a fine indistinct piece of poetical desolation, and my favorite. I was half mad during the time of its composition, between metaphysics, mountains, lakes, love unextinguishable, thoughts unutterable, and the night-mare of my own delinquencies. I should, many a

good day, have blown my brains out, but for the recollection that it would have given pleasure to my mother-in-law; and, even *then,* if I could have been certain to haunt her— but I won't dwell upon these trifling family matters.

Venice is in the *estro*[12] of her carnival, and I have been up these last two nights at the ridotto[13] and the opera, and all that kind of thing. Now for an adventure. A few days ago a gondolier brought me a billet without a subscription,[14] intimating a wish on the part of the writer to meet me either in gondola, or at the island of San Lazaro, or at a third rendezvous, indicated in the note. "I know the country's disposition well,"—in Venice "they do let heaven see those tricks they dare not show"[15] etc. etc.; so, for all response, I said that neither of the three places suited me; but that I would either be at home at ten at night *alone,* or be at the ridotto at midnight, where the writer might meet me masked. At ten o'clock I was at home and alone (Marianna[16] was gone with her husband to a conversazione[17]), when the door of my apartment opened, and in walked a well-looking and (for an Italian) *bionda*[18] girl of about nineteen, who informed me that she was married to the brother of my *amorosa,* and wished to have some conversation with me. I made a decent reply, and we had some talk in Italian and Romaic (her mother being a Greek of Corfu), when, lo! in a very few minutes in marches, to my very great astonishment, Marianna S—, *in propria persona,*[19] and, after making a most polite curtsy to her sister-in-law and to me, without a single word seizes her said sister-in-law by the hair, and bestows upon her some sixteen slaps, which would have made your ear ache only to hear their echo. I need not describe the screaming which ensued. The luckless visitor took flight.

[5] Goddess of retribution.
[6] Legendary king of ancient Britain.
[7] A part of it.
[8] Slightly altered from Shakespeare, *Richard III.*
[9] The *Times* and *Morning Chronicle* were Tory and Whig, respectively. Byron was a Whig.
[10] Moore's poem *Lalla Rookh* was expected in February.
[11] Canto 3.

[12] Excitement.
[13] Masquerade ball.
[14] A note without a signature.
[15] *Othello.*
[16] Marianna Segati, one of Byron's Venetian mistresses. Byron lived in the Segati home.
[17] Social gathering.
[18] Blonde.
[19] "In her very own person."

I seized Marianna, who, after several vain efforts to get away in pursuit of the enemy, fairly went into fits in my arms; and, in spite of reasoning, eau de Cologne, vinegar, half a pint of water, and God knows what other waters beside, continued so till past midnight.

After damning my servants for letting people in without apprizing me, I found that Marianna in the morning had seen her sister-in-law's gondolier on the stairs; and, suspecting that this apparition boded her no good, had either returned of her own accord, or been followed by her maids or some other spy of her people to the conversazione, from whence she returned to perpetrate this piece of pugilism. I had seen fits before, and also some small scenery of the same genus in and out of our island; but this was not all. After about an hour, in comes—who? why, Signor S—, her lord and husband, and finds me with his wife fainting upon a sofa, and all the apparatus of confusion, disheveled hair, hats, handkerchiefs, salts, smelling bottles—and the lady as pale as ashes, without sense or motion. His first question was, "What is all this?" The lady could not reply—so I did. I told him the explanation was the easiest thing in the world; but, in the mean time, it would be as well to recover his wife—at least, her senses. This came about in due time of suspiration and respiration.

You need not be alarmed—jealousy is not the order of the day in Venice, and daggers are out of fashion, while duels, on love mat-ters, are unknown—at least, with the husbands. But, for all this, it was an awkward affair; and though he must have known that I made love to Marianna, yet I believe he was not, till that evening, aware of the extent to which it had gone. It is very well known that almost all the married women have a lover; but it is usual to keep up the forms, as in other nations. I did not, therefore, know what the devil to say. I could not out with the truth, out of regard to her, and I did not choose to lie for my sake;—besides, the thing told itself. I thought the best way would be to let her explain it as she chose (a woman being never at a loss—the devil always sticks by them)—only determining to protect and carry her off, in case of any ferocity on the part of the Signor. I saw that he was quite calm. She went to bed, and next day—how they settled it, I know not, but settle it they did. Well—then I had to explain to Marianna about this never-to-be-sufficiently-confounded sister-in-law; which I did by swearing innocence, eternal constancy, etc. etc. . . . But the sister-in-law, very much discomposed with being treated in such wise, has (not having her own shame before her eyes) told the affair to half Venice, and the servants (who were summoned by the fight and the fainting) to the other half. But, here, nobody minds such trifles, except to be amused by them. I don't know whether you will be so, but I have scrawled a long letter out of these follies.

Believe me ever, etc.

Percy Bysshe Shelley
(1792–1822)

EVEN AS A CHILD SHELLEY WAS A DREAMER AND A REBEL. HE LIVED IN A WORLD OF BRIGHT visions and continual make-believe. At school he revolted against the "fagging" system (under which the older boys tormented the younger ones) and against pedagogical authority. In his reading he went from cheap novels and romances of terror to the literature of science and the skeptics, and preferred bizarre chemical experiments to the more prosaic assignments of the classroom. So radical were his religious views that he was nicknamed "Shelley the Atheist," and the parents of Harriet Grove, his first sweetheart, felt compelled to break up the romance.

At Oxford Shelley continued his nonconformist ways. Scorning the orthodox curriculum, the regular university activities of classroom and playing field, the authority of the professors, and the usual recreations of the undergraduates, he read voraciously on his own and continued his amateur forays into science. The climax of his youthful iconoclasm came when he and his friend Thomas Jefferson Hogg published *The Necessity of Atheism* and were immediately expelled from Oxford for refusing to disavow their authorship.

Shelley's remaining years in England (1811–1818) were chaotic. He met and married Harriet Westbrook, provoking another quarrel with his ultraconservative father, Sir Timothy. He went to Ireland, where he spoke and wrote for reform. In 1813 appeared his first important poem, *Queen Mab,* the most complete statement of his early radicalism. Shelley and Harriet grew further and further apart as she found it impossible to keep up with his wide-ranging intellectual interests. He met William Godwin and his intelligent daughter Mary, with whom he soon fell in love. They eloped to France in 1814. He returned to find debts piling up and friends alienated, but in 1815 a bequest from his grandfather eased his financial burdens. In this same year appeared *Alastor,* the first poem to show Shelley's shift from propaganda to poetry and from a materialistic skepticism to idealism. In 1816, he and Mary, now the parents of two children, went to Switzerland, where he was in close contact with Lord Byron. He came back to England in the fall, and Harriet drowned herself later in the year. Shelley was refused the custody of his and Harriet's two children because of his radical views. In 1818, fearing that his children by Mary (whom he had legally married after Harriet's suicide) might also be taken from him, he left England, never to return.

Shelley spent the last four years of his life in Italy writing poetry, making new friends, visiting Byron, interesting himself in the Spanish and Greek revolutions, and planning a magazine with Byron and Leigh Hunt. Among the important works written during these creative years are *Prometheus Unbound,* a lyrical drama which symbolically states the need for the mind of man to be dominated by brotherly love before tyranny and evil can be overthrown and the perfect society can be achieved; *The Cenci,* a powerful play, based on Elizabethan models, of murder and incest; the *Philosophical View of Reform,* an uncompleted prose tract urging certain reform measures; *Hellas,* a lyrical drama inspired by the Greek fight for independence; *Adonais,* the great elegy on Keats; the *Defense of Poetry,* his finest piece of prose; *The Triumph of Life,* an unfinished vision-poem; and many excellent shorter works.

In July, 1822, Shelley and a friend, Edward Williams, went sailing on the Gulf of Spezia in Shelley's boat, the *Don Juan.* A storm arose, the boat capsized, and both men were drowned. When Shelley's body was washed up on shore, it was cremated according to Italian regulations, and the ashes were buried in the Protestant Cemetery in Rome, where Keats also was buried.

Shelley's poetry is an interesting mingling of the lyrical and the philosophical. The fluid melody of his lines and the preponderance of imagery drawn from the realms of the insubstantial and amorphous—light, cloud, wind, air, and water—have led some readers to regard Shelley as a vague dreamer. Behind all his verse, however, is the keen mind of a vigorous thinker. With Shelley lyricism was a means to change the hearts of men, and

so to hasten the millennium. His statement of the ideals of love and beauty and human brotherhood makes an eloquent appeal to us today.

It has been conjectured that if Byron and Shelley had survived to old age, Byron would have turned conservative at last, like Wordsworth and Coleridge, but Shelley would have remained a zealous reformer to the end. For Byron the conjecture is questionable; for Shelley it seems altogether likely. Although Shelley altered his philosophical position from materialism to Platonic idealism, his enthusiasm for liberal causes never abated, and his passion for human brotherhood and for a Utopian society based on universal love was as strong in 1822 as it was in 1811. His hope for mankind remained constant; what changed was his concept of how the hope could be realized. During these eleven years the poet came gradually to dominate the propagandist, and the idealist to supplant the materialistic skeptic.

Hymn to Intellectual Beauty

By intellectual beauty Shelley means ideal beauty—that supreme ideal beauty of which particular earthly beauties are but imperfect representations. It is real, eternal, unchanging; they are apparent, transitory, mutable. This is a Platonic doctrine which is found in many of Shelley's poems and which he often symbolizes in the form of a lovely woman. Shelley makes little or no distinction between ideal beauty and ideal love; and it is his passionate conviction that only as men seek out this ideal, only as they allow its influence to pervade their hearts and minds, will there be any improvement in the human lot.

I

The awful shadow of some unseen Power [1]
  Floats though unseen among us—visiting
  This various world with as inconstant wing
As summer winds that creep from flower to
    flower—
Like moonbeams that behind some piny
    mountain shower,   5
    It visits with inconstant glance
    Each human heart and countenance;
Like hues and harmonies of evening—
    Like clouds in starlight widely spread—
    Like memory of music fled—   10
    Like aught that for its grace may be
Dear, and yet dearer for its mystery.[2]

2

Spirit of Beauty, that dost consecrate
  With thine own hues all thou dost shine
    upon

Of human thought or form—where art
    thou gone?   15
Why dost thou pass away and leave our state,
This dim vast vale of tears, vacant and desolate?
    Ask why [3] the sunlight not forever
    Weaves rainbows o'er yon mountain
      river;
Why aught should fail and fade that once is
    shown;   20
    Why fear and dream and death and birth
    Cast on the daylight of this earth
    Such gloom; why man has such a scope
For love and hate, despondency and hope.[4]

3

No voice from some sublimer world hath
    ever   25
  To sage or poet these responses [5] given;

[1] Intellectual Beauty.
[2] One of Shelley's favorite poetical devices is a catalogue of SIMILES. How are these similes (in ll. 4–12) appropriate to the meaning? What do they have in common?

[3] I.e., one might as well ask why.
[4] This stanza is Shelley's expression of the inconstancy of the visitations of Intellectual Beauty in terms of the problems of suffering, evil, change, and death.
[5] Responses to what?

Therefore the names of demon, ghost, and
heaven,
Remain the records of their vain endeavor,
Frail spells, whose uttered charm might not
avail to sever,
    From all we hear and all we see,   30
    Doubt, chance, and mutability.
Thy light alone, like mist o'er mountains
driven,
    Or music by the night wind sent
    Through strings of some still instrument,
    Or moonlight on a midnight stream, 35
Gives grace and truth to life's unquiet dream.

4

Love, hope, and self-esteem, like clouds depart
    And come, for some uncertain moments
lent.
Man were immortal, and omnipotent,
Didst thou, unknown and awful as thou
art,   40
Keep with thy glorious train firm state within
his heart.
    Thou messenger of sympathies,
    That wax and wane in lovers' eyes!
Thou, that to human thought art nourishment,
    Like darkness to a dying flame,   45
    Depart not as thy shadow came,
    Depart not, lest the grave should be,
Like life and fear, a dark reality!

5

While yet a boy I sought for ghosts, and sped
    Through many a listening chamber, cave
and ruin,   50
    And starlight wood, with fearful steps pur-
suing
Hopes of high talk with the departed dead.
I called on poisonous names with which our
youth is fed:
    I was not heard—I saw them not—
    When musing deeply on the lot   55
Of life, at that sweet time when winds are
wooing
    All vital things that wake to bring
    News of birds and blossoming,—
    Sudden, thy shadow fell on me;

I shrieked, and clasped my hands in
    ecstasy! [6]   60

6

I vowed that I would dedicate my powers
    To thee and thine—have I not kept the
vow?
    With beating heart and streaming eyes,
even now
I call the phantoms of a thousand hours [7]
Each from his voiceless grave: they have in
visioned bowers   65
    Of studious zeal or love's delight
    Outwatched with me the envious night—
They know that never joy illumed my brow
    Unlinked with hope that thou wouldst
free
    This world from its dark slavery,[8]   70
    That thou, O awful Loveliness,
Wouldst give whate'er these words cannot
express.

7

The day becomes more solemn and serene [9]
    When noon is past; there is a harmony
    In autumn, and a luster in its sky,   75
Which through the summer is not heard or
seen,
As if it could not be, as if it had not been!
    Thus let thy power, which like the truth
    Of nature on my passive youth
Descended, to my onward life supply   80
    Its calm,—to one who worships thee,
    And every form containing thee,[10]
    Whom, Spirit fair, thy spells did bind
To fear himself, and love all humankind.
(1816; 1817)

STUDY AIDS: 1. The FIGURATIVE LAN-
GUAGE of this poem is fairly typical of Shelley's
imagery. How does it differ from Byron's (e.g.,
in *Childe Harold's Pilgrimage*)? How is it appropriate to the content of this particular poem?

[6] The contrast in this stanza is between superstition and orthodoxy (l. 53) on the one hand
and the true religion of Intellectual Beauty on the
other.
[7] The past hours of his own life.
[8] Lines 69–70: Shelley's idealism and his passion
for social reform were closely linked.
[9] Work out the IMAGERY of this final stanza.
[10] Why the distinction in ll. 81–82?

2. SCAN a stanza and put down its RHYME SCHEME. Why is it an effective metrical form for the subject matter?

3. Does this "religion" of Shelley seem to you vague and impractical? How can Intellectual Beauty "free This world from its dark slavery"?

Ozymandias

Ozymandias (probably Rameses II) was an ancient Egyptian tyrant. On the pedestal of his ruined statue is this inscription: "I am Ozymandias, king of kings. If anyone would know how great I am and where I lie, let him surpass one of my works."

I met a traveler from an antique land
Who said: "Two vast and trunkless legs of
   stone
Stand in the desert. Near them, on the sand,
Half sunk, a shattered visage lies, whose
   frown,
And wrinkled lip, and sneer of cold com-
   mand,   5
Tell that its sculptor well those passions read
Which yet survive, stamped on these lifeless
   things,
The hand that mocked them, and the heart
   that fed: [1]
And on the pedestal these words appear:

'My name is Ozymandias, king of kings: [2] 10
Look on my works, ye mighty, and despair!'
Nothing beside remains. Round the decay
Of that colossal wreck, boundless and bare
The lone and level sands stretch far away." [3]
(1817; 1818)

STUDY AIDS: 1. What is the THEME of this sonnet? How is it developed? What effect does Shelley gain by quoting a traveler? Does Shelley moralize directly?

2. Analyze the character of Ozymandias as suggested by the poem. Who are his twentieth-century counterparts?

Stanzas Written in Dejection, Near Naples

The main cause of Shelley's melancholy in 1818 was the death of his young daughter. But there were other causes: ill health; separation from his English friends; the hostile reception of his poetry by the critics and its neglect by the public; and perhaps a temporary estrangement from his wife.

The sun is warm, the sky is clear,
   The waves are dancing fast and bright,
Blue isles and snowy mountains wear
   The purple noon's transparent might;

The breath of the moist earth is light 5
   Around its unexpanded buds;
   Like many a voice of one delight,
   The winds', the birds', the ocean-floods',
The city's voice itself is soft like Solitude's.[1]

[1] "Hand" (whose hand?) and "heart" (whose heart?) are the direct objects of "survive" (l. 7). "Mocked" can mean merely "imitated" or "derided by mimicry." Which do you think is the better reading here? What is gained by the ambiguity?
[2] In ll. 10–11, note that Shelley has altered the actual inscription. Does a poet have a right to make such changes? How is Shelley's version an improvement? Why should the "mighty" "despair"?
[3] What effect is given by the shifting, in the last three lines, to the vista of the boundlessly

stretching sands? What is the IRONY? Note the ASSONANCE of "round"–"boundless," "wreck"–"stretch"; and the ALLITERATION of "boundless and bare," "lone and level."

[1] Personified "solitude" is here used to point up the beauty of the noontime scene, but it also looks ahead to Shelley's own feelings of isolation as given in the final three stanzas. So, too, the word "alone" of l. 14.

I see the deep's untrampled floor   10
  With green and purple sea-weeds strown;
I see the waves upon the shore
  Like light dissolved in star-showers
    thrown;
  I sit upon the sands alone—
The lightning of the noon-tide ocean   15
  Is flashing round me, and a tone
Arises from its measured motion,
How sweet! did any heart now share in my
  emotion.

Alas! I have nor hope nor health,
  Nor peace within nor calm around,   20
Nor that content, surpassing wealth,
  The sage in meditation found,
    And walked with inward glory crowned—
Nor fame, nor power, nor love, nor leisure.
  Others I see whom these surround—   25
Smiling they live, and call life pleasure;
To me that cup has been dealt in another
  measure.[2]

Yet now despair itself is mild,
  Even as the winds and waters are;

I could lie down like a tired child,   30
  And weep away the life of care
  Which I have borne, and yet must bear,
Till death like sleep might steal on me,
  And I might feel in the warm air
My cheek grow cold, and hear the sea   35
Breathe o'er my dying brain its last
  monotony.

Some might lament that I were cold,[3]
  As I, when this sweet day is gone,
Which my lost heart, too soon grown old,
  Insults with this untimely moan;   40
  They might lament—for I am one
Whom men love not,—and yet regret,
  Unlike this day, which, when the sun
Shall on its stainless glory set,
Will linger, though enjoyed, like joy in mem-
  ory yet.   45

(1818; 1824)

STUDY AIDS: What is the contrast between the first two stanzas and the rest of the poem? How is the transition between the two parts made?

Song to the Men of England

This poem and the sonnet which follows are expressions of Shelley's indignation over the "Peterloo Massacre" of 1819. A crowd of Manchester citizens, gathered on St. Peter's Field to urge certain Parliamentary reforms, was set upon by the militia. A number of people were killed or wounded. Because of this incident Shelley was more convinced than ever that revolution in England was imminent.

Men of England, wherefore plough
For the lords who lay ye low?
Wherefore weave with toil and care
The rich robes your tyrants wear?

Wherefore feed, and clothe, and save,   5
From the cradle to the grave,
Those ungrateful drones who would
Drain your sweat—nay, drink your blood?

Wherefore, bees of England, forge
Many a weapon, chain, and scourge,   10
That these stingless drones may spoil
The forced produce of your toil?

Have ye leisure, comfort, calm,
Shelter, food, love's gentle balm?
Or what is it ye buy so dear   15
With your pain and with your fear?

[2] SCAN this line. How does its rhythm fit the mood?

[3] The same "cold" of l. 35—the coldness of death. The general meaning of this difficult final stanza is this: "Some people might be sorry when I am dead, just as I lament the passing of this day (which

I am insulting with my moans). They might be sorry, for I am not loved; they might regret that I ever lived, unlike the way I feel about this day, which will be enjoyed in memory long after it is gone." Can you justify this more than usually tortured syntax?

The seed ye sow, another reaps;
The wealth ye find, another keeps;
The robes ye weave, another wears;
The arms ye forge, another bears.   20

Sow seed—but let no tyrant reap;
Find wealth—let no impostor heap;
Weave robes—let not the idle wear;
Forge arms—in your defense to bear.

Shrink to your cellars, holes, and cells;   25
In halls ye deck another dwells.
Why shake the chains ye wrought? Ye see
The steel ye tempered glance on ye.

With plough and spade, and hoe and loom,
Trace your grave and build your tomb,   30
And weave your winding-sheet, till fair
England be your sepulcher.
(1819; 1839)

STUDY AIDS: 1. This is a poem of insurgency, a stirring rhetorical appeal for action. Properly read aloud under certain conditions, it would be very effective. In accounting for its effectiveness, consider the verse form, the words (their length, connotation, and familiarity), and the rhythm. Can you think of other features of the poem that contribute to its rousing effect?

2. What is the effect of the many questions of the first four stanzas?

Sonnet: England in 1819

An old, mad, blind, despised, and dying
     king [1]—
Princes,[2] the dregs of their dull race, who flow
Through public scorn—mud from a muddy
     spring—
Rulers who neither see, nor feel, nor know,
But leech-like to their fainting country cling, 5
Till they drop, blind in blood, without a
     blow—
A people starved and stabbed in the untilled
     field [3]—

An army, which liberticide and prey
Makes as a two-edged sword to all who
     wield—
Golden and sanguine laws which tempt and
     slay;   10
Religion, Christless, Godless—a book sealed;
A senate—Time's worst statute unrepealed—
Are graves, from which a glorious phantom
     may
Burst to illumine our tempestuous day.
(1819; 1839)

Ode to the West Wind

I

O wild west wind, thou breath of autumn's
     being,
Thou, from whose unseen presence the leaves
     dead
Are driven, like ghosts from an enchanter
     fleeing,

Yellow, and black, and pale, and hectic red,
Pestilence-stricken multitudes! O thou,   5
Who chariotest to their dark wintry bed

The wingèd seeds, where they lie cold and
     low,

Each like a corpse within its grave, until
Thine azure sister of the spring shall blow

Her clarion o'er the dreaming earth, and fill 10
(Driving sweet buds like flocks to feed in air)
With living hues and odors plain and hill: [1]

[1] George III, who died in 1820 after ten years of blindness and insanity.
[2] Especially the pleasure-loving Prince Regent, the future George IV.
[3] A reference to the Peterloo Massacre.

[1] The west wind is presented as destroyer (ll. 1–5) and as preserver (ll. 5–8). Lines 9–12 describe the future rebirth resulting from the west wind's dual role. Note the death-burial-resurrection imagery here, with the blowing of the "clarion" like Gabriel's final trumpet.

Wild spirit, which art moving everywhere;
Destroyer and preserver; hear, oh hear!

2

Thou on whose stream, 'mid the steep sky's
    commotion,   15
Loose clouds like earth's decaying leaves are
    shed,
Shook from the tangled boughs of heaven and
    ocean,

Angels of rain and lightning! there are spread
On the blue surface of thine airy surge,
Like the bright hair uplifted from the
    head   20

Of some fierce Mænad,[2] even from the dim
    verge
Of the horizon to the zenith's height,
The locks of the approaching storm. Thou
    dirge

Of the dying year, to which this closing
    night [3]
Will be the dome of a vast sepulcher,   25
Vaulted with all thy congregated might

Of vapors, from whose solid atmosphere
Black rain, and fire, and hail, will burst: Oh
    hear!

3

Thou who didst waken from his summer-
    dreams
The blue Mediterranean, where he lay,   30
Lulled by the coil of his crystàlline streams,

Beside a pumice [4] isle in Baiae's bay,[5]
And saw in sleep old palaces and towers [6]
Quivering within the wave's intenser day,

All overgrown with azure moss and flowers   35
So sweet, the sense faints picturing them!
    Thou
For whose path the Atlantic's level powers

[2] A priestess of Bacchus.
[3] The night sky.
[4] Volcanic.
[5] Near Naples.
[6] These ruins of old Roman baths are down in
the water.

Cleave themselves into chasms, while far be-
    low
The sea-blooms and the oozy woods which
    wear [7]
The sapless foliage of the ocean know   40

Thy voice, and suddenly grow gray with fear
And tremble and despoil themselves: Oh
    hear!

4

If I were a dead leaf thou mightest bear;
If I were a swift cloud to fly with thee;
A wave to pant beneath thy power, and
    share   45

The impulse of thy strength, only less free
Than thou, O uncontrollable! If even
I were as in my boyhood, and could be

The comrade of thy wanderings over heaven,
As then, when to outstrip thy skyey speed 50
Scarce seemed a vision; I would ne'er have
    striven

As thus with thee in prayer in my sore need.
Oh! lift me as a wave, a leaf, a cloud!
I fall upon the thorns of life! I bleed! [8]

A heavy weight of hours has chained and
    bowed   55
One too like thee—tameless, and swift, and
    proud.

5

Make me thy lyre, even as the forest is:
What if my leaves are falling like its own!
The tumult of thy mighty harmonies

Will take from both a deep, autumnal tone, 60
Sweet though in sadness. Be thou, Spirit
    fierce,
My spirit! Be thou me, impetuous one!

[7] In a note Shelley called attention to the scientific accuracy of ll. 39-41: "The vegetation at the
bottom of the sea, of rivers, and of lakes, sympathizes
with that of the land in the change of seasons, and
is consequently influenced by the winds which
announce it." Shelley had a lifelong interest in
science, an interest reflected in much of his poetry.
[8] Is this line in keeping with the rest of the
poem?

Drive my dead [9] thoughts over the universe
Like withered leaves to quicken a new birth!
And, by the incantation of this verse,   65

Scatter, as from an unextinguished hearth
Ashes and sparks, my words among mankind!
Be through my lips to unawakened earth

The trumpet of a prophecy! O wind,
If winter comes, can spring be far behind? [10]   70
(1819; 1820)

STUDY AIDS: 1. This poem is beautifully constructed. Each stanza performs a distinct function. Determine in each case what it is.
2. In addition to analyzing his subject, the poet in several ways has also synthesized it—i.e., bound the parts together into a whole. Note, e.g., how "stream" (l. 15) and "blue surface" (l. 19) look ahead to st. 3; and how "boughs" (l. 17) and "foliage" (l. 40) look back to st. 1. Find other instances of such verbal linkings.

3. The synthesis is also thematic. The west wind is invoked in the first stanza as "destroyer and preserver"—the old leaves must be destroyed before the new leaves come. How is this theme carried through the poem? How is this dual role reflected in the effect of the wind on the clouds and waves? How reflected in the prayer for identification? What does the poet wish to destroy, what preserve?
4. Rhyme and rhythm also contribute to the synthesis. Shelley has made Dante's TERZA RIMA the metrical basis for a stanza of fourteen lines, concluding with a COUPLET. Why is the rhyme scheme appropriate to the subject matter? Note the long, carefully molded sentences (e.g., the first stanza is one sentence) combined with pauses of various lengths and at varied intervals. How do these flowing rhythms fit the content? Are the lines mostly END-STOPPED or RUN-ON? What is the effect of the final couplet at the end of each stanza?
5. This is an intensely emotional poem. How is the emotion brought under control? Does it get out of control at any point in the poem?

The Cloud

This poem is an excellent illustration of Shelley's poetical use of scientific (here meteorological) phenomena and of his facility in versification. Note the complicated stanza form with its internal rhymes.

I bring fresh showers for the thirsting flowers,
   From the seas and the streams;
I bear light shade for the leaves when laid
   In their noonday dreams.
From my wings are shaken the dews that
   waken   5
   The sweet buds every one,
When rocked to rest on their mother's breast,
   As she dances about the sun.
I wield the flail of the lashing hail,
   And whiten the green plains under,   10
And then again I dissolve it in rain,
   And laugh as I pass in thunder.

I sift the snow on the mountains below,
   And their great pines groan aghast;

And all the night 'tis my pillow white,   15
   While I sleep in the arms of the blast.
Sublime on the towers of my skyey bowers,
   Lightning my pilot sits;
In a cavern under is fettered the thunder,
   It struggles and howls at fits;   20
Over earth and ocean, with gentle motion,
   This pilot is guiding me,
Lured by the love of the genii that move
   In the depths of the purple sea;
Over the rills, and the crags, and the hills,   25
   Over the lakes and the plains,

[10] In this line, "winter" and "spring" repeat the idea of st. 1 ("the dark wintry bed" and "thine azure sister of the spring"); but in the light of the last two stanzas of personal application they have taken on a larger significance than their merely natural one. What do they now symbolize?

[9] In what way does Shelley regard his thoughts as "dead"? Cf. the "ashes and sparks" of l. 67.

Wherever he dream, under mountain or
    stream,[1]
    The spirit he loves remains;[2]
And I all the while bask in heaven's blue
    smile,
    Whilst he is dissolving in rains.   30

The sanguine sunrise, with his meteor eyes,
    And his burning plumes outspread,
Leaps on the back of my sailing rack,[3]
    When the morning star shines dead;
As on the jag of a mountain crag,   35
    Which an earthquake rocks and swings,
An eagle alit one moment may sit
    In the light of its golden wings.
And when sunset may breathe, from the lit
    sea beneath,
    Its ardors of rest and of love,   40
And the crimson pall of eve may fall
    From the depth of heaven above,
With wings folded I rest, on mine airy nest,
    As still as a brooding dove.

That orbèd maiden with white fire laden,   45
    Whom mortals call the moon,
Glides glimmering o'er my fleece-like floor,
    By the midnight breezes strewn;
And wherever the beat of her unseen feet,
    Which only the angels hear,   50
May have broken the woof of my tent's thin
    roof,
    The stars peep behind her and peer;
And I laugh to see them whirl and flee,
    Like a swarm of golden bees,
When I widen the rent in my wind-built
    tent,   55
    Till the calm rivers, lakes, and seas,
Like strips of the sky fallen through me on
    high,
    Are each paved with the moon and these.[4]

I bind the sun's throne with a burning zone,
    And the moon's with a girdle of pearl;   60
The volcanoes are dim, and the stars reel and
    swim,
    When the whirlwinds my banner unfurl.

---

[1] "Under mountain or stream" modifies "remains."
[2] This line is the direct object of "[may] dream"
above.
[3] A broken part of the cloud.
[4] The stars.

From cape to cape, with a bridge-like shape,
    Over a torrent sea,
Sunbeam-proof, I hang like a roof—   65
    The mountains its columns be.
The triumphal arch, through which I march,
    With hurricane, fire, and snow,
When the powers of the air are chained to my
    chair,
    Is the million-colored bow;   70
The sphere-fire above its soft colors wove,
    While the moist earth was laughing below.

I am the daughter of earth and water,
    And the nursling of the sky;
I pass through the pores of the ocean and
    shores,   75
    I change, but I cannot die.[5]
For after the rain when with never a stain
    The pavilion of heaven is bare,
And the winds and sunbeams with their con-
    vex [6] gleams
    Build up the blue dome of air,   80
I silently laugh at my own cenotaph,[7]
    And out of the caverns of rain,
Like a child from the womb, like a ghost from
    the tomb,[8]
    I arise and unbuild it again.
(1820)

STUDY AIDS: 1. Is Shelley's attempt in this
poem to invest the cloud and other meteorological
phenomena with human attributes convincing?
Is the poem unified by a central mood to which
all the images contribute? Or do these images
seem to be merely decorative, and to lack unity?
    2. Does the metrical scheme give the effect of
lightness and swiftness that it is obviously intended to? How? Is it varied or monotonous?
Would the poem have been better if Shelley had
changed his stanza pattern throughout?

---

[5] This line perhaps states the central idea of the
poem: the notion of the eternal behind the ephemeral—a typical Shelleyan (and Platonic) notion.
[6] "Convex" because the light rays are refracted by
the air.
[7] An empty tomb (commemorating someone lost
or buried elsewhere). Why is this an appropriate
metaphor for "the blue dome of air"?
[8] One critic says that the two images in this line
do not work in harmony, that "if we try to see
the figure, the figure breaks down completely."
What do you think?

To a Skylark

Shelley prayed to the west wind for its regenerating power; here he seeks from the skylark the secret of its aerial music. The two poems thus illustrate two major aspects of Shelley's poetical nature: his reforming zeal and his lyrical intensity.

Hail to thee, blithe spirit!
  Bird thou never wert,
That from heaven, or near it,
  Pourest thy full heart
In profuse strains of unpremeditated art. 5

Higher still and higher
  From the earth thou springest
Like a cloud of fire;
  The blue deep thou wingest,
And singing still dost soar, and soaring ever
    singest. 10

In the golden lightning
  Of the sunken sun,
O'er which clouds are bright'ning,
  Thou dost float and run;
Like an unbodied joy whose race is just be-
    gun. 15

The pale purple even
  Melts around thy flight;
Like a star of heaven,
  In the broad daylight
Thou art unseen, but yet I hear thy shrill
    delight, 20

Keen as are the arrows
  Of that silver sphere,[1]
Whose intense lamp narrows
  In the white dawn clear
Until we hardly see—we feel that it is there. 25

All the earth and air
  With thy voice is loud,
As, when night is bare,
  From one lonely cloud
The moon rains out her beams, and heaven is
    overflowed. 30

[1] The morning star (Venus).

What thou art we know **not**;
  What is most like thee?
From rainbow clouds there flow **not**
  Drops so bright to see
As from thy presence showers a rain of
    melody. 35

Like a poet hidden
  In the light of thought,
Singing hymns unbidden,
  Till the world is wrought
To sympathy with hopes and fears it heeded
    not: 40

Like a high-born maiden
  In a palace tower,
Soothing her love-laden
  Soul in secret hour
With music sweet as love, which overflows
    her bower: 45

Like a glowworm golden
  In a dell of dew,
Scattering unbeholden
  Its aerial hue
Among the flowers and grass, which screen it
    from the view! 50

Like a rose embowered
  In its own green leaves,
By warm winds deflowered,
  Till the scent it gives
Makes faint with too much sweet those heavy-
    wingèd thieves: [2] 55

Sound of vernal showers
  On the twinkling grass,

[2] What characteristic is common to all of the subjects of the preceding SIMILES (ll. 36–55)?

Rain-awakened flowers,
  All that ever was
Joyous, and clear, and fresh, thy music doth
    surpass: 60

Teach us, sprite or bird,
  What sweet thoughts are thine:
I have never heard
  Praise of love or wine
That panted forth a flood of rapture so di-
    vine.   65

Chorus hymeneal,[3]
  Or triumphal chant,
Matched with thine would be all
  But an empty vaunt,
A thing wherein we feel there is some hidden
    want.   70

What objects are the fountains
  Of thy happy strain?
What fields, or waves, or mountains?
  What shapes of sky or plain?
What love of thine own kind? what ignorance
    of pain?   75

With thy clear keen joyance
  Languor cannot be:
Shadow of annoyance
  Never came near thee:
Thou lovest—but ne'er knew love's sad
    satiety.   80

Waking or asleep,
  Thou of death must deem
Things more true and deep
  Than we mortals dream,
Or how could thy notes flow in such a crystal
    stream?   85

We [4] look before and after,
  And pine for what is not:
Our sincerest laughter
  With some pain is fraught;
Our sweetest songs are those that tell of sad-
    dest thought.   90

[3] Pertaining to marriage.
[4] Man, in contrast to the skylark.

Yet if we could scorn [5]
  Hate, and pride, and fear;
If we were things born
  Not to shed a tear,
I know not how thy joy we ever should come
    near.   95

Better than all measures
  Of delightful sound,
Better than all treasures
  That in books are found,
Thy skill to poet were, thou scorner of the
    ground!   100

Teach me half the gladness [6]
  That thy brain must know,
Such harmonious madness
  From my lips would flow
The world should listen then—as I am listen-
    ing now.   105
(1820)

STUDY AIDS: 1. Throughout this poem Shelley emphasizes the skylark as a symbol and practically ignores its natural qualities except those of its soaring flight and lilting song. Is the comment in Aldous Huxley's *Point Counter Point* justified: "Shelley? Don't talk to me of Shelley . . . Blithe spirit! . . . Just pretending, just lying to himself as usual. The lark couldn't be allowed to be a mere bird . . ."?

2. Is this a poem of escapism: Does Shelley seem to be running away from the problems of the real world? Does the skylark inhabit an ideal world which man, try as he may, can never reach? Is the final stanza, then, hopeful or despairing?

3. Wordsworth wrote a poem on the skylark, ending:

Type of the wise, who soar, but never roam,
True to the kindred points of heaven and home.

What is the difference between Wordsworth's conception and Shelley's?

[5] What is the PARADOX expressed in this stanza? Is this paradox resolved?
[6] Is there any point of comparison between this stanza and the final section of *Kubla Khan*, ll. 37–54 (p. 570)? Cf. also the last stanza of the *Ode to the West Wind* (p. 659).

Adonais

John Keats died in Rome on February 23, 1821. Although he died of tuberculosis, it was commonly believed that the unsympathetic review of his poem *Endymion* in the *Quarterly Review* had caused—or at least had hastened—his death. This false report was probably the main reason for Shelley's writing the elegy *Adonais*, since the vehemence of the attacks upon the reviewers, especially upon the anonymous critic of the *Quarterly*, is one of the dominant notes of the poem. This vehemence arises not only from an outraged sense of injustice done against a fellow-poet, but also from Shelley's regarding himself as a similar victim of hostile reviewers. Were it not for this self-identification of author with subject, the elegy would probably never have been written, for the two poets were by no means close friends.

The result is that *Adonais* is a curious mixture of elegiac mourning, philosophic consolation, and sharp invective. Beginning with stanza 39, the poem affirms for Adonais a dual immortality of earthly fame and of absorption into the eternal beauty, and for Shelley a similar victory over the forces of evil, change, and death.

1

I weep for Adonais [1]—he is dead!
O, weep for Adonais! though our tears
Thaw not the frost which binds so dear a head!
And thou, sad Hour,[2] selected from all years
To mourn our loss, rouse thy obscure compeers,[3]   5
And teach them thine own sorrow, say: "With me
Died Adonais; till the Future dares
Forget the Past, his fate and fame shall be
An echo and a light unto eternity!"

2

Where wert thou, mighty Mother,[4] when he lay,   10

3

Oh, weep for Adonais—he is dead!
Wake, melancholy Mother, wake and weep! 20
Yet wherefore? Quench within their burning bed [8]
Thy fiery tears, and let thy loud heart keep
Like his, a mute and uncomplaining sleep;
For he is gone, where all things wise and fair

When thy son lay, pierced by the shaft [5] which flies
In darkness? where was lorn Urania
When Adonais died? With veilèd eyes,[6]
'Mid listening Echoes, in her paradise
She sat, while one,[7] with soft enamored breath,   15
Rekindled all the fading melodies,
With which, like flowers that mock the corpse beneath,
He had adorned and hid the coming bulk of Death.

[1] A form of Adonis, who was a Greek youth beloved of Aphrodite (Venus). When he was killed by a boar, Venus rushed to his side and bewailed his death.

[2] The hour of Adonais' death.

[3] Hours of lesser importance.

[4] Urania. Venus, goddess of love, had two surnames, emphasizing two kinds of love: Venus Pandemos, standing for earthly, physical love (the Venus of the Adonis legend); and Venus Urania, standing for heavenly or spiritual love. Urania was also the Greek muse of astronomy. All these elements are merged in Shelley's figure; Urania becomes another one of his female symbols for Intellectual Beauty (or Love). Note also that Shelley has spiritualized the relationship by making Urania the *mother* of Adonais.

[5] The anonymous reviewer in the *Quarterly Review*. Shelley is not consistent in his symbolic references to the reviewer or his review. As you proceed, note the various things the reviewer or his criticism is called.

[6] Note the IRONY of ll. 13–18: When Adonais was killed, Urania was listening to one of the Echoes reciting Adonais' poetry.

[7] One Echo.

[8] Lines 21–27: The futility of mourning is a common theme in the elegy.

Descend;—oh, dream not that the amorous deep   25
Will yet restore him to the vital air;
Death feeds on his mute voice, and laughs at our despair.

4

Most musical of mourners, weep again! [9]
Lament anew, Urania!—He [10] died,
Who was the sire of an immortal strain,   30
Blind, old, and lonely, when his country's pride,[11]
The priest, the slave, and the liberticide,[12]
Trampled and mocked with many a loathèd rite
Of lust and blood; he went, unterrified,
Into the gulf of death; but his clear sprite   35
Yet reigns o'er earth; the third [13] among the sons of light.

5

Most musical of mourners, weep anew!
Not all to that bright station dared to climb;
And happier they their happiness who knew,[14]
Whose tapers yet burn through that night of time   40
In which suns perished; other more sublime,
Struck by the envious wrath of man or god,
Have sunk, extinct in their refulgent prime;
And some yet live, treading the thorny road,
Which leads, through toil and hate, to Fame's serene abode.   45

[9] Weep now for Adonais as before for Milton. What is the implication?
[10] Milton.
[11] "Pride" is the object of "trampled and mocked" (l. 33).
[12] Lines 32–34 refer to the Restoration and its reaction against Puritanism.
[13] The first two are probably Homer and Dante, both great epic poets like Milton.
[14] In ll. 39–45, three classes of poets are suggested: (1) lesser poets than Milton who were happier in achieving a certain popularity (ll. 39–41); (2) greater poets (like Keats) than those of class one, cut off in their prime (ll. 41–43); (3) poets yet alive (like Shelley), still struggling towards fame (ll. 44–45).

6

But now, thy youngest, dearest one, has perished—
The nursling of thy widowhood, who grew,
Like a pale flower by some sad maiden cherished,
And fed with true-love tears, instead of dew;
Most musical of mourners, weep anew!   50
Thy extreme [15] hope, the loveliest and the last,
The bloom, whose petals nipped before they blew
Died on the promise of the fruit, is waste;
The broken lily lies—the storm is overpast.

7

To that high capital,[16] where kingly Death   55
Keeps his pale court in beauty and decay,
He came; and bought, with price of purest breath,
A grave among the eternal.—Come away! [17]
Haste, while the vault of blue Italian day
Is yet his fitting charnel-roof! while still   60
He lies, as if in dewy sleep he lay;
Awake him not! surely he takes his fill
Of deep and liquid rest, forgetful of all ill.

8

He will awake no more, oh, never more!—
Within the twilight chamber spreads apace 65
The shadow of white Death, and at the door
Invisible Corruption [18] waits to trace
His [19] extreme way to her [20] dim dwelling-place;
The eternal Hunger [21] sits, but pity and awe
Soothe her pale rage, nor dares she to deface   70
So fair a prey, till darkness,[22] and the law
Of change, shall o'er his sleep the mortal curtain draw.

[15] Last.
[16] Rome.
[17] From heaven to the body of Keats.
[18] Bodily decay.
[19] Adonais' way.
[20] Corruption's.
[21] Corruption.
[22] Of the grave.

9

Oh, weep for Adonais!—The quick Dreams,[23]
The passion-wingèd ministers of thought,
Who were his flocks, whom near the living
    streams   75
Of his young spirit he fed, and whom he
    taught
The love which was its music, wander not—
Wander no more, from kindling brain to
    brain,[24]
But droop there, whence they sprung; and
    mourn their lot
Round the cold heart, where, after their
    sweet pain,   80
They ne'er will gather strength, or find a
    home again.

10

And one with trembling hands clasps his cold
    head,
And fans him with her moonlight wings, and
    cries;
"Our love, our hope, our sorrow, is not dead;
See, on the silken fringe of his faint eyes, 85
Like dew upon a sleeping flower, there lies
A tear some Dream has loosened from his
    brain."
Lost angel of a ruined paradise!
She knew not 'twas her own; as with no stain
She faded, like a cloud which had outwept
    its rain.   90

11

One from a lucid urn of starry dew
Washed his light limbs as if embalming them;
Another clipped her profuse locks, and threw
The wreath upon him, like an anadem,[25]
Which frozen tears instead of pearls begem; 95
Another in her wilful grief would break
Her bow and wingèd reeds, as if to stem
A greater loss with one which was more weak;
And dull the barbèd fire against his frozen
    cheek.

[23] In ll. 73–117, the first group of mourners is
the poetical imaginings of Adonais himself, a group
of personified abstractions. They perform various
rites over the corpse, preparing it for burial.
[24] From the brain of Adonais to that of a reader
of his poetry.
[25] Garland.

12

Another Splendor on his mouth alit,   100
That mouth, whence it was wont to draw the
    breath
Which gave it strength to pierce the guarded
    wit,[26]
And pass into the panting heart beneath
With lightning and with music: the damp
    death
Quenched its caress upon his icy lips;   105
And, as a dying meteor stains a wreath
Of moonlight vapor, which the cold night
    clips,[27]
It flushed through his pale limbs, and passed
    to its eclipse.

13

And others came—Desires and Adorations,
Wingèd Persuasions and veiled Destinies, 110
Splendors, and Glooms, and glimmering In-
    carnations
Of hopes and fears, and twilight Phantasies;
And Sorrow, with her family of Sighs,
And Pleasure, blind with tears, led by the
    gleam
Of her own dying smile instead of eyes, 115
Came in slow pomp;—the moving pomp might
    seem
Like pageantry of mist on an autumnal
    stream.

14

All he had loved, and molded into thought,
From shape, and hue, and odor, and sweet
    sound,
Lamented Adonais. Morning sought   120
Her eastern watch-tower, and her hair un-
    bound,
Wet with the tears which should adorn the
    ground,
Dimmed the aërial eyes that kindle day;
Afar the melancholy thunder moaned,
Pale Ocean in unquiet slumber lay,   125
And the wild Winds flew round, sobbing in
    their dismay.[28]

[26] Intellect (of the reader).
[27] Embraces.
[28] What images in sts. 7–14 indicate the passage
of time?

15

Lost Echo [29] sits amid the voiceless mountains,
And feeds her grief with his remembered lay,
And will no more reply to winds or fountains,
Or amorous birds perched on the young green
    spray,   130
Or herdsman's horn, or bell at closing day;
Since she can mimic not his lips, more dear
Than those for whose disdain she pined away
Into a shadow of all sounds—a drear
Murmur, between their songs, is all the wood-
    men hear.   135

16

Grief made the young Spring wild, and she
    threw down
Her kindling buds, as if she Autumn were,
Or they dead leaves; since her delight is flown,
For whom should she have waked the sullen
    year?
To Phoebus [30] was not Hyacinth so dear   140
Nor to himself [31] Narcissus, as to both [32]
Thou, Adonais: wan they stand and sere
Amid the faint companions of their youth,
With dew all turned to tears; odor, to sighing
    ruth.[33]

17

Thy spirit's sister, the lorn nightingale [34] 145
Mourns not her mate with such melodious
    pain;
Not so the eagle, who like thee could scale
Heaven, and could nourish in the sun's do-
    main
Her mighty youth with morning, doth com-
    plain,

[29] A mountain nymph in love with Narcissus
(see l. 141). Her love was not returned, and she
pined away into "a shadow of all sounds" (l. 134).
Shelley has here adapted the legend to his poem.
[30] Apollo, who loved and accidentally killed the
boy Hyacinthus, from whose blood he caused the
flower (hyacinth) to spring up.
[31] Adonais. Narcissus is referred to in Keats's
Endymion; he fell in love with his own image in a
pool and was turned into a flower that bears his
name.
[32] Both flowers, symbolizing all of nature.
[33] Pity.
[34] Shelley is conceivably thinking of Keats's
Ode to a Nightingale.

Soaring and screaming round her empty
    nest,   150
As Albion [35] wails for thee: the curse of Cain
Light on his [36] head who pierced thy inno-
    cent breast,
And scared the angel soul that was its earthly
    guest!

18

Ah, woe is me! Winter is come and gone,[37]
But grief returns with the revolving year; 155
The airs and streams renew their joyous tone;
The ants, the bees, the swallows reappear;
Fresh leaves and flowers deck the dead Sea-
    sons' bier;
The amorous birds now pair in every brake,
And build their mossy homes in field and
    brere; [38]   160
And the green lizard, and the golden snake,
Like unimprisoned flames, out of their trance
    awake.

19

Through wood and stream and field and hill
    and ocean
A quickening life from the earth's heart has
    burst
As it has ever done, with change and mo-
    tion,   165
From the great morning of the world when
    first
God dawned on chaos; in its stream immersed,
The lamps of heaven flash with a softer light;
All baser things pant with life's sacred thirst;
Diffuse themselves; and spend in love's de-
    light,   170
The beauty and the joy of their renewèd
    might.

20

The leprous corpse, touched by this spirit
    tender,
Exhales itself in flowers of gentle breath;

[35] England.
[36] The *Quarterly* reviewer's.
[37] In the next four stanzas the contrast is between
the renewed life of springtime and the unrenewable
life of Adonais.
[38] Bush.

Like incarnations of the stars, when splendor
Is changed to fragrance, they illumine
    death   175
And mock the merry worm that wakes be-
    neath;
Nought [39] we know, dies. Shall that [40] alone
    which knows
Be as a sword consumed before the sheath
By sightless lightning?—the intense atom [41]
    glows
A moment, then is quenched in a most cold
    repose.   180

21

Alas! that all we loved of him should be,
But for our grief, as if it had not been,
And grief itself be mortal! Woe is me!
Whence are we, and why are we? of what
    scene [42]
The actors or spectators? Great and mean 185
Meet massed in death, who lends what life
    must borrow.[43]
As long as skies are blue, and fields are green,
Evening must usher night, night urge the
    morrow,
Month follow month with woe, and year
    wake year to sorrow.

22

He will awake no more, oh, never more! 190
"Wake thou," cried Misery, "childless Mother,
    rise
Out of thy sleep, and slake, in thy heart's
    core,
A wound more fierce than his, with tears and
    sighs."
And all the Dreams that watched Urania's
    eyes,

[39] In the physical world.
[40] The human mind or spirit. Shelley is posing
the question: Shall matter and energy be imperishable and yet the human mind be completely annihilated? In the intensity of his grief, Shelley
admits that it would seem so (ll. 179–180).
[41] The mind or spirit.
[42] In ll. 184–189, personal grief is momentarily
absorbed in the sense of the larger human tragedy,
the question of the meaning of human sorrow.
[43] I.e., life is nourished on dead things; or, Death
is the all-powerful capitalist, and Life the dependent
borrower.

And all the Echoes whom their sister's song 195
Had held in holy silence, cried: "Arise!"
Swift as a Thought by the snake Memory
    stung,
From her ambrosial rest the fading Splendor [44]
    sprung.

23

She rose like an autumnal night, that springs
Out of the east, and follows wild and drear 200
The golden day, which, on eternal wings,
Even as a ghost abandoning a bier,
Had left the earth a corpse. Sorrow and fear
So struck, so roused, so rapt Urania;
So saddened round her like an atmosphere 205
Of stormy mist; so swept her on her way
Even to the mournful place where Adonais
    lay.

24

Out of her secret paradise she sped,
Through camps and cities rough with stone,
    and steel,
And human hearts, which to her aëry tread 210
Yielding not, wounded the invisible
Palms [45] of her tender feet where'er they fell:
And barbèd tongues, and thoughts more sharp
    than they,
Rent the soft form they never could repel,
Whose sacred blood, like the young tears of
    May,   215
Paved with eternal flowers that undeserving
    way.

25

In the death-chamber for a moment Death,
Shamed by the presence of that living might,
Blushed to annihilation,[46] and the breath
Revisited those lips, and Life's pale light 220
Flashed through those limbs, so late her dear
    delight.

[44] Urania. The next seven stanzas present Urania's
journey to the death-chamber of Adonais and her
speech over his body.
[45] Soles.
[46] A vivid, paradoxical IMAGE. "The nature of
Death is to be pallid: therefore Death, in blushing,
abnegates his very nature, and almost ceases to be
Death" (Rossetti).

"Leave me not wild and drear and comfort-
less,
As silent lightning leaves the starless night!
Leave me not!" cried Urania: her distress
Roused Death: Death rose and smiled, and
met her vain caress.   225

26

"Stay yet awhile! speak to me once again;
Kiss me, so long but as a kiss may live;
And in my heartless [47] breast and burning
brain
That word, that kiss, shall all thoughts else
survive,
With food of saddest memory kept alive, 230
Now thou art dead, as if it were a part
Of thee, my Adonais! I would give
All that I am to be as thou now art!
But I am chained to Time, and cannot thence
depart!

27

"O gentle child, beautiful as thou wert,   235
Why didst thou leave the trodden paths of
men
Too soon,[48] and with weak hands though
mighty heart
Dare the unpastured dragon [49] in his den?
Defenseless as thou wert, oh, where was then
Wisdom the mirrored shield, or scorn the
spear?   240
Or hadst thou waited the full cycle, when
Thy spirit should have filled its crescent
sphere,
The monsters [50] of life's waste had fled from
thee like deer.

28

"The herded wolves, bold only to pursue;
The obscene ravens, clamorous o'er the
dead;   245
The vultures to the conqueror's banner true
Who feed where Desolation first has fed,

---

[47] She has bestowed her heart upon Adonais.
[48] Shelley warned Keats not to rush into publication.
[49] The reviewer.
[50] The critics. Note what they are called in the
next three lines.

And whose wings rain contagion;—how they
fled,
When, like Apollo, from his golden bow
The Pythian [51] of the age one arrow sped 250
And smiled!—The spoilers tempt no second
blow,
They fawn on the proud feet that spurn
them lying low.

29

"The sun comes forth, and many reptiles
spawn;
He sets, and each ephemeral insect then
Is gathered into death without a dawn,   255
And the immortal stars awake again;
So is it in the world of living men:
A godlike mind soars forth, in its delight
Making earth bare and veiling heaven, and
when
It sinks, the swarms that dimmed or shared
its light   260
Leave to its kindred lamps the spirit's awful
night." [52]

30

Thus ceased she: and the mountain shepherds
came,[53]
Their garlands sere, their magic mantles rent;
The Pilgrim of Eternity,[54] whose fame
Over his living head like heaven is bent,   265
An early but enduring monument,
Came, veiling all the lightnings of his song
In sorrow; from her wilds Ierne [55] sent
The sweetest lyrist [56] of her saddest wrong,
And Love taught Grief to fall like music
from his tongue.   270

---

[51] Apollo, so-called because he slew the Python,
a fabulous serpent. Here it refers to Byron, who
replied to the critics' attack on one of his youthful
volumes of poems with a devastating satire, *English
Bards and Scotch Reviewers* (the "arrow" of l. 250).
But ll. 251–252 are not true.
[52] The general idea of this stanza is that the
critics (reptiles, insects) are dependent upon the
creative artist for their petty existence.
[53] The next six stanzas describe the coming of
fellow poets to mourn over Adonais.
[54] Byron, who gave the name of Pilgrim to his
own Childe Harold. Byron, however, was hardly a
friend of Keats.
[55] Ireland.
[56] Tom Moore, Irish poet.

31

Midst others of less note, came one frail
   form,[57]
A phantom among men; companionless
As the last cloud of an expiring storm
Whose thunder is its knell; he, as I guess,
Had gazed on Nature's naked loveliness,   275
Actaeon-like,[58] and now he fled astray
With feeble steps o'er the world's wilderness,
And his own thoughts, along that rugged way,
Pursued, like raging hounds, their father and
   their prey.

32

A pardlike [59] spirit beautiful and swift—   280
A love in desolation masked;—a power
Girt around with weakness; it can scarce up-
   lift
The weight of the superincumbent hour;
It is a dying lamp, a falling shower,
A breaking billow;—even whilst we speak   285
Is it not broken? On the withering flower
The killing sun smiles brightly: on a cheek
The life can burn in blood, even while the
   heart may break.

33

His head was bound with pansies overblown,
And faded violets, white, and pied, and
   blue;   290
And a light spear [60] topped with a cypress
   cone,
Round whose rude shaft dark ivy-tresses grew
Yet dripping with the forest's noonday dew,
Vibrated, as the ever-beating heart

Shook the weak hand that grasped it; of that
   crew   295
He came the last, neglected and apart;
A herd-abandoned deer struck by the
   hunter's dart.

34

All stood aloof, and at his partial moan
Smiled through their tears; well knew that
   gentle band
Who in another's fate now wept his own,   300
As in the accents of an unknown land [61]
He sung new sorrow; sad Urania scanned
The stranger's mien, and murmured: "Who
   art thou?"
He answered not, but with a sudden hand
Made bare his branded and ensanguined
   brow,   305
Which was like Cain's or Christ's [62]—oh! that
   it should be so!

35

What softer voice is hushed over the dead?
Athwart what brow is that dark mantle
   thrown?
What form leans sadly o'er the white death-
   bed,
In mockery of monumental stone,   310
The heavy heart heaving without a moan?
If it be he,[63] who, gentlest of the wise,
Taught, soothed, loved, honored the departed
   one,
Let me not vex, with inharmonious sighs,
The silence of that heart's accepted sacri-
   fice.   315

[57] Shelley himself. Shelley devotes four stanzas to himself. Why does he give himself so much attention? Is this a flaw in the poem? Is the self-portrait one of pride or humility?

[58] Actaeon was a hunter who looked upon the bathing Diana and was therefore transformed by the indignant goddess into a stag that was chased and torn apart by his own dogs. Likewise, Shelley had gazed upon the intimate secrets of nature (the vision of the ideal) and so had been ever after-wards tormented by the intensity of that vision.

[59] Leopard-like.

[60] The thyrsus, sacred to Dionysus and appropriate to poets.

[61] Either: (1) England, "unknown" because it was not known to the Greek deities or because the English tongue was unknown in Italy; or (2) the world of ideal beauty, "unknown" to an indifferent age.

[62] A bold phrase that horrified the reviewers. Shelley is thinking of himself as an outcast and is reminding the reader that the populace down through the ages has condemned its saviors as well as its sinners. Is this an effective climax to the self-portrait, or is it too melodramatic?

[63] Leigh Hunt, poet and critic, and, of the four figures mentioned here, Keats's closest friend.

36

Our Adonais has drunk poison—oh!
What deaf [64] and viperous murderer could crown
Life's early cup with such a draught of woe?
The nameless worm [65] would now itself disown:
It felt, yet could escape, the magic tone 320
Whose prelude [66] held all envy, hate, and wrong,
But what was howling in one breast alone,
Silent with expectation of the song,
Whose master's hand is cold, whose silver lyre unstrung.

37

Live thou, whose infamy is not thy fame! 325
Live! fear no heavier chastisement from me,
Thou noteless blot on a remembered name!
But be thyself, and know thyself to be!
And ever at thy season be thou free
To spill the venom when thy fangs o'er-
flow: 330
Remorse and Self-contempt shall cling to thee;
Hot Shame shall burn upon thy secret brow,
And like a beaten hound tremble thou shalt
—as now.

38

Nor let us weep that our delight is fled [67]
For from these carrion kites that scream be-
low; 335
He wakes or sleeps [68] with the enduring dead;
Thou [69] canst not soar where he is sitting now—
Dust to the dust! but the pure spirit shall flow
Back to the burning fountain whence it came,
A portion of the Eternal, which must glow 340

[64] Because he could not hear the beauty of Keats's verses.
[65] The anonymous reviewer of the *Quarterly*.
[66] Keats had only begun his poetical career.
[67] St. 38 is the transitional stanza to the final part of the poem, the part that gives the answer to the troubled question of ll. 177–179.
[68] Shelley does not commit himself on the question of personal immortality. Keats will have the immortality of fame and of his spirit's reunion with the spirit of love and beauty.
[69] The reviewer.

Through time and change, unquenchably the same,
Whilst thy cold embers choke the sordid hearth of shame.

39

Peace, peace! he is not dead, he doth not sleep [70]—
He hath awakened from the dream of life—
'Tis we, who lost in stormy visions, keep 345
With phantoms an unprofitable strife,
And in mad trance, strike with our spirit's knife
Invulnerable nothings.—We decay
Like corpses in a charnel; fear and grief
Convulse us and consume us day by day, 350
And cold hopes swarm like worms within our living clay.

40

He has outsoared the shadow of our night;
Envy and calumny and hate and pain,
And that unrest which men miscall delight,
Can touch him not and torture not again; 355
From the contagion of the world's slow stain
He is secure, and now can never mourn
A heart grown cold, a head grown gray in vain;
Nor, when the spirit's self has ceased to burn,
With sparkless ashes load an unlamented urn. 360

41

He lives, he wakes—'tis Death is dead, not he;
Mourn not for Adonais.—Thou young Dawn,
Turn all thy dew to splendor, for from thee
The spirit thou lamentest is not gone;
Ye caverns and ye forests, cease to moan! 365
Cease, ye faint flowers and fountains, and thou Air,

[70] The theme of this and the following stanza is the paradoxical one that mortal life is death, from which we awaken into the true life. Stanzas 39, 40, 42, and 43 are the eloquent expression of Shelley's confidence that Keats's soul will be merged with the spirit of love and beauty which inspired his life as a poet on earth. Since Urania is a symbol of this spirit, she unites the two sections of the poem, being not only the mother of Adonais who mourns over his death but also the ultimate reality to which he returns.

Which like a mourning veil thy scarf hadst
  thrown
O'er the abandoned earth, now leave it bare
Even to the joyous stars which smile on its
  despair!

42

He is made one with nature: there is
  heard   370
His voice in all her music, from the moan
Of thunder, to the song of night's sweet bird;
He is a presence to be felt and known
In darkness and in light, from herb and stone,
Spreading itself where'er that power [71] may
  move   375
Which has withdrawn his being to its own;
Which wields the world with never-wearied
  love,
Sustains it from beneath, and kindles it
  above.

43

He is a portion of the loveliness
Which once he made more lovely: he doth
  bear   380
His part, while the one spirit's plastic stress [72]
Sweeps through the dull dense world, com-
  pelling there,
All new successions to the forms they wear;
Torturing th' unwilling dross that checks its
  flight
To its own likeness, as each mass may
  bear;   385
And bursting in its beauty and its might
From trees and beasts and men into the
  heaven's light.[73]

44

The splendors of the firmament of time [74]
May be eclipsed, but are extinguished not;

Like stars to their appointed height they
  climb,   390
And death is a low mist which cannot blot
The brightness it may veil. When lofty
  thought
Lifts a young heart above its mortal lair,
And love and life contend in it, for what
Shall be its earthly doom, the dead live
  there   395
And move like winds of light on dark and
  stormy air.

45

The inheritors of unfulfilled renown [75]
Rose from their thrones, built beyond mortal
  thought,
Far in the unapparent. Chatterton [76]
Rose pale—his solemn agony had not   400
Yet faded from him; Sidney,[77] as he fought
And as he fell and as he lived and loved
Sublimely mild, a spirit without spot,
Arose; and Lucan,[78] by his death approved:
Oblivion as they rose shrank like a thing re-
  proved.   405

46

And many more, whose names on earth are
  dark,
But whose transmitted effluence cannot die
So long as fire outlives the parent spark,
Rose, robed in dazzling immortality.
"Thou art become as one of us," they cry, 410
"It was for thee yon kingless sphere has long
Swung blind in unascended majesty,
Silent alone amid an heaven of song.
Assume thy wingèd throne, thou Vesper [79]
  of our throng!"

[71] Intellectual beauty (or love).
[72] Lines 381–387 express the neo-Platonic notion that the Ideal attempts to shape the resisting actual into forms as nearly perfect as possible.
[73] What is the gradation here?
[74] Sts. 44–46 depict the immortality of fame that Adonais has achieved through his poetry. The recurrent symbolism is that he has become one of the stars in the firmament of time: note the "sons of light" (l. 36) referred to in ll. 388–392, and ll. 411–414.
[75] In sts. 45–46, the picture of "the inheritors of unfulfilled renown" (young poets who died before achieving their deserved fame) receiving Adonais as their king is not to be taken as a statement of Shelley's belief in personal immortality. It is FIGURATIVE LANGUAGE only.
[76] English poet who committed suicide when he was 17.
[77] English man of letters who died at 32.
[78] Roman poet who committed suicide at 26.
[79] The evening star.

47

Who mourns for Adonais? Oh, come forth, 415
Fond wretch! [80] and know thyself and him
  aright.
Clasp with thy panting soul the pendulous
  earth;
As from a center, dart thy spirit's light
Beyond all worlds, until its spacious might
Satiate the void circumference: then
  shrink   420
Even to a point within our day and night;
And keep thy heart light lest it make thee
  sink
When hope has kindled hope, and lured thee
  to the brink.

48

Or go to Rome, which is the sepulcher,
Oh, not of him, but of our joy: 'tis nought 425
That ages, empires, and religions there
Lie buried in the ravage they have wrought;
For such as he can lend—they borrow not
Glory from those who made the world their
  prey;
And he is gathered to the kings of thought 430
Who waged contention with their time's
  decay,
And of the past are all that cannot pass away.

49

Go thou to Rome—at once the paradise,
The grave, the city, and the wilderness;
And where its wrecks like shattered moun-
  tains rise,   435
And flowering weeds, and fragrant copses
  dress
The bones of Desolation's nakedness
Pass, till the spirit of the spot shall lead
Thy footsteps to a slope of green access [81]
Where, like an infant's smile, over the
  dead   440

[80] He who foolishly ("fond" means "foolish" here) mourns for Adonais. This is a difficult stanza. It seems to mean that such a person should attempt to project his soul through all the universe in order to realize how small a part of it he is, but not to let this mystical awareness overwhelm him.
[81] The Protestant Cemetery in Rome, where Keats is buried.

A light of laughing flowers along the grass is
  spread;

50

And gray walls molder round, on which dull
  Time
Feeds, like slow fire upon a hoary brand;
And one keen pyramid [82] with wedge sublime,
Pavilioning the dust of him who planned 445
This refuge for his memory, doth stand
Like flame transformed to marble; and be-
  neath,
A field is spread, on which a newer band
Have pitched in heaven's smile their camp of
  death,
Welcoming him we lose with scarce ex-
  tinguished breath.   450

51

Here pause: these graves are all too young as
  yet
To have outgrown the sorrow which con-
  signed
Its charge to each; and if the seal is set,
Here, on one fountain of a mourning mind,
Break it not thou! too surely shalt thou
  find   455
Thine own well full, if thou returnest home,
Of tears and gall. From the world's bitter wind
Seek shelter in the shadow of the tomb.
What Adonais is, why fear we to become?

52

The One remains, the many change and
  pass; [83]   460
Heaven's light forever shines, earth's shadows
  fly;
Life, like a dome of many-colored glass,
Stains the white radiance of Eternity,
Until Death tramples it to fragments.—Die,
If thou wouldst be with that which thou dost
  seek!   465

[82] The tomb of Caius Cestius, a Roman tribune.
[83] Lines 460–464 are five of the most often quoted lines in Shelley's poetry and his "finest expression of ultimate reality as distinguished from its earthly shadow," with death the gateway from the temporal to the eternal. Work out the image in detail.

Follow where all is fled!—Rome's azure sky,
Flowers, ruins, statues, music, words are weak
The glory they transfuse with fitting truth to
    speak.

53

Why linger, why turn back, why shrink, my
    heart?
Thy hopes are gone before: from all things
    here   470
They have departed; thou shouldst now de-
    part!
A light is passed from the revolving year,
And man, and woman; and what still is dear
Attracts to crush, repels to make thee wither.
The soft sky smiles—the low wind whispers
    near: 475
'Tis Adonais calls! oh, hasten thither,
No more let Life divide what Death can join
    together.

54

That Light whose smile kindles the uni-
    verse,[84]
That Beauty in which all things work and
    move,
That Benediction which the eclipsing
    curse   480
Of birth can quench not, that sustaining Love
Which through the web of being blindly
    wove
By man and beast and earth and air and sea,
Burns bright or dim, as each are mirrors of

The fire for which all thirst; now beams on
    me,   485
Consuming the last clouds of cold mortality.

55

The breath whose might I have invoked in
    song
Descends on me; my spirit's bark is driven,
Far from the shore, far from the trembling
    throng
Whose sails were never to the tempest
    given;   490
The massy earth and sphered skies are riven!
I am borne darkly, fearfully, afar;
Whilst, burning through the inmost veil of
    heaven,
The soul of Adonais, like a star,
Beacons from the abode where the Eternal
    are.   495
(1821)

STUDY AIDS: 1. How would you justify
the inclusion, in an elegy, of the frequent attacks upon the critics and especially upon the
anonymous reviewer who supposedly "killed"
Keats? Are they any more inappropriate than
Milton's attack upon the clergy in *Lycidas*, ll.
113–131 (p. 254)?
    2. Does Shelley seem sincere in his tribute
to Keats? Why does he put so much of himself
into the poem?
    3. Consider the various views of immortality
presented in the poem. Are they reconcilable
one with another?

Hymn of Apollo

1

The sleepless Hours who watch me as I lie,[1]
    Curtained with star-inwoven tapestries
From the broad moonlight of the sky,
    Fanning the busy dreams from my dim
        eyes,—

---

[84] This stanza defines the "One" of l. 460 in its
many aspects. Cf. the *Hymn to Intellectual Beauty*
(p. 665).

[1] Apollo was first of all the sun-god, and in this
role Shelley celebrates him in sts. 1, 2, and 4 as
he makes his daily journey across the sky.

Waken me when their mother, the gray
        Dawn,   5
Tells them that dreams and that the moon
        is gone.

2

Then I arise, and climbing heaven's blue
        dome,
    I walk over the mountains and the waves,
Leaving my robe upon the ocean foam;
    My footsteps pave the clouds with fire; the
        caves   10

Are filled with my bright presence, and the
air
Leaves the green earth to my embraces bare.

3

The sunbeams are my shafts, with which I kill
Deceit, that loves the night and fears the
day;
All men who do or even imagine ill   15
Fly me, and from the glory of my ray
Good minds and open actions take new might,
Until diminished by the reign of night.[2]

4

I feed the clouds, the rainbows and the
flowers
With their ethereal colors; the moon's
globe   20
And the pure stars [3] in their eternal bowers
Are cinctured with my power as with a
robe;
Whatever lamps on earth or heaven may
shine
Are portions of one power, which is mine.[4]

5

I stand at noon upon the peak of heaven,   25
Then with unwilling steps I wander down
Into the clouds of the Atlantic even;
For grief that I depart they weep and
frown:
What look is more delightful than the smile
With which I soothe them from the western
isle?   30

6

I am the eye with which the universe
Beholds itself and knows itself divine; [5]
All harmony of instrument or verse,
All prophecy, all medicine are mine,[6]
All light of art or nature;—to my song   35
Victory and praise in its [7] own right belong.
(1820; 1824)

STUDY AIDS: This lyric is an excellent illustration of Shelley's ability to adapt ancient
myth to his own purposes. Compare this poem
to *The Cloud* and the *Ode to the West Wind*
in the natural, scientific, and symbolic handling
of the subject.

To Night

Swiftly walk o'er the western wave,
    Spirit of Night!
Out of the misty eastern cave,
Where, all the long and lone daylight,
Thou wovest dreams of joy and fear,   5
Which make thee terrible and dear—
    Swift be thy flight!

Wrap thy form in a mantle gray,
    Star-inwrought!
Blind with thine hair the eyes of Day;   10
Kiss her until she be wearied out,
Then wander o'er city, and sea, and land,
Touching all with thine opiate wand—
    Come, long-sought!

When I arose and saw the dawn,   15
    I sighed for thee;
When light rode high, and the dew was gone,
And noon lay heavy on flower and tree,
And the weary Day turned to his rest,
Lingering like an unloved guest,   20
    I sighed for thee.

Thy brother Death came, and cried,
    "Wouldst thou me?"
Thy sweet child Sleep, the filmy-eyed,
Murmured like a noontide bee,   25

[2] In this stanza Apollo becomes the symbol of
imagination or intellectual beauty.
[3] Probably the planets, which reflect the sun's
light.

[4] In this stanza Apollo is scientifically pictured as
the source of all light and color.
[5] In ll. 31–32, the sun is a symbol of the ultimate
reality (the absolute).
[6] In ll. 33–34 we are reminded that Apollo was
also the god of poetry, prophecy, and medicine.
[7] Refers to "song" (l. 35).

"Shall I nestle near thy side?
Wouldst thou me?"—And I replied,
    "No, not thee!"

Death will come when thou art dead,
    Soon, too soon—   30

Sleep will come when thou art fled;
Of neither would I ask the boon
I ask of thee, belovèd Night—
Swift be thine approaching flight,
    Come soon, soon!   35
(1821; 1824)

To ——

One word is too often profaned
    For me to profane it,
One feeling too falsely disdained
    For thee to disdain it;
One hope is too like despair   5
    For prudence to smother,
And pity from thee more dear
    Than that from another.

I can give not what men call love,
    But wilt thou accept not   10
The worship the heart lifts above
    And the heavens reject not,—
The desire of the moth for the star,
    Of the night for the morrow,
The devotion to something afar   15
    From the sphere of our sorrow?
(1824)

To ——

Music, when soft voices die,
Vibrates in the memory—
Odors, when sweet violets sicken,
Live within the sense they quicken.

Rose leaves, when the rose is dead,   5
Are heaped for the belovèd's bed;
And so thy thoughts,[1] when thou art gone,
Love itself shall slumber on.
(1821; 1824)

Lines: "When the Lamp Is Shattered"

1

When the lamp is shattered,
The light in the dust lies dead;
    When the cloud is scattered,
The rainbow's glory is shed.
    When the lute is broken,   5
Sweet tones are remembered not;
    When the lips have spoken,
Loved accents are soon forgot.

2

    As music and splendor
Survive not the lamp and the lute,   10

The heart's echoes render
No song when the spirit is mute:
    No song but sad dirges,
Like the wind through a ruined cell,
    Or the mournful surges   15
That ring the dead seaman's knell.

3

    When hearts have once mingled,
Love first leaves the well-built nest;
    The weak one is singled
To endure what it once possessed.   20
    O love! who bewailest
The frailty of all things here,
    Why choose you the frailest
For your cradle, your home, and your bier?

[1] I.e., thoughts of thee. "Thoughts" is the object
of "on" in the next line.

4

Its [1] passions will rock thee,[2]   25
As the storms rock the ravens on high;
  Bright reason will mock thee,
Like the sun from a wintry sky.
  From thy nest every rafter

Will rot, and thine eagle home   30
  Leave thee naked to laughter,
When leaves fall and cold winds come.
(1824)

STUDY AIDS: State in a single phrase the theme of the lyric.

John Keats
(1795–1821)

THE BRILLIANT THOUGH TRAGICALLY BRIEF CAREER OF KEATS IS ONE OF THE GREAT CHAPTERS in English literature. Although few poets have risen higher, few have begun life more humbly than John Keats, who was born the son of a livery stable operator and an innkeeper's daughter. Orphaned at fifteen, Keats left school to become an apprentice of an apothecary-surgeon. He seemed headed for a career in medicine, but gave it up suddenly in favor of poetry, for which he had developed a passion since discovering the poetry of Spenser a few years before. He was encouraged by the essayist and poet Leigh Hunt, who welcomed young Keats to his circle of literary friends, introducing him to Wordsworth, Shelley, Hazlitt, and other eminent literary people.

In 1817 Keats published *Poems,* a volume of youthful verse. Although it included the celebrated sonnet, "On First Looking into Chapman's Homer," most of the poems were imitative. Realizing he was too much the disciple of Hunt, he began, through an intensive study of Shakespeare, to work out an "independent system of poetry" and to express it in his first long poem, *Endymion* (1818). The poem was not completely successful, but it contains many passages of rare beauty and many more that hint of future mastery. It certainly did not deserve the slashing criticism it received from the *Quarterly Review* and *Blackwood's Magazine.*

This poet, however, was not to be "snuffed out by an article," as Byron put it. He set about improving his poetical craftsmanship through working on *Hyperion,* and continued his painstaking composition of shorter works. But he was working against odds, for he began to show signs of the tuberculosis that had killed his mother, and was also to claim the life of his brother Tom. Furthermore, he was tortured by his love for Fanny Brawne, since he soon realized that marriage, for one in his financial and physical condition, was hopeless. These discouraging experiences helped to produce the mature poet of 1819, the year of *The Eve of St. Agnes, La Belle Dame Sans Merci, Hyperion, Lamia, To Autumn,* and the "great odes." Most of these poems appeared in his third volume of poems in 1820.

But time was running out for John Keats. By the end of 1819 he was in wretched condition, and the spring and summer of 1820 found him failing rapidly. In September he

---

[1] Referring to the heart of "the frailest" (l. 23) or "the weak one" (l. 19) as distinguished from "the well-built nest" (l. 18).
  [2] Love (l. 21).

sailed for Italy in search of new health, but it was too late, and he died in Rome in February, 1821. Although he once said, "I think I shall be among the English poets after my death," in the despondency of his final illness he doubted the security of his fame. At his request these words, which time and posterity have quite contradicted, were carved on his gravestone: "Here lies one whose name was writ in water."

His personal letters and the testimony of friends show Keats to have been a vigorous, zestful, warm-hearted person. He had a tough, even profound, mind, and there is a sturdy intellectual fiber in some of his poems. Also he was far from insensitive to the social and political evils of his time. Yet Keats is distinguished and best remembered for his devotion to beauty. He saw the world not as a symbol of religious truth, as Wordsworth did, and not as the mere tangible manifestation of ideal beauty, as did Shelley. Rather he resembles the Elizabethan poets in his celebration of the beauties and joys of the world as excellent in themselves. For pure sensuous beauty in verse one must go to Shakespeare to find his superior. Keats was a dedicated artist. His fertile, inventive mind discovered new resources for the language of poetry, an enrichment of the medium that put later poets in his debt. Also he was a meticulous craftsman. Inspired he was, no doubt, but many of his fine effects he achieved through hard work, as the studied revisions in his manuscripts show. Art and nature are perfectly joined in this poet, who loved the world he lived in and wished to reveal it to us in all its beauty.

The Eve of St. Agnes

In no other poem of Keats is his painstaking care better illustrated. He was determined to get the exact word, the precise image, the right effects of sound and color. This tale of romantic love in a rich medieval setting is remarkable for its sensuous appeal.

1

St. Agnes' Eve [1]—Ah, bitter chill it was!
The owl, for all his feathers, was a-cold;
The hare limped trembling through the frozen grass,
And silent was the flock in woolly fold:
Numb were the beadsman's [2] fingers, while he told   5
His rosary,[3] and while his frosted breath,
Like pious incense from a censer old,
Seemed taking flight for heaven,[4] without a death,
Past the sweet Virgin's picture, while his prayer he saith.

2

His prayer he saith, this patient, holy man;   10
Then takes his lamp, and riseth from his knees,
And back returneth, meager, barefoot, wan,
Along the chapel aisle by slow degrees:
The sculptured dead, on each side, seem to freeze,[5]
Emprisoned in black, purgatorial rails:[6]   15
Knights, ladies, praying in dumb orat'ries,[7]
He passeth by; and his weak spirit fails
To think how they may ache in icy hoods and mails.

[1] January 20, supposedly the coldest day of the year. Note the artistry with which Keats establishes the icy atmosphere through a succession of "cold" images.

[2] A beadsman was a man hired to pray for his benefactor.

[3] I.e., counted the beads of his rosary.

[4] According to ancient superstition, at the moment of death the soul left the body in the form of a vapor. Why is this image particularly appropriate here?

[5] Leigh Hunt remarked that "the very architecture seems to be taking part in the action." Watch for other examples of this effect.

[6] Garments.

[7] Small prayer chapels. Why "dumb"?

3

Northward he turneth through a little door,
And scarce three steps, ere music's golden
  tongue   20
Flattered to tears this agèd man and poor;
But no—already had his death-bell rung:
The joys of all his life were said and sung:
His was harsh penance on St. Agnes' Eve:
Another way he went, and soon among   25
Rough ashes sat he for his soul's reprieve,
And all night kept awake, for sinners' sake
  to grieve.

4

That ancient beadsman heard the prelude
  soft;
And so it chanced, for many a door was
  wide,[8]
From hurry to and fro. Soon, up aloft,   30
The silver, snarling trumpets 'gan to chide:
The level chambers, ready with their pride,
Were glowing to receive a thousand guests:
The carvèd angels, ever eager-eyed,
Stared, where upon their heads the cornice
  rests,   35
With hair blown back, and wings put cross-
  wise on their breasts.[9]

5

At length burst in the argent [10] revelry,
With plume, tiara, and all rich array,
Numerous as shadows haunting faerily
The brain, new-stuffed, in youth, with tri-
  umphs gay   40
Of old romance. These let us wish away,[11]
And turn, sole-thoughted, to one lady there,
Whose heart had brooded, all that wintry
  day,
On love, and winged St. Agnes' saintly care,
As she had heard old dames full many times
  declare.   45

[8] Note the quick shift to a sharply contrasting
scene: the noise and color of the festive ball in the
castle.
[9] Cf. ll. 34–36 with ll. 14–18 above.
[10] Shining (literally "silver").
[11] Note the fairy-wand touch.

6

They told her how, upon St. Agnes' Eve,
Young virgins might have visions of delight,
And soft adorings from their loves receive
Upon the honeyed middle of the night,
If ceremonies due they did aright;   50
As, supperless to bed they must retire,
And couch supine their beauties, lily white;
Nor look behind, nor sideways, but require
Of heaven with upward eyes for all that they
  desire.

7

Full of this whim was thoughtful Made-
  line: 55
The music, yearning like a god in pain,
She scarcely heard: her maiden eyes divine,
Fixed on the floor, saw many a sweeping
  train
Pass by—she heeded not at all: in vain
Came many a tiptoe, amorous cavalier,   60
And back retired; not cooled by high disdain,
But she saw not: her heart was otherwhere;
She sighed for Agnes' dreams, the sweetest
  of the year.

8

She danced along with vague, regardless
  eyes,
Anxious her lips, her breathing quick and
  short: [12]   65
The hallowed hour was near at hand: she
  sighs
Amid the timbrels,[13] and the thronged resort
Of whisperers in anger, or in sport;
'Mid looks of love, defiance, hate, and scorn,
Hoodwinked with faery fancy; all amort, [14] 70
Save to St. Agnes and her lambs unshorn,[15]
And all the bliss to be before tomorrow
  morn.

[12] This line originally read: "Her anxious mouth
full pulped with rosy thought." Why is the final
version superior?
[13] Small hand drums.
[14] Dead.
[15] On the saint's day, the wool of two sacrificed
lambs was woven by the nuns.

9

So, purposing each moment to retire,
She lingered still. Meantime, across the moors,
Had come young Porphyro, with heart on
    fire   75
For Madeline. Beside the portal doors,
Buttressed from moonlight,[16] stands he, and
    implores
All saints to give him sight of Madeline,
But for one moment in the tedious hours,
That he might gaze and worship all un-
    seen;   80
Perchance speak, kneel, touch, kiss—in sooth
    such things have been.

10

He ventures in: let no buzzed whisper tell:
All eyes be muffled, or a hundred swords
Will storm his heart, love's fev'rous citadel:
For him, those chambers held barbarian
    hordes,   85
Hyena foemen, and hot-blooded lords,
Whose very dogs would execrations howl
Against his lineage: [17] not one breast affords
Him any mercy, in that mansion foul,
Save one old beldame,[18] weak in body and in
    in soul.   90

11

Ah, happy chance! the agèd creature came,
Shuffling along with ivory-headed wand,
To where he stood, hid from the torch's
    flame,
Behind a broad hall-pillar, far beyond
The sound of merriment and chorus bland: 95
He startled her; but soon she knew his face,
And grasped his fingers in her palsied hand,
Saying, "Mercy, Porphyro! hie thee from this
    place;
They are all here tonight, the whole blood-
    thirsty race!

12

"Get hence! get hence! there's dwarfish Hilde-
    brand;   100
He had a fever late, and in the fit
He cursèd thee and thine, both house and
    land:
Then there's that old Lord Maurice, not a
    whit
More tame for his gray hairs—Alas me! flit!
Flit like a ghost away."—"Ah, Gossip [19]
    dear,   105
We're safe enough; here in this armchair sit,
And tell me how"—"Good saints! not here, not
    here;
Follow me, child, or else these stones will be
    thy bier."

13

He followed through a lowly archèd way,
Brushing the cobwebs with his lofty
    plume;   110
And as she muttered, "Well-a—well-a-day!"
He found him in a little moonlight room,
Pale, latticed, chill, and silent as a tomb.
"Now tell me where is Madeline," said he,
"O tell me, Angela, by the holy loom   115
Which none but secret sisterhood may see,
When they St. Agnes' wool are weaving,
    piously."

14

"St. Agnes! Ah! it is St. Agnes' Eve—
Yet men will murder upon holy days:
Thou must hold water in a witch's sieve,[20] 120
And be liege-lord of all the elves and fays,
To venture so: it fills me with amaze
To see thee, Porphyro!—St. Agnes' Eve!
God's help! my lady fair the conjuror plays
This very night: good angels her deceive! 125
But let me laugh awhile, I've mickle [21] time
    to grieve."

15

Feebly she laugheth in the languid moon,
While Porphyro upon her face doth look,

[16] Note the effectiveness of this picture. Why is "buttressed" an excellent word here? (Why not "hidden" or "sheltered"?)
[17] Lines 85–88 echo the famous feud in *Romeo and Juliet*. What does the enmity between the two families add to the story?
[18] An old (usually ugly) woman.

[19] Godmother.
[20] A sieve that will magically hold water.
[21] Much.

Like puzzled urchin on an aged crone
Who keepeth closed a wond'rous riddle-
book,   130
As spectacled she sits in chimney nook.[22]
But soon his eyes grew brilliant, when she
told
His lady's purpose; and he scarce could brook
Tears, at the thought of those enchantments
cold,
And Madeline asleep in lap of legends old. 135

16

Sudden a thought came like a full-blown
rose,
Flushing his brow, and in his painèd heart
Made purple riot: [23] then doth he propose
A stratagem, that makes the beldame start:
"A cruel man and impious thou art: 140
Sweet lady, let her pray, and sleep, and
dream
Alone with her good angels, far apart
From wicked men like thee. Go, go! I deem
Thou canst not surely be the same that thou
didst seem."

17

"I will not harm her, by all saints I swear," 145
Quoth Porphyro: "O may I ne'er find grace
When my weak voice shall whisper its last
prayer,
If one of her soft ringlets I displace,
Or look with ruffian passion in her face:
Good Angela, believe me by these tears; 150
Or I will, even in a moment's space,
Awake, with horrid shout, my foemen's ears,
And beard them, though they be more fanged
than wolves and bears."

18

"Ah! why wilt thou affright a feeble soul?
A poor, weak, palsy-stricken, churchyard
thing,   155
Whose passing-bell may ere the midnight toll;
Whose prayers for thee, each morn and
evening,

Were never missed." Thus plaining, doth she
bring
A gentler speech from burning Porphyro;
So woeful, and of such deep sorrowing,   160
That Angela gives promise she will do
Whatever he shall wish, betide her weal or
woe.

19

Which was, to lead him, in close secrecy,
Even to Madeline's chamber, and there hide
Him in a closet, of such privacy   165
That he might see her beauty unespied,
And win perhaps that night a peerless bride,
While legioned faeries paced the coverlet,
And pale enchantment held her sleepy-eyed.
Never on such a night have lovers met,   170
Since Merlin paid his demon all the mon-
strous debt.[24]

20

"It shall be as thou wishest," said the dame:
"All cates [25] and dainties shall be storèd there
Quickly on this feast-night: by the tambour
frame [26]
Her own lute thou wilt see: no time to
spare,   175
For I am slow and feeble, and scarce dare
On such a catering trust my dizzy head.
Wait here, my child, with patience; kneel in
prayer
The while: Ah! thou must needs the lady
wed,
Or may I never leave my grave among the
dead."   180

21

So saying, she hobbled off with busy fear.
The lover's endless minutes slowly passed;
The dame returned, and whispered in his
ear

---

[22] Note the picture-book effect in ll. 127-131.
[23] What is startling—and yet effective—about this combination of adjective and noun?
[24] Merlin, the wizard of Arthurian legend, was begotten by a demon, whom he repaid by wicked deeds.
[25] Delicacies. According to the legend of St. Agnes's Eve, the lover appearing to his lady would feed her delicious food and (l. 175) play soft music for her.
[26] An embroidery frame shaped like a drum.

To follow her—with agèd eyes aghast
From fright of dim espial. Safe at last, 185
Through many a dusky gallery, they gain
The maiden's chamber, silken, hushed, and
chaste;
Where Porphyro took covert, pleased amain.[27]
His poor guide hurried back with agues in her
brain.

22

Her faltering hand upon the balustrade, 190
Old Angela was feeling for the stair,
When Madeline, St. Agnes' charmèd maid,
Rose, like a missioned spirit, unaware:
With silver taper's light, and pious care,
She turned, and down the agèd gossip led 195
To a safe level matting. Now prepare,
Young Porphyro, for gazing on that bed;
She comes, she comes again, like ring-dove
frayed [28] and fled.

23

Out went the taper as she hurried in;
Its little smoke, in pallid moonshine, died: 200
She closed the door, she panted, all akin
To spirits of the air, and visions wide:
No uttered syllable, or, woe betide!
But to her heart, her heart was voluble,
Paining with eloquence her balmy side; 205
As though a tongueless nightingale should
swell
Her throat in vain, and die, heart-stifled in
her dell.

24

A casement high and triple-arched there was,
All garlanded with carven imageries
Of fruits, and flowers, and bunches of knot-
grass, 210
And diamonded with panes of quaint device,
Innumerable of stains and splendid dyes,
As are the tiger-moth's deep-damasked wings;
And in the midst, 'mong thousand heraldries,
And twilight saints, and dim emblazon-
ings, 215

[27] Greatly.
[28] Frightened.

A shielded scutcheon blushed with blood of
queens and kings.

25

Full on this casement shone the wintry moon,
And threw warm gules [29] on Madeline's fair
breast,
As down she knelt for heaven's grace and
boon;
Rose-bloom fell on her hands, together
pressed, 220
And on her silver cross soft amethyst,
And on her hair a glory, like a saint:
She seemed a splendid angel,[30] newly dressed,
Save wings, for heaven—Porphyro grew faint:
She knelt, so pure a thing, so free from mortal
taint. 225

26

Anon his heart revives: her vespers done,
Of all its wreathèd pearls her hair she frees;
Unclasps her warmèd jewels one by one;
Loosens her fragrant bodice; by degrees
Her rich attire creeps rustling to her knees: 230
Half-hidden, like a mermaid in sea-weed,
Pensive awhile she dreams awake, and sees,
In fancy, fair St. Agnes in her bed,
But dares not look behind, or all the charm is
fled.[31]

27

Soon, trembling, in her soft and chilly
nest, 235
In sort of wakeful swoon, perplexed she lay,
Until the poppied warmth of sleep oppressed
Her soothèd limbs, and soul fatigued away;
Flown, like a thought, until the morrow-day;
Blissfully havened both from joy and pain; 240

[29] An heraldic term for "reds." Keats used "reds"
in his first version. Why is "gules" better? Note
the use of color throughout.
[30] What purpose does this comparison serve? Cf.
also l. 219, the pressing of her hands together in
l. 220, the cross of l. 221, "like a saint" of l. 222,
and l. 225. What does this total image do to the
sensuality of Madeline's disrobing?
[31] Sts. 24–26, arrived at after extensive revision,
are excellent illustrations of Keats's ability at rich
description.

Clasped like a missal where swart Paynims
  pray; [32]
Blinded alike from sunshine and from rain,
As though a rose should shut, and be a bud
  again.

28

Stol'n to this paradise, and so entranced,
Porphyro gazed upon her empty dress,   245
And listened to her breathing, if it chanced
To wake into a slumberous tenderness;
Which when he heard, that minute did he
  bless,
And breathed himself: then from the closet
  crept,
Noiseless as fear in a wide wilderness,   250
And over the hushèd carpet, silent, stepped,
And 'tween the curtains peeped, where, lo!—
  how fast she slept.

29

Then by the bedside, where the faded moon
Made a dim, silver twilight, soft he set
A table, and, half anguished, threw there-
  on   255
A cloth of woven crimson, gold, and jet—
O for some drowsy Morphean [33] amulet!
The boisterous, midnight, festive clarion,[34]
The kettle-drum, and far-heard clarionet,
Affray his ears, though but in dying tone— 260
The hall door shuts again, and all the noise
  is gone.

30

And still she slept an azure-lidded sleep,
In blanchèd linen, smooth, and lavendered,[35]
While he from forth the closet brought a
  heap

[32] The meaning of the line is: "Shut like a
prayer book in a pagan land." The prayer book
(missal) would be shut (clasped) either because
pagans (Paynims) would have no reason to open
it or because Christians would keep it clasped in
secrecy or fright.
[33] Pertaining to Morpheus, god of sleep. An
amulet is a charm.
[34] Why does the poet momentarily let us hear
the sound of the ball below at this point?
[35] Perfumed with lavender.

Of candied apple, quince, and plum, and
  gourd;   265
With jellies soother than the creamy curd,
And lucent syrups, tinct with cinnamon;
Manna and dates, in argosy transferred
From Fez; and spicèd dainties, every one,
From silken Samarcand to cedared Leba-
  non.[36]   270

31

These delicates he heaped with glowing hand
On golden dishes and in baskets bright
Of wreathèd silver: sumptuous they stand
In the retirèd quiet of the night,
Filling the chilly room with perfume
  light.—   275
"And now, my love, my seraph fair, awake!
Thou art my heaven, and I thine eremite.[37]
Open thine eyes, for meek St. Agnes' sake,
Or I shall drowse beside thee, so my soul doth
  ache."

32

Thus whispering, his warm, unnervèd arm 280
Sank in her pillow. Shaded was her dream
By the dusk curtains—'twas a midnight charm
Impossible to melt as icèd stream:
The lustrous salvers [38] in the moonlight
  gleam;
Broad golden fringe upon the carpet lies: 285
It seemed he never, never could redeem
From such a steadfast spell his lady's eyes;
So mused awhile, entoiled in woofèd phan-
  tasies.

33

Awakening up, he took her hollow lute—
Tumultuous—and, in chords that tenderest
  be,   290
He played an ancient ditty, long since mute,
In Provence [39] called "La belle dame sans
  merci"; [40]

[36] What do the proper names of ll. 269–270 add
to the description?
[37] Hermit.
[38] Trays.
[39] A region of southern France.
[40] "The beautiful lady without mercy." This is
the title of a poem by Alain Chartier, a medieval
Provençal poet. Note Keats's own poem with this
title.

Close to her ear touching the melody;—
Wherewith disturbed, she uttered a soft
  moan:
He ceased—she panted quick—and sud-
  denly   295
Her blue affrayèd eyes wide open shone:
Upon his knees he sank, pale as smooth-
  sculptured stone.

34

Her eyes were open, but she still beheld,
Now wide awake, the vision of her sleep:
There was a painful change, that nigh ex-
  pelled   300
The blisses of her dream so pure and deep
At which fair Madeline began to weep,
And moan forth witless words with many a
  sigh;
While still her gaze on Porphyro would keep;
Who knelt, with joinèd hands and piteous
  eye,   305
Fearing to move or speak, she looked so
  dreamingly.

35

"Ah, Porphyro!" said she, "but even now
Thy voice was at sweet tremble in mine ear,
Made tuneable with every sweetest vow;
And those sad eyes were spiritual and
  clear: 310
How changed thou art! how pallid, chill, and
  drear!
Give me that voice again, my Porphyro,
Those looks immortal, those complainings
  dear!
Oh, leave me not in this eternal woe,
For if thou diest, my love, I know not where
  to go."   315

36

Beyond a mortal man impassioned far
At these voluptuous accents, he arose,
Ethereal, flushed, and like a throbbing star
Seen mid the sapphire heaven's deep repose;
Into her dream he melted, as the rose   320
Blendeth its odor with the violet—
Solution sweet; meantime the frost-wind
  blows

Like love's alarum pattering the sharp sleet
Against the window-panes; St. Agnes' moon
  hath set.

37

'Tis dark; quick pattereth the flaw-blown [41]
  sleet;   325
"This is no dream, my bride, my Madeline!"
'Tis dark; the icèd gusts still rave and beat;
"No dream, alas! alas! and woe is mine!
Porphyro will leave me here to fade and
  pine.—
Cruel! what traitor could thee hither bring? 330
I curse not, for my heart is lost in thine,
Though thou forsakest a deceivèd thing;—
A dove forlorn and lost with sick unprunèd
  wing."

38

"My Madeline! sweet dreamer! lovely bride!
Say, may I be for aye thy vassal blest?   335
Thy beauty's shield, heart-shaped and ver-
  meil [42]-dyed?
Ah, silver shrine, here will I take my rest
After so many hours of toil and quest,
A famished pilgrim—saved by miracle.
Though I have found, I will not rob thy
  nest   340
Saving of thy sweet self; if thou think'st well
To trust, fair Madeline, to no rude infidel.

39

"Hark! 'tis an elfin storm from faery land,
Of haggard seeming, [43] but a boon indeed:
Arise—arise! the morning is at hand—   345
The bloated wassailers [44] will never heed—
Let us away, my love, with happy speed;
There are no ears to hear, or eyes to see—
Drowned all in Rhenish [45] and the sleepy
  mead;[46]
Awake! arise! my love, and fearless be,   350
For o'er the southern moors I have a home for
  thee."

[41] Wind-blown.
[42] Vermilion.
[43] Wild appearance.
[44] Drinkers.
[45] Rhine wine.
[46] A fermented drink.

40

She hurried at his words, beset with fears,
For there were sleeping dragons all around,
At glaring watch, perhaps, with ready spears—
Down the wide stairs a darkling way they
    found.—   355
In all the house was heard no human sound.
A chain-drooped lamp was flickering by each
    door;
The arras,[47] rich with horseman, hawk, and
    hound,
Fluttered in the besieging wind's uproar;
And the long carpets rose along the gusty
    floor.   360

41

They glide, like phantoms, into the wide
    hall;
Like phantoms to the iron porch they glide,
Where lay the porter, in uneasy sprawl,
With a huge empty flagon by his side;
The wakeful bloodhound rose, and shook his
    hide,   365
But his sagacious eye an inmate owns:
By one, and one, the bolts full easy slide—
The chains lie silent on the footworn stones;—
The key turns, and the door upon its hinges
    groans.[48]

42

And they are gone: aye, ages long ago   370
These lovers fled away into the storm.
That night the Baron dreamt of many a woe,
And all his warrior-guests, with shade and
    form

Of witch, and demon, and large coffin-worm,
Were long be-nightmared. Angela the old 375
Died palsy-twitched, with meager face de-
    form;
The beadsman, after thousand aves told,
For aye unsought-for slept among his ashes
    cold.[49]

(1819; 1820)

STUDY AIDS: 1. This is a poem of vivid
contrasts. List the various pairs of contrasts in
the poem ranging from the simplest (such as
the cold of the night outside over against the
warmth of Madeline's room) to the most complex and subtle. How many can you find, and
how has Keats used them to build up the pattern
and atmosphere of the poem? In this respect,
what role is played by the beadsman and Angela?
Particularly why is so much attention paid to
the beadsman, who takes no part in the story?

2. Is *The Eve of St. Agnes* a completely
"happy" poem? Presumably the lovers escape
and "live happily ever after." Is this the dominant mood? Go through the poem and see how
often the motif of death is stated or suggested
(e.g., ll. 8, 14, 22, 84, 105, etc.). If this is an
undertone of the poem, does it enrich the mood
or harm it? One critic suggests that the lovers
go out to almost immediate certain death. Do
you agree? Can the poem in any sense of the
word be considered a tragedy?

3. Is the Spenserian stanza appropriate to
this poem? What does it do to the pace of the
narrative?

4. Consider the poem as a story. Are the
characters sufficiently developed? Is the setting
more important than the characters? Is there a
climax? Does the story have a THEME? Does
Keats's treatment of the story make any implied
comment on life and love?

La Belle Dame Sans Merci [1]

"O, what can ail thee, knight at arms,[2]
    Alone and palely loitering?
The sedge has withered from the lake,
    And no birds sing!

"O, what can ail thee, knight at arms,   5
    So haggard and so woe-begone?
The squirrel's granary is full,
    And the harvest's done.

---

[47] Tapestry.
[48] What effect is gained by focusing our attention
on the arras, the lamp, the carpets, the hall, the
porch, the porter, the flagon, the bloodhound, and,
especially, at the end, the bolts, the chains, the key,
and the door?

[49] What purpose is served by this gruesome final
stanza? Does the beadsman die?

---

[1] "The beautiful lady without mercy." See *The
Eve of St. Agnes*, l. 292, note (p. 694).
[2] The later version substituted "wretched wight"
for "knight at arms." Which is superior and why?

"I see a lily on thy brow,
  With anguish moist and fever dew,   10
And on thy cheeks a fading rose
  Fast withereth too."

"I met a lady in the meads,[3]
  Full beautiful—a faery's child;
Her hair was long, her foot was light,   15
  And her eyes were wild.

"I made a garland for her head,
  And bracelets too, and fragrant zone; [4]
She looked at me as she did love,
  And made sweet moan.   20

"I set her on my pacing steed,
  And nothing else saw all day long;
For sidelong would she bend, and sing
  A faery's song.

"She found me roots of relish sweet,   25
  And honey wild and manna-dew;
And sure in language strange she said,
  'I love thee true.'

"She took me to her elfin grot,[5]
  And there she gazed and sighed full sore, 30
And there I shut her wild, wild eyes—
  With kisses four.[6]

"And there she lullèd me asleep,
  And there I dreamed—ah, woe betide!—

The latest dream I ever dreamed   35
  On the cold hill's side.

"I saw pale kings, and princes too,
  Pale warriors, death-pale were they all:
They cried—'La Belle Dame sans Merci
  Hath thee in thrall!'   40

"I saw their starved lips in the gloam
  With horrid warning gapèd wide,
And I awoke, and found me here
  On the cold hill's side.

"And this is why I sojourn here   45
  Alone and palely loitering,
Though the sedge is withered from the lake,
  And no birds sing."[7]
(1819; 1888)

STUDY AIDS: 1. In this poem what is Keats's most striking modification of the standard BALLAD STANZA? What total effect does this change have upon the poem? Does Keats get any variety throughout the poem in the fourth line of each stanza? Compare this literary ballad with one of the old popular ballads (e.g., p. 116). How are they alike, how different?

2. What particular words and images enable Keats to achieve his weird and haunting effect? Is the result pure poetry, or does it suggest some relation to life? Is this effect all he is seeking, or does the poem have some allegorical meaning (such as the lady symbolizing Fanny Brawne, or love, or tuberculosis, or the most beautiful poetry)?

Ode to a Nightingale

In the three great odes of May, 1819, Keats is seeking a solution to the problem of a world heavy with sorrow and tragedy: the mortal world of pain, impermanence, decay, and death.

I

My heart aches, and a drowsy numbness pains
  My sense, as though of hemlock [1] I had
    drunk,

Or emptied some dull opiate to the drains [2]
  One minute past, and Lethe-wards [3] had
    sunk:

[3] From this point on, the knight speaks.
[4] Belt.
[5] Fairy cave.
[6] Keats jokingly wrote: "Why four Kisses—you will say—why four because . . . I was obliged to choose an even number that both eyes might have fair play. . . . I think two a piece quite sufficient. Suppose I had seven; there would have been three and a half a piece—a very awkward affair."

[7] Note how the last stanza repeats and intensifies the atmosphere of desolation established in the opening stanza. Does the poet gain anything by making the slight changes?

---

[1] A poison. (Socrates was executed by the use of hemlock.)
[2] Dregs.
[3] Toward Lethe, the river of forgetfulness in Hades.

'Tis not through envy of thy happy lot,   5
But being too happy [4] in thine happiness—
That thou, light-wingèd dryad [5] of the
trees,
In some melodious plot
Of beechen green, and shadows number-
less,
Singest of summer in full-throated
ease.   10

2

O, for a draught of vintage! [6] that hath been
Cooled a long age in the deep-delvèd earth,
Tasting of Flora [7] and the country green,
Dance, and Provençal [8] song, and sunburnt
mirth! [9]
O for a beaker full of the warm south,   15
Full of the true, the blushful Hippocrene,[10]
With beaded bubbles winking at the
brim,
And purple-stainèd mouth;
That I might drink, and leave the world
unseen,
And with thee fade away into the forest
dim: 20

3

Fade far away, dissolve, and quite forget [11]
What thou among the leaves hast never
known,
The weariness, the fever, and the fret
Here, where men sit and hear each other
groan;
Where palsy shakes a few, sad, last gray
hairs,   25

Where youth grows pale, and specter-thin,
and dies; [12]
Where but to think is to be full of sorrow
And leaden-eyed despairs,
Where Beauty cannot keep her lustrous
eyes,
Or new Love pine at them beyond tomor-
row.   30

4

Away! away! [13] for I will fly to thee,
Not charioted by Bacchus and his pards,[14]
But on the viewless [15] wings of poesy,
Though the dull brain perplexes and re-
tards:
Already with thee! [16] tender is the night, 35
And haply the Queen-Moon is on her
throne,
Clustered around by all her starry fays;
But here there is no light,
Save what from heaven is with the breezes
blown
Through verdurous glooms and winding
mossy ways.   40

5

I cannot see what flowers are at my feet,
Nor what soft incense hangs upon the
boughs,
But, in embalmèd [17] darkness, guess each
sweet
Wherewith the seasonable month endows
The grass, the thicket, and the fruit-tree
wild;   45
White hawthorn, and the pastoral eglan-
tine;
Fast fading violets covered up in leaves;
And mid-May's eldest child,

[4] Note that the poet's feeling is a mixture of pain and pleasure: he is "too happy," but his "heart aches" and numbness "pains" his sense (l. 1). Watch for the reappearance of this pleasure-pain (happi-ness-sorrow) motif throughout the ode.

[5] In Greek myth, a tree-nymph.

[6] In this stanza the poet wishes for escape through wine.

[7] Goddess of flowers.

[8] Provence is a region of southern France noted in medieval times as the home of singing trouba-dours.

[9] Literally, "mirth" cannot be "sunburnt." What does the phrase mean?

[10] A fountain sacred to the Muses.

[11] This stanza gives the reason why the poet wishes for the escape to be afforded by wine.

[12] This line gains added poignancy when one remembers that Keats's brother Tom had just died of tuberculosis five months earlier and that Keats recognized the symptoms of consumption in him-self.

[13] The poet dismisses the idea of wine. What does he substitute for it?

[14] Leopards, who drew the car of Bacchus, god of wine.

[15] Invisible.

[16] The poetic imagination has done its work.

[17] "Embalmèd" means "fragrant" here, but it carries other associations. What are they? Note their appropriateness when you read the next stanza.

The coming musk-rose, full of dewy wine,
The murmurous haunt of flies on summer
eves.   50

6

Darkling I listen; and, for many a time,
I have been half in love with easeful
Death,[18]
Called him soft names in many a musèd rime,
To take into the air my quiet breath;
Now more than ever seems it rich to die, 55
To cease upon the midnight with no pain,
While thou art pouring forth thy soul
abroad
In such an ecstasy!
Still wouldst thou sing, and I have ears in
vain—
To thy high requiem become a sod. 60

7

Thou wast not born for death, immortal [19]
bird!
No hungry generations tread thee down;
The voice I hear this passing night was heard
In ancient days by emperor and clown:
Perhaps the self-same song that found a
path   65
Through the sad heart of Ruth, when, sick
for home,
She stood in tears amid the alien [20] corn;
The same that oft-times hath
Charmed magic casements, opening on the
foam
Of perilous seas, in faery lands for-
lorn.[21]   70

[18] What is the difference between the attitude toward death here and that of st. 3? Why the difference? What is the PARADOX involved?
[19] In what sense is the nightingale (whose actual life span is brief) immortal?
[20] Why "alien"? (See Ruth 1:15–18).
[21] Lines 68–70 are among the most magical in English poetry. What makes them so haunting? Note, for example, the ALLITERATION; the increase in vagueness as one moves from "magic casements" to "perilous seas" to "faery lands forlorn" (a kind of fading-away effect); and the hypnotic rhythms (read the lines aloud). Keats first wrote "keel-less" for "perilous." "Keel-less" is more specific. Why is "perilous" better?

8

Forlorn! the very word is like a bell
To toll me back from thee to my sole
self!
Adieu! the fancy cannot cheat so well
As she is famed to do, deceiving elf.
Adieu! adieu! thy plaintive anthem [22] fades 75
Past the near meadows, over the still
stream,
Up the hillside; and now 'tis buried [23]
deep
In the next valley glades:
Was it a vision, or a waking dream?
Fled is that music—Do I wake or
sleep?   80
(1819; 1820)

STUDY AIDS: 1. At least part of the richness of this ode lies in the tension set up between sets of opposites: pleasure—pain; life—death; the world of the nightingale—the world of reality. And yet in the poem these opposites are partially reconciled, as intense pleasure becomes a kind of pain, as death is seen to be a way of supreme escape from a world of death, and as the poet himself transfers his own conscious life momentarily into the ideal world symbolized by the bird's song. Analyze in detail st. 1 with reference to the pain-pleasure motif and st. 6 with reference to the life-death motif.

2. Note the rich suggestiveness of the words, phrases, and IMAGERY used throughout the poem: "Lethe-wards," "light-wingèd dryad," "sunburnt mirth," "blushful Hippocrene," "leaden-eyed despairs," "charioted by Bacchus and his pards," "viewless wings of poesy," etc. Pick out others that seem to you particularly striking and try to explain why they are effective.

3. Why is Keats not successful in his attempt to escape from the world of harsh reality? Is there in the poem any expression of acceptance of the human lot? Was his experience a moment of insight into fundamental truth or just a fantasy with little or no value ("a vision, or a waking dream")?

[22] Previously, the bird's song seems to have been a happy song (note ll. 5–6, 58); here it is a "plaintive anthem." Is this contradictory? What has happened?
[23] Again, death is suggested. What is the poet's attitude toward this suggested death?

Ode on Melancholy

In this ode, as in the *Ode to a Nightingale,* a poem which is suffused with melancholy, Keats is concerned with the problem of earthly change, decay, and death, and of a world compounded of both joy and sorrow. He is interested in the melancholy mood itself and in whether it can paradoxically be made to serve the cause of high aesthetic enjoyment.

1

No, no, go not to Lethe,[1] neither twist
  Wolf's-bane,[2] tight-rooted, for its poisonous
      wine;
Nor suffer thy pale forehead to be kissed
  By nightshade,[3] ruby grape of Proserpine; [4]
Make not your rosary of yew-berries,[5]   5
  Nor let the beetle,[6] nor the death-moth [7] be
    Your mournful Psyche,[8] nor the downy
      owl [9]
A partner in your sorrow's mysteries;
  For shade to shade will come too drowsily,
    And drown the wakeful anguish of the
      soul.[10]   10

2

But when the melancholy fit shall fall [11]
  Sudden from heaven like a weeping cloud,
That fosters the droop-headed flowers all,
  And hides the green hill in an April
      shroud; [12]
Then glut thy sorrow on a morning rose, 15
  Or on the rainbow of the salt sand-wave,
  Or on the wealth of globèd peonies;

Or if thy mistress some rich anger shows,
  Emprison her soft hand, and let her rave,
    And feed deep, deep upon her peerless
      eyes.[13]   20

3

She [14] dwells with Beauty—Beauty that must
    die;
  And Joy, whose hand is ever at his lips
Bidding adieu; and aching Pleasure [15] nigh,
  Turning to poison while the bee-mouth
    sips:
Ay, in the very temple of Delight   25
  Veiled Melancholy has her sovran shrine,
    Though seen of none save him whose
      strenuous tongue
Can burst Joy's grape against his palate
    fine;
His soul shall taste the sadness of her might,
  And be among her cloudy trophies
    hung.   30
(1819; 1820)

---

[1] River of forgetfulness in Hades.
[2] A poisonous plant.
[3] Also a poisonous plant.
[4] Wife of Hades (Pluto) and so queen of the underworld.
[5] The yew-tree is a symbol of mourning.
[6] In Egypt the sacred beetle, a symbol of resurrection, was put in coffins.
[7] A moth with skull-like markings.
[8] Goddess of the soul, often pictured as a girl with butterfly wings.
[9] A bird with mournful associations.
[10] What has the poet said in this stanza? What do all the images have in common? What is the implied "if" of this stanza?
[11] What light does this line shed on the previous stanza?
[12] What do you think of when you think of April? What do you think of when you think of a shroud? Why has Keats put the two together?

STUDY AIDS: 1. How does the final stanza bring together and reconcile the opposing elements of sts. 1 and 2? What two lines of the final stanza most directly state the theme of the ode?

2. In one of his letters Keats wrote: "Do you not see how necessary a world of pains and troubles is to school an intelligence and make it a soul? A place where the heart must feel and suffer in a thousand diverse ways." How is the same philosophy of acceptance which is expressed here reflected also in the *Ode on Melancholy?*

[13] What has the poet said in this stanza? How do the images differ from those in st. 1? What do these have in common?
[14] What is the antecedent, the "mistress" of l. 18, or personified melancholy?
[15] Do you see any comparison between "aching Pleasure" and "April shroud" (l. 14)?

3. Which is the more melancholy poem, the *Ode to a Nightingale* or the *Ode on Melancholy*? Why? What part is played by the mood of melancholy in each poem? Which offers the more successful "solution" to the problem of a world of life versus death, a world where joy and sorrow are ever mixed?

4. Study carefully the rich images of this ode. How does each one relate to the theme? How are they related to each other?

5. In the eighteenth century the love of melancholy became a kind of cult, the mood of melancholy being cultivated in an artificial and sentimental way. Is Keats's cultivation of melancholy similar? To what more important truth about life does he relate it?

Ode on a Grecian Urn

In this ode Keats seeks in the permanence of art a solution to his recurrent problem, the problem of mutability and death. Men and women live and die; the human figures on a preserved urn live forever, unchanged in youth and beauty. More important, their lives and passions are continually relived from generation to generation, as sensitive observers like Keats penetrate their static immobility and re-create in imagination the feelings and experiences caught and "frozen" by the original artist.

1

Thou still unravished bride of quietness,
  Thou foster-child of silence and slow time,
Sylvan historian,[1] who canst thus express
  A flowery tale more sweetly than our
      rhyme:
What leaf-fringed legend haunts about thy
      shape   5
  Of deities or mortals, or of both,
    In Tempe or the dales of Arcady?[2]
What men or gods are these? What maid-
    ens loth?
What mad pursuit? What struggle to escape?
  What pipes and timbrels? What wild
     ecstasy?   10

2

Heard melodies are sweet, but those unheard[3]
  Are sweeter; therefore, ye soft pipes, play
    on;
Not to the sensual[4] ear, but, more endeared,
  Pipe to the spirit ditties of no tone:
Fair youth, beneath the trees, thou canst not
    leave   15

Thy song, nor ever can those trees be bare;
  Bold lover, never, never canst thou kiss,
Though winning near the goal—yet, do not
    grieve;
  She cannot fade, though thou hast not
    thy bliss,
For ever wilt thou love, and she be fair! 20

3

Ah, happy, happy boughs! that cannot shed
  Your leaves, nor ever bid the spring adieu;
And, happy melodist, unwearied,
  For ever piping songs for ever new.
More happy love! more happy, happy love! 25
  For ever warm and still to be enjoyed,
    For ever panting, and for ever young;
All breathing human passion far above,[5]
  That leaves a heart high-sorrowful and
    cloyed,
    A burning forehead, and a parching
     tongue.   30

4

Who are these coming to the sacrifice?[6]
  To what green altar, O mysterious priest,

[1] The poet begins the ode by addressing the urn (in ll. 1–3) as an "unravished bride," a "foster-child of silence and slow time," and a "sylvan historian." Why is each of these appropriate to the urn?

[2] Tempe and Arcady (Arcadia) are picturesque regions of Greece.

[3] I.e., heard only in imagination.

[4] Sensuous.

[5] Up to this point, the contrast between this ideal world-out-of-time and the actual world-in-time has only been suggested or implied; in ll. 28–30 it is made explicit as the real world intrudes directly.

[6] St. 4 introduces, again by a series of questions, another scene on the urn (it is as if the poet were turning the vase in his hands). What is this scene and how does it differ from the first one?

Lead'st thou that heifer lowing at the skies,
And all her silken flanks with garlands
drest?
What little town by river or sea shore,   35
Or mountain-built with peaceful citadel,
Is emptied of this folk, this pious morn?
And, little town, thy streets for evermore
Will silent be; and not a soul to tell
Why thou art desolate, can e'er re-
turn.[7]   40

5

O Attic shape! Fair attitude! with brede [8]
Of marble men and maidens overwrought,
With forest branches and the trodden weed;
Thou, silent form! dost tease us out of
thought
As doth eternity: [9] Cold pastoral! [10]   45
When old age shall this generation waste,
Thou shalt remain, in midst of other woe
Than ours, a friend to man, to whom thou
say'st,
"Beauty is truth, truth beauty,"—that is all
Ye know on earth, and all ye need to
know.   50
(1819; 1820)

STUDY AIDS: 1. The most famous lines of the poem are the last two, especially the statement: "Beauty is truth, truth beauty." Ruskin objected that Keats was confusing two separate ideas: a proposition, he said, can be true (such as "It is raining outside") but not beautiful; an object (such as a rose) may be beautiful, but hardly "true." Is this what Keats means by "truth" here? T. S. Eliot regards the last two lines as "a serious blemish on a beautiful poem" and confesses that they seem to him "meaningless." What do they mean to you? Keats once wrote in a letter: "What the imagination seizes as beauty must be truth"; does this statement help to clarify his meaning in the poem? The statement is spoken by the urn. Is it all right, then, to consider it as a general proposition, or must we think of it as a dramatic pronouncement of the urn and in its relation only to the poem itself?

2. Which poem seems to you the more successful "solution" to the problem of decay and death, the *Ode on a Grecian Urn* or the *Ode on Melancholy*? Why? What is the difference in the approach of each ode to the problem?

To Autumn

Having wrestled with the problems of pain and pleasure, change and permanence, life and death in the three great odes of May, 1819, Keats seems to have arrived at a stoical acceptance of what he called this "Vale of Soul-making," where joy and sorrow are inextricably intermingled and where all we can know is that "beauty is truth, truth beauty." In such a mood of acceptance he could write (in September, 1819) the ode *To Autumn*, "the most calm, the most perfectly serene of all his poems."

1

Season of mists and mellow fruitfulness,[1]
Close bosom-friend of the maturing sun;
Conspiring with him how to load and bless

With fruit the vines that round the thatch-
eaves run;
To bend with apples the mossed cottage-
trees,   5

[8] Embroidery.
[9] I.e., the idea of eternity.
[10] "Cold," of course, because made of marble. But what else does the image suggest in terms of the development of the poem (also "silent form" of the preceding line)? What has happened to the poet in his relation to the figures on the urn? Why is it now a "cold" pastoral?

[7] After the first group of scenes, the poet commented upon the immortality of the life presented on the urn as contrasted with the mortality of actual life, to the disadvantage of the latter. Here, in ll. 38–40, what does he do? Is the "little town" actually depicted on the urn, do you think, or is this an extension of the poet's imagination? What effect is given by the adjective "desolate" in l. 40? How have the two worlds (the world of the urn, the world of actuality) somehow come together?

[1] The effect of this stanza is one of fullness and ripeness. Note the sounds and images that build up this effect.

And fill all the fruit with ripeness to the
    core;
    To swell the gourd, and plump the
      hazel shells
With a sweet kernel; to set budding more,
And still more, later flowers for the bees,
Until they think warm days will never
    cease,   10
    For summer has o'er-brimmed their
      clammy cells.

2

Who hath not seen thee oft amid thy store?
    Sometimes whoever seeks abroad may find
Thee sitting careless on a granary floor,
    Thy hair soft-lifted by the winnowing
      wind;   15
Or on a half-reaped furrow sound asleep,
    Drowsed with the fume of poppies, while
      thy hook
    Spares the next swath and all its twinèd
      flowers:
And sometime like a gleaner thou dost keep
    Steady thy laden head across a brook; 20
    Or by a cider-press, with patient look,
    Thou watchest the last oozings, hours by
      hours.[2]

3

Where are the songs of spring? Ay, where are
    they?
    Think not of them, thou hast thy music
      too,—
While barrèd clouds bloom the soft-dying
    day,   25
    And touch the stubble-plains with rosy hue;
Then in a wailful choir the small gnats
    mourn
    Among the river sallows,[3] borne aloft
    Or sinking as the light wind lives or
      dies;
And full-grown lambs loud bleat from hilly
    bourn;   30
    Hedge-crickets sing; and now with treble
      soft
    The redbreast whistles from a garden-croft,
    And gathering swallows twitter in the
      skies.
(1819; 1820)

STUDY AIDS: 1. Is this a purely descriptive
poem, or does it have some philosophic significance?
    2. What is the tempo of the poem? SCAN
several lines. How is this tempo achieved?

Sonnets

On First Looking into Chapman's Homer

Keats knew no Greek. A friend introduced him to the poetry of Homer through the vivid
translation of George Chapman, the Elizabethan poet. The experience prompted this sonnet.

Much have I traveled in the realms of gold,
And many goodly states and kingdoms seen;
Round many western islands have I been
Which bards in fealty [1] to Apollo [2] hold.
Oft of one wide expanse had I been told   5
That deep-browed Homer ruled as his
    demesne: [3]

Yet did I never breathe its pure serene [4]
Till I heard Chapman speak out loud and
    bold:
Then felt I like some watcher of the skies
When a new planet swims [5] into his ken; [6] 10
Or like stout Cortez [7] when with eagle eyes

[2] St. 2 is built up around what figurative device?
How is this device prepared for in st. 1?
[3] Willows.

[1] Faithfulness of a feudal vassal to his lord.
[2] God of poetry and of the founding of states.
[3] Domain.

[4] The first version of this line was: "Yet never
could I judge what men could mean." How is the
revision an improvement? What part of speech is
"serene"?
[5] Why is this verb particularly appropriate?
[6] Range of sight.
[7] Balboa, of course, discovered the Pacific. Does
Keats's "mistake" mar the poem?

He stared at the Pacific—and all his men
Looked at each other with a wild surmise—
Silent, upon a peak in Darien.[8]
(1815; 1816)

STUDY AIDS: 1. This SONNET (what kind
is it?) is built around the theme of exploration
and discovery. The OCTAVE is an elaborated
METAPHOR telling what was explored and discovered; the SESTET consists of two SIMILES expressing how Keats felt about the discovery.
2. Precisely what is Keats saying by means of
the extended metaphor of the octave? What is
the symbolism of the various words and phrases
in the first eight lines? (E.g., in the first line

Keats is saying: "Much have I read in great
literature.")
3. What are the two similes of the sestet?
How are they related to each other and to the
extended metaphor of the octave? What is gained
by the shift of the field of exploration from
earth to sky and then back to earth again? How
does the poem reach a kind of climax in the final
image?
4. Chapman was a poet of the Renaissance.
How is this exciting period of world history
suggested throughout the sonnet?
5. The mood of the sonnet is not restricted
to the excitement of discovering Homer in a
fine translation. How does the theme have a
more universal application?

On the Grasshopper and the Cricket

The poetry of earth is never dead:
When all the birds are faint with the hot sun,
And hide in cooling trees, a voice will run
From hedge to hedge about the new-mown
    mead;
That is the grasshopper's—he takes the lead 5
In summer luxury,—he has never done
With his delights; for when tired out with
    fun

He rests at ease beneath some pleasant weed.
The poetry of earth is ceasing never:
On a lone winter evening, when the frost 10
Has wrought a silence, from the stove there
    shrills
The cricket's song, in warmth increasing ever,
And seems to one in drowsiness half lost,
The grasshopper's among some grassy hills.
(1816; 1817)

On the Sea

It keeps eternal whisperings around
Desolate shores, and with its mighty swell
Gluts twice ten thousand caverns, till the spell
Of Hecate[1] leaves them their old shadowy
    sound.
Often 'tis in such gentle temper found,   5
That scarcely will the very smallest shell
Be moved for days from whence it sometime
    fell,
When last the winds of heaven were un-
    bound.
Oh ye! who have your eye-balls vexed and
    tired,
Feast them upon the wideness of the sea; 10
Oh ye! whose ears are dinned with uproar
    rude,

Or fed too much with cloying melody—
Sit ye near some old cavern's mouth and brood
Until ye start, as if the sea-nymphs quired![2]
(1817; 1848)

STUDY AIDS: What is the division of subject matter between the OCTAVE and the SESTET?
What contrasting images are found within the
octave? To what sense does the sonnet primarily
appeal? How do ll. 10, 13, and 14 go back to
the beginning of the sonnet?

[8] Darien is a former province of Panama. Note
the meter and structure of this line. How do they
fit the picture here represented?

[1] Dark goddess of magic.
[2] Sang in a chorus (choired).

When I Have Fears

When I have fears that I may cease to be
Before my pen has gleaned my teeming
  brain,
Before high pilèd books, in charactry,
Hold like rich garners the full-ripened grain;
When I behold, upon the night's starred
  face,   5
Huge cloudy symbols of a high romance,
And think that I may never live to trace
Their shadows, with the magic hand of
  chance;
And when I feel, fair creature of an hour!
That I shall never look upon thee more,   10
Never have relish in the faery power
Of unreflecting love!—then on the shore
Of the wide world I stand alone, and think
Till love and fame to nothingness do sink.
(1818; 1848)

How Fevered Is the Man

How fevered is the man who cannot look
Upon his mortal days with temperate blood,
Who vexes all the leaves of his life's book,
And robs his fair name of its maidenhood;
It is as if the rose should pluck herself, 5
Or the ripe plum finger its misty bloom,
As if a Naiad,[1] like a meddling elf,
Should darken her pure grot with muddy
  gloom.
But the rose leaves herself upon the briar,
For winds to kiss and grateful bees to feed, 10
And the ripe plum still wears its dim attire;
The undisturbèd lake has crystal space;
Why then should man, teasing the world for
  grace,
Spoil his salvation for a fierce miscreed?[2]
(1819; 1848)

STUDY AIDS: What is the theme of this sonnet? How do the images of the rose, the plum, and the Naiad help to develop this theme?

Bright Star, Would I Were Steadfast as Thou Art

This sonnet is often called Keats's "last sonnet," since he copied it down on his way to Italy in September, 1820. However, it was almost certainly composed before this, probably early in 1819.

Bright star! would I were steadfast as thou
  art—
Not in lone splendor hung aloft the night,
And watching, with eternal lids apart,
Like nature's patient sleepless eremite,[3]
The moving waters at their priestlike task 5
Of pure ablution round earth's human shores,
Or gazing on the new soft fallen mask
Of snow upon the mountains and the moors—
No—yet still steadfast, still unchangeable,
Pillowed upon my fair love's ripening
  breast,   10
To feel forever its soft fall and swell,
Awake forever in a sweet unrest,
Still, still to hear her tender-taken breath,
And so live ever—or else swoon to death.
(1846)

STUDY AIDS: Here is an earlier version of the same sonnet:

Bright star! would I were steadfast as thou art!
Not in lone splendor hung amid the night;
Not watching, with eternal lids apart
Like nature's devout sleepless eremite

[1] A water nymph.
[2] This is one of two sonnets on fame. What then is the "fierce miscreed" of the last line?
[3] Religious recluse; hermit.

The morning waters at their priestlike task
Of pure ablution round earth's human shores;
Or gazing on the new soft fallen mask
Of snow upon the mountains and the moors:—
No;—yet still steadfast, still unchangeable
Cheek-pillowed on my love's white ripening
   breast,

To touch, forever, its warm sink and swell,
Awake, forever, in a sweet unrest;
To hear, to feel her tender-taken breath,
Half-passionless, and so swoon on to death.

How have the various changes improved the poem?

Letters

To Benjamin Bailey

November 22, 1817.

My dear Bailey,

. . . .

O I wish I was as certain of the end of all your troubles as that of your momentary start about the authenticity of the imagination. I am certain of nothing but of the holi- [10] ness of the heart's affections, and the truth of imagination. What the imagination seizes as beauty must be truth—whether it existed before or not—for I have the same idea of all our passions as of love: they are all, in their [15] sublime, creative of essential beauty. In a word, you may know my favorite speculation by my first book, and the little song I sent in my last, which is a representation from the fancy of the probable mode of operating [20] in these matters. The imagination may be compared to Adam's dream [1]—he awoke and found it truth. I am more zealous in this affair, because I have never yet been able to perceive how anything can be known for [25] truth by consecutive reasoning—and yet it must be. Can it be that even the greatest philosopher ever arrived at his goal without putting aside numerous objections? However it may be, O for a life of sensations rather [30] than of thoughts! It is "a vision in the form of youth," a shadow of reality to come. And this consideration has further convinced me—for it has come as auxiliary to another favorite speculation of mine—that we shall [35] enjoy ourselves hereafter by having what we called happiness on earth repeated in a finer tone. And yet such a fate can only befall

[1] Of the creation of Eve (in *Paradise Lost*).

those who delight in sensation, rather than hunger as you do after truth. Adam's dream will do here, and seems to be a conviction that imagination and its empyreal reflection is the [5] same as human life and its spiritual repetition. But, as I was saying, the simple imaginative mind may have its rewards in the repetition of its own silent working coming continually on the spirit with a fine suddenness. To [10] compare great things with small, have you never by being surprised with an old melody, in a delicious place by a delicious voice, *felt* over again your very speculations and surmises at the time it first operated on your [15] soul? Do you not remember forming to yourself the singer's face, more beautiful than it was possible, and yet with the elevation of the moment you did not think so? Even then you were mounted on the wings of imagination, [20] so high that the prototype must be hereafter— that delicious face you will see. What a time! I am continually running away from the subject. Sure this cannot be exactly the case with a complex mind—one that is imaginative, and [25] at the same time careful of its fruits, who would exist partly on sensation, partly on thought, to whom it is necessary that years should bring the philosophic mind? Such a one I consider yours, and therefore it is neces- [30] sary to your eternal happiness that you not only drink this old wine of heaven, which I shall call the redigestion of our most ethereal musings upon earth, but also increase in knowledge and know all things. I am glad to [35] hear that you are in a fair way for Easter. You will soon get through your unpleasant reading, and then!—but the world is full of troubles, and I have not much reason to think myself pestered with many. . . .

You perhaps at one time thought there was such a thing as worldly happiness to be arrived at, at certain periods of time marked out. You have of necessity from your disposition been thus led away. I scarcely remember counting upon any happiness. I look not for it if it be not in the present hour—nothing startles me beyond the moment. The setting sun will always set me to rights, or if a sparrow come before my window, I take part in its existence and pick about the gravel. The first thing that strikes me on hearing a misfortune having befallen another is this— "Well, it cannot be helped: he will have the pleasure of trying the resources of his spirit." And I beg now, my dear Bailey, that hereafter should you observe anything cold in me not to put it to the account of heartlessness, but abstraction—for I assure you I sometimes feel not the influence of a passion or affection during a whole week. And so long this sometimes continues, I begin to suspect myself, and the genuineness of my feelings at other times, thinking them a few barren tragedy tears. . . .

To John Hamilton Reynolds

February 3, 1818.

. . . .

It may be said that we ought to read our contemporaries, that Wordsworth, etc. should have their due from us. But, for the sake of a few fine imaginative or domestic passages, are we to be bullied into a certain philosophy engendered in the whims of an egotist? Every man has his speculations, but every man does not brood and peacock over them till he makes a false coinage and deceives himself. Many a man can travel to the very bourn of heaven, and yet want confidence to put down his half-seeing. Sancho [1] will invent a journey heavenward as well as anybody. We hate poetry that has a palpable design upon us, and, if we do not agree, seems to put its hand into its breeches pocket. Poetry should be great and unobtrusive, a thing which enters into one's soul, and does not startle it or amaze it with itself—but with its subject. How beautiful are the retired flowers! How would they lose their beauty were they to throng into the highway, crying out, "Admire me, I am a violet! Dote upon me, I am a primrose!" Modern poets differ from the Elizabethans in this: each of the moderns like an elector of Hanover governs his petty state and knows how many straws are swept daily from the causeways in all his dominions, and has a continual itching that all the housewives should have their coppers well scoured: The ancients were emperors of vast provinces; they had only heard of the remote ones and scarcely cared to visit them. I will cut all this —I will have no more of Wordsworth or Hunt [2] in particular. Why should we be of the tribe of Manasseh, when we can wander with Esau? [3] Why should we kick against the pricks,[4] when we can walk on roses? Why should we be owls, when we can be eagles? Why be teased with "nice-eyed wagtails," [5] when we have in sight "the cherub contemplation"? [6] Why with Wordsworth's 'Matthew with a bough of wilding in his hand,' [7] when we can have Jacques 'under an oak,' [8] etc.? The secret of the bough of wilding will run through your head faster than I can write it. Old Matthew spoke to him some years ago on some nothing, and because he happens in an evening walk to imagine the figure of the old man, he must stamp it down in black and white, and it is henceforth sacred. I don't mean to deny Wordsworth's grandeur and Hunt's merit, but I mean to say we need not be teased with grandeur and merit when we can have them uncontaminated and unobtrusive. Let us have the old poets and Robin Hood. . . .

[1] The earthy squire of Don Quixote.

[2] Leigh Hunt, poet and essayist, friend of Keats.

[3] Esau, oldest son of Isaac, was cheated out of his birthright by his brother Jacob. Manasseh was the first-born son of Joseph.

[4] I.e., why should we hurt ourselves by vain resistance? Quoted from Acts. 9:5. ("Pricks" are "goads.")

[5] A phrase from Leigh Hunt's The Nymphs.

[6] Milton, Il Penseroso.

[7] The Two April Mornings. "Wilding" is a wild plant, particularly the wild apple.

[8] As You Like It.

To John Hamilton Reynolds

May 3, 1818.

. . . .

Were I to study physic or rather medicine again, I feel it would not make the
least difference in my poetry; when the mind
is in its infancy a bias is in reality a bias,
but when we have acquired more strength, a 10
bias becomes no bias. Every department of
knowledge we see excellent and calculated
towards a great whole. I am so convinced of
this that I am glad at not having given away
my medical books, which I shall again look 15
over to keep alive the little I know thither-
wards. . . . An extensive knowledge is needful to thinking people—it takes away the
heat and fever; and helps, by widening
speculation, to ease the burden of the mys- 20
tery, a thing which I begin to understand a
little, and which weighed upon you in the
most gloomy and true sentence in your letter.
The difference of high sensations with and
without knowledge appears to me this: in 25
the latter case we are falling continually ten
thousand fathoms deep and being blown up
again, without wings, and with all horror of
a bare-shouldered creature—in the former case,
our shoulders are fledged, and we go through 30
the same air and space without fear. . . .
You may perhaps be anxious to know for
fact to what sentence in your letter I allude.
You say, "I fear there is little chance of anything else in this life." You seem by that to 35
have been going through with a more painful
and acute zest the same labyrinth that I
have. I have come to the same conclusion thus
far. My branchings out therefrom have been
numerous: one of them is the consideration 40
of Wordsworth's genius and as a help, in the
manner of gold being the meridian line of
worldly wealth, how he differs from Milton.
And here I have nothing but surmises, from
an uncertainty whether Milton's apparently 45
less anxiety for humanity proceeds from his
seeing further or not than Wordsworth. And
whether Wordsworth has in truth epic passion, and martyrs himself to the human heart,
the main region of his song. In regard to his 50

genius alone, we find what he says true as
far as we have experienced, and we can
judge no further but by larger experience; for
axioms in philosophy are not axioms until
they are proved upon our pulses. We read
fine things, but never feel them to the full
until we have gone the same steps as the
author. I know this is not plain; you will
know exactly my meaning when I say that
now I shall relish Hamlet more than I ever
have done. Or, better, you are sensible no
man can set down venery[1] as a bestial or
joyless thing until he is sick of it, and therefore all philosophizing on it would be mere
wording. Until we are sick, we understand
not; in fine, as Byron says, "Knowledge is
sorrow";[2] and I go on to say that "Sorrow is
wisdom"—and further for aught we can know
for certainty, "Wisdom is folly." So you see
how I have run away from Wordsworth and
Milton, and shall still run away from what
was in my head, to observe that some kind of
letters are good squares, others handsome
ovals, and other some orbicular, others sphe-
roid—and why should not there be another
species with two rough edges like a rat-trap?
I hope you will find all my long letters of
that species, and all will be well; for by
merely touching the spring delicately and
ethereally, the rough-edged will fly immediately into a proper compactness; and thus
you may make a good wholesome loaf, with
your own leaven in it, of my fragments. If
you cannot find this said rat-trap sufficiently
tractable, alas for me, it being an impossibility
in grain for my ink to stain otherwise. If I
scribble long letters I must play my vagaries.
I must be too heavy, or too light, for whole
pages. I must be quaint and free of tropes[3]
and figures. I must play my draughts[4] as I
please, and for my advantage and your erudition, crown a white with a black, or a black
with a white, and move into black or white,
far and near as I please. I must go from Hazlitt
to Patmore,[5] and make Wordsworth and Cole-

[1] Sexual intercourse.
[2] *Manfred*.
[3] Figures of speech.
[4] Checkers.
[5] Early nineteenth-century writer.

man [6] play at leap-frog, or keep one of them down a whole half-holiday at fly-the-garter [7]—"From Gray to Gay, from Little to Shakespeare." [8] Also as a long cause requires two or more sittings of the court, so a long letter will require two or more sittings of the breech, wherefore I shall resume after dinner.

Have you not seen a gull, an orc,[9] a sea-mew, or anything to bring this line to a proper length, and also fill up this clear part; that like the gull I may dip [10]—I hope, not out of sight—and also, like a gull, I hope to be lucky in a good-sized fish. This crossing a letter is not without its association, for checker-work leads us naturally to a milk-maid, a milkmaid to Hogarth, Hogarth to Shakespeare, Shakespeare to Hazlitt, Hazlitt to Shakespeare—and thus by merely pulling an apron-string we set a pretty peal of chimes at work. Let them chime on while, with your patience, I will return to Wordsworth—whether or no he has an extended vision or a circumscribed grandeur—whether he is an eagle in his nest or on the wing. And to be more explicit and to show you how tall I stand by the giant, I will put down a simile of human life as far as I now perceive it; that is, to the point to which I say we both have arrived at. Well, I compare human life to a large mansion of many apartments, two of which I can only describe, the doors of the rest being as yet shut upon me. The first we step into we call the infant or thoughtless chamber, in which we remain as long as we do not think. We remain there a long while, and notwithstanding the doors of the second chamber remain wide open, showing a bright appearance, we care not to hasten to it; but are at length imperceptibly impelled by the awakening of the thinking principle within us. We no sooner get into the second chamber, which I shall call the chamber of maiden-

thought, than we become intoxicated with the light and the atmosphere, we see nothing but pleasant wonders, and think of delaying there for ever in delight. However, among the effects this breathing is father of is that tremendous one of sharpening one's vision into the heart and nature of man, of convincing one's nerves that the world is full of misery and heart-break, pain, sickness, and oppression—whereby this chamber of maiden-thought becomes gradually darkened, and at the same time, on all sides of it, many doors are set open—but all dark, all leading to dark passages. We see not the balance of good and evil—we are in a mist—we are now in that state—we feel the "burden of the mystery." To this point was Wordsworth come, as far as I can conceive, when he wrote "Tintern Abbey," and it seems to me that his genius is explorative of those dark passages. Now, if we live, and go on thinking, we too shall explore them. He is a genius and superior to us, in so far as he can, more than we, make discoveries, and shed a light in them. Here I must think Wordsworth is deeper than Milton, though I think it has depended more upon the general and gregarious advance of intellect, than individual greatness of mind. From the *Paradise Lost* and the other works of Milton, I hope it is not too presuming, even between ourselves, to say, that his philosophy, human and divine, may be tolerably understood by one not much advanced in years. In his time Englishmen were just emancipated from a great superstition, and men had got hold of certain points and resting-places in reasoning which were too newly born to be doubted, and too much opposed by the mass of Europe not to be thought ethereal and authentically divine. Who could gainsay his ideas on virtue, vice, and chastity in *Comus* just at the time of the dismissal of cod-pieces and a hundred other disgraces? Who would not rest satisfied with his hintings at good and evil in the *Paradise Lost*, when just free from the Inquisition and burning in Smithfield? The Reformation produced such immediate and great benefits that Protestantism was considered under the immediate eye of heaven, and its own remaining

[6] Contemporary playwright.

[7] A variety of leapfrog.

[8] Cf. Pope: "From grave to gay, from lively to severe" (*Essay on Man*).

[9] A sea animal.

[10] Keats is writing vertically up and down the page as well as horizontally. At this point, the word "dip" is crossed by the vertical writing and partially obscured.

dogmas and superstitions then, as it were, regenerated, constituted those resting-places and seeming sure points of reasoning. From that I have mentioned, Milton, whatever he may have thought in the sequel, appears to have been content with these by his writings. He did not think into the human heart as Wordsworth has done. Yet Milton as a philosopher had sure as great powers as Wordsworth.

What is then to be inferred? O many things. It proves there is a really grand march of intellect; it proves that a mighty providence subdues the mightiest minds to the service of the time being, whether it be in human knowledge or religion. . . .

To George and Georgiana Keats

April 28, 1919.

. . . .

The whole appears to resolve into this —that man is originally a poor forked creature subject to the same mischances as the beasts of the forest, destined to hardships and disquietude of some kind or other. If he improves by degrees his bodily accommodations and comforts, at each stage, at each ascent there are waiting for him a fresh set of annoyances—he is mortal, and there is still a heaven with its stars above his head. The most interesting question that can come before us is, How far by the persevering endeavors of a seldom appearing Socrates mankind may be made happy. I can imagine such happiness carried to an extreme, but what must it end in?—death—and who could in such a case bear with death? The whole troubles of life, which are now frittered away in a series of years, would then be accumulated for the last days of a being who instead of hailing its approach would leave this world as Eve left paradise. But in truth I do not at all believe in this sort of perfectibility—the nature of the world will not admit of it—the inhabitants of the world will correspond to itself. Let the fish philosophize the ice away from the rivers in winter time, and they shall be at continual play in the tepid delight of summer. Look at the poles and at the sands of Africa, whirlpools and volcanoes—let men exterminate them and I will say that they may arrive at earthly happiness. The point at which man may arrive is as far as the parallel state in inanimate nature, and no further. For instance, suppose a rose to have sensation; it blooms on a beautiful morning, it enjoys itself. But then comes a cold wind, a hot sun —it cannot escape it, it cannot destroy its annoyances—they are as native to the world as itself. No more can man be happy in spite, the worldly elements will prey upon his nature. The common cognomen of this world among the misguided and superstitious is "a vale of tears," from which we are to be redeemed by a certain arbitrary interposition of God and taken to heaven. What a little, circumscribed, straitened notion! Call the world, if you please, "The vale of soul-making." Then you will find out the use of the world (I am speaking now in the highest terms for human nature admitting it to be immortal, which I will here take for granted for the purpose of showing a thought which has struck me concerning it). I say *"soul-making"*—soul as distinguished from an intelligence. There may be intelligences or sparks of the divinity in millions, but they are not souls till they acquire identities, till each one is personally itself. Intelligences are atoms of perception—they know and they see and they are pure. In short they are God. How then are the souls to be made? How then are these sparks which are God to have identity given them so as ever to possess a bliss peculiar to each one's individual existence? How but by the medium of a world like this? . . .

Do you not see how necessary a world of pains and troubles is to school an intelligence and make it a soul? . . .

If what I have said should not be plain enough, as I fear it may not be, I will put you in the place where I began in this series of thoughts. I mean I began by seeing how man was formed by circumstances—and what are circumstances but touchstones of his heart? And what are touchstones but provings of his heart, but fortifiers or alterers of his nature? And what is his altered nature but his soul? And what was his soul before it came into the world and had these provings and alterations and perfectionings? An intelligence without identity. And how is this identity to be made? Through the medium of the heart. And how is the heart to become this medium but in a world of circumstances? . . .

Thomas Carlyle
(1795-1881)

WHEN WALT WHITMAN HEARD THAT CARLYLE WAS DEAD, HE SAID THAT WITHOUT HIM "the array of British thought . . . of the last fifty years" would have been "like an army with no artillery." Certainly, for many years Carlyle's voice was like a big gun roaring over England, exhorting, warning, denouncing.

Before 1837 it seemed that the voice would command little or no hearing. After leaving the University of Edinburgh in 1814 without taking a degree, Carlyle entered upon a period of struggle against poverty, religious doubts, dyspepsia, and misgivings about his role in the world, a struggle that would have defeated a less rugged spirit. His reading of the skeptics undermined the Calvinistic Christianity he had inherited from his stern father and pious mother; and he had to pass through the dolorous region of the "Everlasting No" before he could recapture and reform his faith, and emerge into the triumphant affirmation of the "Everlasting Yea." This spiritual victory he achieved through his study of German idealism, which convinced him of the reality of a spiritual world and of the value of work, worship, renunciation, faith, and duty. Indeed, Carlyle began his literary career as a translator and interpreter of German literature, and his debt to his German masters remained great throughout his life.

After a tempestuous courtship he married Jane Welsh, a witty and strong-minded woman, and for six years the couple lived on her isolated farm at Craigenputtock. There Carlyle wrote some of his finest essays and developed his major ideas. There, too, he composed that most unusual and highly individual autobiography, Sartor Resartus. But the turning point of his literary career did not come until 1837, with the publication of The French Revolution, which had been written under a hardship (the first draft of volume one, lent to John Stuart Mill, was destroyed in a fire through the carelessness of a servant). This history, which interprets the Revolution as a dramatic revelation of Providence working in human affairs and which has all the graphic immediacy of a reporter's eyewitness account, was a great success. Carlyle's days of grim struggle were over.

For the next twenty years or more, according to his biographer Froude, "amidst the controversies, the arguments, the doubts, the crowding uncertainties . . . Carlyle's voice was to the young generation of Englishmen like the sound of 'Ten thousand trumpets' in their ears." Sartor Resartus, already published in the United States under the supervision of his friend Emerson, was reissued; his essays appeared in book form; he gave a number of successful lectures, including a series which later appeared as Heroes and Hero-Worship; he wrote massive biographies of Oliver Cromwell and Frederick the Great and a shorter study of his disciple John Sterling; and he continued his analysis and condemnation of the contemporary social scene with *Chartism* (1840), *Past and Present* (1843), and *Latter-Day Pamphlets* (1850).

The final period of his life began with the death of his wife in 1866. It was a period of solitude and disillusionment, though many honors came to him and his books continued to sell. During these bitter years he wrote little. After the passage of the Reform Bill of 1867, which elicited from him another outburst against democracy and a prophecy of impending doom in *Shooting Niagara: and After?*, Carlyle seemed to feel that there was little hope for England or America.

Today many readers find Carlyle unattractive both in form and content. His style, with its violence and dogmatism, its imperatives, hyperboles, and other "shock" techniques, they often regard as grotesque. They also find unpalatable his aversion to science, his antidemocratic bias, and his exaltation of the "great leader." Our experiences with twentieth-century dictatorships have made us understandably impatient with excessive hero-worship.

And yet Carlyle can teach us a great deal. He reminds us that life is more than "Mechanics" and man something better than a "more or less incompetent digestive-apparatus." In a voice as tonic and compelling as that of the Hebrew prophets, he calls us back to the bedrock virtues of faith and worship, work and duty. And though we can hardly approve his prescription of a dedicated aristocracy that will lead a nation in the path it should go, he alerts us to the dangers of a democracy that, in the leveling process, loses its reverence for great men and its recognition of an aristocracy of talent. "What we can learn from Carlyle," says Basil Willey, "is that 'democracy,' in order to survive, must be born again; it must unlearn its economic idolatries, cease to be self-seeking and mechanical, and recapture its soul by returning to its own inmost ideas. . . ."

On Heroes, Hero-worship, and the Heroic in History

Between 1837 and 1840 Carlyle gave a series of four groups of lectures in London. The last group, *On Heroes, Hero-worship, and the Heroic in History*, consisting of six lectures, discussed the hero as divinity (Odin), as prophet (Mahomet), as poet (Dante, Shakespeare), as priest (Luther, Knox), as man of letters (Johnson, Rousseau, Burns), and as king (Cromwell, Napoleon).

These lectures vividly illustrate and elaborate Carlyle's theory of history as "the essence of innumerable biographies." Stressing the role of the great man in history, he stands squarely opposed to those who see history primarily as an expression of impersonal forces and who thus relegate the individual to a place of little importance.

The Hero as Divinity . . .

We have undertaken to discourse here for a little on Great Men, their manner of appearance in our world's business, how they have shaped themselves in the world's history, what ideas men formed of them, what work they did;—on Heroes, namely, and on their reception and performance; what I call Hero-worship and the Heroic in human affairs. Too evidently this is a large topic; deserving quite other treatment than we can expect to give 5 it at present. A large topic; indeed, an illimitable one; wide as Universal History itself. For, as I take it, Universal History, the history of what man has accomplished in this world, is at bottom the History of the Great Men who have worked here. They were the leaders of men, these great ones; the modelers, patterns, and in a wide sense creators, of whatsoever the general mass of men contrived to do or to attain; all things that we see standing accomplished in the world are properly the outer material result, the practical realization and embodiment, of Thoughts that dwelt in the Great Men sent into the world: the soul of the whole world's history, it may justly be considered, were the history of these. Too clearly it is a topic we shall do no justice to in this place!

One comfort is, that Great Men, taken up in any way, are profitable company. We cannot look, however imperfectly, upon a great man, without gaining something by him. He is the living light-fountain, which it is good and pleasant to be near. The light which enlightens, which has enlightened the darkness of the world; and this not as a kindled lamp only, but rather as a natural luminary shining by the gift of Heaven; a flowing light-fountain, as I say, of native original insight, of manhood and heroic nobleness;— in whose radiance all souls feel that it is well with them. On any terms whatsoever, you will not grudge to wander in such neighborhood for a while. These Six classes [1] of Heroes, chosen out of widely-distant countries and epochs, and in mere external figure differing altogether, ought, if we look faithfully at them, to illustrate several things for us. Could we see *them* well, we should get some glimpses into the very marrow of the world's history. How happy, could I but, in any measure, in such times as these, make manifest to you the meanings of Heroism; the divine relation (for I may well call it such) which in all times unites a Great Man to other men; and thus, as it were, not exhaust my subject, but so much as break ground on it! At all events, I must make the attempt.

It is well said, in every sense, that a man's religion is the chief fact with regard to him. A man's, or a nation of men's. By religion I do not mean here the church-creed which he professes, the articles of faith which he will

[1] See headnote.

sign and, in words or otherwise, assert; not this wholly, in many cases not this at all. We see men of all kinds of professed creeds attain to almost all degrees of worth or worthlessness under each or any of them. This is not what I call religion, this profession and assertion; which is often only a profession and assertion from the outworks of the man, from the mere argumentative region of him, if even so deep as that. But the thing a man does practically believe (and this is often enough *without* asserting it even to himself, much less to others); the thing a man does practically lay to heart, and know for certain, concerning his vital relations to this mysterious Universe, and his duty and destiny there, that is in all cases the primary thing for him, and creatively determines all the rest. That is his *religion;* or, it may be, his mere skepticism and *no-religion:* the manner it is in which he feels himself to be spiritually related to the Unseen World or No-World; and I say, if you tell me what that is, you tell me to a very great extent what the man is, what the kind of things he will do is. Of a man or of a nation we inquire, therefore, first of all, What religion they had? Was it Heathenism—plurality of gods, mere sensuous representation of this Mystery of Life, and for chief recognized element therein Physical Force? Was it Christianism; faith in an Invisible, not as real only, but as the only reality; Time, through every meanest moment of it, resting on Eternity; Pagan empire of Force displaced by a nobler supremacy, that of Holiness? Was it Skepticism, uncertainty and inquiry whether there was an Unseen World, any Mystery of Life except a mad one;—doubt as to all this, or perhaps unbelief and flat denial? Answering of this question is giving us the soul of the history of the man or nation. The thoughts they had were the parents of the actions they did; their feelings were parents of their thoughts: it was the unseen and spiritual in them that determined the outward and actual; —their religion, as I say, was the great fact about them. In these Discourses, limited as we are, it will be good to direct our survey chiefly to that religious phasis of the matter. That once known well, all is known. We have chosen as the first Hero in our series, Odin the central figure of Scandinavian Paganism; an emblem to us of a most extensive province of things. Let us look for a little at the Hero as Divinity, the oldest primary form of Heroism.

Surely it seems a very strange-looking thing this Paganism; almost inconceivable to us in these days. A bewildering, inextricable jungle of delusions, confusions, falsehoods and absurdities, covering the whole field of Life! A thing that fills us with astonishment, almost, if it were possible, with incredulity— for truly it is not easy to understand that sane men could ever calmly, with their eyes open, believe and live by such a set of doctrines. That men should have worshiped their poor fellow-man as a God, and not him only, but stocks and stones, and all manner of animate and inanimate objects; and fashioned for themselves such a distracted chaos of hallucinations by way of Theory of the Universe: all this looks like an incredible fable. Nevertheless it is a clear fact that they did it. Such hideous inextricable jungle of misworships, misbeliefs, men, made as we are, did actually hold by, and live at home in. This is strange. Yes, we may pause in sorrow and silence over the depths of darkness that are in man; if we rejoice in the heights of purer vision he has attained to. Such things were and are in man; in all men; in us too.

Some speculators have a short way of accounting for the Pagan religion: mere quackery, priestcraft, and dupery, say they; no sane man ever did believe it—merely contrived to persuade other men, not worthy of the name of sane, to believe it! It will be often our duty to protest against this sort of hypothesis about men's doings and history; and I here, on the very threshold, protest against it in reference to Paganism, and to all other *isms* by which man has ever for a length of time striven to walk in this world. They have all had a truth in them, or men would not have taken them up. Quackery and dupery do abound; in religions, above all in the more advanced decaying stages of religions, they have fearfully abounded; but quackery was never the originating influence in such things; it was not the health and life of such things, but their disease, the sure precursor of their being about to die! Let us never forget this. It seems to me a most mournful hypothesis, that of quackery giving birth to any faith even in savage men. Quackery gives birth to nothing; gives death to all things. We shall not see into the true heart of anything, if we look merely at the quackeries of it; if we do not reject the quackeries altogether; as mere diseases, corruptions, with which our and all men's sole duty is to have done with them, to sweep them out of our thoughts as out of our practice. Man everywhere is the born enemy of lies.——We shall begin to have a chance of understanding Paganism, when we first admit that to its followers it was, at one time, earnestly true. Let us consider it very certain that men did believe in Paganism; men with open eyes, sound senses, men made altogether like ourselves; that we, had we been there, should have believed in it. Ask now, What Paganism could have been?

Another theory, somewhat more respectable, attributes such things to Allegory. It was a play of poetic minds, say these theorists; a shadowing-forth, in allegorical fable, in personification and visual form, of what such poetic minds had known and felt of this Universe. Which agrees, add they, with a primary law of human nature, still everywhere observably at work, though in less important things. That what a man feels intensely, he struggles to speak-out of him, to see represented before him in visual shape, and as if with a kind of life and historical reality in it. Now doubtless there is such a law, and it is one of the deepest in human nature; neither need we doubt that it did operate fundamentally in this business. The hypothesis which ascribes Paganism wholly or mostly to this agency, I call a little more respectable; but I cannot yet call it the true hypothesis. Think, would *we* believe, and take with us as our life-guidance, an allegory, a poetic sport? Not sport but earnest is what we should require. It is a most earnest thing to be alive in this world; to die is not sport for a man. Man's life never was a sport to him; it was a stern reality, altogether a serious matter to be alive!

I find, therefore, that though these Allegory theorists are on the way towards truth in this matter, they have not reached it either. Pagan Religion is indeed an Allegory, a Symbol of what men felt and knew about the Universe; and all Religions are Symbols of that, altering always as that alters: but it seems to me a radical perversion, and even *in*version, of the business, to put that forward as the origin and moving cause, when it was rather the result and termination. To get beautiful allegories, a perfect poetic symbol, was not the want of men; but to know what they were to believe about this Universe, what course they were to steer in it; what, in this mysterious Life of theirs, they had to hope and to fear, to do and to forbear doing. The *Pilgrim's Progress* is an Allegory, and a beautiful, just and serious one: but consider whether Bunyan's Allegory could have *preceded* the Faith it symbolizes! The Faith had to be already there, standing believed by everybody;—of which the Allegory could *then* become a shadow; and, with all its seriousness, we may say a *sportful shadow*, a mere play of the Fancy, in comparison with that awful Fact and scientific certainty which it poetically strives to emblem. The Allegory is the product of the certainty, not the producer of it; not in Bunyan's, nor in any other case. For Paganism, therefore, we have still to inquire, Whence came that scientific certainty, the parent of such a bewildered heap of allegories, errors and confusions? How was it, what was it?

Surely it were a foolish attempt to pretend "explaining," in this place, or in any place, such a phenomenon as that far-distant distracted cloudy imbroglio [2] of Paganism— more like a cloudfield than a distant continent of firm land and facts! It is no longer a reality, yet it was one. We ought to understand that this seeming cloudfield was once a reality; that not poetic allegory, least of all that dupery and deception was the origin of it. Men, I say, never did believe idle songs,

[2] Complicated situation.

never risked their soul's life on allegories; men in all times, especially in early earnest times, have had an instinct for detecting quacks, for detesting quacks. Let us try if, leaving out both the quack theory and the allegory one, and listening with affectionate attention to that far-off confused rumor of the Pagan ages, we cannot ascertain so much as this at least, That there was a kind of fact at the heart of them; that they too were not mendacious and distracted, but in their own poor way true and sane!

You remember that fancy of Plato's,[3] of a man who had grown to maturity in some dark distance, and was brought on a sudden into the upper air to see the sun rise. What would his wonder be, his rapt astonishment at the sight we daily witness with indifference! With the free open sense of a child, yet with the ripe faculty of a man, his whole heart would be kindled by that sight, he would discern it well to be Godlike, his soul would fall down in worship before it. Now, just such a childlike greatness was in the primitive nations. The first Pagan Thinker among rude men, the first man that began to think, was precisely this child-man of Plato's. Simple, open as a child, yet with the depth and strength of a man. Nature had as yet no name to him; he had not yet united under a name the infinite variety of sights, sounds, shapes and motions, which we now collectively name Universe, Nature, or the like,—and so with a name dismiss it from us. To the wild deep-hearted man all was yet new, not veiled under names or formulas; it stood naked, flashing-in on him there, beautiful, awful, unspeakable. Nature was to this man, what to the Thinker and Prophet it forever is, *preter*natural. [4] . . .

Worship is transcendent wonder; wonder for which there is now no limit or measure; that is worship. To these primeval men, all things and everything they saw exist beside them were an emblem of the Godlike, of some God.

And look what perennial fiber of truth was in that. To us also, through every star, through

[3] The famous allegory of the cave, found in the *Republic*, Bk. 7.
[4] Beyond the natural.

every blade of grass, is not a God made visible, if we will open our minds and eyes? We do not worship in that way now: but is it not reckoned still a merit, proof of what we call a "poetic nature," that we recognize how every object has a divine beauty in it; how every object still verily is "a window through which we may look into Infinitude itself"? He that can discern the loveliness of things, we call him Poet, Painter, Man of Genius, gifted, lovable. These poor Sabeans [5] did even what he does—in their own fashion. That they did it, in what fashion soever, was a merit: better than what the entirely stupid man did, what the horse and camel did— namely, nothing!

But now if all things whatsoever that we look upon are emblems to us of the Highest God, I add that more so than any of them is man such an emblem. You have heard of St. Chrysostom's [6] celebrated saying in reference to the Shekinah,[7] or Ark of Testimony, visible Revelation of God, among the Hebrews: "The true Shekinah is Man!" Yes, it is even so: this is no vain phrase; it is veritably so. The essence of our being, the mystery in us that calls itself "I"—ah, what words have we for such things?—is a breath of Heaven; the Highest Being reveals himself in man. This body, these faculties, this life of ours, is it not all as a vesture for that Unnamed? "There is but one Temple in the Universe," says the devout Novalis,[8] "and that is the Body of Man. Nothing is holier than that high form. Bending before men is a reverence done to this Revelation in the Flesh. We touch Heaven when we lay our hand on a human body!" This sounds much like a mere flourish of rhetoric; but it is not so. If well meditated, it will turn out to be a scientific fact; the expression, in such words as can be had, of the actual truth of the thing. *We* are the miracle of miracles—the great inscrutable mystery of God. We cannot understand it, we know not how to speak of it; but we may feel and know, if we like, that it is verily so.

Well; these truths were once more readily felt than now. The young generations of the world, who had in them the freshness of young children, and yet the depth of earnest men, who did not think they had finished-off all things in Heaven and Earth by merely giving them scientific names, but had to gaze direct at them there, with awe and wonder: they felt better what of divinity is in man and Nature;—they, without being mad, could *worship* Nature, and man more than anything else in Nature. Worship, that is, as I said above, admire without limit: this, in the full use of their faculties, with all sincerity of heart, they could do. I consider Hero-worship to be the grand modifying element in that ancient system of thought. What I called the perplexed jungle of Paganism sprang, we may say, out of many roots: every admiration, adoration of a star or natural object, was a root or fiber of a root; but Hero-worship is the deepest root of all; the tap-root, from which in a great degree all the rest were nourished and grown.

And now if worship even of a star had some meaning in it, how much more might that of a Hero! Worship of a Hero is transcendent admiration of a Great Man. I say great men are still admirable; I say there is, at bottom, nothing else admirable! No nobler feeling than this of admiration for one higher than himself dwells in the breast of man. It is to this hour, and at all hours, the vivifying influence in man's life. Religion I find stands upon it; not Paganism only, but far higher and truer religions—all religion hitherto known. Hero-worship, heartfelt prostrate admiration, submission, burning, boundless, for a noblest godlike Form of Man—is not that the germ of Christianity itself? The greatest of all Heroes in One—whom we do not name here! Let sacred silence meditate that sacred matter; you will find it the ultimate perfection of a principle extant throughout man's whole history on earth.

Or coming into lower, less *un*speakable provinces, is not all Loyalty akin to religious Faith also? Faith is loyalty to some inspired

[5] Syrian inhabitants of Mesopotamia who worshiped celestial bodies.

[6] Chrysostom, early Church father.

[7] Manifestation of the divine presence.

[8] Pseudonym of Friedrich von Hardenberg, German romantic writer and mystic.

Teacher, some spiritual Hero. And what therefore is loyalty proper, the life-breath of all society, but an effluence of Hero-worship, submissive admiration for the truly great? Society is founded on Hero-worship. All dignities of rank, on which human association rests, are what we may call a *Hero*-archy (Government of Heroes)—or a Hierarchy, for it is "sacred" enough withal! The Duke means *Dux,* Leader; King is *Kön-ning, Kan-ning,*[9] Man that *knows* or *cans.* Society everywhere is some representation, not *in*supportably inaccurate, of a graduated Worship of Heroes; —reverence and obedience done to men really great and wise. Not *in*supportably inaccurate, I say! They are all as bank-notes, these social dignitaries, all representing gold;—and several of them, alas, always are *forged* notes. We can do with some forged false notes; with a good many even; but not with all, or the most of them forged! No: there have to come revolutions then; cries of Democracy,[10] Liberty, and Equality, and I know not what:—the notes being all false, and no gold to be had for *them,* people take to crying in their despair that there is no gold, that there never was any!—"Gold," Hero-worship, *is* nevertheless, as it was always and everywhere, and cannot cease till man himself ceases.

I am well aware that in these days Hero-worship, the thing I call Hero-worship, professes to have gone out, and finally ceased. This, for reasons which it will be worth while some time to inquire into, is an age that as it were denies the existence of great men; denies the desirableness of great men. Show our critics a great man, a Luther for example, they begin to what they call "account" for him; not to worship him, but take dimensions of him—and bring him out to be a little kind of man! He was the "creature of the Time," they say; the Time called him forth, the Time did everything, he nothing—but what we the little

critic could have done too! This seems to me but melancholy work. The Time call forth? Alas, we have known Times *call* loudly enough for their great man; but not find him when they called! He was not there; Providence had not sent him; the Time, *calling* its loudest, had to go down to confusion and wreck because he would not come when called.

For if we will think of it, no Time need have gone to ruin, could it have *found* a man great enough, a man wise and good enough: wisdom to discern truly what the Time wanted, valor to lead it on the right road thither; these are the salvation of any Time. But I liken common languid Times, with their unbelief, distress, perplexity, with their languid doubting characters and embarrassed circumstances, impotently crumbling down into ever worse distress towards final ruin;— all this I liken to dry dead fuel, waiting for the lightning out of Heaven that shall kindle it. The great man, with his free force direct out of God's own hand, is the lightning. His word is the wise healing word which all can believe in. All blazes round him now, when he has once struck on it, into fire like his own. The dry moldering sticks are thought to have called him forth. They did want him greatly; but as to calling him forth—!—Those are critics of small vision, I think, who cry: "See, is it not the sticks that made the fire?" No sadder proof can be given by a man of his own littleness than disbelief in great men. There is no sadder symptom of a generation than such general blindness to the spiritual lightning, with faith only in the heap of barren dead fuel. It is the last consummation of unbelief. In all epochs of the world's history, we shall find the Great Man to have been the indispensable savior of his epoch;— the lightning, without which the fuel never would have burnt. The History of the World, I said already, was the Biography of Great Men.

Such small critics do what they can to promote unbelief and universal spiritual paralysis; but happily they cannot always completely succeed. In all times it is possible for a man to arise great enough to feel that

[9] Carlyle is wrong here; "king" has a different derivation.
[10] Carlyle had little use for democracy, which he once defined as the "despair of finding any Heroes to govern you, and the contented putting up with the want of them."

they and their doctrines are chimeras and cobwebs. And what is notable, in no time whatever can they entirely eradicate out of living men's hearts a certain altogether peculiar reverence for Great Men; genuine admiration, loyalty, adoration, however dim and perverted it may be. Hero-worship endures for ever while man endures. . . .

Yes, from Norse Odin to English Samuel Johnson, from the divine Founder of Christianity to the withered Pontiff [11] of Encyclopedism, in all times and places, the Hero has been worshiped. It will ever be so. We all love great men; love, venerate, and bow down submissive before great men: nay can we honestly bow down to anything else? Ah, does not every true man feel that he is himself made higher by doing reverence to what is really above him? No nobler or more blessed feeling dwells in man's heart. And to me it is very cheering to consider that no skeptical logic, or general triviality, insincerity and aridity of any Time and its influences can destroy this noble inborn loyalty and worship that is in man. In times of unbelief, which soon have to become times of revolution, much down-rushing, sorrowful decay and ruin is visible to everybody. For myself in these days, I seem to see in this indestructibility of Hero-worship the everlasting adamant lower than which the confused wreck of revolutionary things cannot fall. The confused wreck of things crumbling and even crashing and tumbling all round us in these revolutionary ages, will get down so far; *no* farther. It is an eternal corner-stone, from which they can begin to build themselves up again. That man, in some sense or other, worships Heroes; that we all of us reverence and must ever reverence Great Men: this is, to me, the living rock amid all rushings-down whatsoever;—the one fixed point in modern revolutionary history, otherwise as if bottomless and shoreless. . . .

(1841)

STUDY AIDS: 1. What two theories about the origin of pagan religion does Carlyle refute? How does he refute each? What is his own theory? What is the relation of this theory to his doctrine of Heroes?

2. Carlyle has been condemned as a kind of ideological father of Nazism and Fascism. What ideas in this lecture might justify such an accusation? How would you defend Carlyle against the charge? Is Carlyle's view of history (as primarily determined by great men) adequate? In our day, are we guilty of excessive "debunking" of great men?

Past and Present

Past and Present is Carlyle's most important work of social criticism. Growing out of his deep concern with the condition of the poor in Great Britain, it was, as he put it, a most "red hot, indignant thing."

The work is in four books, one of which deals with the past—specifically with the feudal days of the thirteenth century. For Carlyle this was a period of social health, when leaders took their responsibilities seriously, when each man knew his place and his work in the closely knit order, when loyalty to heroes was a real dynamic force, and when sincere religious faith permeated all of society. Two books treat of the present, with its lack of responsibility in the rulers, its trust in political panaceas like democracy, its substitution of the Quack for the Hero, its devotion to "liberty," "Cash-Payment," and "laissez faire," and its replacement of true religious faith by materialism, cant, and hypocrisy.

The final book suggests the cure. Society must be ordered like an army, with a true aristocracy providing responsible leadership. The "Captains of Industry" must learn to apply the same energy to the solution of social problems that they now do to the making of money. The State must become more powerful, and education must be more carefully directed. Above all, a radical

---

[11] Voltaire, the great French satirist, who contributed to the famous French Encyclopedia and who embraced the rationalistic, skeptical doctrines which found expression in that work.

regeneration of the national soul must take place, in which the "Gospel of Mammonism" is superseded by a true gospel of work, worship, faith, and duty.

Gospel of Mammonism [1]

Reader, even Christian Reader as thy title goes, hast thou any notion of Heaven and Hell? I rather apprehend not. Often as the words are on our tongue, they have got a fabulous or semi-fabulous character for most of us, and pass on like a kind of transient similitude, like a sound signifying little.

Yet it is well worth while for us to know, once and always, that they are not a similitude, nor a fable nor semifable; that they are an everlasting highest fact! "No Lake of Sicilian or other sulphur [2] burns now anywhere in these ages," sayest thou? Well, and if there did not! Believe that there does not; believe it if thou wilt, nay hold by it as a real increase, a rise to higher stages, to wider horizons and empires. All this has vanished, or has not vanished; believe as thou wilt as to all this. But that an Infinite of Practical Importance, speaking with strict arithmetical exactness, an *Infinite,* has vanished or can vanish from the Life of any Man—this thou shalt not believe! O brother, the Infinite of Terror, of Hope, of Pity, did it not at any moment disclose itself to thee, indubitable, unnamable? Came it never, like the gleam of *preter*natural [3] eternal Oceans, like the voice of old Eternities, far-sounding through thy heart of hearts? Never? Alas, it was not thy Liberalism, then; it was thy Animalism! The Infinite is more sure than any other fact. But only men can discern it; mere building beavers, spinning arachnes, [4] much more the predatory vulturous and vulpine species, do not discern it well!—

"The word Hell," says Sauerteig, [5] "is still frequently in use among the English people; but I could not without difficulty ascertain what they meant by it. Hell generally signifies the Infinite Terror, the thing a man *is* infinitely afraid of, and shudders and shrinks from, struggling with his whole soul to escape from it. There is a Hell therefore, if you will consider, which accompanies man, in all stages of his history, and religious or other development; but the Hells of men and Peoples differ notably. With Christians it is the infinite terror of being found guilty before the Just Judge. With old Romans, I conjecture, it was the terror not of Pluto, [6] for whom probably they cared little, but of doing unworthily, doing unvirtuously, which was their word for un*man*fully. And now what is it, if you pierce through his Cants, [7] his oft-repeated Hearsays, what he calls his Worships and so forth—what is it that the modern English soul does, in very truth, dread infinitely, and contemplate with entire despair? What *is* his Hell, after all these reputable, oft-repeated Hearsays, what is it? With hesitation, with astonishment, I pronounce it to be: The terror of 'Not succeeding'—of not making money, fame, or some other figure in the world—chiefly of not making money! Is not that a somewhat singular Hell?"

Yes, O Sauerteig, it is very singular. If we do not "succeed," where is the use of us? We had better never have been born. "Tremble intensely," as our friend the Emperor of China says; *there* is the black Bottomless of Terror; what Sauerteig calls the "Hell of the English"!—But indeed this Hell belongs naturally to the Gospel of Mammonism, which also has its corresponding Heaven. For there *is* one Reality among so many Phantasms; about one thing we are entirely in earnest: The making of money. Working Mammonism does divide the world with idle game-preserving Dilettantism [8]—thank Heaven that

[1] From Book 3, ch. 2. Mammon is the personification of wealth; hence, "Mammonism" is the greedy pursuit of riches.

[2] Sulphur was one of the main exports of Sicily.

[3] Out of the ordinary course of nature.

[4] Spiders. Arachne was a Lydian maiden who challenged Athena to a weaving contest. Because of her presumption she was turned into a spider.

[5] "Sour-dough"—the name of a professor invented by Carlyle to be his occasional spokesman.

[6] Ruling deity of Hades.

[7] Insincere speeches, especially those of a pious nature.

[8] I.e., the activities of the sports-loving aristocracy.

there is even a Mammonism, *anything* we are in earnest about! Idleness is worst, Idleness alone is without hope; [9] work earnestly at anything, you will by degrees learn to work at almost all things. There is endless hope in work, were it even work at making money.

True, it must be owned, we for the present, with our Mammon-Gospel, have come to strange conclusions. We call it a Society; and go about professing openly the totalest separation, isolation. Our life is not a mutual helpfulness; but rather, cloaked under due laws-of-war, named "fair competition" and so forth, it is a mutual hostility. We have profoundly forgotten everywhere that *Cash-payment* is not the sole relation of human beings; we think, nothing doubting, that *it* absolves and liquidates all engagements of man. "My starving workers?" answers the rich mill-owner; "Did not I hire them fairly in the market? Did I not pay them, to the last sixpence, the sum covenanted for? What have I to do with them more?"—Verily Mammon-worship is a melancholy creed. When Cain, for his own behoof, had killed Abel, and was questioned, "Where is thy brother?" he too made answer, "Am I my brother's keeper?" Did I not pay my brother *his* wages, the thing he had merited from me?

O sumptuous Merchant-Prince, illustrious game-preserving Duke, is there no way of "killing" thy brother but Cain's rude way! "A good man by the very look of him, by his very presence with us as a fellow wayfarer in this Life-pilgrimage, *promises* so much." Woe to him if he forget all such promises, if he never know that they were given! To a deadened soul, seared with the brute Idolatry of Sense, to whom going to Hell is equivalent to not making money, all "promises," and moral duties, that cannot be pleaded for in Courts of Requests,[10] address themselves in vain. Money he can be ordered to pay, but nothing more. I have not heard in all Past History, and expect not to hear in all Future History, of any Society anywhere under God's Heaven supporting itself on

such Philosophy. The Universe is not made so; it is made otherwise than so. The man or nation of men that thinks it is made so, marches forward nothing doubting, step after step; but marches—whither we know! In these last two centuries of Atheistic Government (near two centuries now, since the blessed restoration of his Sacred Majesty, and Defender of the Faith, Charles Second), I reckon that we have pretty well exhausted what of "firm earth" there was for us to march on—and are now, very ominously, shuddering, reeling, and let us hope trying to recoil, on the cliff's edge!—

For out of this that we call Atheism come so many other *isms* and falsities, each falsity with its misery at its heels!—A soul is not like wind (*spiritus,* or breath) contained within a capsule; the ALMIGHTY MAKER is not like a Clockmaker that once, in old immemorial ages, having *made* his Horologe [11] of a Universe, sits ever since and sees it go! Not at all. Hence comes Atheism; come, as we say, many other *isms;* and as the sum of all, comes Valetism, the *reverse* of Heroism; sad root of all woes whatsoever. For indeed, as no man ever saw the above-said wind-element enclosed within its capsule, and finds it at bottom more deniable than conceivable; so too he finds, in spite of Bridgewater Bequests,[12] your Clockmaker Almighty an entirely questionable affair, a deniable affair—and accordingly denies it, and along with it so much else. Alas, one knows not what and how much else! For the faith in an Invisible, Unnamable, Godlike, present everywhere in all that we see and work and suffer, is the essence of all faith whatsoever; and that once denied, or still worse, asserted with lips only, and out of bound prayer-books only, what other thing remains believable? That Cant well-ordered is marketable Cant; that Heroism means gas-lighted Histrionism,[13] that seen

[9] In another place Carlyle says: "One monster there is in the world: the idle man."
[10] Local small-debt courts.
[11] Any instrument for telling time. This conception of an "absentee" Creator was a common one in the eighteenth century.
[12] Through a bequest of the last Earl of Bridgewater, eight treatises were published between 1833 and 1840 on "The Power, Wisdom, and Goodness of God as Manifested in the Creation."
[13] Play-acting.

with "clear eyes" (as they call Valet-eyes), no man is a Hero, or ever was a Hero, but all men are Valets and Varlets.[14] The accursed practical quintessence of all sorts of Unbelief! For if there be now no Hero, and the Histrio himself begin to be seen into, what hope is there for the seed of Adam here below? We are the doomed everlasting prey of the Quack; who, now in this guise, now in that, is to filch us, to pluck and eat us, by such modes as are convenient for him. For the modes and guises I care little. The Quack once inevitable, let him come swiftly, let him pluck and eat me—swiftly, that I may at least have done with him; for in his Quack-world I can have no wish to linger. Though he slay me, yet will I *not* trust in him.[15] Though he conquer nations, and have all the Flunkies of the Universe shouting at his heels, yet will I know well that *he* is an Inanity; that for him and his there is no continuance appointed, save only in Gehenna [16] and the Pool. Alas, the Atheist world, from its utmost summits of Heaven and Westminster-Hall, downwards through poor seven-feet Hats [17] and "Unveracities fallen hungry," down to the lowest cellars and neglected hunger-dens of it, is very wretched.

One of Dr. Alison's [18] Scotch facts struck us much. A poor Irish Widow, her husband having died in one of the Lanes of Edinburgh, went forth with her three children, bare of all resource, to solicit help from the Charitable Establishments of that City. At this Charitable Establishment and then at that she was refused; referred from one to the other, helped by none—till she had exhausted them all; till her strength and heart

failed her; she sank down in typhus fever; died, and infected her Lane with fever, so that "seventeen other persons" died of fever there in consequence. The human Physician asks thereupon, as with a heart too full for speaking, Would it not have been *economy* to help this poor Widow? She took typhus fever, and killed seventeen of you!—Very curious. The forlorn Irish Widow applies to her fellow-creatures, as if saying, "Behold I am sinking, bare of help; ye must help me! I am your sister, bone of your bone; one God made us; ye must help me!" They answer, "No, impossible; thou art no sister of ours." But she proves her sisterhood; her typhus fever kills *them*—they actually were her brothers, though denying it! Had human creature ever to go lower for a proof?

For, as indeed was very natural in such case, all government of the Poor by the Rich has long ago been given over to Supply-and-demand, *Laissez faire*,[19] and suchlike, and universally declared to be "impossible." "You are no sister of ours; what shadow of proof is there? Here are our parchments, our padlocks, proving indisputably our money-safes to be *ours*, and you to have no business with them. Depart! It is impossible!"—Nay what wouldst thou thyself have us do? cry indignant readers. Nothing, my friends—till you have got a soul for yourselves again. Till then all things are "impossible." Till then I cannot even bid you buy, as the old Spartans would have done,[20] twopence worth of powder and lead, and compendiously [21] shoot to death this poor Irish Widow—even that is "impossible" for you. Nothing is left but that she prove her sisterhood by dying, and infecting you with typhus. Seventeen of you lying dead will not deny such proof that she *was* flesh of your flesh; and perhaps some of the living may lay it to heart.

"Impossible—" Of a certain two-legged animal with feathers it is said, if you draw a

[14] Scoundrels.

[15] Cf. Job 13:15: "Though he slay me, yet will I trust in him. . . ."

[16] A New Testament name for Hell; actually a place of refuse near Jerusalem.

[17] In the previous chapter Carlyle tells of a London hatter who advertises his wares by having a "huge lath-and-plaster Hat, seven-feet high, upon wheels," rolled through the streets. For Carlyle the hatter "has not attempted to make better hats . . . but his whole industry is turned to *persuade* us that he has made such!"

[18] W. P. Alison, *Observations on the Management of the Poor in Scotland.*

[19] "Let do"—that is, let people do what they choose; the theory that government should interfere as little as possible with economic activities.

[20] Plutarch says that the slaves (helots) of the Spartans were killed when they were old and useless, since they could not be sold or freed.

[21] Summarily.

distinct chalk-circle round him, he sits imprisoned, as if girt with an iron ring of Fate; and will die there, though within sight of victuals—or sit in sick misery there, and be fatted to death. The name of this poor two-legged animal is—Goose; and they make of him, when well fattened, *Pâté de foie gras*,[22] much prized by some!

Labor

For there is a perennial nobleness, and even sacredness, in Work. Were he never so benighted, forgetful of his high calling, there is always hope in a man that actually and earnestly works: in Idleness alone is there perpetual despair. Work, never so Mammonish, mean, *is* in communication with Nature; the real desire to get Work done will itself lead one more and more to truth, to Nature's appointments and regulations, which are truth.

The latest Gospel in this world is, Know thy work and do it. "Know thyself":[1] long enough has that poor "self" of thine tormented thee; thou wilt never get to "know" it, I believe! Think it not thy business, this of knowing thyself; thou art an unknowable individual: know what thou canst work at; and work at it, like a Hercules![2] That will be thy better plan.

It has been written, "an endless significance lies in Work"; a man perfects himself by working. Foul jungles are cleared away, fair seedfields rise instead, and stately cities; and withal the man himself first ceases to be a jungle and foul unwholesome desert thereby. Consider how, even in the meanest sorts of Labor, the whole soul of a man is composed into a kind of real harmony, the instant he sets himself to work! Doubt, Desire, Sorrow, Remorse, Indignation, Despair itself, all these like helldogs lie beleaguering the soul of the poor dayworker, as of every man: but he bends himself with free valor against his task,

and all these are stilled, all these shrink murmuring far off into their caves. The man is now a man. The blessed glow of Labor in him, is it not as purifying fire, wherein all poison is burnt up, and of sour smoke itself there is made bright blessed flame!

Destiny, on the whole, has no other way of cultivating us. A formless Chaos, once set it *revolving,* grows round and ever rounder; ranges itself, by mere force of gravity, into strata, spherical courses; is no longer a Chaos, but a round compacted World. What would become of the Earth, did she cease to revolve? In the poor old Earth, so long as she revolves, all inequalities, irregularities disperse themselves; all irregularities are incessantly becoming regular. Hast thou looked on the Potter's wheel—one of the venerablest objects; old as the Prophet Ezekiel and far older? Rude lumps of clay, how they spin themselves up, by mere quick whirling, into beautiful circular dishes. And fancy the most assiduous Potter, but without his wheel; reduced to make dishes or rather amorphous botches, by mere kneading and baking! Even such a Potter were Destiny, with a human soul that would rest and lie at ease, that would not work and spin! Of an idle unrevolving man the kindest Destiny, like the most assiduous Potter without wheel, can bake and knead nothing other than a botch; let her spend on him what expensive coloring, what gilding and enameling she will, he is but a botch. Not a dish; no, a bulging, kneaded, crooked, shambling, squint-cornered,[3] amorphous botch —a mere enameled vessel of dishonor! Let the idle think of this.

Blessed is he who has found his work; let him ask no other blessedness. He has a work, a life-purpose; he has found it, and will follow it! How, as a free-flowing channel, dug and torn by noble force through the sour mud-swamp of one's existence, like an ever-deepening river there, it runs and flows;—draining off the sour festering water, gradually from the root of the remotest grass-blade; making, instead of pestilential swamp, a green fruitful meadow with its clear-flowing stream. How blessed for the meadow itself, let the stream

---

[22] A paste made with fattened goose livers.

[1] A fundamental precept of Greek philosophy.
[2] Son of Jupiter, noted for his strength and for accomplishing twelve gigantic labors.

[3] Irregular.

and *its* value be great or small! Labor is Life: from the inmost heart of the Worker rises his god-given Force, the sacred celestial Life-essence breathed into him by Almighty God; from his inmost heart awakens him to all nobleness—to all knowledge, "self-knowledge" and much else, so soon as Work fitly begins. Knowledge? The knowledge that will hold good in working, cleave thou to that; for Nature herself accredits that, says Yea to that. Properly thou hast no other knowledge but what thou hast got by working: the rest is yet all a hypothesis of knowledge; a thing to be argued of in schools, a thing floating in the clouds, in endless logic-vortices, till we try it and fix it. "Doubt, of whatever kind, can be ended by Action alone." [4]

And again, hast thou valued Patience, Courage, Perseverance, Openness to light; readiness to own thyself mistaken, to do better next time? All these, all virtues in wrestling with the dim brute Powers of Fact, in ordering of thy fellows in such wrestle, there and elsewhere not at all, thou wilt continually learn. Set down a brave Sir Christopher [5] in the middle of black ruined Stone-heaps, of foolish unarchitectural Bishops, redtape Officials, idle Nell-Gwyn [6] Defenders of the Faith; and see whether he will ever raise a Paul's Cathedral out of all that, yea or no! Rough, rude, contradictory are all things and persons, from the mutinous masons and Irish hodmen, up to the idle Nell-Gwyn Defenders, to blustering redtape Officials, foolish unarchitectural Bishops. All these things and persons are there not for Christopher's sake and his Cathedral's; they are there for their own sake mainly! Christopher will have to conquer and constrain all these—if he be able. All these are against him. Equitable Nature herself, who carries her mathematics and architectonics not on the face of her, but deep in the hidden heart of her—Nature herself is but partially for him; will be wholly against him, if he constrain her not! His very

money, where is it to come from? The pious munificence of England lies far-scattered, distant, unable to speak, and say, "I am here"; —must be spoken to before it can speak. Pious munificence, and all help, is so silent, invisible like the gods; impediment, contradictions manifold are so loud and near! O brave Sir Christopher, trust thou in those notwithstanding, and front all these; understand all these; by valiant patience, noble effort, insight, by man's-strength, vanquish and compel all these —and, on the whole, strike down victoriously the last topstone of that Paul's Edifice; thy monument for certain centuries, the stamp "Great Man" impressed very legibly on Portland-stone [7] there!—

Yes, all manner of help, and pious response from Men or Nature, is always what we call silent; cannot speak or come to light, till it be seen, till it be spoken to. Every noble work is at first "impossible." In very truth, for every noble work the possibilities will lie diffused through Immensity; inarticulate, undiscoverable except to faith. Like Gideon [8] thou shalt spread out thy fleece at the door of thy tent; see whether under the wide arch of Heaven there be any bounteous moisture, or none. Thy heart and life-purpose shall be as a miraculous Gideon's fleece, spread out in silent appeal to Heaven: and from the kind Immensities, what from the poor unkind Localities and town and country Parishes there never could, blessed dew-moisture to suffice thee shall have fallen!

Work is of a religious nature—work is of a *brave* nature; which it is the aim of all religion to be. All work of man is as the swimmer's: a waste ocean threatens to devour him; if he front it not bravely, it will keep its word. By incessant wise defiance of it, lusty rebuke and buffet of it, behold how it loyally supports him, bears him as its conqueror along. "It is so," says Goethe, "with all things that man undertakes in this world."

[4] A saying of Goethe.
[5] Sir Christopher Wren, the architect who rebuilt much of London after the Great Fire of 1666, notably St. Paul's Cathedral.
[6] Actress, and mistress of Charles II.

[7] A limestone from the Isle of Portland.
[8] Cf. Judges 6:37-40. After Gideon placed a fleece of wool upon the floor, it became wet while the surrounding ground remained dry. Through this miracle he was assured of the Lord's protection of Israel.

Brave Sea-captain, Norse Sea-king—Columbus, my hero, royalest Sea-king of all! it is no friendly environment this of thine, in the waste deep waters; around thee mutinous discouraged souls, behind thee disgrace and ruin, before thee the unpenetrated veil of Night. Brother, these wild water-mountains, bounding from their deep bases (ten miles deep, I am told), are not entirely there on thy behalf! Meseems *they* have other work than 10 floating thee forward—and the huge Winds, that sweep from Ursa Major [9] to the Tropics and Equators, dancing their giant-waltz through the kingdoms of Chaos and Immensity, they care little about filling rightly or 15 filling wrongly the small shoulder-of-mutton sails in this cockle-skiff [10] of thine! Thou art not among articulate-speaking friends, my brother; thou art among immeasurable dumb monsters, tumbling, howling wide as the 20 world here. Secret, far off, invisible to all hearts but thine, there lies a help in them: see how thou wilt get at that. Patiently thou wilt wait till the mad Southwester spend itself saving thyself by dextrous science of defense, 25 the while: valiantly, with swift decision, wilt thou strike in, when the favoring East, the Possible, springs up. Mutiny of men thou wilt sternly repress; weakness, despondency, thou wilt cheerily encourage: thou 30 wilt swallow down complaint, unreason, weariness, weakness of others and thyself;—

how much wilt thou swallow down! There shall be a depth of Silence in thee, deeper than this Sea, which is but ten miles deep: a Silence unsoundable; known to God only. 5 Thou shalt be a Great Man. Yes, my World-Soldier, thou of the World Marine-service—thou wilt have to be *greater* than this tumultuous unmeasured World here round thee is; thou, in thy strong soul, as with wrestler's arms, shalt embrace it, harness it down; and make it bear thee on—to new Americas, or whither God wills!

(1843)

STUDY AIDS: 1. Carlyle's style has been compared to that of the Old Testament prophets. What elements of his style make the comparison apt? Is it a style appropriate to his purpose?
2. Define fully the "Gospel of Mammonism." What is its Hell, its Heaven? How does the incident of the Irish widow who died of typhoid illustrate one of Carlyle's points? What is the meaning of the final parable about the goose?
3. Why does Carlyle place such a high value on labor? What images does he use to bring out his ideas? Why is work a form of worship for Carlyle? Why do you think he chooses Sir Christopher Wren and Columbus as illustrations of true workers?
4. Are any of Carlyle's comments in these two essays still applicable to society? What do you think of his suggested solutions to the problems he is concerned with?

Thomas Babington Macaulay
(1800–1859)

THE QUALITIES OF MIND THAT SERVED MACAULAY IN LATER YEARS WERE EVIDENT FROM his childhood. As a small boy he read with extreme rapidity, and he had an incredibly tenacious memory. If all the copies of *Paradise Lost* and *Pilgrim's Progress* were destroyed, he once said, he would try "to reproduce them both from recollection," and it was probably no idle boast.

After his graduation from Cambridge, Macaulay leaped into prominence with a brilliant essay on Milton in the *Edinburgh Review* (1825). In 1830 he entered Parliament, mak-

---

[9] The Great Bear or Big Dipper, a constellation.
[10] A small, fragile boat.

ing his first speech the next year in favor of the Reform Bill. For four years he was in India, where he helped prepare a new penal code and encouraged native education.

Returning to England, he continued his political life, which became less demanding with the fall of the Whigs in 1841 and ceased for a while with the loss of his Edinburgh seat in 1847. He then completed his four-volume *History of England* (1848–1855). Again he was returned to Parliament (1852–1856), was appointed Lord Rector of the University of Glasgow, and was made Baron Macaulay.

Carlyle said of Macaulay that "he had no vision," and Arnold spoke of his "confident shallowness." It is true that Macaulay was not a man of deep and subtle insights and that his was a practical mind, contemptuous of speculative philosophy, believing that "an acre in Middlesex is better than a principality in Utopia." Undoubtedly he was too dogmatic, too sure of his own position.

But with all his shortcomings Macaulay was sensible, vigorous, direct. And whether we agree with his philosophy or not, we have to admire his style, one of the most distinctive prose styles in English. Fond of parallels and antitheses, dramatic contrasts of blacks and whites, and concrete illustrations, Macaulay is always clear and vivid. He could also make history come alive. His account of England in 1685 (the famous third chapter of volume one of his *History of England*), with its graphic detail and sharp contrasts, is a brilliantly successful effort to picture and interpret a bygone era.

Francis Bacon

The following selection is something less than half of the extensive article that Macaulay contributed to the *Edinburgh Review* (July, 1837) as a review of a new edition of Bacon's works.

. . . .

Two words form the key of the Baconian doctrine, utility and progress. The ancient philosophy disdained to be useful, and was content to be stationary. It dealt largely in 5 theories of moral perfection, which were so sublime that they never could be more than theories; in attempts to solve insoluble enigmas; in exhortations to the attainment of unattainable frames of mind. It could not con- 10 descend to the humble office of ministering to the comfort of human beings. All the schools contemned that office as degrading; some censured it as immoral. Once indeed Posidonius, a distinguished writer of the age 15 of Cicero and Caesar, so far forgot himself as to enumerate, among the humbler blessings which mankind owed to philosophy, the discovery of the principle of the arch, and the introduction of the use of metals. This 20 eulogy was considered as an affront, and was taken up with proper spirit. Seneca[1] ve-

[1] Roman Stoic philosopher.

hemently disclaims these insulting compliments. Philosophy, according to him, has nothing to do with teaching men to rear arched roofs over their heads. The true philosopher does not care whether he has an arched roof or any roof. Philosophy has nothing to do with teaching men the uses of metals. She teaches us to be independent of all material substances, of all mechanical contrivances. The wise man lives according to nature. Instead of attempting to add to the physical comforts of his species, he regrets that his lot was not cast in that golden age when the human race had no protection against the cold but the skins of wild beasts, no screen from the sun but a cavern. To impute to such a man any share in the invention or improvement of a plough, a ship, or a mill is an insult. "In my own time," says Seneca, "there have been inventions of this sort, transparent windows, tubes for diffusing warmth equally through all parts of a building, shorthand, which has been carried to such a perfection that a writer can keep pace with the most rapid speaker. But the inventing of such things is drudgery for the lowest slaves; philosophy lies deeper. It is not her office to teach men how to use their hands. The object of her lessons is to form the soul. *Non est, inquam, instrumentorum ad usus necessarios opifex."* [2] If the *non* were left out, this last sentence would be no bad description of the Baconian philosophy, and would, indeed, very much resemble several expressions in the *Novum Organum.* "We shall next be told," exclaims Seneca, "that the first shoemaker was a philosopher." For our own part, if we are forced to make our choice between the first shoemaker and the author of the three books "On Anger," we pronounce for the shoemaker. It may be worse to be angry than to be wet. But shoes have kept millions from being wet; and we doubt whether Seneca ever kept anybody from being angry.

It is very reluctantly that Seneca can be brought to confess that any philosopher had ever paid the smallest attention to anything that could possibly promote what vulgar people would consider as the well-being of mankind. He labors to clear Democritus [3] from the disgraceful imputation of having made the first arch, and Anacharsis [4] from the charge of having contrived the potter's wheel. He is forced to own that such a thing might happen; and it may also happen, he tells us, that a philosopher may be swift of foot. But it is not in his character of philosopher that he either wins a race or invents a machine. No, to be sure. The business of a philosopher was to declaim in praise of poverty with two millions sterling out at usury, to meditate epigrammatic conceits about the evils of luxury, in gardens which moved the envy of sovereigns, to rant about liberty, while fawning on the insolent and pampered freedmen of a tyrant, to celebrate the divine beauty of virtue with the same pen which had just be-

fore written a defense of the murder of a mother by a son.[5]

From the cant of this philosophy, a philosophy meanly proud of its own unprofitableness, it is delightful to turn to the lessons of the great English teacher. We can almost forgive all the faults of Bacon's life when we read that singularly graceful and dignified passage: *"Ego certe, ut de me ipso, quod res est, loquar, et in iis quæ nunc edo, et in iis quæ in posterum meditor, dignitatem ingenii et nominis mei, si qua sit, sæpius sciens et volens projicio, dum commodis humanis inserviam; quique architectus fortasse in philosophia et scientiis esse debeam, etiam operarius, et bajulus, et quidvis demum fio, cum haud pauca quæ omnino fieri necesse sit, alii autem ob innatam superbiam subterfugiant, ipsi sustineam et exsequar."* [6] This *philanthropia,* which, as he said in one of the most remarkable of his early letters, "was so fixed in his mind, as it could not be removed," this majestic humility, this persuasion that nothing can be too insignificant for the attention of the wisest, which is not too insignificant to give pleasure or pain to the meanest, is the great characteristic distinction, the essential spirit of the Baconian philosophy. We trace it in all that Bacon has written on physics, on laws, on morals. And we conceive that from this peculiarity all the other peculiarities of his system directly and almost necessarily sprang.

The spirit which appears in the passage of Seneca to which we have referred tainted the whole body of the ancient philosophy from the time of Socrates downwards, and took possession of intellects with which that of Seneca cannot for a moment be compared. It

---

[2] "She is not, I say, the maker of instruments for necessary purposes."

[3] Greek philosopher of 5th–4th century B.C.

[4] A Scythian prince who visited Athens in the 6th century B.C. in search of knowledge.

[5] All the foregoing comments are directed against Seneca.

[6] "To say truly how the matter stands with me, both in regard to the works I am now publishing and in those I am planning, I often knowingly and willingly ignore the glory of my wit and fame (if I have any) in my efforts to advance human welfare; so that although I should perhaps be an architect in philosophy and the sciences, I become an ordinary workman and laborer, whatever is needed, since there are many things that must be done in building the structure, things which others, because of a natural disdain, shrink from and refuse to do."

pervades the dialogues of Plato. It may be distinctly traced in many parts of the works of Aristotle. Bacon has dropped hints from which it may be inferred that, in his opinion, the prevalence of this feeling was in a great measure to be attributed to the influence of Socrates. Our great countryman evidently did not consider the revolution which Socrates effected in philosophy as a happy event, and constantly maintained that the earlier Greek speculators, Democritus in particular, were, on the whole, superior to their more celebrated successors.

Assuredly if the tree which Socrates planted and Plato watered is to be judged of by its flowers and leaves, it is the noblest of trees. But if we take the homely test of Bacon, if we judge of the tree by its fruits, our opinion of it may perhaps be less favorable. When we sum up all the useful truths which we owe to that philosophy, to what do they amount? We find, indeed, abundant proofs that some of those who cultivated it were men of the first order of intellect. We find among their writings incomparable specimens both of dialectical and rhetorical art. We have no doubt that the ancient controversies were of use, in so far as they served to exercise the faculties of the disputants; for there is no controversy so idle that it may not be of use in this way. But, when we look for something more, for something which adds to the comforts or alleviates the calamities of the human race, we are forced to own ourselves disappointed. We are forced to say with Bacon that this celebrated philosophy ended in nothing but disputation, that it was neither a vineyard nor an olive-ground, but an intricate wood of briars and thistles, from which those who lost themselves in it brought back many scratches and no food.

We readily acknowledge that some of the teachers of this unfruitful wisdom were among the greatest men that the world has ever seen. . . .

But in truth the very admiration which we feel for the eminent philosophers of antiquity forces us to adopt the opinion that their powers were systematically misdirected. For how else could it be that such powers should effect so little for mankind? A pedestrian may show as much muscular vigor on a treadmill as on the highway road. But on the road his vigor will assuredly carry him forward; and on the treadmill he will not advance an inch. The ancient philosophy was a treadmill, not a path. It was made up of revolving questions, of controversies which were always beginning again. . . . What is the highest good, whether pain be an evil, whether all things be fated, whether we can be certain of anything, whether we can be certain that we are certain of nothing, whether a wise man can be unhappy, whether all departures from right be equally reprehensible; these, and other questions of the same sort, occupied the brains, the tongues, and the pens of the ablest men in the civilized world during several centuries. This sort of philosophy, it is evident, could not be progressive. It might indeed sharpen and invigorate the minds of those who devoted themselves to it; and so might the disputes of the orthodox Lilliputians and the heretical Blefuscudians about the big ends and the little ends of eggs.[7] But such disputes could add nothing to the stock of knowledge. The human mind accordingly, instead of marching, merely marked time. It took as much trouble as would have sufficed to carry it forward; and yet remained on the same spot. There was no accumulation of truth, no heritage of truth acquired by the labor of one generation and bequeathed to another, to be again transmitted with large additions to a third. Where this philosophy was in the time of Cicero, there it continued to be in the time of Seneca, and there it continued to be in the time of Favorinus.[8] The same sects were still battling with the same unsatisfactory arguments, about the same interminable questions. There had been no want of ingenuity, of zeal, of industry. Every trace of intellectual cultivation was there, except a harvest. There had been plenty of ploughing, harrowing, reaping, threshing. But the garners contained only smut and stubble.

The ancient philosophers did not neglect

[7] See Swift, *Gulliver's Travels*, Part I (p. 396).
[8] Greek philosopher of 2nd century A.D.

natural science; but they did not cultivate it for the purpose of increasing the power and ameliorating the condition of man. The taint of barrenness had spread from ethical to physical speculations. Seneca wrote largely on natural philosophy, and magnified the importance of that study. But why? Not because it tended to assuage suffering, to multiply the conveniences of life, to extend the empire of man over the material world; but solely because it tended to raise the mind above low cares, to separate it from the body, to exercise its subtlety in the solution of very obscure questions. Thus natural philosophy was considered in the light merely of a mental exercise. It was made subsidiary to the art of disputation; and it consequently proved altogether barren of useful discoveries. . . .

At length the time arrived when the barren philosophy which had, during so many ages, employed the faculties of the ablest of men, was destined to fall. . . .

At this time Bacon appeared. . . . The philosophy which he taught was essentially new. It differed from that of the celebrated teachers, not merely in method, but also in object. Its object was the good of mankind, in the sense in which the mass of mankind always have understood and always will understand the word good. . . .

The difference between the philosophy of Bacon and that of his predecessors cannot, we think, be better illustrated than by comparing his views on some important subjects with those of Plato. We select Plato, because we conceive that he did more than any other person towards giving to the minds of speculative men that bent which they retained till they received from Bacon a new impulse in a diametrically opposite direction.

It is curious to observe how differently these great men estimated the value of every kind of knowledge. Take arithmetic for example. Plato, after speaking slightly of the convenience of being able to reckon and compute in the ordinary transactions of life, passes to what he considers as a far more important advantage. The study of the properties of numbers, he tells us, habituates the mind to the contemplation of pure truth, and raises

us above the material universe. He would have his disciples apply themselves to this study, not that they may be able to buy or sell, not that they may qualify themselves to be shopkeepers or traveling merchants, but that they may learn to withdraw their minds from the ever-shifting spectacle of this visible and tangible world, and to fix them on the immutable essences of things.

Bacon, on the other hand, valued this branch of knowledge, only on account of its uses with reference to that visible and tangible world which Plato so much despised. He speaks with scorn of the mystical arithmetic of the later Platonists, and laments the propensity of mankind to employ, on mere matters of curiosity, powers the whole exertion of which is required for purposes of solid advantage. He advises arithmeticians to leave these trifles, and to employ themselves in framing convenient expressions, which may be of use in physical researches.

The same reasons which led Plato to recommend the study of arithmetic led him to recommend also the study of mathematics. The vulgar crowd of geometricians, he says, will not understand him. They have practice always in view. They do not know that the real use of the science is to lead men to the knowledge of abstract, essential, eternal truth. Indeed, if we are to believe Plutarch,[9] Plato carried this feeling so far that he considered geometry as degraded by being applied to any purpose of vulgar utility. Archytas,[10] it seems, had framed machines of extraordinary power on mathematical principles. Plato remonstrated with his friend, and declared that this was to degrade a noble intellectual exercise into a low craft, fit only for carpenters and wheelwrights. The office of geometry, he said, was to discipline the mind, not to minister to the base wants of the body. His interference was successful; and from that time, according to Plutarch, the science of mechanics was considered as unworthy of the attention of a philosopher.

Archimedes[11] in a later age imitated and

[9] Greek biographer.
[10] Greek philosopher and inventor.
[11] Greek mathematician of Syracuse.

surpassed Archytas. But even Archimedes was not free from the prevailing notion that geometry was degraded by being employed to produce anything useful. It was with difficulty that he was induced to stoop from speculation to practice. He was half ashamed of those inventions which were the wonder of hostile nations, and always spoke of them slightingly as mere amusements, as trifles in which a mathematician might be suffered to relax his mind after intense application to the higher parts of his science.

The opinion of Bacon on this subject was diametrically opposed to that of the ancient philosophers. He valued geometry chiefly, if not solely, on account of those uses, which to Plato appeared so base. And it is remarkable that the longer Bacon lived the stronger this feeling became. When in 1605 he wrote the two books on the *Advancement of Learning,* he dwelt on the advantages which mankind derived from mixed mathematics; [12] but he at the same time admitted that the beneficial effect produced by mathematical study on the intellect, though a collateral advantage, was "no less worthy than that which was principal and intended." But it is evident that his views underwent a change. When, near twenty years later, he published the *De Augmentis,* which is the *Treatise on the Advancement of Learning,* greatly expanded and carefully corrected, he made important alterations in the part which related to mathematics. He condemned with severity the high pretensions of the mathematicians, *delicias et fastum mathematicorum.*[13] Assuming the well-being of the human race to be the end of knowledge, he pronounced that mathematical science could claim no higher rank than that of an appendage or auxiliary to other sciences. Mathematical science, he says, is the handmaid of natural philosophy; she ought to demean herself as such; and he declares that he cannot conceive by what ill chance it has happened that she presumes to claim precedence over her mistress. He predicts—a pre-

diction which would have made Plato shudder —that as more and more discoveries are made in physics, there will be more and more branches of mixed mathematics. Of that collateral advantage the value of which, twenty years before, he rated so highly, he says not one word. This omission cannot have been the effect of mere inadvertence. His own treatise was before him. From that treatise he deliberately expunged whatever was favorable to the study of pure mathematics, and inserted several keen reflections on the ardent votaries of that study. This fact, in our opinion, admits of only one explanation. Bacon's love of those pursuits which directly tend to improve the condition of mankind, and his jealousy of all pursuits merely curious, had grown upon him, and had, it may be, become immoderate. He was afraid of using any expression which might have the effect of inducing any man of talents to employ in speculations, useful only to the mind of the speculator, a single hour which might be employed in extending the empire of man over matter. If Bacon erred here, we must acknowledge that we greatly prefer his error to the opposite error of Plato. We have no patience with a philosophy which, like those Roman matrons who swallowed abortives in order to preserve their shapes, takes pains to be barren for fear of being homely.

Let us pass to astronomy. This was one of the sciences which Plato exhorted his disciples to learn, but for reasons far removed from common habits of thinking. "Shall we set down astronomy," says Socrates,[14] "among the subjects of study?" "I think so," answers his young friend Glaucon: "to know something about the seasons, the months, and the years is of use for military purposes, as well as for agriculture and navigation." "It amuses me," says Socrates, "to see how afraid you are, lest the common herd of people should accuse you of recommending useless studies." He then proceeds, in that pure and magnificent diction which, as Cicero said, Jupiter would use if Jupiter spoke Greek, to explain, that the use of astronomy is not to add to the vulgar comforts of life, but to assist in raising

[12] Mathematics that is a mixture of the theoretical and the applied.

[13] "The daintiness and arrogance of mathematicians."

[14] In Plato's *Republic.*

the mind to the contemplation of things which are to be perceived by the pure intellect alone. The knowledge of the actual motions of the heavenly bodies Socrates considers as of little value. The appearances which make the sky beautiful at night are, he tells us, like the figures which a geometrician draws on the sand, mere examples, mere helps to feeble minds. We must get beyond them; we must neglect them; we must attain to an astronomy which is as independent of the actual stars as geometrical truth is independent of the lines of an ill-drawn diagram. This is, we imagine, very nearly, if not exactly, the astronomy which Bacon compared to the ox of Prometheus, a sleek, well-shaped hide, stuffed with rubbish, goodly to look at, but containing nothing to eat. He complained that astronomy had, to its great injury, been separated from natural philosophy, of which it was one of the noblest provinces, and annexed to the domain of mathematics. The world stood in need, he said, of a very different astronomy, of a living astronomy, of an astronomy which should set forth the nature, the motion, and the influences of the heavenly bodies, as they really are.

On the greatest and most useful of all human inventions, the invention of alphabetical writing, Plato did not look with much complacency. He seems to have thought that the use of letters had operated on the human mind as the use of the go-cart in learning to walk, or of corks in learning to swim, is said to operate on the human body. It was a support which, in his opinion, soon became indispensable to those who used it, which made vigorous exertion first unnecessary and then impossible. The powers of the intellect would, he conceived, have been more fully developed without this delusive aid. Men would have been compelled to exercise the understanding and the memory, and, by deep and assiduous meditation, to make truth thoroughly their own. Now, on the contrary, much knowledge is traced on paper, but little is engraved in the soul. A man is certain that he can find information at a moment's notice when he wants it. He therefore suffers it to fade from his mind. Such a man cannot in strictness be said to know anything. He has the show without the reality of wisdom. These opinions Plato has put into the mouth of an ancient king of Egypt.[15] But it is evident from the context that they were his own; and so they were understood to be by Quintilian.[16] Indeed they are in perfect accordance with the whole Platonic system.

Bacon's views, as may easily be supposed, were widely different. The powers of the memory, he observes, without the help of writing, can do little towards the advancement of any useful science. He acknowledges that the memory may be disciplined to such a point as to be able to perform very extraordinary feats. But on such feats he sets little value. The habits of his mind, he tells us, are such that he is not disposed to rate highly any accomplishment, however rare, which is of no practical use to mankind. As to these prodigious achievements of the memory, he ranks them with the exhibitions of rope-dancers and tumblers. "These two performances," he says, "are much of the same sort. The one is an abuse of the powers of the body; the other is an abuse of the powers of the mind. Both may perhaps excite our wonder; but neither is entitled to our respect."

To Plato, the science of medicine appeared to be of very disputable advantages. He did not indeed object to quick cures for acute disorders, or for injuries produced by accidents. But the art which resists the slow sap of a chronic disease, which repairs frames enervated by lust, swollen by gluttony, or inflamed by wine, which encourages sensuality by mitigating the natural punishment of the sensualist, and prolongs existence when the intellect has ceased to retain its entire energy, had no share of his esteem. A life protracted by medical skill he pronounced to be a long death. The exercise of the art of medicine ought, he said, to be tolerated, so far as that art may serve to cure the occasional distempers of men whose constitutions are good. As to those who have bad constitutions, let them die; and the sooner the better. Such men are

[15] In the *Phaedrus.*
[16] Roman orator and rhetorician.

unfit for war, for magistracy, for the management of their domestic affairs, for severe study and speculation. If they engage in any vigorous mental exercise, they are troubled with giddiness and fulness of the head, all which they lay to the account of philosophy. The best thing that can happen to such wretches is to have done with life at once. He quotes mythical authority in support of this doctrine; and reminds his disciples that the practice of the sons of Aesculapius,[17] as described by Homer, extended only to the cure of external injuries.

Far different was the philosophy of Bacon. Of all the sciences, that which he seems to have regarded with the greatest interest was the science which, in Plato's opinion, would not be tolerated in a well-regulated community. To make men perfect was no part of Bacon's plan. His humble aim was to make imperfect men comfortable. The beneficence of his philosophy resembled the beneficence of the common Father, whose sun rises on the evil and the good, whose rain descends for the just and the unjust. In Plato's opinion man was made for philosophy; in Bacon's opinion philosophy was made for man; it was a means to an end; and that end was to increase the pleasures and to mitigate the pains of millions who are not and cannot be philosophers. That a valetudinarian who took great pleasure in being wheeled along his terrace, who relished his boiled chicken and his weak wine and water, and who enjoyed a hearty laugh over the Queen of Navarre's tales,[18] should be treated as a *caput lupinum* [19] because he could not read the *Timaeus* [20] without a headache, was a notion which the humane spirit of the English school of wisdom altogether rejected. Bacon would not have thought it beneath the dignity of a philosopher to contrive an improved garden chair for such a valetudinarian, to devise some way of rendering his medicines more palatable, to invent repasts which he might enjoy, and pillows on which he might sleep soundly; and this though there might not be the smallest hope that the mind of the poor invalid would ever rise to the contemplation of the ideal beautiful and the ideal good. As Plato had cited the religious legends of Greece to justify his contempt for the more recondite parts of the art of healing, Bacon vindicated the dignity of that art by appealing to the example of Christ, and reminded men that the great Physician of the soul did not disdain to be also the physician of the body.

When we pass from the science of medicine to that of legislation, we find the same difference between the systems of these two great men. Plato, at the commencement of the *Dialogue on Laws*, lays it down as a fundamental principle that the end of legislation is to make men virtuous. It is unnecessary to point out the extravagant conclusions to which such a proposition leads. Bacon well knew to how great an extent the happiness of every society must depend on the virtue of its members; and he also knew what legislators can and what they cannot do for the purpose of promoting virtue. The view which he has given of the end of legislation, and of the principal means for the attainment of that end, has always seemed to us eminently happy, even among the many happy passages of the same kind with which his works abound. *Finis et scopus quem leges intueri atque ad quem jussiones et sanctiones suas dirigere debent, non alius est quam ut cives feliciter degant. Id fiet si pietate et religione recte instituti, moribus honesti, armis adversus hostes externos tuti, legum auxilio adversus seditiones et privatas injurias muniti, imperio et magistratibus obsequentes, copiis et opibus locupletes et florentes fuerint.*[21] The end is the

---

[17] The god of healing. Physicians, therefore, are called his "sons."
[18] The *Heptameron,* a collection of lively love stories.
[19] An outlaw ("wolf's head").
[20] One of Plato's dialogues.

[21] "The end and scope which laws should hold in view, and to which they should direct their decrees and sanctions, is none other than that citizens should live happily. This will be brought about if the citizens are rightly trained in piety and religion, sound in morality, protected by arms against foreign foes, defended by the help of the laws against civil discords and private injuries, obedient to the government and the magistrates, and rich and flourishing in goods and wealth."

well-being of the people. The means are the imparting of moral and religious education; the providing of everything necessary for defense against foreign enemies; the maintaining of internal order; the establishing of a judicial, financial, and commercial system, under which wealth may be rapidly accumulated and securely enjoyed.

Even with respect to the form in which laws ought to be drawn, there is a remarkable difference of opinion between the Greek and the Englishman. Plato thought a preamble essential; Bacon thought it mischievous. Each was consistent with himself. Plato, considering the moral improvement of the people as the end of legislation, justly inferred that a law which commanded and threatened, but which neither convinced the reason, nor touched the heart, must be a most imperfect law. He was not content with deterring from theft a man who still continued to be a thief at heart, with restraining a son who hated his mother from beating his mother. The only obedience on which he set much value was the obedience which an enlightened understanding yields to reason, and which a virtuous disposition yields to precepts of virtue. He really seems to have believed that, by prefixing to every law an eloquent and pathetic exhortation, he should, to a great extent, render penal enactments superfluous. Bacon entertained no such romantic hopes; and he well knew the practical inconveniences of the course which Plato recommended. *Neque nobis,* says he, *prologi legum qui inepti olim habiti sunt, et leges introducunt disputantes non jubentes, utique placerent, si priscos mores ferre possemus. . . . Quantum fieri potest prologi evitentur, et lex incipiat a jussione.*[22]

Each of the great men whom we have compared intended to illustrate his system by a philosophical romance; and each left his romance imperfect. Had Plato lived to finish the *Critias,* a comparison between that noble fiction and the *New Atlantis*[23] would probably have furnished us with still more striking instances than any which we have given. It is amusing to think with what horror he would have seen such an institution as Solomon's House[24] rising in his republic: with what vehemence he would have ordered the brew-houses, the perfume-houses, and the dispensatories to be pulled down; and with what inexorable rigor he would have driven beyond the frontier all the Fellows of the college, merchants of light and depredators, lamps and pioneers.

To sum up the whole, we should say that the aim of the Platonic philosophy was to exalt man into a god. The aim of the Baconian philosophy was to provide man with what he requires while he continues to be man. The aim of the Platonic philosophy was to raise us far above vulgar wants. The aim of the Baconian philosophy was to supply our vulgar wants. The former aim was noble; but the latter was attainable. Plato drew a good bow; but, like Acestes in Virgil, he aimed at the stars; and therefore, though there was no want of strength or skill, the shot was thrown away. His arrow was indeed followed by a track of dazzling radiance, but it struck nothing.

*Volans liquidis in nubibus arsit arundo
Signavitque viam flammis, tenuisque recessit
Consumpta in ventos.*[25]

Bacon fixed his eye on a mark which was placed on the earth, and within bow-shot, and hit it in the white. The philosophy of Plato began in words and ended in words, noble words indeed, words such as were to be expected from the finest of human intellects exercising boundless dominion over the finest of human languages. The philosophy

[22] "Nor are we at all pleased by preambles to laws, which were formerly regarded as impertinent, and which present the laws as arguing rather than commanding, if only we could endure the ancient practices. . . . As far as possible, let preambles be avoided, and let the law begin with an enactment."

[23] Bacon's *New Atlantis,* in which he tells of a visit to an imaginary island in the Pacific and of the ideal social conditions there.

[24] An ideal college described in the *New Atlantis,* "dedicated to the study of the works and creatures of God" from a practical point of view.

[25] "Flying through liquid clouds the arrow blazed, And marked its trail with flame, then burned away, Vanishing amid the winds" (*Aeneid*).

of Bacon began in observations and ended in arts.

The boast of the ancient philosophers was that their doctrine formed the minds of men to a high degree of wisdom and virtue. This was indeed the only practical good which the most celebrated of those teachers even pretended to effect; and undoubtedly, if they had effected this, they would have deserved far higher praise than if they had discovered the most salutary medicines or constructed the most powerful machines. But the truth is that, in those very matters in which alone they professed to do any good to mankind, in those very matters for the sake of which they neglected all the vulgar interests of mankind, they did nothing or worse than nothing. They promised what was impracticable; they despised what was practicable; they filled the world with long words and long beards; and they left it as wicked and as ignorant as they found it.

An acre in Middlesex is better than a principality in Utopia. The smallest actual good is better than the most magnificent promises of impossibilities. The wise man of the Stoics would, no doubt, be a grander object than a steam-engine. But there are steam-engines. And the wise man of the Stoics is yet to be born. A philosophy which should enable a man to feel perfectly happy while in agonies of pain would be better than a philosophy which assuages pain. But we know that there are remedies which will assuage pain; and we know that the ancient sages liked the toothache just as little as their neighbors. A philosophy which should extinguish cupidity would be better than a philosophy which should devise laws for the security of property. But it is possible to make laws which shall, to a very great extent, secure property. And we do not understand how any motives which the ancient philosophy furnished could extinguish cupidity. We know indeed that the philosophers were no better than other men. From the testimony of friends as well as of foes, from the confessions of Epictetus [26] and Seneca, as well as from the sneers of Lucian [27] and the fierce invectives of Juvenal,[28] it is plain that these teachers of virtue had all the vices of their neighbors, with the additional vice of hypocrisy. Some people may think the object of the Baconian philosophy a low object, but they cannot deny that, high or low, it has been attained. They cannot deny that every year makes an addition to what Bacon called "fruit." They cannot deny that mankind have made, and are making, great and constant progress in the road which he pointed out to them. Was there any such progressive movement among the ancient philosophers? After they had been declaiming eight hundred years, had they made the world better than when they began? Our belief is that, among the philosophers themselves, instead of a progressive improvement there was a progressive degeneracy. An abject superstition which Democritus or Anaxagoras [29] would have rejected with scorn, added the last disgrace to the long dotage of the Stoic and Platonic schools. Those unsuccessful attempts to articulate which are so delightful and interesting in a child, shock and disgust in an aged paralytic; and in the same way, those wild and mythological fictions which charm us, when we hear them lisped by Greek poetry in its infancy, excite a mixed sensation of pity and loathing, when mumbled by Greek philosophy in its old age. We know that guns, cutlery, spy-glasses, clocks, are better in our time than they were in the time of our fathers, and were better in the time of our fathers than they were in the time of our grandfathers. We might, therefore, be inclined to think that, when a philosophy which boasted that its object was the elevation and purification of the mind, and which for this object neglected the sordid office of ministering to the comforts of the body, had flourished in the highest honor during many hundreds of years, a vast moral amelioration must have taken place. Was it so? Look at the schools of this wisdom four centuries before the Christian era and four centuries after that era. Compare the men whom those schools formed at those two periods. Compare Plato

[26] Stoic philosopher.
[27] A Greek satirist.
[28] A Roman satirist.
[29] Early Greek philosopher.

and Libanius.[30] Compare Pericles and Julian.[31] This philosophy confessed, nay boasted, that for every end but one it was useless. Had it attained that one end?

Suppose that Justinian,[32] when he closed the schools of Athens, had called on the last few sages who still haunted the Portico,[33] and lingered round the ancient plane-trees, to show their title to public veneration: suppose that he had said: "A thousand years have elapsed since, in this famous city, Socrates posed Protagoras and Hippias;[34] during those thousand years a large proportion of the ablest men of every generation has been employed in constant efforts to bring to perfection the philosophy which you teach; that philosophy has been munificently patronized by the powerful; its professors have been held in the highest esteem by the public; it has drawn to itself almost all the sap and vigor of the human intellect: and what has it effected? What profitable truth has it taught us which we should not equally have known without it? What has it enabled us to do which we should not have been equally able to do without it?" Such questions, we suspect, would have puzzled Simplicius and Isidore.[35] Ask a follower of Bacon what the new philosophy, as it was called in the time of Charles the Second, has effected for mankind, and his answer is ready: "It has lengthened life; it has mitigated pain; it has extinguished diseases; it has increased the fertility of the soil; it has given new securities to the mariner; it has furnished new arms to the warrior; it has spanned great rivers and estuaries with bridges of form unknown to our fathers; it

has guided the thunderbolt innocuously from heaven to earth; it has lighted up the night with the splendor of day; it has extended the range of the human vision; it has multiplied the power of the human muscles; it has accelerated motion; it has annihilated distance; it has facilitated intercourse, correspondence, all friendly offices, all despatch of business; it has enabled man to descend to the depths of the sea, to soar into the air, to penetrate securely into the noxious recesses of the earth, to traverse the land in cars which whirl along without horses, and the ocean in ships which run ten knots an hour against the wind. These are but a part of its fruits, and of its first fruits. For it is a philosophy which never rests, which has never attained, which is never perfect. Its law is progress. A point which yesterday was invisible is its goal today, and will be its starting-post to-morrow."

Great and various as the powers of Bacon were, he owes his wide and durable fame chiefly to this, that all those powers received their direction from common sense. His love of the vulgar useful, his strong sympathy with the popular notions of good and evil, and the openness with which he avowed that sympathy, are the secret of his influence. There was in his system no cant, no illusion. He had no anointing for broken bones, no fine theories *de finibus*,[36] no arguments to persuade men out of their senses. He knew that men, and philosophers as well as other men, do actually love life, health, comfort, honor, security, the society of friends, and do actually dislike death, sickness, pain, poverty, disgrace, danger, separation from those to whom they are attached. He knew that religion, though it often regulates and moderates these feelings, seldom eradicates them; nor did he think it desirable for mankind that they should be eradicated. The plan of eradicating them by conceits like those of Seneca, or syllogisms like those of Chrysippus,[37] was too preposterous to be for a moment

[30] Greek sophist and rhetorician of the 4th century A.D.

[31] Roman emperor of the 4th century A.D., called "the Apostate" because he renounced his Christian upbringing and attempted to revive paganism. Macaulay contrasts him with Pericles, the great statesman under whose leadership Athens reached the height of her glory in the 5th century B.C.

[32] Emperor in 6th century A.D.

[33] The "Painted Porch," a colonnade in Athens where Zeno, the founder of Stoicism, taught his disciples.

[34] Characters in Plato's dialogue *Protagoras*.

[35] Among the last of the neo-Platonists (6th century A.D.).

[36] Concerning final ends.

[37] A Stoic philosopher who stated many of his ideas in the form of the syllogism, a logical argument consisting of a major premise, a minor premise, and a conclusion.

entertained by a mind like his. He did not understand what wisdom there could be in changing names where it was impossible to change things; in denying that blindness, hunger, the gout, the rack, were evils, and calling them ἀποπροήγμενα;[38] in refusing to acknowledge that health, safety, plenty, were good things, and dubbing them by the name of ἀδιάφορα.[39] In his opinions on all these subjects, he was not a Stoic, nor an Epicurean, nor an Academic, but what would have been called by Stoics, Epicureans, and Academics a mere ἰδιώτης, a mere common man. And it was precisely because he was so that his name makes so great an era in the history of the world. It was because he dug deep that he was able to pile high. It was because, in order to lay his foundations, he went down into those parts of human nature which lie low, but which are not liable to change, that the fabric which he reared has risen to so stately an elevation, and stands with such immovable strength.

We have sometimes thought that an amusing fiction might be written, in which a disciple of Epictetus and a disciple of Bacon should be introduced as fellow-travelers. They come to a village where the small-pox has just begun to rage, and find houses shut up, intercourse suspended, the sick abandoned, mothers weeping in terror over their children. The Stoic assures the dismayed population that there is nothing bad in the small-pox, and that to a wise man disease, deformity, death, the loss of friends, are not evils. The Baconian takes out a lancet and begins to vaccinate. They find a body of miners in great dismay. An explosion of noisome vapors has just killed many of those who were at work; and the survivors are afraid to venture into the cavern. The Stoic assures them that such an accident is nothing but a mere ἀποπροήγμενον.[40] The Baconian, who has no such fine word at his command, contents himself with devising a safety-lamp. They find a shipwrecked merchant wringing his hands on the shore. His vessel with an inestimable cargo has just gone down, and he is reduced in a moment from opulence to beggary. The Stoic exhorts him not to seek happiness in things which lie without himself, and repeats the whole chapter of Epictetus πρὸς τοὺς τὴν ἀπορίαν δεδοικότας.[41] The Baconian constructs a diving-bell, goes down in it, and returns with the most precious effects from the wreck. It would be easy to multiply illustrations of the difference between the philosophy of thorns and the philosophy of fruit, the philosophy of words and the philosophy of works. . . .

(1837)

STUDY AIDS: 1. In analyzing Macaulay's prose style, the following terms are often used: balance, ANTITHESIS, concrete language, and parallelism. Point to outstanding examples of each of these qualities in the essay on Bacon. How does his style compare with that of Carlyle in *Past and Present?* Which do you prefer and why?

2. What is Macaulay's basic THEME in this essay? Is he fair to Plato and the theoretical philosophers? How would you answer Macaulay's arguments against this group? What does Macaulay mean by the two terms "utility" and "progress"? Measured by the Macaulayan definitions of these terms, of what value are poetry, religion, the fine arts?

[38] "Things relatively evil."
[39] "Things indifferent."

[40] "Relative evil."
[41] "To those who fear poverty."

John Henry Newman
(1801–1890)

NEWMAN'S LONG LIFE DIVIDES SHARPLY INTO TWO ALMOST EVEN PARTS, SEPARATED BY his acceptance of Roman Catholicism in 1845.

The first half was a period of calm until the beginning of the Oxford Movement in 1833. Newman was a sensitive, precocious boy who was the product of a deeply religious Evangelical household. At Oxford he abandoned his plans for the bar and determined to become a churchman. Two years' study as a fellow of Oriel College led to his ordination in the Church of England and his appointment as curate of St. Clement's Church in Oxford. In 1828 he was made vicar of St. Mary's, the official University Church, a position which he held for the next fifteen years.

After traveling to Italy in the winter of 1832–1833, when he wrote many lyrics (including the well-known hymn "Lead, Kindly Light"), Newman returned to England in time to hear his friend Keble preach on "National Apostasy," a sermon which initiated the Oxford Movement. Newman was thereby inspired to launch a series of essays, *Tracts for the Times* (1833–1841), in which the tenets of the Oxford Movement found expression.

Essentially, the Oxford Movement was an attempt to stem the tide of religious liberalism, which to Newman and his friends was devitalizing the church and religion in England. It sought to purify the Anglican Church by a return to the theology and ritual of the early church (that of the fourth and fifth centuries). In *Tract 90,* however, published in 1841, Newman advanced arguments so close to those of Roman Catholicism that he was required to discontinue the series. The next year he resigned his vicarage and, after two years of meditation in rural retirement, embraced Roman Catholicism.

On his return from his ordination in Rome, Newman set up an Oratory near Birmingham, where he lived the rest of his life, writing, speaking, and carrying on his priestly duties. For many years both Catholics and Protestants looked upon him with some suspicion, but on the publication in 1864 of his frank, sincere, and moving autobiography, *Apologia Pro Vita Sua* ("Justification of His Life")—the climax of a long quarrel between him and Charles Kingsley—Newman was recognized for the honestly dedicated person that he was. The crowning event of his life was his being made a cardinal by Pope Leo XIII in 1879.

Although Newman wrote two novels and some lyrics, his greatness as a writer lies in his superb autobiography and in his essays and sermons. In reading Newman, one becomes quickly aware of an amazing intellectual subtlety exercising itself in prose of rare sinewy strength. Newman has no superior as a stylist; he is a rhetorician who knows the devices of color and concreteness, of vividness and variety. But the rhetoric is not mere surface brilliance; it is the outer form of an inner logic as compelling as a mathematical demonstration. Whether he is discoursing on grace and free will, or is defining the nature of a liberal education, he brings to bear upon the subject originality of thought as well as power of expression.

The Idea of a University

In 1851 Newman was asked to become rector of a projected Catholic University in Dublin. The next year he went to that city to deliver a series of nine lectures on *The Scope and Nature of a University Education,* later published, with some related essays, as *The Idea of a University.* These discourses, which contain insights still valid for the twentieth century, constitute a brilliant analysis and defense of liberal education as opposed to merely utilitarian instruction.

Knowledge Its Own End

A university may be considered with reference either to its students or to its studies; and the principle, that all knowledge is a whole and the separate sciences[1] parts of one, which I have hitherto been using in behalf of its studies, is equally important when we direct our attention to its students. Now then I turn to the students, and shall consider the education which, by virtue of this principle, a university will give them; and thus I shall be introduced, gentlemen, to the second question, which I proposed to discuss, viz., whether and in what sense its teaching, viewed relatively to the taught, carries the attribute of utility along with it.

I

I have said that all branches of knowledge are connected together, because the subject-matter of knowledge is intimately united in itself, as being the acts and the work of the Creator. Hence it is that the sciences, into which our knowledge may be said to be cast, have multiplied bearings one on another, and an internal sympathy, and admit, or rather demand, comparison and adjustment. They complete, correct, balance, each other. This consideration, if well-founded, must be taken into account, not only as regards the attainment of truth, which is their common end, but as regards the influence which they exercise upon those whose education consists in the study of them. I have said already, that to give undue prominence to one is to be unjust to another; to neglect or supersede these is to divert those from their proper object. It is to unsettle the boundary lines between science and science, to disturb their action, to destroy the harmony which binds them together. Such a proceeding will have a corresponding effect when introduced into a place of education. There is no science but tells a different tale, when viewed as a portion of a whole, from what it is likely to suggest when taken by itself, without the safeguard, as I may call it, of others.

Let me make use of an illustration. In the combination of colors, very different effects are produced by a difference in their selection and juxtaposition; red, green, and white change their shades, according to the contrast to which they are submitted. And, in like manner, the drift and meaning of a branch of knowledge varies with the company in which it is introduced to the student. If his reading is confined simply to one subject, however such division of labor may favor the advancement of a particular pursuit, a point into which I do not here enter, certainly it has a tendency to contract his mind. If it is incorporated with others, it depends on those others as to the kind of influence which it exerts upon him. Thus the classics, which in England are the means of refining the taste, have in France subserved the spread of revolutionary and deistical doctrines.[2] In metaphysics, again, Butler's *Analogy of Religion*[3] which has had so much to do with the conversion to the Catholic faith of members of the University of Oxford, appeared to Pitt[4]

[1] Departments of systematized knowledge.

[2] The Catholic University in France attacked classical learning, since Greek was regarded as the devil's tongue. Thus many lovers of the classics opposed the Church.

[3] A theological treatise by Joseph Butler, eighteenth-century English churchman. It opposed deism by defending revealed religion.

[4] Whig statesman.

and others, who had received a different training, to operate only in the direction of infidelity. And so again, Watson, Bishop of Llandaff, as I think he tells us in the narrative of his life, felt the science of mathematics to indispose the mind to religious belief, while others see in its investigations the best parallel, and thereby defense, of the Christian mysteries. In like manner, I suppose, Arcesilaus [5] would not have handled logic as Aristotle, nor Aristotle have criticized poets as Plato; yet reasoning and poetry are subject to scientific rules.

It is a great point then to enlarge the range of studies which a university professes, even for the sake of the students; and, though they cannot pursue every subject which is open to them, they will be the gainers by living among those and under those who represent the whole circle. This I conceive to be the advantage of a seat of universal learning, considered as a place of education. An assemblage of learned men, zealous for their own sciences, and rivals of each other, are brought, by familiar intercourse and for the sake of intellectual peace, to adjust together the claims and relations of their respective subjects of investigation. They learn to respect, to consult, to aid each other. Thus is created a pure and clear atmosphere of thought, which the student also breathes, though in his own case he only pursues a few sciences out of the multitude. He profits by an intellectual tradition, which is independent of particular teachers, which guides him in his choice of subjects, and duly interprets for him those which he chooses. He apprehends the great outlines of knowledge, the principles on which it rests, the scale of its parts, its lights and its shades, its great points and its little, as he otherwise cannot apprehend them. Hence it is that his education is called "liberal." A habit of mind is formed which lasts through life, of which the attributes are, freedom, equitableness, calmness, moderation, and wisdom; or what in a former discourse I have ventured to call a philosophical habit. This then I would assign as the special fruit of the education furnished at a university,

[5] Greek skeptical philosopher.

as contrasted with other places of teaching or modes of teaching. This is the main purpose of a university in its treatment of its students.

And now the question is asked me, What is the *use* of it? And my answer will constitute the main subject of the discourses which are to follow.

2

Cautious and practical thinkers, I say, will ask of me, what, after all, is the gain of this philosophy, of which I make such account, and from which I promise so much. Even supposing it to enable us to give the degree of confidence exactly due to every science respectively, and to estimate precisely the value of every truth which is anywhere to be found, how are we better for this master view of things, which I have been extolling? Does it not reverse the principle of the division of labor? will practical objects be obtained better or worse by its cultivation? to what then does it lead? where does it end? what does it do? how does it profit? what does it promise? Particular sciences are respectively the basis of definite arts, which carry on to results tangible and beneficial the truths which are the subjects of the knowledge attained; what is the art of this science of sciences? what is the fruit of such a philosophy? what are we proposing to effect, what inducements do we hold out to the Catholic community, when we set about the enterprise of founding a university?

I am asked what is the end of university education, and of the liberal or philosophical knowledge which I conceive it to impart: I answer, that what I have already said has been sufficient to show that it has a very tangible, real, and sufficient end, though the end cannot be divided from that knowledge itself. Knowledge is capable of being its own end. Such is the constitution of the human mind, that any kind of knowledge, if it be really such, is its own reward. And if this is true of all knowledge, it is true also of that special philosophy, which I have made to consist in a comprehensive view of truth in all its branches, of the relations of science to science, of their mutual bearings, and their respective values. What the worth of such an acquirement is, compared with other objects which we seek—wealth or power or honor or the conveniences and comforts of life, I do not profess here to discuss; but I would maintain, and mean to show, that it is an object, in its own nature so really and undeniably good, as to be the compensation of a great deal of thought in the compassing, and a great deal of trouble in the attaining.

Now, when I say that knowledge is, not merely a means to something beyond it, or the preliminary of certain arts into which it naturally resolves, but an end sufficient to rest in and to pursue for its own sake, surely I am uttering no paradox, for I am stating what is both intelligible in itself, and has ever been the common judgment of philosophers and the ordinary feeling of mankind. I am saying what at least the public opinion of this day ought to be slow to deny, considering how much we have heard of late years, in opposition to religion, of entertaining, curious, and various knowledge. I am but saying what whole volumes have been written to illustrate, by a "selection from the records of philosophy, literature, and art, in all ages and countries, of a body of examples, to show how the most unpropitious circumstances have been unable to conquer an ardent desire for the acquisition of knowledge." [6] That further advantages accrue to us and redound to others by its possession, over and above what it is in itself, I am very far indeed from denying; but, independent of these, we are satisfying a direct need of our nature in its very acquisition; and, whereas our nature, unlike that of the inferior creation, does not at once reach its perfection, but depends, in order to it, on a number of external aids and appliances, knowledge, as one of the principal gifts or accessories by which it is completed, is valuable for what its very presence in us does for us after the manner of a habit, even though it be turned to no further account, nor subserve any direct end.

[6] *The Pursuit of Knowledge under Difficulties*, by George Lillie Craik.

3

Hence it is that Cicero, in enumerating the various heads of mental excellence, lays down the pursuit of knowledge for its own sake, as the first of them. "This pertains most of all to human nature," he says, "for we are all of us drawn to the pursuit of knowledge; in which to excel we consider excellent, whereas to mistake, to err, to be ignorant, to be deceived, is both an evil and a disgrace." [7] And he considers knowledge the very first object to which we are attracted, after the supply of our physical wants. After the calls and duties of our animal existence, as they may be termed, as regards ourselves, our family, and our neighbors, follows, he tells us, "the search after truth. Accordingly, as soon as we escape from the pressure of necessary cares, forthwith we desire to see, to hear, to learn; and consider the knowledge of what is hidden, or is wonderful, a condition of our happiness."

This passage, though it is but one of many similar passages in a multitude of authors, I take for the very reason that it is so familiarly known to us; and I wish you to observe, gentlemen, how distinctly it separates the pursuit of knowledge from those ulterior objects to which certainly it can be made to conduce, and which are, I suppose, solely contemplated by the persons who would ask of me the use of a university or liberal education. So far from dreaming of the cultivation of knowledge directly and mainly in order to our physical comfort and enjoyment, for the sake of life and person, of health, of the conjugal and family union, of the social tie and civil security, the great orator implies, that it is only after our physical and political needs are supplied, and when we are "free from necessary duties and cares," that we are in a condition for "desiring to see, to hear, and to learn." Nor does he contemplate in the least degree the reflex or subsequent action of knowledge, when acquired, upon those material goods which we set out by securing before we seek it; on the contrary, he expressly denies its bearing upon social life altogether, strange as such a procedure is to

[7] *De Officiis* ("Concerning Duties").

those who live after the rise of the Baconian philosophy,[8] and he cautions us against such a cultivation of it as will interfere with our duties to our fellow-creatures. "All these methods," he says, "are engaged in the investigation of truth; by the pursuit of which to be carried off from public occupations is a transgression of duty. For the praise of virtue lies altogether in action; yet intermissions often occur, and then we recur to such pursuits; not to say that the incessant activity of the mind is vigorous enough to carry us on in the pursuit of knowledge, even without any exertion of our own." The idea of benefiting society by means of "the pursuit of science and knowledge" did not enter at all into the motives which he would assign for their cultivation.

This was the ground of the opposition which the elder Cato [9] made to the introduction of Greek philosophy among his countrymen, when Carneades [10] and his companions, on occasion of their embassy, were charming the Roman youth with their eloquent expositions of it. The fit representative of a practical people, Cato estimated everything by what it produced; whereas the pursuit of knowledge promised nothing beyond knowledge itself. He despised that refinement or enlargement of mind of which he had no experience.

4

Things, which can bear to be cut off from everything else and yet persist in living, must have life in themselves; pursuits, which issue in nothing, and still maintain their ground for ages, which are regarded as admirable, though they have not as yet proved themselves to be useful, must have their sufficient end in themselves, whatever it turn out to be. And we are brought to the same conclusion by considering the force of the epithet, by which the knowledge under consideration is popularly designated. It is common to speak of "liberal knowledge," of the "liberal arts and studies," and of a "liberal education," as the especial characteristic or property of a university and of a gentleman; what is really meant by the word? Now, first, in its grammatical sense it is opposed to servile; and by "servile work" is understood, as our catechisms inform us, bodily labor, mechanical employment, and the like, in which the mind has little or no part. Parallel to such works are those arts, if they deserve the name, of which the poet speaks, which owe their origin and their method to hazard, not to skill; as, for instance, the practice and operations of an empiric.[11] As far as this contrast may be considered as a guide into the meaning of the word, liberal knowledge and liberal pursuits are exercises of mind, of reason, of reflection.

But we want something more for its explanation, for there are bodily exercises which are liberal, and mental exercises which are not so. For instance, in ancient times the practitioners in medicine were commonly slaves; yet it was an art as intellectual in its nature, in spite of the pretense, fraud, and quackery with which it might then, as now, be debased, as it was heavenly in its aim. And so in like manner, we contrast a liberal education with a commercial education or a professional; yet no one can deny that commerce and the professions afford scope for the highest and most diversified powers of mind. There is then a great variety of intellectual exercises, which are not technically called "liberal"; on the other hand, I say, there are exercises of the body which do receive that appellation. Such, for instance, was the palæstra,[12] in ancient times; such the Olympic games,[13] in which strength and dexterity of body as well as of mind gained the prize. In Xenophon [14] we read of the young Persian nobility being taught to ride on horseback and to speak the truth; both being among the accomplishments of a gentleman. War, too, however rough a profession, has ever been accounted liberal,

[8] To Newman the Baconian philosophy was primarily a philosophy of practical utility.
[9] Roman statesman.
[10] Greek skeptical philosopher.
[11] One who bases his knowledge on practical experience.
[12] A school for wrestling and gymnastics.
[13] Games held every fourth year at Olympia.
[14] Greek general and historian.

unless in cases when it becomes heroic, which would introduce us to another subject.

Now comparing these instances together, we shall have no difficulty in determining the principle of this apparent variation in the application of the term which I am examining. Manly games, or games of skill, or military prowess, though bodily, are, it seems, accounted liberal; on the other hand, what is merely professional, though highly intellectual, nay, though liberal in comparison of trade and manual labor, is not simply called liberal, and mercantile occupations are not liberal at all. Why this distinction? because that alone is liberal knowledge, which stands on its own pretensions, which is independent of sequel, expects no complement, refuses to be *informed*[15] (as it is called) by any end, or absorbed into any art, in order duly to present itself to our contemplation. The most ordinary pursuits have this specific character, if they are self-sufficient and complete; the highest lose it, when they minister to something beyond them. It is absurd to balance, in point of worth and importance, a treatise on reducing fractures with a game of cricket or a fox-chase; yet of the two the bodily exercise has that quality which we call "liberal," and the intellectual has not. And so of the learned professions[16] altogether, considered merely as professions; although one of them be the most popularly beneficial, and another the most politically important, and the third the most intimately divine of all human pursuits, yet the very greatness of their end, the health of the body, or of the commonwealth, or of the soul, diminishes, not increases, their claim to the appellation "liberal," and that still more, if they are cut down to the strict exigencies of that end. If, for instance, theology, instead of being cultivated as a contemplation, be limited to the purposes of the pulpit or be represented by the catechism, it loses—not its usefulness, not its divine character, not its meritoriousness (rather it increases these qualities by such charitable condescension)—but it does lose the particular attribute which I

am illustrating; just as a face worn by tears and fasting loses its beauty, or a laborer's hand loses its delicateness;—for theology thus exercised is not simple knowledge, but rather is an art or a business making use of theology. And thus it appears that even what is supernatural need not be liberal, nor need a hero be a gentleman, for the plain reason that one idea is not another idea. And in like manner the Baconian philosophy, by using its physical sciences in the service of man, does thereby transfer them from the order of liberal pursuits to, I do not say the inferior, but the distinct class of the useful. And, to take a different instance, hence again, as is evident, whenever personal gain is the motive, still more distinctive an effect has it upon the character of a given pursuit; thus racing, which was a liberal exercise in Greece, forfeits its rank in times like these, so far as it is made the occasion of gambling.

All that I have been now saying is summed up in a few characteristic words of the great philosopher.[17] "Of possessions," he says, "those rather are useful, which bear fruit; those *liberal, which tend to enjoyment*. By fruitful, I mean, which yield revenue; by enjoyable, where *nothing accrues of consequence beyond the use*."[18]

5

Do not suppose, gentlemen, that in thus appealing to the ancients, I am throwing back the world two thousand years, and fettering philosophy with the reasonings of paganism. While the world lasts, will Aristotle's doctrine on these matters last, for he is the oracle of nature and of truth. While we are men, we cannot help, to a great extent, being Aristotelians, for the great master does but analyze the thoughts, feelings, views, and opinions of human kind. He has told us the meaning of our own words and ideas, before we were born. In many subject-matters, to think correctly, is to think like Aristotle; and we are his disciples whether we will or no, though we may not know it. Now, as to the

[15] Given form.
[16] As described by the rest of the sentence, what would these be?
[17] Aristotle.
[18] The *Rhetoric*.

particular instance before us, the word "liberal" as applied to knowledge and education, expresses a specific idea, which ever has been, and ever will be, while the nature of man is the same, just as the idea of the beautiful is specific, or of the sublime, or of the ridiculous, or of the sordid. It is in the world now, it was in the world then; and, as in the case of the dogmas of faith, it is illustrated by a continuous historical tradition, and never was out of the world, from the time it came into it. There have indeed been differences of opinion from time to time, as to what pursuits and what arts came under that idea, but such differences are but an additional evidence of its reality. That idea must have a substance in it, which has maintained its ground amid these conflicts and changes, which has ever served as a standard to measure things withal, which has passed from mind to mind unchanged, when there was so much to color, so much to influence any notion or thought whatever, which was not founded in our very nature. Were it a mere generalization, it would have varied with the subjects from which it was generalized; but though its subjects vary with the age, it varies not itself. The palæstra may seem a liberal exercise to Lycurgus,[19] and illiberal to Seneca;[20] coach-driving and prize-fighting may be recognized in Elis,[21] and be condemned in England; music may be despicable in the eyes of certain moderns, and be in the highest place with Aristotle and Plato—(and the case is the same in the particular application of the idea of beauty, or of goodness, or of moral virtue, there is a difference of tastes, a difference of judgments)—still these variations imply, instead of discrediting, the archetypal [22] idea, which is but a previous hypothesis or condition, by means of which issue is joined between contending opinions, and without which there would be nothing to dispute about.

I consider, then, that I am chargeable with no paradox, when I speak of a knowledge which is its own end, when I call it liberal knowledge, or a gentleman's knowledge, when I educate for it, and make it the scope of a university. And still less am I incurring such a charge, when I make this acquisition consist, not in knowledge in a vague and ordinary sense, but in that knowledge which I have especially called philosophy or, in an extended sense of the word, science; for whatever claims knowledge has to be considered as a good, these it has in a higher degree when it is viewed not vaguely, not popularly, but precisely and transcendently as philosophy. Knowledge, I say, is then especially liberal, or sufficient for itself, apart from every external and ulterior object, when and so far as it is philosophical, and this I proceed to show.

6

Now bear with me, gentlemen, if what I am about to say, has at first sight a fanciful appearance. Philosophy, then, or science, is related to knowledge in this way:—knowledge is called by the name of science or philosophy, when it is acted upon, informed, or if I may use a strong figure, impregnated by reason. Reason is the principle of that intrinsic fecundity of knowledge, which, to those who possess it, is its especial value, and which dispenses with the necessity of their looking abroad for any end to rest upon external to itself. Knowledge, indeed, when thus exalted into a scientific form, is also power; not only is it excellent in itself, but whatever such excellence may be, it is something more, it has a result beyond itself. Doubtless; but that is a further consideration, with which I am not concerned. I only say that, prior to its being a power, it is a good; that it is, not only an instrument, but an end. I know well it may resolve itself into an art, and terminate in a mechanical process, and in tangible fruit; but it also may fall back upon that reason, which informs it, and resolve itself into philosophy. In one case it is called useful knowledge, in the other liberal. The same person may cultivate it in both ways at once; but this again is a matter foreign to

[19] Famous Spartan lawgiver.
[20] Roman Stoic philosopher.
[21] A part of ancient Greece.
[22] Constituting a model or pattern.

my subject; here I do but say that there are two ways of using knowledge, and in matter of fact those who use it in one way are not likely to use it in the other, or at least in a very limited measure. You see, then, here are two methods of education; the end of the one is, to be philosophical, of the other to be mechanical; the one rises towards general ideas, the other is exhausted upon what is particular and external. Let me not be thought to deny the necessity, or to decry the benefit, of such attention to what is particular and practical, as belongs to the useful or mechanical arts; life could not go on without them; we owe our daily welfare to them; their exercise is the duty of the many, and we owe to the many a debt of gratitude for fulfilling that duty. I only say that knowledge, in proportion as it tends more and more to to be particular, ceases to be knowledge. It is a question whether knowledge can in any proper sense be predicated of the brute creation; without pretending to metaphysical exactness of phraseology, which would be unsuitable to an occasion like this, I say, it seems to me improper to call that passive sensation, or perception of things, which brutes seem to possess, by the name of knowledge. When I speak of knowledge, I mean something intellectual, something which grasps what it perceives through the senses; something which takes a view of things; which sees more than the senses convey; which reasons upon what it sees, and while it sees; which invests it with an idea. It expresses itself, not in a mere enunciation, but by an enthymeme: [23] it is of the nature of science from the first, and in this consists its dignity. The principle of real dignity in knowledge, its worth, its desirableness, considered irrespectively of its results, is this germ within it of a scientific or a philosophical process. This is how it comes to be an end in itself; this is why it admits of being called liberal. Not to know the relative disposition of things is the state of slaves or children; to have mapped

[23] A logical argument (such as a syllogism) with one of its steps left unstated. E.g., John will never make high marks, for playboys never do. (What premise is omitted?)

out the universe is the boast, or at least the ambition, of philosophy.

Moreover, such knowledge is not a mere extrinsic or accidental advantage, which is ours to-day and another's to-morrow, which may be got up from a book, and easily forgotten again, which we can command or communicate at our pleasure, which we can borrow for the occasion, carry about in our hand, and take into the market; it is an acquired illumination, it is a habit, a personal possession, and an inward endowment. And this is the reason, why it is more correct, as well as more usual, to speak of a university as a place of education, than of instruction, though, when knowledge is concerned, instruction would at first sight have seemed the more appropriate word. We are instructed, for instance, in manual exercises, in the fine and useful arts, in trades, and in ways of business; for these are methods, which have little or no effect upon the mind itself, are contained in rules committed to memory, to tradition, or to use, and bear upon an end external to themselves. But education is a higher word; it implies an action upon our mental nature, and the formation of a character; it is something individual and permanent, and is commonly spoken of in connection with religion and virtue. When, then, we speak of the communication of knowledge as being education, we thereby really imply that that knowledge is a state or condition of mind; and since cultivation of mind is surely worth seeking for its own sake, we are thus brought once more to the conclusion, which the word "liberal" and the word "philosophy" have already suggested, that there is a knowledge, which is desirable, though nothing come of it, as being of itself a treasure, and a sufficient remuneration of years of labor.

7

This, then, is the answer which I am prepared to give to the question with which I opened this discourse. Before going on to speak of the object of the Church in taking up philosophy, and the uses to which she puts it, I am prepared to maintain that philosophy is its own end, and, as I conceive, I have now begun proving it. I am prepared to maintain that there is a knowledge worth possessing for what it is, and not merely for what it does; and what minutes remain to me to-day I shall devote to the removal of some portion of the indistinctness and confusion with which the subject may in some minds be surrounded.[24]

It may be objected then, that, when we profess to seek knowledge for some end or other beyond itself, whatever it be, we speak intelligibly; but that, whatever men may have said, however obstinately the idea may have kept its ground from age to age, still it is simply unmeaning to say that we seek knowledge for its own sake, and for nothing else; for that it ever leads to something beyond itself, which therefore is its end, and the cause why it is desirable;—moreover, that this end is twofold, either of this world or of the next; that all knowledge is cultivated either for secular objects or for eternal; that if it is directed to secular objects, it is called useful knowledge, if to eternal, religious or Christian knowledge;—in consequence, that if, as I have allowed, this liberal knowledge does not benefit the body or estate, it ought to benefit the soul; but if the fact be really so, that it is neither a physical or a secular good on the one hand, nor a moral good on the other, it cannot be a good at all, and is not worth the trouble which is necessary for its acquisition.

And then I may be reminded that the professors of this liberal or philosophical knowledge have themselves, in every age, recognized this exposition of the matter, and have submitted to the issue in which it terminates; for they have ever been attempting to make men virtuous; or, if not, at least have assumed that refinement of mind was virtue, and that they themselves were the virtuous portion of mankind. This they have professed on the one hand; and on the other, they have utterly failed in their professions, so as ever to make themselves a proverb among men, and a laughing-stock both to the grave and the dissipated portion of mankind, in consequence of them. Thus they have furnished against themselves both the ground and the means of their own exposure, without any trouble at all to any one else. In a word, from the time that Athens was the university of the world, what has philosophy taught men, but to promise without practising, and to aspire without attaining? What has the deep and lofty thought of its disciples ended in but eloquent words? Nay, what has its teaching ever meditated, when it was boldest in its remedies for human ill, beyond charming us to sleep by its lessons, that we might feel nothing at all? like some melodious air, or rather like those strong and transporting perfumes, which at first spread their sweetness over everything they touch, but in a little while do but offend in proportion as they once pleased us. Did philosophy support Cicero [25] under the disfavor of the fickle populace, or nerve Seneca [26] to oppose an imperial tyrant? It abandoned Brutus,[27] as he sorrowfully confessed, in his greatest need, and it forced Cato,[28] as his panegyrist strangely boasts, into the false position of defying heaven. How few can be counted among its professors, who, like Polemon,[29] were thereby converted from a profligate course, or like Anaxagoras,[30] thought the world well lost in exchange for its possession? The philosopher in *Rasselas* [31] taught a superhuman doctrine, and then succumbed without an effort to a trial of human affection.

[24] In sections 7 and 8, Newman persuasively develops the arguments of objectors to his position. Is he fair in this presentation?

[25] It was said of Cicero, Roman orator and statesman, that he was too easily elated by good fortune and too easily disheartened by adversity. He was assassinated.

[26] Seneca was accused of conspiring against Nero and was ordered to commit suicide.

[27] Brutus, one of the assassins of Julius Caesar, was deserted by many of his followers and later, after his defeat by Octavius, killed himself.

[28] Cato committed suicide rather than surrender to the conquering Julius Caesar.

[29] An Athenian philosopher who was "converted from a profligate course" by hearing a lecture on temperance in the school of Xenocrates.

[30] Greek philosopher who gave up rich possessions in order to study philosophy. Later he was exiled for views deemed antireligious.

[31] A philosophical romance by Samuel Johnson.

"He discoursed," we are told, "with great energy on the government of the passions. His look was venerable, his action graceful, his pronunciation clear, and his diction elegant. He showed, with great strength of sentiment and variety of illustration, that human nature is degraded and debased, when the lower faculties predominate over the higher. He communicated the various precepts given, from time to time, for the conquest of passion, and displayed the happiness of those who had obtained the important victory, after which man is no longer the slave of fear, nor the fool of hope. . . . He enumerated many examples of heroes immovable by pain or pleasure, who looked with indifference on those modes or accidents to which the vulgar give the names of good and evil."

Rasselas in a few days found the philosopher in a room half darkened, with his eyes misty, and his face pale. "Sir," said he, "you have come at a time when all human friendship is useless; what I suffer cannot be remedied, what I have lost cannot be supplied. My daughter, my only daughter, from whose tenderness I expected all the comforts of my age, died last night of a fever." "Sir," said the prince, "mortality is an event by which a wise man can never be surprised; we know that death is always near, and it should therefore always be expected." "Young man," answered the philosopher, "you speak like one who has never felt the pangs of separation." "Have you, then, forgot the precept," said Rasselas, "which you so powerfully enforced? . . . consider that external things are naturally variable, but truth and reason are always the same." "What comfort," said the mourner, "can truth and reason afford me? Of what effect are they now, but to tell me that my daughter will not be restored?"

8

Better, far better, to make no professions, you will say, than to cheat others with what we are not, and to scandalize them with what we are. The sensualist, or the man of the world, at any rate is not the victim of fine words, but pursues a reality and gains it. The philos-

ophy of utility, you will say, gentlemen, has at least done its work; and I grant it,—it aimed low, but it has fulfilled its aim. If that man [32] of great intellect who has been its prophet in the conduct of life played false to his own professions, he was not bound by his philosophy to be true to his friend or faithful in his trust. Moral virtue was not the line in which he undertook to instruct men; and though, as the poet [33] calls him, he were the "meanest" of mankind, he was so in what may be called his private capacity, and without any prejudice to the theory of induction. He had a right to be so, if he chose, for anything that the idols [34] of the den or the theater had to say to the contrary. His mission was the increase of physical enjoyment and social comfort; and most wonderfully, most awfully has he fulfilled his conception and his design. Almost day by day have we fresh and fresh shoots, and buds, and blossoms, which are to ripen into fruit, on that magical tree of knowledge which he planted, and to which none of us perhaps, except the very poor, but owes, if not his present life, at least his daily food, his health, and general well-being. He was the divinely provided minister of temporal benefits to all of us so great, that, whatever I am forced to think of him as a man, I have not the heart, from mere gratitude, to speak of him severely. And, in spite of the tendencies of his philosophy, which are, as we see at this day, to depreciate, or to trample on theology, he has himself, in his writings, gone out of his way, as if with a prophetic misgiving of those tendencies, to insist on it as the instrument of that beneficent Father, who, when He came on earth in visible form, took on Him first and most prominently the office of assuaging the bodily wounds of human nature. And truly, like the old mediciner in

[32] Francis Bacon, who formulated the charges of treason against his patron, the Earl of Essex, and who himself was later convicted of taking bribes.
[33] Pope.
[34] In the *Novum Organum* Bacon discusses four kinds of false thinking which he terms "idols." The "idols of the den" are personal prejudices and circumstances; those of the "theater" are traditional dogmas. (See p. 192.)

the tale, "he sat diligently at his work, and hummed, with cheerful countenance, a pious song"; and then in turn "went out singing into the meadows so gaily, that those who had seen him from afar might well have thought it was a youth gathering flowers for his beloved, instead of an old physician gathering healing herbs in the morning dew." [35]

Alas, that men, in the action of life or in their heart of hearts, are not what they seem to be in their moments of excitement, or in their trances or intoxications of genius—so good, so noble, so serene! Alas, that Bacon too in his own way should after all be but the fellow of those heathen philosophers who in their disadvantages had some excuse for their inconsistency, and who surprise us rather in what they did say than in what they did not do! Alas, that he too, like Socrates or Seneca,[36] must be stripped of his holy-day coat, which looks so fair, and should be but a mockery amid his most majestic gravity of phrase; and, for all his vast abilities, should, in the littleness of his own moral being, but typify the intellectual narrowness of his school! However, granting all this, heroism after all was not his philosophy: I cannot deny he has abundantly achieved what he proposed. His is simply a method whereby bodily discomforts and temporal wants are to be most effectually removed from the greatest number; and already, before it has shown any signs of exhaustion, the gifts of nature, in their most artificial shapes and luxurious profusion and diversity, from all quarters of the earth, are, it is undeniable, by its means brought even to our doors, and we rejoice in them.

9

Useful knowledge then, I grant, has done its work; and liberal knowledge as certainly has not done its work—supposing, that is, as

[35] *The Unknown Patient,* by Friedrich Fouqué, German poet.

[36] Socrates, charged with corrupting the minds of Athenian youth, was condemned to die by drinking hemlock. Seneca, denouncing riches even while he enjoyed his own great wealth, was regarded by many as a hypocrite.

the objectors assume, its direct end, like religious knowledge, is to make men better; but this I will not for an instant allow, and unless I allow it, those objectors have said nothing to the purpose. I admit, rather I maintain, what they have been urging, for I consider knowledge to have its end in itself. For all its friends, or its enemies, may say, I insist upon it, that it is as real a mistake to burden it with virtue or religion as with the mechanical arts. Its direct business is not to steel the soul against temptation, or to console it in affliction, any more than to set the loom in motion, or to direct the steam carriage; be it ever so much the means or the condition of both material and moral advancement, still, taken by and in itself, it as little mends our hearts as it improves our temporal circumstances. And if its eulogists claim for it such a power, they commit the very same kind of encroachment on a province not their own as the political economist who should maintain that his science educated him for casuistry or diplomacy. Knowledge is one thing, virtue is another; good sense is not conscience, refinement is not humility, nor is largeness and justness of view faith. Philosophy, however enlightened, however profound, gives no command over the passions, no influential motives, no vivifying principles. Liberal education makes not the Christian, not the Catholic, but the gentleman. It is well to be a gentleman, it is well to have a cultivated intellect, a delicate taste, a candid, equitable, dispassionate mind, a noble and courteous bearing in the conduct of life;—these are the connatural [37] qualities of a large knowledge; they are the objects of a university; I am advocating, I shall illustrate and insist upon them; but still, I repeat, they are no guarantee for sanctity or even for conscientiousness, they may attach to the man of the world, to the profligate, to the heartless—pleasant, alas, and attractive as he shows when decked out in them. Taken by themselves, they do but seem to be what they are not; they look like virtue at a distance, but they are detected by close observers, and on the long run; and hence it is that they are popularly accused

[37] Connected by nature.

of pretense and hypocrisy, not, I repeat, from their own fault, but because their professors and their admirers persist in taking them for what they are not, and are officious in arrogating for them a praise to which they have no claim. Quarry the granite rock with razors, or moor the vessel with a thread of silk; then may you hope with such keen and delicate instruments as human knowledge and human reason to contend against those giants, the passion and the pride of man.

Surely we are not driven to theories of this kind in order to vindicate the value and dignity of liberal knowledge. Surely the real grounds on which its pretensions rest are not so very subtle or abstruse, so very strange or improbable. Surely it is very intelligible to say, and that is what I say here, that liberal education, viewed in itself, is simply the cultivation of the intellect as such, and its object is nothing more or less than intellectual excellence. Every thing has its own perfection, be it higher or lower in the scale of things; and the perfection of one is not the perfection of another. Things animate, inanimate, visible, invisible, all are good in their kind, and have a *best* of themselves, which is an object of pursuit. Why do you take such pains with your garden or your park? You see to your walks and turf and shrubberies; to your trees and drives; not as if you meant to make an orchard of the one, or corn or pasture land of the other, but because there is a special beauty in all that is goodly in wood, water, plain, and slope, brought all together by art into one shape, and grouped into one whole. Your cities are beautiful, your palaces, your public buildings, your territorial mansions, your churches; and their beauty leads to nothing beyond itself. There is a physical beauty and a moral: there is a beauty of person, there is a beauty of our moral being, which is natural virtue; and in like manner there is a beauty, there is a perfection, of the intellect. There is an ideal perfection in these various subject-matters, towards which individual instances are seen to rise, and which are the standards for all instances whatever. The Greek divinities and demigods, as the statuary has molded them, with their symmetry of figure, and their high forehead and their regular features, are the perfection of physical beauty. The heroes, of whom history tells, Alexander, or Caesar, or Scipio,[38] or Saladin,[39] are the representatives of that magnanimity or self-mastery which is the greatness of human nature. Christianity too has its heroes, and in the supernatural order, and we call them saints. The artist puts before him beauty of feature and form; the poet, beauty of mind; the preacher, the beauty of grace: then intellect too, I repeat, has its beauty, and it has those who aim at it. To open the mind, to correct it, to refine it, to enable it to know, and to digest, master, rule, and use its knowledge, to give it power over its own faculties, application, flexibility, method, critical exactness, sagacity, resource, address, eloquent expression, is an object as intelligible (for here we are inquiring, not what the object of a liberal education is worth, nor what use the church makes of it, but what it is in itself), I say, an object as intelligible as the cultivation of virtue, while, at the same time, it is absolutely distinct from it.

10

This indeed is but a temporal object, and a transitory possession: but so are other things in themselves which we make much of and pursue. The moralist will tell us that man, in all his functions, is but a flower which blossoms and fades, except so far as a higher principle breathes upon him, and makes him and what he is immortal. Body and mind are carried on into an eternal state of being by the gifts of divine munificence; but at first they do but fail in a failing world; and if the powers of intellect decay, the powers of the body have decayed before them, and, as an hospital or an almshouse, though its end be ephemeral, may be sanctified to the service of religion, so surely may a university, even

---

[38] There were many famous Scipios, a noble Roman family. The reference is probably to Publius Cornelius Scipio, who defeated Hannibal.

[39] Noted sultan of Egypt and Syria who opposed the Crusades.

were it nothing more than I have as yet described it. We attain to heaven by using this world well, though it is to pass away; we perfect our nature, not by undoing it, but by adding to it what is more than nature, and directing it towards aims higher than its own. (1852; 1873)

STUDY AIDS: 1. Try to sum up Newman's argument in two or three sentences. Which sentences in his discourse seem to you to be key sentences, summarizing his thought? (E.g., the sentence on p. 738/2, ll. 43–44.) What does he mean by "liberal" studies? How does he meet the objection that liberal studies are not useful? What does he mean by saying that knowledge is its own end? How does Newman

meet the argument that liberal knowledge has not made men better and so has not done its work, whereas the philosophy of utility has fulfilled its promises?

2. Do we place our educational emphasis today on liberal, or nonliberal studies, as Newman defines them? Does the average American college or university fit Newman's ideal as set forth on p. 738/1, l. 22 ff.? Are college studies related so as to give students a "master view" of things? Is a liberal education as Newman defines it a luxury in a technological age?

3. Consider these elements of Newman's prose style: his use of balance, antithesis, parallelism; his use of illustration and allusion; his handling of prose rhythms; his logical persuasiveness. What is his argumentative method in sections 7 and 8? Why is it effective?

Alfred, Lord Tennyson
(1809–1892)

WHEN THE REACTION AGAINST VICTORIANISM SET IN AT THE END OF THE NINETEENTH century, Tennyson became one of the prime targets for hostile criticism. The Laureate, almost as much of an institution as the Queen herself, seemed to embody all the qualities that the anti-Victorians found so annoying—moral earnestness, sentimentalism, shallow thinking, a tendency to compromise. So Tennyson's reputation went into a decline from which it has only recently begun to recover.

Tennyson was born and reared in Lincolnshire, the son of a somber clergyman-father whose moody temperament was reflected in the boy's own disposition. After an early education largely under the tutelage of his father, Tennyson went up to Cambridge. There he joined the society of The Apostles, a group of earnest young men who came together to discuss literature, philosophy, and politics. Among them he made close friends, especially Arthur Henry Hallam, the brilliant son of a well-known historian.

The death of his father in 1831 made it impossible for Tennyson to return to the University for a degree. By this time, however, he was determined to be a poet, and in 1832 published his second important volume of poems (the first had appeared in 1830). Because of the adverse criticism leveled at this offering and because of the sudden death of his friend Hallam, Tennyson entered upon what has been called his "Ten Years' Period of Silence." During this decade (1833–1842) he published practically no poetry except for two magazine contributions. But he continued to write and revise, and he followed a rigorous program of studies that enlarged and matured his thinking.

The silence was broken in 1842 with *Poems in Two Volumes,* the first volume containing revisions of older pieces, the second containing new poems. These two volumes received favorable comment and marked Tennyson as one of the outstanding poets of the day. In 1845 he received a pension of £200 from the government. In 1847 he published *The Princess,* a long poem on education for women which is a "medley" of song, narrative, and didactic comment.

The turning point in Tennyson's career was 1850. He published *In Memoriam,* the great elegy on which he had worked intermittently for almost seventeen years; he was made Poet Laureate upon the death of Wordsworth; and he finally married after a long engagement. From this time on, Tennyson rose rapidly to fame. His residence at Farringford on the Isle of Wight became such a tourist attraction that he was forced to take a second home at Aldworth. He received many honors, such as degrees from both Oxford and Cambridge and a peerage from the Queen.

Poem after poem continued to flow from his pen: among them *The Ode on the Death of the Duke of Wellington,* his first public performance as Laureate (1852); *Maud,* a long monodrama of lyrical and psychological interest (1855); *Idylls of the King,* a re-working of the Arthurian legends (1859), later to be expanded; and *Enoch Arden,* one of his most popular poems (1864).

After a decade dedicated to a none-too-successful attempt to master the drama (Tennyson wrote a total of seven plays), he returned to lyric, narrative, and philosophical poetry, recapturing much of the vigor of his earlier art. The collections of poems which appeared between 1885 and 1892 contain many fine pieces, especially those stressing narrative or meditative elements.

Some critics have disparaged Tennyson's philosophic insight or profundity of thought. It is true that Tennyson's poetry sheds no startling new light on age-old questions nor provides no brilliant solutions to the specific problems of his age. Rejecting the "falsehood of extremes," Tennyson is cautious, conservative, compromising. Sometimes his theological musings tread perilously close to shallowness; and when he pontificates he may justly be put aside for more rigorous thinkers. Many readers regret that Tennyson the incomparable lyrist is too frequently submerged in Tennyson the self-appointed poet-prophet of the age.

But there is no denying Tennyson's lyrical genius. At their best his images are fresh and compelling. His reworking of classical themes into fresh romantic molds is, more often than not, brilliantly successful. His evocation of mood is matched by few poets. His command of narrative and dialect poetry is frequently vigorous. His mastery of technical forms and devices is sure.

But it is wrong to set up a black-and-white opposition between Tennyson's lyrical gifts and his penchant for philosophic and religious comment. Depth and originality Tennyson's thinking may not have, and perhaps he moralizes too much for modern taste. But even his platitudes often have poetic interest, losing something of their banality in the freshness of expression; and when he explores the age-old conflict between faith and doubt—as he does in *In Memoriam* and many a shorter poem—his ideas are not without value to the twentieth-century reader caught up in a similar struggle.

The Poet

The poet in a golden clime was born,
  With golden stars above;
Dowered with the hate of hate, the scorn of
    scorn,[1]
  The love of love.

He saw through life and death, through good
    and ill,   5
  He saw through his own soul.
The marvel of the everlasting will,
  An open scroll,

Before him lay; with echoing feet he threaded
  The secretest walks of fame: 10
The viewless arrows of his thoughts were
    headed
  And winged with flame,

Like Indian reeds[2] blown from his silver
    tongue,
  And of so fierce a flight,
From Calpe unto Caucasus[3] they sung,   15
  Filling with light

And vagrant melodies the winds which bore
  Them earthward till they lit;
Then, like the arrow-seeds of the field flower,[4]
  The fruitful wit   20

Cleaving took root, and springing forth anew
  Where'er they fell, behold,
Like to the mother plant in semblance, grew
  A flower all gold,

And bravely[5] furnished all abroad to fling 25
  The wingèd shafts of truth,

To throng with stately blooms the breathing
    spring
  Of hope and youth.

So many minds did gird their orbs with beams,
  Though one did fling the fire;   30
Heaven flowed upon the soul in many dreams
  Of high desire.

Thus truth was multiplied on truth, the world
  Like one great garden showed,
And through the wreaths of floating dark
    upcurled,   35
  Rare sunrise flowed.

And Freedom reared in that august sunrise
  Her beautiful bold brow,
When rites and forms before his burning eyes
  Melted like snow.   40

There was no blood upon her maiden robes
  Sunned by those orient skies;
But round about the circles of the globes
  Of her keen eyes

And in her raiment's hem was traced in
    flame   45
  Wisdom, a name to shake
All evil dreams of power—a sacred name.
  And when she spake,

Her words did gather thunder as they ran,
  And as the lightning to the thunder   50
Which follows it, riving the spirit of man,
  Making earth wonder,

So was their meaning to her words. No sword
  Of wrath her right arm whirled,
But one poor poet's scroll, and with his
    word   55
  She shook the world.

(1830)

[1] There are two possible meanings for these parallel phrases in ll. 3–4. What are they, and which is better?

[2] Darts blown from pipes. Follow the extension of the figure through the succeeding lines.

[3] From Gibraltar to the Caucasus Mountains, eastern and western extremes of Europe.

[4] The dandelion.

[5] Gloriously.

STUDY AIDS: 1. This poem is one of Tennyson's earliest expressions of what he believed to be the mission of the poet. According to the poem, what are the endowments of the poet (ll. 1–16)? What are the effects of his words (ll. 17–56)?

2. Does Tennyson give any attention in this poem to the poet's aesthetic function? Would he agree with Shelley's pronouncement: "Poets are the unacknowledged legislators of the world"? In this poem how does Tennyson relate poetry to freedom?

The Lady of Shalott

This is Tennyson's first poem derived from Arthurian legend and one of his most successful experiments in melody and in sensuous imagery.

Part 1

On either side the river lie
Long fields of barley and of rye,
That clothe the wold [1] and meet the sky;
And through the field the road runs by
    To many-towered Camelot,[2]   5
And up and down the people go,
Gazing where the lilies blow [3]
Round an island there below,
    The island of Shalott.

Willows whiten,[4] aspens quiver,   10
Little breezes dusk and shiver
Through the wave that runs for ever
By the island in the river
    Flowing down to Camelot.
Four gray walls, and four gray towers,   15
Overlook a space of flowers,
And the silent isle imbowers
    The Lady of Shalott.

By the margin, willow-veiled,
Slide the heavy barges trailed   20
By slow horses; and unhailed
The shallop [5] flitteth silken-sailed
    Skimming down to Camelot:
But who hath seen her wave her hand?
Or at the casement seen her stand?   25
Or is she known in all the land,
    The Lady of Shalott?

[1] An upland plain.
[2] King Arthur's capital city.
[3] Bloom.
[4] I.e., the wind reveals the white underside of the leaves. Note the condensation in the image and the accuracy of observation.
[5] A small boat.

Only reapers, reaping early
In among the bearded barley,
Hear a song that echoes cheerly   30
From the river winding clearly,
    Down to towered Camelot;
And by the moon the reaper weary,
Piling sheaves in uplands airy,
Listening, whispers " 'Tis the fairy   35
    Lady of Shalott."

Part 2

There she weaves by night and day
A magic web with colors gay.
She has heard a whisper say,
A curse is on her if she stay   40
    To look down to Camelot.
She knows not what the curse may be,
And so she weaveth steadily,
And little other care hath she,
    The Lady of Shalott.   45

And moving through a mirror clear
That hangs before her all the year,
Shadows of the world appear.
There she sees the highway near
    Winding down to Camelot;   50
There the river eddy whirls,
And there the surly village-churls,
And the red cloaks of market girls,
    Pass onward from Shalott.

Sometimes a troop of damsels glad,   55
An abbot on an ambling pad,[6]
Sometimes a curly shepherd-lad,
Or long-haired page in crimson clad,
    Goes by to towered Camelot;

[6] An easy-paced horse.

And sometimes through the mirror blue 60
The knights come riding two and two;
She hath no loyal knight and true,
    The Lady of Shalott.

But in her web she still delights
To weave the mirror's magic sights, 65
For often through the silent nights
A funeral, with plumes and lights
    And music, went to Camelot;
Or when the moon was overhead,
Came two young lovers lately wed; 70
"I am half-sick of shadows," said
    The Lady of Shalott.[7]

Part 3

A bow-shot from her bower-eaves,
He rode between the barley-sheaves;
The sun came dazzling through the leaves, 75
And flamed upon the brazen greaves [8]
    Of bold Sir Lancelot.
A redcross knight for ever kneeled
To a lady in his shield,
That sparkled on the yellow field, 80
    Beside remote Shalott.

The gemmy bridle glittered free,
Like to some branch of stars we see
Hung in the golden galaxy.[9]
The bridle bells rang merrily 85
    As he rode down to Camelot;
And from his blazoned baldric [10] slung
A mighty silver bugle hung,
And as he rode his armor rung,
    Beside remote Shalott. 90

All in the blue unclouded weather
Thick-jewelled shone the saddle-leather,
The helmet and the helmet-feather
Burned like one burning flame together,
    As he rode down to Camelot; 95

[7] Tennyson said that the clue to the symbolic meaning of the poem is in ll. 71–72: "The new-born love for something, for some one in the wide world from which she has been so long secluded, takes her out of the region of shadows into that of realities."

[8] Leg armor.

[9] The Milky Way.

[10] A shoulder belt to hold a bugle or sword.

As often through the purple night,
Below the starry clusters bright,
Some bearded meteor,[11] trailing light,
    Moves over still Shalott.

His broad clear brow in sunlight glowed; 100
On burnished hooves his war-horse trode;
From underneath his helmet flowed
His coal-black curls as on he rode,
    As he rode down to Camelot.
From the bank and from the river 105
He flashed into the crystal mirror,
"Tirra lirra," by the river
    Sang Sir Lancelot.

She left the web, she left the loom,
She made three paces through the room, 110
She saw the water-lily bloom,
She saw the helmet and the plume,
    She looked down to Camelot.
Out flew the web and floated wide;
The mirror cracked from side to side; 115
"The curse is come upon me," cried
    The Lady of Shalott.

Part 4

In the stormy east-wind straining,
The pale yellow woods were waning,
The broad stream in his banks complain-
    ing, 120
Heavily the low sky raining
    Over towered Camelot;
Down she came and found a boat
Beneath a willow left afloat,
And round about the prow she wrote 125
    The Lady of Shalott.

And down the river's dim expanse—
Like some bold seër in a trance,
Seeing all his own mischance—
With a glassy countenance 130
    Did she look to Camelot.
And at the closing of the day
She loosed the chain, and down she lay;
The broad stream bore her far away,
    The Lady of Shalott. 135

Lying, robed in snowy white
That loosely flew to left and right—

[11] Comet.

The leaves upon her falling light—
Through the noises of the night
   She floated down to Camelot;   140
And as the boat-head wound along
The willowy hills and fields among,
They heard her singing her last song,
   The Lady of Shalott.

Heard a carol, mournful, holy,   145
Chanted loudly, chanted lowly,
Till her blood was frozen slowly,
And her eyes were darkened wholly,
   Turned to towered Camelot;
For ere she reached upon the tide   150
The first house by the water-side,
Singing in her song she died,
   The Lady of Shalott.

Under tower and balcony,
By garden-wall and gallery,   155
A gleaming shape she floated by,
Dead pale between the houses high,
   Silent into Camelot.
Out upon the wharfs they came,
Knight and burgher, lord and dame,   160
And round the prow they read her name,
   The Lady of Shalott.

Who is this? and what is here?
And in the lighted palace near
Died the sound of royal cheer;   165
And they crossed themselves for fear,
   All the knights at Camelot:
But Lancelot mused a little space;
He said, "She has a lovely face;

God in his mercy lend her grace,   170
   The Lady of Shalott."
(1832)

STUDY AIDS: 1. Part of the exquisite melody of this poem is achieved through the stanza form. What is unusual about it? Does Tennyson handle the rhymes with ease, or do they seem forced? Which of the many descriptive images seem to you particularly graphic?

2. Tennyson greatly revised this poem between 1832 and 1842. The first version of the last stanza was as follows:

They crossed themselves, their stars they blest,
Knight, minstrel, abbot, squire, and guest,
There lay a parchment on her breast,
That puzzled more than all the rest
   The well-fed wits at Camelot.
"The web was woven curiously,
The charm is broken utterly,
Draw near and fear not—this is I,
   The Lady of Shalott."

Consider the differences in the two versions: What is gained by the questions at the beginning? By the elimination of the series in the second line? By the omission of "the well-fed wits at Camelot"? What dramatic irony is achieved by shifting the focus from the parchment to Lancelot—his musing and his comment? What other improvements can you find?

3. Does Tennyson's suggestion of the symbolic meaning of the poem (see the note to ll. 71–72) satisfy you? Is the Lady to be condemned for not facing up to reality long before, or is she blameworthy for leaving her work and trying to become a part of real life? Could she in any way symbolize the poet and his calling?

The Lotos-Eaters

Homer's *Odyssey* tells how Odysseus (Ulysses) visited the land of the lotos-eaters, where some of his men, eating of the lotos blossom, wished never to return home but to stay in lotos-land forever. Odysseus had to force them back to the ships and tie them up. This poem catches perfectly, in its opening Spenserian stanzas, the soft and dreamy quality of lotos-land, and, in the choric song, the lazy cry of his lotos-filled men, alternating between lush description and complaint against ceaseless and senseless activity.

"Courage!" he [1] said, and pointed toward the
   land,
"This mounting wave will roll us shoreward
   soon."

[1] Ulysses.

In the afternoon they came unto a land,[2]
In which it seemed always afternoon.

[2] Note that ll. 1 and 3 have the same end-word. Tennyson said that the "no-rhyme" is "lazier." Note the similar "lazy" effect of the repetition of "afternoon."

All round the coast the languid air did
  swoon,   5
Breathing like one that hath a weary dream.
Full-faced above the valley stood the moon;
And like a downward smoke, the slender
  stream [3]
Along the cliff to fall and pause and fall did
  seem.

A land of streams! some, like a downward
  smoke,   10
Slow-dropping veils of thinnest lawn,[4] did go;
And some through wavering lights and
  shadows broke,
Rolling a slumbrous sheet of foam below.
They saw the gleaming river seaward flow
From the inner land; far off, three mountain-
  tops,   15
Three silent pinnacles of aged snow,
Stood sunset-flushed; and, dewed with show-
  ery drops,
Up-clomb the shadowy pine above the woven
  copse.[5]

The charmèd sunset lingered low adown
In the red west; through mountain clefts the
  dale   20
Was seen far inland, and the yellow down
Bordered with palm, and many a winding
  vale
And meadow, set with slender galingale;[6]
A land where all things always seemed the
  same!
And round about the keel with faces pale,   25
Dark faces pale against that rosy flame,
The mild-eyed melancholy Lotos-eaters came.

Branches they bore of that enchanted stem,
Laden with flower and fruit, whereof they
  gave
To each, but whoso did receive of them   30
And taste, to him the gushing of the wave
Far, far away did seem to mourn and rave
On alien shores; and if his fellow spake,

[3] The effect of ll. 8–9 is like that of a slow-motion picture.
[4] A fine, sheer linen or cotton fabric.
[5] What effect is given by the "s"-sounds in this stanza? And by the "l"-sounds in the following stanza?
[6] A kind of herb.

His voice was thin, as voices from the grave;
And deep-asleep he seemed, yet all awake,   35
And music in his ears his beating heart did
  make.

They sat them down upon the yellow sand,
Between the sun and moon upon the shore;
And sweet it was to dream of fatherland,
Of child, and wife, and slave; but evermore   40
Most weary seemed the sea, weary the oar,
Weary the wandering fields of barren foam.
Then some one said, "We will return no
  more";
And all at once they sang, "Our island home [7]
Is far beyond the wave; we will no longer
  roam."   45

Choric Song

I

There is sweet music here that softer falls
Than petals from blown roses on the grass,
Or night-dews on still waters between walls
Of shadowy granite, in a gleaming pass;
Music that gentlier on the spirit lies,   50
Than tired eyelids upon tired eyes;
Music that brings sweet sleep down from the
  blissful skies.
Here are cool mosses deep,
And through the moss the ivies creep,
And in the stream the long-leaved flowers
  weep,   55
And from the craggy ledge the poppy hangs
  in sleep.

2

Why are we weighed upon with heaviness,
And utterly consumed with sharp distress,
While all things else have rest from weariness?
All things have rest: why should we toil
  alone,   60
We only toil, who are the first of things,
And make perpetual moan,
Still from one sorrow to another thrown;
Nor ever fold our wings,
And cease from wanderings,   65
Nor steep our brows in slumber's holy balm;
Nor harken what the inner spirit sings,

[7] Ithaca, an island off the west coast of Greece.

"There is no joy but calm!"—
Why should we only toil, the roof and crown
of things?

3

Lo! in the middle of the wood,   70
The folded leaf is wooed from out the bud
With winds upon the branch, and there
Grows green and broad, and takes no care,
Sun-steeped at noon, and in the moon
Nightly dew-fed; and turning yellow   75
Falls, and floats adown the air.
Lo! sweetened with the summer light,
The full-juiced apple, waxing over-mellow,
Drops in a silent autumn night.
All its allotted length of days   80
The flower ripens in its place,
Ripens and fades, and falls, and hath no toil,
Fast-rooted in the fruitful soil.

4

Hateful is the dark-blue sky,
Vaulted o'er the dark-blue sea.   85
Death is the end of life; ah, why
Should life all labor be?
Let us alone. Time driveth onward fast,
And in a little while our lips are dumb.
Let us alone. What is it that will last?   90
All things are taken from us, and become
Portions and parcels of the dreadful past.
Let us alone. What pleasure can we have
To war with evil? Is there any peace
In ever climbing up the climbing wave?   95
All things have rest, and ripen toward the
grave
In silence—ripen, fall and cease:
Give us long rest or death, dark death, or
dreamful ease.

5

How sweet it were, hearing the downward
stream,
With half-shut eyes ever to seem   100
Falling asleep in a half-dream!
To dream and dream, like yonder amber light,
Which will not leave the myrrh-bush on the
height;

To hear each other's whispered speech;
Eating the lotos day by day,   105
To watch the crisping ripples on the beach,
And tender curving lines of creamy spray;
To lend our hearts and spirits wholly
To the influence of mild-minded melancholy;
To muse and brood and live again in mem-
ory,   110
With those old faces of our infancy
Heaped over with a mound of grass,
Two handfuls of white dust, shut in an urn
of brass!

6

Dear is the memory of our wedded lives,
And dear the last embraces of our wives   115
And their warm tears; but all hath suffered
change;
For surely now our household hearths are
cold,
Our sons inherit us, our looks are strange,
And we should come like ghosts to trouble
joy.
Or else the island princes over-bold   120
Have eat our substance, and the minstrel sings
Before them of the ten-years' war in Troy,
And our great deeds, as half-forgotten things.
Is there confusion in the little isle?
Let what is broken so remain.   125
The gods are hard to reconcile;
'Tis hard to settle order once again.
There *is* confusion worse than death,
Trouble on trouble, pain on pain,
Long labor unto agèd breath,   130
Sore task to hearts worn out by many wars
And eyes grown dim with gazing on the
pilot-stars.[8]

7

But, propped on beds of amaranth[9] and
moly,[10]
How sweet (while warm airs lull us, blowing
lowly)

[8] Note the several excuses the men give (ll.
114–132) for not returning home.
[9] A fictitious flower, supposed never to fade.
[10] A magic flower, used by Odysseus to protect
himself against the enchantress Circe.

With half-dropped eyelids still,   135
Beneath a heaven dark and holy,
To watch the long bright river drawing slowly
His waters from the purple hill—
To hear the dewy echoes calling
From cave to cave through the thick-twined
    vine—   140
To watch the emerald-colored water falling
Through many a woven acanthus-wreath [11]
    divine!
Only to hear and see the far-off sparkling
    brine,
Only to hear were sweet, stretched out be-
    neath the pine.

8

The lotos blooms below the barren peak, [12] 145
The lotos blows by every winding creek;
All day the wind breathes low with mellower
    tone;
Through every hollow cave and alley lone
Round and round the spicy downs the yellow
    lotos-dust is blown.
We have had enough of action, and of motion
    we,   150
Rolled to starboard, rolled to larboard, when
    the surge was seething free,
Where the wallowing monster spouted his
    foam-fountains in the sea.
Let us swear an oath, and keep it with an
    equal mind,
In the hollow Lotos-land to live and lie re-
    clined
On the hills like gods together, careless of
    mankind.   155
For they lie beside their nectar, and the bolts
    are hurled
Far below them in the valleys, and the clouds
    are lightly curled

Round their golden houses, girdled with the
    gleaming world;
Where they smile in secret, looking over
    wasted lands,
Blight and famine, plague and earthquake,
    roaring deeps and fiery sands,   160
Clanging fights, and flaming towns, and sink-
    ing ships, and praying hands.
But they smile, they find a music centered in
    a doleful song
Steaming up, a lamentation and an ancient
    tale of wrong,
Like a tale of little meaning though the words
    are strong;
Chanted from an ill-used race of men that
    cleave the soil,   165
Sow the seed, and reap the harvest with
    enduring toil,
Storing yearly little dues of wheat, and wine
    and oil;
Till they perish and they suffer—some, 'tis
    whispered—down in hell
Suffer endless anguish, others in Elysian val-
    leys dwell,
Resting weary limbs at last on beds of as-
    phodel. [13]   170
Surely, surely, slumber is more sweet than
    toil, the shore
Than labor in the deep mid-ocean, wind and
    wave and oar;
O, rest ye, brother mariners, we will not
    wander more.
(1832)

STUDY AIDS: 1. Why is the Spenserian
stanza an effective choice for the opening description of the land of the lotos-eaters? Point out
the various means by which Tennyson achieves
a lazy, dreamy atmosphere.
    2. Do you see any similarity between the
theme of this poem and that of *The Lady of
Shalott* in terms of the problem of facing reality?

[11] The acanthus was a plant sacred to the Greek
gods.
[12] Notice the change of rhyme-scheme in the
last section.

[13] According to Homer, the Elysian Fields (the
Greek paradise) were filled with asphodel (of the
lily family).

St. Agnes' Eve [1]

Deep on the convent-roof the snows
  Are sparkling to the moon;
My breath to heaven like vapor goes; [2]
  May my soul follow soon!
The shadows of the convent-towers   5
  Slant down the snowy sward,
Still creeping with the creeping hours
  That lead me to my Lord.
Make Thou my spirit pure and clear
  As are the frosty skies,   10
Or this first snowdrop of the year
  That in my bosom lies.

As these white robes are soiled and dark,
  To yonder shining ground;
As this pale taper's earthly spark,   15
  To yonder argent round; [3]
So shows my soul before the Lamb, [4]
  My spirit before Thee;
So in mine earthly house I am,
  To that I hope to be.   20
Break up the heavens, O Lord! and far,
  Through all yon starlight keen,

Draw me, thy bride, a glittering star,
  In raiment white and clean.

He lifts me to the golden doors;   25
  The flashes come and go;
All heaven bursts her starry floors,
  And strows her lights below,
And deepens on and up! the gates
  Roll back, and far within   30
For me the Heavenly Bridegroom [5] waits,
  To make me pure of sin.
The sabbaths of eternity,
  One sabbath deep and wide—
A light upon the shining sea—   35
  The Bridegroom with his bride!
(1837)

STUDY AIDS: 1. Who is speaking in the poem? What images reveal her piety?
2. What is the basic difference between Tennyson's treatment of the legend and Keats's (in *The Eve of St. Agnes*)?

Morte d'Arthur [1]

This poem, which was later revised and incorporated into the *Idylls of the King* as *The Passing of Arthur*, was written about 1834, long before Tennyson had conceived of a full, allegorical treatment of the Arthurian legends.

So all day long the noise of battle rolled
Among the mountains by the winter sea,
Until King Arthur's table, man by man,
Had fallen in Lyonness [2] about their lord,
King Arthur; then, because his wound was deep,   5
The bold Sir Bedivere uplifted him,
Sir Bedivere, the last of all his knights,

And bore him to a chapel nigh the field,
A broken chancel with a broken cross,
That stood on a dark strait of barren land.   10
On one side lay the ocean and on one
Lay a great water, and the moon was full.
  Then spake King Arthur to Sir Bedivere:
"The sequel of to-day unsolders all
The goodliest fellowship of famous knights   15
Whereof this world holds record. Such a sleep

---

[1] St. Agnes was a martyred Christian virgin of the third century. It was superstitiously believed that on St. Agnes' Eve (January 20) a young girl, by observing the proper ritual, could gain a vision of her future husband.
[2] Cf. Keats's *The Eve of St. Agnes*, l. 8 (p. 689).
[3] The silver moon.

[4] Christ.
[5] Christ.

---

[1] "The death of Arthur."
[2] A mythical district next to Cornwall. According to legend, it sank beneath the sea.

They sleep—the men I loved. I think that we
Shall never more, at any future time,
Delight our souls with talk of knightly deeds,
Walking about the gardens and the halls 20
Of Camelot,[3] as in the days that were.
I perish by this people which I made,—
Though Merlin [4] sware that I should come again
To rule once more—but let what will be, be,
I am so deeply smitten through the helm 25
That without help I cannot last till morn.
Thou therefore take my brand Excalibur,
Which was my pride; for thou rememberest how
In those old days, one summer noon, an arm
Rose up from out the bosom of the lake, 30
Clothed in white samite,[5] mystic, wonderful,
Holding the sword—and how I rowed across
And took it, and have worn it, like a king;
And, wheresoever I am sung or told
In aftertime, this also shall be known. 35
But now delay not; take Excalibur,
And fling him far into the middle mere; [6]
Watch what thou seest, and lightly bring me word."
To him replied the bold Sir Bedivere:
"It is not meet, Sir King, to leave thee thus, 40
Aidless, alone, and smitten through the helm.
A little thing may harm a wounded man.
Yet I thy hest will all perform at full,
Watch what I see, and lightly bring thee word."
So saying, from the ruined shrine he stepped 45
And in the moon athwart the place of tombs,
Where lay the mighty bones of ancient men,
Old knights, and over them the sea-wind sang
Shrill, chill, with flakes of foam. He, stepping down
By zigzag paths, and juts of pointed rock, 50
Came on the shining levels of the lake.
There drew he forth the brand Excalibur,
And o'er him, drawing it, the winter moon,
Brightening the skirts of a long cloud, ran forth

And sparkled keen with frost against the hilt; 55
For all the haft twinkled with diamond sparks,
Myriads of topaz-lights, and jacinth [7]-work
Of subtlest jewelry. He gazed so long
That both his eyes were dazzled, as he stood,
This way and that dividing the swift mind, 60
In act to throw; but at the last it seemed
Better to leave Excalibur concealed
There in the many-knotted water-flags,
That whistled stiff and dry about the marge.
So strode he back slow to the wounded king. 65
Then spake King Arthur to Sir Bedivere:
"Hast thou performed my mission which I gave?
What is it thou hast seen? or what hast heard?"
And answer made the bold Sir Bedivere:
"I heard the ripple washing in the reeds, 70
And the wild water lapping on the crag."
To whom replied King Arthur, faint and pale:
"Thou hast betrayed thy nature and thy name,
Not rendering true answer, as beseemed
Thy fealty, nor like a noble knight; 75
For surer sign had followed, either hand,
Or voice, or else a motion of the mere.
This is a shameful thing for men to lie.
Yet now, I charge thee, quickly go again
As thou art lief [8] and dear, and do the thing 80
I bade thee, watch, and lightly bring me word."
Then went Sir Bedivere the second time
Across the ridge, and paced beside the mere,
Counting the dewy pebbles, fixed in thought;
But when he saw the wonder of the hilt, 85
How curiously and strangely chased,[9] he smote
His palms together, and he cried aloud:
"And if indeed I cast the brand away,
Surely a precious thing, one worthy note,
Should thus be lost forever from the earth, 90
Which might have pleased the eyes of many men.
What good should follow this, if this were done?

[3] King Arthur's capital.
[4] The magician of Arthur's court.
[5] A heavy silk fabric.
[6] Middle of the lake.

[7] A kind of gem.
[8] Beloved.
[9] Engraved.

What harm, undone? deep harm to disobey,
Seeing obedience is the bond of rule.
Were it well to obey then, if a king de-
    mand   95
An act unprofitable, against himself?
The king is sick, and knows not what he
    does.
What record, or what relic of my lord
Should be to aftertime, but empty breath
And rumors of a doubt? but were this kept, 100
Stored in some treasure-house of mighty kings,
Some one might show it at a joust of arms,
Saying, 'King Arthur's sword, Excalibur,
Wrought by the lonely maiden of the lake;
Nine years she wrought it, sitting in the
    deeps   105
Upon the hidden bases of the hills.'
So might some old man speak in the after-
    time
To all the people, winning reverence;
But now much honor and much fame were
    lost." [10]
    So spake he, clouded with his own con-
    ceit,[11]   110
And hid Excalibur the second time,
And so strode back slow to the wounded king.
    Then spoke King Arthur, breathing heav-
    ily:
"What is it thou has seen? or what hast
    heard?"
    And answer made the bold Sir Bedivere: 115
"I heard the water lapping on the crag,
And the long ripple washing in the reeds."
    To whom replied King Arthur, much in
    wrath:
"Ah, miserable and unkind, untrue,
Unknightly, traitor-hearted! Woe is me! 120
Authority forgets a dying king,
Laid widowed of the power in his eye
That bowed the will. I see thee what thou
    art,
For thou, the latest-left of all my knights,
In whom should meet the offices of all, 125
Thou wouldst betray me for the precious hilt;
Either from lust of gold, or like a girl
Valuing the giddy pleasure of the eyes.

[10] Note that Bedivere has a harder mental struggle this time. What arguments does he use to convince himself?
[11] Thought.

Yet, for a man may fail in duty twice,
And the third time may prosper, get thee
    thence;   130
But, if thou spare to fling Excalibur,
I will arise and slay thee with my hands."
    Then quickly rose Sir Bedivere, and ran,
And, leaping down the ridges lightly, plunged
Among the bulrush-beds, and clutched the
    sword,   135
And strongly wheeled and threw it. The great
    brand
Made lightnings in the splendor of the moon,
And flashing round and round, and whirled
    in an arch,
Shot like a streamer of the northern morn,[12]
Seen where the moving isles of winter [13]
    shock   140
By night, with noises of the northern sea.
So flashed and fell the brand Excalibur;
But ere he dipped the surface, rose an arm
Clothed in white samite, mystic, wonderful,
And caught him by the hilt, and brandished
    him   145
Three times, and drew him under in the
    mere.
And lightly went the other to the king.
    Then spoke King Arthur, drawing thicker
    breath:
"Now see I by thine eyes that this is done.
Speak out; what is it thou hast heard, or
    seen?"   150
    And answer made the bold Sir Bedivere:
"Sir King, I closed mine eyelids, lest the gems
Should blind my purpose, for I never saw,
Nor shall see, here or elsewhere, till I die,
Not though I live three lives of mortal
    men,   155
So great a miracle as yonder hilt.
Then with both hands I flung him, wheeling
    him;
But when I looked again, behold an arm,
Clothed in white samite, mystic, wonderful,
That caught him by the hilt, and brandished
    him   160
Three times, and drew him under in the
    mere."
    And answer made King Arthur, breathing
    hard:

[12] I.e., northern lights.
[13] I.e., icebergs.

"My end draws nigh; 'tis time that I were
    gone.
Make broad thy shoulders to receive my
    weight,
And bear me to the margin; yet I fear   165
My wound hath taken cold, and I shall die."
    So saying, from the pavement he half rose,
Slowly, with pain, reclining on his arm,
And looking wistfully with wide blue eyes
As in a picture. Him Sir Bedivere   170
Remorsefully regarded through his tears,
And would have spoken, but he found not
    words,
Then took with care, and kneeling on one
    knee,
O'er both his shoulders drew the languid
    hands,
And rising bore him through the place of
    tombs.   175
    But, as he walked, King Arthur panted
    hard,
Like one that feels a nightmare on his bed
When all the house is mute. So sighed the
    king,
Muttering and murmuring at his ear, "Quick,
    quick!
I fear it is too late, and I shall die."   180
But the other swiftly strode from ridge to
    ridge,
Clothed with his breath, and looking, as he
    walked,
Larger than human on the frozen hills.
He heard the deep behind him, and a cry
Before. His own thought drove him like a
    goad.   185
Dry [14] clashed his harness in the icy caves
And barren chasms, and all to left and right
The bare black cliff clanged round him, as
    he based
His feet on juts of slippery crag that rang
Sharp-smitten with the dint of armèd
    heels—   190
And on a sudden, lo! the level lake,
And the long glories of the winter moon.
    Then saw they how there hove a dusky
    barge,
Dark as a funeral scarf from stem to stern,
Beneath them; and descending they were
    ware   195

    [14] Harsh.

That all the decks were dense with stately
    forms
Black-stoled, black-hooded, like a dream—by
    these
Three queens with crowns of gold—and from
    them rose
A cry that shivered to the tingling stars,
And, as it were one voice, an agony   200
Of lamentation, like a wind, that shrills
All night in a waste land, where no one
    comes,
Or hath come, since the making of the world.
    Then murmured Arthur, "Place me in the
    barge,"
And to the barge they came. There those three
    queens   205
Put forth their hands, and took the king, and
    wept.
But she, that rose the tallest of them all
And fairest, laid his head upon her lap,
And loosed the shattered casque, and chafed
    his hands,
And called him by his name, complaining
    loud,   210
And dropping bitter tears against his brow
Striped with dark blood; for all his face was
    white
And colorless, and like the withered moon
Smote by the fresh beam of the springing
    east;
And all his greaves and cuisses [15] dashed with
    drops   215
Of onset; and the light and lustrous curls—
That made his forehead like a rising sun
High from the dais-throne—were parched with
    dust;
Or, clotted into points and hanging loose,
Mixed with the knightly growth that fringed
    his lips.   220
So like a shattered column lay the king;
Not like that Arthur who, with lance in
    rest,
From spur to plume a star of tournament,
Shot through the lists at Camelot, and charged
Before the eyes of ladies and of kings.   225
    Then loudly cried the bold Sir Bedivere:
"Ah! my Lord Arthur, whither shall I go?
Where shall I hide my forehead and my eyes?
For now I see the true old times are dead,

    [15] I.e., leg and thigh armor.

When every morning brought a noble
    chance,   230
And every chance brought out a noble knight.
Such times have been not since the light [16]
    that led
The holy Elders with the gift of myrrh.
But now the whole Round Table is dissolved
Which was an image of the mighty world; 235
And I, the last, go forth companionless,
And the days darken round me, and the
    years,
Among new men, strange faces, other minds."
    And slowly answered Arthur from the
    barge:
"The old order changeth, yielding place to
    new,[17]   240
And God fulfils himself in many ways,
Lest one good custom should corrupt the
    world.
Comfort thyself: what comfort is in me?
I have lived my life, and that which I have
    done
May He within himself make pure! but
    thou,   245
If thou shouldst never see my face again,
Pray for my soul. More things are wrought
    by prayer
Than this world dreams of. Wherefore, let
    thy voice
Rise like a fountain for me night and day.
For what are men better than sheep or
    goats   250
That nourish a blind life within the brain,
If, knowing God, they lift not hands of
    prayer

Both for themselves and those who call them
    friend?
For so the whole round earth is every way
Bound by gold chains about the feet of
    God.   255
But now farewell. I am going a long way
With these thou seest—if indeed I go—
(For all my mind is clouded with a doubt)
To the island-valley of Avilion; [18]
Where falls not hail, or rain, or any snow, 260
Nor ever wind blows loudly; but it lies
Deep-meadowed, happy, fair with orchard
    lawns
And bowery hollows crowned with summer
    sea,
Where I will heal me of my grievous wound."
    So said he, and the barge with oar and
    sail   265
Moved from the brink, like some full-breasted
    swan
That, fluting a wild carol ere her death,[19]
Ruffles her pure cold plume, and takes the
    flood
With swarthy webs. Long stood Sir Bedivere
Revolving many memories, till the hull   270
Looked one black dot against the verge of
    dawn,
And on the mere the wailing died away.
(1842)

STUDY AIDS: 1. What is the verse form?
What effect is given by the many RUN-ON LINES?
    2. Is there any psychological interest in the
story? Are Bedivere's actions made credible?
"Some think that King Arthur may be taken
to typify conscience" (Tennyson). How?

Ulysses

As Homer's *Odyssey* tells us, Ulysses (Odysseus) wandered ten years after the fall of Troy but
finally reached his home in Ithaca and killed the suitors who were plaguing his wife, Penelope.
Tennyson's poem, however, is based upon a passage in Dante's *Inferno*, in which Ulysses says
that neither affection for his son, nor respect for his old father, nor love for Penelope could
conquer his desire to gain experience of the world and of human vice and virtue. So he sets forth

[16] The Star of Bethlehem.
[17] The "old order" was indeed changing when the *Morte d'Arthur* was published: Parliamentary
reform and Catholic Emancipation had taken place; the Oxford Movement, the Corn Law agitation, and
Chartism were in full swing; new social and industrial problems were demanding new solutions.
[18] Avalon, the earthly paradise of the Arthurian legends.
[19] According to legend, the swan sings only just as it is about to die.

upon the sea again with a small, faithful band, and after long wandering they reach the extremities of the world. Whereupon Ulysses urges his men to go on, reminding them that they were not "made to live like beasts, but to follow virtue and knowledge."

Tennyson said that *Ulysses* expressed his need "of going forward and braving the struggle of life" after the death of his close friend Hallam.

It little profits that an idle king,
By this still hearth, among these barren crags,[1]
Matched with an agèd wife,[2] I mete and dole
Unequal laws unto a savage race,
That hoard, and sleep, and feed, and know not me.   5
I cannot rest from travel; I will drink
Life to the lees. All times I have enjoyed
Greatly, have suffered greatly, both with those
That loved me, and alone; on shore, and when
Through scudding drifts the rainy Hyades [3] 10
Vexed the dim sea. I am become a name;
For always roaming with a hungry heart
Much have I seen and known,—cities of men
And manners, climates, councils, governments,
Myself not least, but honored of them all,— 15
And drunk delight of battle with my peers,
Far on the ringing plains of windy Troy.
I am a part of all that I have met;
Yet all experience is an arch wherethrough [4]
Gleams that untraveled world, whose margin fades   20
For ever and for ever when I move.
How dull it is to pause, to make an end,
To rust unburnished, not to shine in use!
As though to breathe were life! Life piled on life
Were all too little, and of one to me   25
Little remains; but every hour is saved
From that eternal silence, something more,
A bringer of new things; and vile it were
For some three suns to store and hoard myself,
And this gray spirit yearning in desire   30
To follow knowledge, like a sinking star,

Beyond the utmost bound of human thought.
    This is my son, mine own Telemachus,
To whom I leave the scepter and the isle,—
Well-loved of me, discerning to fulfil   35
This labor, by slow prudence to make mild
A rugged people, and through soft degrees
Subdue them to the useful and the good.
Most blameless is he, centered in the sphere
Of common duties, decent not to fail   40
In offices of tenderness, and pay
Meet adoration to my household gods,
When I am gone. He works his work, I mine.
    There lies the port; the vessel puffs her sail;
There gloom the dark, broad seas. My mariners,   45
Souls that have toiled, and wrought, and thought with me,—
That ever with a frolic welcome took
The thunder and the sunshine, and opposed
Free hearts, free foreheads,—you and I are old;
Old age hath yet his honor and his toil.   50
Death closes all; but something ere the end,
Some work of noble note, may yet be done,
Not unbecoming men that strove with gods.
The lights begin to twinkle from the rocks;
The long day wanes; the slow moon climbs; the deep   55
Moans round with many voices. Come, my friends,
'Tis not too late to seek a newer world.
Push off, and sitting well in order smite
The sounding furrows; for my purpose holds
To sail beyond the sunset, and the baths   60
Of all the western stars, until I die.
It may be that the gulfs will wash us down;
It may be we shall touch the Happy Isles,[5]
And see the great Achilles,[6] whom we knew.

[1] Of Ithaca, Ulysses' kingdom.
[2] Penelope.
[3] A star cluster believed to cause rain when it rose with the sun. Tennyson borrowed the phrase from Virgil ("pluvias Hyades"). What does this borrowing add to the poem?
[4] Explain the image in ll. 19–21.

[5] The Islands of the Blest (later identified with the Elysian Fields), the dwelling place of good men after death.
[6] The outstanding Greek hero in the Trojan War.

Though much is taken, much abides; and though 65
We are not now that strength which in old days
Moved earth and heaven, that which we are, we are,—
One equal temper of heroic hearts,
Made weak by time and fate, but strong in will
To strive, to seek, to find, and not to yield. 70
(1842)

STUDY AIDS: 1. What is the threefold structure of the poem? How does this structure add to the dramatic quality? Note the number of RUN-ON LINES and the stops within the lines. What does this treatment of the blank verse add to the poem?

2. Is Ulysses speaking to his men throughout the poem, or only from l. 45 on? What qualities of a persuasive speech does the poem have? What use does Ulysses make of contrast?

3. What is Ulysses' attitude toward his wife, his son, his people, and his mariners? Why does he have these attitudes? Would you call him a restless wanderer who wants new adventures and who cannot stay home and face his royal responsibilities?

4. Contrast the mood and tone of *Ulysses* with those of *The Lotos-Eaters*. Is Ulysses essentially a character sketch, is it a statement of a philosophy of life, or is it both?

Tithonus

Tithonus was loved by Aurora (Eos), goddess of the dawn, who asked the gods to grant him immortality but who forgot to request eternal youth. Her petition was granted, and although Tithonus did not die, he grew older and weaker and more withered.

The woods decay, the woods decay and fall,
The vapors weep their burthen to the ground,
Man comes and tills the field and lies beneath,
And after many a summer dies the swan.
Me only cruel immortality 5
Consumes; I wither slowly in thine [1] arms,
Here at the quiet limit of the world,
A white-haired shadow roaming like a dream
The ever-silent spaces of the east,
Far-folded mists, and gleaming halls of morn. 10
Alas! for this gray shadow, once a man—
So glorious in his beauty and thy choice,
Who madest him thy chosen, that he seemed
To his great heart none other than a god!
I asked thee, "Give me immortality." 15
Then didst thou grant mine asking with a smile,
Like wealthy men who care not how they give.
But thy strong Hours [2] indignant worked their wills,

And beat me down and marred and wasted me,
And though they could not end me, left me maimed 20
To dwell in presence of immortal youth,
Immortal age beside immortal youth,
And all I was in ashes. Can thy love,
Thy beauty, make amends, though even now,
Close over us, the silver star, [3] thy guide, 25
Shines in those tremulous eyes that fill with tears
To hear me? Let me go; take back thy gift.
Why should a man desire in any way
To vary from the kindly [4] race of men,
Or pass beyond the goal of ordinance 30
Where all should pause, as is most meet for all?
A soft air fans the cloud apart; there comes
A glimpse of that dark world where I was born.
Once more the old mysterious glimmer steals
From thy pure brows, and from thy shoulders pure, 35
And bosom beating with a heart renewed.

[1] Aurora's.
[2] The goddesses who see to it that all things go through their appointed cycles of birth, growth, decay, and death.
[3] The morning star (Venus).
[4] Natural.

Thy cheek begins to redden through the
    gloom,
Thy sweet eyes brighten slowly close to mine,
Ere yet they blind the stars, and the wild
    team [5]
Which love thee, yearning for thy yoke,
    arise,   40
And shake the darkness from their loosened
    manes,
And beat the twilight into flakes of fire.
    Lo! ever thus thou growest beautiful
In silence, then before thine answer given
Departest, and thy tears are on my cheek.   45
    Why wilt thou ever scare me with thy tears;
And make me tremble lest a saying learned,
In days far-off, on that dark earth, be true?
"The gods themselves cannot recall their gifts."
    Ay me! ay me! with what another heart   50
In days far-off, and with what other eyes
I used to watch—if I be he that watched—
The lucid outline forming round thee; saw
The dim curls kindle into sunny rings;
Changed with thy mystic change, and felt
    my blood   55
Glow with the glow that slowly crimsoned all
Thy presence and thy portals, while I lay,
Mouth, forehead, eyelids, growing dewy-warm

With kisses balmier than half-opening buds
Of April, and could hear the lips that
    kissed   60
Whispering I knew not what of wild and
    sweet,
Like that strange song I heard Apollo sing,
While Ilion [6] like a mist rose into towers.
    Yet hold me not for ever in thine east;
How can my nature longer mix with thine? 65
Coldly thy rosy shadows bathe me, cold
Are all thy lights, and cold my wrinkled feet
Upon thy glimmering thresholds, when the
    steam
Floats up from those dim fields about the
    homes
Of happy men that have the power to die,   70
And grassy barrows [7] of the happier dead.
Release me, and restore me to the ground.
Thou seest all things, thou wilt see my grave;
Thou wilt renew thy beauty morn by morn,
I earth in earth forget these empty courts,   75
And thee returning on thy silver wheels.
(1833–34?; 1860)

STUDY AIDS: Contrast the TONE of this
poem with that of *Ulysses*. How is this difference
in tone achieved?

Locksley Hall

Locksley Hall is a study in the psychology of youth. The young man who is the speaker in the
poem has been disappointed in love; his sweetheart, Amy, has been forced by her parents to
marry a richer man. How shall he handle this disappointment?—here is the problem to which the
poem suggests various solutions.

Comrades, leave me here a little, while as yet
    'tis early morn;
Leave me here, and when you want me,
    sound upon the bugle-horn.

'Tis the place, and all around it, as of old,
    the curlews [1] call,
Dreary gleams [2] about the moorland flying
    over Locksley Hall;

Locksley Hall, that in the distance overlooks
    the sandy tracts,   5
And the hollow ocean-ridges roaring into
    cataracts.

Many a night from yonder ivied casement,
    ere I went to rest,
Did I look on great Orion [3] sloping slowly to
    the west.

[5] The team that pulled Aurora's chariot up to
Mt. Olympus each day to announce the dawn.
[6] Troy, which, according to legend, was built by
the music of Apollo's lyre.

[7] Large sepulchral mounds.
_____
[1] Large, brownish birds.
[2] Of light, not in apposition with "curlews."
[3] The constellation of "The Hunter."

Many a night I saw the Pleiads,[4] rising
  through the mellow shade,
Glitter like a swarm of fire-flies tangled in a
  silver braid.   10

Here about the beach I wandered, nourishing a youth sublime
With the fairy tales of science, and the long
  result of time;

When the centuries behind me like a fruitful
  land reposed;
When I clung to all the present for the
  promise that it closed;

When I dipped into the future far as human
  eye could see,   15
Saw the vision of the world, and all the
  wonder that would be.—[5]

In the spring a fuller crimson comes upon the
  robin's breast;
In the spring the wanton lapwing [6] gets himself another crest;

In the spring a livelier iris [7] changes on the
  burnished dove;
In the spring a young man's fancy lightly
  turns to thoughts of love.   20

Then her cheek was pale and thinner than
  should be for one so young,
And her eyes on all my motions with a mute
  observance hung.

And I said, "My cousin Amy, speak, and
  speak the truth to me,
Trust me, cousin, all the current of my being
  sets to thee."

On her pallid cheek and forehead came a
  color and a light,   25
As I have seen the rosy red flushing in the
  northern night.

And she turned—her bosom shaken with a
  sudden storm of sighs—
All the spirit deeply dawning in the dark of
  hazel eyes—

Saying, "I have hid my feelings, fearing they
  should do me wrong";
Saying, "Dost thou love me, cousin?" weeping, "I have loved thee long."   30

Love took up the glass of time, and turned
  it in his glowing hands;
Every moment, lightly shaken, ran itself in
  golden sands.

Love took up the harp of life, and smote on
  all the chords with might;
Smote the chord of self, that, trembling,
  passed in music out of sight.[8]

Many a morning on the moorland did we
  hear the copses [9] ring,   35
And her whisper thronged my pulses with the
  fullness of the spring.

Many an evening by the waters did we watch
  the stately ships,
And our spirits rushed together at the touching of the lips.

O my cousin, shallow-hearted! O my Amy,
  mine no more!
O the dreary, dreary moorland! O the barren,
  barren shore!   40

Falser than all fancy fathoms, falser than all
  songs have sung,
Puppet to a father's threat, and servile to a
  shrewish tongue!

Is it well to wish thee happy?—having known
  me—to decline
On a range of lower feelings and a narrower
  heart than mine!

Yet it shall be; thou shalt lower to his level
  day by day,   45

---

[4] A group of stars in the constellation Taurus.
[5] What kind of young man is revealed by ll. 11-16?
[6] A crested bird of the plover family.
[7] During the mating season the colors on the dove's neck become more brilliant.
[8] Explain the meaning of the two images in ll. 31-34.
[9] Groves of small trees.

What is fine within thee growing coarse to
sympathize with clay.

As the husband is, the wife is; thou art mated
with a clown,
And the grossness of his nature will have
weight to drag thee down.

He will hold thee, when his passion shall
have spent its novel force,
Something better than his dog, a little dearer
than his horse. 50

What is this? his eyes are heavy; think not
they are glazed with wine.
Go to him, it is thy duty; kiss him, take his
hand in thine.

It may be my lord is weary, that his brain is
overwrought;
Soothe him with thy finer fancies, touch him
with thy lighter thought.

He will answer to the purpose, easy things
to understand— 55
Better thou wert dead before me, though I
slew thee with my hand!

Better thou and I were lying, hidden from
the heart's disgrace,
Rolled in one another's arms, and silent in a
last embrace.

Cursèd be the social wants that sin against
the strength of youth!
Cursèd be the social lies that warp us from
the living truth! 60

Cursèd be the sickly forms that err from
honest nature's rule!
Cursèd be the gold that gilds the straitened
forehead of the fool!

Well—'tis well that I should bluster!—Hadst
thou less unworthy proved—
Would to God—for I had loved thee more
than ever wife was loved.

Am I mad, that I should cherish that which
bears but bitter fruit? 65

I will pluck it from my bosom, though my
heart be at the root.

Never, though my mortal summers to such
length of years should come
As the many-wintered crow that leads the
clanging rookery home.

Where is comfort? in division of the records
of the mind?
Can I part her from herself, and love her, as
I knew her, kind? 70

I remember one that perished; sweetly did
she speak and move;
Such a one do I remember, whom to look at
was to love.

Can I think of her as dead, and love her for
the love she bore?
No—she never loved me truly; love is love for
evermore.

Comfort? comfort scorned of devils! this is
truth the poet [10] sings, 75
That a sorrow's crown of sorrow is remembering happier things.

Drug thy memories, lest thou learn it, lest
thy heart be put to proof,
In the dead unhappy night, and when the
rain is on the roof.

Like a dog, he [11] hunts in dreams, and thou
art staring at the wall,
Where the dying night-lamp flickers, and the
shadows rise and fall. 80

Then a hand shall pass before thee, pointing
to his drunken sleep,
To thy widowed marriage-pillows, to the
tears that thou wilt weep.

Thou shalt hear the "Never, never," whispered by the phantom years,
And a song from out the distance in the
ringing of thine ears;

[10] Dante.
[11] Amy's husband.

And an eye shall vex thee, looking ancient
    kindness on thy pain.   85
Turn thee, turn thee on thy pillow; get thee
    to thy rest again.

Nay, but nature brings thee solace; for a
    tender voice will cry.
'Tis a purer life than thine, a lip to drain thy
    trouble dry.

Baby lips will laugh me down; my latest rival
    brings thee rest.
Baby fingers, waxen touches, press me from
    the mother's breast.   90

O, the child too clothes the father with a
    dearness not his due.
Half is thine and half is his; it will be worthy
    of the two.

O, I see thee old and formal, fitted to thy
    petty part,
With a little hoard of maxims preaching down
    a daughter's heart.

"They were dangerous guides the feelings—
    she herself was not exempt—   95
Truly, she herself had suffered"—Perish in
    thy self-contempt!

Overlive it—lower yet—be happy! wherefore
    should I care?
I myself must mix with action, lest I wither
    by despair.

What is that which I should turn to, lighting
    upon days like these?
Every door is barred with gold, and opens but
    to golden keys.   100

Every gate is thronged with suitors, all the
    markets overflow.
I have but an angry fancy; what is that which
    I should do?

I had been content to perish, falling on the
    foeman's ground,

[12] It was an old notion that heavy cannon fire
quieted the winds.

When the ranks are rolled in vapor, and the
    winds are laid with sound.[12]

But the jingling of the guinea helps the hurt
    that honor feels,   105
And the nations do but murmur, snarling at
    each other's heels.

Can I but relive in sadness? I will turn that
    earlier page.
Hide me from my deep emotion, O thou
    wondrous mother-age!

Make me feel the wild pulsation that I felt
    before the strife,
When I heard my days before me, and the
    tumult of my life;   110

Yearning for the large excitement that the
    coming years would yield,
Eager-hearted as a boy when first he leaves
    his father's field,

And at night along the dusky highway near
    and nearer drawn,
Sees in heaven the light of London flaring
    like a dreary dawn;

And his spirit leaps within him to be gone
    before him then,   115
Underneath the light he looks at, in among
    the throngs of men;

Men, my brothers, men the workers, ever
    reaping something new;
That which they have done but earnest of
    the things that they shall do.

For I dipped into the future, far as human
    eye could see,
Saw the vision of the world, and all the won-
    der that would be;   120

Saw the heavens fill with commerce, argosies
    of magic sails,
Pilots of the purple twilight, dropping down
    with costly bales;

Heard the heavens fill with shouting, and
    there rained a ghastly dew

From the nations' airy navies grappling in
the central blue;

Far along the world-wide whisper of the
southwind rushing warm,   125
With the standards of the peoples plunging
through the thunder storm;

Till the war-drum throbbed no longer, and
the battle flags were furled
In the parliament of man, the federation of
the world.

There the common sense of most shall hold
a fretful realm in awe,
And the kindly earth shall slumber, lapped
in universal law.   130

So I triumphed, ere my passion sweeping
through me left me dry,
Left me with the palsied heart, and left me
with the jaundiced [13] eye;

Eye, to which all order festers, all things here
are out of joint.
Science moves, but slowly, slowly, creeping
on from point to point;

Slowly comes a hungry people,[14] as a lion,
creeping nigher,   135
Glares at one that nods and winks behind a
slowly-dying fire.

Yet I doubt not through the ages one increasing purpose runs,
And the thoughts of men are widened with
the process of the suns.

What is that to him that reaps not harvest of
his youthful joys,
Though the deep heart of existence beat for
ever like a boy's?   140

Knowledge comes, but wisdom lingers, and I
linger on the shore,

[13] Prejudiced.
[14] A reference to the various revolutionary activities of the 1840's, especially to those on the
Continent in 1848.

And the individual withers, and the world
is more and more.

Knowledge comes, but wisdom lingers, and
he bears a laden breast,
Full of sad experience, moving toward the
stillness of his rest.

Hark, my merry comrades call me, sounding
on the bugle-horn,   145
They to whom my foolish passion were a
target for their scorn.

Shall it not be scorn to me to harp on such
a moldered string?
I am shamed through all my nature to have
loved so slight a thing.

Weakness to be wroth with weakness!
woman's pleasure, woman's pain—
Nature made them blinder motions bounded
in a shallower brain.   150

Woman is the lesser man, and all thy passions, matched with mine,
Are as moonlight unto sunlight, and as water
unto wine—

Here at least, where nature sickens, nothing.
Ah, for some retreat
Deep in yonder shining orient, where my life
began to beat,

Where in wild Mahratta-battle fell my father
evil-starred;—   155
I was left a trampled orphan, and a selfish
uncle's ward.

Or to burst all links of habit—there to
wander far away,
On from island unto island at the gateways
of the day—

Larger constellations burning, mellow moons
and happy skies,
Breadths of tropic shade and palms in cluster,
knots of paradise;   160

Never comes the trader, never floats an
European flag,

Slides the bird o'er lustrous woodland, swings
  the trailer [15] from the crag;

Droops the heavy-blossomed bower, hangs the
  heavy-fruited tree—
Summer isles of Eden lying in dark-purple
  spheres of sea.

There methinks would be enjoyment more
  than in this march of mind,   165
In the steamship, in the railway, in the
  thoughts that shake mankind.

There the passions cramped no longer shall
  have scope and breathing-space;
I will take some savage woman, she shall rear
  my dusky race.

Iron-jointed, supple-sinewed, they shall dive,
  and they shall run,
Catch the wild goat by the hair, and hurl
  their lances in the sun;   170

Whistle back the parrot's call, and leap the
  rainbows of the brooks,
Not with blinded eyesight poring over miserable books—

Fool, again the dream, the fancy! but I *know*
  my words are wild,
But I count the gray barbarian lower than the
  Christian child.

I, to herd with narrow foreheads, vacant of
  our glorious gains,   175
Like a beast with lower pleasures, like a beast
  with lower pains!

Mated with a squalid savage—what to me
  were sun or clime?
I the heir of all the ages, in the foremost
  files of time—

I that rather held it better men should perish
  one by one,
Than that earth should stand at gaze like
  Joshua's moon [16] in Ajalon!   180

Not in vain the distance beacons. Forward,
  forward, let us range,

[15] Trailing vine.
[16] See Joshua 10:12-13.

Let the great world spin for ever down the
  ringing grooves [17] of change.

Through the shadow of the globe we sweep
  into the younger day;
Better fifty years of Europe than a cycle of
  Cathay.[18]

Mother-age,—for mine [19] I knew not,—help
  me as when life begun;   185
Rift the hills, and roll the waters, flash the
  lightnings, weigh the sun.

O, I see the crescent promise of my spirit
  hath not set.
Ancient founts of inspiration well through all
  my fancy yet.

Howsoever these things be, a long farewell
  to Locksley Hall!
Now for me the woods may wither, now for
  me the roof-tree fall.   190

Comes a vapor from the margin, blackening
  over heath and holt,
Cramming all the blast before it, in its breast
  a thunderbolt.

Let it fall on Locksley Hall, with rain or hail,
  or fire or snow;
For the mighty wind arises, roaring seaward,
  and I go.
(1842)

STUDY AIDS: 1. From l. 65 on, the youth
considers several solutions to his problem. Locate
the proposed solutions and his evaluations of
them.
  2. What is the unusual metrical line in which
the poem is cast? Is it an effective choice? There
is more than one way to SCAN the line. Is one
better?
  3. How does the poem illustrate Tennyson's
interest in social, political, and scientific events?
Assuming that the positive ideas are Tennyson's,
does the poet show too much faith in progress?
Is he too much the self-satisfied Englishman?

[17] Literally, "railroad tracks," a figure based on
the poet's early belief that train wheels ran in
grooves.
[18] What is the meaning of this line, which sums
up one of the important ideas of the poem?
[19] I.e., my mother (see l. 156).

Break, Break, Break

Break, break, break,
  On thy cold gray stones, O sea!
And I would that my tongue could utter
  The thoughts that arise in me.

O well for the fisherman's boy,   5
  That he shouts with his sister at play!
O well for the sailor lad,
  That he sings in his boat on the bay!

And the stately ships go on
  To their haven under the hill;   10

But O for the touch of a vanished hand,
  And the sound of a voice that is still!

Break, break, break,
  At the foot of thy crags, O sea!
But the tender grace of a day that is dead 15
  Will never come back to me.
(1842)

STUDY AIDS: How do the three images of ll. 5–10 serve to "utter the thoughts that arise" in the poet? How are they more effective in this respect than the more direct statement of ll. 11–12?

Songs from "The Princess"

The Princess is a long poem in which Tennyson treats, in narrative, the theme of the rights of women, an important question in Victorian England. Although as a whole this work is of only slight interest to modern readers, the interspersed songs are fine instances of Tennyson's skill in lyric verse.

The Splendor Falls on Castle Walls

The splendor falls on castle walls
  And snowy summits old in story;
The long light shakes across the lakes,
  And the wild cataract leaps in glory.
Blow, bugle, blow, set the wild echoes fly-
  ing,   5
Blow, bugle; answer, echoes, dying, dying,
  dying.

O, hark, O, hear! how thin and clear,
  And thinner, clearer, farther going!
O, sweet and far from cliff and scar
  The horns of elfland faintly blowing! 10
Blow, let us hear the purple glens replying,
Blow, bugle; answer, echoes, dying, dying,
  dying.

O love, they die in yon rich sky,
  They faint on hill or field or river;
Our echoes roll from soul to soul,   15
  And grow for ever and for ever.

Blow, bugle, blow, set the wild echoes flying,
And answer, echoes, answer, dying, dying,
  dying.
(1850)

Tears, Idle Tears

Tears, idle tears, I know not what they
  mean,
Tears from the depth of some divine despair
Rise in the heart, and gather to the eyes,
In looking on the happy autumn-fields,
And thinking of the days that are no more. 5

Fresh as the first beam glittering on a sail,
That brings our friends up from the under-
  world,
Sad as the last which reddens over one
That sinks with all we love below the verge;
So sad, so fresh, the days that are no more. 10

Ah, sad and strange as in dark summer
  dawns

The earliest pipe of half-awakened birds
To dying ears, when unto dying eyes
The casement slowly grows a glimmering
    square;
So sad, so strange, the days that are no
    more.   15

Dear as remembered kisses after death,
And sweet as those by hopeless fancy feigned
On lips that are for others; deep as love,
Deep as first love, and wild with all regret;
O death in life, the days that are no more! 20
(1847)

STUDY AIDS: 1. Note adjectives describing
"the days that are no more": "fresh," "sad,"
"strange," "dear," "sweet," "deep," and "wild."
How are the various images of the poem appropriate to these adjectives?
2. Show how the idea of death becomes increasingly prominent as the poem proceeds,
reaching a climax in l. 20.

Now Sleeps the Crimson Petal

Now sleeps the crimson petal, now the
    white,
Nor waves the cypress in the palace walk;
Nor winks the gold fin in the porphyry font.
The fire-fly wakens; waken thou with me.

Now droops the milkwhite peacock like a
    ghost,   5
And like a ghost she glimmers on to me.

Now lies the earth all Danaë [1] to the stars,
And all thy heart lies open unto me.

Now slides the silent meteor on, and leaves
A shining furrow, as thy thoughts in me. 10

Now folds the lily all her sweetness up,
And slips into the bosom of the lake.
So fold thyself, my dearest, thou, and slip
Into my bosom and be lost in me.
(1847)

[1] A Greek princess who, despite her imprisonment
by her father, was visited by Zeus in the form of
a golden shower.

Come Down, O Maid

Come down, O maid, from yonder moun-
    tain height:
What pleasure lives in height (the shepherd
    sang)
In height and cold, the splendor of the hills?
But cease to move so near the heavens, and
    cease
To glide a sunbeam by the blasted pine, 5
To sit a star upon the sparkling spire;
And come, for love is of the valley, come,
For love is of the valley, come thou down
And find him; by the happy threshold, he,
Or hand in hand with plenty in the maize, 10
Or red with spirted purple of the vats,
Or foxlike in the vine; nor cares to walk
With death and morning on the silver horns,[2]
Nor wilt thou snare him in the white ravine
Nor find him dropped upon the firths of
    ice,[3]   15
That huddling slant in furrow-cloven [4] falls
To roll the torrent out of dusky doors.[5]
But follow; let the torrent dance thee down
To find him in the valley; let the wild
Lean-headed eagles yelp alone, and leave 20
The monstrous ledges there to slope, and spill
Their thousand wreaths of dangling water-
    smoke,
That like a broken purpose waste in air.
So waste not thou, but come; for all the vales
Await thee; azure pillars of the hearth   25
Arise to thee; the children call, and I
Thy shepherd pipe, and sweet is every sound,
Sweeter thy voice, but every sound is sweet;
Myriads of rivulets hurrying through the
    lawn,
The moan of doves in immemorial elms, 30
And murmuring of innumerable bees.
(1847)

STUDY AIDS: This song is apparently sung
by a Swiss shepherd to his sweetheart. What is
he asking her to do? How are the images appropriate to his request?

[2] The snow-capped peaks of the mountains.
[3] Glaciers.
[4] Split by crevasses.
[5] Debris through which the stream emerges at
the foot of the glacier.

In Memoriam

When Arthur Henry Hallam died suddenly in Vienna on September 15, 1833, not only was Tennyson robbed of his dearest friend but his religious faith was shaken. Soon he began to write the various lyrics that were to make up *In Memoriam*, and for seventeen years he composed them, at first with no thought of weaving them together into an elegiac whole.

Because his mourning was so personal, Tennyson ignored the formal convention of the pastoral elegy and wrote directly of his grief and of his consequent spiritual problems. However, Tennyson himself reminds us that "this is a poem, not an actual biography. . . . It was meant to be a kind of Divina Commedia, ending with happiness. . . . The different moods of sorrow as in a drama are dramatically given, and my conviction that fear, doubts, and suffering will find answer and relief only through Faith in a God of Love. *I* is not always the author speaking of himself, but the voice of the human race speaking through him."

The poem consists of a Prologue, 131 sections (of which 22 are here reprinted), and an Epilogue. It is divided into four parts by three Christmas sections. Although Tennyson thought he had invented the stanza form, an unusual one rhyming abba, it had been used occasionally before his time.

Prologue [1]

Strong Son of God, immortal love,
  Whom we, that have not seen thy face,
  By faith, and faith alone, embrace,
Believing where we cannot prove;

Thine are these orbs of light and shade; 5
  Thou madest life in man and brute;
  Thou madest death; and lo, thy foot
Is on the skull which thou hast made.

Thou wilt not leave us in the dust:
  Thou madest man, he knows not why, 10
  He thinks he was not made to die;
And thou hast made him; thou art just.

Thou seemest human and divine,
  The highest, holiest manhood, thou.
  Our wills are ours, we know not how; 15
Our wills are ours, to make them thine.

Our little systems have their day;
  They have their day and cease to be;
  They are but broken lights of thee,
And thou, O Lord, art more than they. 20

[1] The Prologue was one of the last sections of *In Memoriam* to be written and thus reflects Tennyson's attitude at the end of his spiritual conflict.

We have but faith; we cannot know,
  For knowledge is of things we see;
  And yet we trust it comes from thee,
A beam in darkness; let it grow.

Let knowledge grow from more to more, 25
  But more of reverence in us dwell;
  That mind and soul, according well,
May make one music as before,

But vaster. We are fools and slight;
  We mock thee when we do not fear. 30
  But help thy foolish ones to bear;
Help thy vain worlds to bear thy light.

Forgive what seemed my sin in me,
  What seemed my worth since I began;
  For merit lives from man to man, 35
And not from man, O Lord, to thee.

Forgive my grief for one removed,
  Thy creature, whom I found so fair.
  I trust he lives in thee, and there
I find him worthier to be loved. 40

Forgive these wild and wandering cries,
  Confusions of a wasted youth;
  Forgive them where they fail in truth,
And in thy wisdom make me wise.
(1849; 1850)

I

I held it truth, with him [2] who sings
  To one clear harp in divers tones,
  That men may rise on stepping-stones
Of their dead selves to higher things.

But who shall so forecast the years   5
  And find in loss a gain to match?
  Or reach a hand through time to catch
The far-off interest of tears?

Let love clasp grief lest both be drowned,[3]
  Let darkness keep her raven gloss.   10
  Ah, sweeter to be drunk with loss,
To dance with death, to beat the ground,

Than that the victor hours should scorn
  The long result of love, and boast,
  "Behold the man that loved and lost,   15
But all he was is overworn."

3

O sorrow, cruel fellowship,[4]
  O priestess in the vaults of death,
  O sweet and bitter in a breath,
What whispers from thy lying lip?

"The stars," she whispers, "blindly run;   5
  A web is woven across the sky;
  From out waste places comes a cry,
And murmurs from the dying sun;

"And all the phantom, nature, stands—
  With all her music in her tone,   10
  A hollow echo of my own,—
A hollow form with empty hands."

And shall I take a thing so blind,
  Embrace her as my natural good;
  Or crush her, like a vice of blood,   15
Upon the threshold of the mind?

[2] Perhaps Goethe.
[3] This line states the theme of this section.
[4] In this section, Tennyson is saying that since sorrow brings him a message of universal purposelessness, he hesitates to yield to her any more.
[5] Where Hallam lived in London.
[6] SCAN this line. Note the effect of the meter, the monosyllables, and the alliteration.

7

Dark house,[5] by which once more I stand
  Here in the long unlovely street,
  Doors, where my heart was used to beat
So quickly, waiting for a hand,

A hand that can be clasped no more—   5
  Behold me, for I cannot sleep,
  And like a guilty thing I creep
At earliest morning to the door.

He is not here; but far away
  The noise of life begins again,   10
  And ghastly through the drizzling rain
On the bald street breaks the blank day.[6]

19

The Danube [7] to the Severn [8] gave
  The darkened heart that beat no more;
  They laid him by the pleasant shore,
And in the hearing of the wave.

There twice a day the Severn fills;   5
  The salt sea-water passes by,
  And hushes half the babbling Wye,[9]
And makes a silence in the hills.

The Wye is hushed nor moved along,
  And hushed my deepest grief of all,   10
  When filled with tears that cannot fall,
I brim with sorrow drowning song.

The tide flows down, the wave again
  Is vocal in its wooded walls;
  My deeper anguish also falls,   15
And I can speak a little then.

21

I sing to him that rests below,
  And, since the grasses round me wave,
  I take the grasses of the grave,
And make them pipes whereon to blow.

[7] The Danube River flows by Vienna, where Hallam died.
[8] The Severn River, in England, flows by Clevedon, where Hallam was buried, and empties into the Bristol Channel (see l. 4).
[9] The Wye River joins the Severn just above Clevedon. Work out the comparison in ll. 5–16.

The traveler hears me now and then,   5
    And sometimes harshly will he speak:
    "This fellow would make weakness weak,
And melt the waxen hearts of men."

Another answers: "Let him be,
    He loves to make parade of pain,   10
    That with his piping he may gain
The praise that comes to constancy."

A third is wroth: "Is this an hour
    For private sorrow's barren song,
    When more and more the people
        throng [10]   15
The chairs and thrones of civil power?

"A time to sicken and to swoon,
    When Science reaches forth her arms
    To feel from world to world, and charms
Her secret from the latest moon?" [11]   20

Behold, ye speak an idle thing;
    Ye never knew the sacred dust.
    I do but sing because I must,
And pipe but as the linnets sing;

And one is glad; her note is gay,   25
    For now her little ones have ranged;
    And one is sad; her note is changed,
Because her brood is stolen away. [12]

27

I envy not in any moods
    The captive void of noble rage:
    The linnet born within the cage,
That never knew the summer woods;

I envy not the beast that takes   5
    His license in the field of time,
    Unfettered by the sense of crime,
To whom a conscience never wakes;

Nor, what may count itself as blest,
    The heart that never plighted troth   10
    But stagnates in the weeds of sloth;
Nor any want-begotten rest.

I hold it true, whate'er befall;
    I feel it, when I sorrow most—
    'Tis better to have loved and lost   15
Than never to have loved at all.

30

With trembling fingers did we weave
    The holly round the Christmas hearth;
    A rainy cloud possessed the earth,
And sadly fell our Christmas-eve. [13]

At our old pastimes in the hall   5
    We gamboled, making vain pretense
    Of gladness, with an awful sense
Of one mute shadow watching all.

We paused: the winds were in the beech;
    We heard them sweep the winter land; 10
    And in a circle hand-in-hand
Sat silent, looking each at each.

Then echo-like our voices rang;
    We sung, though every eye was dim,
    A merry song we sang with him   15
Last year; impetuously we sang.

We ceased; a gentler feeling crept
    Upon us: surely rest is meet.
    "They [14] rest," we said, "their sleep is
        sweet,"
And silence followed, and we wept.   20

Our voices took a higher range;
    Once more we sang: "They do not die
    Nor lose their mortal sympathy,
Nor change to us, although they change;

"Rapt [15] from the fickle and the frail   25
    With gathered power, yet the same,
    Pierces the keen seraphic flame
From orb to orb, from veil to veil."

[10] Lines 15–16 allude to the many demands in the 1840's (such as those of the Chartists) for political and economic reform.
[11] Neptune was discovered in 1846; the eighth satellite of Saturn in 1848.
[12] In this section the poet defends his poems against imagined attacks. Note these attacks (ll. 7–20) and the poet's reply (ll. 21–28).
[13] 1833, the first Christmas Eve after Hallam's death. Note how the mood changes from the first part of the section to the last.
[14] The dead.
[15] Freed.

Rise, happy morn, rise, holy morn,
   Draw forth the cheerful day from night: 30
   O Father, touch the east, and light
The light that shone when hope was born.

34

My own dim life should teach me this,
   That life shall live for evermore,
   Else earth is darkness at the core,
And dust and ashes all that is;

This round [16] of green, this orb [17] of flame, 5
   Fantastic beauty; such as lurks
   In some wild poet, when he works
Without a conscience or an aim.

What then were God to such as I?
   'Twere hardly worth my while to choose 10
   Of things all mortal, or to use
A little patience ere I die;

'Twere best at once to sink to peace,
   Like birds the charming serpent draws
   To drop head-foremost in the jaws 15
Of vacant darkness and to cease.

50

Be near me when my light is low,
   When the blood creeps, and the nerves
     prick
   And tingle; and the heart is sick,
And all the wheels of being slow.

Be near me when the sensuous frame 5
   Is racked with pangs that conquer trust;
   And Time, a maniac scattering dust,
And Life, a fury slinging flame.[18]

Be near me when my faith is dry,
   And men the flies of latter spring, 10
   That lay their eggs, and sting and sing
And weave their petty cells and die.

Be near me when I fade away,
   To point the term of human strife,
   And on the low dark verge of life 15
The twilight of eternal day.

[16] The earth.
[17] The sun.
[18] The Furies are depicted as bearing torches.

54

O, yet we trust that somehow good
   Will be the final goal of ill,
   To pangs of nature, sins of will,
Defects of doubt, and taints of blood;

That nothing walks with aimless feet; 5
   That not one life shall be destroyed,
   Or cast as rubbish to the void,
When God hath made the pile complete;

That not a worm is cloven in vain;
   That not a moth with vain desire 10
   Is shriveled in a fruitless fire,
Or but subserves another's gain.

Behold, we know not anything;
   I can but trust that good shall fall
   At last—far off—at last, to all, 15
And every winter change to spring.

So runs my dream; but what am I?
   An infant crying in the night;
   An infant crying for the light,
And with no language but a cry. 20

55

The wish, that of the living whole
   No life may fail beyond the grave,
   Derives it not from what we have
The likest God within the soul?

Are God and Nature then at strife, 5
   That Nature lends such evil dreams?
   So careful of the type [19] she seems,
So careless of the single life,

That I, considering everywhere
   Her secret meaning in her deeds, 10
   And finding that of fifty seeds
She often brings but one to bear,

I falter where I firmly trod,
   And falling with my weight of cares
   Upon the great world's altar-stairs 15
That slope through darkness up to God,

[19] Species. Here and in the next section Tennyson shows his acquaintance with evolutionary philosophy, soon to be substantiated scientifically in Darwin's *Origin of Species* (1859).

I stretch lame hands of faith, and grope,
  And gather dust and chaff, and call
    To what I feel is Lord of all,
And faintly trust the larger hope.   20

56

"So careful of the type?"[20] but no.
  From scarpèd[21] cliff and quarried stone
  She[22] cries, "A thousand types are gone;
I care for nothing, all shall go.

"Thou makest thine appeal to me.   5
  I bring to life, I bring to death;
  The spirit does but mean the breath.
I know no more." And he, shall he,[23]

Man, her last work, who seemed so fair,
  Such splendid purpose in his eyes,   10
  Who rolled the psalm to wintry skies,
Who built him fanes of fruitless prayer,

Who trusted God was love indeed
  And love creation's final law—
  Though nature, red in tooth and claw   15
With ravine, shrieked against his creed—

Who loved, who suffered countless ills,
  Who battled for the true, the just,
  Be blown about the desert dust,
Or sealed within the iron hills?   20

No more?[24] A monster then, a dream,
  A discord. Dragons of the prime,[25]
  That tare each other in their slime,
Were mellow music matched with him.

O life as futile, then, as frail!   25
  O for thy[26] voice to soothe and bless!

[20] See l. 7 in section 55 above. Nature is concerned not even with species; she cares for nothing.
[21] Cut down vertically. Tennyson was acquainted with the geologic evidence of the birth and death of many different forms of life.
[22] Nature.
[23] "He" is a subject. Where is the predicate?
[24] The speaker questions Nature's statement in line 8.
[25] Monsters of primeval ages. Tennyson is saying that if man, with all his accomplishments, idealism, religious faith (ll. 9–18), comes to nothing at death (ll. 19–20), then primeval beasts, who showed no such promise, are preferable to him (l. 24).
[26] Hallam's.

What hope of answer, or redress?
Behind the veil, behind the veil.

67

When on my bed the moonlight falls,
  I know that in thy place[27] of rest
  By that broad water of the west
There comes a glory on the walls:

Thy marble bright in dark appears,   5
  As slowly steals a silver flame
  Along the letters of thy name,
And o'er the number of thy years.

The mystic glory swims away,
  From off my bed the moonlight dies;   10
  And closing eaves of wearied eyes
I sleep till dusk is dipped in gray;

And then I know the mist is drawn
  A lucid veil from coast to coast,
  And in the dark church like a ghost   15
Thy tablet glimmers to the dawn.

70

I cannot see the features right,
  When on the gloom I strive to paint
  The face I know; the hues are faint
And mix with hollow masks of night;

Cloud-towers by ghostly masons wrought,   5
  A gulf that ever shuts and gapes,
  A hand that points, and pallèd shapes
In shadowy thoroughfares of thought;

And crowds that stream from yawning doors,
  And shoals of puckered faces drive;   10
  Dark bulks that tumble half alive,
And lazy lengths on boundless shores;

Till all at once beyond the will
  I hear a wizard music roll,
  And through a lattice on the soul   15
Looks thy fair face and makes it still.[28]

[27] The church at Clevedon. (See n. 8, p. 773.)
[28] In section 70 the poet says that in the moments before sleep he finds it difficult to picture Hallam's features clearly in the midst of all the shapes that throng "the shadowy thoroughfares of thought." Then (in the last stanza) sleep finally comes, and with it the face of his friend. Note the effectiveness of the imagery in depicting this interesting psychological phenomenon.

78

Again at Christmas [29] did we weave
  The holly round the Christmas hearth;
  The silent snow possessed the earth,
And calmly fell our Christmas-eve.

The yule-clog [30] sparkled keen with frost,   5
  No wing of wind the region swept,
  But over all things brooding slept
The quiet sense of something lost.

As in the winters left behind,
  Again our ancient games had place,   10
  The mimic picture's [31] breathing grace,
And dance and song and hoodman-blind. [32]

Who showed a token of distress?
  No single tear, no mark of pain—
  O sorrow, then can sorrow wane?   15
O grief, can grief be changed to less?

O last regret, regret can die!
  No—mixed with all this mystic frame,
  Her deep relations are the same,
But with long use her tears are dry.

95

By night we lingered on the lawn,
  For underfoot the herb was dry;
  And genial warmth; and o'er the sky
The silvery haze of summer drawn;

And calm that let the tapers burn   5
  Unwavering; not a cricket chirred;
  The brook alone far-off was heard,
And on the board the fluttering urn. [33]

And bats went round in fragrant skies,
  And wheeled or lit the filmy shapes [34]   10
  That haunt the dusk, with ermine capes
And woolly breasts and beaded eyes;

While now we sang old songs that pealed
  From knoll to knoll, where, couched at
    ease,
  The white kine glimmered, and the trees   15
Laid their dark arms about the field.

But when those others, one by one,
  Withdrew themselves from me and night,
  And in the house light after light   20
Went out, and I was all alone,

A hunger seized my heart; I read
  Of that glad year which once had been,
  In those fallen leaves [35] which kept their
    green,
The noble letters of the dead.

And strangely on the silence broke   25
  The silent-speaking words, and strange
  Was love's dumb cry defying change
To test his worth; and strangely spoke

The faith, the vigor, bold to dwell
  On doubts that drive the coward back,   30
  And keen through wordy snares to track
Suggestion to her inmost cell.

So word by word, and line by line, [36]
  The dead man touched me from the past,
  And all at once it seemed at last   35
The living soul was flashed on mine,

And mine in this was wound, and whirled
  About empyreal [37] heights of thought,
  And came on that which is, and caught
The deep pulsations of the world,   40

Æonian [38] music measuring out
  The steps of time—the shocks of chance—
  The blows of death. At length my trance
Was canceled, stricken through with doubt.

[29] The Christmas of 1834. Compare this section
with section 30. What do the differences in details
reveal of the poet's changing attitude?
[30] "Clog" is a dialectical variant of "log."
[31] A game like charades.
[32] Blindman's-buff.
[33] The simmering tea urn.
[34] Moths.

[35] Pages of Hallam's letters.
[36] A mystical experience is described in the next
three stanzas. Cf. a somewhat similar attempt of
Wordsworth to describe a mystical experience in
Tintern Abbey, ll. 35–49 (p. 523).
[37] Celestial.
[38] Of the ages. Lines 41–42 mean that time,
chance, and death were harmonized ("measured
out") by this eternal music.

Vague words! but ah, how hard to frame 45
In matter-molded forms of speech,[39]
Or even for intellect to reach
Through memory that which I became;

Till now the doubtful dusk revealed [40]
The knolls once more where, couched at
ease, 50
The white kine glimmered, and the trees
Laid their dark arms about the field;

And sucked from out the distant gloom
A breeze began to tremble o'er
The large leaves of the sycamore, 55
And fluctuate all the still perfume,

And gathering freshlier overhead
Rocked the full-foliaged elms, and swung
The heavy-folded rose, and flung
The lilies to and fro, and said, 60

"The dawn, the dawn," and died away;
And East and West, without a breath,
Mixed their dim lights, like life and death,
To broaden into boundless day.[41]

96

You [42] say, but with no touch of scorn,
Sweet-hearted, you, whose light-blue eyes
Are tender over drowning flies,
You tell me, doubt is devil-born.

I know not. One indeed I knew 5
In many a subtle question versed,
Who touched a jarring lyre at first,
But ever strove to make it true;

Perplexed in faith, but pure in deeds,
At last he beat his music out. 10

[39] Mystics agree that their mystical experiences
cannot be adequately communicated.
[40] Lines 49–64: Note how this intense experience is framed by two exquisite descriptions of a
calm and beautiful natural scene.
[41] In a way section 95 is climactic. The poet, left
alone in the garden, reads over some old letters of
Hallam and suddenly has a mystical experience of
communion with his friend's spirit.
[42] A tender-hearted person of simple faith.

There lives more faith in honest doubt,[43]
Believe me, than in half the creeds.

He fought his doubts, and gathered strength,
He would not make his judgment blind,
He faced the specters of the mind 15
And laid them; thus he came at length

To find a stronger faith his own,
And power was with him in the night,
Which makes the darkness and the light,
And dwells not in the light alone, 20

But in the darkness and the cloud,[44]
As over Sinaï's peaks of old,
While Israel made their gods of gold,
Although the trumpet blew so loud.

106

Ring out, wild bells, to the wild sky,[45]
The flying cloud, the frosty light;
The year is dying in the night;
Ring out, wild bells, and let him die.

Ring out the old, ring in the new, 5
Ring, happy bells, across the snow;
The year is going, let him go;
Ring out the false, ring in the true.

Ring out the grief that saps the mind,
For those that here we see no more; 10
Ring out the feud of rich and poor,
Ring in redress to all mankind.

Ring out a slowly dying cause,
And ancient forms of party strife;
Ring in the nobler modes of life, 15
With sweeter manners, purer laws.

Ring out the want, the care, the sin,
The faithless coldness of the times;
Ring out, ring out my mournful rhymes,
But ring the fuller minstrel in. 20

[43] Lines 11–12 are often quoted. What do they
mean?
[44] See Exodus 19:16–25; 32:1–6.
[45] This section is a New Year's song. Contrast its
mood with those of the Christmas sections (30 and
78).

Ring out false pride in place and blood,
  The civic slander and the spite;
Ring in the love of truth and right,
Ring in the common love of good.

Ring out old shapes of foul disease;   25
  Ring out the narrowing lust of gold;
  Ring out the thousand wars of old,
Ring in the thousand years of peace.[46]

Ring in the valiant man and free,
  The larger heart, the kindlier hand;   30
  Ring out the darkness of the land,
Ring in the Christ that is to be.[47]

118

Contemplate all this work of Time,
  The giant [48] laboring in his youth;
  Nor dream of human love and truth,
As dying nature's earth and lime; [49]

But trust that those we call the dead   5
  Are breathers of an ampler day
  For ever nobler ends. They [50] say,
The solid earth whereon we tread

In tracts of fluent heat began,
  And grew to seeming-random forms,   10
  The seeming prey of cyclic storms,
Till at the last arose the man;

Who throve and branched from clime to
    clime,
  The herald of a higher race,[51]
  And of himself in higher place,[52]   15
If so he type this work of time

Within himself, from more to more;
  Or, crowned with attributes of woe
  Like glories, move his course, and show
That life is not as idle ore,   20

But iron dug from central gloom,
  And heated hot with burning fears,
  And dipped in baths of hissing tears,
And battered with the shocks of doom

To shape and use. Arise and fly   25
  The reeling faun,[53] the sensual feast;
  Move upward, working out the beast,
And let the ape and tiger die.[54]

124

That which we dare invoke to bless;
  Our dearest faith; our ghastliest doubt;
  He, they, one, all; within, without;
The power in darkness whom we guess—

I found him not in world or sun,   5
  Or eagle's wing, or insect's eye,
  Nor through the questions men may try,
The petty cobwebs we have spun.

If e'er when faith had fallen asleep,
  I heard a voice, "believe no more,"   10
  And heard an ever-breaking shore
That tumbled in the Godless deep,

A warmth within the breast would melt
  The freezing reason's colder part,
  And like a man in wrath the heart   15
Stood up and answered, "I have felt." [55]

[46] See Rev. 20.

[47] A reference, Tennyson said, to the time "when Christianity without bigotry will triumph, when the controversies of creeds shall have vanished."

[48] The Titan Cronus, who came to be called the god of time.

[49] I.e., as mortal, like the body.

[50] The scientists, particularly Laplace, whose nebular hypothesis of the origin of the solar system Tennyson refers to in ll. 8–11.

[51] On earth.

[52] The after-life.

[53] A mythical beast, half goat and half man, here symbolizing man's lower nature, as do "ape" and "tiger" in l. 28.

[54] Section 118 is climactic, and is to be compared and contrasted with section 56, which also deals with the theme of evolution. In this section the poet applies the concept to man's spiritual growth. In ll. 16–28 he says that man, if he will, can match this natural evolution within himself by subduing his lower nature and turning the sufferings of life to spiritual advantage. Show how the images express this idea.

[55] In ll. 5–16 Tennyson says that he found God not in nature (ll. 5–6) or in intellectual theorizing (ll. 7–8), but, even when doubt was strongest (ll. 9–12), in the deep feelings of the heart (ll. 13–16).

No, like a child in doubt and fear:
  But that blind clamor made me wise;
  Then was I as a child that cries,
But, crying, knows his father near;   20

And what I am beheld again
  What is, and no man understands;
  And out of darkness came the hands
That reach through nature, molding men.

130

Thy [56] voice is on the rolling air;
  I hear thee where the waters run;
  Thou standest in the rising sun,
And in the setting thou art fair.

What art thou then? I cannot guess;   5
  But though I seem in star and flower
  To feel thee some diffusive power,
I do not therefore love thee less.

My love involves the love before;
  My love is vaster passion now;   10
  Though mixed with God and nature thou,
I seem to love thee more and more.

Far off thou art, but ever nigh;
  I have thee still, and I rejoice;

I prosper, circled with thy voice;   15
I shall not lose thee though I die.

  Ring in the love of truth and right,
  Ring in the common love of good.

131

O living will [57] that shalt endure
  When all that seems [58] shall suffer shock,
  Rise in the spiritual rock,[59]
Flow through our deeds and make them pure,

That we may lift from out of dust   5
  A voice as unto him that hears,
  A cry above the conquered years [60]
To one that with us works, and trust,

With faith that comes of self-control,
  The truths that never can be proved   10
  Until we close with all we loved,
And all we flow from, soul in soul.
(1850)

STUDY AIDS: 1. Where can you find evidences in *In Memoriam* of Tennyson's efforts to reconcile science and religion? Is he successful?
  2. Is Tennyson at his best when writing purely lyrical or descriptive verse, or when dealing with problems of faith and doubt? Are his solutions to these problems convincing?

The Eagle

He clasps the crag with crooked hands;
Close to the sun in lonely lands,
Ringed with the azure world, he stands.

The wrinkled sea beneath him crawls;
He watches from his mountain walls,
And like a thunderbolt he falls.
(1851)

STUDY AIDS: 1. What impression of the eagle do we get from this poem? What details build up this impression? How is the meaning of ll. 1–2 reinforced by the ALLITERATION? By the use of "hands" instead of "claws"?
  2. Why is the sea "wrinkled"? Does the eagle seem to have human (or even superhuman) qualities? What is the effect of "his mountain walls"? Note how the last line, with explosive force, shatters the majestic immobility of the picture.

[56] Hallam's. Cf. the idea of the first two stanzas with sts. 42–43 of *Adonais* (p. 683).
[57] Tennyson said that this meant "free will, the higher and enduring part of man."
[58] I.e., the material creation.

[59] In 1 Cor. 10:4 Christ is called a "spiritual rock."
[60] What is the contrast between "conquered years" and the "victor hours" of section 1, l. 13 (p. 773)?

Crossing the Bar

A few days before his death, Tennyson said to his son: "Mind you put *Crossing the Bar* at the end of all editions of my poems."

Sunset and evening star,
    And one clear call for me!
And may there be no moaning of the bar,[1]
    When I put out to sea,

But such a tide as moving seems asleep,   5
    Too full for sound and foam,
When that which drew from out the bound-
    less deep
    Turns again home.

Twilight and evening bell,
    And after that the dark!   10
And may there be no sadness of farewell,
    When I embark;

For though from out our bourn[2] of time and
    place
    The flood may bear me far,
I hope to see my Pilot[3] face to face   15
    When I have crossed the bar.
(1889)

Robert Browning
(1812–1889)

MANY OF THE QUALITIES EXPRESSED IN THE POETRY OF ROBERT BROWNING OWE MUCH TO his parentage and early environment. His father, a bank clerk, was an amateur artist and cultured litterateur, who fostered in his son an interest in books, poetry, and painting. His mother combined a fine musical talent with a strong religious commitment; from her Browning got his great love for music and his religious convictions. The well-stocked Browning library contained both standard and out-of-the-way volumes, and only two miles away was the Dulwich gallery of paintings, one of the best collections in England. It is little wonder, then, that Robert Browning received most of his education at home, from tutors or under the intelligent supervision of his father. His formal training in school or college was sporadic and slight.

Browning's first published poem, *Pauline* (1833), enjoyed only a few slight notices; but his second, *Paracelsus* (1835), made a successful impression upon the intelligentsia, and soon Browning was moving in a circle of prominent literary figures. Among these was Macready, the famous tragic actor, who asked Browning to write a play for him. Thereafter, during the decade of 1837–1846, Browning wrote a number of plays, in which it became increasingly obvious that his talents did not lie in the direction of stageworthy drama.

In 1840 Browning published *Sordello*, a poem of such obscurity that the small reputation he had built up was almost ruined. To regain it, his publishers issued his next works in

[1] Any bank of gravel, sand, or the like across a river's mouth.
[2] Limits.
[3] "That Divine and Unseen Who is alway guiding us" (Tennyson).

pamphlet form, designed to reach a wide market. Most of these are plays, but two of them are collections of lyrics containing some of his best known pieces.

The next chapter of Browning's life began in 1844, when he first wrote to Elizabeth Barrett, praising her poetry and initiating a correspondence that brought about an early meeting, a persistent courtship, which ended with a romantic elopement to Italy. Elizabeth Barrett was a well-known poet, a semi-invalid under the domination of a tyrannical father who would hear nothing of her marrying. But Browning was deterred by no obstacles, and Elizabeth found her dark misgivings and trepidations vanishing in the strong light of her lover's determination and enthusiasm.

The fifteen years in Italy (1846–1861) were, on the whole, very happy years, with Elizabeth's frail health improving under the stimulus of her husband's devotion and energy. She quickly interested herself in Italian politics; Browning was more fascinated by the art shops and book stalls of Florence, the city where they made their home. In 1850 he published *Christmas Eve* and *Easter Day,* in which most of his basic religious convictions are stated; and in 1855 appeared his best collection of poems, *Men and Women,* two volumes showing his mastery of the dramatic monologue, his intense absorption in Italian life and culture, and his penetrating psychological insight.

Browning's Italian residence came to an end with the death of Elizabeth in 1861. He returned to England, both to get away from a place of sharp memories and to supervise the education of his son. Living a life of seclusion for some time, he overcame his depression and plunged into an active social life. From 1864 until his death he was a familiar figure in important gatherings and something of a man-about-town. As his reputation grew, many honors were bestowed upon him; and he was both amused and pleased by the establishment of Browning Societies during the latter years of his life.

Browning's greatest work, *The Ring and the Book,* was published in 1868 and 1869. It is a long blank-verse poem in twelve books, based upon a seventeenth-century murder trial. It tells the story from many points of view and with a sustained interest remarkable in so extensive a work. During the 1870's Browning published many other long poems, but they do not measure up to the excellence of *The Ring and the Book.*

In his collections of shorter poems, however, he once again reached a high standard, though his metrics become increasingly rough, and the domination of "gray argument" over lyricism is too frequent. Nevertheless, there are many fine pieces in these volumes, especially in the *Dramatis Personae* of 1864, the two series of *Dramatic Idyls* of 1879 and 1880, and the final volume, *Asolando,* which appeared on the very day of his death in 1889. Despite some falling off in poetical excellence, Browning maintained his creative vigor to the end.

To a number of people in our disillusioned time, Browning's resolute optimism has become a little suspect. In poem after poem Browning emphasizes God's love, presents evil as a necessary configuration in the total pattern, affirms the afterlife as essential to the fulfillment of thwarted aspirations in this life, and stresses this world as a testing-ground where men can grow because they are gloriously imperfect, constantly reaching out toward goals they can never quite attain.

Perhaps Browning is greatest as a psychological poet. In his poems all kinds of people come to life before our eyes, people whose true, inner selves are laid bare in moments of crisis, or who, in casual monologue, unwittingly reveal their deepest urges and convictions. Browning was especially fascinated by the abnormal and the grotesque. He was also deeply interested in the passion of love and its opposite, hate.

There is great variety in his work—religious poems, poems of heroic action, poems on painting and music, poems depicting an historical epoch, poems of Italian life, poems of love and hate, narrative poems, lyric poems, dramatic poems. There are few areas of human life that Robert Browning did not explore.

My Last Duchess

Ferrara

In this dramatic monologue, the Duke of Ferrara, a nobleman of Renaissance Italy, is showing a portrait of his last duchess to an envoy of the count whose daughter he is negotiating to marry. He is explaining why the former duchess proved to be an unsatisfactory wife.

That's my last Duchess painted on the wall,
Looking as if she were alive. I call
That piece a wonder, now: Frà Pandolf's [1]
    hand
Worked busily a day, and there she stands.
Will't please you sit and look at her? I said 5
"Frà Pandolf" by design, for never read
Strangers like you that pictured countenance,
The depth and passion of its earnest glance,
But to myself they turned (since none puts
    by
The curtain I have drawn for you, but I) [2] 10
And seemed as they would ask me, if they
    durst,
How such a glance came there; so, not the
    first
Are you to turn and ask thus. Sir, 'twas not
Her husband's presence only, called that spot
Of joy into the Duchess' cheek: perhaps 15
Frà Pandolf chanced to say, "Her mantle laps
Over my lady's wrist too much," or "Paint
Must never hope to reproduce the faint
Half-flush that dies along her throat"; such
    stuff
Was courtesy, she thought, and cause
    enough   20
For calling up that spot of joy. She had
A heart—how shall I say? [3]—too soon made
    glad,
Too easily impressed: she liked whate'er

She looked on, and her looks went every-
    where.
Sir, 'twas all one! My favor at her breast, 25
The dropping of the daylight in the west,
The bough of cherries some officious fool
Broke in the orchard for her, the white mule
She rode with round the terrace—all and each
Would draw from her alike the approving
    speech,   30
Or blush, at least. She thanked men,—good!
    but thanked
Somehow—I know not how—as if she ranked
My gift of a nine-hundred-years-old name
With anybody's gift. Who'd stoop to blame
This sort of trifling? Even had you skill   35
In speech—which I have not [4]—to make your
    will
Quite clear to such an one, and say, "Just this
Or that in you disgusts me; here you miss,
Or there exceed the mark"—and if she let
Herself be lessoned so, nor plainly set   40
Her wits to yours, forsooth, and made excuse,
—E'en then would be some stooping; and I
    choose
Never to stoop. Oh sir, she smiled, no doubt,
Whene'er I passed her; but who passed with-
    out
Much the same smile? This grew; I gave com-
    mands;   45
Then all smiles stopped together. [5] There she
    stands
As if alive. Will't please you rise? We'll meet

---

[1] An imaginary painter who is also a monk or friar.
[2] What insight do we get into the Duke's character through the parenthetical statement in ll. 9–10?
[3] Is the Duke's difficulty in expressing himself here a pretense, or are there reasons for the difficulty? Cf. also l. 32.

[4] Is the "which I have not" sincere modesty?
[5] Questioned, Browning said he meant that the Duke had his wife put to death or shut up in a convent. Which seems the more likely? Why is the indefiniteness preferable to a precise statement?

The company below, then. I repeat,
The count your master's known munificence [6]
Is ample warrant that no just pretense   50
Of mine for dowry will be disallowed;
Though his fair daughter's self, as I avowed [7]
At starting, is my object. Nay, we'll go
Together down, sir.[8] Notice Neptune,
   though,
Taming a sea-horse,[9] thought a rarity,   55
Which Claus of Innsbruck [10] cast in bronze
   for me!
(1842)

STUDY AIDS: 1. In this DRAMATIC MONO-
LOGUE, what is the character of the Duke as
revealed by his own words? Enumerate his
various traits. What remarks bring them out? Is
his impression of himself the same as the impression we get of him? Is there IRONY here?
Is the Duke a true art lover? Why does he tell
the envoy all these things about his former
wife? Is he clever in so doing? What relation
does his revelation have to the hoped-for marriage?
   2. What is the character of the Duchess as
revealed by the Duke? Again, is our final impression of her the same as his? If not, what is
the difference? Why was he dissatisfied with her?
   3. The poem is in rhyme, but it doesn't
seem to be. Why not? How does this "playing
down" of the rhyme add to the effectiveness of
the poem?

Soliloquy of the Spanish Cloister

Gr-r-r—there go, my heart's abhorrence! [1]
   Water your damned flower-pots, do!
If hate killed men, Brother Lawrence,
   God's blood, would not mine kill you!
What? your myrtle-bush wants trimming?   5
   Oh, that rose has prior claims—
Needs its leaden vase filled brimming?
   Hell dry you up with its flames!

At the meal we sit together:
   Salve tibi! [2] I must hear   10
Wise talk of the kind of weather,
   Sort of season, time of year:
Not a plenteous cork-crop: scarcely [3]
   Dare we hope oak-galls,[4] *I doubt:*
What's the Latin name for "parsley"?   15
   What's the Greek name for swine's snout?

Whew! We'll [5] have our platter burnished,
   Laid with care on our own shelf!
With a fire-new spoon we're furnished,
   And a goblet for ourself,   20
Rinsed like something sacrificial
   Ere 'tis fit to touch our chaps [6]
Marked with L for our initial!
   (He-he! There his lily snaps!)

Saint, forsooth! While brown Dolores [7]   25
   Squats outside the convent bank
With Sanchicha, telling stories,
   Steeping tresses in the tank,
Blue-black, lustrous, thick like horsehairs,
   —Can't I see his dead eye glow,   30
Bright as 'twere a Barbary corsair's? [8]
   (That is, if he'd let it show!)

When he finishes refection [9]
   Knife and fork he never lays
Cross-wise, to my recollection,   35
   As do I, in Jesu's praise.

---

[6] What do ll. 49–51 show about the Duke's
interest in his wife-to-be?
   [7] Are ll. 52–53 an honest statement?
   [8] What does this sentence mean? Has the envoy
rushed ahead (anxious to get away from this man),
or is he meekly waiting to follow the Duke down?
The meaning would determine the tone of voice
in which the Duke speaks. What do you think
it is? In either case, what is shown about the Duke's
character?
   [9] Is the "taming a sea-horse" possibly symbolic?
What do ll. 54–56 contribute to the poem?
   [10] An imaginary sculptor.

[1] What is the difference between the way the
speaker expresses his hatred of Brother Lawrence
in ll. 1–4 and in ll. 5–7?

[2] "Hail to thee!"
   [3] Why are ll. 13–15 in italics?
   [4] Oak apples, used in the production of ink.
   [5] What is the effect of the plural pronoun in this
stanza?
   [6] Jaws.
   [7] What sin is imputed to Brother Lawrence in
this stanza? What is revealed about the speaker?
   [8] A pirate of the North African coast.
   [9] Regular meal. What characteristic of the speaker
is revealed in this stanza? Of Brother Lawrence?

I the Trinity illustrate,
  Drinking watered orange-pulp—
In three sips the Arian [10] frustrate;
  While he drains his at one gulp.   40

Oh, those melons! If he's able
  We're to have a feast! so nice!
One goes to the Abbot's table,
  All of us get each a slice.
How go on your flowers? None double?   45
  Not one fruit-sort can you spy?
Strange!—And I, too, at such trouble
  Keep them close-nipped on the sly!

There's a great text in Galatians,
  Once you trip on it, entails   50
Twenty-nine distinct damnations,
  One sure, if another fails: [11]
If I trip him just a-dying,
  Sure of heaven as sure can be,
Spin him round and send him flying   55
  Off to hell, a Manichee? [12]

Or, my scrofulous [13] French novel
  On gray paper with blunt type!
Simply glance at it, you grovel
  Hand and foot in Belial's gripe: [14]   60
If I double down its pages
  At the woeful sixteenth print,[15]

When he gathers his greengages,[16]
  Ope a sieve and slip it in't?

Or, there's Satan!—one might venture   65
  Pledge one's soul to him, yet leave
Such a flaw in the indenture [17]
  As he'd miss till, past retrieve,
Blasted lay that rose-acacia
  We're so proud of! Hy, Zy, Hine . . .[18] 70
'St, there's Vespers! [19] *Plena gratiâ*,
  Ave, Virgo! [20] Gr-r-r you swine!
(1843)

STUDY AIDS: 1. Characterize both the speaker and Brother Lawrence. What is the speaker's dominant emotion? What other emotions does he display? Why does he hate Brother Lawrence so? Do you have any sympathy for the speaker at all?

2. This poem, like *My Last Duchess*, is a psychological study. What are the main differences in the technique of revelation? Would you call this poem primarily humorous or sinister? Why? What kinds of revenge has the speaker been taking on Brother Lawrence? What other kinds does he consider? What ironic climax of these plans is reached in the last stanza?

3. Browning had little use for asceticism. How does this poem reveal that attitude?

The Lost Leader

Browning had Wordsworth in mind when he wrote this poem. In 1842 Wordsworth accepted a pension from the government; in 1843 he was appointed Poet Laureate. These two events brought to a kind of climax the increasing conservatism of the once liberal Wordsworth, and Browning, like many another Englishman, deplored the change. Browning, however, later regretted the sharpness of his attack.

Just for a handful of silver [1] he left us,
  Just for a riband [2] to stick in his coat—

Found the one gift of which fortune bereft
  us,[3]
  Lost all the others she lets us devote;

[10] The Arians denied the Trinity.
[11] Probably a reference to Galatians 5:18–21, which, however, enumerates only seventeen sins.
[12] A follower of Mani, a Persian who founded the religion of Manicheism, which spread from Babylonia in the fourth century and was pronounced heretical by the Christian church.
[13] I.e., morally contaminated.
[14] The devil's grip.
[15] Illustration. What does this specific knowledge reveal about the speaker?
[16] Greenish-yellow plums.

[17] An agreement in writing. What kind of agreement with Satan does the speaker contemplate?
[18] The meaning of these words is not known; they may be a fragment of a necromantic curse.
[19] Evening religious services.
[20] "Hail, Virgin, full of grace" (the Ave Maria, a form of prayer). What is the IRONY here?

[1] Suggesting the pension of 1842. Who else betrayed for a handful of silver?
[2] Suggesting the appointment to the laureateship.
[3] All supporters of a liberal program.

They, with the gold to give, doled him out
 silver,   5
So much was theirs who so little allowed:
How all our copper had gone for his service!
 Rags—were they purple, his heart had been
 proud!
We that had loved him so, followed him,
 honored him,
 Lived in his mild and magnificent eye,   10
Learned his great language, caught his clear
 accents,
 Made him our pattern to live and to die!
Shakespeare was of us, Milton was for us,[4]
 Burns, Shelley, were with us,—they watch
 from their graves!
He alone breaks from the van and the free-
 men,—   15
 He alone sinks to the rear and the slaves!

We shall march prospering,—not through his
 presence;
 Songs may inspirit us,—not from his lyre;
Deeds will be done,—while he boasts his
 quiescence,
 Still bidding crouch whom[5] the rest bade
 aspire: 20
Blot out his name, then, record one lost soul
 more,[6]

One task more declined, one more footpath
 untrod,
One more devils'-triumph and sorrow for
 angels,
 One wrong more to man, one more insult
 to God!
Life's night begins: let him never come back
 to us!   25
 There would be doubt, hesitation and pain,
Forced praise on our part—the glimmer of
 twilight,
 Never glad confident morning again!
Best fight on well, for we taught him—strike
 gallantly,[7]
 Menace our heart ere we master his own; 30
Then let him receive the new knowledge and
 wait us,
 Pardoned in heaven, the first by the throne!
(1842)

STUDY AIDS: 1. Of what value is it to
know that Browning had Wordsworth in mind
in writing this poem? Is Browning's attitude
here primarily one of regret, indignation, or
hostility?
 2. What does Mrs. Browning mean when
she said of this poem that it was "worth all the
journalizing and pamphleteering in the world"?

Night and Morning

These two lyrics were originally published as one poem with the above title. Browning later
published them as two poems with separate titles. In both lyrics the man is speaking.

Meeting at Night

The gray sea and the long black land;[1]
And the yellow half-moon large and low;
And the startled little waves that leap
In fiery ringlets from their sleep,
As I gain the cove with pushing prow,   5
And quench its speed in the slushy sand.

Then a mile of warm sea-scented beach;
Three fields to cross till a farm appears;
A tap at the pane, the quick sharp scratch
And blue spurt of a lighted match,   10
And a voice less loud, through its joys and
 fears,
Than the two hearts beating each to each!
(1845)

[4] Why did Browning single out the four poets
mentioned in ll. 13–14? Do you approve of his
selection?
 [5] The people, especially the downtrodden masses.
 [6] Scan this line. How does the rhythm fit the
meaning? Note the rhetorical effectiveness of ll.
17–24.

[7] What do ll. 29–32 mean?

[1] Note the impressionistic use of sounds and
colors throughout the poem. Note, too, the grammatical structure. How does it help to build up the
suspense?

Parting at Morning

Round the cape of a sudden came the sea,
And the sun looked over the mountain's rim:
And straight was a path of gold for him,[2]
And the need of a world of men for me.[3]
(1845)

STUDY AIDS: 1. What narrative is implied in these two brief lyrics? What aspect of it is Browning interested in? How do the images build up the emotional effect?
2. What is the difference in emphasis between the two lyrics? Is there a conflict of ideas between them? What various statements about love are suggested in the poems?

The Bishop Orders His Tomb at St. Praxed's Church

Rome, 15—

"I know of no other piece of modern English, prose or poetry, in which there is so much told, as in these lines, of the Renaissance spirit—its worldliness, inconsistency, pride, hypocrisy, ignorance of itself, love of art, of luxury, and of good Latin" (John Ruskin).

Vanity, saith the preacher, vanity![1]
Draw round my bed: is Anselm keeping back?
Nephews [2]—sons mine . . . ah God, I know not! Well—
She, men would have to be your mother once,
Old Gandolf [3] envied me, so fair she was!   5
What's done is done, and she is dead beside,
Dead long ago, and I am bishop since,
And as she died so must we die ourselves,
And thence ye may perceive the world's a dream.
Life, how and what is it? As here I lie   10
In this state-chamber, dying by degrees,
Hours and long hours in the dead night, I ask
"Do I live, am I dead?" Peace, peace seems all.[4]
Saint Praxed's [5] ever was the church for peace;
And so, about this tomb of mine. I fought   15
With tooth and nail to save my niche, ye know:
—Old Gandolf cozened [6] me, despite my care;
Shrewd was that snatch from out the corner south

He graced his carrion with, God curse the same!
Yet still my niche is not so cramped but thence   20
One sees the pulpit o' the epistle-side,[7]
And somewhat of the choir, those silent seats,
And up into the aery dome where live
The angels, and a sunbeam's sure to lurk:
And I shall fill my slab of basalt [8] there,   25
And 'neath my tabernacle [9] take my rest,
With those nine columns round me, two and two.
The odd one at my feet where Anselm stands:
Peach-blossom marble all, the rare, the ripe
As fresh-poured red wine of a mighty pulse.   30
—Old Gandolf with his paltry onion-stone,[10]
Put me where I may look at him! True peach,
Rosy and flawless: how I earned the prize!
Draw close: that conflagration of my church
—What then? So much was saved if aught were missed!   35
My sons, ye would not be my death? Go dig
The white-grape vineyard where the oil-press stood,
Drop water gently till the surface sink,
And if ye find . . . Ah God, I know not, I! . . .

[2] The sun.
[3] What does this line mean?

[1] Eccl. 1:2.
[2] Why does the Bishop call his sons "nephews"? What is revealed here about the Bishop and about the Church of the late Italian Renaissance?
[3] The Bishop's detested predecessor and rival.
[4] What is the shift in time in ll. 4–13?
[5] San Prassede is an actual church in Rome. The characters, however, are all imaginary.
[6] Tricked.

[7] The right-hand side as one faces the altar.
[8] A hard, dark-colored rock.
[9] Canopy.
[10] A cheap marble that peels into layers like an onion.

Bedded in store of rotten fig-leaves soft,　40
And corded up in a tight olive-frail,[11]
Some lump, ah God, of *lapis lazuli*,[12]
Big as a Jew's head cut off at the nape,
Blue as a vein o'er the Madonna's breast . . .[13]
Sons, all have I bequeathed you, villas, all,　45
That brave Frascati [14] villa with its bath,
So, let the blue lump poise between my knees,
Like God the Father's globe on both his hands
Ye worship in the Jesu Church [15] so gay,
For Gandolf shall not choose but see and
　　burst!　50
Swift as a weaver's shuttle fleet our years: [16]
Man goeth to the grave, and where is he?
Did I say basalt for my slab, sons? Black—
'Twas ever antique-black [17] I meant! How
　　else
Shall ye contrast my frieze [18] to come be-
　　neath?　55
The bas-relief [19] in bronze ye promised me,
Those Pans and nymphs ye wot of, and per-
　　chance
Some tripod,[20] thyrsus,[21] with a vase or so,
The Savior at his sermon on the mount,
Saint Praxed [22] in a glory, and one Pan　60
Ready to twitch the nymph's last garment off,
And Moses with the tables . . . but I know
Ye mark me not! What do they whisper thee,

[11] Olive-basket.
[12] A semiprecious blue stone.
[13] Lines 34–44: What did the Bishop do during the church fire?
[14] A fashionable Roman suburb.
[15] Jesuit Church, Rome.
[16] Job 7:6.
[17] A very expensive black marble. The Bishop has decided he wants something even finer than basalt (l. 25).
[18] An ornamented band.
[19] Low-relief—that is, carving or sculpture only slightly raised from the background to which it is attached, as on modern coins.
[20] A three-legged stool. The priestess of Apollo at Delphi sat on a tripod.
[21] A staff borne by the followers of Bacchus. What is the significance of these pagan symbols and their being mingled with Christian elements?
[22] A Roman virgin of the third century who gave her wealth to the poor. What is ironic about: (1) the Bishop's wanting her likeness on the frieze along with the other items (especially the one which follows); (2) his promise (ll. 73–75) to pray to her for mistresses for his sons; and (3) his being buried in the church named after her?

Child of my bowels, Anselm? Ah, ye hope
To revel down my villas while I gasp　65
Bricked o'er with beggar's moldy travertine [23]
Which Gandolf from his tomb-top chuckles
　　at!
Nay, boys, ye love me—all of jasper, then!
'Tis jasper [24] ye stand pledged to, lest I grieve
My bath must needs be left behind, alas!　70
One block, pure green as a pistachio-nut,
There's plenty jasper somewhere in the
　　world—
And have I not Saint Praxed's ear to pray
Horses for ye, and brown [25] Greek manu-
　　scripts,
And mistresses with great smooth marbly
　　limbs?　75
—That's if ye carve my epitaph aright,
Choice Latin, picked phrase, Tully's [26] every
　　word,
No gaudy ware like Gandolf's second line—
Tully, my masters? Ulpian [27] serves his
　　need!
And then how I shall lie through centuries,　80
And hear the blessed mutter of the mass,
And see God made and eaten [28] all day long,
And feel the steady candle-flame, and taste
Good strong thick stupefying incense-smoke!
For as I lie here, hours of the dead night,　85
Dying in state and by such slow degrees,
I fold my arms as if they clasped a crook,[29]
And stretch my feet forth straight as stone can
　　point,
And let the bedclothes, for a mortcloth,[30]
　　drop
Into great laps and folds of sculptor's-work:　90
And as yon tapers dwindle, and strange
　　thoughts
Grow, with a certain humming in my ears,
About the life before I lived this life,
And this life too, popes, cardinals and priests,

[23] A kind of inexpensive limestone.
[24] A green stone.
[25] With age.
[26] Cicero's—i.e., pure, classical Latin.
[27] A Roman jurist, whose Latin was less elegant than Cicero's.
[28] During the mass, according to the Catholic doctrine of transubstantiation, the bread is miraculously transformed into the body of Christ. Is the Bishop's interest in the sacrament spiritual?
[29] The bishop's crozier, symbol of his rank.
[30] Funeral pall.

Saint Praxed at his sermon on the mount,[31] 95
Your tall pale mother with her talking eyes,
And new-found agate urns as fresh as day,
And marble's language, Latin pure, discreet,
—Aha, *elucescebat*[32] quoth our friend?
No Tully, said I, Ulpian at the best!   100
Evil and brief hath been my pilgrimage.
All *lapis*, all, sons! Else I give the Pope
My villas! Will ye ever eat my heart?
Ever your eyes were as a lizard's quick,
They glitter like your mother's for my soul, 105
Or ye would heighten my impoverished frieze,
Piece out its starved design, and fill my vase
With grapes, and add a visor[33] and a term,[34]
And to the tripod ye would tie a lynx
That in his struggle throws the thyrsus
      down,   110
To comfort me on my entablature
Whereon I am to lie till I must ask
"Do I live, am I dead?" There, leave me,
      there!
For ye have stabbed me with ingratitude
To death—ye wish it—God, ye wish it!
      Stone—   115
Gritstone,[35] a-crumble! Clammy squares which
      sweat

As if the corpse they keep were oozing
      through—
And no more *lapis* to delight the world!
Well, go! I bless ye. Fewer tapers there,
But in a row: and, going, turn your backs 120
—Ay, like departing altar-ministrants,
And leave me in my church, the church for
      peace,
That I may watch at leisure if he leers—
Old Gandolf—at me, from his onion-stone,
As still he envied me, so fair she was!   125
(1845)

STUDY AIDS: 1. Reread the comment of
Ruskin in the headnote. Find in the poem
all those things that illustrate the Renaissance
"worldliness, inconsistency, pride, hypocrisy, ignorance of itself, love of art, of luxury, and of
good Latin." How do the various images build
up the picture of an age?
      2. Characterize the Bishop. Is he altogether
condemnable? Why does he confess some of his
sins to his sons? What signs do we have of his
mental weakness as he lies on his deathbed?
Do we have any suggestions of the attitudes
taken toward him by his sons?
      3. Is there any similarity of method between
this poem and *My Last Duchess*?

Love Among the Ruins

Where the quiet-colored end of evening
      smiles,
      Miles and miles,
On the solitary pastures where our sheep
      Half-asleep
Tinkle homeward through the twilight, stray
      or stop   5
      As they crop—
Was the site once of a city great and gay,
      (So they say)
Of our country's very capital, its prince
      Ages since   10
Held his court in, gathered councils, wielding
      far
      Peace or war.

Now—the country does not even boast a tree,
      As you see,
To distinguish slopes of verdure, certain
      rills   15
      From the hills
Intersect and give a name to, (else they run
      Into one,)
Where the domed and daring palace shot its
      spires
      Up like fires   20
O'er the hundred-gated circuit of a wall
      Bounding all,
Made of marble, men might march on nor
      be pressed,
      Twelve abreast.

[31] An obvious error; Jesus preached the sermon
on the mount. What is the matter with the Bishop?
[32] "He was famous." The classic Ciceronian form
would be "elucebat."

[33] Mask.
[34] Bust.
[35] A coarse sandstone. Why doesn't the Bishop
trust his sons?

And such plenty and perfection, see, of
    grass   25
    Never was!
Such a carpet as, this summer-time, o'er-
    spreads
    And embeds
Every vestige of the city, guessed alone,
    Stock or stone—   30
Where a multitude of men breathed joy and
    woe
    Long ago;
Lust of glory pricked their hearts up, dread of
    shame
    Struck them tame;
And that glory and that shame alike, the
    gold   35
    Bought and sold.

Now—the single little turret that remains
    On the plains,
By the caper [1] overrooted, by the gourd
    Overscored,   40
While the patching houseleek's [2] head of blos-
    som winks
    Through the chinks—
Marks the basement whence a tower in an-
    cient time
    Sprang sublime,
And a burning ring, all round, the chariots
    traced   45
    As they raced,
And the monarch and his minions [3] and his
    dames
    Viewed the games.

And I know, while thus the quiet-colored eve
    Smiles to leave   50
To their folding, all our many-tinkling fleece
    In such peace,
And the slopes and rills in undistinguished
    gray
    Melt away—
That a girl with eager eyes and yellow hair   55
    Waits me there
In the turret whence the charioteers caught
    soul
    For the goal,

[1] A small, prickly bush.
[2] The houseleek is a pink-flowered plant.

When the king looked, where she looks now,
    breathless, dumb
    Till I come.   60

But he looked upon the city, every side,
    Far and wide,
All the mountains topped with temples, all
    the glades'
    Colonnades,
All the causeys,[4] bridges, aqueducts—and
    then,   65
    All the men!
When I do come, she will speak not, she will
    stand,
    Either hand
On my shoulder, give her eyes the first em-
    brace
    Of my face,   70
Ere we rush, ere we extinguish sight and
    speech
    Each on each.

In one year they sent a million fighters forth
    South and north,
And they built their gods a brazen pillar
    high   75
    As the sky,
Yet reserved a thousand chariots in full force—
    Gold, of course.
Oh heart! oh blood that freezes, blood that
    burns!
    Earth's returns   80
For whole centuries of folly, noise and sin!
    Shut them in,
With their triumphs and their glories and the
    rest!
    Love is best.
(1855)

STUDY AIDS: 1. One of the two major
contrasts in this poem is obviously that between
the past and the present. What is the other major
contrast? How are they related? At what point
in the poem is the second one introduced? How
is each stanza structurally related to these contrasts? How and why does the structural order
shift in st. 6 (ll. 49–60)? How does the stanza
structure reach a climax in the final stanza?

[3] Favorite subjects.
[4] Causeways.

2. One critic speaks of this poem as having "a meter made out of the cadence of sheep-bells." Explain.

3. What would you say is the central idea of this poem? What line of the poem best sums it up? Is there any IRONY in the poem?

"Childe Roland to the Dark Tower Came"
See Edgar's Song [1] in *Lear*

This weird, nightmarish poem, written by Browning in a single day, came to him, he tells us, "as a kind of dream. I had to write it. . . . I did not know then what I meant beyond that, and I'm sure I don't know now." Despite this disclaimer, many ingenious interpretations of the poem have been made. Late in his life, when he was asked if he agreed with one of these analyses, Browning said: "Oh, no, not at all. Understand, I don't repudiate it, either; I only mean I was conscious of no allegorical intention." The nearest he ever came to approving a meaning was the time he responded to a man who asked him whether the central idea of the poem could not be summed up in the sentence: "He that endureth to the end shall be saved." Browning said, "Yes, just about that."

A poem like this is important not so much for what it means as for what it is. Browning has taken memories of a tower he once saw in the Carrara mountains, of a painting he later viewed in Paris, of a picture of a gaunt horse in his own drawing room, of details from his favorite book on painting, and of Edgar's mad song in *King Lear,* and from these and the products of a rich imagination he has created a masterpiece of the macabre and the grotesque. Surrealistic, anticipatory of the stream-of-consciousness technique, obscure in its possible symbolism and suggestion, *Childe Roland* is Browning's most "modern" poem; and yet it is as old as the bad dreams of men.

My first thought was, he lied in every word,
  That hoary cripple, with malicious eye
  Askance to watch the working of his lie
On mine, and mouth scarce able to afford
Suppression of the glee, that pursed and
    scored [2]   5
  Its edge, at one more victim gained thereby.

What else should he be set for, with his staff?
  What, save to waylay with his lies, ensnare
  All travelers that might find him posted
    there,
And ask the road? I guessed what skull-like
    laugh   10
Would break, what crutch 'gin write my epi-
    taph

For pastime in the dusty thoroughfare,
If at his counsel I should turn aside
  Into that ominous tract which, all agree,
  Hides the Dark Tower. Yet acquiesc-
    ingly [3]   15
I did turn as he pointed; neither pride
Nor hope rekindling at the end descried,
  So much as gladness that some end might
    be.

For, what with my whole world-wide wander-
    ing,
  What with my search drawn out through
    years, my hope   20
Dwindled into a ghost not fit to cope
With that obstreperous joy success would
    bring,—
I hardly tried now to rebuke the spring
  My heart made, finding failure in its scope.

[1] In *King Lear,* III, iv, Edgar, disguised as a mad beggar, sings this song:
"Childe Rowland to the dark tower came,
  His word was still—Fie, foh, and fum
I smell the blood of a British man."

What does this reference add to the TONE of the poem?

[2] Throughout the poem note the emphasis upon ugly words, harsh sounds, and grotesque images.
[3] Some readers see in this horrible old man a symbol of the devil.

As when a sick man very near to death [4]   25
  Seems dead indeed, and feels begin and
    end
  The tears, and takes the farewell of each
    friend,
And hears one bid the other go, draw breath
Freelier outside, ("since all is o'er," he saith,
  "And the blow fallen no grieving can
    amend;")   30

While some discuss if near the other graves
  Be room enough for this, and when a day
  Suits best for carrying the corpse away,
With care about the banners, scarves and
    staves:
And still the man hears all, and only craves   35
  He may not shame such tender love and
    stay.

Thus, I had so long suffered in this quest,
  Heard failure prophesied so oft, been
    writ
  So many times among "The Band"—to wit,
The knights who to the Dark Tower's search
    addressed   40
  Their steps—that just to fail as they, seemed
    best,
  And all the doubt was now—should I be
    fit?

So, quiet as despair, I turned from him,
  That hateful cripple, out of his highway
  Into the path he pointed. All the day   45
Had been a dreary one at best, and dim
Was settling to its close, yet shot one grim
  Red leer to see the plain catch its estray.[5]

For mark! no sooner was I fairly found
  Pledged to the plain, after a pace or two,   50
  Than, pausing to throw backward a last
    view
O'er the safe road, 'twas gone; gray plain all
    round:
Nothing but plain to the horizon's bound.
  I might go on; naught else remained to
    do.

So, on I went. I think I never saw   55
  Such starved ignoble nature; nothing
    throve:
  For flowers—as well expect a cedar grove!
But cockle, spurge, according to their law
Might propagate their kind, with none to
    awe,
  You'd think; a burr had been a treasure
    trove.   60

No! penury, inertness and grimace,
  In some strange sort, were the land's por-
    tion. "See
  Or shut your eyes," said nature peevishly,
"It nothing skills; [6] I cannot help my case:
'Tis the last judgment's fire must cure this
    place,   65
  Calcine [7] its clods and set my prisoners
    free."

If there pushed any ragged thistle-stalk
  Above its mates, the head was chopped;
    the bents [8]
  Were jealous else. What made those holes
    and rents
In the dock's harsh swarth leaves, bruised as
    to balk   70
All hope of greenness? 'tis a brute must walk
  Pashing their life out, with a brute's in-
    tents.

As for the grass, it grew as scant as hair
  In leprosy; thin dry blades pricked the
    mud
  Which underneath looked kneaded up with
    blood.   75
One stiff blind horse, his every bone a-stare,
Stood stupefied, however he came there:
  Thrust out past service from the devil's
    stud!

Alive? he might be dead for aught I know,
  With that red gaunt and colloped [9] neck
    a-strain,   80
  And shut eyes underneath the rusty mane;

[4] Explain this comparison, extended through two
stanzas.
[5] A strayed animal (here, Childe Roland).

[6] Avails.
[7] Turn into powder by heat.
[8] Coarse grasses.
[9] Marked with folds or ridges.

Seldom went such grotesqueness with such
    woe;
I never saw a brute I hated so;
    He must be wicked to deserve such pain.

I shut my eyes and turned them on my
    heart. 85
    As a man calls for wine before he fights,
    I asked one draught of earlier, happier
    sights,
Ere fitly I could hope to play my part.
Think first, fight afterwards—the soldier's art:
    One taste of the old time sets all to rights. 90

Not it! I fancied Cuthbert's reddening face
    Beneath its garniture of curly gold,
    Dear fellow, till I almost felt him fold
An arm in mine to fix me to the place,
That way he used. Alas, one night's dis-
    grace! 95
    Out went my heart's new fire and left it
    cold.

Giles then, the soul of honor—there he stands
    Frank as ten years ago when knighted first.
    What honest man should dare (he said) he
    durst.
Good—but the scene shifts—faugh! what hang-
    man hands 100
Pin to his breast a parchment? His own bands
    Read it. Poor traitor, spit upon and curst!

Better this present than a past like that;
    Back therefore to my darkening path again!
    No sound, no sight as far as eye could
    strain. 105
Will the night send a howlet [10] or a bat?
I asked: when something on the dismal flat
    Came to arrest my thoughts and change
    their train.

A sudden little river crossed my path
    As unexpected as a serpent comes. 110
    No sluggish tide congenial to the glooms;
This, as it frothed by, might have been a bath
For the fiend's glowing hoof—to see the wrath
    Of its black eddy bespate [11] with flakes and
    spumes.

[10] Owl.
[11] Spattered.

So petty yet so spiteful! All along, 115
    Low scrubby alders kneeled down over it;
    Drenched willows flung them headlong in
    fit
Of mute despair, a suicidal throng:
The river which had done them all the
    wrong,
    Whate'er that was, rolled by, deterred no
    whit. 120

Which, while I forded,—good saints, how I
    feared
    To set my foot upon a dead man's cheek,
    Each step, or feel the spear I thrust to
    seek
For hollows, tangled in his hair or beard!
—It may have been a water-rat I speared, 125
    But, ugh! it sounded like a baby's shriek.

Glad was I when I reached the other bank.
    Now for a better country. Vain presage!
    Who were the strugglers, what war did they
    wage,
Whose savage trample thus could pad [12] the
    dank 130
Soil to a plash? [13] Toads in a poisoned tank,
    Or wild cats in a red-hot iron cage—

The fight must so have seemed in that fell
    cirque. [14]
    What penned them there, with all the
    plain to choose? [15]
    No footprint leading to that horrid
    mews, [16] 135
None out of it. Mad brewage set to work
Their brains, no doubt, like galley-slaves the
    Turk
    Pits for his pastime, Christians against
    Jews.

And more than that—a furlong on—why, there!
    What bad use was that engine for, that
    wheel, 140

[12] Trample down.
[13] Puddle.
[14] Fierce arena.
[15] What do the questions in ll. 129–134 add to
the TONE?
[16] Enclosure.

Or brake, not wheel—that harrow fit to
reel [17]
Men's bodies out like silk? with all the air
Of Tophet's [18] tool, on earth left unaware,
   Or brought to sharpen its rusty teeth of
steel.

Then came a bit of stubbed ground, once a
   wood,   145
   Next a marsh, it would seem, and now
   mere earth
   Desperate and done with: (so a fool finds
   mirth,
Makes a thing and then mars it, till his mood
Changes and off he goes!) within a rood—
   Bog, clay and rubble,[19] sand and stark
   black dearth.   150

Now blotches rankling, colored gay and grim,
   Now patches where some leanness of the
   soil's
   Broke into moss or substances like boils;
Then came some palsied [20] oak, a cleft in him
Like a distorted mouth that splits its rim 155
   Gaping at death, and dies while it recoils.

And just as far as ever from the end!
   Naught in the distance but the evening,
   naught
   To point my footstep further! At the
   thought,
A great black bird, Apollyon's [21] bosom-
   friend,   160
Sailed past, nor beat his wide wing dragon-
   penned [22]
   That brushed my cap—perchance the guide
   I sought.

For, looking up, aware I somehow grew,
   'Spite of the dusk, the plain had given
   place

[17] I.e., the thing seemed like some instrument of
torture.
[18] Hell's.
[19] Broken rock. Note the intense ugliness of this
line in sound and imagery. This ugliness continues
unabated through the next stanza.
[20] Paralyzed.
[21] The devil's (see Rev. 9:11).
[22] Feathered like the wing of a dragon.

All round to mountains—with such name
   to grace   165
Mere ugly heights and heaps now stolen in
   view.
How thus they had surprised me,—solve it,
   you!
   How to get from them was no clearer case.

Yet half I seemed to recognize some trick
   Of mischief happened to me, God knows
   when—   170
   In a bad dream perhaps. Here ended,
   then,
Progress this way. When, in the very nick
Of giving up, one time more, came a click
   As when a trap shuts—you're inside the
   den!

Burningly it came on me all at once,   175
   This was the place! those two hills on the
   right,
   Crouched like two bulls locked horn in
   horn in fight;
While to the left, a tall scalped [23] moun-
   tain . . . Dunce,
Dotard, a-dozing at the very nonce,[24]
   After a life spent training for the sight! 180

What in the midst lay but the Tower itself?
   The round squat turret, blind as the fool's
   heart,
   Built of brown stone, without a counter-
   part
In the whole world. The tempest's mocking
   elf
Points to the shipman thus the unseen
   shelf   185
   He strikes on, only when the timbers start.

Not see? because of night perhaps?—why, day
   Came back again for that! before it left,
   The dying sunset kindled through a cleft:
The hills, like giants at a hunting, lay,   190
Chin upon hand, to see the game at bay,—
   "Now stab and end the creature—to the
   heft!" [25]

[23] Bare-peaked.
[24] Moment.
[25] Handle.

Not hear? when noise was everywhere! it
 tolled
Increasing like a bell. Names in my ears,
Of all the lost adventurers my peers,— 195
How such a one was strong, and such was
 bold,
And such was fortunate, yet each of old
Lost, lost! one moment knelled the woe of
 years.

There they stood, ranged along the hillsides,
 met
To view the last of me, a living frame 200
For one more picture! in a sheet of flame
I saw them and I knew them all. And yet
Dauntless the slug-horn [26] to my lips I set,
 And blew. *"Childe Roland to the Dark
 Tower came."*
(1855)

STUDY AIDS: 1. William Lyon Phelps suggests three different interpretations of this poem: "First, the Tower is the quest, and Success is found only in the moment of Failure. Second, the Tower is the quest, and when found is worth nothing: the hero has spent his life searching something that in the end is seen to be only a round, squat, blind turret. . . . Third, the Tower is not the quest at all—it is damnation, and when the knight turns *aside* from the true road to seek the Tower, he is a lost soul steadily slipping through increasing darkness to hell." Does any one of these interpretations best fit the poem?
 2. This poem is filled with ugly images, words, and sounds. We think of a work of art as beautiful. Is there a contradiction here? In what sense is *Childe Roland* a "beautiful" poem?

Fra Lippo Lippi [1]

The central portion of this zestful monologue contains not only a presentation of the artistic creed of this realistic painter of the early Italian Renaissance but also a statement of Browning's vigorous philosophy of life and poetry.

I am poor brother Lippo, by your leave!
You need not clap your torches to my face.
Zooks,[2] what's to blame? you think you see a
 monk!
What, 'tis past midnight, and you go the
 rounds,
And here you catch me at an alley's end 5
Where sportive ladies leave their doors ajar?
The Carmine's [3] my cloister: hunt it up,
Do,—harry out, if you must show your zeal,
Whatever rat, there, haps on his wrong hole,
And nip each softling of a wee white
 mouse, 10
Weke, weke, that's crept to keep him company!

Aha, you know your betters! Then, you'll take
Your hand away that's fiddling on my throat,
And please to know me likewise. Who am I?
Why, one, sir, who is lodging with a friend 15
Three streets off—he's a certain . . . how
 d'ye call?
Master—a . . . Cosimo of the Medici,[4]
In the house that caps the corner. Boh! you
 were best! [5]
Remember and tell me, the day you're
 hanged,
How you affected such a gullet's-gripe! 20
But you, sir, it concerns you that your knaves
Pick up a manner nor discredit you:
Zooks, are we pilchards,[6] that they sweep the
 streets
And count fair prize what comes into their
 net?

[26] Trumpet. Does Childe Roland blow his trumpet in triumph or as a warning?

[1] A fifteenth-century Florentine painter. In Browning's poem he has just been caught up by the city guards as he is returning to his room in the Medici palace after a night of frolicking.
 [2] A short form of the oath "Gadzooks."
 [3] The monastery of the Carmelite friars.

[4] Lippo's patron, the most powerful man in Florence. Is Lippo really having trouble remembering his name?
 [5] Best to take your hands off my throat.
 [6] Small, cheap fish.

He's Judas [7] to a tittle, that man is!   25
Just such a face! Why, sir, you make amends.
Lord, I'm not angry! Bid your hangdogs go
Drink out this quarter-florin to the health
Of the munificent house that harbors me
(And many more beside, lads! more be-
    side!)   30
And all's come square again. I'd like his face—
His, elbowing on his comrade in the door
With the pike and lantern,—for the slave that
    holds
John Baptist's head [8] a-dangle by the hair
With one hand ("Look you, now," as who
    should say)   35
And his weapon in the other, yet unwiped!
It's not your chance to have a bit of chalk,
A wood-coal or the like? or you should see!
Yes, I'm the painter, since you style me so.
What, brother Lippo's doings, up and
    down,   40
You know them and they take you? like
    enough!
I saw the proper twinkle in your eye—
'Tell you, I liked your looks at very first.
Let's sit and set things straight now, hip to
    haunch.
Here's spring come, and the nights one makes
    up bands   45
To roam the town and sing out carnival,[9]
And I've been three weeks shut within my
    mew,[10]
A-painting for the great man, saints and saints
And saints again. I could not paint all night—
Ouf! I leaned out of window for fresh air. 50
There came a hurry of feet and little feet,
A sweep of lute-strings, laughs, and whiffs of
    song,—
Flower o' the broom,[11]
Take away love, and our earth is a tomb!
Flower o' the quince,   55
I let Lisa go, and what good in life since?
Flower o' the thyme—and so on. Round they
    went.

[7] Lippo sees one of the guards with the eye of
a painter. Cf. also ll. 31–38.
[8] After it had been cut off by order of King
Herod.
[9] The gay season just before Lent.
[10] Coop.
[11] The following song is a typical Florentine folk
song, known as a *stornello*.

Scarce had they turned the corner when a
    titter
Like the skipping of rabbits by moonlight,—
    three slim shapes,
And a face that looked up . . . zooks, sir,
    flesh and blood,   60
That's all I'm made of! Into shreds it went,
Curtain and counterpane and coverlet,
All the bed-furniture—a dozen knots,
There was a ladder! Down I let myself,
Hands and feet, scrambling somehow, and so
    dropped,   65
And after them. I came up with the fun
Hard by Saint Laurence,[12] hail fellow, well
    met,—
Flower o' the rose,
If I've been merry, what matter who knows?
And so, as I was stealing back again,   70
To get to bed and have a bit of sleep
Ere I rise up to-morrow and go work
On Jerome [13] knocking at his poor old breast
With his great round stone to subdue the
    flesh,
You snap me of the sudden. Ah, I see!   75
Though your eye twinkles still, you shake
    your head—
Mine's shaved [14]—a monk, you say—the sting's
    in that!
If Master Cosimo announced himself,
Mum's the word naturally; but a monk!
Come, what am I a beast for? tell us, now! 80
I was a baby when my mother died
And father died and left me in the street.
I starved there, God knows how, a year or two
On fig-skins, melon-parings, rinds and shucks,
Refuse and rubbish. One fine frosty day,   85
My stomach being empty as your hat,
The wind doubled me up, and down I went.
Old Aunt Lapaccia [15] trussed me with one
    hand,
(Its fellow was a stinger as I knew)
And so along the wall, over the bridge, 90
By the straight cut to the convent. Six words
    there,

[12] The Church of San Lorenzo.
[13] An early Church Father who was often painted
in this act of penance. What is the IRONY of the
reference?
[14] Monks had shaved heads.
[15] Mona Lapacia, the sister of Lippo's father.

While I stood munching my first bread that
   month:
"So boy, you're minded," quoth the good fat
   father,
Wiping his own mouth, 'twas refection-
   time,[16]—
"To quit this very miserable world?   95
Will you renounce" . . . "the mouthful of
   bread?" thought I;
By no means! Brief, they made a monk of
   me;
I did renounce the world, its pride and
   greed,
Palace, farm, villa, shop, and banking-house,
Trash, such as these poor devils of Medici 100
Have given their hearts to—all at eight years
   old.
Well, sir, I found in time, you may be sure,
'Twas not for nothing—the good bellyful,
The warm serge and the rope that goes all
   round,
And day-long blessed idleness beside!   105
"Let's see what the urchin's fit for"—that
   came next.
Not overmuch their way, I must confess.
Such a to-do! They tried me with their books;
Lord, they'd have taught me Latin in pure
   waste!
Flower o' the clove,   110
All the Latin I construe is "amo," I love!
But, mind you, when a boy starves in the
   streets
Eight years together, as my fortune was,
Watching folk's faces to know who will fling
The bit of half-stripped grape-bunch he de-
   sires,   115
And who will curse or kick him for his
   pains,—
Which gentleman processional [17] and fine,
Holding a candle to the sacrament,
Will wink and let him lift a plate and catch
The droppings of the wax to sell again, 120
Or holla for the Eight [18] and have him
   whipped,—
How say I?—nay, which dog bites, which lets
   drop

His bone from the heap of offal in the street,—
Why, soul and sense of him grow sharp alike;
He learns the look of things, and none the
   less   125
For admonition from the hunger-pinch.
I had a store of such remarks,[19] be sure,
Which, after I found leisure, turned to use.
I drew men's faces on my copy-books,
Scrawled them within the antiphonary's
   marge,[20]   130
Joined legs and arms to the long music-notes,
Found eyes and nose and chin for A's and B's,
And made a string of pictures of the world
Betwixt the ins and outs of verb and noun,
On the wall, the bench, the door. The monks
   looked black.   135
"Nay," quoth the prior, "turn him out, d'ye
   say?
In no wise. Lose a crow and catch a lark.
What if at last we get our man of parts,
We Carmelites, like those Camaldolese
And Preaching Friars,[21] to do our church up
   fine   140
And put the front on it that ought to be!"
And hereupon he bade me daub away.
Thank you! my head being crammed, the
   walls a blank,
Never was such prompt disemburdening.
First, every sort of monk, the black and
   white,   145
I drew them, fat and lean: then, folk at
   church,
From good old gossips waiting to confess
Their cribs [22] of barrel-droppings,[23] candle-
   ends,—
To the breathless fellow at the altar-foot,
Fresh from his murder, safe [24] and sitting
   there   150
With the little children round him in a
   row
Of admiration, half for his beard and half
For that white anger of his victim's son
Shaking a fist at him with one fierce arm,

[16] Mealtime. What is the IRONY here?
[17] I.e., a gentleman marching in a religious procession.
[18] The governing magistrates of Florence.
[19] Things noticed.
[20] Margin of the choir-book.
[21] The Dominicans, an order of friars like the
Carmelites and the Camaldolese in l. 139.
[22] Petty thefts.
[23] Drops of wine.
[24] "Safe" because neither the law nor his victim's
son could seize him in a church.

Signing himself with the other because of
Christ   155
(Whose sad face on the cross sees only this
After the passion [25] of a thousand years)
Till some poor girl, her apron o'er her head,
(Which the intense eyes looked through)
came at eve
On tiptoe, said a word, dropped in a loaf, 160
Her pair of earrings and a bunch of flowers
(The brute took growling), prayed, and so
was gone.
I painted all; then cried, " 'Tis ask and have;
Choose, for more's ready!"—laid the ladder
flat,
And showed my covered bit of cloister-
wall.   165
The monks closed in a circle and praised loud
Till checked, taught what to see and not to
see,
Being simple bodies,—"That's the very man!
Look at the boy who stoops to pat the dog!
That woman's like the prior's niece who
comes   170
To care about his asthma: it's the life!"
But there my triumph's straw-fire flared and
funked; [26]
Their betters took their turn to see and say:
The prior and the learned pulled a face
And stopped all that in no time. "How?
what's here?   175
Quite from the mark of painting, bless us all!
Faces, arms, legs, and bodies like the true
As much as pea and pea! it's devil's-game!
Your business is not to catch men with show,
With homage to the perishable clay,   180
But lift them over it, ignore it all,
Make them forget there's such a thing as
flesh.
Your business is to paint the souls of men—
Man's soul, and it's a fire, smoke . . . no, it's
not [27] . . .
It's vapor done up like a new-born babe— 185
(In that shape when you die it leaves your
mouth)
It's . . . well, what matters talking, it's the
soul!

[25] Suffering.
[26] Went out.
[27] In ll. 184–187 the Prior is having difficulty in
describing the indescribable.

Give us no more of body than shows soul!
Here's Giotto,[28] with his saint a-praising God,
That sets us praising,—why not stop with
him?   190
Why put all thoughts of praise out of our
head
With wonder at lines, colors, and what not?
Paint the soul, never mind the legs and
arms! [29]
Rub all out, try at it a second time.
Oh, that white smallish female with the
breasts,   195
She's just my niece . . . Herodias,[30] I would
say,—
Who went and danced and got men's heads
cut off!
Have it all out!" Now, is this sense, I ask? [31]
A fine way to paint soul, by painting body
So ill, the eye can't stop there, must go
further   200
And can't fare worse! Thus, yellow does for
white
When what you put for yellow's simply black,
And any sort of meaning looks intense
When all beside itself means and looks
naught.
Why can't a painter lift each foot in turn, 205
Left foot and right foot, go a double step,
Make his flesh liker and his soul more like,
Both in their order? Take the prettiest face,
The prior's niece . . . patron-saint—is it so
pretty
You can't discover if it means hope, fear, 210
Sorrow or joy? won't beauty go with these?
Suppose I've made her eyes all right and
blue,

[28] A famous medieval Florentine painter who,
with a technique less realistic than that of later
painters, was able, the Prior believes, to "paint
the soul."
[29] Lines 175–193 present the ecclesiastical idea of
painting against which Fra Lippo Lippi (and the
Renaissance) rebelled. Note the satire.
[30] The mother of Salome, who danced for the
head of John the Baptist (see Matt. 14:1–12).
Browning has the Prior confuse the two women.
Why?
[31] In ll. 198–219, Browning states not only
Lippo's artistic creed (and so that of the Renaissance
revolt against medieval asceticism) but also his own.
What is this creed? Lines 217–218 are particularly
noteworthy.

Can't I take breath and try to add life's flash,
And then add soul and heighten them three-
    fold?
Or say there's beauty with no soul at all— 215
(I never saw it—put the case the same);
If you get simple beauty and naught else,
You get about the best thing God invents:
That's somewhat: and you'll find the soul you
    have missed,
Within yourself, when you return him
    thanks.   220
"Rub all out!" Well, well, there's my life, in
    short,
And so the thing has gone on ever since.
I'm grown a man no doubt, I've broken
    bounds:
You should not take a fellow eight years old
And make him swear to never kiss the
    girls.   225
I'm my own master, paint now as I please—
Having a friend, you see, in the corner-
    house!
Lord, it's fast holding by the rings in front—
Those great rings [32] serve more purposes than
    just
To plant a flag in, or tie up a horse!   230
And yet the old schooling sticks, the old grave
    eyes
Are peeping o'er my shoulder as I work,
The heads shake still—"It's art's decline, my
    son!
You're not of the true painters, great and
    old;
Brother Angelico's [33] the man, you'll find; 235
Brother Lorenzo [34] stands his single peer:
Fag on at flesh, you'll never make the third!"
Flower o' the pine,
You keep your mistr . . . manners, and I'll
*   stick to mine!*
I'm not the third, then: bless us, they must
    know!   240
Don't you think they're the likeliest to know,
They with their Latin? So, I swallow my
    rage,
Clench my teeth, suck my lips in tight, and
    paint

To please them—sometimes do and sometimes
    don't; [35]
For, doing most, there's pretty sure to
    come   245
A turn, some warm eve finds me at my
    saints—
A laugh, a cry, the business of the world—
(*Flower o' the peach,*
Death for us all, and his own life for each!)
And my whole soul revolves, the cup runs
    over,   250
The world and life's too big to pass for a
    dream,
And I do these wild things in sheer despite,
And play the fooleries you catch me at,
In pure rage! The old mill-horse, out at grass
After hard years, throws up his stiff heels
    so,   255
Although the miller does not preach to him
The only good of grass is to make chaff.
What would men have? Do they like grass
    or no—
May they or mayn't they? all I want's the
    thing
Settled for ever one way. As it is,   260
You tell too many lies and hurt yourself:
You don't like what you only like too much,
You do like what, if given you at your
    word,
You find abundantly detestable.
For me, I think I speak as I was taught; 265
I always see the garden and God there
A-making man's wife: and, my lesson learned,
The value and significance of flesh,
I can't unlearn ten minutes afterwards. [36]

You understand me: I'm a beast, I
    know.   270
But see, now—why, I see as certainly
As that the morning-star's about to shine,
What will hap some day. We've a youngster
    here
Comes to our convent, studies what I do,
Slouches and stares and lets no atom drop: 275

[32] These rings helped Lippo to climb in and out of his room.

[33] A devout monastic painter of religious subjects.

[34] Lorenzo Monaco was also a "painter of souls."

[35] Lines 242–244 point up the transitional character of Lippo's painting.

[36] In ll. 250–269 Lippo's (and Browning's) anti-asceticism reaches a climax. How does the image of the mill-horse turned "out at grass" illuminate the meaning of the passage?

His name is Guidi [37]—he'll not mind the
    monks—
They call him Hulking Tom, he lets them
    talk—
He picks my practice up—he'll paint apace,
I hope so—though I never live so long,
I know what's sure to follow. You be
    judge!   280
You speak no Latin more than I, belike;
However, you're my man, you've seen the
    world
—The beauty and the wonder and the power,
The shapes of things, their colors, lights and
    shades,
Changes, surprises,—and God made it all! 285
—For what? Do you feel thankful, ay or no,
For this fair town's face, yonder river's line,
The mountain round it and the sky above,
Much more the figures of man, woman, child,
These are the frame to? What's it all
    about?   290
To be passed over, despised? or dwelt upon,
Wondered at? oh, this last of course!—you say.
But why not do as well as say,—paint these
Just as they are, careless what comes of it?
God's works—paint any one, and count it
    crime   295
To let a truth slip. Don't object, "His works
Are here already; nature is complete:
Suppose you reproduce her—(which you
    can't)
There's no advantage! you must beat her,
    then."
For, don't you mark? we're made so that we
    love   300
First when we see them painted, things we
    have passed
Perhaps a hundred times nor cared to see;
And so they are better, painted—better to us,
Which is the same thing. Art was given for
    that;
God uses us to help each other so,   305
Lending our minds out. [38] Have you noticed,
    now,
Your cullion's [39] hanging face? A bit of chalk,

And trust me but you should, though! How
    much more,
If I drew higher things with the same truth!
That were to take the prior's pulpit-place, 310
Interpret God to all of you! Oh, oh,
It makes me mad to see what men shall do
And we in our graves! This world's no blot
    for us,
Nor blank; it means intensely, and means
    good:
To find its meaning is my meat and
    drink. [40]   315
"Ay, but you don't so instigate to prayer!"
Strikes in the prior: "when your meaning's
    plain
It does not say to folk—remember matins,
Or, mind you fast next Friday!" Why, for
    this
What need of art at all? A skull and
    bones,   320
Two bits of stick nailed crosswise, or, what's
    best,
A bell to chime the hour with, does as well.
I painted a Saint Laurence [41] six months
    since
At Prato, [42] splashed the fresco in fine style:
"How looks my painting, now the scaffold's
    down?"   325
I ask a brother: "Hugely," he returns—
"Already not one phiz [43] of your three slaves
Who turn the Deacon off his toasted side,
But's scratched and prodded to our heart's
    content,
The pious people have so eased their own 330
With coming to say prayers there in a rage:
We get on fast to see the bricks beneath.
Expect another job this time next year,
For pity and religion grow i' the crowd—
Your painting serves its purpose!" Hang the
    fools!   335

—That is—you'll not mistake an idle word
Spoke in a huff by a poor monk, God wot,
Tasting the air this spicy night which turns

---

[37] Tommaso Guidi, or Masaccio, actually Lippo's
master, not his pupil.
[38] Lines 283–306 give another eloquent statement
of the realist's creed.
[39] Rascal's.
[40] Browning's own zest for life was never better
stated than in this sentence.
[41] A painting of St. Laurence, who was martyred
by being burned on a gridiron.
[42] A town near Florence.
[43] Face (a short, slangy form of "physiognomy").

The unaccustomed head like Chianti [44] wine!
Oh, the church knows! don't misreport me,
    now!   340
It's natural a poor monk out of bounds
Should have his apt word to excuse himself:
And hearken how I plot to make amends.
I have bethought me: I shall paint a piece
. . . There's for you! Give me six months,
    then go, see   345
Something in Sant' Ambrogio's! [45] Bless the
    nuns!
They want a cast o' my office.[46] I shall paint
God in the midst, Madonna and her babe,
Ringed by a bowery, flowery angel-brood,
Lilies and vestments and white faces,
    sweet   350
As puff on puff of grated orris-root [47]
When ladies crowd to church at midsummer.
And then in the front, of course a saint or
    two—
Saint John,[48] because he saves the Florentines,
Saint Ambrose,[49] who puts down in black and
    white   355
The convent's friends and gives them a long
    day,
And Job, I must have him there past mistake,
The man of Uz (and Us without the z,
Painters who need his patience). Well, all
    these
Secured at their devotion, up shall come   360
Out of a corner when you least expect,
As one by a dark stair into a great light,
Music and talking, who but Lippo! [50] I!—
Mazed, motionless and moonstruck—I'm the
    man!
Back I shrink—what is this I see and hear? 365
I, caught up with my monk's-things by mis-
    take,

My old serge gown and rope that goes all
    round,
I, in this presence, this pure company!
Where's a hole, where's a corner for escape?
Then steps a sweet angelic slip of a thing 370
Forward, puts out a soft palm—"Not so fast!"
—Addresses the celestial presence, "Nay,
He made you and devised you, after all,
Though he's none of you! Could Saint John
    there draw—
His camel-hair [51] make up a painting-
    brush?   375
We come to brother Lippo for all that,
Iste perfecit opus!" [52] So, all smile—
I shuffle sideways with my blushing face
Under the cover of a hundred wings
Thrown like a spread of kirtles [53] when you're
    gay   380
And play hot cockles,[54] all the doors being
    shut,
Till, wholly unexpected, in there pops
The hothead husband! Thus I scuttle off
To some safe bench behind, not letting go
The palm of her, the little lily thing   385
That spoke the good word for me in the nick,
Like the prior's niece . . . Saint Lucy, I
    would say.
And so all's saved for me, and for the church
A pretty picture gained. Go, six months
    hence!
Your hand, sir, and good-by: no lights, no
    lights!   390
The street's hushed, and I know my own way
    back,
Don't fear me! There's the gray beginning.
    Zooks!
(1855)

STUDY AIDS: 1. In an expertly fashioned
DRAMATIC MONOLOGUE, the "audience" plays an

---

[44] A popular Italian table wine named from the Chianti mountains.

[45] The convent of St. Ambrose in Florence. For this church Lippo did *The Coronation of the Virgin,* described in ll. 347–377.

[46] A work of my creation.

[47] Iris-root ground into a fragrant powder.

[48] John the Baptist, patron saint of Florence.

[49] Saint Ambrose, the patron saint of the convent, is depicted in the painting as writing down the names of donors to the convent.

[50] As Renaissance painters often did, Lippo plans to put himself into the picture.

[51] John was "clothed with camel's hair" (Mark 1:6).

[52] "This one created the work." These words are inscribed on a scroll in the lower right corner of the painting near the head of the man supposedly representing Lippo.

[53] Women's skirts.

[54] A game in which a blindfolded player is struck from behind and then tries to guess who hit him. Lippo's meaning here, however (see ll. 382–383), is probably not quite so innocent.

important part; the reader is frequently reminded of its presence, and it determines much of what the speaker says and how he says it. How are these conditions fulfilled in *Fra Lippo Lippi*? Would Fra Lippo Lippi have said the same things, in the same way, to a group of monks, or to Cosimo de Medici, or to other painters?

2. What are some of the characteristics of Lippo as Browning has depicted him? How are these characteristics presented in the poem?

When is Lippo serious, when is he not? Does he have any unlikable traits?

3. Lippo's artistic and philosophical creeds are summed up especially in ll. 198–220, 251–269, and 313–315. What are the main points of his ideas about art? Of his philosophy of life? How are the two creeds related? To what degree are Lippo's own life and experiences responsible for these ideas? Do you agree with them? How can they be related to Browning and his poetry?

Andrea del Sarto
(Called "The Faultless Painter")

In striking contrast to the racy vigor of *Fra Lippo Lippi* is this equally brilliant monologue, *Andrea del Sarto*, based on the career of the Renaissance painter, Andrea d'Agnolo di Francesco di Luca (1486–1531), called "del Sarto" because he was the son of a tailor ("sarto"). In 1512 he married Lucrezia del Fede, "an artful woman who made him do as she pleased in all things." The poem is a psychological study and also an exploration of the relation of art to life.

But do not let us quarrel any more,
No, my Lucrezia; bear with me for once:
Sit down and all shall happen as you wish.
You turn your face, but does it bring your heart?
I'll work then for your friend's friend, never fear,   5
Treat his own subject after his own way,
Fix his own time, accept too his own price,
And shut the money into this small hand
When next it takes mine. Will it? tenderly?
Oh, I'll content him,—but to-morrow, love! 10
I often am much wearier than you think,
This evening more than usual, and it seems
As if—forgive now—should you let me sit
Here by the window with your hand in mine
And look a half-hour forth on Fiesole,[1]   15
Both of one mind, as married people use,[2]
Quietly, quietly the evening through,
I might get up to-morrow to my work
Cheerful and fresh as ever. Let us try.
To-morrow, how you shall be glad for this! 20
Your soft hand is a woman of itself,
And mine the man's bared breast she curls inside.
Don't count the time lost, neither; you must serve

For each of the five pictures we require:
It saves a model. So! keep looking so—   25
My serpentining beauty, rounds on rounds!
—How could you ever prick those perfect ears,
Even to put the pearl there! oh, so sweet—
My face, my moon, my everybody's moon,
Which everybody looks on and calls his,   30
And, I suppose, is looked on by in turn,
While she looks—no one's: very dear, no less.
You smile? why, there's my picture ready made,
There's what we painters call our harmony!
A common grayness silvers everything,—   35
All in a twilight, you and I alike
—You, at the point of your first pride in me
(That's gone you know),—but I, at every point;
My youth, my hope, my art, being all toned down
To yonder sober pleasant Fiesole.   40
There's the bell clinking from the chapel-top;
That length of convent-wall across the way
Holds the trees safer, huddled more inside;
The last monk leaves the garden;[3] days decrease,
And autumn grows, autumn in everything. 45
Eh? the whole seems to fall into a shape

[1] A suburb of Florence.
[2] Are accustomed to do.

[3] In ll. 41–44 note that Andrea sees the scene with a painter's eye.

Alinari Photo, reprinted by permission of the Uffizi Gallery, Florence.

Filippo Lippi's "Coronation of the Virgin," described in lines 347 ff.
of Browning's "Fra Lippo Lippi."

Byron, a watercolor by William Blake.

Bettmann Archive.

Robert Browning in 1859.

The Bettmann Archive.

Hyde Park Corner, 1888.

As if I saw alike my work and self
And all that I was born to be and do,
A twilight-piece. Love, we are in God's hand.
How strange now looks the life he makes us
    lead;   50
So free we seem, so fettered fast we are!
I feel he laid the fetter: let it lie! [4]
This chamber for example—turn your head—
All that's behind us! You don't understand
Nor care to understand about my art,   55
But you can hear at least when people speak:
And that cartoon, the second from the door
—It is the thing, love! so such thing should
    be—
Behold Madonna!—I am bold to say.
I can do with my pencil what I know,   60
What I see, what at bottom of my heart
I wish for, if I ever wish so deep—
Do easily, too—when I say, perfectly,
I do not boast, perhaps: yourself are judge,
Who listened to the legate's [5] talk last
    week,   65
And just as much they used to say in France.
At any rate 'tis easy, all of it!
No sketches first, no studies,—that's long past;
I do what many dream of all their lives,
—Dream? strive to do, and agonize to do, 70
And fail in doing. I could count twenty such
On twice your fingers, and not leave this
    town,
Who strive—you don't know how the others
    strive
To paint a little thing like that you smeared
Carelessly passing with your robes afloat [6]— 75
Yet do much less, so much less, someone says,
(I know his name, no matter)—so much less!
Well, less is more, Lucrezia: I am judged.
There burns a truer light of God in them,
In their vexed, beating, stuffed, and stopped-
    up brain,   80
Heart, or whate'er else, than goes on to
    prompt
This low-pulsed forthright craftsman's hand
    of mine.

Their works drop groundward, but them-
    selves, I know,
Reach many a time a heaven that's shut to
    me,
Enter and take their place there sure
    enough,   85
Though they come back and cannot tell the
    world.
My works are nearer heaven, but I sit here.
The sudden blood of these men! at a word—
Praise them, it boils, or blame them, it boils
    too.
I, painting from myself and to myself,   90
Know what I do, am unmoved by men's
    blame
Or their praise either. Somebody remarks
Morello's [7] outline there is wrongly traced,
His hue mistaken; what of that? or else,
Rightly traced and well ordered; what of
    that?   95
Speak as they please, what does the moun-
    tain care?
Ah, but a man's reach should exceed his
    grasp,
Or what's a heaven for? [8] All is silver-gray
Placid and perfect with my art: the worse!
I know both what I want and what might
    gain,   100
And yet how profitless to know, to sigh
"Had I been two, another and myself,
Our head would have o'erlooked the world!"
    No doubt.
Yonder's a work now, of that famous youth
The Urbinate [9] who died five years ago. 105
'Tis copied; George Vasari [10] sent it me.)
Well, I can fancy how he did it all,
Pouring his soul, with kings and popes to
    see,
Reaching, that heaven might so replenish
    him,

---

[4] Why does Andrea find this fatalism consoling?
[5] The legate was the Pope's representative.
[6] Lines 60–75: Andrea recognizes his perfect craftsmanship—his technical skill, which many artists would give anything to possess. Note the ironic touch in ll. 74–75.

[7] Morello is a mountain near Florence.
[8] Lines 76–98: And yet, with all his technical expertness, Andrea sees that many of the inferior craftsmen are greater than he, for they have aspirations outrunning their capacities; and so their works have "soul."
[9] Raphael, a famous Italian Renaissance painter, born in Urbino.
[10] A student of Andrea and the author of a book from which Browning got much of his biographical material about painters.

Above and through his art—for it gives
way: 110
That arm is wrongly put—and there again—
A fault to pardon in the drawing's lines,
Its body, so to speak: its soul is right,
He means right—that, a child may under-
stand.
Still, what an arm! and I could alter it: 115
But all the play, the insight and the stretch—
Out of me, out of me! And wherefore out?
Had you enjoined them on me, given me
soul,
We might have risen to Rafael, I and you!
Nay, love, you did give all I asked, I
think—   120
More than I merit, yes, by many times.
But had you—oh, with the same perfect brow,
And perfect eyes, and more than perfect
mouth,
And the low voice my soul hears, as a bird
The fowler's pipe, and follows to the
snare—   125
Had you, with these the same, but brought
a mind!
Some women do so. Had the mouth there
urged
"God and the glory! never care for gain.
The present by the future, what is that?
Live for fame, side by side with Agnolo![11] 130
Rafael is waiting: up to God, all three!"
I might have done it for you. So it seems:[12]
Perhaps not. All is as God overrules.
Besides, incentives come from the soul's self;
The rest avail not. Why do I need you?   135
What wife had Rafael, or has Agnolo?
In this world, who can do a thing, will not;
And who would do it, cannot, I perceive:
Yet the will's somewhat—somewhat, too, the
power—
And thus we half-men struggle. At the
end,   140
God, I conclude, compensates, punishes.
'Tis safer for me, if the award be strict,
That I am something underrated here,
Poor this long while, despised, to speak the
truth.

[11] Michelangelo, another great Italian Renaissance
artist.
[12] In ll. 132–135 Andrea suggests three possible
reasons for his failure.

I dared not, do you know, leave home all
day,   145
For fear of chancing on the Paris lords.
The best is when they pass and look aside;
But they speak sometimes; I must bear it all.
Well may they speak! That Francis,[13] that
first time,
And that long festal year at Fontaine-
bleau![14]   150
I surely then could sometimes leave the
ground,
Put on the glory, Rafael's daily wear,
In that humane great monarch's golden
look,—
One finger in his beard or twisted curl
Over his mouth's good mark that made the
smile,   155
One arm about my shoulder, round my neck,
The jingle of his gold chain in my ear,
I painting proudly with his breath on me,
All his court round him, seeing with his eyes,
Such frank French eyes, and such a fire of
souls   160
Profuse, my hand kept plying by those
hearts—
And, best of all, this, this, this face beyond,
This in the background, waiting on my
work,
To crown the issue with a last reward!
A good time, was it not, my kingly days? 165
And had you not grown restless . . . but I
know—
'Tis done and past; 'twas right, my instinct
said;
Too live the life grew, golden and not gray,
And I'm the weak-eyed bat no sun should
tempt
Out of the grange whose four walls make his
world.   170
How could it end in any other way?
You called me, and I came home to your
heart.
The triumph was—to reach and stay there;
since

[13] Francis I, king of France, who had given
Andrea money to buy art works for him. Instead,
Andrea bought a house for Lucrezia.
[14] The location of one of the palaces of the
French king. Andrea did some of his best work
there.

I reached it ere the triumph, what is lost?
Let my hands frame your face in your hair's
gold,   175
You beautiful Lucrezia that are mine!
"Rafael did this, Andrea painted that;
The Roman's[15] is the better when you
pray,
But still the other's Virgin was his wife"[16]—
Men will excuse me. I am glad to judge   180
Both pictures in your presence; clearer grows
My better fortune, I resolve to think.
For, do you know, Lucrezia, as God lives,
Said one day Agnolo, his very self,
To Rafael . . . I have known it all these
years . . .   185
(When the young man was flaming out his
thoughts
Upon a palace-wall for Rome to see,
Too lifted up in heart because of it)
"Friend, there's a certain sorry little scrub
Goes up and down our Florence, none cares
how,   190
Who, were he set to plan and execute
As you are, pricked on by your popes and
kings,
Would bring the sweat into that brow of
yours!"
To Rafael's!—And indeed the arm is wrong.
I hardly dare . . . yet, only you to see,   195
Give the chalk here—quick, thus the line
should go!
Ay, but the soul! he's Rafael! rub it out!
Still, all I care for, if he spoke the truth,
(What he? why, who but Michel Agnolo?
Do you forget already words like those?)   200
If really there was such a chance, so lost,—
Is, whether you're—not grateful—but more
pleased.
Well, let me think so. And you smile indeed!
This hour has been an hour! Another smile?
If you would sit thus by me every night   205
I should work better, do you comprehend?
I mean that I should earn more, give you
more.
See, it is settled dusk now; there's a star;
Morello's gone, the watch-lights show the
wall,

The cue-owls speak the name we call them
by.   210
Come from the window, love,—come in, at
last,
Inside the melancholy little house
We built to be so gay with. God is just.
King Francis may forgive me: oft at nights
When I look up from painting, eyes tired
out,   215
The walls become illumined, brick from
brick
Distinct, instead of mortar, fierce bright gold,
That gold of his I did cement them with!
Let us but love each other. Must you go?
That cousin[17] here again? he waits out-
side?   220
Must see you—you, and not with me? Those
loans?
More gaming debts to pay? you smiled for
that?
Well, let smiles buy me! have you more to
spend?
While hand and eye and something of a heart
Are left me, work's my ware, and what's it
worth?   225
I'll pay my fancy. Only let me sit
The gray remainder of the evening out,
Idle, you call it, and muse perfectly
How I could paint, were I but back in France,
One picture, just one more—the Virgin's
face,   230
Not yours this time! I want you at my side
To hear them—that is, Michel Agnolo—
Judge all I do and tell you of its worth.
Will you? To-morrow, satisfy your friend.
I take the subjects for his corridor,   235
Finish the portrait out of hand—there, there,
And throw him in another thing or two
If he demurs; the whole should prove enough
To pay for this same cousin's freak. Beside,
What's better and what's all I care about, 240
Get you the thirteen scudi[18] for the ruff!
Love, does that please you? Ah, but what does
he,
The cousin! what does he to please you more?

I am grown peaceful as old age tonight.
I regret little, I would change still less.   245

[15] Raphael's.
[16] Andrea used his wife as a model for the Virgin
Mary. Note the IRONY.
[17] Actually a lover.
[18] Plural of "scudo," an Italian coin.

Since there my past life lies, why alter it?
The very wrong to Francis!—it is true
I took his coin, was tempted and complied,
And built this house and sinned, and all is
said.
My father and my mother died of want. 250
Well, had I riches of my own? you see
How one gets rich! Let each one bear his lot.
They were born poor, lived poor, and poor
they died:
And I have labored somewhat in my time
And not been paid profusely. Some good
son   255
Paint my two hundred pictures—let him try!
No doubt, there's something strikes a balance.
Yes,
You loved me quite enough, it seems tonight.
This must suffice me here. What would one
have?
In heaven, perhaps, new chances, one more
chance—   260
Four great walls in the New Jerusalem,[19]
Meted [20] on each side by the angel's reed,
For Leonard,[21] Rafael, Agnolo and me
To cover—the three first without a wife,

While I have mine! So—still they overcome   265
Because there's still Lucrezia—as I choose.

Again the cousin's whistle! Go, my love.
(1855)

STUDY AIDS: 1. What characteristics of
Andrea del Sarto are revealed in his monologue?
What do you think is the underlying reason
for his weariness and plaintiveness? Do you feel
pity for him, or contempt? At what points in
the poem does he show something of his old
spark and fire?
2. How are Lucrezia's characteristics revealed
in the poem? Precisely at what points in the
poem are her actions and reactions suggested?
Why does Andrea continue to love her?
3. Browning believed strongly in the "glory
of the imperfect." In what respect is the imperfect glorious? Andrea is "the faultless painter."
What is wrong with his "perfection"? How could
a less technically perfect painter be a greater
artist than Andrea? What does Browning mean
by the famous lines (97–98): "Ah, but a man's
reach should exceed his grasp, Or what's a heaven
for?"

[19] See Rev. 21:10–21.
[20] Measured.
[21] Leonardo da Vinci, another famous Italian
Renaissance artist.

Prospice [1]

Shortly after the death of his wife, Browning wrote this stirring poem, which expresses not
only his love for her but also his courage and his faith in personal immortality.

Fear death? [2]—to feel the fog in my throat,
    The mist in my face,
When the snows begin, and the blasts denote
    I am nearing the place,
The power of the night, the press of the
    storm,   5
    The post of the foe;

Where he stands, the Arch Fear [3] in a visible
    form,
    Yet the strong man must go:
For the journey is done and the summit at-
    tained,
    And the barriers fall,   10
Though a battle's to fight ere the guerdon [4]
    be gained,
    The reward of it all.
I was ever a fighter, so—one fight more,
    The best and the last!
I would hate that death bandaged my eyes,
    and forbore,   15
    And bade me creep past.

[1] "Look forward" (pronounced prŏs'-pi-see).
[2] What effect is gained by starting with this brief
question?
[3] Death.
[4] Reward.

No! let me taste the whole of it, fare like my
    peers
  The heroes of old,
Bear the brunt, in a minute pay life's glad
    arrears
  Of pain, darkness and cold.   20
For sudden the worst turns the best to the
    brave,
  The black minute's at end,[5]
And the elements' rage, the fiend-voices that
    rave,
  Shall dwindle, shall blend,
Shall change, shall become first a peace out
    of pain,[6]   25
  Then a light, then thy [7] breast,

O thou soul of my soul! I shall clasp thee
    again,
  And with God be the rest!
(1864)

STUDY AIDS: 1. This poem is highly personal. What universal significance, then, does it have?
  2. What is the dominant image of the poem?
  3. What is the TONE of the poem? Do you get the impression of boastfulness or the pretended courage of one "whistling in the graveyard"? If not, why not? What qualities of Browning emerge?
  4. How does Browning avoid sentimentality in the poem?

Epilogue to Asolando

This poem was the final poem in the collection *Asolando: Facts and Fancies,* which was published on the day (December 12, 1889) that Browning died in Venice.

At the midnight in the silence of the sleep-
    time,
  When you [1] set your fancies free,
Will they pass to where—by death, fools think,
    imprisoned—
Low he [2] lies who once so loved you, whom
    you loved so—
  —Pity me? [3]   5

Oh, to love so, be so loved, yet so mistaken!
  What had I on earth to do
With the slothful, with the mawkish, the un-
    manly?
Like the aimless, helpless, hopeless, did I
    drivel
  —Being—who?   10

One who never turned his back but marched
    breast forward,
  Never doubted clouds would break,
Never dreamed, though right were worsted,
    wrong would triumph,
Held we fall to rise, are baffled to fight better,
  Sleep to wake.   15

No, at noonday in the bustle of man's work-
    time [4]
  Greet the unseen with a cheer!
Bid him forward, breast and back as either
    should be,
"Strive and thrive!" cry "Speed—fight on, fare
    ever
    There as here!" [5]   20
(1889)

STUDY AIDS: Compare this poem with Tennyson's *Crossing the Bar* (p. 781).

[5] Note the appropriate images and metrical pattern by which Browning expresses the transition from the pain of death to the peace of immortality.
[6] "Out of pain" was originally "then a joy." Why is the change an improvement?
[7] Mrs. Browning's.

[1] A reader who admires Browning.
[2] Browning.
[3] I.e., will your fancies pity me for being dead?

[4] This stanza expresses what the "you" of st. 1 should do. Note the points of contrast between the two stanzas.
[5] I.e., in the after-life as on earth.

Edward Fitzgerald
(1809–1883)

SOMETIMES A TRANSLATOR DOES HIS JOB SO WELL THAT THE RESULT DESERVES TO BE CLASSED among original, creative works of literature. Such is the case with Edward Fitzgerald and the *Rubáiyát of Omar Khayyám*. Instead of a literal, precise translation, losing in life what it achieves in scholarly accuracy, Fitzgerald's *Rubáiyát* is more of an imaginative re-rendering of the old Persian poem into English verse, capturing the spirit of the original even as it expresses the poetic genius of the translator.

Fitzgerald, who is remembered only as a translator and letter-writer, lived a quiet, uneventful life. He attended Cambridge, where he was a friend of Thackeray. A few years after graduation he became interested in Persian poetry, and in 1859 published his translation of the *Rubáiyát* anonymously. He spent his later years quietly at his home near Woodbridge, Suffolk, reading, tending his flowers, and making leisurely excursions on a nearby estuary in his small boat. He died two years before the appearance of the volume of his friend Tennyson's poetry, which contained an introductory tribute to him and praised his

> golden Eastern lay,
> Than which I know no version done
> In English more divinely well.

The Rubáiyát of Omar Khayyám [1]

Fitzgerald's anonymous translation was at first ignored. A year after its publication Rossetti found a copy in a London bookstall and through his praise brought it to public attention. Since then it has been one of the most popular and often-quoted of nineteenth-century poems, expressing in subtle music and rich imagery the hedonism, pessimism, skepticism, and fatalism which, singly or collectively, have at one time or another dominated the moods of all men.

At Rossetti's prompting, Fitzgerald made many revisions of the poem. The present text is the final version of 1879.

1

Wake! for the sun who scattered into flight
The stars before him from the field of night,
  Drives night along with them from heaven,
    and strikes
The sultan's turret with a shaft of light. . . .

3

And, as the cock crew, those who stood before
The tavern shouted—"Open, then, the door! 10

[1] Omar Khayyám was an eleventh-century Persian poet-astronomer, whose verse was couched in "rubáiyát" or "quatrains."

You know how little while we have to
  stay,
And, once departed, may return no more." . . .

7

Come, fill the cup, and in the fire of spring 25
Your winter-garment of repentance fling:
  The bird of time has but a little way
To flutter—and the bird is on the wing.

8

Whether at Naishápúr or Babylon,
Whether the cup with sweet or bitter run, 30

The wine of life keeps oozing drop by
    drop,
The leaves of life keep falling one by one.

9

Each morn a thousand roses brings, you say;
Yes, but where leaves the rose of yesterday?
    And this first summer month that brings
      the rose   35
Shall take Jamshyd and Kaikobád [2] away. . . .

12

A book of verses underneath the bough,   45
A jug of wine, a loaf of bread—and thou
    Beside me singing in the wilderness—
Ah, wilderness were paradise enow! [3]

13

Some for the glories of this world; and some
Sigh for the prophet's [4] paradise to come;   50
    Ah, take the cash, and let the credit go,
Nor heed the rumble of a distant drum! . . .

16

The worldly hope men set their hearts upon
Turns ashes—or it prospers; and anon,
    Like snow upon the desert's dusty face,
Lighting a little hour or two—is gone.

17

Think, in this battered caravanserai [5]   65
Whose portals are alternate night and day,
    How sultan after sultan with his pomp
Abode his destined hour, and went his
    way. . . .

19

I sometimes think that never blows so red
The rose as where some buried Caesar bled;
    That every hyacinth [6] the garden wears   75
Dropped in her lap from some once lovely
    head.

20

And this reviving herb whose tender green
Fledges the river-lip on which we lean—
    Ah, lean upon it lightly! for who knows
From what once lovely lip it springs unseen! 80

21

Ah, my belovèd, fill the cup that clears
To-day of past regret and future fears:
    To-morrow!—Why, to-morrow I may be
Myself with yesterday's seven thousand years.[7]

22

For some we loved, the loveliest and the
    best   85
That from his vintage rolling time has prest,
    Have drunk their cup a round or two be-
      fore,
And one by one crept silently to rest.

23

And we, that now make merry in the room
They left, and summer dresses in new
    bloom,   90
    Ourselves must we beneath the couch of
    earth
Descend—ourselves to make a couch—for
    whom?

24

Ah, make the most of what we yet may spend,
Before we too into the dust descend;
    Dust into dust, and under dust, to lie,   95
Sans [8] wine, sans song, sans singer, and—
    sans end!

25

Alike for those who to-day prepare,
And those that after some to-morrow stare,
    A muezzin [9] from the tower of darkness
    cries,
"Fools, your reward is neither here nor
    there."   100

---

[2] Jamshyd and Kaikobád are legendary Persian
kings.
[3] Enough.
[4] Mohammed's.
[5] An inn where caravans stop for the night. Of
what is it a symbol here?

[6] According to Greek myth, Hyacinth was a
youth whom Apollo accidentally killed. From his
blood sprang the flower that bears his name.
[7] A thousand years for each of the planets known
to Omar.
[8] Without.
[9] A crier who calls Mohammedans to prayer.

26

Why, all the saints and sages who discussed
Of the two worlds so wisely—they are thrust
   Like foolish prophets forth; their words to
    scorn
Are scattered, and their mouths are stopped
   with dust.

27

Myself when young did eagerly frequent 105
Doctor and saint, and heard great argument
   About it and about: but evermore
Came out by the same door where in I went.

28

With them the seed of wisdom did I sow,
And with my own hand wrought to make it
    grow; 110
   And this was all the harvest that I reaped—
"I came like water, and like wind I go."

29

Into this universe, and why not knowing,
Nor whence, like water willy-nilly flowing;
   And out of it, as wind along the waste, 115
I know not whither, willy-nilly blowing. . . .

31

Up from earth's center through the seventh
    gate
I rose, and on the throne of Saturn [10] sate,
   And many a knot unraveled by the road;
But not the master-knot of human fate.

32

There was the door to which I found no
    key; 125
There was the veil through which I could
   not see:
   Some little talk awhile of me and thee [11]
There was—and then no more of thee and me.

[10] "The Lord of the Seventh Heaven" (Fitzgerald). According to ancient astronomy, nine concentric spheres (Heavens) surrounded the earth.
[11] "Me and thee": "Of some dividual Existence or
Personality distinct from the Whole" (Fitzgerald).

33

Earth could not answer; nor the seas that
   mourn
In flowing purple, of their lord forlorn; 130
   Nor rolling heaven, with all his signs [12]
    revealed
And hidden by the sleeve of night and
   morn. . . .

35

Then to the lip of this poor earthen urn
I leaned, the secret of my life to learn:
   And lip to lip it murmured—"While you
    live,
Drink!—for, once dead, you never shall re-
   turn." . . . 140

41

Perplexed no more with human or divine,
To-morrow's tangle to the winds resign,
   And lose your fingers in the tresses of
The cypress-slender minister [13] of wine.

42

And if the wine you drink, the lip you
    press, 165
End in what all begins and ends in—Yes;
   Think that you are to-day what yesterday
You were—to-morrow you shall not be less.

43

So when the angel [14] of the darker drink
At last shall find you by the river-brink, 170
   And, offering his cup, invite your soul
Forth to your lips to quaff—you shall not
   shrink. . . .

46

And fear not lest existence closing your
Account, and mine, should know the like no
   more;
   The eternal Saki [15] from that bowl has
    poured
Millions of bubbles like us, and will pour.

[12] Of the zodiac.
[13] The girl who pours the wine.
[14] Azrael, the Angel of Death.
[15] Wine-bearer. What is the symbolism?

47

When you and I behind the veil are past, 185
Oh but the long long while the world shall
last,
  Which of our coming and departure heeds
As the seven seas should heed a pebble-cast.

48

A moment's halt—a momentary taste
Of being from the well amid the waste— 190
  And lo!—the phantom caravan has reached
The nothing it set out from—Oh, make haste!

49

Would you that spangle of existence spend
About the secret—quick about it, friend!
  A hair perhaps divides the false and
  true— 195
And upon what, prithee, does life de-
pend? . . .

54

Waste not your hour, nor in the vain pursuit
Of this and that endeavor and dispute;
  Better be jocund with the fruitful grape 215
Than sadden after none, or bitter, fruit.

55

You know, my friends, with what a brave
  carouse
I made a second marriage in my house;
  Divorced old barren reason from my bed,
And took the daughter of the vine to
  spouse. . . . 220

59

The grape that can with logic absolute
The two-and-seventy jarring sects [16] confute;
  The sovereign alchemist that in a trice 235
Life's leaden metal into gold transmute. . . .

[16] "The seventy-two religions supposed to divide
the world" (Fitzgerald).
[17] I.e., since this juice is. What is the "argument"
of the stanza?
[18] Caused by the illumination of a candle placed
in a so-called "magic lantern," an early form of
picture projector.

61

Why, be this juice [17] the growth of God, who
  dare 241
Blaspheme the twisted tendril as a snare?
  A blessing, we should use it, should we not?
And if a curse—why, then, who set it
  there? . . .

63

O threats of hell and hopes of paradise!
One thing at least is certain—this life flies; 250
  One thing is certain and the rest is lies;
The flower that once has blown forever dies.

64

Strange, is it not? that of the myriads who
Before us passed the door of darkness through,
  Not one returns to tell us of the road, 255
Which to discover we must travel too.

65

The revelations of devout and learned
Who rose before us, and as prophets burned,
  Are all but stories, which, awoke from
  sleep
They told their fellows, and to sleep re-
  turned. 260

66

I sent my soul through the invisible,
Some letter of that after-life to spell:
  And by and by my soul returned to me,
And answered "I myself am heaven and hell."

67

Heaven but the vision of fulfilled desire, 265
And hell the shadow of a soul on fire,
  Cast on the darkness into which ourselves,
So late emerged from, shall so soon expire.

68

We are no other than a moving row
Of magic shadow-shapes [18] that come and
  go 270
  Round with this sun-illumined lantern held
In midnight by the Master of the Show;

69

Impotent pieces of the game He plays
Upon this checker-board of nights and days;
   Hither and thither moves, and checks, and
     slays,   275
And one by one back in the closet lays.

70

The ball [19] no question makes of ayes and noes
But here or there as strikes the player goes;
   And He that tossed you down into the field,
He knows about it all—He knows—HE
     knows!   280

71

The Moving Finger writes; and, having writ,
Moves on: nor all your piety nor wit
   Shall lure it back to cancel half a line,
Nor all your tears wash out a word of it.

72

And that inverted bowl they call the sky,   285
Whereunder crawling cooped we live and die,
   Lift not your hands to it for help—for it
As impotently rolls as you or I.

73

With earth's first clay they did the last man
   knead,
And there of the last harvest sowed the
   seed: 290
   And the first morning of creation wrote
What the last dawn of reckoning shall read.

74

Yesterday this day's madness did prepare;
To-morrow's silence, triumph, or despair:
   Drink! for you know not whence you came,
     nor why: 295
Drink! for you know not why you go, nor
     where. . . .

[19] In polo.
[20] Snare. The poet rebels against the injustice
of imperfectly made creatures being punished for
sins which, through "predestined evil," they cannot
help committing. Note, too, the philosophic arguments of the preceding two stanzas.

77

And this I know: whether the one true
   light   305
Kindle to love, or wrath—consume me quite,
   One flash of it within the tavern caught
Better than in the temple lost outright.

78

What! out of senseless nothing to provoke
A conscious something to resent the yoke 310
   Of unpermitted pleasure, under pain
Of everlasting penalties, if broke!

79

What, from this helpless creature be repaid
Pure gold for what he lent him dross-allayed—
   Sue for a debt we never did contract,   315
And cannot answer—Oh the sorry trade!

80

Oh Thou, who didst with pitfall and with
   gin [20]
Beset the road I was to wander in,
   Thou wilt not with predestined evil round
Enmesh, and then impute my fall to
     sin! . . .   320

82

As under cover of departing day   325
Slunk hunger-stricken Ramazan [21] away,
   Once more within the Potter's house alone
I stood, surrounded by the shapes of clay.

83

Shapes of all sorts and sizes, great and small,
That stood along the floor and by the wall; 330
   And some loquacious vessels were; and some
Listened perhaps, but never talked at all.

84

Said one among them [22]—"Surely not in vain
My substance of the common earth was taken
   And to this figure molded, to be broke, 335
Or trampled back to shapeless earth again."

[21] The Mohammedan month of fasting.
[22] The speeches of the various pots represent
different philosophies of life. What are they?

85

Then said a second—"Never a peevish boy
Would break the bowl from which he drank
    in joy:
  And He that with his hand the vessel made
Will surely not in after wrath destroy."   340

86

After a momentary silence spake
Some vessel of a more ungainly make;
  "They sneer at me for leaning all awry:
What! did the hand then of the Potter shake?"

87

Whereat some one of the loquacious lot— 345
I think a Sufi [23] pipkin—waxing hot—
  "All this of pot and Potter—Tell me then,
Who is the Potter, pray, and who the pot?"

88

"Why," said another, "Some there are who
  tell
Of one who threatens He will toss to hell 350
  The luckless pots He marred in making—
    pish!
He's a good fellow, and 'twill all be well."

89

"Well," murmured one, "Let whoso make or
  buy,
My clay with long oblivion is gone dry:
  But fill me with the old familiar juice, 355
Methinks I might recover by and by." . . .

91

Ah, with the grape my fading life provide,
And wash the body whence the life has died,
  And lay me, shrouded in the living leaf,
By some not unfrequented garden-side—

92

That even my buried ashes such a snare 365
Of vintage shall fling up into the air
  As not a true-believer passing by
But shall be overtaken unaware.

[23] One of a Persian sect of mystics.

93

Indeed the idols [24] I have loved so long
Have done my credit in this world much
    wrong: 370
  Have drowned my glory in a shallow cup,
And sold my reputation for a song.

94

Indeed, indeed, repentance oft before
I swore—but was I sober when I swore?
  And then and then came spring, and rose-
    in-hand   375
My thread-bare penitence apieces tore.

95

And much as wine has played the infidel,
And robbed me of my robe of honor—well,
  I wonder often what the vintners [25] buy
One half so precious as the stuff they sell. 380

96

Yet ah, that spring should vanish with the
  rose!
That youth's sweet-scented manuscript should
  close!
  The nightingale that in the branches sang,
Ah whence, and whither flown again, who
  knows! . . .

99

Ah love! could you and I with Him conspire
To grasp this sorry scheme of things entire,
  Would not we shatter it to bits—and
    then   395
Re-mold it nearer to the heart's desire!

100

Yon rising moon that looks for us again—
How oft hereafter will she wax and wane;
  How oft hereafter rising look for us
Through this same garden—and for one in
  vain!   400

[24] What are Omar's "idols"?
[25] Wine-merchants.

101

And when like her, oh Saki, you shall pass
Among the guests star-scattered on the grass,
  And in your blissful errand reach the spot
Where I made one—turn down an empty
    glass!

(1859)

STUDY AIDS: 1. What is unusual about
the rhyme-scheme of the stanza? What effect
does this feature have upon the atmosphere of
the poem?

2. Under what different images does the poet
represent God (or fate), life, man, the after-life,
philosophy, death, and pleasure? Which of these
images seem to you particularly effective, and
why?

3. In this poem are expressed the philosophies
of hedonism, fatalism, pessimism, and skepticism.
Pick out passages in which these various philosophies are presented. Since the poet upholds a
philosophy of pleasure, why is he not happy?

Thomas Henry Huxley
(1825–1895)

THE FACT THAT THOMAS HENRY HUXLEY INVENTED THE TERM "AGNOSTIC," WHICH HE
applied to himself, reveals much about the intellectual temper of the man. Agnosticism
asserts, he said, "that it is wrong for a man to say that he is certain of the objective truth
of any proposition unless he can produce evidence which logically justifies that certainty."
Huxley was preëminently a seeker after truth, and his way to truth is the scientific way
—through observation, experiment, and verification, with rigorous thinking controlling every
phase of the process.

After taking a degree in medicine and serving a four-year stint in the Royal Navy as
assistant surgeon, Huxley was appointed to a lectureship in natural history at the Royal
School of Mines in London. Later he became Naturalist to the Government Geological
Survey. Thereafter his fame as a scientist grew, as he published technical papers and essays, lectured widely to both learned and popular audiences, and received many honors.

Huxley was one of the first to accept the evolutionary theory of Charles Darwin. He did
much to explain and popularize the theory, and, as "Darwin's bulldog," to defend it against
its many adversaries, scientific and clerical. For years he fought vigorous battles, on the
lecture platform and in the printed page, against the stodgy churchmen and educators
who were blocking the progress of science. Furthermore, he met these opponents on their
own ground, for he was a cultivated scholar, and could quote Shakespeare and the Bible
quite as aptly as they could. "Science and literature," he said, "are not two things, but two
sides of one thing." This opinion is embodied in the man and in his forceful essays.

Science and Culture

This essay—with a few introductory paragraphs which are here omitted—was delivered by
Huxley as an address at the opening of Sir Josiah Mason's Science College at Birmingham in 1880,
and was published the next year. It is a persuasive plea for the inclusion of science in the

curriculum and for the recognition of the cultural value of scientific studies. One of its most famous results was to call forth Matthew Arnold's brilliant reply in *Literature and Science*.

. . . From the time that the first suggestion to introduce physical science into ordinary education was timidly whispered, until now, the advocates of scientific education have met with opposition of two kinds. On the one hand, they have been pooh-poohed by the men of business who pride themselves on being the representatives of practicality; while, on the other hand, they have been excommunicated by the classical scholars, in their capacity of Levites[1] in charge of the ark of culture and monopolists of liberal education.

The practical men believed that the idol whom they worship—rule of thumb—has been the source of the past prosperity, and will suffice for the future welfare of the arts and manufactures. They were of opinion that science is speculative rubbish; that theory and practice have nothing to do with one another; and that the scientific habit of mind is an impediment, rather than an aid, in the conduct of ordinary affairs.

I have used the past tense in speaking of the practical men—for although they were very formidable thirty years ago, I am not sure that the pure species has not been extirpated. In fact, so far as mere argument goes, they have been subjected to such a *feu d'enfer*[2] that it is a miracle if any have escaped. But I have remarked that your typical practical man has an unexpected resemblance to one of Milton's angels. His spiritual wounds, such as are inflicted by logical weapons, may be as deep as a well and as wide as a church door,[3] but beyond shedding a few drops of ichor,[4] celestial or otherwise, he is no whit the worse. So, if any of these opponents be left, I will not waste time in vain repetition of the demonstrative evidence of the practical value of science; but knowing

that a parable will sometimes penetrate where syllogisms fail to effect an entrance, I will offer a story for their consideration.

Once upon a time, a boy,[5] with nothing to depend upon but his own vigorous nature, was thrown into the thick of the struggle for existence in the midst of a great manufacturing population. He seems to have had a hard fight, inasmuch as, by the time he was thirty years of age, his total disposable funds amounted to twenty pounds. Nevertheless, middle life found him giving proof of his comprehension of the practical problems he had been roughly called upon to solve, by a career of remarkable prosperity.

Finally, having reached old age with its well-earned surroundings of "honor, troops of friends,"[6] the hero of my story bethought himself of those who were making a like start in life, and how he could stretch out a helping hand to them.

After long and anxious reflection this successful practical man of business could devise nothing better than to provide them with the means of obtaining "sound, extensive, and practical scientific knowledge." And he devoted a large part of his wealth and five years of incessant work to this end.

I need not point the moral of a tale which, as the solid and spacious fabric of the Scientific College assures us, is no fable, nor can anything which I could say intensify the force of this practical answer to practical objections.

We may take it for granted then, that, in the opinion of those best qualified to judge, the diffusion of thorough scientific education is an absolutely essential condition of industrial progress; and that the college which has been opened to-day will confer an inestimable boon upon those whose livelihood is to be gained by the practice of the arts and manufactures of the district.

The only question worth discussion is, whether the conditions, under which the work

[1] In Old Testament times, those who helped guard the Ark of the Lord.

[2] "Fire of Hell."

[3] Cf. *Romeo and Juliet*: "No, 'tis not so deep as a well, nor so wide as a church-door; but 'tis enough, 'twill serve."

[4] An ethereal fluid believed to flow in the veins of the gods.

[5] Josiah Mason.

[6] An echo of a line in *Macbeth*.

of the college is to be carried out, are such as to give it the best possible chance of achieving permanent success.

Sir Josiah Mason, without doubt most wisely, has left very large freedom of action to the trustees, to whom he proposes ultimately to commit the administration of the college, so that they may be able to adjust its arrangements in accordance with the changing conditions of the future. But, with respect to three points, he has laid most explicit injunctions upon both administrators and teachers.

Party politics are forbidden to enter into the minds of either, so far as the work of the college is concerned; theology is as sternly banished from its precincts; and finally, it is especially declared that the college shall make no provision for "mere literary instruction and education."

It does not concern me at present to dwell upon the first two injunctions any longer than may be needful to express my full conviction of their wisdom. But the third prohibition brings us face to face with those other opponents of scientific education, who are by no means in the moribund condition of the practical man, but alive, alert, and formidable.

It is not impossible that we shall hear this express exclusion of "literary instruction and education" from a college which, nevertheless, professes to give a high and efficient education, sharply criticized. Certainly the time was that the Levites of culture would have sounded their trumpets against its walls as against an educational Jericho.[7]

How often have we not been told that the study of physical science is incompetent to confer culture; that it touches none of the higher problems of life; and, what is worse, that the continual devotion to scientific studies tends to generate a narrow and bigoted belief in the applicability of scientific methods to the search after truth of all kinds? How frequently one has reason to observe that no reply to a troublesome argument tells so well as calling its author a "mere scientific specialist." And, as I am afraid it is not permissible to speak of this form of opposition to scientific education in the past tense, may we not expect to be told that this, not only omission, but prohibition, of "mere literary instruction and education" is a patent example of scientific narrow-mindedness?

I am not acquainted with Sir Josiah Mason's reasons for the action which he has taken; but if, as I apprehend is the case, he refers to the ordinary classical course of our schools and universities by the name of "mere literary instruction and education," I venture to offer sundry reasons of my own in support of that action.

For I hold very strongly by two convictions —The first is, that neither the discipline nor the subject-matter of classical education is of such direct value to the student of physical science as to justify the expenditure of valuable time upon either; and the second is, that for the purpose of attaining real culture, an exclusively scientific education is at least as effectual as an exclusively literary education.

I need hardly point out to you that these opinions, especially the latter, are diametrically opposed to those of the great majority of educated Englishmen, influenced as they are by school and university traditions. In their belief, culture is obtainable only by a liberal education; and a liberal education is synonymous, not merely with education and instruction in literature, but in one particular form of literature, namely, that of Greek and Roman antiquity. They hold that the man who has learned Latin and Greek, however little, is educated; while he who is versed in other branches of knowledge, however deeply, is a more or less respectable specialist, not admissible into the cultured caste. The stamp of the educated man, the university degree, is not for him.

I am too well acquainted with the generous catholicity of spirit, the true sympathy with scientific thought, which pervades the writings of our chief apostle [8] of culture to identify him with these opinions; and yet one may cull from one and another of those epistles

[7] In Joshua it is told how the walls of Jericho were brought down by the blowing of the Levites' trumpets. What is the point of the comparison?

[8] Matthew Arnold.

to the Philistines,[9] which so much delight all who do not answer to that name, sentences which lend them some support.

Mr. Arnold tells us that the meaning of culture is "to know the best that has been thought and said in the world." [10] It is the criticism of life contained in literature. That criticism regards "Europe as being, for intellectual and spiritual purposes, one great confederation, bound to a joint action and working to a common result; and whose members have, for their common outfit, a knowledge of Greek, Roman, and Eastern antiquity, and of one another. Special, local, and temporary advantages being put out of account, that modern nation will in the intellectual and spiritual sphere make most progress, which most thoroughly carries out this program. And what is that but saying that we too, all of us, as individuals, the more thoroughly we carry it out, shall make the more progress?"

We have here to deal with two distinct propositions. The first, that a criticism of life is the essence of culture; the second, that literature contains the materials which suffice for the construction of such criticism.

I think that we must all assent to the first proposition. For culture certainly means something quite different from learning or technical skill. It implies the possession of an ideal, and the habit of critically estimating the value of things by comparison with a theoretic standard. Perfect culture should supply a complete theory of life, based upon a clear knowledge alike of its possibilities and of its limitations.

But we may agree to all this, and yet strongly dissent from the assumption that literature alone is competent to supply this knowledge. After having learned all that Greek, Roman, and Eastern antiquity have thought and said, and all that modern literature has to tell us, it is not self-evident that we have laid a sufficiently broad and deep

foundation for that criticism of life, which constitutes culture.

Indeed, to any one acquainted with the scope of physical science, it is not at all evident. Considering progress only in the "intellectual and spiritual sphere," I find myself wholly unable to admit that either nations or individuals will really advance, if their common outfit draws nothing from the stores of physical science. I should say that an army, without weapons of precision and with no particular base of operations, might more hopefully enter upon a campaign on the Rhine, than a man, devoid of a knowledge of what physical science has done in the last century, upon a criticism of life.

When a biologist meets with an anomaly,[11] he instinctively turns to the study of development to clear it up. The rationale of contradictory opinions may with equal confidence be sought in history.

It is, happily, no new thing that Englishmen should employ their wealth in building and endowing institutions for educational purposes. But, five or six hundred years ago, deeds of foundation expressed or implied conditions as nearly as possible contrary to those which have been thought expedient by Sir Josiah Mason. That is to say, physical science was practically ignored, while a certain literary training was enjoined as a means to the acquirement of knowledge which was essentially theological.

The reason of this singular contradiction between the actions of men alike animated by a strong and disinterested desire to promote the welfare of their fellows, is easily discovered.

At that time, in fact, if any one desired knowledge beyond such as could be obtained by his own observation, or by common conversation, his first necessity was to learn the Latin language, inasmuch as all the higher knowledge of the western world was contained in works written in that language. Hence, Latin grammar, with logic and rhetoric, studied through Latin, were the fundamentals of education. With respect to the substance of the knowledge imparted through this channel, the Jewish and Christian Scrip-

---

[9] The name which Arnold commonly uses for the materialistic enemies of culture. The Philistines were the foremost enemy of the Hebrews in the early days of settling in Canaan.

[10] This quotation and the one which follows are from Arnold's well-known essay *The Function of Criticism at the Present Time.*

[11] A deviation from the common forms.

tures, as interpreted and supplemented by the Romish Church, were held to contain a complete and infallibly true body of information.

Theological dicta were, to the thinkers of those days, that which the axioms and definitions of Euclid are to the geometers of these. The business of the philosophers of the middle ages was to deduce from the data furnished by the theologians, conclusions in accordance with the ecclesiastical decrees. They were allowed the high privilege of showing, by logical process, how and why that which the church said was true, must be true. And if their demonstrations fell short of or exceeded this limit, the church was maternally ready to check their aberrations; if need were, by the help of the secular arm.

Between the two, our ancestors were furnished with a compact and complete criticism of life. They were told how the world began and how it would end; they learned that all material existence was but a base and insignificant blot upon the fair face of the spiritual world, and that nature was, to all intents and purposes, the play-ground of the devil; they learned that the earth is the center of the visible universe, and that man is the cynosure [12] of things terrestrial, and more especially was it inculcated that the course of nature had no fixed order, but that it could be, and constantly was, altered by the agency of innumerable spiritual beings, good and bad, according as they were moved by the deeds and prayers of men. The sum and substance of the whole doctrine was to produce the conviction that the only thing really worth knowing in this world was how to secure that place in a better which, under certain conditions, the church promised.

Our ancestors had a living belief in this theory of life, and acted upon it in their dealings with education, as in all other matters. Culture meant saintliness—after the fashion of the saints of those days; the education that led to it was, of necessity, theological; and the way to theology lay through Latin.

That the study of nature—further than was requisite for the satisfaction of everyday wants

[12] Center of attraction.

—should have any bearing on human life was far from the thoughts of men thus trained. Indeed, as nature had been cursed for man's sake, it was an obvious conclusion that those who meddled with nature were likely to come into pretty close contact with Satan. And, if any born scientific investigator followed his instincts, he might safely reckon upon earning the reputation, and probably upon suffering the fate, of a sorcerer.

Had the western world been left to itself in Chinese isolation, there is no saying how long this state of things might have endured. But, happily, it was not left to itself. Even earlier than the thirteenth century, the development of Moorish civilization in Spain and the great movement of the crusades had introduced the leaven which, from that day to this, has never ceased to work. At first, through the intermediation of Arabic translations, afterwards by the study of the originals, the western nations of Europe became acquainted with the writings of the ancient philosophers and poets, and, in time, with the whole of the vast literature of antiquity.

Whatever there was of high intellectual aspiration or dominant capacity in Italy, France, Germany, and England, spent itself for centuries in taking possession of the rich inheritance left by the dead civilizations of Greece and Rome. Marvelously aided by the invention of printing, classical learning spread and flourished. Those who possessed it prided themselves on having attained the highest culture then within the reach of mankind.

And justly. For, saving Dante on his solitary pinnacle, there was no figure in modern literature at the time of the Renaissance to compare with the men of antiquity; there was no art to compete with their sculpture; there was no physical science but that which Greece had created. Above all, there was no other example of perfect intellectual freedom —of the unhesitating acceptance of reason as the sole guide to truth and the supreme arbiter of conduct.

The new learning necessarily soon exerted a profound influence upon education. The language of the monks and schoolmen seemed little better than gibberish to scholars fresh from Virgil and Cicero, and the study of Latin was placed upon a new foundation. Moreover, Latin itself ceased to afford the sole key to knowledge. The student who sought the highest thought of antiquity, found only a secondhand reflection of it in Roman literature, and turned his face to the full light of the Greeks. And after a battle, not altogether dissimilar to that which is at present being fought over the teaching of physical science, the study of Greek was recognized as an essential element of all higher education.

Then the humanists, as they were called, won the day; and the great reform which they effected was of incalculable service to mankind. But the Nemesis [13] of all reformers is finality; and the reformers of education, like those of religion, fell into the profound, however common, error of mistaking the beginning for the end of the work of reformation.

The representatives of the humanists, in the nineteenth century, take their stand upon classical education as the sole avenue to culture, as firmly as if we were still in the age of Renaissance. Yet, surely, the present intellectual relations of the modern and the ancient worlds are profoundly different from those which obtained three centuries ago. Leaving aside the existence of a great and characteristically modern literature, of modern painting, and, especially, of modern music, there is one feature of the present state of the civilized world which separates it more widely from the Renaissance, than the Renaissance was separated from the middle ages.

This distinctive character of our own times lies in the vast and constantly increasing part which is played by natural knowledge. Not only is our daily life shaped by it; not only does the prosperity of millions of men depend upon it, but our whole theory of life has long been influenced, consciously or unconsciously, by the general conceptions of the universe, which have been forced upon us by physical science.

In fact, the most elementary acquaintance with the results of scientific investigation

[13] Ancient Greek goddess of retributive justice.

shows us that they offer a broad and striking contradiction to the opinion so implicitly credited and taught in the middle ages.

The notions of the beginning and the end of the world entertained by our forefathers are no longer credible. It is very certain that the earth is not the chief body in the material universe, and that the world is not subordinated to man's use. It is even more certain that nature is the expression of a definite order with which nothing interferes, and that the chief business of mankind is to learn that order and govern themselves accordingly. Moreover this scientific "criticism of life" presents itself to us with different credentials from any other. It appeals not to authority, nor to what anybody may have thought or said, but to nature. It admits that all our interpretations of natural fact are more or less imperfect and symbolic, and bids the learner seek for truth not among words but among things. It warns us that the assertion which outstrips evidence is not only a blunder but a crime.

The purely classical education advocated by the representatives of the humanists in our day, gives no inkling of all this. A man may be a better scholar than Erasmus,[14] and know no more of the chief causes of the present intellectual fermentation than Erasmus did. Scholarly and pious persons, worthy of all respect, favor us with allocutions upon the sadness of the antagonism of science to their medieval way of thinking, which betray an ignorance of the first principles of scientific investigation, an incapacity for understanding what a man of science means by veracity, and an unconsciousness of the weight of established scientific truths, which is almost comical.

There is no great force in the *tu quoque* [15] argument, or else the advocates of scientific education might fairly enough retort upon the modern humanists that they may be learned specialists, but that they possess no such sound foundation for a criticism of life as deserves the name of culture. And, indeed, if we were disposed to be cruel, we might

[14] Dutch humanistic scholar in the Renaissance.
[15] "You too."

urge that the humanists have brought this reproach upon themselves, not because they are too full of the spirit of the ancient Greek, but because they lack it.

The period of the Renaissance is commonly called that of the "revival of letters," as if the influences then brought to bear upon the mind of Western Europe had been wholly exhausted in the field of literature. I think it is very commonly forgotten that the revival of science, effected by the same agency, although less conspicuous, was not less momentous.

In fact, the few and scattered students of nature of that day picked up the clue to her secrets exactly as it fell from the hands of the Greeks a thousand years before. The foundations of mathematics were so well laid by them, that our children learn their geometry from a book written for the schools of Alexandria two thousand years ago. Modern astronomy is the natural continuation and development of the work of Hipparchus and of Ptolemy;[16] modern physics of that of Democritus and of Archimedes;[17] it was long before modern biological science outgrew the knowledge bequeathed to us by Aristotle, by Theophrastus, and by Galen.[18]

We cannot know all the best thoughts and sayings of the Greeks unless we know what they thought about natural phenomena. We cannot fully apprehend their criticism of life unless we understand the extent to which that criticism was affected by scientific conceptions. We falsely pretend to be the inheritors of their culture, unless we are penetrated, as the best minds among them were, with an unhesitating faith that the free employment of reason, in accordance with scientific method, is the sole method of reaching truth.

Thus I venture to think that the preten-

[16] Hipparchus was a Greek astronomer, Ptolemy a later Greco-Egyptian astronomer.
[17] Democritus was an early Greek natural philosopher who formulated an atomic theory of matter; Archimedes was a Greek mathematician and inventor.
[18] Aristotle did work in anatomical studies and in biological classification; Theophrastus, pupil of Plato and Aristotle, studied botany; Galen was a Greek medical scientist.

sions of our modern humanists to the possession of the monopoly of culture and to the exclusive inheritance of the spirit of antiquity must be abated, if not abandoned. But I should be very sorry that anything I have said should be taken to imply a desire on my part to depreciate the value of classical education, as it might be and as it sometimes is. The native capacities of mankind vary no less than their opportunities; and while culture is one, the road by which one man may best reach it is widely different from that which is most advantageous to another. Again, while scientific education is yet inchoate and tentative, classical education is thoroughly well organized upon the practical experience of generations of teachers. So that, given ample time for learning and estimation for ordinary life, or for a literary career, I do not think that a young Englishman in search of culture can do better than follow the course usually marked out for him, supplementing its deficiencies by his own efforts.

But for those who mean to make science their serious occupation; or who intend to follow the profession of medicine; or who have to enter early upon the business of life; for all these, in my opinion, classical education is a mistake; and it is for this reason that I am glad to see "mere literary education and instruction" shut out from the curriculum of Sir Josiah Mason's College, seeing that its inclusion would probably lead to the introduction of the ordinary smattering of Latin and Greek.

Nevertheless, I am the last person to question the importance of genuine literary education, or to suppose that intellectual culture can be complete without it. An exclusively scientific training will bring about a mental twist as surely as an exclusively literary training. The value of the cargo does not compensate for a ship's being out of trim; and I should be very sorry to think that the Scientific College would turn out none but lopsided men.

There is no need, however, that such a catastrophe should happen. Instruction in English, French, and German is provided, and thus the three greatest literatures of the modern world are made accessible to the student.

French and German, and especially the latter language, are absolutely indispensable to those who desire full knowledge in any department of science. But even supposing that the knowledge of these languages acquired is not more than sufficient for purely scientific purposes, every Englishman has, in his native tongue, an almost perfect instrument of literary expression; and, in his own literature, models of every kind of literary excellence. If an Englishman cannot get literary culture out of his Bible, his Shakespeare, his Milton, neither, in my belief, will the profoundest study of Homer and Sophocles, Virgil and Horace, give it to him.

Thus, since the constitution of the college makes sufficient provision for literary as well as for scientific education, and since artistic instruction is also contemplated, it seems to me that a fairly complete culture is offered to all who are willing to take advantage of it.

But I am not sure that at this point the "practical" man, scotched but not slain, may ask what all this talk about culture has to do with an institution, the object of which is defined to be "to promote the prosperity of the manufactures and the industry of the country." He may suggest that what is wanted for this end is not culture, nor even a purely scientific discipline, but simply a knowledge of applied science.

I often wish that this phrase, "applied science," had never been invented. For it suggests that there is a sort of scientific knowledge of direct practical use, which can be studied apart from another sort of scientific knowledge, which is of no practical utility, and which is termed "pure science." But there is no more complete fallacy than this. What people call applied science is nothing but the application of pure science to particular classes of problems. It consists of deductions from those general principles, established by reasoning and observation, which constitute pure science. No one can safely make these deductions until he has a firm grasp of the principles; and he can obtain that grasp only by personal experience of the operations of observation and of reasoning on which they are founded.

Almost all the processes employed in the arts and manufactures fall within the range either of physics or of chemistry. In order to improve them, one must thoroughly understand them; and no one has a chance of really understanding them, unless he has obtained that mastery of principles and that habit of dealing with facts, which is given by long-continued and well-directed purely scientific training in the physical and the chemical laboratory. So that there really is no question as to the necessity of purely scientific discipline, even if the work of the college were limited by the narrowest interpretation of its stated aims.

And, as to the desirableness of a wider culture than that yielded by science alone, it is to be recollected that the improvement of manufacturing processes is only one of the conditions which contribute to the prosperity of industry. Industry is a means and not an end; and mankind work only to get something which they want. What that something is depends partly on their innate, and partly on their acquired, desires.

If the wealth resulting from prosperous industry is to be spent upon the gratification of unworthy desires, if the increasing perfection of manufacturing processes is to be accompanied by an increasing debasement of those who carry them on, I do not see the good of industry and prosperity.

Now it is perfectly true that men's views of what is desirable depend upon their characters; and that the innate proclivities to which we give that name are not touched by any amount of instruction. But it does not follow that even mere intellectual education may not, to an indefinite extent, modify the practical manifestation of the characters of men in their actions, by supplying them with motives unknown to the ignorant. A pleasure-loving character will have pleasure of some sort; but, if you give him the choice, he may prefer pleasures which do not degrade him to those which do. And this choice is offered to every man, who possesses in literary or artistic culture a never-failing source of pleasures, which are neither withered by age, nor staled by custom,[19] nor embittered in the recollection by the pangs of self-reproach.

If the institution opened to-day fulfils the 5 intention of its founder, the picked intelligences among all classes of the population of this district will pass through it. No child born in Birmingham, henceforward, if he have the capacity to profit by the opportunities 10 offered to him, first in the primary and other schools, and afterwards in the Scientific College, need fail to obtain, not merely the instruction, but the culture most appropriate to the conditions of his life. 15

Within these walls, the future employer and the future artisan may sojourn together for a while, and carry, through all their lives, the stamp of the influences then brought to bear upon them. Hence, it is not beside the 20 mark to remind you, that the prosperity of industry depends not merely upon the improvement of manufacturing processes, not merely upon the ennobling of the individual character, but upon a third condition, namely, 25 a clear understanding of the conditions of social life, on the part of both the capitalist and the operative, and their agreement upon common principles of social action. They must learn that social phenomena are as much the 30 expression of natural laws as any others; that no social arrangements can be permanent unless they harmonize with the requirements of social statics and dynamics; and that, in the nature of things, there is an arbiter whose 35 decisions execute themselves.

But this knowledge is only to be obtained by the application of the methods of investigation adopted in physical researches to the investigation of the phenomena of society. 40 Hence, I confess, I should like to see one addition made to the excellent scheme of education propounded for the college, in the shape of provision for the teaching of sociology. For though we are all agreed that party 45 politics are to have no place in the instruction of the college; yet in this country, prac-

tically governed as it is now by universal suffrage, every man who does his duty must exercise political functions. And, if the evils which are inseparable from the good of political liberty are to be checked, if the perpetual oscillation of nations between anarchy and despotism is to be replaced by the steady march of self-restraining freedom; it will be because men will gradually bring themselves to deal with political, as they now deal with scientific questions; to be as ashamed of undue haste and partisan prejudice in the one case as in the other; and to believe that the machinery of society is at least as delicate as that of a spinning-jenny, and as little likely to be improved by the meddling of those who have not taken the trouble to master the principles of its action.

In conclusion, I am sure that I make myself the mouthpiece of all present in offering to the venerable founder of the institution, which now commences its beneficent career, our congratulations on the completion of his work; and in expressing the conviction, that the remotest posterity will point to it as a crucial instance of the wisdom which natural piety leads all men to ascribe to their ancestors. (1880)

STUDY AIDS: 1. For Huxley, who are the two main enemies of scientific education? How does he meet the objections of each?

2. In Huxley's opinion, what is wrong with "an exclusively literary education"? On what point does he agree with Matthew Arnold? On what point does he disagree?

3. How does Huxley explain the fact that five or six hundred years ago, men actuated by motives as benevolent as those of Josiah Mason would have set up conditions for a new college directly opposite to those that Mason stipulated? What does Huxley mean when he says the modern humanists are hardly apostles of a true culture "not because they are too full of the spirit of the ancient Greek, but because they lack it"? What values, if any, does Huxley find in a classical, or literary, education?

4. What three conditions does Huxley list for the prosperity of industry, and what is the relation of a scientific education to each? What is his objection to the phrase "applied science"?

---

[19] Cf. Shakespeare on Cleopatra: "Age cannot wither her, nor custom stale Her infinite variety" (*Antony and Cleopatra*).

Why does he want sociology added to the curriculum of the new college?

5. If Huxley were alive today, do you think he would be satisfied with the nature and extent of scientific education in the modern world? What criticisms would he probably offer?

Matthew Arnold
(1822–1888)

MATTHEW ARNOLD IS REMEMBERED AS BOTH POET AND CRITIC. THE SON OF DR. THOMAS Arnold, the famous headmaster of Rugby School, he went from Rugby to Oxford, becoming, on his graduation, a fellow of Oriel College. He devoted much of his time to poetry, and by 1853 had published three volumes of verse, which include many of his best poems. In 1851, the year of his marriage, he was appointed inspector of schools, a position he held the rest of his life. The year 1857, when he was named Professor of Poetry at Oxford, was something of a turning point in his career. Although he lectured on literary subjects, Arnold became more and more concerned with the great cultural problems demanding solutions from thoughtful minds. Feeling he could not give to poetry the dedication it required, he all but abandoned it in favor of prose criticism. Between 1861 and 1888 he published several critical volumes—*Culture and Anarchy* and two series of *Essays in Criticism* being the most notable.

Before turning from poetry to criticism, however, Arnold had produced a body of verse that entitles him to high rank among the Victorian poets. Primarily it is a poetry of doubt and disillusionment, of quest and questioning, of melancholy and loneliness. As a young man Arnold was beset with many conflicts—between faith and reason, between his romantic inclinations and his classical outlook, between a desire to withdraw from the world and a realization of the need for active participation—and these conflicts find expression in his verse. There is, however, a strong strain of stoical acceptance and endurance in Arnold which will never let his inner self be mastered by the outward event or allow him to go to pieces under the pressure of conflict.

Arnold's self-mastery is mirrored in the great body of prose work which he produced after 1860, works in which he brought his luminous intelligence to bear upon subjects literary, social, and religious. In his literary criticism Arnold proceeds from certain large definitions, arrived at through the experience of a wide and cultivated taste, and by means of "touchstones" (literary passages of unquestioned excellence) used as standards of evaluation. Whether he is discussing the grand style in poetry, the Celtic influence on English verse, the function of criticism, the achievements of Continental authors, or the art of translating Homer, one senses the presence of an unerring good taste, keen powers of discrimination, and a grasp which, rising far above the insular and provincial, considers the whole world, past and present, as its intellectual arena.

Arnold's social criticism is closely related to his literary comment. The function of criticism, he said, is a disinterested endeavor to know and to propagate the best that has been thought and said in the world. But he saw around him a society indifferent to this best. It was a society that worshiped forms and institutions of all kinds ("machinery," he called it) and was satisfied to follow the dictates of the class self, "doing as one likes," instead of obeying the demands of the "best self." So, through his religion of culture, the "harmonious expansion of all the powers that go to make up the beauty and worth of human life," Arnold set about to humanize the self-satisfied Mammon-worshipers of his day. He reminded his countrymen that without the "sweetness and light" of this true culture, without more emphasis on thinking and less on doing, all the political devices and religious institutions in the world were in vain.

Arnold's religious essays attempt to strike a balance between the scoffings of the skeptic and the dogmatism of the fanatic. He wrote for those whose intellectual seriousness made it impossible for them to accept the old creeds but who, on the other hand, were not satisfied with agnosticism and denial. Defining religion as "morality touched with emotion," Arnold decries a Christianity of miracle, dogma, supernaturalism, literal adherence to the Bible, and emphasis on ritual. He gives us instead a Christianity which stresses ethical perfection and the "sweet reasonableness" of Jesus, a Bible which has the deep insights of great symbolic literature, and a God who is the "not-ourselves that makes for righteousness."

Lionel Trilling writes: "Of the literary men of the great English nineteenth century there are few who have stayed quite so fresh, so immediate, and so relevant as Matthew Arnold. . . . As a poet he reaches us not more powerfully but, we sometimes feel, more intimately than any other. As a critic he provided us with the essential terms for our debate in matters of taste and judgment."

Quiet Work

One lesson, nature, let me learn of thee,
One lesson which in every wind is blown,
One lesson of two duties kept at one
Though the loud world proclaim their enmity—
Of toil unsevered from tranquility!   5
Of labor, that in lasting fruit outgrows
Far noisier schemes, accomplished in repose,
Too great for haste, too high for rivalry!

Yes, while on earth a thousand discords ring,
Man's fitful uproar mingling with his toil,   10
Still do thy sleepless ministers move on,
Their glorious tasks in silence perfecting;
Still working, blaming still our vain turmoil,
Laborers that shall not fail, when man is gone.
(1849)

The Forsaken Merman

Using a familiar situation of old folk tales—the marriage of a human being to a mermaid or merman—Arnold created this musical, melancholy poem, which has, in the words of Swinburne, "all the fanciful, pitiful beauty of dreams and legends born in gray, windy lands on shores and hillsides whose life is quiet and wild."

Come, dear children, let us away;
Down and away below!
Now my brothers call from the bay,
Now the great winds shorewards blow,

Now the salt tides seawards flow,   5
Now the wild white horses [1] play,
Champ and chafe and toss in the spray.

[1] What are the "wild white horses"?

Children dear, let us away!
This way, this way!

Call her once before you go— 10
Call once yet!
In a voice that she will know:
"Margaret! Margaret!"
Children's voices should be dear
(Call once more) to a mother's ear; 15
Children's voices, wild with pain—
Surely she will come again!
Call her once and come away;
This way, this way!
"Mother dear, we cannot stay! 20
The wild white horses foam and fret."
Margaret! Margaret!

Come, dear children, come away down;
Call no more!
One last look at the white-walled town, 25
And the little gray church on the windy
    shores;
Then come down!
She will not come though you call all day;
Come away, come away!

Children dear, was it yesterday 30
We heard the sweet bells over the bay?
In the caverns where we lay,
Through the surf and through the swell,
The far-off sound of a silver bell?
Sand-strewn caverns, cool and deep, 35
Where the winds are all asleep;
Where the spent lights quiver and gleam,
Where the salt weed sways in the stream,
Where the sea-beasts, ranged all round,
Feed in the ooze of their pasture-ground; 40
Where the sea-snakes coil and twine,
Dry their mail[2] and bask in the brine;
Where great whales come sailing by,
Sail and sail, with unshut eye,
Round the world for ever and aye? 45
When did music come this way?
Children dear, was it yesterday?

Children dear, was it yesterday
(Call yet once) that she went away?
Once she sate with you and me, 50
On a red gold throne in the heart of the sea,

[2] Scales, which look like armor (coats of mail).

And the youngest sate on her knee.
She combed its bright hair, and she tended
    it well,
When down swung the sound of the far-off
    bell.
She sighed, she looked up through the clear
    green sea. 55
She said: "I must go, for my kinsfolk pray
In the little gray church on the shore to-day.
'Twill be Easter-time in the world—ah me!
And I lose my poor soul, merman, here with
    thee."
I said: "Go up, dear heart, through the
    waves; 60
Say thy prayer, and come back to the kind
    seacaves."
She smiled, she went up through the surf in
    the bay.
Children dear, was it yesterday?

Children dear, were we long alone?
"The sea grows stormy, the little ones
    moan. 65
Long prayers," I said, "in the world they say;
Come!" I said; and we rose through the surf
    in the bay.
We went up the beach, by the sandy down
Where the sea-stocks[3] bloom, to the white-
    walled town;
Through the narrow paved streets, where all
    was still, 70
To the little gray church on the windy hill.
From the church came a murmur of folk at
    their prayers,
But we stood without in the cold blowing
    airs.
We climbed on the graves, on the stones worn
    with rains,
And we gazed up the aisle through the small
    leaded panes. 75
She sate by the pillar; we saw her clear:
"Margaret, hist! come quick, we are here!
Dear heart," I said, "we are long alone;
The sea grows stormy, the little ones moan."
But, ah, she gave me never a look, 80
For her eyes were sealed to the holy book!
Loud prays the priest; shut stands the door.
Come away, children, call no more!
Come away, come down, call no more!

[3] Flowers of the stock family.

Down, down, down! 85
Down to the depths of the sea!
She sits at her wheel in the humming town,
Singing most joyfully.
Hark, what she sings: "O joy, O joy,
For the humming street, and the child with
    its toy! 90
For the priest, and the bell, and the holy
    well; [4]
For the wheel where I spun,
And the blessèd light of the sun!"
And so she sings her fill,
Singing most joyfully, 95
Till the spindle falls from her hand,
And the whizzing wheel stands still.
She steals to the window, and looks at the
    sand,
And over the sand at the sea;
And her eyes are set in a stare; 100
And anon there breaks a sigh,
And anon there drops a tear,
From a sorrow-clouded eye,
And a heart sorrow-laden,
A long, long sigh, 105
For the cold strange eyes of a little mermaiden
And the gleam of her golden hair. [5]

Come away, away children;
Come children, come down!
The hoarse wind blows coldly; 110
Lights shine in the town.
She will start from her slumber
When gusts shake the door;
She will hear the winds howling,
Will hear the waves roar. 115

We shall see, while above us
The waves roar and whirl,
A ceiling of amber,
A pavement of pearl.
Singing, "Here came a mortal, 120
But faithless was she!
And alone dwell for ever
The kings of the sea."

But, children, at midnight,
When soft the winds blow, 125
When clear falls the moonlight,
When spring-tides are low;
When sweet airs come seaward
From heaths starred with broom,
And high rocks throw mildly 130
On the blanched sands a gloom;
Up the still, glistening beaches,
Up the creeks we will hie,
Over banks of bright seaweed
The ebb-tide leaves dry. 135
We will gaze, from the sand-hills,
At the white, sleeping town;
At the church on the hill-side—
And then come back down.
Singing, "There dwells a loved one, 140
But cruel is she!
She left lonely for ever
The kings of the sea."
(1849)

STUDY AIDS: This poem gains a great
deal by being read aloud. How are the sound-
qualities in keeping with the subject matter?
What are some of the means by which the sound
effects are achieved?

[4] The church font, filled with holy water.
[5] As an illustration of the effective repetition in
this poem, note the number of lines beginning with
"and" in ll. 93–107. Find similar examples in the
rest of the poem.

The Buried Life

Light flows our war of mocking words, and
    yet,
Behold, with tears mine eyes are wet!
I feel a nameless sadness o'er me roll.

Yes, yes, we know that we can jest,
We know, we know that we can smile! 5
But there's a something in this breast,
To which thy light words bring no rest,
And thy gay smiles no anodyne.
Give me thy hand, and hush awhile,
And turn those limpid eyes on mine, 10
And let me read there, love! thy inmost
    soul.

Alas! is even love too weak
To unlock the heart, and let it speak?
Are even lovers powerless to reveal
To one another what indeed they feel?   15
I knew the mass of men concealed
Their thoughts, for fear that if revealed
They would by other men be met
With blank indifference, or with blame re-
     proved;
I knew they lived and moved   20
Tricked in disguises, alien to the rest
Of men, and alien to themselves—and yet
The same heart beats in every human breast!

But we, my love!—doth a like spell benumb
Our hearts, our voices?—must we too be
     dumb?   25
Ah! well for us, if even we,
Even for a moment, can get free
Our heart, and have our lips unchained;
For that which seals them hath been deep-
     ordained!

Fate, which foresaw   30
How frivolous a baby man would be—
By what distractions he would be possessed,
How he would pour himself in every strife,
And well-nigh change his own identity—
That it might keep from his capricious play 35
His genuine self, and force him to obey
Even in his own despite his being's law,
Bade through the deep recesses of our breast
The unregarded river of our life
Pursue with indiscernible flow its way;   40
And that we should not see
The buried stream, and seem to be
Eddying at large in blind uncertainty,
Though driving on with it eternally.

But often, in the world's most crowded
     streets,   45
But often, in the din of strife,
There rises an unspeakable desire
After the knowledge of our buried life;
A thirst to spend our fire and restless force
In tracking out our true, original course;   50
A longing to inquire
Into the mystery of this heart which beats
So wild, so deep in us—to know
Whence our lives come and where they go.

And many a man in his own breast then
     delves,   55
But deep enough, alas! none ever mines.
And we have been on many thousand lines,
And we have shown, on each, spirit and
     power;
But hardly have we, for one little hour,
Been on our own line, have we been our-
     selves—   60
Hardly had skill to utter one of all
The nameless feelings that course through our
     breast,
But they course on forever unexpressed.
And long we try in vain to speak and act
Our hidden self, and what we say and do 65
Is eloquent, is well—but 'tis not true!
And then we will no more be racked
With inward striving, and demand
Of all the thousand nothings of the hour
Their stupefying power;   70
Ah yes, and they benumb us at our call!
Yet still, from time to time, vague and forlorn,
From the soul's subterranean depth upborne
As from an infinitely distant land,
Come airs, and floating echoes, and convey 75
A melancholy into all our day.

Only—but this is rare—
When a belovèd hand is laid in ours,
When, jaded with the rush and glare
Of the interminable hours,   80
Our eyes can in another's eyes read clear,
When our world-deafened ear
Is by the tones of a loved voice caressed—
A bolt is shot back somewhere in our breast,
And a lost pulse of feeling stirs again;   85
The eye sinks inward, and the heart lies
     plain,
And what we mean, we say, and what we
     would, we know.
A man becomes aware of his life's flow,
And hears its winding murmur; and he sees
The meadows where it glides, the sun, the
     breeze.   90

And there arrives a lull in the hot race
Wherein he doth forever chase
That flying and elusive shadow, rest.
An air of coolness plays upon his face,
And an unwonted calm pervades his breast. 95

And then he thinks he knows
The hills where his life rose,
And the sea where it goes.
(1852)

STUDY AIDS: 1. What does Arnold mean by "the buried life"? With what life is it contrasted?

2. By what means is this buried life occasionally known and understood?

To Marguerite

Yes: in the sea of life enisled,
With echoing straits between us thrown,
Dotting the shoreless watery wild,
We mortal millions live alone.
The islands feel the enclasping flow,   5
And then their endless bounds they know.

But when the moon their hollows lights
And they are swept by balms of spring,
And in their glens, on starry nights
The nightingales divinely sing,   10
And lovely notes, from shore to shore,
Across the sounds and channels pour;

Oh then a longing like despair
Is to their farthest caverns sent;
For surely once, they feel, we were   15
Parts of a single continent.
Now round us spreads the watery plain—
Oh might our marges meet again!

Who ordered, that their longing's fire
Should be, as soon as kindled, cooled?   20
Who renders vain their deep desire?
A God, a God their severance ruled;
And bade betwixt their shores to be
The unplumbed, salt, estranging sea.
(1852)

Philomela [1]

Hark! ah, the nightingale—
The tawny-throated!
Hark, from that moonlit cedar what a burst!
What triumph! hark!—what pain!

O wanderer from a Grecian shore,   5
Still, after many years, in distant lands,
Still nourishing in thy bewildered brain
That wild, unquenched, deep-sunken, old-
world pain—
Say, will it never heal?

[1] According to one version of the legend, Tereus, king of Thrace (or of Daulis in Phocis), tired of his wife Procne, and tore out her tongue to insure her silence. Then, pretending she was dead, he married Philomela, Procne's sister. But Procne, through her weaving, told Philomela the truth; and the two sisters, in revenge, killed Itylus, the son of Tereus, and served him to his father for food. As Tereus pursued the fleeing women, the gods turned Philomela into a nightingale, Procne into a swallow, and Tereus into a hawk.

And can this fragrant lawn   10
With its cool trees, and night,
And the sweet, tranquil Thames,
And moonshine, and the dew,
To thy racked heart and brain
Afford no balm?   15

Dost thou to-night behold,
Here, through the moonlight on this English
grass,
The unfriendly palace in the Thracian wild?
Dost thou again peruse
With hot cheeks and seared eyes   20
The too clear web, and thy dumb sister's
shame?
Dost thou once more assay
Thy flight, and feel come over thee,
Poor fugitive, the feathery change
Once more, and once more seem to make re-
sound   25

With love and hate, triumph and agony,
Lone Daulis, and the high Cephissian [2] vale?
Listen, Eugenia [3]—
How thick the bursts come crowding through
  the leaves!
Again—thou hearest?   30

Eternal passion!
Eternal pain!
(1853)

STUDY AIDS: Much of the poem is a series of questions, addressed to Philomela. How do these questions affect the mood of the poem?

The Scholar-Gypsy

The story of the Scholar-Gypsy is found in Joseph Glanvil's *The Vanity of Dogmatizing* (1661), referred to by Arnold in ll. 31–32. A young Oxford student, forced to leave the University because of poverty, joined a troop of gypsies and studied their magical arts. When some old friends came upon him and questioned him, he spoke of the occult powers of the gypsies and said that when he had mastered all their secrets he intended to tell the world what he had learned.

Go, for they call you, shepherd,[1] from the
  hill;
  Go, shepherd, and untie the wattled cotes! [2]
    No longer leave thy wistful flock unfed,
  Nor let thy bawling fellows rack their
    throats,
    Nor the cropped herbage shoot another
      head.   5
      But when the fields are still,
  And the tired men and dogs all gone to
    rest,
    And only the white sheep are sometimes
      seen
    Cross and recross the strips of moon-
      blanched green,
  Come, shepherd, and again begin the
    quest! [3]   10

Here, where the reaper was at work of late,
  In this high field's dark corner, where he
    leaves
    His coat, his basket, and his earthen
      cruse,[4]
  And in the sun, all morning, binds the
    sheaves,

Then here, at noon, comes back his
  stores to use—   15
    Here will I sit and wait,
  While to my ear from uplands far away
    The bleating of the folded flocks is borne,
    With distant cries of reapers in the corn—
  All the live murmur of a summer's day. 20

Screened is this nook, o'er the high half-reaped
  field,
  And here till sun-down, shepherd! will I be.
    Through the thick corn the scarlet pop-
      pies peep,
  And round green roots and yellowing stalks,
    I see
    Pale pink convolvulus [5] in tendrils
      creep;   25
    And air-swept lindens yield
  Their scent, and rustle down their per-
    fumed showers
    Of bloom on the bent grass where I am
      laid,
  And bower me from the August sun with
    shade;
  And the eye travels down to Oxford's
    towers.   30

And near me on the grass lies Glanvil's book.
  Come let me read the oft-read tale again!
    The story of the Oxford scholar poor,
  Of pregnant parts [6] and quick inventive
    brain,

[2] The Cephissus was a river in Phocis.
[3] An imagined friend.

---

[1] The function of the shepherd in the poem is not clear.
[2] Sheepfolds built of wattles—i.e., interwoven twigs and branches.
[3] I.e., search for the Scholar-Gypsy, still thought to haunt the neighborhood.
[4] Jar.
[5] Morning-glory or bindweed.
[6] I.e., promising talents.

Who, tired of knocking at preferment's
　　door,　　　　　　　　　　　35
　One summer morn forsook
His friends, and went to learn the gypsy-
　　lore,
　And roamed the world with that wild
　　brotherhood,
And came, as most men deemed, to little
　　good,
　But came to Oxford and his friends no
　　more.　　　　　　　　　　　40

But once, years after, in the country-lanes,
　Two scholars, whom at college erst [7] he
　　knew,
Met him, and of his way of life enquired;
　Whereat he answered that the gypsy-crew,
　His mates, had arts to rule as they de-
　　sired　　　　　　　　　　　45
　　The workings of men's brains,
And they can bind them to what thoughts
　　they will.
　"And I," he said, "the secret of their art,
When fully learned, will to the world
　　impart;
　But it needs heaven-sent [8] moments for
　　this skill."　　　　　　　　　50

This said, he left them, and returned no more.
　But rumors hung about the countryside,
　　That the lost scholar long was seen to
　　stray,
　Seen by rare glimpses, pensive and tongue-
　　tied,
　In hat of antique shape, and cloak of
　　gray,　　　　　　　　　　　55
　　The same the gypsies wore.
Shepherds had met him on the Hurst [9] in
　　spring;
　At some lone alehouse in the Berkshire
　　moors,
　On the warm ingle-bench,[10] the smock-
　　frocked boors [11]

Had found him seated at their entering;　60
But, 'mid their drink and clatter, he would
　　fly.—
　And I myself seem half to know thy looks,
　And put the shepherds, wanderer! on thy
　　trace;
　And boys who in lone wheatfields scare
　　the rooks,[12]
　I ask if thou hast passed their quiet
　　place;　　　　　　　　　　　65
　　Or in my boat I lie
Moored to the cool bank in the summer-
　　heats,
　'Mid wide grass meadows which the sun-
　　shine fills,
　And watch the warm, green-muffled
　　Cumner hills,
And wonder if thou hauntest their shy
　　retreats.　　　　　　　　　70

For most, I know, thou lovest retired ground:
　Thee, at the ferry, Oxford riders blithe,
　　Returning home on summer-nights, have
　　met
　Crossing the stripling [13] Thames at Bab-
　　lockhithe,
　　Trailing in the cool stream thy fingers
　　wet,　　　　　　　　　　　75
　　As the punt's rope chops round; [14]
And leaning backward in a pensive dream,
　And fostering [15] in thy lap a heap of
　　flowers
　Plucked in shy fields and distant Wych-
　　wood bowers,
And thine eyes resting on the moonlit
　　stream.　　　　　　　　　80

And then they land, and thou art seen no
　　more!—
　Maidens who from the distant hamlets come
　To dance around the Fyfield elm in May,
　Oft through the darkening fields have seen
　　thee roam,

---

[7] Formerly.
[8] Arnold originally had "happy." Why is "heaven-sent" an improvement?
[9] A hill near Oxford. Unless otherwise identified, the proper names used in the next seven stanzas refer to places near Oxford.
[10] Bench in the corner by the chimney.
[11] Peasants.

[12] Crow-like birds.
[13] The Thames is near its source at this point and so is still a "stripling" or "young fellow."
[14] The ferry boat ("punt") is pulled across by a rope, which jumps or darts around ("chops").
[15] Cherishing.

Or cross a stile into the public way.   85
    Oft thou hast given them store
Of flowers: the frail-leafed white anemone,
Dark bluebells drenched with dews of
        summer eves,
And purple orchises with spotted leaves;
But none hath words she can report of
        thee.   90

And, above Godstow Bridge, when haytime's
        here
    In June, and many a scythe in sunshine
        flames,
    Men who through those wide fields of
        breezy grass,
Where black-winged swallows haunt the
        glittering Thames,
    To bathe in the abandoned lasher [16]
        pass,   95
    Have often passed thee near,
Sitting upon the river bank o'ergrown;
    Marked thine outlandish garb, thy figure
        spare,
    Thy dark vague eyes, and soft abstracted
        air—
But when they came from bathing, thou
        wast gone!   100

At some lone homestead in the Cumner hills,
    Where at her open door the housewife
        darns,
    Thou hast been seen; or hanging on a
        gate,
    To watch the threshers in the mossy
        barns.
    Children, who early range these slopes,
        and late,   105
    For cresses from the rills,
Have known thee eying, all an April day,
    The springing pastures and the feeding
        kine;
And marked thee, when the stars come
        out and shine,
Through the long dewy grass move slow
        away.   110

In autumn, on the skirts of Bagley Wood,
    (Where most the gypsies by the turf-edged
        way
    [16] A pool below a dam.

Pitch their smoked tents, and every bush
        you see
With scarlet patches tagged, and shreds of
        gray,[17]
    Above the forest-ground called Thes-
        saly),   115
    The blackbird, picking food,
Sees thee, nor steps his meal, nor fears at
        all;
    So often has he known thee past him
        stray,
    Rapt, twirling in thy hand a withered
        spray,
And waiting for the spark from heaven [18]
        to fall.   120

And once, in winter,[19] on the causeway
        chill,
    Where home through flooded fields foot-
        travelers go,
    Have I not passed thee on the wooden
        bridge,
Wrapped in thy cloak and battling with the
        snow,
    Thy face toward Hinksey and its wintry
        ridge?   125
    And thou hast climbed the hill,
And gained the white brow of the Cumner
        range;
    Turned once to watch, while thick the
        snowflakes fall,
    The line of festal light in Christ-Church
        hall; [20]
Then sought thy straw in some sequestered
        grange.   130

But what—I dream! [21] Two hundred years are
        flown,
    Since first thy story ran through Oxford
        halls,
    And the grave Glanvil did the tale in-
        scribe

[17] I.e., the tattered but gaily colored clothes of
the gypsies were hung on the bushes.
[18] See ll. 48–50.
[19] Does Arnold use all the four seasons in ll.
51–130?
[20] The dining hall of Christ Church College,
Oxford.
[21] In this stanza Arnold denies the apparent
immortality of the Scholar-Gypsy.

That thou wert wandered from the studious
walls
  To learn strange arts, and join a gypsy-
tribe;   135
    And thou from earth art gone
Long since, and in some quiet churchyard
laid:
  Some country-nook, where o'er thy unknown grave
  Tall grasses and white flowering nettles
wave,
Under a dark red-fruited yew-tree's
shade.   140

No, No,[22] thou hast not felt the lapse of
hours!
For what wears out the life of mortal men?
  'Tis that from change to change their
being rolls;
  'Tis that repeated shocks, again, again,
Exhaust the energy of strongest souls, 145
    And numb the elastic powers.
Till, having used our nerves with bliss and
teen,[23]
  And tired upon a thousand schemes our
wit,
To the just-pausing Genius [24] we remit
Our worn-out life, and are—what we have
been.   150

Thou hast not lived, why shouldst thou perish,
so? [25]
  Thou hadst one aim, one business, one desire;

[22] But now Arnold denies the denial of the previous stanza.
[23] Sorrow.
[24] Various interpretations of "just-pausing Genius"
have been suggested: (1) man's guardian spirit,
which pauses a moment before leaving him at death;
(2) the Spirit of the Universe, which pauses in
man for that brief period of his life; (3) the impartial Supreme Spirit ("just" meaning "with
justice"), which pauses to deal out death equitably
to men; (4) the Soul of the Universe, which pauses
briefly to summon man at death and to which man's
spirit returns.
[25] "So" (i.e., in the manner described in the
previous stanza) modifies both "lived" and "perish."
The Scholar-Gypsy is then contrasted with ordinary
men.

Else wert thou long since numbered with
the dead!
Else hadst thou spent, like other men, thy
fire!
The generations of thy peers are fled, 155
  And we ourselves shall go;
But thou possessest an immortal lot,
  And we imagine thee exempt from age
  And living as thou livest on Glanvil's
page,
Because thou hadst what we, alas! have
not.   160

For early didst thou leave the world, with
powers
Fresh, undiverted to the world without,
  Firm to their mark, not spent on other
things;
  Free from the sick fatigue, the languid
doubt,
  Which much to have tried, in much been
baffled, brings.   165
    O life unlike to ours!
Who [26] fluctuate idly without term or
scope,
  Of whom each strives, nor knows for
what he strives,
  And each half-lives a hundred different
lives;
Who wait like thee, but not, like thee, in
hope.   170

Thou waitest for the spark from heaven! and
we,
  Light half-believers of our casual creeds,
  Who never deeply felt, nor clearly
willed,
Whose insight never has borne fruit in
deeds,
  Whose vague resolves never have been
fulfilled;   175
    For whom each year we see
Breeds new beginnings, disappointments
new;
  Who hesitate and falter life away,
  And lose tomorrow the ground won to-
day:
Ah! do not we, wanderer! await it too? 180

[26] Refers to the implied "we" of "ours."

Yes, we await it! but it still delays,
  And then we suffer! and amongst us,
      one [27]
    Who most has suffered, takes dejectedly
His seat upon the intellectual throne;
    And all his store of sad experience he 185
      Lays bare of wretched days;
  Tells us his misery's birth and growth and
      signs,
    And how the dying spark of hope was
      fed,
    And how the breast was soothed, and
      how the head,
And all his hourly-varied anodynes.[28] 190

This for our wisest! and we others pine,
  And wish the long unhappy dream would
      end,
    And waive all claim to bliss, and try to
      bear,
With close-lipped patience for our only
      friend,
    Sad patience, too near neighbor to de-
      spair. 195
    But none has hope like thine!
Thou through the fields and through the
      woods dost stray,
  Roaming the country-side, a truant boy,
  Nursing thy project in unclouded joy,
  And every doubt long blown by time
      away. 200

O born in days when wits were fresh and
      clear,
  And life ran gaily as the sparkling Thames,
    Before this strange disease of modern
      life,
With its sick hurry, its divided aims,
    Its heads o'ertaxed, its palsied hearts, was
      rife— 205
    Fly hence, our contact fear!
  Still fly, plunge deeper in the bowering
      wood!

Averse, as Dido [29] did, with gesture stern,
  From her false friend's approach in
      Hades turn,
Wave us away; and keep thy solitude! 210

Still nursing the unconquerable hope,[30]
  Still clutching the inviolable shade,
    With a free onward impulse brushing
      through,
  By night, the silvered branches of the
      glade,
    Far on the forest-skirts, where none pur-
      sue, 215
      On some mild pastoral slope
Emerge; and resting on the moonlit pales,
Freshen thy flowers, as in former years,
With dew, or listen with enchanted ears,
From the dark dingles,[31] to the nightin-
      gales! 220

But fly our paths, our feverish contact fly!
  For strong the infection of our mental strife,
    Which, though it gives no bliss, yet spoils
      for rest;
  And we should win thee from thy own fair
      life,
    Like us distracted, and like us un-
      blessed. 225
      Soon, soon thy cheer would die,
Thy hopes grow timorous, and unfixed thy
      powers,
    And thy clear aims be cross and shifting
      made;
  And then thy glad perennial youth would
      fade,
Fade, and grow old at last, and die like
      ours.[32] 230

Then fly our greetings, fly our speech and
      smiles!

---

[27] Tennyson, Carlyle, Coleridge, and Goethe have
each been suggested. Although in 1883 Arnold is
reported to have said that he meant Goethe, the
evidence of the stanza itself (ll. 185–190 are
descriptive of *In Memoriam*) points to Tennyson
as the person Arnold originally had in mind.

[28] Drugs to ease (not cure) pain.

[29] In the *Aeneid* Virgil tells how Aeneas descended into Hades and met the shade of Dido,
Queen of Carthage, who had killed herself when
Aeneas abandoned her. She turned away and refused to speak to him.

[30] See l. 171.

[31] Small, wooded valleys.

[32] This stanza gives the reason why the Scholar-
Gypsy should fly from modern life. What is that
reason?

As some grave Tyrian [33] trader, from the
    sea,
Descried at sunrise an emerging prow,
Lifting the cool-haired creepers stealthily,[34]
The fringes of a southward-facing
    brow   235
    Among the Ægæan [35] isles;
And saw the merry Grecian [36] coaster come,
Freighted with amber grapes and
    Chian [37] wine,
Green bursting figs, and tunnies [38]
    steeped in brine,
And knew the intruders on his ancient
    home,   240

The young light-hearted masters of the waves!
And snatched his rudder, and shook out
    more sail;
And day and night held on indignantly
O'er the blue Midland waters [39] with the
    gale,
Betwixt the Syrtes [40] and soft Sicily, 245
    To where the Atlantic raves
Outside the western straits; [41] and unbent
    sails
There, where down cloudy cliffs, through
    sheets of foam,

Shy traffickers, the dark Iberians [42] come;
And on the beach undid his corded
    bales.   250
(1853)

STUDY AIDS: 1. Arnold's poem is in five
parts: (1) introduction; (2) the story of the
Scholar-Gypsy and imaginings about him; (3)
a denial of his immortality; (4) a reaffirmation of
his immortality and the reasons for it; (5) warning advice to the Scholar-Gypsy. Mark off the
divisions between these parts.

2. How does the TONE of the poem change
as the subject is developed? After l. 141, the
Scholar-Gypsy takes on symbolic importance. Of
what is he a symbol? What criticism is Arnold
making of the world of his day? Does this
criticism apply as well to the twentieth century?

3. The final two stanzas recapture something
of the quiet, romantic note of the first part of
the poem. But they do more than this; they
constitute an extended SIMILE. Explain the simile. (For example, what does the Tyrian trader
stand for, what the Grecian coaster?)

4. Do the many allusions to specific places
near Oxford add to or detract from the poem?
How does the descriptive part of the poem prepare the way for the later criticism of modern
life?

The Progress of Poesy

Youth rambles on life's arid mount,
And strike the rock,[43] and finds the vein,
And brings the water from the fount,
The fount which shall not flow again.

The man mature with labor chops   5
For the bright stream a channel grand,
And sees not that the sacred drops
Ran off and vanished out of hand.

And then the old man totters nigh,
And feebly rakes among the stones.   10
The mount is mute, the channel dry; [44]
And down he lays his weary bones.
(1867)

STUDY AIDS: This poem is about youth,
manhood, and old age. What does it have to do
with "the progress of poesy," which is not even
mentioned? Explain the imagery. How does the
note of pessimism increase from stanza to stanza?

[33] Pertaining to Tyre, a Phoenician city noted
for its trading activities in the ancient world.
[34] I.e., pushing aside the foliage ("creepers")
overhanging the shore.
[35] The sea between Greece and Asia Minor.
[36] The Greeks gradually displaced the Phoenicians
as traders.
[37] Pertaining to Chios, an Aegean island.
[38] A variety of large fish.
[39] Mediterranean.

[40] The ancient name of Sidra and Cabes, two
gulfs on the northeastern coast of Africa, opposite
the island of Sicily.
[41] Strait of Gibraltar.
[42] Early inhabitants of the Spanish Peninsula.
[43] Cf. Ex. 17:1–7, where Moses strikes the rock
to bring forth water for the thirsting Israelites.
[44] How does this line refer back to the first two
stanzas?

An afternoon in Hyde Park, 1889.

The Blessed Damozel, from the painting by Rossetti.

Dover Beach

The sea is calm to-night.
The tide is full, the moon lies fair
Upon the straits; on the French coast the light
Gleams and is gone; the cliffs of England stand,
Glimmering and vast, out in the tranquil bay.   5
Come to the window, sweet is the night-air!
Only, from the long line of spray
Where the sea meets the moon-blanched land,
Listen! you hear the grating roar
Of pebbles which the waves draw back, and fling,   10
At their return, up the high strand,
Begin, and cease; and then again begin,
With tremulous cadence slow; and bring
The eternal note of sadness in.[1]

Sophocles,[2] long ago,   15
Heard it on the Ægæan, and it brought
Into his mind the turbid ebb and flow
Of human misery; we
Find also in the sound a thought,
Hearing it by this distant northern sea.   20

The sea of faith
Was once, too, at the full, and round earth's shore
Lay like the folds of a bright girdle furled;
But now I only hear
Its melancholy, long, withdrawing roar,   25
Retreating, to the breath
Of the night-wind, down the vast edges drear
And naked shingles[3] of the world.

Ah, love, let us be true[4]
To one another! for the world, which seems   30
To lie before us like a land of dreams,
So various, so beautiful, so new,
Hath really neither joy, nor love, nor light,
Nor certitude, nor peace, nor help for pain;
And we are here as on a darkling plain,[5]   35
Swept with confused alarms of struggle and flight,
Where ignorant armies clash by night.
(1867)

STUDY AIDS: 1. How does each stanza of this poem mark a progression in the thought? Are the four stanzas structurally related in any other way? What two seas are mentioned, and how are they related?

2. What is the basic conflict set forth, and how is it resolved? To whom is Arnold speaking? What part does this person play in the resolution of the conflict?

3. Note the gradual increase in emotional intensity from the quiet gentleness of the opening description through a philosophic melancholy to a kind of controlled desperation. How is this shift in tone related to the progression of thought?

4. What is the function of moonlight in the poem? How is moonlight related to the theme and particularly to the image of the last three lines?

5. Arnold wrote of a man who was "Wandering between two worlds, one dead, The other powerless to be born." What did he mean, and how is his comment applicable to Dover Beach?

---

[1] How has Arnold caught the rhythm of the sea in this stanza? Note, for example, the subtle use of pauses, of an irregular RHYME-SCHEME, and of variation in line-lengths .

[2] Famous Greek tragic dramatist. In his Antigone, the chorus compares the prospect of family ruin to the sound of an angry sea. What does the reference to this ancient writer of tragedy (5th century B.C.) add to the poem?

[3] Large, coarse gravel, such as is found on a sea beach.

[4] There is no reference to the sea in this last stanza. What, then, is the relation of ll. 29–37 to ll. 1–28?

[5] Note the details of this final image (ll. 35–37). What is its total effect? What are the "confused alarms" and "ignorant armies"?

Rugby Chapel
November, 1857

Dr. Thomas Arnold, the poet's father, was the headmaster of Rugby School, in the chapel of which he was buried in 1842. More than fifteen years later Matthew Arnold was led to write this elegy by some remarks of a critic accusing Dr. Arnold of fanaticism and humorlessness.

Coldly, sadly descends
The autumn evening. The field
Strewn with its dank yellow drifts
Of withered leaves, and the elms,
Fade into dimness apace,   5
Silent—hardly a shout
From a few boys late at their play!
The lights come out in the street,
In the schoolroom windows;—but cold,
Solemn, unlighted, austere,   10
Through the gathering darkness, arise
The chapel walls, in whose bound
Thou, my father! art laid.

There thou dost lie, in the gloom
Of the autumn evening. But ah!   15
That word, *gloom*, to my mind
Brings thee back, in the light
Of thy radiant vigor, again;
In the gloom of November we passed
Days not dark at thy side;   20
Seasons impaired not the ray
Of thy buoyant cheerfulness clear.
Such thou wast! and I stand
In the autumn evening, and think
Of by-gone autumns with thee.   25

Fifteen years have gone round
Since thou arosest to tread,
In the summer morning, the road
Of death, at a call unforeseen,
Sudden. For fifteen years,   30
We who till then in thy shade
Rested as under the boughs
Of a mighty oak, have endured
Sunshine and rain as we might,
Bare, unshaded, alone,   35
Lacking the shelter of thee.

O strong soul, by what shore
Tarriest thou now? For that force,

Surely, has not been left vain!
Somewhere, surely, afar,   40
In the sounding labor-house vast
Of being, is practiced that strength,
Zealous, beneficent, firm!

Yes, in some far-shining sphere,
Conscious or not of the past,   45
Still thou performest the word
Of the Spirit in whom thou dost live—
Prompt, unwearied, as here!
Still thou upraisest with zeal
The humble good from the ground,   50
Sternly repressest the bad!
Still, like a trumpet, dost rouse
Those who with half-open eyes
Tread the border-land dim
'Twixt vice and virtue; revivest,   55
Succorest!—this was thy work,
This was thy life upon earth.

What is the course of the life
Of mortal men on the earth?—
Most men eddy about   60
Here and there—eat and drink,
Chatter and love and hate,
Gather and squander, are raised
Aloft, are hurled in the dust,
Striving blindly, achieving   65
Nothing; and then they die—
Perish;—and no one asks
Who or what they have been,
More than he asks what waves,
In the moonlit solitudes mild   70
Of the midmost ocean, have swelled,
Foamed for a moment, and gone.

And there are some, whom a thirst
Ardent, unquenchable, fires,
Not with the crowd to be spent,   75
Not without aim to go round

In an eddy of purposeless dust,
Effort unmeaning and vain.
Ah, yes! some of us strive
Not without action to die 80
Fruitless, but something to snatch
From dull oblivion, nor all
Glut the devouring grave!
We, we have chosen our path—
Path to a clear-purposed goal, 85
Path of advance!—but it leads
A long, steep journey, through sunk
Gorges, o'er mountains in snow.
Cheerful, with friends, we set forth—
Then, on the height, comes the storm. 90
Thunder crashes from rock
To rock, the cataracts reply,
Lightnings dazzle our eyes.
Roaring torrents have breached
The track, the stream-bed descends 95
In the place where the wayfarer once
Planted his footstep—the spray
Boils o'er its borders! aloft
The unseen snow-beds dislodge
Their hanging ruin; alas, 100
Havoc is made in our train!
Friends, who set forth at our side,
Falter, are lost in the storm.
We, we only are left!
With frowning foreheads, with lips 105
Sternly compressed, we strain on,
On—and at nightfall at last
Come to the end of our way,
To the lonely inn 'mid the rocks;
Where the gaunt and taciturn host [1] 110
Stands on the threshold, the wind
Shaking his thin white hairs—
Holds his lantern to scan
Our storm-beat figures, and asks:
Whom in our party we bring? 115
Whom we have left in the snow?

Sadly we answer: We bring
Only ourselves! we lost
Sight of the rest in the storm.
Hardly ourselves we fought through, 120
Stripped, without friends, as we are.
Friends, companions, and train,
The avalanche swept from our side.

[1] Death.

But thou would'st not alone
Be saved, my father! alone 125
Conquer and come to thy goal,
Leaving the rest in the wild.
We were weary, and we
Fearful, and we in our march
Fain to drop down and to die. 130
Still thou turnedst, and still
Beckonedst the trembler, and still
Gavest the weary thy hand.

If, in the paths of the world,
Stones might have wounded thy feet, 135
Toil or dejection have tried
Thy spirit, of that we saw
Nothing—to us thou wast still
Cheerful, and helpful, and firm!
Therefore to thee it was given 140
Many to save with thyself;
And, at the end of thy day,
O faithful shepherd! to come,
Bringing thy sheep in thy hand.
And through thee I believe 145
In the noble and great who are gone;
Pure souls honored and blessed
By former ages, who else—
Such, so soulless, so poor,
Is the race of men whom I see— 150
Seemed but a dream of the heart,
Seemed but a cry of desire.
Yes! I believe that there lived
Others like thee in the past,
Not like the men of the crowd 155
Who all round me today
Bluster or cringe, and make life
Hideous, and arid, and vile;
But souls tempered with fire,
Fervent, heroic, and good, 160
Helpers and friends of mankind.

Servants of God!—or sons
Shall I not call you? because
Not as servants ye knew
Your Father's innermost mind, 165
His, who unwillingly sees
One of His little ones lost—
Yours is the praise, if mankind
Hath not as yet in its march
Fainted, and fallen, and died! 170

See! In the rocks of the world
Marches the host of mankind,
A feeble, wavering line.
Where are they tending?—A God
Marshaled them, gave them their goal.   175
Ah, but the way is so long!
Years they have been in the wild!
Sore thirst plagues them, the rocks,
Rising all round, overawe;
Factions divide them, their host   180
Threatens to break, to dissolve.
—Ah, keep, keep them combined!
Else, of the myriads who fill
That army, not one shall arrive;
Sole they shall stray; in the rocks   185
Stagger forever in vain,
Die one by one in the waste.

Then, in such an hour of need
Of your fainting, dispirited race,
Ye,[2] like angels, appear,   190
Radiant with ardor divine!
Beacons of hope, ye appear!
Languor is not in your heart,
Weakness is not in your word,

Weariness not on your brow.   195
Ye alight in our van! at your voice,
Panic, despair, flee away.
Ye move through the ranks, recall
The stragglers, refresh the outworn,
Praise, re-inspire the brave!   200
Order, courage, return.
Eyes rekindling, and prayers,
Follow your steps as ye go.
Ye fill up the gaps in our files,
Strengthen the wavering line,   205
Stablish, continue our march,
On, to the bound of the waste,
On, to the City of God.
(1867)

STUDY AIDS: 1. In ll. 58–170, Arnold describes three classes of men. Who are they? In which group does he place his father? In which himself?

2. How does the mood of the poem's ending differ from that of its beginning? Is this shift abrupt or gradual? How does the ending contrast with the ending of *Dover Beach?*

3. What metrical form is used? Is it appropriate to this elegy?

Culture and Anarchy

"Hebraism and Hellenism" is the fourth chapter of *Culture and Anarchy,* a book composed of six articles that had first appeared in *Cornhill Magazine.* In this book Arnold criticizes England for her faith in "machinery," by which he means any exterior or material thing set up as a goal in itself. To this he opposes "culture," defined as "a study of perfection"—that is, "a harmonious expansion of *all* the powers which make the beauty and worth of human nature." Culture brings together "sweetness and light," sweetness being "the moral and social passion for doing good," and light "the scientific passion for pure knowledge." Culture thus holds up before us the authority of the "best self," whereas the average Englishman hates all authority and idolizes freedom ("doing as one likes") as the ultimate good.

Hebraism and Hellenism

This fundamental ground [1] is our preference of doing to thinking. Now, this preference is a main element in our nature, and as we study it we find ourselves opening up a number of large questions on every side.

Let me go back for a moment to Bishop

[2] The "helpers and friends of mankind" of l. 161.

[1] In the previous chapter—"Barbarians, Philistines, and Populace" (standing respectively for the upper, middle, and lower classes of England)—Arnold has reproved his countrymen for their lack of "intellectual flexibility," particularly for their inability to

see the difference between restraint for its own sake and restraint in the interests of "right reason." His final sentence is: "But now let us try to go a little deeper, and to find, beneath our actual habits and practice, the very ground and cause out of which they spring." "Hebraism and Hellenism" continues from this point.

Wilson,[2] who says, "First, never go against the best light you have; secondly, take care that your light be not darkness." We show, as a nation, laudable energy and persistence in walking according to the best light we have, but are not quite careful enough, perhaps, to see that our light be not darkness. This is only another version of the old story that energy is our strong point and favorable characteristic, rather than intelligence. But we may give to this idea a more general form still, in which it will have a yet larger range of application. We may regard this energy driving at practice, this paramount sense of the obligation of duty, self-control, and work, this earnestness in going manfully with the best light we have, as one force. And we may regard the intelligence driving at those ideas which are, after all, the basis of right practice, the ardent sense for all the new and changing combinations of them which man's development brings with it, the indomitable impulse to know and adjust them perfectly, as another force. And these two forces we may regard as in some sense rivals—rivals, not by the necessity of their own nature, but as exhibited in man and his history; and rivals dividing the empire of the world between them. And to give these forces names from the two races of men who have supplied the most signal and splendid manifestations of them, we may call them respectively the forces of Hebraism and Hellenism. Hebraism and Hellenism—between these two points of influence moves our world. At one time it feels more powerfully the attraction of one of them, at another time of the other; and it ought to be, though it never is, evenly and happily balanced between them.

The final aim of both Hellenism and Hebraism, as of all great spiritual disciplines, is no doubt the same: man's perfection, or salvation. The very language which they both of them use in schooling us to reach this aim is often identical. Even when their language indicates by variation—sometimes a broad variation, often a but slight and subtle variation—the different courses of thought which

are uppermost in each discipline, even then the unity of the final end and aim is still apparent. To employ the actual words of that discipline with which we ourselves are all of us most familiar, and the words of which, therefore, come most home to us, that final end and aim is "that we might be partakers of the divine nature." [3] These are the words of a Hebrew apostle; but of Hellenism and Hebraism alike this is, I say, the aim. When the two are confronted, as they very often are confronted, it is nearly always with what I may call a rhetorical purpose: the speaker's whole design is to exalt and enthrone one of the two, and he uses the other only as a foil and to enable him the better to give effect to his purpose. Obviously, with us, it is usually Hellenism which is thus reduced to minister to the triumph of Hebraism. There is a sermon on Greece and the Greek spirit by a man never to be mentioned without interest and respect, Frederick Robertson,[4] in which this rhetorical use of Greece and the Greek spirit, and the inadequate exhibition of them necessarily consequent upon this, is almost ludicrous, and would be censurable if it were not to be explained by the exigencies of a sermon. On the other hand, Heinrich Heine [5] and other writers of his sort give us the spectacle of the tables completely turned, and of Hebraism brought in just as a foil and contrast to Hellenism and to make the superiority of Hellenism more manifest. In both these cases there is injustice and misrepresentation. The aim and end of both Hebraism and Hellenism is, as I have said, one and the same, and this aim and end is august and admirable.

Still, they pursue this aim by very different courses. The uppermost idea with Hellenism is to see things as they really are; the uppermost idea with Hebraism is conduct and obedience. Nothing can do away with this ineffaceable difference. The Greek quarrel with the body and its desires is that they hinder right thinking; the Hebrew quarrel with them is that they hinder right acting.

---

[3] 2 Peter 1:4.
[4] A liberal Anglican clergyman of great influence.
[5] Famous German lyric poet.

[2] Thomas Wilson, Bishop of Sodor and Man. The quotation which follows is from his *Maxims*.

"He that keepeth the law, happy is he"; [6] "Blessed is the man that feareth the Eternal, that delighteth greatly in His commandments"; [7]—that is the Hebrew notion of felicity; and, pursued with passion and tenacity, this notion would not let the Hebrew rest till, as is well known, he had at last got out of the law a network of prescriptions to enwrap his whole life, to govern every moment of it, every impulse, every action. The Greek notion of felicity, on the other hand, is perfectly conveyed in these words of a great French moralist: *"C'est le bonheur des hommes"* [8]—when? when they abhor that which is evil? [9] no;—when they exercise themselves in the law of the Lord day and night? [10] no;—when they die daily?[11] no;—when they walk about the New Jerusalem with palms in their hands? [12] no;—but when they think aright, when their thought hits: *"quand ils pensent juste."* [13] At the bottom of both the Greek and the Hebrew notion is the desire, native in man, for reason and the will of God, the feeling after the universal order—in a word, the love of God. But while Hebraism seizes upon certain plain, capital intimations of the universal order, and rivets itself, one may say, with unequaled grandeur of earnestness and intensity on the study and observance of them, the bent of Hellenism is to follow, with flexible activity, the whole play of the universal order, to be apprehensive of missing any part of it, of sacrificing one part to another, to slip away from resting in this or that intimation of it, however capital. An unclouded clearness of mind, an unimpeded play of thought, is what this bent drives at. The governing idea of Hellenism is *spontaneity of consciousness;* that of Hebraism, *strictness of conscience.*

Christianity changed nothing in this essential bent of Hebraism to set doing above knowing. Self-conquest, self-devotion, the fol-lowing not our own individual will but the will of God, *obedience,* is the fundamental idea of this form, also, of the discipline to which we have attached the general name of Hebraism. Only, as the old law and the network of prescriptions with which it enveloped human life were evidently a motive-power not driving and searching enough to produce the result aimed at—patient continuance in well-doing, self-conquest—Christianity substituted for them boundless devotion to that inspiring and affecting pattern of self-conquest offered by Jesus Christ; and by the new motive-power, of which the essence was this, though the love and admiration of Christian churches have for centuries been employed in varying, amplifying, and adorning the plain description of it, Christianity, as St. Paul truly says, "establishes the law," [14] and, in the strength of the ampler power which she has thus supplied to fulfill it, has accomplished the miracles, which we all see, of her history.

So long as we do not forget that both Hellenism and Hebraism are profound and admirable manifestations of man's life, tendencies, and powers, and that both of them aim at a like final result, we can hardly insist too strongly on the divergence of line and of operation with which they proceed. It is a divergence so great that it most truly, as the prophet Zechariah says, "has raised up thy sons, O Zion, against thy sons, O Greece!" [15] The difference whether it is by doing or by knowing that we set most store, and the practical consequences which follow from this difference, leave their mark on all the history of our race and of its development. Language may be abundantly quoted from both Hellenism and Hebraism to make it seem that one follows the same current as the other toward the same goal. They are, truly, borne towards the same goal; but the currents which bear them are infinitely different. It is true, Solomon will praise knowing: "Understanding is a well-spring of life unto him that hath it." [16] And in the New Testament, again,

[6] Prov. 29:18.
[7] Psalms 112:1.
[8] "It is the good fortune of men."
[9] From Rom. 12:9.
[10] From Psalms 1:2.
[11] From 1 Cor. 15:31.
[12] From Rev. 3:12; 7:9.
[13] "When they think rightly."

[14] Rom. 3:31.
[15] Zech. 9:13.
[16] Prov. 16:22.

Jesus Christ is a "light," and "truth makes us free." [17] It is true, Aristotle will undervalue knowing: "In what concerns virtue," says he, "three things are necessary—knowledge, deliberate will, and perseverance; but whereas the two last are all-important, the first is a matter of little importance." [18] It is true that with the same impatience with which St. James enjoins a man to be not a forgetful hearer but a "doer of the word," [19] Epictetus [20] exhorts us to *do* what we have demonstrated to ourselves we ought to do; or he taunts us with futility, for being armed at all points to prove that lying is wrong, yet all the time continuing to lie. It is true, Plato,[21] in words which are almost the words of the New Testament or the *Imitation*,[22] calls life a learning to die. But underneath the superficial agreement the fundamental divergence still subsists. The "understanding" of Solomon is "the walking in the way of the commandments"; [23] this is "the way of peace," [24] and it is of this that blessedness comes. In the New Testament, the truth which gives us the peace of God and makes us free is the love of Christ constraining us to crucify, as he did, and with a like purpose of moral regeneration, the flesh with its affections and lusts, and thus establishing, as we have seen, the law. The moral virtues, on the other hand, are with Aristotle but the porch and access to the intellectual, and with these last is blessedness. That partaking of the divine life, which both Hellenism and Hebraism, as we have said, fix as their crowning aim, Plato expressly denies to the man of practical virtue merely, of self-conquest with any other motive than that of perfect intellectual vision. He reserves it for the lover of pure knowledge, of seeing things as they really are—the φιλομαθής.[25]

Both Hellenism and Hebraism arise out of the wants of human nature, and address themselves to satisfying those wants. But their methods are so different, they lay stress on such different points, and call into being by their respective disciplines such different activities, that the face which human nature presents when it passes from the hands of one of them to those of the other is no longer the same. To get rid of one's ignorance, to see things as they are, and by seeing them as they are to see them in their beauty, is the simple and attractive ideal which Hellenism holds out before human nature; and from the simplicity and charm of this ideal, Hellenism, and human life in the hands of Hellenism, is invested with a kind of aërial ease, clearness, and radiancy; they are full of what we call sweetness and light.[26] Difficulties are kept out of view, and the beauty and rationalness of the ideal have all our thoughts. "The best man is he who most tries to perfect himself, and the happiest man is he who most feels that he *is* perfecting himself"—this account of the matter by Socrates, the true Socrates [27] of the *Memorabilia*, has something so simple, spontaneous, and unsophisticated about it that it seems to fill us with clearness and hope when we hear it. But there is a saying which I have heard attributed to Mr. Carlyle [28] about Socrates—a very happy saying, whether it is really Mr. Carlyle's or not —which excellently marks the essential point in which Hebraism differs from Hellenism. "Socrates," this saying goes, "is terribly *at ease in Zion*." [29] Hebraism—and here is the source of its wonderful strength—has always been severely preoccupied with an awful sense of the impossibility of being at ease in Zion; of the difficulties which oppose themselves to man's pursuit or attainment of that perfection of which Socrates talks so hopefully, and, as from this point of view one

---

[17] From John 8:12, 32.

[18] Aristotle's *Ethics*.

[19] From James 1:25.

[20] Stoic philosopher. The reference is to his *Discourses*.

[21] The reference is to his *Phaedo*.

[22] *Imitation of Christ*, fifteenth-century religious work attributed to the German writer Thomas à Kempis.

[23] Psalms 119:32–35.

[24] Isa. 59:8.

[25] "The lover of knowledge."

[26] See the headnote. Arnold took this phrase from Swift's *Battle of the Books*.

[27] The "true Socrates" is that presented by Xenophon's *Memorabilia* as distinguished from the Socrates of Plato's dialogues, who is partly a mouthpiece for Plato himself.

[28] Thomas Carlyle. See p. 710.

[29] Cf. Amos 6:1.

might almost say, so glibly. It is all very well to talk of getting rid of one's ignorance, of seeing things in their reality, seeing them in their beauty; but how is this to be done when there is something which thwarts and spoils all our efforts?

This something is sin; and the space which sin fills in Hebraism, as compared with Hellenism, is indeed prodigious. This obstacle to perfection fills the whole scene, and perfection appears remote and rising away from earth, in the background. Under the name of sin, the difficulties of knowing oneself and conquering oneself which impede man's passage to perfection become, for Hebraism, a positive, active entity hostile to man, a mysterious power which I heard Dr. Pusey [30] the other day, in one of his impressive sermons, compare to a hideous hunchback seated on our shoulders, and which it is the main business of our lives to hate and oppose. The discipline of the Old Testament may be summed up as a discipline teaching us to abhor and flee from sin; the discipline of the New Testament, as a discipline teaching us to die to it. As Hellenism speaks of thinking clearly, seeing things in their essence and beauty, as a grand and precious feat for man to achieve, so Hebraism speaks of becoming conscious of sin, of awakening to a sense of sin, as a feat of this kind. It is obvious to what wide divergence these differing tendencies, actively followed, must lead. As one passes and repasses from Hellenism to Hebraism, from Plato to St. Paul, one feels inclined to rub one's eyes and ask oneself whether man is indeed a gentle and simple being, showing the traces of a noble and divine nature, or an unhappy chained captive,[31] laboring with groanings that cannot be uttered to free himself from the body of this death.

Apparently it was the Hellenic conception of human nature which was unsound, for the world could not live by it. Absolutely to call it unsound, however, is to fall into the common error of its Hebraizing enemies; but it was unsound at that particular moment of man's development, it was premature. The indispensable basis of conduct and self-control, the platform upon which alone the perfection aimed at by Greece can come into bloom, was not to be reached by our race so easily; centuries of probation and discipline were needed to bring us to it. Therefore the bright promise of Hellenism faded, and Hebraism ruled the world. Then was seen that astonishing spectacle, so well marked by the often-quoted words of the prophet Zechariah, when men of all languages and nations took hold of the skirt of him that was a Jew, saying, "We will go with you, for we have heard that God is with you." [32] And the Hebraism which thus received and ruled a world all gone out of the way, and altogether become unprofitable, was and could not but be the later, the more spiritual, the more attractive development of Hebraism. It was Christianity; that is to say, Hebraism aiming at self-conquest and rescue from the thrall of vile affections, not by obedience to the letter of a law, but by conformity to the image of a self-sacrificing example. To a world stricken with moral enervation Christianity offered its spectacle of an inspired self-sacrifice; to men who refused themselves nothing, it showed one who refused himself everything;—"my Savior banished joy!" says George Herbert.[33] When the *alma Venus*,[34] the life-giving and joy-giving power of nature, so fondly cherished by the pagan world, could not save her followers from self-dissatisfaction and ennui, the severe words of the apostle came bracingly and refreshingly: "Let no man deceive you with vain words, for because of these things cometh the wrath of God upon the children of disobedience." [35] Through age after age and generation after generation, our race, or all that part of our race which was most living and progressive, was "baptized into a

---

[30] Edward B. Pusey, scholarly Anglican clergyman, was one of the leaders of the Oxford Movement (see p. 517), whose members were often referred to as "Puseyites."
[31] Cf. Rom. 8:26.

[32] Zech. 8:23.
[33] Seventeenth-century religious poet (see p. 222). The quotation is from his poem *The Size*.
[34] "Fostering Venus."
[35] Eph. 5:6.

death"; [36] and endeavored, by suffering in the flesh, to cease from sin. Of this endeavor, the animating labors and afflictions of early Christianity, the touching asceticism of medieval Christianity, are the great historical manifestations. Literary monuments of it, each in its own way incomparable, remain in the *Epistles* of St. Paul, in St. Augustine's *Confessions*, and in the two original and simplest books of the *Imitation*.

Of two disciplines laying their main stress, the one on clear intelligence, the other on firm obedience; the one on comprehensively knowing the ground of one's duty, the other on diligently practicing it; the one on taking all possible care (to use Bishop Wilson's words again) that the light we have be not darkness, the other that according to the best light we have we diligently walk, the priority naturally belongs to that discipline which braces all man's moral powers and founds for him an indispensable basis of character. And, therefore, it is justly said of the Jewish people, who were charged with setting powerfully forth that side of the divine order to which the words "conscience" and "self-conquest" point, that they were "entrusted with the oracles of God"; [37] as it is justly said of Christianity, which followed Judaism and which set forth this side with a much deeper effectiveness and a much wider influence, that the wisdom of the old pagan world was foolishness [38] compared to it. No words of devotion and admiration can be too strong to render thanks to these beneficent forces which have so borne forward humanity in its appointed work of coming to the knowledge and possession of itself; above all, in those great moments when their action was the wholesomest and the most necessary.

But the evolution of these forces, separately and in themselves, is not the whole evolution of humanity, their single history is not the whole history of man; whereas their admirers are always apt to make it stand for the whole history. Hebraism and Hellenism are, neither of them, the law of human development, as their admirers are prone to make them; they are, each of them, contributions to human development, august contributions, invaluable contributions, and each showing itself to us more august, more invaluable, more preponderant over the other, according to the moment in which we take them and the relation in which we stand to them. The nations of our modern world, children of that immense and salutary movement [39] which broke up the pagan world, inevitably stand to Hellenism in a relation which dwarfs it and to Hebraism in a relation which magnifies it. They are inevitably prone to take Hebraism as the law of human development, and not as simply a contribution to it, however precious. And yet the lesson must perforce be learned, that the human spirit is wider than the most priceless of the forces which bear it onward, and that to the whole development of man Hebraism itself is, like Hellenism, but a contribution.

Perhaps we may help ourselves to see this clearer by an illustration drawn from the treatment of a single great idea which has profoundly engaged the human spirit, and has given it eminent opportunities for showing its nobleness and energy. It surely must be perceived that the idea of immortality, as this idea rises in its generality before the human spirit, is something grander, truer, and more satisfying than it is in the particular forms by which St. Paul, in the famous fifteenth chapter of the *Epistle to the Corinthians*, and Plato, in the *Phaedo*, endeavor to develop and establish it. Surely we cannot but feel that the argumentation with which the Hebrew apostle goes about to expound this great idea is, after all, confused and inconclusive; and that the reasoning, drawn from analogies of likeness and equality, which is employed upon it by the Greek philosopher, is over-subtle and sterile. Above and beyond the inadequate solutions which Hebraism and Hellenism here attempt, extends the immense and august problem itself, and the human spirit which gave birth to it. And this single illustration may suggest to us how the same thing happens in other cases also.

[36] From Rom. 6:3.
[37] Rom. 3:2.
[38] Cf. 1 Cor. 3:19.
[39] Christianity.

But meanwhile, by alternations of Hebraism and Hellenism, of a man's intellectual and moral impulses, of the effort to see things as they really are and the effort to win peace by self-conquest, the human spirit proceeds; and each of these two forces has its appointed hours of culmination and seasons of rule. As the great movement of Christianity was a triumph of Hebraism and man's moral impulses, so the great movement which goes by the name of the Renaissance was an uprising and reinstatement of man's intellectual impulses and of Hellenism. We in England, the devoted children of Protestantism, chiefly know the Renaissance by its subordinate and secondary side of the Reformation. The Reformation has been often called a Hebraizing revival, a return to the ardor and sincereness of primitive Christianity. No one, however, can study the development of Protestantism and of Protestant churches without feeling that into the Reformation too—Hebraizing child of the Renaissance, and offspring of its fervor rather than its intelligence, as it undoubtedly was—the subtle Hellenic leaven of the Renaissance found its way, and that the exact respective parts, in the Reformation, of Hebraism and of Hellenism are not easy to separate. But what we may with truth say is that all which Protestantism was to itself clearly conscious of, all which it succeeded in clearly setting forth in words, had the characters of Hebraism rather than of Hellenism. The Reformation was strong in that it was an earnest return to the Bible and to doing from the heart the will of God as there written. It was weak in that it never consciously grasped or applied the central idea of the Renaissance—the Hellenic idea of pursuing, in all lines of activity, the law and science, to use Plato's words, of things as they really are. Whatever direct superiority, therefore, Protestantism had over Catholicism was a moral superiority, a superiority arising out of its greater sincerity and earnestness—at the moment of its apparition, at any rate—in dealing with the heart and conscience. Its pretensions to an intellectual superiority are in general quite illusory. For Hellenism, for the thinking side in man as distinguished from

the acting side, the attitude of mind of Protestantism towards the Bible in no respect differs from the attitude of mind of Catholicism towards the Church. The mental habit of him who imagines that Balaam's ass spoke,[40] in no respect differs from the mental habit of him who imagines that a Madonna of wood or stone winked; and the one, who says that God's Church makes him believe what he believes, and the other, who says that God's Word makes him believe what he believes, are for the philosopher perfectly alike in not really and truly knowing, when they say "God's Church" and "God's Word," what it is they say or whereof they affirm.

In the sixteenth century, therefore, Hellenism reëntered the world, and again stood in presence of Hebraism—a Hebraism renewed and purged. Now, it has not been enough observed, how, in the seventeenth century, a fate befell Hellenism in some respects analogous to that which befell it at the commencement of our era. The Renaissance, that great reawakening of Hellenism, that irresistible return of humanity to nature and to seeing things as they are, which in art, in literature, and in physics produced such splendid fruits, had, like the anterior Hellenism of the pagan world, a side of moral weakness and of relaxation or insensibility of the moral fiber, which in Italy showed itself with the most startling plainness, but which in France, England, and other countries was very apparent too. Again this loss of spiritual balance, this exclusive preponderance given to man's perceiving and knowing side, this unnatural defect of his feeling and acting side, provoked a reaction. Let us trace that reaction where it most nearly concerns us.

Science has now made visible to everybody the great and pregnant elements of difference which lie in race, and in how signal a manner they make the genius and history of an Indo-European people vary from those of a Semitic people. Hellenism is of Indo-European growth, Hebraism is of Semitic growth; and we English, a nation of Indo-European stock, seem to belong naturally to the movement of

[40] See Num. 22:21–35.

Hellenism. But nothing more strongly marks the essential unity of man than the affinities we can perceive, in this point or that, between members of one family of peoples and members of another. And no affinity of this kind is more strongly marked than that likeness in the strength and prominence of the moral fiber, which, notwithstanding immense elements of difference, knits in some special sort the genius and history of us English, and our American descendants across the Atlantic, to the genius and history of the Hebrew people. Puritanism, which has been so great a power in the English nation, and in the strongest part of the English nation, was originally the reaction in the seventeenth century of the conscience and moral sense of our race against the moral indifference and lax rule of conduct which in the sixteenth century came in with the Renaissance. It was a reaction of Hebraism against Hellenism; and it powerfully manifested itself, as was natural, in a people with much of what we call a Hebraizing turn, with a signal affinity for the bent which was the master-bent of Hebrew life. Eminently Indo-European by its humor,[41] by the power it shows, through this gift, of imaginatively acknowledging the multiform aspects of the problem of life and of thus getting itself unfixed from its own over-certainty, of smiling at its own over-tenacity, our race has yet (and a great part of its strength lies here), in matters of practical life and moral conduct, a strong share of the assuredness, the tenacity, the intensity of the Hebrews. This turn manifested itself in Puritanism, and has had a great part in shaping our history for the last two hundred years. Undoubtedly it checked and changed amongst us that movement of the Renaissance which we see producing in the reign of Elizabeth such wonderful fruits. Undoubtedly it stopped the prominent rule and direct development of that order of ideas which we call by the name of Hellenism, and gave the first rank to a different order of ideas. Apparently, too, as we said of the former defeat of Hellenism, if Hellenism was defeated this shows that Hellenism was imperfect and that its ascendency

[41] Dominant trait.

at that moment would not have been for the world's good.

Yet there is a very important difference between the defeat inflicted on Hellenism by Christianity eighteen hundred years ago, and the check given to the Renaissance by Puritanism. The greatness of the difference is well measured by the difference in force, beauty, significance, and usefulness between primitive Christianity and Protestantism. Eighteen hundred years ago it was altogether the hour of Hebraism. Primitive Christianity was legitimately and truly the ascendant force in the world at that time, and the way of mankind's progress lay through its full development. Another hour in man's development began in the fifteenth century, and the main road of his progress then lay for a time through Hellenism. Puritanism was no longer the central current of the world's progress; it was a side stream crossing the central current and checking it. The cross and the check may have been necessary and salutary, but that does not do away with the essential difference between the main stream of man's advance and a cross or side stream. For more than two hundred years the main stream of man's advance has moved towards knowing himself and the world, seeing things as they are, spontaneity of consciousness; the main impulse of a great part, and that the strongest part, of our nation has been towards strictness of conscience. They have made the secondary the principal at the wrong moment, and the principal they have at the wrong moment treated as secondary. This contravention of the natural order has produced, as such contravention always must produce, a certain confusion and false movement, of which we are now beginning to feel, in almost every direction, the inconvenience. In all directions our habitual courses of action seem to be losing efficaciousness, credit, and control, both with others and even with ourselves. Everywhere we see the beginnings of confusion, and we want a clue to some sound order and authority. This we can only get by going back upon the actual instincts and forces which rule our life, seeing them as they really are, connecting them with other instincts and forces, and enlarging our whole view and rule of life.

(1867–1868)

Discourses in America

Arnold delivered this essay as a lecture during his American tour of 1883–1884 and published it—along with two other lectures—in his *Discourses in America,* 1885.

In our day, when the humanistic studies are seriously threatened by an increasing emphasis upon technical and vocational training, Arnold's eloquent and persuasive defense of a liberal education based upon "literature" (which he defines in a broad sense) is even more timely than it was in the 1880's.

Literature and Science

Practical people talk with a smile of Plato and of his absolute ideas,[1] and it is impossible to deny that Plato's ideas do often seem impractical and impracticable, and especially 5 when one views them in connection with the life of a great work-a-day world like the United States. The necessary staple of the life of such a world Plato [2] regards with dis- 10 dain; handicraft and trade and the working professions he regards with disdain; but what becomes of the life of an industrial modern community if you take handicraft and trade and the working professions out of it? The 15 base mechanic arts and handicrafts, says Plato, bring about a natural weakness in the principle of excellence in a man, so that he cannot govern the ignoble growths in him, but nurses them, and cannot understand fos- 20

tering any other. Those who exercise such arts and trades, as they have their bodies, he says, marred by their vulgar businesses, so they have their souls, too, bowed and broken 5 by them. And if one of these uncomely people has a mind to seek self-culture and philosophy, Plato compares him to a bald little tinker, who has scraped together money, and has got his release from service, and has had 10 a bath, and bought a new coat, and is rigged out like a bridegroom about to marry the daughter of his master who has fallen into poor and helpless estate.

Nor do the working professions fare any 15 better than trade at the hands of Plato. He draws for us an inimitable picture of the working lawyer, and of his life of bondage; he shows how this bondage from his youth up has stunted and warped him, and made 20 him small and crooked of soul, encompassing him with difficulties which he is not man enough to rely on justice and truth as means to encounter, but has recourse, for help out of them, to falsehood and wrong. And so, 25 says Plato, this poor creature is bent and broken, and grows up from boy to man with-

---

[1] Plato believed in two worlds: the transitory, changing world of sense experience; and the eternal, unchanging world of absolute ideas. The former was but a dim, imperfect reflection of the latter.

[2] The following notions of Plato concerning education are taken largely from his *Republic.*

out a particle of soundness in him, although exceedingly smart and clever in his own esteem.

One cannot refuse to admire the artist who draws these pictures. But we say to ourselves that his ideas show the influence of a primitive and obsolete order of things, when the warrior caste and the priestly caste were alone in honor, and the humble work of the world was done by slaves. We have now changed all that; the modern majesty consists in work, as Emerson [3] declares; and in work, we may add, principally of such plain and dusty kind as the work of cultivators of the ground, handicraftsmen, men of trade and business, men of the working professions. Above all is this true in a great industrious community such as that of the United States.

Now education, many people go on to say, is still mainly governed by the ideas of men like Plato, who lived when the warrior caste and the priestly or philosophical class were alone in honor, and the really useful part of the community were slaves. It is an education fitted for persons of leisure in such a community. This education passed from Greece and Rome to the feudal communities of Europe, where also the warrior caste and the priestly caste were alone held in honor, and where the really useful and working part of the community, though not nominally slaves as in the pagan world, were practically not much better off than slaves, and not more seriously regarded. And how absurd it is, people end by saying, to inflict this education upon an industrious modern community, where very few indeed are persons of leisure, and the mass to be considered has not leisure, but is bound, for its own great good, and for the great good of the world at large, to plain labor and to industrial pursuits, and the education in question tends necessarily to make men dissatisfied with these pursuits and unfitted for them!

That is what is said. So far I must defend Plato as to plead that his view of education and studies is in the general, as it seems to me, sound enough, and fitted for all sorts and conditions of men, whatever their pursuits may be. "An intelligent man," says Plato,

"will prize those studies which result in his soul getting soberness, righteousness, and wisdom, and will less value the others." [4] I cannot consider that a bad description of the aim of education, and of the motives which should govern us in the choice of studies, whether we are preparing ourselves for a hereditary seat in the English House of Lords or for the pork trade in Chicago.

Still I admit that Plato's world was not ours, that his scorn of trade and handicraft is fantastic, that he had no conception of a great industrial community such as that of the United States, and that such a community must and will shape its education to suit its own needs. If the usual education handed down to it from the past does not suit it, it will certainly before long drop this and try another. The usual education in the past has been mainly literary. The question is whether the studies which were long supposed to be the best for all of us are practically the best now; whether others are not better. The tyranny of the past, many think, weighs on us injuriously in the predominance given to letters in education. The question is raised whether, to meet the needs of our modern life, the predominance ought not now to pass from letters to science; and naturally the question is nowhere raised with more energy than here in the United States. The design of abasing what is called "mere literary instruction and education," and of exalting what is called "sound, extensive, and practical scientific knowledge," [5] is, in this intensely modern world of the United States, even more perhaps than in Europe, a very popular design, and makes great and rapid progress.

I am going to ask whether the present movement for ousting letters from their old predominance in education, and for transferring the predominance in education to the

[3] *Literary Ethics.*
[4] The *Republic.*
[5] Josiah Mason, a self-made man of wealth, gave a great deal of money to establish the Science College at Birmingham, stipulating that the College should make no provision for "mere literary instruction and education" but should concern itself, instead, with "sound, extensive, and practical scientific knowledge."

natural sciences, whether this brisk and flourishing movement ought to prevail, and whether it is likely that in the end it really will prevail. An objection may be raised which I will anticipate. My own studies have been almost wholly in letters, and my visits to the field of the natural sciences have been very slight and inadequate, although those sciences have always strongly moved my curiosity. A man of letters, it will perhaps be said, is not competent to discuss the comparative merits of letters and natural science as means of education. To this objection I reply, first of all, that his incompetence, if he attempts the discussion but is really incompetent for it, will be abundantly visible; nobody will be taken in; he will have plenty of sharp observers and critics to save mankind from that danger. But the line I am going to follow is, as you will soon discover, so extremely simple that perhaps it may be followed without failure even by one who for a more ambitious line of discussion would be quite incompetent.

Some of you may possibly remember a phrase of mine which has been the object of a good deal of comment; an observation to the effect that in our culture, the aim being "to know ourselves and the world," we have, as the means to this end, "to know the best which has been thought and said in the world." [6] A man of science, who is also an excellent writer and the very prince of debaters, Professor Huxley,[7] in a discourse at the opening of Sir Josiah Mason's college at Birmingham,[8] laying hold of this phrase, expanded it by quoting some more words of mine, which are these:

The civilized world is to be regarded as now being, for intellectual and spiritual purposes, one great confederation, bound to a joint action and working to a common result; and whose members have for their proper outfit a knowledge of Greek, Roman, and Eastern antiquity, and of one another. Special local and temporary advantages being put out of account, that modern nation will in the intellectual and spiritual sphere make most progress, which most thoroughly carries out this program.[9]

Now on my phrase, thus enlarged, Professor Huxley remarks that when I speak of the above-mentioned knowledge as enabling us to know ourselves and the world, I assert literature to contain the materials which suffice for thus making us know ourselves and the world. But it is not by any means clear, says he, that, after having learned all which ancient and modern literatures have to tell us, we have laid a sufficiently broad and deep foundation for that criticism of life, that knowledge of ourselves and the world, which constitutes culture. On the contrary, Professor Huxley declares that he finds himself "wholly unable to admit that either nations or individuals will really advance, if their outfit draws nothing from the stores of physical science. An army without weapons of precision, and with no particular base of operations, might more hopefully enter upon a campaign on the Rhine, than a man, devoid of a knowledge of what physical science has done in the last century, upon a criticism of life."

This shows how needful it is for those who are to discuss any matter together, to have a common understanding as to the sense of the terms they employ—how needful, and how difficult. What Professor Huxley says, implies just the reproach which is so often brought against the study of belles-lettres,[10] as they are called: that the study is an elegant one, but slight and ineffectual; a smattering of Greek and Latin and other ornamental things, of little use for anyone whose object is to get at truth, and to be a practical man. So, too, M. Renan [11] talks of the "superficial

---

[6] From Arnold's famous essay *The Function of Criticism at the Present Time.*

[7] Thomas Henry Huxley, noted nineteenth-century scientist and essayist. The "discourse" to which Arnold refers is *Science and Culture.* (See p. 814.)

[8] See n. 5 above.

[9] *The Function of Criticism at the Present Time.*

[10] Literature emphasizing aesthetic as distinguished from informational values—poetry, drama, fiction, etc., as distinguished from technical and scientific writing.

[11] Ernest Renan, nineteenth-century French critic and historian.

humanism" of a school-course which treats us as if we were all going to be poets, writers, preachers, orators, and he opposes this humanism to positive science, or the critical search after truth. And there is always a tendency in those who are remonstrating against the predominance of letters in education, to understand by letters belles-lettres, and by belles-lettres a superficial humanism, the opposite of science or true knowledge.

But when we talk of knowing Greek and Roman antiquity, for instance, which is the knowledge people have called the humanities, I for my part mean a knowledge which is something more than a superficial humanism, mainly decorative. "I call all teaching scientific," says Wolf,[12] the critic of Homer, "which is systematically laid out and followed up to its original sources. For example: a knowledge of classical antiquity is scientific when the remains of classical antiquity are correctly studied in the original languages." There can be no doubt that Wolf is perfectly right; that all learning is scientific which is systematically laid out and followed up to its original sources, and that genuine humanism is scientific.

When I speak of knowing Greek and Roman antiquity, therefore, as a help to knowing ourselves and the world, I mean more than a knowledge of so much vocabulary, so much grammar, so many portions of authors in the Greek and Latin languages. I mean knowing the Greeks and Romans, and their life and genius, and what they were and did in the world; what we get from them, and what is its value. That, at least, is the ideal; and when we talk of endeavoring to know Greek and Roman antiquity, as a help to knowing ourselves and the world, we mean endeavoring so to know them as to satisfy this ideal, however much we may still fall short of it.

The same also as to knowing our own and other modern nations, with the like aim of getting to understand ourselves and the world. To know the best that has been thought

[12] Friedrich August Wolf, German scholar and critic.

and said by the modern nations, is to know, says Professor Huxley, "only what modern literatures have to tell us; it is the criticism of life contained in modern literature." And yet "the distinctive character of our times," he urges, "lies in the vast and constantly increasing part which is played by natural knowledge." And how, therefore, can a man, devoid of knowledge of what physical science has done in the last century, enter hopefully upon a criticism of modern life?

Let us, I say, be agreed about the meaning of the terms we are using. I talk of knowing the best which has been thought and uttered in the world; Professor Huxley says this means knowing literature. Literature is a large word; it may mean everything written with letters or printed in a book. Euclid's *Elements* and Newton's *Principia* are thus literature. All knowledge that reaches us through books is literature. But by literature Professor Huxley means belles-lettres. He means to make me say, that knowing the best which has been thought and said by the modern nations is knowing their belles-lettres and no more. And this is no sufficient equipment, he argues, for a criticism of modern life. But as I do not mean, by knowing ancient Rome, knowing merely more or less of Latin belles-lettres, and taking no account of Rome's military, and political, and legal, and administrative work in the world; and as, by knowing ancient Greece, I understand knowing her as the giver of Greek art, and the guide to a free and right use of reason and to scientific method, and the founder of our mathematics and physics and astronomy and biology,—I understand knowing her as all this, and not merely knowing certain Greek poems, and histories, and treatises, and speeches,—so as to the knowledge of modern nations also. By knowing modern nations, I mean not merely knowing their belles-lettres, but knowing also what has been done by such men as Copernicus, Galileo, Newton, Darwin. "Our ancestors learned," says Professor Huxley, "that the earth is the center of the visible universe, and that man is the cynosure [13] of things terrestrial; and more especially was it inculcated that the

[13] Center of attention or interest.

course of nature had no fixed order, but that it could be, and constantly was, altered." But for us now, continues Professor Huxley, "the notions of the beginning and the end of the world entertained by our forefathers are no longer credible. It is very certain that the earth is not the chief body in the material universe, and that the world is not subordinated to man's use. It is even more certain that nature is the expression of a definite order, with which nothing interferes." "And yet," he cries, "the purely classical education advocated by the representatives of the humanists in our day gives no inkling of all this!"

In due place and time I will just touch upon that vexed question of classical education, but at present the question is as to what is meant by knowing the best which modern nations have thought and said. It is not knowing their belles-lettres merely which is meant. To know Italian belles-lettres is not to know Italy, and to know English belles-lettres is not to know England. Into knowing Italy and England there comes a great deal more, Galileo and Newton among it. The reproach of being a superficial humanism, a tincture of belles-lettres, may attach rightly enough to some other disciplines; but to the particular discipline recommended when I proposed knowing the best that has been thought and said in the world, it does not apply. In that best I certainly include what in modern times has been thought and said by the great observers and knowers of nature.

There is, therefore, really no question between Professor Huxley and me as to whether knowing the great results of the modern scientific study of nature is not required as a part of our culture, as well as knowing the products of literature and art. But to follow the processes by which those results are reached, ought, say the friends of physical science, to be made the staple of education for the bulk of mankind. And here there does arise a question between those whom Professor Huxley calls with playful sarcasm "the

Levites [14] of culture," and those whom the poor humanist is sometimes apt to regard as its Nebuchadnezzars.[15]

The great results of the scientific investigation of nature we are agreed upon knowing, but how much of our study are we bound to give to the processes by which those results are reached? The results have their visible bearing on human life. But all the processes, too, all the items of fact, by which those results are reached and established, are interesting. All knowledge is interesting to a wise man, and the knowledge of nature is interesting to all men. It is very interesting to know, that, from the albuminous white of the egg, the chick in the egg gets the materials for its flesh, bones, blood, and feathers; while, from the fatty yolk of the egg, it gets the heat and energy which enable it at length to break its shell and begin the world. It is less interesting, perhaps, but still it is interesting, to know that when a taper burns, the wax is converted into carbonic acid and water. Moreover, it is quite true that the habit of dealing with facts, which is given by the study of nature, is, as the friends of physical science praise it for being, an excellent discipline. The appeal, in the study of nature, is constantly to observation and experiment; not only is it said that the thing is so, but we can be made to see that it is so. Not only does a man tell us that when a taper burns the wax is converted into carbonic acid and water, as a man may tell us, if he likes, that Charon [16] is punting his ferryboat on the river Styx, or that Victor Hugo is a sublime poet, or Mr. Gladstone the most admirable of statesmen; but we are made to see that the conversion into carbonic acid and water does actually happen. This reality of natural knowledge it is, which makes the friends of physical science contrast it, as a knowledge of things, with the humanist's knowledge, which is, say they, a knowledge of words. And hence Professor Huxley is moved to lay it down that, "for the purpose

[14] The Levites were an ancient Hebrew group who helped the priests with the traditional rites and ceremonial customs. By employing this figure, what accusation does Huxley imply?

[15] Nebuchadnezzar was the Babylonian king who captured Jerusalem and enslaved the Hebrews. What does Arnold mean here?

[16] The creature who ferries the souls of the dead across the Styx into Hades.

of attaining real culture, an exclusively scientific education is at least as effectual as an exclusively literary education." And a certain president of the Section for Mechanical Science in the British Association [17] is, in Scripture phrase, "very bold," and declares that if a man, in his mental training, "has substituted literature and history for natural science, he has chosen the less useful alternative." But whether we go these lengths or not, we must all admit that in natural science the habit gained of dealing with facts is a most valuable discipline, and that everyone should have some experience of it.

More than this, however, is demanded by the reformers. It is proposed to make the training in natural science the main part of education, for the great majority of mankind at any rate. And here, I confess, I part company with the friends of physical science, with whom up to this point I have been agreeing. In differing from them, however, I wish to proceed with the utmost caution and diffidence.[18] The smallness of my own acquaintance with the disciplines of natural science is ever before my mind, and I am fearful of doing these disciplines an injustice. The ability and pugnacity of the partisans of natural science make them formidable persons to contradict. The tone of tentative inquiry, which befits a being of dim faculties and bounded knowledge, is the tone I would wish to take and not to depart from. At present it seems to me, that those who are for giving to natural knowledge, as they call it, the chief place in the education of the majority of mankind, leave one important thing out of their account: the constitution of human nature. But I put this forward on the strength of some facts not at all recondite, very far from it; facts capable of being stated in the simplest possible fashion, and to which, if I so state them, the man of science will, I am sure, be willing to allow their due weight.

Deny the facts altogether, I think, he hardly can. He can hardly deny that when we set ourselves to enumerate the powers [19] which go to the building up of human life, and say that they are the power of conduct, the power of intellect and knowledge, the power of beauty, and the power of social life and manners—he can hardly deny that this scheme, though drawn in rough and plain lines enough, and not pretending to scientific exactness, does yet give a fairly true representation of the matter. Human nature is built up by these powers; we have the need for them all. When we have rightly met and adjusted the claims of them all, we shall then be in a fair way for getting soberness and righteousness, with wisdom. This is evident enough, and the friends of physical science would admit it.

But perhaps they may not have sufficiently observed another thing: namely, that the several powers just mentioned are not isolated, but there is, in the generality of mankind, a perpetual tendency to relate them one to another in divers ways. With one such way of relating them I am particularly concerned now. Following our instinct for intellect and knowledge, we acquire pieces of knowledge; and presently, in the generality of men, there arises the desire to relate these pieces of knowledge to our sense for conduct, to our sense for beauty—and there is weariness and dissatisfaction if the desire is balked. Now in this desire lies, I think, the strength of that hold which letters have upon us.

All knowledge is, as I said just now, interesting; and even items of knowledge which from the nature of the case cannot well be related, but must stand isolated in our thoughts, have their interest. Even lists of exceptions have their interest. If we are studying Greek accents, it is interesting to know that *pais* and *pas*, and some other monosyllables of the same form of declension, do not take the circumflex upon the last syllable of the genitive plural, but vary, in this respect, from the common rule. If we are studying physiology, it is interesting to know that the pulmonary

[17] The British Association for the Advancement of Science.

[18] Is Arnold's professed "diffidence" here—and in the next three sentences—sincere, or is it argumentative strategy?

[19] From Arnold's essay *Sweetness and Light* it is clear that by "powers" he means "desires and capacities."

artery carries dark blood and the pulmonary vein carries bright blood, departing in this respect from the common rule for the division of labor between the veins and the arteries. But everyone knows how we seek naturally to combine the pieces of our knowledge together, to bring them under general rules, to relate them to principles; and how unsatisfactory and tiresome it would be to go on forever learning lists of exceptions, or accumulating items of fact which must stand isolated.

Well, that same need of relating our knowledge, which operates here within the sphere of our knowledge itself, we shall find operating, also, outside that sphere. We experience, as we go on learning and knowing,—the vast majority of us experience,—the need of relating what we have learned and known to the sense which we have in us for conduct, to the sense which we have in us for beauty.

A certain Greek prophetess of Mantineia in Arcadia, Diotima by name, once explained to the philosopher Socrates that love, and impulse, and bent of all kinds, is, in fact, nothing else but the desire in men that good should for ever be present to them.[20] This desire for good, Diotima assured Socrates, is our fundamental desire, of which fundamental desire every impulse in us is only some one particular form. And therefore this fundamental desire it is, I suppose,—this desire in men that good should be for ever present to them,—which acts in us when we feel the impulse for relating our knowledge to our sense for conduct and to our sense for beauty. At any rate, with men in general the instinct exists. Such is human nature. And the instinct, it will be admitted, is innocent, and human nature is preserved by our following the lead of its innocent instincts. Therefore, in seeking to gratify this instinct in question, we are following the instinct of self-preservation in humanity.

But, no doubt, some kinds of knowledge cannot be made to directly serve the instinct in question, cannot be directly related to the sense for beauty, to the sense for conduct. These are instrument-knowledges; they lead

[20] The myth of Diotima is recounted by Socrates in Plato's *Symposium*.

on to other knowledges, which can. A man who passes his life in instrument-knowledges is a specialist. They may be invaluable as instruments to something beyond, for those who have the gift thus to employ them; and they may be disciplines in themselves wherein it is useful for every one to have some schooling. But it is inconceivable that the generality of men should pass all their mental life with Greek accents or with formal logic. My friend Professor Sylvester, who is one of the first mathematicians in the world, holds transcendental doctrines as to the virtue of mathematics, but those doctrines are not for common men. In the very Senate House and heart of our English Cambridge I once ventured, though not without an apology for my profaneness, to hazard the opinion that for the majority of mankind a little of mathematics, even, goes a long way. Of course this is quite consistent with their being of immense importance as an instrument to something else; but it is the few who have the aptitude for thus using them, not the bulk of mankind.

The natural sciences do not, however, stand on the same footing with these instrument-knowledges. Experience shows us that the generality of men will find more interest in learning that, when a taper burns, the wax is converted into carbonic acid and water, or in learning the explanation of the phenomenon of dew, or in learning how the circulation of the blood is carried on, than they find in learning that the genitive plural of *pais* and *pas* does not take the circumflex on the termination. And one piece of natural knowledge is added to another, and others are added to that, and at last we come to propositions so interesting as Mr. Darwin's famous proposition that "our ancestor was a hairy quadruped furnished with a tail and pointed ears, probably arboreal in his habits."[21] Or we come to propositions of such reach and magnitude as those which Professor Huxley delivers, when he says that the notions of our forefathers about the beginning and the end of the world were all wrong, and that nature is the expression of a definite order with which nothing interferes.

[21] *The Descent of Man.*

Interesting, indeed, these results of science are, important they are, and we should all of us be acquainted with them. But what I now wish you to mark is, that we are still, when they are propounded to us and we receive them, we are still in the sphere of intellect and knowledge. And for the generality of men there will be found, I say, to arise, when they have duly taken in the proposition that their ancestor was "a hairy quadruped furnished with a tail and pointed ears, probably arboreal in his habits," there will be found to arise an invincible desire to relate this proposition to the sense in us for conduct, and to the sense in us for beauty. But this the men of science will not do for us, and will hardly even profess to do. They will give us other pieces of knowledge, other facts, about other animals and their ancestors, or about plants, or about stones, or about stars; and they may finally bring us to those great "general conceptions of the universe, which are forced upon us all," says Professor Huxley, "by the progress of physical science." But still it will be knowledge only which they give us; knowledge not put for us into relation with our sense for conduct, our sense for beauty, and touched with emotion by being so put; not thus put for us, and therefore, to the majority of mankind, after a certain while, unsatisfying, wearying.

Not to the born naturalist, I admit. But what do we mean by a born naturalist? We mean a man in whom the zeal for observing nature is so uncommonly strong and eminent, that it marks him off from the bulk of mankind. Such a man will pass his life happily in collecting natural knowledge and reasoning upon it, and will ask for nothing, or hardly anything, more. I have heard it said that the sagacious and admirable naturalist whom we lost not very long ago, Mr. Darwin, once owned to a friend that for his part he did not experience the necessity for two things which most men find so necessary to them— religion and poetry; science and the domestic affections, he thought, were enough. To a born naturalist, I can well understand that this should seem so. So absorbing is his occupation with nature, so strong his love for his occupation, that he goes on acquiring natural knowledge and reasoning upon it, and has little time or inclination for thinking about getting it related to the desire in man for conduct, the desire in man for beauty. He relates it to them for himself as he goes along, so far as he feels the need; and he draws from the domestic affections all the additional solace necessary. But then Darwins are extremely rare. Another great and admirable master of natural knowledge, Faraday,[22] was a Sandemanian. That is to say, he related his knowledge to his instinct for conduct and to his instinct for beauty, by the aid of that respectable Scottish sectary, Robert Sandeman. And so strong, in general, is the demand of religion and poetry to have their share in a man, to associate themselves with his knowing, and to relieve and rejoice it, that, probably, for one man amongst us with the disposition to do as Darwin did in this respect, there are at least fifty with the disposition to do as Faraday.

Education lays hold upon us, in fact, by satisfying this demand. Professor Huxley holds up to scorn medieval education, with its neglect of the knowledge of nature, its poverty even of literary studies, its formal logic devoted to "showing how and why that which the Church said was true must be true." But the great medieval universities were not brought into being, we may be sure, by the zeal for giving a jejune [23] and contemptible education. Kings have been their nursing fathers, and queens have been their nursing mothers, but not for this. The medieval universities came into being because the supposed knowledge, delivered by Scripture and the Church, so deeply engaged men's hearts, by so simply, easily, and powerfully relating itself to their desire for conduct, their desire for beauty. All other knowledge was dominated by this supposed knowledge and was subordinated to it, because of the surpassing strength of the hold which it gained upon the

---

[22] Distinguished chemist and physicist, who belonged to the Sandemanian sect of Protestantism founded by the Scottish clergyman Robert Sandeman.

[23] Empty, vapid.

affections of men, by allying itself profoundly with their sense for conduct, their sense for beauty.

But now, says Professor Huxley, conceptions of the universe fatal to the notions held by our forefathers have been forced upon us by physical science. Grant to him that they are thus fatal, that the new conceptions must and will soon become current everywhere, and that everyone will finally perceive them to be fatal to the beliefs of our forefathers. The need of humane letters, as they are truly called, because they serve the paramount desire in men that good should be forever present to them—the need of humane letters, to establish a relation between the new conceptions, and our instinct for beauty, our instinct for conduct, is only the more visible. The Middle Ages could do without humane letters, as it could do without the study of nature, because its supposed knowledge was made to engage its emotions so powerfully. Grant that the supposed knowledge disappears, its power of being made to engage the emotions will of course disappear along with it—but the emotions themselves, and their claim to be engaged and satisfied, will remain. Now if we find by experience that humane letters have an undeniable power of engaging the emotions, the importance of humane letters in a man's training becomes not less, but greater, in proportion to the success of modern science in extirpating what it calls "medieval thinking."

Have humane letters, then, have poetry and eloquence, the power here attributed to them of engaging the emotions, and do they exercise it? And if they have it and exercise it, how do they exercise it, so as to exert an influence upon man's sense for conduct, his sense for beauty? Finally, even if they both can and do exert an influence upon the senses in question, how are they to relate to them the results—the modern results—of natural science? All these questions may be asked. First, have poetry and eloquence the power of calling out the emotions? The appeal is to experience. Experience shows that for the vast majority of men, for mankind in general, they have the power. Next, do they exercise

it? They do. But then, how do they exercise it so as to affect man's sense for conduct, his sense for beauty? And this is perhaps a case for applying the Preacher's words: "Though a man labor to seek it out, yet he shall not find it; yea, farther, though a wise man think to know it, yet shall he not be able to find it." [24] Why should it be one thing, in its effect upon the emotions, to say, "Patience is a virtue," and quite another thing, in its effect upon the emotions, to say with Homer,

τλητὸν γὰρ Μοῖραι θυμὸν θέσαν ἀνθρώποισιν

"for an enduring heart have the destinies appointed to the children of men"? [25] Why should it be one thing, in its effect upon the emotions, to say with the philosopher Spinoza, *Felicitas in eo consistit quod homo suum esse conservare potest*—"Man's happiness consists in his being able to preserve his own essence," [26] and quite another thing, in its effect upon the emotions, to say with the Gospel, "What is a man advantaged, if he gain the whole world, and lose himself, forfeit himself?" [27] How does this difference of effect arise? [28] I cannot tell, and I am not much concerned to know; the important thing is that it does arise, and that we can profit by it. But how, finally, are poetry and eloquence to exercise the power of relating the modern results of natural science to man's instinct for conduct, his instinct for beauty? And here again I answer that I do not know how they will exercise it, but that they can and will exercise it I am sure. I do not mean that modern philosophical poets and modern philosophical moralists are to come and relate for us, in express terms, the results of modern scientific research to our instinct for conduct, our instinct for beauty. But I mean that we shall find, as a matter of experience, if we know the best that has been thought and uttered in the world, we

[24] Eccl. 8:17.
[25] The *Iliad*.
[26] The *Ethics*.
[27] Luke 9:25. What distinction is Arnold making in the foregoing pairs of quotations?
[28] Is Arnold "ducking" the questions in the next three sentences—or are the answers unnecessary to his argument?

shall find that the art and poetry and eloquence of men who lived, perhaps, long ago, who had the most limited natural knowledge, who had the most erroneous conceptions about many important matters, we shall find that this art, and poetry, and eloquence, have in fact not only the power of refreshing and delighting us, they have also the power,—such is the strength and worth, in essentials, of their authors' criticism of life,—they have a fortifying, and elevating, and quickening, and suggestive power, capable of wonderfully helping us to relate the results of modern science to our need for conduct, our need for beauty. Homer's conceptions of the physical universe were, I imagine, grotesque; but really, under the shock of hearing from modern science that "the world is not subordinated to man's use, and that man is not the cynosure of things terrestrial," I could, for my own part, desire no better comfort than Homer's line which I quoted just now,

τλητὸν γὰρ Μοῖραι θυμὸν θέσαν ἀνθρώποισιν—

"for an enduring heart have the destinies appointed to the children of men"!

And the more that men's minds are cleared, the more that the results of science are frankly accepted, the more that poetry and eloquence come to be received and studied as what in truth they really are—the criticism of life by gifted men, alive and active with extraordinary power at an unusual number of points—so much the more will the value of humane letters, and of art also, which is an utterance having a like kind of power with theirs, be felt and acknowledged, and their place in education be secured.

Let us therefore, all of us, avoid indeed as much as possible any invidious comparison between the merits of humane letters, as means of education, and the merits of the natural sciences. But when some President of a Section for Mechanical Science insists on making the comparison, and tells us that "he who in his training has substituted literature and history for natural science has chosen the less useful alternative," let us make answer to him that the student of humane letters only, will, at least, know also the great general conceptions brought in by modern physical science; for science, as Professor Huxley says, forces them upon us all. But the student of the natural sciences only, will, by our very hypothesis, know nothing of humane letters; not to mention that in setting himself to be perpetually accumulating natural knowledge, he sets himself to do what only specialists have in general the gift of doing genially.[29] And so he will probably be unsatisfied, or at any rate incomplete, and even more incomplete than the student of humane letters only.

I once mentioned in a school-report, how a young man in one of our English training colleges having to paraphrase the passage in *Macbeth* beginning,

Canst thou not minister to a mind diseased?

turned this line into, "Can you not wait upon the lunatic?" And I remarked what a curious state of things it would be, if every pupil of our national schools knew, let us say, that the moon is two thousand one hundred and sixty miles in diameter, and thought at the same time that a good paraphrase for

Canst thou not minister to a mind diseased?

was, "Can you not wait upon the lunatic?" If one is driven to choose, I think I would rather have a young person ignorant about the moon's diameter, but aware that "Can you not wait upon the lunatic?" is bad, than a young person whose education had been such as to manage things the other way.[30]

Or to go higher than the pupils of our national schools. I have in my mind's eye a member of our British Parliament who comes to travel here in America, who afterwards relates his travels, and who shows a really masterly knowledge of the geology of this great country and of its mining capabilities but who ends by gravely suggesting that the United States should borrow a prince from our Royal Family, and should make him their king, and should create a House of Lords of great landed proprietors after the pattern of ours; and then America, he thinks, would

[29] Naturally; according to their genius.
[30] What has been Arnold's point in this paragraph?

have her future happily and perfectly secured. Surely, in this case, the President of the Section for Mechanical Science would himself hardly say that our member of Parliament, by concentrating himself upon geology and mineralogy, and so on, and not attending to literature and history, had "chosen the more useful alternative."

If then there is to be separation and option between humane letters on the one hand, and the natural sciences on the other, the great majority of mankind, all who have not exceptional and overpowering aptitudes for the study of nature, would do well, I cannot but think, to choose to be educated in humane letters rather than in the natural sciences. Letters will call out their being at more points, will make them live more.

I said that before I ended I would just touch on the question of classical education, and I will keep my word. Even if literature is to retain a large place in our education, yet Latin and Greek, say the friends of progress, will certainly have to go. Greek is the grand offender in the eyes of these gentlemen. The attackers of the established course of study think that against Greek, at any rate, they have irresistible arguments. Literature may perhaps be needed in education, they say; but why on earth should it be Greek literature? Why not French or German? Nay, "has not an Englishman models in his own literature of every kind of excellence?" [31] As before, it is not on any weak pleadings of my own that I rely for convincing the gainsayers; it is on the constitution of human nature itself, and on the instinct of self-preservation in humanity. The instinct for beauty is set in human nature, as surely as the instinct for knowledge is set there, or the instinct for conduct. If the instinct for beauty is served by Greek literature and art as it is served by no other literature and art, we may trust to the instinct of self-preservation in humanity for keeping Greek as part of our culture. We may trust to it for even making the study of Greek more prevalent than it is now. Greek will come, I hope, some day to be studied more rationally than at present, but it will be increasingly

[31] Huxley, *Science and Culture*.

studied as men increasingly feel the need in them for beauty, and how powerfully Greek art and Greek literature can serve this need. Women will again study Greek, as Lady Jane Grey [32] did; I believe that in that chain of forts, with which the fair host of the Amazons [33] are now engirdling our English universities, I find that here in America, in colleges like Smith College in Massachusetts, and Vassar College in the state of New York, and in the happy families of the mixed universities out west, they are studying it already.

Defuit una mihi symmetria prisca—"The antique symmetry was the one thing wanting to me," said Leonardo da Vinci, and he was an Italian. I will not presume to speak for the Americans, but I am sure that, in the Englishman, the want of this admirable symmetry of the Greeks is a thousand times more great and crying than in any Italian. The results of the want show themselves most glaringly, perhaps, in our architecture, but they show themselves, also, in all our art. Fit details strictly combined, in view of a large general result nobly conceived; that is just the beautiful *symmetria prisca* of the Greeks, and it is just where we English fail, where all our art fails. Striking ideas we have, and well-executed details we have; but that high symmetry which, with satisfying and delightful effect, combines them, we seldom or never have. The glorious beauty of the Acropolis [34] at Athens did not come from single fine things stuck about on that hill, a statue here, a gateway there; no, it arose from all things being perfectly combined for a supreme total effect. What must not an Englishman feel about our deficiencies in this respect, as the sense for beauty, whereof this symmetry is an essential element, awakens and strengthens within him! what will not one day be his respect and desire for Greece and its *symmetria prisca,* when the scales drop from his eyes as he walks the London

[32] Descendant of Henry VII and queen of England for nine days in 1553.
[33] Ancient female warriors. Arnold is referring to the rise of women's colleges in England.
[34] The hill on which the Parthenon and other stately Athenian buildings were located.

streets, and he sees such a lesson in meanness as the Strand,[35] for instance, in its true deformity! But here we are coming to our friend Mr. Ruskin's province,[36] and I will not intrude upon it, for he is its very sufficient guardian.

And so we at last find, it seems, we find flowing in favor of the humanities the natural and necessary stream of things, which seemed against them when we started. The "hairy quadruped furnished with a tail and pointed ears, probably arboreal in his habits," this good fellow carried hidden in his nature, apparently, something destined to develop into a necessity for humane letters. Nay, more; we seem finally to be even led to the further conclusion that our hairy ancestor carried in his nature, also, a necessity for Greek.

And therefore, to say the truth, I cannot really think that humane letters are in much actual danger of being thrust out from their leading place in education, in spite of the array of authorities against them at this moment. So long as human nature is what it is, their attractions will remain irresistible. As with Greek, so with letters generally: they will some day come, we may hope, to be studied more rationally, but they will not lose their place. What will happen will rather be that there will be crowded into education other matters besides, far too many; there will be, perhaps, a period of unsettlement and confusion and false tendency; but letters will not in the end lose their leading place. If they lose it for a time, they will get it back again. We shall be brought back to them by our wants and aspirations. And a poor humanist

may possess his soul in patience, neither strive nor cry, admit the energy and brilliancy of the partisans of physical science, and their present favor with the public, to be far greater than his own, and still have a happy faith that the nature of things works silently on behalf of the studies which he loves, and that, while we shall all have to acquaint ourselves with the great results reached by modern science, and to give ourselves as much training in its disciplines as we can conveniently carry, yet the majority of men will always require humane letters; and so much the more, as they have the more and the greater results of science to relate to the need in man for conduct, and to the need in him for beauty.

(1885)

STUDY AIDS: 1. This essay is largely a reply to Huxley's *Science and Culture,* which argued that science should be the staple of education. On what point does Arnold agree with Huxley? On what point does he disagree? Which one do you think has the better of the argument, and why?

2. What is Arnold's distinction between "belles-lettres" and "literature"? Is it a valid distinction? How does it serve his argument? Does Arnold have any use for belles-lettres?

3. State the central idea of Arnold's essay in a single sentence. Do you agree with it? Are we in danger today of placing too much emphasis on scientific technology, vocational training, and intense specialization, and not enough on "literature" in Arnold's sense of the term? Are Arnold's arguments for a literary education and even for the study of the Greek classics applicable today?

4. Compare this essay with Newman's discussion of a liberal education (pp. 736–748). How are the approaches of the two men alike, how different?

---

[35] A busy London street.
[36] John Ruskin, the Victorian essayist and critic, was the author of several books on the relation of aesthetics to social and economic problems.

Dante Gabriel Rossetti
(1828–1882)

THE PRE-RAPHAELITE MOVEMENT, LIKE THE OXFORD MOVEMENT, WAS A COUNTERCURRENT in the broad stream of nineteenth-century thought. A group of painters, dissatisfied with the conventionalism of Victorian art, rebelled against the prevailing modes and went back to the artists before Raphael for their inspiration. In them they found "a manifest emotional sincerity," a loving eye for detail, a grace and decorative charm, and a combination of child-like freshness with spiritual depth, that prompted their enthusiasm and their discipleship.

The leader of this movement was Dante Gabriel Rossetti, a painter as well as a poet, who brought to his poetry a number of the qualities expressed in his visual art. His early schooling (the best of it at home under the supervision of his scholarly Italian father) was followed by training in various art schools, where he grew increasingly impatient with the conventionalized ideals of art. In 1848 he and some fellow painters of kindred mind expressed their dissatisfaction by forming the Pre-Raphaelite Brotherhood and by publishing, two years later, a magazine called *The Germ,* in which they presented their views on art and literature. In this periodical appeared some of Rossetti's early poems.

Also about this time began Rossetti's tragic romance with Elizabeth Siddal, a beautiful, talented model whom he finally married in 1860 and who died (possibly by suicide) two years later. In morbid despair and self-reproach Rossetti ordered some of his manuscript poems to be buried with her, but was persuaded to have them dug up in 1870, when they were published.

Rossetti's later life was unhappy. The poet quarreled with a critic who condemned Rossetti as the leader of "the Fleshly School of Poetry," he suffered feelings of persecution, and his life was shortened by addiction to drugs. But his fame as painter and poet continued to grow; and the year before his death he put out a new edition of his 1870 *Poems* and a suc-cessful volume of *Ballads and Sonnets* containing, among other fine pieces, his completed sonnet series, *The House of Life.*

In Rossetti the poet and the painter merge. In his painting is the soul of the poet; in his poetry is the eye of the painter. But there is more to Rossetti's poetry than careful visual detail, high coloration, and decorative imagery. In his best verse, the poet's luxuriance and emotionalism are subject to an austere intellectual control, and his sensuousness is tempered by deep spirituality.

The Blessed Damozel

This graphic poem, oscillating delicately between nearness and distance, is a haunting combina-tion of the childlike and the mystical. Its theme was suggested by Poe's *The Raven:* "I saw at once," said Rossetti, "that Poe had done the utmost it was possible to do with the grief of the lover on earth, and I determined to reverse the conditions and give utterance to the yearnings of the loved one in heaven."

The blessed damozel[1] leaned out
  From the gold bar of heaven;
Her eyes were deeper than the depth
  Of waters stilled at even;
She had three lilies in her hand,   5
  And the stars in her hair were seven.[2]

Her robe, ungirt from clasp to hem,
  No wrought flowers did adorn,
But a white rose of Mary's gift,
  For service meetly[3] worn;   10
Her hair that lay along her back
  Was yellow like ripe corn.

Herseemed[4] she scarce had been a day
  One of God's choristers;
The wonder was not yet quite gone   15
  From that still look of hers;
Albeit, to them she left, her day
  Had counted as ten years.

(To one, it is ten years of years.[5]
  . . . Yet now, and in this place,   20
Surely she leaned o'er me—her hair
  Fell all about my face. . . .
Nothing: the autumn fall of leaves.
  The whole year sets apace.)

It was the rampart of God's house   25
  That she was standing on;
By God built over the sheer depth
  The which is space begun;
So high, that looking downward thence
  She scarce could see the sun.   30

It lies in heaven, across the flood
  Of ether, as a bridge.
Beneath, the tides of day and night
  With flame and darkness ridge
The void, as low as where this earth   35
  Spins like a fretful midge.[6]

Around her, lovers, newly met
  'Mid deathless love's acclaims,
Spoke evermore among themselves
  Their heart-remembered names;   40
And the souls mounting up to God[7]
  Went by her like thin flames.

And still she bowed herself and stooped
  Out of the circling charm;
Until her bosom must have made   45
  The bar she leaned on warm,
And the lilies lay as if asleep
  Along her bended arm.

From the fixed place of heaven she saw
  Time,[8] like a pulse, shake fierce   50
Through all the worlds. Her gaze still strove
  Within the gulf to pierce
Its path; and now she spoke as when
  The stars sang in their spheres.[9]

The sun was gone now; the curled moon   55
  Was like a little feather
Fluttering far down the gulf; and now
  She spoke through the still weather.
Her voice was like the voice the stars
  Had when they sang together.   60

(Ah sweet! Even now, in that bird's song,
  Strove not her accents there,
Fain to be hearkened? When those bells
  Possessed the mid-day air,
Strove not her steps to reach my side   65
  Down all the echoing stair?)

"I wish that he were come to me,
  For he will come," she said.
"Have I not prayed in heaven?—on earth,
  Lord, Lord, has he not prayed?   70
Are not two prayers a perfect strength?
  And shall I feel afraid?

[1] Damsel; lady.
[2] What effect is produced by numbering the lilies and the stars?
[3] Appropriately.
[4] It seemed to her.
[5] The words—or thoughts—of the earthly lover are given in the parenthetical portions. What effect does this device have?
[6] Small gnat or fly.

[7] The imagery of ll.41–42 is reminiscent of medieval painting.
[8] Time, like space in l. 28, is regarded as a purely human conception. God and his world are timeless and spaceless.
[9] Rossetti has combined Job 38:7 ("When the morning stars sang together") and the ancient belief in the music of the spheres.

"When round his head the aureole clings,
  And he is clothed in white,
I'll take his hand and go with him   75
  To the deep wells of light;
As unto a stream we will step down,
  And bathe there in God's sight.

"We two will stand beside that shrine,
  Occult, withheld, untrod,   80
Whose lamps are stirred continually
  With prayers sent up to God;
And see our old prayers, granted, melt
  Each like a little cloud.

"We two will lie in the shadow of   85
  That living mystic tree [10]
Within whose secret growth the Dove [11]
  Is sometimes felt to be,
While every leaf that His plumes touch
  Saith His name audibly.   90

"And I myself will teach to him,
  I myself, lying so,
The songs I sing here; which his voice
  Shall pause in, hushed and slow,
And find some knowledge at each pause,   95
  Or some new thing to know."

(Alas! We two, we two, thou say'st!
  Yea, one wast thou with me
That once of old. But shall God lift
  To endless unity   100
The soul whose likeness with thy soul
  Was but its love for thee?)

"We two," she said, "will seek the groves
  Where the lady Mary is,
With her five handmaidens, whose names   105
  Are five sweet symphonies,
Cecily, Gertrude, Magdalen,
  Margaret, and Rosalys. [12]

"Circlewise sit they, with bound locks
  And foreheads garlanded;   110
Into the fine cloth, white like flame
  Weaving the golden thread,

To fashion the birth-robes for them
  Who are just born, being dead.

"He shall fear, haply, and be dumb: 115
  Then will I lay my cheek
To his, and tell about our love,
  Not once abashed or weak;
And the dear Mother will approve
  My pride, and let me speak.   120

"Herself shall bring us, hand in hand,
  To Him round whom all souls
Kneel, the clear-ranged unnumbered heads
  Bowed with their aureoles;
And angels meeting us shall sing   125
  To their citherns and citoles. [13]

"There will I ask of Christ the Lord
  Thus much for him and me:—
Only to live as once on earth
  With love,—only to be,   130
As then awhile, forever now
  Together, I and he."

She gazed and listened and then said,
  Less sad of speech than mild,—
"All this is when he comes." She ceased. 135
  The light thrilled towards her, filled
With angels in strong level flight. [14]
  Her eyes prayed, and she smiled.

(I saw her smile.) But soon their path
  Was vague in distant spheres: 140
And then she cast her arms along
  The golden barriers,
And laid her face between her hands,
  And wept. (I heard her tears.)
(1847; 1850)

STUDY AIDS: 1. What are the medieval elements in the poem? In what ways does the author reveal himself to be a painter?

2. What is the difference between the thoughts of the lover and the utterances of the blessed damozel? What is her hope? What is

[10] The tree of life, as described in Rev. 22:2.
[11] Symbol of the Holy Spirit.
[12] These five names, selected for their musical sounds, are the names of Christian saints.

[13] Citherns and citoles are medieval musical instruments.
[14] How is the image of the flying angels appropriate to the smile, and then to the tears, of the blessed damozel?

his reaction to her expectations? Why does the poem end with her tears? Why is she sad?

3. One critic says that "it is the combination of vastness and nearness in the poem which lends it an incomparable charm." Point to the images that give the effect of vastness, and those which give the effect of nearness. How does Rossetti achieve a childlike quality in the poem? How is the union of the sensuous and the spiritual achieved?

My Sister's Sleep [1]

She fell asleep on Christmas Eve:
  At length the long-ungranted shade
  Of weary eyelids overweighed
The pain nought else might yet relieve.

Our mother, who had leaned all day   5
  Over the bed from chime to chime,
  Then raised herself for the first time,
And as she sat her down, did pray.

Her little work-table was spread
  With work to finish. For the glare   10
  Made by her candle, she had care
To work some distance from the bed.

Without, there was a cold moon up,
  Of winter radiance sheer and thin;
  The hollow halo it was in   15
Was like an icy crystal cup.

Through the small room, with subtle sound
  Of flame, by vents the fireshine drove
  And reddened. In its dim alcove
The mirror shed a clearness round.   20

I had been sitting up some nights,
  And my tired mind felt weak and blank;
  Like a sharp strengthening wine it drank
The stillness and the broken lights.

Twelve struck. That sound, by dwindling
    years [2]   25
  Heard in each hour, crept off; and then
  The ruffled silence spread again,
Like water that a pebble stirs.

Our mother rose from where she sat:
  Her needles, as she laid them down,   30

Met lightly, and her silken gown
Settled: no other noise than that.

"Glory unto the Newly Born!"
  So, as said angels, she did say;
  Because we were in Christmas Day,   35
Though it would still be long till morn.

Just then in the room over us
  There was a pushing back of chairs,
  As some who had sat unawares
So late, now heard the hour, and rose.   40

With anxious softly-stepping haste
  Our mother went where Margaret lay,
  Fearing the sounds o'erhead—should they
Have broken her long watched-for rest!

She stooped an instant, calm, and turned; 45
  But suddenly turned back again;
  And all her features seemed in pain
With woe, and her eyes gazed and yearned.

For my part, I but hid my face,
  And held my breath, and spoke no
    word: 50
  There was none spoken; but I heard
The silence for a little space.

Our mother bowed herself and wept:
  And both my arms fell, and I said,
  "God knows I knew that she was dead." 55
And there, all white, my sister slept.

Then kneeling, upon Christmas morn
  A little after twelve o'clock,
  We said, ere the first quarter struck,
"Christ's blessing on the newly born!"   60
(1847; 1850)

[1] The incident recounted in this poem is imaginary.
[2] Old people, because they are light sleepers or because they are so conscious of the passing of time, are said to hear each stroke of the hour.

STUDY AIDS: 1. What means has Rossetti used to prevent this poem from being over-sentimental?

2. As in *The Blessed Damozel*, can you find in this poem examples of "the painter's eye"?

Sister Helen

Sister Helen is based upon the old superstition that burning or injuring the image of a person while performing certain magical rites will bring upon him suffering or death. As Helen melts the waxen image of her faithless lover, Keith of Ewern (l. 87), she carries on a chilling dialogue with her little brother.

"Why did you melt your waxen man,
　　　Sister Helen?
To-day is the third since you began."
"The time was long, yet the time ran,
　　　Little brother." 5
　　　(*O Mother, Mary Mother,*
Three days to-day, between Hell and
Heaven!)

"But if you have done your work aright,
　　　Sister Helen,
You'll let me play, for you said I might." 10
"Be very still in your play to-night,
　　　Little brother."
　　　(*O Mother, Mary Mother,*
Third night, to-night, between Hell and
Heaven!)

"You said it must melt ere vesper-bell, 15
　　　Sister Helen;
If now it be molten, all is well."
"Even so,—nay, peace! you cannot tell,
　　　Little brother."
　　　(*O Mother, Mary Mother,* 20
Oh what is this, between Hell and
Heaven?)

"Oh the waxen knave was plump to-day,
　　　Sister Helen;
How like dead folk he has dropped away!"
"Nay now, of the dead what can you say, 25
　　　Little brother?"
　　　(*O Mother, Mary Mother,*
What of the dead, between Hell and
Heaven?)

"See, see, the sunken pile of wood,
　　　Sister Helen, 30
Shines through the thinned wax red as
　　blood!"

"Nay now, when looked you yet on blood,
　　　Little brother?"
　　　(*O Mother, Mary Mother,*
How pale she is, between Hell and
Heaven!) 35

"Now close your eyes, for they're sick and
　　sore,
　　　Sister Helen,
And I'll play without the gallery door."
"Ay, let me rest,—I'll lie on the floor,
　　　Little brother." 40
　　　(*O Mother, Mary Mother,*
What rest to-night, between Hell and
Heaven?)

"Here high up in the balcony,
　　　Sister Helen,
The moon flies face to face with me." 45
"Ay, look and say whatever you see,
　　　Little brother."
　　　(*O Mother, Mary Mother,*
What sight to-night, between Hell and
Heaven?)

"Outside it's merry in the wind's wake, 50
　　　Sister Helen;
In the shaken trees the chill stars shake."
"Hush, heard you a horse-tread as you spake,
　　　Little brother?"
　　　(*O Mother, Mary Mother,* 55
What sound to-night, between Hell and
Heaven?)

"I hear a horse-tread, and I see,
　　　Sister Helen,
Three horsemen that ride terribly."
"Little brother, whence come the three, 60
　　　Little brother?"
　　　(*O Mother, Mary Mother,*
Whence should they come, between Hell and
Heaven?)

"They come by the hill-verge from Boyne
  Bar,[1]
        Sister Helen,   65
And one draws nigh, but two are afar."
"Look, look, do you know them who they are,
  Little brother?"
(O Mother, Mary Mother,
Who should they be, between Hell and
  Heaven?)   70

"Oh, it's Keith of Eastholm rides so fast,
        Sister Helen,
For I know the white mane on the blast."
"The hour has come, has come at last,
  Little brother!"   75
(O Mother, Mary Mother,
Her hour at last, between Hell and Heaven!)

"He has made a sign and called 'Halloo!'
        Sister Helen,
And he says that he would speak with
  you."   80
"Oh tell him I fear the frozen dew,
  Little brother."
(O Mother, Mary Mother,
Why laughs she thus, between Hell and
  Heaven?)

"The wind is loud, but I hear him cry,   85
        Sister Helen,
That Keith of Ewern's like to die."
"And he and thou, and thou and I,
  Little brother."
(O Mother, Mary Mother,   90
And they and we, between Hell and
  Heaven!)

"Three days ago, on his marriage-morn,
        Sister Helen,
He sickened, and lies since then forlorn."
"For bridegroom's side is the bride a thorn, 95
  Little brother?"
(O Mother, Mary Mother,
Cold bridal cheer, between Hell and
  Heaven!)

"Three days and nights he has lain abed,
        Sister Helen,   100
And he prays in torment to be dead."

[1] A sandbar at the mouth of the Boyne River,
in Ireland.

"The thing may chance, if he have prayed,
  Little brother!"
(O Mother, Mary Mother,
If he have prayed, between Hell and
  Heaven!)   105

"But he has not ceased to cry to-day,
        Sister Helen,
That you should take your curse away."
"My prayer was heard,—he need but pray,
  Little brother!"   110
(O Mother, Mary Mother,
Shall God not hear, between Hell and
  Heaven?)

"But he says, till you take back your ban,[2]
        Sister Helen,
His soul would pass, yet never can."   115
"Nay then, shall I slay a living man,
  Little brother?"
(O Mother, Mary Mother,
A living soul, between Hell and Heaven!)

"But he calls forever on your name,   120
        Sister Helen,
And says that he melts before a flame."
"My heart for his pleasure fared the same,
  Little brother."
(O Mother, Mary Mother,   125
Fire at the heart, between Hell and Heaven!)

"Here's Keith of Westholm riding fast,
        Sister Helen,
For I know the white plume on the blast."
"The hour, the sweet hour I forecast,   130
  Little brother!"
(O Mother, Mary Mother,
Is the hour sweet, between Hell and
  Heaven?)

"He stops to speak, and he stills his horse,
        Sister Helen;   135
But his words are drowned in the wind's
  course."
"Nay hear, nay hear, you must hear perforce,
  Little brother!"
(O Mother, Mary Mother,
What word now heard, between Hell and
  Heaven?)   140

[2] Curse.

"Oh he says that Keith of Ewern's cry,
      Sister Helen,
Is ever to see you ere he die."
"In all that his soul sees, there am I,
      Little brother!"   145
    (*O Mother, Mary Mother,*
The soul's one sight, between Hell and
   Heaven!)

"He sends a ring and a broken coin,[3]
      Sister Helen,
And bids you mind the banks of Boyne." 150
"What else he broke will he ever join,
      Little brother?"
    (*O Mother, Mary Mother,*
No, never joined, between Hell and
   Heaven!)

"He yields you these and craves full fain, 155
      Sister Helen,
You pardon him in his mortal pain."
"What else he took will he give again,
      Little brother?"
    (*O Mother, Mary Mother,*   160
Not twice to give, between Hell and
   Heaven!)

"He calls your name in an agony,
      Sister Helen,
That even dead love must weep to see."
"Hate, born of love, is blind as he,   165
      Little brother!"
    (*O Mother, Mary Mother,*
Love turned to hate, between Hell and
   Heaven!)

"Oh it's Keith of Keith now that rides fast,
      Sister Helen,   170
For I know the white hair on the blast."
"The short, short hour will soon be past,
      Little brother!"
    (*O Mother, Mary Mother,*
Will soon be past, between Hell and
   Heaven!)   175

"He looks at me and he tries to speak,
      Sister Helen,
But oh! his voice is sad and weak!"

"What here should the mighty baron seek,
      Little brother?"   180
    (*O Mother, Mary Mother,*
Is this the end, between Hell and Heaven?)

"Oh his son still cries, if you forgive,
      Sister Helen,
The body dies, but the soul shall live."   185
"Fire [4] shall forgive me as I forgive,
      Little brother!"
    (*O Mother, Mary Mother,*
As she forgives, between Hell and Heaven!)

"Oh he prays you, as his heart would rive, 190
      Sister Helen,
To save his dear son's soul alive."
"Fire cannot slay it, it shall thrive,
      Little brother!"
    (*O Mother, Mary Mother,*   195
Alas, alas, between Hell and Heaven!)

"He cries to you, kneeling in the road,
      Sister Helen,
To go with him for the love of God!"
"The way is long to his son's abode,   200
      Little brother."
    (*O Mother, Mary Mother,*
The way is long, between Hell and Heaven!)

"A lady's here, by a dark steed brought,
      Sister Helen,   205
So darkly clad, I saw her not."
"See her now or never see aught,
      Little brother!"
    (*O Mother, Mary Mother,*
What more to see, between Hell and
   Heaven?)   210

"Her hood falls back, and the moon shines
   fair,
      Sister Helen,
On the Lady of Ewern's golden hair."
"Blest hour of my power and her despair,
      Little brother!"   215
    (*O Mother, Mary Mother,*
Hour blest and banned, between Hell and
   Heaven!)

[3] Each of the two lovers had kept half of a broken coin as a pledge.

[4] Sister Helen anticipates being burned at the stake for witchcraft.

"Pale, pale her cheeks, that in pride did glow,
        Sister Helen,
'Neath the bridal-wreath three days ago." 220
"One morn for pride and three days for woe,
        Little brother!"
        (*O Mother, Mary Mother,*
Three days, three nights, between Hell and
Heaven!)

"Her clasped hands stretch from her bending
        head,   225
                Sister Helen;
With the loud wind's wail her sobs are wed."
"What wedding-strains hath her bridal-bed,
        Little brother?"
        (*O Mother, Mary Mother,*   230
What strain but death's, between Hell and
Heaven?)

"She may not speak, she sinks in a swoon,
        Sister Helen,—
She lifts her lips and gasps on the moon."
"Oh! might I but hear her soul's blithe
        tune,   235
        Little brother!"
        (*O Mother, Mary Mother,*
Her woe's dumb cry, between Hell and
Heaven!)

"They've caught her to Westholm's saddle-
        bow,
                Sister Helen,   240
And her moonlit hair gleams white in its
        flow."
"Let it turn whiter than winter snow,
        Little brother!"
        (*O Mother, Mary Mother,*
Woe-withered gold, between Hell and
Heaven!)   245

"O Sister Helen, you heard the bell,
        Sister Helen;
More loud than the vesper-chime it fell."
"No vesper-chime, but a dying knell,
        Little brother!"   250
        (*O Mother, Mary Mother,*
His dying knell, between Hell and Heaven!)

"Alas! but I fear the heavy sound,
        Sister Helen;

Is it in the sky or in the ground?"   255
"Say, have they turned their horses round,
        Little brother?"
        (*O Mother, Mary Mother,*
What would she more, between Hell and
Heaven?)

"They have raised the old man from his
        knee,   260
                Sister Helen,
And they ride in silence hastily."
"More fast the naked soul doth flee,
        Little brother!"
        (*O Mother, Mary Mother,*   265
The naked soul, between Hell and Heaven!)

"Flank to flank are the three steeds gone,
        Sister Helen,
But the lady's dark steed goes alone."
"And lonely her bridegroom's soul hath
        flown,   270
        Little brother."
        (*O Mother, Mary Mother,*
The lonely ghost, between Hell and
Heaven!)

"Oh the wind is sad in the iron chill,
        Sister Helen,   275
And weary sad they look by the hill."
"But Keith of Ewern's sadder still,
        Little brother!"
        (*O Mother, Mary Mother,*
Most sad of all, between Hell and
Heaven!)   280

"See, see, the wax has dropped from its place,
        Sister Helen,
And the flames are winning up apace!"
"Yet here they burn but for a space,
        Little brother!"   285
        (*O Mother, Mary Mother,*
Here for a space, between Hell and Heaven!)

"Ah! what white thing at the door has
        crossed,
                Sister Helen,
Ah! what is this that sighs in the frost?" 290
"A soul that's lost as mine is lost,
        Little brother!"
        (*O Mother, Mary Mother,*

Lost, lost, all lost, between Hell and
  Heaven!)
(1853)

STUDY AIDS: 1. What does the poem gain
by being cast in dialogue form? What characteristics of Sister Helen emerge from the dialogue? What characteristics of the little boy?
What is the contrast between the two?
  2. What effect is produced by the refrain
(italicized in parentheses)? Is there any connection between this refrain and the evil ritualism

of Helen's witchcraft? Does the refrain get in
the way of the story?
  3. Who comes to plead with Helen? What
is the effect of having the little boy report to
his sister what is said and done? How do Helen's
comments in this section contrast with his? At
what point is the climax of her revenge? What
is the meaning of the final stanza?
  4. One critic has described the mood of the
poem as one of "chilly and restrained horror."
What images in the poem help to produce this
mood?

The House of Life [1]

  The curious combination of eroticism and mysticism in Rossetti's poetry, a combination more
Renaissance than Victorian and perhaps more Italian than English, reaches its height in his
sonnet series, *The House of Life,* a collection of over one hundred sonnets written throughout a
period of more than thirty years.
  Although the tragic love between Rossetti and Elizabeth Siddal is undoubtedly reflected in many
of the sonnets (and perhaps his later love for the wife of William Morris), it is a mistake to probe
the poems for autobiographical detail or to identify with a single person all the women who are
mentioned. More important are the exotic atmosphere, the intense passion, and the employment
of complex imagery and subtle symbolism.

The Sonnet

A sonnet is a moment's monument—
Memorial from the soul's eternity
To one dead deathless [2] hour. Look that it be,
Whether for lustral [3] rite or dire portent,
Of its own arduous fullness reverent: 5
Carve it in ivory or in ebony,
As day or night may rule; and let time see
Its flowering crest impearled and orient.
A sonnet is a coin: its face reveals
The soul—its converse, to what power 'tis
  due:—   10
Whether for tribute to the august appeals
Of life, or dower in love's high retinue,
It serve; or, 'mid the dark wharf's cavernous
  breath,
In Charon's [4] palm it pay the toll to death.
(1881)

  [1] The title is taken from astrology, which divides
the heavens into twelve "houses," one of which
is the house of (human) life.
  [2] How can an hour be both "dead" and "deathless"?
  [3] Pertaining to purification.
  [4] Charon ferried the dead across the river Styx
into Hades.

STUDY AIDS: 1. What are the two META-
PHORS elaborated respectively in the octave and
in the sestet?
  2. What advice is Rossetti giving about writing the sonnet? Is it to deal with important
subject matter? What are the "powers" which
should inspire it? Is a particular form of the
sonnet referred to by "face" and "converse" in
ll. 9–10?

71. The Choice—1

Eat thou and drink; to-morrow thou shalt die.
Surely the earth, that's wise being very old,
Needs not our help. Then loose me, love, and
  hold
Thy sultry hair up from my face; that I
May pour for thee this golden wine; brim-
  high,   5
Till round the glass thy fingers glow like
  gold.
We'll drown all hours: thy song, while hours
  are tolled,
Shall leap, as fountains veil the changing sky.
Now kiss, and think that there are really
  those,

My own high-bosomed beauty, who increase   10
Vain gold, vain lore, and yet might choose
  our way!
Through many years they toil; then on a day
They die not—for their life was death—but
  cease;
And round their narrow lips the mold falls
  close.
(1848; 1870)

72. The Choice—2

Watch thou and fear; to-morrow thou shalt
  die.
Or art thou sure thou shalt have time for
  death?
Is not the day which God's word promiseth
To come man knows not when? In yonder
  sky,
Now while we speak, the sun speeds forth:
  can I   5
Or thou assure him of his goal? God's breath
Even at this moment haply quickeneth
The air to a flame; till spirits, always nigh
Though screened and hid, shall walk the day-
  light here.
And dost thou prate of all that man shall
  do?   10
Canst thou, who hast but plagues, presume to
  be
Glad in his gladness that comes after thee?
Will *his* strength slay *thy* worm in hell?
  Go to:
Cover thy countenance, and watch, and fear.
(1848; 1870)

73. The Choice—3

Think thou and act; to-morrow thou shalt die.
Outstretched in the sun's warmth upon the
  shore,
Thou say'st: "Man's measured path is all
  gone o'er;
Up all his years, steeply, with strain and sigh,
Man clomb until he touched the truth; and
  I,   5
Even I, am he whom it was destined for."
How should this be? Art thou, then, so much
  more
Than they who sowed, that thou shouldst
  reap thereby?

Nay, come up hither. From this wave-washed
  mound
Unto the furthest flood-brim look with me; 10
Then reach on with thy thought till it be
  drowned.
Miles and miles distant though the last line
  be,
And though thy soul sail leagues and leagues
  beyond,
Still, leagues beyond those leagues, there is
  more sea.
(1848; 1870)

STUDY AIDS: These three sonnets are to be considered together. Three philosophies of life are presented by the three poems. What are they? How are the images in each sonnet appropriate to the philosophy presented? What role does death play in each sonnet?

78. Body's Beauty

Of Adam's first wife, Lilith,[5] it is told
(The witch he loved before the gift of Eve)
That, ere the snake's, her sweet tongue could
  deceive,
And her enchanted hair was the first gold.
And still she sits, young while the earth is
  old,   5
And, subtly of herself contemplative,
Draws men to watch the bright web [6] she can
  weave,
Till heart and body and life are in its hold.
The rose and poppy [7] are her flowers; for
  where
Is he not found, O Lilith, whom shed scent 10
And soft-shed kisses and soft sleep shall snare?
Lo! as that youth's [8] eyes burned at thine, so
  went
Thy spell through him, and left his straight
  neck bent
And round his heart one strangling golden
  hair.
(1864; 1870)

STUDY AIDS: Of what does Lilith seem to be a symbol?

[5] In Jewish and medieval popular belief, Adam's first wife. She was also a famous witch.
[6] Of her hair (see l. 14).
[7] The rose is a symbol of love; the poppy, of sleep.
[8] Adam's.

86. Lost Days

The lost days of my life until today,
What were they, could I see them on the
   street
Lie as they fell? Would they be ears of wheat
Sown once for food but trodden into clay?
Or golden coins squandered and still to
   pay?   5
Or drops of blood dabbling the guilty feet?
Or such spilled water as in dreams must cheat
The undying throats of hell, athirst alway?
I do not see them here; but after death
God knows I know the faces I shall see, 10
Each one a murdered self, with low last
   breath.
"I am thyself—what hast thou done to me?"
"And I—and I—thyself" (lo! each one saith),
"And thou thyself to all eternity!"
(1858; 1869)

STUDY AIDS: 1. What is meant by "lost
days"? The octave is a series of questions; the
sestet a grim affirmation. What are the questions
about? Does the sestet answer the opening general question?
   2. Why is each lost day a "murdered self"?
Why will this be truly known only after death?
State the central idea of this sonnet in a single
declarative sentence.

97. A Superscription

Look in my face; my name is Might-have-
   been;
I am also called No-more, Too-late, Fare-well;
Unto thine ear I hold the dead-sea shell [9]
Cast up thy life's foam-fretted [10] feet between;
Unto thine eyes the glass where that is seen 5
Which had life's form and love's, but by my
   spell
Is now a shaken shadow intolerable,
Of ultimate things unuttered the frail screen.
Mark me, how still I am! But should there
   dart
One moment through thy soul the soft sur-
   prise   10
Of that winged Peace which lulls the breath
   of sighs,—
Then shalt thou see me smile, and turn apart
Thy visage to mine ambush at thy heart
Sleepless with cold commemorative eyes.
(1869)

STUDY AIDS: Is there any kinship between
the theme of this sonnet and that of *Lost Days?*
What is the personified figure in the octave?
What is his relation to death? At what moments
is he particularly active (sestet)?

George Meredith
(1828–1909)

MEREDITH'S EARLY EDUCATION WAS IN PRIVATE SCHOOLS, AND HE NEVER ATTENDED A
college or university. After studying at a Moravian school in Germany, he returned to
England to work in a London law office. But literature appealed to him more than the
law, and in 1851 he published his first book, a volume of poems. In the meantime he had
married the daughter of Thomas Love Peacock, the novelist. The marriage turned out
badly; in 1858 Mrs. Meredith ran away with a painter, leaving her husband to take care
of their son. The unhappy story is reflected in *Modern Love,* a series of sixteen-line, son-
net-like poems that Meredith published the year after his wife's death.
   Although Meredith had published an Oriental fantasy and a Gothic novel before 1859,

---

[9] A shell from the sea of death.
[10] The dead-sea image continues—but why "life's foam-fretted feet"?

his career as a novelist really began in that year with *The Ordeal of Richard Feverel,* one of the best loved of English novels. During the next fifty years he wrote many other novels, the most notable of which are *The Egoist* (1879), *The Tragic Comedians* (1880), and *Diana of the Crossways* (1885). Among his other writings is the brilliant essay on *The Idea of Comedy and the Uses of the Comic Spirit,* delivered as a lecture in 1877.

Since Meredith regarded fiction as "philosophy's elect handmaid," his novels are primarily psychological studies characterized by intellectual subtlety, an often difficult style, and a disregard for plot. He therefore was not immediately popular, and he relied on journalism to earn a living. He wrote reviews, served as a foreign correspondent, read for a publishing house, and for a time acted as editor of the *Fortnightly Magazine.*

Meredith's poetry has the same faults as his fiction. It tends to be over-analytical and obscure, with a style frequently mannered and involved. But at its best it is fresh and intellectually stimulating. The philosophy reflected in his verse is one of healthy optimism, which welcomes the findings of science and sees nature as a stern but beneficent mother, under whose rigorous tutelage man has achieved his supreme faculty of critical intelligence.

Love in the Valley

Under yonder beech-tree single on the greens-
    ward,
  Couched with her arms behind her golden
    head,
Knees and tresses folded to slip and ripple
    idly,
  Lies my young love sleeping in the
    shade.
Had I the heart to slide an arm beneath
    her,   5
  Press her parting lips as her waist I gather
    slow,
Waking in amazement she could not but
    embrace me:
  Then would she hold me and never let me
    go?

Shy as the squirrel and wayward as the swal-
    low,
  Swift as the swallow along the river's
    light   10
Circleting the surface to meet his mirrored
    winglets,
  Fleeter she seems in her stay than in her
    flight.
Shy as the squirrel that leaps among the
    pine-tops,
  Wayward as the swallow overhead at set of
    sun,

She whom I love is hard to catch and con-
    quer,   15
  Hard, but O the glory of the winning were
    she won!

When her mother tends her before the laugh-
    ing mirror,
  Tying up her laces, looping up her hair,
Often she thinks, were this wild thing
    wedded,
  More love should I have, and much less
    care.   20
When her mother tends her before the
    lighted mirror,
  Loosening her laces, combing down her
    curls,
Often she thinks, were this wild thing
    wedded,
  I should miss but one for many boys and
    girls.

Heartless she is as the shadow in the mead-
    ows,   25
  Flying to the hills on a blue and breezy
    noon.
No, she is athirst and drinking up her won-
    der:
  Earth to her is young as the slip of the new
    moon.

Deals she an unkindness, 'tis but her rapid
  measure,
  Even as in a dance; and her smile can heal
  no less: 30
Like the swinging May-cloud that pelts the
  flowers with hailstones
  Off a sunny border, she was made to bruise
  and bless.

Lovely are the curves of the white owl sweeping
  Wavy in the dusk lit by one large star.
Lone on the fir-branch, his rattle-note unvaried,   35
  Brooding o'er the gloom, spins the brown
  eve-jar.[1]
Darker grows the valley, more and more forgetting:
  So were it with me if forgetting could be
  willed.
Tell the grassy hollow that holds the bubbling
  well-spring,
  Tell it to forget the source that keeps it
  filled.   40

Stepping down the hill with her fair companions,
  Arm in arm, all against the raying west,
Boldly she sings, to the merry tune she
  marches,
  Brave in her shape, and sweeter unpossessed.
Sweeter, for she is what my heart first awaking   45
  Whispered the world was; morning light is
  she.
Love that so desires would fain keep her
  changeless;
  Fain would fling the net, and fain have her
  free.

Happy happy time, when the white star hovers
  Low over dim fields fresh with gloomy
  dew,   50
Near the face of dawn, that draws athwart
  the darkness,
  Threading it with color, like yewberries the
  yew.

[1] A night bird like the whippoorwill.

Thicker crowd the shades as the grave east
  deepens
  Glowing, and with crimson a long cloud
  swells.
Maiden still the morn is; and strange she is,
  and secret;   55
  Strange her eyes; her cheeks are cold as
  cold sea-shells.

Sunrays, leaning on our southern hills and
  lighting
  Wild cloud-mountains that drag the hills
  along,
Oft ends the day of your shifting brilliant
  laughter
  Chill as a dull face frowning on a song. 60
Ay, but shows the south-west a ripple-
  feathered bosom
  Blown to silver while the clouds are shaken
  and ascend
Scaling the mid-heavens as they stream, there
  comes a sunset
  Rich, deep like love in beauty without
  end.

When at dawn she sighs, and like an infant
  to the window   65
  Turns grave eyes craving light, released
  from dreams,
Beautiful she looks, like a white water-lily
  Bursting out of bud in havens of the
  streams.
When from bed she rises clothed from neck
  to ankle
  In her long nightgown sweet as boughs of
  May,   70
Beautiful she looks, like a tall garden lily
  Pure from the night, and splendid for the
  day.

Mother of the dews, dark eye-lashed twilight,
  Low-lidded twilight, o'er the valley's brim,
Rounding on thy breast sings the dew-
  delighted skylark,   75
  Clear as though the dewdrops had their
  voice in him.
Hidden where the rose-flush drinks the ray-
  less planet,[2]

[2] The morning star—actually the planet Venus—
robbed of its rays by the dawn's light.

Fountain-full he pours the spraying foun-
tain-showers.
Let me hear her laughter, I would have her
ever
  Cool as dew in twilight, the lark above the
  flowers.   80

All the girls are out with their baskets for
the primrose;
  Up lanes, woods through, they troop in
  joyful bands.
My sweet leads: she knows not why, but now
she loiters,
  Eyes the bent anemones, and hangs her
  hands.
Such a look will tell that the violets are peep-
ing,   85
  Coming the rose: and unaware a cry
Springs in her bosom for odors and for color,
  Covert and the nightingale; she knows not
  why.

Kerchiefed head and chin she darts between
her tulips,
  Streaming like a willow gray in arrowy
  rain: 90
Some bend beaten cheek to gravel, and their
angel
  She will be; she lifts them, and on she
  speeds again.
Black the driving raincloud breasts the iron
gateway:
  She is forth to cheer a neighbor lacking
  mirth.
So when sky and grass met rolling dumb for
thunder   95
  Saw I once a white dove, sole light of earth.

Prim little scholars are the flowers of her
garden,
  Trained to stand in rows, and asking if they
  please.
I might love them well but for loving more
the wild ones:
  O my wild ones! they tell me more than
  these.   100
You, my wild one, you tell of honied field-
rose,
  Violet, blushing eglantine in life; and even
  as they,

They by the wayside are earnest of your goodness,
  You are of life's, on the banks that line the
  way.

Peering at her chamber the white crowns the
red rose,   105
  Jasmine winds the porch with stars two
  and three.
Parted is the window; she sleeps; the starry
jasmine
  Breathes a falling breath that carries
  thoughts of me.
Sweeter unpossessed, have I said of her my
sweetest?
  Not while she sleeps: while she sleeps the
  jasmine breathes,   110
Luring her to love; she sleeps; the starry
jasmine
  Bears me to her pillow under white rose-
  wreaths.

Yellow with birdfoot-trefoil [3] are the grass-
glades;
  Yellow with cinquefoil [4] of the dew-gray
  leaf;
Yellow with stonecrop; [5] the moss-mounds are
yellow;   115
  Blue-necked the wheat sways, yellowing to
  the sheaf.
Green-yellow bursts from the copse the laughing yaffle: [6]
  Sharp as a sickle is the edge of shade and
  shine:
Earth in her heart laughs looking at the
heavens,
  Thinking of the harvest: I look and think
  of mine.   120

This I may know: her dressing and undress-
ing
  Such a change of light shows as when the
  skies in sport
Shift from cloud to moonlight; or edging over
thunder
  Slips a ray of sun; or sweeping into port

---

[3] A plant with a leaf like the foot of a bird.
[4] A plant with leaves divided into five leaflets.
[5] A mosslike plant with yellow flowers.
[6] The green woodpecker.

White sails furl; or on the ocean borders 125
  White sails lean along the waves leaping
    green.
Visions of her shower before me, but from
  eyesight
  Guarded she would be like the sun were
    she seen.

Front door and back of the mossed old farm-
  house
  Open with the morn, and in a breezy
    link [7]   130
Freshly sparkles garden to stripe-shadowed
  orchard,
  Green across a rill where on sand the min-
    nows wink.
Busy in the grass the early sun of summer
  Swarms, and the blackbird's mellow fluting
    notes
Call my darling up with round and roguish
  challenge: 135
  Quaintest, richest carol of all the singing
    throats!

Cool was the woodside; cool as her white
  dairy
  Keeping sweet the cream-pan; and there
    the boys from school,
Cricketing below, rushed brown and red with
  sunshine;
  O the dark translucence of the deep-eyed
    cool!   140
Spying from the farm, herself she fetched a
  pitcher
  Full of milk, and tilted for each in turn the
    beak.
Then a little fellow, mouth up and on tiptoe,
  Said, "I will kiss you": she laughed and
    leaned her cheek.

Doves of the fir-wood walling high our red
  roof   145
  Through the long noon coo, crooning
    through the coo.
Loose droop the leaves, and down the sleepy
  roadway
  Sometimes pipes a chaffinch; loose droops
    the blue.

   [7] Part of a winding stream and its adjoining
ground.

Cows flap a slow tail knee-deep in the river,
  Breathless, given up to sun and gnat and
    fly.   150
Nowhere is she seen; and if I see her no-
  where,
  Lightning may come, straight rains and
    tiger sky.

O the golden sheaf, the rustling treasure-arm-
  ful!
  O the nutbrown tresses nodding interlaced!
O the treasure-tresses one another over   155
  Nodding! O the girdle slack about the
    waist!
Slain are the poppies that shot their random
  scarlet
  Quick amid the wheatears: wound about
    the waist,
Gathered, see these brides of earth one blush
  of ripeness!
  O the nutbrown tresses nodding inter-
    laced!   160

Large and smoky red the sun's cold disk
  drops,
  Clipped by naked hills, on violet shaded
    snow:
Eastward large and still lights up a bower of
  moonrise,
  Whence at her leisure steps the moon
    aglow.
Nightlong on black print-branches [8] our
  beech-tree   165
  Gazes in this whiteness: nightlong could I.
Here may life on death or death on life be
  painted.
  Let me clasp her soul to know she cannot
    die!

Gossips count her faults; they scour a narrow
  chamber
  Where there is no window, read not heaven
    or her.   170
"When she was tiny," one aged woman
  quavers,
  Plucks at my heart and leads me by the
    ear.
Faults she had once as she learned to run and
  tumbled:

   [8] The shadows of the beech-tree branches.

Faults of feature some see, beauty not complete.
Yet, good gossips, beauty that makes holy 175
Earth and air, may have faults from head
to feet.

Hither she comes; she comes to me; she
lingers,
Deepens her brown eyebrows, while in new
surprise
High rise the lashes in wonder of a stranger;
Yet am I the light and living of her
eyes.   180
Something friends have told her fills her heart
to brimming,
Nets her in her blushes, and wounds her,
and tames.—
Sure of her haven, O like a dove alighting,
Arms up, she dropped: our souls were in
our names.

Soon will she lie like a white-frost sunrise. 185
Yellow oats and brown wheat, barley pale
as rye,
Long since your sheaves have yielded to the
thresher,
Felt the girdle loosened, seen the tresses fly.
Soon will she lie like a blood-red sunset.
Swift with the to-morrow, green-winged
Spring!   190
Sing from the south-west, bring her back the
truants,

Nightingale and swallow, song and dipping
wing.

Soft new beech-leaves, up to beamy April
Spreading bough on bough a primrose
mountain, you,
Lucid in the moon, raise lilies to the sky-
fields,   195
Youngest green transfused in silver shining
through:
Fairer than the lily, than the wild white
cherry:
Fair as in image my seraph love appears
Borne to me by dreams when dawn is at my
eyelids:
Fair as in the flesh she swims to me on
tears.   200

Could I find a place to be alone with heaven,
I would speak my heart out: heaven is my
need.
Every woodland tree is flushing like the dogwood,
Flashing like the whitebeam,[9] swaying like
the reed.
Flushing like the dogwood crimson in October;   205
Streaming like the flag-reed south-west
blown;
Flashing as in gusts the sudden-lighted whitebeam:
All seem to know what is for heaven alone.
(1851)

Lucifer [1] in Starlight

On a starred night Prince Lucifer uprose.
Tired of his dark dominion swung the fiend
Above the rolling ball in cloud part screened,
Where sinners hugged their specter of repose.
Poor prey to his hot fit of pride were those. 5
And now upon his western wing he leaned,
Now his huge bulk o'er Afric's sands
careened,

Now the black planet shadowed Arctic snows.
Soaring through wider zones that pricked his
scars
With memory of the old revolt from Awe, 10
He reached a middle height, and at the
stars,
Which are the brain of heaven, he looked,
and sank.
Around the ancient track marched, rank on
rank,
The army of unalterable law.
(1883)

[9] A tree whose leaves are white underneath.

[1] The archangel who, in his pride, rebelled against
God and was therefore cast out of heaven to
become Satan, the ruler of hell.

STUDY AIDS: 1. Why is Lucifer making this particular flight? Why does he ignore the earth ("the rolling ball") and its "sinners" hugging "their specter of repose"? What impression of him do we get in ll. 6–8?

2. Why does the view of the stars cause him to cease his upward flight? What is symbolized by the stars, as distinguished from Lucifer? What, then, is the general THEME of the sonnet?

William Morris
(1834–1896)

WILLIAM MORRIS ONCE SAID THAT A MAN WASN'T WORTH MUCH WHO COULD NOT WEAVE A tapestry and compose an epic poem at the same time. The statement is indicative of Morris's energy, productivity, and versatility. At one time or another, he was an architect, a painter, a designer, a printer, a poet, an essayist, an editor, a translator, an active socialist, and a manufacturer of tapestries, furniture, wallpaper, chintzes, metalwork, carpets, and stained-glass windows.

Morris went up to Oxford planning to enter the church. He changed his mind and decided to become an architect. Then his friendship with Rossetti turned him to painting and poetry. In 1858 he published *The Defense of Guenevere and Other Poems,* showing the influence of Rossetti and Browning and reflecting his interest in medieval life. When Morris was married and discovered that he could not furnish a house for his wife according to his tastes, he set up a firm to produce things for the home which would combine grace with utility. "Have nothing in your houses," he once said, inspired by Ruskin, "that you do not know to be useful, or believe to be beautiful." The same desire for beauty in everyday objects led him, late in life, to establish the Kelmscott Press, which put out a number of handsome volumes, including the famous Kelmscott Chaucer. Morris became a socialist for a similar reason: the ugliness he saw around him he believed to be ultimately the product of a capitalistic and competitive social system; to get rid of the ugliness, he thought, man must change the society.

Although he wrote a few propagandistic poems, the great bulk of Morris's poetry does not reflect his social ideas. It is basically escapist poetry—romantic, decorative, usually narrative. Ancient tales had a fascination for him. His major poetic work is *The Earthly Paradise* (1868–1870), in which two groups of travelers, Greek and Scandinavian, come together to tell old stories. In *The Life and Death of Jason* (1867) he retold the myth of the Golden Fleece as a medievalist might tell it. And in *Sigurd the Volsung* (1876), his last long poem and in his opinion the best, he turned to the Volsunga saga for his inspiration. In addition, Morris did many translations from the *Odyssey,* the *Aeneid, Beowulf,* and Scandinavian sagas. During the final years of his life he wrote a series of prose fantasies on medieval themes, bearing such bewitching titles as *The Well at the World's End, The Roots of the Mountains,* and *The Water of the Wondrous Isles.*

The Haystack in the Floods

The story of this poem takes place in the fourteenth century during the Hundred Years' War. Shortly after the battle of Poitiers (1356) Robert de Marny, an English knight, is attempting to escape with his mistress, Jehane, across the border into Gascony, which was then English territory. But their way is barred by a French knight, Godmar, whose ambush marks the start of the poem.

Had she come all the way for this,
To part at last without a kiss?
Yea, had she borne the dirt and rain
That her own eyes might see him slain
Beside the haystack in the floods?   5

Along the dripping leafless woods,
The stirrup touching either shoe,
She rode astride as troopers do;
With kirtle kilted [1] to her knee,
To which the mud splashed wretchedly;   10
And the wet dripped from every tree
Upon her head and heavy hair,
And on her eyelids broad and fair;
The tears and rain ran down her face.

By fits and starts they rode apace,   15
And very often was his place
Far off from her; he had to ride
Ahead, to see what might betide
When the roads crossed; and sometimes, when
There rose a murmuring from his men,   20
Had to turn back with promises;
Ah me! she had but little ease;
And often for pure doubt and dread
She sobbed, made giddy in the head
By the swift riding; while, for cold,   25
Her slender fingers scarce could hold
The wet reins; yea, and scarcely, too,
She felt the foot within her shoe
Against the stirrup: all for this,
To part at last without a kiss   30
Beside the haystack in the floods.

For when they neared that old soaked hay,
They saw across the only way
That Judas, Godmar, and the three
Red running lions dismally   35
Grinned from his pennon,[2] under which,
In one straight line along the ditch,
They counted thirty heads.

                             So then,
While Robert turned round to his men,
She saw at once the wretched end,   40
And, stooping down, tried hard to rend
Her coif [3] the wrong way from her head,
And hid her eyes; while Robert said:
"Nay, love, 'tis scarcely two to one,
At Poictiers [4] where we made them run   45
So fast—why, sweet my love, good cheer,
The Gascon frontier is so near,
Nought after this."

                      But, "O," she said,[5]
"My God! my God! I have to tread
The long way back without you; then   50
The court at Paris; those six men;
The gratings of the Chatelet;
The swift Seine on some rainy day
Like this, and people standing by,
And laughing, while my weak hands try   55
To recollect how strong men swim.
All this, or else a life with him,
For which I should be damned at last,
Would God that this next hour were past!"

[1] Skirt tucked up.
[2] Banner.
[3] A tight-fitting cap tied under the chin. Why does she hide her eyes?
[4] A great victory for the English, despite the five-to-one numerical superiority of the French.
[5] Jehane quickly foresees the tragic result with its terrible alternative for her: trial for witchcraft or a life with Godmar. The "six men" would be her judges; the Chatelet was a Paris prison; and ll. 53–56 refer to a medieval method of testing accused witches by throwing them into water: if they swam they were guilty; if they drowned they were innocent. Note the swift compression.

He answered not, but cried his cry,   60
"St. George [6] for Marny!" cheerily;
And laid his hand upon her rein.
Alas! no man of all his train [7]
Gave back that cheery cry again;
And, while for rage his thumb beat fast   65
Upon his sword-hilt, some one cast
About his neck a kerchief long,
And bound him.

               Then they went along
To Godmar; who said: "Now, Jehane,
Your lover's life is on the wane   70
So fast, that if this very hour
You yield not as my paramour,
He will not see the rain leave off—
Nay, keep your tongue from gibe and scoff,
Sir Robert, or I slay you now."   75

She laid her hand upon her brow,
Then gazed upon the palm, as though
She thought her forehead bled, and—"No,"
She said, and turned her head away,
As there were nothing else to say,   80
And everything were settled: red
Grew Godmar's face from chin to head:
"Jehane, on yonder hill there stands
My castle, guarding well my lands:
What hinders me from taking you,   85
And doing that I list to do
To your fair wilful body, while
Your knight lies dead?"

              A wicked smile
Wrinkled her face, her lips grew thin,
A long way out she thrust her chin: 90
"You know that I should strangle you
While you were sleeping; or bite through
Your throat, by God's help—ah!" she said,
"Lord Jesus, pity your poor maid!
For in such wise they hem me in,   95
I cannot choose but sin and sin,
Whatever happens: yet I think
They could not make me eat or drink,
And so should I just reach my rest."
"Nay, if you do not my behest,   100
O Jehane! though I love you well,"
Said Godmar, "would I fail to tell

All that I know." "Foul lies," she said.
"Eh? lies, my Jehane? by God's head,
At Paris folks would deem them true!   105
Do you know, Jehane, they cry for you,
'Jehane the brown! Jehane the brown!
Give us Jehane to burn or drown!'—
Eh—gag me Robert!—sweet my friend,
This were indeed a piteous end   110
For those long fingers, and long feet,
And long neck, and smooth shoulders sweet;
An end that few men would forget
That saw it—So, an hour yet:
Consider, Jehane, which to take   115
Of life or death!"

             So, scarce awake,
Dismounting, did she leave that place,
And totter some yards: with her face
Turned upward to the sky she lay,
Her head on a wet heap of hay,   120
And fell asleep: and while she slept,
And did not dream, the minutes crept
Round to the twelve again; but she,
Being waked at last, sighed quietly
And strangely childlike came, and said: 125
"I will not." Straightway Godmar's head,
As though it hung on strong wires,[8] turned
Most sharply round, and his face burned.

For Robert—both his eyes were dry,
He could not weep, but gloomily   130
He seemed to watch the rain; yea, too,
His lips were firm; he tried once more
To touch her lips; she reached out, sore
And vain desire so tortured them,
The poor gray lips, and now the hem   135
Of his sleeve brushed them.

             With a start
Up Godmar rose, thrust them apart;
From Robert's throat he loosed the bands
Of silk and mail; with empty hands
Held out, she stood and gazed, and saw,   140
The long bright blade without a flaw
Glide out from Godmar's sheath, his hand
In Robert's hair; she saw him bend
Back Robert's head; she saw him send
The thin steel down; the blow told well,   145

[6] The patron saint of England.
[7] What is the implication of ll. 63–64?

[8] Note how this image is in keeping with the taut atmosphere of the poem.

Right backward the knight Robert fell,
And moaned as dogs do, being half dead,
Unwitting, as I deem: so then
Godmar turned grinning to his men,
Who ran, some five or six, and beat   150
His head to pieces at their feet.

Then Godmar turned again and said:
"So, Jehane, the first fitte [9] is read!
Take note, my lady, that your way
Lies backward to the Chatelet!"   155
She shook her head and gazed awhile
At her cold hands with a rueful smile,
As though this thing had made her mad.

This was the parting that they had
Beside the haystack in the floods.   160
(1858)

STUDY AIDS: 1. One critic cites this poem
as an illustration of Morris's ability "to visualize
an anguished scene . . . and create a sense of
intense actuality in his medieval narratives." By
what means does Morris do this?
2. What does the story gain by being told
from Jehane's point of view? What does her
being accused of witchcraft add to the atmosphere? Do any of her words or actions support
the accusation?

The Defense of Guenevere

According to Malory, the great fifteenth-century chronicler of the Arthurian legends, Modred
and Agravaine conspired against Launcelot and Queen Guenevere. They persuaded King Arthur
to go on a hunting trip and to send back word that he would not return that night. As they had
hoped, Guenevere then sent for Launcelot, whereupon Modred and Agravaine, with twelve armed
knights, trapped the lovers in the Queen's room. Allowing only one of the knights to slip into the
room, Launcelot slew him, put on his armor, and went out and killed all of the band except
Modred, who fled wounded to Arthur. The King then ordered Guenevere to be burned at the
stake.

In this poem the Queen is defending herself against the charge of adultery. Gauwaine, whom
Morris (departing from Malory) makes her chief accuser, has just spoken.

But, knowing now that they would have her
    speak,
She threw her wet hair backward from her
    brow,
Her hand close to her mouth touching her
    cheek,

As though she had had there a shameful blow,
And feeling it shameful to feel aught but
    shame   5
All through her heart, yet felt her cheek
    burned so,

She must a little touch it; like one lame
She walked away from Gauwaine, with her
    head
Still lifted up; and on her cheek of flame

The tears dried quick; she stopped at last
    and said: 10

"O knights and lords, it seems but little skill [1]
To talk of well-known things past now and
    dead.

"God wot [2] I ought to say, I have done ill,
And pray you all forgiveness heartily!
Because you must be right, such great lords;
    still   15

"Listen—suppose your time were come to die,
And you were quite alone and very weak;
Yea, laid a-dying, while very mightily

"The wind was ruffling up the narrow streak
Of river through your broad lands running
    well;   20
Suppose a hush should come, then someone
    speak:

[9] Division in a poem; part of a story.

[1] Use.
[2] Knows.

" 'One of these cloths is heaven, and one is
hell;
Now choose one cloth forever—which they
be,
I will not tell you; you must somehow tell

" 'Of your own strength and mightiness; here,
see!'   25
Yea, yea, my lord,[3] and you to ope your eyes,
At foot of your familiar bed to see

"A great God's angel standing, with such dyes,
Not known on earth, on his great wings, and
hands,
Held out two ways, light from the inner
skies   30

"Showing him well, and making his commands
Seem to be God's commands, moreover, too,
Holding within his hands the cloths on
wands;

"And one of these strange choosing cloths
was blue,
Wavy and long, and one cut short and red; 35
No man could tell the better of the two.

"After a shivering half-hour you said:
'God help! heaven's color, the blue'; and he
said, 'hell.' [4]
Perhaps you would then roll upon your bed,

"And cry to all good men that loved you
well,   40
'Ah, Christ! if only I had known, known,
known';
Launcelot went away, then I could tell,

"Like wisest man how all things would be,
moan,
And roll and hurt myself, and long to die,
And yet fear much to die for what was
sown.   45

---

[3] Gauwaine.
[4] Noting that the color blue signifies faithfulness,
and red passion, what is the meaning of the image
that Guenevere develops in ll. 22–38? Why did
the choice of "heaven's color, the blue," turn out
to be "hell"?

"Nevertheless you, O Sir Gauwaine, lie;
Whatever may have happened through these
years,

God knows I speak truth, saying that you lie."
Her voice was low at first, being full of tears,
But as it cleared, it grew full loud and shrill, 50
Growing a windy shriek in all men's ears,

A ringing in their startled brains, until
She said that Gauwaine lied, then her voice
sunk,
And her great eyes began again to fill,

Though still she stood right up, and never
shrunk,   55
But spoke on bravely, glorious lady fair!
Whatever tears her full lips may have drunk,

She stood, and seemed to think, and wrung
her hair,
Spoke out at last with no more trace of shame,
With passionate twisting of her body there: 60

"It chanced upon a day that Launcelot came
To dwell at Arthur's court: at Christmas-time
This happened; when the heralds sung his
name,

" 'Son of King Ban of Benwick,' seemed to
chime
Along with all the bells that rang that day, 65
O'er the white roofs, with little change of
rhyme.

"Christmas and whitened winter passed away,
And over me the April sunshine came,
Made very awful with black hail-clouds; yea

"And in the summer I grew white with
flame,   70
And bowed my head down—autumn, and the
sick
Sure knowledge things would never be the
same,

"However often spring might be most thick
Of blossoms and buds, smote on me, and I
grew
Careless of most things, let the clock tick,
tick,   75

"To my unhappy pulse, that beat right through
My eager body: while I laughed out loud,
And let my lips curl up at false or true,

"Seemed cold and shallow without any cloud.
Behold, my judges, then the cloths [5] were brought: 80
While I was dizzied thus, old thoughts would crowd,

"Belonging to the time ere I was bought
By Arthur's great name and his little love;
Must I give up for ever then, I thought,

"That which I deemed would ever round me move   85
Glorifying all things; for a little word,[6]
Scarce ever meant at all, must I now prove

"Stone-cold for ever? Pray you, does the Lord
Will that all folks should be quite happy and good?
I love God now a little, if this cord [7]   90

"Were broken, once for all what striving could
Make me love anything in earth or heaven?
So day by day it grew, as if one should

"Slip slowly down some path worn smooth and even,
Down to a cool sea on a summer day;   95
Yet still in slipping was there some small leaven

"Of stretched hands catching small stones by the way,
Until one surely reached the sea at last,
And felt strange new joy as the worn head lay

"Back, with the hair like sea-weed; yea, all past   100
Sweat of the forehead, dryness of the lips,
Washed utterly out by the dear waves o'ercast

[5] Referring to the image of ll. 22–38.
[6] The marriage vows. What does Guenevere mean by ll. 86–88?
[7] The tie between her and Launcelot.

"In the lone sea, far off from any ships!
Do I not know now of a day in spring?
No minute of that wild day ever slips   105

"From out my memory; I hear thrushes sing,
And wheresoever I may be, straightway
Thoughts of it all come up with most fresh sting;

"I was half mad with beauty on that day,
And went without my ladies all alone,   110
In a quiet garden walled round every way;

"I was right joyful of that wall of stone,
That shut the flowers and trees up with the sky,
And trebled all the beauty: to the bone,

"Yea right through to my heart, grown very shy   115
With weary thoughts, it pierced, and made me glad;
Exceedingly glad, and I knew verily,

"A little thing just then had made me mad;
I dared not think, as I was wont to do,
Sometimes, upon my beauty; if I had   120

"Held out my long hand up against the blue,
And, looking on the tenderly darkened fingers,
Thought that by rights one ought to see quite through,

"There, see you, where the soft still light yet lingers,
Round by the edges; what should I have done,   125
If this had joined with yellow spotted singers,

"And startling green drawn upward by the sun?
But shouting, loosed out, see now! all my hair,
And trancedly stood watching the west wind run

"With faintest half-heard breathing sound; why there   130
I lose my head e'en now in doing this;
But shortly listen: In that garden fair

"Came Launcelot walking; this is true, the
kiss
Wherewith we kissed in meeting that spring
day,
I scarce dare talk of the remembered bliss, 135

"When both our mouths went wandering in
one way,
And aching sorely, met among the leaves;
Our hands being left behind strained far
away.

"Never within a yard of my bright sleeves
Had Launcelot come before: and now, so
nigh!   140
After that day why is it Guenevere grieves?

"Nevertheless you, O Sir Gauwaine, lie,
Whatever happened on through all those
years,
God knows I speak truth, saying that you
lie.

"Being such a lady could I weep these tears 145
If this were true? A great queen such as I
Having sinned this way, straight her con-
science sears;

"And afterwards she liveth hatefully,
Slaying and poisoning, certes never weeps,—
Gauwaine, be friends now, speak me lov-
ingly.   150

"Do I not see how God's dear pity creeps
All through your frame, and trembles [8] in
your mouth?
Remember in what grave your mother sleeps,

"Buried in some place far down in the south,
Men are forgetting as I speak to you;   155
By her head, severed in that awful drouth

"Of pity that drew Agravaine's fell blow,
I pray your pity! let me not scream out
For ever after, when the shrill winds blow

[8] I.e., should creep and should tremble if he would
but remember (ll. 153–157) how his brother
Agravaine killed their mother because of her un-
faithfulness to her husband. In other words, Agravaine's cruel lack of pity should move Gauwaine to
act just the opposite.

"Through half your castle-locks! let me not
shout   160
For ever after in the winter night
When you ride out alone! in battle-rout

"Let not my rusting tears make your sword
light!
Ah! God of mercy, how he turns away!
So, ever must I dress [9] me to the fight, 165

"So: let God's justice work! Gauwaine, I say,
See me hew down your proofs: yea all men
know
Even as you said how Mellyagraunce [10] one
day,

"One bitter day in la Fausse Garde,[11] for so
All good knights held it after, saw: 170
Yea, sirs, by cursed unknightly outrage;[12]
though

"You, Gauwaine, held his word without a
flaw,
This Mellyagraunce saw blood upon my bed—
Whose blood then pray you? is there any law

[9] Address.
[10] In ll. 168–221, Guenevere gives her account
of a previous incident in which she was accused of
adultery, an incident obviously just used by Gauwaine to support his present accusation. As told
by Malory, Mellyagraunce, who was in love with
the Queen, seized Guenevere while she was on a
May-day expedition, wounding some of her knights
in the attack. She agreed to go to his castle if he
would let her take along her wounded knights and
tend to them. In the meantime, a child from the
May-day expedition had fled to Launcelot and told
him what had happened. He rode to the castle
and would have killed Mellyagraunce immediately
if Guenevere had not interceded. During the night
Launcelot broke the bars of a window in Guenevere's
room, cutting his arm in the act, and came to her.
The next morning, his blood was found upon the
Queen's bed, and Mellyagraunce accused her of
adultery with one of her wounded knights. Launcelot defended Guenevere against the charge, challenged Mellyagraunce to trial by combat, and killed
him.
[11] "The False Prison." Guenevere gives this name
to Mellyagraunce's castle because he had attacked
her unarmed knights (see l. 189) and forced her
to be his prisoner.
[12] Mellyagraunce had come into the Queen's bedroom and pulled aside her bed curtains before she
had arisen.

"To make a queen say why some spots of
red   175
Lie on her coverlet? or will you say,
'Your hands are white, lady, as when you
wed,

" 'Where did you bleed?' and must I stammer
out—'Nay,
I blush indeed, fair lord, only to rend
My sleeve up to my shoulder, where there
lay   180

" 'A knife-point last night:' so must I defend
The honor of the lady Guenevere?
Not so, fair lords, even if the world should
end

"This very day, and you were judges here
Instead of God. Did you see Mellyagraunce   185
When Launcelot stood by him? what white
fear

"Curdled his blood, and how his teeth did
dance,
His side sink in? as my knight cried and
said,
'Slayer of unarmed men, here is a chance!

" 'Setter of traps,¹³ I pray you guard your
head,   190
By God I am so glad to fight with you,
Stripper of ladies, that my hand feels lead

" 'For driving weight; hurrah now! draw and
do
For all my wounds are moving in my breast,
And I am getting mad with waiting so.'   195

"He struck his hands together o'er the beast,
Who fell down flat, and grovelled at his
feet,
And groaned at being slain so young—'at
least.'

"My knight said, 'Rise you, sir, who are so
fleet

¹³ Launcelot had fallen into a dungeon through
a floor trap set by Mellyagraunce but had escaped
just in time to save Guenevere.

At catching ladies, half-armed ¹⁴ will I
fight,   200
My left side all uncovered!' then I weet,¹⁵

"Up sprang Sir Mellyagraunce with great
delight
Upon his knave's face; not until just then
Did I quite hate him, as I saw my knight

"Along the lists look to my stake and pen 205
With such a joyous smile, it made me sigh
From agony beneath my waist-chain,¹⁶ when

"The fight began, and to me they drew
nigh;
Ever Sir Launcelot kept him on the right,
And traversed warily, and ever high   210

"And fast leaped caitiff's ¹⁷ sword, until my
knight
Sudden threw up his sword to his left hand,
Caught it, and swung it; that was all the
fight,

"Except a spout of blood on the hot land;
For it was hottest summer; and I know   215
I wondered how the fire, while I should stand,

"And burn, against the heat, would quiver so,
Yards above my head; thus these matters
went;
Which things were only warnings of the woe

"That fell on me. Yet Mellyagraunce was
shent,¹⁸   220
For Mellyagraunce had fought against the
Lord;
Therefore, my lords, take heed lest you be
blent ¹⁹

"With all this wickedness; say no rash word
Against me, being so beautiful; my eyes,

¹⁴ In order to provoke the frightened Mellyagraunce into combat, Launcelot said he would fight
only half-armed.
¹⁵ Know.
¹⁶ Guenevere was chained by the waist to the
stake at which she was to be burned.
¹⁷ A caitiff is a base, despicable person.
¹⁸ Destroyed.
¹⁹ Blended, involved.

Wept all away to gray, may bring some
   sword   225

"To drown you in your blood; see my breast
   rise,
Like waves of purple sea, as here I stand;
And how my arms are moved in wonderful
   wise;

"Yea also at my full heart's strong command,
See through my long throat how the words
   go up   230
In ripples to my mouth; how in my hand

"The shadow lies like wine within a cup
Of marvelously colored gold; yea now
This little wind is rising, look you up,

"And wonder how the light is falling so   235
Within my moving tresses: will you dare,
When you have looked a little on my brow,

"To say this thing is vile? or will you care
For any plausible lies of cunning woof,
When you can see my face with no lie
   there   240

"For ever? am I not a gracious proof—
'But in your chamber Launcelot was found'—
Is there a good knight then would stand aloof,

"When a queen says with gentle queenly
   sound,
'O true as steel, come now and talk with
   me;   245
I love to see your step upon the ground

" 'Unwavering; also well I love to see
That gracious smile light up your face, and
   hear
Your wonderful words, that all mean verily

" 'The thing they seem to mean. Good friend,
   so dear   250
To me in everything, come here tonight,
Or else the hours will pass most dull and
   drear.

" 'If you come not, I fear this time I might
Get thinking overmuch of times gone by,
When I was young, and green hope was in
   sight;   255

" 'For no man cares now to know why I sigh;
And no man comes to sing me pleasant songs,
Nor any brings me the sweet flowers that
   lie

" 'So thick in the gardens; therefore one so
   longs
To see you, Launcelot, that we may be   260
Like children once again, free from all wrongs

" 'Just for one night.' Did he not come to me?
What thing could keep true Launcelot away
If I said, 'Come'? There was one less than
   three

"In my quiet room that night, and we were
   gay;   265
Till sudden I rose up, weak, pale, and sick,
Because a bawling [20] broke our dream up; yea,

"I looked at Launcelot's face and could not
   speak,
For he looked helpless too, for a little while;
Then I remember how I tried to shriek,   270

"And could not, but fell down; from tile to
   tile
The stones they threw up rattled o'er my head
And made me dizzier; till within awhile

"My maids were all about me, and my head
On Launcelot's breast was being soothed
   away   275
From its white chattering, until Launcelot
   said—

"By God! I will not tell you more to-day,
Judge any way you will—what matters it?
You know quite well the story of that fray,

"How Launcelot stilled their bawling, the
   mad fit   280
That caught up Gauwaine—all, all, verily,
But just that which would save me; these
   things flit.

"Nevertheless you, O Sir Gauwaine, lie;
Whatever may have happened these long
   years,
God knows I speak truth, saying that you
   lie!   285
   [20] The noise of the knights who had discovered
her and Launcelot together.

"All I have said is truth, by Christ's dear
   tears."
She would not speak another word, but stood
Turned sideways; listening, like a man who
   hears

His brother's trumpet sounding through the
   wood
Of his foes' lances. She leaned eagerly,   290
And gave a slight spring sometimes, as she
   could

At last hear something really; joyfully
Her cheek grew crimson, as the headlong
   speed

Of the roan charger drew all men to see,
The knight who came was Launcelot at good
   need.   295
(1858)

STUDY AIDS: 1. What personal traits of
Guenevere are revealed in her speech? In what
ways are they revealed? Is her defense convincing? What arguments does she use? To what
fine audacity does she rise in ll. 222–241?

2. One cannot fully understand or appreciate
The Defense of Guenevere without knowing
something of the story. Is this a flaw in the
poem?

Algernon Charles Swinburne
(1837–1909)

NEO-PAGAN, REBEL, SENSUALIST, APOSTLE OF LIBERTY, EXQUISITE MUSICIAN IN WORDS—
Swinburne is a striking figure among the Victorians. "Violence," it has been said, "is his
unique contribution to Victorian poetry," and Ruskin labeled him a "demoniac youth."
Born of an aristocratic family, Swinburne went to Eton with assorted enthusiasms—for the
sea, for the French and Italian languages, for strenuous exercise, and for heroes. His radicalism and heavy drinking led to his being withdrawn from school and privately tutored.
For the same reasons his stay at Oxford was short, but he made friends at the University,
including the future Pre-Raphaelites, who influenced his literary tastes.

After writing two undistinguished plays, Swinburne published *Atalanta in Calydon*
(1865), which was quite successful with the many readers who welcomed a poetry different from that of Browning and Tennyson. The next year, however, fame turned to
notoriety with the appearance of his *Poems and Ballads*. These verses were rather too
pagan and suggestive even for the anti-Tennysonians, and a reviewer called Swinburne
"the libidinous laureate of a pack of satyrs."

Always a hater of monarchy, Swinburne turned his attention to the cause of liberty,
especially to the fight for freedom in Italy. He saw in the Italian patriot Mazzini, visiting
England at the time, a symbol of man's eternal struggle against tyranny. The poet's devotion to liberty found expression in *Songs before Sunrise* (1871) and *Songs of Two Nations* (1875). He continued to write and to publish for the rest of his life, which undoubtedly was prolonged through the kind attentions of a friend, who encouraged the
poet to lead a sane and sober existence. Most of these later writings, however, lack the
fire and inspiration of his earlier work.

Tennyson identified the main element in Swinburne's poetical genius when he called
him "a reed through which all things blow into music." Music, sounds, words, form—these
are the keys to his perennial appeal. He is not devoid of ideas, but it is melody, not meaning, that is Swinburne's forte. Although at times his absorption in words and sound effects
is excessive, at its best his verse is wonderfully musical.

Atalanta in Calydon

Atalanta in Calydon is a lyrical drama in which Swinburne says he has tried to "reproduce for English readers the likeness of a Greek tragedy with . . . something . . . of its true life and charm. . . ." It is particularly memorable for its many musical lyrics.

When the Hounds of Spring

When the hounds of spring are on winter's
　　traces,
　The mother of months[1] in meadow or
　　plain
Fills the shadows and windy places
　With lisp of leaves and ripple of rain;
And the brown bright nightingale amorous 5
Is half assuaged for Itylus,[2]
For the Thracian ships and the foreign faces,
　The tongueless vigil and all the pain.

Come with bows bent and with emptying of
　　quivers,
　Maiden most perfect, lady of light,　　　10
With a noise of winds and many rivers,
　With a clamor of waters, and with might;
Bind on thy sandals, O thou most fleet,
Over the splendor and speed of thy feet;
For the faint east quickens, the wan west
　　shivers,　　　　　　　　　　　　　15
　Round the feet of the day and the feet of
　　the night.

Where shall we find her, how shall we sing
　　to her,
　Fold our hands round her knees, and cling?
O that man's heart were as fire and could
　　spring to her,
　Fire, or the strength of the streams that
　　spring!　　　　　　　　　　　　　20
For the stars and the winds are unto her
As raiment, as songs of the harp-player;
For the risen stars and the fallen cling to her,
　And the southwest-wind and the west-wind
　　sing.

[1] Artemis (Diana), goddess of the moon.
[2] Son of Procne and Tereus, king of Thrace.
(See n. 1, p. 828.)
[3] What does this line mean?
[4] The shepherd's pipe of straw.
[5] Sylvan demigod, half goat and half man.
[6] God of flocks and pastures,
[7] God of wine,

For winter's rains and ruins are over,　　25
　And all the season of snows and sins;
The days dividing lover and lover,
　The light that loses, the night that wins;[3]
And time remembered is grief forgotten,
And frosts are slain and flowers begotten, 30
And in green underwood and cover
　Blossom by blossom the spring begins.

The full streams feed on flower of rushes,
　Ripe grasses trammel a traveling foot,
The faint fresh flame of the young year
　　flushes　　　　　　　　　　　　35
　From leaf to flower and flower to fruit;
And fruit and leaf are as gold and fire,
And the oat[4] is heard above the lyre,
And the hoofed heel of a satyr[5] crushes
　The chestnut-husk at the chestnut-root. 40

And Pan[6] by noon and Bacchus[7] by night,
　Fleeter of foot than the fleet-foot kid,
Follows with dancing and fills with delight
　The Mænad and the Bassarid;[8]
And soft as lips that laugh and hide,　　45
The laughing leaves of the trees divide,[9]
And screen from seeing and leave in sight
　The god pursuing, the maiden hid.

The ivy falls with the Bacchanal's[10] hair
　Over her eyebrows hiding her eyes;　　50
The wild vine slipping down leaves bare
　Her bright breast shortening into sighs;
The wild vine slips with the weight of its
　　leaves,
But the berried ivy catches and cleaves
To the limbs that glitter, the feet that scare 55
　The wolf that follows, the fawn that flies.
(1865)

[8] The Mænad and the Bassarid were female followers of Bacchus.
[9] Lines 46–48: As the god chases the maiden, they are alternately revealed and hidden by the tree leaves.
[10] A Bacchanal is a worshiper of Bacchus,

Before the Beginning of Years

Before the beginning of years
  There came to the making of man
Time, with a gift of tears;
  Grief, with a glass that ran;
Pleasure, with pain for leaven;   5
  Summer, with flowers that fell;
Remembrance fallen from heaven,
  And madness risen from hell;
Strength without hands to smite;
  Love that endures for a breath: 10
Night, the shadow of light,
  And life, the shadow of death.

And the high gods took in hand
  Fire, and the falling of tears,
And a measure of sliding sand   15
  From under the feet of the years;
And froth and drift of the sea;
  And dust of the laboring earth;
And bodies of things to be
  In the houses of death and of birth;   20
And wrought with weeping and laughter,
  And fashioned with loathing and love,

With life before and after
  And death beneath and above,
For a day and a night and a morrow,   25
  That his strength might endure for a span
With travail and heavy sorrow,
  The holy spirit of man.

From the winds of the north and the south
  They gathered as unto strife;   30
They breathed upon his mouth,
  They filled his body with life;
Eyesight and speech they wrought
  For the veils of the soul therein,
A time for labor and thought,   35
  A time to serve and to sin:
They gave him light in his ways,
  And love, and a space for delight,
And beauty and length of days,
  And night, and sleep in the night.   40
His speech is a burning fire;
  With his lips he travaileth;
In his heart is a blind desire,
  In his eyes foreknowledge of death;
He weaves, and is clothed with derision; 45
  Sows, and he shall not reap;
His life is a watch or a vision
  Between a sleep and a sleep.
(1865)

Hymn to Proserpine [1]
(After the Proclamation [2] in Rome of the Christian Faith)
Vicisti, Galilaee [3]

In this poem a pagan Roman is lamenting the overthrow of the Greek deities by the new, colorless religion of Christianity.

I have lived long enough, having seen one
  thing, that love hath an end;
Goddess and maiden and queen, be near me
  now and befriend.
Thou art more than the day or the morrow,
  the seasons that laugh or that weep;
For these give joy and sorrow, but thou,
  Proserpina, sleep.

Sweet is the treading of wine, [4] and sweet the
  feet of the dove; [5]   5
But a goodlier gift [6] is thine than foam of the
  grapes or love.

[1] Wife of Pluto and so queen of the underworld.

[2] The Edict of Milan, 313 A.D., by which the emperor Constantine officially recognized Christianity.

[3] "You have conquered, Galilean." These words were supposedly uttered by the dying emperor Julian (331–363), called "the Apostate" because of his renunciation of Christianity. During his reign paganism revived for a time.

[4] A reference to Bacchus, god of wine.

[5] The dove was sacred to Venus.

[6] Death.

Yea, is not even Apollo,[7] with hair and harp-
string of gold,
A bitter god to follow, a beautiful god to behold?
I am sick of singing: the bays [8] burn deep and
chafe: I am fain
To rest a little from praise and grievous pleasure and pain.   10
For the gods we know not of, who give us our
daily breath,
We know they are cruel as love or life, and
lovely as death.
O gods dethroned and deceased, cast forth,
wiped out in a day!
From your wrath is the world released, redeemed from your chains, men say.
New gods are crowned in the city; their flowers have broken your rods;   15
They are merciful, clothed with pity, the
young compassionate gods.
But for me their new device is barren, the
days are bare;
Things long past over suffice, and men forgotten that were.
Time and the gods are at strife; ye dwell in
the midst thereof,
Draining a little life from the barren breasts
of love.   20
I say to you, cease, take rest; yea, I say to you
all, be at peace,
Till the bitter milk of her breast and the
barren bosom shall cease.
Wilt thou yet take all, Galilean? but these
thou shalt not take,
The laurel, the palms [9] and the pæan, the
breasts of the nymphs in the brake;
Breasts more soft than a dove's, that tremble
with tenderer breath;   25
And all the wings of the Loves,[10] and all
the joy before death;
All the feet of the hours that sound as a single
lyre,
Dropped and deep in the flowers, with strings
that flicker like fire.

More than these wilt thou give, things fairer
than all these things?
Nay, for a little we live, and life hath mutable wings.   30
A little while and we die; shall life not thrive
as it may?
For no man under the sky lives twice, out-
living his day.
And grief is a grievous thing, and a man hath
enough of his tears:
Why should he labor, and bring fresh grief
to blacken his years?
Thou hast conquered, O pale Galilean; the
world has grown gray from thy breath; 35
We have drunken of things Lethean,[11] and
fed on the fullness of death.
Laurel is green for a season, and love is sweet
for a day;
But love grows bitter with treason, and laurel
outlives not May.
Sleep, shall we sleep after all? for the world
is not sweet in the end;
For the old faiths loosen and fall, the new
years ruin and rend.   40
Fate is a sea without shore, and the soul is a
rock that abides;
But her ears are vexed with the roar and her
face with the foam of the tides.
O lips that the live blood faints in, the leavings
of racks and rods! [12]
O ghastly glories of saints, dead limbs of gib-
beted gods! [13]
Though all men abase them before you in
spirit, and all knees bend,   45
I kneel not, neither adore you, but standing,
look to the end.[14]
All delicate days and pleasant, all spirits and
sorrows are cast
Far out with the foam of the present that
sweeps to the surf of the past:

[7] Among other things, the god of music and
poetry.
[8] Laurel, with which a poet is crowned.
[9] The laurel and palms were sacred to the gods.
[10] Cupid and Venus, god and goddess of love.

[11] Causing forgetfulness, as the waters of Lethe,
a river of Hades, were supposed to do.
[12] A reference to the persecutions and self-tortures
of the early Christians. The speaker condemns
Christianity for its asceticism and lack of vitality.
[13] Line 44 refers to the Christian veneration of
martyrdom and the Crucifixion.
[14] The death, ages hence, of the Christian gods.
In the next section of the poem, ll. 47–74, this
vision of the ceaseless roll of the ages is presented
under the image of a limitless ocean.

Where beyond the extreme sea-wall, and between the remote sea-gates,
Waste water washes, and tall ships founder,
and deep death waits: 50
Where, mighty with deepening sides, clad
about with the seas as with wings,
And impelled of invisible tides, and fulfilled
of unspeakable things,
White-eyed and poisonous-finned, shark-
toothed and serpentine-curled,
Rolls, under the whitening wind of the future,
the wave of the world.
The depths stand naked in sunder behind it,
the storms flee away;   55
In the hollow before it the thunder is taken
and snared as a prey;
In its sides is the north-wind bound; and its
salt is of all men's tears;
With light of ruin, and sound of changes, and
pulse of years:
With travail of day after day, and with trouble
of hour upon hour;
And bitter as blood is the spray; and the crests
are as fangs that devour: 60
And its vapor and storm of its steam as the
sighing of spirits to be;
And its noise as the noise in a dream; and its
depth as the roots of the sea:
And the height of its heads as the height of
the utmost stars of the air:
And the ends of the earth at the might thereof
tremble, and time is made bare.
Will ye bridle the deep sea with reins, will ye
chasten the high sea with rods?   65
Will ye take her to chain her with chains, who
is older than all ye gods?
All ye as a wind shall go by, as a fire shall ye
pass and be past;
Ye are gods, and behold, ye shall die, and
the waves be upon you at last.
In the darkness of time, in the deeps of the
years, in the changes of things,
Ye shall sleep as a slain man sleeps, and the
world shall forget you for kings.   70
Though the feet of thine [15] high priests tread
where thy lords and our forefathers trod,
Though these that were gods are dead, and
thou being dead art a god,

Though before thee the throned Cytherean [16]
be fallen, and hidden her head,
Yet thy kingdom shall pass, Galilean, thy dead
shall go down to thee dead.
Of the maiden thy mother men sing as a goddess with grace clad around;   75
Thou art throned where another was king;
where another was queen she is crowned.
Yea, once we had sight of another: but now
she is queen, say these.
Not as thine, not as thine was our mother, a
blossom of flowering seas,
Clothed round with the world's desire as with
raiment, and fair as the foam,
And fleeter than kindled fire, and a goddess
and mother of Rome.[17]   80
For thine came pale and a maiden, and sister
to sorrow; but ours,
Her deep hair heavily laden with odor, and
color of flowers,
White rose of the rose-white water, a silver
splendor, a flame,
Bent down unto us that besought her, and
earth grew sweet with her name.
For thine came weeping, a slave among slaves,
and rejected; but she   85
Came flushed from the full-flushed wave, and
imperial, her foot on the sea.
And the wonderful waters knew her, the
winds and the viewless ways,
And the roses grew rosier, and bluer the sea-
blue stream of the bays.
Ye are fallen, our lords, by what token? we
wist that ye should not fall.
Ye were all so fair that are broken; and one
more fair than ye all.   90
But I turn to her [18] still, having seen she shall
surely abide in the end;
Goddess and maiden and queen, be near me
now and befriend.
O daughter of earth,[19] of my mother, her
crown and blossom of birth,

[15] Jesus is now addressed directly.

[16] Venus (Aphrodite), who, according to one
legend, was born out of the foam of the sea near the
island of Cythera.
[17] Venus was the mother of Aeneas, legendary
ancestor of the Romans. The contrast here is between Venus and Mary the mother of Christ.
[18] Proserpine.
[19] Proserpine was the daughter of Ceres (Deme-
ter), goddess of earth.

I am also, I also thy brother; I go as I came
  unto earth.
In the night where thine eyes are as moons are
  in heaven, the night where thou art,   95
Where the silence is more than all tunes,
  where sleep overflows from the heart,
Where the poppies [20] are sweet as the rose in
  our world, and the red rose is white,
And the wind falls faint as it blows with the
  fume of the flowers of the night,
And the murmur of spirits that sleep in the
  shadow of gods from afar
Grows dim in thine ears and deep as the deep
  dim soul of a star,   100
In the sweet low light of thy face, under
  heavens untrod by the sun,
Let my soul with their souls find place, and
  forget what is done and undone.
Thou art more than the gods who number the
  days of our temporal breath;
For these give labor and slumber; but thou,
  Proserpina, death.

Therefore now at thy feet I abide for a season
  in silence. I know   105
I shall die as my fathers died, and sleep as they
  sleep; even so.
For the glass of the years is brittle wherein we
  gaze for a span;
A little soul for a little bears up this corpse
  which is man.[21]
So long I endure, no longer; and laugh not
  again, neither weep.
For there is no god found stronger than death;
  and death is a sleep.   110
(1866)

STUDY AIDS: 1. Why is the poem addressed
to Proserpine? Why does the speaker prefer
paganism to Christianity? As he laments over
the triumph of the new religion, what is his
consolation? Is he fair to Christianity?
  2. The speaker has been called an Epicurean
—that is, one who lives to achieve pleasure, or
the absence of pain. What passages of the poem
support this view?

The Garden of Proserpine

The Garden of Proserpine, wrote Swinburne, expresses "that brief total pause of passion and thought, when the spirit, without fear or hope of good things or evil, hungers and thirsts only after the perfect sleep."

Here, where the world is quiet;
  Here, where all trouble seems
Dead winds' and spent waves' riot
  In doubtful dreams of dreams,[1]
I watch the green field growing   5
For reaping folk and sowing,
For harvest time and mowing,
  A sleepy world of streams.

I am tired of tears and laughter,
  And men that laugh and weep,   10
Of what may come hereafter
  For men that sow to reap:

I am weary of days and hours,
Blown [2] buds of barren flowers,
Desires and dreams and powers,   15
  And every thing but sleep.

Here life has death for neighbor,
  And far from eye or ear
Wan waves and wet winds labor,
  Weak ships and spirits steer;   20
They drive adrift, and whither
They wot [3] not who make thither;
But no such winds blow hither,
  And no such things grow here.

[20] Causing deep sleep, they are especially sacred to Proserpine.
[21] Line 108 is derived from a sentence of Epictetus, Greek Stoic philosopher: "Thou art a little soul bearing up a corpse."

[1] What does this phrase "dreams of dreams" mean? What is its effect?
[2] Having blossomed.
[3] Know.

No growth of moor or coppice,   25
  No heather-flower or vine,
But bloomless buds of poppies,
  Green grapes of Proserpine,[4]
Pale beds of blowing rushes
Where no leaf blooms or blushes,   30
Save this whereout she crushes
  For dead men deadly wine.

Pale, without name or number,
  In fruitless fields of corn,
They bow themselves and slumber   35
  All night till light is born;
And like a soul belated,
In hell and heaven unmated,
By cloud and mist abated
  Comes out of darkness morn.   40

Though one were strong as seven,
  He too with death shall dwell,
Nor wake with wings in heaven,
  Nor weep for pains in hell;
Though one were fair as roses,   45
His beauty clouds and closes;
And well though love reposes,
  In the end it is not well.

Pale, beyond porch and portal,[5]
  Crowned with calm leaves,[6] she stands 50
Who gathers all things mortal
  With cold immortal hands;
Her languid lips are sweeter
Than love's, who fears to greet her,
To men that mix and meet her   55
  From many times and lands.

She waits for each and other,
  She waits for all men born;
Forgets the earth her mother,[7]
  The life of fruits and corn;   60
And spring and seed and swallow

[4] See n. 1, p. 885.
[5] The entrance to the underworld.
[6] Of the poppy.
[7] See n. 19, p. 887.

Take wing for her, and follow
Where summer song rings hollow,
  And flowers are put to scorn.

There go the loves that wither,   65
  The old loves with wearier wings,[8]
And all dead years draw thither,
  And all disastrous things;
Dead dreams of days forsaken,
Blind buds that snows have shaken,   70
Wild leaves that winds have taken,
  Red strays of ruined springs.

We are not sure of sorrow,
  And joy was never sure;
To-day will die to-morrow;   75
  Time stoops to no man's lure;
And love, grown faint and fretful,
With lips but half regretful
Sighs, and with eyes forgetful
  Weeps that no loves endure.   80

From too much love of living,
  From hope and fear set free,
We thank with brief thanksgiving
  Whatever gods may be
That no life lives forever;   85
That dead men rise up never;
That even the weariest river
  Winds somewhere safe to sea.

Then star nor sun shall waken,
  Nor any change of light;   90
Nor sound of waters shaken,
  Nor any sound or sight;
Nor wintry leaves nor vernal,
Nor days nor things diurnal:
Only the sleep eternal   95
  In an eternal night.
(1866)

STUDY AIDS: What is the MOOD of this
poem? How do the images, sound effects, and
metrical form create this mood? What do the
FEMININE ENDINGS of many lines contribute?

[8] How does the meter of this line fit the meaning?

Francis Thompson
(1859–1907)

OCCASIONALLY A MINOR POET WILL PRODUCE A MAJOR POEM. SUCH IS THE CASE WITH Francis Thompson. Although he published three volumes of poetry and a fair amount of prose, he remains for most readers the author of *The Hound of Heaven*, one of the great religious poems of our literature.

Thompson's early years were miserable. After attempts to become a Catholic priest and then a doctor had both failed, he went to London, where he spent three years in extreme poverty, fighting tuberculosis and becoming increasingly addicted to opium. He was rescued from this pathetic state by a magazine editor and his wife, Wilfrid and Alice Meynell, who befriended him. It was with their help and encouragement that he wrote his celebrated poem.

The Hound of Heaven [1]

I fled Him, down the nights and down the
    days;
  I fled Him, down the arches of the years;
I fled Him, down the labyrinthine ways
  Of my own mind; and in the mist of
    tears
I hid from Him, and under running laugh-
    ter.   5
      Up vistaed hopes I sped;
      And shot, precipitated,
Adown titanic [2] glooms of chasmèd fears,
  From those strong feet that followed, fol-
    lowed after.
      But with unhurrying chase,   10
      And unperturbèd pace,
    Deliberate speed, majestic instancy,[3]
      They beat—and a voice beat
      More instant than the feet—

"All things betray thee, who betrayest
    Me."   15

    I pleaded, outlaw-wise,
By many a hearted casement, curtained red,
  Trellised with intertwining charities
(For, though I knew His love who followèd,
    Yet was I sore adread   20
Lest, having Him, I must have naught be-
    side);
But, if one little casement parted wide,
  The gust of His approach would clash it to.
Fear wist [4] not to evade, as love wist to pur-
    sue.
Across the margent [5] of the world I fled, 25
  And troubled the gold gateways of the stars,
  Smiting for shelter on their clangèd bars;
    Fretted to dulcet jars
And silvern chatter the pale ports of the
    moon.[6]

[1] This image may have been suggested to Thompson by Shelley, who wrote of "Heaven's winged hound" in *Prometheus Unbound*.

[2] Gigantic (the Titans were giants).

[3] Insistency.

[4] Knew.

[5] Edge.

[6] I.e., beat upon the gates of the moon until they gave forth sweet music.

I said to dawn, Be sudden; to eve, Be soon; 30
  With thy young skyey blossoms heap me
    over
  From this tremendous lover!
Float thy vague veil about me, lest He see!
  I tempted all His servitors,[7] but to find
My own betrayal in their constancy, 35
In faith to Him their fickleness to me,
  Their traitorous trueness, and their loyal
    deceit.
To all swift things for swiftness did I sue;
  Clung to the whistling mane of every
    wind.
    But whether they swept, smoothly
      fleet, 40
    The long savannahs [8] of the blue;
    Or whether, thunder-driven,
      They clanged his chariot athwart a
        heaven
Plashy with flying lightnings round the
  spurn [9] of their feet—
  Fear wist not to evade as love wist to pur-
    sue. 45
    Still with unhurrying chase,
    And unperturbèd pace,
    Deliberate speed, majestic instancy,
    Came on the following feet,
    And a voice above their beat— 50
  "Naught shelters thee, who wilt not shel-
    ter Me."

I sought no more that after which I strayed
  In face of man or maid;
But still within the little children's eyes
  Seems something, something that re-
    plies; 55
They at least are for me, surely for me!
I turned me to them very wistfully;
But, just as their young eyes grew sudden
  fair

With dawning answers there,
Their angel plucked them from me by the
  hair. 60
"Come then, ye other children, nature's—
  share
With me" (said I) "your delicate fellowship;
  Let me greet you lip to lip,
  Let me twine with you caresses,
    Wantoning 65
  With our Lady-Mother's [10] vagrant
    tresses,
    Banqueting
  With her in her wind-walled palace,
  Underneath her azured daïs,
  Quaffing, as your taintless way is, 70
    From a chalice
Lucent-weeping [11] out of the dayspring."
  So it was done;
I in their delicate fellowship was one—
Drew the bolt of nature's secrecies. 75
I knew all the swift importings [12]
  On the willful face of skies;
  I knew how the clouds arise
  Spumèd of the wild sea-snortings; [13]
    All that's born or dies 80
    Rose and drooped with—made them shap-
      ers
Of mine own moods, or wailful or divine—
  With them joyed and was bereaven.
  I was heavy with the even,
  When she lit her glimmering tapers 85
  Round the day's dead sanctities.
  I laughed in the morning's eyes.
I triumphed and I saddened with all weather,
  Heaven and I wept together,
And its sweet tears were salt with mortal
  mine; 90
Against the red throb of its sunset-heart
    I laid my own to beat,
    And share commingling heat;
But not by that, by that, was eased my human
  smart.
In vain my tears were wet on Heaven's gray
  cheek. 95

[7] Noting that "servitors" would be God's various creatures, what do ll. 34–37 mean? How can their faith be fickleness, their trueness traitorous, their deceit loyal? This kind of verbal self-contradiction is called an "oxymoron."
[8] Plains.
[9] Kick.

[10] Nature's.
[11] Dripping bright drops.
[12] Meanings.
[13] Formed by the spray thrown up by the waves.

For ah! we know not what each other says,
　　These things and I; in sound I speak—
Their sound is but their stir, they speak by
　　　　silences.
Nature, poor stepdame, cannot slake my
　　drouth;
　　Let her, if she would owe [14] me,　　100
Drop yon blue bosom-veil of sky, and show me
　　The breasts of her tenderness;
Never did any milk of hers once bless
　　My thirsting mouth.
　　Nigh and nigh draws the chase,　　105
　　With unperturbèd pace,
　　Deliberate speed, majestic instancy;
　　And past those noisèd feet
　　A voice comes yet more fleet—
"Lo! naught contents thee, who content'st not
　　Me."　　　　　　　　　　　　　　110

Naked I wait Thy love's uplifted stroke!
My harness piece by piece Thou hast hewn
　　from me,
　　And smitten me to my knee;
　　I am defenseless utterly.
　　I slept, methinks, and woke,　　115
And, slowly gazing, find me stripped in sleep.
In the rash lustihead of my young powers,
　　I shook the pillaring hours
And pulled my life upon me; [15] grimed with
　　smears,
I stand amid the dust of the mounded
　　years—　　　　　　　　　　　　120
My mangled youth lies dead beneath the heap.
My days have crackled and gone up in smoke,
Have puffed and burst as sun-starts on a
　　stream.
　　Yea, faileth now even dream
The dreamer, and the lute the lutanist;　　125
Even the linked fantasies,[16] in whose blossomy
　　twist
I swung the earth a trinket at my wrist,
Are yielding; cords of all too weak account
For earth with heavy griefs so overplussed.
　　Ah! is Thy love indeed　　　　130
A weed, albeit an amaranthine [17] weed,

[14] Own.
[15] As Samson pulled down the roof of the temple
upon his head.
[16] Poems.
[17] Immortal, like the amaranth (a flower), which
is said to grow in heaven.

Suffering no flowers except its own to mount?
　　Ah! must—
　　Designer infinite!—
Ah! must Thou char the wood ere Thou canst
　　limn [18] with it?　　　　　　135
My freshness spent its wavering shower in the
　　dust;
And now my heart is as a broken fount,
Wherein tear-drippings stagnate, spilled down
　　ever
　　From the dank thoughts that shiver
Upon the sighful branches of my mind.　　140
　　Such is; what is to be?
The pulp so bitter, how shall taste the rind?
I dimly guess what time in mists confounds:
Yet ever and anon a trumpet sounds
From the hid battlements of eternity;　　145
Those shaken mists a space unsettle, then
Round the half-glimpsèd turrets slowly wash
　　again.
　　But not ere him who summoneth
　　I first have seen, enwound
With glooming robes purpureal, cypress-
　　crowned; [19]　　　　　　　150
His name I know, and what his trumpet saith.
Whether man's heart or life it be which yields
　　Thee harvest, must Thy harvest fields
　　Be dunged with rotten death?

　　Now of that long pursuit　　155
　　Comes on at hand the bruit; [20]
That voice is round me like a bursting
　　sea:
　　"And is thy earth so marred,
　　Shattered in shard [21] on shard?
Lo, all things fly thee, for thou fliest
　　Me!　　　　　　　　　　160
　　Strange, piteous, futile thing,
Wherefore should any set thee love apart?
Seeing none but I makes much of naught"
　　(He said),
"And human love needs human meriting,　165
　　How hast thou merited—
Of all man's clotted clay the dingiest clot?
　　Alack, thou knowest not
How little worthy of any love thou art!

[18] Draw.
[19] Symbol of mourning and death.
[20] Noise.
[21] Fragment.

Whom wilt thou find to love ignoble thee 170
    Save Me, save only Me?
All which I took from thee I did but take,
    Not for thy harms,
But just that thou might'st seek it in my arms.
    All which thy child's mistake   175
Fancies as lost, I have stored for thee at home;
    Rise, clasp my hand, and come!"

    Halts by me that footfall;
    Is my gloom, after all,
    Shade of His hand, outstretched caress-
        ingly?   180
    "Ah, fondest, blindest, weakest,
    I am He whom thou seekest!
Thou dravest [22] love from thee, who dravest
    Me."
(1891; 1893)

STUDY AIDS: 1. Quite obviously, the speaker of the poem is trying to escape from "the hound of heaven." What or who is the hound of heaven? Why is the poet trying to get away from him? What various means does he use to escape the hound? Why is he not successful? What, then, is the THEME of the poem?

2. In ll. 61–110 Thompson is concerned with a single way of "escape." What is it? Why is it futile?

3. Why is l. 111 the turning-point of the poem? Analyze carefully the succession of images in ll. 111–154. How do they fit together?

4. What is the shift in TONE at the close of the poem, and how is it justified?

5. Read the opening stanza aloud. What is the effect of the rhythm?

Gerard Manley Hopkins
(1844–1889)

HOPKINS ENTERED OXFORD UNIVERSITY TO PREPARE HIMSELF FOR THE ANGLICAN MINISTRY. While there, however, he came under the influence of John Henry Newman (later Cardinal Newman) and was converted to Roman Catholicism. When he entered the Jesuit order in 1868 he burned his poems and wrote no more for seven years. But the desire to express himself in poetry was too strong, and he began writing once more. At his death, his manuscripts were given to his friend and fellow-poet, Robert Bridges, who published them in 1918.

Hopkins' poetry has had considerable influence on twentieth-century poets, who find in it an emotional vitality and intensity akin to their own. His versification is difficult. It is based, for the most part, on medieval and Anglo-Saxon poetic practices. Hopkins called it "sprung rhythm": four or five stressed syllables with an indefinite number of unstressed syllables to one line (in contrast to the regular patterns of traditional poetry). He also made other experiments: breaking a word at the end of a line in order to use the half-word as a rhyme; placing phrases between a word and its modifier; and above all, tying the two halves of a line with alliteration.

His poetry is almost exclusively religious. In expressing his personal devotion to God, Hopkins is closer in spirit and practice to modern religious poets than to his own contemporaries of the 1870's–1880's.

[22] Drovest.

The Windhover

To Christ Our Lord

A windhover is a variety of hawk noted for its habit of flying straight into the wind, matching its speed with the wind's, and then plummeting earthward.

The poem discusses Hopkins' admiration for a balance maintained in the midst of violent force and motion. The life and actions of Christ (symbolized by the windhover) best reveal this balance to men.

I caught this morning morning's minion,[1] king-
    dom of daylight's dauphin,[2] dapple-
    dawn-drawn Falcon, in his riding
Of the rolling level underneath him steady
    air,[3] and striding
High there, how he rung upon the rein of a
    wimpling [4] wing
In his ecstasy! then off, off forth on swing,
    As a skate's heel sweeps smooth on a bow-
    bend: [5] the hurl [6] and gliding   5
Rebuffed the big wind. My heart in hiding
Stirred [7] for a bird—the achieve of, the mastery
    of the thing!

Brute beauty [8] and valor and act, oh, air,
    pride,[9] plume here
    Buckle! and the fire [10] that breaks from
    thee then, a billion
Times told lovelier, more dangerous, O my
    chevalier! [11]   10

No wonder of it: [12] shéer plód makes plow
    down sillion [13]
Shine, and blue-bleak embers,[14] ah, my dear,
    Fall, gall themselves, and gash gold-ver-
    milion.

(1877; 1918)

STUDY AIDS: 1. The poem develops Hopkins' admiration and feelings for the windhover. Note the subtitle of the poem. To what is the poet comparing the windhover? What words in the poem apply equally to the bird and to Christ? What does the poet mean by saying that the Falcon (Christ) "rebuffed the big wind"? What act of violence in Christ's life gave beauty and significance to him? What relation do the words "gall" and "gash" (l. 14) have to this act of violence?

2. How do alliteration, twisted syntax, and inverted word order contribute to Hopkins' meaning and emotion in the poem?

3. What kind of poem is The Windhover: epic, sonnet, or ode?

[1] Servant.

[2] Heir apparent, crown prince.

[3] Hopkins' meaning is not difficult if you re-arrange the line into normal word order: "I caught (saw) this morning (the) minion of morning, (the) dauphin of (the) kingdom of daylight, (the) Falcon, drawn (by the) dapple-dawn, in his riding of the rolling air, level (and) steady underneath him." Although this arrangement makes the meaning clearer, does it create the same effect as the original? Try to explain why there is a difference.

[4] Rippling; to lay in folds. What is the IMAGE used in ll. 4–5? What two things are compared?

[5] The bending or bowing of the knee in skating.

[6] Hopkins is fond of creating verbal nouns. Notice other examples in the poem. How does this one illustrate the poem's subject and Hopkins' feelings?

[7] Why is Hopkins moved by the sight of the windhover?

[8] Why is "beauty" modified by "Brute"?

[9] The peak of the falcon's climb before his plunge earthward.

[10] The bird's plumage shows color (fire) as the air forces the feathers apart.

[11] Knight. Why is this apt? What is its relation to "achieve," "valor," "act"?

[12] Hopkins now gives the reason for his admiration through two images: the shining plowshare and the glowing embers.

[13] A furrow or the ridge of earth between. What makes the plowshare shine?

[14] What makes the almost dead embers glow? In these two images and in the windhover itself, is violence necessary for beauty (note "Brute beauty," l. 8)?

No Worst, There Is None

There seems little doubt that Hopkins, when he wrote this sonnet, had been reading or remembering Shakespeare's *King Lear*. The poem is not about the play, but Hopkins uses the grief of Edgar (a character in *Lear*) to express his own grief. In the play, the aged Gloucester has had his eyes gouged out as an indirect consequence of his own spiritual blindness: he had cast off his virtuous son, Edgar, in favor of his ignoble son, Edmund. He accepts his physical blindness as a fitting retribution for his sins, especially that against Edgar. In *King Lear,* IV, i, Gloucester asks a beggar (his good son, Edgar, in disguise) to lead him to the cliffs of Dover, where he intends to commit suicide. Edgar speaks to himself:

> Edgar (*aside*)   O gods! Who is 't can say 'I am at the worst'?
> And worse than e'er I was . . .
> And worse I may be yet: the worst is not
> So long as we can say 'This is the worst.'

Eventually Edgar succeeds in convincing Gloucester that an evil spirit has put the idea of suicide into his mind, but that God has preserved him from this final sin by wafting him down to the base of the cliff. Gloucester replies:

> I do remember now: henceforth I'll bear
> Affliction till it do cry out itself
> 'Enough, enough, and die.'

No worst, there is none. Pitched past pitch of grief,
More pangs will, schooled at forepangs, wilder wring.
Comforter, where, where is your comforting?
Mary, mother of us, where is your relief?
My cries heave, herds-long; huddle in a main, a chief   5
Woe, world-sorrow; on an age-old anvil wince and sing—
Then lull, then leave off. Fury had shrieked "No lingering! Let me be fell: [1] force I must be brief."

O the mind, mind has mountains; cliffs of fall
Frightful, sheer, no-man-fathomed. Hold them cheap   10
May who ne'er hung there. Nor does long our small
Durance deal with that steep or deep. Here! creep,
Wretch, under a comfort serves in a whirlwind: all
Life death does end and each day dies with sleep.

(1885–1887; 1918)

STUDY AIDS: Is the last line optimistic or pessimistic?

[1] Fallen.

Spring and Fall: to a young child

Márgarét, are you gríeving
Over Goldengrove unleaving?
Leáves, líke the things of man, you
With your fresh thoughts care for, can you?
Ah! ás the heart grows older   5
It will come to such sights colder

By and by, nor spare a sigh
Though worlds of wanwood [1] leafmeal [2] lie;
And yet you wíll weep and know why.
Now no matter, child, the name: 10

[1] Dying, colorless leaves.
[2] Leaf by leaf, as piece by piece of "piecemeal."

Sórrow's spríngs áre the same,
Nor mouth had, no nor mind, expressed
What heart heard of, ghost guessed:
It ís the blight man was born for,[3]
It is Margaret you mourn for.   15
(1880; 1918)

Heaven-Haven

(A Nun Takes the Veil)

I have desired to go
    Where springs not fail,
To fields where flies no sharp and sided
        hail,
    And a few lilies blow.

And I have asked to be
    Where no storms come,
Where the green swell is in the haven dumb,
    And out of the swing of the sea.
(ca. 1866; 1918)

Felix Randal

Felix Randal the farrier,[1] O he is dead then?
    my duty all ended,
Who have watched his mold of man, big-
    boned and hardy-handsome
Pining, pining, till time when reason rambled
    in it and some
Fatal four disorders, fleshed there, all con-
    tended?

Sickness broke him. Impatient he cursed at
    first, but mended   5
Being anointed[2] and all; though a heavenlier
    heart began some
Months earlier, since I had our sweet reprieve
    and ransom[3]
Tendered to him. Ah well, God rest him all
    road ever he offended!

This seeing the sick endears them to us, us
    too it endears.
My tongue had taught thee comfort, touch
    had quenched thy tears,   10
Thy tears that touched my heart, child, Felix,
    poor Felix Randal;

How far from then forethought of, all thy
    more boisterous years,
When thou at the random[4] grim forge, power-
    ful amidst peers,[5]
Didst fettle for the great gray drayhorse his
    bright and battering sandal!
(1880; 1918)

---

[3] This is the statement of the poem—man's mortality. Margaret "mourns for Margaret" (l. 15), because she has felt but not understood that all life must eventually die.

---

[1] Blacksmith.
[2] I.e., having received extreme unction.
[3] The communion which had saved Felix.

[4] Constructed of rough stones.
[5] Equals.

Pied [1] Beauty

Glory be to God for dappled things—
  For skies as couple [2]-color as a brinded [3]
    cow;
  For rose-moles all in stipple upon trout that
    swim;
Fresh-firecoal chestnut-falls; [4] finches' wings;
  Landscape plotted and pieced—fold, fallow,
    and plough; [5]   5
    And áll trádes, their gear and tackle and
    trim.

All things counter,[6] original, spare,[7] strange;
  Whatever [8] is fickle, freckled (who knows
    how?)

With swift, slow; sweet, sour; adazzle, dim;
He fathers-forth whose beauty is past
    change: 10
          Praise him.

(1877; 1918)

STUDY AIDS: 1. Work out the rhyme scheme. Work out the ALLITERATION. Read the poem aloud. Why is it more effective when read aloud?

2. What aspects of nature seem to appeal to Hopkins? How would you describe his sense of beauty as seen in nature (take into consideration all of his poems you have read)?

[1] Variegated.
[2] Two.
[3] Streaked.
[4] Roasted chestnut husks.
[5] Plowed fields.
[6] Opposite.
[7] Rare.
[8] Direct object of verb "fathers-forth" (l. 10).

Pied Beauty

Glory be to God for dappled things—
For skies of couple-colour as a brinded[2]
    cow;
For rose-moles all in stipple upon trout that
    swim;
Fresh-firecoal chestnut-falls; finches' wings;
Landscape plotted and pieced—fold, fallow,
    and plough;
    And all trádes, their gear and tackle and
    trim.

All things counter, original, spare, strange;
Whatever is fickle, freckled (who knows
    how?)
        With swift, slow; sweet, sour; adazzle, dim;
He fathers-forth whose beauty is past
    change:
                Praise him.
                                            (1877; 1918)

STUDY AIDS: 1. Work out the rhyme scheme. Work out the alliteration. Read the poem aloud. Why is it more effective when read aloud?
    2. What aspects of nature seem to appeal to Hopkins? How would you describe his sense of beauty as seen in nature (take into consideration all of the poems you have read)?

[1] Piece of cloth.
[2] Brindled. Streaked.
[3] Roasted chestnut husks.
[4] Direct object of verb "fathers-forth" (l. 10).

The Twentieth Century

READERS OF ENGLISH LITERATURE OFTEN REGARD AS "CONTEMPO-
rary" only the writings of the last forty years. While it is true
that the First World War serves as a convenient point of chronological demarcation, literature since that time cannot be dis-
sociated from that of the later nineteenth century. It inherits the
ideas and social problems bequeathed it by the Victorians. Indeed,
if there is any consistent pattern or order in twentieth-century
literature, it is the attempt to solve the problems that nineteenth-
century thought had posed.

Chief among the inherited ideas are: (1) Darwinism, or the
theory of biological evolution, and its attendant philosophy of
determinism; (2) Marxism, or the doctrine of dialectical materialism; and (3) Freudianism, or the psychology of Freud, which
attempts to describe the growth and function of the mind. These
ideas, coupled with the rapid technological advances of the nineteenth-century Industrial Revolution and a staggering increase
in the whole body of scientific knowledge, produced even greater
confusion in the areas of moral and ethical values for the twentieth-
century writer than they had for his Victorian forebears.

Modern man's confusion grew to disillusionment and despair as he witnessed the political violence and upheaval of
his century. The First World War broke out in 1914. For five

899

exhausting years the struggle continued, until finally England and her allies emerged victorious over Germany and dictated the Peace Treaty of Versailles (1919). But the war "to make the world safe for democracy" solved little. Between 1918 and 1939 minor wars were fought in all parts of the world: Japan invaded China; Italy devoured Ethiopia; France subjugated Morocco and Syria; Spain almost destroyed herself by civil war. New forms of anti-democratic government were spreading: Fascism in Germany, Italy, and Spain; Communism in Russia; a rampant militarism in Japan. In 1939 Great Britain was again involved in war with Germany, this time a total war which quickly engulfed the whole world. Although Britain once more emerged victorious, she was considerably weakened in the aftermath of the conflict. Her empire was shrunken, her domestic economy was shattered, and the ensuing national poverty brought into power the Labor Party, which instituted a regime of socialism to cure the ills of the country. The old way of life, together with the moral and cultural standards which had been the basis of English literature, was passing away.

The new writer had to find a new basis for literature, new values for mankind. He was faced with a bewildering array of nostrums for the ailments of the day, but he found none satisfactory. His age had no homogeneity, no common temper; it was molded by no dominant idea, such as the faith in reason which had shaped the eighteenth century or the belief in progress which had shaped the nineteenth. It was an age of tension, which W. H. Auden characterized in 1947 in the title of a volume of poems, *The Age of Anxiety*.

As the new writer surveyed his immediate past he could see ample evidence that the "old order changeth, yielding place to new," but he had no certainty as to which new order would prevail. Some writers pleaded that the old tradition of liberal Christian humanism was still valid; others insisted that the secular scientific world had rendered that tradition impotent. Those writers who rejected the scientific tradition as the guide of life could not agree on any system of values which might be used to interpret man's experience. Even those who did accept science and the machine disagreed as to how they could be incorporated in literature. The tension of the new age was apparent in its many divisions and hostilities, each one of which diametrically opposed another; in politics, the individual vs. society, and Fascism or Communism vs. Democracy; in religion, fundamentalism vs. modernism, traditional humanism vs. deism; in philosophy, past vs. experimental present, civilization vs. primitivism; in art, conformity vs. nonconformity, strict form vs. experimental form, realism vs. romanticism.

Each writer chose his own standard and for the most part seemed unaware of others. Occasionally a few (and they were lesser luminaries) banded together into literary groups and published small magazines and volumes, which were short-lived. From 1911 to 1922 the "Georgians" issued their anthologies of verse. Their best known contributors were Rupert Brooke, John Drinkwater, and John Masefield. There was little agreement even among avowed Georgians as to what their program was. They opposed the formally religious, philosophic, and didactic themes of Victorian poetry and the "sad and wicked themes" of the 1890 aesthetes; they were to write on simple subjects like "Nature, love, old age, childhood, animals . . . unemotional subjects." In general the Georgians' reaction to the complexity of the modern world was a return to an adulterated Wordsworthianism stripped of sentiment and mysticism.

Of more significance and lasting influence were the "Imagists," an Anglo-American group of poets who published their views in *The Imagists* from 1914 to 1917. Like the

Georgians, the Imagists also found their program too restrictive. The American members —Ezra Pound, Amy Lowell, and H. D. (Hilda Doolittle)—were better known poets than their English colleagues—Osbert Sitwell, Richard Aldington, and Frank S. Flint. However, the group indelibly imprinted itself on future literature through the anti-romantic criticism of T. E. Hulme. The Imagists aimed at a hard clarity and precision of language in rendering objects and ideas in poetry; they rigorously avoided all exuberance, sentiment, or lushness. T. S. Eliot, Virginia Woolf, James Joyce, as well as several contemporary critics, were indebted to the imagist poets.

These and other vaguely defined groups, however, seemed only remotely aware of the moral and intellectual ferment of the new century. An awareness of the spirit of an age is the mark of a higher talent, and such talent had made its appearance toward the end of the Victorian era. Matthew Arnold, William Morris, John Ruskin, and Samuel Butler, four prophets of the new era, had set themselves against the limited optimism of the earlier Victorians and had voiced discontent with England's industrialism and with the smugness and complacency of her middle class.

By the turn of the century the skepticism of Arnold had deepened into the pessimism expressed in the writings of Thomas Hardy and A. E. Housman, and, later, in those of Aldous Huxley, and in the earlier work of T. S. Eliot. Hardy, in denying Christianity and immortality, accepted the evolutionary thesis of Darwin and the determinism of science, doctrines explaining the new world as he saw it. In his novels *Tess of the D'Urbervilles* (1891) and *Jude the Obscure* (1895), blind destiny destroys the innocent and the guilty with impartiality. Human beings are the too self-conscious victims of the "social mold civilization fits us into." A. E. Housman, unlike Hardy, does not cry out against God and man, but the tempers of the two men are akin. Aware that the older, accepted standards were crumbling, Housman replaced them with a stoicism bred of classical study. A dark fatalism stains his view of life, which saw life's frustrations more clearly than its satisfactions. *A Shropshire Lad* (1896) urges youth to enjoy itself because death comes quickly. The same view, with less force, is expressed in *Last Poems* (1922) and the posthumous *More Poems* (1936).

Aldous Huxley's reaction to contemporary society is not so much one of pessimism as of disgust and cynicism. He has rejected his Victorian grandfather's hope in scientific progress. Huxley finds little hope in life: conventional religion is a sham, sensual joys are delusions, action produces only frustration. The brilliant, comic wit of his early novels, *Antic Hay* (1923) and *Point Counter Point* (1928), turns to a satiric indictment of modern science in *Brave New World* (1932) and finally to bitter contempt in *After Many a Summer Dies the Swan* (1939). It is small wonder that Huxley has withdrawn from the contemporary world to pursue mysticism and the contemplative life.

Wystan Hugh Auden, although considerably younger than Huxley or Eliot, shares their pessimism. Of all contemporary poets, none is so socially conscious as Auden. No other poet has worried so much about man as a social creature or has more earnestly sought relief from man's social tensions. His poetry of the thirties pictured the social system as outworn and decayed. With other young writers—Louis MacNeice, Stephen Spender, Julian Bell, and Christopher Caudwell, among others—Auden embraced Marxism as a way to free himself from "the brute force of this world." But he soon learned that a political program, which he had embraced out of idealism, offered no real cure for the psychological and moral disorders of the twentieth century. In his attempts to resolve his dilemma, Auden vacillated between the Marxian and Freudian views: does social injustice produce psychological disorder, or does psychic evil produce social evil? Auden has not yet solved his problem. A later poem, "In Time of War" (1939), is still pessimistic in its presentation of a humanity thwarted: modern man's intelligence is more fertile than before, but his heart is more stunted. Perhaps because of this basic pessimism, Auden has, for himself, accepted a religious solution to the problem.

While it is true that T. S. Eliot in his early writing shared the pessimistic views of Hardy and Housman, his total vision is far less fatalistic than theirs. *The Love-Song of J. Alfred Prufrock* (1917), *The Waste Land* (1922), and *The Hollow Men* (1925) present the modern world and its inhabitants as desolate and sordid, lacking purpose or direction. But Eliot's literary criticism complements this poetic disenchantment by presenting affirmative views. *The Sacred Wood* (1920) and *Selected Essays* (1932) develop his belief in classicism and tradition. Eliot's classicism does not involve a return to the older standards, nor is to be achieved by following rules or imitating older literature. He argues that literature is a continuous process, emerging from the past and containing it. Fresh creation expresses itself not in terms of the older world but of the new, changing world; it modifies the past and helps complete it. In preserving tradition the new writer will use a language "which is struggling to digest and express new objects, new groups of objects, new feelings, new aspects." In this approach to literature Eliot presents an answer to his century's problems. Unlike Hardy, with his theoretical hope that mankind might ameliorate its condition through a kind of evolution, and unlike Housman, who would stoically accept the new world because he could do nothing else, Eliot seeks a solution to the ills of his time. He is not content merely to expose the hypocrisy, stupidity, and desolation of the modern man. He would make us aware of the whole history of the human soul, which is alone in a wasteland unless it is redeemed by courage and faith. Perhaps this tentative answer to the questioning of the twentieth century explains why Eliot has been the influential poet and critic of the day. Younger writers have found in him an inspiration they could not find elsewhere.

Eliot's statement that modern literature "repudiates, or is wholly ignorant of, our most fundamental and important beliefs" ("the primacy of the supernatural over the natural life") implies the subject of his major poems: the spiritual world of man's being. The method by which Eliot turns this intellectual conviction into something that can be perceived—that is, into poetry—is one of myth. In myth the present fades into the past and the past into the present. While Eliot is not directly influenced by Freud's research into the psyche of man, the modifications of Freud's work by Jung and Havelock Ellis and its application to anthropology by Jessie Weston (*From Ritual to Romance,* 1920), suggested to him recurring myths in several civilizations. These provide the scaffolding of many of his poems.

A similar use of myth and symbol for metaphor is to be seen in the poetry of William Butler Yeats. His early romantic verse employed universal symbols much as the Romantics had. But as Yeats became acquainted with Irish mythology, the Celtic myths became the symbols for expressing his dislike and distrust of a scientific and naturalistic world. They stood for the world of the imagination, which for Yeats is the true world, just as they represent what for Eliot is the true world, the world of the intellect. Still later, Yeats's studies in mysticism, theosophy, clairvoyance, and oriental art forms led him to create myths to express the basic tension between paganism and Christianity, the natural and the supernatural, the soul and the senses. Perhaps, because like Eliot, Yeats found a personal solution to modern confusion, he has proved an inspiration to younger writers.

The influence of Freudian psychology can be seen more or less directly in the work of D. H. Lawrence, James Joyce, Dylan Thomas, Virginia Woolf, Katherine Mansfield, and Henry James. In these writers, it is not Freud's pioneering work in myth that is important; rather, it is his exploration and explanation of the human mind and psyche that opened up new areas of human experience to be recorded.

Lawrence stumbled on ideas which were becoming current and proclaimed them in his novels because they best fitted his personal experience that life was a conflict between emotion and intellect, body and spirit. Lawrence was seemingly never conscious of the unity of the two, only their opposition. His preoccupation with sex is often attributed to Freud's interpretation of the sexual instinct as the motivating drive behind human behavior. But Lawrence's interest in sex and its roots in the unconscious predates his reading of Freud, who only substantiated Lawrence's firmly-held belief that the flesh is wiser than the intellect. In essence, he is a confirmed romantic, somewhat akin to the eighteenth–century primitivists but unlike them in his use of primitivism to explain the "life urge," the "old life modes" inherited by modern man from his primitive ancestors, the primitive unconscious which modern civilization has buried.

Like Lawrence, James Joyce also plumbed the depths of the unconscious, that vast abyss into which Freud had looked. Joyce also resembled Lawrence in his romanticism, in his belief that the vision of truth is interior and individual. It is true that Joyce was in revolt against the accepted order of society and religion, but he did not undertake to set it right; rather he tried to obtain a clear impression of the substance of life and to render it in language appropriate to the true inner vision. His greatest contribution was one of style and language. To express the flux of sensations and ideas, which constitutes the life of the mind, Joyce resorted to a succession of images indicated by single words, half-phrases, new coined words ("Manorwombanborn"), and twisted quotations ("To see life foully"). This is the way the mind works before it imposes order upon the flux of imagery and sensation. The external, the conscious, the subconscious, and the unconscious are mixed in disorder. Beneath the surface of the civilized world are the dark inner secrets, and these constitute the true nature of modern man, that wanderer, Ulysses, the Leopold Bloom of *Ulysses* (1922).

Most clearly Freudian of all contemporaries was the Welsh poet, Dylan Thomas, who saw the world in sexual terms and gave a psychopathological interpretation of it in his poetry. Thomas seemed preoccupied with the conflict between the creative and destructive elements in sex, and using sex as a myth he explored good and evil. Even with this modern approach to man and his nature, the older values lurk beneath the surface of Thomas' startling language and thought: he has an Old Testament consciousness of sin which amounts to near obsession. Thomas, too, shares the tension of his age.

The shadow of Joyce fell across the path of Virginia Woolf. Her writing until that moment had been conventional, but in Joyce she found life unfolded in a succession of images just as experience itself occurs. Her novels are built of this material but not on the grand scale of Joyce. Her subject is crystallized in a situation or in a moment of time; her art is to arrange life (the true inner stream of consciousness) in a pattern suggested by her intuition. The pattern gives form to the flux of life, but the life thus represented is that of a limited world. It is not the turbulent, modern world, and Virginia Woolf offers no lessening of the tensions of modern man.

Katherine Mansfield shares Joyce's and Virginia Woolf's concern for artistic perfection and their interest in the inner mind as the true state of existence. Miss Mansfield wrote short stories only. Her best examples of the form deal with a single fragment of emotional experience which she observes minutely, objectively, and with great insight into character.

Fiction of this sort had earlier been the special province of Henry James. In novels and stories James treats the members of a small, restricted segment of society—international, wealthy, sophisticated, self-conscious, and living according to set social codes. He regards this group not from his own point of view as its creator, but from the viewpoints of the characters involved. His handling of point of view not only influenced Virginia Woolf, Katherine Mansfield, and Joseph Conrad, but also has marked the direction taken by many writers of prose fiction since his time. If James was not absorbed in the social problems of his day, it is partly because art offered a substitute for life. He defined art as "the one corner of human life in which we may take our ease. To justify our presence there the only thing demanded of us is that we shall have felt the representational impulse. . . . Wherever her shining standard floats, the need for apology and compromise is over; there it is enough simply that we please or are pleased. There the tree is judged only by its fruits. If these are sweet the tree is justified. . . ."

Although Joseph Conrad learned much from Henry James in matters of technique, his interest in the social scene and the whole range of human experience was much greater than that of James. As a man of his century he was interested in the problem of good and evil. Life was a spectacle of pity, terror, and beauty. Conrad's novels explore this problem by placing man in conflict with natural forces and with forces within his own nature: Lord Jim in *Lord Jim* (1900), Mr. Kurtz in *Heart of Darkness* (1902), and Heyst in *Victory* (1915). Thus Conrad, too, writes of the inner life of man, its tensions and conflicts. Although external action is often abundant in his novels and stories, it is of secondary importance: Conrad is chiefly concerned with the nature of man, as revealed in the choice made within his mind and heart.

Possibly because drama responds more quickly to contemporary problems than does poetry or fiction, there was a resurgence of dramatic literature in the twentieth century. Many writers in the modern era have experimented with dramatic writing: Auden, Joyce, Henry James, D. H. Lawrence, T. S. Eliot, Yeats, Christopher Isherwood, Sean O'Casey, Synge, and even Dylan Thomas, who wrote radio plays for the British Broadcasting Corporation. In the immediate background of this revival was the drama of the Norwegian dramatist Ibsen, who had combined the structure of the "well-made play" with subject matter drawn from the contemporary world in order to dramatize the inner conflicts of man. His work inaugurated a new era in English drama, superior to any since the Renaissance. One of the first to reflect Ibsen's influence was George Bernard Shaw, then a young man who felt that Fabian socialism offered the best solution for the economic and social disorders of the day. Shaw created the "discussion play" to present his many ideas. His plays have little action, but they serve as vehicles for his brilliant wit, which illuminates many subjects: slum-landlordism, armament making, the newly-emancipated woman, prostitution, creative evolution which will produce the super-race, archaic laws of marriage and divorce, war, pacifism, and the romantic hero.

Shaw's "discussion play" was not a radical departure from existing dramatic traditions. Other dramatists experimented more widely. Two attempts are particularly noteworthy for the future of drama. One was the Irish Literary Revival. Although drama was not the sole concern of the Irish group, the founding of the Abbey Theater and the plays of Synge, Yeats, and O'Casey may well be its most enduring contributions to modern literature. Yeats's drama is poetic, symbolic, and impressionistic; O'Casey's technique ranges from realism to extreme forms of expressionism. The other attempt, which may point a new direction, is the revival of verse drama. Yeats had pioneered in this field, but Eliot and Christopher Fry are more successful. Eliot's drama is philosophical, usually offering Eliot's own religious views as a solution to modern doubt and confusion. Fry is less serious. His plays, compounded of exuberant rhetoric and flashing imagery, seldom allow disenchantment to sully their moods. For Fry, the very joy of living defies time and despair.

Contemporary literature, especially poetry and fiction, is often criticized for its obscurity and difficulty. Conscious of the political, social, and moral chaos of the twentieth century, cut off from the older humane values and traditions of literature, the modern writer tries to portray the tension of this century. As Eliot stated in an essay of 1926, the modern poet is the spokesman of "a generation for whom the dissolution of value had in itself a positive value." This sense of dissolution and confusion, which the writer attempts to communicate, is reflected in the communication itself.

Admittedly, modern literature is obscure, its poets often deserving the epithet, "the cerebral school of poetry." It could hardly be otherwise. The search for new values, the search for new techniques and language to express those values, and the feeling that the writer is living in a world hostile to his work creates a brilliant but often esoteric literature. The great increase in knowledge, which forced specialization upon modern man, broke down communication. A writer could no longer assume that his audience shared a common body of knowledge and cultural and moral values. To whom, then, could he address his work? Often, it was to his own fellow-writers, and the result was a private language of coteries. If he was not satisfied with this, he could create his own system of values through myth or symbol and hope to establish an audience. Although this method, too, occasionally produced obscurity, it was at least partially successful in the work of Eliot, Yeats, and Joyce.

Even if most contemporary literature proves ephemeral, its influence will have been healthy. These writers are exacting critics of the contemporary world. They have offered no easy solutions to reduce modern tension, but they have restored a vigorous intelligence and grit to the practice of art. They have broken with tradition and made a fresh start, which will be the foundation of the structure yet to be built by the future.

Thomas Hardy
(1840–1928)

THOMAS HARDY WAS ONE OF THE LAST OF THE VICTORIAN NOVELISTS AND ONE OF THE FIRST of modern poets. He wrote novels for over twenty-five years (1868–1895), abandoned the form when *Jude the Obscure* (1896) was widely denounced for its shocking realism ("Jude the Obscene" it was called), and then turned to poetry, which he wrote and published until his death. Actually poetry was his first love; during his early years as a young architect he composed many poems. But since no publisher would accept them, he began to write prose fiction. Among his best known novels are *Far from the Madding Crowd* (1874), *The Return of the Native* (1878), *The Mayor of Casterbridge* (1886), *The Woodlanders* (1887), *Tess of the D'Urbervilles* (1891), and *Jude the Obscure.* All these works are characterized by a tragic pessimism as they depict individuals battling hopelessly against an inexorable fate.

Pessimism and ironic tragedy suffuse Hardy's poetry, too, from the *Wessex Poems* of 1898 to the *Winter Words* of 1928, although the dominant notes of gloom, bitterness, and senseless suffering are occasionally lightened by an expression of hope or at least harmonized by a stoical and courageous acceptance of life's ironies. Indeed, Hardy once defined his "pessimism" as only "questionings in the exploration of reality," and then quoted himself:

> If a way to the better there be, it exacts a
> full look at the worst.

In form, Hardy's poetry tends to be rather rough and crude, its diction blunt and colloquial, its metrics lacking in polished smoothness, its verse patterns original and varied. Most of his poems are short, philosophical lyrics expressing his dominant outlook, or concentrated narratives that point up the sardonic irony of the human drama. Some of the titles of his collections are revealing: *Time's Laughingstocks* (1909), *Satires of Circumstance* (1914), and *Human Shows* (1925). Hardy also wrote one long epic poem, *The Dynasts,* which was published in three parts between 1903 and 1908. Little regarded when it first appeared, this powerful dramatic treatment of the Napoleonic period is now recognized as Hardy's poetical masterpiece.

The Darkling [1] Thrush

I leant upon a coppice [2] gate
  When frost was specter-gray,
And winter's dregs made desolate
  The weakening eye of day.
The tangled bine-stems scored the sky   5
  Like strings of broken lyres,

And all mankind that haunted nigh
  Had sought their household fires.

The land's sharp features seemed to be
  The Century's corpse [3] outleant,   10

[1] In the dark; hence obscure, not clearly understood.

[2] Thicket.

[3] What is the meaning of this phrase (note the date of the poem)?

His crypt [4] the cloudy canopy,
  The wind his death lament.
The ancient pulse of germ and birth
  Was shrunken hard and dry,
And every spirit upon earth 15
  Seemed fervorless as I.

At once a voice arose among
  The bleak twigs overhead
In a full-hearted evensong [5]
  Of joy illimited; 20
An aged thrush, frail, gaunt, and small,
  In blast-beruffled plume,
Had chosen thus to fling his soul
  Upon the growing gloom.

So little cause for carolings 25
  Of such ecstatic sound
Was written on terrestrial things
  Afar or nigh around,
That I could think there trembled through
  His happy good-night air 30
Some blessed hope, whereof he knew
  And I was unaware.
(1900)

STUDY AIDS: 1. What is the atmosphere of the first two stanzas? What words and images create this atmosphere? Why a "darkling" thrush? 2. In such an atmosphere as this, does the thrush's song seem hopeful or hopeless? Is the thrush a SYMBOL? If so, of what?

Drummer Hodge

Drummer Hodge is an imagined English boy killed in the Boer War of 1899–1902, fought between British and Dutch settlers in South Africa.

They throw in Drummer Hodge, to rest
  Uncoffined—just as found:
His landmark is a kopje-crest [1]
  That breaks the veldt [2] around;
And foreign constellations [3] west 5
  Each night above his mound.

Young Hodge the Drummer never knew—
  Fresh from his Wessex [4] home—
The meaning of the broad Karoo,[5]
  The Bush,[6] the dusty loam,[7] 10
And why uprose to nightly view
  Strange stars amid the gloam.[8]

Yet portion of that unknown plain
  Will Hodge forever be;

His homely Northern breast and brain [9] 15
  Grow to some Southern tree,
And strange-eyed constellations reign
  His stars eternally.
(1902)

STUDY AIDS: 1. What is the shift in time-sequence from stanza to stanza? Why is the shift in this particular order? 2. Within each stanza there is a kind of widening progression, marked by each two of the six lines. What is it? 3. What part do the stars play in each stanza? Is the reference to them in the final stanza different in any way from the previous references? Is there a shift in point of view? 4. What is the tragedy (or pathos) of Drummer Hodge? Is the pathos resolved in any way in the last stanza? What is the curious triumph of this fallen drummer? How are intimacy and remote distance brought together by the imagery of the final stanza?

[4] Vault.
[5] "Evensong" suggests a religious service. Why is this appropriate here?

[1] Top of a small hill.
[2] A grass-covered field.
[3] Those seen in the southern hemisphere. Note the striking use of "west" as a verb.
[4] A general area in the south of England, the setting in Hardy's novels.
[5] A dry plateau in South Africa.
[6] A vast area covered with scrubby vegetation.

[7] Soil.
[8] Twilight.
[9] Note the alliteration. Hardy could have used "heart and head." Why is "breast and brain" better? What does it reveal about the attitude of the poet toward Drummer Hodge?

The Man He Killed

"Had he and I but met
By some old ancient inn,
We should have sat us down to wet
Right many a nipperkin! [1]

"But ranged as infantry,   5
And staring face to face,
I shot at him as he at me,
And killed him in his place.

"I shot him dead because—
Because he was my foe,   10
Just so—my foe of course he was;
That's clear enough; although

"He thought he'd 'list, perhaps,
Off-hand-like—just as I—

Was out of work—had sold his traps—   15
No other reason why.

"Yes; quaint and curious war is!
You shoot a fellow down
You'd treat if met where any bar is,
Or help to half-a-crown."   20
(1909)

STUDY AIDS: 1. What is gained by putting
this poem in monologue form? What ironies of
war are brought out as the speaker talks? What
kind of man is he?
    2. What purpose is served by the repetition of
"because" in ll. 9–10 and of the reason in l. 11?

---

[1] A half pint, or less, of liquor.

Channel-Firing

That night your great guns, unawares,
Shook all our coffins as we lay,
And broke the chancel [1] window-squares,
We thought it was the Judgment-day

And sat upright. While drearisome   5
Arose the howl of wakened hounds:
The mouse let fall the altar-crumb,
The worms drew back into the mounds,

The glebe [2] cow drooled. Till God called,
    "No;
It's gunnery practice out at sea   10
Just as before you went below;
The world is as it used to be:

"All nations striving strong to make
Red war yet redder. Mad as hatters
They do no more for Christès sake   15
Than you who are helpless in such matters.

"That this is not the judgment-hour
For some of them's a blessed thing,
For if it were they'd have to scour
Hell's floor for so much threatening . . .   20

"Ha, ha. It will be warmer when
I blow the trumpet (if indeed
I ever do; for you are men,
And rest eternal sorely need)."

So down we lay again. "I wonder,   25
Will the world ever saner be,"
Said one, "than when He sent us under
In our indifferent century!"

And many a skeleton shook his head.
"Instead of preaching forty year,"   30
My neighbor Parson Thirdly said,
"I wish I had stuck to pipes and beer." [3]

---

[1] Part of the church around the altar.

[2] Land assigned to a clergyman as part of his
benefice. Note the alternation of the funereal and
the commonplace in ll. 6–9.
[3] Why does the Parson say this?

Again the guns disturbed the hour,
Roaring their readiness to avenge,
As far inland as Stourton Tower,[4]   35
And Camelot,[5] and starlit Stonehenge.[6]
(1914)

STUDY AIDS: 1. Precisely what is the situation described in the poem? Who is speaking? What does the conversational tone of the first eight stanzas do to the horrible and gruesome details? How is this conversational tone achieved? (Note, for instance, the running over of st. 1

into st. 2, and 2 into 3; God's speech; and the talk among the skeletons.)
2. What is the shift of tone in the last stanza? Are the proper names here merely decoration?
3. This poem has been called "a little fable, or parable." Fables and parables teach us something through a brief story. What is taught here; i.e., what is the central idea of the poem? Is there IRONY in the poem?
4. Compare and contrast *Drummer Hodge, The Man He Killed,* and *Channel-Firing* as anti-war poems.

The Convergence of the Twain

On April 15, 1912, the ocean liner *Titanic,* then the world's largest ship, struck an iceberg on her maiden voyage from Southampton to New York and sank within three hours. Over 1500 people lost their lives. This poem expresses Hardy's reaction to the disaster.

1

In a solitude of the sea
Deep from human vanity,
And the pride of life that planned her, stilly
  couches she.

2

Steel chambers, late the pyres
Of her salamandrine fires,   5
Cold currents thrid,[1] and turn to rhythmic
  tidal lyres.

3

Over the mirrors meant
To glass the opulent
The sea-worm crawls—grotesque, slimed,
  dumb, indifferent.

4

Jewels in joy designed   10
To ravish the sensuous mind
Lie lightless, all their sparkles bleared and
  black and blind.

5

Dim moon-eyed fishes near
Gaze at the gilded gear
And query: "What does this vainglorious-
  ness down here?" . . .   15

6

Well: while was fashioning
This creature of cleaving wing,
The Immanent Will that stirs and urges
  everything

7

Prepared a sinister mate
For her—so gaily great—   20
A shape of ice, for the time far and dissociate.

8

And as the smart ship grew
In stature, grace, and hue,
In shadowy silent distance grew the iceberg
  too.

[4] A tower on the border of Wiltshire and Somerset, known also as "Alfred's Tower," and presumably dating from the time of King Alfred.
[5] Capital of King Arthur's kingdom.
[6] A group of upright prehistoric stones on Salisbury Plain, England. What is the effect of these

proper names, one associated with Saxon times, one with the days of King Arthur, and the last going back to prehistoric ages?

------

[1] Pass through; thread their way.

9

Alien they seemed to be;   25
  No mortal eye could see
The intimate welding of their later history,

10

Or sign that they were bent
  By paths coincident
On being anon twin halves of one august
  event,   30

11

Till the Spinner of the Years
  Said "Now!" And each one hears,

And consummation comes, and jars two hemispheres.
(1913; 1914)

STUDY AIDS: 1. What picture is presented in the first five stanzas? What contrast is expressed in each of these stanzas? What images are used to express the contrast? What is the IRONY?
2. What shift in time takes place in the next five stanzas (6–10)? What is the relation of this part of the poem to the first five stanzas? Why is the picture of the iceberg more general, less distinct, than the picture of the ship?
3. How does the final stanza climactically bring together the preceding parts of the poem (sts. 1–5, and sts. 6–10)?
4. What is the philosophy of life that pervades this poem?

The Oxen

This poem is based upon an old folk belief that at midnight on Christmas Eve the oxen will kneel as they did in the stable at Bethlehem when Christ was born.

Christmas Eve, and twelve of the clock.
  "Now they are all on their knees,"
An elder said as we sat in a flock
  By the embers in hearthside ease.

We pictured the meek mild creatures where   5
  They dwelt in their strawy pen,
Nor did it occur to one of us there
  To doubt they were kneeling then.

So fair a fancy few would weave
  In these years! Yet, I feel,   10
If someone said on Christmas Eve,
  "Come; see the oxen kneel,

"In the lonely barton [1] by yonder coomb [2]
  Our childhood used to know,"
I should go with him in the gloom,   15
  Hoping it might be so.
(1915; 1917)

STUDY AIDS: 1. What is the time shift between the first two stanzas and the last two? What change has taken place between the two periods? Does the speaker regret the change?
2. Is the mood of the poem bitter, sorrowful, satirical, gay, wistful, or what? Why?

[1] Farmyard.
[2] Steep, narrow valley.

Alfred Edward Housman
(1859–1936)

FEW ENGLISH POETS HAVE ATTAINED SO HIGH A DEGREE OF FAME WITH SO SLENDER AN output as did A. E. Housman, the shy, scholarly Cambridge professor who spent most of his intellectual energies on the editing of Latin texts. The slim volume on which that fame primarily rests—*A Shropshire Lad*—was published in 1896; *Last Poems* came out in 1922; and after his death his brother Laurence published *More Poems* in 1936.

Moreover, the range of his verse is as narrow as the quantity is small. Scorning metrical experiment and innovation, Housman employed the simplest of verse forms to sing over and over again his haunting tunes of pessimism, death, and stoical courage in facing up to "Whatever brute and blackguard made the world." In the poetical world of Housman, life is brief and joy is fleeting. Death often comes violently in the form of murder or suicide. Beauty fades, lovers are unfaithful, friends forget. For A. E. Housman as for Samuel Johnson, life is a state in which much is to be endured and little enjoyed. But the endurance is important. The game must be played with chin up even though the losing of it is assured; and meanwhile there are the pleasures of the Shropshire hillside and meadow, of love and drinking, of song and laughter—pleasures which, though transient, will help to turn our minds from the ultimate futility. For, after all,

> Malt does more than Milton can
> To justify God's ways to man.

Housman's poetical craftsmanship is impeccable. He uses simple, common words, but they are in the right place at the right time. He has the true classicist's love of balance and order, of neatness and precision, of economy of means to ends. At their best, his little poems are like carefully cut and polished diamonds, the product of painstaking workmanship and infinite patience. "The height of art," said an ancient critic, "is to conceal art." Such is the art of A. E. Housman.

Loveliest of Trees

Loveliest of trees, the cherry now
Is hung with bloom along the bough,
And stands about the woodland ride
Wearing white for Eastertide.

Now, of my threescore years and ten,[1]   5
Twenty will not come again,
And take from seventy springs a score,
It only leaves me fifty more.

And since to look at things in bloom
Fifty springs are little room,   10
About the woodlands I will go
To see the cherry hung with snow.[2]
(1896)

[1] Psalms 90:10: "The days of our years are threescore years and ten." How old is the speaker of the poem?

[2] Of what is "snow" a SYMBOL? Why is it used?

STUDY AIDS: Note the careful organization of this little lyric: the first stanza makes a statement about the English countryside; the second stanza makes a statement about the poet; the third stanza brings the two together. Elaborate this development. What is the central idea?

To an Athlete Dying Young

The time you won your town the race
We chaired you through the market-place;
Man and boy stood cheering by,
And home we brought you shoulder-high.

Today, the road all runners come,   5
Shoulder-high we bring you home,
And set you at your threshold down,
Townsman of a stiller town.

Smart lad, to slip betimes away
From fields where glory does not stay   10
And early though the laurel grows
It withers quicker than the rose.

Eyes the shady night has shut
Cannot see the record cut,[1]
And silence sounds no worse than cheers   15
After earth has stopped the ears.

Now you will not swell the rout[2]
Of lads that wore their honors out,
Runners whom renown outran
And the name died before the man.   20

So set, before its echoes fade,
The fleet foot on the sill[3] of shade,
And hold to the low lintel[4] up
The still-defended challenge-cup.

And round that early-laureled head   25
Will flock to gaze the strengthless dead,
And find unwithered on its curls
The garland briefer than a girl's.
(1896)

STUDY AIDS: 1. Why is the dead athlete
being congratulated? In what sense has he been
victorious in another race? The THEME of the
poem is thus a PARADOX. What is it?
 2. Explain the SYMBOLISM of "laurel" (l. 11)
and "rose" (l. 12). What is the poet saying by
means of these symbols? How are these two
symbols used again in the final stanza? Explain
also the symbolism of "sill of shade" (l. 22) and
"lintel" (l. 23).
 3. How does the simple, conversational tone
("Smart lad") affect the pathos of the poem?
How do symbolism and paradox help the poet
to avoid sentimentality?

Is My Team Plowing?

"Is my team plowing,
  That I was used to drive
And hear the harness jingle.
  When I was man alive?"

Aye, the horses trample,   5
  The harness jingles now;
No change though you lie under
  The land you used to plow.

"Is football playing
  Along the river shore,   10
With lads to chase the leather,
  Now I stand up no more?"

Aye, the ball is flying,
  The lads play heart and soul;
The goal stands up, the keeper   15
  Stands up to keep the goal.

"Is my girl happy,
  That I thought hard to leave,
And has she tired of weeping
  As she lies down at eve?"   20

Aye, she lies down lightly,
  She lies not down to weep;
Your girl is well contented.
  Be still, my lad, and sleep.

[1] Broken.
[2] Number.

[3] Threshold of a door.
[4] Top of a doorway.

"Is my friend hearty,   25
  Now I am thin and pine,
And has he found to sleep in
  A better bed than mine?"

Yes, lad, I lie easy,
  I lie as lads would choose;   30
I cheer a dead man's sweetheart—
  Never ask me whose.
(1896)

STUDY AIDS: 1. The poem is cast in the form of a dialogue. What two people are speaking? What is the attitude of each speaker?

2. What is the IRONY of the ending? In the light of this ending, what previous parts of the poem are suddenly revealed to be also ironic?

3. What are the various meanings of sleep suggested in the last three stanzas?

4. How would you characterize the TONES of this poem?

Into My Heart an Air That Kills

Into my heart an air that kills
  From yon far country blows;
What are those blue remembered hills,
  What spires, what farms are those?

That is the land of lost content,   5
  I see it shining plain,
The happy highways where I went
  And cannot come again.
(1896)

With Rue My Heart Is Laden

With rue [1] my heart is laden
  For golden [2] friends I had,
For many a rose-lipped maiden
  And many a lightfoot lad.

By brooks too broad for leaping   5
  The lightfoot boys [3] are laid;
The rose-lipped girls are sleeping
  In fields where roses fade.
(1896)

Terence, This Is Stupid Stuff

"Terence,[1] this is stupid stuff:
You eat your victuals fast enough;
There can't be much amiss, 'tis clear,
To see the rate you drink your beer.
But oh, good Lord, the verse you make,   5
It gives a chap the bellyache.
The cow, the old cow, she is dead;
It sleeps well, the horned head:
We poor lads, 'tis our turn now

To hear such tunes as killed the cow.   10
Pretty friendship 'tis to rhyme
Your friends to death before their time
Moping melancholy mad.
Come, pipe a tune to dance to, lad."

[3] In this stanza, the "maiden" and "lad" have become "boys" and "girls." What is the effect of the change? What do "lightfoot" and "rose-lipped" suggest?

[1] Sorrow.

[2] Cf. Shakespeare's "Golden lads and girls all must, As chimney-sweepers, come to dust." What does the echo of Shakespeare add to the poem?

[1] Housman first called A Shropshire Lad by the title Poems by Terence Hearsay. Terence, therefore, is Housman himself.

Why, if 'tis dancing you would be,　15
There's brisker pipes than poetry.
Say, for what were hop [2]-yards meant,
Or why was Burton [3] built on Trent?
Oh, many a peer of England brews
Livelier liquor than the Muse,　20
And malt [4] does more than Milton can
To justify God's ways to man.
Ale, man, ale's the stuff to drink
For fellows whom it hurts to think:
Look into the pewter pot　25
To see the world as the world's not.
And faith, 'tis pleasant till 'tis past:
The mischief is that 'twill not last.
Oh, I have been to Ludlow [5] Fair
And left my necktie God knows where,　30
And carried half way home, or near,
Pints and quarts of Ludlow beer.
Then the world seemed none so bad,
And I myself a sterling lad;
And down in lovely muck I've lain,　35
Happy till I woke again.
Then I saw the morning sky—
Heigho, the tale was all a lie;
The world, it was the old world yet,
I was I, my things were wet,　40
And nothing now remained to do
But begin the game anew.

Therefore, since the world has still
Much good, but much less good than ill,
And while the sun and moon endure　45
Luck's a chance, but trouble's sure,
I'd face it as a wise man would,
And train for ill and not for good.
'Tis true, the stuff I bring for sale
Is not so brisk a brew as ale;　50
Out of a stem that scored [6] the hand

I wrung it in a weary land.
But take it—if the smack is sour,
The better for the embittered hour;
It should do good to heart and head　55
When your soul is in my soul's stead;
And I will friend you, if I may,
In the dark and cloudy day.

There was a king reigned in the East;
There, when kings will sit to feast,　60
They get their fill before they think
With poisoned meat and poisoned drink.
He gathered all that springs to birth
From the many-venomed earth;
First a little, thence to more,　65
He sampled all her killing store;
And easy, smiling, seasoned sound,
Sate the king when healths went round.
They put arsenic in his meat
And stared aghast to watch him eat;　70
They poured strychnine in his cup
And shook to see him drink it up.
They shook, they stared as white's their shirt,
Them it was their poison hurt.
—I tell the tale that I heard told.
Mithridates, he died old.
(1896)

STUDY AIDS: 1. The poem is in four sections. In the first section, a speaker voices an objection. What is it? The remaining sections are given over to Terence's (Housman's) reply. What is Terence's defense? Is it convincing?

2. The final section adds nothing to Terence's argument, but is a parable. What is the relation of the parable to Terence's argument? Could the final section of the poem have been omitted without loss?

3. Why does Terence compare poetry with beer (malt)? Does this comparison fit in with the final parable?

[2] A plant used in brewing.
[3] A town (on the river Trent), a center of the English brewing industry.
[4] Beer. Lines 21–22 are often quoted. What do they mean? See Milton's *Paradise Lost*, Bk. 1, 26 (p. 259).

[5] A town in southern Shropshire.
[6] Cut. Housman is saying that his poetry has been "wrung" from sharp, stinging experience.

Henry James
(1843–1916)

BOTH ENGLAND AND AMERICA CLAIM HENRY JAMES. HE WAS BORN IN NEW YORK, LIVED also in Cambridge, Boston, and Newport, and wrote of America and Americans in his fiction. But he also belongs to English literature both because he lived in England most of his adult life, becoming a British citizen in 1915, and because his contributions to the art of fiction have had such widespread influence on the English novel.

James first saw Europe at an early age. His wealthy father, a man of independent mind who wanted the best for his children, took the family to Europe, where Henry and his older brother William were educated by tutors and introduced to the culture of the Old World. When Henry grew up and knew he wanted to write, he lived for a while in Paris, associating with Flaubert and the Russian novelist Turgenev. Soon, however, he was attracted to England where, except for several trips to the United States, he spent the rest of his life.

A writer of great energy and complete devotion to his craft. James produced significant work in several genres. Although he failed in his determined effort to become a playwright, he succeeded brilliantly in the short story and also in criticism; indeed, his critical essay "The Art of Fiction" (1884) is still one of the best statements ever made on the subject. But his most ambitious work was in the novel, for him the noblest of literary forms. The novels, in the following partial list fall into three groups. His early books treat of the American in Europe—*Roderick Hudson* (1876), *The American* (1877), and *The Portrait of a Lady* (1881). Later he turned to a study of English life in *The Princess Casamassima* (1886), *The Tragic Muse* (1890), and *The Spoils of Poynton* (1897). Finally, after the unsuccessful venture with the theater, he entered the "major phase" of his career, again picturing the American abroad in the three rich, tightly woven novels that are usually considered to be his greatest achievement—*The Wings of the Dove* (1902), *The Ambassadors* (1903), and *The Golden Bowl* (1904).

In the international novels, his most characteristic work, James confronts his Americans with the older, more traditional, more refined culture of Europe. In their ignorance, brashness, and naïvete they seem at a disadvantage, and no doubt reflect their author's distress at the rawness of American life. But if they are culturally deficient, usually they are morally superior to the Europeans. In presenting this conflict between manners and morals James leaves us in no real doubt as to where he stands; cosmopolitan manners, worldliness, urbanity, though desirable, are no substitute for moral probity and essential decency.

James was a specialist in the drama of human relationships. He gives us little overt, physical action; indeed some readers, including his brother William, the philosopher, have felt that "nothing happens" in a James story. But James believed that a good deal happens when a person discovers a truth about himself, about another, about human nature, and it is incident of this kind that he gives us. His stories are usually discoveries. A character faces a person, a problem, a situation, which he (and the reader) does not understand; the unfolding of the story permits his (and the reader's) gradual enlightenment. If we are confused in the early portions of a James story, we must be patient and must try, together with the "central intelligence" from whose restricted point of view all is seen, to understand the meaning of the data presented by events. Much of James's alleged difficulty is overcome if one remembers that the story is a deliberate process of gradual revelation. It is worth remembering, too, that in reading a James story we learn as we learn in life, and that herein lies the realism of his method.

The Tree of Knowledge

As often with James, this story grew from a chance remark of an acquaintance. A woman had spoken to him about Gordon Greenough and his father, Horatio Greenough, the American sculptor whose thinking on aesthetics far outran his talent with mallet and chisel. James made no effort, however, to base his story on Greenough's life.

We do well to read a James story at least twice. Having, on a first reading, satisfied our curiosity about the outcome of events, we are free on a second reading to pick up hints, allusions, nuances, which escaped us earlier. Each reading brings its own kind of pleasure.

It was one of the secret opinions, such as we all have, of Peter Brench that his main success in life would have consisted in his never having committed himself about the work, as it was called, of his friend Morgan Mallow. This was a subject on which it was, to the best of his belief, impossible with veracity to quote him, and it was nowhere on record that he had, in the connection, on any occasion and in any embarrassment, either lied or spoken the truth. Such a triumph had its honor even for a man of other triumphs —a man who had reached fifty, who had escaped marriage, who had lived within his means, who had been in love with Mrs. Mallow for years without breathing it, and who, last but not least, had judged himself once for all. He had so judged himself in fact that he felt an extreme and general humility to be his proper portion; yet there was nothing that made him think so well of his parts as the course he had steered so often through the shallows just mentioned. It became thus a real wonder that the friends in whom he had most confidence were just those with whom he had most reserves. He couldn't tell Mrs. Mallow— or at least he supposed, excellent man, he couldn't—that she was the one beautiful reason he had never married; any more than he could tell her husband that the sight of the multiplied marbles in that gentleman's studio was an affliction of which even time had never blunted the edge. His victory, however, as I have intimated, in regard to these productions, was not simply in his not having let it out that he deplored them; it was, remarkably, in his not having kept it in by anything else.

The whole situation, among these good people, was verily a marvel, and there was probably not such another for a long way from the spot that engages us—the point at which the soft declivity of Hampstead began at that time to confess in broken accents to Saint John's Wood. He despised Mallow's statues and adored Mallow's wife, and yet was distinctly fond of Mallow, to whom, in turn, he was equally dear. Mrs. Mallow rejoiced in the statues—though she preferred, when pressed, the busts; and if she was visibly attached to Peter Brench it was because of his affection for Morgan. Each loved the other moreover for the love borne in each case to Lancelot, whom the Mallows respectively cherished as their only child and whom the friend of their fireside identified as the third—but decidedly the handsomest—of his godsons. Already in the old years it had come to that—that no one, for such a relation, could possibly have occurred to any of them, even to the baby itself, but Peter. There was luckily a certain independence, of the pecuniary sort, all round: the Master could never otherwise have spent his solemn *Wander-jahre* in Florence and Rome, and continued by the Thames as well as by the Arno and the Tiber to add unpurchased group to group and model, for what was too apt to prove in the event mere love, fancy-heads of celebrities either too busy or too buried—too much of the age or too little of it—to sit. Neither could Peter, lounging in almost daily, have found time to keep the whole complicated tradition so alive by his presence. He was massive but mild, the depositary of these mysteries—large and loose and ruddy and curly, with deep tones, deep eyes, deep pockets, to say nothing of the habit of long pipes, soft hats and brownish grayish weather-faded clothes, apparently always the same.

He had "written," it was known, but had never spoken, never spoken in particular of that; and he had the air (since, as was believed, he continued to write) of keeping it up in order to have something more—as if he hadn't at the worst enough—to be silent about. Whatever his air, at any rate, Peter's occasional unmentioned prose and verse were quite truly the result of an impulse to maintain the purity of his taste by establishing still more firmly the right relation of fame to feebleness. The little green door of his domain was in a garden-wall on which the discolored stucco made patches, and in the small detached villa behind it everything was old, the furniture, the servants, the books, the prints, the immemorial habits and the new improvements. The Mallows, at Carrara Lodge,[1] were within ten minutes, and the studio there was on their little land, to which they had added, in their happy faith, for building it. This was the good fortune, if it was not the ill, of her having brought him in marriage a portion that put them in a manner at their ease and enabled them thus, on their side, to keep it up. And they did keep it up—they always had—the infatuated sculptor and his wife, for whom nature had refined on the impossible by relieving them of the sense of the difficult. Morgan had at all events everything of the sculptor but the

spirit of Phidias [2]—the brown velvet, the becoming *beretto,* [3] the "plastic" presence, the fine fingers, the beautiful accent in Italian and the old Italian factotum. He seemed to make up for everything when he addressed Egidio with the "tu" [4] and waved him to turn one of the rotary pedestals of which the place was full. They were tremendous Italians at Carrara Lodge, and the secret of the part played by this fact in Peter's life was in a large degree that it gave him, sturdy Briton as he was, just the amount of "going abroad" he could bear. The Mallows were all his Italy, but it was in a measure for Italy he liked them. His one worry was that Lance—to which they had shortened his godson—was, in spite of a public school,[5] perhaps a shade too Italian. Morgan meanwhile looked like somebody's flattering idea of somebody's own person as expressed in the great room provided at the Uffizzi Museum for the general illustration of that idea by eminent hands. The Master's sole regret that he hadn't been born rather to the brush than to the chisel sprang from his wish that he might have contributed to that collection.

It appeared with time at any rate to be to the brush that Lance had been born; for Mrs. Mallow, one day when the boy was turning twenty, broke it to their friend, who shared, to the last delicate morsel, their problems and pains, that it seemed as if nothing would really do but that he should embrace the career. It had been impossible longer to remain blind to the fact that he was gaining no glory at Cambridge, where Brench's own college had for a year tempered its tone to him as for Brench's own sake. Therefore why renew the vain form of preparing him for the impossible? The impossible—it had become clear—was that he should be anything but an artist.

"Oh dear, dear!" said poor Peter.

"Don't you believe in it?" asked Mrs. Mallow, who still, at more than forty, had

---

[1] Carrara, Italy, is the source of a fine-quality marble used in sculpture.

[2] The outstanding sculptor of ancient Greece.

[3] Beret, or cap.

[4] The familiar pronoun, second person singular.

[5] English public schools resemble American private schools.

her violet velvet eyes, her creamy satin skin and her silken chestnut hair.

"Believe in what?"

"Why in Lance's passion."

"I don't know what you mean by 'believing in it.' I've never been unaware, certainly, of his disposition, from his earliest time, to daub and draw; but I confess I've hoped it would burn out."

"But why should it," she sweetly smiled, "with his wonderful heredity? Passion is passion—though of course indeed *you*, dear Peter, know nothing of that. Has the Master's ever burned out?"

Peter looked off a little and, in his familiar formless way, kept up for a moment, a sound between a smothered whistle and a subdued hum. "Do you think he's going to be another Master?"

She seemed scarce prepared to go that length, yet she had on the whole a marvelous trust. "I know what you mean by that. Will it be a career to incur the jealousies and provoke the machinations that have been at times almost too much for his father? Well—say it may be, since nothing but clap-trap, in these dreadful days, *can*, it would seem, make its way, and since, with the curse of refinement and distinction, one may easily find one's self begging one's bread. Put it at the worst— say he *has* the misfortune to wing his flight further than the vulgar taste of his stupid countrymen can follow. Think, all the same, of the happiness—the same the Master has had. He'll *know*."

Peter looked rueful. "Ah but *what* will he know?"

"Quiet joy!" cried Mrs. Mallow, quite impatient and turning away.

2

He had of course before long to meet the boy himself on it and to hear that practically everything was settled. Lance was not to go up [6] again, but to go instead to Paris where, since the die was cast, he would find the best advantages. Peter had always felt he must be taken as he was, but had never perhaps

[6] I.e., go back to Cambridge.

found him so much of that pattern as on this occasion. "You chuck Cambridge then altogether? Doesn't that seem rather a pity?"

Lance would have been like his father, to his friend's sense, had he had less humor, and like his mother had he had more beauty. Yet it was a good middle way for Peter that, in the modern manner, he was, to the eye, rather the young stockbroker than the young artist. The youth reasoned that it was a question of time—there was such a mill to go through, such an awful lot to learn. He had talked with fellows and had judged. "One has got, today," he said, "don't you see? to know."

His interlocutor, at this, gave a groan. "Oh hang it, *don't* know!"

Lance wondered. " 'Don't'? Then what's the use—?"

"The use of what?"

"Why of anything. Don't you think I've talent?"

Peter smoked away for a little in silence; then went on: "It isn't knowledge, it's ignorance that—as we've been beautifully told—is bliss."

"Don't you think I've talent?" Lance repeated.

Peter, with his trick of queer kind demonstrations, passed his arm round his godson and held him a moment. "How do I know?"

"Oh," said the boy, "if it's your own ignorance you're defending—!"

Again, for a pause, on the sofa, his godfather smoked. "It isn't. I've the misfortune to be omniscient."

"Oh well," Lance laughed again, "if you know *too* much—!"

"That's what I do, and it's why I'm so wretched."

Lance's gaiety grew. "Wretched? Come, I say!"

"But I forgot," his companion went on— "you're not to know about that. It would indeed for you, too, make the too much. Only I'll tell you what I'll do." And Peter got up from the sofa. "If you'll go up again I'll pay your way at Cambridge."

Lance stared, a little rueful in spite of being

still more amused. "Oh Peter! You disapprove so of Paris?"

"Well, I'm afraid of it."

"Ah I see!"

"No, you don't see—yet. But you will—that is you would. And you mustn't."

The young man thought more gravely. "But one's innocence, already—!"

"Is considerably damaged? Ah that won't matter," Peter persisted—"we'll patch it up here."

"Here? Then you want me to stay at home?"

Peter almost confessed to it. "Well, we're so right—we four together—just as we are. We're so safe. Come, don't spoil it."

The boy, who had turned to gravity, turned from this, on the real pressure in his friend's tone, to consternation. "Then what's a fellow to be?"

"My particular care. Come, old man"—and Peter now fairly pleaded—"I'll look out for you."

Lance, who had remained on the sofa with his legs out and his hands in his pockets, watched him with eyes that showed suspicion. Then he got up. "You think there's something the matter with me—that I can't make a success."

"Well, what do you call a success?"

Lance thought again. "Why the best sort, I suppose, is to please one's self. Isn't that the sort that, in spite of cabals and things, is —in his own peculiar line—the Master's?"

There were so much too many things in this question to be answered at once that they practically checked the discussion, which became particularly difficult in the light of such renewed proof that, though the young man's innocence might, in the course of his studies, as he contended, somewhat have shrunken, the finer essence of it still remained. That was indeed exactly what Peter had assumed and what above all he desired; yet perversely enough it gave him a chill. The boy believed in the cabals and things, believed in the peculiar line, believed, to be brief, in the Master. What happened a month or two later wasn't that he went up again at the expense of his godfather, but that a fortnight

after he had got settled in Paris this personage sent him fifty pounds.

He had meanwhile at home, this personage, made up his mind to the worst; and what that might be had never yet grown quite so vivid to him as when, on his presenting himself one Sunday night, as he never failed to do, for supper, the mistress of Carrara Lodge met him with an appeal as to—of all things in the world—the wealth of the Canadians. She was earnest, she was even excited. "Are many of them *really* rich?"

He had to confess he knew nothing about them, but he often thought afterwards of that evening. The room in which they sat was adorned with sundry specimens of the Master's genius, which had the merit of being, as Mrs. Mallow herself frequently suggested, of an unusually convenient size. They were indeed of dimensions not customary in the products of the chisel, and they had the singularity that, if the objects and features intended to be small looked too large, the objects and features intended to be large looked too small. The Master's idea, either in respect to this matter or to any other, had in almost any case, even after years, remained undiscoverable to Peter Brench. The creations that so failed to reveal it stood about on pedestals and brackets, on tables and shelves, a little staring white population, heroic, idyllic, allegoric, mythic, symbolic, in which "scale" had so strayed and lost itself that the public square and the chimney-piece seemed to have changed places, the monumental being all diminutive and the diminutive all monumental; branches at any rate, markedly, of a family in which stature was rather oddly irrespective of function, age and sex. They formed, like the Mallows themselves, poor Brench's own family—having at least to such a degree the note of familiarity. The occasion was one of those he had long ago learned to know and to name—short flickers of the faint flame, soft gusts of a kinder air. Twice a year regularly the Master believed in his fortune, in addition to believing all the year round in his genius. This time it was to be made by a bereaved couple from Toronto, who had given him the handsomest order for a tomb to three lost children, each of whom they desired to see, in the composition, emblematically and characteristically represented.

Such was naturally the moral of Mrs. Mallow's question: if their wealth was to be assumed, it was clear, from the nature of their admiration, as well as from mysterious hints thrown out (they were a little odd!) as to other possibilities of the same mortuary sort, that their further patronage might be; and not less evident that should the Master become at all known in those climes nothing would be more inevitable than a run of Canadian custom. Peter had been present before at runs of custom, colonial and domestic— present at each of those of which the aggregation had left so few gaps in the marble company round him; but it was his habit never at these junctures to prick the bubble in advance. The fond illusion, while it lasted, eased the wound of elections never won, the long ache of medals and diplomas carried off, on every chance, by every one but the Master; it moreover lighted the lamp that would glimmer through the next eclipse. They lived, however, after all—as it was always beautiful to see—at a height scarce susceptible of ups and downs. They strained a point at times charmingly, strained it to admit that the public was here and there not too bad to buy; but they would have been nowhere without their attitude that the Master was always too good to sell. They were at all events deliciously formed, Peter often said to himself, for their fate; the Master had a vanity, his wife had a loyalty, of which success, depriving these things of innocence, would have diminished the merit and the grace. Any one could be charming under a charm, and as he looked about him at a world of prosperity more void of proportion even than the Master's museum he wondered if he knew another pair that so completely escaped vulgarity.

"What a pity Lance isn't with us to rejoice!" Mrs. Mallow on this occasion sighed at supper.

"We'll drink to the health of the absent," her husband replied, filling his friend's glass and his own and giving a drop to their companion; "but we must hope he's preparing himself for a happiness much less like this of ours this evening—excusable as I grant it to be!—than like the comfort we have always (whatever has happened or has not happened) been able to trust ourselves to enjoy. The comfort," the Master explained, leaning back in the pleasant lamplight and firelight, holding up his glass and looking round at his marble family, quartered more or less, a monstrous brood, in every room—"the comfort of art in itself!"

Peter looked a little shyly at his wine. "Well—I don't care what you may call it when a fellow doesn't—but Lance must learn to *sell*, you know. I drink to his acquisition of the secret of a base popularity!"

"Oh, yes, *he* must sell," the boy's mother, who was still more, however, this seemed to give out, the Master's wife, rather artlessly allowed.

"Ah," the sculptor after a moment confidently pronounced, "Lance *will*. Don't be afraid. He'll have learned."

"Which is exactly what Peter," Mrs. Mallow gaily returned—"why in the world were you so perverse, Peter?—wouldn't when he told him hear of."

Peter, when this lady looked at him with accusatory affection—a grace on her part not infrequent—could never find a word; but the Master, who was always all amenity and tact, helped him out now as he had often helped him before. "That's his old idea, you know —on which we've so often differed: his theory that the artist should be all impulse and instinct. *I* go in of course for a certain amount of school. Not too much—but a due proportion. There's where his protest came in," he continued to explain to his wife, "as against what *might*, don't you see? be in question for Lance."

"Ah well"—and Mrs. Mallow turned the violet eyes across the table at the subject of this discourse—"he's sure to have meant of course nothing but good. Only that wouldn't have prevented him, if Lance *had* taken his advice, from being in effect horribly cruel."

They had a sociable way of talking of him to his face as if he had been in the clay or —at most—in the plaster, and the Master was unfailingly generous. He might have been waving Egidio to make him revolve. "Ah but poor Peter wasn't so wrong as to what it may after all come to that he *will* learn."

"Oh but nothing artistically bad," she urged —still, for poor Peter, arch and dewy.

"Why just the little French tricks," said the Master: on which their friend had to pretend to admit, when pressed by Mrs. Mallow, that these aesthetic vices had been the objects of his dread.

3

"I know now," Lance said to him the next year, "why you were so much against it." He had come back supposedly for a mere interval and was looking about him at Carrara Lodge, where indeed he had already on two or three occasions since his expatriation briefly reappeared. This had the air of a longer holiday. "Something rather awful has happened to me. It *isn't* so very good to know."

"I'm bound to say high spirits don't show in your face," Peter was rather ruefully forced to confess. "Still, are you very sure you do know?"

"Well, I at least know about as much as I can bear." These remarks were exchanged in Peter's den, and the young man, smoking cigarettes, stood before the fire with his back against the mantel. Something of his bloom seemed really to have left him.

Poor Peter wondered. "You're clear then as to what in particular I wanted you not to go for?"

"In particular?" Lance thought. "It seems to me that in particular there can have been only one thing."

They stood for a little sounding each other. "Are you quite sure?"

"Quite sure I'm a beastly duffer? Quite—by this time."

"Oh!"—and Peter turned away as if almost with relief.

"It's *that* that isn't pleasant to find out."

"Oh I don't care for 'that,'" said Peter presently coming round again. "I mean I personally don't."

"Yet I hope you can understand a little that I myself should!"

"Well, what do you mean by it?" Peter sceptically asked.

And on this Lance had to explain—how the upshot of his studies in Paris had inexorably proved a mere deep doubt of his means. These studies had so waked him up that a new light was in his eyes; but what the new light did was really to show him too much. "Do you know what's the matter with me? I'm too horribly intelligent. Paris was really the last place for me. I've learned what I can't do."

Poor Peter stared—it was a staggerer; but even after they had had, on the subject, a longish talk in which the boy brought out to the full the hard truth of his lesson, his friend betrayed less pleasure than usually breaks into a face to the happy tune of "I told you so!" Poor Peter himself made now indeed so little a point of having told him so that Lance broke ground in a different place a day or two after. "What was it then that—before I went —you were afraid I should find out?" This, however, Peter refused to tell him—on the ground that if he hadn't yet guessed perhaps he never would, and that in any case nothing at all for either of them was to be gained by giving the thing a name. Lance eyed him on this an instant with the bold curiosity of youth—with the air indeed of having in his mind two or three names, of which one or other would be right. Peter nevertheless, turning his back again, offered no encouragement, and when they parted afresh it was with some show of impatience on the side of the boy. Accordingly on their next encounter Peter saw at a glance that he had now, in the interval, divined and that, to sound his note, he was only waiting till they should find themselves alone. This he had soon arranged and he then broke straight out. "Do you know your conundrum has been keeping me awake? But in the watches of the night the answer came over me—so that, upon my honor, I quite laughed out. Had you been supposing I had to go to Paris to learn *that?*" Even now, to see him still so sublimely on his guard, Peter's young friend had to laugh afresh. "You won't give a sign till you're sure? Beautiful old Peter!" But Lance at last produced it.

"Why, hang it, the truth about the Master."

It made between them for some minutes a lively passage, full of wonder for each at the wonder of the other. "Then how long have you understood—"

"The true value of his work? I understood it," Lance recalled, "as soon as I began to understand anything. But I didn't begin fully to do that, I admit, till I got *là-bas*."[7]

"Dear, dear!"—Peter gasped with retrospective dread.

"But for what have you taken me? I'm a hopeless muff—that I *had* to have rubbed in. But I'm not such a muff as the Master!" Lance declared.

"Then why did you never tell me—?"

"That I hadn't, after all"—the boy took him up—"remained such an idiot? Just because I never dreamed *you* knew. But I beg your pardon. I only wanted to spare you. And what I don't now understand is how the deuce then for so long you've managed to keep bottled."

Peter produced his explanation, but only after some delay and with a gravity not void of embarrassment. "It was for your mother."

"Oh!" said Lance.

"And that's the great thing now—since the murder *is* out. I want a promise from you. I mean"—and Peter almost feverishly followed it up—"a vow from you, solemn and such as you owe me here on the spot, that you'll sacrifice anything rather than let her ever guess—"

"That *I've* guessed?"—Lance took it in. "I see." He evidently after a moment had taken in much. "But what is it you've in mind that I may have a chance to sacrifice?"

"Oh one has always something."

Lance looked at him hard. "Do you mean that *you've* had—?" The look he received back, however, so put the question by that he found soon enough another. "Are you really sure my mother doesn't know?"

Peter, after renewed reflection, was really sure. "If she does she's too wonderful."

"But aren't we all too wonderful?"

"Yes," Peter granted—"but in different ways. The things so desperately important because

[7] "Over there," i.e., Paris.

your father's little public consists only, as you know then," Peter developed—"well, of how many?"

"First of all," the Master's son risked, "of himself. And last of all too. I don't quite see of whom else."

Peter had an approach to impatience. "Of your mother, I say—*always*."

Lance cast it all up. "You absolutely feel that?"

"Absolutely."

"Well then with yourself that makes three."

"Oh *me!*"—and Peter, with a wag of his kind old head, modestly excused himself. "The number's at any rate small enough for any individual dropping out to be too dreadfully missed. Therefore, to put it in a nutshell, take care, my boy—that's all—that *you're* not!"

"I've got to keep on humbugging?" Lance wailed.

"It's just to warn you of the danger of your failing of that that I've seized this opportunity."

"And what do you regard in particular," the young man asked, "as the danger?"

"Why this certainty: that the moment your mother, who feels so strongly, should suspect your secret—well," said Peter desperately, "the fat would be on the fire."

Lance for a moment seemed to stare at the blaze. "She'd throw me over?"

"She'd throw *him* over."

"And come round to us?"

Peter, before he answered, turned away. "Come round to *you*." But he had said enough to indicate—and, as he evidently trusted, to avert—the horrid contingency.

4

Within six months again, none the less, his fear was on more occasions than one all before him. Lance had returned to Paris for another trial; then had reappeared at home and had had, with his father, for the first time in his life, one of the scenes that strike sparks. He described it with much expression to Peter, touching whom (since they had never done so before) it was the sign of a new reserve on the part of the pair at Carrara Lodge that they at present failed, on a matter of intimate interest, to open themselves—if not in joy then in sorrow—to their good friend. This produced perhaps practically between the parties a shade of alienation and a slight intermission of commerce—marked mainly indeed by the fact that to talk at his ease with his old playmate Lance had in general to come to see him. The closest if not quite the gayest relation they had yet known together was thus ushered in. The difficulty for poor Lance was a tension at home—begotten by the fact that his father wished him to be at least the sort of success he himself had been. He hadn't "chucked" Paris—though nothing appeared more vivid to him than that Paris had chucked him: he would go back again because of the fascination in trying, in seeing, in sounding the depths—in learning one's lesson, briefly, even if the lesson were simply that of one's impotence in the presence of one's larger vision. But what did the Master, all aloft in his senseless fluency, know of impotence, and what vision—to be called such—had he in all his blind life ever had? Lance, heated and indignant, frankly appealed to his godparent on this score.

His father, it appeared, had come down on him for having, after so long, nothing to show, and hoped that on his next return this deficiency would be repaired. *The* thing, the Master complacently set forth was—for any artist, however inferior to himself—at least to "do" something. "What can you do? That's all I ask!" *He* had certainly done enough, and there was no mistake about what he had to show. Lance had tears in his eyes when it came thus to letting his old friend know how great the strain might be on the "sacrifice" asked of him. It wasn't so easy to continue humbugging—as from son to parent —after feeling one's self despised for not groveling in mediocrity. Yet a noble duplicity was what, as they intimately faced the situation, Peter went on requiring; and it was still for a time what his young friend, bitter and sore, managed loyally to comfort him with. Fifty pounds more than once again, it was true, rewarded both in London and in Paris the young friend's loyalty; none the less sensibly, doubtless, at the moment, that the money was a direct advance on a decent sum for which Peter had long since privately prearranged an ultimate function. Whether by these arts or others, at all events, Lance's just resentment was kept for a season—but only for a season—at bay. The day arrived when he warned his companion that he could hold out—or hold in—no longer. Carrara Lodge had had to listen to another lecture delivered from a great height—an infliction really heavier at last than, without striking back or in some way letting the Master have the truth, flesh and blood could bear.

"And what I don't see is," Lance observed with a certain irritated eye for what was after all, if it came to that, owing to himself too; "what I don't see is, upon my honor, how *you,* as things are going, can keep the game up."

"Oh the game for me is only to hold my tongue," said placid Peter. "And I have my reason."

"Still my mother?"

Peter showed a queer face as he had often shown it before—that is by turning it straight away. "What will you have? I haven't ceased to like her."

"She's beautiful—she's a dear of course," Lance allowed; "but what is she to you, after all, and what is it to you that, as to anything whatever, she should or she shouldn't?"

Peter, who had turned red, hung fire a little. "Well—it's all simply what I make of it."

There was now, however, in his young friend a strange, an adopted insistence. "What are you after all to *her?*"

"Oh nothing. But that's another matter."

"She cares only for my father," said Lance the Parisian.

"Naturally—and that's just why."

"Why you've wished to spare her?"

"Because she cares so tremendously much."

Lance took a turn about the room, but with his eyes still on his host. "How awfully—always—you must have liked her!"

"Awfully. Always," said Peter Brench.

The young man continued for a moment to muse—then stopped again in front of him.

"Do you know how much she cares?" Their eyes met on it, but Peter, as if his own found something new in Lance's, appeared to hesitate, for the first time in an age, to say he did know. *"I've* only just found out," said Lance. "She came to my room last night, after being present, in silence and only with her eyes on me, at what I had had to take from him; she came—and she was with me an extraordinary hour."

He had paused again and they had again for a while sounded each other. Then something—and it made him suddenly turn pale—came to Peter. "She *does* know?"

"She does know. She let it all out to me—so as to demand of me no more than 'that,' as she said, of which she herself had been capable. She has always, always known," said Lance without pity.

Peter was silent a long time; during which his companion might have heard him gently breathe, and on touching him might have felt within him the vibration of a long low sound suppressed. By the time he spoke at last he had taken everything in. "Then I do see how tremendously much."

"Isn't it wonderful?" Lance asked.

"Wonderful," Peter mused.

"So that if your original effort to keep me from Paris was to keep me from knowledge——!" Lance exclaimed as if with a sufficient indication of this futility.

It might have been at the futility Peter appeared for a little to gaze. "I think it must have been—without my quite at the time knowing it—to keep *me!*" he replied at last as he turned away.

(1900)

STUDY AIDS: 1. In what sense is "the Master" the center of interest in the story? In what sense is he not? With what feeling are we made to regard him—pity, contempt, amusement?

2. Mrs. Mallow, Brench, and Lance all know the truth about the Master, but none knows the other two know. When does each of them learn the truth? At what point in the story do we learn that they know the truth? At what point in the story does each of them learn that he shares his knowledge with another? What precipitates this revelation among the three characters? What motive prompts each character to keep the knowledge to himself? Does Brench understand his motive as well as we do? Where in the story does he fully understand it?

3. James had a tendency to spin his stories out to such a length as to make them unmarketable. His effort to keep this story short was, he felt, a heroic one, because the story cried out for fuller treatment. On the basis of the story itself can you imagine how, if he had expanded it, he might have developed it beyond the present conclusion? What will life at Carrara Lodge be like, now that some of the inhabitants are no longer innocent but knowing?

4. James made much of POINT OF VIEW in his fiction. What he called the "central intelligence," the person to whom things are revealed, is Brench. The narrator, however, is not Brench but one imagined to stand next to Brench in the story and to see what he sees. In the narrative portions of the story he is allowed to reveal what Brench—but only Brench—is thinking. Does he do this also in the dramatic scenes, involving dialogue, or is his method wholly objective—a report only of what people say and what may be inferred from their remarks?

5. The title alludes to the story of Adam and Eve. Said the Lord: "But of the tree of the knowledge of good and evil, thou shalt not eat of it: for in the day that thou eatest thereof thou shalt surely die" (Gen. 2:17). In what respects, if any, does James's story parallel the account of the Fall in Genesis?

Joseph Conrad
(1857–1924)

THE WRITER OF SOME OF THE MOST DISTINGUISHED PROSE FICTION IN ENGLISH WAS BORN not in England but in Poland. Joseph Conrad (his full name is Teodor Josef Konrad Korzeniowski) learned the language and literature of England from his father, an aristocrat, who was a poet, critic, and translator of Shakespeare. Educated for a profession at Cracow, Conrad preferred a seaman's life and shipped at the age of sixteen. He was at sea for twenty-one years, the last ten as master in the British Merchant Marine. In 1894, having become a British subject, he quit the sea, married an Englishwoman, and settled down to a life of writing.

After an uncertain start in *Almayer's Folly* (1895), he went on to write a succession of remarkable novels, perhaps the best of which are *The Nigger of the Narcissus* (1897), *Lord Jim* (1900), *Nostromo* (1904), and *Victory* (1915). He was equally successful in such admired stories as *Youth* and *Heart of Darkness* (1902), *Typhoon* (1903), and *The Secret Sharer* (1912). Much of the appeal of these tales lies in Conrad's remote settings—ships at sea, Africa, the East Indian tropics. His stories are full of vividly rendered scenes ("My task is," he said, "to make you *see*"). Sights, sounds, and smells of life on shipboard or in fetid jungle create the scenic atmosphere that always counts for much in Conrad's work.

Enchanting as they are in themselves, Conrad's settings also do much to influence character. He favored remote settings, not only because he knew them from experience, but also because they allowed him to isolate his characters from the ordinary world, the better to examine their essential natures. The world these characters inhabit is a world of strong forces, both natural and man-made, which exert pressures on men. Conrad is interested in how a man meets the challenge of these pressures. Often he succumbs to them; but often, too, he withstands them. By opposing the force, chance, brutality, and betrayal in life with order, courage, and virtue, particularly the virtue of fidelity, a man can preserve his dignity and, as it were, save his soul.

The fidelity Conrad valued in life was also a central feature of his literary philosophy. As an artist he tried earnestly to render the truth of life. To do this he abandoned the plot of conventional fiction because he felt that its artificiality obscured the truth. The imagination, he held, should be used "to describe human hearts—and not to create events that are, properly speaking, accidents only." Another way he achieved the truth, or the illusion of it, was to tell the story through a narrator; events are seen and reported not by an all-knowing author but usually by a character in the story. This close adherence to a restricted point of view, as in the fiction of Henry James, enhances the plausibility of the story and compels our belief. The narrator may analyze and interpret events, but Conrad keeps analysis at a minimum, preferring to allow events to speak for themselves. This objective narrative method means that significances in a Conrad story are not spelled out for us, but must often be inferred from the action. Here style is important. Conrad chooses words not alone for their precise meaning, but, like a poet, for the suggestive power of their sound and arrangement. Style, for him, was the means of blending form and content.

Il Conde

This story grew from an actual experience related to the author by a Polish friend, a Count Czembek. It is representative of Conrad's art in its concern with passion hidden beneath the rational surfaces of life, in its functional use of setting, in its philosophical overtones, and in its use of a narrator and manipulated time. Although seemingly simple and direct, the story on close reading will be found to be richly suggestive.

Vedi Napoli e poi mori

"See Naples and then die"

The first time we got into conversation was in the National Museum in Naples, in the rooms on the ground floor containing the famous collection of bronzes from Herculaneum and Pompeii: that marvelous legacy of antique art whose delicate perfection has been preserved for us by the catastrophic 10 fury of a volcano.

He addressed me first, over the celebrated Resting Hermes which we had been looking at side by side. He said the right things about the wholly admirable piece. Nothing 15 profound. His taste was natural rather than cultivated. He had obviously seen many fine things in his life and appreciated them: but he had no jargon of a dilettante or the connoisseur. A hateful tribe. He spoke like a 20 fairly intelligent man of the world, a perfectly unaffected gentleman.

We had known each other by sight for some few days past. Staying in the same hotel—good, but not extravagantly up to date—I had 25 noticed him in the vestibule going in and out. I judged he was an old and valued client. The bow of the hotel-keeper was cordial in its deference, and he acknowledged it with familiar courtesy. For the servants he was *Il* 30 *Conde.* There was some squabble over a man's parasol—yellow silk with white lining sort of thing—the waiters had discovered abandoned outside the dining-room door. Our gold-laced door-keeper recognized it and I 35 heard him directing one of the lift boys to run after *Il Conde* with it. Perhaps he was the only Count staying in the hotel, or perhaps he had the distinction of being *the* Count *par excellence,* conferred upon him because 40 of his tried fidelity to the house.

Having conversed at the Museo—(and by the by he had expressed his dislike of the busts and statues of Roman emperors in the gallery of marbles: their faces were too vigorous, too pronounced for him)—having conversed already in the morning, I did not think I was intruding when in the evening, finding the dining-room very full, I proposed to share his little table. Judging by the quiet urbanity of his consent he did not think so either. His smile was very attractive.

He dined in an evening waistcoat and a "smoking" (he called it so) with a black tie. All this of very good cut, not new—just as these things should be. He was, morning or evening, very correct in his dress. I have no doubt that his whole existence had been correct, well ordered and conventional, undisturbed by startling events. His white hair brushed upward off a lofty forehead gave him the air of an idealist, of an imaginative man. His white moustache, heavy but carefully trimmed and arranged, was not unpleasantly tinted a golden yellow in the middle. The faint scent of some very good perfume, and of good cigars (that last odor quite remarkable to come upon in Italy) reached me across the table. It was in his eyes that his age showed most. They were a little weary with creased eyelids. He must have been sixty or a couple of years more. And he was communicative. I would not go so far as to call it garrulous—but distinctly communicative.

He had tried various climates, of Abbazia, of the Riviera, of other places, too, he told me, but the only one which suited him was the climate of the Gulf of Naples. The ancient Romans, who, he pointed out to me, were men expert in the art of living, knew very well what they were doing when they built their villas on these shores, in Baiæ, in

Vico, in Capri. They came down to this seaside in search of health, bringing with them their trains of mimes and flute-players to amuse their leisure. He thought it extremely probable that the Romans of the higher classes were specially predisposed to painful rheumatic affections.

This was the only personal opinion I heard him express. It was based on no special erudition. He knew no more of the Romans than an average informed man of the world is expected to know. He argued from personal experience. He had suffered himself from a painful and dangerous rheumatic affection till he found relief in this particular spot of southern Europe.

This was three years ago, and ever since he had taken up his quarters on the shores of the gulf, either in one of the hotels in Sorrento or hiring a small villa in Capri. He had a piano, a few books: picked up transient acquaintances of a day, week, or month in the stream of travelers from all Europe. One can imagine him going out for his walks in the streets and lanes, becoming known to beggars, shopkeepers, children, country people; talking amiably over the walls to the contadini [1]— and coming back to his rooms or his villa to sit before the piano, with his white hair brushed up and his thick orderly moustache, "to make a little music for myself." And, of course, for a change there was Naples near by—life, movement, animation, opera. A little amusement, as he said, is necessary for health. Mimes and flute-players, in fact. Only, unlike the magnates of ancient Rome, he had no affairs of the city to call him away from these moderate delights. He had no affairs at all. Probably he had never had any grave affairs to attend to in his life. It was a kindly existence, with its joys and sorrows regulated by the course of nature—marriages, births, deaths —ruled by the prescribed usages of good society and protected by the state.

He was a widower; but in the months of July and August he ventured to cross the Alps for six weeks on a visit to his married daughter. He told me her name. It was that of a very aristocratic family. She had a castle—in

[1] Country folk.

Bohemia, I think. This is as near as I ever came to ascertaining his nationality. His own name, strangely enough, he never mentioned. Perhaps he thought I had seen it on the published list. Truth to say, I never looked. At any rate, he was a good European—he spoke four languages to my certain knowledge —and a man of fortune. Not of great fortune, evidently and appropriately. I imagine that to be extremely rich would have appeared to him improper, outré—too blatant altogether. And obviously, too, the fortune was not of his making. The making of a fortune cannot be achieved without some roughness. It is a matter of temperament. His nature was too kindly for strife. In the course of conversation he mentioned his estate quite by the way, in reference to that painful and alarming rheumatic affection. One year, staying incautiously beyond the Alps as late as the middle of September, he had been laid up for three months in that lonely country house with no one but his valet and the caretaking couple to attend to him. Because, as he expressed it, "he kept no establishment there." He had only gone for a couple of days to confer with his land agent. He promised himself never to be so imprudent in the future. The first weeks of September would find him on the shores of his beloved gulf.

Sometimes in traveling one comes upon such lonely men, whose only business is to wait for the unavoidable. Deaths and marriages have made a solitude round them, and one really cannot blame their endeavors to make the waiting as easy as possible. As he remarked to me: "At my time of life freedom from physical pain is a very important matter."

It must not be imagined that he was a wearisome hypochondriac. He was really much too well-bred to be a nuisance. He had an eye for the small weaknesses of humanity. But it was a good-natured eye. He made a restful, easy, pleasant companion for the hours between dinner and bedtime. We spent three evenings together, and then I had to leave Naples in a hurry to look after a friend who had fallen seriously ill in Taormina. Having nothing to do, Il Conde came to see me off at the station. I was somewhat upset, and his idleness was always ready to take a kindly form. He was by no means an indolent man.

He went along the train peering into the carriages for a good seat for me, and then remained talking cheerily from below. He declared he would miss me that evening very much and announced his intention of going after dinner to listen to the band in the public garden, the Villa Nazionale. He would amuse himself by hearing excellent music and looking at the best society. There would be a lot of people, as usual.

I seem to see him yet—his raised face with a friendly smile under the thick moustaches, and his kind, fatigued eyes. As the train began to move, he addressed me in two languages: first in French, saying, *"Bon voyage"*; then, in his very good, somewhat emphatic English, encouragingly, because he could see my concern: "All will—be—well—yet!"

My friend's illness having taken a favorable turn, I returned to Naples on the tenth day. I cannot say I had given much thought to *Il Conde* during my absence, but entering the dining-room I looked for him in his habitual place. I had an idea he might have gone back to Sorrento to his piano and his books and his fishing. He was great friends with all the boatmen, and fished a good deal with lines from a boat. But I made out his white head in a crowd of heads, and even from a distance noticed something unusual in his attitude. Instead of sitting erect, gazing all round with alert urbanity, he drooped over his plate. I stood opposite him for some time before he looked up, a little wildly, if such a strong word can be used in connection with his correct appearance.

"Ah, my dear sir! Is it you?" he greeted me. "I hope all is well."

He was very nice about my friend. Indeed, he was always nice, with the niceness of people whose hearts are genuinely humane. But this time it cost him an effort. His attempts at general conversation broke down into dulness. It occurred to me he might have been indisposed. But before I could frame the inquiry he muttered:

"You find me here very sad."

"I am sorry for that," I said. "You haven't had bad news, I hope?"

It was very kind of me to take an interest. No. It was not that. No bad news, thank God. And he became very still, as if holding his breath. Then, leaning forward a little, and in an odd tone of awed embarrassment, he took me into his confidence.

"The truth is that I have had a very—a very —how shall I say?—abominable adventure happen to me."

The energy of the epithet was sufficiently startling in that man of moderate feelings and toned-down vocabulary. The word unpleasant I should have thought would have fitted amply the worst experience likely to befall a man of his stamp. And an adventure, too. Incredible! But it is in human nature to believe the worst, and I confess I eyed him stealthily, wondering what he had been up to. In a moment, however, my unworthy suspicions vanished. There was a fundamental refinement of nature about the man which made me dismiss all idea of some more or less disreputable scrape.

"It is very serious. Very serious." He went on nervously. "I will tell you after dinner, if you will allow me."

I expressed my perfect acquiescence by a little bow, nothing more. I wished him to understand that I was not likely to hold him to that offer, if he thought better of it later on. We talked of indifferent things, but with a sense of difficulty quite unlike our former easy, gossipy intercourse. The hand raising a piece of bread to his lips, I noticed, trembled slightly. This symptom, in regard of my reading of the man, was no less than startling.

In the smoking-room he did not hang back at all. Directly we had taken our usual seats he leaned sideways over the arm of his chair and looked straight into my eyes earnestly.

"You remember," he began, "that day you went away? I told you then I would go to the Villa Nazionale to hear some music in the evening."

I remembered. His handsome old face, so fresh for his age, unmarked by any trying experience, appeared haggard for an instant. It was like the passing of a shadow. Returning his steadfast gaze, I took a sip of my black coffee. He was systematically minute in his narrative, simply in order, I think, not to let his excitement get the better of him.

After leaving the railway station, he had an ice, and read the paper in a café. Then he went back to the hotel, dressed for dinner, and dined with a good appetite. After dinner he lingered in the hall (there were chairs and tables there) smoking his cigar; talked to the little girl of the Primo Tenore of the San Carlo theater, and exchanged a few words with that "amiable lady," the wife of the Primo Tenore. There was no performance that evening, and these people were going to the Villa also. They went out of the hotel. Very well.

At the moment of following their example —it was half-past nine already—he remembered he had a rather large sum of money in his pocket-book. He entered, therefore, the office and deposited the greater part of it with the book-keeper of the hotel. This done, he took a carozella and drove to the seashore. He got out of the cab and entered the Villa on foot from the Largo di Vittoria end.

He stared at me very hard. And I understood then how really impressionable he was. Every small fact and event of that evening stood out in his memory as if endowed with mystic significance. If he did not mention to me the color of the pony which drew the carozella, and the aspect of the man who drove, it was a mere oversight arising from his agitation, which he repressed manfully.

He had then entered the Villa Nazionale from the Largo di Vittoria end. The Villa Nazionale is a public pleasure-ground laid out in grass plots, bushes, and flower-beds between the houses of the Riviera di Chiaja and the waters of the bay. Alleys of trees, more or less parallel, stretch its whole length—which is considerable. On the Riviera di Chiaja side the electric tramcars run close to the railings. Between the garden and the sea is the fashionable drive, a broad road bordered by a low wall, beyond which the Mediterranean splashes with gentle murmurs when the weather is fine.

As life goes on late at night in Naples, the broad drive was all astir with a brilliant swarm of carriage lamps moving in pairs, some creeping slowly, others running rapidly under the thin, motionless line of electric lamps defining the shore. And a brilliant swarm of stars hung above the land humming with voices, piled up with houses, glittering with lights—and over the silent flat shadows of the sea.

The gardens themselves are not very well lit. Our friend went forward in the warm gloom, his eyes fixed upon a distant luminous region extending nearly across the whole width of the Villa, as if the air had glowed there with its own cold, bluish, and dazzling light. This magic spot, behind the black trunks of trees and masses of inky foliage, breathed out sweet sounds mingled with bursts of brassy roar, sudden clashes of metal, and grave, vibrating thuds.

As he walked on, all these noises combined together into a piece of elaborate music whose harmonious phrases came persuasively through a great disorderly murmur of voices and shuffling of feet on the gravel of that open space. An enormous crowd immersed in the electric light, as if in a bath of some radiant and tenuous fluid shed upon their heads by luminous globes, drifted in its hundreds round the band. Hundreds more sat on chairs in more or less concentric circles, receiving unflinchingly the great waves of sonority that ebbed out into the darkness. The Count penetrated the throng, drifted with it in tranquil enjoyment, listening and looking at faces. All people of good society: mothers with their daughters, parents and children, young men and young women all talking, smiling, nodding to each other. Very many pretty faces, and very many pretty toilettes. There was, of course, a quantity of diverse types: showy old fellows with white moustaches, fat men, thin men, officers in uniform; but what predominated, he told me, was the South Italian type of young man, with a colorless, clear complexion, red lips, jet-black little moustache and liquid black eyes so wonderfully effective in leering or scowling.

Withdrawing from the throng, the Count shared a little table in front of the café with a young man of just such a type. Our friend had some lemonade. The young man was sitting moodily before an empty glass. He looked up once, and then looked down again. He also tilted his hat forward. Like this——

The Count made a gesture of a man pulling his hat down over his brow, and went on:

"I think to myself: he is sad; something is wrong with him; young men have their troubles. I take no notice of him, of course. I pay for my lemonade, and go away."

Strolling about in the neighborhood of the band, the Count thinks he saw twice that young man wandering alone in the crowd. Once their eyes met. It must have been the same young man, but there were so many there of that type that he could not be certain. Moreover, he was not very much concerned except in so far that he had been struck by the marked, peevish discontent of that face.

Presently, tired of the feeling of confinement one experiences in a crowd, the Count edged away from the band. An alley, very somber by contrast, presented itself invitingly with its promise of solitiude and coolness. He entered it, walking slowly on till the sound of the orchestra became distinctly deadened. Then he walked back and turned about once more. He did this several times before he noticed that there was somebody occupying one of the benches.

The spot being midway between two lamp-posts the light was faint.

The man lolled back in the corner of his seat, his legs stretched out, his arms folded and his head drooping on his breast. He never stirred, as though he had fallen asleep there, but when the Count passed by next time he had changed his attitude. He sat leaning forward. His elbows were propped on his knees, and his hands were rolling a cigarette. He never looked up from that occupation.

The Count continued his stroll away from the band. He returned slowly, he said. I can imagine him enjoying to the full, but with his usual tranquillity, the balminess of this southern night and the sounds of music softened delightfully by the distance.

Presently, he approached for the third time the man on the garden seat, still leaning forward with his elbows on his knees. It was a dejected pose. In the semi-obscurity of the alley his high shirt collar and his cuffs made small patches of vivid whiteness. The Count said that he had noticed him getting up brusquely as if to walk away, but almost before he was aware of it the man stood before him asking in a low, gentle tone whether the signore would have the kindness to oblige him with a light.

The Count answered this request by a polite "Certainly," and dropped his hands with the intention of exploring both pockets of his trousers for the matches.

"I dropped my hands," he said, "but I never put them in my pockets. I felt a pressure there——"

He put the tip of his finger on a spot close under his breastbone, the very spot of the human body where a Japanese gentleman begins the operation of the harakiri, which is a form of suicide following upon dishonor, upon an intolerable outrage to the delicacy of one's feelings.

"I glance down," the Count continued in an awe-struck voice, "and what do I see? A knife! A long knife——"

"You don't mean to say," I exclaimed amazed, "that you have been held up like this in the Villa at half-past ten o'clock, within a stone's throw of a thousand people!"

He nodded several times, staring at me with all his might.

"The clarinet," he declared solemnly, "was finishing his solo, and I assure you I could hear every note. Then the band crashed *fortissimo,* and that creature rolled its eyes and gnashed its teeth, hissing at me with the greatest ferocity, 'Be silent! No noise or——' "

I could not get over my astonishment.

"What sort of knife was it?" I asked stupidly.

"A long blade. A stiletto—perhaps a kitchen knife. A long narrow blade. It gleamed. And his eyes gleamed. His white teeth, too. I could see them. He was very ferocious. I thought to myself: 'If I hit him he will kill me.' How could I fight with him? He had the knife and I had nothing. I am nearly seventy, you know, and that was a young man. I seemed even to recognize him. The moody young man of the café. The young man I met in the crowd. But I could not tell. There are so many like him in this country."

The distress of that moment was reflected in his face. I should think that physically he must have been paralyzed by surprise. His thoughts, however, remained extremely active. They ranged over every alarming possibility. The idea of setting up a vigorous shouting for help occurred to him, too. But he did nothing of the kind, and the reason why he refrained gave me a good opinion of his mental self-possession. He saw in a flash that nothing prevented the other from shouting, too.

"That young man might in an instant have thrown away his knife and pretended I was the aggressor. Why not? He might have said I attacked him. Why not? It was one incredible story against another! He might have said anything—bring some dishonoring charge against me—what do I know? By his dress he was no common robber. He seemed to belong to the better classes. What could I say? He was an Italian—I am a foreigner. Of course I have my passport, and there is our consul—but to be arrested, dragged at night to the police office like a criminal!"

He shuddered. It was in his character to shrink from scandal much more than from mere death. And certainly for many people this would have always remained—considering certain peculiarities of Neapolitan manners—a deucedly queer story. The Count was no fool. His belief in the respectable placidity of life having received this rude shock, he thought that now anything might happen. But also a notion came into his head that this young man was perhaps merely an infuriated lunatic.

This was for me the first hint of his attitude toward this adventure. In his exaggerated delicacy of sentiment he felt that nobody's self-esteem need be affected by what a madman may choose to do to one. It became apparent, that the Count was to be denied that consolation. He enlarged upon the abominably savage way in which that young man rolled his glistening eyes and gnashed his white teeth. The band was going now through a slow movement of solemn braying by all the trombones, with deliberately repeated bangs of the big drum.

"But what did you do?" I asked, greatly excited.

"Nothing," answered the Count. "I let my hands hang down very still. I told him quietly I did not intend making a noise. He snarled like a dog, then said in an ordinary voice:

" *'Vostro portofolio.'*

"So I naturally," continued the Count—and from this point acted the whole thing in pantomime. Holding me with his eyes, he went through all the motions of reaching into his inside breast pocket, taking out a pocket-book, and handing it over. But that young man, still bearing steadily on the knife, refused to touch it.

He directed the Count to take the money out himself, received it into his left hand, motioned the pocket-book to be returned to the pocket, all this being done to the sweet thrilling of flutes and clarinets sustained by the emotional drone of the hautboys. And the "young man," as the Count called him, said: "This seems very little."

"It was, indeed, only 340 or 360 lire," the Count pursued. "I had left my money in the hotel, as you know. I told him this was all I had on me. He shook his head impatiently and said:

" *'Vostro orologio.'* "

The Count gave me the dumb show of pulling out his watch, detaching it. But, as it happened, the valuable gold half-chronometer he possessed had been left at a watch-maker's for cleaning. He wore that evening (on a leather guard) the Waterbury fifty-franc thing he used to take with him on his fishing expeditions. Perceiving the nature of this booty, the well-dressed robber made a contemptuous clicking sound with his tongue like this, "Tse-Ah!" and waved it away hastily. Then, as the Count was returning the disdained object to his pocket, he demanded with a threateningly increased pressure of the knife on the epigastrum, by way of reminder:

"Vostri anelli."

"One of the rings," went on the Count, "was given me many years ago by my wife; the other is the signet ring of my father. I said, 'No. *That* you shall not have!'"

Here the Count reproduced the gesture corresponding to that declaration by clapping one hand upon the other, and pressing both thus against his chest. It was touching in its resignation. "That you shall not have," he repeated firmly and closed his eyes, fully expecting—I don't know whether I am right in recording that such an unpleasant word had passed his lips—fully expecting to feel himself being—I really hesitate to say—being disembowelled by the push of the long, sharp blade resting murderously against the pit of his stomach—the very seat, in all human beings, of anguishing sensations.

Great waves of harmony went on flowing from the band.

Suddenly the Count felt the nightmarish pressure removed from the sensitive spot. He opened his eyes. He was alone. He had heard nothing. It is probable that the "young man" had departed, with light steps, some time before, but the sense of the horrid pressure had lingered even after the knife had gone. A feeling of weakness came over him. He had just time to stagger to the garden seat. He felt as though he had held his breath for a long time. He sat all in a heap, panting with the shock of the reaction.

The band was executing, with immense bravura, the complicated finale. It ended with a tremendous crash. He heard it unreal and remote, as if his ears had been stopped, and then the hard clapping of a thousand, more or less, pairs of hands, like a sudden hail-shower passing away. The profound silence which succeeded recalled him to himself.

A tramcar, resembling a long glass box wherein people sat with their heads strongly lighted, ran along swiftly within sixty yards of the spot where he had been robbed. Then another rustled by, and yet another going the other way. The audience about the band had broken up, and were entering the alley in small conversing groups. The Count sat up straight and tried to think calmly of what had happened to him. The vileness of it took his breath away again. As far as I can make it out he was disgusted with himself.

I do not mean to say with his behavior. Indeed, if his pantomimic rendering of it for my information was to be trusted, it was simply perfect. No, it was not that. He was not ashamed. He was shocked at being the selected victim, not of robbery so much as of contempt. His tranquility had been wantonly desecrated. His lifelong, kindly nicety of outlook had been defaced.

Nevertheless, at that stage, before the iron had time to sink deep, he was able to argue himself into comparative equanimity. As his agitation calmed down somewhat, he became aware that he was frightfully hungry. Yes, hungry. The sheer emotion had made him simply ravenous. He left the seat and, after walking for some time, found himself outside the gardens and before an arrested tramcar, without knowing very well how he came there. He got in as if in a dream, by a sort of instinct. Fortunately he found in his trouser pocket a copper to satisfy the conductor. Then the car stopped, and as everybody was getting out he got out, too. He recognized the Piazza San Ferdinando, but apparently it did not occur to him to take a cab and drive to the hotel. He remained in distress on the Piazza like a lost dog, thinking vaguely of the best way of getting something to eat at once.

Suddenly he remembered his twenty-franc piece. He explained to me that he had that piece of French gold for something like three years. He used to carry it about with him as a sort of reserve in case of accident. Anybody is liable to have his pocket picked—a quite different thing from a brazen and insulting robbery.

The monumental arch of the Galleria Umberto faced him at the top of a noble flight of stairs. He climbed these without loss of time, and directed his steps toward the Café Umberto. All the tables outside were occupied by a lot of people who were drinking. But as he wanted something to eat, he went into the café, which is divided into aisles by square pillars set all round with long looking-glasses. The Count sat down on a red plush bench against one of these pillars, waiting for his risotto. And his mind reverted to his abominable adventure.

He thought of the moody, well-dressed young man, with whom he had exchanged glances in the crowd around the bandstand, and who, he felt confident, was the robber. Would he recognize him again? Doubtless. But he did not want ever to see him again. The best thing was to forget this humiliating episode.

The Count looked round anxiously for the coming of his risotto, and, behold! to the left against the wall—there sat the young man. He was alone at a table, with a bottle of some sort of wine or syrup and a carafe of iced water before him. The smooth olive cheeks, the red lips, the little jet-black moustache turned up gallantly, the fine black eyes a little heavy and shaded by long eyelashes, that peculiar expression of cruel discontent to be seen only in the busts of some Roman emperors—it was he, no doubt at all. But that was a type. The Count looked away hastily. The young officer over there reading a paper was like that, too. Same type. Two young men farther away playing draughts also resembled——

The Count lowered his head with the fear in his heart of being everlastingly haunted by the vision of that young man. He began to eat his risotto. Presently he heard the young man on his left call the waiter in a bad-tempered tone.

At the call, not only his own waiter, but two other idle waiters belonging to a quite different row of tables, rushed toward him with obsequious alacrity, which is not the general characteristic of the waiters in the Café Umberto. The young man muttered something and one of the waiters walking rapidly to the nearest door called out into the Galleria: "Pasquale! O! Pasquale!"

Everybody knows Pasquale, the shabby old fellow who, shuffling between the tables, offers for sale cigars, cigarettes, picture postcards, and matches to the clients of the café. He is in many respects an engaging scoundrel. The Count saw the gray-haired, unshaven ruffian enter the café, the glass case hanging from his neck by a leather strap, and, at a word from the waiter, make his shuffling way with a sudden spurt to the young man's table. The young man was in need of a cigar with which Pasquale served him fawningly. The old peddler was going out, when the Count, on a sudden impulse, beckoned to him.

Pasquale approached, the smile of deferential recognition combining oddly with the cynical, searching expression of his eyes. Leaning his case on the table, he lifted the glass lid without a word. The Count took a box of cigarettes and urged by a fearful curiosity, asked as casually as he could——

"Tell me, Pasquale, who is that young signore sitting over there?"

The other bent over his box confidentially.

"That, *Signor Conde,*" he said, beginning to rearrange his wares busily and without looking up, "that is a young *Cavaliere* of a very good family from Bari. He studies in the University here, and is the chief, *capo,* of an association of young men—of very nice young men."

He paused, and then, with mingled discretion and pride of knowledge, murmured the explanatory word "Camorra"[2] and shut down the lid. "A very powerful Camorra," he breathed out. "The professors themselves respect it greatly . . . *una lira e cinquanti centesimi, Signor Conde.*"[3]

Our friend paid with the gold piece. While Pasquale was making up the change, he observed that the young man, of whom he had heard so much in a few words, was watching the transaction covertly. After the old vagabond had withdrawn with a bow, the Count settled with the waiter and sat still. A numbness, he told me, had come over him.

The young man paid, too, got up and crossed over, apparently for the purpose of looking at himself in the mirror set in the pillar nearest to the Count's seat. He was dressed all in black with a dark green bow tie. The Count looked round, and was startled by meeting a vicious glance out of the corners of the other's eyes. The young *Cavaliere* from Bari (according to Pasquale; but Pasquale is, of course, an accomplished liar) went on arranging his tie, settling his hat before the

[2] A clique or gang.
[3] "One lire and fifty cents, Signor Conde."

glass, and meantime he spoke just loud enough to be heard by the Count. He spoke through his teeth with the most insulting venom of contempt and gazing straight into the mirror.

"Ah! So you have some gold on you—you old liar—you old *birba* [4]—you *furfante!* [5] But you are not done with me yet."

The fiendishness of his expression vanished like lightning, and he lounged out of the café with a moody, impassive face.

The poor Count, after telling me this last episode, fell back trembling in his chair. His forehead broke into perspiration. There was a wanton insolence in the spirit of this outrage which appalled even me. What it was to the Count's delicacy I won't attempt to guess. I am sure that if he not been too refined to do such a blatantly vulgar thing as dying from apoplexy in a café, he would have had a fatal stroke there and then. All irony apart, my difficulty was to keep him from seeing the full extent of my commiseration. He shrank from every excessive sentiment, and my commiseration was practically unbounded. It did not surprise me to hear that he had been in bed a week. He had got up to make his arrangements for leaving southern Italy for good and all.

And the man was convinced that he could not live through a whole year in any other climate!

No argument of mine had any effect. It was not timidity, though he did say to me once: "You do not know what a Camorra is, my dear sir. I am a marked man." He was not afraid of what could be done to him. His delicate conception of his dignity was defiled by a degrading experience. He couldn't stand that. No Japanese gentleman, outraged in his exaggerated sense of honor, could have gone about his preparations for harakiri with greater resolution. To go home really amounted to suicide for the poor Count.

There is a saying of Neapolitan patriotism, intended for the information of foreigners, I presume: "See Naples and then die." *Vedi Napoli e poi mori.* It is a saying of excessive vanity, and everything excessive was abhorrent to the nice moderation of the poor Count. Yet, as I was seeing him off at the railway station, I thought he was behaving with singular fidelity to its conceited spirit. *Vedi Napoli!* . . . He had seen it! He had seen it with startling thoroughness—and now he was going to his grave. He was going to it by the *train de luxe* of the International Sleeping Car Company, *via* Trieste and Vienna. As the four long, somber coaches pulled out of the station I raised my hat with the solemn feeling of paying the last tribute of respect to a funeral *cortège. Il Conde's* profile, much aged already, glided away from me in stony immobility, behind the lighted pane of glass— *Vedi Napoli e poi mori!*

(1908)

STUDY AIDS: 1. The Count is shown to be worldly, civilized, cultivated, above all a man of moderation. In what ways is he moderate? Why does Conrad devote so much space to establishing this trait of character? How is it related to the meaning of the story?

2. Why does the Count finally leave Naples? Is it because he fears for his life, or is there another reason? Although the Count is a sympathetic character, it seems likely that Conrad is making an implicit judgment of him. What is the judgment?

3. Between the suggestive terminal tableaux of the Museum at the beginning and the "funeral *cortège*" at the end, Conrad gives us many vivid scenes: the beautiful city of Naples in general, and the Villa Nazionale, with its well-kept formal gardens and parallel rows of trees in particular. How is this setting appropriate to the Count and his terrifying experience? In the passage recounting the assault, what use does Conrad make of light and dark? Why does he tell us so much about the band and its "harmony"?

4. Although Conrad's details are convincing as straight facts in the story, many of them also have symbolic overtones. For instance, the Count's rheumatism, a physical disability, also suggests the paralysis of his will. What similar overtones do you discover in: (1) the young man's pointing his knife at the pit of the Count's stomach; (2) the description of the young man —his gleaming eyes and glistening teeth, his

---

[4] Scoundrel.
[5] Rascal.

hissing his words, his "venom of contempt," his "fiendishness"?

5. Conrad made notable advances in the handling of time in fiction. Draw up a list of events in the order in which they occur in time, and then compare it with the order in which Conrad presents them. Why does he depart from a normal chronological ordering of events?

6. Conrad does not tell the story himself but tells it through a narrator, the "I" in the story.

What is the advantage of this POINT OF VIEW? The assault on the Count occurs while the narrator is absent from Naples; the Count tells him about it when he returns. Conrad, instead of reporting the Count's telling of his experience, makes the narrator *retell* it. Why not have the Count himself tell it? Notice how we are kept aware that it is a retelling from the Count's frequent interruption of the narrative, with a consequent shifting back and forth in time.

William Butler Yeats
(1865–1939)

T. S. ELIOT HAS STATED THAT YEATS WAS THE GREATEST POET OF THE MODERN WORLD—"certainly the greatest in this language, and as far as I am able to judge, in any language." Whatever posterity may think of Eliot's evaluation, it will not be able to deny Yeats's influence on twentieth-century literature.

Yeats was born in Dublin, the son of an Anglo-Irish, Protestant portrait painter. He attended school in London and later studied art in Dublin, but abandoned it because of his interest in literature. At the invitation of Oscar Wilde he went to London, where he remained for eight years (1888–1896). While there he actively participated in various groups concerned with aesthetics, mysticism, and art. His early poetry, written between 1888 and 1900 under the influence of Blake, the French Symbolists, Pater, and Ruskin, often expresses the desire to escape into fantasy or a mystic world.

Shortly after his return to Dublin in 1896 he met Lady Gregory. This was probably the turning point of his career. Two years later, with Lady Gregory, Edward Martyn, and George Moore he founded the Irish Literary Theater, which in 1904 became the famous Abbey Theater. This theater was the vehicle of the Irish Renaissance, that flowering of cultural nationalism which made the world more aware of Irish folklore and Celtic culture than it had been since the beginning of romanticism in the later eighteenth century. Although the poetic dramas which Yeats wrote for the Theater are not equal to his lyric verse nor to the plays of J. M. Synge and Sean O'Casey, *The Countess Cathleen* (1892), *The Land of Heart's Desire* (1894), and *Deirdre* (1907) were highly successful.

As Yeats grew older, a more realistic and pessimistic strain replaced the earlier one of escape into romantic fantasy. His earlier mysticism, however, deepened. In his later volumes of poetry, notably *The Tower* (1928) and *Last Poems* (1936–1939), he expresses his strong faith in an ideal world which transcends this physical one, a permanent world of the imagination, which can be entered only through art or intuition. Few, if any, poets other than Yeats have evoked this world with such imaginative power and mastery of language.

The Lake Isle of Innisfree [1]

I will arise and go now, and go to Innisfree,
And a small cabin build there, of clay and
    wattles [2] made:
Nine [3] bean-rows will I have there, a hive for
    the honey-bee.
And live alone in the bee-loud glade.

And I shall have some peace there, for peace
    comes dropping slow,   5
Dropping from the veils of the morning to
    where the cricket sings;
There midnight's all a glimmer, and noon a
    purple glow,
And evening full of linnet's wings.

I will arise and go now, for always night and
    day

I hear lake water lapping with low sounds by
    the shore;   10
While I stand on the roadway, or on the
    pavements gray,
I hear it in the deep heart's core.
(1893)

STUDY AIDS: 1. In l. 3 Yeats is creating an
aura of mystery by the use of "Nine bean-rows."
If the line were changed to "Some bean rows,"
what effect, other than that of mystery, would
be lost?
    2. Notice the sharp contrast between "bee-
loud glade" (l. 4) and "pavements gray" (l. 11).
How is this reminiscent of Wordsworth's views?
    3. The poem expresses a romantic longing for
peace and solitude. What other human desires
are expressed?

The White Birds

I would that we were, my belovèd, white
    birds on the foam of the sea!
We tire of the flame of the meteor, before it
    can fade and flee;
And the flame of the blue star of twilight,
    hung low on the rim of the sky,
Has awaked in our hearts, my belovèd, a sad-
    ness that may not die.

A weariness comes from those dreamers, dew
    dabbled, the lily and rose;   5
Ah, dream not of them, my belovèd, the flame
    of the meteor that goes,
Or the flame of the blue star that lingers, hung
    low in the fall of the dew:
For I would we were changed to white birds
    on the wandering foam: I and you!

I am haunted by numberless islands, and
    many a Danaän [4] shore,
Where Time would surely forget us, and Sor-
    row come near us no more;   10
Soon far from the rose and the lily, and fret
    of the flames would we be,
Were we only white birds, my belovèd,
    buoyed out on the foam of the sea!
(1893)

STUDY AIDS: 1. The flame of the star
and meteor and the lily and the rose seem to
represent the beauty of physical, sensory things
in this world. What do the white birds represent?
    2. If the beauty of this world creates a "sad-
ness" (l. 4) and a "weariness" (l. 5) in man,
what is Yeats saying about: (1) beauty; and
(2) the completeness of man's experience?

[1] Innisfree is a lake in County Sligo, Ireland.
[2] Sticks.
[3] In medieval belief, numbers had mystical significance (cf. use of "five" in *Sir Gawain and the
Green Knight*).

[4] The place of eternal happiness in Celtic mythology.

When You Are Old

When you are old and gray and full of sleep,
And nodding by the fire, take down this book,
And slowly read, and dream of the soft look
Your eyes had once, and of their shadows
  deep;

How many loved your moments of glad
  grace,   5
And loved your beauty with love false or true;
But one man loved the pilgrim soul in you,
And loved the sorrows of your changing face.

And bending down beside the glowing bars
Murmur, a little sadly, how love fled   10
And paced upon the mountains overhead
And hid his face amid a crowd of stars.
(1893)

STUDY AIDS: 1. What is a "pilgrim soul"
(l. 7)?
    2. How did "one man's" love (l. 7) differ
from that of the "many" (l. 5)?

Never Give All the Heart

Never give all the heart, for love
Will hardly seem worth thinking of
To passionate women if it seem
Certain, and they never dream
That it fades out from kiss to kiss;   5
For everything that's lovely is
But a brief, dreamy, kind delight.
O never give the heart outright,

For they, for all smooth lips can say,
Have given their hearts up to the play.   10
And who could play it well enough
If deaf and dumb and blind with love?
He that made this knows all the cost,
For he gave all his heart and lost.
(1904)

The Collar-Bone of a Hare

Would I could cast a sail on the water
Where many a king has gone
And many a king's daughter,
And alight at the comely trees and the lawn,
The playing upon pipes and the dancing,   5
And learn that the best thing is
To change my loves while dancing
And pay but a kiss for a kiss.

I would find by the edge of that water
The collar-bone of a hare   10
Worn thin by the lapping of water,
And pierce it through with a gimlet, and stare
At the old bitter world where they marry in
  churches,
And laugh over the untroubled water
At all who marry in churches,   15
Through the white thin bone of a hare.
(1919)

An Irish Airman Foresees His Death

I know that I shall meet my fate
Somewhere among the clouds above;
Those that I fight I do not hate,

Those that I guard I do not love;
My country is Kiltartan Cross,   5
My countrymen Kiltartan's poor,

No likely end could bring them loss
Or leave them happier than before.
Nor law, nor duty bade me fight,
Nor public men, nor cheering crowds, 10
A lonely impulse of delight
Drove to this tumult in the clouds;
I balanced all, brought all to mind,
The years to come seemed waste of breath,

A waste of breath the years behind 15
In balance with this life, this death.
(1919)

STUDY AIDS: 1. Why did the Irish pilot enlist?
2. What is the pilot's view of life? Of death?

The Second Coming [1]

The poem presents Yeats's belief that some unknown yet felt evil threatens to destroy modern civilization. The first stanza gives the poet's impression of the present world; the second, the terrible vision forced on him by the present.

Turning and turning in the widening gyre [2]
The falcon cannot hear the falconer;
Things fall apart: the center cannot hold;
Mere anarchy is loosed upon the world,
The blood-dimmed tide is loosed, and every-
where 5
The ceremony of innocence is drowned;
The best lack all conviction, while the
worst
Are full of passionate intensity.

Surely some revelation is at hand;
Surely the Second Coming is at hand. 10
The Second Coming! Hardly are those words
out
When a vast image out of *Spiritus Mundi* [3]
Troubles my sight: somewhere in sands of the
desert
A shape [4] with lion body and the head of a
man,
A gaze blank and pitiless as the sun, 15
Is moving its slow thighs, while all about it
Reel shadows of the indignant desert birds.
The darkness drops again; but now I know
That twenty centuries of stony sleep

Were vexed to nightmare by a rocking
cradle, [5] 20
And what rough beast, its hour come round
at last,
Slouches towards Bethlehem to be born?
(1921)

STUDY AIDS: 1. The opening image is very effective. The falcon in its characteristic flight (in ever-widening circles) cannot hear its master's voice. What is implied about the motion of the world of human beings? How do the images of ll. 4–8 illustrate the statement, "the center cannot hold"? What is the "blood-dimmed tide" and "ceremony of innocence"?
2. Since the "center" of the modern world "cannot hold," it threatens to fly off in all directions. Some great event, such as the second coming, must be at hand. Is this a Christian poem prophesying the coming of the Son of God to judge and destroy the world? Note that the *Spiritus Mundi* is a pagan concept used to evaluate Christianity. What does this IRONY do to Christianity?
3. Many poets have equated Christianity with significant human history and have then lamented that Christianity has not been as good as it ought to have been. Notice the image in ll. 18–20. In the image "twenty centuries of stony

[1] The "second coming" of Christ.
[2] A favorite image of Yeats: turning in circles as a gyroscope turns.
[3] "The soul of the world." It is a phrase used by Yeats to express his belief that all experience as well as past, present, and future history are contained in racial memory. The human mind in moments of mystical intuition can penetrate this memory, but it cannot be touched through sensory perception.

[4] The beast is described in terms of the Sphinx. Some critics believe it refers to the "Anti-Christ" described in the Book of Revelation. Whatever specific "rough beast" Yeats may have had in mind, ll. 13–22 undoubtedly create a sense of evil in a disintegrating world.
[5] The manger in Bethlehem.

sleep" does Yeats equate Christianity with human history, or is Christianity only one of many such phases in the world's life? According to Yeats, what kind of history has Christianity produced? What is the meaning of the last two lines? Has this birth yet come to pass? Is the poem optimistic or pessimistic?

4. One might say that Yeats uses Christianity as one half of his major METAPHOR or myth in this poem. What is the other half?

A Prayer for My Daughter

Once more the storm is howling, and half hid
Under this cradle-hood and coverlid
My child sleeps on. There is no obstacle
But Gregory's wood and one bare hill
Whereby the haystack- and roof-leveling
    wind,   5
Bred on the Atlantic, can be stayed;
And for an hour I have walked and prayed
Because of the great gloom that is in my
    mind.

I have walked and prayed for this young child
    an hour
And heard the sea-wind scream upon the
    tower,   10
And under the arches of the bridge, and
    scream
In the elms above the flooded stream;
Imagining in excited reverie
That the future years had come,
Dancing to a frenzied drum,   15
Out of the murderous innocence of the sea.

May she be granted beauty and yet not
Beauty to make a stranger's eye distraught,
Or hers before a looking-glass, for such,
Being made beautiful overmuch,   20
Consider beauty a sufficient end,
Lose natural kindness and maybe
The heart-revealing intimacy
That chooses right, and never find a friend.

Helen being chosen found life flat and dull 25
And later had much trouble from a fool,[1]

While that great Queen,[2] that rose out of the
    spray,
Being fatherless could have her way
Yet chose a bandy-leggèd smith for man.
It's certain that fine women eat   30
A crazy salad with their meat
Whereby the Horn of Plenty [3] is undone.

In courtesy I'd have her chiefly learned;
Hearts are not had as a gift but hearts are
    earned
By those that are not entirely beautiful;   35
Yet many, that have played the fool
For beauty's very self, has charm made wise,
And many a poor man that has roved,
Loved and thought himself beloved,
From a glad kindness cannot take his
    eyes.   40

May she become a flourishing hidden tree
That all her thoughts may like the linnet [4] be,
And have no business but dispensing round
Their magnanimities of sound,
Nor but in merriment begin a chase,   45
Nor but in merriment a quarrel.
O may she live like some green laurel
Rooted in one dear perpetual place.

My mind, because the minds that I have
    loved,
The sort of beauty that I have approved,   50
Prosper but little, has dried up of late,
Yet knows that to be choked with hate
May well be of all evil chances chief.
If there's no hatred in a mind
Assault and battery of the wind   55
Can never tear the linnet from the leaf.

[1] Helen of Troy, who married the Greek prince Menelaus. Later she was abducted by Paris ("fool"), and according to legend the incident caused the Trojan war.
[2] Venus, the goddess of beauty and love, married Hephaestus, the god of fire and metalworking. Zeus, in jealous anger, had thrown him from Mt. Olympus. The fall broke the fire god's leg; thereafter he walked with a limp ("bandy-leggèd").

[3] The horn of Amalthea, the nurse of Zeus. It became filled with whatever its possessor wished, and hence is an emblem of plenty, or happiness.
[4] A small bird of the finch family.

An intellectual hatred is the worst,
So let her think opinions are accursed.
Have I not seen the loveliest woman born
Out of the mouth of Plenty's horn,   60
Because of her opinionated mind
Barter that horn and every good
By quiet natures understood
For an old bellows full of angry wind?

Considering that, all hatred driven hence,   65
The soul recovers radical innocence
And learns at last that it is self-delighting,
Self-appeasing, self-affrighting,
And that its own sweet will is Heaven's will;

She can, though every face should scowl   70
And every windy quarter howl
Or every bellows burst, be happy still.

And may her bridegroom bring her to a
     house
Where all's accustomed, ceremonious;
For arrogance and hatred are the wares   75
Peddled in the thoroughfares.
How but in custom and in ceremony
Are innocence and beauty born?
Ceremony's a name for the rich horn,
And custom for the spreading laurel tree.   80
(1919; 1921)

Leda and the Swan

In Greek mythology Zeus, enamored of Leda, wife of the king of Sparta, came to her in the form of a swan. Of their union was born a blue egg, from which was hatched Helen of Troy, the most beautiful woman of the ancient world. Yeats was fond of this myth and used it several times in his poetry to symbolize the union of mortal and immortal, flesh and spirit.

A sudden blow: the great wings beating still
Above the staggering girl, her thighs caressed
By the dark webs, her nape caught in his bill,
He holds her helpless breast upon his breast.

How can those terrified vague fingers push 5
The feathered glory from her loosening
     thighs?
And how can body, laid in that white rush,
But feel the strange heart beating where it
     lies?

A shudder in the loins engenders there
The broken wall, the burning roof and
     tower   10
And Agamemnon dead.[1]
          Being so caught up,
So mastered by the brute blood of the air,

Did she put on his knowledge with his power
Before the indifferent beak could let her drop?
(1925)

STUDY AIDS: 1. What kind of poem is
Leda and the Swan? The first eight lines describe
the mating of Zeus and Leda. What do the last
six lines imply as the result of the union of the
divine and mortal, the flesh and spirit?

2. If the swan symbolizes inspiration, spirit,
or the divine spark in the human imagination,
what is Yeats saying about poetry?

3. If the union of Zeus and Leda symbolizes
the union of flesh and spirit, what is Yeats saying in the final two lines about man's knowledge
and power?

4. Who is the ultimate cause of the "broken
wall, the burning roof and tower And Agamemnon dead"?

Sailing to Byzantium

Yeats here expresses his views on art (poetry) and its relation to man's life. This relationship
is presented symbolically in terms of an old who, weary and slightly regretful that sensuous
enjoyment is no longer possible, seeks compensation for his loss. He finds his repose in the intel-

[1] Helen's abduction by Paris led to the Trojan war (ll. 10–11).

lectual environment of Byzantium (now Istanbul). Yeats has explained his choice of Byzantium as symbol in the following statement: "In early Byzantium, maybe never before or since in recorded history, religion, aesthetic, and practical life were one."

That[1] is no country for old men. The young
In one another's arms, birds in the trees
(Those dying generations) at their song,
The salmon-falls, the mackerel-crowded seas,[2]
Fish, flesh, or fowl, commend all summer
    long   5
Whatever is begotten, born, and dies.
Caught in that sensual music, all neglect
Monuments of unaging intellect.[3]

An aged man is but a paltry thing,
A tattered coat upon a stick, unless   10
Soul clap its hands and sing, and louder sing
For every tatter in its mortal dress;[4]
Nor is there singing school[5] but studying
Monuments of its own magnificence;
And therefore I have sailed the seas and
    come   15
To the holy city of Byzantium.[6]

O sages, standing in God's holy fire
As in the gold mosaic of a wall,
Come from the holy fire, perne in a gyre,[7]
And be the singing-masters of my soul.   20
Consume my heart away—sick with desire
And fastened to a dying animal
It knows not what it is—and gather me
Into the artifice of eternity.[8]

Once out of nature I shall never take   25
My bodily form from any natural thing,

But such a form as Grecian goldsmiths make
Of hammered gold and gold enamelling
To keep a drowsy emperor awake;
Or set upon a golden bough[9] to sing   30
To lords and ladies of Byzantium
Of what is past, or passing, or to come.[10]
(1928)

STUDY AIDS: 1. Byzantium, among other things, is used as a symbol for things of the mind and spirit as opposed to sensuous experience. Yeats believed that the art of Byzantium was inspired by mind and spirit, not by emotion. As such it was timeless and permanent. If artists do not imitate nature, what, according to the poem, should they imitate?

2. How does man study "Monuments of its own magnificence" (l. 14)? Why is art that is copied from nature inadequate?

3. What is the value of the kind of art described in the poem? What other values does it have than the two mentioned in ll. 29–32?

4. Although the poem is primarily a poet's views on his own artistic inspiration, what values of interest to the non-poet are implied in the poem?

5. Yeats disliked science, especially when it tried to explain eternal values of human life. What evidences of his distrust do you see in the poem? What is the connection between his distrust and the theme of the poem?

[1] I.e., the sensuous world of the young. The use of the demonstrative indicates that the speaker has arrived at Byzantium.

[2] Notice that each image in ll. 1–5 emphasizes the fertility of all nature ("fish, flesh, fowl"). This aspect of nature finds its contrast in ll. 7–8.

[3] Works of art, like those of Byzantium in the fifth and sixth centuries: an abstract, intellectual art not dependent on the world of the senses.

[4] Since age precludes sensuous experience (the raw material of much art), man must sing the louder to compensate for the loss; he must find another kind of inspiration.

[5] I.e., inspiration. Man's poetic nature must learn to sing (find inspiration) in the works of the soul itself; these are works of art (l. 14).

[6] Notice that the works of art which inspire are in Byzantium. That art which is inspired by nature is not adequate.

[7] I.e., descend in a spiral motion.

[8] Cf. ll. 8, 14. Notice the word "artifice."

[9] Yeats's own note states, "I have read somewhere that in the Emperor's palace at Byzantium was a tree made of gold and silver, and artificial birds that sang."

[10] Contrast the time span here with that of this world in l. 6.

James Joyce
(1882–1941)

JAMES JOYCE WAS BORN IN DUBLIN AND EDUCATED IN JESUIT SCHOOLS BEFORE TAKING HIS degree at the Royal University in 1902. Feeling the restricting influences of home, country, and religion—like his hero, Stephen Dedalus, in the autobiographical novel, *The Portrait of the Artist as a Young Man*—Joyce left Ireland in 1902, never to return except for short visits, like that occasioned by the death of his mother in 1903. The rest of his life was spent in Rome, Trieste, Zurich, and especially Paris, his home during most of these years.

Joyce's literary career began in 1907 with the appearance of a volume of poems, *Chamber Music*. His collection of short stories, *Dubliners,* came out in 1914, *Exiles* (a play) in 1915, and *The Portrait of the Artist* in 1916. His two major novels, *Ulysses* and *Finnegans Wake,* were published in book form in 1922 and 1940 respectively.

Joyce found that his forte was not in poetry or drama. It is in prose fiction that Joyce's genius truly expresses itself, prose fiction that has exerted a tremendous influence on twentieth-century writing. As one goes from *Dubliners* through *The Portrait of the Artist* and *Ulysses* to *Finnegans Wake,* he discovers a fascinating evolution of complexity of form and subjectivity of content. *Dubliners* is fairly straightforward and direct. *The Portrait of the Artist* makes much fuller use of symbols, of linguistic nuances, and of the stream-of-consciousness technique (an attempt to approximate in language the random, unorganized flow of thought—the free associations of both the conscious and the subconscious mind).

In *Ulysses,* which T. S. Eliot has called "the most considerable work of imagination in English in our time," these devices are carried much farther and new ones added. This novel (whose unmitigated frankness brought it into frequent conflict with the censors) is the record of a single day in the lives of a few Dubliners, especially of one Leopold Bloom, the Ulysses of this odyssey. Many detailed and ingenious parallels to Homer's characters, episodes, and descriptions are employed; an amazing variety of styles appears; symbolism and allusion are profuse and difficult; and all the inner processes of thought and half-thought are laid bare in full and candid detail. Most astonishing, perhaps, is the sheer linguistic virtuosity of this word artist who has been termed the greatest master of language since Milton.

But *Ulysses* is a first-grade reader compared to *Finnegans Wake,* which was seventeen years in the making and which has been called everything from "a triumph of free association" to "a stupendous and erudite hoax." *Finnegans Wake,* even more than *Ulysses,* explores the conscious and the subconscious, employing for the purpose a language concocted of linguistic borrowings, coined words with subtle connotations, combined forms, familiar words in new and bizarre combinations, ingenious malapropisms, and outrageous puns.

A Little Cloud

"A Little Cloud" and the other stories that make up *Dubliners* were ready for publication in 1906, but the collection did not appear until 1914, since Joyce had difficulty in getting it printed. The publishers were repelled by this realistic presentation of the drab and seamy side of Irish life.

"My intention," Joyce explained in a letter, "was to write a chapter of the moral history of my country, and I chose Dublin for the scene because that city seemed to me the center of paralysis. . . . I have written it for the most part in a style of scrupulous meanness. . . ."

Eight years before he had seen his friend off at the North Wall and wished him godspeed. Gallaher had got on. You could tell that at once by his traveled air, his well-cut tweed suit, and fearless accent. Few fellows 5 had talents like his and fewer still could remain unspoiled by such success. Gallaher's heart was in the right place and he had deserved to win. It was something to have a friend like that. 10

Little Chandler's thoughts ever since lunchtime had been of his meeting with Gallaher, of Gallaher's invitation and of the great city London where Gallaher lived. He was called Little Chandler because, though he was but 15 slightly under the average stature, he gave one the idea of being a little man. His hands were white and small, his frame was fragile, his voice was quiet and his manners were refined. He took the greatest care of his fair 20 silken hair and moustache and used perfume discreetly on his handkerchief. The half-moons of his nails were perfect and when he smiled you caught a glimpse of a row of childish white teeth. 25

As he sat at his desk in the King's Inns he thought what changes those eight years had brought. The friend whom he had known under a shabby and necessitous guise had become a brilliant figure on the London Press. 30 He turned often from his tiresome writing to gaze out of the office window. The glow of a late autumn sunset covered the grass plots and walks. It cast a shower of kindly golden dust on the untidy nurses and decrepit old 35 men who drowsed on the benches; it flickered upon all the moving figures—on the children who ran screaming along the gravel paths and on everyone who passed through the gardens. He watched the scene and thought of life; and (as always happened when he thought of life) he became sad. A gentle melancholy took possession of him. He felt how useless it was to struggle against fortune, this being the burden of wisdom which the ages had bequeathed to him.

He remembered the books of poetry upon his shelves at home. He had bought them in his bachelor days and many an evening, as he sat in the little room off the hall, he had been tempted to take one down from the bookshelf and read out something to his wife. But shyness had always held him back; and so the books had remained on their shelves. At times he repeated lines to himself and this consoled him.

When his hour had struck he stood up and took leave of his desk and of his fellow-clerks punctiliously. He emerged from under the feudal arch of the King's Inns, a neat modest figure, and walked swiftly down Henrietta Street. The golden sunset was waning and the air had grown sharp. A horde of grimy children populated the street. They stood or ran in the roadway or crawled up the steps before the gaping doors or squatted like mice upon the thresholds. Little Chandler gave them no thought. He picked his way deftly through all that minute vermin-like life and under the shadow of the gaunt spectral mansions in which the old nobility of Dublin had roistered. No memory of the past touched him, for his mind was full of a present joy.

He had never been in Corless's but he knew the value of the name. He knew that people went there after the theater to eat oysters and drink liqueurs; and he had heard that the waiters there spoke French and German. Walking swiftly by at night he had seen cabs drawn up before the door and richly dressed ladies, escorted by cavaliers, alight and enter quickly. They wore noisy dresses and many wraps. Their faces were powdered and they caught up their dresses, when they touched earth, like alarmed Atalantas.[1] He had always passed without turning his head to look. It was his habit to walk swiftly in the street even by day and whenever he found himself in the city late at night he hurried on his way apprehensively and excitedly. Sometimes, however, he courted the causes of his fear. He chose the darkest and narrowest streets and, as he walked boldly forward, the silence that was spread about his footsteps troubled him, the wandering, silent figures troubled him; and at times a sound of low fugitive laughter made him tremble like a leaf.

He turned to the right toward Capel Street. Ignatius Gallaher on the London Press! Who would have thought it possible eight years before? Still, now that he reviewed the past, Little Chandler could remember many signs of future greatness in his friend. People used to say that Ignatius Gallaher was wild. Of course, he did mix with a rakish set of fellows at that time, drank freely and borrowed money on all sides. In the end he had got mixed up in some shadowy affair, some money transaction; at least, that was one version of his flight. But nobody denied him talent. There was always a certain . . . something in Ignatius Gallaher that impressed you in spite of yourself. Even when he was out at elbows and at his wit's end for money he kept up a bold face. Little Chandler remembered (and the remembrance brought a slight flush of pride to his cheek) one of Ignatius Gallaher's sayings when he was in a tight corner:

"Half time now, boys," he used to say light-heartedly. "Where's my considering cap?"

That was Ignatius Gallaher all out; and, damn it, you couldn't but admire him for it.

Little Chandler quickened his pace. For the first time in his life he felt himself

[1] Atalanta was a virgin huntress of Greek mythology.

superior to the people he passed. For the first time his soul revolted against the dull inelegance of Capel Street. There was no doubt about it: if you wanted to succeed you had to go away. You could do nothing in Dublin. As he crossed Grattan Bridge he looked down the river towards the lower quays and pitied the poor stunted houses. They seemed to him a band of tramps, huddled together tramps, huddled together along the river-banks, their old coats covered with dust and soot, stupefied by the panorama of sunset and waiting for the first chill of night to bid them arise, shake themselves and begone. He wondered whether he could write a poem to express his idea. Perhaps Gallaher might be able to get it into some London paper for him. Could he write something original? He was not sure what idea he wished to express but the thought that a poetic moment had touched him took life within him like an infant hope. He stepped onward bravely.

Every step brought him nearer to London, farther from his own sober inartistic life. A light began to tremble on the horizon of his mind. He was not so old—thirty-two. His temperament might be said to be just at the point of maturity. There were so many different moods and impressions that he wished to express in verse. He felt them within him. He tried to weigh his soul to see if it was a poet's soul. Melancholy was the dominant note of his temperament, he thought, but it was a melancholy tempered by recurrences of faith and resignation and simple joy. If he could give expression to it in a book of poems perhaps men would listen. He would never be popular: he saw that. He could not sway the crowd but he might appeal to a little circle of kindred minds. The English critics, perhaps, would recognize him as one of the Celtic school by reason of the melancholy tone of his poems; besides that, he would put in allusions. He began to invent sentences and phrases from the notice which his book would get. *"Mr. Chandler has the gift of easy and graceful verse."* . . . *"A wistful sadness pervades these poems."* . . . *"The Celtic note."* It was a pity his name was not more Irish-looking. Perhaps it would be better to insert his mother's name before the surname: Thomas Malone Chandler, or better still: T. Malone Chandler. He would speak to Gallaher about it.

He pursued his revery so ardently that he passed his street and had to turn back. As he came near Corless's his former agitation began to overmaster him and he halted before the door in indecision. Finally he opened the door and entered.

The light and noise of the bar held him at the doorways for a few moments. He looked about him, but his sight was confused by the shining of many red and green wineglasses. The bar seemed to him to be full of people and he felt that the people were observing him curiously. He glanced quickly to right and left (frowning slightly to make his errand appear serious), but when his sight cleared a little he saw that nobody had turned to look at him: and there, sure enough, was Ignatius Gallaher leaning with his back against the counter and his feet planted far apart.

"Hallo, Tommy, old hero, here you are! What is it to be? What will you have? I'm taking whisky: better stuff than we get across the water. Soda? Lithia?[2] No mineral? I'm the same. Spoils the flavor. . . . Here, garçon, bring us two halves of malt whisky, like a good fellow. . . . Well, and how have you been pulling along since I saw you last? Dear God, how old we're getting! Do you see any signs of aging in me—eh, what? A little gray and thin on the top—what?"

Ignatius Gallaher took off his hat and displayed a large closely cropped head. His face was heavy, pale and clean-shaven. His eyes, which were of bluish slate-color, relieved his unhealthy pallor and shone out plainly above the vivid orange tie he wore. Between these rival features the lips appeared very long and shapeless and colorless. He bent his head and felt with two sympathetic fingers the thin hair at the crown. Little Chandler shook his head as a denial. Ignatius Gallaher put on his hat again.

"It pulls you down," he said. "Press life. Always hurry and scurry, looking for copy and sometimes not finding it: and then, always to have something new in your stuff. Damn proofs and printers, I say, for a few days. I'm deuced glad, I can tell you, to get back to the old country. Does a fellow good, a bit of a holiday. I feel a ton better since I landed again in dear dirty Dublin. . . . Here you are, Tommy. Water? Say when."

Little Chandler allowed his whisky to be very much diluted.

"You don't know what's good for you, my boy," said Gallaher. "I drink mine neat."[3]

"I drink very little as a rule," said Little Chandler modestly. "An odd half-one or so when I meet any of the old crowd: that's all."

"Ah, well," said Ignatius Gallaher, cheerfully, "here's to us and to old times and old acquaintance."

They clinked glasses and drank the toast.

"I met some of the old gang today," said Ignatius Gallaher. "O'Hara seems to be in a bad way. What's he doing?"

"Nothing," said Little Chandler. "He's gone to the dogs."

"But Hogan has a good sit, hasn't he?"

"Yes; he's in the Land Commission."

"I met him one night in London and he seemed to be very flush. . . . Poor O'Hara! Booze, I suppose?"

"Other things, too," said Little Chandler shortly.

Ignatius Gallaher laughed.

"Tommy," he said, "I see you haven't changed an atom. You're the very same serious person that used to lecture me on Sunday mornings when I had a sore head and a fur on my tongue. You'd want to knock about a bit in the world. Have you never been anywhere even for a trip?"

"I've been to the Isle of Man,"[4] said Little Chandler.

Ignatius Gallaher laughed.

"The Isle of Man!" he said. "Go to London or Paris: Paris, for choice. That'd do you good."

"Have you seen Paris?"

"I should think I have! I've knocked about there a little."

[2] A mineral water.

[3] Undiluted, "straight."

[4] An island in the Irish Sea.

"And is it really so beautiful as they say?" asked Little Chandler.

He sipped a little of his drink while Ignatius Gallaher finished his boldly.

"Beautiful?" said Ignatius Gallaher, pausing on the word and on the flavor of his drink. "It's not so beautiful, you know. Of course, it is beautiful. . . . But it's the life of Paris; that's the thing. Ah, there's no city like Paris for gaiety, movement, excitement. . . ."

Little Chandler finished his whisky and, after some trouble, succeeded in catching the barman's eye. He ordered the same again.

"I've been to the Moulin Rouge," Ignatius Gallaher continued when the barman had removed their glasses, "and I've been to all the Bohemian cafés. Hot stuff! Not for a pious chap like you, Tommy."

Little Chandler said nothing until the barman returned with two glasses: then he touched his friend's glass lightly and reciprocated the former toast. He was beginning to feel somewhat disillusioned. Gallaher's accent and way of expressing himself did not please him. There was something vulgar in his friend which he had not observed before. But perhaps it was only the result of living in London amid the bustle and competition of the Press. The old personal charm was still there under this new gaudy manner. And, after all, Gallaher had lived, he had seen the world. Little Chandler looked at his friend enviously.

"Everything in Paris is gay," said Ignatius Gallaher. "They believe in enjoying life—and don't you think they're right? If you want to enjoy yourself properly you must go to Paris. And, mind you, they've a great feeling for the Irish there. When they heard I was from Ireland they were ready to eat me, man."

Little Chandler took four or five sips from his glass.

"Tell me," he said, "is it true that Paris is so . . . immoral as they say?"

Ignatius Gallaher made a catholic gesture with his right arm.

"Every place is immoral," he said. "Of course you do find spicy bits in Paris. Go to one of the students' balls, for instance. That's lively, if you like, when the *cocottes*[5] begin to let themselves loose. You know what they are, I suppose?"

"I've heard of them," said Little Chandler.

Ignatius Gallaher drank off his whisky and shook his head.

"Ah," he said, "you may say what you like. There's no woman like the Parisienne—for style, for go."

"Then it is an immoral city," said Little Chandler, with timid insistence—"I mean, compared with London or Dublin?"

"London!" said Ignatius Gallaher. "It's six of one and half-a-dozen of the other. You ask Hogan, my boy. I showed him a bit about London when he was over there. He'd open your eye. . . . I say, Tommy, don't make punch of that whisky: liquor up."

"No, really. . . ."

"O, come on, another one won't do you any harm. What is it? The same again, I suppose?"

"Well . . . all right."

"*François,* the same again. . . . Will you smoke, Tommy?"

Ignatius Gallaher produced his cigar-case. The two friends lit their cigars and puffed at them in silence until their drinks were served.

"I'll tell you my opinion," said Ignatius Gallaher, emerging after some time from the clouds of smoke in which he had taken refuge, "it's a rum world. Talk of immorality! I've heard of cases—what am I saying?—I've known them: cases of . . . immorality. . . ."

Ignatius Gallaher puffed thoughtfully at his cigar and then in a calm historian's tone he proceeded to sketch for his friend some pictures of the corruption which was rife abroad. He summarized the vices of many capitals and seemed inclined to award the palm to Berlin. Some things he could not vouch for (his friends had told him), but of others he had had personal experience. He spared neither rank nor caste. He revealed many of the secrets of religious houses on the Continent and described some of the practices which were fashionable in high society

[5] Young women of questionable morals.

and ended by telling, with details, a story about an English duchess—a story which he knew to be true. Little Chandler was astonished.

"Ah, well," said Ignatius Gallaher, "here we are in old jog-along Dublin where nothing is known of such things."

"How dull you must find it," said Little Chandler, "after all the other places you've seen!"

"Well," said Ignatius Gallaher, "it's a relaxation to come over here, you know. And, after all, it's the old country, as they say, isn't it? You can't help having a certain feeling for it. That's human nature. . . . But tell me something about yourself. Hogan told me you had . . . tasted the joys of connubial bliss. Two years ago, wasn't it?"

Little Chandler blushed and smiled.

"Yes," he said. "I was married last May twelve months."

"I hope it's not too late in the day to offer my best wishes," said Ignatius Gallaher. "I didn't know your address or I'd have done so at the time."

He extended his hand, which Little Chandler took.

"Well, Tommy," he said, "I wish you and yours every joy in life, old chap, and tons of money, and may you never die till I shoot you. And that's the wish of a sincere friend, an old friend. You know that?"

"I know that," said Little Chandler.

"Any youngsters?" said Ignatius Gallaher.

Little Chandler blushed again.

"We have one child," he said.

"Son or daughter?"

"A little boy."

Ignatius Gallaher slapped his friend sonorously on the back.

"Bravo," he said, "I wouldn't doubt you, Tommy."

Little Chandler smiled, looked confusedly at his glass and bit his lower lip with three childishly white front teeth.

"I hope you'll spend an evening with us," he said, "before you go back. My wife will be delighted to meet you. We can have a little music and—"

"Thanks awfully, old chap," said Ignatius Gallaher. "I'm sorry we didn't meet earlier. But I must leave tomorrow night."

"Tonight, perhaps . . . ?"

"I'm awfully sorry, old man. You see I'm over here with another fellow, clever young chap he is too, and we arranged to go to a little card-party. Only for that . . ."

"Oh, in that case . . ."

"But who knows?" said Ignatius Gallaher considerately. "Next year I may take a little skip over here now that I've broken the ice. It's only a pleasure deferred."

"Very well," said Little Chandler, "the next time you come we must have an evening together. That's agreed now, isn't it?"

"Yes, that's agreed," said Ignatius Gallaher. "Next year if I come, *parole d'honneur.*" [6]

"And to clinch the bargain," said Little Chandler, "we'll just have one more now."

Ignatius Gallaher took out a large gold watch and looked at it.

"Is it to be the last?" he said. "Because you know, I have an a.p." [7]

"Oh, yes, positively," said Little Chandler.

"Very well, then," said Ignatius Gallaher, "let us have one as a *deoc an doruis* [8]—that's good vernacular for a small whisky, I believe."

Little Chandler ordered the drinks. The blush which had risen to his face a few moments before was establishing itself. A trifle made him blush at any time: and now he felt warm and excited. Three small whiskies had gone to his head and Gallaher's strong cigar had confused his mind, for he was a delicate and abstinent person. The adventure of meeting Gallaher after eight years, of finding himself with Gallaher in Corless's surrounded by lights and noise, of listening to Gallaher's stories and of sharing for a brief space Gallaher's vagrant and triumphant life, upset the equipoise of his sensitive nature. He felt acutely the contrast between his own life and his friend's, and it seemed to him unjust. Gallaher was his inferior in birth and education. He was sure that he could do something better than his friend had ever done, or could ever do, something higher

[6] "Word of honor."
[7] Appointment.
[8] "Drink of the door" (Gaelic); a parting drink.

than mere tawdry journalism if he only go
the chance. What was it that stood in his way?
His unfortunate timidity! He wished to vindicate himself in some way, to assert his manhood. He saw behind Gallaher's refusal of 5
his invitation. Gallaher was only patronizing
him by his friendliness just as he was patronizing Ireland by his visit.

The barman brought their drinks. Little
Chandler pushed one glass towards his friend 10
and took up the other boldly.

"Who knows?" he said, as they lifted their
glasses. "When you come next year I may
have the pleasure of wishing long life and
happiness to Mr. and Mrs. Ignatius Gallaher." 15

Ignatius Gallaher in the act of drinking
closed one eye expressively over the rim of
his glass. When he had drunk he smacked
his lips decisively, set down his glass and said:

"No blooming fear of that, my boy. I'm 20
going to have my fling first and see a bit of
life and the world before I put my head in
the sack—if I ever do."

"Some day you will," said Little Chandler
calmly. 25

Ignatius Gallaher turned his orange tie and
slate-blue eyes full upon his friend.

"You think so?" he said.

"You'll put your head in the sack," repeated Little Chandler stoutly, "like every- 30
one else if you can find the girl."

He had slightly emphasized his tone and
he was aware that he had betrayed himself;
but, though the color had heightened in his
cheek, he did not flinch from his friend's 35
gaze. Ignatius Gallaher watched him for a
few moments and then said:

"If ever it occurs, you may bet your bottom
dollar there'll be no mooning and spooning
about it. I mean to marry money. She'll have 40
a good fat account at the bank or she won't
do for me."

Little Chandler shook his head.

"Why, man alive," said Ignatius Gallaher,
vehemently, "do you know what it is? I've 45
only to say the word and tomorrow I can
have the woman and the cash. You don't believe it? Well, I know it. There are hundreds
—what am I saying?—thousands of rich Ger-
mans and Jews, rotten with money, that'd 50

only be too glad. . . . You wait a while, my
boy. See if I don't play my cards properly.
When I go about a thing I mean business, I
tell you. You just wait."

He tossed his glass to his mouth, finished
his drink and laughed loudly. Then he looked
thoughtfully before him and said in a calmer
tone:

"But I'm in no hurry. They can wait. I
don't fancy tying myself up to one woman,
you know."

He imitated with his mouth the act of tasting and made a wry face.

"Must get a bit stale, I should think," he
said.

Little Chandler sat in the room off the
hall, holding a child in his arms. To save
money they kept no servant, but Annie's
young sister Monica came for an hour or so
in the morning and an hour or so in the evening to help. But Monica had gone home
long ago. It was a quarter to nine. Little
Chandler had come home late for tea and,
moreover, he had forgotten to bring Annie
home the parcel of coffee from Bewley's. Of
course she was in a bad humor and gave him
short answers. She said she would do without
any tea but when it came near the time at
which the shop at the corner closed she decided to go out herself for a quarter of a
pound of tea and two pounds of sugar. She
put the sleeping child deftly in his arms and
said:

"Here. Don't waken him."

A little lamp with a white china shade
stood upon the table and its light fell over a
photograph which was enclosed in a frame
of crumpled horn. It was Annie's photograph.
Little Chandler looked at it, pausing at the
thin tight lips. She wore the pale blue summer blouse which he had brought her home
as a present one Saturday. It had cost him
ten and elevenpence; but what an agony of
nervousness it had cost him! How he had
suffered that day, waiting at the shop door
until the shop was empty, standing at the
counter and trying to appear at his ease while
the girl piled ladies' blouses before him, pay-

ing at the desk and forgetting to take up the odd penny of his change, being called back by the cashier, and finally striving to hide his blushes as he left the shop by examining the parcel to see if it was securely tied. When he brought the blouse home Annie kissed him and said it was very pretty and stylish; but when she heard the price she threw the blouse on the table and said it was a regular swindle to charge ten and elevenpence for it. At first she wanted to take it back but when she tried it on she was delighted with it, especially with the make of the sleeves, and kissed him and said he was very good to think of her.

Hm!

He looked coldly into the eyes of the photograph and they answered coldly. Certainly they were pretty and the face itself was pretty. But he found something mean in it. Why was it so unconscious and ladylike? The composure of the eyes irritated him. They repelled him and defied him: there was no passion in them, no rapture. He thought of what Gallaher had said about rich Jewesses. Those dark Oriental eyes, he thought, how full they are of passion, of voluptuous longing! . . . Why had he married the eyes in the photograph?

He caught himself up at the question and glanced nervously round the room. He found something mean in the pretty furniture which he had bought for his house on the hire system. Annie had chosen it herself and it reminded him of her. It was too prim and pretty. A dull resentment against his life awoke within him. Could he not escape from his little house? Was it too late for him to try to live bravely like Gallaher? Could he go to London? There was the furniture still to be paid for. If he could only write a book and get it published, that might open the way for him.

A volume of Byron's poems lay before him on the table. He opened it cautiously with his left hand lest he should waken the child and began to read the first poem in the book:

Hushed are the winds and still the eve-
ning gloom,

Not e'en a Zephyr wanders through
the grove,
Whilst I return to view my Margaret's
tomb
And scatter flowers on the dust I
love.[9]

He paused. He felt the rhythm of the verse about him in the room. How melancholy it was! Could he, too, write like that, express the melancholy of his soul in verse? There were so many things he wanted to describe: his sensation of a few hours before on Grattan Bridge, for example. If he could get back again into that mood. . . .

The child awoke and began to cry. He turned from the page and tried to hush it: but it would not be hushed. He began to rock it to and fro in his arms but its wailing cry grew keener. He rocked it faster while his eyes began to read the second stanza:

Within this narrow cell reclined her clay,
That clay where once . . .

It was useless. He couldn't read. He couldn't do anything. The wailing of the child pierced the drum of his ear. It was useless, useless! He was a prisoner for life. His arms trembled with anger and suddenly bending to the child's face he shouted:

"Stop!"

The child stopped for an instant, had a spasm of fright and began to scream. He jumped up from his chair and walked hastily up and down the room with the child in his arms. It began to sob piteously, losing its breath for four or five seconds, and then bursting out anew. The thin walls of the room echoed the sound. He tried to soothe it but it sobbed more convulsively. He looked at the contracted and quivering face of the child and began to be alarmed. He counted seven sobs without a break between them and caught the child to his breast in fright. If it died! . . .

The door was burst open and a young woman ran in, panting.

"What is it? What is it?" she cried.

The child, hearing its mother's voice, broke out into a paroxysm of sobbing.

[9] Byron, *On the Death of a Young Lady.*

"It's nothing, Annie . . . it's nothing. . . .
He began to cry . . ."

She flung her parcels on the floor and
snatched the child from him.

"What have you done to him?" she cried,
glaring into his face.

Little Chandler sustained for one moment
the gaze of her eyes and his heart closed
together as he met the hatred in them. He
began to stammer:

"It's nothing. . . . He . . . he began to
cry. . . . I couldn't . . . I didn't do anything. . . . What?"

Giving no heed to him she began to walk
up and down the room, clasping the child
tightly in her arms and murmuring:

"My little man! My little mannie! Was 'ou
frightened, love? . . . There now, love! There
now! . . . Lambabaun! Mamma's little lamb
of the world! . . . There now!"

Little Chandler felt his cheeks suffused
with shame and he stood back out of the
lamplight. He listened while the paroxysm
of the child's sobbing grew less and less; and
tears of remorse started to his eyes.

(1914)

STUDY AIDS: 1. This short story is constructed like a little play, in three separate
"scenes" or "acts." In the first, we find Little
Chandler anticipating his meeting with Gallaher;
in the second, Little Chandler and Gallaher
drinking and talking at Corless's; in the third,
Little Chandler at home that same evening with
his sleeping child. What is the setting of each
of these scenes, and of what importance is each
setting to its scene?

2. The story obviously centers around Little
Chandler. What kind of man is he? What details of description, dialogue, and action does
Joyce use to bring out his personality? What
kind of person is Gallaher? How is his character
brought out? Which of the two characters is
the more interesting? Is Gallaher likable or not?
Do you feel sympathy for Little Chandler? Is he
pitiful, tragic, ridiculous?

3. What is the basic CONFLICT of the story?
Is it one between two personalities, between a
man and his environment, or between two ways
of life? Or is the main conflict within Little
Chandler himself?

4. The CLIMAX of the story is that point
where Little Chandler shouts "Stop!" to his
wailing child. Is it an appropriate climax? Why
does not Little Chandler beat or even murder
his wife, or rob his firm, or run away from
home? What does the DENOUEMENT add to the
story?

5. What is the significance of the title, "A
Little Cloud"?

Virginia Woolf
(1882–1941)

SINCE VIRGINIA WOOLF WAS THE DAUGHTER OF SIR LESLIE STEPHEN, FAMOUS EDITOR
and essayist, she was introduced early into the world of literature and its writers. It was
a world she loved, and one in which she lived at first obscurely, as book reviewer for
the *London Times Literary Supplement,* but later as a novelist with considerable fame.
She created this world after her own image and peopled it with well-known intellectuals
and writers, such as E. M. Forster, Lytton Strachey, the Sitwells—Edith, Osbert, and
Sacheverell—and Victoria Sackville-West. Most of these friends published their books
through The Hogarth Press, which was founded by Mrs. Woolf and her husband,
Leonard Woolf. When the cruelties and physical destruction of the Second World War
threatened civilization and the world she loved, she committed suicide by drowning.

Virginia Woolf stands among the foremost novelists of the twentieth century. Influenced by James Joyce's *Ulysses* and Marcel Proust's *Remembrance of Things Past,* she turned away from the nineteenth-century traditional novelists, whom she considered "materialists" interested only in an external portrayal of men, and sought to reveal the inner consciousness of characters. This inner reality is presented through sensations, thought processes, emotions, and above all through the effect which time works on individual personality. External action, which is restricted by space relationships, receives little attention in Virginia Woolf's novels; it is replaced by time, the one thing that controls and measures the consciousness of man. Time is the real protagonist of the four novels upon which her fame rests: *Jacob's Room* (1922), *Mrs. Dalloway* (1925), *To the Lighthouse* (1927), and *The Waves* (1931).

Kew Gardens

Kew Gardens at first reading appears to be an impressionistic sketch, emphasizing mood, but it is actually a completely achieved nontraditional story. Our attention is focused upon an oval flower bed in Kew Gardens and particularly upon a snail, which slowly but unremittingly crosses the bed toward some unknown but certain goal. The snail is described as a human being usually would be, and the slight action of the human beings who pause at the flower bed we watch from the snail's point of view.

From the oval-shaped flower-bed there rose perhaps a hundred stalks spreading into heart-shaped or tongue-shaped leaves half-way up and unfurling at the tip red or blue or yellow petals marked with spots of color raised upon the surface; and from the red, blue or yellow gloom of the throat emerged a straight bar, rough with gold dust and slightly clubbed at the end. The petals were voluminous enough to be stirred by the summer breeze, and when they moved, the red, blue and yellow lights passed one over the other, staining an inch of the brown earth beneath with a spot of the most intricate color. The light fell either upon the smooth, gray back of a pebble, or, the shell of a snail with its brown, circular veins, or falling into a raindrop, it expanded with such intensity of red, blue and yellow the thin walls of water that one expected them to burst and disappear. Instead, the drop was left in a second silver gray once more, and the light now settled upon the flesh of a leaf, revealing the branching thread of fiber beneath the surface, and again it moved on and spread its illumination in the vast green spaces beneath the dome of the heart-shaped and tongue-shaped leaves.

Then the breeze stirred rather more briskly overhead and the color was flashed into the air above, into the eyes of the men and women who walk in Kew Gardens in July. The figures of these men and women straggled past the flowerbed with a curiously irregular movement not unlike that of the white and blue butterflies who crossed the turf in zig-zag flights from bed to bed. The man was about six inches in front of the woman, strolling carelessly, while she bore on with greater purpose, only turning her head now and then to see that the children were not too far behind. The man kept this distance in front of the woman purposely, though perhaps unconsciously, for he wished to go on with his thoughts.

"Fifteen years ago I came here with Lily," he thought. "We sat somewhere over there by a lake and I begged her to marry me all through the hot afternoon. How the dragonfly kept circling round us: how clearly I see the dragonfly and her shoe with the square silver buckle at the toe. All the time I spoke I saw her shoe and when it moved impatiently I knew without looking up what she was going to say: the whole of her seemed to be in her shoe. And my love, my desire, were in the dragonfly; for some reason I thought that if it settled there, on that leaf, the broad one with the red flower in the middle of it, if the dragonfly settled on the leaf she would say 'Yes' at once. But the dragonfly went round and round: it never settled anywhere —of course not, happily not, or I shouldn't be walking here with Eleanor and the children. Tell me, Eleanor. D'you ever think of the past?"

"Why do you ask, Simon?"

"Because I've been thinking of the past. I've been thinking of Lily, the woman I might have married. . . . Well, why are you silent? Do you mind my thinking of the past?"

"Why should I mind, Simon? Doesn't one always think of the past, in a garden with men and women lying under the trees? Aren't they one's past, all that remains of it, those men and women, those ghosts lying under the trees, . . . one's happiness, one's reality?"

"For me, a square silver shoe buckle and a dragonfly——"

"For me, a kiss. Imagine six little girls sitting before their easels twenty years ago, down by the side of a lake, painting the water-lilies, the first red water-lilies I'd ever seen. And suddenly a kiss, there on the back of my neck. And my hand shook all the afternoon so that I couldn't paint. I took out my watch and marked the hour when I would allow myself to think of the kiss for five minutes only—it was so precious—the kiss of an old gray-haired woman with a wart on her nose, the mother of all my kisses all my life. Come, Caroline, come, Herbert."

They walked on past the flower-bed, now walking four abreast, and soon diminished in size among the trees and looked half transparent as the sunlight and shade swam over their backs in large trembling irregular patches.

In the oval flower-bed the snail, whose shell had been stained red, blue and yellow for the space of two minutes or so, now appeared to be moving very slightly in its shell, and next began to labor over the crumbs of loose earth which broke away and rolled down as it passed over them. It appeared to have a definite goal in front of it, differing in this respect from the singular high-stepping angular green insect who attempted to cross in front of it, and waited for a second with its antennae trembling as if in deliberation, and then stepped off as rapidly and strangely in the opposite direction. Brown cliffs with deep green lakes in the hollows, flat, bladelike trees that waved from root to tip, round boulders of gray stone, vast crumpled surfaces of thin crackling texture—all the objects lay across the snail's progress between one stalk and another to his goal. Before he had decided whether to circumvent the arched tent of a dead leaf or to breast it there came past the bed the feet of other human beings.

This time they were both men. The younger of the two wore an expression of perhaps unnatural calm; he raised his eyes and fixed them very steadily in front of him while his companion spoke, and directly his companion had done speaking he looked on the ground again and sometimes opened his lips only after a long pause and sometimes did not open them at all. The elder man had a curiously uneven and shaky method of walking, jerking his hand forward and throwing up his head abruptly, rather in the manner of an impatient carriage horse tired of waiting outside a house; but in the man these gestures were irresolute and pointless. He talked almost incessantly; he smiled to himself and again began to talk, as if the smile had been an answer. He was talking about spirits—the spirits of the dead, who, according to him, were even now telling him all sorts of odd things about their experiences in Heaven.

"Heaven was known to the ancients as Thessaly, William, and now, with this war, the spirit matter is rolling between the hills like thunder." He paused, seemed to listen, smiled, jerked his head and continued:

"You have a small electric battery and a piece of rubber to insulate the wire—isolate? —insulate?—well, we'll skip the details, no good going into details that wouldn't be understood—and in short the little machine stands in any convenient position by the head of the bed, we will say, on a neat mahogany stand. All arrangements being properly fixed by workmen under my direction, the widow applies her ear and summons the spirit by sign as agreed. Woman! Widows! Women in black——"

Here he seemed to have caught sight of a woman's dress in the distance, which in the shade looked a purple black. He took off his hat, placed his hand upon his heart, and hurried towards her muttering and gesticulating feverishly. But William caught him by the sleeve and touched a flower with the tip of his walking-stick in order to divert the old man's attention. After looking at it for a moment in some confusion the old man bent his ear to it and seemed to answer a voice speaking from it, for he began talking about the forests of Uruguay which he had visited hundreds of years ago in company with the most beautiful young woman in Europe. He could be heard murmuring about forests of Uruguay blanketed with the wax petals of tropical roses, nightingales, sea beaches, mermaids, and women drowned at sea, as he suffered himself to be moved on by William, upon whose face the look of stoical patience grew slowly deeper and deeper.

Following his steps so closely as to be slightly puzzled by his gestures came two elderly women of the lower middle class, one stout and ponderous, the other rosy cheeked and nimble. Like most people of their station they were frankly fascinated by any signs of eccentricity betokening a disordered brain, especially in the well-to-do; but they were too far off to be certain whether the gestures were merely eccentric or genuinely mad. After they had scrutinized the old man's back in silence for a moment and given each other a queer, sly look, they went on energetically piecing together their very complicated dialogue:

"Nell, Bert, Lot, Cess, Phil, Pa, he says, I says, she says, I says, I says——"

"My Bert, Sis, Bill, Grandad, the old man, sugar,

Sugar, flour, kippers, greens,
Sugar, sugar, sugar."

The ponderous woman looked through the pattern of falling words at the flowers standing cool, firm, and upright in the earth, with a curious expression. She saw them as a sleeper waking from a heavy sleep sees a brass candlestick reflecting the light in an unfamiliar way, and closes his eyes and opens them, and seeing the brass candlestick again, finally starts broad awake and stares at the candlestick with all his powers. So the heavy woman came to a standstill opposite the oval-shaped flower-bed, and ceased even to pretend to listen to what the other woman was saying. She stood there letting the words fall over her, swaying the top part of her body slowly backwards and forwards, looking at the flowers. Then she suggested that they should find a seat and have their tea.

The snail had now considered every possible method of reaching his goal without going round the dead leaf or climbing over it. Let alone the effort needed for climbing a leaf, he was doubtful whether the thin texture which vibrated with such an alarming crackle when touched even by the tips of his horns would bear his weight; and this determined him finally to creep beneath it, for there was a point where the leaf curved high enough from the ground to admit him. He had just inserted his head in the opening and was taking stock of the high brown roof and was getting used to the cool brown light when two other people came past outside on the turf. This time they were both young, a young man and a young woman. They were both in the prime of youth, or even in that season which precedes the prime of youth, the season before the smooth pink folds of the flower have burst their gummy case, when the wings of the butterfly, though fully grown, are motionless in the sun.

"Lucky it isn't Friday," he observed.

"Why? D'you believe in luck?"

"They make you pay sixpence on Friday."

"What's sixpence anyway? Isn't it worth sixpence?"

"What's 'it'—what do you mean by 'it'?"

"O, anything—I mean—you know what I mean."

Long pauses came between each of these remarks; they were uttered in toneless and monotonous voices. The couple stood still on the edge of the flowerbed, and together pressed the end of her parasol deep down into the soft earth. The action and the fact that his hand rested on the top of hers ex-[5]pressed their feelings in a strange way, as these short insignificant words also expressed something, words with short wings for their heavy body of meaning, inadequate to carry them far and thus alighting awkwardly upon [10]the very common objects that surrounded them, and were to their inexperienced touch so massive; but who knows (so they thought as they pressed the parasol into the earth) what precipices aren't concealed in them, or [15]what slopes of ice don't shine in the sun on the other side? Who knows? Who has ever seen this before? Even when she wondered what sort of tea they gave you at Kew, he felt that something loomed up behind her words, [20]and stood vast and solid behind them; and the mist very slowly rose and uncovered— O, Heavens, what were those shapes?—little white tables, and waitresses who looked first at her and then at him; and there was a bill [25]that he would pay with a real two shilling piece, and it was real, all real, he assured himself, fingering the coin in his pocket, real to everyone except to him and to her; even to him it began to seem real; and then—but it [30]was too exciting to stand and think any longer, and he pulled the parasol out of the earth with a jerk and was impatient to find the place where one had tea with other peo- ple, like other people.

"Come along, Trissie; it's time we had [35]our tea."

"Wherever *does* one have one's tea?" she asked with the oddest thrill of excitement in her voice, looking vaguely round and letting [40]herself be drawn on down the grass path, trailing her parasol; turning her head this way and that way forgetting her tea, wishing to go down there and then down there, re- membering orchids and cranes among wild [45]flowers, a Chinese pagoda and a crimson crested bird; but he bore her on.

Thus one couple after another with much the same irregular and aimless movement passed the flower-bed and were enveloped in [50]layer after layer of green blue vapor, in which at first their bodies had substance and a dash of color, but later both substance and color dissolved in the green-blue atmosphere. How hot it was! So hot that even the thrush chose to hop, like a mechanical bird, in the shadow of the flowers, with long pauses be- tween one movement and the next; instead of rambling vaguely the white butterflies danced one above another, making with their white shifting flakes the outline of a shat- tered marble column above the tallest flowers; the glass roofs of the palm house shone as if a whole market full of shiny green umbrellas had opened in the sun; and in the drone of the airplane the voice of the summer sky murmured its fierce soul. Yellow and black, pink and snow white, shapes of all these colors, men, women, and children were spotted for a second upon the horizon, and then, seeing the breadth of yellow that lay upon the grass, they wavered and sought shade beneath the trees, dissolving like drops of water in the yellow and green atmosphere, staining it faintly with red and blue. It seemed as if all gross and heavy bodies had sunk down in the heat motionless and lay huddled upon the ground, but their voices went wavering from them as if they were flames lolling from the thick waxen bodies of candles. Voices. Yes, voices. Wordless voices, breaking the silence suddenly with such depth of contentment, such passion of desire, or, in the voices of children, such freshness of surprise; breaking the silence? But there was no silence; all the time the motor omnibuses were turning their wheels and changing their gear; like a vast nest of Chinese boxes all of wrought steel turning ceaselessly one within another the city mur- mured; on the top of which the voices cried aloud and the petals of myriads of flowers flashed their colors into the air.

(1921)

STUDY AIDS: 1. What human beings pause to look at or pass the flower bed? What ages do they represent? What social classes do they represent? What scope do they give to the story (i.e., what areas of human life does the story explore)?

2. The climax of the story comes in the final paragraph. Reread it carefully. Persons, flowers, trees, and insects dissolve into color. Only the wordless "voices went wavering from them as if they were flames lolling from the thick waxen bodies of candles." This "flame-candle" image is used in several of Mrs. Woolf's works to illustrate her belief in a spirit-matter dualism. The "gross and heavy bodies," "the thick waxen bodies of candles" are matter; in opposition to these are the "voices," and "the flames"—spirit. Like Henri Bergson, Mrs. Woolf considers "life" an intuitive, spiritual force, a vital drive, equal to an awareness of eternal as distinct from chronological time. Life is a battle between eternity and chronological time. When consciousness attains this awareness of eternity (not measurable by time or space) it is spirit or life; when awareness is surrendered, life becomes matter. *Kew Gardens,* then, shows this vital force battling against matter in vegetable, insect, and human life. Are the human beings moving toward spirit or matter? Toward what is the snail moving? Is the snail more purposeful than human beings? How does IRONY operate in the contrast?

3. Notice how the human beings are always described in terms of insects, animals, or flowers (p. 951/2, l. 5 ff.; p. 952/2, l. 26 ff.; p. 954/1, l. 48 ff.). This is an obvious contrast to the snail, whose assiduous journey is told in terms of human effort. What is the meaning of this contrast?

4. Since life is measured in terms of consciousness or awareness of the eternal moment in any given moment of chronological time, of what significance are action and "things" in the story? What is the significance of the final sentence?

Katherine Mansfield
(1888–1923)

KATHERINE MANSFIELD PUBLISHED HER FIRST STORY WHEN SHE WAS NINE—IN A SCHOOL paper in Wellington, New Zealand, where she was born Kathleen Mansfield Beauchamp in 1888. In 1903 she went to London to complete her education, returned reluctantly to New Zealand in 1906, and then went back to London in 1909 to begin the literary career which by that time she had definitely chosen. She had difficulty in getting anything into print until finally the editor of *The New Age* recognized her talent and published a series of her short stories in 1910–1911, stories written while she had been convalescing in Germany after a severe illness. They appeared in book form, *In a German Pension* (1911), the turning point of Katherine Mansfield's career.

In 1913 she married the English critic John Middleton Murry. During the next three years they put out two short-lived magazines, the second with the help of D. H. Lawrence. The last nine years of her life were spent fighting physical sickness and spiritual unrest. Her chronic illness, diagnosed as tuberculosis in 1914, was aggravated by the death of her brother in the war. She sojourned in the south of France, London, Switzerland, her condition becoming progressively worse. In France she wrote the beautiful story of her childhood published as *Prelude;* in England she contributed critical reviews to *The Athenaeum,* under Murry's editorship; in Switzerland she wrote her most famous stories, those published in 1922 as *The Garden Party and Other Stories.* She spent her last year near Paris under the tutelage of a Russian mystic, seeking a cure through intense spiritual discipline. But her condition was desperate, and early in 1923 she died of a violent hemorrhage at Fontainebleau.

In Katherine Mansfield's short stories there is a minimum of external incident but a great deal of psychological insight, of fine sensitiveness to the nuances of personality and character relationships. Plot yields to mood and atmosphere; events are less important than the subtle use of symbolism, the skilful combination of tenderness and irony; and there is a kind of feminine fragility in both style and content. But slight as the material often is, there is always the exquisite "purity" of which Murry speaks, a purity which bears witness to the passion for perfection that was one of Katherine Mansfield's dominant traits.

The Daughters of the Late Colonel

I

The week after was one of the busiest weeks of their lives. Even when they went to bed it was only their bodies that lay down and rested; their minds went on, thinking things out, talking things over, wondering, deciding, trying to remember where . . .

Constantia lay like a statue, her hands by her sides, her feet just overlapping each other, the sheet up to her chin. She stared at the ceiling.

"Do you think father would mind if we gave his top-hat to the porter?"

"The porter?" snapped Josephine. "Why ever the porter? What a very extraordinary idea!"

"Because," said Constantia slowly, "he must often have to go to funerals. And I noticed at—at the cemetery that he only had a bowler." She paused. "I thought then how very much he'd appreciate a top-hat. We ought to give him a present, too. He was always very nice to father."

"But," cried Josephine, flouncing on her pillow and staring across the dark at Constantia, "father's head!" And suddenly, for one awful moment, she nearly giggled. Not, of course, that she felt in the least like giggling. It must have been habit. Years ago, when they had stayed awake at night talking, their beds had simply heaved. And now the porter's head, disappearing, popped out, like a candle, under father's hat. . . . The giggle mounted, mounted; she clenched her hands; she fought it down; she frowned fiercely at the dark and said "Remember" terribly sternly.

"We can decide to-morrow," she sighed.

Constantia had noticed nothing; she sighed.

"Do you think we ought to have our dressing-gowns dyed as well?"

"Black?" almost shrieked Josephine.

"Well, what else?" said Constantia. "I was thinking—it doesn't seem quite sincere, in a way, to wear black out of doors and when we're fully dressed, and then when we're at home——"

"But nobody sees us," said Josephine. She gave the bedclothes such a twitch that both her feet became uncovered, and she had to creep up the pillows to get them well under again.

"Kate does," said Constantia. "And the postman very well might."

Josephine thought of her dark-red slippers, which matched her dressing-gown, and of Constantia's favorite indefinite green ones which went with hers. Black! Two black dressing-gowns and two pairs of black wooly slippers, creeping off to the bathroom like black cats.

"I don't think it's absolutely necessary," said she.

Silence. Then Constantia said, "We shall have to post the papers with the notice in them tomorrow to catch the Ceylon mail. . . . How many letters have we had up till now?"

"Twenty-three."

Josephine had replied to them all, and twenty-three times when she came to "We miss our dear father so much," she had broken down and had to use her handkerchief, and on some of them even to soak up a very light-blue tear with an edge of blotting-paper. Strange! She couldn't have put it on—but twenty-three times. Even now, though, when she said over to herself sadly, "We miss our dear father *so* much" she could have cried if she'd wanted to.

"Have you got enough stamps?" came from Constantia.

"Oh, how could I tell?" said Josephine crossly. "What's the good of asking me that now?"

"I was just wondering," said Constantia mildly.

Silence again. There came a little rustle, a scurry, a hop.

"A mouse," said Constantia.

"It can't be a mouse because there aren't any crumbs," said Josephine.

"But it doesn't know there aren't," said Constantia.

A spasm of pity squeezed her heart. Poor little thing! She wished she'd left a tiny piece of biscuit on the dressing-table. It was awful to think of it not finding anything. What would it do?

"I can't think of how they manage to live at all," she said slowly.

"Who?" demanded Josephine.

And Constantia said more loudly than she meant to, "Mice."

Josephine was furious. "Oh, what nonsense, Con!" she said. "What have mice got to do with it? You're asleep."

"I don't think I am," said Constantia. She shut her eyes to make sure. She was.

Josephine arched her spine, pulled up her knees, folded her arms so that her fists came under her ears, and pressed her cheek hard against the pillow.

2

Another thing that complicated matters was they had Nurse Andrews staying on with them that week. It was their own fault; they had asked her. It was Josephine's idea. On the morning—well, on the last morning, when the doctor had gone, Josephine had said to Constantia, "Don't you think it would be rather nice if we asked Nurse Andrews to stay on for a week as our guest?"

"Very nice," said Constantia.

"I thought," went on Josephine quickly, "I should just say this afternoon, after we've paid her, 'My sister and I would be very pleased, after all you've done for us, Nurse Andrews, if you would stay on for a week as our guest.' I'd have to put that in about being our guest in case—"

"Oh, but she could hardly expect to be paid!" cried Constantia.

"One never knows," said Josephine sagely.

Nurse Andrews had, of course, jumped at the idea. But it was a bother. It meant that they had to have regular sit-down meals at the proper times, whereas if they'd been alone they could have just asked Kate if she wouldn't have minded bringing them a tray wherever they were. And meal-times now that the strain was over were rather a trial.

Nurse Andrews was simply fearful about butter. Really they couldn't help feeling that about butter, at least, she took advantage of their kindness. And she had that maddening habit of asking for just an inch more bread to finish what she had on her plate, and then, at the last mouthful, absent-mindedly—of course it wasn't absent-mindedly—taking another helping. Josephine got very red when this happened, and she fastened her small, bead-like eyes on the tablecloth as if she saw a minute strange insect creeping through the web of it. But Constantia's long, pale face lengthened and set, and she gazed away—away—far over the desert, to where that line of camels unwound like a thread of wool. . . .

"When I was with Lady Tukes," said Nurse Andrews, "she had such a dainty little contrayvance for the buttah. It was a silvah Cupid balanced on the—on the bordah of a glass dish, holding a tayny fork. And when you wanted some buttah you simply pressed his foot and he bent down and speared you a piece. It was quite a gayme."

Josephine could hardly bear that. But "I think those things are very extravagant" was all she said.

"But whey?" asked Nurse Andrews, beaming through her eyeglasses. "No one, surely, would take more buttah than one wanted—would one?"

"Ring, Con," cried Josephine. She couldn't trust herself to reply.

And proud young Kate, the enchanted

princess, came in to see what the old tabbies wanted now. She snatched away their plates of mock something or other and slapped down a white, terrified blanc-mange.

"Jam, please, Kate," said Josephine kindly.

Kate knelt and burst open the sideboard, lifted the lid of the jam-pot, saw it was empty, put it on the table, and stalked off.

"I'm afraid," said Nurse Andrews a moment later, "there isn't any."

"Oh, what a bother!" said Josephine. She bit her lip. "What had we better do?"

Constantia looked dubious. "We can't disturb Kate again," she said softly.

Nurse Andrews waited, smiling at them both. Her eyes wandered, spying at everything behind her eye-glasses. Constantia in despair went back to her camels. Josephine frowned heavily—concentrated. If it hadn't been for this idiotic woman she and Con would, of course, have eaten their blanc-mange without. Suddenly the idea came.

"I know," she said. "Marmalade. There's some marmalade in the sideboard. Get it, Con."

"I hope," laughed Nurse Andrews, and her laugh was like a spoon tinkling against a medicine-glass—"I hope it's not very bittah marmalayde."

3

But, after all, it was not long now, and then she'd be gone for good. And there was no getting over the fact that she had been very kind to father. She had nursed him day and night at the end. Indeed, both Constantia and Josephine felt privately she had rather overdone the not leaving him at the very last. For when they had gone in to say good-bye Nurse Andrews had sat beside his bed the whole time, holding his wrist and pretending to look at her watch. It couldn't have been necessary. It was so tactless, too. Supposing father had wanted to say something—something private to them. Not that he had. Oh, far from it! He lay there, purple, a dark, angry purple in the face, and never even looked at them when they came in. Then, as they were standing there, wondering what to do, he had suddenly opened one eye. Oh,

what a difference it would have made, what a difference to their memory of him, how much easier to tell people about it, if he had only opened both! But no—one eye only. It glared at them a moment and then . . . went out.

4

It had made it very awkward for them when Mr. Farolles, of St. John's, called the same afternoon.

"The end was quite peaceful, I trust?" were the first words he said as he glided towards them through the dark drawing-room.

"Quite," said Josephine faintly. They both hung their heads. Both of them felt certain that eye wasn't at all a peaceful eye.

"Won't you sit down?" said Josephine.

"Thank you, Miss Pinner," said Mr. Farolles gratefully. He folded his coat-tails and began to lower himself into father's armchair, but just as he touched it he almost sprang up and slid into the next chair instead.

He coughed. Josephine clasped her hands; Constantia looked vague.

"I want you to feel, Miss Pinner," said Mr. Farolles, "and you, Miss Constantia, that I'm trying to be helpful. I want to be helpful to you both, if you will let me. These are the times," said Mr. Farolles, very simply and earnestly, "when God means us to be helpful to one another."

"Thank you very much, Mr. Farolles," said Josephine and Constantia.

"Not at all," said Mr. Farolles gently. He drew his kid gloves through his fingers and leaned a little forward. "And if either of you would like a little Communion, either or both of you, here *and* now, you have only to tell me. A little Communion is often very helpful—a great comfort," he added tenderly.

But the idea of a little Communion terrified them. What! In the drawing-room by themselves—with no—no altar or anything! The piano would be much too high, thought Constantia, and Mr. Farolles could not possibly lean over it with the chalice. And Kate would be sure to come bursting in and interrupt them, thought Josephine. And supposing the bell rang in the middle? It might be somebody important—about their mourning.

Would they get up reverently and go out, or would they have to wait . . . in torture?

"Perhaps you will send round a note by your good Kate if you would care for it later," said Mr. Farolles.

"Oh yes, thank you very much!" they both said.

Mr. Farolles got up and took his black straw hat from the round table.

"And about the funeral," he said softly. "I may arrange that—as your dear father's old friend and yours, Miss Pinner—and Miss Constantia?"

Josephine and Constantia got up too.

"I should like it to be quite simple," said Josephine firmly, "and not too expensive. At the same time, I should like——"

"A good one that will last," thought dreamy Constantia, as if Josephine were buying a nightgown. But of course Josephine didn't say that. "One suitable to our father's position." She was very nervous.

"I'll run round to our good friend Mr. Knight," said Mr. Farolles soothingly. "I will ask him to come and see you. I am sure you will find him very helpful indeed."

5

Well, at any rate, all that part of it was over, though neither of them could possibly believe that father was never coming back. Josephine had had a moment of absolute terror at the cemetery, while the coffin was lowered, to think that she and Constantia had done this thing without asking his permission. What would father say when he found out? For he was bound to find out sooner or later. He always did. "Buried. You two girls had me *buried!*" She heard his stick thumping. Oh, what would they say? What possible excuse could they make? It sounded such an appallingly heartless thing to do. Such a wicked advantage to take of a person because he happened to be helpless at the moment. The other people seemed to treat it all as a matter of course. They were strangers; they couldn't be expected to understand that father was the very last person for such a thing to happen to. No, the entire blame for it all would fall on her and Constantia. And the

expense, she thought, stepping into the tight-buttoned cab. When she had to show him the bills. What would he say then?

She heard him absolutely roaring, "And do you expect me to pay for this gimcrack excursion of yours?"

"Oh," groaned poor Josephine aloud, "we shouldn't have done it, Con!"

And Constantia, pale as a lemon in all that blackness, said in a frightened whisper, "Done what, Jug?"

"Let them bu-bury father like that," said Josephine, breaking down and crying into her new, queer-smelling mourning handkerchief.

"But what else could we have done?" asked Constantia wonderingly. "We couldn't have kept him, Jug—we couldn't have kept him unburied. At any rate, not in a flat that size."

Josephine blew her nose; the cab was dreadfully stuffy.

"I don't know," she said forlornly. "It is all so dreadful. I feel we ought to have tried to, just for a time at least. To make perfectly sure. One thing's certain"—and her tears sprang out again—"father will never forgive us for this—never!"

6

Father would never forgive them. That was what they felt more than ever when, two mornings later, they went into his room to go through his things. They had discussed it quite calmly. It was even down on Josephine's list of things to be done. *Go through father's things and settle about them.* But that was a very different matter from saying after breakfast:

"Well, are you ready, Con?"

"Yes, Jug—when you are."

"Then I think we'd better get it over."

It was dark in the hall. It had been a rule for years never to disturb father in the morning, whatever happened. And now they were going to open the door without knocking even. . . . Constantia's eyes were enormous at the idea; Josephine felt weak in the knees.

"You—you go first," she gasped, pushing Constantia.

But Constantia said, as she always had said on those occasions, "No, Jug, that's not fair. You're eldest."

Josephine was going to say—what at other times she wouldn't have owned to for the world—what she kept for her very last weapon, "But you're tallest," when they noticed that the kitchen door was open, and there stood Kate. . . .

"Very stiff," said Josephine, grasping the door-handle and doing her best to turn it. As if anything ever deceived Kate.

It couldn't be helped. That girl was . . . Then the door was shut behind them, but— but they weren't in father's room at all. They might have suddenly walked through the wall by mistake into a different flat altogether. Was the door just behind them? They were too frightened to look. Josephine knew that if it was it was holding itself tight shut; Constantia felt that, like the doors in dreams, it hadn't any handle at all. It was the coldness which made it so awful. Or the whiteness— which? Everything was covered. The blinds were down, a cloth hung over the mirror, a sheet hid the bed; a huge fan of white paper filled the fireplace. Constantia timidly put out her hand; she almost expected a snowflake to fall. Josephine felt a queer tingling in her nose, as if her nose was freezing. Then a cab klop-klopped over the cobbles below, and the quiet seemed to shake into little pieces.

"I had better pull up a blind," said Josephine bravely.

"Yes, it might be a good idea," whispered Constantia.

They only gave the blind a touch, but it flew up and the cord flew after, rolling round the blind-stick, and the little tassel tapped as if trying to get free. That was too much for Constantia.

"Don't you think—don't you think we might put it off for another day?" she whispered.

"Why?" snapped Josephine, feeling, as usual, much better now that she knew for certain Constantia was terrified. "It's got to be done. But I do wish you wouldn't whisper, Con."

"I didn't know I was whispering," whispered Constantia.

"And why do you keep on staring at the bed?" said Josephine, raising her voice almost defiantly.

"Oh, Jug, don't say so!" said poor Connie. "At any rate, not so loudly."

Josephine felt herself that she had gone too far. She took a wide swerve over to the chest of drawers, put out her hand, but quickly drew it back again.

"Connie!" she gasped, and she wheeled round and leaned with her back against the chest of drawers.

"Oh, Jug—what?"

Josephine could only glare. She had the most extraordinary feeling that she had just escaped something simply awful. But how could she explain to Constantia that father was in the chest of drawers? He was in the top drawer with his handkerchiefs and neckties, or in the next with his shirts and pajamas, or in the lowest of all with his suits. He was watching there, hidden away—just behind the door-handle—ready to spring.

She pulled a funny old-fashioned face at Constantia, just as she used to in the old days when she was going to cry.

"I can't open," she nearly wailed.

"No, don't, Jug," whispered Constantia earnestly. "It's much better not to. Don't let's open anything. At any rate, not for a long time."

"But—but it seems so weak," said Josephine, breaking down.

"But why not be weak for once, Jug?" argued Constantia, whispering quite fiercely. "If it is weak." And her pale stare flew from the locked writing-table—so safe—to the huge glittering wardrobe, and she began to breathe in a queer, panting way. "Why shouldn't we be weak for once in our lives, Jug? It's quite excusable. Let's be weak—be weak, Jug. It's much nicer to be weak than to be strong."

And then she did one of those amazingly bold things that she'd done about twice before in their lives; she marched over to the wardrobe, turned the key, and took it out of the lock. Took it out of the lock and held it up to Josephine, showing Josephine by her extraordinary smile that she knew what she'd done, she'd risked deliberately father being in there among his overcoats.

If the huge wardrobe had lurched forward, had crashed down on Constantia, Josephine wouldn't have been surprised. On the contrary, she would have thought it the only suitable thing to happen. But nothing happened. Only the room seemed quieter than ever, and bigger flakes of cold air fell on 10 Josephine's shoulders and knees. She began to shiver.

"Come, Jug," said Constantia, still with that awful callous smile, and Josephine followed just as she had that last time, when Con- 15 stantia had pushed Benny into the round pond.

7

But the strain told on them when they were 20 back in the dining-room. They sat down, very shaky, and looked at each other.

"I don't feel I can settle to anything," said Josephine, "until I've had something. Do you think we could ask Kate for two cups of hot 25 water?"

"I really don't see why we shouldn't," said Constantia carefully. She was quite normal again. "I won't ring. I'll go to the kitchen door and ask her." 30

"Yes, do," said Josephine, sinking down into a chair. "Tell her, just two cups, Con, nothing else—on a tray."

"She needn't even put the jug on, need she?" said Constantia, as though Kate might 35 very well complain if the jug had been there.

"Oh, no, certainly not! The jug's not at all necessary. She can pour direct out of the kettle," cried Josephine, feeling that would 40 be a labor-saving indeed.

Their cold lips quivered at the greenish brims. Josephine curved her small red hands round the cup; Constantia sat up and blew on the wavy stream, making it flutter from one 45 side to the other.

"Speaking of Benny," said Josephine.

And though Benny hadn't been mentioned Constantia immediately looked as though he had. 50

"He'll expect us to send him something of father's, of course. But it's so difficult to know what to send to Ceylon."

"You mean things get unstuck so on the voyage," murmured Constantia. 5

"No, lost," said Josephine sharply. "You know there's no post. Only runners."

Both paused to watch a black man in white linen drawers running through the pale fields for dear life, with a large brown- 10 paper parcel in his hands. Josephine's black man was tiny; he scurried along glistening like an ant. But there was something blind and tireless about Constantia's tall, thin fellow which made him, she decided, a very 15 unpleasant person indeed . . . On the veranda, dressed all in white and wearing a cork helmet, stood Benny. His right hand shook up and down, as father's did when he was impatient. And behind him, not in the 20 least interested, sat Hilda, the unknown sister-in-law. She swung in a cane rocker and flicked over the leaves of the *Tatler*.

"I think his watch would be the most suitable present," said Josephine. 25

Constantia looked up; she seemed surprised.

"Oh, would you trust a gold watch to a native?"

"But of course I'd disguise it," said Jose- 30 phine. "No one would know it was a watch." She liked the idea of having to make a parcel such a curious shape that no one could possibly guess what it was. She even thought for a moment of hiding the watch in a nar- 35 row cardboard corset-box that she'd kept by her for a long time, waiting for it to come in for something. It was such beautiful firm cardboard. But, no, it wouldn't be appropriate for this occasion. It had lettering on it: 40 *Medium Women's 28. Extra Firm Busks.* It would be almost too much of a surprise for Benny to open that and find father's watch inside.

"And of course it isn't as though it would 45 be going—ticking, I mean," said Constantia, who was still thinking of the native love of jewelry. "At least," she added, "it would be very strange if after all that time 50 it was."

8

Josephine made no reply. She had flown off on one of her tangents. She had suddenly thought of Cyril. Wasn't it more usual for the only grandson to have the watch? And then dear Cyril was so appreciative, and a gold watch meant so much to a young man. Benny, in all probability, had quite got out of the habit of watches; men so seldom wore waistcoats in those hot climates. Whereas Cyril in London wore them from year's end to year's end. And it would be so nice for her and Constantia, when he came to tea, to know it was there. "I see you've got on grand-father's watch, Cyril." It would be somehow so satisfactory.

Dear boy! What a blow his sweet, sympa-thetic little note had been! Of course they quite understood; but it was most unfortunate.

"It would have been such a point, having him," said Josephine.

"And he would have enjoyed it so," said Constantia, not thinking what she was saying.

However, as soon as he got back he was coming to tea with his aunties. Cyril to tea was one of their rare treats.

"Now, Cyril, you mustn't be frightened of our cakes. Your Auntie Con and I bought them at Buzzard's this morning. We know what a man's appetite is. So don't be ashamed of making a good tea."

Josephine cut recklessly into the rich dark cake that stood for her winter gloves or the soling and heeling of Constantia's only re-spectable shoes. But Cyril was most unman-like in appetite.

"I say, Aunt Josephine, I simply can't. I've only just had lunch, you know."

"Oh, Cyril, that can't be true! It's after four," cried Josephine. Constantia sat with her knife poised over the chocolate-roll.

"It is, all the same," said Cyril, "I had to meet a man at Victoria,[1] and he kept me hanging about till . . . there was only time to get lunch and to come on here. And he gave me—phew"—Cyril put his hand to his forehead—"a terrific blowout," he said.

[1] A London railway station.

It was disappointing—today of all days. But still he couldn't be expected to know.

"But you'll have a meringue, won't you, Cyril?" said Aunt Josephine. "These me-ringues were bought specially for you. Your dear father was so fond of them. We were sure you are, too."

"I *am*, Aunt Josephine," cried Cyril ar-dently. "Do you mind if I take half to begin with?"

"Not at all, dear boy; but we mustn't let you off with that."

"Is your dear father still so fond of me-ringues?" asked Auntie Con gently. She winced faintly as she broke through the shell of hers.

"Well, I don't quite know, Auntie Con," said Cyril breezily.

At that they both looked up.

"Don't know?" almost snapped Josephine. "Don't know a thing like that about your own father, Cyril?"

"Surely," said Auntie Con softly.

Cyril tried to laugh it off. "Oh, well," he said, "it's such a long time since—" He fal-tered. He stopped. Their faces were too much for him.

"Even *so*," said Josephine.

And Auntie Con looked.

Cyril put down his teacup. "Wait a bit," he cried. "Wait a bit, Aunt Josephine. What am I thinking of?"

He looked up. They were beginning to brighten. Cyril slapped his knee.

"Of course," he said, "it was meringues. How could I have forgotten? Yes, Aunt Josephine, you're perfectly right. Father's most frightfully keen on meringues."

They didn't only beam. Aunt Josephine went scarlet with pleasure; Auntie Con gave a deep, deep sigh.

"And now, Cyril, you must come and see father," said Josephine. "He knows you were coming today."

"Right," said Cyril, very firmly and heartily. He got up from his chair; suddenly he glanced at the clock.

"I say, Auntie Con, isn't your clock a bit slow? I've got to meet a man at—at Paddington just after five. I'm afraid I shan't be able to stay very long with grandfather."

"Oh, he won't expect you to stay *very* long!" said Aunt Josephine.

Constantia was still gazing at the clock. She couldn't make up her mind if it was fast or slow. It was one or the other, she felt almost certain of that. At any rate, it had been.

Cyril still lingered. "Aren't you coming along, Auntie Con?"

"Of course," said Josephine, "we shall all go. Come on, Con."

9

They knocked at the door, and Cyril followed his aunts into grandfather's hot, sweetish room.

"Come on," said Grandfather Pinner. "Don't hang about. What is it? What've you been up to?"

He was sitting in front of a roaring fire, clasping his stick. He had a thick rug over his knees. On his lap there lay a beautiful pale yellow silk handkerchief.

"It's Cyril, father," said Josephine shyly. And she took Cyril's hand and led him forward.

"Good afternoon, grandfather," said Cyril, trying to take his hand out of Aunt Josephine's. Grandfather Pinner shot his eyes at Cyril in the way he was famous for. Where was Auntie Con? She stood on the other side of Aunt Josephine; her long arms hung down in front of her; her hands were clasped. She never took her eyes off grandfather.

"Well," said Grandfather Pinner, beginning to thump, "what have you got to tell me?"

What had he, what had he got to tell him? Cyril felt himself smiling like a perfect imbecile. The room was stifling, too.

But Aunt Josephine came to his rescue. She cried brightly, "Cyril says his father is still very fond of meringues, father dear."

"Eh?" said Grandfather Pinner, curving his hand like a purple meringue-shell over one ear.

Josephine repeated, "Cyril says his father is still very fond of meringues."

"Can't hear," said old Colonel Pinner. And he waved Josephine away with his stick, then pointed to Cyril. "Tell me what she's trying to say," he said.

(My God!) "Must I?" said Cyril, blushing and staring at Aunt Josephine.

"Do, dear," she smiled. "It will please him so much."

"Come on, out with it!" cried Colonel Pinner testily, beginning to thump again.

And Cyril leaned forward and yelled, "Father's still very fond of meringues."

At that Grandfather Pinner jumped as though he had been shot.

"Don't shout!" he cried. "What's the matter with the boy? *Meringues!* What about 'em?"

"Oh, Aunt Josephine, must we go on?" groaned Cyril desperately.

"It's quite all right, dear boy," said Aunt Josephine, as though he and she were at the dentist's together. "He'll understand in a minute." And she whispered to Cyril, "He's getting a bit deaf, you know." Then she leaned forward and really bawled at Grandfather Pinner, "Cyril only wanted to tell you, father dear, that *his* father is still very fond of meringues."

Colonel Pinner heard that time, heard and brooded, looking Cyril up and down.

"What an esstrordinary thing!" said old Grandfather Pinner. "What an esstrordinary thing to come all this way here to tell me!"

And Cyril felt it *was*.

"Yes, I shall send Cyril the watch," said Josephine.

"That would be very nice," said Constantia. "I seem to remember last time he came there was some little trouble about the time."

10

They were interrupted by Kate bursting through the door in her usual fashion, as though she had discovered some secret panel in the wall.

"Fried or boiled?" asked the bold voice.

Fried or boiled? Josephine and Constantia were quite bewildered for the moment. They could hardly take it in.

"Fried or boiled what, Kate?" asked Josephine, trying to begin to concentrate.

Kate gave a loud sniff. "Fish."

"Well, why didn't you say so immediately?" Josephine reproached her gently. "How could you expect us to understand, Kate? There are a great many things in this world, you know, which are fried or boiled." And after such a display of courage she said quite brightly to Constantia, "Which do you prefer, Con?"

"I think it might be nice to have it fried," said Constantia. "On the other hand, of course boiled fish is very nice. I think I prefer both equally well . . . Unless you . . . In that case——"

"I shall fry it," said Kate, and she bounced back, leaving their door open and slamming the door of her kitchen.

Josephine gazed at Constantia; she raised her pale eyebrows until they rippled away into her pale hair. She got up. She said in a very lofty, imposing way, "Do you mind following me into the drawing-room, Constantia? I've something of great importance to discuss with you."

For it was always to the drawing-room they retired when they wanted to talk over Kate.

Josephine closed the door meaningly. "Sit down, Constantia," she said, still very grand. She might have been receiving Constantia for the first time. And Con looked round vaguely for a chair, as though she felt indeed quite a stranger.

"Now, the question is," said Josephine, bending forward, "whether we shall keep her or not."

"That is the question," agreed Constantia.

"And this time," said Josephine firmly, "we must come to a definite decision."

Constantia looked for a moment as though she might begin going over all the other times, but she pulled herself together and said, "Yes, Jug."

"You see, Con," explained Josephine, "everything is so changed now." Constantia looked up quickly. "I mean," went on Josephine, "we're not dependent on Kate as we were." And she blushed faintly. "There's not father to cook for."

"That is perfectly true," agreed Constantia. "Father certainly doesn't want any cooking now, whatever else—"

Josephine broke in sharply, "You're not sleepy, are you, Con?"

"Sleepy, Jug?" Constantia was wide-eyed.

"Well, concentrate more," said Josephine sharply, and she returned to the subject. "What it comes to is, if we did"—and this she barely breathed, glancing at the door—"give Kate notice"—she raised her voice again—"we could manage our own food."

"Why not?" cried Constantia. She couldn't help smiling. The idea was so exciting. She clasped her hands. "What should we live on, Jug?"

"Oh, eggs in various forms!" said Jug, lofty again. "And besides, there are all the cooked foods."

"But I've always heard," said Constantia, "they are considered so very expensive."

"Not if one buys them in moderation," said Josephine. But she tore herself away from the fascinating bypath and dragged Constantia after her.

"What we've got to decide now, however, is whether we really do trust Kate or not."

Constantia leaned back. Her flat little laugh flew from her lips.

"Isn't it curious, Jug," said she, "that just on this one subject I've never been able to quite make up my mind."

II

She never had. The whole difficulty was to prove anything. How did one prove things, how could one? Suppose Kate had stood in front of her and deliberately made a face. Mightn't she very well have been in pain? Wasn't it impossible, at any rate, to ask Kate if she was making a face at her? If Kate answered "No"—and of course she would say "No"—what a position! How undignified. Then again Constantia suspected, she was almost certain that Kate went to her chest of drawers when she and Josephine were out, not to take things but to spy. Many times she had come back to find her amethyst cross in the most unlikely places, under her lace ties or on top of her evening Bertha. More than once she had laid a trap for Kate. She had arranged things in a special order and then called Josephine to witness.

"You see, Jug?"

"Quite, Con."

"Now we shall be able to tell."

But, oh, dear, when she did go to look, she was as far off from a proof as ever! If anything was displaced, it might so very well have happened as she closed the drawer; a jolt might have done it so easily.

"You come, Jug, and decide. I really can't. It's too difficult."

But after a long pause and a long glare Josephine would sigh, "Now you've put the doubt into my mind, Con, I'm sure I can't tell myself."

"Well, we can't postpone it again," said Josephine. "If we postpone it this time—"

12

But at that moment in the street below a barrel-organ struck up. Josephine and Constantia sprang to their feet together.

"Run, Con," said Josephine. "Run quickly. There's sixpence on the——"

Then they remembered. It didn't matter. They would never have to stop the organ-grinder again. Never again would she and Constantia be told to make that monkey take his noise somewhere else. Never would sound that loud, strange bellow when father thought they were not hurrying enough. The organ-grinder might play there all day and the stick would not thump.

> *It never will thump again,*
> *It never will thump again,*

played the barrel-organ.

What was Constantia thinking? She had such a strange smile; she looked different. She couldn't be going to cry.

"Jug, Jug," said Constantia softly, pressing her hands together. "Do you know what day it is? It's Saturday. It's a week to-day, a whole week."

> *A week since father died,*
> *A week since father died,*

cried the barrel-organ. And Josephine, too, forgot to be practical and sensible; she smiled faintly, strangely. On the Indian carpet there fell a square of sunlight, pale red; it came and went and came—and stayed, deepened—until it shone almost golden.

"The sun's out," said Josephine, as though it really mattered.

A perfect fountain of bubbling notes shook from the barrel-organ, round, bright notes, carelessly scattered.

Constantia lifted her big, cold hands as if to catch them, and then her hands fell again. She walked over to the mantelpiece to her favorite Buddha. And the stone and gilt image, whose smile always gave her such a queer feeling, almost a pain and yet a pleasant pain, seemed to-day to be more than smiling. He knew something; he had a secret. "I know something that you don't know," said her Buddha. Oh, what was it, what could it be? And yet she had always felt there was . . . something.

The sunlight pressed through the windows, thieved its way in, flashed its light over the furniture and the photographs. Josephine watched it. When it came to mother's photograph, the enlargement over the piano, it lingered as though puzzled to find so little remained of mother, except the earrings shaped like tiny pagodas and a black feather boa. Why did the photographs of dead people always fade so? wondered Josephine. As soon as a person was dead their photograph died too. But, of course, this one of mother was very old. It was thirty-five years old. Josephine remembered standing on a chair and pointing out that feather boa to Constantia and telling her that it was a snake that had killed their mother in Ceylon. . . . Would everything have been different if mother hadn't died? She didn't see why. Aunt Florence had lived with them until they had left school, and they had moved three times and had their yearly holiday and . . . and there'd been changes of servants, of course.

Some little sparrows, young sparrows they sounded, chirped on the window-ledge. *Yeep—eyeep—yeep.* But Josephine felt they were not sparrows, not on the window-ledge. It was inside her, that queer little crying noise. *Yeep—eyeep—yeep.* Ah, what was it crying, so weak and forlorn?

If mother had lived, might they have married? But there had been nobody for them to marry. There had been father's Anglo-Indian friends before he quarreled with them. But after that she and Constantia never met a single man except clergymen. How did one meet men? Or even if they'd met them, how could they have got to know men well enough to be more than strangers? One read of people having adventures, being followed, and so on. But nobody had ever followed Constantia and her. Oh yes, there had been one year at Eastbourne a mysterious man at their boarding-house who had put a note on the jug of hot water outside their bedroom door! But by the time Connie had found it the steam had made the writing too faint to read; they couldn't even make out to which of them it was addressed. And he had left next day. And that was all. The rest had been looking after father, and at the same time keeping out of father's way. But now? But now? The thieving sun touched Josephine gently. She lifted her face. She was drawn over to the window by gentle beams. . . .

Until the barrel-organ stopped playing Constantia stayed before the Buddha, wondering, but not as usual, not vaguely. This time her wonder was like longing. She remembered the times she had come in here, crept out of bed in her nightgown when the moon was full, and lain on the floor with her arms outstretched, as though she was crucified. Why? The big, pale moon had made her do it. The horrible dancing figures on the carved screen had leered at her and she hadn't minded. She remembered too how, whenever they were at the seaside, she had gone off by herself and got as close to the sea as she could, and sung something, something she had made up, while she gazed all over that restless water. There had been this other life, running out, bringing things home in bags, getting things on approval, discussing them with Jug, taking then back to get more things on approval, and arranging father's trays and trying not to annoy father. But it all seemed to have happened in a kind of tunnel. It wasn't real. It was only when she came out of the tunnel into the moonlight or by the sea or into a thunderstorm that she really felt herself. What did it mean? What did it all lead to? Now? Now?

She turned away from the Buddha with one of her vague gestures. She went over to where Josephine was standing. She wanted to say something to Josephine, something frightfully important, about—about the future and what . . .

"Don't you think perhaps—" she began.

But Josephine interrupted her. "I was wondering if now—" she murmured. They stopped; they waited for each other.

"Go on, Con," said Josephine.

"No, no, Jug; after you," said Constantia.

"No, say what you were going to say. You began," said Josephine.

"I . . . I'd rather hear what you were going to say first," said Constantia.

"Don't be absurd, Con."

"Really, Jug."

"Connie!"

"Oh, *Jug!*"

A pause. Then Constantia said faintly, "I can't say what I was going to say, Jug, because I've forgotten what it was . . . that I was going to say."

Josephine was silent for a moment. She stared at a big cloud where the sun had been. Then she replied shortly, "I've forgotten too."

(1922)

STUDY AIDS: 1. This is a typical Katherine Mansfield story: not much seems to happen; there is apparently no climax; the conflict is vague. The entire "action" is taken up with the trivial thoughts and doings of two sisters after the death of their father.

Obviously the attention of the story is upon the characters of the two sisters. What are their personalities like? What incidents point up their childlike helplessness and vagueness? Why do they have so much trouble making decisions? Are they differentiated at all?

2. Other characters play a part in the story. Characterize Nurse Andrews (how does she contrast with the two sisters?), Mr. Farolles, their brother Benny, their nephew Cyril. How do the sections involving these characters throw

further light on the personalities and background of Josephine and Constantia?

Especially important is the presence of the dead Colonel. How is his dominating influence established? What kind of man was he? In what way is he responsible for the personalities and present difficulties of his daughters?

3. Throughout the story Katherine Mansfield uses symbolic and suggestive detail. The two girls, for instance, have little sense of time. How is this brought out (note, e.g., the many references to clocks and watches, and the apparently aimless time-shifts in the story)? They move in a timeless, unreal world. The final episode is especially rich in symbolism. Note, for instance, the "tunnel"-image on p. 996/1, l. 50 ff. What qualities does a tunnel suggest? How is this image prepared for by the preceding episodes (find touches that bring out darkness, confine-

ment, narrowness, loneliness, isolation, and fear)? In the final section, the "thieving" sunlight steals through the room, begins to light things up, then falls on a faded photograph, and finally vanishes behind a cloud. What is symbolized here? Is the ending one of hope or futile despair?

4. What, then, is the basic conflict of the story? Is it one between the two girls and the dead Colonel, or between the unreal world of the sisters and the world of harsh reality? Or is it a conflict within the girls' own minds?

5. Are the two sisters primarily pathetic or comic? Much of the story is close to farce (illustrate this), but is farcical humor the dominant element? How is the blend of pathos and comedy achieved throughout the story? Does one of these elements finally triumph, or is the delicate balance maintained to the very end?

David Herbert Lawrence
(1885–1930)

PROBABLY THE MOST IMPORTANT INFLUENCES ON THE LIFE OF D. H. LAWRENCE WERE his parents. His father, a coal-miner, was an uneducated, easy-going, impulsive man of great vitality; in contrast, his mother was an intelligent, aggressive schoolteacher who dominated her son to such an extent that he was never to find complete happiness with another woman. As Lawrence came to recognize this maternal tie, he rejected the rational way of life, which he felt his mother represented, and preached of the happy life afforded by his father's intuitive, irrational approach.

Lawrence quit high school at the age of sixteen and began to teach school. During his career as a teacher he wrote poetry, and in 1909 some of his early poems saw print, largely through the efforts of a young woman with whom he had fallen in love. She later was to appear as Miriam in *Sons and Lovers* (1913), a novel which traces Lawrence's inner conflicts as a young man. When his first novel, *The White Peacock*, was published in 1911, he resigned his teaching appointment to live by his writing. The next year he eloped with Frieda von Richthofen, whom he could not marry until she received a divorce.

Trouble plagued Lawrence. Because his wife was German and he himself was not in sympathy with World War I, he was suspected of disloyalty to England; his elopement had created a scandal; and he was stricken with tuberculosis. With Frieda he began an odyssey around the world, hoping to find health and ease of mind, but his wanderings over the face of the earth led only to his untimely death in France in 1930.

Lawrence was a prolific writer in several genres: the novel, poetry, the short story, the essay, and the drama. Although his poetry is frequently anthologized, his novels and short stories are better known. Among his novels are *The Rainbow* (1915), *Women in Love* (1920), *The Plumed Serpent* (1926), and his last novel, *Lady Chatterley's Lover* (1928), which until recently was banned in the United States. A few of his short story collections are *The Prussian Officer* (1914), *The Captain's Doll* (1923), and *The Lovely Lady* (1933). The experience of life which Lawrence presents is much the same, whether the medium is prose or poetry. Man can live only through the senses, the true sources of imagination and emotion; reason, science, education, and wealth have nothing to contribute to man's spirit, to his real vitality. This vitality lies in the subconscious and even unconscious mind of mind and makes him one with the beginnings of nature, with the dark gods of the blood, before civilization corrupted him. Lawrence, in *Apocalypse,* defines this awareness as the "cosmic sense":

What we want is to destroy our false, inorganic connections, especially those related to money, and reëstablish the living organic connections with the cosmos, the sun and earth, with mankind and nation and family. Start with the sun, and the rest will slowly happen.

The Rocking-Horse Winner

Hobbyhorses have an ancient history. They are common in folklore, and there is evidence among primitive peoples of rituals in which the riders rocked themselves into a trance in order to attain the power of prophecy.

There was a woman who was beautiful, who started with all the advantages, yet she had no luck. She married for love, and the love turned to dust. She had bonny children, yet she felt they had been thrust upon her, and she could not love them. They looked at her coldly, as if they were finding fault with her. And hurriedly she felt she must cover up some fault in herself. Yet what it was that she must cover up she never knew. Nevertheless, when her children were present, she always felt the center of her heart go hard. This troubled her, and in her manner she was all the more gentle and anxious for her children, as if she loved them very much. Only she herself knew that at the center of her heart was a hard little place that could not feel love, no, not for anybody. Everybody else said of her: "She is such a good mother. She adores her children." Only she herself, and her children themselves, knew it was not so. They read it in each other's eyes.

There were a boy and two little girls. They lived in a pleasant house, with a garden, and they had discreet servants, and felt themselves superior to anyone in the neighborhood.

Although they lived in style, they felt always an anxiety in the house. There was never enough money. The mother had a small income, and the father had a small income, but not nearly enough for the social position which they had to keep up. The father went in to town to some office. But though he had good prospects, these prospects never materialized. There was always the grinding sense of the shortage of money, though the style was always kept up.

At last the mother said: "I will see if I can't make something." But she did not know where to begin. She racked her brains, and tried this thing and the other, but could not find anything successful. The failure made deep lines come into her face. Her children were growing up, they would have to go to school. There must be more money, there must be more money. The father, who was always very handsome and expensive in his tastes, seemed as if he never *would* be able to do anything worth doing. And the mother, who had a great belief in herself, did not succeed any better, and her tastes were just as expensive.

And so the house came to be haunted by the unspoken phrase: *There must be more money! There must be more money!* The children could hear it all the time, though nobody said it aloud. They heard it at Christmas, when the expensive and splendid toys filled the nursery. Behind the shining modern rocking-horse, behind the smart doll's-house, a voice would start whispering: "There *must* be more money! There *must* be more money!" And the children would stop playing to listen for a moment. They would look into each other's eyes, to see if they had all heard. And each one saw in the eyes of the other two that they too had heard. "There *must* be more money! There *must* be more money!"

It came whispering from the springs of the still-swaying rocking-horse, and even the horse, bending his wooden, champing head, heard it. The big doll, sitting so pink and smirking in her new pram, could hear it quite plainly, and seemed to be smirking all the more self-consciously because of it. The foolish puppy, too, that took the place of the teddy-bear, he was looking so extraordinarily foolish for no other reason but that he heard the secret whisper all over the house: "There *must* be more money!"

Yet nobody ever said it aloud. The whisper was everywhere, and therefore no one spoke it. Just as no one ever says: "We are breathing!" in spite of the fact that breath is coming and going all the time.

"Mother," said the boy Paul one day, "why don't we keep a car of our own? Why do we always use uncle's, or else a taxi?"

"Because we're the poor members of the family," said the mother.

"But why *are* we, mother?"

"Well—I suppose," she said slowly and bitterly, "it's because your father has no luck."

The boy was silent for some time.

"Is luck money, mother?" he asked, rather timidly.

"No, Paul. Not quite. It's what causes you to have money."

"Oh!" said Paul vaguely. "I thought when Uncle Oscar said *filthy lucker,* it meant money."

"*Filthy lucre* does mean money," said the mother. "But it's lucre, not luck."

"Oh!" said the boy. "Then what *is* luck, mother?"

"It's what causes you to have money. If you're lucky you have money. That's why it's better to be born lucky than rich. If you're rich, you may lose your money. But if you're lucky, you will always get more money."

"Oh! Will you? And is father not lucky?"

"Very unlucky, I should say," she said bitterly.

The boy watched her with unsure eyes.

"Why?" he asked.

"I don't know. Nobody ever knows why one person is lucky and another unlucky."

"Don't they? Nobody at all? Does *nobody* know?"

"Perhaps God. But He never tells."

"He ought to, then. And aren't you lucky either, Mother?"

"I can't be, if I married an unlucky husband."

"But by yourself, aren't you?"

"I used to think I was, before I married. Now I think I am very unlucky indeed."

"Why?"

"Well—never mind! Perhaps I'm not really," she said.

The child looked at her, to see if she meant it. But he saw, by the lines of her mouth, that she was only trying to hide something from him.

"Well, anyhow," he said stoutly, "I'm a lucky person."

"Why?" said his mother, with a sudden laugh.

He stared at her. He didn't even know why he had said it.

"God told me," he asserted, brazening it out.

"I hope He did, dear!" she said, again with a laugh, but rather bitter.

"He did, mother!"

"Excellent!" said the mother, using one of her husband's exclamations.

The boy saw she did not believe him; or, rather, that she paid no attention to his assertion. This angered him somewhat, and made him want to compel her attention.

He went off by himself, vaguely, in a childish way, seeking for the clue to "luck." Absorbed, taking no heed of other people, he went about with a sort of stealth, seeking inwardly for luck. He wanted luck, he wanted it, he wanted it. When the two girls were playing dolls in the nursery, he would sit on his big rocking-horse, charging madly into space, with a frenzy that made the little girls peer at him uneasily. Wildly the horse careered, the waving dark hair of the boy tossed, his eyes had a strange glare in them. The little girls dared not speak to him.

When he had ridden to the end of his mad little journey, he climbed down and stood in front of his rocking-horse, staring fixedly into its lowered face. Its red mouth was slightly open, its big eye was wide and glassy-bright.

"Now!" he would silently command the snorting steed. "Now, take me to where there is luck! Now take me!"

And he would slash the horse on the neck with the little whip he had asked Uncle Oscar for. He *knew* the horse could take him to where there was luck, if only he forced it. So he would mount again, and start on his furious ride, hoping at last to get there. He knew he could get there.

"You'll break your horse, Paul!" said the nurse.

"He's always riding like that! I wish he'd leave off!" said his elder sister Joan.

But he only glared down on them in silence. Nurse gave him up. She could make nothing of him. Anyhow he was growing beyond her.

One day his mother and his Uncle Oscar came in when he was on one of his furious rides. He did not speak to them.

"Hallo, you young jockey! Riding a winner?" said his uncle.

"Aren't you growing too big for a rocking-horse? You're not a very little boy any longer, you know," said his mother.

But Paul only gave a blue glare from his big, rather close-set eyes. He would speak to nobody when he was in full tilt. His mother watched him with an anxious expression on her face.

At last he suddenly stopped forcing his horse into the mechanical gallop, and slid down.

"Well, I got there!" he announced fiercely, his blue eyes still flaring, and his sturdy long legs straddling apart.

"Where did you get to?" asked his mother.

"Where I wanted to go," he flared back at her.

"That's right, son!" said Uncle Oscar. "Don't you stop till you get there. What's the horse's name?"

"He doesn't have a name," said the boy.

"Gets on without all right?" asked the uncle.

"Well, he has different names. He was called Sansovino last week."

"Sansovino, eh? Won the Ascot. How did you know his name?"

"He always talks about horse-races with Bassett," said Joan.

The uncle was delighted to find that his small nephew was posted with all the racing news. Bassett, the young gardener, who had been wounded in the left foot in the war and had got his present job through Oscar Cresswell, whose batman he had been, was a perfect blade of the "turf." He lived in the racing events, and the small boy lived with him.

Oscar Cresswell got it all from Bassett.

"Master Paul comes and asks me, so I can't do more than tell him, sir," said Bassett, his face terribly serious, as if he were speaking of religious matters.

"And does he ever put anything on a horse he fancies?"

"Well—I don't want to give him away—he's a young sport, a fine sport, sir. Would you mind asking him himself? He sort of takes a pleasure in it, and perhaps he'd feel I was giving him away, sir, if you don't mind."

Bassett was serious as a church.

The uncle went back to his nephew, and took him off for a ride in the car.

"Say, Paul, old man, do you ever put anything on a horse?" the uncle asked.

The boy watched the handsome man closely.

"Why, do you think I oughtn't to?" he parried.

"Not a bit of it! I thought perhaps you might give me a tip for the Lincoln."

The car sped on into the country, going down to Uncle Oscar's place in Hampshire.

"Honor bright?" said the nephew.

"Honor bright, son!" said the uncle.

"Well, then, Daffodil."

"Daffodil! I doubt it, sonny. What about Mirza?"

"I only know the winner," said the boy. "That's Daffodil."

"Daffodil, eh?"

There was a pause. Daffodil was an obscure horse comparatively.

"Uncle!"

"Yes, son?"

"You won't let it go any further, will you? I promised Bassett."

"Bassett be damned, old man! What's he got to do with it?"

"We're partners. We've been partners from the first. Uncle, he lent me my first five shillings, which I lost. I promised him, honor bright, it was only between me and him; only you gave me that ten-shilling note I started winning with, so I thought you were lucky. You won't let it go any further, will you?"

The boy gazed at his uncle from those big, hot, blue eyes, set rather close together. The uncle stirred and laughed uneasily.

"Right you are, son! I'll keep your tip private. Daffodil, eh? How much are you putting on him?"

"All except twenty pounds," said the boy. "I keep that in reserve."

The uncle thought it a good joke.

"You keep twenty pounds in reserve, do you, you young romancer? What are you betting, then?"

"I'm betting three hundred," said the boy gravely. "But it's between you and me, Uncle Oscar! Honor bright?"

The uncle burst into a roar of laughter.

"It's between you and me all right, you young Nat Gould," he said, laughing. "But where's your three hundred?"

"Bassett keeps it for me. We're partners."

"You are, are you! And what is Bassett putting on Daffodil?"

"He won't go quite as high as I do, I expect. Perhaps he'll go a hundred and fifty."

"What, pennies?" laughed the uncle.

"Pounds," said the child, with a surprised look at his uncle. "Bassett keeps a bigger reserve than I do."

Between wonder and amusement Uncle Oscar was silent. He pursued the matter no further, but he determined to take his nephew with him to the Lincoln races.

"Now, son," he said, "I'm putting twenty on Mirza, and I'll put five for you on any horse you fancy. What's your pick?"

"Daffodil, uncle."

"No, not the fiver on Daffodil!"

"I should if it was my own fiver," said the child.

"Good! Good! Right you are! A fiver for me and a fiver for you on Daffodil."

The child had never been to a race-meeting before, and his eyes were blue fire. He pursed his mouth tight, and watched. A Frenchman just in front had put his money on Lancelot. Wild with excitement, he flayed his arms up and down, yelling *Lancelot! Lancelot!* in his French accent.

Daffodil came in first, Lancelot second, Mirza third. The child, flushed and with eyes blazing, was curiously serene. His uncle brought him four five-pound notes, four to one.

"What am I to do with these?" he cried, waving them before the boy's eyes.

"I suppose we'll talk to Bassett," said the boy. "I expect I have fifteen hundred now; and twenty in reserve; and this twenty."

His uncle studied him for some moments.

"Look here, son!" he said. "You're not serious about Bassett and that fifteen hundred, are you?"

"Yes, I am. But it's between you and me, uncle. Honor bright!"

"Honor bright all right, son! But I must talk to Bassett."

"If you'd like to be a partner, uncle, with Bassett and me, we could all be partners. Only, you'd have to promise, honor bright, uncle, not to let it go beyond us three. Bassett and I are lucky, and you must be lucky, because it was your ten shillings I started winning with. . . ."

Uncle Oscar took both Bassett and Paul into Richmond Park for an afternoon, and there they talked.

"It's like this, you see, sir," Bassett said. "Master Paul would get me talking about racing events, spinning yarns, you know, sir. And he was always keen on knowing if I'd made or if I'd lost. It's about a year since, now, that I put five shilling on Blush of Dawn for him—and we lost. Then the luck turned, with that ten shillings he had from you, that we put on Singhalese. And since that time, it's been pretty steady, all things considering. What do you say, Master Paul?"

"We're all right when we're sure," said Paul. "It's when we're not quite sure that we go down."

"Oh, but we're careful then," said Bassett.

"But when are you *sure?*" smiled Uncle Oscar.

"It's Master Paul, sir," said Bassett, in a secret, religious voice. "It's as if he had it from heaven. Like Daffodil, now, for the Lincoln. That was as sure as eggs."

"Did you put anything on Daffodil?" asked Oscar Cresswell.

"Yes, sir. I made my bit."

"And my nephew?"

Bassett was obstinately silent, looking at Paul.

"I made twelve hundred, didn't I, Bassett? I told uncle I was putting three hundred on Daffodil."

"That's right," said Bassett, nodding.

"But where's the money?" asked the uncle.

"I keep it safe locked up, sir. Master Paul he can have it any minute he likes to ask for it."

"What, fifteen hundred pounds?"

"And twenty! And *forty,* that is, with the twenty he made on the course."

"It's amazing!" said the uncle.

"If Master Paul offers you to be partners, sir, I would, if I were you; if you'll excuse me," said Bassett.

Oscar Cresswell thought about it.

"I'll see the money," he said.

They drove home again, and sure enough, Bassett came round to the garden-house with fifteen hundred pounds in notes. The twenty pounds reserve was left with Joe Glee, in the Turf Commission deposit.

"You see, it's all right, uncle, when I'm *sure!* Then we go strong, for all we're worth. Don't we, Bassett?"

"We do that, Master Paul."

"And when are you sure?" said the uncle, laughing.

"Oh, well, sometimes I'm *absolutely* sure, like about Daffodil," said the boy; "and sometimes I have an idea; and sometimes I haven't even an idea, have I, Bassett? Then we're careful, because we mostly go down."

"You do, do you! And when you're sure, like about Daffodil, what makes you sure, sonny?"

"Oh, well, I don't know," said the boy uneasily. "I'm sure, you know, uncle; that's all."

"It's as if he had it from heaven, sir," Bassett reiterated.

"I should say so!" said the uncle.

But he became a partner. And when the Leger was coming on, Paul was "sure" about Lively Spark, which was a quite inconsiderable horse. The boy insisted on putting a thousand on the horse, Bassett went for five hundred, and Oscar Cresswell two hundred. Lively Spark came in first, and the betting had been ten to one against him. Paul had made ten thousand.

"You see," he said, "I was absolutely sure of him."

Even Oscar Cresswell had cleared two thousand.

"Look here, son," he said, "this sort of thing makes me nervous."

"It needn't, uncle! Perhaps I shan't be sure again for a long time."

"But what are you going to do with your money?" asked the uncle.

"Of course," said the boy, "I started it for

mother. She said she had no luck, because father is unlucky, so I thought if *I* was lucky, it might stop whispering."

"What might stop whispering?"

"Our house. I *hate* our house for whispering."

"What does it whisper?"

"Why—why"—the boy fidgeted—"why, I don't know. But it's always short of money, you know, uncle."

"I know it, son, I know it."

"You know people send mother writs, don't you, uncle?"

"I'm afraid I do," said the uncle.

"And then the house whispers, like people laughing at you behind your back. It's awful, that is! I thought if I was lucky . . ."

"You might stop it," added the uncle.

The boy watched him with big blue eyes, that had an uncanny cold fire in them, and he said never a word.

"Well, then!" said the uncle. "What are we doing?"

"I shouldn't like mother to know I was lucky," said the boy.

"Why not, son?"

"She'd stop me."

"I don't think she would."

"Oh!"—and the boy writhed in an odd way —"I *don't* want her to know, uncle."

"All right, son! We'll manage it without her knowing."

They managed it very easily. Paul, at the other's suggestion, handed over five thousand pounds to his uncle, who deposited it with the family lawyer, who was then to inform Paul's mother that a relative had put five thousand pounds into his hands, which sum was to be paid out a thousand pounds at a time, on the mother's birthday, for the next five years.

"So she'll have a birthday present of a thousand pounds for five successive years," said Uncle Oscar. "I hope it won't make it all the harder for her later."

Paul's mother had her birthday in November. The house had been "whispering" worse than ever lately, and, even in spite of his luck, Paul could not bear up against it. He was very anxious to see the effect of the birthday letter, telling his mother about the thousand pounds.

When there were no visitors, Paul now took his meals with his parents, as he was beyond the nursery control. His mother went into town nearly every day. She had discovered that she had an odd knack of sketching furs and dress materials, so she worked secretly in the studio of a friend who was the chief "artist" for the leading drapers. She drew the figures of ladies in furs and ladies in silk and sequins for the newspaper advertisements. This young woman artist earned several thousand pounds a year, but Paul's mother only made several hundreds, and she was again dissatisfied. She so wanted to be first in something, and she did not succeed, even in making sketches for drapery advertisements.

She was down to breakfast on the morning of her birthday. Paul watched her face as she read her letters. He knew the lawyer's letter. As his mother read it, her face hardened and became more expressionless. Then a cold, determined look came on her mouth. She hid the letter under the pile of others, and said not a word about it.

"Didn't you have anything nice in the post for your birthday, mother?" said Paul.

"Quite moderately nice," she said, her voice cold and absent.

She went away to town without saying more.

But in the afternoon Uncle Oscar appeared. He said Paul's mother had had a long interview with the lawyer, asking if the whole five thousand could not be advanced at once, as she was in debt.

"What do you think, uncle?" said the boy.

"I leave it to you, son."

"Oh, let her have it, then! We can get some more with the other," said the boy.

"A bird in the hand is worth two in the bush, laddie!" said Uncle Oscar.

"But I'm sure to *know* for the Grand National; or the Lincolnshire; or else the Derby. I'm sure to know for *one* of them," said Paul.

So Uncle Oscar signed the agreement, and Paul's mother touched the whole five thousand. Then something very curious happened.

The voices in the house suddenly went mad, like a chorus of frogs on a spring evening. There were certain new furnishings, and Paul had a tutor. He was *really* going to Eton, his father's school, in the following autumn. There were flowers in the winter, and a blossoming of the luxury Paul's mother had been used to. And yet the voices in the house, behind the sprays of mimosa and almond blossom, and from under the piles of iridescent cushions, simply trilled and screamed in a sort of ecstasy: "There *must* be more money! Oh-h-h; there *must* be more money. Oh, now, now-w! Now-w-w—there *must* be more money!—more than ever! More than ever!"

It frightened Paul terribly. He studied away at his Latin and Greek with his tutors. But his intense hours were spent with Bassett. The Grand National had gone by: he had not "known," and had lost a hundred pounds. Summer was at hand. He was in agony for the Lincoln. But even for the Lincoln he didn't "know," and he lost fifty pounds. He became wild-eyed and strange, as if something were going to explode in him.

"Let it alone, son! Don't you bother about it!" urged Uncle Oscar. But it was as if the boy couldn't really hear what his uncle was saying.

"I've got to know for the Derby! I've got to know for the Derby!" the child reiterated, his big blue eyes blazing with a sort of madness.

His mother noticed how overwrought he was.

"You'd better go to the seaside. Wouldn't you like to go now to the seaside, instead of waiting? I think you'd better," she said, looking down at him anxiously, her heart curiously heavy because of him.

But the child lifted his uncanny blue eyes. "I couldn't possibly go before the Derby, mother!" he said. "I couldn't possibly!"

"Why not?" she said, her voice becoming heavy when she was opposed. "Why not? You can still go from the seaside to see the Derby with your Uncle Oscar, if that's what you wish. No need for you to wait here. Besides, I think you care too much about these races. It's a bad sign. My family has been a gambling family, and you won't know till you grow up how much damage it has done. But it has done damage. I shall have to send Bassett away, and ask Uncle Oscar not to talk racing to you, unless you promise to be reasonable about it; go away to the seaside and forget it. You're all nerves!"

"I'll do what you like, mother, so long as you don't send me away till after the Derby," the boy said.

"Send you away from where? Just from this house?"

"Yes," he said, gazing at her.

"Why, you curious child, what makes you care about this house so much, suddenly? I never knew you loved it."

He gazed at her without speaking. He had a secret within a secret, something he had not divulged, even to Bassett or to his Uncle Oscar.

But his mother, after standing undecided and a little bit sullen for some moments, said:

"Very well, then! Don't go to the seaside till after the Derby, if you don't wish it. But promise me you won't let your nerves go to pieces. Promise you won't think so much about horse-racing and *events,* as you call them!"

"Oh, no," said the boy casually. "I won't think much about them, mother. You needn't worry. I wouldn't worry, mother, if I were you."

"If you were me and I were you," said his mother, "I wonder what we *should* do!"

"But you know you needn't worry, mother, don't you?" the boy repeated.

"I should be awfully glad to know it," she said wearily.

"Oh, well, you *can,* you know. I mean, you *ought* to know you needn't worry," he insisted.

"Ought I? Then I'll see about it," she said.

Paul's secret of secrets was his wooden horse, that which had no name. Since he was emancipated from a nurse and a nursery-governess, he had had his rocking-horse removed to his own bedroom at the top of the house.

"Surely, you're too big for a rocking-horse!" his mother had remonstrated.

"Well, you see, mother, till I can have a *real* horse, I like to have *some* sort of animal about," had been his quaint answer.

"Do you feel he keeps you company?" she laughed.

"Oh, yes! He's very good, he always keeps me company, when I'm there," said Paul.

So the horse, rather shabby, stood in an arrested prance in the boy's bedroom.

The Derby was drawing near, and the boy grew more and more tense. He hardly heard what was spoken to him, he was very frail, and his eyes were really uncanny. His mother had sudden strange seizures of uneasiness about him. Sometimes, for half-an-hour, she would feel a sudden anxiety about him that was almost anguish. She wanted to rush to him at once, and know he was safe.

Two nights before the Derby, she was at a big party in town, when one of her rushes of anxiety about her boy, her first-born, gripped her heart till she could hardly speak. She fought with the feeling, might and main, for she believed in common sense. But it was too strong. She had to leave the dance and go downstairs to telephone to the country. The children's nursery-governess was terribly surprised and startled at being rung up in the night.

"Are the children all right, Miss Wilmot?"

"Oh, yes, they are quite all right."

"Master Paul? Is he all right?"

"He went to bed as right as a trivet. Shall I run up and look at him?"

"No," said Paul's mother reluctantly. "No! Don't trouble. It's all right. Don't sit up. We shall be home fairly soon." She did not want her son's privacy intruded upon.

"Very good," said the governess.

It was about one o'clock when Paul's mother and father drove up to their house. All was still. Paul's mother went to her room and slipped off her white fur cloak. She had told her maid not to wait up for her. She heard her husband downstairs, mixing a whisky-and-soda.

And then, because of the strange anxiety at her heart, she stole upstairs to her son's room. Noiselessly she went along the upper corridor. Was there a faint noise? What was it?

She stood, with arrested muscles, outside his door, listening. There was a strange, heavy, and yet not loud noise. Her heart stood still. It was a soundless noise, yet rushing and powerful. Something huge, in violent, hushed motion. What was it? What in God's name was it? She ought to know. She felt that she knew the noise. She knew what it was.

Yet she could not place it. She couldn't say what it was. And on and on it went, like a madness.

Softly, frozen with anxiety and fear, she turned the door-handle.

The room was dark. Yet in the space near the window, she heard and saw something plunging to and fro. She gazed in fear and amazement.

Then suddenly she switched on the light, and saw her son, in his green pajamas, madly surging on the rocking-horse. The blaze of light suddenly lit him up, as he urged the wooden horse, and lit her up, as she stood, blonde, in her dress of pale green and crystal, in the doorway.

"Paul!" she cried. "Whatever are you doing?"

"It's Malabar!" he screamed, in a powerful, strange voice. "It's Malabar!"

His eyes blazed at her for one strange and senseless second, as he ceased urging his wooden horse. Then he fell with a crash to the ground, and she, all her tormented motherhood flooding upon her, rushed to gather him up.

But he was unconscious, and unconscious he remained, with some brain-fever. He talked and tossed, and his mother sat stonily by his side.

"Malabar! It's Malabar! Bassett, Bassett, I *know*! It's Malabar!"

So the child cried, trying to get up and urge the rocking-horse that gave him his inspiration.

"What does he mean by Malabar?" asked the heart-frozen mother.

"I don't know," said the father stonily.

"What does he mean by Malabar?" she asked her brother Oscar.

"It's one of the horses running for the Derby," was the answer.

And, in spite of himself, Oscar Cresswell spoke to Bassett, and himself put a thousand on Malabar: at fourteen to one.

The third day of the illness was critical: they were waiting for a change. The boy, with his rather long, curly hair, was tossing ceaselessly on the pillow. He neither slept nor regained consciousness, and his eyes were like blue stones. His mother sat, feeling her heart had gone, turned actually into a stone.

In the evening, Oscar Cresswell did not come, but Bassett sent a message, saying could he come up for one moment, just one moment? Paul's mother was very angry at the intrusion, but on second thought she agreed. The boy was the same. Perhaps Bassett might bring him to consciousness.

The gardener, a shortish fellow with a little brown moustache, and sharp little brown eyes, tiptoed into the room, touched his imaginary cap to Paul's mother, and stole to the bedside, staring with glittering, smallish eyes, at the tossing, dying child.

"Master Paul!" he whispered. "Master Paul! Malabar came in first all right, a clean win. I did as you told me. You've made over seventy thousand pounds, you have; you've got over eighty thousand. Malabar came in all right, Master Paul."

"Malabar! Malabar! Did I say Malabar, mother? Did I say Malabar? Do you think I'm lucky, mother? I knew Malabar, didn't I? Over eighty thousand pounds! I call that lucky, don't you, mother? Over eighty thousand pounds! I knew, didn't I know I knew? Malabar came in all right. If I ride my horse till I'm sure, then I tell you, Bassett, you can go as high as you like. Did you go for all you were worth, Bassett?"

"I went a thousand on it, Master Paul."

"I never told you, mother, that if I can ride my horse, and *get there*, then I'm absolutely sure—oh, absolutely! Mother, did I ever tell you? I *am* lucky!"

"No, you never did," said the mother.

But the boy died in the night.

And even as he lay dead, his mother heard her brother's voice saying to her: "My God, Hester, you're eighty-odd thousand to the good, and a poor devil of a son to the bad. But, poor devil, poor devil, he's best gone out of a life where he rides his rocking-horse to find a winner."

(1933)

STUDY AIDS: 1. All fiction embodies a conflict, either between persons, or between men and nature. In this story Paul, a sensitive boy, is the protagonist. With what is he in conflict— himself, his mother, or "voices" haunting his home?

2. Who is responsible for filling the house with whispers? What attitude toward life starts the boy down the road to death? How does Lawrence relate this attitude to the values placed upon life by society (see the final paragraph of the story)? Is this final statement a criticism of Paul or of society's practical attitude as represented by his mother and uncle? Who, then, is the real antagonist of the story (note the opening paragraph, particularly the recurring phrase "the center of her heart")?

3. Is Paul destroyed because he made contact with the dark god Luck through unconscious, supernatural forces, or because he degraded these vital forces to practical (monetary) ends? After what action do the voices become louder and more insistent?

4. Note details in the story which make plausible the symbolism of the rocking-horse as a link between the visible and invisible worlds. Why are religious words and phrases used in describing Bassett? Why is the story told in the style of a fairy tale?

5. An author's attitude toward his subject matter is related to the "meaning" of the story. Often this attitude is achieved by POINT OF VIEW. What point of view does Lawrence use in this story? How does this point of view help Lawrence interpret and give meaning to his subject matter?

6. Is Lawrence attacking money as an evil in itself?

Thomas Stearns Eliot

(1888–   )

T. S. ELIOT WAS BORN IN ST. LOUIS, MISSOURI. HE WAS GRADUATED FROM HARVARD University in 1910 and then went to Europe for further study at the Sorbonne and Merton College, Oxford. In 1914 he settled permanently in London, where he worked as a bank teller, as editor of the magazine *Criterion,* and later as a member of the publishing house of Faber and Faber, which position he still holds. In 1927 he became a British citizen.

Eliot's fame as a poet came early with the publication of *The Love Song of J. Alfred Prufrock* (1915) and *The Waste Land* (1922). Although the amount of poetry he has written is small, his reputation has remained consistently high, despite some formidable and acute opposition from other poet-critics. That it has done so is perhaps the result of his more voluminous criticism, which, for the most part, supplements his poetic practice.

Like Milton, Eliot evidently prefers a "fit audience, though few." His poetry is difficult, but the difficulty usually arises from his technique: a scarcity of transitions in order to achieve compression; the frequent use of myth to indicate the continuity of human experience; and innumerable quotations and contexts from earlier poets, a knowledge of which is essential for a full understanding of his poetry. Despite its difficulty, Eliot's writing continues to attract new readers who are willing to take the time and effort necessary to enjoy it.

In addition to his reputation as critic and poet, Eliot is also in the forefront of those modern dramatists who have attempted to restore poetry to drama. His first success in this field was the religious drama *Murder in the Cathedral* (1935). He later turned his attention to comedy in *The Cocktail Party* (1949), *The Confidential Clerk* (1954), and *The Elder Statesman* (1958).

Tradition and the Individual Talent

Although Eliot's poetry has had great influence on modern poets, his critical theories have been equally important in revaluing all English poetry. This particular essay pronounced a view which has become a shibboleth among many critics, poets, and readers. Eliot states that a poem is impersonal, an object in itself, distinct and separate from the personality of the poet who wrote it (see below, p. 981/1, l. 22 ff.). He is even more explicit in *The Sacred Wood* (1928):

"We can only say that a poem, in some sense, has its own life; that its parts form something quite different from a body of neatly ordered biographical data; that the feeling, or emotion, or vision resulting from the poem is something different from the feeling or emotion or vision in the mind of the poet."

Eliot is insisting that one pay attention to the poem, not to the poet. Using this view as a starting point, several modern critics have gone on to develop critical systems based upon Eliot's thesis.

I

In English writing we seldom speak of tradition, though we occasionally apply its name in deploring its absence. We cannot refer to "the tradition" or to "a tradition"; at most, we employ the adjective in saying that the poetry of So-and-so is "traditional" or even "too traditional." Seldom, perhaps, does the word appear except in a phrase of censure. If otherwise, it is vaguely approbative, with the implication, as to the work approved, of some pleasing archaeological reconstruction. You can hardly make the word agreeable to English ears without this comfortable reference to the reassuring science of archaeology.

Certainly the word is not likely to appear in our appreciations of living or dead writers. Every nation, every race, has not only its own creative, but its own critical turn of mind; and is even more oblivious of the shortcomings and limitations of its critical habits than of those of its creative genius. We know, or think we know, from the enormous mass of critical writing that has appeared in the French language the critical method or habit of the French; we only conclude (we are such unconscious people) that the French are "more critical" than we, and sometimes even plume ourselves a little with the fact, as if the French were the less spontaneous. Perhaps they are; but we might remind ourselves that criticism is as inevitable as breathing, and that we should be none the worse for articulating what passes in our minds when we read a book and feel an emotion about it, for criticizing our own minds in their work of criticism. One of the facts that might come to light in this process is our tendency to insist, when we praise a poet, upon those aspects of his work in which he least resembles anyone else. In these aspects or parts of his work we pretend to find what is individual, what is the peculiar essence of the man. We dwell with satisfaction upon the poet's difference from his predecessors, especially his immediate predecessors; we endeavor to find something that can be isolated in order to be enjoyed. Whereas if we approach a poet without this prejudice we shall often find that not only the best, but the most individual parts of his work may be those in which the dead poets, his ancestors, assert their immortality most vigorously. And I do not mean the impressionable period of adolescence, but the period of full maturity.

Yet if the only form of tradition, of handing down, consisted in following the ways of the immediate generation before us in a blind or timid adherence to its successes, "tradition" should positively be discouraged. We have seen many such simple currents soon lost in the sand; and novelty is better than repetition. Tradition is a matter of much wider significance. It cannot be inherited, and if you want it you must obtain it by great labor. It involves, in the first place, the historical sense, which we may call nearly indispensable to anyone who would continue to be a poet beyond his twenty-fifth year; and the historical sense involves a perception, not only of the pastness of the past, but of its presence; the historical sense compels a man to write not merely with his own generation in his bones, but with a feeling that the whole of the literature of Europe from Homer and within it the whole of the literature of his own country has a simultaneous existence and composes a simultaneous order. This historical sense, which is a sense of the timeless as well as of the temporal and of the timeless and of the temporal together, is what makes a writer traditional. And it is at the same time what makes a writer most acutely conscious of his place in time, of his own contemporaneity.

No poet, no artist of any art, has his complete meaning alone. His significance, his appreciation is the appreciation of his relation to the dead poets and artists. You cannot value him alone; you must set him, for contrast and comparison, among the dead. I mean this as a principle of aesthetic, not merely historical, criticism. The necessity that he shall conform, that he shall cohere, is not one-sided; what happens when a new work of art is created is something that happens simultaneously to all the works of art which preceded it. The existing monuments form an ideal order among themselves, which is modified by the introduction of the new (the really new) work of art among them. The existing order is complete before the new work arrives; for order to persist after the supervention of novelty, the *whole* existing order must be, if ever so slightly, altered; and so the relations, proportions, values of each work of art toward the whole are readjusted;

and this is conformity between the old and the new. Whoever has approved this idea of order, of the form of European, of English literature will not find it preposterous that the past should be altered by the present as much as the present is directed by the past. And the poet who is aware of this will be aware of great difficulties and responsibilities.

In a peculiar sense he will be aware also that he must inevitably be judged by the standards of the past. I say judged, not amputated, by them; not judged to be as good as, or worse or better than, the dead; and certainly not judged by the canons of dead critics. It is a judgment, a comparison, in which two things are measured by each other. To conform merely would be for the new work not really to conform at all; it would not be new, and would therefore not be a work of art. And we do not quite say that the new is more valuable because it fits in; but its fitting in is a test of its value—a test, it is true, which can only be slowly and cautiously applied, for we are none of us infallible judges of conformity. We say: it appears to conform, and is perhaps individual, or it appears individual, and may conform; but we are hardly likely to find that it is one and not the other.

To proceed to a more intelligible exposition of the relation of the poet to the past: he can neither take the past as a lump, an indiscriminate bolus,[1] nor can he form himself wholly on one or two private admirations, nor can he form himself wholly upon one preferred period. The first course is inadmissible, the second is an important experience of youth, and the third is a pleasant and highly desirable supplement. The poet must be very conscious of the main current, which does not at all flow invariably through the most distinguished reputations.[2] He must be quite aware of the obvious fact that art never improves, but that the material of art is never

quite the same. He must be aware that the mind of Europe—the mind of his own country—a mind which he learns in time to be much more important than his own private mind—is a mind which changes, and that this change is a development which abandons nothing en route, which does not superannuate either Shakespeare, or Homer, or the rock drawing of the Magdalenian draughtsmen. That this development, refinement perhaps, complication certainly, is not, from the point of view of the artist, any improvement. Perhaps not even an improvement from the point of view of the psychologist or not to the extent which we imagine; perhaps only in the end based upon a complication in economics and machinery. But the difference between the present and the past is that the conscious present is an awareness of the past in a way and to an extent which the past's awareness of itself cannot show.

Someone said: "The dead writers are remote from us because we know so much more than they did." Precisely, and they are that which we know.

I am alive to a usual objection to what is clearly part of my program for the métier[3] of poetry. The objection is that the doctrine requires a ridiculous amount of erudition (pedantry), a claim which can be rejected by appeal to the lives of poets in any pantheon. It will even be affirmed that much learning deadens or perverts poetic sensibility. While, however, we persist in believing that a poet ought to know as much as will not encroach upon his necessary receptivity and necessary laziness, it is not desirable to confine knowledge to whatever can be put into a useful shape for examinations, drawing-rooms, or the still more pretentious modes of publicity. Some can absorb knowledge, the more tardy must sweat for it. Shakespeare acquired more essential history from Plutarch than most men could from the whole British Museum. What is to be insisted upon is that the poet must develop or procure the consciousness of the past and that he should continue to develop this consciousness throughout his career.

---

[1] A large pill or dose of medicine.

[2] One of Eliot's central tenets: the true tradition of English poetry after Shakespeare descends through the seventeenth-century metaphysical poets—rather than through the better-known Milton—to Dryden, Dr. Johnson, Coleridge, and Arnold.

[3] Profession, trade.

What happens is a continual surrender of himself as he is at the moment to something which is more valuable. The progress of an artist is a continual self-sacrifice, a continual extinction of personality.

There remains to define this process of depersonalization and its relation to the sense of tradition. It is in this depersonalization that art may be said to approach the condition of science. I therefore invite you to consider, as a suggestive analogy, the action which takes place when a bit of finely filiated platinum is introduced into a chamber containing oxygen and sulphur dioxide.

2

Honest criticism and sensitive appreciation is directed not upon the poet but upon the poetry. If we attend to the confused cries of the newspaper critics and the susurrus [4] of popular repetition that follows, we shall hear the names of poets in great numbers; if we seek not Blue-book knowledge but the enjoyment of poetry, and ask for a poem, we shall seldom find it. I have tried to point out the importance of the relation of the poem to other poems by other authors, and suggested the conception of poetry as a living whole of all the poetry that has ever been written. The other aspect of this impersonal theory of poetry is the relation of the poem to its author. And I hinted, by an analogy, that the mind of the mature poet differs from that of the immature one not precisely in any valuation of "personality," not being necessarily more interesting, or having "more to say," but rather by being a more finely perfected medium in which special, or very varied, feelings are at liberty to enter into new combinations.

The analogy was that of the catalyst. When the two gases previously mentioned are mixed in the presence of a filament of platinum, they form sulphurous acid. This combination takes place only if the platinum is present; nevertheless the newly formed acid contains no trace of platinum, and the platinum itself is apparently unaffected: has remained inert, neutral, and unchanged. The mind of the poet is the shred of platinum. It may partly

[4] Soft, murmuring sound.

or exclusively operate upon the experience of the man himself; but, the more perfect the artist, the more completely separate in him will be the man who suffers and the mind which creates; the more perfectly will the mind digest and transmute the passions which are its material.

The experience, you will notice, the elements which enter the presence of the transforming catalyst, are of two kinds: emotions and feelings. The effect of a work of art upon the person who enjoys it is an experience different in kind from any experience not of art. It may be formed out of one emotion, or may be a combination of several; and various feelings, inhering for the writer in particular words or phrases or images, may be added to compose the final result. Or great poetry may be made without the direct use of any emotion whatever: composed out of feelings solely. Canto xv of the *Inferno* (Brunetto Latini) is a working up of the emotion evident in the situation; but the effect, though single as that of any work of art, is obtained by considerable complexity of detail. The last quatrain gives an image, a feeling attaching to an image, which "came," which did not develop simply out of what precedes, but which was probably in suspension in the poet's mind until the proper combination arrived for it to add itself to. The poet's mind is in fact a receptacle for seizing and storing up numberless feelings, phrases, images, which remain there until all the particles which can unite to form a new compound are present together.

If you compare several representative passages of the greatest poetry you see how great is the variety of types of combination, and also how completely any semi-ethical criterion of "sublimity" misses the mark. For it is not the "greatness," the intensity, of the emotions, the components, but the intensity of the artistic process, the pressure, so to speak, under which the fusion takes place, that counts. The episode of Paolo and Francesca employs a definite emotion, but the intensity of the poetry is something quite different from whatever intensity in the supposed experience it may give the impression of. It is no more intense, furthermore, than Canto xxvi, the voyage of Ulysses, which has not the direct dependence upon an emotion. Great variety is possible in the process of transmutation of emotion: the murder of Agamemnon, or the agony of Othello, gives an artistic effect apparently closer to a possible original than the scenes from Dante. In the *Agamemnon,* the artistic emotion approximates to the emotion of an actual spectator; in *Othello* to the emotion of the protagonist himself. But the difference between art and the event is always absolute; the combination which is the murder of Agamemnon is probably as complex as that which is the voyage of Ulysses. In either case there has been a fusion of elements. The ode of Keats contains a number of feelings which have nothing particular to do with the nightingale, but which the nightingale, partly perhaps because of its attractive name, and partly because of its reputation, served to bring together.

The point of view which I am struggling to attack is perhaps related to the metaphysical theory of the substantial unity of the soul: for my meaning is, that the poet has, not a "personality" to express, but a particular medium, which is only a medium and not a personality, in which impressions and experiences combine in peculiar and unexpected ways. Impressions and experiences which are important for the man may take no place in the poetry, and those which become important in the poetry may play quite a negligible part in the man, the personality.

I will quote a passage which is unfamiliar enough to be regarded with fresh attention in the light—or darkness—of these observations:

And now methinks I could even chide myself
For doating on her beauty, though her death
Shall be revenged after no common action.
Does the silkworm expend her yellow labors
For thee? For thee does she undo herself?
Are lordships sold to maintain ladyships
For the poor benefit of a bewildering minute?
Why does yon fellow falsify highways,
And put his life between the judge's lips,
To refine such a thing—keeps horse and men
To beat their valors for her? . . . [5]

In this passage (as is evident if it is taken in its context) there is a combination of positive and negative emotions: an intensely strong attraction toward beauty and an equally intense fascination by the ugliness which is contrasted with it and which destroys it. This balance of contrasted emotion is in the dramatic situation to which the speech is pertinent, but that situation alone is inadequate to it. This is, so to speak, the structural emotion, provided by the drama. But the whole effect, the dominant tone, is due to the fact that a number of floating feelings, having an affinity to this emotion by no means superficially evident, have combined with it to give us a new art emotion.

It is not in his personal emotions, the emotions provoked by particular events in his life, that the poet is in any way remarkable or interesting. His particular emotions may be simple, or crude, or flat. The emotion in his poetry will be a very complex thing, but not with the complexity of the emotions of people who have very complex or unusual emotions in life. One error, in fact, of eccentricity in poetry is to seek for new human emotions to express; and in this search for novelty in the wrong place it discovers the perverse. The business of the poet is not to find new emotions, but to use the ordinary ones and, in working them up into poetry, to express feelings which are not in actual emotions at all. And emotions which he has never experienced will serve his turn as well as those familiar to him. Consequently, we must believe that "emotion recollected in tranquility" is an inexact formula. For it is neither emotion, nor recollection, nor, without distortion of meaning, tranquility. It is a concentration, and a new thing resulting from the concentration, of a very great number of experiences which to the practical and active person would not seem to be experiences at all; it is a concentration which does not happen consciously or of deliberation. These experiences are not "recollected," and they finally unite in an atmosphere which is "tranquil" only in that it is a passive attending upon the event. Of course this is not quite the whole story.

[5] C. Tourneur, *Revenger's Tragedy,* III, v.

There is a great deal, in the writing of poetry, which must be conscious and deliberate. In fact, the bad poet is usually unconscious where he ought to be conscious, and conscious where he ought to be unconscious. Both errors tend to make him "personal." Poetry is not a turning loose of emotion, but an escape from emotion; it is not the expression of personality, but an escape from personality. But, of course, only those who have personality and emotions know what it means to want to escape from these things.

3

ὁ δὲ νοῦς ἴσως θειότερόν τι καὶ ἀπαθές ἐστιν.[6]

This essay proposes to halt at the frontier of metaphysics or mysticism, and confine itself to such practical conclusions as can be applied by the responsible person interested in poetry. To divert interest from the poet to the poetry is a laudable aim: for it would conduce to a juster estimation of actual poetry, good and bad. There are many people who appreciate the expression of sincere emotion in verse, and there is a smaller number of people who can appreciate technical excellence. But very few know when there is an expression of *significant* emotion, emotion which has its life in the poem and not in the history of the poet. The emotion of art is impersonal. And the poet cannot reach this impersonality without surrendering himself wholly to the work to be done. And he is not likely to know what is to be done unless he lives in what is not merely the present, but the present moment of the past, unless he is conscious, not of what is dead, but of what is already living.

(1920)

STUDY AIDS: 1. Part 1 discusses the poet's relation to tradition, the past. Part 2 discusses the "impersonality" of the poet. What is the relationship of the two parts of the essay?

2. In Eliot's view, what makes a poem effective—the poet's own feelings or emotion in the poem, the reader's feelings or emotion upon reading the poem, or the artistic fusion of everything which is the poem itself? Does this view make reading a poem an objective or a subjective experience?

3. Study carefully the two paragraphs beginning on p. 981/1, l. 35. What does Eliot mean by the emotion aroused by art? Can this "new" emotion be stated factually? Does it come from the poet's own inner emotions or from the fact that these have been given order or structure in a poem? Is Eliot saying that subjective feeling must be given an objective form if poetry is to result?

4. What is literary "tradition" to Eliot? Does he simply mean that a poet must know what has been written before his own day? How is past literature reordered by a new work of art?

5. Is Eliot a classicist or a romantic? Why?

6. What evidence do you see in *Sweeney among the Nightingales* that illustrates Eliot's view of tradition as stated here—the modern poet must write "with a feeling that the whole of the literature of Europe . . . has a simultaneous existence"?

The Love Song of J. Alfred Prufrock

S'io credesse che mia risposta fosse
A persona che mai tornasse al mondo,
Questa fiamma staria senza piu scosse.

Ma perciocche giammai di questo fondo
Non torno vivo alcun, s'i'odo il vero,
Senza tema d'infamia ti rispondo.[1]

[6] "The mind is no doubt something more divine and unaffected" (Aristotle, *De Anima*).

[1] "If I thought my answer were to one who ever could return to the world, this flame should shake no more; but since none ever did return alive from this depth, if what I hear be true, without fear of infamy I answer thee" (Dante, *Inferno*, 27: 61–66).

The speaker here is Guido da Montefeltro who, upon being asked to identify himself in hell, at first refuses to answer Dante lest his words go back to the real world. In like manner Prufrock speaks the poem to himself because he cannot reveal his thoughts to the world without.

Let us go then, you [2] and I,
When the evening is spread out against the
    sky
Like a patient etherized upon a table; [3]
Let us go, through certain half-deserted streets,
The muttering retreats   5
Of restless nights in one-night cheap hotels
And sawdust restaurants with oyster-shells:
Streets that follow like a tedious argument
Of insidious intent
To lead you to an overwhelming ques-
    tion . . .   10
Oh, do not ask, "What is it?"
Let us go and make our visit. [4]

In the room the women come and go
Talking of Michelangelo. [5]

The yellow fog that rubs its back upon the
    window-panes, [6]   15
The yellow smoke that rubs its muzzle on the
    window-panes
Licked its tongue into the corners of the
    evening,
Lingered upon the pools that stand in drains,
Let fall upon its back the soot that falls from
    chimneys,
Slipped by the terrace, made a sudden leap, 20
And seeing that it was a soft October night,
Curled once about the house, and fell asleep.

And indeed there will be time [7]
For the yellow smoke that slides along the
    street,
Rubbing its back upon the window-panes; 25
There will be time, there will be time
To prepare a face to meet the faces that you
    meet;

There will be time to murder and create,
And time for all the works and days of
    hands
That lift and drop a question on your plate; 30
Time for you and time for me,
And time yet for a hundred indecisions,
And for a hundred visions and revisions,
Before the taking of a toast and tea.

In the room the women come and go   35
Talking of Michelangelo.

And indeed there will be time
To wonder, "Do I dare?" and, "Do I dare?"
Time to turn back and descend the stair,
With a bald spot in the middle of my hair— 40
(They will say: "How his hair is growing
    thin!")
My morning coat, my collar mounting firmly
    to the chin,
My necktie rich and modest, but asserted by
    a simple pin—
(They will say: "But how his arms and legs
    are thin!")
Do I dare   45
Disturb the universe?
In a minute there is time
For decisions and revisions which a minute
    will reverse.

For I have known them all already, known
    them all:—
Have known the evenings, mornings, after-
    noons,   50
I have measured out my life with coffee
    spoons;
I know [8] the voices dying with a dying fall
Beneath the music from a farther room.
    So how should I presume?

[2] The outer Prufrock ("I") addresses the inner suppressed self ("you"). The poem, then, is the soliloquy of a man suspended in isolation, unable to commit himself to action or emotion. It is a poem of dramatized frustration.
[3] How is the image of ll. 2–3 appropriate to the character of Prufrock?
[4] Although the reason given for going through the streets is to "make our visit," does the atmosphere of ll. 1–12 imply that this is evasion? What is evaded?
[5] Lines 13–14 recall that the object of his visit is the "room." After this brief interruption he resumes his walk and interior monologue in l. 15.

[6] How does the "cat-fog" image reflect Prufrock's mental state? Is action or inertia suggested by the image?
[7] Note the reiteration of "time" in the many emotions and states of mind expressed in ll. 23–34. What does this word imply about Prufrock's facing his "overwhelming question" (l. 10)? Does it suggest that he is "etherized" (l. 3)? When must he finally face this question (see l. 34)? Where must he face it (see ll. 35–36; 12–13)?
[8] The present tense indicates that Prufrock is within sound of the voices; he is approaching the "room" where he must face the "question."

And I have known the eyes already, known
    them all—   55
The eyes that fix you in a formulated phrase,
And when I am formulated, sprawling on a
    pin,
When I am pinned and wriggling on the
    wall,
Then how should I begin
To spit out all the butt-ends of my days and
    ways?   60
    And how should I presume?

And I have known the arms already, known
    them all—
Arms that are braceleted and white and bare
(But in the lamplight, downed with light
    brown hair!)
Is it perfume from a dress   65
That makes me so digress?
Arms that lie along a table, or wrap about a
    shawl.
    And should I then presume?
    And how should I begin? [9]

. . . .

Shall I say, I have gone at dusk through nar-
    row streets   70
And watched the smoke that rises from the
    pipes
Of lonely men in shirt-sleeves, leaning out of
    windows? . . .

I should have been a pair of ragged claws
Scuttling across the floors of silent seas.[10]

. . . .

And the afternoon, the evening, sleeps so
    peacefully!   75
Smoothed by long fingers,
Asleep . . . tired . . . or it malingers,

Stretched on the floor, here beside you and
    me.[11]
Should I, after tea and cakes and ices,[12]
Have the strength to force the moment to its
    crisis?   80
But though I have wept and fasted, wept and
    prayed,
Though I have seen my head (grown slightly
    bald) brought in upon a platter,
I am no prophet—and here's no great matter;
I have seen the moment of my greatness
    flicker,
And I have seen the eternal Footman hold my
    coat, and snicker,   85
And in short, I was afraid.

And would it have been worth it, after all,
After the cups, the marmalade, the tea,
Among the porcelain, among some talk of you
    and me,
Would it have been worth while,   90
To have bitten off the matter with a smile,
To have squeezed the universe into a ball
To roll it toward some overwhelming question,
To say: "I am Lazarus, come from the dead,
Come back to tell you all, I shall tell you
    all"—   95
If one, settling a pillow by her head,
    Should say: "That is not what I meant at
    all.
    That is not it, at all."

And would it have been worth it, after all,
Would it have been worth while,   100
After the sunsets and the dooryards and the
    sprinkled streets,
After the novels, after the teacups, after the
    skirts that trail along the floor—
And this, and so much more?—
It is impossible to say just what I mean!
But as if a magic lantern threw the nerves in
    patterns on a screen: 105
Would it have been worth while

---

[9] In ll. 48–69 the images have progressed from
voices through eyes and arms to this climax (l. 69),
which is both a question and an answer. What does
the progression indicate as to the nature of the
"question"?
    The ellipsis marks throughout are the poet's.
[10] His attempt to face the question breaks down,
and Prufrock concludes by conjecturing what kind
of creature he should have been (ll. 73–74). Would
such a creature have argued with himself about
what course of action to take?

[11] I.e., Prufrock. The lady is referred to as "one"
(ll. 96, 107). Notice the cat image recurring in
ll. 75–78.
[12] Lines 79–80 begin a series of heroic parallels
to Prufrock which produce a mock-heroic tone.
Who is the figure in ll. 82–83; in ll. 94–95; in l.
111? How is each of these appropriate to Prufrock's
situation and character?

If one, settling a pillow or throwing off a
    shawl,
And turning toward the window, should say:
    "That is not it at all,
    That is not what I meant, at all."   110

.   .   .   .

No! [13] I am not Prince Hamlet, nor was meant
    to be;
Am an attendant lord, one that will do
To swell a progress, start a scene or two,
Advise the prince; no doubt, an easy tool,
Deferential, glad to be of use,   115
Politic, cautious, and meticulous;
Full of high sentence, but a bit obtuse;
At times, indeed, almost ridiculous—
Almost, at times, the Fool.

I grow old . . . I grow old . . .   120
I shall wear the bottoms of my trousers rolled.

Shall I part my hair behind? Do I dare to eat
    a peach?
I shall wear white flannel trousers, and walk
    upon the beach.
I have heard the mermaids singing, each to
    each.

I do not think that they will sing to me.   125

I have seen them riding seaward on the
    waves

Combing the white hair of the waves blown
    back
When the wind blows the water white and
    black.

We have lingered in the chambers of the sea
By sea-girls wreathed with seaweed red and
    brown   130
Till human voices wake us, and we drown.
(1917)

STUDY AIDS: 1. What is the setting of the
poem? Why is this appropriate?
    2. What is the "overwhelming question"
Prufrock dare not ask? Why does he not resolve
his conflict?
    3. Do you have sympathy for Prufrock?
Where in the poem does he reveal that he perceives beauty, understands love and sympathy?
    4. Which part of Prufrock's personality is
represented by sea-imagery ("oyster shells," "lob-
ters," "mermaids singing" to Ulysses)? What
other kinds of imagery express his divided consciousness (e.g., hair imagery, crude and polite
society, etc.)?
    5. Does Eliot's imagery tell us more about the
one who perceives or the things perceived; i.e.,
do we learn more about Prufrock's mood or his
visit to "the room"?
    6. Is there any justification in the poem for
calling Prufrock a representative of modern
man?

Sweeney among the Nightingales
ὤμοι, πέπληγημαι καιρίαν πληγήν ἔσω.[1]

Eliot once commented that all he consciously wanted to do in this poem was to create a sense
of foreboding. Sweeney, however, is one of Eliot's symbols for the vulgarity of the present century,
a time degraded by unheroic action and lack of faith in anything. Sweeney appears as a character
in two other poems: Sweeney Erect and Sweeney Agonistes.

APENECK [2] SWEENEY spreads his knees
Letting his arms hang down to laugh,

The zebra stripes along his jaw
Swelling to maculate [3] giraffe.

[13] By l. 120 Prufrock has reached a decision: no
more "overwhelming questions" for him. How does
he indicate this resignation?

[1] "Ah me! I have been smitten deep with a mortal
blow." This quotation is from Agamemnon, a play
by Aeschylus; it is the cry of Agamemnon (Greek
ruler and leader of the attack against Troy), when

his wife, Clytemnestra, and her lover, Aegisthus,
murder him.
    [2] Notice how Sweeney is dehumanized. In what
metaphoric terms does Eliot present him? Does he
ever speak? What single human-like sound does he
utter (see l. 2)?
    [3] Spotted; defiled, stained.

The circles of the stormy moon [4] 5
Slide westward toward the River Plate,
Death and the Raven [5] drift above
And Sweeney guards the hornèd gate.

Gloomy Orion and the Dog [6]
Are veiled; and hushed the shrunken seas; 10
The person in the Spanish cape [7]
Tries to sit on Sweeney's knees

Slips and pulls the table cloth
Overturns a coffee-cup,
Reorganized upon the floor 15
She yawns and draws a stocking up;

The silent man [8] in mocha brown
Sprawls at the window-sill and gapes;
The waiter brings in oranges
Banana figs and hothouse grapes; 20

The silent vertebrate [9] in brown
Contracts and concentrates, withdraws;
Rachel *née* [10] Rabinovitch
Tears at the grapes with murderous paws;

She and the lady in the cape 25
Are suspect, thought to be in league;

Therefore the man with heavy eyes
Declines the gambit,[11] shows fatigue,

Leaves the room and reappears
Outside the window, leaning in, 30
Branches of wisteria [12]
Circumscribe a golden grin;

The host with someone indistinct
Converses at the door apart,
The nightingales [13] are singing near 35
The Convent of the Sacred Heart,

And sang [14] within the bloody wood
When Agamemnon cried aloud,
And let their liquid siftings fall
To stain the stiff dishonored shroud. 40
(1920)

STUDY AIDS: 1. An oversimplified statement of the poem's central idea might be this: Life, isolated from the natural and spiritual forces alive around it, is death. Symbolism plays a major part in presenting connotations which enrich the poem's theme. How do the connotations of the following contribute to this theme: (1) the

[4] Lines 5–10 place Sweeney (in the contemporary world of a tavern or night club) against the ordered patterns of nature and myth (which were ancient explanations of man's relationship with nature). What verbs and adjectives in these lines subtly suggest that while nature is still the same, it has little meaning to Sweeney and his companions?
[5] The constellations listed in ll. 5–10 are also connected with myths which treat of death (usually because of lechery). The "moon" (l. 5) is Diana, goddess of chastity, who "slides" to her setting; the "Raven" (l. 7) is the constellation Corvus; the "hornèd gate" (l. 8) is related to Orion, who met death at the hand of Diana, because of his lechery (*Aeneid*, 6). Agamemnon was also murdered because of lechery.
[6] Stanzas 1 and 2 set the scene. Lines 9–40 (one sentence) describe the action which takes place in this setting.
[7] A prostitute who tries to seduce Sweeney. How is she dehumanized, isolated from mankind, i.e., without identity?
[8] One of Sweeney's murderers.
[9] Notice the amoeba-like, rather than human, movement.
[10] "Born." Rachel has disassociated herself from her origins, and since unidentified, is dehumanized ("tears . . . paws," l. 24).
[11] A move in chess in which a pawn is sacrificed to gain an advantage. Sweeney backs away from the woman's overtures; he declines to be a sacrifice. What figures earlier presented in the poem were sacrifices to lechery? Why does Sweeney reject the offer?
[12] The wisteria vine frames ("circumscribes") the grin. It forms an "outside," and picks up through its color imagery "grapes" (l. 20), the "Sacred Heart" (l. 36), the "bloody wood" (l. 37), and "stain" (l. 40). This blood imagery carries connotations of sacrifice, and ironically implies that true sacrifice is unrelated ("outside") to Sweeney—it is nothing but a "stain" on his "dishonored shroud" (l. 40), because like everyone else he is "apart" (l. 34), aloof and unidentified with life and vitality.
[13] The myth of Philomela, another bloody betrayal. She was raped by her brother-in-law, who ordered her tongue torn out that she might not tell. The gods gave her a beautiful, inviolate voice as a reward for her torment and betrayal, i.e., mercy and beauty resulted from her sacrifice. What is the myth's association with "Sacred Heart" (l. 36) and "bloody wood" (l. 37)?
[14] The shift in tense from "are singing" (l. 35) to "sang" juxtaposes the contemporary Sweeney with ancient Agamemnon and other heroic figures from the past.

animal imagery which describes Sweeney; (2) the astronomical imagery which describes the night of his betrayal; (3) the nightingales; (4) The Convent of the Sacred Heart; (5) "the bloody wood When Agamemnon cried aloud"?

2. Is Sweeney more moral and heroic than Orion because he rejects the woman's advances? How will Sweeney be literally betrayed (see ll. 25–28, 33–34)? How symbolically; i.e., why is he defenseless in the face of betrayal? Will his sacrifice have meaning?

3. There are definite parallels between Sweeney's betrayal and that of Christ in Gethsemane.

What are some of them in the poem? Is Eliot implying that Sweeney is a Christ-like figure? What is the ironic contrast between the two betrayals? What, then, is the purpose of the parallel?

4. How is the poem a criticism of contemporary life? How many characters are in this scene? Does anyone have a distinct identity? What does this fact imply about modern life and society?

5. In what external details do Sweeney and Prufrock differ? What basic trait do they have in common?

The Hollow Men
A penny for the Old Guy [1]

This poem is Eliot's most pessimistic one and, together with *The Waste Land* (1922), earned him the epithet, "poet of the lost generation." Considerable doubt has been cast on this labeling by recent scholarship and criticism. Nevertheless, the poem is dark and despairing—no hope for the future penetrates its gloom. Its theme is the frustration by fear of any form of action men might take.

I

We [2] are the hollow men
We are the stuffed men
Leaning together
Headpiece filled with straw. Alas!
Our dried voices, when   5
We whisper together
Are quiet and meaningless
As wind in dry grass
Or rats' feet over broken glass
In our dry cellar [3]   10

Shape without form, shade without color,
Paralyzed force, gesture without motion; [4]

Those who have crossed
With direct eyes, to death's other kingdom
Remember us—if at all—not as lost   15
Violent souls, but only
As the hollow men
The stuffed men.

2

Eyes [5] I dare not meet in dreams
In death's dream kingdom [6]   20
These do not appear:

[1] Guy Fawkes tried to blow up the House of Commons with gunpowder in 1605. He was detected, and the day, November 5, is celebrated as Guy Fawkes Day. Children beg pennies for fireworks by carrying straw-filled effigies of Fawkes through the streets and crying, "A penny for the Old Guy." Eliot uses the figure with a double meaning: (1) modern men are hollow effigies like those straw figures of Fawkes; and (2) modern men are not like Fawkes, who was willing to die in the explosion to carry out his "action."

[2] The identification of men and Fawkes' effigy is made explicit here in the beginning.

[3] The images of ll. 1–10 suggest worship: "Leaning together . . . whisper together" with voices "quiet and meaningless." Again, the word "kingdom" (l. 14) and the debased ritual and Lord's Prayer at the end of the poem imply that Eliot feels our "hollowness" is somehow related to our lack of faith in God, in mankind, in ourselves individually. Lack of faith in anything would preclude any action.

[4] Lines 11–12 present four PARADOXES, which describe men afraid to act, i.e., hollow, straw men.

[5] See l. 14.

[6] This is not "death's *other* kingdom" (l. 14); it is "death's *dream* kingdom"—this actual life which, without faith or action, is a death-in-life, a living death, a life without meaning.

There,[7] the eyes are
Sunlight on a broken column
There, is a tree swinging
And voices are   25
In the wind's singing
More distant and more solemn
Than a fading star.

Let me be no nearer [8]
In death's dream kingdom   30
Let me also wear
Such deliberate disguises
Rat's coat, crowskin, crossed staves
In a field
Behaving as the wind behaves   35
No nearer—

Not that final meeting
In the twilight kingdom

3

This is the dead land [9]
This is cactus land   40
Here the stone images
Are raised, here they receive
The supplication of a dead man's hand
Under the twinkle of a fading star.[10]

Is it like this [11]   45
In death's other kingdom
Waking alone
At the hour when we are
Trembling with tenderness
Lips that would kiss   50
Form prayers to broken stone.

4

The eyes are not here [12]
There are no eyes here
In this valley of dying stars
In this hollow valley   55
This broken jaw of our lost kingdoms

In this last of meeting places
We grope together
And avoid speech
Gathered on this beach of the tumid river 60

Sightless, unless [13]
The eyes reappear
As the perpetual star
Multifoliate rose
Of death's twilight kingdom   65
The hope only [14]
Of empty men.

5

Here we go round the prickly pear [15]
Prickly pear prickly pear
Here we go round the prickly pear   70
At five o'clock in the morning.

Between the idea
And the reality
Between the motion
And the act   75
Falls the Shadow [16]
For Thine is the Kingdom [17]

[7] The antecedent is vague but probably refers to "death's dream kingdom."

[8] I.e., to the "direct eyes," since I cannot face them. Let me be a scarecrow (ll. 31–36), a hollow man.

[9] Part 3 describes the worship of the hollow men in "death's dream kingdom"; instead of a living God, there are only "stone images" (l. 41) worshiped by dead men's "hands." What is the implication of this?

[10] What ATMOSPHERE does this line produce?

[11] Lines 45–51 image the frustration of love. What is the object of this love, man or God (see ll. 50–51)?

[12] Part 4 creates the feeling of existence in a "valley of dying stars," where without eyes there can be no "vision." What kind of existence is described by the imagery of ll. 55–60?

[13] The only hope possible is for the "eyes" to return as the "perpetual," not the "fading" or "dying" star. To help communicate his meaning, the poet identifies these "eyes" as the "multifoliate rose," a term from Dante's *Paradiso*. Dante, bathed in Beatrice's smiling "eyes of light," saw Paradise unfold as a "multifoliate rose of saints." This was possible because Dante, urged on by faith, had climbed (action) the mountain of Purgatory out of "death's twilight kingdom" (l. 65).

[14] What do ll. 66–67 suggest as to the possibility of regeneration? In the context of the poem are they better read as "the hope only . . ." or "the only hope . . ."?

[15] Part 5 returns to actual existence and does not develop the "hope" of l. 66. Devoid of hope, life is as meaningless as a child's game (ll. 68–71).

[16] The term is possibly taken from Jung, a disciple of the psychologist Freud, who used it to describe the inner darkness of man, his spirit paralyzed by a fear of acting, his will negated.

[17] The "Shadow" affects religion.

Between the conception
And the creation
Between the emotion   80
And the response
Falls the Shadow
       Life is very long [18]

Between the desire
And the spasm   85
Between the potency
And the existence
Between the essence
And the descent
Falls the Shadow   90
       For Thine is the Kingdom [19]

For Thine is [20]
Life is
For Thine is the

This is the way the world ends   95
This is the way the world ends

This is the way the world ends
Not with a bang but a whimper. [21]
(1925)

STUDY AIDS: 1. Does the poem interpret
hope, or faith as religious faith only, and the
"Shadow" as religious skepticism?
   2. What evidences can you see in society
which would substantiate Eliot's criticism of
modern man as a straw effigy, reduced to inac-
tion because of fear (e.g., the overwhelming
desire for financial security, etc.)?
   3. Do you think Eliot would agree with
Dante and Baudelaire that to do anything is
better than to do nothing?
   4. Eliot is often criticized for omitting grammatical transitions and connectives. Does this
compression render *The Hollow Men* unintelligible? Is there a psychological sequence from
one stanza to another in the poem?
   5. Why does the poem end on a pessimistic
note?

Macavity: the Mystery Cat [1]

Macavity's a Mystery Cat: he's called the
   Hidden Paw—
For he's the master criminal who can defy the
   Law.
He's the bafflement of Scotland Yard, the
   Flying Squad's despair:
For when they reach the scene of crime—
   Macavity's not there!

Macavity, Macavity, there's no one like
   Macavity,   5
He's broken every human law, he breaks the
   law of gravity.
His powers of levitation would make a fakir
   stare,
And when you reach the scene of crime—
   Macavity's not there!

You may seek him in the basement, you may
   look up in the air—
But I tell you once and once again, *Macavity's*
   not there!   10

Macavity's a ginger cat, he's very tall and
   thin;
You would know him if you saw him, for his
   eyes are sunken in.
His brow is deeply lined with thought, his
   head is highly domed;
His coat is dusty from neglect, his whiskers
   are uncombed.
He sways his head from side to side, with
   movements like a snake;   15
And when you think he's half asleep, he's
   always wide awake.

[18] The "Shadow" affects life, making it long
and burdensome. Even procreation is affected (ll.
78–87).
[19] The "Shadow" makes the Kingdom of God
difficult to attain.
[20] In ll. 92–94 the predicates of the responses are
missing. How does this illustrate the effect of the
Shadow described in ll. 72–91?

[21] Hollow men end their lives with the whimper
of fear, not with the "bang" of Guy Fawkes or of the
"lost, Violent souls."

[1] In 1939 Eliot published *Old Possum's Book of
Practical Cats,* a volume of whimsical verse about
cats. He has been known to remark that of his
earlier verse these poems are his favorites.

Macavity, Macavity, there's no one like
   Macavity,
For he's a fiend in feline shape, a monster of
   depravity.
You may meet him in a by-street, you may
   see him in the square—
But when a crime's discovered, then *Macav-*
   ity's not there!   20

He's outwardly respectable. (They say he
   cheats at cards.)
And his footprints are not found in any file of
   Scotland Yard's.
And when the larder's looted, or the jewel-
   case is rifled,
Or when the milk is missing, or another Peke's
   been stifled,
Or the greenhouse glass is broken, and the
   trellis past repair—   25
Ay, there's the wonder of the thing! *Macavity's*
   not there!

And when the Foreign Office find a Treaty's
   gone astray,
Or when the Admiralty lose some plans and
   drawings by the way,
There may be a scrap of paper in the hall or
   on the stair—

But it's useless to investigate—*Macavity's not*
   there!   30
And when the loss has been disclosed, the
   Secret Service say:
'It *must* have been Macavity!'—but he's a mile
   away.
You'll be sure to find him resting, or a-licking
   of his thumbs,
Or engaged in doing complicated long division
   sums.

Macavity, Macavity, there's no one like
   Macavity,   35
There never was a cat of such deceitfulness
   and suavity.
He always has an alibi, and one or two to
   spare:
At whatever time the deed took place—
   MACAVITY WASN'T THERE!
And they say that all the cats whose wicked
   deeds are widely known
(I might mention Mungojerrie, I might men-
   tion Griddlebone)   40
Are nothing more than agents for the cat who
   all the time
Just controls their operations: The Napoleon
   of Crime!
(1939)

Aldous Huxley
(1894-   )

THE GRANDSON OF THOMAS H. HUXLEY, THE FAMOUS NINETEENTH-CENTURY SCIENTIST AND essayist; the great-nephew of Matthew Arnold; the son of Leonard Huxley, well-known writer and educator; and the younger brother of Julian Huxley, the renowned biologist— Aldous Huxley is a member of a distinguished family.

At Oxford, Huxley turned to literature when eye disease made it impossible for him to pursue a medical career. Beginning with *The Burning Wheel* (1916), a book of poetry, he has published volume after volume of poems, novels, essays, short stories, and travel accounts. He has also done a great deal of journalistic work, edited the letters of his friend D. H. Lawrence, turned out movie scenarios, and written a book on the improvement of eyesight. For many years Huxley and his Belgian wife traveled widely but in the late 1930's settled down in California.

The early Huxley was a cynic and satirist, writing bitter, disillusioned poetry and then novels noted for their acid and irony. The best known of these brilliant, caustic novels are

Crome Yellow (1921), *Antic Hay* (1923), *Those Barren Leaves* (1925), *Point Counter Point* (1928), and *Brave New World* (1932).

Later, however, Huxley gradually abandoned his sharp, satirical attacks and became the increasingly devoted proponent of an affirmative philosophy of mysticism. This change was due in part to his contact, in 1935, with a Dr. W. H. Bates, whose success in improving human vision convinced Huxley of the "possibility of becoming the master of one's circumstances instead of their slave." The change is reflected in novels like *Eyeless in Gaza* (1936), *After Many a Summer Dies the Swan* (1939), and *Time Must Have a Stop* (1944), and is stated explicitly in his more recent philosophical essays. Huxley has even taken up the practice of yoga, an ascetic Eastern technique of bodily position and control which enables the practitioner to achieve a kind of spiritual contact with ultimate reality. Such techniques, he believes, teach us "the art of obtaining freedom from the fundamental disability of egotism," and, he says, "it is with the problem of personal, psychological freedom that I find myself predominantly concerned."

Brave New World [1]

Huxley's satirical attack upon the values of modern life reached its climax in *Brave New World* (1932), his devastating picture of a future society in which some of the grimmer promises of the twentieth century have reached their logical fulfilment. Here is a completely planned, mechanical world in which the word "Ford" has supplanted "God," dating is reckoned in terms of B. F. (Before Ford) and A. F. (After Ford), and the earth is divided into districts ruled over by Fordships. Babies are decanted out of test tubes, "mother" is an obscene word, and sex relations are as common and matter of fact as eating. The movies have developed into "feelies," where one can enjoy vicarious sensations without the dangers or the inconveniences of the real thing. Education has become a process of mass-conditioning, so that everyone is happy and satisfied with his appointed level in society, whether he is one of the Alpha Plus Intellectuals at the top or one of the Epsilon Minus Morons at the bottom. And in case of any emotional disturbance, there is the wonder drug soma—the culmination of the tranquilizing pill—which routs all pain and quickly restores both bodily and mental harmony.

The opening chapters describe the processes of birth and education in this "brave new world."

Chapter 2

Mr. Foster was left in the Decanting Room. The D.H.C.[2] and his students stepped into the nearest lift and were carried up to the fifth floor.

INFANT NURSERIES. NEO-PAVLOVIAN [3] CONDITIONING ROOMS, announced the notice board.

[1] "O brave new world, / That has such people in it!" (*The Tempest*, V, i).
[2] The Director of Hatcheries and Conditioning, in the Central London Hatchery and Conditioning Center.
[3] Pavlov was the Russian scientist who made pioneer studies in conditioned reflexes.

The Director opened a door. They were in a large bare room, very bright and sunny; for the whole of the southern wall was a single window. Half a dozen nurses, trousered and 5 jacketed in the regulation white viscose-linen uniform, their hair aseptically hidden under white caps, were engaged in setting out bowls of roses in a long row across the floor. Big bowls, packed tight with blossom. Thousands 10 of petals, ripe-blown and silkily smooth, like the cheeks of innumerable little cherubs, but of cherubs, in that bright light, not exclusively pink and Aryan, but also luminously Chinese, also Mexican, also apoplectic with too much 15 blowing of celestial trumpets, also pale as death, pale with the posthumous whiteness of marble.[4]

The nurses stiffened to attention as the D.H.C. came in.

"Set out the books," he said curtly.

In silence the nurses obeyed his command. Between the rose bowls the books were duly set out—a row of nursery quartos opened invitingly each at some gaily colored image of beast or fish or bird.

"Now bring in the children."

They hurried out of the room and returned in a minute or two, each pushing a kind of tall dumb-waiter laden, on all its four wire-netted shelves, with eight-month-old babies, all exactly alike (a Bokanovsky Group,[5] it was evident) and all (since their caste was Delta) dressed in khaki.

"Put them down on the floor."

The infants were unloaded.

"Now turn them so that they can see the flowers and books."

Turned, the babies at once fell silent, then began to crawl toward those clusters of sleek colors, those shapes so gay and brilliant on the white pages. As they approached, the sun came out of a momentary eclipse behind a cloud. The roses flamed up as though with a sudden passion from within; a new and profound significance seemed to suffuse the shining pages of the books. From the ranks of the crawling babies came little squeals of excitement, gurgles and twitterings of pleasure.

The Director rubbed his hands. "Excellent!" he said. "It might almost have been done on purpose."

The swiftest crawlers were already at their goal. Small hands reached out uncertainly, touched, grasped, unpetaling the transfigured roses, crumpling the illuminated pages of the books. The Director waited until all were happily busy. Then, "Watch carefully," he said. And, lifting his hand, he gave the signal.

[4] What is the effect of the description in this paragraph?

[5] In "Bokanovsky's Process," the fertilized ovum is caused to divide, and to continue to divide, until as many as 96 perfectly formed embryos may result from a single egg.

The Head Nurse, who was standing by a switchboard at the other end of the room, pressed down a little lever.

There was a violent explosion. Shriller and ever shriller, a siren shrieked. Alarm bells maddeningly sounded.

The children started, screamed; their faces were distorted with terror.

"And now," the Director shouted (for the noise was deafening), "now we proceed to rub in the lesson with a mild electric shock."

He waved his hand again, and the Head Nurse pressed a second lever. The screaming of the babies suddenly changed its tone. There was something desperate, almost insane, about the sharp spasmodic yelps to which they now gave utterance. Their little bodies twitched and stiffened; their limbs moved jerkily as if to the tug of unseen wires.

"We can electrify that whole strip of floor," bawled the Director in explanation. "But that's enough," he signaled to the nurse.

The explosions ceased, the bells stopped ringing, the shriek of the siren died down from tone to tone into silence. The stiffly twitching bodies relaxed, and what had become the sob and yelp of infant maniacs broadened out once more into a normal howl of ordinary terror.

"Offer them the flowers and the books again."

The nurses obeyed; but at the approach of the roses, at the mere sight of those gaily-colored images of pussy and cock-a-doodle-do and baa-baa black sheep, the infants shrank away in horror; the volume of their howling suddenly increased.

"Observe," said the Director triumphantly, "observe."

Books and loud noises, flowers and electric shocks—already in the infant mind these couples were compromisingly linked; and after two hundred repetitions of the same or a similar lesson would be wedded indissolubly. What man has joined, nature is powerless to put asunder.

"They'll grow up with what the psychologists used to call an 'instinctive' hatred of books and flowers. Reflexes unalterably conditioned. They'll be safe from books and botany all their lives." The Director turned to his nurses. "Take them away again."

Still yelling, the khaki babies were loaded on to their dumb-waiters and wheeled out, leaving behind them the smell of sour milk and a most welcome silence.

One of the students held up his hand; and though he could see quite well why you couldn't have lower-caste people wasting the Community's time over books, and that there was always the risk of their reading something which might undesirably decondition one of their reflexes, yet . . . well, he couldn't understand about the flowers. Why go to the trouble of making it psychologically impossible for Deltas to like flowers?

Patiently the D.H.C. explained. If the children were made to scream at the sight of a rose, that was on grounds of high economic policy. Not so very long ago (a century or thereabouts), Gammas, Deltas, even Epsilons, had been conditioned to like flowers—flowers in particular and wild nature in general. The idea was to make them want to be going out into the country at every available opportunity, and so compel them to consume transport.

"And didn't they consume transport?" asked the student.

"Quite a lot," the D.H.C. replied. "But nothing else."

Primroses and landscapes, he pointed out, have one grave defect: they are gratuitous. A love of nature keeps no factories busy. It was decided to abolish the love of nature, at any rate among the lower classes; to abolish the love of nature, but *not* the tendency to consume transport. For of course it was essential that they should keep on going to the country, even though they hated it. The problem was to find an economically sounder reason for consuming transport than a mere affection for primroses and landscapes. It was duly found.

"We condition the masses to hate the country," concluded the Director. "But simultaneously we condition them to love all country sports. At the same time, we see to it that all country sports shall entail the use of elaborate apparatus. So that they consume

manufactured articles as well as transport. Hence those electric shocks."

"I see," said the student, and was silent, lost in admiration.

There was a silence; then, clearing his throat, "Once upon a time," the Director began, "while our Ford was still on earth, there was a little boy called Reuben Rabinovitch. Reuben was the child of Polish-speaking parents." The Director interrupted himself. "You know what Polish is, I suppose?"

"A dead language."

"Like French and German," added another student, officiously showing off his learning.

"And 'parent'?" questioned the D.H.C.

There was an uneasy silence. Several of the boys blushed. They had not yet learned to draw the significant but often very fine distinction between smut and pure science. One, at last, had the courage to raise a hand.

"Human beings used to be . . ." he hesitated; the blood rushed to his cheeks. "Well, they used to be viviparous." [6]

"Quite right." The Director nodded approvingly.

"And when the babies were decanted . . ."

"'Born,'" came the correction.

"Well, then they were the parents—I mean, not the babies, of course; the other ones." The poor boy was overwhelmed with confusion.

"In brief," the Director summed up, "the parents were the father and the mother." The smut that was really science fell with a crash into the boys' eye-avoiding silence. "Mother," he repeated loudly rubbing in the science; and, leaning back in his chair, "These," he said gravely, "are unpleasant facts; I know it. But then most historical facts *are* unpleasant."

He returned to Little Reuben—to Little Reuben, in whose room, one evening, by an oversight, his father and mother (crash, crash!) happened to leave the radio turned on.

("For you must remember that in those days of gross viviparous reproduction, children were always brought up by their parents and not in State Conditioning Centers.")

[6] Producing living young rather than eggs.

While the child was asleep, a broadcast program from London suddenly started to come through; and the next morning, to the astonishment of his crash and crash (the more daring of the boys ventured to grin at one another), Little Reuben woke up repeating word for word a long lecture by that curious old writer ("one of the very few whose works have been permitted to come down to us"), George Bernard Shaw, who was speaking, according to a well-authenticated tradition, about his own genius. To Little Reuben's wink and snigger, this lecture was, of course, perfectly incomprehensible and, imagining that their child had suddenly gone mad, they sent for a doctor. He, fortunately, understood English, recognized the discourse as that which Shaw had broadcasted the previous evening, realized the significance of what had happened, and sent a letter to the medical press about it.

"The principle of sleep-teaching, or hypnopaedia, had been discovered." The D. H. C. made an impressive pause.

The principle had been discovered; but many, many years were to elapse before that principle was usefully applied.

"The case of Little Reuben occurred only twenty-three years after Our Ford's first T-Model was put on the market." (Here the Director made a sign of the T on his stomach and all the students reverently followed suit.) "And yet . . ."

Furiously the students scribbled. "Hypnopaedia, first used officially in A.F. 214. Why not before? Two reasons. (a) . . ."

"These early experimenters," the D.H.C. was saying, "were on the wrong track. They thought that hypnopaedia could be made an instrument of intellectual education . . ."

(A small boy asleep on his right side, the right arm stuck out, the right hand hanging limp over the edge of the bed. Through a round grating in the side of a box a voice speaks softly.

"The Nile is the longest river in Africa and the second in length of all the rivers of the globe. Although falling short of the length of the Mississippi-Missouri, the Nile is at the head of all rivers as regards the length of its basin, which extends through 35 degrees of latitude . . ."

At breakfast the next morning, "Tommy," someone says, "do you know which is the longest river in Africa?" A shaking of the head. "But don't you remember something that begins: The Nile is the . . ."

"The — Nile — is — the — longest — river — in — Africa — and — the — second — in — length — of — all — the — rivers — of — the — globe . . ." The words come rushing out. "Although — falling — short — of . . ."

"Well now, which is the longest river in Africa?"

The eyes are blank. "I don't know."

"But the Nile, Tommy."

"The — Nile — is — the — longest — river — in — Africa — and — second . . ."

"Then which river is the longest, Tommy?"

Tommy burst into tears. "I don't know," he howls.)

That howl, the Director made it plain, discouraged the earliest investigators. The experiments were abandoned. No further attempt was made to teach children the length of the Nile in their sleep. Quite rightly. You can't learn a science unless you know what it's all about.

"Whereas, if they'd only started on *moral* education," said the Director, leading the way towards the door. The students followed him, desperately scribbling as they walked and all the way up in the lift. "Moral education, which ought never, in any circumstances, to be rational."

"Silence, silence," whispered a loud speaker as they stepped out at the fourteenth floor, and "Silence, silence," the trumpet mouths indefatigably repeated at intervals down every corridor. The students and even the Director himself rose automatically to the tips of their toes. They were Alphas, of course; but even Alphas have been well conditioned. "Silence, silence." All the air of the fourteenth floor was sibilant with the categorical imperative.

Fifty yards of tiptoeing brought them to a door which the Director cautiously opened. They stepped over the threshold into the twilight of a shuttered dormitory. Eighty cots stood in a row against the wall. There was a

William Butler Yeats.

James Joyce.

James Joyce with Sylvia Beach, the publisher of *Ulysses*.

sound of light regular breathing and a continuous murmur, as of very faint voices remotely whispering.

A nurse rose as they entered and came to attention before the Director.

"What's the lesson this afternoon?" he asked.

"We had Elementary Sex for the first forty minutes," she answered. "But now it's switched over to Elementary Class Consciousness."

The Director walked slowly down the long line of cots. Rosy and relaxed with sleep, eighty little boys and girls lay softly breathing. There was a whisper under every pillow. The D.H.C. halted and, bending over one of the little beds, listened attentively.

"Elementary Class Consciousness, did you say? Let's have it repeated a little louder by the trumpet."

At the end of the room a loud speaker projected from the wall. The Director walked up to it and pressed a switch.

". . . all wear green," said a soft but very distinct voice, beginning in the middle of a sentence, "and Delta Children wear khaki. Oh no, I don't want to play with Delta children. And Epsilons are still worse. They're too stupid to be able to read or write. Besides they wear black, which is such a beastly color. I'm *so* glad I'm a Beta."

There was a pause; then the voice began again.

"Alpha children wear gray. They work much harder than we do, because they're so frightfully clever. I'm really awfully glad I'm a Beta, because I don't work so hard. And then we are much better than the Gammas and Deltas. Gammas are stupid. They all wear green, and Delta children wear khaki. Oh no, I *don't* want to play with Delta children. And Epsilons are still worse. They're too stupid to be able . . ."

The Director pushed back the switch. The voice was silent. Only its thin ghost continued to mutter from beneath the eighty pillows.

"They'll have that repeated forty or fifty times more before they wake; then again on Thursday, and again on Saturday. A hundred and twenty times three times a week for thirty months. After which they go on to a more advanced lesson."

Roses and electric shocks, the khaki of Deltas and a whiff of asafoetida—wedded indissolubly before the child can speak. But wordless conditioning is crude and wholesale; cannot bring home the finer distinctions, cannot inculcate the more complex courses of behavior. For that there must be words, but words without reason. In brief, hypnopaedia.

"The greatest moralizing and socializing force of all time."

The students took it down in their little books. Straight from the horse's mouth.

Once more the Director touched the switch.

". . . so frightfully clever," the soft, insinuating, indefatigable voice was saying, "I'm really awfully glad I'm a Beta, because . . ."

Not so much like drops of water, though water, it is true, can wear holes in the hardest granite; rather, drops of liquid sealing-wax, drops that adhere, incrust, incorporate themselves with what they fall on, till finally the rock is all one scarlet blob.

"Till at last the child's mind *is* these suggestions, and the sum of the suggestions *is* the child's mind. And not the child's mind only. The adult's mind too—all his life long. The mind that judges and desires and decides—made up of these suggestions. But all these suggestions are *our* suggestions!" The Director almost shouted in his triumph. "Suggestions from the State." He banged the nearest table. "It therefore follows . . ."

A noise made him turn round.

"Oh, Ford!" he said in another tone, "I've gone and wakened the children."

[Into this well-ordered, antiseptic world is suddenly thrust "the Savage," a throwback to a previous age who has been born and brought up in the old-fashioned way. He finds himself incapable of adjusting to the mechanical perfection around him, rebels violently against it, and finally commits suicide. Before he does, however, he is brought before Mustapha Mond, the Resident World Controller for Western Europe. The Controller explains to the Savage the facts of life in the new society, where Shakespeare is no longer understood ("you can't make tragedies without social instability"), individualism cannot be tolerated, and even science itself must be carefully restricted ("every discovery in pure science is potentially subversive"). Their discussion continues in chapter 17.]

Chapter 17

"Art, science—you seem to have paid a fairly high price for your happiness," said the Savage, when they were alone. "Anything else?" [5]

"Well, religion, of course," replied the Controller. "There used to be something called God—before the Nine Years' War. But I was forgetting; you know all about God, I suppose." [10]

"Well . . ." The Savage hesitated. He would have liked to say something about solitude, about night, about the mesa lying pale under the moon, about the precipice, the [15] plunge into shadowy darkness, about death. He would have liked to speak; but there were no words. Not even in Shakespeare.

The Controller, meanwhile, had crossed to the other side of the room and was unlocking [20] a large safe set into the wall between the bookshelves. The heavy door swung open. Rummaging in the darkness within, "It's a subject," he said, "that has always had a great interest for me." He pulled out a thick [25] black volume. "You've never read this, for example."

The Savage took it. *"The Holy Bible, containing the Old and New Testaments,"* he read aloud from the title-page. [30]

"Nor this." It was a small book and had lost its cover.

"The Imitation of Christ." [7]

"Nor this." He handed out another volume.

"The Varieties of Religious Experience. By [35] William James."

"And I've got plenty more," Mustapha Mond continued, resuming his seat. "A whole collection of pornographic old books. God in the safe and Ford on the shelves." He pointed [40] with a laugh to his avowed library—to the shelves of books, the rack full of reading-machine bobbins and sound-track rolls.

[7] A famous devotional book of the fifteenth century.

"But if you know about God, why don't you tell them?" asked the Savage indignantly. "Why don't you give them these books about God?"

"For the same reason as we don't give them *Othello*: they're old; they're about God hundreds of years ago. Not about God now."

"But God doesn't change."

"Men do, though."

"What difference does that make?"

"All the difference in the world," said Mustapha Mond. He got up again and walked to the safe. "There was a man called Cardinal Newman," he said. "A cardinal," he exclaimed parenthetically, "was a kind of Arch-Community-Songster."

"'I Pandulph, of fair Milan, cardinal.' [8] I've read about them in Shakespeare."

"Of course you have. Well, as I was saying, there was a man called Cardinal Newman. Ah, here's the book." He pulled it out. "And while I'm about it I'll take this one too. It's by a man called Maine de Biran. [9] He was a philosopher, if you know what that was."

"A man who dreams of fewer things than there are in heaven and earth," [10] said the Savage promptly.

"Quite so. I'll read you one of the things he *did* dream of in a moment. Meanwhile, listen to what this old Arch-Community-Songster said." He opened the book at the place marked by a slip of paper and began to read. "'We are not our own any more than what we possess is our own. We did not make ourselves, we cannot be supreme over ourselves. We are not our own masters. We are God's property. Is it not our happiness thus to view the matter? Is it any happiness or any comfort, to consider that we *are* our own? It may be thought so by the young and prosperous. These may think it a great

[8] Shakespeare, *King John.*
[9] Marie François Pierre Gonthier (1766–1824), French mystical philosopher.
[10] Shakespeare, *Hamlet.*

thing to have everything, as they suppose, their own way—to depend on no one—to have to think of nothing out of sight, to be without the irksomeness of continual acknowledgment, continual prayer, continual reference of what they do to the will of another. But as time goes on, they, as all men, will find that independence was not made for man—that it is an unnatural state—will do for a while, but will not carry us on safely to the end . . .'" Mustapha Mond paused, put down the first book and, picking up the other, turned over the pages. "Take this, for example," he said, and in his deep voice once more began to read: "'A man grows old; he feels in himself that radical sense of weakness, of listlessness, of discomfort, which accompanies the advance of age; and, feeling thus, imagines himself merely sick, lulling his fears with the notion that this distressing condition is due to some particular cause, from which, as from an illness, he hopes to recover. Vain imaginings! That sickness is old age; and a horrible disease it is. They say that it is the fear of death and of what comes after death that makes men turn to religion as they advance in years. But my own experience has given me the conviction that, quite apart from any such terrors or imaginings, the religious sentiment tends to develop as we grow older; to develop because, as the passions grow calm, as the fancy and sensibilities are less excited and less excitable, our reason becomes less troubled in its working, less obscured by the images, desires and distractions, in which it used to be absorbed; whereupon God emerges as from behind a cloud; our soul feels, sees, turns towards the source of all light; turns naturally and inevitably; for now that all that gave to the world of sensations its life and charms has begun to leak away from us, now that phenomenal existence is no more bolstered up by impressions from within or from without, we feel the need to lean on something that abides, something that will never play us false—a reality, an absolute and everlasting truth. Yes, we inevitably turn to God; for this religious sentiment is of its nature so pure, so delightful to the soul that experiences it, that it makes up to us for all our other losses.'" Mustapha Mond shut the book and leaned back in his chair. "One of the numerous things in heaven and earth that these philosophers didn't dream about was this" (he waved his hand), "us, the modern world. 'You can only be independent of God while you've got youth and prosperity; independence won't take you safely to the end.' Well, we've now got youth and prosperity right up to the end. What follows? Evidently, that we can be independent of God. 'The religious sentiment will compensate us for all our losses.' But there aren't any losses for us to compensate; religious sentiment is superfluous. And why should we go hunting for a substitute for youthful desires, when youthful desires never fail? A substitute for distractions, when we go on enjoying all the old fooleries to the very last? What need have we of repose when our minds and bodies continue to delight in activity? of consolation, when we have *soma?* of something immovable, where there is the social order?"

"Then you think there is no God?"

"No, I think there quite probably is one."

"Then why? . . ."

Mustapha Mond checked him. "But he manifests himself in different ways to different men. In premodern times he manifested himself as the being that's described in these books. Now . . ."

"How does he manifest himself now?" asked the Savage.

"Well, he manifests himself as an absence; as though he weren't there at all."

"That's your fault."

"Call it the fault of civilization. God isn't compatible with machinery and scientific medicine and universal happiness. You must make your choice. Our civilization has chosen machinery and medicine and happiness. That's why I have to keep these books locked up in the safe. They're smut. People would be shocked if . . ."

The Savage interrupted him. "But isn't it *natural* to feel there's a God?"

"You might as well ask if it's natural to do up one's trousers with zippers," said the Controller sarcastically. "You remind me of

another of those old fellows called Bradley.[11]
He defined philosophy as the finding of bad
reason for what one believes by instinct. As
if one believed anything by instinct! One
believes things because one has been conditioned to believe them. Finding bad reasons
for what one believes for other bad reasons—
that's philosophy. People believe in God because they've been conditioned to believe in
God."

"But all the same," insisted the Savage, "it
is natural to believe in God when you're
alone—quite alone, in the night, thinking
about death . . ."

"But people never are alone now," said
Mustapha Mond. "We make them hate solitude; and we arrange their lives so that it's
almost impossible for them ever to have it."

The Savage nodded gloomily. At Malpais
he had suffered because they had shut him
out from the communal activities of the
pueblo, in civilized London he was suffering
because he could never escape from those
communal activities, never be quietly alone.

"Do you remember that bit in *King Lear?*"
said the Savage at last. " 'The gods are just
and of our pleasant vices make instruments
to plague us; the dark and vicious place where
thee he got cost him his eyes,' and Edmund [12]
answers—you remember, he's wounded, he's
dying—'Thou hast spoken right; 'tis true. The
wheel has come full circle; I am here.' What
about that now? Doesn't there seem to be a
God managing things, punishing, reward-
ing?"

"Well, does there?" questioned the Controller in his turn. "You can indulge in any
number of pleasant vices with a freemartin [13]
and run no risks of having your eyes put out
by your son's mistress. 'The wheel has come
full circle; I am here.' But where would
Edmund be nowadays? Sitting in a pneu-
matic chair, with his arm round a girl's waist,
sucking away at his sex-hormone chewing-
gum and looking at the feelies. The gods are
just. No doubt. But their code of law is

dictated, in the last resort, by the people who
organize society; Providence takes its cue from
men."

"Are you sure?" asked the Savage. "Are
you quite sure that Edmund in that pneu-
matic chair hasn't been just as heavily punished as the Edmund who's wounded and
bleeding to death? The gods are just. Haven't
they used his pleasant vices as an instrument
to degrade him?"

"Degrade him from what position? As a
happy, hard-working, goods-consuming citizen
he's perfect. Of course, if you choose some
other standard than ours, then perhaps you
might say he was degraded. But you've got to
stick to one set of postulates. You can't play
Electro-magnetic Golf according to the rules
of Centrifugal Bumble-puppy."

"But value dwells not in particular will,"
said the Savage. "It holds his estimate and
dignity as well wherein 'tis precious of itself
as in the prizer." [14]

"Come, come," protested Mustapha Mond,
"that's going rather far, isn't it?"

"If you allowed yourselves to think of God,
you wouldn't allow yourselves to be degraded
by pleasant vices. You'd have a reason for
bearing things patiently, for doing things with
courage. I've seen it with the Indians."

"I'm sure you have," said Mustapha Mond.
"But then we aren't Indians. There isn't
any need for a civilized man to bear anything
that's seriously unpleasant. And as for doing
things—Ford forbid that he should get the
idea into his head. It would upset the whole
social order if men started doing things on
their own."

"What about self-denial, then? If you had
a God, you'd have a reason for self-denial."

"But industrial civilization is only possible
when there's no self-denial. Self-indulgence
up to the very limits imposed by hygiene and
economics. Otherwise the wheels stop turning."

"You'd have a reason for chastity!" said
the Savage, blushing a little as he spoke the
words.

"But chastity means passion, chastity means
neurasthenia. And passion and neurasthenia

[11] English philosopher of the nineteenth and
twentieth centuries.
[12] One of the chief villains in *King Lear.*
[13] A sterile woman.
[14] Shakespeare's *Troilus and Cressida.*

mean instability. And instability means the end of civilization. You can't have a lasting civilization without plenty of pleasant vices."

"But God's the reason for everything noble and fine and heroic. If you had a God . . ."

"My dear young friend," said Mustapha Mond, "civilization has absolutely no need of nobility or heroism. These things are symptoms of political inefficiency. In a properly organized society like ours, nobody has any opportunities for being noble or heroic. Conditions have got to be thoroughly unstable before the occasion can arise. Where there are wars, where there are divided allegiances, where there are temptations to be resisted, objects of love to be fought for or defended —there, obviously, nobility and heroism have some sense. But there aren't any wars nowadays. The greatest care is taken to prevent you from loving any one too much. There's no such thing as a divided allegiance; you're so conditioned that you can't help doing what you ought to do. And what you ought to do is on the whole so pleasant, so many of the natural impulses are allowed free play, that there really aren't any temptations to resist. And if ever, by some unlucky chance, anything unpleasant should somehow happen, why, there's always *soma* to give you a holiday from the facts. And there's always *soma* to calm your anger, to reconcile you to your enemies, to make you patient and long-suffering. In the past you could only accomplish these things by making a great effort and after years of hard moral training. Now, you swallow two or three half-gram tablets, and there you are. Anybody can be virtuous now. You can carry at least half your morality about in a bottle. Christianity without tears —that's what *soma* is."

"But the tears are necessary. Don't you remember what Othello said? 'If after every tempest came such calms, may the winds blow till they have wakened death.' There's a story one of the old Indians used to tell us, about the Girl of Mátaski. The young men who wanted to marry her had to do a morning's hoeing in her garden. It seemed easy; but there were flies and mosquitoes, magic ones. Most of the young men simply couldn't stand the biting and stinging. But the one that could—he got the girl."

"Charming! But in civilized countries," said the Controller, "you can have girls without hoeing for them; and there aren't any flies or mosquitoes to sting you. We got rid of them all centuries ago."

The Savage nodded, frowning. "You got rid of them. Yes, that's just like you. Getting rid of everything unpleasant instead of learning to put up with it. Whether 'tis better in the mind to suffer the slings and arrows of outrageous fortune, or to take arms against a sea of troubles and by opposing end them.[15] . . . But you don't do either. Neither suffer nor oppose. You just abolish the slings and arrows. It's too easy." . . .

"What you need," the Savage went on, "is something *with* tears for a change. Nothing costs enough here."

("Twelve and a half million dollars," Henry Foster had protested when the Savage told him that. "Twelve and a half million—that's what the new Conditioning Center cost. Not a cent less.")

"Exposing what is mortal and unsure to all that fortune, death and danger dare, even for an eggshell. Isn't there something in that?" he asked, looking up at Mustapha Mond. "Quite apart from God—though of course God would be a reason for it. Isn't there something in living dangerously?"

"There's a great deal in it," the Controller replied. "Men and women must have their adrenals stimulated from time to time."

"What?" questioned the Savage, uncomprehending.

"It's one of the conditions of perfect health. That's why we've made the V.P.S. treatments compulsory."

"V.P.S.?"

"Violent Passion Surrogate. Regularly once a month. We flood the whole system with adrenin. It's the complete physiological equivalent of fear and rage. All the tonic effects of murdering Desdemona and being murdered by Othello, without any of the inconveniences."

"But I like the inconveniences."

[15] *Hamlet.*

"We don't," said the Controller. "We prefer to do things comfortably."

"But I don't want comfort. I want God, I want poetry, I want real danger, I want freedom, I want goodness. I want sin."

"In fact," said Mustapha Mond, "you're claiming the right to be unhappy."

"All right then," said the Savage defiantly, "I'm claiming the right to be unhappy."

"Not to mention the right to grow old and ugly and impotent; the right to have syphilis and cancer; the right to have too little to eat; the right to be lousy; the right to live in constant apprehension of what may happen to-morrow; the right to catch typhoid; the right to be tortured by unspeakable pains of every kind." There was a long silence.

"I claim them all," said the Savage at last.

Mustapha Mond shrugged his shoulders. "You're welcome," he said.

(1932)

STUDY AIDS: 1. What is the difference in TONE between chapters 2 and 17? Which is the more effective satire, and why?

2. Who has the better of the argument in chapter 17, the Controller or the Savage? On whose side, if either, is Huxley?

3. In *Brave New World Revisited* (1958) Huxley points out how many of his "prophecies" in *Brave New World* have very nearly been realized. What present-day practices and accomplishments seem to you to match pretty well the picture of Huxley's "brave new world" as presented in chapters 2 and 17?

4. What are some of the condemnations, stated or implied, of modern life in *Brave New World*? Are these criticisms valid?

Wystan Hugh Auden
(1907–　　)

AUDEN IS DIFFICULT TO "PLACE." THIS IS SO, NOT ONLY BECAUSE WE LACK THE PERSPECtive of history, but also because his work so clearly represents the multiplicity and complexity of the modern world. There is an astonishing variety in his verse—variety of belief and attitude, and of mood, language, and form. This makes him "unpredictable," as some readers have felt, but it also makes him remarkably interesting. Few modern poets have done so much to extend the range of poetry and to demonstrate its resources.

W. H. Auden was born in York of well-to-do parents and received the education of an English gentleman. As early as his undergraduate days at Christ College, Oxford, however, he became sharply critical of his social class and turned to left-wing politics for a solution to the ills of English social and economic life. His early poems reflect his political interests. He drove an ambulance for the Loyalists in the Spanish Civil War (1936–1939), but with others of his time he lost faith in Marxian Socialism as a social panacea, and in 1939 he came to the United States, later becoming a naturalized citizen. Life in America, he felt, was most representative of the modern world, and here he would have no roots, no ties, no commitments—a free status, which he considered indispensable to an artist. His *Collected Poetry* appeared in 1945, and in 1947 *The Age of Anxiety*, which was later awarded the Pulitzer Prize.

Since his disenchantment with Socialism, Auden has not been closely associated with any group or institution. His poems reflect his acquaintance with modern tendencies in philosophy and religion, but his inherent skepticism prevents his embracing a system. He has called himself an "existentialist"—that is, one who believes man finds significance only within himself, apart from all of his social relations. Auden is thus an analyst and satirist of his time, and a poet of the isolated consciousness of the modern man, who is cut off from the past and from his fellows.

Song 25

"O where are you going?" said reader to rider,
"That valley is fatal when furnaces burn,
Yonder's the midden whose odors will madden,
That gap is the grave where the tall return."

"O do you imagine," said fearer to farer,   5
"That dusk will delay on your path to the pass,
Your diligent looking discover the lacking
Your footsteps feel from granite to grass?"

"O what was that bird," said horror to hearer,
"Did you see that shape in the twisted trees?   10
Behind you swiftly the figure comes softly,
The spot on your skin is a shocking disease?"

"Out of this house"—said rider to reader
"Yours never will"—said farer to fearer

"They're looking for you"—said hearer to horror   15
As he left them there, as he left them there.
(1932)

STUDY AIDS: 1. Work out carefully the way in which the last stanza is related to the preceding ones. Who is the "he" in the last line?

2. Structurally the poem is built around a conflict. What kinds of persons (or forces) are parties to the conflict? How is it resolved?

3. Expanded, st. 2 might read in part: "O do you imagine . . . [that] Your diligent looking [will] discover the lacking [which] Your footsteps feel [as they pass] from granite to grass?" What idea is suggested by the image of passing "from granite to grass"? What idea is suggested by the "shape in the twisted trees" (l. 10)?

Doom is Dark and Deeper Than Any Sea-Dingle

Doom is dark and deeper than any sea-dingle.[1]
Upon what man it fall
In spring, day-wishing flowers appearing,
Avalanche sliding, white snow from rock-face,
That he should leave his house,   5
No cloud-soft hand can hold him, restraint by women;
But ever that man goes
Through place-keepers, through forest trees,
A stranger to strangers over undried sea,
Houses for fishes, suffocating water,   10
Or lonely on fell [2] as chat,[3]
By pot-holed becks [4]
A bird stone-haunting, an unquiet bird.

There head falls forward, fatigued at evening,
And dreams of home,   15
Waving from window, spread of welcome,
Kissing of wife under single sheet;
But waking sees
Bird-flocks nameless to him, through doorway voices
Of new men making another love.   20

Save him from hostile capture,
From sudden tiger's spring at corner;
Protect his house,
His anxious house where days are counted
From thunderbolt protect,   25

[1] A narrow cleft on the ocean floor.
[2] A moor.
[3] A small bird.
[4] Brooks.

From gradual ruin spreading like a stain;
Converting number from vague to certain,
Bring joy, bring day of his returning,
Lucky with day approaching, with leaning
  dawn.
(1934)

STUDY AIDS: 1. In the Anglo-Saxon poem
"The Wanderer," to which the present poem
is clearly related, the spokesman laments that he
has been cast out by his lord and become an exile.
(See p. 33.) Auden's wanderer, however, is not
so much a physical as an intellectual and spiritual
exile. The theme of the poem is close to that
of "Song 25," but it is developed differently.
Describe the difference in development.

2. Auden's style, as here, is often elliptical;
he gains an effect of energy and compression by
omitting connecting words. The syntax of ll. 2–6
becomes clear if one supplies words and re-
arranges phrases as follows: "No cloud-soft hand
[nor] restraint by women can hold him—that
man upon whom it [doom] fall—[or prevent]
That he should leave his house."

3. The terse, compact phrasing and the virtual
absence of end-rhyme suggest Anglo-Saxon
verse. Other Anglo-Saxon poetic devices appear
in the poem: compound, appositive, ALLITERA-
TION. Find instances of each.

Musée des Beaux Arts [1]

About suffering they were never wrong,
The Old Masters: how well they understood
Its human position; how it takes place
While someone else is eating or opening a
  window or just walking dully along;
How, when the aged are reverently, passion-
  ately waiting   5
For the miraculous birth, there always must
  be
Children who did not specially want it to hap-
  pen, skating
On a pond at the edge of the wood:
They never forgot
That even the dreadful martyrdom must run
  its course   10
Anyhow in a corner, some untidy spot
Where the dogs go on with their doggy life
  and the torturer's horse
Scratches its innocent behind on a tree.

In Breughel's [2] *Icarus*,[3] for instance: how
  everything turns away
Quite leisurely from the disaster; the ploughman may   15
Have heard the splash, the forsaken cry,
But for him it was not an important failure;
  the sun shone
As it had to on the white legs disappearing
  into the green
Water; and the expensive delicate ship that
  must have seen
Something amazing, a boy falling out of the
  sky,   20
Had somewhere to get to and sailed calmly
  on.
(1940)

STUDY AIDS: 1. Breughel's painting, referred to in the second part of the poem, prompts
the general observation about the Old Masters
in the first part. State this observation about
life in your own words.

2. In comparison with the previous poem, is
the phrasing of this poem elliptical or full? Is
the language unusual or is it familiar and conversational? How are these stylistic qualities
suitable to the subject of the poem? How can
the surprising detail and diction of l. 13 be
justified in terms of the subject of the poem?

[1] "Museum of Fine Arts," the name of the
gallery in Brussels that houses Pieter Breughel's
painting "Icarus."
[2] Pieter Breughel (1568–1625), the noted realistic Flemish painter.
[3] In Greek legend the youth Icarus tried to
escape from Crete on artificial wings of wax,
fashioned by his father Daedalus. He flew too near
the sun, the wings melted, and he fell into the
sea and was drowned.

In Memory of W. B. Yeats

I

He disappeared in the dead of winter:
The brooks were frozen, the air-ports almost
    deserted,
And snow disfigured the public statues;
The mercury sank in the mouth of the dying
    day.
O all the instruments agree   5
The day of his death was a dark cold day.

Far from his illness
The wolves ran on through the evergreen
    forests,
The peasant river was untempted by the
    fashionable quays;
By mourning tongues   10
The death of the poet was kept from his
    poems.

But for him it was his last afternoon as him-
    self,
An afternoon of nurses and rumors;
The provinces of his body revolted,
The current of his feeling failed: he became
    his admirers.   15

Now he is scattered among a hundred cities
And wholly given over to unfamiliar affec-
    tions;
To find his happiness in another kind of wood
And be punished under a foreign code of con-
    science.
The words of a dead man   20
Are modified in the guts of the living.

But in the importance and noise of tomorrow
When the brokers are roaring like beasts on
    the floor of the Bourse,[1]
And the poor have the sufferings to which
    they are fairly accustomed,
And each in the cell of himself is almost
    convinced of his freedom;   25
A few thousand will think of this day

As one thinks of a day when one did some-
    thing slightly unusual.

O all the instruments agree
The day of his death was a dark cold day.

2

You were silly like us: your gift survived it
    all;   30
The parish of rich women, physical decay,
Yourself; mad Ireland hurt you into poetry.
Now Ireland has her madness and her
    weather still,
For poetry makes nothing happen: it survives
In the valley of its saying where executives 35
Would never want to tamper; it flows south
From ranches of isolation and the busy griefs,
Raw towns that we believe and die in; it sur-
    vives,
A way of happening, a mouth.

3

Earth, receive an honored guest;   40
William Yeats is laid to rest:
Let the Irish vessel lie
Emptied of its poetry.

Time that is intolerant
Of the brave and innocent,   45
And indifferent in a week
To a beautiful physique,

Worships language and forgives
Everyone by whom it lives;
Pardons cowardice, conceit,   50
Lays its honors at their feet.

Time that with this strange excuse
Pardoned Kipling [2] and his views,
And will pardon Paul Claudel,[3]
Pardons him for writing well.   55

[1] The stock exchange in Paris.

[2] Rudyard Kipling (1865–1936), who celebrated
British imperialism in his verse.
[3] I.e., his chauvinism. Paul Claudel (1868–   )
is an eminent French poet and diplomat.

In the nightmare of the dark
All the dogs of Europe bark,
And the living nations wait,
Each sequestered in its hate;

Intellectual disgrace　　　　　　　60
Stares from every human face,
And the seas of pity lie
Locked and frozen in each eye.

Follow, poet, follow right
To the bottom of the night,　　　　65
With your unconstraining voice
Still persuade us to rejoice;

With the farming of a verse
Make a vineyard of the curse,[4]

Sing of human unsuccess　　　　　70
In a rapture of distress;

In the deserts of the heart
Let the healing fountain start,
In the prison of his days
Teach the free man how to praise.　75
(1940)

STUDY AIDS: 1. Note the change in form, from part one to part three, in terms of: (1) line length; (2) regularity of meter; (3) rhyme. How is this change suitable to the poet's subject?

2. An extensive essay on Auden's beliefs about poetry could be derived from the suggestive and highly charged lines of this poem. Mark the passages that you think contain significant opinions, and try to state them in complete sentences.

Stephen Spender
(1909–　　)

AT SEVERAL POINTS THE CAREER OF THE POET STEPHEN SPENDER PARALLELS THAT OF HIS friend Auden. Both attended Oxford, both were convinced of the moral and intellectual bankruptcy of the English upper class, and both turned to Marxian Socialism for salvation. Spender's long didactic poem *Vienna* (1934) and his *Trial of a Judge* (1938) are strongly charged with his political convictions. His faith in radical reform was severely shaken by the Second World War, however, and his later verse, like Auden's, has been less overtly political. He has taught and lectured widely in the United States, but has remained a British subject.

In spite of these similarities, Spender's poetry is quite different from Auden's. Whereas Auden is usually detached and critically objective toward his subject, Spender seems to be personally involved. Auden is frequently harsh, bitter, and satirical; Spender, although equally distressed by modern life, often manages to achieve a soaring lyricism. The two have been compared to two of the English Romantic poets—Auden, with his mocking satire, resembling the Byron of *Don Juan*; Spender, with his deep human sympathy, his idealism, and his lyrical voice, resembling Shelley. The two poems of Spender included below exemplify his theory that "Poetry does not state truth; it states the condition within which something felt is true."

---

[4] The "curse" refers to the expulsion of Adam and Eve from Paradise. What does this couplet imply about the function of poetry?

I Think Continually of Those Who Were Truly Great

I think continually of those who were truly
  great.
Who, from the womb, remembered the soul's
  history
Through corridors of light where the hours
  are suns
Endless and singing. Whose lovely ambition
Was that their lips, still touched with fire, 5
Should tell of the Spirit clothed from head
  to foot in song.
And who hoarded from the Spring branches
The desires falling across their bodies like
  blossoms.

What is precious is never to forget
The essential delight of the blood drawn from
  ageless springs   10
Breaking through rocks in worlds before our
  earth.
Never to deny its pleasure in the morning
  simple light
Nor its grave evening demand for love.
Never to allow gradually the traffic to smother
With noise and fog the flowering of the
  spirit.   15

Near the snow, near the sun, in the highest
  fields
See how these names are feted by the waving
  grass
And by the streamers of white cloud

And whispers of wind in the listening sky.
The names of those who in their lives fought
  for life   20
Who wore at their hearts the fire's center.
Born of the sun they traveled a short while
  towards the sun,
And left the vivid air signed with their honor.
(1933)

STUDY AIDS: 1. The "truly great" probably
refers to artists and writers. What evidence in
the poem supports such an interpretation? Why
are they great?

2. Stanza 2, in contrast to sts. 1 and 3, suggests what it is in life that tends to prevent
greatness. What does "traffic" mean (l. 14)?

3. Notice the Platonic imagery of ll. 2–3, 5
(why "*still* touched"?), 7–8, and 22. How does
this imagery help to define greatness?

4. Although the lines are of unequal length
and are unrhymed, this poem was not merely
"dashed off." Several drafts of it exist, showing
the poet working for the best phrasing. Earlier
versions of the last line are: (1) "For in this
vivid air dwells their peculiar honor"; (2) "Who
on vivid air have signed their peculiar honor";
(3) "Who in vivid air expressed their peculiar
honor"; (4) "In vivid air is expressed the
peculiar honor"; (5) "Left the vivid air signed
with their peculiar honor." Although one can
not be sure why the poet settled on the final
reading, can you think of reasons why it is
better than the earlier ones?

The Express

After the first powerful plain manifesto
The black statement of pistons, without more
  fuss
But gliding like a queen, she leaves the sta-
  tion.
Without bowing and with restrained uncon-
  cern
She passes the houses which humbly crowd
  outside,   5
The gasworks and at last the heavy page

Of death, printed by gravestones in the
  cemetery.
Beyond the town there lies the open country
Where, gathering speed, she acquires
  mystery,
The luminous self-possession of ships on
  ocean.   10
It is now she begins to sing—at first quite low
Then loud, and at last with a jazzy madness—
The song of her whistle screaming at curves,

Of deafening tunnels, brakes, innumerable
  bolts.
And always light, aerial, underneath   15
Goes the elate meter of her wheels.
Steaming through metal landscape on her
  lines
She plunges new eras of wild happiness
Where speed throws up strange shapes, broad
  curves
And parallels clean like the steel of guns.   20
At last, further than Edinburgh or Rome,
Beyond the crest of the world, she reaches
  night
Where only a low streamline brightness
Of phosphorus on the tossing hills is white.
Ah, like a comet through flames she moves
  entranced   25

Wrapped in her music no bird song, no, nor
  bough
Breaking with honey buds, shall ever equal.
(1934)

STUDY AIDS: 1. The poem is a brilliant,
vivid description of a train, but it is something
more, too. Notice the progress of the train: From
a standstill it begins to move, passes houses and
graves, gathers speed and becomes "light, aerial,"
goes beyond "Edinburgh or Rome," and "reaches
night." This progress prepares for the final three
lines of the poem. What is the importance of
these final lines?
2. Instead of "elate" in l. 16, the poet in
earlier versions had written "tapping" and "raving." Is "elate" an improvement? Why or why
not?

George Orwell
(1903-1950)

ALTHOUGH HIS BOOKS BEGAN TO APPEAR AS EARLY AS 1933, GEORGE ORWELL WAS NOT
well known in the United States until the publication of *Animal Farm* (1945), a satire
on dictatorships. That book and the even more influential *Nineteen Eighty-Four* (1949)
won him many readers and established him as one of the most provocative social critics of
our time.

All his life Orwell was interested in social and political arrangements, particularly the
way in which they affect the lives of individual human beings. He was born in India (his
real name was Eric Blair) and educated at Eton, where he experienced the petty tyrannies
of English public school life, later recounted in *Such, Such Were the Joys* (1953). His experiences when he returned to the Orient are the subject of *Burmese Days* (1934) and
the essay "Shooting an Elephant." For a time he lived a hand-to-mouth existence in European cities, compulsively undergoing a self-imposed poverty that showed him how the
poor live and die; he described the experience vividly in *Down and Out in Paris and
London* (1933). *Homage to Catalonia* (1938) is based on his service with the Loyalist
army in the Spanish Civil War. His alarm at the growing menace of totalitarianism
prompted the influential satires mentioned above.

Orwell's sympathies were with the political "left." He was always skeptical of systems,
programs, and parties, however, because he felt that they tended to lose sight of the needs
of individuals. It was this feeling, at first only a suspicion with Orwell but later a real
fear, that informs *Nineteen Eighty-Four*. He believed that governments, increasingly more
highly organized and more efficient, are becoming ends in themselves; although their
reforms are ostensibly made for the benefit of the people, their chief aim is the perpetu-

ation of their own power. Indifferent to the individual at first, they come more and more to regard him as a threat that must be suppressed. This tendency is probably further advanced in some countries than in others; but one seriously misreads Orwell's book if he thinks it applies to those countries alone. It presents a twentieth-century dilemma which knows no national boundaries.

Orwell wanted to make political writing an art. Seriously interested in language and prose style, he deplored the tendency of modern prose to favor the abstract over the concrete term, the flabby or pretentious expression over the direct and honest one. His concern was not only aesthetic; he discerned a real relationship between language habits and political development. In the world of *Nineteen Eighty-Four* one of the state's chief instruments in maintaining an absolute tyranny is "Newspeak," a language from which have been excluded all words necessary to the formulation of a free thought. Orwell himself wrote a vivid, concrete prose that enabled him, in the words of the *Partisan Review's* citation of merit in 1949, to achieve "a scrupulous fidelity to his experience that has placed him in that very valuable class of the writer who is a witness of his time."

Nineteen Eighty-Four

When the story opens, the super state is already in operation. How it came into being is best revealed in "the book," a historical account by one Emmanuel Goldstein, once a respected party leader, but long since out of favor. In fact Goldstein, who escaped from the state some time before the story takes place, is officially regarded as the state's chief betrayer. As such, he is often the central object of the "two-minute hate."

I

It was a bright cold day in April, and the clocks were striking thirteen. Winston Smith, his chin muzzled into his breast in an effort 5 to escape the vile wind, slipped quickly through the glass doors of Victory Mansions, though not quickly enough to prevent a swirl of gritty dust from entering along with him.

The hallway smelled of boiled cabbage and 10 old rag mats. At one end of it a colored poster, too large for indoor display, had been tacked to the wall. It depicted simply an enormous face, more than a meter wide: the face of a man of about forty-five, with a heavy 15 black mustache and ruggedly handsome features. Winston made for the stairs. It was no use trying the lift. Even at the best of times it was seldom working, and at present the electric current was cut off during daylight 20 hours. It was part of the economy drive in preparation for Hate Week. The flat was seven flights up, and Winston, who was thirty-nine, and had a varicose ulcer above his right ankle, went slowly, resting several times on the way. On each landing, opposite the lift shaft, the poster with the enormous face gazed from the wall. It was one of those pictures which are so contrived that the eyes follow you about when you move. BIG BROTHER IS WATCHING YOU, the caption beneath it ran.

Inside the flat a fruity voice was reading out a list of figures which had something to do with the production of pig iron. The voice came from an oblong metal plaque like a dulled mirror which formed part of the surface of the right-hand wall. Winston turned a switch and the voice sank somewhat, though the words were still distinguishable. The instrument (the telescreen, it was called) could be dimmed, but there was no way of shutting it off completely. He moved over to the window: a smallish, frail figure, the meagerness of his body merely emphasized by the blue overalls which were the uniform of the Party. His hair was very fair, his face naturally sanguine, his skin roughened by coarse soap and blunt razor blades and the cold of the winter that had just ended.

Outside, even through the shut window pane, the world looked cold. Down in the street little eddies of wind were whirling dust and torn paper into spirals, and though the sun was shining and the sky a harsh blue, there seemed to be no color in anything except the posters that were plastered everywhere. The black-mustachioed face gazed down from every commanding corner. There was one on the house front immediately opposite. BIG BROTHER IS WATCHING YOU, the caption said, while the dark eyes looked deep into Winston's own. Down at street level another poster, torn at one corner, flapped fitfully in the wind, alternately covering and uncovering the single word INGSOC. In the far distance a helicopter skimmed down between the roofs, hovered for an instant like a blue-bottle, and darted away again with a curving flight. It was the Police Patrol, snooping into people's windows. The patrols did not matter, however. Only the Thought Police mattered.

Behind Winston's back the voice from the telescreen was still babbling away about pig iron and the overfulfilment of the Ninth Three-Year Plan. The telescreen received and transmitted simultaneously. Any sound that Winston made, above the level of a very low whisper, would be picked up by it; moreover, so long as he remained within the field of vision which the metal plaque commanded, he could be seen as well as heard. There was of course no way of knowing whether you were being watched at any given moment. How often, or on what system, the Thought Police plugged in on any individual wire was guesswork. It was even conceivable that they watched everybody all the time. But at any rate they could plug in your wire whenever they wanted to. You had to live—did live, from habit that became instinct—in the assumption that every sound you made was overheard, and, except in darkness, every movement scrutinized.

Winston kept his back turned to the telescreen. It was safer; though, as he well knew, even a back can be revealing. A kilometer away the Ministry of Truth, his place of work, towered vast and white above the grimy landscape. This, he thought with a sort of vague distaste—this was London, chief city of Airstrip One, itself the third most populous of the provinces of Oceania. He tried to squeeze out some childhood memory that should tell him whether London had always been quite like this. Were there always these vistas of rotting nineteenth-century houses, their sides shored up with balks of timber, their windows patched with cardboard and their roofs with corrugated iron, their crazy garden walls sagging in all directions? And the bombed sites where the plaster dust swirled in the air and the willow herb straggled over the heaps of rubble; and the places where the bombs had cleared a larger patch and there had sprung up sordid colonies of wooden dwellings like chicken houses? But it was no use, he could not remember: nothing remained of his childhood except a series of bright-lit tableaux, occurring against no background and mostly unintelligible.

The Ministry of Truth—Minitrue, in Newspeak [1] was startlingly different from any other object in sight. It was an enormous pyramidal structure of glittering white concrete, soaring up, terrace after terrace, three hundred meters into the air. From where Winston stood it was just possible to read, picked out on its white face in elegant lettering, the three slogans of the Party:

WAR IS PEACE
FREEDOM IS SLAVERY
IGNORANCE IS STRENGTH.

The Ministry of Truth contained, it was said, three thousand rooms above ground level, and

[1] "Newspeak was the official language of Oceania." [Orwell's note.] In an Appendix, "The Principles of Newspeak," Orwell explains this language. "It was intended," he says, "that when Newspeak had been adopted once and for all and Oldspeak forgotten, a heretical thought—that is, a thought diverging from the principles of Ingsoc—should be literally unthinkable, at least so far as thought is dependent on words." The word "free" existed in Newspeak, but only in the sense of "This dog is free from lice." It could not be used in such a phrase as "intellectually free," since intellectual freedom did not exist and so no word for it was needed.

corresponding ramifications below. Scattered about London there were just three other buildings of similar appearance and size. So completely did they dwarf the surrounding architecture that from the roof of Victory Mansions you could see all four of them simultaneously. They were the homes of the four Ministries between which the entire apparatus of government was divided: the Ministry of Truth, which concerned itself with news, entertainment, education, and the fine arts; the Ministry of Peace, which concerned itself with war; the Ministry of Love, which maintained law and order; and the Ministry of Plenty, which was responsible for economic affairs. Their names, in Newspeak: Minitrue, Minipax, Miniluv, and Miniplenty.

The Ministry of Love was the really frightening one. There were no windows in it at all. Winston had never been inside the Ministry of Love, nor within half a kilometer of it. It was a place impossible to enter except on official business, and then only by penetrating through a maze of barbed-wire entanglements, steel doors, and hidden machine-gun nests. Even the streets leading up to its outer barriers were roamed by gorilla-faced guards in black uniforms, armed with jointed truncheons.

Winston turned round abruptly. He had set his features into the expression of quiet optimism which it was advisable to wear when facing the telescreen. He crossed the room into the tiny kitchen. By leaving the Ministry at this time of day he had sacrificed his lunch in the canteen, and he was aware that there was no food in the kitchen except a hunk of dark-colored bread which had got to be saved for tomorrow's breakfast. He took down from the shelf a bottle of colorless liquid with a plain white label marked VICTORY GIN. It gave off a sickly, oily smell, as of Chinese rice-spirit. Winston poured out nearly a teacupful, nerved himself for a shock, and gulped it down like a dose of medicine.

Instantly his face turned scarlet and the water ran out of his eyes. The stuff was like nitric acid, and moreover, in swallowing it one had the sensation of being hit on the back of the head with a rubber club. The next moment, however, the burning in his belly died down and the world began to look more cheerful. He took a cigarette from a crumpled packet marked VICTORY CIGARETTES and incautiously held it upright, whereupon the tobacco fell out onto the floor. With the next he was more successful. He went back to the living room and sat down at a small table that stood to the left of the telescreen. From the table drawer he took out a penholder, a bottle of ink, and a thick, quarto-sized blank book with a red back and a marbled cover.

For some reason the telescreen in the living room was in an unusual position. Instead of being placed, as was normal, in the end wall, where it could command the whole room, it was in the longer wall, opposite the window. To one side of it there was a shallow alcove in which Winston was now sitting, and which, when the flats were built, had probably been intended to hold bookshelves. By sitting in the alcove, and keeping well back, Winston was able to remain outside the range of the telescreen, so far as sight went. He could be heard, of course, but so long as he stayed in his present position he could not be seen. It was partly the unusual geography of the room that had suggested to him the thing that he was now about to do.

But it had also been suggested by the book that he had just taken out of the drawer. It was a peculiarly beautiful book. Its smooth creamy paper, a little yellowed by age, was of a kind that had not been manufactured for at least forty years past. He could guess, however, that the book was much older than that. He had seen it lying in the window of a frowsy little junk shop in a slummy quarter of the town (just what quarter he did not now remember) and had been stricken immediately by an overwhelming desire to possess it. Party members were supposed not to go into ordinary shops ("dealing on the free market," it was called), but the rule was not strictly kept, because there were various things such as shoelaces and razor blades which it was impossible to get hold of in any other way. He had given a quick glance up and down the street and then had slipped inside and bought the book for two dollars fifty. At the time he was not conscious of wanting it for any particular purpose. He had carried it guiltily home in his brief case. Even with nothing written in it, it was a compromising possession.

The thing that he was about to do was to open a diary. This was not illegal (nothing was illegal, since there were no longer any laws), but if detected it was reasonably certain that it would be punished by death, or at least by twenty-five years in a forced-labor camp. Winston fitted a nib into the penholder and sucked it to get the grease off. The pen was an archaic instrument, seldom used even for signatures, and he had procured one, furtively and with some difficulty, simply because of a feeling that the beautiful creamy paper deserved to be written on with a real nib instead of being scratched with an ink pencil. Actually he was not used to writing by hand. Apart from very short notes, it was usual to dictate everything into the speak-write, which was of course impossible for his present purpose. He dipped the pen into the ink and then faltered for just a second. A tremor had gone through his bowels. To mark the paper was the decisive act. In small clumsy letters he wrote:

April 4th, 1984.

He sat back. A sense of complete helplessness had descended upon him. To begin with, he did not know with any certainty that this *was* 1984. It must be round about that date, since he was fairly sure that his age was thirty-nine, and he believed that he had been born in 1944 or 1945; but it was never possible nowadays to pin down any date within a year or two.

For whom, it suddenly occurred to him to wonder, was he writing this diary? For the future, for the unborn. His mind hovered for a moment round the doubtful date on the page, and then fetched up with a bump against the Newspeak word *doublethink*. For the first time the magnitude of what he had undertaken came home to him. How could you communicate with the future? It was of its nature impossible. Either the future

would resemble the present, in which case it would not listen to him, or it would be different from it, and his predicament would be meaningless.

For some time he sat gazing stupidly at the paper. The telescreen had changed over to strident military music. It was curious that he seemed not merely to have lost the power of expressing himself, but even to have forgotten what it was that he had originally intended to say. For weeks past he had been making ready for this moment, and it had never crossed his mind that anything would be needed except courage. The actual writing would be easy. All he had to do was to transfer to paper the interminable restless monologue that had been running inside his head, literally for years. At this moment, however, even the monologue had dried up. Moreover, his varicose ulcer had begun itching unbearably. He dared not scratch it, because if he did so it always became inflamed. The seconds were ticking by. He was conscious of nothing except the blankness of the page in front of him, the itching of the skin above his ankle, the blaring of the music, and a slight booziness caused by the gin.

Suddenly he began writing in sheer panic, only imperfectly aware of what he was setting down. His small but childish handwriting straggled up and down the page, shedding first its capital letters and finally even its full stops:

April 4th; 1984. Last night to the flicks. All war films. One very good one of a ship full of refugees being bombed somewhere in the Mediterranean. Audience much amused by shots of a great huge fat man trying to swim away with a helicopter after him. first you saw him wallowing along in the water like a porpoise, then you saw him through the helicopters gunsights, then he was full of holes and the sea round him turned pink and he sank as suddenly as though the holes had let in the water. audience shouting with laughter when he sank. then you saw a lifeboat full of children with a helicopter hovering over it. there was a middleaged woman might have been a jewess sitting up in the bow with a little boy about three years old in her arms. little boy screaming with fright and hiding his head between her breasts as if he was trying to burrow right into her and the woman putting her arms around him and comforting him although she was blue with fright herself. all the time covering him up as much as possible as if she thought her arms could keep the bullets off him. then the helicopter planted a 20 kilo bomb in among them terrific flash and the boat went all to matchwood. then there was a wonderful shot of a childs arm going up up up right up into the air a helicopter with a camera in its nose must have followed it up and there was a lot of applause from the party seats but a woman down in the prole part of the house suddenly started kicking up a fuss and shouting they didn't oughter of showed it not in front of the kids they didnt it aint right not in front of kids it aint until the police turned her turned her out i don't suppose anything happened to her nobody cares what the proles say typical prole reaction they never—

Winston stopped writing, partly because he was suffering from cramp. He did not know what had made him pour out this stream of rubbish. But the curious thing was that while he was doing so a totally different memory had clarified itself in his mind, to the point where he almost felt equal to writing it down. It was, he now realized, because of this other incident that he had suddenly decided to come home and begin the diary today.

It had happened that morning at the Ministry, if anything so nebulous could be said to happen.

It was nearly eleven hundred, and in the Records Department, where Winston worked, they were dragging the chairs out of the cubicles and grouping them in the center of the hall, opposite the big telescreen, in preparation for the Two Minutes Hate. Winston was just taking his place in one of the middle rows when two people whom he knew by sight, but had never spoken to, came unexpectedly into the room. One of them was a girl whom he often passed in the corridors. He did not know her name, but he knew that she worked in the Fiction Department. Pre-

sumably—since he had sometimes seen her with oily hands and carrying a spanner—she had some mechanical job on one of the novel-writing machines. She was a bold-looking girl of about twenty-seven, with thick dark hair, a freckled face, and swift, athletic movements. A narrow scarlet sash, emblem of the Junior Anti-Sex League, was wound several times around the waist of her overalls, just tightly enough to bring out the shapeliness of her hips. Winston had disliked her from the very first moment of seeing her. He knew the reason. It was because of the atmosphere of hockey fields and cold baths and community hikes and general clean-mindedness which she managed to carry about with her. He disliked nearly all women, and especially the young and pretty ones. It was always the women, and above all the young ones, who were the most bigoted adherents of the Party, the swallowers of slogans, the amateur spies and nosers-out of unorthodoxy. But this particular girl gave him the impression of being more dangerous than most. Once when they passed in the corridor she had given him a quick sidelong glance which seemed to pierce right into him and for a moment had filled him with black terror. The idea had even crossed his mind that she might be an agent of the Thought Police. That, it was true, was very unlikely. Still, he continued to feel a peculiar uneasiness, which had fear mixed up in it as well as hostility, whenever she was anywhere near him.

The other person was a man named O'Brien, a member of the Inner Party and holder of some post so important and remote that Winston had only a dim idea of its nature. A momentary hush passed over the group of people round the chairs as they saw the black overalls of an Inner Party member approaching. O'Brien was a large, burly man with a thick neck and a coarse, humorous, brutal face. In spite of his formidable appearance he had a certain charm of manner. He had a trick of resetting his spectacles on his nose which was curiously disarming—in some indefinable way, curiously civilized. It was a gesture which, if anyone had still thought in such terms, might have recalled an eighteenth-century nobleman offering his snuffbox. Winston had seen O'Brien perhaps a dozen times in almost as many years. He felt deeply drawn to him, and not solely because he was intrigued by the contrast between O'Brien's urbane manner and his prizefighter's physique. Much more it was because of a secretly held belief—or perhaps not even a belief, merely a hope—that O'Brien's political orthodoxy was not perfect. Something in his face suggested it irresistibly. And again, perhaps it was not even unorthodoxy that was written in his face, but simply intelligence. But at any rate he had the appearance of being a person that you could talk to, if somehow you could cheat the telescreen and get him alone. Winston had never made the smallest effort to verify this guess; indeed, there was no way of doing so. At this moment O'Brien glanced at his wristwatch, saw that it was nearly eleven hundred, and evidently decided to stay in the Records Department until the Two Minutes Hate was over. He took a chair in the same row as Winston, a couple of places away. A small, sandy-haired woman who worked in the next cubicle to Winston was between them. The girl with dark hair was sitting immediately behind.

The next moment a hideous, grinding screech, as of some monstrous machine running without oil, burst from the big telescreen at the end of the room. It was a noise that set one's teeth on edge and bristled the hair at the back of one's neck. The Hate had started.

As usual, the face of Emmanuel Goldstein, the Enemy of the People, had flashed onto the screen. There were hisses here and there among the audience. The little sandy-haired woman gave a squeak of mingled fear and disgust. Goldstein was the renegade and backslider who once, long ago (how long ago, nobody quite remembered), had been one of the leading figures of the Party, almost on a level with Big Brother himself, and then had engaged in counter-revolutionary activities, had been condemned to death, and had mysteriously escaped and disappeared. The program of the Two Minutes Hate varied from day to day, but there was none in which

Goldstein was not the principal figure. He was the primal traitor, the earliest defiler of the Party's purity. All subsequent crimes against the Party, all treacheries, acts of sabotage, heresies, deviations, sprang directly out of his teaching. Somewhere or other he was still alive and hatching his conspiracies: perhaps somewhere beyond the sea, under the protection of his foreign paymasters; perhaps even—so it was occasionally rumored—in some hiding place in Oceania itself.

Winston's diaphragm was constricted. He could never see the face of Goldstein without a painful mixture of emotions. It was a lean Jewish face, with a great fuzzy aureole of white hair and a small goatee beard—a clever face, and yet somehow inherently despicable, with a kind of senile silliness in the long thin nose near the end of which a pair of spectacles was perched. It resembled the face of a sheep, and the voice, too, had a sheeplike quality. Goldstein was delivering his usual venomous attack upon the doctrines of the Party—an attack so exaggerated and perverse that a child should have been able to see through it, and yet just plausible enough to fill one with an alarmed feeling that other people, less level-headed than oneself, might be taken in by it. He was abusing Big Brother, he was denouncing the dictatorship of the Party, he was demanding the immediate conclusion of peace with Eurasia, he was advocating freedom of speech, freedom of the press, freedom of assembly, freedom of thought, he was crying hysterically that the revolution had been betrayed—and all this in rapid polysyllabic speech which was a sort of parody of the habitual style of the orators of the Party, and even contained Newspeak words: more Newspeak words, indeed, than any Party member would normally use in real life. And all the while, lest one should be in any doubt as to the reality which Goldstein's specious claptrap covered, behind his head on the telescreen there marched the endless columns of the Eurasian army—row after row of solid-looking men with expressionless Asiatic faces, who swam up to the surface of the screen and vanished, to be replaced by others exactly similar. The dull, rhythmic tramp of the soldiers' boots formed the background to Goldstein's bleating voice.

Before the Hate had proceeded for thirty seconds, uncontrollable exclamations of rage were breaking out from half the people in the room. The self-satisfied sheeplike face on the screen, and the terrifying power of the Eurasian army behind it, were too much to be borne; besides, the sight or even the thought of Goldstein produced fear and anger automatically. He was an object of hatred more constant than either Eurasia or Eastasia, since when Oceania was at war with one of these powers it was generally at peace with the other. But what was strange was that although Goldstein was hated and despised by everybody, although every day, and a thousand times a day, on platforms, on the telescreen, in newspapers, in books, his theories were refuted, smashed, ridiculed, held up to the general gaze for the pitiful rubbish that they were—in spite of all this, his influence never seemed to grow less. Always there were fresh dupes waiting to be seduced by him. A day never passed when spies and saboteurs acting under his directions were not unmasked by the Thought Police. He was the commander of a vast shadowy army, an underground network of conspirators dedicated to the overthrow of the State. The Brotherhood, its name was supposed to be. There were also whispered stories of a terrible book, a compendium of all the heresies, of which Goldstein was the author and which circulated clandestinely here and there. It was a book without a title. People referred to it, if at all, simply as *the book*. But one knew of such things only through vague rumors. Neither the Brotherhood nor *the book* was a subject that any ordinary Party member would mention if there was a way of avoiding it.

In its second minute the Hate rose to a frenzy. People were leaping up and down in their places and shouting at the tops of their voices in an effort to drown the maddening bleating voice that came from the screen. The little sandy-haired woman had turned bright pink, and her mouth was opening and shutting like that of a landed fish. Even O'Brien's heavy face was flushed. He was sitting very straight in his chair, his powerful chest swelling and quivering as though he were standing up to the assault of a wave. The dark-haired girl behind Winston had begun crying out "Swine! Swine! Swine!" and suddenly she picked up a heavy Newspeak dictionary and flung it at the screen. It struck Goldstein's nose and bounced off; the voice continued inexorably. In a lucid moment Winston found that he was shouting with the others and kicking his heel violently against the rung of his chair. The horrible thing about the Two Minutes Hate was not that one was obliged to act a part, but that it was impossible to avoid joining in. Within thirty seconds any pretense was always unnecessary. A hideous ecstasy of fear and vindictiveness, a desire to kill, to torture, to smash faces in with a sledge hammer, seemed to flow through the whole group of people like an electric current, turning one even against one's will into a grimacing, screaming lunatic. And yet the rage that one felt was an abstract, undirected emotion which could be switched from one object to another like the flame of a blowlamp. Thus, at one moment Winston's hatred was not turned against Goldstein at all, but, on the contrary, against Big Brother, the Party, and the Thought Police; and at such moments his heart went out to the lonely, derided heretic on the screen, sole guardian of truth and sanity in a world of lies. And yet the very next instant he was at one with the people about him, and all that was said of Goldstein seemed to him to be true. At those moments his secret loathing of Big Brother changed into adoration, and Big Brother seemed to tower up, an invincible, fearless protector, standing like a rock against the hordes of Asia, and Goldstein, in spite of his isolation, his helplessness, and the doubt that hung about his very existence, seemed like some sinister enchanter, capable by the mere power of his voice of wrecking the structure of civilization.

It was even possible, at moments, to switch one's hatred this way or that by a voluntary act. Suddenly, by the sort of violent effort with which one wrenches one's head away from the pillow in a nightmare, Winston succeeded in transferring his hatred from the face on the screen to the dark-haired girl behind him. Vivid, beautiful hallucinations flashed through his mind. He would flog her to death with a rubber truncheon. He would tie her naked to a stake and shoot her full of arrows like Saint Sebastian. He would ravish her and cut her throat at the moment of climax. Better than before, moreover, he realized *why* it was that he hated her. He hated her because she was young and pretty and sexless, because he wanted to go to bed with her and would never do so, because round her sweet supple waist, which seemed to ask you to encircle it with your arm, there was only the odious scarlet sash, aggressive symbol of chastity.

The Hate rose to its climax. The voice of Goldstein had become an actual sheep's bleat, and for an instant the face changed into that of a sheep. Then the sheep-face melted into the figure of a Eurasian soldier who seemed to be advancing, huge and terrible, his submachine gun roaring, and seeming to spring out of the surface of the screen, so that some of the people in the front row actually flinched backwards in their seats. But in the same moment, drawing a deep sigh of relief from everybody, the hostile figure melted into the face of Big Brother, black-haired, black mustachioed, full of power and mysterious calm, and so vast that it almost filled up the screen. Nobody heard what Big Brother was saying. It was merely a few words of encouragement, the sort of words that are uttered in the din of battle, not distinguishable individually but restoring confidence by the fact of being spoken. Then the face of Big Brother faded away again, and instead the three slogans of the Party stood out in bold capitals:

WAR IS PEACE
FREEDOM IS SLAVERY
IGNORANCE IS STRENGTH.

But the face of Big Brother seemed to persist for several seconds on the screen, as though the impact that it had made on everyone's eyeballs were too vivid to wear off immediately. The little sandy-haired woman had flung herself forward over the back of the chair in front of her. With a tremulous murmur that sounded like "My Savior!" she extended her arms toward the screen. Then she buried her face in her hands. It was apparent that she was uttering a prayer.

At this moment the entire group of people broke into a deep, slow, rhythmical chant of "B-B! . . . B-B! . . . B-B!" over and over again, very slowly, with a long pause between the first "B" and the second—a heavy, murmurous sound, somehow curiously savage, in the background of which one seemed to hear the stamp of naked feet and the throbbing of tom-toms. For perhaps as much as thirty seconds they kept it up. It was a refrain that was often heard in moments of overwhelming emotion. Partly it was a sort of hymn to the wisdom and majesty of Big Brother, but still more it was an act of self-hypnosis, a deliberate drowning of consciousness by means of rhythmic noise. Winston's entrails seemed to grow cold. In the Two Minutes Hate he could not help sharing in the general delirium, but this sub-human chanting of "B-B! . . . B-B!" always filled him with horror. Of course he chanted with the rest: it was impossible to do otherwise. To dissemble your feelings, to control your face, to do what everyone else was doing, was an instinctive reaction. But there was a space of a couple of seconds during which the expression in his eyes might conceivably have betrayed him. And it was exactly at this moment that the significant thing happened —if, indeed, it did happen.

Momentarily he caught O'Brien's eye. O'Brien had stood up. He had taken off his spectacles and was in the act of resetting them on his nose with his characteristic gesture. But there was a fraction of a second when their eyes met, and for as long as it took to happen Winson knew—yes, he *knew!* —that O'Brien was thinking the same thing as himself. An unmistakable message had passed. It was as though their two minds had opened and the thoughts were flowing from one into the other through their eyes. "I am with you," O'Brien seemed to be saying to him. "I know precisely what you are feeling. I know all about your contempt, your hatred, your disgust. But don't worry, I am on your side!" And then the flash of intelligence was gone, and O'Brien's face was as inscrutable as everybody else's.

That was all, and he was already uncertain whether it had happened. Such incidents never had any sequel. All that they did was to keep alive in him the belief, or hope, that others besides himself were the enemies of the Party. Perhaps the rumors of vast underground conspiracies were true after all—perhaps the Brotherhood really existed! It was impossible, in spite of the endless arrests and confessions and executions, to be sure that the Brotherhood was not simply a myth. Some days he believed in it, some days not. There was no evidence, only fleeting glimpses that might mean anything or nothing: snatches of overheard conversation, faint scribbles on lavatory walls—once, even, when two strangers met, a small movement of the hands which had looked as though it might be a signal of recognition. It was all guesswork: very likely he had imagined everything. He had gone back to his cubicle without looking at O'Brien again. The idea of following up their momentary contact hardly crossed his mind. It would have been inconceivably dangerous even if he had known how to set about doing it. For a second, two seconds, they had exchanged an equivocal glance, and that was the end of the story. But even that was a memorable event, in the locked loneliness in which one had to live.

Winston roused himself and sat up straighter. He let out a belch. The gin was rising from his stomach.

His eyes refocused on the page. He discovered that while he sat helplessly musing he had also been writing, as though by automatic action. And it was no longer the same cramped awkward handwriting as before. His pen had slid voluptuously over the smooth paper, printing in large neat capitals—

DOWN WITH BIG BROTHER
DOWN WITH BIG BROTHER
DOWN WITH BIG BROTHER
DOWN WITH BIG BROTHER
DOWN WITH BIG BROTHER

over and over again, filling half a page.

He could not help feeling a twinge of panic. It was absurd, since the writing of those particular words was not more dangerous than the initial act of opening the diary; but for a moment he was tempted to tear out the spoiled pages and abandon the enterprise altogether.

But he did not do so, however, because he knew that it was useless. Whether he wrote DOWN WITH BIG BROTHER, or whether he refrained from writing it, made no difference. Whether he went on with the diary, or whether he did not go on with it, made no difference. The Thought Police would get him just the same. He had committed—would still have committed, even if he had never set pen to paper—the essential crime that contained all others in itself. Thoughtcrime, they called it. Thoughtcrime was not a thing that could be concealed forever. You might dodge successfully for a while, even for years, but sooner or later they were bound to get you.

It was always at night—the arrests invariably happened at night. The sudden jerk out of sleep, the rough hand shaking your shoulder, the lights glaring in your eyes, the ring of hard faces round the bed. In the vast majority of cases there was no trial, no report of the arrest. People simply disappeared, always during the night. Your name was removed from the registers, every record of everything you had ever done was wiped out, your one-time existence was denied and then forgotten. You were abolished, annihilated: *vaporized* was the usual word.

For a moment he was seized by a kind of hysteria. He began writing in a hurried untidy scrawl:

theyll shoot me i dont care theyll shoot me in the back of the neck i dont care down with big brother they always shoot you in the back of the neck i dont care down with big brother

He sat back in his chair, slightly ashamed of himself, and laid down his pen. The next moment he started violently. There was a knocking at his door.

Already! He sat as still as a mouse, in the futile hope that whoever it was might go away after a single attempt. But no, the knocking was repeated. The worst thing of all would be to delay. His heart was thumping like a drum, but his face, from long habit, was probably expressionless. He got up and moved heavily toward the door.

[Later, Winston meets Julia, who appears to be a loyal member of the Party, but who loathes the New Order quite as much as he. They often meet secretly. In the following passage Winston reads to her from the banned book, *The Theory and Practice of Oligarchical Collectivism,* by Emmanuel Goldstein.]

The clock's hands said six, meaning eighteen. They had three or four hours ahead of them. He propped the book against his knees and began reading:

Chapter 1.

IGNORANCE IS STRENGTH.

Throughout recorded time, and probably since the end of the Neolithic Age, there have been three kinds of people in the world, the High, the Middle, and the Low. They have been subdivided in many ways, they have borne countless different names, and their relative numbers, as well as their attitude toward one another, have varied from age to age; but the essential structure of society has never altered. Even after enormous upheavals and seemingly irrevocable changes, the same pattern has always reasserted itself, just as a gyroscope will always return to equilibrium, however far it is pushed one way or the other.

"Julia, are you awake?" said Winston.

"Yes, my love, I'm listening. Go on. It's marvelous."

He continued reading:

The aims of these three groups are entirely irreconcilable. The aim of the High is to remain where they are. The aim of the Middle is to change places with the High. The aim of the Low, when they have an aim— for it is an abiding characteristic of the Low that they are too much crushed by drudgery to be more than intermittently conscious of anything outside their daily lives—is to abolish all distinctions and create a society in which all men shall be equal. Thus throughout history a struggle which is the same in its main outlines recurs over and over again. For long periods the High

seem to be securely in power, but sooner or later there always comes a moment when they lose either their belief in themselves, or their capacity to govern efficiently, or both. They are then overthrown by the Middle, who enlist the Low on their side by pretending to them that they are fighting for liberty and justice. As soon as they have reached their objective, the Middle thrust the Low back into their old position of servitude, and themselves become the High. Presently a new Middle group splits off from one of the other groups, or from both of them, and the struggle begins over again. Of the three groups, only the Low are never even temporarily successful in achieving their aims. It would be an exaggeration to say that throughout history there had been no progress of a material kind. Even today, in a period of decline, the average human being is physically better off than he was a few centuries ago. But no advance in wealth, no softening of manners, no reform or revolution has ever brought human equality a millimeter nearer. From the point of view of the Low, no historic change has ever meant much more than a change in the name of their masters.

By the late nineteenth century the recurrences of this pattern had become obvious to many observers. There then arose schools of thinkers who interpreted history as a cyclical process and claimed to show that inequality was the unalterable law of human life. This doctrine, of course, had always had its adherents, but in the manner in which it was now put forward there was a significant change. In the past the need for a hierarchical form of society had been the doctrine specifically of the High. It had been preached by kings and aristocrats and by the priests, lawyers, and the like who were parasitical upon them, and it had generally been softened by promises of compensation in an imaginary world beyond the grave. The Middle, so long as it was struggling for power, had always made use of such terms as freedom, justice, and fraternity. Now, however, the concept of human brotherhood began to be assailed by people who were not yet in positions of command, but merely hoped to be so before long. In the past the Middle had made revolutions under the banner of equality, and then had established a fresh tyranny as soon as the old one was overthrown. The new Middle groups in effect proclaimed their tyranny beforehand. Socialism, a theory which appeared in the early nineteenth century and was the last link in a chain of thought stretching back to the slave rebellions of antiquity, was still deeply infected by the Utopianism of past ages. But in each variant of Socialism that appeared from about 1900 onwards the aim of establishing liberty and equality was more and more openly abandoned. The new movements which appeared in the middle years of the century, Ingsoc in Oceania, Neo-Bolshevism in Eurasia, Death-worship, as it is commonly called, in Eastasia, had the conscious aim of perpetuating *un*freedom and *in*equality. These new movements, of course, grew out of the old ones and tended to keep their names and pay lip-service to their ideology. But the purpose of all of them was to arrest progress and freeze history at a chosen moment. The familiar pendulum swing was to happen once more, and then stop. As usual, the High were to be turned out by the Middle, who would then become the High; but this time, by conscious strategy, the High would be able to maintain their position permanently.

The new doctrines arose partly because of the accumulation of historical knowledge, and the growth of the historical sense, which had hardly existed before the nineteenth century. The cyclical movement of history was now intelligible, or appeared to be so; and if it was intelligible, then it was alterable. But the principal, underlying cause was that, as early as the beginning of the twentieth century, human equality had become technically possible. It was still true that men were not equal in their native talents and that functions had to be specialized in ways that favored some individuals against others; but there was no longer any real need for class distinctions or for large differences of wealth. In earlier ages, class distinctions had been not only inevitable but desirable. Inequality was the price of civilization. With the development of machine production, however, the case was altered. Even if it was still necessary for human beings to do different kinds of work, it was no longer necessary for them to live at different social or economic levels. Therefore, from the point of view of the new groups who were on the point of seizing power, human equality was no longer an ideal to be striven after, but a danger to be averted. In more primitive ages, when a just and peaceful society was in fact not possible, it had been fairly easy to believe in it. The idea of an earthly paradise in which men should live together in a state of brotherhood, without laws and without brute labor, had haunted the human imagination for thousands of years. And this vision had had a certain hold even on the groups who actually profited by each historic change. The heirs of the French, English, and American revolutions had partly believed in their own phrases about the rights of man, freedom of speech, equality before the law, and the like, and had even allowed their conduct to be influenced by them to some extent. But by the fourth decade of the twentieth century all the main currents of political thought were authoritarian. The earthly paradise had been discredited at exactly the moment when it became realizable. Every new political theory, by whatever name it called itself, led back to hierarchy and regimentation. And in the general hardening of outlook that set in round about 1930, practices which had been long abandoned, in some cases for hundreds of years—imprisonment without trial, the use of war prisoners as slaves, public executions, torture to extract confessions, the use of hostages and the deportation of whole populations—not only became common again, but were tolerated and even defended by people who considered themselves enlightened and progressive.

It was only after a decade of national wars, civil wars, revolutions and counterrevolutions in all parts of the world that Ingsoc and its rivals emerged as fully worked-out political theories. But they had been foreshadowed by the various systems, generally called totalitarian, which had appeared earlier in the century, and the main outlines of the world which would emerge from the prevailing chaos had long been obvious. What kind of people would control this world had been equally obvious. The new aristocracy was made up for the most part of bureaucrats, scientists, technicians, trade-union organizers, publicity experts, sociologists, teachers, journalists, and professional politicians. These people, whose origins lay in the salaried middle class and the upper grades of the working class, had been shaped and brought together by the barren world of monopoly industry and centralized government. As compared with their opposite numbers in the past ages, they were less avaricious, less tempted by luxury, hungrier for pure power, and, above all, more conscious of what they were doing and more intent on crushing opposition. This last difference was cardinal. By comparison with that existing today, all the tyrannies of the past were half-hearted and inefficient. The ruling groups were always infected to some extent by liberal ideas, and were content to leave loose ends everywhere, to regard only the overt act, and to be uninterested in what their subjects were thinking. Even the Catholic Church of the Middle Ages was tolerant by modern standards. Part of the reason for this was that in the past no government had the power to keep its citizens under constant surveillance. The invention of print, however, made it easier to manipulate public opinion, and the film and the radio carried the process further. With the development of television, and the technical advance which made it possible to receive and transmit simultaneously on the same instrument, private life came to an end. Every citizen, or at least every citizen important enough to be worth watching, could be kept for twenty-four hours a day under the eyes of the police and in the sound of official propaganda, with all other channels of communication closed. The possibility of enforcing not only complete obedience to the will of the State, but complete uniformity of opinion on all subjects, now existed for the first time.

After the revolutionary period of the Fifties and Sixties, society regrouped itself, as always, into High, Middle, and Low. But the new High group, unlike all its forerunners, did not act upon instinct but knew what was needed to safeguard its position. It had long been realized that the only secure basis for oligarchy is collectivism. Wealth and privilege are most easily defended when they are possessed jointly. The so-called "abolition of private property" which took place in the middle years of the century meant, in effect, the concentration of property in far fewer hands than before; but with this difference, that the new owners were a group instead of a mass of individuals. Individually, no member of the Party owns anything, except petty personal belongings. Collectively, the Party owns everything in Oceania, because it controls everything and disposes of the products as it thinks fit. In the years following the Revolution it was able to step into this commanding position almost unopposed, because the whole process was represented as an act of collectivization. It had always been assumed that if the capitalist class were expropriated, Socialism must follow; and unquestionably the capitalists had been expropriated. Factories, mines, land, houses, transport—everything had been taken away from them; and since these things were no longer private property, it followed that they must be public property. Ingsoc, which grew out of the earlier Socialist movement and inherited its phraseology, has in fact carried out the main item in the Socialist program, with the result, foreseen and intended beforehand, that economic inequality has been made permanent.

But the problems of perpetuating a hierarchical society go deeper than this. There are only four ways in which a ruling group can fall from power. Either it is conquered from without, or it governs so inefficiently that the masses are stirred to revolt, or it allows a strong and discontented Middle Group to come into being, or it loses its own self-confidence and willingness to govern. These causes do not operate singly, and as a rule all four of them are present in some degree. A ruling class which could guard against all of them would remain in power permanently. Ultimately the determining factor is the mental attitude of the ruling class itself.

After the middle of the present century, the first danger had in reality disappeared. Each of the three powers which now divide the world is in fact unconquerable, and could only become conquerable through slow demographic changes which a government with wide powers can easily avert. The second danger, also, is only a theoretical one. The masses never revolt of their own accord, and they never revolt merely because they are oppressed. Indeed, so long as they are not permitted to have standards of comparison they never even become aware that they are oppressed. The recurrent economic crises of past times were totally unnecessary and are not now permitted to happen, but other and equally large dislocations can and do happen without having political results, because there is no way in which discontent can become articulate. As for the problem of overproduction, which has been latent in our society since the development of machine technique, it is solved by the device of continuous warfare (see Chapter 3), which is also useful in keying up public morale to the necessary pitch. From the point of view of our present rulers, therefore, the only genuine dangers are the splitting-off of a new group of able, underemployed, power-hungry people, and the growth of liberalism and skepticism in their own ranks. The problem, that is to say, is educational. It is a problem of continuously molding the consciousness both of the directing group and of the larger executive group that lies immediately below it. The consciousness of the masses needs only to be influenced in a negative way.

Given this background, one could infer, if one did not know it already, the general structure of Oceanic society. At the apex of the pyramid comes Big Brother. Big Brother is infallible and all-powerful. Every success, every achievement, every victory, every scientific discovery, all knowledge, all wisdom, all happiness, all virtue, are held to issue directly from his leadership and inspiration. Nobody has ever seen Big Brother. He is a face on the hoardings, a voice on the telescreen. We may be reasonably sure that he will never die, and there is already considerable uncertainty as to when he was born. Big Brother is the guise in which the Party chooses to exhibit itself to the world. His function is to act as a focusing point for love, fear, and reverence, emotions which are more easily felt toward an individual than toward an organization. Below Big Brother comes the Inner Party, its numbers limited to six millions, or something less than two per cent of the population of Oceania. Below the Inner Party comes the Outer Party, which, if the Inner Party is described as the brain of the State, may be justly likened to the hands. Below that come the dumb masses whom we habitually refer to as "the proles," numbering perhaps eighty-five per cent of the population. In the terms of our earlier classification, the proles are the Low, for the slave populations of the equatorial lands, who pass constantly from conqueror to conqueror, are not a permanent or necessary part of the structure.

In principle, membership in these three groups is not hereditary. The child of Inner Party parents is in theory not born into the Inner Party. Admission to either branch of the Party is by examination, taken at the age of sixteen. Nor is there any racial discrimination, or any marked domination of one province by another. Jews, Negroes, South Americans of pure Indian blood are to be found in the highest ranks of the Party, and the administrators of any area are always drawn from the inhabitants of that area. In no part of Oceania do the inhabitants have the feeling that they are a colonial population ruled from a distant capital. Oceania has no capital, and its titular head is a person whose whereabouts nobody knows. Except that English is its chief *lingua franca* and Newspeak its official language, it is not centralized in any way. Its rulers are not held together by blood ties but by adherence to a common doctrine. It is true that our society is stratified, and very rigidly stratified, on what at first sight appear to be hereditary lines. There is far less to-and-fro movement between the different groups than happened under capitalism or even in the pre-industrial ages. Between the two branches of the Party there is a certain amount of interchange, but only so much as will ensure that weaklings are excluded from the Inner Party and that ambitious members of the Outer Party are made harmless by allowing them to rise. Proletarians, in practice, are not allowed to graduate into the Party. The most gifted among them, who might possibly become nuclei of discontent, are simply marked down by the Thought Police and eliminated. But this state of affairs is not necessarily permanent, nor is it a matter of principle. The Party is not a class in the old sense of the word. It does not aim at transmitting power to its own children, as such; and if there were no other way of keeping the ablest people at the top, it would be perfectly prepared to recruit an entire new generation from the ranks of the proletariat. In the crucial years, the fact that the Party was not a hereditary body did a great deal to neutralize opposition. The older kind of Socialist, who had been trained to fight against something called "class privilege," assumed that what is not hereditary cannot be permanent. He did not see that the continuity of an oligarchy need not be physical, nor did he pause to reflect that hereditary aristocracies have always been shortlived, whereas adoptive organizations such as the Catholic Church have sometimes lasted for hundreds or thousands of years. The essence of oligarchical rule is not father-to-son inheritance, but the persistence of a certain world-view and a certain way of life, imposed by the dead upon the living. A ruling group is a ruling group so long as it can nominate its successors. The Party is not concerned with perpetuating its blood but with perpetuating itself. *Who* wields power is not important, provided that the hierarchical structure remains always the same.

All the beliefs, habits, tastes, emotions, mental attitudes that characterize our time are really designed to sustain the mystique of the Party and prevent the true nature of present-day society from being perceived. Physical rebellion, or any preliminary move toward rebellion, is at present not possible. From the proletarians nothing is to be feared. Left to themselves, they will continue from generation to generation and from century to century, working, breeding, and dying, not only without any impulse to rebel, but without the power of grasping that the world could be other than it is. They could only become dangerous if the advance of industrial technique made it necessary to educate them more highly; but, since military and commercial rivalry are no longer important, the level of popular education is actually declining. What opinions the masses hold, or do not hold, is looked on as a matter of indifference. They can be granted intellectual liberty because they have no intellect. In a Party member, on the other hand, not even the smallest deviation of opinion on the most unimportant subject can be tolerated.

A Party member lives from birth to death under the eye of the Thought Police. Even when he is alone he can never be sure that he is alone. Wherever he may be, asleep or awake, working or resting, in his bath or in bed, he can be inspected without warning and without knowing that he is being inspected. Nothing that he does is indifferent. His friendships, his relaxations, his behavior toward his wife and children, the expression of his face when he is alone, the words he mutters in sleep, even the characteristic movements of his body, are all jealously scrutinized. Not only any actual misdemeanor, but any eccentricity, however small, any change of habits, any nervous mannerism that could possibly be the symptom of an inner struggle, is certain to be detected. He has no freedom of choice in any direction whatever. On the other hand, his actions are not regulated by law or by any clearly formulated code of behavior. In Oceania there is no law. Thoughts and actions which, when detected, mean certain death are not formally forbidden, and the endless purges, arrests, tortures, imprisonments, and vaporizations are not inflicted as punishment for crimes which have actually been committed, but are merely the wiping-out of persons who might perhaps commit a crime at some time in the future. A Party member is required to have not only the right opinions, but the right instincts. Many of the beliefs and attitudes demanded of him are never plainly stated, and could not be stated without laying bare the contradictions inherent in Ingsoc. If he is a person naturally orthodox (in Newspeak, a *goodthinker*), he will in all circumstances know, without taking thought, what is the true belief or the desirable emotion. But in any case an elaborate mental training, undergone in childhood and grouping itself round the Newspeak words *crimestop, blackwhite,* and *doublethink,* makes him unwilling and unable to think too deeply on any subject whatever.

A Party member is expected to have no private emotions and no respites from enthusiasm. He is supposed to live in a continuous frenzy of hatred of foreign enemies and internal traitors, triumph over victories, and self-abasement before the power and wisdom of the Party. The discontents produced by his bare, unsatisfying life are deliberately turned outwards and dissipated by such devices as the Two Minutes Hate, and the speculations which might possibly induce a skeptical or rebellious attitude are killed in advance by his early acquired inner discipline. The first and simplest stage in the discipline, which can be taught even to young children, is called, in Newspeak, *crimestop. Crimestop* means the faculty of stopping short, as though by instinct, at the threshold of any dangerous thought. It includes the power of not grasping analogies, of failing to perceive logical errors, of misunderstanding the simplest arguments if they are inimical to Ingsoc, and of being bored or repelled by any train of thought which is capable of leading in a heretical direction. *Crimestop,* in short, means protective stupidity. But stupidity is not enough. On the contrary, orthodoxy in the full sense demands a control over one's own mental processes as complete as that of a contortionist over his body. Oceanic society

rests ultimately on the belief that Big Brother is omnipotent and that the Party is infallible. But since in reality Big Brother is not omnipotent and the Party is not infallible, there is need for an unwearying, moment-to-moment flexibility in the treatment of facts. The key word here is *blackwhite.* Like so many Newspeak words, this word has two mutually contradictory meanings. Applied to an opponent, it means the habit of impudently claiming that black is white, in contradiction of the plain facts. Applied to a Party member, it means a loyal willingness to say that black is white when Party discipline demands this. But it means also the ability to *believe* that black is white, and more, to *know* that black is white, and to forget that one has ever believed the contrary. This demands a continuous alteration of the past, made possible by the system of thought which really embraces all the rest, and which is known in Newspeak as *doublethink.*

The alteration of the past is necessary for two reasons, one of which is subsidiary and, so to speak, precautionary. The subsidiary reason is that the Party member, like the proletarian, tolerates present-day conditions partly because he has no standards of comparison. He must be cut off from the past, just as he must be cut off from the foreign countries, because it is necessary for him to believe that he is better off than his ancestors and that the average level of material comfort is constantly rising. But by far the more important reason for the readjustment of the past is the need to safeguard the infallibility of the Party. It is not merely that speeches, statistics, and records of every kind must be constantly brought up to date in order to show that the predictions of the Party were in all cases right. It is also that no change of doctrine or in political alignment can ever be admitted. For to change one's mind, or even one's policy, is a confession of weakness. If, for example, Eurasia or Eastasia (whichever it may be) is the enemy today, then that country must always have been the enemy. And if the facts say otherwise, then the facts must be altered. Thus history is continuously rewritten. This day-to-day falsification of the past, carried out by the Ministry of Truth, is as necessary to the stability of the regime as the work of repression and espionage carried out by the Ministry of Love.

The mutability of the past is the central tenet of Ingsoc. Past events, it is argued, have no objective existence, but survive only in written records and in human memories. The past is whatever the records and the memories agree upon. And since the Party is in full control of all records, and in equally full control of the minds of its members, it follows that the past is whatever the Party chooses to make it. It also follows that though the past is alterable, it never has been altered in any specific instance. For when it has been recreated in whatever shape is needed at the moment, then this new version *is* the past, and no different past can ever have existed. This holds good even when, as often happens, the same event has to be altered out of recognition several times in the course of a year. At all times the Party is in possession of absolute truth, and clearly the absolute can never have been different from what it is now. It will be seen that the control of the past depends above all on the training of memory. To make sure that all written records agree with the orthodoxy of the moment is merely a mechanical act. But it is also necessary to *remember* that events happened in the desired manner. And if it is necessary to rearrange one's memories or to tamper with written records, then it is necessary to *forget* that one has done so. The trick of doing this can be learned like any other mental technique. It *is* learned by the majority of Party members, and certainly by all who are intelligent as well as orthodox. In Oldspeak it is called, quite frankly, "reality control." In Newspeak it is called *doublethink*, although *doublethink* comprises much else as well.

Doublethink means the power of holding two contradictory beliefs in one's mind simultaneously, and accepting both of them. The Party intellectual knows in which direction his memories must be altered; he therefore knows that he is playing tricks with reality; but by the exercise of *doublethink* he also satisfies himself that reality is not violated.

The process has to be conscious, or it would not be carried out with sufficient precision, but it also has to be unconscious, or it would bring with it a feeling of falsity and hence of guilt. *Doublethink* lies at the very heart of Ingsoc, since the essential act of the Party is to use conscious deception while retaining the firmness of purpose that goes with complete honesty. To tell deliberate lies while genuinely believing in them, to forget any fact that has become inconvenient, and then, when it becomes necessary again, to draw it back from oblivion for just so long as it is needed, to deny the existence of objective reality and all the while to take account of the reality which one denies—all this is indispensably necessary. Even in using the word *doublethink* it is necessary to exercise *doublethink*. For by using the word one admits that one is tampering with reality; by a fresh act of *doublethink* one erases this knowledge; and so on indefinitely, with the lie always one leap ahead of the truth. Ultimately it is by means of *doublethink* that the Party has been able—and may, for all we know, continue to be able for thousands of years—to arrest the course of history.

All past oligarchies have fallen from power either because they ossified or because they grew soft. Either they became stupid and arrogant, failed to adjust themselves to changing circumstances, and were overthrown, or they became liberal and cowardly, made concessions when they should have used force, and once again were overthrown. They fell, that is to say, either through consciousness or through unconsciousness. It is the achievement of the Party to have produced a system of thought in which both conditions can exist simultaneously. And upon no other intellectual basis could the dominion of the Party be made permanent. If one is to rule, and to continue ruling, one must be able to dislocate the sense of reality. For the secret of rulership is to combine a belief in one's own infallibility with the power to learn from past mistakes.

It need hardly be said that the subtlest practitioners of *doublethink* are those who invented *doublethink* and know that it is a vast system of mental cheating. In our society, those who have the best knowledge of what is happening are also those who are furthest from seeing the world as it is. In general, the greater the understanding, the greater the delusion: the more intelligent, the less sane. One clear illustration of this is the fact that war hysteria increases in intensity as one rises in the social scale. Those whose attitude toward the war is most nearly rational are the subject peoples of the disputed territories. To these people the war is simply a continuous calamity which sweeps to and fro over their bodies like a tidal wave. Which side is winning is a matter of complete indifference to them. They are aware that a change of overlordship means simply that they will be doing the same work as before for new masters who treat them in the same manner as the old ones. The slightly more favored workers whom we call "the proles" are only intermittently conscious of the war. When it is necessary they can be prodded into frenzies of fear and hatred, but when left to themselves they are capable of forgetting for long periods that the war is happening. It is in the ranks of the Party, and above all of the Inner Party, that the true war enthusiasm is found. World-conquest is believed in most firmly by those who know it to be impossible. This peculiar linking-together of opposites—knowledge with ignorance, cynicism with fanaticism—is one of the chief distinguishing marks of Oceanic society. The official ideology abounds with contradictions even where there is no practical reason for them. Thus, the Party rejects and vilifies every principle for which the Socialist movement originally stood, and it chooses to do this in the name of Socialism. It preaches a contempt for the working class unexampled for centuries past, and it dresses its members in a uniform which was at one time peculiar to manual workers and was adopted for that reason. It systematically undermines the solidarity of the family, and it calls its leader by a name which is a direct appeal to the sentiments of family loyalty. Even the names of the four Ministries by which we are governed exhibit a sort of impudence in their deliberate reversal of the

facts. The Ministry of Peace concerns itself with war, the Ministry of Truth with lies, the Ministry of Love with torture, and the Ministry of Plenty with starvation. These contradictions are not accidental, nor do they result from ordinary hypocrisy: they are deliberate exercises in *doublethink*. For it is only by reconciling contradictions that power can be retained indefinitely. In no other way could the ancient cycle be broken. If human equality is to be forever averted—if the High, as we have called them, are to keep their places permanently—then the prevailing mental condition must be controlled insanity.

But there is one question which until this moment we have almost ignored. It is: *why* should human equality be averted? Supposing that the mechanics of the process have been rightly described, what is the motive for this huge, accurately planned effort to freeze history at a particular moment of time?

Here we reach the central secret. As we have seen, the mystique of the Party, and above all of the Inner Party, depends upon *doublethink*. But deeper than this lies the original motive, the never-questioned instinct that first led to the seizure of power and brought *doublethink*, the Thought Police, continuous warfare, and all the other necessary paraphernalia into existence afterwards. This motive really consists . . .

Winston became aware of silence, as one becomes aware of a new sound. It seemed to him that Julia had been very still for some time past. She was lying on her side, naked from the waist upwards, with her cheek pillowed on her hand and one dark lock tumbling across her eyes. Her breast rose and fell slowly and regularly.

"Julia."

No answer.

"Julia, are you awake?"

No answer. She was asleep. He shut the book, put it carefully on the floor, lay down, and pulled the coverlet over both of them.

He had still, he reflected, not learned the ultimate secret. He understood *how*; he did not understand *why*. Chapter 1, like Chapter 3, had not actually told him anything that he did not know; it had merely systematized the knowledge that he possessed already. But after reading it he knew better than before that he was not mad. Being in a minority, even a minority of one, did not make you 5 mad. There was truth and there was untruth, and if you clung to the truth even against the whole world, you were not mad. A yellow beam from the sinking sun slanted in through the window and fell across the pillow. He 10 shut his eyes. The sun on his face and the girl's smooth body touching his own gave him a strong, sleepy, confident feeling. He was safe, everything was all right. He fell asleep murmuring "Sanity is not statistical," 15 with the feeling that this remark contained in it a profound wisdom.

(1949)

STUDY AIDS: 1. Chapter 1 is related with a minimum of explanation or comment by the author; mostly he records behavior. Nevertheless a good deal is implied about how the state operates and why. What are some of its methods? Is Winston Smith sympathetic with the aims of the state? What evidence supports your opinion?

2. What is the meaning of these "Newspeak" terms: "blackwhite," "doublethink," "crimestop"?

3. What is the nature of the orthodoxy found in Ingsoc? (See p. 1020/1, l. 26 ff.)? What is a "goodthinker"? Do you know of any evidence in modern life of a tendency toward the kind of orthodoxy the author describes?

4. How does Orwell's story compare, in content and in form, with other imaginative social visions included in this book: More's *Utopia*, Swift's *Gulliver's Travels*, Huxley's *Brave New World*?

Dylan Thomas
(1914-1953)

WHEN DYLAN THOMAS DIED IN NEW YORK, HE HAD BECOME, UNLIKE MOST POETS IN their lifetimes, a legend. Despite the difficulty of his poetry, he was familiar to many people and represented for them the popular view of what a poet should be: gregarious, warm, bohemian visionary. The legend has harmed the poet; it is Thomas's writing that counts, not his personality.

He was born in Swansea, Wales, the son of a schoolmaster. Although he did not know the Welsh language, and in fact was anti-Welsh in many respects, his Celtic background profoundly influenced him, particularly in his extravagant rhetoric and in his emotionally religious attitude toward life. Thomas's first volume, *Eighteen Poems* (1934), written in his teens, treats of the frustrations and erotic imaginings that obsess the adolescent. His second volume, *Twenty-Five Poems* (1936), was more broadly significant. It contains a series of ten sonnets which present, often through sexual myth, the orthodox Christian feelings of despair and hope. This theme was to become more prevalent in the later poetry, which appeared in four volumes: *The Map of Love* (1939), *New Poems* (1943), *Deaths and Entrances* (1946), and *Twenty-six Poems* (1950). On the whole, these volumes show the poet becoming more interested in nature and landscape, and creating an imagery less packed and concentrated.

There are many readers who prefer Thomas's prose to his poetry. He has written two collections of short stories, *Portrait of the Artist as a Young Dog* (1940) and *Adventures in the Skin Trade* (1955), as well as film scenarios, radio broadcasts, and a play, *Under Milk Wood* (1954). His prose is rambling, vividly anecdotal, and conversational, marked by a humor and pathos lacking in his verse.

Light Breaks Where No Sun Shines

Light breaks where no sun shines;
Where no sea runs, the waters of the heart
Push in their tides;
And, broken ghosts with glowworms in their
heads,
The things of light 5
File through the flesh where no flesh decks
the bones.

A candle in the thighs
Warms youth and seed and burns the seeds
of age;
Where no seed stirs,
The fruit of man unwrinkles in the stars, 10
Bright as a fig;
Where no wax [1] is, the candle shows its hairs.

Dawn breaks behind the eyes;
From poles of skull and toe the windy blood
Slides like a sea; 15
Nor fenced, nor staked, the gushers of the sky
Spout to the rod
Divining in a smile the oil of tears.

Night in the sockets rounds,
Like some pitch moon, the limit of the
globes; 20
Day lights the bone;
Where no cold is, the skinning gales unpin
The winter's robes;
The film of spring is hanging from the lids.

Light breaks on secret lots, 25
On tips of thought where thoughts smell in
the rain;
When logics die,
The secret of the soil grows through the eye,
And blood jumps in the sun;
Above the waste allotments the dawn
halts. 30

(1934)

STUDY AIDS: The poem works out the relation of man to the external universe: Thomas sees man (the little universe) as containing within himself the characteristics of the greater external universe. What parallels between the two worlds does the poet draw in each stanza?

Fern Hill

Now as I was young and easy under the
apple boughs
About the lilting house and happy as the
grass was green,
The night above the dingle starry,
Time let me hail and climb
Golden in the heydays of his eyes, 5
And honored among wagons I was prince
of the apple towns
And once below a time I lordly had the trees
and leaves
Trail with daisies and barley
Down the rivers of the windfall light.

And as I was green and carefree, famous
among the barns 10

About the happy yard and singing as the
farm was home,
In the sun that is young once only,
Time let me play and be
Golden in the mercy of his means,
And green and golden I was huntsman and
herdsman, the calves 15
Sang to my horn, the foxes on the hills
barked clear and cold,
And the sabbath rang slowly
In the pebbles of the holy streams.

All the sun long it was running, it was lovely,
the hay-
Fields high as the house, the tunes from the
chimneys, it was air, 20
And playing, lovely and watery
And fire green as grass.
And nightly under the simple stars

[1] Thomas frequently uses "wax" as a symbol for mortal or dead flesh.

As I rode to sleep the owls were bearing the
  farm away,
All the moon long I heard, blessed among
  stables, the nightjars   25
    Flying with the ricks, and the horses
      Flashing into the dark.

And then to awake, and the farm, like a
  wanderer white
With the dew, come back, the cock on his
  shoulder: it was all
    Shining, it was Adam and maiden,   30
      The sky gathered again
And the sun grew round that very day.
So it must have been after the birth of the
  simple light
In the first, spinning place, the spellbound
  horses walking warm
    Out of the whinnying green stable   35
On to the fields of praise.

And honored among foxes and pheasants by
  the gay house
Under the new made clouds and happy as
  the heart was long,
    In the sun born over and over,
      I ran my heedless ways,   40
My wishes raced through the house high
  hay

And nothing I cared, at my sky blue trades,
  that time allows
In all his tuneful turning so few and such
  morning songs
    Before the children green and golden
      Follow him out of grace,   45

Nothing I cared, in the lamb white days,
  that time would take me
Up to the swallow thronged loft by the shadow
  of my hand,
    In the moon that is always rising,
      Nor that riding to sleep
    I should hear him fly with the high
      fields   50
And wake to the farm forever fled from
  the childless land.
Oh as I was young and easy in the mercy of
  his means,
      Time held me green and dying
    Though I sang in my chains like the sea.
(1943)

STUDY AIDS: *Fern Hill* is often compared
with Wordsworth's *Tintern Abbey*. How are
the poems similar? Dissimilar? How do the
philosophies of the two poems differ?

Poem in October

It was my thirtieth year to heaven
Woke to my hearing [1] from harbor and
  neighbor wood
And the mussel pooled and the heron
    Priested shore
  The morning beckon   5

With water praying and call of seagull and
  rook
And the knock of sailing boats on the net-
  webbed wall
      Myself to set foot
        That second
  In the still sleeping town and set forth.   10

My birthday began with the water——[2]
Birds and the birds of the winged trees flying
  my name
  Above the farms and the white horses
      And I rose
    In rainy autumn   15

[1] One must read the poetry of Thomas slowly
if one is to savor its taste. His syntax builds pitfalls
for the cursory reader. For example, the object of
"hearing" (l. 2) is the infinitive phrase "the morning
beckon" (l. 5), which in turn takes for its object,
"Myself" (l. 8). Many words intervene. If one
reads slowly, however, making all possible grammatical, denotative, and connotative connections
with other words and sentence elements, the poetry
becomes a rich experience, well worth the trouble.

[2] The word "dylan" means "water" in Welsh.

T. S. Eliot.

Dylan Thomas, from a portrait by Augustus John.

By permission of the National Museum of Wales, Cardiff.

"Ennui" by Walter Sickert.

By permission of the City of York Art Gallery, York, England.

"Winter Sea" by Paul Nash.

By permission of the Tate Gallery, London, and of Miss Catherine Powell.

And walked abroad in a shower of all my days.
High tide and the heron dived when I took
    the road
        Over the border
        And the gates
Of the town closed as the town awoke.   20

A springful of larks in a rolling
Cloud and the roadside bushes brimming with
    whistling
    Blackbirds and the sun of October
        Summery
        On the hill's shoulder,   25
Here were fond climates and sweet singers
    suddenly
Come in the morning where I wandered and
    listened
    To the rain wringing
        Wind blow cold
In the wood faraway under me.   30

Pale rain over the dwindling harbor
And over the sea-wet church the size of a
    snail
    With its horns through mist and the castle
        Brown as owls,
But all the gardens   35
Of spring and summer were blooming in the
    tall tales
Beyond the border and under the lark-full
    cloud.
    There could I marvel
        My birthday
Away but the weather turned around.   40

It turned away from the blithe country,
And down the other air and the blue altered
    sky
    Streamed again a wonder of summer
        With apples
    Pears and red currants,   45
And I saw in the turning so clearly a
    child's
Forgotten mornings when he walked with his
    mother
    Through the parables
        Of sunlight
And the legends of the green chapels   50

And the twice told fields of infancy

That his tears burned my cheeks and his heart
    moved in mine.
These were the woods the river and the sea
        Where a boy
    In the listening   55
Summertime of the dead whispered the truth
    of his joy
To the trees and the stones and the fish in
    the tide.
    And the mystery
        Sang alive
Still in the water and singing birds.   60

And there could I marvel my birthday
Away but the weather turned around. And
    the true
    Joy of the long-dead child sang burning
        In the sun.
    It was my thirtieth   65
Year to heaven stood there then in the sum-
    mer noon
Though the town below lay leaved with
    October blood.
    O may my heart's truth
        Still be sung
On this high hill in a year's turning.   70
(1946)

STUDY AIDS: 1. The poem recounts a walk
the poet took on his thirtieth birthday. Where
did he walk? How much time did his walk
take?

2. Like *Fern Hill*, this poem deals with childhood. The two poems are also built on contrast.
What is contrasted here?

3. "The weather turned around" (l. 40) indicates a change in the weather during the walk.
What psychological change in the poet does the
phrase indicate? Who is the "long-dead child"
(l. 63)?

4. Thomas is justly famous for his phrases.
Explain the following: (1) "thirtieth year to
heaven" (l. 1); (2) "Summery On the hill's
shoulder" (ll. 24–25); (3) "parables Of sunlight" (ll. 48–49); (4) "legends of the green
chapels" (l. 50); (5) "October blood" (l. 67).

5. Although the poem is written in a set
stanza pattern, there is no actual rhyme used.
There are, however, approximate rhymes, though
not arranged in any pattern. Find several of
these.

Do Not Go Gentle into That Good Night

This poem was addressed by Thomas to his dying father.

Do not go gentle into that good night,
Old age should burn and rave at close of day;
Rage, rage against the dying of the light.

Though wise men at their end know dark is right,
Because their words had forked no lightning they   5
Do not go gentle into that good night.

Good men, the last wave by, crying how bright
Their frail deeds might have danced in a green bay,
Rage, rage against the dying of the light.

Wild men who caught and sang the sun in flight,   10
And learn, too late, they grieved it on its way,
Do not go gentle into that good night.

Grave men, near death, who see with blinding sight
Blind eyes could blaze like meteors and be gay,
Rage, rage against the dying of the light.   15

And you, my father, there on the sad height,
Curse, bless, me now with your fierce tears, I pray.
Do not go gentle into that good night.
Rage, rage against the dying of the light.

(1952)

STUDY AIDS: 1. From the poem, what kind of man does the poet's father appear to have been? What is the dominant emotion expressed by the poet at his father's death?
2. The poem is a villanelle. Describe its rhyme scheme and metrical pattern.

Old Garbo

This story is from *Portrait of the Artist as a Young Dog* (1940), a collection of sketches and short stories based on childhood and adolescent experiences of Dylan Thomas.

Mr. Farr trod delicately and disgustedly down the dark, narrow stairs like a man on mice. He knew, without looking or slipping, that vicious boys had littered the darkest corners with banana peel; and when he reached the lavatory, the basins would be choked and the chains snapped on purpose. He remembered "Mr. Farr, no father" scrawled in brown, and the day the sink was full of blood that nobody admitted having lost. A girl rushed past him up the stairs, knocked the papers out of his hand, did not apologize, and the loose meg of his cigarette burned his lower lip as he failed to open the lavatory door. I heard from inside his protest and rattlings, the sing-song whine of his voice, the stamping of his small, patent-leather shoes, his favorite swear-words —he swore, violently and privately, like a collier [1] used to thinking in the dark—and I let him in.

"Do you always lock the door?" he asked, scurrying to the tiled wall.

"It stuck," I said.

He shivered and buttoned.

He was the senior reporter, a great shorthand writer, a chain-smoker, a bitter [2] drinker, very humorous, round-faced and round-bellied, with dart holes in his nose. Once, I thought as I stared at him then in the lavatory of the offices of the *Tawe News*, he might have been a mincing-mannered man,

[1] Miner.
[2] Ale.

with a strut and a cane to balance it, a watch-chain across the waistcoat, a gold tooth, even, perhaps a flower from his own garden in his button-hole. But now each attempt at a precise gesture was caked and soaked before it began; when he placed the tips of his thumb and forefinger together, you saw only the cracked nails in mourning and the Woodbine stains. He gave me a cigarette and shook his coat to hear matches.

"Here's a light, Mr. Farr," I said.

It was good to keep in with him; he covered all the big stories, the occasional murder, such as when Thomas O'Connor used a bottle on his wife—but that was before my time—the strikes, the best fires. I wore my cigarette as he did, a hanging badge of bad habits.

"Look at that word on the wall," he said. "Now that's ugly. There's a time and a place."

Winking at me, scratching his bald patch as though the thought came from there, he said: "Mr. Solomon wrote that."

Mr. Solomon was the news editor and a Wesleyan.

"Old Solomon," said Mr. Farr, "he'd cut every baby in half just for pleasure."

I smiled and said: "I bet he would!" But I wished that I could have answered in such a way as to show for Mr. Solomon the disrespect I did not feel. This was a great male moment, and the most enjoyable since I had begun work three weeks before: leaning against the cracked wall, smoking and smiling, looking down at my shoe scraping circles on the wet floor, sharing a small wickedness with an old, important man. I should have been writing up last night's performance of *The Crucifixion* or loitering, with my new hat on one side, through the Christmas-Saturday-crowded town in the hopes of an accident.

"You must come along with me one night," Mr. Farr said slowly. "We'll go down the 'Fishguard' on the docks; you can see the sailors knitting there in the public bar. Why not to-night? And there's shilling women in the 'Lord Jersey.' You stick to Woodbines, like me."

He washed his hands as a young boy does, wiping the dirt on the roll-towel, stared in

the mirror over the basin, twirled the ends of his moustache, and saw them droop again immediately after.

"Get to work," he said.

I walked into the lobby, leaving him with his face pressed to the glass and one finger exploring his bushy nostrils.

It was nearly eleven o'clock, and time for a cocoa or a Russian tea in the Cafe Royal, above a tobacconist's in High Street, where junior clerks and shop assistants and young men working in their fathers' offices or articled [3] to stockbrokers and solicitors met every morning for gossip and stories. I made my way through the crowds: the Valley men, up for the football; the country shoppers; the window gazers; the silent, shabby men at the corners of the packed streets, standing in isolation in the rain; the press of mothers and prams; old women in black, brooched dresses carrying frails; [4] smart girls with shining mackintoshes and splashed stockings; little, dandy lascars, [5] bewildered by the weather; business men with wet spats; through a mushroom forest of umbrellas; and all the time I thought of the paragraphs I would never write. I'll put you all in a story by and by.

Mrs. Constable, laden and red with shopping, recognized me as she charged out of Woolworth's like a bull. "I haven't seen your mother for ages! Oh! this Christmas rush! Remember me to Florrie. I'm going to have a cup of tea at the 'Modern.' There," she said, "I've lost a pan!"

I saw Percy Lewis, who put chewing gum in my hair at school.

A tall man stared at the doorway of a hat shop, resisting the crowds, standing hard and still. All the moving irrelevancies of good news grew and acted around me as I reached the cafe entrance and climbed the stairs.

"What's for you, Mr. Swaffer?"

"The usual, please." Cocoa and free biscuit.

Most of the boys were there already. Some wore the outlines of moustaches, others had sideboards [6] and crimped hair, some smoked

---

[3] Apprenticed.
[4] Baskets.
[5] East Indian sailors.
[6] Sideburns.

curved pipes and talked with them gripped between their teeth, there were pin-stripe trousers and hard collars, one daring bowler.

"Sit by here," said Leslie Bird. He was in the boots [7] at Dan Lewis's.

"Been to the flicks this week, Thomas?"

"Yes. The Regal. *White Lies*. Damned good show, too! Connie Bennett was great! Remember her in the foam-bath, Leslie?"

"Too much foam for me, old man."

The broad vowels of the town were narrowed in, the rise and fall of the family accent was caught and pressed.

At the top window of the International Stores across the street a group of uniformed girls were standing with tea-cups in their hands. One of them waved a handkerchief. I wondered if she waved it to me. "There's that dark piece again," I said. "She's got her eye on you."

"They all look all right in their working clothes," he said. "You catch them when they're all dolled up, they're awful. I knew a little nurse once, she looked a peach in her uniform, really refined; no, really, I mean. I picked her up on the prom [8] one night. She was in her Sunday best. There's a difference; she looked like a bit of Marks and Spencer's." [9] As he talked he was looking through the window with the corners of his eyes.

The girl waved again, and turned away to giggle.

"Pretty cheap!" he said.

I said: "And little Audrey laughed and laughed."

He took out a plated cigarette case. "Present," he said. "I bet my uncle with three balls [10] has it in a week. Have a best Turkish."

His matches were marked Allsopps. "Got them from behind the 'Carlton,'" he said. "Pretty girl behind the bar; knows her onions. You've never been there, have you? Why don't you drop in for one to-night? Gil Morris'll be there, too. There's a hop at the 'Melba.'"

"Sorry," I said. "I'm going out with our senior reporter. Some other time, Leslie. So long!"

I paid my threepence.

"Good morning, Cassie."

"Good morning, Hannen."

The rain had stopped and High Street shone. Walking on the tram-lines, a neat man held his banner high and prominently feared the Lord. I knew him as a Mr. Matthews, who had been saved some years ago from British port and who now walked every night, in rubber shoes with a prayer book and a flashlight, through the lanes. There went Mr. Evans the Produce [11] through the side-door of the "Bugle." Three typists rushed by for lunch, poached egg and milkshake, leaving a lavender scent. Should I take the long way through the Arcade, and stop to look at the old man with the broken, empty pram, who always stood there, by the music store, and who would take off his cap and set his hair alight for a penny? It was only a trick to amuse boys, and I took the short cut down Chapel Street, on the edge of the slum called the Strand, past the enticing Italian chip shop where young men who had noticing parents bought twopennyworth on late nights to hide their breath before the last tram home. Then up the narrow office stairs and into the reporters' room.

Mr. Solomon was shouting down the telephone. I heard the last words: "You're just a dreamer, Williams." He put the receiver down. "That boy's a buddy dreamer," he said to no one. He never swore.

I finished my report of *The Crucifixion* and handed it to Mr. Farr.

"Too much platitudinous verbosity."

Half an hour later, Ted Williams, dressed to golf, sidled in, smiling, thumbed his nose at Mr. Solomon's back, and sat quietly in a corner with a nail-file.

I whispered: "What was he slanging you for?"

"I went out on a suicide, a tram conductor called Hopkins, and the widow made me stay and have a cup of tea. That's all." He was very winning in his ways, more like a girl than a man who dreamed of Fleet Street and

---

[7] I.e., he sold shoes.

[8] Sidewalk.

[9] Chain store which sold cheap clothing.

[10] Pawn-shop.

[11] A grocer who specializes in vegetables.

spent his summer fortnight walking up and down past the *Daily Express* office and looking for celebrities in the pubs.

Saturday was my free afternoon. It was one o'clock and time to leave, but I stayed on; Mr. Farr said nothing. I pretended to be busy, scribbling words and caricaturing with no likeness Mr. Solomon's toucan profile and the snub copy-boy who whistled out of tune behind the windows of the telephone box. I wrote my name, "Reporters' Room, *Tawe News,* Tawe, South Wales, England, Europe, The Earth." And a list of books I had not written: "Land of My Fathers, a Study of the Welsh Character in all its aspects"; "Eighteen, a Provincial Autobiography"; "The Merciless Ladies, a Novel." Still Mr. Farr did not look up. I wrote "Hamlet." Surely Mr. Farr, stubbornly transcribing his council notes had not forgotten. I heard Mr. Solomon mutter, leaning over his shoulder: "To aitch [12] with Alderman Daniels." Half past one. Ted was in a dream. I spent a long time putting on my overcoat, tied my Old Grammarian's [13] scarf one way and then another.

"Some people are too lazy to take their half-days off," said Mr. Farr suddenly. "Six o'clock in the 'Lamps'' back bar." He did not turn around nor stop writing.

"Going for a nice walk?" asked my mother.

"Yes, on the common. Don't keep tea waiting."

I went to the Plaza. "Press," I said to the girl with the Tyrolean hat and skirt.

"There's been two reporters this week."

"Special notice."

She showed me to a seat. During the educational film, with the rude seeds hugging and sprouting in front of my eyes and plants like arms and legs, I thought of the bob women and the pansy sailors in the dives. There might be a quarrel with razors, and once Ted Williams found a lip outside the Mission to Seamen. It had a small moustache. The sinuous plants danced on the screen. If only Tawe were a larger seatown, there would be curtained rooms underground with blue films. The potato's life came to an end.

[12] Hell.
[13] Grammar school.

Then I entered an American college and danced with the president's daughter. The hero, called Lincoln, tall and dark with good teeth, I displaced quickly, and the girl spoke my name as she held his shadow, the singing college chorus in sailors' hats and bathing dresses called me big boy and king, Jack Oakie and I sped up the field, and on the shoulders of the crowd the president's daughter and I brought across the shifting-colored curtain with a kiss that left me giddy and bright-eyed as I walked out of the cinema into the strong lamplight and the new rain.

A whole wet hour to waste in the crowds. I watched the queue outside the Empire and studied the posters of *Nuit de Paris,* and thought of the chorus girls I had seen walking arm in arm, earlier that week, up and down the streets in the winter sunshine, their mouths, I remembered remarking and treasuring for the first page of "The Merciless Ladies" that was never begun, like crimson scars, their hair raven-black or silver; their scent and paint reminded me of the hot and chocolate-colored East, their eyes were pools. Lola de Kenway, Babs Courcey, Ramona Day would be with me all my life. Until I died, of a wasting, painless disease, and spoke my prepared last words, they would always walk with me, recalling me to my dead youth in the vanished High Street nights when the shop windows were blazing, and singing came out of the pubs, and sirens from the Hafod sat in the steaming chip shops with their handbags on their knees and their earrings rattling. I stopped to look at the window of Dirty Black's, the Fancy Man, but it was innocent; there were only itching and sneezing powders, stink bombs, rubber pens, and Charlie masks; all the novelties were inside, but I dared not go in for fear a woman would serve me, Mrs. Dirty Black with a moustache and knowing eyes, or a thin, dog-faced girl I saw there once, who winked and smelled of seaweed. In the market I bought pink cachous.[14] You never knew.

The back room of "The Three Lamps" was full of elderly men. Mr. Farr had not arrived. I leaned against the bar, between

[14] A pill to sweeten the breath.

an alderman and a solicitor, drinking bitter, wishing that my father could see me now and glad, at the same time, that he was visiting Uncle A. in Aberavon. He could not fail to see that I was a boy no longer, nor fail to be angry at the angle of my fag and my hat and the threat of the clutched tankard. I liked the taste of beer, its live, white lather, its brass-bright depths, the sudden world through the wet-brown walls of the glass, the tilted rush to the lips and the slow swallowing down to the lapping belly, the salt on the tongue, the foam at the corners.

"Same again, miss." She was middle-aged. "One for you, miss?"

"Not during hours, ta [15] all the same."

"You're welcome."

Was that an invitation to drink with her afterwards, to wait at the back door until she glided out, and then to walk through the night, along the promenade and sands, on to a soft dune where couples lay loving under their coats and looking at the Mumbles lighthouse? She was plump and plain, her netted hair was auburn and wisped with gray. She gave me my change like a mother giving her boy pennies for the pictures, and I would not go out with her if she put cream on it.

Mr. Farr hurried down High Street, savagely refusing laces and matches, averting his eyes from the shabby crowds. He knew that the poor and the sick and the ugly, unwanted people were so close around him that, with one look of recognition, one gesture of sympathy, he would be lost among them and the evening would be spoiled for ever.

"You're a pint man then," he said at my elbow.

"Good evening, Mr. Farr. Only now and then for a change. What's yours? Dirty night," I said.

Safe in a prosperous house, out of the way of the rain and the unsettling streets, where the poor and the past could not touch him, he took his glass lazily in the company of business and professional men and raised it to the light. "It's going to get dirtier," he said. "You wait till the 'Fishguard.' Here's health! You can see the sailors knitting there.

And the old fish-girls in the 'Jersey.' Got to go to the w.[16] for a breath of fresh air."

Mr. Evans the Produce came in quickly through a side door hidden by curtains, whispered his drink, shielded it with his overcoat, swallowed it in secrecy.

"Similar," said Mr. Farr, "and half for his nibs."

The bar was too high class to look like Christmas. A notice said "No Ladies."

We left Mr. Evans gulping in his tent.

Children screamed in Goat Street, and one boy, out of season, pulled my sleeve, crying: "Penny for the guy!" [17] Big women in men's caps barricaded their doorways, and a posh [18] girl gave us the wink at the corner of the green iron convenience opposite the Carlton Hotel. We entered to music, the bar was hung with ribbons and balloons, a tubercular tenor clung to the piano, behind the counter Leslie Bird's pretty barmaid was twitting a group of young men who leaned far over and asked to see her garters and invited her to gins and limes and lonely midnight walks and moist adventures in the cinema. Mr. Farr sneered down his glass as I watched the young men enviously and saw how much she liked their ways, how she slapped their hands lightly and wriggled back, in pride of her prettiness and gaiety, to pull the beer-handles.

"Toop little Twms from the Valleys. There'll be some puking to-night," he said with pleasure.

Other young men, sleek-haired, pale, and stocky, with high cheekbones and deep eyes, bright ties, double-breasted waistcoats and wide trousers, some pocked from the pits, their broad hands scarred and damaged, all exultantly half-drunk, stood singing round the piano, and the tenor with the fallen chest led in a clear voice. Oh! to be able to join in the suggestive play or the rocking choir, to shout *Bread of Heaven,* with my shoulders back and my arms linked with Little Moscow, or to be called "saucy" and "a one" as I joked and ogled at the counter,

[16] Water-closet, toilet.
[17] See p. 987, n. 1.
[18] Fancy.

[15] Thanks.

making innocent, dirty love that could come to nothing among the spilt beer and piling glasses.

"Let's get away from the bloody nightingales," said Mr. Farr.

"Too much bloody row," I said.

"Now we're coming to somewhere." We crawled down Strand alleys by the side of the mortuary, through a gas-lit lane where hidden babies cried together, and reached the "Fishguard" door as a man, muffled like Mr. Evans, slid out in front of us with a bottle or a black-jack in one gloved hand. The bar was empty. An old man whose hands trembled sat behind the counter, staring at his turnip watch.

"Merry Christmas, Pa."

"Good evening, Mr. F."

"Drop of rum, Pa."

A red bottle shook over two glasses.

"Very special poison, son."

"This'll make your eyes bulge," said Mr. Farr.

My iron head stood high and firm, no sailors' rum could rot the rock of my belly. Poor Leslie Bird the port-sipper, and little Gil Morris who marked dissipation under his eyes with a blacklead every Saturday night, I wished they could have seen me now, in the dark, stunted room with photographs of boxers peeling on the wall.

"More poison, Pa," I said.

"Where's the company to-night? gone to the Riviera?"

"They're in the snuggery, Mr. F., there's a party for Mrs. Prothero's daughter."

In the back room, under a damp royal family, a row of black-dressed women on a hard bench sat laughing and crying, short glasses lined by their Guinnesses.[19] On an opposite bench two men in jerseys drank appreciatively, nodding at the emotions of the women. And on the one chair, in the middle of the room, an old woman, with a bonnet tied under her chins, a feather boa and white gym shoes, tittered and wept above the rest. We sat on the men's bench. One of the two touched his cap with a sore hand.

[19] A kind of ale.

"What's the party, Jack?" asked Mr. Farr. "Meet my colleague, Mr. Thomas; this is Jack Stiff, the mortuary keeper."

Jack Stiff spoke from the side of his mouth. "It's Mrs. Prothero there. We call her Old Garbo because she isn't like her, see. She had a message from the hospital about an hour ago, Mrs. Harris's Winifred brought it here, to say her second daughter's died in pod."

"Baby girl dead, too," said the man at his side.

"So all the old girls came round to sympathize, and they made a big collection for her, and now she's beginning to drink it up and treating round. We've had a couple of pints from her already."

"Shameful!"

The rum burned and kicked in the hot room, but my head felt tough as a hill and I could write twelve books before morning and roll the "Carlton" barmaid, like a barrel, the length of Tawe sands.

"Drinks for the troops!"

Before a new audience, the women cried louder, patting Mrs. Prothero's knees and hands, adjusting her bonnet, praising her dead daughter.

"What'll you have, Mrs. Prothero, dear?"

"No, have it with me, dear, best in the house."

"Well, a Guinness tickles my fancy."

"And a little something in it, dear."

"Just for Margie's sake, then."

"Think if she was here now, dear, singing *One of the Ruins* or *Cockles and Mussels*; she had a proper madam's voice."

"Oh, don't, Mrs. Harris!"

"There, we're only bucking you up. Grief killed the cat, Mrs. Prothero. Let's have a song together, dear."

"The pale moon was rising above the gray mountain,
The sun was declining beneath the blue sea,
When I strolled with my love to the pure crystal fountain,"

Mrs. Prothero sang.

"It was her daughter's favorite song," said Jack Stiff's friend.

Mr. Farr tapped me on the shoulder; his hand fell slowly from a great height and his thin, bird's voice from a whirring circle on the ceiling. "A drop of out-of-doors for you and me." The gamps [20] and bonnets, the white gym-shoes, the bottles and the mildew king, the singing mortuary man, the *Rose of Tralee,* swam together in the snuggery; two small men, Mr. Farr and his twin brother, led me on an ice-rink to the door, and the night air slapped me down. The evening happened suddenly. A wall slumped over and knocked off my trilby; Mr. Farr's brother disappeared under the cobbles. Here came a wall like a buffalo; dodge him, son. Have a drop of angostura, have a drop of brandy, Fernet Branca, Polly, Ooo! the mother's darling! have a hair of the dog.

"Feeling better now?"

I sat in a plush chair I had never seen before, sipping a mothball drink and appreciating an argument between Ted Williams and Mr. Farr. Mr. Farr was saying sternly: "You came in here to look for sailors."

"No, I didn't then," said Ted. "I came for local color."

The notices on the wall were: " 'The Lord Jersey.' Prop.: Titch Thomas." "No Betting." "No Swearing, B—— you." "The Lord helps Himself, but you mustn't." "No Ladies allowed, except Ladies."

"This is a funny pub," I said. "See the notices?"

"Okay now?"

"I'm feeling upsydaisy."

"There's a pretty girl for you. Look, she's giving you the glad."

"But she's got no nose."

My drink, like winking, had turned itself into beer. A hammer tapped. "Order! order!" At a sound in a new saloon a collarless chairman with a cigar called on Mr. Jenkins to provide *The Lily of Laguna.*

"By request," said Mr. Jenkins.

"Order! order! for Katie Sebastopol Street. What is it, Katie?"

She sang the National Anthem.

"Mr. Fred Jones will supply his usual dirty one."

[20] Umbrellas.

A broken baritone voice spoiled the chorus: I recognized it as my own, and drowned it.

A girl of the Salvation Army avoided the arms of two firemen and sold them a *War Cry.*

A young man with a dazzling handkerchief round his head, black and white holiday shoes with holes for the toes, and no socks, danced until the bar cried: "Mabel!"

Ted clapped at my side. "That's style! 'Nijinsky of the Night-world,' there's a story! Wonder if I can get an interview?"

"Half a crack," said Mr. Farr.

"Don't make me cross."

A wind from the docks tore up the street, I heard the rowdy dredger in the bay and a boat blowing to come in, the gas-lamps bowed and bent, then again smoke closed about the stained walls with George and Mary dripping above the women's bench, and Jack Stiff whispered, holding his hand in front of him like the paw of an animal: "Old Garbo's gone."

The sad and jolly women huddled together.

"Mrs. Harris's little girl got the message wrong. Old Garbo's daughter's right as rain, the baby was born dead. Now the old girls want their money back, but they can't find Garbo anywhere." He licked his hand. "I know where she's gone."

His friend said: "To a boozer over the bridge."

In low voices the women reviled Mrs. Prothero, liar, adulteress, mother of bastards, thief.

"She got you know what."

"Never cured it."

"Got Charlie tattooed on her."

"Three and eight she owes me."

"Two and ten."

"Money for my teeth."

"One and a tanner out of my Old Age."

Who kept filling my glass? Beer ran down my cheek and my collar. My mouth was full of saliva. The bench spun. The cabin of the "Fishguard" tilted. Mr. Farr retreated slowly; the telescope twisted, and his face, with wide and hairy nostrils, breathed against mine.

"Mr. Thomas is going to get sick."

"Mind your brolly,[21] Mrs. Arthur."

[21] Braw: Scots or Welsh word for "fine clothes."

"Take his head."

The last tram clanked home. I did not have the penny for the fare. "You get off here. Careful!" The revolving hill to my father's house reached to the sky. Nobody was up. I crept to a wild bed, and the wallpaper lakes converged and sucked me down.

Sunday was a quiet day, though St. Mary's bells, a mile away, rang on, long after church time, in the holes of my head. Knowing that I would never drink again, I lay in bed until midday dinner and remembered the unsteady shapes and far-off voices of the ten o'clock town. I read the newspapers. All news was bad that morning, but an article called "Our Lady was a Flower-lover" moved me to tears of bewilderment and contrition. I excused myself from the Sunday joint [22] and three vegetables.

In the park in the afternoon I sat alone near the deserted bandstand. I caught a ball of waste paper that the wind blew down the gravel path towards the rockery, and, straightening it out and holding it on my knee, wrote the first three lines of a poem without hope. A dog nosed me out where I crouched, behind a bare tree in the cold, and rubbed its nose against my hand. "My only friend," I said. It stayed with me up to the early dusk, sniffing and scratching.

On Monday morning, with shame and hate, afraid to look at them again, I destroyed the article and the poem, throwing the pieces on to the top of the wardrobe, and I told Leslie Bird in the tram to the office: "You should have been with us, Saturday. Christ!"

Early on Tuesday night, which was Christmas Eve, I walked, with a borrowed half-crown, into the back room of the "Fishguard." Jack Stiff was alone. The women's bench was covered with sheets of newspaper. A bunch of balloons hung from the lamp.

[22] Of mutton.

"Here's health!"

"Merry Christmas!"

"Where's Mrs. Prothero?"

His hand was bandaged now. "Oh! You haven't heard? She spent all the collection money. She took it over the bridge to the 'Heart's Delight.' It was over a pound. She'd spent a lot of it before they found her daughter wasn't dead. She couldn't face them then. Have this one with me. So she finished it up by stop-tap Monday. Then a couple of men from the banana boats saw her walking across the bridge, and she stopped half-way. But they weren't in time."

"Merry Christmas!"

"We got a pair of gym shoes on our slab."

None of Old Garbo's friends came in that night.

When I showed this story a long time later to Mr. Farr, he said: "You got it all wrong. You got the people mixed. The boy with the handkerchief danced in the 'Jersey.' Fred Jones was singing in the 'Fishguard.' Never mind. Come and have one to-night in the 'Nelson.' There's a girl down there who'll show you where the sailor bit her. And there's a policeman who knew Jack Johnson."

"I'll put them all in a story by and by," I said.

(1940)

STUDY AIDS: 1. Why is this a short story rather than just a character sketch?

2. What irony is at the base of the story?

3. What is the function of Mr. Farr in the story?

4. Is the story about Mrs. Prothero (Old Garbo) or the "I" who narrates the action?

5. Try to determine how the author characterizes people. For example, read the opening paragraph carefully and analyze the character of Mr. Farr.

Appendix One

ON PROSODY

When we speak of a poem's *meaning*, we have in mind more than the central idea or feeling that can be stated in a prose paraphrase. The meaning does include the central idea or feeling, of course, but it includes more besides. It certainly includes rhythm, an obvious but at the same time a subtle element in a poem. Rhythm contributes so much to the total effect of a poem that we will do well to give it careful attention in our study. The important thing always is to feel the rhythm, and readers with a strong rhythmic sense can do this without analyzing what they hear. Even for such readers, however, metrical analysis is valuable, not because it gives names to what one may feel instinctively, but because sometimes it is only through such analysis that one can notice the part rhythm plays in conveying meaning. Let us consider the matter in two stages, the first a preparation for the second: (1) determining the normal metrical pattern; and (2) discovering the deviations from that pattern.

I

Rhythm, or the recurrence of phenomena at intervals of time, is everywhere about us. The succession of the seasons, the alternation of day and night, the breaking of waves on a shore, our steps in walking, our breathing, the very beat of our hearts—all such natural events are rhythmic, as are also the ticking of clocks and the clickety-clack of trains over the rails. Language, too, is rhythmical, since several features of the spoken language (volume or intensity, pitch, pauses, etc.) recur at intervals as one speaks. The recurrent feature that interests us is volume, or, as we say, stress or accent. When we pronounce English words of two syllables, we usually emphasize (i.e., speak louder and more distinctly) either the first or the second syllable. The accepted pronunciation of "teacher," "college," and "pulley," for instance, requires us to emphasize or accent the first syllable —a fact we can represent with capitals (TEACHer, COLlege, PULley) or by the more conventional accent marks (téacher, cóllege, púlley). Other two-syllable words require the heavy accent on the second syllable: attáck, defér, avénge. With some two-syllable words the accent is fairly evenly divided: jáckknĭfe, básebăll, sídewălk. The accenting of part of a word applies likewise to words of three syllables (béautĭfŭl, íntervăl, párămount, and óvertŭrn, ŭnăttáched, dĭsăllów) and of four and even five syllables.

This stress that we give to a part of a word, a habit we acquire very early as we are learning the language, is called *word accent*. A second principle determining how we place the accent in speaking the language has to do with accenting not parts of words but certain whole words within a sentence. It is the meaning of the sentence that determines how much stress we give to the individual words in it. If we say "He didn't do it; I did it," the meaning requires us to stress "I" and to give little accent to "did." But suppose a person finally succeeds in doing something he has often attempted; he says "I did it!" In this case "I" is not accented, but "did" is. Such emphasis, which is as natural as word accent, we call *rhetorical accent*. To sum up, we can say that whenever a person speaks, he utters a mixture of accented and unaccented syllables, the differences between the two depending on recognized pronunciation (word accent) and on the function of words in the sentence (rhetorical accent).

Both poetry and prose are rhythmical in that in both there is a recurrence of accented syllables. In poetry, however, the recurrence is regular; the succession of accented and unaccented syllables makes a definite and regular pattern which we call the *meter* (i.e., measure). Consider the following lines:

> Alone she cuts and binds the grain,
> And sings a melancholy strain.

For the two words here of more than one syllable, word accent would reveal how the stresses fall: ălóne and mélănchŏlў. To find how the stresses fall on the rest of the words, all monosyllables, we notice the rhetorical accent—i.e., where the sense of the lines forces us to place stress. Normally we do not stress such words as "and," "a," and "the," nor would we feel we should stress them in reading these lines. We would, however, want to stress the rest of the words, the ones in this case that carry the meaning: "cuts," "binds," "grain," "sings," and "strain." If we indicate these accent marks accordingly, the lines would look like this:

> Ălóne shĕ cúts ănd bínds thĕ gráin,
> Ănd síngs ă mélănchŏlў stráin.

What the accent marks show is a pattern of alternation—an unaccented syllable, an accented one, an unaccented one, and so on. Now we ask, How often is the cycle of alternation repeated? That is, What constitutes a unit in this cycle? In these lines the unit (or *foot*, as it is called) is composed of two syllables—one unaccented and one accented; after these two are sounded (as in "alone") the pattern is repeated (in "she cuts"). The other question we ask is, How many times does the pattern appear in one line? If we draw a vertical line after each unit, or foot, thus,

> Ălóne | shĕ cúts | ănd bínds | thĕ gráin,
> Ănd síngs | ă mĕl|ănchŏl|ў stráin

we see that it appears four times, or each line contains four feet. We have, then, in scanning the lines in this way, noted two things about their meter: (1) the nature of the foot (one unaccented syllable followed by an accented one), and (2) the number of such feet in the line.

These two facts, taken together, designate the meter of the line. It is customary, in naming a meter, to use the Greek terms for both the kind and number of feet in the line. The most common kinds of feet are as follows:

Name of foot (adjectival form in parenthesis)	Accent pattern	Examples
iamb (iambic)	˘ ´	alone, today
anapest (anapestic)	˘ ˘ ´	overturn, all alone
trochee (trochaic)	´ ˘	busy, trouble
dactyl (dactylic)	´ ˘ ˘	fabulous, vanity

Another kind of foot, used only singly and rarely constituting an entire line, is this:

| spondee (spondaic) | ´ ´ | jackknife, Go Slow! |

The second fact involved in naming a meter—the number of feet in a line—is also designated by Greek terms, the roots of which are familiar to us in such words as "*tri*cycle" and "*penta*gon." We have "monometer" for a line of one foot, "dimeter" for a line of two feet, and at the other end of the scale, "heptameter" for a line of seven feet, and "octameter" for a line of eight feet. Lines of seven and eight feet, though, are much less common than the following:

trimeter (trim-e-ter)	three feet in the line
tetrameter (te-tram-e-ter)	four " " " "
pentameter (pen-tam-e-ter)	five " " " "
hexameter (hex-am-e-ter)	six " " " "

What, then, is the name of the meter of the line quoted above, "Alone she cuts and binds the grain"? The feet are iambic, and there are four of them in the line; so the line is written, we say, in iambic tetrameter. Samples of some of the more common meters are as follows:

Grow old | along | with me!   iambic trimeter
The best | is yet | to be.

I wan|dered lone|ly as | a cloud   iambic tetrameter

For fools | rush in | where an|gels fear | to tread   iambic pentameter

Heard a | carol, | mournful, | holy,   trochaic tetrameter
Chanted | loudly, | chanted | lowly.

Once up | on a | midnight | dreary, | while I | pondered, | trochaic octameter
  weak and | weary,
Over | many a | quaint and | curious | volume | of for | gotten | lore

The Assyr | rian came down | like the wolf | on the fold   anapestic tetrameter

We that had | loved him so, | followed him, | honored him   dactylic tetrameter

Determine the meter of the following lines and check your answer in the footnotes:

1. Just for a handful of silver he left us [1]
2. She walks in beauty, like the night [2]
3. Double, double, toil and trouble
   Fire burn and cauldron bubble [3]
4. When I consider how my light is spent [4]
5. Perishing gloomily,
   Spurred by contumely,
   Cold inhumanity,
   Burning insanity.[5]
6. And no voice but was praising this Roland of mine,
   As I poured down his throat our last measure of wine.[6]

2

After we read the first few lines of a poem we "get the feel" of its meter; that is, we sense the pattern of accented and unaccented syllables. Once we sense it we may feel we should go on to try to force all of the words into the pattern. If the metrical pattern calls for a heavy accent on a word at a given point in the line, we may feel we should stress the word, whether the sense demands it or not, in order to conform to the pattern. Perhaps we would not go far wrong in so doing, provided the metrical pattern of accents always coincided with the word accent and rhetorical accent that we considered earlier. The fact is that often it does not so coincide. This means that if we stress words according to the metrical pattern, we often will be ignoring the sense of the line; our reading will be mechanical and forced.

To see how true this is, try emphasizing the predominant pattern of iambic pentameter in the following lines from *Paradise Lost*. Satan, recovering from his fall to hell, is breathing defiance and asserting his determination to maintain his integrity in spite of defeat.

> hail,
> Infernal world! and thou, profoundest hell,
> Receive thy new possessor—one who brings
> A mind not to be changed by place or time.
> The mind is its own place, and in itself
> Can make a heaven of hell, a hell of heaven.

The reading you get can be represented with capitals as follows:

> HAIL,
> InFERnal WORLD! and THOU, proFOUNDest HELL,
> ReCEIVE thy NEW posSESsor—ONE who BRINGS
> A MIND not TO be CHANGED by PLACE or TIME.
> The MIND is ITS own PLACE, and IN itSELF
> Can MAKE a HEAVEN of HELL, a HELL of HEAVEN.

---

[1] Dactylic tetrameter.
[2] Iambic tetrameter.
[3] Trochaic tetrameter.

[4] Iambic pentameter.
[5] Dactylic dimeter.
[6] Anapestic tetrameter.

Such a reading is proper for most of the passage, but is quite unsatisfactory at two points: (1) in l. 4 it emphasizes the preposition "to" (which, according to rhetorical accent, deserves no stress), and it fails to emphasize "not" (which, according to the sense of the line, demands stress); (2) in l. 5, a strict iambic reading places emphasis on "its," which is desirable, but it fails to stress "own," a word that requires stress. We get a better reading of the two lines if we pay less attention to metrical accent (the five-footed iambic pattern) and more to rhetorical accent—in other words, if we read the line more naturally, paying attention to the sense. Such a reading of the passage would be represented like this:

> hail,
> Infer|nal world! | and thou, | profound|est hell,
> Receive | thy new | possess|or—one | who brings
> A mind | not to | be changed | by place | and time.
> The mind| is its | own place, | and in | itself
> Can make | a heaven | of hell, | a hell | of heaven.

In l. 4, the second foot is not an iamb, but a trochee; in l. 5, the third foot is not an iamb but a spondee. This *substitution* of one type of foot for another is very common in poetry. It may occur rarely in a poem or it may occur so frequently as to be a metrical principle of the poem. Note, for example, the mixing of iambic and anapestic feet in the following stanza:

> For a breeze | of morn|ing moves,
>   And the plan|et of love|is on high,
> Begin|ning to faint|in the light|that she loves
>   On a bed | of daf|fodil sky,
> To faint | in the light | of the sun | she loves,
>   To faint | in his light, | and to die.

At the beginning of our discussion we divided our topic into two parts—discovering and naming the meter, and noting deviations from that meter. Naming the meter is part of the process of describing the poem, but merely naming it does not tell us much about the poem. A truly important question about metrics, probably the most important question, is, How does the poet use the meter he has chosen, or, more particularly, How is his meter made to deviate from the normal metrical pattern he has established? If we note the deviations and if we can detect reasons for their being introduced, then we are in a position to say something significant about the way meter helps the poet convey his meaning.

At first glance it may seem presumptuous of us to try to "detect reasons" why metrical variations are introduced. We are not mind readers, it may be argued; how can we tell what the poet intended? The answer is that of course we cannot tell what he intended. To admit this, however, is not to admit we are unjustified in noting features of the poet's achievement. We shall be safe so long as we say, not "the poet introduced this metrical variation because he wanted to suggest such and such," but rather "since this metrical variation is suitable to the sense of the line, it is a valuable feature of the poem."

Certainly one happy result of departing from the metrical norm is a pleasing variety.

The movement of a poem would be a deadly mechanical progress if it followed a completely regular pattern. Variation, simply for the sake of variation, is enjoyable. Consider the analogous case of music. A circus calliope, grinding out a march tune, sounds metrically as mechanical and unsubtle as a steam engine. By contrast, a gifted musician produces a metrical pattern of infinite variation. Perhaps this is most noticeable with some jazz musicians, since improvising variations is so important a feature of their art. A jazz drummer establishes the beat, but he will later depart from it with a hundred intricate and subtle deviations. All the time he is off the regular beat we can feel that beat, without hearing it; in fact we appreciate his departure from it (knowing he will return to it) because we can sense the discrepancy between the heard sound and the basic beat, which we feel. Meter in poetry operates in much the same way. The basic beat is the predominant meter, established early and adhered to through most of the poem. Occasionally, though, the poet departs from the norm by introducing substitute feet. When this happens we have, as with the drummer, two metrical lines: the heard one (variation) and the felt one (norm). Sensing the relationship of these two lines, now identical, now diverging, is one of the pleasures poetry can give.

Granted that metrical variation for its own sake is pleasant, with the best poets the variation usually contributes in some way to the poem's meaning. For one thing, the variation can throw stress on important words and make them stand out. Consider once more the lines from *Paradise Lost,* scanned to show metrical variation:

> háil,
> Ínfer|năl worĺd! | and thóu, | prŏfoúnd | ešt heĺl,
> Receĭve | thў néw | posséss | or—oné | whŏ briñgs
> Ă miñd | nŏt tŏ | bĕ chañged | bў plắce | ŏr tíme.
> The miñd | iš its | own plắce, | and iń | itseĺf
> Căn mắke | ă heaveň | ŏf heĺl, | ă heĺl | ŏf heáven.

The deviation from the norm in l. 4 throws the vocal emphasis, and hence our attention, on "not," a word which, considering the meaning of the lines, is an important one. Similarly in l. 5 the substitution of spondee for iamb in the third foot serves to emphasize the thought. If Milton had written

> The mind is of itself, and in itself

the meter would have been regular, but the line would have been less vigorous and emphatic. "The mind is *its own* place," he wrote, and the departure from the iambic flow helps to emphasize the idea of personal autonomy.

Another value of metrical variation is that it enables the poet to adapt the movement of the line to its sense. A few examples will make this clear. Lines in Tennyson's *Ulysses* give a sense of the passing of time:

> The loñg | dắy waňes; | the slów | moón clímbs; | the deép
> Moans round with many voices.

The pauses contribute to the slow movement of the line; but equally important is the use of substitute feet—spondees for iambs in the second and fourth feet. Each word in "long day wanes" and in "slow moon climbs" is accented so as to slow down the line to a pace suitable to the sense. Or consider lines from *Romeo and Juliet,* in which Montague is speaking of his son Romeo's behavior as a sighing, pining lover:

> Many a morning hath he there been seen,
> With tears augmenting the fresh morning's dew,
> Adding | to clouds | more clouds | with his | deep sighs.

The spondees, "more clouds" and "deep sighs," suit the sense of brooding melancholy suggested by the words. Or, again, notice this line from *Othello;* Iago is telling how, as part of his scheme against Cassio, he has made drunk three of the guards. "Three lads of Cyprus," he says,

> Have I | to-night | fluster'd | with flow|ing cups.

The word "fluster'd," a trochaic foot, breaks the normal iambic meter. This variation not only throws emphasis on the crucial word in the line; it is also possible to regard this metrical deviation as reinforcing the notion of social deviation (i.e., drunkenness) referred to in the line.

Such, then, are some of the ways metrical variation can become a means of expression. Metrics in poetry is a more complicated matter than this short discussion has been able to indicate. Still, one can make a good start toward understanding it if he will ask of each poem he studies the following questions:

1. What is the predominant meter?
2. Where does the poet deviate from the metrical norm?
3. In what ways is it appropriate for him to deviate at these points?

Appendix Two

A GLOSSARY OF TERMS

The following brief definitions are limited to technical and critical terms used in the Study Aids.

ALEXANDRINE. A line of iambic hexameter, introduced into pentameter lines for variety or used to round out an iambic stanza. See SPENSERIAN STANZA.

ALLEGORY. A narrative in which objects, characters, and actions have a secondary (general or abstract) meaning beyond the literal one. Allegory operates as metaphor does: it can be thought of as metaphor extended until it becomes systematic symbolism. See SYMBOL.

ALLITERATION. The repetition of the initial sounds of two or more consecutive words or words near each other:
> "The fair breeze blew, the white foam flew,
> The furrow followed free."
> (Coleridge, *The Ancient Mariner*)

ANALOGY. (1) A general term denoting a comparison between two things essentially different but resembling each other in one or more significant respects. Analogy in this broad sense includes SIMILE and METAPHOR. (2) In a more restricted sense, analogy is a comparison used in exposition and in argument. (a) In exposition it is used to clarify difficult or unfamiliar matter, as "A communal society is like a colony of ants." A writer might develop the analogy by detailing the points of similarity. (b) In argument, analogy involves an inference: if A is like B in some respects, then it must be like B in other respects. Such an argument may sound persuasive but is often fallacious.

ANAPEST. See Appendix One.

ANTITHESIS. A contrast or opposition of two items—words, clauses, sentences, or thoughts— expressed so that each is balanced against the other. True antithesis requires that the opposition be expressed through similar grammatical structure:
> "God made the country, and man made the town."
> (Cowper, *The Task*)

ASSONANCE. The repetition of stressed vowel sounds in two or more syllables:
> "Thin glittering textures of the filmy dew,
> Dipped in the richest tincture of the sky."
> (Pope, *The Rape of the Lock*)

ATMOSPHERE. The mood pervading a story, poem, or play. Often it derives from the setting, or physical surroundings, and in narrative it is likely to suggest the nature and outcome of events.

BALLAD. A simple narrative poem, of anonymous authorship, originally intended to be sung. Its stanza is usually four lines, rhyming abcb, with lines one and three composed of four feet, lines two and four of three feet. The "literary" or "art" ballad is a conscious imitation of the folk ballad.

BLANK VERSE. Unrhymed iambic pentameter. See Appendix One.

CAESURA. A rhythmic pause or break in a line of verse:
> "If thou beest he: // but O how fallen! how changed"
> (Milton, *Paradise Lost*)

CLASSIC (adj.). (1) Referring to the literature of ancient Greece and Rome. (2) Referring to any literature which emphasizes restraint, dominance of reason, sense of form, simplicity of style, respect for tradition, conservatism. Classic literature accepts as truth the accumulated knowledge of all past civilized periods, particularly that of Greece and Rome. In this meaning, "classic" is the opposite of ROMANTIC. (3) often used for "neoclassic," referring to English literature of the Restoration and eighteenth century, which sought to emulate and imitate the writings of the ancient Greek and Roman eras.

CLIMAX. In fiction and drama, climax is the point of highest emotional tension, or the point at which the outcome of events is clearly determined.

CONCEIT. A figure of speech, occasionally overdeveloped or strained. Metaphysical poetry is characterized by frequent and ingenious use of conceits. The phrase "Petrarchan conceit" has a specialized use: it refers to those conventionalized images used by writers of Petrarchan sonnets, especially in the Elizabethan period.

CONFLICT. A significant opposition between two characters, or between one character and an external force, or within a character. At the end of stories and plays, conflicts are usually resolved. See DENOUEMENT.

CONNOTATION (and DENOTATION). The denotation of a word is its precise, dictionary meaning; the connotation is its emotional coloring or associative meanings, which it suggests or implies beyond its literal definition. Thus, "female parent" and "mother" denote the same thing; but the term "mother" is rich in connotative values and so may evoke an emotional response from a hearer or reader. Keats uses "gules" for "red" in *The Eve of St. Agnes* mainly because, since it is an heraldic term, it connotes the whole atmosphere of feudal days, with their knights, castles, and code of loyalty and love.

CONVENTION. A device or style which through custom or usage has become traditional in technique.

COUPLET. Two successive lines of poetry rhyming with each other:
> "A little learning is a dangerous thing;
> Drink deep, or taste not the Pierian spring."
> (Pope, *Essay on Criticism*)

DACTYL. See Appendix One.

DENOTATION. See CONNOTATION.

DENOUEMENT. The unraveling of the plot or story in drama and fiction; the explanation or outcome.

DIDACTIC. Referring to a piece of writing the major purpose of which is to instruct.

DIMETER. See Appendix One.

DRAMATIC MONOLOGUE. A poem in which a single speaker "talks" the poem at a significant moment in his life, revealing his own character and actions. The difference between a dramatic and an ordinary monologue is that in the former an audience (one or more listeners) is clearly present and affects the TONE and content of the speech.

ELEGY. A lyric poem, usually written in conventional language, which sets forth the poet's meditations on death.

END-STOPPED. An end-stopped line of poetry is one in which the thought of the line comes to a definite stop at the end of the line. The second line of an HEROIC COUPLET (the form favored by Pope and Dryden and other neoclassical poets) was commonly end-stopped, forming the closed couplet. If a line is not end-stopped, it is a RUN-ON LINE.

EPIC. A long narrative poem presenting a central character of heroic proportions, and usually tracing the development or death of a nation. The epic makes considerable use of conventions: *in medias res* beginning, supernatural intervention, catalogues, heroic similes, elevated language, battles, journeys to the underworld, etc.

FEMININE ENDING. In iambic or anapestic meter, a final foot followed by an unaccented, "extra" syllable: "To be or not to be, that is the ques*tion*." (Shakespeare, *Hamlet*)

FEMININE RHYME. A rhyme of words of two or more syllables, the last of which is unaccented, as in ll. 1 and 3 in the following quotation:
"So, we'll go no more a roving
　So late into the night,
Though the heart be still as loving,
　And the moon be still as bright."
　(Byron, *So We'll Go No More A Roving*)

FIGURATIVE LANGUAGE. Expression which departs from normal, literal language by using figures of speech. The most commonly used figures of speech are apostrophe, HYPERBOLE, UNDERSTATEMENT, METAPHOR, METONYMY, PARADOX, PERSONIFICATION, SIMILE, and synecdoche. See METAPHOR and IMAGERY. The difference between figurative and nonfigurative language may be illustrated by two simple sentences:
1. His razor-sharp mind cut the problem neatly into three slices.
2. His capable mind divided the problem quickly into three parts.
Both sentences say about the same thing. But in the first, the meaning is carried—and intensified—by a figure or image, that of a sharp razor cutting a block of material into three portions. In the second, no such figure or image is present; no comparison is made between the capable mind and some other thing. Figurative language, skilfully employed, illuminates the idea and often "emotionalizes" it. It not only states a meaning but often suggests an attitude toward the meaning or an emotion about the meaning. Poets use figurative language because they wish to communicate experience, and experience involves more than factual statement.

FOOT. In versification, a combination of stressed and unstressed syllables making up a basic unit in the METER. See Appendix One.

FORESHADOWING. Details in a narrative that give the reader an intimation of some event which is to come later in the action.

HEROIC COUPLET. A rhyming, iambic pentameter couplet which is END-STOPPED.

HEXAMETER. See Appendix One.

HYPERBOLE. Exaggeration for literary effect: "His mind was a million miles away." See FIGURATIVE LANGUAGE.

IAMB(ic). See Appendix One.

IMAGE. A representation of sense experience. We think of imagery as "mental pictures," and this is its most common usage; but there is also sound imagery, taste imagery, touch imagery, and odor imagery. Imagery brings concreteness and suggestiveness to literature, especially to poetry, by making comparisons between things and illuminating literal and abstract statements. Imagery often employs FIGURATIVE LANGUAGE and is at the very heart of poetic expression. While it may present factual truth, imagery makes the reader feel the truth, since it forces him to recreate the imaginative act with which the poet created.

IMPRESSIONISM. (1) A highly subjective manner of writing, in which the author presents things as they seem to him, not necessarily as they are in actuality. (2) A kind of criticism or subjective appreciation of a work of art, which treats the work in terms of the responses it evokes in the perceiver.

IRONY. On the simplest level, irony is a statement that literally says one thing but intends another. Usually the intended meaning is directly opposed to the literal statement, as in the sentence, "Oh, no, you never tell a lie!" where the obviously intended meaning is that the person addressed is a liar. On a higher level, irony takes note of the discrepancy that often exists between aspiration and fulfillment, promises and results, expectations and consequences, ideals and actualities. To point up this discrepancy, irony usually employs figures of speech which are based on contrast, such as PARADOX and UNDERSTATEMENT. The reader should not take the term only in a restricted, literal sense, however, since irony has as many shades of intensity as authors have attitudes toward the idea being presented.

LYRIC. Originally a poem to be sung (to a lyre); now used to denote a short poem marked by subjective emotion and melody.

METAPHOR. (1) A figure of speech stating one thing in terms of another. The comparison is implied rather than stated explicitly, as in the SIMILE; simile says one thing is *like* another, but metaphor says one thing *is* something else:
"Beauty is but a flower,
Which wrinkles will devour."
(Nashe, *Litany in Time of Plague*)
(2) In a more generic sense, metaphor is the over-all idea, impression, or experience that a poem produces in the reader when he analyzes the poem's imagery. It is the new combined experience the writer wishes us to think of in terms of a subject explored through imagery. For example, the subject of Keats's *To Autumn* (p. 702) is an awareness of Autumn. The imagery of stanza one asks that we think of the season as the "close bosom-friend of the maturing sun." This basic image is developed by many images of pregnancy in the stanza. The over-all metaphor which emerges in stanza one is an awareness of Autumn, the season, as a woman about to give birth to offspring—the offspring being a metaphoric representation of the riches of the harvest. This stanza along with the second and third (each with its own over-all metaphor) gives rise to the central metaphor of the total poem —the figure of Autumn humanly realized and emotionally experienced. Metaphor may be explicit (i.e., subject and image stated) or implicit (i.e., the subject of the poem or comparison may be implied by the image). When the central subject of a poem is implied, the poem is symbolic.

METAPHYSICAL. A term first applied by Dryden (and popularized by Dr. Johnson) to the poetry of John Donne and his followers among seventeenth-century poets. Metaphysical poetry is characterized primarily by the "metaphysical conceit," an image which usually compares dissimilar things by finding a logical point at which the things compared are similar:
"If they be two [i.e., lovers' souls], they are
two so
As stiff twin compasses are two,
Thy soul the fixed foot, makes no show
To move, but doth, if the other do."
(Donne, *A Valediction: Forbidding Mourning*)
Such a technique makes the poem (which is an emotional experience) intellectual. Metaphysical poetry tends to be analytical, psychological, unconventional, and logical. It was in its day an honest attempt to express the paradoxical complexities of human nature and life.

METER. A regular or nearly regular rhythmical pattern established by the repetition of a dominant foot. See Appendix One.

METONYMY. A figure of speech (see FIGURATIVE LANGUAGE) in which the name of one thing is used for that of another which it suggests, or with which it is commonly associated: "There was no appeal from the chair." (Here "chair" is used for "chairman.")

MOCK EPIC. A form of SATIRE, in which trivial subjects are treated in the lofty, dignified manner of the EPIC.

OCTAVE. Eight lines of poetry considered as a unit. The term is most often used to refer to the first eight lines of a Petrarchan SONNET.

OCTOSYLLABIC. A line of verse containing eight syllables. See Appendix One.

ODE. An elaborate lyric poem, written in dignified language, on a serious subject, and usually in a complicated metrical form.

ONOMATOPOEIA. The use of words which, supposedly, sound like what they mean, such as *splash, buzz, murmur,* etc. When effectively used, onomatopoeia enables a writer to express sense through sound.

OVERSTATEMENT. See HYPERBOLE.

PARADOX. A statement which apparently contradicts itself or is untrue if taken literally, but which is true on a figurative level:
"The child is father of the man"
(Wordsworth, *My Heart Leaps Up*)
The statement is literally impossible; yet in the deeper sense that the experiences of the child determine the temper of the man he will become, the statement is true. Often in a poem the paradox is not explicitly stated as a proposition but emerges in the development of the poem's ideas and imagery.

PARAPHRASE. A restatement of the meaning of a piece of prose or poetry in words different from those of the original. Although paraphrase is a useful analytical tool, one must realize that a paraphrase of a poem is not the poem; it is only a rephrasing of the ideas in the original piece, and is by no means a substitute for the original. Every original literary statement "says" more than the most satisfactory paraphrase of it.

PASTORAL. (1) A poem which treats of rural life by using conventional figures and artificial language, as Marlowe's *The Passionate Shepherd to His Love.* (2) Any poem which treats of actual rural people or life, as Goldsmith's *The Deserted Village.*

PENTAMETER. See Appendix One.

PERSONIFICATION. A figure of speech in which an inanimate object or abstract idea is represented as having human characteristics:
"Thou still unravished bride of quietness"
(Keats, *Ode on a Grecian Urn*)

PETRARCHAN CONCEIT. See CONCEIT.

POETIC DICTION. Words different from those in everyday use, which are felt to have qualities (including their uncommonness) that make them appropriate to poetry. In an effort to avoid homely words, poets of the eighteenth century used a poetic diction which included obscure Latinate terms ("umbrageous") and terms of circumlocution. (For an example of poetic diction as metaphor, see p. 419, l. 80.) Many later poets have deplored using a special vocabulary for poetry, and consequently have tended to use words drawn from the normal English vocabulary.

POETIC JUSTICE. Ideal justice, satisfied, at the conclusion of a narrative, when good conduct is rewarded and evil conduct punished.

POINT OF VIEW. In fiction, point of view is the position, psychological as well as physical, from which events are seen by the narrator. He may be a part of the story or outside it; and he may presume to know the thoughts of one or all characters, or of none. Thus point of view has a great deal to do with determining the nature of a story.

QUATRAIN. A four-line stanza.

REALISM. As a literary term realism means the representation, in art or literature, of life as it is, instead of as it might or ought to be. Realism tends to stress everyday life and manners and to include the ugly as well as the beautiful elements of existence. When a work emphasizes the sordid, the ugly, the brutal—presenting man only as a physical entity—it is said to be in the mode of "naturalism."

REFRAIN. A line or phrase which is repeated at regular intervals throughout a poem—usually at the end of stanzas.

RHYME SCHEME. The pattern of rhymes used in a poem or part of a poem.

RHYTHM. In poetry, the recurrence, in a more or less regular pattern, of stressed and unstressed syllables in a line. See Appendix One.

ROMANTIC. (1) Referring to that body of English literature produced by the "romantics" of the late eighteenth and early nineteenth centuries. (2) Referring to any art which is the opposite of CLASSIC. Romantic literature is marked by one or more of the following qualities and characteristics: a subjective, individual vision of truth, uniqueness, the free use of the imagination, emotion, occasional looseness of form because of experimentation, love of external nature, interest in the past, especially in more primitive societies, and interest in human rights and social change.

RUN-ON LINE. A line of poetry which is not END-STOPPED—that is, a line in which the sense continues into the next line without a pause or break. The following lines indicate the effective use of run-on lines to achieve a fluidity of motion appropriate to the content:

"As one that in a silver vision floats
Obedient to the sweep of odorous winds
Upon resplendent clouds, so rapidly
Along the dark and ruffled waters fled
The straining boat."
(Shelley, *Prometheus Unbound*)

SATIRE. A form of literature in which the vices and follies of mankind are treated with ridicule or contempt. The methods of satire are commonly sarcasm, IRONY, wit, HYPERBOLE, and UNDERSTATEMENT. Satire is not merely destructive; although its main object is to attack and unmask, it holds up, at least by implication, a better way of life than the one criticized. Its primary object, therefore, is to reform.

SCAN(sion). To scan a poem is to analyze it into its metrical components. See Appendix One.

SENTIMENTALISM. In literature, sentimentalism is the indulgence in emotion for its own sake, an indulgence unjustified by the content of the work or passage. Sentimentalism is thus a derogatory term (and so, usually, is the corresponding adjective, "sentimental"), to be distinguished from "sentiment," which means a mental attitude that is highly responsive to feeling and emotion and which carries no derogatory tinge.

SESTET. The last six lines of a Petrarchan SONNET.

SIMILE. A figure of speech (see FIGURATIVE LANGUAGE) in which a comparison is made between two things essentially unlike but resembling each other in one or more aspects. The comparison is indicated explicitly by the use of *like* or *as*:

"O, my love is like a red, red rose,
That's newly sprung in June."
(Burns, *A Red, Red Rose*)

SONNET. A poem of fourteen lines of iambic pentameter. There are two major forms of the sonnet, forms determined by the arrangement of thought and by the RHYME-SCHEME. The first is the Petrarchan (or

Italian, or "regular") sonnet, with the OCTAVE rhyming abba abba, and the SESTET in any of several fashions. The second form is the Shakespearean (or English, or Elizabethan) sonnet, rhyming abab cdcd efef gg. It is thus composed of three QUATRAINS and a COUPLET.

A "sonnet sequence" is a group of sonnets held together (often quite loosely) by some dominant theme or subject matter. Such a grouping is more unified than a "sonnet series," which is merely a number of sonnets published together.

SPENSERIAN STANZA. A stanza created by Edmund Spenser for his *Faerie Queene*. It is a nine-line iambic stanza, the first eight lines being pentameter, the ninth a hexameter, or ALEXANDRINE, rhyming ababbcbcc.

SPONDEE. A poetical foot consisting of two accented syllables. See Appendix One.

SYMBOL(ism). Any image which stands for the unnamed subject of the passage (see METAPHOR). It may be any object, character, or incident, which is so emphasized as to have a range of meaning beyond itself. Blake's tiger, in his poem of that title, is probably a symbol of evil.

SYNTAX. The relationship of words in a sentence. Determining the syntax of a sentence means finding the subject, predicate, modifiers, etc. In poetry unusual syntax is sometimes used for rhythmical or rhetorical effect.

TERZA RIMA. A three-line stanza of iambic pentameter, with interlocking rhyme: aba bcb cdc, etc.

TETRAMETER. See Appendix One.

THEME. The central idea, attitude, or total significance which the piece of literature develops or illustrates. Some critics distinguish between theme and central idea by saying that theme is the broader subject treated by the piece, and should be stated in discussion as a noun or noun phrase, whereas the central idea is more definite, and can be stated in the form of a sentence. In Marvell's *To His Coy Mistress* (p. 243), the theme is "the brevity of life"; the central idea is "Since life is so short, let's make love while we can."

TONE. The author's own attitude toward what he is presenting. In spoken language tone is indicated by inflection of the voice, by facial expression, and by gesture. Every poem is dramatic—someone is speaking to someone else. The voice we hear is not the poet's own voice speaking in his own person, just as the person spoken to is never the actual "you" of the reader. To determine "who" is speaking in a poem, the reader must consider *how* the speaker speaks, i.e., his tone. This is often difficult to determine, but if one notes the social relationship between speaker and the one spoken to, the tone the speaker adopts is more easily determined. Tone is thus based upon the social relationship within the total dramatic context of the poem: a lover speaking to his beloved, a husband to his wife, a worshiper to God, a servant to his master, etc. Tone is further determined by the *manner* the speaker adopts within this social relationship. His manner depends upon the dramatic situation being developed in the poem: the lover may praise, chide, or argue with his beloved. His tone may then be intimate, angry, formal, casual, chivalric, etc., according to the dramatic situation of the poem and the social relationship between the speaker and the one spoken to.

TRIMETER. See Appendix One.

TROCHEE. See Appendix One.

UNDERSTATEMENT. Understatement is HYPER-BOLE in reverse, i.e., stating the idea less vigorously than literal accuracy demands. Most often understatement serves the cause of IRONY.

Index of Authors, Titles, and First Lines of Poetry

A little black thing among the snow, 506
A slumber did my spirit seal, 527
A sonnet is a moment's monument, 866
A sudden blow: the great wings beating still, 940
About suffering they were never wrong, 1002
ADDISON, JOSEPH, and STEELE, RICHARD, 332–52
Adonais, 675
Adventures of a Shilling (Tatler 249), 335
After the first powerful plain manifesto, 1005
After-Thought, 549
Alexander Pope (from Lives of the English Poets), 445
Alexander's Feast; or, the Power of Music, 313
Alysoun, 111
An old, mad, blind, despised, and dying king, 669
Ancient Mariner, The Rime of the, 551
Andrea del Sarto, 802
Apeneck Sweeney spreads his knees, 985
Areopagitica, 293
Argument of his Book, The, 232
ARNOLD, MATTHEW, 823–57
As an unperfect actor on the stage, 169
As I was walking all alane, 114
As virtuous men pass mildly away, 204
As when a tree's cut down, the secret root, 311
At the midnight in the silence of the sleep-time, 807
Atalanta in Calydon, 884
AUDEN, WYSTAN HUGH, 1000–1004
Avenge, O Lord, thy slaughtered saints, whose bones, 257
Awake, my St. John! leave all meaner things, 373

Bachelor's Complaint of the Behavior of Married People, A, 587
BACON, FRANCIS, 180–94
Bard, The, 428
Batter my heart, three-personed God, for you, 206
Before the beginning of years, 885
Behold her, single in the field, 541
Beowulf, 7
Bermudas, 244
Biographia Literaria, 582
Bishop Orders His Tomb at St. Praxed's Church, The, 787
Blacksmiths, The, 112
BLAKE, WILLIAM, 501–507
Blessed Damozel, The, 858

Body's Beauty (from The House of Life), 867
Book, The, 231
BOSWELL, JAMES, 447–71
Brave New World, 991
Break, break, break, 770
Bright star! would I were steadfast as thou art, 705
BROWNING, ROBERT, 781–807
Buried Life, The, 826
BURNS, ROBERT, 484–501
But do not let us quarrel any more, 802
But, knowing now that they would have her speak, 877
But you who seek to give and merit fame, 353
BYRON, GEORGE GORDON, LORD, 609–63
Bytuene Mersh and Averil, 111

Calm was the day, and through the trembling air, 159
CAMPION, THOMAS, 177–80
Canonization, The, 202
CARLYLE, THOMAS, 711–24
Channel-Firing, 908
CHAUCER, GEOFFREY, 54–109, 112
Cherry-Ripe, 233
Cherry-ripe, ripe, ripe, I cry, 233
Childe Harold's Pilgrimage, 611
"Childe Roland to the Dark Tower Came," 791
Chimney-Sweeper, The, 506
Choice—1, The (from The House of Life), 866
Choice—2, The (from The House of Life), 867
Choice—3, The (from The House of Life), 867
Christabel, 570
Christmas Eve, and twelve of the clock, 910
Citizen of the World, The, 472
Clod and the Pebble, The, 507
Cloud, The, 671
Coldly, sadly descends, 836
COLERIDGE, SAMUEL TAYLOR, 550–86
Collar, The, 222
Collar-Bone of a Hare, The, 937
COLLINS, WILLIAM, 423–25
Come, dear children, let us away, 824
Come down, O maid, from yonder mountain height, 771
Come live with me, and be my love, 165
Come, my Celia, let us prove, 211
Come, Sleep! O Sleep, the certain knot of peace, 143

Come, we shepherds whose blest sight, 225
Complaint of Chaucer to His Empty Purse, 112
Composed upon Westminster Bridge, 545
Comrades, leave me here a little, while as yet 'tis early morn, 764
CONRAD, JOSEPH, 925–34
Convergence of the Twain, The, 909
Corinna's Going a-Maying, 235
Cotter's Saturday Night, The, 489
"Courage!" he said, and pointed toward the land, 753
CRASHAW, RICHARD, 225–27
Crossing the Bar, 781
Cuckoo Song, 110
Culture and Anarchy, 838

Daedalus, or Mechanical Skill, 188
Darkling Thrush, The, 906
Daughters of the Late Colonel, The, 956
Death, be not proud, though some have callèd thee, 205
Deep on the convent-roof the snows, 757
Defense of Guenevere, The, 877
Defense of Poesy, The, 144
DEFOE, DANIEL, 318–32
Dejection: An Ode, 579
DEKKER, THOMAS, 195–98
Demon Lover, The, 116
Denial, 224
Deserted Village, The, 477
Devotions upon Emergent Occasions, 208
Diary of Samuel Pepys, The, 304
Discourse on Idols, 191
Discourses in America, 846
Divers doth use, as I have heard and know, 139
Divine Image, The, 504
Do not go gentle into that good night, 1028
Don Juan, 634
DONNE, JOHN, 198–210
Doom is dark and deeper than any sea-dingle, 1001
Dover Beach, 835
DRAYTON, MICHAEL, 162–65
Drink to me only with thine eyes, 212
Drummer Hodge, 907
DRYDEN, JOHN, 308–18

Eagle, The, 780
Earth has not anything to show more fair, 545
Eat thou and drink; tomorrow thou shalt die, 866
Elegy IX, 206
Elegy Written in a Country Churchyard, 425
ELIOT, THOMAS STEARNS, 977–90
Eloïsa to Abelard, 368
Epilogue to Asolando, 807
Epistle to J. Lapraik, 485
Epitaph on Elizabeth, L. H., 212
Epithalamion, 153
Essay on Criticism, An, 353
Essay on Man, An, 373
Eternal God! Maker of all, 231

Eve of St. Agnes, The, 689
Even such is time, that takes in trust, 167
Expostulation and Reply, 521
Express, The, 1005

Fables, Ancient and Modern, 316
Fair daffodils, we weep to see, 235
Fair seed-time had my soul, and I grew up, 535
Fair stood the wind for France, 163
Farewell, thou child of my right hand, and joy, 212
Fear death?—to feel the fog in my throat, 806
Fear no more the heat o' the sun, 176
Felix Randal, 896
Felix Randal the farrier, O he is dead then? my duty all ended, 896
Fern Hill, 1025
FITZGERALD, EDWARD, 808–14
Five years have past; five summers, with the length, 522
Fly, The, 505
Folk Ballads, 113–18
Follow your saint, follow with accents sweet, 178
For God's sake hold your tongue, and let me love, 202
For those my unbaptized rimes, 238
Forsaken Merman, The, 824
Fra Lippo Lippi, 795
Francis Bacon, 725
From harmony, from heavenly harmony, 312
Full many a glorious morning have I seen, 171

Garden, The, 245
Garden of Proserpine, The, 888
Gather ye rosebuds while ye may, 234
General Prologue (to *The Canterbury Tales*), 56
Get Up and Bar the Door, 118
Get up, get up for shame, the blooming morn, 235
Glory be to God for dappled things, 897
Go and catch a falling star, 199
Go, for they call you, shepherd, from the hill, 829
GOLDSMITH, OLIVER, 471–84
Good-Morrow, The, 201
GRAY, THOMAS, 425–33
Gr-r-r—there go, my heart's abhorrence! 784
Gulliver's Travels, 380
Gull's Hornbook, The, 195

Ha! whare ye gaun, ye crowlin' ferlie? 488
"Had he and I but met," 908
Had she come all the way for this, 875
Had we but world enough, and time, 243
Hag, The, 237
Hail to thee, blithe spirit! 673
Happy those early days, when I, 228
HARDY, THOMAS, 906–10
Hark! ah, the nightingale, 828
Hark, hark! the lark at heaven's gate sings, 176
Having this day my horse, my hand, my lance, 143
Haystack in the Floods, The, 875
HAZLITT, WILLIAM, 598–609

He clasps the crag with crooked hands, 780
He disappeared in the dead of winter, 1003
Heaven-Haven, 896
Hebraism and Hellenism (from *Culture and Anarchy*), 838
Hence, loathed Melancholy, 248
Hence, vain deluding joys, 250
HERBERT, GEORGE, 222–24
Here, where the world is quiet, 888
HERRICK, ROBERT, 231–38
His Poetry His Pillar, 237
His Prayer for Absolution, 238
His Prayer to Ben Jonson, 233
Hollow Men, The, 987
Holy Sonnets, The, 205
Holy Thursday (Is this a holy thing to see), 506
Holy Thursday ('Twas on a Holy Thursday, their innocent faces clean), 503
Holy Willie's Prayer, 494
HOPKINS, GERARD MANLEY, 893–97
Hound of Heaven, The, 890
House of Life, The, 866
HOUSMAN, ALFRED EDWARD, 911–14
How fevered is the man who cannot look, 705
How Roses Came Red, 233
How sleep the brave, who sink to rest, 424
How soon hath time, the subtle thief of youth, 256
How sweet I roamed from field to field, 502
How vainly men themselves amaze, 245
How Violets Came Blue, 234
How Women Pass Their Time (*Spectator* 323), 349
HUXLEY, ALDOUS, 990–1000
HUXLEY, THOMAS HENRY, 814–22
Hymn of Apollo, 685
Hymn to God, My God, in My Sickness, 207
Hymn to Intellectual Beauty, 665
Hymn to Proserpine, 885

I am a little world made cunningly, 205
I am poor brother Lippo, by your leave! 795
I bring fresh showers for the thirsting flowers, 671
I can love both fair and brown, 200
I caught this morning's morning minion, kingdom of daylight's dauphin, dapple-dawn-drawn Falcon, in his riding, 894
I fled Him, down the nights and down the days, 890
I have desired to go, 896
I have lived long enough, having seen one thing, that love hath an end, 885
I held it truth, with him who sings, 773
I know that I shall meet my fate, 937
I leant upon a coppice gate, 906
I met a traveler from an antique land, 667
I saw Eternity the other night, 228
I sing of brooks, of blossoms, birds, and bowers, 232
I struck the board, and cried, "No more; I will abroad!" 222
I think continually of those who were truly great, 1005
I traveled among unknown men, 526

I walked the other day to spend my hour, 230
I wander through each chartered street, 506
I want a hero: an uncommon want, 634
I weep for Adonais—he is dead! 675
I will arise and go now, and go to Innisfree, 936
I wonder, by my troth, what thou and I, 201
I would that we were, my beloved, white birds on the foam of the sea, 936
Icham of Irlande, 110
Idea of a University, The, 736
If all the world and love were young, 166
If aught of oaten stop, or pastoral song, 423
If from the public way you turn your steps, 527
If thou survive my well-contented day, 170
Il Conde, 926
Il Penseroso, 250
In a solitude of the sea, 909
"In churches," said the Pardoner, "when I preach," 85
In Memoriam, 772
In Memory of W. B. Yeats, 1003
In sober mornings do not thou rehearse, 232
In the Holy Nativity of Our Lord God, 225
In these deep solitudes and awful cells, 368
In Xanadu did Kubla Khan, 569
Indifferent, The, 200
Infant Sorrow, 507
Into my heart an air that kills, 913
Irish Airman Foresees His Death, An, 937
Irish Dancer, The, 110
Is my team plowing, 912
Is there for honest poverty, 495
Is this a holy thing to see, 506
Is thy face like thy mother's, my fair child! 611
It fell about the Martinmass time, 118
It is a beauteous evening, calm and free, 546
It is an ancient Mariner, 551
It keeps eternal whisperings around, 704
It little profits that an idle king, 761
It was a lover and his lass, 176
It was my thirtieth year to heaven, 1026

Jack and Joan they think no ill, 179
JAMES, HENRY, 915–24
Jesu, Swetë Sonë Derë, 110
JOHNSON, SAMUEL, 433–47
JONSON, BEN, 210–21
Joseph Addison (from *Lives of the English Poets*), 443
Journal of the Plague Year, A, 324
JOYCE, JAMES, 942–50
Just for a handful of silver he left us, 785

KEATS, JOHN, 688–711
Kew Gardens, 950
Kubla Khan, 569

La Belle Dame Sans Merci, 696
Lady of Shalott, The, 751
LAMB, CHARLES, 586–98

Lamb, The, 502
Lake Isle of Innisfree, The, 936
L'Allegro, 248
LAWRENCE, D. H., 967–76
Leda and the Swan, 940
Let me not to the marriage of true minds, 173
Let those who are in favor with their stars, 169
Let us go then, you and I, 983
Letter to the Earl of Chesterfield, 437
Letters (Byron), 658
Letters (Gray), 431
Letters (Keats), 706
Letters (Lamb), 594
Life of Samuel Johnson, The, 448
Light breaks where no sun shines, 1025
Light flows our war of mocking words, and yet, 826
Like as the waves make towards the pebbled shore, 171
Lines: Composed a Few Miles above Tintern Abbey, 522
Lines: "When the Lamp Is Shattered," 687
Literature and Science (from Discourses in America), 846
Little Black Boy, The, 503
Little Cloud, A, 943
Little fly, 505
Little Lamb, who made thee? 502
Lives of the English Poets, 443
Locksley Hall, 764
London, 506
London, 1802, 547
London Journal, 1762–1763, The, 465
Look in my face; my name is Might-have-been, 868
Lord Randal, 118
Lost Days (from The House of Life), 868
Lost Leader, The, 785
Lotos-Eaters, The, 753
Love, 224
Love Among the Ruins, 789
Love bade me welcome; yet my soul drew back, 224
Love in the Valley, 869
Love on a day, wise poets tell, 234
"Love seeketh not itself to please," 507
Love Song of J. Alfred Prufrock, The, 982
LOVELACE, RICHARD, 240–41
Loveliest of trees, the cherry now, 911
Loving in truth, and fain in verse my love to show, 141
Lucifer in Starlight, 873
Lycidas, 252

MACAULAY, THOMAS BABINGTON, 724–35
Macavity: the Mystery Cat, 989
Macavity's a Mystery Cat: he's called the Hidden Paw, 989
Man He Killed, The, 908
MANSFIELD, KATHERINE, 955–67
Márgarét, are you grieving, 895
MARLOWE, CHRISTOPHER, 165–66
MARVELL, ANDREW, 242–46

May I for my own self song's truth reckon, 32
Meditation 17, 209
Meeting at Night, 786
Men of England, wherefore plough, 668
MEREDITH, GEORGE, 868–74
Michael, 527
Middle English Lyrics, 109–113
MILTON, JOHN, 246–98
Milton! thou shouldst be living at this hour, 547
Modest Proposal, A, 412
MORE, SIR THOMAS, 127–37
MORRIS, WILLIAM, 874–83
Morte d'Arthur, 757
Mower's Song, The, 242
My first thought was, he lied in every word, 791
My galley chargèd with forgetfulness, 138
My heart aches, and a drowsy numbness pains, 697
My Last Duchess, 783
My loved, my honored, much respected friend, 489
My lute, awake! perform the last, 139
My mind was once the true survey, 242
My mistress' eyes are nothing like the sun, 174
My mother bore me in the southern wild, 503
My mother groaned, my father wept, 507
My Sister's Sleep, 861
My sweetest Lesbia, let us live and love, 177
Much have I traveled in the realms of gold, 703
Musée des Beaux Arts, 1002
Music, when soft voices die, 687

Never give all the heart, for love, 937
Never seek to tell thy love, 507
NEWMAN, JOHN HENRY, 736–48
Night and Morning, 786
Nineteen Eighty-Four, 1007
No longer mourn for me when I am dead, 172
No, no, go not to Lethe, neither twist, 700
No spring nor summer beauty hath such grace, 206
No worst, there is none. Pitched past pitch of grief, 895
Not marble, nor the gilded monuments, 171
Now as I was young and easy under the apple boughs, 1025
Now sleeps the crimson petal, now the white, 771
Nuns fret not at their convent's narrow room, 548
Nun's Priest's Tale, The, 75
Nymph's Reply to the Shepherd, The, 166

O for some honest lover's ghost, 239
O, mistress mine, where are you roaming? 176
O, my luve's like a red, red rose, 500
O Rose, thou art sick! 505
O thou wha in the heavens does dwell, 494
O, wert thou in the cauld blast, 500
"O, what can ail thee, knight at arms," 696
" 'O where are you going?' said reader to rider," 1001
"O where hae ye been, Lord Randal, my son?" 118
"O where have you been, my long, long love," 116
O wild west wind, thou breath of autumn's being, 669

O, Willie Brew'd a Peck o' Maut, 496
Ode: Intimations of Immortality, 542
Ode on a Grecian Urn, 701
Ode on Melancholy, 700
Ode to a Nightingale, 697
Ode to Evening, 423
Ode to the West Wind, 669
Ode Written in the Beginning of the Year 1746, 424
Of Adam's first wife, Lilith, it is told, 867
Of Great Place, 183
Of man's first disobedience, and the fruit, 259
Of Marriage and Single Life, 185
Of Studies, 184
Of Truth, 181
Oft to the Wanderer, weary of exile, 33
Old China, 590
Old Garbo, 1028
On a starred night Prince Lucifer uprose, 873
On either side the river lie, 751
On Familiar Style, 598
On First Looking into Chapman's Homer, 703
On Going a Journey, 603
On Heroes, Hero-worship and the Heroic in History, 712
On Italian Opera (*Spectator 18*), 343
On My First Son, 212
On Paradise Lost (*Spectator 267*), 347
On the Extinction of the Venetian Republic, 546
On the Grasshopper and the Cricket, 704
On the Late Massacre in Piedmont, 257
On the Sea, 704
On Witchcraft (*Spectator 117*), 345
Once a poor widow, aging year by year, 76
Once did she hold the gorgeous East in fee, 546
Once more the storm is howling, and half hid, 939
One lesson, nature, let me learn of thee, 824
One word is too often profaned, 687
Only a little more, 237
ORWELL, GEORGE, 1006–1024
Out upon it! I have loved, 240
Oxen, The, 910
Ozymandias, 667

Paradise Lost, 258
Pardoner's Tale, The, 87
Parting at Morning, 787
Passionate Shepherd to His Love, The, 165
Past and Present, 718
PEPYS, SAMUEL, 302–308
Philomela, 828
Pied Beauty, 897
Poem in October, 1026
Poet, The, 750
Poison Tree, A, 505
Poor soul, the center of my sinful earth, 175
POPE, ALEXANDER, 352–78
Prayer for My Daughter, A, 939
Preface (to *Fables, Ancient and Modern*), 316
Preface to Shakespeare, 438
Preface (to *The Wisdom of the Ancients*), 187

Prelude, The, 534
Progress of Poesy, The, 834
Prologue, General (to *The Canterbury Tales*), 56
Prologue (to *In Memoriam*), 772
Prologue to the Pardoner's Tale, 85
Prologue to "The Tempest," 311
Prospice, 806
Prothalamion, 159
Pulley, The, 223
Purpose of The Spectator Papers, The (*Spectator 10*), 340

Queen and Huntress, chaste and fair, 211
Quiet Work, 824

RALEIGH, SIR WALTER, 166–67
Rambler No. 4, The, 434
Rape of the Lock, The, 355
Recollections of Sorrow (*Tatler 181*), 333
Red, Red Rose, A, 500
Resolution and Independence, 538
Retreat, The, 228
Rime of the Ancient Mariner, The, 551
Rocking-Horse Winner, The, 968
Rose-cheeked Laura, come, 178
Roses at first were white, 233
ROSSETTI, DANTE GABRIEL, 858–68
Round the cape of a sudden came the sea, 787
Rubáiyát of Omar Khayyám, The, 808
Rugby Chapel, 836
"Ruin seize thee, ruthless King!" 428

Sailing to Byzantium, 940
St. Agnes' Eve, 757
St. Agnes' Eve—Ah, bitter chill it was! 689
Science and Culture, 814
Scholar-Gypsy, The, 829
Scorn not the sonnet; critic, you have frowned, 549
Seafarer, The, 32
Season of mists and mellow fruitfulness, 702
Seasons, The (*Winter*), 418
Second Coming, The, 938
See, Winter comes, to rule the varied year, 418
SHAKESPEARE, WILLIAM, 167–77
Shall I compare thee to a summer's day? 169
She fell asleep on Christmas Eve, 861
She walks in beauty, like the night, 610
SHELLEY, PERCY BYSSHE, 663–88
Sick Rose, The, 505
SIDNEY, SIR PHILIP, 141–52
Since I am coming to that holy room, 207
Sir Gawain and the Green Knight, 35
Sir Patrick Spens, 115
Sister Helen, 862
So all day long the noise of battle rolled, 757
So, we'll go no more a-roving, 633
Soliloquy of the Spanish Cloister, 784
Solitary Reaper, The, 541
Song (Go and catch a falling star), 199
Song: "How Sweet I Roamed," 502

Song (Sweetest love, I do not go), 203
Song to Celia (Drink to me only with thine eyes), 212
Song: To Celia (Come, my Celia, let us prove), 211
Song to the Men of England, 668
Song 25, 1001
Songs (from The Princess), 770
Songs of Experience, 504
Songs of Innocence, 502
Sonnet: England in 1819, 669
Sonnet, The (from The House of Life), 866
Spectator 2 (The Spectator Club), 337
Spectator 10 (The Purpose of The Spectator Papers), 340
Spectator 18 (On Italian Opera), 343
Spectator 117 (On Witchcraft), 345
Spectator 267 (On Paradise Lost), 347
Spectator 323 (How Women Pass Their Time), 349
Spectator Club, The (Spectator 2), 337
SPENDER, STEPHEN, 1004–1006
SPENSER, EDMUND, 152–62
Sphinx, or Science, 190
Spring and Fall: to a young child, 895
She dwelt among the untrodden ways, 526
Stanzas for Music, 633
Stanzas Written in Dejection, Near Naples, 667
STEELE, RICHARD, and ADDISON, JOSEPH, 332–52
Still to be neat, still to be drest, 211
Strange fits of passion have I known, 525
Strong Son of God immortal love, 772
Swart, sweaty smiths, smutched with smoke, 112
Sweeney among the Nightingales, 985
SUCKLING, SIR JOHN, 238–40
Sumer is icumen in, 110
Sunset and evening star, 781
Superscription, A (from The House of Life), 868
Sweet Auburn! loveliest village of the plain, 477
Sweetest love, I do not go, 203
SWIFT, JONATHAN, 379–417
Swiftly walk o'er the western wave, 686
SWINBURNE, ALGERNON CHARLES, 883–89

Tables Turned, The, 522
Tam o'Shanter: A Tale, 497
Tatler 181 (Recollections of Sorrow), 333
Tatler 249 (Adventures of a Shilling), 335
Tears, idle tears, I know not what they mean, 770
Tell me not, sweet, I am unkind, 241
TENNYSON, ALFRED, LORD, 748–81
"Terence, this is stupid stuff," 913
That is no country for old men. The young, 941
That night your great guns, unawares, 908
That time of year thou mayst in me behold, 173
That's my last Duchess painted on the wall, 783
The awful shadow of some unseen Power, 665
The blessed damozel leaned out, 859
The curfew tolls the knell of parting day, 425
The expense of spirit in a waste of shame, 174
The gray sea and the long black land, 786

The hag is astride, 237
The king sits in Dumferling toune, 115
The longest tyranny that ever swayed, 309
The lost days of my life until today, 868
The poet in a golden clime was born, 750
The poetry of earth is never dead, 704
The sea is calm tonight, 835
The sleepless Hours who watch me as I lie, 685
The splendor falls on castle walls, 770
The sun is warm, the sky is clear, 667
The time you won your town the race, 912
The wind doth blow today, my love, 114
The woods decay, the woods decay and fall, 763
The world is too much with us; late and soon, 547
There be none of beauty's daughters, 633
There is a garden in her face, 180
There lived a wife at Usher's Well, 117
There was a roaring in the wind all night, 538
There was a time, when meadow, grove, and stream, 542
They flee from me that sometime did me seek, 140
They throw in Drummer Hodge to rest, 907
Think thou and act; tomorrow thou shalt die, 867
THOMAS, DYLAN, 1024–35
THOMPSON, FRANCIS, 890–93
THOMSON, JAMES, 417–23
Thou still unravished bride of quietness, 701
Thoughts of a Briton on the Subjugation of Switzerland, 548
Three things there be that prosper all apace, 167
Three years she grew in sun and shower, 526
Tiger, The, 504
Tiger! Tiger! burning bright, 504
Timber; or Discoveries, 214
Tintern Abbey, 522
Tired with all these, for restful death I cry, 172
'Tis now, since I sat down before, 239
'Tis the middle of the night by the castle clock, 570
Tithonus, 763
To— (Music, when soft voices die), 687
To— (One word is too often profaned), 687
To a Louse: On Seeing One on a Lady's Bonnet at Church, 488
To a Mouse: On Turning Her up in Her Nest with the Plough, 493
To a Skylark, 673
To Althea, from Prison, 241
To an Athlete Dying Young, 912
To Autumn, 702
To Daffodils, 235
To draw no envy, Shakespeare, on thy name, 213
To His Coy Mistress, 243
To His Son, 167
To Lucasta, Going to the Wars, 241
To Marguerite, 828
To Mercy, Pity, Peace, and Love, 504
To My Honored Friend, Dr. Charleton, 309
To Night, 686
To the Cambro-Britons and Their Harp, His Ballad of Agincourt, 162

KEY TO A MAP OF THE BRITISH ISLES

The Yeats Country A11
Deirdre's Country A13
Ossian's Country A8-9
Kingsley Country B3
The Hardy Country C4
Shakespeare Country C6
The Ivanhoe Country C10
The George Eliot Country B8
The Wordsworth Country B12
The Burns Country B14
The Scott Country B14-15

Abbotsford B15
Aberdeen B19
Aldwinkle C7
Alfoxden B4
Alloway B14
Ambleside B12
Armada route 1-22
Auchinleck B15
Avon River B6

Bath B4
Beaconsfield C5
Bedford C6
Belfast A12
Ben Lomond B16
Ben Nevis B18
Birmingham B7
Birnam Wood B17
Boar's Hill C5
Boston C8
Bosworth Field C7
Bournemouth C2
Boyne River A10
Bristol B4
Bromley C4
Bury St. Edmunds C7

Caerleon B5
Cambridge C6
Canterbury C4

Cardiff B4
Castleconnell A8
Cawdor Castle B20
Chester B9
Chevy Chase B14
Chichester C3
Clyde River B16
Cockermouth B13
Cork A6
Coventry C7
Craigenputtock B14
Culloden B20

Dee River B8
Dirby C8
Derwent Water B12
Donegal A13
Dover C4
Drogheda A10
Dromore A12
Dublin A9
Dunfermline B16
Dumfries B14
Dunsany Castle A10
Durham C13

Ecclefechan B14
Edinburgh B16
Edmonton C5
Elstow C6
Eton C4
Exeter B2

Firth of Clyde B14-15
Firth of Forth B16
Flodden Field B15
Fountain Abbey C11

Giant's Causeway A14
Glamis B18
Glasgow B16
Glastonbury B3
Gloucester B5

Grasmere B12
Gravesend C4
Great Yarmouth C7

Hampstead C4
Harrow C5
Hastings C3
Hebrides A19-22
Higher Bockhampton B3
Holyhead B9
Humber River C10

Ilchester B3
Inverness B20
Iona A17
Ipswich C6
Isle of Man B11-12
Isle of Wight C2
Islington C10

Jarrow C13

Kelmscott C5
Kenilworth Castle C7
Keswick B12
Kilcolman Castle A6
Kilkenny A8
Kirkcaldy B16

Ledbury B6
Leeds C10
Lichfield B8
Limerick A7
Lincoln C9
Lissoy A10
Liverpool B9
Llandaff B4
Loch Katrine B17
Loch Lomond B16
London C4
Ludlow B7
Lutterworth C7

Maidstone C4
Malmesbury B5
Malvern B6
Manchester B9
Margate C4
Melrose B15
Mersey River B9
Mossgiel B15

Nether Stowey B3
Newcastle B13
Norwich C7
Nottingham C8
Nuneaton C7

Olney C6
Otterburn B14
Ottery St. Mary B2
Oxford C5

Penshurst C4
Penzance A1
Perth B17
Plymouth B1
Pomfret Castle C5
Pook's Hill C3
Portsmouth C3
Preston B10

Queenstown A6

Racedown B3
Ramsgate C4
Rochester C4
Roman Wall B13
Rotherwood C9
Roxborough A9
Rugby C7
Rydal Mount B12

St. Albans C5
Salisbury C3
Selkirk B15

Severn River B5
Shannon River A9
Sheffield C9
Skiddaw B13
Shrewsbury B7
Skye A20
Snowdon B8
Solway Firth B13
Southampton C3
Stirling B16
Stoke Poges C5
Stonehenge C3
Stratford-on-Avon C6

Thames River C4
Tara A10
Tamworth C7
Tavistock B2
Tewkesbury B6
Tintagel B2
Tintern Abbey B5
Torquay B2
The Trossachs B17
Tweed River B15
Tyne River B13

Wakefield C10
Wantage C5
Warwick C7
The Wash C8
Wearmouth C13
Whitby C12
Wick B22
Widecombe B2
Winchester C3
Windermere Lake B12
Windsor C4
Woodstock C5
Wotton C4
Wye River B6

Yarrow River B15
York C11

NORTH SEA

Route of the Spanish Armada

ATLANTIC OCEAN

IRISH SEA

Wick

Inverness

Culloden *Cawdor Castle*

Aberdeen

Ben Nevis

Birnam Wood *Glamis*

Perth *Loch Katrine*

Ben Lomond

Loch Lomond

Stirling *Kirkcaldy*

Dunfermline FIRTH OF FORTH

EDINBURGH

Glascow *Clyde R.*

FIRTH of CLYDE

IONA

SKYE

HEBRIDES

Berwick

Flodden Field

Melrose

R. Tweed *Abbotsford* The Selkirks

SCOTT COUNTRY

Auchinleck *Craigenputtock*

Mossgiel *Ecclefechan*

Alloway *Dumfries*

The BURNS COUNTRY

SOLWAY FIRTH

Otterburn *Chevy Chase*

Newcastle

Roman Wall *Jarrow* *Wearmouth*

R. Tyne

Durham

Cockermouth *Skiddaw*

Derwent Water *Keswick*

The WORDSWORTH *Rydal Mount*

Grasmere *Ambleside*

Lake Windemere COUNTRY

Whitby

Fountain Abbey

York

Islington

ISLE OF MAN

Belfast *Dromore*

Giant's Causeway

DEIRDRÈS COUNTRY

Donegal

The YEATS COUNTRY

Route of the Spanish Armada